W9-ARN-653

THE PRENTICE HALL
PEARSON Prentice Hall **PEARSON** Custom Publishing

Just-In-Time program

Just-In-Time

YOU CAN CUSTOMIZE YOUR TEXTBOOK WITH CHAPTERS FROM ANY OF THE FOLLOWING PRENTICE HALL TITLES: *

BUSINESS STATISTICS

- Berenson/Levine/Krehbiel, BASIC BUSINESS STATISTICS, 10/e
- Groebner/Shannon/Fry/Smith, BUSINESS STATISTICS: A DECISION-MAKING APPROACH, 6/e
- Levine/Stephan/Krehbiel/Berenson, STATISTICS FOR MANAGERS USING MICROSOFT EXCEL, 4/e
- Levine/Krehbiel/Berenson, BUSINESS STATISTICS: A FIRST COURSE, 4/e
- Newbold/Carlson/Thorne, STATISTICS FOR BUSINESS AND ECONOMICS, 5/e
- Groebner/Shannon/Fry/Smith, A COURSE IN BUSINESS STATISTICS, 4/e

OPERATIONS MANAGEMENT

- Anupindi/Chopra/Deshmukh/Van Mieghem/Zemel, MANAGING BUSINESS PROCESS FLOWS, 2/e
- Bozarth/Handfield, INTRODUCTION TO OPERATIONS AND SUPPLY CHAIN MANAGEMENT
- Chopra/Meindl, SUPPLY CHAIN MANAGEMENT, 2e
- Foster, MANAGING QUALITY, 2/e
- Handfield/Nichols, Jr., SUPPLY CHAIN MANAGEMENT
- Hanna/Newman, INTEGRATED OPERATIONS MANAGEMENT
- Heineke/Meile, GAMES AND EXERCISES FOR OPERATIONS MANAGEMENT
- Heizer/Render, OPERATIONS MANAGEMENT, 7/e
- Heizer/Render, PRINCIPLES OF OPERATIONS MANAGEMENT, 5/e
- Krajewski/Ritzman, OPERATIONS MANAGEMENT, 7/e
- Latona/Nathan, CASES AND READINGS IN PRODUCTION AND OPERATIONS MANAGEMENT
- Ritzman/Krajewski, FOUNDATIONS OF OPERATIONS MANAGEMENT
- Schmenner, PLANT AND SERVICE TOURS IN OPERATIONS MANAGEMENT, 5/e

MANAGEMENT SCIENCE/SPREADSHEET MODELING

- Eppen/Gould/Schmidt/Moore/Weatherford, INTRODUCTORY MANAGEMENT SCIENCE, 5/e
- Render/Stair/Hanna, QUANTITATIVE ANALYSIS FOR MANAGEMENT, 9/e
- Render/Stair/Balakrishnan, MANAGERIAL DECISION MODELING WITH SPREADSHEETS
- Render/Greenberg/Stair, CASES AND READINGS IN MANAGEMENT SCIENCE, 2e
- Taylor, INTRODUCTION TO MANAGEMENT SCIENCE, 8/e

For more information, or to speak to a customer service representative, contact us at 1-800-777-6872.

www.prenhall.com/custombusiness

* Selection of titles on the JIT program is subject to change.

QUANTITATIVE ANALYSIS FOR MANAGEMENT

NINTH EDITION

Barry Render

Charles Harwood Professor of Management Science
Graduate School of Business, Rollins College

Ralph M. Stair, Jr.

Professor of Information and Management Sciences
Florida State University

Michael E. Hanna

Professor of Decision Sciences
University of Houston—Clear Lake

PEARSON

Prentice
Hall

Upper Saddle River, NJ 07458

To my family – BR

To Lila and Leslie – RMS

To Susan, Mickey, and Katie – MEH

Library of Congress Cataloging-in-Publication Data
Render, Barry.
  Quantitative analysis for management / Barry Render, Ralph M. Stair, Jr., Michael E. Hanna.—9th ed.
    p. cm.
  Includes bibliographical references and index.
  ISBN 0-13-153688-5
    1. Management science. 2. Operations research. I. Stair, Ralph M. II. Hanna, Michael E. III. Title.

  T56.R544 2006
  658.4′03—dc22

                                                            2004060096

AVP/Executive Editor: Mark Pfaltzgraff
VP/Editorial Director: Jeff Shelstad
Senior Sponsoring Editor: Alana Bradley
Senior Editorial Assistant: Jane Avery
Senior Media Project Manager: Nancy Welcher
Marketing Manager: Debbie Clare
Marketing Assistant: Joanna Sabella
Managing Editor (Production): Cynthia Regan
Permissions Coordinator: Charles Morris
Production Manager: Arnold Vila

Designer Director: Maria Lange
Interior Design: Blair Brown
Cover Design: Michael Fruhbeis
Cover Photo: Richard Cummins/Corbis
Composition/Illustration:
  GGS Book Services, Atlantic Highlands
Full-Service Project Management:
  GGS Book Services, Atlantic Highlands
Printer/Binder: Courier/Westford
Typeface: 10/12 Minion

Credits and acknowledgments borrowed from other sources and reproduced, with permission, in this textbook appear on appropriate page within text.

Microsoft® and Windows® are registered trademarks of the Microsoft Corporation in the U.S.A. and other countries. Screen shots and icons reprinted with permission from the Microsoft Corporation. This book is not sponsored or endorsed by or affiliated with the Microsoft Corporation.

Pearson Prentice Hall™ is a trademark of Pearson Eduction, Inc.
Pearson® is a registered trademark of Pearson plc
Prentice Hall® is a registered trademark of Pearson Education, Inc.

Pearson Education LTD.
Pearson Education Singapore, Pte. Ltd
Pearson Education, Canada, Ltd
Pearson Education–Japan

Pearson Education Australia PTY, Limited
Pearson Education North Asia Ltd
Pearson Educación de Mexico, S.A. de C.V.
Pearson Education Malaysia, Pte. Ltd

10 9 8 7 6 5 4 3
ISBN 0-13-153688-5

ABOUT THE AUTHORS

Barry Render is the Charles Harwood Distinguished Professor of Management Science at the Roy E. Crummer Graduate School of Business at Rollins College in Winter Park, Florida. He received his M.S. in Operations Research and his Ph.D. in Quantitative Analysis at the University of Cincinnati. He previously taught at George Washington University, the University of New Orleans, Boston University, and George Mason University, where he held the GM Foundation Professorship in Decision Sciences and was Chair of the Decision Science Department. Dr. Render has also worked in the aerospace industry for General Electric, McDonnell Douglas, and NASA.

Professor Render has co-authored ten textbooks with Prentice-Hall, including *Managerial Decision Modeling with Spreadsheets, Operations Management, Principles of Operations Management, Service Management, Introduction to Management Science*, and *Cases and Readings in Management Science*. His more than one hundred articles on a variety of management topics have appeared in *Decision Sciences, Production and Operations Management, Interfaces, Information and Management*, the *Journal of Management Information Systems, Socio-Economic Planning Sciences*, and *Operations Management Review*, among others.

Dr. Render has also been honored as an AACSB Fellow and named as a Senior Fulbright Scholar in 1982 and again in 1993. He was twice vice-president of the Decision Science Institute Southeast Region and served as Software Review Editor for Decision Line from 1989 to 1995. He has also served as Editor of the *New York Times* Operations Management special issues from 1996 to 2001. Finally, Professor Render has been actively involved in consulting for government agencies and for many corporations, including NASA; the FBI; the U.S. Navy; Fairfax County, Virginia; and C&P Telephone.

He teaches operations management courses in Rollins College's MBA and Executive MBA programs. In 1995 he was named as that school's Professor of the Year, and in 1996 was selected by Roosevelt University to receive the St. Claire Drake Award for Outstanding Scholarship.

Ralph Stair is a retired professor in the College of Business at Florida State University. He received a B.S. in Chemical Engineering from Purdue University and an MBA from Tulane University. Under the guidance of Ken Ramsing and Alan Eliason, he received his Ph.D. in operations management from the University of Oregon.

He has taught at the University of Oregon, the University of Washington, the University of New Orleans, and Florida State University. He has twice taught in Florida State University's Study Abroad Program in London. Over the years, his teaching has been concentrated in the areas of information systems, operations research, and operations management.

Dr. Stair is a member of several academic organizations, including the Decision Sciences Institute and INFORMS, and he regularly participates at national meetings. He has published numerous articles and books, including *Managerial Decision Modeling with Spreadsheets, Introduction to Management Science, Cases and Readings in Management Science, Production and Operations Management: A Self-Correction Approach, Fundamentals of Information Systems, Principles of Information Systems, Introduction to Information Systems, Computers in Today's World, Principles of Data Processing, Learning to Live with Computers, Programming in BASIC, Essentials of BASIC Programming, Essentials of FORTRAN Programming,* and *Essentials of COBOL Programming.*

Dr. Stair divides his time between Florida and Colorado. He enjoys skiing, biking, kayaking, and other outdoor activities.

Michael E. Hanna is Professor of Decision Sciences at the University of Houston—Clear Lake (UHCL). He has a B.A. in Economics, an M.S. in Mathematics, and a Ph.D. in Operations Research from Texas Tech University. For over twenty years, he has been teaching courses in statistics, management science, forecasting, and other quantitative methods. His dedication to teaching has been recognized with the Beta Alpha Psi teaching award in 1995.

Professor Hanna has authored a textbook in management science, published over thirty articles and professional papers, and has served on the Editorial Advisory Board of *Computers and Operations Research.* In 1996, the UHCL Chapter of Beta Gamma Sigma presented him with the Outstanding Scholar Award.

At UHCL, Professor Hanna has served as program coordinator of the Decision Sciences unit and as Director of the Center for Economic Development and Research. In 2001, he received the UHCL President's Distinguished Service Award. He recently completed a second term as Vice-President of the Decision Sciences Institute (DSI). He has been active in DSI serving on the Innovative Education Committee, the Regional Advisory Committee, and the Nominating Committee. For the Southwest DSI, he has held several positions including President, and he received the Southwest DSI Distinguished Service Award in 1997.

BRIEF CONTENTS

CONTENTS

PREFACE

OVERVIEW

The ninth edition of *Quantitative Analysis for Management* maintains the focus on the application of mathematical models in decision-making. Emphasis is placed on model building and computer applications so that students see how these models are used in business today. The mathematical details of more complex algorithms (such as the simplex and transportation algorithms) are presented in separate chapters making it easy for instructors to omit these if they so chose. The modeling aspects and computer solutions associated with these algorithms are contained in other chapters.

In the presentation of new techniques, a managerial problem that students can appreciate is first presented. This provides motivation for learning the mathematical techniques that follow. Then the mathematical model with all the necessary assumptions is provided. Plentiful examples illustrate the use of these techniques. With over 40 years of experience teaching quantitative methods, the authors have found that this is an effective pedagogy that students appreciate.

The only mathematical prerequisite for this textbook is algebra. We use standard notation, terminology, and equations throughout the book. Careful verbal explanation is provided for the mathematical notation and equations used.

Computer output is provided for many examples. The use of QM for Windows, Excel QM, and Excel allow the instructors to choose the software that works best in their situations.

NEW AND UPDATED FEATURES

The features that have been popular in previous editions have been updated and expanded. These are summarized here.

- *Modeling in the Real World* boxes demonstrate the application of the quantitative analysis approach to every technique discussed in the book.

- *Procedure* boxes summarize the more complex quantitative techniques, presenting them as a series of easily understandable steps.

- *Margin notes* highlight the important topics in the text.

- *History* boxes provide interesting asides related to the development of techniques and the people who originated them.

- *QA in Action* boxes summarize published articles illustrating how real organizations have used quantitative analysis to solve problems. The QA in Action boxes have been updated with many new applications.

- *Solved Problems*, included at the end of each chapter, serve as models for students in solving their own homework problems.

- *Discussion Questions* are presented at the end of each chapter to test the student's understanding of the concepts and definitions.

- *Problems* included in every chapter are applications-oriented and test the student's ability to solve exam-type problems. These are graded by level of difficulty: introductory (one bullet), moderate (two bullets), and challenging (three bullets). Many new problems have been added.

- *Internet Homework Problems* provide additional problems for students to work. These are available on the Companion Website.
- *Self Tests* allow students to test their knowledge of important terms and concepts in preparation for quizzes and examinations.
- *Case Studies*, at the end of each chapter, provide additional challenging managerial applications.
- *Glossaries*, at the end of each chapter, define important terms.
- *Key Equations*, provided at the end of each chapter, list the equations presented in that chapter.
- *End-of-Chapter Bibliographies* provide a current selection of more advanced books and articles.
- The software *QM for Windows*, developed by Professor Howard Weiss, uses the full capabilities of Windows to solve quantitative analysis problems. Instructions and screen captures are presented either in the chapters or in the appendices.
- *Excel QM* and *Excel* are used to solve problems throughout the ninth edition. Instructions and screen captures are given either in the chapters or in the appendices.
- *CD-ROM Modules* provide additional coverage of topics in quantitative analysis.
- The Companion Website at www.prenhall.com/render provides additional problems, cases, and other material for almost every chapter.

MAJOR CHANGES TO NINTH EDITION

Cohesive Treatment of Decision Models.
All models for decision theory have been combined into one chapter. Decision trees and utility theory are now presented along with decision tables.

New Chapter on Regression Analysis.
Due to requests by numerous users of previous editions, we have added a chapter on regression analysis. This includes simple linear regression, multiple regression, and brief discussion of nonlinear regression. Statistical inference on the overall model is presented. Other topics include dummy or indicator variables, model building, and cautions and pitfalls of using regression analysis.

Expanded Coverage of Forecasting.
With the new chapter on regression providing an introduction to dummy variables, the forecasting chapter has been expanded to include the additive approach to decomposition. Dummy variables are used in regression models to incorporate seasonal variations into the forecasts.

Enhanced Inventory Chapter.
Responding to user demand, we have now included just-in-time (JIT), materials requirements planning (MRP), and enterprise resource planning (ERP) in the inventory chapter. This provides a more complete introduction to inventory models in one chapter.

CD-ROM MODULES

To streamline the book, six topics are contained in modules available on the student CD-ROM included with the book. The six modules are:

- Analytic Hierarchy Process
- Dynamic Programming

- Decision Theory and the Normal Distribution
- Game Theory
- Mathematical Tools: Matrices and Determinants
- Calculus-Based Optimization

SOFTWARE

Excel. Excel is the featured software tool of the ninth edition. For students already familiar with Excel, instructions and screen captures are provided to highlight functions and tools that are directly related to quantitative analysis. New appendices provide succinct instructions and examples in several chapters. Excel is used for computations with the normal distribution, the binomial distribution, Bayes' theorem, simple and multiple regression, the analytic hierarchy process, Markov analysis, matrix operations, and other models. From the previous edition, Excel is also used for linear and nonlinear programming, simulation, and forecasting.

Excel QM. Excel QM is an Excel add-in that makes the use of Excel even easier. It is used to solve many of the problems and examples found in the text. The use of Excel QM is integrated into most chapters.

QM for Windows. QM for Windows, developed by Professor Howard Weiss, has long been a preferred software package for quantitative techniques. It is menu-driven and very easy-to-use so that students with limited computer experience find it very user friendly. The full version of this software is on the Student CD-ROM and updates to this valuable package are available to the student at www.prenhall.com/weiss.

COMPANION WEBSITE

Our updated Companion Website may be accessed at www.prenhall.com/render. Internet Homework Problems are available to provide more opportunities for students to practice the techniques they have learned.

SUPPLEMENTS

The supplements have been updated to provide the students and instructors with the best teaching and learning package available. Here is a brief list of these supplements.

- *Instructor's Resource CD-ROM.* The Instructor's Resource CD-ROM includes electronic files for the complete Instructor's Solutions Manual, the Test Item File in Word, the computerized Test Item File (TestGen), and updated PowerPoint presentations.
- *Student CD-ROM.* The Student CD-ROM includes Excel QM, QM for Windows, and modules with six additional topics.
- *Instructor's Solutions Manual.* The Instructor's Solutions Manual, updated by the authors, is available to adopters in print form, on the Instructor's Resource CD-ROM and can be accessed online at the Prentice Hall Instructor Resource Center. Solutions to all Internet Homework Problems and Internet Case Studies are also included in this manual.
- *Test Item File.* The updated Test Item File is available to adopters in print form, on the Instructor's Resource CD-ROM and online at the Prentice Hall Instructor Resource Center.

- *Test Generator.* The print test item file is designed for use with the test-generating software. This computerized package allows instructors to custom design, save, and generate classroom tests. The test program permits instructors to: edit, add, or delete questions from the test banks; edit existing graphics and create new graphics; analyze test results; and organize a database of tests and student results. This software allows for greater flexibility and ease of use. It provides many options for organizing and displaying tests, along with a search and sort feature.

ACKNOWLEDGMENTS

We gratefully thank the users of previous editions. Your feedback is valuable in our efforts for continuous improvement. The continued success of *Quantitative Analysis for Management* is a direct result of instructor and student feedback, and it is truly appreciated. Special thanks to the reviewers who provided valuable suggestions and ideas for this edition:

Nicholas G. Hall, *The Ohio State University*
Andrew Tiger, *Southeastern Oklahoma State University*
Bruce K. Blaylock, *Radford University*
Stephen H. Goodman, *University of Central Florida*
Dane Peterson, *Southwest Missouri State University*
Vassilios Karavas, *University of Massachusetts*

The authors are indebted to many people who have made important contributions to this project. Special thanks go to Professors Jerry Kinard, F. Bruce Simmons III, Khala Chand Seal, Victor E. Sower, Michael Ballot, Curtis P. McLaughlin, and Zbigniew H. Przanyski their contributions to the excellent cases included in this edition.

We thank Howard Weiss for providing Excel QM and QM for Windows, two of the most outstanding packages in the field of quantitative methods. We are indebted to Lee Revere (University of Houston—Clear Lake) and John Large (University of South Florida) for providing the wonderful PowerPoint slides and the Test Item File. We are very appreciative of the work of Vijay Gupta in error checking the textbook and solutions manual.

We would also like to thank the reviewers who have helped to make this one of the most widely used textbooks in the field of quantitative analysis.

Stephen Achtenhagen, *San Jose University*
M. Jill Austin, *Middle Tennessee State University*
Raju Balakrishnan, *Clemson University*
Hooshang Beheshti, *Radford University*
Rodney L. Carlson, *Tennessee Technological University*
Edward Chu, *California State University, Dominguez Hills*
John Cozzolino, *Pace University–Pleasantville*
Shad Dowlatshahi, *University of Wisconsin, Platteville*
Ike Ehie, *Southeast Missouri State University*
Ephrem Eyob, *Virginia State University*
Wade Ferguson, *Western Kentucky University*
Robert Fiore, *Springfield College*
Frank G. Forst, *Loyola University of Chicago*
Ed Gillenwater, *University of Mississippi*
Stephen H. Goodman, *University of Central Florida*
Irwin Greenberg, *George Mason University*

Nicholas G. Hall, *Ohio State University*
Robert R. Hill, *University of Houston–Clear Lake*
Gordon Jacox, *Weber State University*
Bharat Jain, *Towson State University*
Vassilios Karavas, *University of Massachusetts–Amherst*
Darlene R. Lanier, *Louisiana State University*
Jooh Lee, *Rowan College*
Richard D. Legault, *University of Massachusetts–Dartmouth*
Douglas Lonnstrom, *Siena College*
Daniel McNamara, *University of St. Thomas*
Robert C. Meyers, *University of Louisiana*
Peter Miller, *University of Windsor*
Ralph Miller, *California State Polytechnic University*
Shahriar Mostashari, *Campbell University*
David Murphy, *Boston College*
Robert Myers, *University of Louisville*

Barin Nag, *Towson State University*

Harvey Nye, *Central State University*

Alan D. Olinsky, *Bryant College*

Savas Ozatalay, *Widener University*

Young Park, *California University of Pennsylvania*

Cy Peebles, *Eastern Kentucky University*

Dane K. Peterson, *Southwest Missouri State University*

Ranga Ramasesh, *Texas Christian University*

William Rife, *West Virginia University*

Bonnie Robeson, *Johns Hopkins University*

Grover Rodich, *Portland State University*

L. Wayne Shell, *Nicholls State University*

Richard Slovacek, *North Central College*

John Swearingen, *Bryant College*

F. S. Tanaka, *Slippery Rock State University*

Jack Taylor, *Portland State University*

Madeline Thimmes, *Utah State University*

M. Keith Thomas, *Olivet College*

Andrew Tiger, *Southeastern Oklahoma State University*

Chris Vertullo, *Marist College*

James Vigen, *California State University, Bakersfield*

William Webster, *The University of Texas at San Antonio*

Larry Weinstein, *Eastern Kentucky University*

We are very grateful to all the people at Prentice Hall who worked so hard to make this book a success. These include Mark Pfaltzgraff, our Executive Editor; Alana Bradley, Senior Sponsoring Editor; Jane Avery, Editorial Assistant; Debbie Clare, Executive Marketing Manager, and Cynthia Regan, Managing Editor. Thank you all!

Barry Render

407-646-2657 (phone)

407-646-1550 (FAX)

brender@rollins.edu (e-mail)

Ralph Stair

rstair@cob.fsu.edu (e-mail)

Michael Hanna

281-283-3201 (phone)

281-226-7304 (FAX)

hanna@uhcl.edu (e-mail)

CHAPTER 1

INTRODUCTION TO QUANTITATIVE ANALYSIS

LEARNING OBJECTIVES

After completing this chapter, students will be able to:

1. Describe the quantitative analysis approach.
2. Understand the application of quantitative analysis in a real situation.
3. Describe the use of modeling in quantitative analysis.
4. Use computers and spreadsheet models to perform quantitative analysis.
5. Discuss possible problems in using quantitative analysis.
6. Perform a break-even analysis.

CHAPTER OUTLINE

1.1   INTRODUCTION

People have been using mathematical tools to help solve problems for thousands of years; however, the formal study and application of quantitative techniques to practical decision making is largely a product of the twentieth century. The techniques we study in this book have been applied successfully to an increasingly wide variety of complex problems in business, government, health care, education, and many other areas. Many such successful uses are discussed throughout this book.

It isn't enough, though, just to know the mathematics of how a particular quantitative technique works; you must also be familiar with the limitations, assumptions, and specific applicability of the technique. The successful use of quantitative techniques usually results in a solution that is timely, accurate, flexible, economical, reliable, and easy to understand and use.

In this and other chapters, there are QA (Quantitative Analysis) in Action boxes that will provide success stories on the applications of management science. These will show how organizations have used quantitative techniques to make better decisions, operate more efficiently, and generate more profits. Taco Bell has reported saving over $150 million with better forecasting of demand and better scheduling of employees. NBC television increased advertising revenue by over $200 million between 1996 and 2000 by using a model to help develop sales plans for advertisers. Continental Airlines saves over $40 million per year by using mathematical models to quickly recover from disruptions caused by weather delays and other factors. These are but a few of the many companies discussed in QA in Action boxes throughout this book.

1.2   WHAT IS QUANTITATIVE ANALYSIS?

Quantitative analysis uses a scientific approach to decision making.

Quantitative analysis is the scientific approach to managerial decision making. Whim, emotions, and guesswork are not part of the quantitative analysis approach. The approach starts with data. Like raw material for a factory, these data are manipulated or processed into information that is valuable to people making decisions. This processing and manipulating of raw data into meaningful information is the heart of quantitative analysis. Computers have been instrumental in the increasing use of quantitative analysis.

In solving a problem, managers must consider both qualitative and quantitative factors. For example, we might consider several different investment alternatives, including certificates of deposit at a bank, investments in the stock market, and an investment in real estate. We can use quantitative analysis to determine how much our investment will be worth in the future when deposited at a bank at a given interest rate for a certain number of years. Quantitative analysis can also be used in computing financial ratios from the balance sheets for several companies whose stock we are considering. Some real estate companies have developed computer programs that use quantitative analysis to analyze cash flows and rates of return for investment property.

In addition to quantitative analysis, *qualitative* factors should also be considered. The weather, state and federal legislation, new technological breakthroughs, the outcome of an election, and so on may all be factors that are difficult to quantify.

Both qualitative and quantitative factors must be considered.

Because of the importance of qualitative factors, the role of quantitative analysis in the decision-making process can vary. When there is a lack of qualitative factors and when the problem, model, and input data remain the same, the results of quantitative analysis can *automate* the decision-making process. For example, some companies use quantitative inventory models to determine automatically *when* to order additional new materials. In most cases, however, quantitative analysis will be an *aid* to the decision-making process. The results of quantitative analysis will be combined with other (qualitative) information in making decisions.

HISTORY   The Origin of Quantitative Analysis

Quantitative analysis has been in existence since the beginning of recorded history, but it was Frederick W. Taylor who in the early 1900s pioneered the principles of the scientific approach to management. During World War II, many new scientific and quantitative techniques were developed to assist the military. These new developments were so successful that after World War II many companies started using similar techniques in managerial decision making and planning. Today, many organizations employ a staff of operations research or management science personnel or consultants to apply the principles of scientific management to problems and opportunities. In this book, we use the terms *management science*, *operations research*, and *quantitative analysis* interchangeably.

The origin of many of the techniques discussed in this book can be traced to individuals and organizations that have applied the principles of scientific management first developed by Taylor; they are discussed in *History* boxes scattered throughout the book.

1.3   THE QUANTITATIVE ANALYSIS APPROACH

Defining the problem can be the most important step.

Concentrate on only a few problems.

The quantitative analysis approach consists of defining a problem, developing a model, acquiring input data, developing a solution, testing the solution, analyzing the results, and implementing the results (see Figure 1.1). One step does not have to be finished completely before the next is started; in most cases one or more of these steps will be modified to some extent before the final results are implemented. This would cause all of the subsequent steps to be changed. In some cases, testing the solution might reveal that the model or the input data are not correct. This would mean that all steps that follow defining the problem would need to be modified.

Defining the Problem

The first step in the quantitative approach is to develop a clear, concise statement of the *problem*. This statement will give direction and meaning to the following steps.

In many cases, defining the problem is the most important and the most difficult step. It is essential to go beyond the symptoms of the problem and identify the true causes. One problem may be related to other problems; solving one problem without regard to other related problems can make the entire situation worse. Thus, it is important to analyze how the solution to one problem affects other problems or the situation in general.

It is likely that an organization will have several problems. However, a quantitative analysis group usually cannot deal with all of an organization's problems at one time. Thus, it is usually necessary to concentrate on only a few problems. For most companies, this means selecting those problems whose solutions will result in the greatest increase in profits or reduction in costs to the company. The importance of selecting the right problems to solve cannot be overemphasized. Experience has shown that bad problem definition is a major reason for failure of management science or operations research groups to serve their organizations well.

When the problem is difficult to quantify, it may be necessary to develop *specific*, *measurable* objectives. A problem might be inadequate health care delivery in a hospital. The objectives might be to increase the number of beds, reduce the average number of days a patient spends in the hospital, increase the physician-to-patient ratio, and so on. When objectives are used, however, the real problem should be kept in mind. It is important to avoid obtaining specific and measurable objectives that may not solve the real problem.

Developing a Model

Once we select the problem to be analyzed, the next step is to develop a *model*. Simply stated, a model is a representation (usually mathematical) of a situation.

Even though you might not have been aware of it, you have been using models most of your life. You may have developed models about people's behavior. Your model might be that friendship is based on reciprocity, an exchange of favors. If you need a favor such as a small loan, your model would suggest that you ask a good friend.

FIGURE 1.1

The Quantitative Analysis Approach

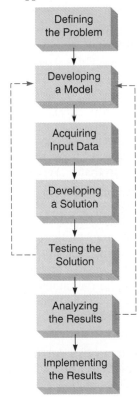

IN ACTION   The Management Science Group Is Bullish at Merrill Lynch

Management science groups at corporations can make a huge difference in reducing costs and increasing profits. At Merrill Lynch, the management science group was established in 1986. Its overall mission is to provide high-quality quantitative analysis, modeling, and decision support. The group analyzes a variety of problems and opportunities related to client services, products, and the marketplace. In the past, this group has helped Merrill Lynch develop asset allocation models, mutual fund portfolio optimization solutions, investment strategy development and research tools, financial planning models, and cross-selling approaches. Currently, there are 20 members of this management science group at Merrill Lynch.

In the late 1990s, Merrill Lynch faced increasing pressure from discount brokers, such as Fidelity, Schwab, and others. These discount brokers threatened to severely cut into the business and profits at traditionally full-service firms like Merrill Lynch. Should Merrill Lynch offer discount online trading and face the possibility of alienating its nearly 14,000 financial consultants? With the help of the management science group,

Merrill Lynch made its decision to offer a new service, called Integrated Choice. The new offering would allow clients to choose the level of service and advice they wanted. One ad read, "By mouse, by phone, by human being." An important aspect of the new service, Unlimited Advantage, gives clients access to a large array of services for a fixed fee. The new offerings have been a resounding success.

In order to provide meaningful assistance to Merrill Lynch, the management science group has concentrated on mathematical models that focus on client satisfaction. What are the keys to continued success for the management science group? Although skill and technical expertise in quantitative methods is essential, the management science group has identified the following four critical success factors: (1) objective analysis, (2) focus on business impact and implementation, (3) teamwork, and (4) adopting a disciplined consultative approach.

Source: Nigam, Raj et al. "Bullish on Management Science," *OR/MS Today* (June 2000), pp. 48–51.

The types of models include physical, scale, schematic, and mathematical models.

Of course, there are many other types of models. Architects sometimes make a *physical model* of a building that they will construct. Engineers develop *scale models* of chemical plants, called pilot plants. A *schematic model* is a picture, drawing, or chart of reality. Automobiles, lawn mowers, gears, fans, typewriters, and numerous other devices have schematic models (drawings and pictures) that reveal how these devices work. What sets quantitative analysis apart from other techniques is that the models that are used are mathematical. A *mathematical model* is a set of mathematical relationships. In most cases, these relationships are expressed in equations and inequalities, as they are in a spreadsheet model that computes sums, averages, or standard deviations.

Although there is considerable flexibility in the development of models, most of the models presented in this book contain one or more variables and parameters. A *variable*, as the name implies, is a measurable quantity that may vary or is subject to change. Variables can be *controllable* or *uncontrollable*. A controllable variable is also called a *decision variable*. An example would be how many inventory items to order. A *parameter* is a measurable quantity that is inherent in the problem. The cost of placing an order for more inventory items is an example of a parameter. In most cases, variables are unknown quantities, while parameters are known quantities. All models should be developed carefully. They should be solvable, realistic, and easy to understand and modify, and the required *input data* should be obtainable. The model developer has to be careful to include the appropriate amount of detail to be solvable yet realistic.

Acquiring Input Data

Once we have developed a model, we must obtain the data that are used in the model (*input data*). Obtaining accurate data for the model is essential; even if the model is a perfect representation of reality, improper data will result in misleading results. This situation is called garbage in, garbage out. For a larger problem, collecting accurate data can be one of the most difficult steps in performing quantitative analysis.

Garbage in, garbage out means that improper data will result in misleading results.

There are a number of sources that can be used in collecting data. In some cases, company reports and documents can be used to obtain the necessary data. Another source is interviews with employees or other persons related to the firm. These individuals can sometimes provide excellent information, and their experience and judgment can be invaluable. A production supervisor, for example, might be able to tell you with a great degree of accuracy the amount of time that it takes to produce a particular product. Sampling and direct measurement provide other sources of data for the model. You may need to know how many pounds of raw material are used in producing a new photochemical product. This information can be obtained by going to the plant and actually measuring with scales the amount of raw material that is being used. In other cases, statistical sampling procedures can be used to obtain data.

Developing a Solution

Developing a solution involves manipulating the model to arrive at the best (optimal) solution to the problem. In some cases, this requires that an equation be solved for the best decision. In other cases, you can use a *trial and error* method, trying various approaches and picking the one that results in the best decision. For some problems, you may wish to try all possible values for the variables in the model to arrive at the best decision. This is called *complete enumeration*. This book will also show you how to solve very difficult and complex problems by repeating a few simple steps until you find the best solution. A series of steps or procedures that are repeated is called an *algorithm*, named after Algorismus, an Arabic mathematician of the ninth century.

The input data and model determine the accuracy of the solution.

The accuracy of the solution depends on the accuracy of the input data and the model. If the input data are accurate to only two significant digits, then the results can be accurate to only two significant digits. For example, the results of dividing 2.6 by 1.4 should be 1.9, not 1.857142857.

Testing the Solution

Before a solution can be analyzed and implemented, it needs to be tested completely. Because the solution depends on the input data and the model, both require testing.

Testing the data and model is done before the results are analyzed.

Testing the input data and the model includes determining the accuracy and completeness of the data used by the model. Inaccurate data will lead to an inaccurate solution. There are several ways to test input data. One method of testing the data is to collect additional data from a different source. If the original data were collected using interviews, perhaps some additional data can be collected by direct measurement or sampling. These additional data can then be compared with the original data, and statistical tests can be employed to determine whether there are differences between the original data and the additional data. If there are significant differences, more effort is required to obtain accurate input data. If the data are accurate but the results are inconsistent with the problem, the model may not be appropriate. The model can be checked to make sure that it is logical and represents the real situation.

Although most of the quantitative techniques discussed in this book have been computerized, you will probably be required to solve a number of problems by hand. To help detect both logical and computational mistakes, you should check the results to make sure that they are consistent with the structure of the problem. For example (1.96) (301.7) is close to (2) (300), which is equal to 600. If your computations are significantly different from 600, you know you have made a mistake.

Analyzing the Results and Sensitivity Analysis

Analyzing the results starts with determining the implications of the solution. In most cases, a solution to a problem will result in some kind of action or change in the way an organization is operating. The implications of these actions or changes must be determined and analyzed before the results are implemented.

Sensitivity analysis determines how the solutions will change with a different model or input data.

Because a model is only an approximation of reality, the sensitivity of the solution to changes in the model and input data is a very important part of analyzing the results. This type of analysis is called *sensitivity analysis* or *postoptimality analysis*. It determines how much the solution will change if there were changes in the model or the input data. When the solution is sensitive to changes in the input data and the model specification, additional testing should be performed to make sure that the model and input data are accurate and valid. If the model or data are wrong, the solution could be wrong, resulting in financial losses or reduced profits.

⟱➡ MODELING IN THE REAL WORLD   **Planning China's Coal and Electricity Delivery System**

Defining the Problem	China produces about 1.1 billion tons of coal each year. Demand, however, is estimated to be about 1.6 billion tons. In addition, China faced air pollution problems that could threaten its high gross national product (GNP) growth rate. These problems were identified by the Chinese State Planning Commission and the World Bank as important to the continued growth of the GNP.
Developing a Model	In order to analyze some of the problems associated with the delivery of coal and electricity, the Chinese State Planning Commission developed a comprehensive model, called the Coal Transport Study (CTS) model. The model specified key components in the generation, transmission, and demand for electricity.
Acquiring Input Data	In addition to historical data, the model requires forecasts of future demand and the potential environmental impact of various energy sources and uses. In addition, specific data concerning the various stages of coal and electricity production are needed.
Developing a Solution	Instead of developing and reporting one solution, the quantitative analysis team analyzed 16 different solutions or possibilities. These solutions revealed that the investment in new coal–electricity systems could be as high as $250 billion over a 10-year period. The new system would have to deliver about 2 billion tons of coal.
Testing the Solution	Assumptions of the model and the solution were carefully tested. About a half-a-year was spent in testing the data, the model, and the solutions. This included running a series of tests on the data and model using known data to make sure that the data and model produced results consistent with the current situation. This testing resulted in fine-tuning the data and model to make them more accurate. After testing, corrections and adjustments were made to make sure that the results were as accurate as possible.
Analyzing the Results	The solutions also resulted in major findings. First, the government should plan on an 8% to 9% growth in power needs. Second, railways will continue to be the dominant transportation system for coal. Next, coal distribution can be greatly increased by increasing the volume and length of coastal and inland waterways. The chance of building and using slurry pipelines was slim. In addition, there were a number of specific findings on how coal should be handled and processed into energy to reduce pollution and negative environmental consequences.
Implementing the Results	Implementation of the CTS model resulted in a new steam coal-washing procedure, the construction of improved railway systems and a new port, and the use of coal imports. In addition, the planning commission has developed a sophisticated model for strategic-level investment planning. The model will be extended to perform energy planning to the year 2010.

Source: M. Kuby, et al. "Planning China's Coal and Electricity Delivery System," *Interfaces* 25 (January–February 1995): 41–68.

The importance of sensitivity analysis cannot be overemphasized. Because input data may not always be accurate or model assumptions may not be completely appropriate, sensitivity analysis can become an important part of the quantitative analysis approach. Most of the chapters in the book cover the use of sensitivity analysis as part of the decision-making and problem-solving process.

Implementing the Results

The final step is to *implement* the results. This is the process of incorporating the solution into the company. This can be much more difficult than you would imagine. Even if the solution is optimal and will result in millions of dollars in additional profits, if managers resist the new solution, all of the efforts of the analysis are of no value. Experience has shown that a large number of quantitative analysis teams have failed in their efforts because they have failed to implement a good, workable solution properly.

After the solution has been implemented, it should be closely monitored. Over time, there may be numerous changes that call for modifications of the original solution. A changing economy, fluctuating demand, and model enhancements requested by managers and decision makers are only a few examples of changes that might require the analysis to be modified.

The Quantitative Analysis Approach and Modeling in the Real World

The quantitative analysis approach is used extensively in the real world. These steps, first seen in Figure 1.1 and described in this section, are the building blocks of any successful use of quantitative analysis. As seen in our first *Modeling in the Real World* box, the steps of the quantitative analysis approach can be used to help a large country such as China plan for critical energy needs now and for decades into the future. Throughout this book, you will see how the steps of the quantitative analysis approach are used to help countries and companies of all sizes save millions of dollars, plan for the future, increase revenues, and provide higher-quality products and services. The *Modeling in the Real World* boxes in every chapter will demonstrate to you the power and importance of quantitative analysis in solving real problems for real organizations. Using the steps of quantitative analysis, however, does not guarantee success. These steps must be applied carefully.

1.4 HOW TO DEVELOP A QUANTITATIVE ANALYSIS MODEL

Developing a model is an important part of the quantitative analysis approach. Let's see how we can use the following mathematical model, which represents profits:

$$\text{Profits} = \text{Revenue} - \text{Expenses}$$

Expenses include fixed and variable costs.

In many cases, we can express revenues as price per unit multiplied times the number of units sold. Expenses can often be determined by summing fixed costs and variable cost. Variable cost is often expressed as variable cost per unit multiplied times the number of units. Thus, we can also express profits as the following mathematical model:

$$\text{Profits} = \text{Revenue} - (\text{fixed cost} + \text{variable cost})$$

$$\text{Profits} = (\text{selling price per unit})(\text{number of units sold})$$
$$- [\text{fixed cost} + (\text{variable cost per unit})(\text{number of units sold})]$$

$$\text{Profits} = sX - [f + vX]$$

$$\text{Profits} = sX - f - vX \tag{1-1}$$

where

$$s = \text{selling price per unit}$$

$$f = \text{fixed cost}$$

$$v = \text{variable cost per unit}$$

$$X = \text{number of units sold}$$

The parameters in this model are f, v, and s, as these are inputs that are inherent in the model. The number of units sold (X) is the decision variable of interest.

Example: Pritchett's Precious Time Pieces We will use the Bill Pritchett clock repair shop example to demonstrate the use of mathematical models. Bill's company, Pritchett's Precious Time Pieces, buys, sells, and repairs old clocks and clock parts. Bill sells rebuilt springs for a price per unit of $10. The fixed cost of the equipment to build the springs is $1,000. The variable cost per unit is $5 for spring material. In this example,

$$s = 10$$

$$f = 1,000$$

$$v = 5$$

The number of springs sold is X, and our profit model becomes

$$\text{Profits} = \$10X - \$1,000 - \$5X$$

If sales are 0, Bill will realize a $1,000 loss. If sales are 1,000 units, he will realize a profit of $4,000. ($4,000 = ($10)(1,000) − $1,000 − ($5)(1,000)). See if you can determine the profit for other values of units sold.

The BEP results in $0 profits.   In addition to the profit models shown here, decision makers are often interested in the *break-even point* (BEP). The BEP is the number of units sold that will result in $0 profits. We set profits equal to $0 and solve for X, the number of units at the break-even point:

$$0 = sX - f - vX$$

This can be written as

$$0 = (s - v)X - f$$

Solving for X we have

$$f = (s - v)X$$

$$X = \frac{f}{s - v}$$

This quantity (X) that results in a profit of zero is the BEP, and we now have this model for the BEP:

$$\text{BEP} = \frac{fixed\ cost}{(selling\ price\ per\ unit) - (variable\ cost\ per\ unit)}$$

$$\text{BEP} = \frac{f}{s - v} \tag{1-2}$$

For the Pritchett's Precious Time Pieces example, the BEP can be computed as follows:

$$\text{BEP} = \$1,000/(\$10 - \$5) = 200 \text{ units, or springs, at the break-even point}$$

The Advantages of Mathematical Modeling

There are a number of advantages of using mathematical models:

1. Models can accurately represent reality. If properly formulated, a model can be extremely accurate. A valid model is one that is accurate and correctly represents the problem or system under investigation. The profit model in the example is accurate and valid for many business problems.

2. Models can help a decision maker formulate problems. In the profit model, for example, a decision maker can determine the important factors or contributors to revenues and expenses, such as sales, returns, selling expenses, production costs, transportation costs, and so on.

3. Models can give us insight and information. For example, using the profit model from the preceding section, we can see what impact changes in revenues and expenses will have on profits. As discussed in the previous section, studying the impact of changes in a model, such as a profit model, is called sensitivity analysis.

4. Models can save time and money in decision making and problem solving. It usually takes less time, effort, and expense to analyze a model. We can use a profit model to analyze the impact of a new marketing campaign on profits, revenues, and expenses. In most cases, using models is faster and less expensive than actually trying a new marketing campaign in a real business setting and observing the results.

5. A model may be the only way to solve some large or complex problems in a timely fashion. A large company, for example, may produce literally thousands of sizes of nuts, bolts, and fasteners. The company may want to make the highest profits possible given its manufacturing constraints. A mathematical model may be the only way to determine the highest profits the company can achieve under these circumstances.

6. A model can be used to communicate problems and solutions to others. A decision analyst can share his or her work with other decision analysts. Solutions to a mathematical model can be given to managers and executives to help them make final decisions.

Mathematical Models Categorized by Risk

Deterministic means complete certainty.

Some mathematical models, like the profit and break-even models previously discussed, do not involve risk or chance. We assume that we know all values used in the model with complete certainty. These are called *deterministic models*. A company, for example, might want to minimize manufacturing costs while maintaining a certain quality level. If we know all these values with certainty, the model is deterministic.

Other models involve risk or chance. For example, the market for a new product might be "good" with a chance of 60% (a probability of 0.6) or "not good" with a chance of 40% (a probability of 0.4). Models that involve chance or risk, often measured as a probability value, are called *probabilistic models*. In this book, we will investigate both deterministic and probabilistic models.

1.5 **THE ROLE OF COMPUTERS AND SPREADSHEET MODELS IN THE QUANTITATIVE ANALYSIS APPROACH**

Developing a solution, testing the solution, and analyzing the results are important steps in the quantitative analysis approach. Because we will be using mathematical models, these steps require mathematical calculations. Fortunately, we can use the computer to make these steps easier. Two programs that allow you to solve many of the problems found in this book are provided in the attached CD-ROM:

1. **QM for Windows**, which is an easy-to-use decision support program developed specifically for this text. See Program 1.1. Appendix D and appendices at the end

PROGRAM 1.1   **QM for Windows' Main Menu of Quantitative Models**

of many chapters show how this powerful computer program can be used to solve quantitative analysis problems.

2. **Excel QM**, which can also be used to solve many of the problems discussed in this book, works automatically within Excel spreadsheets. Excel QM makes using a spreadsheet even easier by providing custom menus and solution procedures that guide you through every step. Program 1.2 shows the main menu for Excel QM and the quantitative models this program can solve. Appendix E also provides further details on how to install and use this program. To solve the break-even problem discussed in Section 1.4, we illustrate Excel QM features in Programs 1.3A and 1.3B.

PROGRAM 1.2

Excel QM's Main Menu of Quantitative Models

PROGRAM 1.3A

Excel QM Input Data for the Break-Even Problem

Microsoft Excel - formulas.xls

File Edit View Insert Format Tools Data Window Help

	A	B	C	D	E	F	G	H
1	**Pritchett Clock Repair Shop**							
2								
3	**Breakeven Analysis**							
4	Enter the fixed and variable costs and the selling price in the data area.							
5								
6								
7	Data							
8		Rebuilt Springs						
9	Fixed cost	1000						
10	Variable cost	5						
11	Revenue	10						
12								
13								
14	**Results**							
15	Breakeven points							
16	Units	=B9/(B11-B10)						
17	Dollars	=B9+B10*B16						
18								
19	**Graph**							
20	Units	Costs	Revenue					
21	0	=B9+B10*A21	=B11*A21					
22	=2*B16	=B9+B10*A22	=B11*A22					

Enter the fixed cost, variable cost and revenue.

Compute the breakeven point in units and dollars.

Construct the cost-volume analysis graph.

1.3 / 1.4 / S1.2 / 3.1 / 4.1a / 4.1 / 5.1 / 5.2 / 5.3 / 5.4 / 5.5 / 6.1 / 6.2 / 6

PROGRAM 1.3B

Excel QM Solution to the Break-Even Problem

Microsoft Excel - captures.Excel97.xls

File Edit View Insert Format Tools Data Window Help

	A	B	C	D	E	F	G	H
1	**Pritchett Clock Repair Shop**							
2								
3	**Breakeven Analysis**							
4	Enter the fixed and variable costs and the selling price in the data area.							
5								
6								
7	Data							
8		Rebuilt Springs						
9	Fixed cost	1000						
10	Variable cost	5						
11	Revenue	10						
12								
13								
14	**Results**							
15	Breakeven points							
16	Units	200						
17	Dollars	$ 2,000.00						
18								
19	**Graph**							
20	Units	Costs	Revenue					
21	0	1000	0					
22	400	3000	4000					

Cost-volume analysis

Notes \ 1.3 / 1.4 / 3.1 / 4.2 / 5.1 / 5.2 / 5.3 / 5.4 / 6.1 / 6.2 / 6.3 / 7.2 / 7

PROGRAM 1.4

Using Goal Seek in the Break-Even Problem

The formula in cell B17 computes the break-even point.

Input values in cells B10–B13 only.

Input target break-even point and Excel will find the price that would result in this.

Put any volume in B13 and Excel will compute the profit in B23.

	A	B	C
2			
3	Breakeven Analysis		
4	Enter the fixed and variable costs and the selling price in the data area.		
5			
6			
7			
8	Data		
9		Option 1	
10	Fixed cost	1000	
11	Variable cost	5	
12	Revenue	10.71	
13	Volume(optional)	250	
14			
15	Results		
16	Breakeven points		
17	Units	175	
18	Dollars	$ 1,875.00	
19			
20	Volume Analysis @	250	units
21	Costs	$ 2,250.00	
22	Revenue	$ 2,678.57	
23	Profit	$ 428.57	
24	Graph		
25	Units	Costs	Revenue
26	0	1000	0
27	349.999142	2749.99571	3749.996

B17 = =B10/(B12-B11)

Goal Seek
Set cell: $B$17
To value: 175
By changing cell: $B$12

Add-in programs make Excel, which is already a wonderful tool for modeling, even more powerful in solving quantitative analysis problems. Excel QM and the Excel files used in the examples throughout this text are also included with the CD-ROM that accompanies this text. There are two other powerful Excel built-in features that make solving quantitative analysis problems easier:

1. **Solver.** Solver is an optimization technique that can maximize or minimize a quantity given a set of limitations or constraints. We will be using Solver throughout the text to solve optimization problems. It is described in detail in Chapter 7 and used in Chapters 7, 8, 9, 10, 11, 12, and 13.

2. **Goal Seek.** This feature of Excel allows you to specify a goal or target (Set Cell) and what variable (Changing Cell) that you want Excel to change in order to achieve a desired goal. Bill Pritchett, for example, would like to determine what price he would need to lower the BEP from 200 springs to 175 springs. Program 1.4 shows how Goal Seek can be used to make the necessary calculations.

1.6   POSSIBLE PROBLEMS IN THE QUANTITATIVE ANALYSIS APPROACH

We have presented the quantitative analysis approach as a logical, systematic means of tackling decision-making problems. Even when these steps are followed carefully, there are many difficulties that can hurt the chances of implementing solutions to real-world problems. We now take a look at what can happen during each of the steps.

Defining the Problem

One view of decision makers is that they sit at a desk all day long waiting until a problem arises and then stand up and attack the problem until it is solved. Once it is solved, they sit down, relax, and wait for the next big problem. In the worlds of business, government, and education, problems are, unfortunately, not easily identified. There are four potential roadblocks that quantitative analysts face in defining a problem. We use an application, inventory analysis, throughout this section as an example.

IN ACTION   Better Modeling for Better Pollution Control

It is often difficult to balance economic returns with pollution control. When pollution is a problem, modeling industrial facilities can maintain high profitability while achieving pollution control guidelines and laws. This was the situation in Chile.

Chile is the world's largest producer of copper, producing 2.2 million tons of the metal in 1994. This large copper production represents about 8% of the country's gross domestic product (GDP). Although private businesses operate about 50% of copper mining operations, Chile controls most of the refining. Unfortunately, the production of copper produces solid, liquid, and gas by-products that end up in the environment. As a result, the Chilean government decided to enact pollution and air quality standards for many of the by-products of the copper mining process.

To help meet pollution and air quality standards, a quantitative optimization model was developed. The objective of the model was to minimize the costs of copper mining while maintaining pollution and air quality standards set by the Chilean government. The model resulted in a number of changes. First, the model solution was substantially different from the clean-up plans that were developed before the model solution. As a result, many of the early clean-up plans were delayed, redone, or scrapped. In addition, some previously developed pollution and air quality clean-up plans were approved because they were consistent with the solution from the model. Furthermore, the model provided critical input to a computerized decision support system to analyze the impact of various copper mining strategies on total costs and pollution control. The result of this optimization model is a cleaner environment at minimal cost.

Source: Mondschein, et al. "Optimal Investment Policies for Pollution Control in the Copper Industry," *Interfaces 27* (November–December 1997): 69–87.

All viewpoints should be considered before formally defining the problem.

Conflicting Viewpoints The first difficulty is that quantitative analysts must often consider conflicting viewpoints in defining the problem. For example, there are at least two views that managers take when dealing with inventory problems. Financial managers usually feel that inventory is too high, as inventory represents cash not available for other investments. Sales managers, on the other hand, often feel that inventory is too low, as high levels of inventory may be needed to fill an unexpected order. If analysts assume either one of these statements as the problem definition, they have essentially accepted one manager's perception and can expect resistance from the other manager when the "solution" emerges. So it's important to consider both points of view before stating the problem. Good mathematical models should include all pertinent information. As we shall see in Chapter 6, both of these factors are included in inventory models.

Impact on Other Departments The next difficulty is that problems do not exist in isolation and are not owned by just one department of a firm. Inventory is closely tied with cash flows and various production problems. A change in ordering policy can seriously hurt cash flows and upset production schedules to the point that savings on inventory are more than offset by increased costs for finance and production. The problem statement should thus be as broad as possible and include input from all departments that have a stake in the solution. When a solution is found, the benefits to all areas of the organization should be identified and communicated to the people involved.

An optimal solution to the wrong problem leaves the real problem unsolved.

Beginning Assumptions The third difficulty is that people have a tendency to state problems in terms of solutions. The statement that inventory is too low implies a solution that inventory levels should be raised. The quantitative analyst who starts off with this assumption will probably indeed find that inventory should be raised. From an implementation standpoint, a "good" solution to the *right* problem is much better than an "optimal" solution to the *wrong* problem. If a problem has been defined in terms of a desired solution, the quantitative analyst should ask questions about why this solution is desired. By probing further, the true problem will surface and can be defined properly.

Solution Outdated Even with the best of problem statements, however, there is a fourth danger. The problem can change as the model is being developed. In our rapidly changing business environment, it is not unusual for problems to appear or disappear virtually overnight. The analyst who presents a solution to a problem that no longer exists can't expect credit for providing timely help. However, one of the benefits of mathematical models is that once the original model has been developed, it can be used over and over again whenever similar problems arise. This allows a solution to be found very easily in a timely manner.

Developing a Model

Fitting the Textbook Models One problem in developing quantitative models is that a manager's perception of a problem won't always match the textbook approach. Most inventory models involve minimizing the total of holding and ordering costs. Some managers view these costs as unimportant; instead, they see the problem in terms of cash flow, turnover, and levels of customer satisfaction. Results of a model based on holding and ordering costs are probably not acceptable to such managers. This is why the analyst must completely understand the model and not simply use the computer as a "black box" where data is input and results are given with no understanding of the process. The analyst who understands the process can explain to the manager how the model does consider these other factors when estimating the different types of inventory costs. If other factors are important as well, the analyst can consider these and use sensitivity analysis and good judgment to modify the computer solution before it is implemented.

Understanding the Model A second major concern involves the trade-off between the complexity of the model and ease of understanding. Managers simply will not use the results of a model they do not understand. Complex problems, though, require complex models. One trade-off is to simplify assumptions in order to make the model easier to understand. The model loses some of its reality but gains some acceptance by management.

One simplifying assumption in inventory modeling is that demand is known and constant. This means that probability distributions are not needed and it allows us to build simple, easy-to-understand models. Demand, however, is rarely known and constant, so the model we build lacks some reality. Introducing probability distributions provides more realism but may put comprehension beyond all but the most mathematically sophisticated managers. One approach is for the quantitative analyst to start with the simple model and make sure that it is completely understood. Later, more complex models can be introduced slowly as managers gain more confidence in using the new approach. Explaining the impact of the more sophisticated models (e.g. carrying extra inventory called safety stock) without going into complete mathematical details is sometimes helpful. Managers can understand and identify with this concept, even if the specific mathematics used to find the appropriate quantity of safety stock is not totally understood.

Acquiring Input Data

Gathering the data to be used in the quantitative approach to problem solving is often no simple task. One-fifth of all firms in a recent study had difficulty with data access.

Obtaining accurate input data can be very difficult.

Using Accounting Data One problem is that most data generated in a firm come from basic accounting reports. The accounting department collects its inventory data, for example, in terms of cash flows and turnover. But quantitative analysts tackling an inventory problem need to collect data on holding costs and ordering costs. If they ask for such data, they may be shocked to find that the data were simply never collected for those specified costs.

Professor Gene Woolsey tells a story of a young quantitative analyst sent down to accounting to get "the inventory holding cost per item per day for part 23456/AZ." The accountant asked the young man if he wanted the first-in, first-out figure, the last-in, first-out figure, the lower of cost or market figure, or the "how-we-do-it" figure. The young man replied that the inventory model required only one number. The accountant at the next desk said, "Hell, Joe, give the kid a number." The kid was given a number and departed.

Validity of Data A lack of "good, clean data" means that whatever data are available must often be distilled and manipulated (we call it "fudging") before being used in a model. Unfortunately, the validity of the results of a model is no better than the validity of the data that go into the model. You cannot blame a manager for resisting a model's "scientific" results when he or she knows that questionable data were used as input. This highlights the importance of the analyst understanding other business functions so that good data can be found and evaluated by the analyst. It also emphasizes the importance of sensitivity analysis, which is used to determine the impact of minor changes in input data. Some solutions are very robust and would not change at all for certain changes in the input data.

Developing a Solution

Hard-to-understand mathematics and one answer can be a problem in developing a solution.

Hard-to-Understand Mathematics The first concern in developing solutions is that although the mathematical models we use may be complex and powerful, they may not be completely understood. Fancy solutions to problems may have faulty logic or data. The aura of mathematics often causes managers to remain silent when they should be critical. The well-known operations researcher C. W. Churchman cautions that "because mathematics has been so revered a discipline in recent years, it tends to lull the unsuspecting into believing that he who thinks elaborately thinks well."[1]

Only One Answer Is Limiting The second problem is that quantitative models usually give just one answer to a problem. Most managers would like to have a *range* of options and not be put in a take-it-or-leave-it position. A more appropriate strategy is for an analyst to present a range of options, indicating the effect that each solution has on the objective function. This gives managers a choice as well as information on how much it will cost to deviate from the optimal solution. It also allows problems to be viewed from a broader perspective, since nonquantitative factors can be considered.

Testing the Solution

The results of quantitative analysis often take the form of predictions of how things will work in the future if certain changes are made now. To get a preview of how well solutions will really work, managers are often asked how good the solution looks to them. The problem is that complex models tend to give solutions that are not intuitively obvious. Such solutions tend to be rejected by managers. The quantitative analyst now has the chance to work through the model and the assumptions with the manager in an effort to convince the manager of the validity of the results. In the process of convincing the manager, the analyst will have to review every assumption that went into the model. If there are errors, they may be revealed during this review. In addition, the manager will be casting a critical eye on everything that went into the model, and if he or she can be convinced that the model is valid, there is a good chance that the solution results are also valid.

Assumptions should be reviewed.

Analyzing the Results

Once the solution has been tested, the results must be analyzed in terms of how they will affect the total organization. You should be aware that even small changes in organizations are often difficult to bring about. If the results indicate large changes in organization policy,

[1] C. W. Churchman. "Relativity Models in the Social Sciences," *Interfaces* 4, 1 (November 1973).

Ⓐ IN ACTION   The Indispensable Role of Management Science at Reynolds

As the title of this box implies, quantitative approaches can be indispensable in helping companies such as the Reynolds Metals Company. Headquartered in Richmond, Virginia, Reynolds Metals Company is a Fortune 75 metals producer. Its aluminum operation includes production, mining, and the use of recycled aluminum. Of the company's $6 billion in sales in a recent year, more than 94% was in value-added fabricated products, including aluminum cans, flexible packaging, and a variety of consumer products.

In order to provide a more effective shipping operation, Reynolds decided to use management science to control shipping and reduce transportation costs. The result was the use of an integer programming model (see Chapter 11) that had the minimization of central dispatch freight cost as a primary objective. Using the annual shipping demand patterns, this quantitative analysis technique was able to improve on-time delivery of shipments and reduce freight costs by more than $7 million annually. As a company spokesperson said: "The confidence and respect I have for the management science discipline gave me the resolve to stick to the project plan when others doubted it could be done. I am very pleased to report today that the results that were predicted are being achieved. Management science made the difference between success and failure for this venture."

Source: W. Moore, J. Warmke, and L. Gorban. *Interfaces* 21, 1 (January–February 1991): 107–129.

the quantitative analyst can expect resistance. In analyzing the results, the analyst should ascertain who must change and by how much, if the people who must change will be better or worse off, and who has the power to direct the change.

1.7   IMPLEMENTATION—NOT JUST THE FINAL STEP

We have just presented some of the many problems that can affect the ultimate acceptance of the quantitative analysis approach and use of its models. It should be clear now that implementation isn't just another step that takes place after the modeling process is over. Each one of these steps greatly affects the chances of implementing the results of a quantitative study.

Lack of Commitment and Resistance to Change

Even though many business decisions can be made intuitively, based on hunches and experience, there are more and more situations in which quantitative models can assist. Some managers, however, fear that the use of a formal analysis process will reduce their decision-making power. Others fear that it may expose some previous intuitive decisions as inadequate. Still others just feel uncomfortable about having to reverse their thinking patterns with formal decision making. These managers often argue against the use of quantitative methods.

Many action-oriented managers do not like the lengthy formal decision-making process and prefer to get things done quickly. They prefer "quick and dirty" techniques that can yield immediate results. Once managers see some quick results that have a substantial payoff, the stage is set for convincing them that quantitative analysis is a beneficial tool.[2]

Management support and user involvement are important.

We have known for some time that management support and user involvement are critical to the successful implementation of quantitative analysis projects. A Swedish study found that only 40% of projects suggested by quantitative analysts were ever implemented. But 70% of the quantitative projects initiated by users, and fully 98% of projects suggested by top managers, *were* implemented.

Lack of Commitment by Quantitative Analysts

Just as managers' attitudes are to blame for some implementation problems, analysts' attitudes are to blame for others. When the quantitative analyst is not an integral part of the department facing the problem, he or she sometimes tends to treat the modeling activity as

---

[2] R. Nebike. "Five Suggestions to Save OR," *OR/MS Today* (August 1995): 10–11.

an end in itself. That is, the analyst accepts the problem as stated by the manager and builds a model to solve only that problem. When the results are computed, he or she hands them back to the manager and considers the job done. The analyst who does not care whether these results help make the final decision is not concerned with implementation.

Successful implementation requires that the analyst not *tell* the users what to do, but work with them and take their feelings into account. An article in *Operations Research* describes an inventory control system that calculated reorder points and order quantities. But instead of insisting that computer-calculated quantities be ordered, a manual override feature was installed. This allowed users to disregard the calculated figures and substitute their own. The override was used quite often when the system was first installed. Gradually, however, as users came to realize that the calculated figures were right more often than not, they allowed the system's figures to stand. Eventually, the override feature was used only in special circumstances. This is a good example of how good relationships can aid in model implementation.

SUMMARY

Quantitative analysis is the scientific approach to decision making. The quantitative analysis approach includes defining the problem, developing a model, acquiring input data, developing a solution, testing the solution, analyzing the results, and implementing the results. In using the quantitative approach, however, there can be potential problems, including conflicting viewpoints, the impact of quantitative analysis models on other departments, beginning assumptions, outdated solutions, fitting textbook models, understanding the model, acquiring good input data, hard-to-understand mathematics, obtaining only one answer, testing the solution, and analyzing the results. In using the quantitative analysis approach, implementation is not the final step. There can be a lack of commitment to the approach and resistance to change.

GLOSSARY

Algorithm. A set of logical and mathematical operations performed in a specific sequence.

Break-Even Point. The quantity of sales which results in zero profit.

Deterministic Model. A model in which all values used in the model are known with complete certainty.

Input Data. Data that are used in a model in arriving at the final solution.

Mathematical Model. A model that uses mathematical equations and statements to represent the relationships within the model.

Model. A representation of reality or of a real-life situation.

Parameter. A measurable input quantity that is inherent in the problem.

Probabilistic Model. A model in which all values used in the model are not known with certainty but rather involve some chance or risk, often measured as a probability value.

Problem. A statement, which should come from a manager, that indicates a problem to be solved or an objective or goal to be reached.

Quantitative Analysis or **Management Science.** A scientific approach using quantitative techniques as a tool in decision making.

Sensitivity Analysis. Determining how sensitive a solution is to changes in the formulation of a problem.

Stochastic Model. Another name for a probabilistic model.

Variable. A measurable quantity that is subject to change.

KEY EQUATIONS

(1-1) Profits $= sX - f - vX$

where

s = selling price per unit

f = fixed cost

v = variable cost per unit

X = number of units sold

An equation to determine profits as a function of the selling price per unit, fixed costs, variable costs, and number of units sold.

(1-2) BEP $= \dfrac{f}{s - v}$

An equation to determine the break-even point (BEP) in units as a function of the selling price per unit (s), fixed costs (f), and variable costs (v).

ⅢⅢ➡ SELF-TEST

- Before taking the self-test, refer back to the learning objectives at the beginning of the chapter, the notes in the margins, and the glossary at the end of the chapter.
- Use the key at the back of the book to correct your answers.
- Restudy pages that correspond to any questions that you answered incorrectly or material you feel uncertain about.

1. In analyzing a problem you should normally study
   a. the qualitative aspects.
   b. the quantitative aspects.
   c. both a and b.
   d. neither a nor b.
2. Quantitative analysis is
   a. a logical approach to decision making.
   b. a rational approach to decision making.
   c. a scientific approach to decision making.
   d. all of the above.
3. Frederick Winslow Taylor
   a. was a military researcher during World War II.
   b. pioneered the principles of scientific management.
   c. developed the use of the algorithm for QA.
   d. all of the above.
4. An input (such as variable cost per unit or fixed cost) for a model is an example of a(n)
   a. decision variable.
   b. parameter.
   c. algorithm.
   d. stochastic variable.
5. The point at which the total revenue equals total cost (meaning zero profit) is called the
   a. zero-profit solution.
   b. optimal profit solution.
   c. break-even point.
   d. fixed cost solution.
6. Quantitative analysis is typically associated with the use of
   a. schematic models.
   b. physical models.
   c. mathematical models.
   d. scale models.
7. Sensitivity analysis is most often associated with which step of the quantitative analysis approach?
   a. defining the problem
   b. acquiring input data

   c. implementing the results
   d. analyzing the results
8. A deterministic model is one in which
   a. there is some uncertainty about the parameters used in the model.
   b. there is a measurable outcome.
   c. all parameters used in the model are known with complete certainty.
   d. there is no available computer software.
9. The term *algorithm*
   a. is named after Algorismus.
   b. is named after a ninth-century Arabic mathematician.
   c. describes a series of steps or procedures to be repeated.
   d. all of the above.
10. An analysis to determine how much a solution would change if there are changes in the model or the input data is called
    a. sensitivity or postoptimality analysis.
    b. schematic or iconic analysis.
    c. futurama conditioning.
    d. both b and c.
11. Decision variables are
    a. controllable.
    b. uncontrollable.
    c. parameters.
    d. constant numerical values associated with any complex problem.
12. _____ is the scientific approach to managerial decision making.
13. _____ is the first step in quantitative analysis.
14. A _____ is a picture, drawing, or chart of reality.
15. A series of steps that are repeated until a solution is found is called a(n) _____.

DISCUSSION QUESTIONS AND PROBLEMS

Discussion Questions

1-1 What is the difference between quantitative and qualitative analysis? Give several examples.

1-2 Define *quantitative analysis*. What are some of the organizations that support the use of the scientific approach?

1-3 What is the quantitative analysis process? Give several examples of this process.

1-4 Briefly trace the history of quantitative analysis. What happened to the development of quantitative analysis during World War II?

1-5 Give some examples of various types of models. What is a mathematical model? Develop two examples of mathematical models.

1-6 List some sources of input data.

1-7 What is implementation, and why is it important?

1-8   Describe the use of sensitivity analysis and postoptimality analysis in analyzing the results.

1-9   Managers are quick to claim that quantitative analysts talk to them in a jargon that does not sound like English. List four terms that might not be understood by a manager. Then explain in nontechnical terms what each term means.

1-10   Why do you think many quantitative analysts don't like to participate in the implementation process? What could be done to change this attitude?

1-11   Should people who will be using the results of a new quantitative model become involved in the technical aspects of the problem-solving procedure?

1-12   C. W. Churchman once said that "mathematics . . . tends to lull the unsuspecting into believing that he who thinks elaborately thinks well." Do you think that the best QA models are the ones that are most elaborate and complex mathematically? Why?

1-13   What is the break-even point? What parameters are necessary to find this?

Problems*

1-14   Gina Fox has started her own company, Foxy Shirts, which manufactures imprinted shirts for special occasions. Since she has just begun this operation, she rents the equipment from a local printing shop when necessary. The cost of using the equipment is $350. The materials used in one shirt cost $8, and Gina can sell these for $15 each.
  (a) If Gina sells 20 shirts, what will her total revenue be? What will her total variable cost be?
  (b) How many shirts must Gina sell to break even? What is the total revenue for this?

1-15   Ray Bond sells handcrafted yard decorations at county fairs. The variable cost to make these is $20 each, and he sells them for $50. The cost to rent a booth at the fair is $150. How many of these must Ray sell to break even?

1-16   Ray Bond, from Problem 1-15, is trying to find a new supplier that will reduce his variable cost of production to $15 per unit. If he was able to succeed in reducing this cost, what would the break-even point be?

1-17   Katherine D'Ann is planning to finance her college education by selling programs at the football games for State University. There is a fixed cost of $400 for printing these programs, and the variable cost is $3. There is also a $1,000 fee that is paid to the university for the right to sell these programs. If Katherine was able to sell programs for $5 each, how many would she have to sell in order to break even?

1-18   Katherine D'Ann, from Problem 1-17, has become concerned that sales may fall, as the team is on a terrible losing streak and attendance has fallen off. In fact, Katherine believes that she will sell only 500 programs for the next game. If it was possible to raise the selling price of the program and still sell 500, what would the price have to be for Katherine to break even by selling 500?

1-19   Farris Billiard Supply sells all types of billiard equipment, and is considering manufacturing their own brand of pool cues. Mysti Farris, the production manager, is currently investigating the production of a standard house pool cue that should be very popular. Upon analyzing the costs, Mysti determines that the materials and labor cost for each cue is $25, and the fixed cost that must be covered is $2,400 per week. With a selling price of $40 each, how many pool cues must be sold to break even? What would the total revenue be at this break-even point?

1-20   Mysti Farris (see problem 1-19) is considering raising the selling price of each cue to $50 instead of $40. If this is done while the costs remain the same, what would the new break-even point be? What would the total revenue be at this break-even point?

1-21   Mysti Farris (see problem 1-19) believes that there is a high probability that 120 pool cues can be sold if the selling price is appropriately set. What selling price would cause the break-even point to be 120?

⫸ CASE STUDY

Food and Beverages at Southwestern University Football Games

Southwestern University (SWU), a large state college in Stephenville, Texas, 30 miles southwest of the Dallas/Fort Worth metroplex, enrolls close to 20,000 students. The school is the dominant force in the small city, with more students during fall and spring than permanent residents.

A longtime football powerhouse, SWU is a member of the Big Eleven conference and is usually in the top 20 in college football rankings. To bolster its chances of reaching the elusive and long-desired number-one ranking, in 1999 SWU hired the legendary Bo Pitterno as its head coach. Although the number-one ranking remained out of reach, attendance at the five Saturday home games each year increased. Prior to Pitterno's arrival, attendance generally averaged 25,000–29,000. Season ticket sales bumped up by 10,000 just with the announcement of the new coach's arrival. Stephenville and SWU were ready to move to the big time!

---

* Note: ⫿ means the problem may be solved with QM for Windows; ✖ means the problem may be solved with Excel QM; and ⫿ means the problem may be solved with QM for Windows and/or Excel QM.

With the growth in attendance came more fame, the need for a bigger stadium, and more complaints about seating, parking, long lines, and concession stand prices. Southwestern University's president, Dr. Marty Starr, was concerned not only about the cost of expanding the existing stadium versus building a new stadium, but also about the ancillary activities. He wanted to be sure that these various support activities generated revenue adequate to pay for themselves. Consequently, he wanted the parking lots, game programs, and food service to all be handled as profit centers. At a recent meeting discussing the new stadium, Starr told the stadium manager, Hank Maddux, to develop a break-even chart and related data for each of the centers. He instructed Maddux to have the food service area break-even report ready for the next meeting. After discussion with other facility managers and his subordinates, Maddux developed the following table showing the suggested selling prices, and his estimate of variable costs, and the percent revenue by item. It also provides an estimate of the percentage of the total revenues that would be expected for each of the items based on historical sales data.

ITEM	SELLING PRICE/UNIT	VARIABLE COST/UNIT	PERCENT REVENUE
Soft drink	$1.50	$0.75	25%
Coffee	2.00	0.50	25%
Hot dogs	2.00	0.80	20%
Hamburgers	2.50	1.00	20%
Misc. snacks	1.00	0.40	10%

Maddux's fixed costs are interesting. He estimated that the pro-rated portion of the stadium cost would be as follows: salaries for food services at $100,000 ($20,000 for each of the five home games); 2,400 square feet of stadium space at $2 per square foot per game; and six people in each of the six booths for 5 hours at $7 an hour. These fixed costs will be proportionately allocated to each of the products based on the percentages provided in the table. For example, the revenue from soft drinks would be expected to cover 25% of the total fixed costs.

Maddux wants to be sure that he has a number of things for President Starr: (1) the total fixed cost that must be covered at each of the games; (2) the portion of the fixed cost allocated to each of the items; (3) what his unit sales would be at break-even for each item—that is, what sales of soft drinks, coffee, hot dogs, and hamburgers are necessary to cover the portion of the fixed cost allocated to each of these items; (4) what the dollar sales for each of these would be at these break-even points; and (5) realistic sales estimates per attendee for attendance of 60,000 and 35,000. (In other words, he wants to know how many dollars each attendee is spending on food at his projected break-even sales at present and if attendance grows to 60,000.) He felt this last piece of information would be helpful to understand how realistic the assumptions of his model are, and this information could be compared with similar figures from previous seasons.

Discussion Questions

1. Prepare a brief report with the items noted so it is ready for Dr. Starr at the next meeting.

Adapted from J. Heizer and B. Render. *Operations Management, 6/e.* Upper Saddle River, NJ: Prentice Hall, 2000, pp. 274–275.

BIBLIOGRAPHY

Ackoff, R. L. *Scientific Method: Optimizing Applied Research Decisions.* New York: John Wiley & Sons, Inc., 1962.

Churchman, C. W. "Relativity Models in the Social Sciences," *Interfaces* 4, 1 (November 1973).

Churchman, C. W. *The Systems Approach.* New York: Delacort Press, 1968.

Clements, Dale, et al. "Analytical MS/OR Tools Applied to a Plant Closure," *Interfaces* (March 1994): 1–12.

Dutta, Goutam. "Lessons for Success in OR/MS Practice Gained from Experiences in Indian and U.S. Steel Plants," *Interfaces* 30, 5 (September–October 2000): 23–30.

Ginzberg, M. J. "Finding an Adequate Measure of OR/MS Effectiveness," *Interfaces* 8, 4 (August 1978): 59–62.

Grayson, C. J. "Management Science and Business Practice," *Harvard Business Review* 51 (1973).

Harris, Carl. "Could You Defend Your Model in Court?" *OR/MS Today* (April 1997): 6.

Hueter, Jackie, and William Swart. "An Integrated Labor-Management System for Taco Bell," *Interfaces* 28:1 (January–February 1998): 75–91.

Keskinocak, Pinar, and Sridhar Tayur. "Quantitative Analysis for Internet-Enabled Supply Chains," *Interfaces* 31, 2 (March–April 2001): 70–89.

Kuby, M., et al. "Planning China's Coal and Electricity Delivery System," *Interfaces* 25 (January 1995): 41–68.

Lancaster, Hal. "Re-engineering Authors Reconsider Re-engineering," *The Wall Street Journal* (January 17, 1995): B1.

McFadzean, Elspeth. "Creativity in MS/OR: Choosing the Appropriate Technique," *Interfaces* 29, 5 (September–October 1999): 110–122.

Pidd, Michael. "Just Modeling Through: A Rough Guide to Modeling," *Interfaces* 29, 2 (March–April 1999): 118–132.

Saaty, T. L. "Reflections and Projections on Creativity in Operations Research and Management Science: A Pressing Need for a Shifting Paradigm," *Operations Research*, 46, 1 (1998): 9–16.

Salveson, Melvin. "The Institute of Management Science: A Prehistory and Commentary," *Interfaces* 27, 3 (May–June 1997): 74–85.

Vazsoni, Andrew. "The Purpose of Mathematical Models Is Insight, Not Numbers," *Decision Line* (January 1998): 20–21.

Venkatakrishnan, C. S. "Optimize Your Career Prospects," *OR/MS Today* (April 1997): 28.

Willemain, T. R. "Model Formulation: What Experts Think About and When," *Operations Research*, 43, 6 (1995): 916–932.

CHAPTER 2

PROBABILITY CONCEPTS AND APPLICATIONS

LEARNING OBJECTIVES

After completing this chapter, students will be able to:

1. Understand the basic foundations of probability analysis.
2. Describe statistically dependent and independent events.
3. Use Bayes' theorem to establish posterior probabilities.
4. Describe and provide examples of both discrete and continuous random variables.
5. Explain the difference between discrete and continuous probability distributions.
6. Calculate expected values and variances and use the normal table.

CHAPTER OUTLINE

Summary • Glossary • Key Equations • Solved Problems • Self-Test • Discussion Questions and Problems • Internet Homework Problems • Case Study: Century Chemical Company • Case Study: WTVX • Bibliography

Appendix 2.1: Derivation of Bayes' Theorem

Appendix 2.2: Basic Statistics Using Excel

2.1 INTRODUCTION

Life would be simpler if we knew without doubt what was going to happen in the future. The outcome of any decision would depend only on how logical and rational the decision was. If you lost money in the stock market, it would be because you failed to consider all of the information or to make a logical decision. If you got caught in the rain, it would be because you simply forgot your umbrella. You could always avoid building a plant that was too large, investing in a company that would lose money, running out of supplies, or losing crops because of bad weather. There would be no such thing as a risky investment. Life would be simpler, but boring.

It wasn't until the sixteenth century that people started to quantify risks and to apply this concept to everyday situations. Today, the idea of risk or probability is a part of our lives. "There is a 40% chance of rain in Omaha today." "The Florida State University Seminoles are favored 2 to 1 over the Louisiana State University Tigers this Saturday." "There is a 50-50 chance that the stock market will reach an all-time high next month."

A probability is a numerical statement about the chance that an event will occur.

A **probability** *is a numerical statement about the likelihood that an event will occur.* In this chapter we examine the basic concepts, terms, and relationships of probability and probability distributions that are useful in solving many quantitative analysis problems. Table 2.1 lists some of the topics covered in this book that rely on probability theory. You can see that the study of quantitative analysis would be quite difficult without it.

2.2 FUNDAMENTAL CONCEPTS

There are two basic rules regarding the mathematics of probability:

People often misuse the two basic rules of probabilities when they use such statements as, "I'm 110% sure we're going to win the big game."

1. The probability, P, of any event or state of nature occurring is greater than or equal to 0 and less than or equal to 1. That is,

$$0 \le P(\text{event}) \le 1 \tag{2-1}$$

A probability of 0 indicates that an event is never expected to occur. A probability of 1 means that an event is always expected to occur.

2. The sum of the simple probabilities for all possible outcomes of an activity must equal 1. Both of these concepts are illustrated in Example 1.

TABLE 2.1

Chapters in This Book That Use Probability

CHAPTER	TITLE
3	Decision Analysis
4	Regression Models
5	Forecasting Models
6	Inventory Control Models
13	Project Management Models
14	Waiting Lines and Queuing Theory Models
15	Simulation Modeling
16	Markov Analysis
17	Statistical Quality Control
Module 3	Decision Theory and the Normal Distribution
Module 4	Game Theory

Example 1: Two Rules of Probability Demand for white latex paint at Diversey Paint and Supply has always been 0, 1, 2, 3, or 4 gallons per day. (There are no other possible outcomes and when one occurs, no other can.) Over the past 200 working days, the owner notes the following frequencies of demand.

QUANTITY DEMANDED (GALLONS)	NUMBER OF DAYS
0	40
1	80
2	50
3	20
4	10
	Total 200

If this past distribution is a good indicator of future sales, we can find the probability of each possible outcome occurring in the future by converting the data into percentages of the total:

QUANTITY DEMANDED	PROBABILITY
0	0.20 (= 40/200)
1	0.40 (= 80/200)
2	0.25 (= 50/200)
3	0.10 (= 20/200)
4	0.05 (= 10/200)
	Total 1.00 (= 200/200)

Thus, the probability that sales are 2 gallons of paint on any given day is P(2 gallons) = 0.25 = 25%. The probability of any level of sales must be greater than or equal to 0 and less than or equal to 1. Since 0, 1, 2, 3, and 4 gallons exhaust all possible events or outcomes, the sum of their probability values must equal 1.

Types of Probability

There are two different ways to determine probability: the *objective approach* and the *subjective approach*.

Objective Probability Example 1 provides an illustration of objective probability assessment. The probability of any paint demand level is the *relative frequency* of occurrence of that demand in a large number of trial observations (200 days, in this case). In general,

$$P(\text{event}) = \frac{\text{number of occurrences of the event}}{\text{total number of trials or outcomes}}$$

Objective probability can also be set using what is called the *classical* or *logical method*. Without performing a series of trials, we can often logically determine what the probabilities of various events should be. For example, the probability of tossing a fair coin once and getting a head is

$$P(\text{head}) = \frac{1}{2} \quad \begin{array}{l} \longleftarrow \textit{number of ways of getting a head} \\ \longleftarrow \textit{number of possible outcomes (head or tail)} \end{array}$$

Similarly, the probability of drawing a spade out of a deck of 52 playing cards can be logically set as

$$P(\text{spade}) = \frac{13}{52} \quad \begin{array}{l} \longleftarrow \textit{number of chances of drawing a spade} \\ \longleftarrow \textit{number of possible outcomes} \end{array}$$

$$= \frac{1}{4} = 0.25 = 25\%$$

Subjective Probability When logic and past history are not appropriate, probability values can be assessed *subjectively*. The accuracy of subjective probabilities depends on the experience and judgment of the person making the estimates. A number of probability values cannot be determined unless the subjective approach is used. What is the probability that the price of gasoline will be more than $4 in the next few years? What is the probability that our economy will be in a severe depression in 2015? What is the probability that you will be president of a major corporation within 20 years?

Where do probabilities come from? Sometimes they are subjective and based on personal experiences. Other times they are objectively based on logical observations such as the roll of a die. Often, probabilities are derived from historical data.

There are several methods for making subjective probability assessments. Opinion polls can be used to help in determining subjective probabilities for possible election returns and potential political candidates. In some cases, experience and judgment must be used in making subjective assessments of probability values. A production manager, for example, might believe that the probability of manufacturing a new product without a single defect is 0.85. In the Delphi method, a panel of experts is assembled to make their predictions of the future. This approach is discussed in Chapter 5.

2.3 MUTUALLY EXCLUSIVE AND COLLECTIVELY EXHAUSTIVE EVENTS

Events are said to be *mutually exclusive* if only one of the events can occur on any one trial. They are called *collectively exhaustive* if the list of outcomes includes every possible outcome. Many common experiences involve events that have both of these properties. In tossing a coin, for example, the possible outcomes are a head or a tail. Since both of them cannot occur on any one toss, the outcomes head and tail are mutually exclusive. Since obtaining a head and a tail represent every possible outcome, they are also collectively exhaustive.

Example 2: Rolling a Die Rolling a die is a simple experiment that has six possible outcomes, each listed in the following table with its corresponding probability:

OUTCOME OF ROLL	PROBABILITY
1	$\frac{1}{6}$
2	$\frac{1}{6}$
3	$\frac{1}{6}$
4	$\frac{1}{6}$
5	$\frac{1}{6}$
6	$\frac{1}{6}$
	Total 1

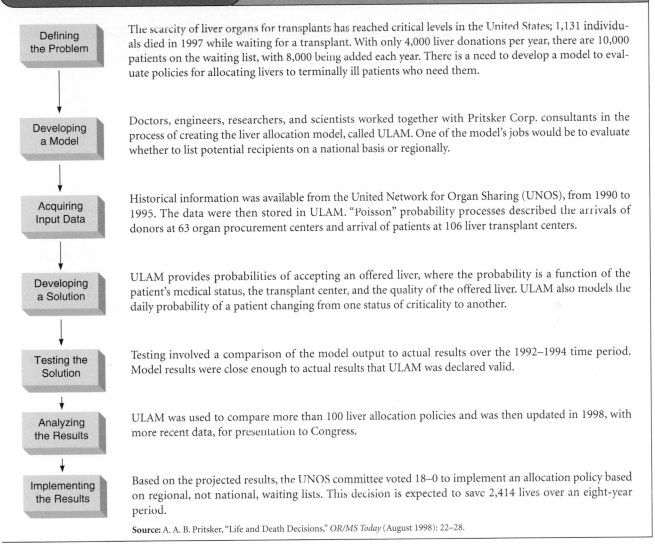

MODELING IN THE REAL WORLD   **Liver Transplants in the United States**

Defining the Problem

The scarcity of liver organs for transplants has reached critical levels in the United States; 1,131 individuals died in 1997 while waiting for a transplant. With only 4,000 liver donations per year, there are 10,000 patients on the waiting list, with 8,000 being added each year. There is a need to develop a model to evaluate policies for allocating livers to terminally ill patients who need them.

Developing a Model

Doctors, engineers, researchers, and scientists worked together with Pritsker Corp. consultants in the process of creating the liver allocation model, called ULAM. One of the model's jobs would be to evaluate whether to list potential recipients on a national basis or regionally.

Acquiring Input Data

Historical information was available from the United Network for Organ Sharing (UNOS), from 1990 to 1995. The data were then stored in ULAM. "Poisson" probability processes described the arrivals of donors at 63 organ procurement centers and arrival of patients at 106 liver transplant centers.

Developing a Solution

ULAM provides probabilities of accepting an offered liver, where the probability is a function of the patient's medical status, the transplant center, and the quality of the offered liver. ULAM also models the daily probability of a patient changing from one status of criticality to another.

Testing the Solution

Testing involved a comparison of the model output to actual results over the 1992–1994 time period. Model results were close enough to actual results that ULAM was declared valid.

Analyzing the Results

ULAM was used to compare more than 100 liver allocation policies and was then updated in 1998, with more recent data, for presentation to Congress.

Implementing the Results

Based on the projected results, the UNOS committee voted 18–0 to implement an allocation policy based on regional, not national, waiting lists. This decision is expected to save 2,414 lives over an eight-year period.

Source: A. A. B. Pritsker, "Life and Death Decisions," *OR/MS Today* (August 1998): 22–28.

These events are both mutually exclusive (on any roll, only one of the six events can occur) and are also collectively exhaustive (one of them must occur and hence they total in probability to 1).

Example 3: Drawing a Card   You are asked to draw one card from a deck of 52 playing cards. Using a logical probability assessment, it is easy to set some of the relationships, such as

$$P(\text{drawing a 7}) = \tfrac{4}{52} = \tfrac{1}{13}$$

$$P(\text{drawing a heart}) = \tfrac{13}{52} = \tfrac{1}{4}$$

We also see that these events (drawing a 7 and drawing a heart) are *not* mutually exclusive since a 7 of hearts can be drawn. They are also *not* collectively exhaustive since there are other cards in the deck besides 7s and hearts.

You can test your understanding of these concepts by going through the following cases:

This table is especially useful in helping to understand the difference between mutually exclusive and collectively exhaustive events.

DRAWS	MUTUALLY EXCLUSIVE?	COLLECTIVELY EXHAUSTIVE?
1. Draw a spade and a club	Yes	No
2. Draw a face card and a number card	Yes	Yes
3. Draw an ace and a 3	Yes	No
4. Draw a club and a nonclub	Yes	Yes
5. Draw a 5 and a diamond	No	No
6. Draw a red card and a diamond	No	No

Adding Mutually Exclusive Events

Often we are interested in whether one event *or* a second event will occur. This is often called the *union* of two events. When these two events are mutually exclusive, the law of addition is simply as follows:

$$P(\text{event } A \text{ or event } B) = P(\text{event } A) + P(\text{event } B)$$

or more briefly,

$$P(A \text{ or } B) = P(A) + P(B) \tag{2-2}$$

For example, we just saw that the events of drawing a spade or drawing a club out of a deck of cards are mutually exclusive. Since $P(\text{spade}) = {}^{13}\!/_{52}$, and $P(\text{club}) = {}^{13}\!/_{52}$, the probability of drawing either a spade or a club is

$$P(\text{spade or club}) = P(\text{spade}) + P(\text{club})$$

$$= {}^{13}\!/_{52} + {}^{13}\!/_{52}$$

$$= {}^{26}\!/_{52} = {}^{1}\!/_{2} = 0.50 = 50\%$$

The *Venn diagram* in Figure 2.1 depicts the probability of the occurrence of mutually exclusive events.

Law of Addition for Events That Are Not Mutually Exclusive

When two events are not mutually exclusive, Equation 2-2 must be modified to account for double counting. The correct equation reduces the probability by subtracting the chance of both events occurring together:

$$P(\text{event } A \text{ or event } B) = P(\text{event } A) + P(\text{event } B)$$

$$- P(\text{event } A \text{ and event } B \text{ both occurring})$$

This can be expressed in shorter form as

$$P(A \text{ or } B) = P(A) + P(B) - P(A \text{ and } B) \tag{2-3}$$

Figure 2.2 illustrates this concept of subtracting the probability of outcomes that are common to both events. When events are mutually exclusive, the area of overlap, called the *intersection*, is 0, as shown in Figure 2.1.

FIGURE 2.1

Addition Law for Events That Are Mutually Exclusive

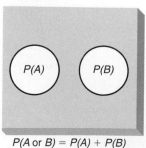

$P(A \text{ or } B) = P(A) + P(B)$

FIGURE 2.2

Addition Law for Events
That Are Not Mutually
Exclusive

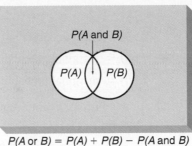

$$P(A \text{ or } B) = P(A) + P(B) - P(A \text{ and } B)$$

The formula for adding events that are not mutually exclusive is P(A or B) = P(A) + P(B) − P(A and B). *Do you understand why we subtract* P(A and B)?

Let us consider the events drawing a 5 and drawing a diamond out of the card deck. These events are not mutually exclusive, so Equation 2-3 must be applied to compute the probability of either a 5 or a diamond being drawn.

$$P(\text{five } or \text{ diamond}) = P(\text{five}) + P(\text{diamond}) - P(\text{five } and \text{ diamond})$$
$$= \tfrac{4}{52} + \tfrac{13}{52} - \tfrac{1}{52}$$
$$= \tfrac{16}{52} = \tfrac{4}{13}$$

2.4 STATISTICALLY INDEPENDENT EVENTS

Events may be either *independent* or *dependent*. When they are *independent*, the occurrence of one event has no effect on the probability of occurrence of the second event. Let us examine four sets of events and determine which are independent:

1. (a) Your education   ⎤ *Dependent events*
    (b) Your income level   ⎦ Can you explain why?

2. (a) Draw a jack of hearts from a full 52-card deck ⎤
    (b) Draw a jack of clubs from a full 52-card deck   ⎦ *Independent events*

3. (a) Chicago Cubs win the National League pennant ⎤
    (b) Chicago Cubs win the World Series   ⎦ *Dependent events*

4. (a) Snow in Santiago, Chile ⎤ *Independent events*
    (b) Rain in Tel Aviv, Israel ⎦

The three types of probability under both statistical independence and statistical dependence are (1) marginal, (2) joint, and (3) conditional. When events are independent, these three are very easy to compute, as we shall see.

A marginal probability is the probability of an event occurring.

A *marginal* (or a *simple*) *probability* is just the probability of an event occurring. For example, if we toss a fair die, the marginal probability of a 2 landing face up is $P(\text{die is a 2}) = \tfrac{1}{6} = 0.166$. Because each separate toss is an independent event (that is, what we get on the first toss has absolutely no effect on any later tosses), the marginal probability for each possible outcome is $\tfrac{1}{6}$.

A joint probability is the product of marginal probabilities.

The *joint probability* of two or more independent events occurring is the product of their marginal or simple probabilities. This may be written as

$$P(AB) = P(A) \times P(B) \tag{2-4}$$

where

$P(AB)$ = joint probability of events A and B occuring together, or one after the other

$P(A)$ = marginal probability of event A

$P(B)$ = marginal probability of event B

The probability, for example, of tossing a 6 on the first roll of a die and a 2 on the second roll is

$$P(\text{6 on first and 2 on second roll})$$

$$= P(\text{tossing a 6}) \times P(\text{tossing a 2})$$

$$= \tfrac{1}{6} \times \tfrac{1}{6} = \tfrac{1}{36}$$

$$= 0.028$$

A conditional probability is the probability of an event occurring given that another event has taken place.

The third type, *conditional probability*, is expressed as $P(B \mid A)$, or "the probability of event B, given that event A has occurred." Similarly, $P(A \mid B)$ would mean "the conditional probability of event A, given that event B has taken place." Since events are independent the occurrence of one in no way affects the outcome of another, $P(A \mid B) = P(A)$ and $P(B \mid A) = P(B)$.

Example 4: Probabilities When Events Are Independent A bucket contains 3 black balls and 7 green balls. We draw a ball from the bucket, replace it, and draw a second ball. We can determine the probability of each of the following events occurring:

1. A black ball is drawn on the first draw.

$$P(B) = 0.30 \textit{ (This is a marginal probability.)}$$

2. Two green balls are drawn.

$$P(GG) = P(G) \times P(G) = (0.7)(0.7) = 0.49$$

(This is a joint probability for two independent events.)

3. A black ball is drawn on the second draw if the first draw is green.

$$P(B \mid G) = P(B) = 0.30 \textit{ (This is a conditional probability but equal to the marginal because the two draws are independent events.)}$$

4. A green ball is drawn on the second draw if the first draw was green.

$$P(G \mid G) = P(G) = 0.70 \textit{ (This is a conditional probability as in event 3.)}$$

2.5 STATISTICALLY DEPENDENT EVENTS

When events are statistically dependent, the occurrence of one event affects the probability of occurrence of some other event. Marginal, conditional, and joint probabilities exist under dependence as they did under independence, but the form of the latter two are changed.

A *marginal probability* is computed exactly as it was for independent events. Again, the marginal probability of the event A occurring is denoted $P(A)$.

Calculating a *conditional probability* under dependence is somewhat more involved than it is under independence. The formula for the conditional probability of A, given that event B has taken place, is stated as

$$P(A\mid B) = \frac{P(AB)}{P(B)}$$

(2-5)

From Equation 2-5, the formula for a joint probability is

$$P(AB) = P(A\mid B)P(B)$$

(2-6)

Example 5: Probabilities When Events Are Dependent   Assume that we have an urn containing 10 balls of the following descriptions:

4 are white (W) and lettered (L).

2 are white (W) and numbered (N).

3 are yellow (Y) and lettered (L).

1 is yellow (Y) and numbered (N).

You randomly draw a ball from the urn and see that it is yellow. What, then, is the probability that the ball is lettered? (See Figure 2.3.)

Since there are 10 balls, it is a simple matter to tabulate a series of useful probabilities.

$$P(WL) = \tfrac{4}{10} = 0.4 \qquad P(YL) = \tfrac{3}{10} = 0.3$$

$$P(WN) = \tfrac{2}{10} = 0.2 \qquad P(YN) = \tfrac{1}{10} = 0.1$$

$$P(W) = \tfrac{6}{10} = 0.6, \ \text{ or } \ P(W) = P(WL) + P(WN) = 0.4 + 0.2 = 0.6$$

$$P(L) = \tfrac{7}{10} = 0.7, \ \text{ or } \ P(L) = P(WL) + P(YL) = 0.4 + 0.3 = 0.7$$

$$P(Y) = \tfrac{4}{10} = 0.4, \ \text{ or } \ P(Y) = P(YL) + P(YN) = 0.3 + 0.1 = 0.4$$

$$P(N) = \tfrac{3}{10} = 0.3, \ \text{ or } \ P(N) = P(WN) + P(YN) = 0.2 + 0.1 = 0.3$$

FIGURE 2.3

Dependent Events of Example 5

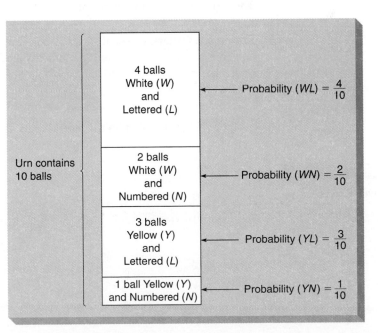

Urn contains 10 balls

4 balls
White (W)
and
Lettered (L)   Probability $(WL) = \dfrac{4}{10}$

2 balls
White (W)
and
Numbered (N)   Probability $(WN) = \dfrac{2}{10}$

3 balls
Yellow (Y)
and
Lettered (L)   Probability $(YL) = \dfrac{3}{10}$

1 ball Yellow (Y)
and Numbered (N)   Probability $(YN) = \dfrac{1}{10}$

We can now calculate the conditional probability that the ball drawn is lettered, given that it is yellow:

$$P(L\,|\,Y) = \frac{P(YL)}{P(Y)} = \frac{0.3}{0.4} = 0.75$$

This equation shows that we divided the probability of *yellow* and *lettered* balls (3 out of 10) by the probability of yellow balls (4 out of 10). There is a 0.75 probability that the yellow ball that you drew is lettered.

We can use the joint probability formula to verify that $P(YL) = 0.3$, which was obtained by inspection in Example 5 by multiplying $P(L\,|\,Y)$ times $P(Y)$.

$$P(YL) = P(L\,|\,Y) \times P(Y) = (0.75)(0.4) = 0.3$$

Example 6: Joint Probabilities When Events Are Dependent Your stockbroker informs you that if the stock market reaches the 12,500-point level by January, there is a 70% probability that Tubeless Electronics will go up in value. Your own feeling is that there is only a 40% chance of the market average reaching 12,500 points by January. Can you calculate the probability that *both* the stock market will reach 12,500 points *and* the price of Tubeless Electronics will go up?

Let M represent the event of the stock market reaching the 12,500 level, and let T be the event that Tubeless goes up in value. Then

$$P(MT) = P(T\,|\,M) \times P(M) = (0.70)(0.40) = 0.28$$

Thus, there is only a 28% chance that *both* events will occur.

2.6   REVISING PROBABILITIES WITH BAYES' THEOREM

Bayes' theorem is used to incorporate additional information as it is made available and help create revised or *posterior probabilities*. This means that we can take new or recent data and then revise and improve upon our old probability estimates for an event (see Figure 2.4). Let us consider the following example.

Example 7: Posterior Probabilities A cup contains two dice identical in appearance. One, however, is fair (unbiased) and the other is loaded (biased). The probability of rolling a 3 on the fair die is $\frac{1}{6}$ or 0.166. The probability of tossing the same number on the loaded die is 0.60.

We have no idea which die is which, but select one by chance and toss it. The result is a 3. Given this additional piece of information, can we find the (revised) probability that the

FIGURE 2.4

Using Bayes' Process

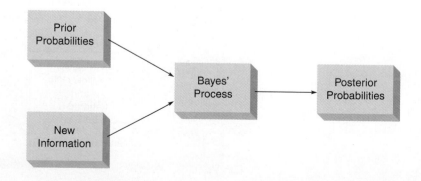

die rolled was fair? Can we determine the probability that it was the loaded die that was rolled?

The answer to these questions is yes, and we do so by using the formula for joint probability under statistical dependence and Bayes' theorem. First, we take stock of the information and probabilities available. We know, for example, that since we randomly selected the die to roll, the probability of it being fair or loaded is 0.50.

$$P(\text{fair}) = 0.50 \quad P(\text{loaded}) = 0.50$$

We also know that

$$P(3\,|\,\text{fair}) = 0.166 \quad P(3\,|\,\text{loaded}) = 0.60$$

Next, we compute joint probabilities $P(3 \text{ and fair})$ and $P(3 \text{ and loaded})$ using the formula $P(AB) = P(A\,|\,B) \times P(B)$.

$$P(3 \text{ and fair}) = P(3\,|\,\text{fair}) \times P(\text{fair})$$

$$= (0.166)(0.50) = 0.083$$

$$P(3 \text{ and loaded}) = P(3\,|\,\text{loaded}) \times P(\text{loaded})$$

$$= (0.60)(0.50) = 0.300$$

A 3 can occur in combination with the state "fair die" or in combination with the state "loaded die." The sum of their probabilities gives the unconditional or marginal probability of a 3 on the toss, namely, $P(3) = 0.083 + 0.300 = 0.383$.

If a 3 does occur, and if we do not know which die it came from, the probability that the die rolled was the fair one is

$$P(\text{fair}\,|\,3) = \frac{P(\text{fair and }3)}{P(3)} = \frac{0.083}{0.383} = 0.22$$

The probability that the die rolled was loaded is

$$P(\text{loaded}\,|\,3) = \frac{P(\text{loaded and }3)}{P(3)} = \frac{0.300}{0.383} = 0.78$$

These two conditional probabilities are called the *revised* or *posterior probabilities* for the next roll of the die.

Before the die was rolled in the preceding example, the best we could say was that there was a 50-50 chance that it was fair (0.50 probability) and a 50-50 chance that it was loaded. After one roll of the die, however, we are able to revise our *prior probability* estimates. The new posterior estimate is that there is a 0.78 probability that the die rolled was loaded and only a 0.22 probability that it was not.

Using a table is often helpful in performing the calculations associated with Bayes Theorem. Table 2.2 provides the general layout for this, and Table 2.3 provides this specific example.

TABLE 2.2	STATE OF NATURE	$P(B\,|\,$ STATE OF NATURE$)$	PRIOR PROBABILITY	JOINT PROBABILITY	POSTERIOR PROBABILITY
Tabular Form of Bayes Calculations Given Event B Has Occurred	A	$P(B\,|\,A)$	$\times P(A)$	$= P(B \text{ and } A)$	$P(B \text{ and } A)/P(B) = P(A\,|\,B)$
	$\overline{A}$	$P(B\,|\,\overline{A})$	$\times P(\overline{A})$	$= P(B \text{ and } \overline{A})$	$P(B \text{ and } \overline{A})/P(B) = P(\overline{A}\,|\,B)$
				$P(B)$	

TABLE 2.3	STATE OF NATURE	P(3 | STATE OF NATURE)	PRIOR PROBABILITY	JOINT PROBABILITY	POSTERIOR PROBABILITY
Bayes Calculations Given a 3 Is Rolled in Example 7	Fair die	0.166	×0.5	= 0.083	0.083/0.383 = 0.22
	Loaded die	0.600	×0.5	= 0.300	0.300/0.383 = 0.78
				P(3) = 0.383	

General Form of Bayes' Theorem

Another way to compute revised probabilities is with Bayes' theorem.

Revised probabilities can also be computed in a more direct way using a general form for *Bayes' theorem*:

$$P(A \mid B) = \frac{P(B \mid A)P(A)}{P(B \mid A)P(A) + P(B \mid \overline{A})P(\overline{A})} \tag{2-7}$$

where

$$\overline{A} = \text{the complement of the event } A; \text{ for example,}$$
$$\text{if } A \text{ is the event "fair die," then } \overline{A} \text{ is "loaded die"}$$

We originally saw in Equation 2-5 the conditional probability of event *A*, given event *B*, is

$$P(A \mid B) = \frac{P(AB)}{P(B)}$$

A Presbyterian minister, Thomas Bayes (1702–1761), did the work leading to this theorem.

Thomas Bayes derived his theorem from this. Appendix 2.1 shows the mathematical steps leading to Equation 2-7. Now let's return to Example 7.

Although it may not be obvious to you at first glance, we used this basic equation to compute the revised probabilities. For example, if we want the probability that the fair die was rolled given the first toss was a 3, namely, *P*(fair die | 3 rolled), we can let

$$\text{event "fair die" replace } A \text{ in Equation 2-7.}$$
$$\text{event "loaded die" replace } \overline{A} \text{ in Equation 2-7.}$$
$$\text{event "3 rolled" replace } B \text{ in Equation 2-7.}$$

We can then rewrite Equation 2-7 and solve as follows:

$$P(\text{fair die} \mid 3 \text{ rolled})$$

$$= \frac{P(3 \mid \text{fair})P(\text{fair})}{P(3 \mid \text{fair})P(\text{fair}) + P(3 \mid \text{loaded})P(\text{loaded})}$$

$$= \frac{(0.166)(0.50)}{(0.166)(0.50) + (0.60)(0.50)}$$

$$= \frac{0.083}{0.383} = 0.22$$

This is the same answer that we computed in Example 7. Can you use this alternative approach to show that *P*(loaded die | 3 rolled) = 0.78? Either method is perfectly acceptable, but when we deal with probability revisions again in Chapter 3, we may find that Equation 2-7 or the tabular approach is easier to apply.

2.7 FURTHER PROBABILITY REVISIONS

Although one revision of prior probabilities can provide useful posterior probability estimates, additional information can be gained from performing the experiment a second time. If it is financially worthwhile, a decision maker may even decide to make several more revisions.

Example 8: A Second Probability Revision Returning to Example 7, we now attempt to obtain further information about the posterior probabilities as to whether the die just rolled is fair or loaded. To do so, let us toss the die a second time. Again, we roll a 3. What are the further revised probabilities?

To answer this question, we proceed as before, with only one exception. The probabilities $P(\text{fair}) = 0.50$ and $P(\text{loaded}) = 0.50$ remain the same, but now we must compute $P(3,3 \mid \text{fair}) = (0.166)(0.166) = 0.027$ and $P(3,3 \mid \text{loaded}) = (0.6)(0.6) = 0.36$. With these joint probabilities of two 3s on successive rolls, given the two types of dice, we may revise the probabilities:

$$P(3, 3 \text{ and fair}) = P(3,3 \mid \text{fair}) \times P(\text{fair})$$

$$= (0.027)(0.5) = 0.013$$

$$P(3, 3 \text{ and loaded}) = P(3,3 \mid \text{loaded}) \times P(\text{loaded})$$

$$= (0.36)(0.5) = 0.18$$

Thus, the probability of rolling two 3s, a marginal probability, is $0.013 + 0.18 = 0.193$, the sum of the two joint probabilities.

$$P(\text{fair} \mid 3, 3) = \frac{P(3, 3 \text{ and fair})}{P(3, 3)}$$

$$= \frac{0.013}{0.193} = 0.067$$

$$P(\text{loaded} \mid 3, 3) = \frac{P(3, 3 \text{ and loaded})}{P(3, 3)}$$

$$= \frac{0.18}{0.193} = 0.933$$

 IN ACTION   Flight Safety and Probability Analysis

With the horrific events of September 11, 2001 and the use of airplanes as weapons of mass destruction, airline safety has become an even more important international issue. How can we reduce the impact of terrorism on air safety? What can be done to make air travel safer overall? One answer is to evaluate various air safety programs and to use probability theory in the analysis of the costs of these programs.

Determining airline safety is a matter of applying the concepts of objective probability analysis. The chance of getting killed in a scheduled domestic flight is about 1 in 5 million. This is probability of about .0000002. Another measure is the number of deaths per passenger mile flown. The number is about 1 passenger per billion passenger miles flown, or a probability of about .000000001. Without question, flying is safer than many other forms of transportation, including driving. For a typical weekend, more people are killed in car accidents than a typical air disaster.

Analyzing new airline safety measures involves costs and the subjective probability that lives will be saved. One airline expert proposed a number of new airline safety measures.

When the costs involved and probability of saving lives were taken into account, the result was about a $1 billion cost for every life saved on average. Using probability analysis will help determine which safety programs will result in the greatest benefit, and these programs can be expanded.

In addition, some proposed safety issues are not completely certain. For example, a Thermal Neutron Analysis device to detect explosives at airports had a probability of .15 of giving a false alarm, resulting in a high cost of inspection and long flight delays. This would indicate that money should be spent on developing more reliable equipment for detecting explosives. The result would be safer air travel with fewer unnecessary delays.

Without question, the use of probability analysis to determine and improve flight safety is indispensable. Many transportation experts hope that the same rigorous probability models used in the airline industry will some day be applied to the much more deadly system of highways and the drivers who use them.

Sources: Robert Machol, "Flying Scared," *OR/MS Today* (October 1997): 32–37 and Arnold Barnett, "The Worst Day Ever," *OR/MS Today* (December 2001): 28–31.

What has this second roll accomplished? Before we rolled the die the first time, we knew only that there was a 0.50 probability that it was either fair or loaded. When the first die was rolled in Example 7, we were able to revise these probabilities:

probability the die is fair = 0.22

probability the die is loaded = 0.78

Now, after the second roll in Example 8, our refined revisions tell us that

probability the die is fair = 0.067

probability the die is loaded = 0.933

This type of information can be extremely valuable in business decision making.

2.8 RANDOM VARIABLES

We have just discussed various ways of assigning probability values to the outcomes of an experiment. Let us now use this probability information to compute the expected outcome, variance, and standard deviation of the experiment. This can help select the best decision among a number of alternatives.

A *random variable* assigns a real number to every possible outcome or event in an experiment. It is normally represented by a letter such as X or Y. When the outcome itself is numerical or quantitative, the outcome numbers can be the random variable. For example, consider refrigerator sales at an appliance store. The number of refrigerators sold during a given day can be the random variable. Using X to represent this random variable, we can express this relationship as follows:

X = number of refrigerators sold during the day

In general, whenever the experiment has quantifiable outcomes, it is beneficial to define these quantitative outcomes as the random variable. Examples are given in Table 2.4.

When the outcome itself is not numerical or quantitative, it is necessary to define a random variable that associates each outcome with a unique real number. Several examples are given in Table 2.5.

There are two types of random variables: *discrete random variables* and *continuous random variables*. Developing probability distributions and making computations based on these distributions depends on the type of random variable.

A random variable is a *discrete random variable* if it can assume only a finite or limited set of values. Which of the random variables in Table 2.4 are discrete random variables?

TABLE 2.4	Examples of Random Variables		
EXPERIMENT	**OUTCOME**	**RANDOM VARIABLES**	**RANGE OF RANDOM VARIABLES**
Stock 50 Christmas trees	Number of Christmas trees sold	X = number of Christmas trees sold	0, 1, 2, . . . , 50
Inspect 600 items	Number of acceptable items	Y = number of acceptable items	0, 1, 2, . . . , 600
Send out 5,000 sales letters	Number of people responding to the letters	Z = number of people responding to the letters	0, 1, 2, . . . , 5,000
Build an apartment building	Percent of building completed after 4 months	R = percent of building completed after 4 months	$0 \leq R \leq 100$
Test the lifetime of a lightbulb (minutes)	Length of time the bulb lasts up to 80,000 minutes	S = time the bulb burns	$0 \leq S \leq 80,000$

TABLE 2.5	EXPERIMENT	OUTCOME	RANDOM VARIABLES	RANGE OF RANDOM VARIABLES
Random Variables for Outcomes That Are Not Numbers	Students respond to a questionnaire	Strongly agree (SA) Agree (A) Neutral (N) Disagree (D) Strongly disagree (SD)	$X = \begin{cases} 5 \text{ if SA} \\ 4 \text{ if A} \\ 3 \text{ if N} \\ 2 \text{ if D} \\ 1 \text{ if SD} \end{cases}$	1, 2, 3, 4, 5
	One machine is inspected	Defective Not defective	$Y = \begin{cases} 0 \text{ if defective} \\ 1 \text{ if not defective} \end{cases}$	0, 1
	Consumers respond to how they like a product	Good Average Poor	$Z = \begin{cases} 3 \text{ if good} \\ 2 \text{ if average} \\ 1 \text{ if poor} \end{cases}$	1, 2, 3

Try to develop a few more examples of discrete random variables to be sure you understand this concept.

Looking at Table 2.4, we can see that stocking 50 Christmas trees, inspecting 600 items, and sending out 5,000 letters are all examples of discrete random variables. Each of these random variables can assume only a finite or limited set of values. The number of Christmas trees sold, for example, can only be integer numbers from 0 to 50. There are 51 values that the random variable X can assume in this example.

A *continuous random variable* is a random variable that has an infinite or an unlimited set of values. Are there any examples of continuous random variables in Tables 2.4 or 2.5? Looking at Table 2.4, we can see that testing the lifetime of a lightbulb is an experiment that can be described with a continuous random variable. In this case, the random variable, S, is the time the bulb burns. It can last for 3,206 minutes, 6,500.7 minutes, 251.726 minutes, or any other value between 0 and 80,000 minutes. In most cases, the range of a continuous random variable is stated as: lower value $\leq S \leq$ upper value, such as $0 \leq S \leq 80,000$. The random variable R in Table 2.4 is also continuous. Can you explain why?

2.9 PROBABILITY DISTRIBUTIONS

Earlier we discussed the probability values of an event. We now explore the properties of *probability distributions*. We see how popular distributions, such as the normal, Poisson, binomial, and exponential probability distributions, can save us time and effort. Since selection of the appropriate probability distribution depends partially on whether the random variable is *discrete* or *continuous*, we consider each of these types separately.

Probability Distribution of a Discrete Random Variable

When we have a *discrete random variable*, there is a probability value assigned to each event. These values must be between 0 and 1, and they must sum to 1. Let's look at an example.

The 100 students in Pat Shannon's statistics class have just completed the instructor evaluations at the end of the course. Dr. Shannon is particularly interested in student response to the textbook because he is in the process of writing a competing statistics book. One of the questions on the evaluation survey was "The textbook was well written and helped me acquire the necessary information."

5. Strongly agree

4. Agree

3. Neutral

2. Disagree

1. Strongly disagree

TABLE 2.6	OUTCOME	RANDOM VARIABLE (X)	NUMBER RESPONDING	PROBABILITY P(X)
Probability Distribution for Textbook Question	Strongly agree	5	10	0.1 = 10/100
	Agree	4	20	0.2 = 20/100
	Neutral	3	30	0.3 = 30/100
	Disagree	2	30	0.3 = 30/100
	Strongly disagree	1	10	0.1 = 10/100
			Total 100	1.0 = 100/100

The students' response to this question in the survey is summarized in Table 2.6. Also shown is the random variable X and the corresponding probability for each possible outcome. This discrete probability distribution was computed using the relative frequency approach presented earlier.

The distribution follows the three rules required of all probability distributions: (1) the events are mutually exclusive and collectively exhaustive, (2) the individual probability values are between 0 and 1 inclusive, and (3) the total of the probability values sum to 1.

Although listing the probability distribution as we did in Table 2.4 is adequate, it can be difficult to get an idea about characteristics of the distribution. To overcome this problem, the probability values are often presented in graph form. The graph of the distribution in Table 2.6 is shown in Figure 2.5.

The graph of this probability distribution gives us a picture of its shape. It helps us identify the central tendency of the distribution, called the mean or *expected value*, and the amount of variability or spread of the distribution, called the *variance.*

Expected Value of a Discrete Probability Distribution

The expected value of a discrete distribution is a weighted average of the values of the random variable.

Once we have established a probability distribution, the first characteristic that is usually of interest is the *central tendency* of the distribution. The expected value, a measure of central tendency, is computed as weighted average of the values of the random variable:

$$E(X) = \sum_{i=1}^{n} X_i P(X_i)$$

$$= X_1 P(X_1) + X_2 P(X_2) + \cdots + X_n P(X_n) \tag{2-8}$$

FIGURE 2.5

Probability Distribution for Dr. Shannon's Class

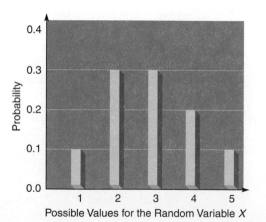

Possible Values for the Random Variable X

where

X_i = random variable's possible values

$P(X_i)$ = probability of each of the random variable's possible values

$\displaystyle\sum_{i=1}^{n}$ = summation sign indicating we are adding all *n* possible values

$E(X)$ = expected value or mean of the random variable

The expected value of any discrete probability distribution can be computed by multiplying each possible value of the random variable, X_i, times the probability, $P(X_i)$, that outcome will occur, and summing the results, Σ. Here is how the expected value can be computed for the textbook question:

$$E(X) = \sum_{i=1}^{5} X_i P(X_i)$$

$$= X_1 P(X_1) + X_2 P(X_2) + X_3 P(X_3) + X_4 P(X_4) + X_5 P(X_5)$$

$$= (5)(0.1) + (4)(0.2) + (3)(0.3) + (2)(0.3) + (1)(0.1)$$

$$= 2.9$$

The expected value of 2.9 implies that the mean response is between disagree (2) and neutral (3), and that the average response is closer to neutral, which is 3. Looking at Figure 2.5, this is consistent with the shape of the probability function.

Variance of a Discrete Probability Distribution

In addition to the central tendency of a probability distribution, most people are interested in the variability or the spread of the distribution. If the variability is low, it is much more likely that the outcome of an experiment will be close to the average or expected value. On the other hand, if the variability of the distribution is high, which means that the probability is spread out over the various random variable values, there is less chance that the outcome of an experiment will be close to the expected value.

A probability distribution is often described by its mean and variance. Even if most of the men in class (or the United States) have heights between 5 feet 6 inches and 6 feet 2 inches, there is still some small probability of outliers.

The *variance* of a probability distribution is a number that reveals the overall spread or dispersion of the distribution. For a discrete probability distribution, it can be computed using the following equation:

$$\sigma^2 = \text{variance} = \sum_{i=1}^{n} \left[X_i - E(X) \right]^2 P(X_i) \tag{2-9}$$

where

X_i = random variable's possible values

$E(X)$ = expected value of the random variable

$[X_i - E(X)]$ = difference between each value of the random variable and the expected value

$P(X_i)$ = probability of each possible value of the random variable

To compute the variance, each value of the random variable is subtracted from the expected value, squared, and multiplied times the probability of occurrence of that value. The results are then summed to obtain the variance. Here is how this procedure is done for Dr. Shannon's textbook question:

$$\text{variance} = \sum_{i=1}^{5} \left[X_i - E(X) \right]^2 P(X_i)$$

$$\begin{aligned}
\text{variance} &= (5 - 2.9)^2(0.1) + (4 - 2.9)^2(0.2) + (3 - 2.9)^2(0.3) + (2 - 2.9)^2(0.3) \\
&\quad + (1 - 2.9)^2(0.1) \\
&= (2.1)^2(0.1) + (1.1)^2(0.2) + (0.1)^2(0.3) + (-0.9)^2(0.3) + (-1.9)^2(0.1) \\
&= 0.441 + 0.242 + 0.003 + 0.243 + 0.361 \\
&= 1.29
\end{aligned}$$

A related measure of dispersion or spread is the *standard deviation*. This quantity is also used in many computations involved with probability distributions. The standard deviation is just the square root of the variance:

$$\sigma = \sqrt{\text{variance}} = \sqrt{\sigma^2} \qquad (2\text{-}10)$$

where

$$\sqrt{} = \text{square root}$$

$$\sigma = \text{standard deviation}$$

The standard deviation for the textbook question is

$$\sigma = \sqrt{\text{variance}}$$

$$= \sqrt{1.29} = 1.14$$

Probability Distribution of a Continuous Random Variable

There are many examples of *continuous random variables*. The time it takes to finish a project, the number of ounces in a barrel of butter, the high temperature during a given day, the exact length of a given type of lumber, and the weight of a railroad car of coal are all examples of continuous random variables. Since random variables can take on an infinite number of values, the fundamental probability rules for continuous random variables must be modified.

As with discrete probability distributions, the sum of the probability values must equal 1. Because there are an infinite number of values of the random variables, however, the probability of each value of the random variable must be 0. If the probability values for the random variable values were greater than 0, the sum would be infinitely large.

A probability density function, f(x), is a mathematical way of describing the probability distribution.

With a continuous probability distribution, there is a continuous mathematical function that describes the probability distribution. This function is called the *probability density function* or simply the *probability function*. It is usually represented by $f(X)$. When working with continuous probability distributions, the probability function can be graphed, and the area underneath the curve represents probability. Thus, to find any probability, we simply find the area under the curve associated with the range of interest.

We now look at the sketch of a sample density function in Figure 2.6. This curve represents the probability density function for the weight of a particular machined part. The weight could vary from 5.06 to 5.30 grams, with weights around 5.18 grams being the most likely. The shaded area represents the probability the weight is between 5.22 and 5.26 grams.

If we wanted to know the probability of a part weighing exactly 5.1300000 grams, for example, we would have to compute the area of a slice of width 0. Of course, this would be 0. This result may seem strange, but if we insist on enough decimal places of accuracy, we are bound to find that the weight differs from 5.1300000 grams *exactly*, be the difference ever so slight.

In this section we have investigated the fundamental characteristics and properties of probability distributions in general. In the next three sections we introduce two important

FIGURE 2.6

Sample Density Function

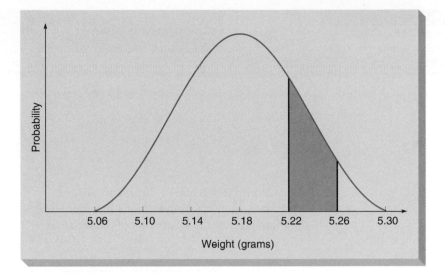

continuous distributions—the normal distribution and the exponential distribution—and two discrete distributions—the Poisson distribution and the binomial distribution.

2.10 THE BINOMIAL DISTRIBUTION

Many business experiments can be characterized by the *Bernoulli process*. The probability of obtaining specific outcomes in a Bernoulli process is described by the binomial probability distribution. In order to be a Bernoulli process, an experiment must have the following characteristics:

1. Each trial in a Bernoulli process has only two possible outcomes. These are typically called a success and a failure, although examples might be yes or no, heads or tails, pass or fail, defective or good, and so on.
2. The probability stays the same from one trial to the next.
3. The trials are statistically independent.
4. The number of trials is a positive integer.

A common example of this process is tossing a coin.

The binomial distribution is used to find the probability of a specific number of successes out of n trials of a Bernoulli process. To find this probability, it is necessary to know the following:

$$n = \text{the number of trials}$$

$$p = \text{the probability of a success on any single trial.}$$

We let

$$r = \text{the number of successes}$$

$$q = 1 - p = \text{the probability of a failure.}$$

The binomial formula is

$$\text{Probability of } r \text{ successes in } n \text{ trials} = \frac{n!}{r!\,(n-r)!}\, p^r q^{n-r} \tag{2-11}$$

The symbol ! means factorial, and $n! = n(n-1)(n-2)\ldots(1)$. For example,

$$4! = (4)(3)(2)(1) = 24$$

Also, $1! = 1$, and $0! = 1$ by definition.

TABLE 2.7		
Binomial Probability Distribution for $n = 5$ and $p = 0.50$	NUMBER OF HEADS (r)	Probability $= \dfrac{5!}{r!(5-r)!}(0.5)^r(0.5)^{5-r}$
	0	$0.03125 = \dfrac{5!}{0!(5-0)!}(0.5)^0(0.5)^{5-0}$
	1	$0.15625 = \dfrac{5!}{1!(5-1)!}(0.5)^1(0.5)^{5-1}$
	2	$0.31250 = \dfrac{5!}{2!(5-2)!}(0.5)^2(0.5)^{5-2}$
	3	$0.31250 = \dfrac{5!}{3!(5-3)!}(0.5)^3(0.5)^{5-3}$
	4	$0.15625 = \dfrac{5!}{4!(5-4)!}(0.5)^4(0.5)^{5-4}$
	5	$0.03125 = \dfrac{5!}{5!(5-5)!}(0.5)^5(0.5)^{5-5}$

Solving Problems with the Binomial Formula

A common example of a binomial distribution is the tossing of a coin and counting the number of heads. For example, if we wished to find the probability of 4 heads in 5 tosses of a coin, we would have

$$n = 5, r = 4, p = 0.5, \quad \text{and} \quad q = 1 - 0.5 = 0.5$$

Thus,

$$P = (4 \text{ successes in 5 trials}) = \frac{5!}{4!(5-4)!} 0.5^4 0.5^{5-4}$$

$$= \frac{5(4)(3)(2)(1)}{4(3)(2)(1)(1!)}(0.0625)(0.5) = 0.15625$$

Thus, the probability of 4 heads in 5 tosses of a coin is 0.15625 or about 16%.

Using Equation 2-11, it is also possible to find the entire probability distribution (all the possible values for r and the corresponding probabilities) for a binomial experiment. The probability distribution for the number of heads in 5 tosses of a fair coin is shown in Table 2.7 and then graphed in Figure 2.7. Appendix 2.2 illustrates how Excel can be used to find these probabilities.

Solving Problems with Binomial Tables

MSA Electronics is experimenting with the manufacture of a new type of transistor that is very difficult to mass produce at an acceptable quality level. Every hour a supervisor takes a

FIGURE 2.7	
Binomial Probability Distribution for $n = 5$ and $p = 0.50$	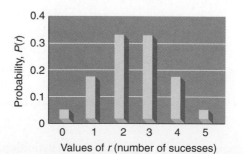

random sample of 5 transistors produced on the assembly line. The probability that any one transistor is defective is considered to be 0.15. MSA wants to know the probability of finding 3, 4, or 5 defectives if the true percentage defective is 15%.

For this problem, $n = 5$, $p = 0.15$, and $r = 3$, 4, or 5. Although we could use the formula for each of these values, it is easier to use binomial tables for this. Appendix B gives a binomial table for a broad range of values for n, r, and p. A portion of this appendix is shown in Table 2.8. To find these probabilities, we look through the $n = 5$ section and find the $p = 0.15$ column. In the row where $r = 3$, we see 0.0244. Thus, $P(r = 3) = 0.0244$. Similarly, $P(r = 4) = 0.0022$, and $P(r = 5) = 0.0001$. By adding these three probabilities we have the probability that the number of defects is 3 or more:

$$P(3 \text{ or more defects}) = P(3) + P(4) + P(5)$$

$$= 0.0244 + 0.0022 + 0.0001 = 0.0267$$

The expected value (or mean) and the variance of a binomial random variable may be easily found. These are

$$\text{Expected value (mean)} = np \qquad (2\text{-}12)$$

$$\text{Variance} = np(1 - p) \qquad (2\text{-}13)$$

TABLE 2.8   **A Sample Table for the Binomial Distribution**

						P					
n	r	0.05	0.10	0.15	0.20	0.25	0.30	0.35	0.40	0.45	0.50
1	0	0.9500	0.9000	0.8500	0.8000	0.7500	0.7000	0.6500	0.6000	0.5500	0.5000
	1	0.0500	0.1000	0.1500	0.2000	0.2500	0.3000	0.3500	0.4000	0.4500	0.5000
2	0	0.9025	0.8100	0.7225	0.6400	0.5625	0.4900	0.4225	0.3600	0.3025	0.2500
	1	0.0950	0.1800	0.2500	0.3200	0.3750	0.4200	0.4550	0.4800	0.4950	0.5000
	2	0.0025	0.0100	0.0225	0.0400	0.0625	0.0900	0.1225	0.1600	0.2025	0.2500
3	0	0.8574	0.7290	0.6141	0.5120	0.4219	0.3430	0.2746	0.2160	0.1664	0.1250
	1	0.1354	0.2430	0.3251	0.3840	0.4219	0.4410	0.4436	0.4320	0.4084	0.3750
	2	0.0071	0.0270	0.0574	0.0960	0.1406	0.1890	0.2389	0.2880	0.3341	0.3750
	3	0.0001	0.0010	0.0034	0.0080	0.0156	0.0270	0.0429	0.0640	0.0911	0.1250
4	0	0.8145	0.6561	0.5220	0.4096	0.3164	0.2401	0.1785	0.1296	0.0915	0.0625
	1	0.1715	0.2916	0.3685	0.4096	0.4219	0.4116	0.3845	0.3456	0.2995	0.2500
	2	0.0135	0.0486	0.0975	0.1536	0.2109	0.2646	0.3105	0.3456	0.3675	0.3750
	3	0.0005	0.0036	0.0115	0.0256	0.0469	0.0756	0.1115	0.1536	0.2005	0.2500
	4	0.0000	0.0001	0.0005	0.0016	0.0039	0.0081	0.0150	0.0256	0.0410	0.0625
5	0	0.7738	0.5905	0.4437	0.3277	0.2373	0.1681	0.1160	0.0778	0.0503	0.0313
	1	0.2036	0.3281	0.3915	0.4096	0.3955	0.3602	0.3124	0.2592	0.2059	0.1563
	2	0.0214	0.0729	0.1382	0.2048	0.2637	0.3087	0.3364	0.3456	0.3369	0.3125
	3	0.0011	0.0081	0.0244	0.0512	0.0879	0.1323	0.1811	0.2304	0.2757	0.3125
	4	0.0000	0.0005	0.0022	0.0064	0.0146	0.0284	0.0488	0.0768	0.1128	0.1563
	5	0.0000	0.0000	0.0001	0.0003	0.0010	0.0024	0.0053	0.0102	0.0185	0.0313
6	0	0.7351	0.5314	0.3771	0.2621	0.1780	0.1176	0.0754	0.0467	0.0277	0.0156
	1	0.2321	0.3543	0.3993	0.3932	0.3560	0.3025	0.2437	0.1866	0.1359	0.0938
	2	0.0305	0.0984	0.1762	0.2458	0.2966	0.3241	0.3280	0.3110	0.2780	0.2344
	3	0.0021	0.0146	0.0415	0.0819	0.1318	0.1852	0.2355	0.2765	0.3032	0.3125
	4	0.0001	0.0012	0.0055	0.0154	0.0330	0.0595	0.0951	0.1382	0.1861	0.2344
	5	0.0000	0.0001	0.0004	0.0015	0.0044	0.0102	0.0205	0.0369	0.0609	0.0938
	6	0.0000	0.0000	0.0000	0.0001	0.0002	0.0007	0.0018	0.0041	0.0083	0.0156

The expected value and variance for the MSA Electronics example are computed as follows:

$$\text{Expected value} = np = 5(0.15) = 0.75$$

$$\text{Variance} = np(1 - p) = 5(0.15)(0.85) = 0.6375$$

2.11   THE NORMAL DISTRIBUTION

The normal distribution affects a large number of processes in our lives (for example, filling boxes of cereal with 32 ounces of corn flakes). Each normal distribution depends on the mean and standard deviation.

One of the most popular and useful continuous probability distributions is the *normal distribution*. The probability density function of this distribution is given by the rather complex formula

$$f(X) = \frac{1}{\sigma\sqrt{2\pi}}\, e^{\frac{-(x-\mu)^2}{2\sigma^2}} \tag{2-14}$$

The normal distribution is specified completely when values for the mean, μ, and the standard deviation, σ, are known. Figure 2.8 shows several different normal distributions with the same standard deviation and different means. As shown, differing values of μ will shift the average or center of the normal distribution. The overall shape of the distribution remains the same. On the other hand, when the standard deviation is varied, the normal curve either flattens out or becomes steeper. This is shown in Figure 2.9.

As the standard deviation, σ, becomes smaller, the normal distribution becomes steeper. When the standard deviation becomes larger, the normal distribution has a tendency to flatten out or become broader.

Area Under the Normal Curve

Because the normal distribution is symmetrical, its midpoint (and highest point) is at the mean. Values on the X axis are then measured in terms of how many standard deviations they lie from the mean. As you may recall from our earlier discussion of probability distributions, the area under the curve (in a continuous distribution) describes the probability that a random variable has a value in a specified interval. When dealing with the uniform distribution, it is easy to compute the area between any points a and b. The normal distribution requires mathematical calculations beyond the scope of this book, but tables that

FIGURE 2.8

Normal Distribution with Different Values for μ

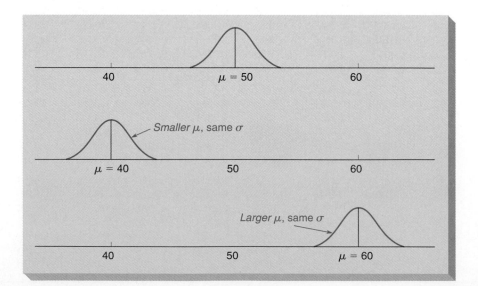

In 1857, most people traveling from California to New York sailed by steamer from San Francisco to the west coast of Panama, crossed the isthmus by train, and took a steamship to New York. The *Central America* operated on the Atlantic side of the Panama route, taking passengers and gold from California to New York. She sank 200 miles off the coast of South Carolina in a hurricane in 1857, taking gold bars and coins worth an estimated $400 million to the ocean bottom almost 8,000 feet below. Some 425 people lost their lives.

In 1985, Lawrence Stone was hired by the Columbus-America Discovery Group to develop a probability distribution map for the location of the *Central America*. The work was to be based on historical information from survivors and ships in the area at the time. The objective was to use the map to design an efficient search plan that would produce a high probability

of finding the target. It would provide specific directions for performing a search and serve as a basis for estimating the amount of time, effort, and money necessary to assure a high probability of success.

Stone's work first involved quantifying all relevant information. He then assigned each scenario a probability distribution and developed the "probability map" as the estimate of the wreck's location from each scenario.

The project was successful. In 1989, the group recovered 1 ton of gold bars and coins from the wreck. Some 39 insurance companies then filed claims to the recovered gold, but all claims were settled in favor of the Columbus-America Discovery Group.

Source: Lawrence D. Stone, "Search for the SS *Central America*," *Interfaces* 22, 1 (January–February 1992): 32–54.

provide areas or probabilities are readily available. For example, Figure 2.10 illustrates three commonly used relationships that have been derived from standard normal tables (to be discussed shortly). The area from point *a* to point *b* in the first drawing represents the probability, 68%, that the random variable will be within 1 standard deviation of the mean. In the middle graph, we see that about 95.4% of the area lies within plus or minus 2 standard deviations of the mean. The third figure shows that 99.7% lies between ±3σ.

95% confidence is actually ±1.96 standard deviations, whereas ±3 standard deviations is actually a 99.7% spread.

Translating Figure 2.10 into an application implies that if IQ in the United States is normally distributed with μ = 100 points, and standard deviation σ = 15 points, we can make the following statements:

1. 68% of the population have IQs between 85 and 115 points (namely, ±1σ).

2. 95.4% of the people have IQs between 70 and 130 points (±2σ).

3. 99.7% of the population have IQs in the range from 55 to 145 points (±3σ).

4. Only 16% of the people have IQs greater than 115 points (from first graph, the area to the right of +1σ).

Normal Distribution with Different Values for σ

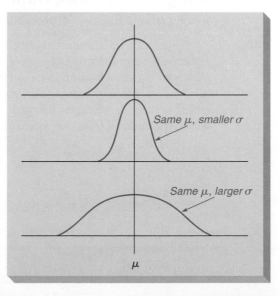

FIGURE 2.10

**Three Common Areas
Under Normal Curves**

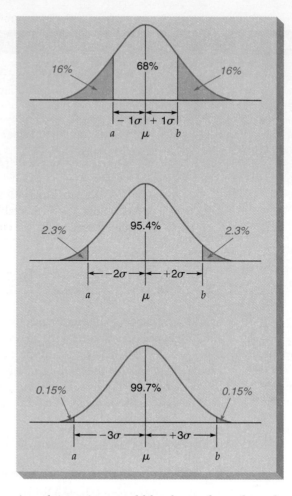

*Figure 2.10 is very important,
and you should comprehend
the meanings of ± 1, 2, and 3
standard deviation symmetrical areas.*

*Managers often speak of 95%
and 99% confidence intervals,
which roughly refer to ± 2 and
3 standard deviation graphs.*

Many more interesting observations could be drawn from these data. Can you tell the probability that a person selected at random has an IQ of less than 70? Greater than 145? Less than 130?

Using the Standard Normal Table

To use a table to find normal probability values, we follow two steps.

Step 1: Convert the normal distribution to what we call a *standard normal distribution.* A standard normal distribution is one that has a mean of 0 and a standard deviation of 1. All normal tables are set up to handle random variables with $\mu = 0$ and $\sigma = 1$. Without a standard normal distribution, a different table would be needed for each pair of μ and σ values. We call the new standard random variable Z. The value for Z for any normal distribution is computed from this equation:

$$Z = \frac{X - \mu}{\sigma}$$

(2-15)

where

X = value of the random variable we want to measure

μ = mean of the distribution

σ = standard deviation of the distribution

Z = number of standard deviations from X to the mean, μ.

For example, if $\mu = 100$, $\sigma = 15$, and we are interested in finding the probability that the random variable X is less than 130, we want $P(X < 130)$:

$$Z = \frac{X - \mu}{\sigma} = \frac{130 - 100}{15}$$

$$= \frac{30}{15} = 2 \text{ standard deviations}$$

This means that the point X is 2.0 standard deviations to the right of the mean. This is shown in Figure 2.11.

Step 2: Look up the probability from a table of normal curve areas. Table 2.9, which also appears as Appendix A, is such a table of areas for the standard normal distribution. It is set up to provide the area under the curve to the left of any specified value of Z.

Let's see how Table 2.9 can be used. The column on the left lists values of Z, with the second decimal place of Z appearing in the top row. For example, for a value of $Z = 2.00$ as just computed, find 2.0 in the left-hand column and 0.00 in the top row. In the body of the table, we find that the area sought is 0.97725, or 97.7%. Thus,

$$P(X < 130) = P(Z < 2.00) = 97.7\%.$$

To be sure you understand the concept of symmetry in Table 2.9, try to find the probability such as P(X < 85). Note that the standard normal table shows only positive Z values.

This suggests that if the mean IQ score is 100, with a standard deviation of 15 points, the probability that a randomly selected person's IQ is less than 130 is 97.7%. By referring back to Figure 2.10, we see that this probability could also have been derived from the middle graph. (Note that $1.0 - 0.977 = 0.023 = 2.3\%$, which is the area in the right-hand tail of the curve.)

To feel comfortable with the use of the standard normal probability table, we need to work a few more examples. We now use the Haynes Construction Company as a case in point.

FIGURE 2.11

Normal Distribution Showing the Relationship Between Z Values and X Values

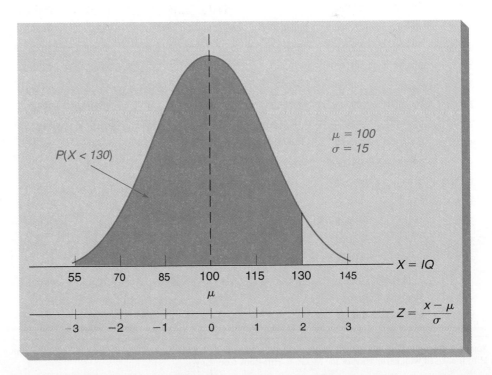

TABLE 2.9   Standardized Normal Distribution Function

| | | | | AREA UNDER THE NORMAL CURVE | | | | | |
Z	0.00	0.01	0.02	0.03	0.04	0.05	0.06	0.07	0.08	0.09
0.0	.50000	.50399	.50798	.51197	.51595	.51994	.52392	.52790	.53188	.53586
0.1	.53983	.54380	.54776	.55172	.55567	.55962	.56356	.56749	.57142	.57535
0.2	.57926	.58317	.58706	.59095	.59483	.59871	.60257	.60642	.61026	.61409
0.3	.61791	.62172	.62552	.62930	.63307	.63683	.64058	.64431	.64803	.65173
0.4	.65542	.65910	.66276	.66640	.67003	.67364	.67724	.68082	.68439	.68793
0.5	.69146	.69497	.69847	.70194	.70540	.70884	.71226	.71566	.71904	.72240
0.6	.72575	.72907	.73237	.73536	.73891	.74215	.74537	.74857	.75175	.75490
0.7	.75804	.76115	.76424	.76730	.77035	.77337	.77637	.77935	.78230	.78524
0.8	.78814	.79103	.79389	.79673	.79955	.80234	.80511	.80785	.81057	.81327
0.9	.81594	.81859	.82121	.82381	.82639	.82894	.83147	.83398	.83646	.83891
1.0	.84134	.84375	.84614	.84849	.85083	.85314	.85543	.85769	.85993	.86214
1.1	.86433	.86650	.86864	.87076	.87286	.87493	.87698	.87900	.88100	.88298
1.2	.88493	.88686	.88877	.89065	.89251	.89435	.89617	.89796	.89973	.90147
1.3	.90320	.90490	.90658	.90824	.90988	.91149	.91309	.91466	.91621	.91774
1.4	.91924	.92073	.92220	.92364	.92507	.92647	.92785	.92922	.93056	.93189
1.5	.93319	.93448	.93574	.93699	.93822	.93943	.94062	.94179	.94295	.94408
1.6	.94520	.94630	.94738	.94845	.94950	.95053	.95154	.95254	.95352	.95449
1.7	.95543	.95637	.95728	.95818	.95907	.95994	.96080	.96164	.96246	.96327
1.8	.96407	.96485	.96562	.96638	.96712	.96784	.96856	.96926	.96995	.97062
1.9	.97128	.97193	.97257	.97320	.97381	.97441	.97500	.97558	.97615	.97670
2.0	.97725	.97784	.97831	.97882	.97932	.97982	.98030	.98077	.98124	.98169
2.1	.98214	.98257	.98300	.98341	.98382	.98422	.98461	.98500	.98537	.98574
2.2	.98610	.98645	.98679	.98713	.98745	.98778	.98809	.98840	.98870	.98899
2.3	.98928	.98956	.98983	.99010	.99036	.99061	.99086	.99111	.99134	.99158
2.4	.99180	.99202	.99224	.99245	.99266	.99286	.99305	.99324	.99343	.99361
2.5	.99379	.99396	.99413	.99430	.99446	.99461	.99477	.99492	.99506	.99520
2.6	.99534	.99547	.99560	.99573	.99585	.99598	.99609	.99621	.99632	.99643
2.7	.99653	.99664	.99674	.99683	.99693	.99702	.99711	.99720	.99728	.99736
2.8	.99744	.99752	.99760	.99767	.99774	.99781	.99788	.99795	.99801	.99807
2.9	.99813	.99819	.99825	.99831	.99836	.99841	.99846	.99851	.99856	.99861
3.0	.99865	.99869	.99874	.99878	.99882	.99886	.99889	.99893	.99896	.99900
3.1	.99903	.99906	.99910	.99913	.99916	.99918	.99921	.99924	.99926	.99929
3.2	.99931	.99934	.99936	.99938	.99940	.99942	.99944	.99946	.99948	.99950
3.3	.99952	.99953	.99955	.99957	.99958	.99960	.99961	.99962	.99964	.99965
3.4	.99966	.99968	.99969	.99970	.99971	.99972	.99973	.99974	.99975	.99976
3.5	.99977	.99978	.99978	.99979	.99980	.99981	.99981	.99982	.99983	.99983
3.6	.99984	.99985	.99985	.99986	.99986	.99987	.99987	.99988	.99988	.99989
3.7	.99989	.99990	.99990	.99990	.99991	.99991	.99992	.99992	.99992	.99992
3.8	.99993	.99993	.99993	.99994	.99994	.99994	.99994	.99995	.99995	.99995
3.9	.99995	.99995	.99996	.99996	.99996	.99996	.99996	.99996	.99997	.99997

Source: Richard I. Levin and Charles A. Kirkpatrick. *Quantitative Approaches to Management*, 4th ed. Copyright © 1978, 1975, 1971, 1965 by McGraw-Hill, Inc. Used with permission of the McGraw-Hill Book Company.

Haynes Construction Company Example

Haynes Construction Company builds primarily three- and four-unit apartment buildings (called triplexes and quadraplexes) for investors, and it is believed that the total construction time in days follows a normal distribution. The mean time to construct a triplex is 100 days, and the standard deviation is 20 days. Recently, the president of Haynes Construction signed a contract to complete a triplex in 125 days. Failure to complete the triplex in 125 days would result in severe penalty fees. What is the probability that Haynes Construction will not be in violation of their construction contract? The normal distribution for the construction of triplexes is shown in Figure 2.12.

To compute this probability, we need to find the shaded area under the curve. We begin by computing Z for this problem:

$$Z = \frac{X - \mu}{\sigma}$$

$$= \frac{125 - 100}{20}$$

$$= \frac{25}{20} = 1.25$$

Looking in Table 2.9 for a Z value of 1.25, we find an area under the curve of 0.89435. (We do this by looking up 1.2 in the left-hand column of the table and then moving to the 0.05 column to find the value for $Z = 1.25$.) Therefore, the probability of not violating the contract is 0.89435, or about an 89% chance.

Now let us look at the Haynes problem from another perspective. If the firm finishes this triplex in 75 days or less, it will be awarded a bonus payment of $5,000. What is the probability that Haynes will receive the bonus?

Figure 2.13 illustrates the probability we are looking for in the shaded area. The first step is again to compute the Z value:

$$Z = \frac{X - \mu}{\sigma}$$

$$= \frac{75 - 100}{20}$$

$$= \frac{-25}{20} = -1.25$$

Normal Distribution for Haynes Construction

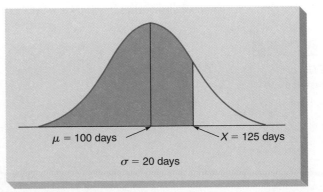

$\mu = 100$ days $X = 125$ days

$\sigma = 20$ days

FIGURE 2.13

Probability That Haynes Will Receive the Bonus by Finishing in 75 Days

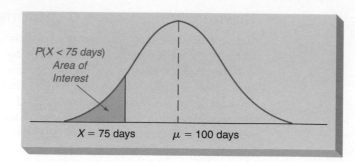

This *Z* value indicates that 75 days is −1.25 standard deviations to the left of the mean. But the standard normal table is structured to handle only positive *Z* values. To solve this problem, we observe that the curve is symmetric. The probability that Haynes will finish in *less than 75 days* is *equivalent* to the probability that it will finish in *more than 125 days*. A moment ago (in Figure 2.12) we found the probability that Haynes will finish in less than 125 days. That value is 0.89435. So the probability it takes more than 125 days is

$$P(X > 125) = 1.0 - P(X < 125)$$

$$= 1.0 - 0.89435 = 0.10565$$

Thus, the probability of completing the triplex in 75 days or less is 0.10565, or about 11%.

One final example: What is the probability that the triplex will take between 110 and 125 days? We see in Figure 2.14 that

$$P(110 < X < 125) = P(X < 125) - P(X < 110)$$

That is, the shaded area in the graph can be computed by finding the probability of completing the building in 125 days or less *minus* the probability of completing it in 110 days or less.

Recall that $P(X < 125\text{ days})$ is equal to 0.89435. To find $P(X < 110\text{ days})$, we follow the two steps developed earlier:

1.
$$Z = \frac{X - \mu}{\sigma} = \frac{110 - 100}{20} = \frac{10}{20}$$

$$= 0.5\text{ standard deviations}$$

2. From Table 2.9, the area for $Z = 0.50$ is 0.69146. So the probability the triplex can be completed in less than 110 days is 0.69146. Finally,

$$P(110 < X < 125) = 0.89435 - 0.69146 = 0.20289$$

The probability that it will take between 110 and 125 days is about 20%.

FIGURE 2.14

Probability of Haynes Completion Between 110 and 125 Days

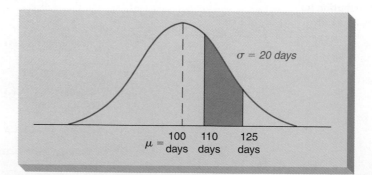

2.12 THE EXPONENTIAL DISTRIBUTION

The *exponential distribution*, also called the *negative exponential distribution*, is used in dealing with queuing problems. The exponential distribution often describes the time required to service a customer. The exponential distribution is a continuous distribution. Its probability function is given by

$$f(X) = \mu e^{-\mu x} \tag{2-16}$$

where

X = random variable (service times)

μ = average number of units the service facility can handle in a specific period of time

e = 2.718 (the base of natural logarithms)

The general shape of the exponential distribution is shown in Figure 2.15. Its expected value and variance can be shown to be

$$\text{expected value} = \frac{1}{\mu} = \text{ average service time} \tag{2-17}$$

$$\text{variance} = \frac{1}{\mu^2} \tag{2-18}$$

The exponential distribution is illustrated again in Chapter 14.

2.13 THE POISSON DISTRIBUTION

An important *discrete* probability distribution is the *Poisson distribution*.[1] We examine it because of its key role in complementing the exponential distribution in queuing theory in Chapter 14. The distribution describes situations in which customers arrive independently during a certain time interval, and the number of arrivals depends on the length of the time interval. Examples are patients arriving at a health clinic, customers arriving at a bank window, passengers arriving at an airport, and telephone calls going through a central exchange.

FIGURE 2.15

Negative Exponential Distribution

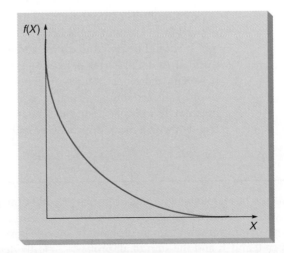

---

[1] This distribution, derived by Simeon Poisson in 1837, is pronounced "pwah-sahn."

FIGURE 2.16

**Sample Poisson
Distribution with $\lambda = 2$**

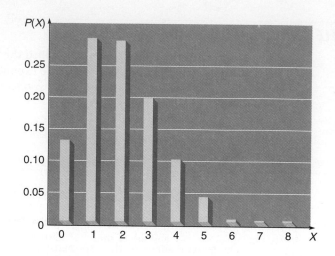

The formula for the Poisson distribution is

$$P(X) = \frac{\lambda^x e^{-\lambda}}{X!}$$

(2-19)

where

$P(X)$ = probability of exactly X arrivals or occurrences

λ = average number of arrivals per unit of time (the mean arrival rate), pronounced "lambda"

$e = 2.718$, the base of the natural logarithms

X = specific value (0, 1, 2, 3, and so on) of the random variable

The mean and variance of the Poisson distribution are equal and are computed simply as

$$\text{expected value} = \lambda$$

(2-20)

$$\text{variance} = \lambda$$

(2-21)

A sample distribution for $\lambda = 2$ arrivals is shown in Figure 2.16. (The values plotted are derived from tables in Appendix C.)

It should be noted that the exponential and Poisson distributions are related. If the number of occurrences per time period follows a Poisson distribution, then the time between occurrences follows an exponential distribution. For example, if the number of phone calls arriving at a customer service center followed a Poisson distribution with a mean of 10 calls per hour, the time between each phone call would be exponentially distributed with a mean time between calls of $\frac{1}{10}$ of an hour (six minutes).

SUMMARY

This chapter presents the fundamental concepts of probability and probability distributions. Probability values can be obtained objectively or subjectively. A single probability value must be between 0 and 1, and the sum of all probability values for all possible outcomes must be equal to 1. In addition, probability values and events can have a number of properties. These properties include mutually exclusive, collectively exhaustive, statistically independent, and statistically dependent events. Rules for computing probability values depend on these fundamental properties. It is also possible to revise probability values when new information becomes available. This can be done using Bayes' theorem.

We also covered the topics of random variables, discrete probability distributions (such as Poisson and binomial), and continuous probability distributions (such as normal and exponential). A probability distribution is any statement of a probability function having a set of collectively exhaustive

and mutually exclusive events. All probability distributions follow the basic probability rules mentioned previously.

The topics presented here will be very important in many of the chapters to come. Basic probability concepts and distributions are used for decision theory, inventory control, Markov analysis, project management, simulation, and statistical quality control.

GLOSSARY

Bayes' Theorem. A formula that is used to revise probabilities based on new information.

Bernoulli Process. A process with two outcomes in each of a series of independent trials in which the probabilities of the outcomes do not change.

Binomial Distribution. A discrete distribution that describes the number of successes in independent trials of a Bernoulli process.

Classical or Logical Approach. An objective way of assessing probabilities based on logic.

Collectively Exhaustive Events. A collection of all possible outcomes of an experiment.

Conditional Probability. The probability of one event occurring given that another has taken place.

Continuous Probability Distribution. A probability distribution with a continuous random variable.

Continuous Random Variable. A random variable that can assume an infinite or unlimited set of values.

Dependent Events. The situation in which the occurrence of one event affects the probability of occurrence of some other event.

Discrete Probability Distribution. A probability distribution with a discrete random variable.

Discrete Random Variable. A random variable that can only assume a finite or limited set of values.

Expected Value. The (weighted) average of a probability distribution.

Independent Events. The situation in which the occurrence of one event has no effect on the probability of occurrence of a second event.

Joint Probability. The probability of events occurring together (or one after the other).

Marginal Probability. The simple probability of an event occurring.

Mutually Exclusive Events. A situation in which only one event can occur on any given trial or experiment.

Negative Exponential Distribution. A continuous probability distribution that describes the time between customer arrivals in a queuing situation.

Normal Distribution. A continuous bell-shaped distribution that is a function of two parameters, the mean and standard deviation of the distribution.

Poisson Distribution. A discrete probability distribution used in queuing theory.

Prior Probability. A probability value determined before new or additional information is obtained. It is sometimes called an a priori probability estimate.

Probability. A statement about the likelihood of an event occurring. It is expressed as a numerical value between 0 and 1, inclusive.

Probability Density Function. The mathematical function that describes a continuous probability distribution. It is represented by $f(X)$.

Probability Distribution. The set of all possible values of a random variable and their associated probabilities.

Random Variable. A variable that assigns a number to every possible outcome of an experiment.

Relative Frequency Approach. An objective way of determining probabilities based on observing frequencies over a number of trials.

Revised or Posterior Probability. A probability value that results from new or revised information and prior probabilities.

Standard Deviation. The square root of the variance.

Subjective Approach. A method of determining probability values based on experience or judgment.

Variance. A measure of dispersion or spread of the probability distribution.

KEY EQUATIONS

(2-1) $0 \le P(\text{event}) \le 1$
A basic statement of probability.

(2-2) $P(A \text{ or } B) = P(A) + P(B)$
Law of addition for mutually exclusive events.

(2-3) $P(A \text{ or } B) = P(A) + P(B) - P(A \text{ and } B)$
Law of addition for events that are not mutually exclusive.

(2-4) $P(AB) = P(A) \times P(B)$
Joint probability for independent events.

(2-5) $P(A \mid B) = \dfrac{P(AB)}{P(B)}$

Conditional probability.

(2-6) $P(AB) = P(A \mid B) \times P(B)$

Joint probability for dependent events.

(2-7) $P(A \mid B) = \dfrac{P(B \mid A)P(A)}{P(B \mid A)P(A) + P(B \mid \overline{A})P(\overline{A})}$

Bayes' law in general form.

(2-8) $E(X) = \displaystyle\sum_{i=1}^{n} X_i P(X_i)$

This equation computes the expected value (mean) of a discrete probability distribution.

(2-9) $\sigma^2 = \text{Variance} = \displaystyle\sum_{i=1}^{n} [X_i - E(X)]^2 P(X_i)$

This equation computes the variance of a discrete probability distribution.

(2-10) $\sigma = \sqrt{\text{variance}} = \sqrt{\sigma^2}$

This equation computes the standard deviation from the variance.

(2-11) Probability of r successes in n trials $= \dfrac{n!}{r!(n-r)!} p^r q^{n-r}$

This formula computes probabilities for the binomial probability distribution.

(2-12) Expected value (mean) $= np$

The expected value of the binomial distribution.

(2-13) Variance $= np(1-p)$

The variance of the binomial distribution.

(2-14) $f(x) = \dfrac{1}{\sigma\sqrt{2\pi}} e^{\frac{-(x-\mu)^2}{2\sigma^2}}$

This is the density function for the normal probability distribution.

(2-15) $Z = \dfrac{X - \mu}{\sigma}$

This equation computes the number of standard deviations, Z, the point X is from the mean μ.

(2-16) $f(X) = \mu e^{-\mu x}$

The exponential distribution.

(2-17) Expected value $= \dfrac{1}{\mu}$

The expected value of an exponential distribution.

(2-18) Variance $= \dfrac{1}{\mu^2}$

The variance of an exponential distribution.

(2-19) $P(X) = \dfrac{\lambda^x e^{-\lambda}}{X!}$

The Poisson distribution.

(2-20) Expected value $= \lambda$

The mean of a Poisson distribution.

(2-21) Variance $= \lambda$

The variance of a Poisson distribution.

SOLVED PROBLEMS

Solved Problem 2-1

In the past 30 days, Roger's Rural Roundup has sold either 8, 9, 10, or 11 lottery tickets. It never sold fewer than 8 or more than 11. Assuming that the past is similar to the future, find the probabilities for the number of tickets sold if sales were 8 tickets on 10 days, 9 tickets on 12 days, 10 tickets on 6 days, and 11 tickets on 2 days.

Solution

SALES	NO. DAYS	PROBABILITY
8	10	0.333
9	12	0.400
10	6	0.200
11	2	0.067
Total	30	1.000

Solved Problem 2-2

A class contains 30 students. Ten are female (F) and U.S. citizens (U); 12 are male (M) and U.S. citizens; 6 are female and non-U.S. citizens (N); 2 are male and non-U.S. citizens.

A name is randomly selected from the class roster and it is female. What is the probability that the student is a U.S. citizen?

Solution

$$P(FU) = {}^{10}\!/_{30} = 0.333$$

$$P(FN) = {}^{6}\!/_{30} = 0.200$$

$$P(MU) = {}^{12}\!/_{30} = 0.400$$

$$P(MN) = {}^{2}\!/_{30} = 0.067$$

$$P(F) = P(FU) + P(FN) = 0.333 + 0.200 = 0.533$$

$$P(M) = P(MU) + P(MN) = 0.400 + 0.067 = 0.467$$

$$P(U) = P(FU) + P(MU) = 0.333 + 0.400 = 0.733$$

$$P(N) = P(FN) + P(MN) = 0.200 + 0.067 = 0.267$$

$$P(U \mid F) = \frac{P(FU)}{P(F)} = \frac{0.333}{0.533} = 0.625$$

Solved Problem 2-3

Your professor tells you that if you score an 85 or better on your midterm exam, then you have a 90% chance of getting an A for the course. You think you have only a 50% chance of scoring 85 or better. Find the probability that *both* your score is 85 or better *and* you receive an A in the course.

Solution

$$P(A \text{ and } 85) = P(A \mid 85) \times P(85) = (0.90)(0.50)$$

$$= 45\%$$

Solved Problem 2-4

A statistics class was asked if it believed that all tests on the Monday following the football game win over their archrival should be postponed automatically. The results were as follows:

Strongly agree	40
Agree	30
Neutral	20
Disagree	10
Strongly disagree	0
	100

Transform this into a numeric score, using the following random variable scale, and find a probability distribution for the results.

Strongly agree	5
Agree	4
Neutral	3
Disagree	2
Strongly disagree	1

Solution

OUTCOME	PROBABILITY, $P(X)$
Strongly agree (5)	$0.4 = 40/100$
Agree (4)	$0.3 = 30/100$
Neutral (3)	$0.2 = 20/100$
Disagree (2)	$0.1 = 10/100$
Strongly disagree (1)	$0.0 = 0/100$
Total	$1.0 = 100/100$

Solved Problem 2-5

For Solved Problem 2-4, let X be the numeric score. Compute the expected value of X.

Solution

$$E(X) = \sum_{i=1}^{5} X_i P(X_i) = X_1 P(X_1) + X_2 P(X_2)$$
$$+ X_3 P(X_3) + X_4 P(X_4) + X_5 P(X_5)$$
$$= 5(0.4) + 4(0.3) + 3(0.2) + 2(0.1) + 1(0)$$
$$= 4.0$$

Solved Problem 2-6

Compute the variance and standard deviation for the random variable X in Solved Problems 2-4 and 2-5.

Solution

$$\text{Variance} = \sum_{i=1}^{5} (x_i - E(x))^2 P(x_i)$$
$$= (5-4)^2(0.4) + (4-4)^2(0.3) + (3-4)^2(0.2) + (2-4)^2(0.1) + (1-4)^2(0.0)$$
$$= (1)^2(0.4) + (0)^2(0.3) + (-1)^2(0.2) + (-2)^2(0.1) + (-3)^2(0.0)$$
$$= 0.4 + 0.0 + 0.2 + 0.4 + 0.0 = 1.0$$

The standard deviation is

$$\sigma = \sqrt{\text{variance}} = \sqrt{1} = 1$$

Solved Problem 2-7

A candidate for public office has claimed that 60% of voters will vote for her. If 5 registered voters were sampled, what is the probability that exactly 3 would say they favor this candidate?

Solution

We use the binomial distribution with $n = 5$, $p = 0.6$, and $r = 3$.

$$P(\text{exactly 3 successes in 5 trials}) = \frac{n!}{r!(n-r)!} p^r q^{n-r} = \frac{5!}{3!(5-3)!}(0.6)^3(0.4)^{5-3} = 0.3456$$

Solved Problem 2-8

The length of the rods coming out of our new cutting machine can be said to approximate a normal distribution with a mean of 10 inches and a standard deviation of 0.2 inch. Find the probability that a rod selected randomly will have a length

a. of less than 10.0 inches.
b. between 10.0 and 10.4 inches.
c. between 10.0 and 10.1 inches.
d. between 10.1 and 10.4 inches.
e. between 9.6 and 9.9 inches.
f. between 9.9 and 10.4 inches.
g. between 9.886 and 10.406 inches.

Solution

First compute the standard normal distribution, the Z-value:

$$Z = \frac{X - \mu}{\sigma}$$

Next, find the area under the curve for the given Z-value by using a standard normal distribution table.

a. $P(X < 10.0) = 0.50000$
b. $P(10.0 < X < 10.4) = 0.97725 - 0.50000 = 0.47725$
c. $P(10.0 < X < 10.1) = 0.69146 - 0.50000 = 0.19146$
d. $P(10.1 < X < 10.4) = 0.97725 - 0.69146 = 0.28579$
e. $P(9.6 < X < 9.9) = 0.97725 - 0.69146 = 0.28579$
f. $P(9.9 < X < 10.4) = 0.19146 + 0.47725 = 0.66871$
g. $P(9.886 < X < 10.406) = 0.47882 + 0.21566 = 0.69448$

⇢ SELF-TEST

■ Before taking the self-test, refer back to the learning objectives at the beginning of the supplement and the glossary at the end of the chapter.

■ Use the key at the back of the book to correct your answers.

■ Restudy pages that correspond to any questions that you answered incorrectly or material you feel uncertain about.

1. If only one event may occur on any one trial, then the events are said to be
   a. independent.
   b. exhaustive.
   c. mutually exclusive.
   d. continuous.

2. New probabilities that have been found using Bayes' theorem are called
   a. prior probabilities.
   b. posterior probabilities.
   c. Bayesian probabilities.
   d. joint probabilities.

3. A measure of central tendency is
   a. expected value.
   b. variance.
   c. standard deviation.
   d. all of the above.

4. To compute the variance, you need to know the
   a. variable's possible values.
   b. expected value of the variable.
   c. probability of each possible value of the variable.
   d. all of the above.

5. The square root of the variance is the
   a. expected value.
   b. standard deviation.
   c. area under the normal curve.
   d. all of the above.

6. Which of the following is an example of a discrete distribution?
   a. the normal distribution
   b. the exponential distribution
   c. the Poisson distribution
   d. the Z-distribution

7. The total area under the curve for any continuous distribution must equal
   a. 1.
   b. 0.
   c. 0.5.
   d. none of the above.

8. Probabilities for all the possible values of a discrete random variable
   a. may be greater than 1.
   b. may be negative on some occasions.
   c. must sum to 1.
   d. are represented by area underneath the curve.

9. In a standard normal distribution, the mean is equal to
   a. 1.
   b. 0.
   c. the variance.
   d. the standard deviation.

10. The probability of two or more independent events occurring is the
    a. marginal probability.
    b. simple probability.
    c. conditional probability.
    d. joint probability.
    e. all of the above.

11. In the normal distribution, 95.45% of the population lies within
    a. 1 standard deviation of the mean.
    b. 2 standard deviations of the mean.
    c. 3 standard deviations of the mean.
    d. 4 standard deviations of the mean.

12. If a normal distribution has a mean of 200 and a standard deviation of 10, 99.7% of the population falls within what range of values?
    a. 170−230
    b. 180−220
    c. 190−210
    d. 175−225
    e. 170−220

13. If two events are mutually exclusive, then the probability of the intersection of these two events will equal
    a. 0.
    b. 0.5.
    c. 1.0.
    d. cannot be determined without more information.

14. If $P(A) = 0.4$ and $P(B) = 0.5$ and $P(A \text{ and } B) = 0.2$, then $P(B \mid A) =$
    a. 0.80.
    b. 0.50.
    c. 0.10
    d. 0.40.
    e. none of the above.

15. If $P(A) = 0.4$ and $P(B) = 0.5$ and $P(A \text{ and } B) = 0.2$, then $P(A \text{ or } B) =$
    a. 0.7.
    b. 0.9.
    c. 1.1.
    d. 0.2.
    e. none of the above.

DISCUSSION QUESTIONS AND PROBLEMS

Discussion Questions

2-1 What are the two basic laws of probability?

2-2 What is the meaning of mutually exclusive events? What is meant by collectively exhaustive? Give an example of each.

2-3 Describe the various approaches used in determining probability values.

2-4 Why is the probability of the intersection of two events subtracted in the sum of the probability of two events?

2-5 What is the difference between events that are dependent and events that are independent?

2-6 What is Bayes' theorem, and when can it be used?

2-7 Describe the characteristics of a Bernoulli process. How is a Bernoulli process associated with the binomial distribution?

2-8 What is a random variable? What are the various types of random variables?

2-9 What is the difference between a discrete probability distribution and a continuous probability distribution? Give your own example of each.

2-10 What is the expected value, and what does it measure? How is it computed for a discrete probability distribution?

2-11 What is the variance, and what does it measure? How is it computed for a discrete probability distribution?

2-12 Name three business processes that can be described by the normal distribution.

2-13 After evaluating student response to a question about a case used in class, the instructor constructed the following probability distribution. What kind of probability distribution is it?

RESPONSE	RANDOM VARIABLE, X	PROBABILITY
Excellent	5	0.05
Good	4	0.25
Average	3	0.40
Fair	2	0.15
Poor	1	0.15

Problems*

2-14 A student taking Management Science 301 at East Haven University will receive one of the five possible grades for the course: A, B, C, D, or F. The distribution of grades over the past two years is as follows:

GRADE	NUMBER OF STUDENTS
A	80
B	75
C	90
D	30
F	25
	Total 300

If this past distribution is a good indicator of future grades, what is the probability of a student receiving a C in the course?

2-15 A silver dollar is flipped twice. Calculate the probability of each of the following occurring:
(a) a head on the first flip
(b) a tail on the second flip given that the first toss was a head
(c) two tails
(d) a tail on the first and a head on the second
(e) a tail on the first and a head on the second or a head on the first and a tail on the second
(f) at least one head on the two flips

2-16 An urn contains 8 red chips, 10 green chips, and 2 white chips. A chip is drawn and replaced, and then a second chip drawn. What is the probability of
(a) a white chip on the first draw?
(b) a white chip on the first draw and a red on the second?
(c) two green chips being drawn?
(d) a red chip on the second, given that a white chip was drawn on the first?

2-17 Evertight, a leading manufacturer of quality nails, produces 1-, 2-, 3-, 4-, and 5-inch nails for various uses. In the production process, if there is an overrun or the nails are slightly defective, they are placed in a common bin. Yesterday, 651 of the 1-inch nails, 243 of the 2-inch nails, 41 of the 3-inch nails, 451 of the 4-inch nails, and 333 of the 5-inch nails were placed in the bin.
(a) What is the probability of reaching into the bin and getting a 4-inch nail?
(b) What is the probability of getting a 5-inch nail?
(c) If a particular application requires a nail that is 3 inches or shorter, what is the probability of getting a nail that will satisfy the requirements of the application?

2-18 Last year, at Northern Manufacturing Company, 200 people had colds during the year. One hundred fifty-five people who did no exercising had colds, and the remainder of the people with colds were involved in a

---

* Note: ✖ means the problem may be solved with Excel using the Basic Statistics Functions described in Appendix 2.2.

weekly exercise program. Half of the 1,000 employees were involved in some type of exercise.

(a) What is the probability that an employee will have a cold next year?

(b) Given that an employee is involved in an exercise program, what is the probability that he or she will get a cold next year?

(c) What is the probability that an employee who is not involved in an exercise program will get a cold next year?

(d) Are exercising and getting a cold independent events? Explain your answer.

2-19 The Springfield Kings, a professional basketball team, has won 12 of its last 20 games and is expected to continue winning at the same percentage rate. The team's ticket manager is anxious to attract a large crowd to tomorrow's game but believes that depends on how well the Kings perform tonight against the Galveston Comets. He assesses the probability of drawing a large crowd to be 0.90 should the team win tonight. What is the probability that the team wins tonight and that there will be a large crowd at tomorrow's game?

2-20 David Mashley teaches two undergraduate statistics courses at Kansas College. The class for Statistics 201 consists of 7 sophomores and 3 juniors. The more advanced course, Statistics 301, has 2 sophomores and 8 juniors enrolled. As an example of a business sampling technique, Professor Mashley randomly selects, from the stack of Statistics 201 registration cards, the class card of one student and then places that card back in the stack. If that student was a sophomore, Mashley draws another card from the Statistics 201 stack; if not, he randomly draws a card from the Statistics 301 group. Are these two draws independent events? What is the probability of

(a) a junior's name on the first draw?

(b) a junior's name on the second draw, given that a sophomore's name was drawn first?

(c) a junior's name on the second draw, given that a junior's name was drawn first?

(d) a sophomore's name on both draws?

(e) a junior's name on both draws?

(f) one sophomore's name and one junior's name on the two draws, regardless of order drawn?

2-21 The oasis outpost of Abu Ilan, in the heart of the Negev desert, has a population of 20 Bedouin tribesmen and 20 Farima tribesmen. El Kamin, a nearby oasis, has a population of 32 Bedouins and 8 Farima. A lost Israeli soldier, accidentally separated from his army unit, is wandering through the desert and arrives at the edge of one of the oases. The soldier has no idea which oasis he has found, but the first person he spots at a distance is a Bedouin. What is the probability that he wandered into Abu Ilan? What is the probability that he is in El Kamin?

2-22 The lost Israeli soldier mentioned in Problem 2-21 decides to rest for a few minutes before entering the desert oasis he has just found. Closing his eyes, he dozes off for 15 minutes, wakes, and walks toward the center of the oasis. The first person he spots this time he again recognizes as a Bedouin. What is the posterior probability that he is in El Kamin?

2-23 Ace Machine Works estimates that the probability its lathe tool is properly adjusted is 0.8. When the lathe is properly adjusted, there is a 0.9 probability that the parts produced pass inspection. If the lathe is out of adjustment, however, the probability of a good part being produced is only 0.2. A part randomly chosen is inspected and found to be acceptable. At this point, what is the posterior probability that the lathe tool is properly adjusted?

2-24 The Boston South Fifth Street Softball League consists of three teams: Mama's Boys, team 1; the Killers, team 2; and the Machos, team 3. Each team plays the other teams just once during the season. The win−loss record for the past five years is as follows:

WINNER	(1)	(2)	(3)
Mama's Boys (1)	X	3	4
The Killers (2)	2	X	1
The Machos (3)	1	4	X

Each row represents the number of wins over the past five years. Mama's Boys beat the Killers 3 times, beat the Machos 4 times, and so on.

(a) What is the probability that the Killers will win every game next year?

(b) What is the probability that the Machos will win at least one game next year?

(c) What is the probability that Mama's Boys will win exactly one game next year?

(d) What is the probability that the Killers will win less than two games next year?

2-25 The schedule for the Killers next year is as follows (refer to Problem 2-24):

Game 1: The Machos

Game 2: Mama's Boys

(a) What is the probability that the Killers will win their first game?

(b) What is the probability that the Killers will win their last game?

(c) What is the probability that the Killers will break even—win exactly one game?

(d) What is the probability that the Killers will win every game?

(e) What is the probability that the Killers will lose every game?

(f) Would you want to be the coach of the Killers?

2-26 The Northside Rifle team has two markspersons, Dick and Sally. Dick hits a bull's-eye 90% of the time, and Sally hits a bull's-eye 95% of the time.

(a) What is the probability that either Dick or Sally or both will hit the bull's-eye if each takes one shot?

(b) What is the probability that Dick and Sally will both hit the bull's-eye?

(c) Did you make any assumptions in answering the preceding questions? If you answered yes, do you think that you are justified in making the assumption(s)?

2-27 In a sample of 1,000 representing a survey from the entire population, 650 people were from Laketown, and the rest of the people were from River City. Out of the sample, 19 people had some form of cancer. Thirteen of these people were from Laketown.

(a) Are the events of living in Laketown and having some sort of cancer independent?

(b) Which city would you prefer to live in, assuming that your main objective was to avoid having cancer?

2-28 Compute the probability of "loaded die, given that a 3 was rolled," as shown in Example 7, this time using the general form of Bayes' theorem from Equation 2-7.

2-29 Which of the following are probability distributions? Why?

(a)

RANDOM VARIABLE X	PROBABILITY
−2	0.1
−1	0.2
0	0.3
1	0.25
2	0.15

(b)

RANDOM VARIABLE Y	PROBABILITY
1	1.1
1.5	0.2
2	0.3
2.5	0.25
3	−1.25

(c)

RANDOM VARIABLE Z	PROBABILITY
1	0.1
2	0.2
3	0.3
4	0.4
5	0.0

2-30 Harrington Health Food stocks 5 loaves of Neutro-Bread. The probability distribution for the sales of Neutro-Bread is listed in the following table. How many loaves will Harrington sell on average?

NUMBER OF LOAVES SOLD	PROBABILITY
0	0.05
1	0.15
2	0.20
3	0.25
4	0.20
5	0.15

2-31 What are the expected value and variance of the following probability distribution?

RANDOM VARIABLE X	PROBABILITY
1	0.05
2	0.05
3	0.10
4	0.10
5	0.15
6	0.15
7	0.25
8	0.15

2-32 There are 10 questions on a true-false test. A student feels unprepared for this test and randomly guesses the answer for each of these.

(a) What is the probability that the student gets exactly 7 correct?

(b) What is the probability that the student gets exactly 8 correct?

(c) What is the probability that the student gets exactly 9 correct?

(d) What is the probability that the student gets exactly 10 correct?

(e) What is the probability that the student gets more than 6 correct?

2-33 Gary Schwartz is the top salesman for his company. Records indicate that he makes a sale on 70% of his sales calls. If he calls on four potential clients, what is the probability that he makes exactly 3 sales? What is the probability that he makes exactly 4 sales?

2-34 If 10% of all disk drives produced on an assembly line are defective, what is the probability that there will be exactly one defect in a random sample of 5 of these? What is the probability that there will be no defects in a random sample of 5?

2-35 Trowbridge Manufacturing produces cases for personal computers and other electronic equipment. The quality control inspector for this company believes that a particular process is out of control. Normally, only 5 percent of all cases are deemed defective due to discolorations. If 6 such cases are sampled, what is the probability that there will be no defective cases if the process is operating correctly? What is the probability that there will be exactly one defective case?

2-36 Refer to the Trowbridge Manufacturing example in Problem 2-35. The quality control inspection procedure is to select 6 items, and if there are 0 or 1 defective cases in the group of 6, the process is said to be in control. If the number of defects is more than 1, the process is out of control. Suppose that the true proportion of defective items is 0.15. What is the probability that there will be 0 or 1 defects in a sample of 6 if the true proportion of defects is 0.15?

2-37 An industrial oven used to cure sand cores for a factory manufacturing engine blocks for small cars is able to maintain fairly constant temperatures. The temperature range of the oven follows a normal distribution with a mean of 450°F and a standard deviation of 25°F. Leslie Larsen, president of the factory, is concerned about the large number of defective cores that have been produced in the past several months. If the oven gets hotter than 475°F, the core is defective. What is the probability that the oven will cause a core to be defective? What is the probability that the temperature of the oven will range from 460° to 470°F?

2-38 Steve Goodman, production foreman for the Florida Gold Fruit Company, estimates that the average sale of oranges is 4,700 and the standard deviation is 500 oranges. Sales follow a normal distribution.

(a) What is the probability that sales will be greater than 5,500 oranges?
(b) What is the probability that sales will be greater than 4,500 oranges?
(c) What is the probability that sales will be less than 4,900 oranges?
(d) What is the probability that sales will be less than 4,300 oranges?

2-39 Susan Williams has been the production manager of Medical Suppliers, Inc., for the past 17 years. Medical Suppliers, Inc., is a producer of bandages and arm slings. During the past 5 years, the demand for No-Stick bandages has been fairly constant. On the average, sales have been about 87,000 packages of No-Stick. Susan has reason to believe that the distribution of No-Stick follows a normal curve, with a standard deviation of 4,000 packages. What is the probability that sales will be less than 81,000 packages?

2-40 Armstrong Faber produces a standard number-two pencil called Ultra-Lite. Since Chuck Armstrong started Armstrong Faber, sales have grown steadily. With the increase in the price of wood products, however, Chuck has been forced to increase the price of the Ultra-Lite pencils. As a result, the demand for Ultra-Lite has been fairly stable over the past 6 years. On the average, Armstrong Faber has sold 457,000 pencils each year. Furthermore, 90% of the time sales have been between 454,000 and 460,000 pencils. It is expected that the sales follow a normal distribution with a mean of 457,000 pencils. Estimate the standard deviation of this distribution. (*Hint:* Work backward from the normal table to find *Z*. Then apply Equation 2-15.)

2-41 The time to complete a construction project is normally distributed with a mean of 60 weeks and a standard deviation of 4 weeks.

(a) What is the probability the project will be finished in 62 weeks or less?
(b) What is the probability the project will be finished in 66 weeks or less?
(c) What is the probability the project will take longer than 65 weeks?

2-42 A new integrated computer system is to be installed worldwide for a major corporation. Bids on this project are being solicited, and the contract will be awarded to one of the bidders. As a part of the proposal for this project, bidders must specify how long the project will take. There will be a significant

penalty for finishing late. One potential contractor determines that the average time to complete a project of this type is 40 weeks with a standard deviation of 5 weeks. The time required to complete this project is assumed to be normally distributed.

(a) If the due date of this project is set at 40 weeks, what is the probability that the contractor will have to pay a penalty (i.e., the project will not be finished on schedule)?
(b) If the due date of this project is set at 43 weeks, what is the probability that the contractor will have to pay a penalty (i.e., the project will not be finished on schedule)?
(c) If the bidder wishes to set the due date in the proposal so that there is only a 5% chance of being late (and consequently only a 5% chance of having to pay a penalty), what due date should be set?

2-43 Patients arrive at the emergency room of Costa Valley Hospital at an average of 5 per day. The demand for emergency room treatment at Costa Valley follows a Poisson distribution.

(a) Using Appendix C, compute the probability of exactly 0, 1, 2, 3, 4, and 5 arrivals per day.
(b) What is the sum of these probabilities, and why is the number less than 1?

2-44 Using the data in Problem 2-43, determine the probability of more than 3 visits for emergency room service on any given day.

2-45 Cars arrive at Carla's Muffler shop for repair work at an average of 3 per hour, following an exponential distribution.

(a) What is the expected time between arrivals?
(b) What is the variance of the time between arrivals?

2-46 A particular test for the presence of steroids is to be used after a professional track meet. If steroids are present, the test will accurately indicate this 95% of the time. However, if steroids are not present, the test will indicate this 90% of the time (so it is wrong 10% of the time and predicts the presence of steroids). Based on past data, it is believed that 2% of the athletes do use steroids. This test is administered to one athlete, and the test is positive for steroids. What is the probability that this person actually used steroids?

2-47 Market Researchers, Inc. has been hired to perform a study to determine if the market for a new product will be good or poor. In similar studies performed in the past, whenever the market actually was good, the market research study indicated that it would be good 85% of the time. On the other hand, whenever the market actually was poor, the market study incorrectly predicted it would be good 20% of the time. Before the study is performed, it is believed there is a 70% chance the market will be good. When Market Researchers, Inc. performs the study for this product, the results predict the market will be good. Given the results of this study, what is the probability that the market actually will be good?

2-48 Policy Pollsters is a market research firm specializing in political polls. Records indicate in past elections, when a candidate was elected, Policy Pollsters had accurately predicted this 80 percent of the time and they were wrong 20% of the time. Records also show for losing candidates, Policy Pollsters accurately predicted they would lose 90 percent of the time and they were only wrong 10% of the time. Before the poll is taken, there is a 50% chance of winning the election. If Policy Pollsters predicts a candidate will win the election, what is the probability that the candidate will actually win? If Policy Pollsters predicts that a candidate will lose the election, what is the probability that the candidate will actually lose?

2-49 Burger City is a large chain of fast-food restaurants specializing in gourmet hamburgers. A mathematical model is now used to predict the success of new restaurants based on location and demographic information for that area. In the past, 70% of all restaurants that were opened were successful. The mathematical model has been tested in the existing restaurants to determine how effective it is. For the restaurants that were successful, 90% of the time the model predicted they would be, while 10% of the time the model predicted a failure. For the restaurants that were not successful, when the mathematical model was applied, 20% of the time it incorrectly predicted a successful restaurant while 80% of the time it was accurate and predicted an unsuccessful restaurant. If the model is used on a new location and predicts the restaurant will be successful, what is the probability that it actually is successful?

INTERNET HOMEWORK PROBLEMS

See our Internet home page at **www.prenhall.com/render** for additional homework problems 2-50 to 2-57.

⫸ CASE STUDY

Century Chemical Company

Century Chemical Company, formed in 1975 as a result of the merger of three smaller firms, produces chlorine and caustic soda through the electrolysis of brine. Century's largest plant, located in St. Gabriel, Louisiana, produces approximately 1,500 tons of chlorine and 1,700 tons of caustic soda daily. The St. Gabriel plant operates at capacity; its entire output is sold.

A major problem confronting Century Chemical Company is associated with its chlorine collection and handling system. The system incorporates headers that collect chlorine gas from the electrolytic cells. The gas then passes through heat exchangers for cooling and condensation of water entrapped in the chlorine. Residual water in the chlorine gas is removed by "scrubbing" with concentrated sulfuric acid. Thereafter, the dry chlorine gas is chilled by being bubbled through liquid chlorine before being fed to the chlorine compressor. The chlorine compressor is the "heart" of the handling system. It pulls the gas from the cells through the cooling and drying system. Then it compresses the gas for liquefaction and storage as liquid chlorine.

A major problem for the production manager of Century Chemical is the gradual deterioration of the plant's compressor capacity because of the fouling of component parts. The reliability of Century's centrifugal compressor at its St. Gabriel complex is 0.92. The 8% downtime includes cleaning and restoration of capacity as well as other mechanical/electrical failures. Heretofore, management at Century has chosen to incur the downtime and lost sales associated with compressor failures. However, from time to time, management considers the installation of a spare compressor. Currently, the cost of such an installation is estimated to total $800,000. The spare compressor is also projected to have a 0.92 reliability factor.

Approximately 12 hours of downtime are required to change over to an installed spare compressor. Profit and overhead contribution for chlorine is estimated at $50 per ton; the profit and overhead contribution for caustic soda is $40 per ton. Century's cost of capital or opportunity cost is estimated to equal 20%. The useful life of the compressor is estimated to be 10 years. Salvage is assumed to be zero. The effective tax rate is 40%.

Discussion Question

Should management of Century Chemical install the spare compressor? Why or why not? (*Hint:* The present value factor of 20% over 10 years is 4.192.)

Source: Professor Jerry Kinard, Western Carolina University.

⇒ CASE STUDY

WTVX

WTVX, Channel 6, is located in Eugene, Oregon, home of the University of Oregon's football team. The station was owned and operated by George Wilcox, a former Duck (University of Oregon football player). Although there were other television stations in Eugene, WTVX was the only station that had a weatherperson who was a member of the American Meteorological Society (AMS). Every night, Joe Hummel would be introduced as the only weatherperson in Eugene who was a member of the AMS. This was George's idea, and he believed that this gave his station the mark of quality and helped with market share.

In addition to being a member of AMS, Joe was also the most popular person on any of the local news programs. Joe was always trying to find innovative ways to make the weather interesting, and this was especially difficult during the winter months when the weather seemed to remain the same over long periods of time. Joe's forecast for next month, for example, was that there would be a 70% chance of rain *every* day, and that what happens on one day (rain or shine) was not in any way dependent on what happened the day before.

One of Joe's most popular features of the weather report was to invite questions during the actual broadcast. Questions would be phoned in, and they were answered on the spot by Joe. Once a ten-year-old boy asked what caused fog, and Joe did an excellent job of describing some of the various causes.

Occasionally, Joe would make a mistake. For example, a high school senior asked Joe what the chances were of getting 15 days of rain in the next month (30 days). Joe made a quick calculation: (70%) × (15 days/30 days) = (70%)(½)= 35%. Joe quickly found out what it was like being wrong in a university town. He had over 50 phone calls from scientists, mathematicians, and other university professors, telling him that he had made a big mistake in computing the chances of getting 15 days of rain during the next 30 days. Although Joe didn't understand all of the formulas the professors mentioned, he was determined to find the correct answer and make a correction during a future broadcast.

Discussion Questions

1. What are the chances of getting 15 days of rain during the next 30 days?
2. What do you think about Joe's assumptions concerning the weather for the next 30 days?

BIBLIOGRAPHY

Berenson, Mark, David Levine, and Timothy Krehbiel. *Basic Business Statistics*, 8/e. Upper Saddle River, NJ: Prentice Hall, 2002.

Campbell, S. *Flaws and Fallacies in Statistical Thinking*. Upper Saddle River, NJ: Prentice Hall, 1974.

Feller, W. *An Introduction to Probability Theory and Its Applications*, Vols. 1 and 2. New York: John Wiley & Sons, Inc., 1957 and 1968.

Hanke, J. E., A. G. Reitsch, and D. W. Wichern. *Business Forecasting*, 7th ed. Upper Saddle River, NJ: Prentice Hall, 2001.

Huff, D. *How to Lie with Statistics*. New York: W. W. Norton & Company, Inc., 1954.

Newbold, Paul, William Carlson, and Betty Thorne. *Statistics for Business and Economics*, 5/e. Upper Saddle River, NJ: Prentice Hall, 2002.

Shannon, Patrick, David Groebner, Phillip Fry, and Kent Smith. *A Course in Business Statistics*, 3/e. Upper Saddle River, NJ: Prentice Hall, 2002.

APPENDIX 2.1: DERIVATION OF BAYES' THEOREM

We know that the following formulas are correct:

$$P(A \mid B) = \frac{P(AB)}{P(B)} \tag{1}$$

$$P(B \mid A) = \frac{P(AB)}{P(A)}$$

[which can be rewritten as $P(AB) = P(B \mid A)P(A)$] and $\tag{2}$

$$P(B \mid \overline{A}) = \frac{P(\overline{A}B)}{P(\overline{A})}$$

[which can be rewritten as $P(\overline{A}B) = P(B \mid \overline{A})P(\overline{A})$]. $\tag{3}$

Furthermore, by definition, we know that

$$P(B) = P(AB) + P(\overline{A}B)$$

$$= P(B \mid A)P(A) + P(B \mid \overline{A})P(\overline{A}) \qquad (4)$$

from (2)   from (3)

Substituting Equations 2 and 4 into Equation 1, we have

$$P(A \mid B) = \frac{P(AB)}{P(B)}$$

from (2)

$$= \frac{P(B \mid A)P(A)}{P(B \mid A)P(A) + P(B \mid \overline{A})P(\overline{A})} \qquad (5)$$

from (4)

This is the general form of Bayes' theorem, shown as Equation 2-7 in this chapter.

APPENDIX 2.2: BASIC STATISTICS USING EXCEL

Statistical Functions

Many statistical functions are available in Excel. All of the functions in Excel can be seen by selecting *fx* from the standard toolbar in Excel and then highlighting the "Statistical" function category. Some of the common functions follow:

- *AVERAGE* computes the average value of a set of numbers
- *VARIANCE* computes the variance of a set of numbers
- *STDEV* computes the standard deviation of a set of numbers
- *STANDARDIZE* computes a *Z*-score
- *NORMDIST* finds a probability for a normal random variable (mean and standard deviation must be input)
- *NORMSDIST* finds a probability associated with a *Z*-score (standard normal).

A brief description of each of these is provided in Excel.

Summary Information

Also in Excel, summary information on a set of data can be quickly found by selecting

TOOLS

DATA ANALYSIS

DESCRIPTIVE STATISTICS (check the summary statistics box)

If the *DATA ANALYSIS* option does not appear when *TOOLS* is selected, it has not yet been installed on the computer. To install this, under *TOOLS*, select *ADD-INS* and check the box next to "Analysis ToolPak" and "Analysis ToolPak—VBA." Click OK; then *DATA ANALYSIS* will appear under *TOOLS*.

Using Excel for Expected Value and Variance

The expected value or mean and variance of a discrete probability distribution can easily be computed in Excel. Program 2.1A gives the formulas for a simple example, and Program 2.1B gives the results. The formula in cell C7 computes the mean, and the formula in cell D7 computes the variance.

PROGRAM 2.1A

Formulas in Excel Spreadsheet for Computing Expected Value and Variance

	A	B	C	D	E	F
	x	P(x)	xP(x)	(x-mean)squared*P(x)		
1	x	P(x)	xP(x)	(x-mean)squared*P(x)		
2	10	0.2	=A2*B2	=(A2-$C$7)^2*B2		
3	20	0.25	=A3*B3	=(A3-$C$7)^2*B3		
4	30	0.25	=A4*B4	=(A4-$C$7)^2*B4		
5	40	0.3	=A5*B5	=(A5-$C$7)^2*B5		
6						
7			=SUM(C2:C5)	=SUM(D2:D5)		
8			Mean	Variance		
9						
10						

*D1 = (x-mean)squared*P(x)*

PROGRAM 2.1B

Values in Excel Spreadsheet for Expected Value and Variance

	A	B	C	D	E	F	G	H	I	J
	x	P(x)	xP(x)	(x-mean)squared*P(x)						
1	x	P(x)	xP(x)	(x-mean)squared*P(x)						
2	10	0.20	2	54.4500						
3	20	0.25	5	10.5625						
4	30	0.25	7.5	3.0625						
5	40	0.30	12	54.6750						
6										
7			26.5	122.75						
8			Mean	Variance						
9										
10										

*D1 = (x-mean)squared*P(x)*

Using Excel for Binomial Probabilities

Excel has a function (*BINOMDIST*) that will compute probabilities for the binomial distribution. For a binomial distribution where

$$n = \text{ the number of trials}$$

$$p = \text{the probability of a success on any single trial}$$

$$r = \text{the number of successes}$$

Excel will provide the probability of exactly r successes with the formula

$$BINOMDIST(r, n, p, FALSE)$$

The fourth parameter of this function (*FALSE*) indicates that exactly r successes is desired. If we wish to find the probability that the number of successes is r or less (a cumulative probability), we use

$$BINOMDIST(r, n, p, TRUE)$$

Program 2.2A provides an example and gives the formulas in cells C6 and C7. This has been written so that you can find new probabilities easily by changing cells B2, B3, and B4. Program 2.2B shows the results.

PROGRAM 2.2A

Formulas in Excel for Binomial Probabilities

A1 = The Binomial Distribution

	A	B	C	D	E
1	The Binomial Distribution				
2	n=	5			
3	p=	0.5			
4	r=	4			
5					
6	Cumulative probability	P(r≤)	=BINOMDIST(B4,B2,B3,TRUE)		
7		P(r)	=BINOMDIST(B4,B2,B3,FALSE)		
8					
9					
10					

Change cells B2, B3, and B4 to find any binomial probability.

The function BINOMDIST(r,n,p,TRUE) returns the cumulative probability.

PROGRAM 2.2B

**Values in Excel for
Binomial Probabilities**

	Microsoft Excel - Book1									
File Edit View Insert Format Tools Data Window Help										
A1		=	The Binomial Distribution							
	A	B	C	D	E	F	G	H	I	J
1	The Binomial Distribution									
2	n=	5								
3	p=	0.5								
4	r=	4								
5										
6	Cumulative probability	P(r≤)	0.9688							
7		P(r)	0.1563							
8										
9										
10										

Using Excel for the Poisson Distribution

Excel also has a function for the Poisson distribution. The probability of exactly x occurrences in a time period is found by the function $POISSON(x, mean, FALSE)$. The cumulative probability is found by the function $POISSON(x, mean, TRUE)$. For example, the probability of exactly 3 occurrences for a Poisson distribution with a mean of 4 ($\lambda = 4$) per time period would be found by using $POISSON(3, 4, FALSE)$.

Using Excel for the Normal Distribution

Two functions in Excel are used with the normal distribution as illustrated here. If X is a normal random variable with $\mu = 40$ and $\sigma = 5$, we find $P(X \leq 45)$ with

$$NORMDIST(x, \mu, \sigma, TRUE) = NORMDIST(45, 40, 5, TRUE) = 0.84134.$$

To find the value of x such that $P(X \leq x) = 0.90$, we use

$$NORMINV(\text{probability}, \mu, \sigma) = NORMINV(0.90, 40, 5) = 46.40775.$$

For a standard normal distribution ($\mu = 0$ and $\sigma = 1$; usually denoted as a z-value), we use $NORMSDIST(z)$ and $NORMSINV(\text{probability})$. For example, to find $P(z \leq 1.0)$, we have

$$NORMSDIST(z) = NORMSDIST(1.0) = 0.84134.$$

To find the z-value such that $P(Z \leq z) = 0.90$, we use

$$NORMSINV(\text{probability}) = NORMSINV(0.90) = 1.28155.$$

DECISION ANALYSIS

LEARNING OBJECTIVES

After completing this chapter, students will be able to:

1. List the steps of the decision-making process.
2. Describe the types of decision-making environments.
3. Make decisions under uncertainty.
4. Use probability values to make decisions under risk.
5. Develop accurate and useful decision trees.
6. Revise probability estimates using Bayesian analysis.
7. Use computers to solve basic decision-making problems.
8. Understand the importance and use of utility theory in decision making.

CHAPTER OUTLINE

3.1 Introduction
3.2 The Six Steps in Decision Making
3.3 Types of Decision-Making Environments
3.4 Decision Making under Uncertainty
3.5 Decision Making under Risk
3.6 Decision Trees
3.7 How Probability Values Are Estimated by Bayesian Analysis
3.8 Utility Theory

Summary • Glossary • Key Equations • Solved Problems • Self-Test •
Discussion Questions and Problems • Internet Homework Problems •
Case Study: Starting Right Corporation • Case Study: Blake Electronics •
Internet Case Studies • Bibliography

Appendix 3.1: Decision Models with QM for Windows

Appendix 3.2: Decision Trees with QM for Windows

Appendix 3.3: Using Excel for Bayes' Theorem

3.1 INTRODUCTION

Decision theory is an analytic and systematic way to tackle problems.

A good decision is based on logic.

To a great extent, the successes or failures that a person experiences in life depend on the decisions that he or she makes. The person who managed the ill-fated space shuttle *Challenger* is no longer working for NASA. The person who designed the top-selling Mustang became president of Ford. Why and how did these people make their respective decisions? In general, what is involved in making good decisions? One decision may make the difference between a successful career and an unsuccessful one. *Decision theory* is an analytic and systematic approach to the study of decision making. In this chapter, we present the mathematical models useful in helping managers make the best possible decisions.

What makes the difference between good and bad decisions? A good decision is one that is based on logic, considers all available data and possible alternatives, and applies the quantitative approach we are about to describe. Occasionally, a good decision results in an unexpected or unfavorable outcome. But if it is made properly, it is *still* a good decision. A bad decision is one that is not based on logic, does not use all available information, does not consider all alternatives, and does not employ appropriate quantitative techniques. If you make a bad decision but are lucky and a favorable outcome occurs, you have *still* made a bad decision. Although occasionally good decisions yield bad results, in the long run, using decision theory will result in successful outcomes.

3.2 THE SIX STEPS IN DECISION MAKING

Whether you are deciding about getting a haircut today, building a multimillion-dollar plant, or buying a new camera, the steps in making a good decision are basically the same:

Six Steps of Decision Making

1. Clearly define the problem at hand.
2. List the possible alternatives.
3. Identify the possible outcomes or states of nature.
4. List the payoff or profit of each combination of alternatives and outcomes.
5. Select one of the mathematical decision theory models.
6. Apply the model and make your decision.

We use the Thompson Lumber Company case as an example to illustrate these decision theory steps. John Thompson is the founder and president of Thompson Lumber Company, a profitable firm located in Portland, Oregon.

The first step is to define the problem.

Step 1. The problem that John Thompson identifies is whether to expand his product line by manufacturing and marketing a new product, backyard storage sheds.

Thompson's second step is to generate the alternatives that are available to him. In decision theory, an *alternative* is defined as a course of action or a strategy that the decision maker can choose.

The second step is to list alternatives.

Step 2. John decides that his alternatives are to construct (1) a large new plant to manufacture the storage sheds, (2) a small plant, or (3) no plant at all (i.e., he has the option of not developing the new product line).

One of the biggest mistakes that decision makers make is to leave out some important alternatives. Although a particular alternative may seem to be inappropriate or of little value, it might turn out to be the best choice.

The next step involves identifying the possible outcomes of the various alternatives. A common mistake is to forget about some of the possible outcomes. Optimistic decision makers tend to ignore bad outcomes, whereas pessimistic managers may discount a favorable outcome. If you don't consider all possibilities, you will not be making a logical decision, and the results may be undesirable. If you do not think the worst can happen, you may design another Edsel automobile. In decision theory, those outcomes over which the decision maker has little or no control are called *states of nature*.

The third step is to identify possible outcomes.

Step 3. Thompson determines that there are only two possible outcomes: the market for the storage sheds could be favorable, meaning that there is a high demand for the product, or it could be unfavorable, meaning that there is a low demand for the sheds.

Once the alternatives and states of nature have been identified, the next step is to express the payoff resulting from each possible combination of alternatives and outcomes. In decision theory, we call such payoffs or profits *conditional values*. Not every decision, of course, can be based on money alone—any appropriate means of measuring benefit is acceptable.

The fourth step is to list payoffs.

Step 4. Because Thompson wants to maximize his profits, he can use *profit* to evaluate each consequence.

John Thompson has already evaluated the potential profits associated with the various outcomes. With a favorable market, he thinks a large facility would result in a net profit of $200,000 to his firm. This $200,000 is a *conditional value* because Thompson's receiving the money is conditional upon both his building a large factory and having a good market. The conditional value if the market is unfavorable would be a $180,000 net loss. A small plant would result in a net profit of $100,000 in a favorable market, but a net loss of $20,000 would occur if the market was unfavorable. Finally, doing nothing would result in $0 profit in either market. The easiest way to present these values is by constructing a *decision table*, sometimes called a *payoff table*. A decision table for Thompson's conditional values is shown in Table 3.1. All of the alternatives are listed down the left side of the table, and all of the possible outcomes or states of nature are listed across the top. The body of the table contains the actual payoffs.

During the fourth step the decision maker can construct decision or payoff tables.

The last two steps are to select and apply the decision theory model.

Steps 5 and 6. The last two steps are to select a decision theory model and apply it to the data to help make the decision. Selecting the model depends on the environment in which you're operating and the amount of risk and uncertainty involved.

TABLE 3.1

Decision Table with Conditional Values for Thompson Lumber

	STATE OF NATURE	
ALTERNATIVE	FAVORABLE MARKET ($)	UNFAVORABLE MARKET ($)
Construct a large plant	200,000	−180,000
Construct a small plant	100,000	−20,000
Do nothing	0	0

Note: It is important to include all alternatives, including "do nothing."

3.3   TYPES OF DECISION-MAKING ENVIRONMENTS

The types of decisions people make depend on how much knowledge or information they have about the situation. There are three decision-making environments:

- Decision making under certainty
- Decision making under uncertainty
- Decision making under risk

Type 1: Decision Making under Certainty In the environment of *decision making under certainty*, decision makers know with certainty the consequence of every alternative or decision choice. Naturally, they will choose the alternative that will maximize their well-being or will result in the best outcome. For example, let's say that you have $1,000 to invest for a one-year period. One alternative is to open a savings account paying 6% interest and

---

ⅢⅢ➡ MODELING IN THE REAL WORLD   *Critical Decisions in a Nuclear World*

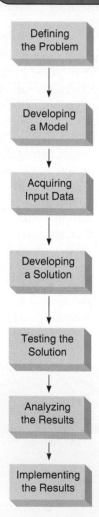

Defining the Problem

Nuclear weapons require that tritium (a radioisotope) be replaced periodically. The supply of tritium is expected to run out in the year 2011. The problem is to determine the best way to produce additional tritium before 2011.

Developing a Model

The decision model used 11 alternatives. Each alternative was one of the feasible ways to produce tritium.

Acquiring Input Data

A number of agencies and individuals were involved in acquiring input data, including the U.S. Department of Energy, the Secretary of Energy, the Office of Defense Programs, and the Weapons Complex Reconfiguration Program.

Developing a Solution

Because there was time to explore various alternatives in more detail, the solution was to further investigate two alternatives previously identified, including the use of an accelerator and a commercial reactor. The testing is continuing and includes schedule, capacity, availability, cost, and environmental analysis.

Testing the Solution

To further analyze the results, the Department of Energy created two new offices: The Office of Commercial Reactor Production and the Office of Accelerator Production.

Analyzing the Results

These offices were funded with hundreds of millions of dollars to investigate the two alternatives.

Implementing the Results

The final results will be implemented before tritium runs out in 2011.

Source: Detlof von Winterdeldt, et al. "An Assessment of Tritium Supply Alternatives in Support of the US Nuclear Weapons Stockpile," *Interfaces* (January–February 1998): 92–112.

another is to invest in a government Treasury bond paying 10% interest. If both investments are secure and guaranteed, there is a certainty that the Treasury bond will pay a higher return. The return after one year will be $100 in interest.

Type 2: Decision Making under Uncertainty In *decision making under uncertainty*, there are several possible outcomes for each alternative, and the decision maker does not know the probabilities of the various outcomes. As an example, the probability that a Democrat will be president of the United States 25 years from now is not known. Sometimes it is impossible to assess the probability of success of a new undertaking or product. The criteria for decision making under uncertainty are explained in Section 3.4.

Probabilities are not known.

Type 3: Decision Making under Risk In *decision making under risk*, there are several possible outcomes for each alternative, and the decision maker knows the probability of occurrence of each outcome. We know, for example, that when playing cards using a standard deck, the probability of being dealt a club is 0.25. The probability of rolling a 5 on a die is 1/6. In decision making under risk, the decision maker usually attempts to maximize his or her expected well-being. Decision theory models for business problems in this environment typically employ two equivalent criteria: maximization of expected monetary value and minimization of expected opportunity loss.

Probabilities are known.

Let's see how decision making under certainty (the type 1 environment) could affect John Thompson. Here we assume that John knows exactly what will happen in the future. If it turns out that he knows with certainty that the market for storage sheds will be favorable, what should he do? Look again at Thompson Lumber's conditional values in Table 3.1. Because the market is favorable, he should build the large plant, which has the highest profit, $200,000.

Few managers would be fortunate enough to have complete information and knowledge about the states of nature under consideration. Decision making under uncertainty, discussed next, is a more difficult situation. We may find that two different people with different perspectives may appropriately choose two different alternatives.

3.4 DECISION MAKING UNDER UNCERTAINTY

Probability data are not available.

When several states of nature exist and a manager *cannot* assess the outcome probability with confidence or when virtually no probability data are available, the environment is called decision making under uncertainty. Several criteria exist for making decisions under these conditions. The ones that we cover in this section are as follows:

1. Maximax (optimistic)
2. Maximin (pessimistic)
3. Criterion of realism (Hurwicz)
4. Equally likely (LaPlace)
5. Minimax regret

The first four criteria can be computed directly from the decision (payoff) table, whereas the minimax regret criterion requires use of the opportunity loss table. Let's take a look at each of the five models and apply them to Thompson Lumber.

Maximax

Maximax is an optimistic approach.

The *maximax* criterion is used to find the alternative that *max*imizes the *max*imum payoff or consequence for every alternative. You first locate the maximum payoff for each alternative, and then pick that alternative with the maximum number. This decision criterion

TABLE 3.2

Thompson's Maximax
Decision

ALTERNATIVE	STATE OF NATURE		
	FAVORABLE MARKET ($)	UNFAVORABLE MARKET ($)	MAXIMUM IN A ROW ($)
Construct a large plant	200,000	−180,000	200,000 ← Maximax
Construct a small plant	100,000	−20,000	100,000
Do nothing	0	0	0

locates the alternative with the *highest* possible gain: therefore it has been called an *optimistic decision criterion*. In Table 3.2 we see that Thompson's maximax choice is the first alternative, "construct a large plant." This is the alternative associated with the maximum of the maximum number within each row or alternative. By using this criterion, the highest of all possible payoffs may be achieved.

Maximin

Maximin is a pessimistic approach.

The *maximin* criterion is used to find the alternative that *max*imizes the *min*imum payoff or consequence for every alternative. You first locate the minimum payoff for each alternative and then pick that alternative with the maximum number. This decision criterion locates the alternative that gives the best of the worst (minimum) payoffs, and thus it has been called a *pessimistic decision criterion*. This criterion guarantees the payoff will be at least the maximin value. Choosing any other alternative may allow a lower (worse) payoff to occur.

Thompson's maximin choice, "do nothing," is shown in Table 3.3. This decision is associated with the maximum of the minimum number within each row or alternative.

Both the maximax and maximin criteria consider only one extreme payoff for each alternative, while all other payoffs are ignored. The next criterion considers both of these extremes.

Criterion of Realism (Hurwicz Criterion)

Criterion of realism uses the weighted average approach.

Often called the *weighted average*, the *criterion of realism* (the *Hurwicz criterion*) is a compromise between an optimistic and a pessimistic decision. To begin with, a *coefficient of realism*, α, is selected; this measures the degree of optimism of the decision maker. This coefficient is between 0 and 1. When α is 1, the decision maker is 100% optimistic about

TABLE 3.3

Thompson's Maximin
Decision

ALTERNATIVE	STATE OF NATURE		
	FAVORABLE MARKET ($)	UNFAVORABLE MARKET ($)	MINIMUM IN A ROW ($)
Construct a large plant	200,000	−180,000	−180,000
Construct a small plant	100,000	−20,000	−20,000
Do nothing	0	0	0 ← Maximin

TABLE 3.4

Thompson's Criterion of Realism Decision

| | STATE OF NATURE | | |
ALTERNATIVE	FAVORABLE MARKET ($)	UNFAVORABLE MARKET ($)	CRITERION OF REALISM OR WEIGHTED AVERAGE ($\alpha = 0.8$) $
Construct a large plant	200,000	−180,000	124,000 ← Realism
Construct a small plant	100,000	−20,000	76,000
Do nothing	0	0	0

the future. When α is 0, the decision maker is 100% pessimistic about the future. The advantage of this approach is that it allows the decision maker to build in personal feelings about relative optimism and pessimism. The weighted average is computed as follows:

$$\text{weighted average} = \alpha(\text{maximum in row}) + (1 - \alpha)(\text{minimum in row})$$

Note that when $\alpha = 1$, this is the same as the optimistic criterion, and when $\alpha = 0$ this is the same as the pessimistic criterion. This value is computed for each alternative, and the alternative with the highest weighted average is then chosen.

If we assume that John Thompson sets his coefficient of realism, α, to be 0.80, the best decision would be to construct a large plant. As seen in Table 3.4, this alternative has the highest weighted average: $124,000 = (0.80) ($200,000) + (0.20) (−$180,000)$.

Because there are only two states of nature in the Thompson Lumber example, only two payoffs for each alternative are present and both are considered. However, if there are more than two states of nature, this criterion will ignore all payoffs except the best and the worst. The next criterion will consider all possible payoffs for each decision.

IN ACTION Decision Analysis Helps Allocate Health Care Funds in the United Kingdom

Individuals and companies have often used decision-making techniques to help them invest or allocate funds to various projects. In some cases, decision-making techniques can be used to determine how millions of dollars are to be spent. This same type of analysis can also be used on a larger scale for countries or governments. This was the case in the allocation of health care funds for the United Kingdom (UK).

Over the years, the United States has debated the possible implementation of a comprehensive national health care program. Although this does not seem likely for the United States in the near future, other countries, such as the UK, have been using some form of national health care system for decades. For the UK, the question is not whether to have a national health care system, but how funds from such a system are to be allocated.

The United Kingdom's National Health Service (NHS) is funded through general tax revenues. The funds are dispersed to about 105 different local health authorities. The annual funding for the NHS is approximately $35 billion. With such a large sum of national funds going to such an important area,

the decision-making process to justly allocate funds can be difficult indeed.

Starting in the 1970s, a formula, based partly on a standardized mortality ratio, was developed to distribute health funds to the local authorities. This formula, however, failed to take into account social deprivation and general health care needs. As a result, the NHS decided to seek a better way to allocate health care dollars to the local authorities.

A team from York University spent about 4 months developing the original allocation model and another 14 months refining the decision-making model. Using decision theory, the team identified a set of key variables to explain health care needs and usage in the UK. This resulted in modifications to the decision-making approach regarding health care funds. Many believe that the new model will more fairly and justly allocate the UK's important national health care funds to those who truly need the assistance.

Source: Nancy Bistritz. "Rx for UK Healthcare Woes," *OR/MS Today* (April 1997): 18.

| | STATE OF NATURE | | |
ALTERNATIVE	FAVORABLE MARKET ($)	UNFAVORABLE MARKET ($)	ROW AVERAGE ($)
Construct a large plant	200,000	−180,000	10,000
Construct a small plant	100,000	−20,000	(40,000) ← Equally likely
Do nothing	0	0	0

Equally Likely (Laplace)

Equally likely criterion uses the average outcome.

One criterion that uses all the payoffs for each alternative is the *equally likely*, also called *Laplace*, decision criterion. This involves finding the average payoff for each alternative, and selecting the alternative with the highest average. The equally likely approach assumes that all probabilities of occurrence for the states of nature are equal, and thus each state of nature is equally likely.

The equally likely choice for Thompson Lumber is the second alternative, "construct a small plant." This strategy, shown in Table 3.5, is the one with the maximum average payoff.

Minimax Regret

Minimax regret criterion is based on opportunity loss.

The next decision criterion that we discuss is based on *opportunity loss* or *regret*. Opportunity loss refers to the difference between the optimal profit or payoff for a given state of nature and the actual payoff received for a particular decision. In other words, it's the amount lost by not picking the best alternative in a given state of nature.

The first step is to create the opportunity loss table by determining the opportunity loss for not choosing the best alternative for each state of nature. Opportunity loss for any state of nature, or any column, is calculated by subtracting each payoff in the column from the *best* payoff in the same column. For a favorable market, the best payoff is $200,000 as a result of the first alternative, "construct a large plant." If the second alternative is selected, a profit of $100,000 would be realized in a favorable market, and this is compared to the best payoff of $200,000. Thus, the opportunity loss is 200,000 − 100,000 = 100,000. Similarly, if "do nothing" is selected, the opportunity loss would be 200,000 − 0 = 200,000.

For an unfavorable market, the best payoff is $0 as a result of the third alternative, "do nothing," so this has 0 opportunity loss. The opportunity losses for the other alternative are found by subtracting the payoffs from this best payoff ($0) in this state of nature as shown in Table 3.6. Thompson's opportunity loss table is shown as Table 3.7.

| STATE OF NATURE | |
FAVORABLE MARKET ($)	UNFAVORABLE MARKET ($)
200,000 − 200,000	0 − (−180,000)
200,000 − 100,000	0 − (−20,000)
200,000 − 0	0 − 0

TABLE 3.7

Opportunity Loss Table for Thompson Lumber

	STATE OF NATURE	
ALTERNATIVE	FAVORABLE MARKET ($)	UNFAVORABLE MARKET ($)
Construct a large plant	0	180,000
Construct a small plant	100,000	20,000
Do nothing	200,000	0

Using the opportunity loss (regret) table, the *minimax regret* criterion finds the alternative that *min*imizes the *max*imum opportunity loss within each alternative. You first find the maximum (worst) opportunity loss for each alternative. Next, looking at these maximum values, pick that alternative with the minimum (or best) number. By doing this, the opportunity loss actually realized is guaranteed to be no more than this minimax value. In Table 3.8, we can see that the minimax regret choice is the second alternative, "construct a small plant." Doing so minimizes the maximum opportunity loss.

We have considered several decision-making criteria to be used when probabilities of the states of nature are not known and cannot be estimated. Now we will see what to do if the probabilities are available.

3.5 DECISION MAKING UNDER RISK

Decision making under risk is a decision situation in which several possible states of nature may occur, and the probabilities of these states of nature are known. In this section we consider one of the most popular methods of making decisions under risk: selecting the alternative with the highest expected monetary value (or simply expected value). We also use the probabilities with the opportunity loss table to minimize the expected opportunity loss.

Expected Monetary Value

EMV is the weighted sum of possible payoffs for each alternative.

Given a decision table with conditional values (payoffs) that are monetary values, and probability assessments for all states of nature, it is possible to determine the *expected monetary value* (EMV) for each alternative. The *expected value*, or the *mean value*, is the long-run average value of that decision. The EMV for an alternative is just the sum of possible

TABLE 3.8

Thompson's Minimax Decision Using Opportunity Loss

	STATE OF NATURE		
ALTERNATIVE	FAVORABLE MARKET ($)	UNFAVORABLE MARKET ($)	MAXIMUM IN A ROW ($)
Construct a large plant	0	180,000	180,000
Construct a small plant	100,000	20,000	(100,000) ← Minimax
Do nothing	200,000	0	200,000

payoffs of the alternative, each weighted by the probability of that payoff occurring. (See the Expected Value material, Section 2.9 of Chapter 2.)

$$
\begin{aligned}
\text{EMV (alternative } i) = {} & \text{(payoff of first state of nature)} \\
& \times \text{(probability of first state of nature)} \\
& + \text{(payoff of second state of nature)} \\
& \times \text{(probability of second state of nature)} \\
& + \ldots + \text{(payoff of last state of nature)} \\
& \times \text{(probability of last state of nature)}
\end{aligned}
\tag{3-1}
$$

The alternative with the maximum EMV is then chosen.

Suppose that John Thompson now believes that the probability of a favorable market is exactly the same as the probability of an unfavorable market; that is, each state of nature has a 0.50 probability. Which alternative would give the greatest expected monetary value? To determine this, John has expanded the decision table, as shown in Table 3.9. His calculations follow:

$$\text{EMV (large plant)} = (0.50)(\$200,000) + (0.50)\,(-\$180,000) = \$10,000$$
$$\text{EMV (small plant)} = (0.50)(\$100,000) + (0.50)(-\$20,000) = \$40,000$$
$$\text{EMV (do nothing)} = (0.50)(\$0) + (0.50)(\$0) = \$0$$

The largest expected value ($40,000) results from the second alternative, "construct a small plant." Thus, Thompson should proceed with the project and put up a small plant to manufacture storage sheds. The EMVs for the large plant and for doing nothing are $10,000 and $0, respectively.

Expected Value of Perfect Information

John Thompson has been approached by Scientific Marketing, Inc., a firm that proposes to help John make the decision about whether to build the plant to produce storage sheds. Scientific Marketing claims that its technical analysis will tell John with certainty whether the market is favorable for his proposed product. In other words, it will change his environment from one of decision making under risk to one of decision making under certainty. This information could prevent John from making a very expensive mistake. Scientific Marketing would charge Thompson $65,000 for the information. What would you recommend to John? Should he hire the firm to make the marketing study? Even if the information from the study is perfectly accurate, is it worth $65,000? What would it be worth? Although some of these questions are difficult to answer, determining the value of such *perfect information* can be very useful. It places an upper bound on what you should be willing to spend on information such as that being sold by Scientific Marketing. In this

---

TABLE 3.9

Decision Table with Probabilities and EMVs for Thompson Lumber

	STATE OF NATURE		
ALTERNATIVE	FAVORABLE MARKET ($)	UNFAVORABLE MARKET ($)	EMV ($)
Construct a large plant	200,000	−180,000	10,000
Construct a small plant	100,000	−20,000	40,000
Do nothing	0	0	0
Probabilities	0.50	0.50	

section, two related terms are investigated: the *expected value of perfect information* (EVPI) and the *expected value with perfect information* (EVwPI). These techniques can help John make his decision about hiring the marketing firm.

The expected value *with* perfect information is the expected or average return, in the long run, if we have perfect information before a decision has to be made. To calculate this value, we choose the best alternative for each state of nature and multiply its payoff times the probability of occurrence of that state of nature.

Expected value *with* perfect information (EVwPI)

$$
\begin{aligned}
&= \text{(best payoff or consequence for first state of nature)} \\
&\times \text{(probability of first state of nature)} \\
&+ \text{(best payoff for second state of nature)} \\
&\times \text{(probability of second state of nature)} \\
&+ \ldots + \text{(best payoff for last state of nature)} \\
&\times \text{(probability of last state of nature)}
\end{aligned}
\tag{3-2}
$$

The expected value *of* perfect information, EVPI, is the expected value *with* perfect information minus the expected value *without* perfect information (i.e., the maximum EMV). Thus, the EVPI is the increase in EMV that results from having perfect information.

$$
\text{EVPI} = \text{expected value } with \text{ perfect information} - \text{maximum EMV} \tag{3-3}
$$

By referring back to Table 3.9, Thompson can calculate the maximum that he would pay for information, that is, the expected value of perfect information, or EVPI. He follows a two-stage process. First, the expected value *with* perfect information is computed. Then, using this result, EVPI is calculated. The procedure is outlined as follows:

1. The best alternative for the state of nature "favorable market" is "build a large plant" with a payoff of $200,000. The best alternative for the state of nature "unfavorable market" is "do nothing," with a payoff of $0.

$$
\text{EVwPI} = (\$200,000)(0.50) + (\$0)(0.50) = \$100,000
$$

Thus, if we had perfect information, the payoff would average $100,000.

2. The maximum EMV without additional information is $40,000 (from Table 3.9). Therefore, the increase in EMV is

$$
\begin{aligned}
\text{EVPI} &= \text{(expected value } with \text{ perfect information)} - \text{(maximum EMV)} \\
&= \$100,000 - \$40,000 \\
&= \$60,000
\end{aligned}
$$

Thus, the *most* Thompson would be willing to pay for perfect information is $60,000. This, of course, is again based on the assumption that the probability of each state of nature is 0.50.

This EVPI also tells us that the most we would pay for any information (perfect or imperfect) is $60,000. In a later section we'll see how to place a value on imperfect or sample information.

Expected Opportunity Loss

An alternative approach to maximizing EMV is to minimize *expected opportunity loss* (EOL). First, an opportunity loss table is constructed. Then the EOL is computed for each alternative by multiplying the opportunity loss by the probability and adding these

		STATE OF NATURE		
TABLE 3.10				
EOL Table for Thompson Lumber	**ALTERNATIVE**	**FAVORABLE MARKET ($)**	**UNFAVORABLE MARKET ($)**	**EOL**
	Construct a large plant	0	180,000	90,000
	Construct a small plant	100,000	20,000	60,000
	Do nothing	200,000	0	100,000
	Probabilities	0.50	0.50	

together. In Table 3.7 we presented the opportunity loss table for the Thompson Lumber example. Using these opportunity losses, we compute the EOL for each alternative by multiplying the probability of each state of nature times the appropriate opportunity loss value and adding these together:

$$\text{EOL(construct large plant)} = (0.5)(\$0) + (0.5)(\$180,000)$$
$$= \$90,000$$
$$\text{EOL(construct small plant)} = (0.5)(\$100,000) + (0.5)(\$20,000)$$
$$= \$60,000$$
$$\text{EOL(do nothing)} = (0.5)(\$200,000) + (0.5)(\$0)$$
$$= (\$100,000)$$

Table 3.10 gives these results. Using minimum EOL as the decision criterion, the best decision would be the second alternative, "construct a small plant."

It is important to note that minimum EOL will always result in the same decision as maximum EMV, and that the EVPI will always equal the minimum EOL. Referring to the Thompson case, we used the payoff table to compute the EVPI to be $60,000. Note that this is the minimum EOL we just computed.

EOL will always result in the same decision as the maximum EMV.

Sensitivity Analysis

In previous sections we determined that the best decision (with the probabilities known) for Thompson Lumber was to construct the small plant, with an expected value of $40,000. This conclusion depends on the values of the economic consequences and the two probability values of a favorable and an unfavorable market. *Sensitivity analysis* investigates how our decision might change given a change in the problem data. In this section, we investigate the impact that a change in the probability values would have on the decision facing Thompson Lumber. We first define the following variable:

Sensitivity analysis investigates how our decision might change with different input data.

$$P = \text{probability of a favorable market}$$

Because there are only two states of nature, the probability of an unfavorable market must be $1-P$.

We can now express the EMVs in terms of P, as shown in the following equations. A graph of these EMV values is shown in Figure 3.1.

$$\text{EMV(large plant)} = \$200,000P - \$180,000(1 - P)$$
$$= \$380,000P - \$180,000$$
$$\text{EMV(small plant)} = \$100,000P - \$20,000(1 - P)$$
$$= \$120,000P - \$20,000$$
$$\text{EMV(do nothing)} = \$0P + \$0(1 - P) = \$0$$

FIGURE 3.1

Sensitivity Analysis

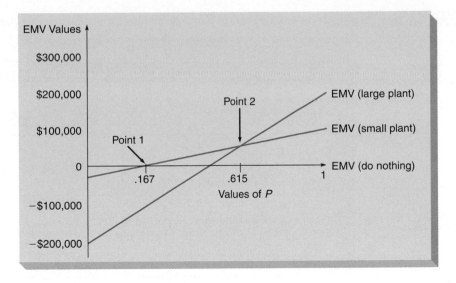

As you can see in Figure 3.1, the best decision is to do nothing as long as P is between 0 and the probability associated with point 1, where the EMV for doing nothing is equal to the EMV for the small plant. When P is between the probabilities for points 1 and 2, the best decision is to build the small plant. Point 2 is where the EMV for the small plant is equal to the EMV for the large plant. When P is greater than the probability for point 2, the best decision is to construct the large plant. Of course, this is what you would expect as P increases. The value of P at points 1 and 2 can be computed as follows:

Point 1: EMV (do nothing) = EMV (small plant)

$$0 = \$120,000P - \$20,000 \qquad P = \frac{20,000}{120,000} = 0.167$$

Point 2: EMV (small plant) = EMV (large plant)

$$\$120,000P - \$20,000 = \$380,000P - \$180,000$$

$$260,000P = 160,000 \qquad P = \frac{160,000}{260,000} = 0.615$$

The results of this sensitivity analysis are displayed in the following table:

BEST ALTERNATIVE	RANGE OF P VALUES
Do nothing	Less than 0.167
Construct a small plant	0.167 − 0.615
Construct a large plant	Greater than 0.615

Using Excel QM to Solve Decision Theory Problems

Excel QM can be used to solve a variety of decision theory problems discussed in this chapter. Programs 3.1A and 3.1B show the use of Excel QM to solve the Thompson Lumber case. Program 3.1A provides the formulas needed to compute the EMV, maximin, maximax, and other measures. Program 3.1B shows the results of these formulas.

PROGRAM 3.1A   Input Data for the Thompson Lumber Problem Using Excel QM

Compute the EMV for each alternative using the SUMPRODUCT function, the worst case using the MIN function, and the best case using the MAX function.

To calculate the EVPI, find the best outcome for each scenario.

Find the best outcome for each measure using the MAX function.

Use SUMPRODUCT to compute the product of the best outcomes by the probabilities and find the difference between this and the best expected value yielding the EVPI.

Thompson Lumber

Decision Tables

Enter the profits or costs in the main body of the data table. Enter probabilities in the first row if you want to compute the expected value.

	A	B	C	D	E	F		
6	Data				Results			
7	Profit	Favorable Market	Unfavorable Market		EMV	Minimum	Maximum	Hurwicz
8	Probability	0.5	0.5					0.8
9	Large Plant	200000	-180000		=SUMPRODUCT(B$8:C$8,B9:C9)	=MIN(B9:C9)	=MAX(B9:C9)	=$I$8*G9+(1-$I$8)*F9
10	Small plant	100000	-20000		=SUMPRODUCT(B$8:C$8,B10:C10)	=MIN(B10:C10)	=MAX(B10:C10)	=$I$8*G10+(1-$I$8)*F10
11	Do nothing	0	0		=SUMPRODUCT(B$8:C$8,B11:C11)	=MIN(B11:C11)	=MAX(B11:C11)	
12					=MAX(E9:E11)	=MAX(F9:F11)	=MAX(G9:G11)	=MAX(I9:I11)
13								
14	Expected Value of Perfect Information							
15	Column best	=MAX(B9:B11)	=MAX(C9:C11)	=SUMPRODUCT(B$8:C$8,B15:C15)	<-Expected value under certainty			
16				=E12	<-Best expected value			
17				=E15-E12	<-Expected value of perfect information			
18								
19	Regret							
20		=B7	=C7		Expected	Maximum		
21	=A8	=B8	=C8					
22	=A9	=B15 - B9	=C15 - C9		=SUMPRODUCT(B$8:C$8,B22:C22)	=MAX(B22:C22)		
23	=A10	=B15 - B10	=C15 - C10		=SUMPRODUCT(B$8:C$8,B23:C23)	=MAX(B23:C23)		
24	=A11	=B15 - B11	=C15 - C11		=SUMPRODUCT(B$8:C$8,B24:C24)	=MAX(B24:C24)		
25					=MIN(E22:E24)	=MIN(F22:F24)		

\ 1.3 / 1.4 / S1.2 \ 3.1

PROGRAM 3.1B   Output Results for the Thompson Lumber Problem Using Excel QM

Thompson Lumber

Decision Tables

Enter the profits or costs in the main body of the data table. Enter probabilities in the first row if you want to compute the expected value.

	A	B	C	D	E	F	G	H	I	J
6	Data				Results					
7	Profit	Favorable Market	Unfavorable Market		EMV	Minimum	Maximum		Hurwicz	
8	Probability	0.5	0.5					coefficient	0.8	
9	Large Plant	200000	-180000		10000	-180000	200000		124000	
10	Small plant	100000	-20000		40000	-20000	100000		76000	
11	Do nothing	0	0		0	0	0			
12				Maximum	40000	0	200000		124000	
13										
14	Expected Value of Perfect Information									
15	Column best	200000	0		100000	<-Expected value under certainty				
16					40000	<-Best expected value				
17					60000	<-Expected value of perfect information				
18										
19	Regret									
20		Favorable Market	Unfavorable Market		Expected	Maximum				
21	Probability	0.5	0.5							
22	Large Plant	0	180000		90000	180000				
23	Small plant	100000	20000		60000	100000				
24	Do nothing	200000	0		100000	200000				
25				Minimum	60000	100000				

\ 1.3 / 1.4 / S1.2 \ 3.1 / 4.1a / 4.1 / 5.1a / 5.1b / 5.2 / 5.3 / 5.4 / 5.4 form

3.6 DECISION TREES

Any problem that can be presented in a decision table can also be graphically illustrated in a *decision tree*. All decision trees are similar in that they contain *decision points* or *decision nodes* and *state-of-nature points* or *state of nature nodes*:

- A decision node from which one of several alternatives may be chosen
- A state-of-nature node out of which one state of nature will occur

In drawing the tree, we begin at the left and move to the right. Thus, the tree presents the decisions and outcomes in sequential order. Lines or branches from the squares (decision nodes) represent alternatives, and branches from the circles represent the states of nature. Figure 3.2 gives the basic decision tree for the Thompson Lumber example. First, John decides whether to construct a large plant, a small plant, or no plant. Then, once that decision is made, the possible states of nature or outcomes (favorable or unfavorable market) will occur. The next step is to put the payoffs and probabilities on the tree and begin the analysis.

Analyzing problems with decision trees involves five steps:

Five Steps of Decision Tree Analysis

1. Define the problem.
2. Structure or draw the decision tree.
3. Assign probabilities to the states of nature.
4. Estimate payoffs for each possible combination of alternatives and states of nature.
5. Solve the problem by computing expected monetary values (EMVs) for each state of nature node. This is done by working backward, that is, starting at the right of the tree and working back to decision nodes on the left. Also, at each decision node, the alternative with the best EMV is selected.

The final decision tree with the payoffs and probabilities for John Thompson's decision situation is shown in Figure 3.3. Note that the payoffs are placed at the right side of each of the tree's branches. The probabilities are shown in parentheses next to each state of nature. Beginning with the payoffs on the right of the figure, the EMVs for each state-of-nature node are then calculated and placed by their respective nodes. The EMV of the first node is $10,000. This represents the branch from the decision node to construct a large plant. The EMV for node 2, to construct a small plant, is $40,000. Building no plant or

FIGURE 3.2

Thompson's Decision Tree

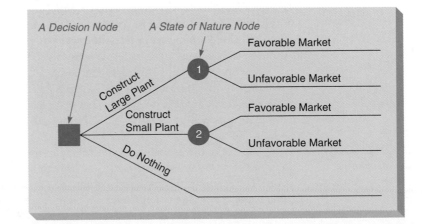

FIGURE 3.3

Completed and Solved
Decision Tree for
Thompson Lumber

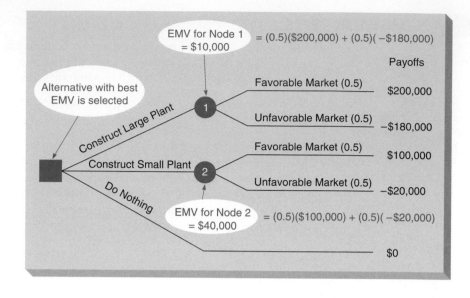

doing nothing has, of course, a payoff of $0. The branch leaving the decision node leading to the state-of-nature node with the highest EMV should be chosen. In Thompson's case, a small plant should be built.

A More Complex Decision for Thompson Lumber—Sample Information When *sequential decisions* need to be made, decision trees are much more powerful tools than decision tables. Let's say that John Thompson has two decisions to make, with the second decision dependent on the outcome of the first. Before deciding about building a new plant, John has the option of conducting his own marketing research survey, at a cost of $10,000. The information from his survey could help him decide whether to construct a large plant, a small plant, or not to build at all. John recognizes that such a market survey will not provide him with *perfect* information, but it may help quite a bit nevertheless.

All outcomes and alternatives must be considered.

John's new decision tree is represented in Figure 3.4. Let's take a careful look at this more complex tree. Note that *all possible outcomes and alternatives* are included in their logical sequence. This is one of the strengths of using decision trees in making decisions. The user is forced to examine all possible outcomes, including unfavorable ones. He or she is also forced to make decisions in a logical, sequential manner.

Examining the tree, we see that Thompson's first decision point is whether to conduct the $10,000 market survey. If he chooses not to do the study (the lower part of the tree), he can either construct a large plant, a small plant, or no plant. This is John's second decision point. The market will either be favorable (0.50 probability) or unfavorable (also 0.50 probability) if he builds. The payoffs for each of the possible consequences are listed along the right side. As a matter of fact, the lower portion of John's tree is *identical* to the simpler decision tree shown in Figure 3.3. Why is this so?

The upper part of Figure 3.4 reflects the decision to conduct the market survey. State-of-nature node 1 has two branches. There is a 45% chance that the survey results will indicate a favorable market for storage sheds. We also note that the probability is 0.55 that the survey results will be negative. The derivation of this probability will be discussed in the next section.

Most of the probabilities are conditional probabilities.

The rest of the probabilities shown in parentheses in Figure 3.4 are all *conditional probabilities* or *posterior probabilities* (these probabilities will also be discussed in the next section). For example, 0.78 is the probability of a favorable market for the sheds given a favorable result from the market survey. Of course, you would expect to find a high probability

FIGURE 3.4   Larger Decision Tree with Payoffs and Probabilities for Thompson Lumber

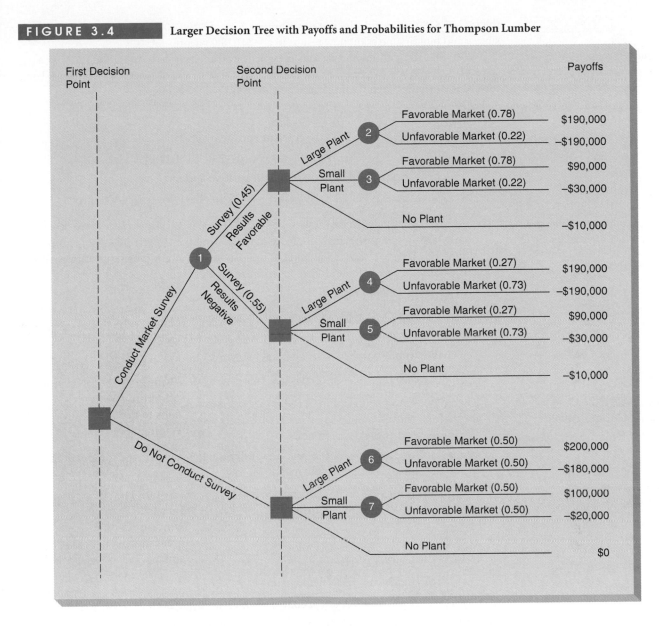

The cost of the survey had to be subtracted from the original payoffs.

of a favorable market given that the research indicated that the market was good. Don't forget, though, there is a chance that John's $10,000 market survey didn't result in perfect or even reliable information. Any market research study is subject to error. In this case, there is a 22% chance that the market for sheds will be unfavorable given that the survey results are positive.

We note that there is a 27% chance that the market for sheds will be favorable given that John's survey results are negative. The probability is much higher, 0.73, that the market will actually be unfavorable given that the survey was negative.

Finally, when we look to the payoff column in Figure 3.4, we see that $10,000, the cost of the marketing study, had to be subtracted from each of the top 10 tree branches. Thus, a large plant with a favorable market would normally net a $200,000 profit. But because the market study was conducted, this figure is reduced by $10,000 to $190,000. In the unfavorable case, the loss of $180,000 would increase to a greater loss of $190,000. Similarly, conducting the survey and building no plant now results in a $-$10,000 payoff.

With all probabilities and payoffs specified, we can start calculating the EMV at each state-of-nature node. We begin at the end, or right side of the decision tree and work back toward the origin. When we finish, the best decision will be known.

We start by computing the EMV of each branch.

1. Given favorable survey results,

$$\text{EMV(node 2)} = \text{EMV(large plant | positive survey)}$$
$$= (0.78)(\$190,000) + (0.22)(-\$190,000) = \$106,400$$
$$\text{EMV(node 3)} = \text{EMV(small plant | positive survey)}$$
$$= (0.78)(\$90,000) + (0.22)(-\$30,000) = \$63,600$$

EMV calculations for favorable survey results are made first.

The EMV of no plant in this case is $-$10,000. Thus, if the survey results are favorable, a large plant should be built. Note that we bring the expected value of this decision ($106,400) to the decision node to indicate that, if the survey results are positive, our expected value will be $106,400. This is shown in Figure 3.5.

2. Given negative survey results,

$$\text{EMV(node 4)} = \text{EMV(large plant | negative survey)}$$
$$= (0.27)(\$190,000) + (0.73)(-\$190,000) = -\$87,400$$
$$\text{EMV(node 5)} = \text{EMV(small plant | negative survey)}$$
$$= (0.27)(\$90,000) + (0.73)(-\$30,000) = \$2,400$$

EMV calculations for unfavorable survey results are done next.

The EMV of no plant is again $-$10,000 for this branch. Thus, given a negative survey result, John should build a small plant with an expected value of $2,400, and this figure is indicated at the decision node.

3. Continuing on the upper part of the tree and moving backward, we compute the expected value of conducting the market survey.

We continue working backward to the origin, computing EMV values.

$$\text{EMV(node 1)} = \text{EMV(conduct survey)}$$
$$= (0.45)(\$106,400) + (0.55)(\$2,400)$$
$$= \$47,880 + \$1,320 = \$49,200$$

4. If the market survey is *not* conducted,

$$\text{EMV(node 6)} = \text{EMV(large plant)}$$
$$= (0.50)(\$200,000) + (0.50)(-\$180,000)$$
$$= \$10,000$$
$$\text{EMV(node 7)} = \text{EMV(small plant)}$$
$$= (0.50)(\$100,000) + (0.50)(-\$20,000)$$
$$= \$40,000$$

The EMV of no plant is $0.

Thus, building a small plant is the best choice, given that the marketing research is not performed, as we saw earlier.

5. We move back to the first decision node and choose the best alternative. The expected monetary value of conducting the survey is $49,200, versus an EMV of $40,000 for not conducting the study, so the best choice is to *seek* marketing information. If the survey results are favorable, John should construct a large plant; but if the research is negative, John should construct a small plant.

FIGURE 3.5   Thompson's Decision Tree with EMVs Shown

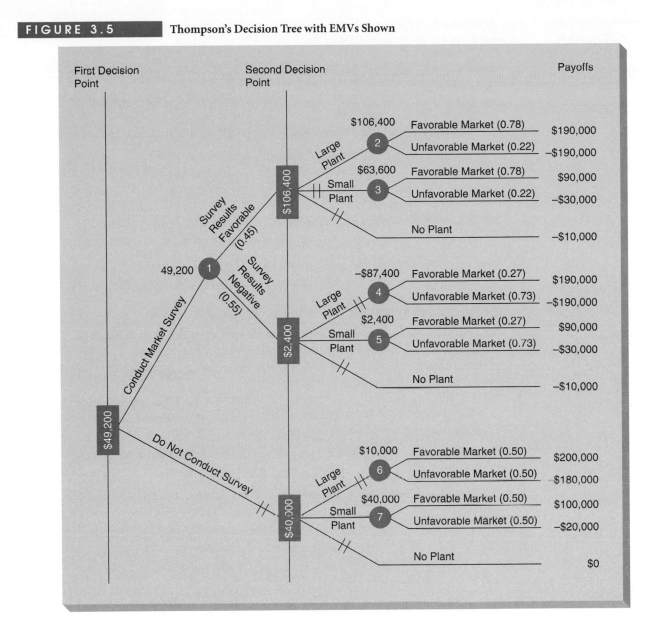

In Figure 3.5, these expected values are placed on the decision tree. Notice on the tree that a pair of slash lines / / through a decision branch indicates that a particular alternative is dropped from further consideration. This is because its EMV is lower than the EMV for the best alternative. After you have solved several decision tree problems, you may find it easier to do all of your computations on the tree diagram.

Expected Value of Sample Information   With the market survey he intends to conduct, John Thompson knows that his best decision will be to build a large plant if the survey is favorable or a small plant if the survey results are negative. But John also realizes that conducting the market research is not free. He would like to know what the actual value of doing a survey is. One way of measuring the value of market information is to compute the

EVSI measures the value of sample information.

expected value of sample information (EVSI) which is the increase in expected value resulting from the sample information.

$$\text{EVSI} = \begin{pmatrix} \text{expected value} \\ \textit{with} \text{ sample} \\ \text{information, assuming} \\ \text{no cost to gather it} \end{pmatrix} - \begin{pmatrix} \text{expected value} \\ \text{of best decision} \\ \textit{without} \text{ sample} \\ \text{information} \end{pmatrix} \qquad (3\text{-}4)$$

= (EV with sample information + cost) − (EV without sample information)

In John's case, his EMV would be $59,200 *if* he hadn't already subtracted the $10,000 study cost from each payoff. (Do you see why this is so? If not, add $10,000 back into each payoff, as in the original Thompson problem, and recompute the EMV of conducting the market study.) From the lower branch of Figure 3.5, we see that the EMV of *not* gathering the sample information is $40,000. Thus,

EVSI = ($49,200 + $10,000) − $40,000 = $59,200 − $40,000 = $19,200

This means that John could have paid up to $19,200 for a market study and still come out ahead. Since it costs only $10,000, the survey is indeed worthwhile.

Sensitivity Analysis

As with payoff tables, sensitivity analysis can be applied to decision trees as well. The overall approach is the same. Consider the decision tree for the expanded Thompson Lumber problem shown in Figure 3.5. How sensitive is our decision (to conduct the marketing survey) to the probability of favorable survey results?

Let p be the probability of favorable survey results. Then $(1 - p)$ is the probability of negative survey results. Given this information, we can develop an expression for the EMV of conducting the survey, which is node 1:

$$\text{EMV(node 1)} = (\$106,400)p + (\$2,400)(1 - p)$$
$$= \$104,000p + \$2,400$$

We are indifferent when the EMV of conducting the marketing survey, node 1, is the same as the EMV of not conducting the survey, which is $40,000. We can find the indifference point by equating EMV(node 1) to $40,000:

$$\$104,000p + \$2,400 = \$40,000$$

$$\$104,000p = \$37,600$$

$$p = \frac{\$37,600}{\$104,000} = 0.36$$

As long as the probability of favorable survey results, p, is greater than 0.36, our decision will stay the same. When p is less than 0.36, our decision will be not to conduct the survey.

We could also perform sensitivity analysis for other problem parameters. For example, we could find how sensitive our decision is to the probability of a favorable market given favorable survey results. At this time, this probability is 0.78. If this value goes up, the large plant becomes more attractive. In this case, our decision would not change. What happens when this probability goes down? The analysis becomes more complex. As the probability of a favorable market given favorable survey results goes down, the small plant becomes more attractive. At some point, the small plant will result in a higher EMV (given favorable survey results) than the large plant. This, however, does not conclude our analysis. As the probability of a favorable market given favorable survey results continues to fall, there will be a point where not conducting the survey, with an EMV of $40,000, will be more attractive than conducting the marketing survey. We leave the actual calculations to you. It is important to note that sensitivity analysis should consider *all* possible consequences.

3.7 HOW PROBABILITY VALUES ARE ESTIMATED BY BAYESIAN ANALYSIS

Bayes' theorem allows decision makers to revise probability values.

There are many ways of getting probability data for a problem such as Thompson's. The numbers (such as 0.78, 0.22, 0.27, 0.73 in Figure 3.4) can be assessed by a manager based on experience and intuition. They can be derived from historical data, or they can be computed from other available data using Bayes' theorem. The advantage of Bayes' Theorem is that it incorporates both our initial estimates of the probabilities as well as information about the accuracy of the information source (e.g. market research survey).

The Bayes' theorem approach recognizes that a decision maker does not know with certainty what state of nature will occur. It allows the manager to revise his or her initial or prior probability assessments based on new information. The revised probabilities are called *posterior probabilities*. (Before continuing, you may wish to review Bayes' theorem in Chapter 2.)

Calculating Revised Probabilities

In the Thompson Lumber case solved in Section 3.6, we made the assumption that the following four conditional probabilities were known:

$$P \text{ (favorable market(FM) | survey results positive)} = 0.78$$
$$P \text{ (unfavorable market(UM) | survey results positive)} = 0.22$$
$$P \text{ (favorable market(FM) | survey results negative)} = 0.27$$
$$P \text{ (unfavorable market(UM) | survey results negative)} = 0.73$$

We now show how John Thompson was able to derive these values with Bayes' theorem. From discussions with market research specialists at the local university, John knows that special surveys such as his can either be positive (i.e., predict a favorable market) or be negative (i.e., predict an unfavorable market). The experts have told John that, statistically, of all new products with a *favorable market* (FM), market surveys were positive and predicted success correctly 70% of the time. Thirty percent of the time the surveys falsely predicted negative results or an *unfavorable market* (UM). On the other hand, when there was actually an unfavorable market for a new product, 80% of the surveys correctly predicted negative results. The surveys incorrectly predicted positive results the remaining 20% of the time. These conditional probabilities are summarized in Table 3.11. They are an indication of the accuracy of the survey that John is thinking of undertaking.

Recall that without any market survey information, John's best estimates of a favorable and unfavorable market are

$$P(\text{FM}) = 0.50$$
$$P(\text{UM}) = 0.50$$

These are referred to as the *prior probabilities*.

TABLE 3.11		STATE OF NATURE	
Market Survey Reliability in Predicting States of Nature	**RESULT OF SURVEY**	**FAVORABLE MARKET (FM)**	**UNFAVORABLE MARKET (UM)**
	Positive (predicts favorable market for product)	$P(\text{survey positive | FM}) = 0.70$	$P(\text{survey positive | UM}) = 0.20$
	Negative (predicts unfavorable market for product)	$P(\text{survey negative | FM}) = 0.30$	$P(\text{survey negative | UM}) = 0.80$

We are now ready to compute Thompson's revised or posterior probabilities. These desired probabilities are the reverse of the probabilities in Table 3.11. We need the probability of a favorable or unfavorable market given a positive or negative result from the market study. The general form of Bayes' theorem presented in Chapter 2 is

$$P(A \mid B) = \frac{P(B \mid A) \cdot P(A)}{P(B \mid A) \cdot P(A) + P(B \mid \overline{A}) \cdot P(\overline{A})}$$ (3-5)

where

$$A, B = \text{any two events}$$

$$\overline{A} = \text{complement of } A$$

We can let A represent a favorable market and B represent a positive survey. Then, substituting the appropriate numbers into this equation, we obtain the conditional probabilities, given that the market survey is positive:

$$P(\text{FM} \mid \text{survey positive})$$

$$= \frac{P(\text{survey positive} \mid \text{FM}) \cdot P(\text{FM})}{P(\text{survey positive} \mid \text{FM}) \cdot P(\text{FM}) + P(\text{survey positive} \mid \text{UM}) \cdot P(\text{UM})}$$

$$= \frac{(0.70)(0.50)}{(0.70)(0.50) + (0.20)(0.50)} = \frac{0.35}{0.45} = 0.78$$

$$P(\text{UM} \mid \text{survey positive})$$

$$= \frac{P(\text{survey positive} \mid \text{UM}) \cdot P(\text{UM})}{P(\text{survey positive} \mid \text{UM}) \cdot P(\text{UM}) + P(\text{survey positive} \mid \text{FM}) \cdot P(\text{FM})}$$

$$= \frac{(0.20)(0.50)}{(0.20)(0.50) + (0.70)(0.50)} = \frac{0.10}{0.45} = 0.22$$

Note that the denominator (0.45) in these calculations is the probability of a positive survey. An alternative method for these calculations is to use a probability table as shown in Table 3.12. An Excel spreadsheet to do this is shown in Appendix 3.3.

| TABLE 3.12 | Probability Revisions Given a Positive Survey | | | |

STATE OF NATURE	CONDITIONAL PROBABILITY P(SURVEY POSITIVE I STATE OF NATURE)	PRIOR PROBABILITY	JOINT PROBABILITY	POSTERIOR PROBABILITY P(STATE OF NATURE I SURVEY POSITIVE)
FM	0.70	× 0.50	= 0.35	0.35/0.45 = 0.78
UM	0.20	× 0.50	= 0.10	0.10/0.45 = 0.22
		P(survey results positive) = 0.45		1.00

The conditional probabilities, given the market survey is negative, are

$$P(\text{FM} \mid \text{survey negative})$$

$$= \frac{P(\text{survey negative} \mid \text{FM}) \cdot P(\text{FM})}{P(\text{survey negative} \mid \text{FM}) \cdot P(\text{FM}) + P(\text{survey negative} \mid \text{UM}) \cdot P(\text{UM})}$$

$$= \frac{(0.30)(0.50)}{(0.30)(0.50) + (0.80)(0.50)} = \frac{0.15}{0.55} = 0.27$$

$$P(\text{UM} \mid \text{survey negative})$$

$$= \frac{P(\text{survey negative} \mid \text{UM}) \cdot P(\text{UM})}{P(\text{survey negative} \mid \text{UM}) \cdot P(\text{UM}) + P(\text{survey negative} \mid \text{FM}) \cdot P(\text{FM})}$$

$$= \frac{(0.80)(0.50)}{(0.80)(0.50) + (0.30)(0.50)} = \frac{0.40}{0.55} = 0.73$$

New probabilities provide valuable information.

Note that the denominator (0.55) in these calculations is the probability of a negative survey. These computations given a negative survey could also have been performed in a table instead, as in Table 3.13.

The posterior probabilities now provide John Thompson with estimates for each state of nature if the survey results are positive or negative. As you know, John's *prior probability* of success without a market survey was only 0.50. Now he is aware that the probability of successfully marketing storage sheds will be 0.78 if his survey shows positive results. His chances of success drop to 27% if the survey report is negative. This is valuable management information, as we saw in the earlier decision tree analysis.

Potential Problem in Using Survey Results

In many decision-making problems, survey results or pilot studies are done before an actual decision (such as building a new plant or taking a particular course of action) is made. As discussed earlier in this section, Bayes' analysis is used to help determine the correct conditional probabilities that are needed to solve these types of decision theory problems. In computing these conditional probabilities, we need to have data about the surveys and their accuracies. If a decision to build a plant or to take another course of action is actually made, we can determine the accuracy of our surveys. Unfortunately, we cannot

TABLE 3.13   Probability Revisions Given a Negative Survey

STATE OF NATURE	CONDITIONAL PROBABILITY P(SURVEY NEGATIVE | STATE OF NATURE)	PRIOR PROBABILITY	JOINT PROBABILITY	POSTERIOR PROBABILITY P(STATE OF NATURE | SURVEY NEGATIVE)
FM	0.30	× 0.50	= 0.15	0.15/0.55 = 0.27
UM	0.80	× 0.50	= 0.40	0.40/0.55 = 0.73
		P(survey results negative) = 0.55		1.00

always get data about those situations in which the decision was not to build a plant or not to take some course of action. Thus, sometimes when we use survey results, we are basing our probabilities only on those cases in which a decision to build a plant or take some course of action is actually made. This means that, in some situations, conditional probability information may not be not quite as accurate as we would like. Even so, calculating conditional probabilities helps to refine the decision-making process and, in general, to make better decisions.

3.8 UTILITY THEORY

We have focused on the EMV criterion for making decisions under risk. However, there are many occasions in which people make decisions that would appear to be inconsistent with the EMV criterion. When people buy insurance, the amount of the premium is greater than the expected payout to them from the insurance company because the premium includes the expected payout, the overhead cost, and the profit for the insurance company. A person involved in a lawsuit may choose to settle out of court rather than go to trial even if the expected value of going to trial is greater than the proposed settlement. A person buys a lottery ticket even though the expected return is negative. Casino games of all types have negative expected returns for the player, and yet millions of people play these games. A businessperson may rule out one potential decision because it could bankrupt the firm if things go bad, even though the expected return for this decision is better than that of all other alternatives.

The overall value of the result of a decision is called utility.

Why do people make decisions that don't maximize their EMV? They do this because the monetary value is not always a true indicator of the overall value of the result of the decision. The overall worth of a particular outcome is called *utility*, and rational people make decisions that maximize the expected utility. Although at times the monetary value is a good indicator of utility, there are other times when it is not. This is particularly true when some of the values involve an extremely large payoff or an extremely large loss. For example, suppose that you are the lucky holder of a lottery ticket. Five minutes from now a fair coin could be flipped, and if it comes up tails, you would win $5 million. If it comes up heads, you would win nothing. Just a moment ago a wealthy person offered you $2 million for your ticket. Let's assume that you have no doubts about the validity of the offer. The person will give you a certified check for the full amount, and you are absolutely sure the check would be good.

A decision tree for this situation is shown in Figure 3.6. The EMV for rejecting the offer indicates that you should hold on to your ticket, but what would you do? Just think, $2 million for *sure* instead of a 50% chance at nothing. Suppose you were greedy enough to hold on to the ticket, and then lost. How would you explain that to your friends? Wouldn't $2 million be enough to be comfortable for a while?

EMV is not always the best approach.

Most people would choose to sell the ticket for $2 million. Most of us, in fact, would probably be willing to settle for a lot less. Just how low we would go is, of course, a matter of personal preference. People have different feelings about seeking or avoiding risk. Using the EMV alone is not always a good way to make these types of decisions.

One way to incorporate your own attitudes toward risk is through *utility theory*. In the next section we explore first how to measure utility and then how to use utility measures in decision making.

Measuring Utility and Constructing a Utility Curve

Utility assessment assigns the worst outcome a utility of 0 and the best outcome, 1.

The first step in using utility theory is to assign utility values to each monetary value in a given situation. It is convenient to begin *utility assessment* by assigning the worst outcome a utility of 0 and the best outcome a utility of 1. Although any values may be used as long as

FIGURE 3.6

**Your Decision Tree for the
Lottery Ticket**

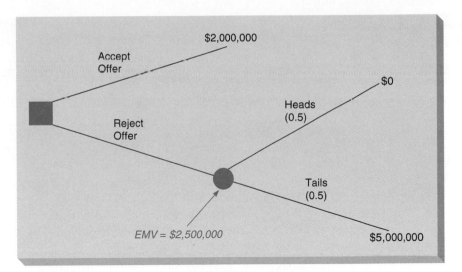

the utility for the best outcome is greater than the utility for the worst outcome, using 0 and 1 has some benefits. Because we have chosen to use 0 and 1, all other outcomes will have a utility value between 0 and 1. In determining the utilities of all outcomes, other than the best or worst outcome, a *standard gamble* is considered. This gamble is shown in Figure 3.7.

In Figure 3.7, p is the probability of obtaining the best outcome, and $(1 - p)$ is the probability of obtaining the worst outcome. Assessing the utility of any other outcome involves determining the probability (p), which makes you indifferent between alternative 1, which is the gamble between the best and worst outcomes, and alternative 2, which is obtaining the other outcome for sure. When you are indifferent between alternatives 1 and 2, the expected utilities for these two alternatives must be equal. This relationship is shown as

*When you are indifferent, the
expected utilities are equal.*

expected utility of alternative 2 = expected utility of alternative 1

utility of other outcome = (p)(utility of *best* outcome, which is 1)

$$+ (1 - p)(\text{utility of the } worst \text{ outcome, which is 0})$$ (3-6)

utility of other outcome = $(p)(1) + (1 - p)(0) = p$

Now all you have to do is to determine the value of the probability (p) that makes you indifferent between alternatives 1 and 2. In setting the probability, you should be aware that utility assessment is completely subjective. It's a value set by the decision maker that can't be measured on an objective scale. Let's take a look at an example.

FIGURE 3.7

**Standard Gamble for
Utility Assessment**

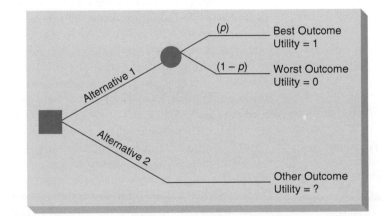

FIGURE 3.8

Utility of $5,000

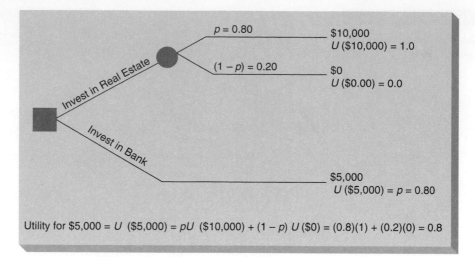

$$\text{Utility for } \$5{,}000 = U(\$5{,}000) = pU(\$10{,}000) + (1-p)U(\$0) = (0.8)(1) + (0.2)(0) = 0.8$$

Once utility values have been determined, a utility curve can be constructed.

Jane Dickson would like to construct a utility curve revealing her preference for money between $0 and $10,000. A *utility curve* is a graph that plots utility value versus monetary value. She can either invest her money in a bank savings account or she can invest the same money in a real estate deal.

If the money is invested in the bank, in three years Jane would have $5,000. If she invested in the real estate, after three years she could either have nothing or $10,000. Jane, however, is very conservative. Unless there is an 80% chance of getting $10,000 from the real estate deal, Jane would prefer to have her money in the bank, where it is safe. What Jane has done here is to assess her utility for $5,000. When there is an 80% chance (this means that p is 0.8) of getting $10,000, Jane is indifferent between putting her money in real estate or putting it in the bank. Jane's utility for $5,000 is thus equal to 0.8, which is the same as the value for p. This utility assessment is shown in Figure 3.8.

Other utility values can be assessed in the same way. For example, what is Jane's utility for $7,000? What value of p would make Jane indifferent between $7,000 and the gamble that would result in either $10,000 or $0? For Jane, there must be a 90% chance of getting the $10,000. Otherwise, she would prefer the $7,000 for sure. Thus, her utility for $7,000 is 0.90. Jane's utility for $3,000 can be determined in the same way. If there were a 50% chance of obtaining the $10,000, Jane would be indifferent between having $3,000 for sure and taking the gamble of either winning the $10,000 or getting nothing. Thus, the utility of $3,000 for Jane is 0.5. Of course, this process can be continued until Jane has assessed her utility for as many monetary values as she wants. These assessments, however, are enough to get an idea of Jane's feelings toward risk. In fact, we can plot these points in a utility curve, as is done in Figure 3.9. In the figure, the assessed utility points of $3,000, $5,000, and $7,000 are shown by dots, and the rest of the curve is inferred from these.

Jane's utility curve is typical of a *risk avoider*. A risk avoider is a decision maker who gets less utility or pleasure from a greater risk and tends to avoid situations in which high losses might occur. As monetary value increases on her utility curve, the utility increases at a slower rate.

The shape of a person's utility curve depends on many factors.

Figure 3.10 illustrates that a person who is a *risk seeker* has an opposite-shaped utility curve. This decision maker gets more utility from a greater risk and higher potential payoff. As monetary value increases on his or her utility curve, the utility increases at an increasing rate. A person who is *indifferent* to risk has a utility curve that is a straight line. The shape of a person's utility curve depends on the specific decision being considered, the monetary values involved in the situation, the person's psychological frame of mind, and

FIGURE 3.9

Utility Curve for Jane Dickson

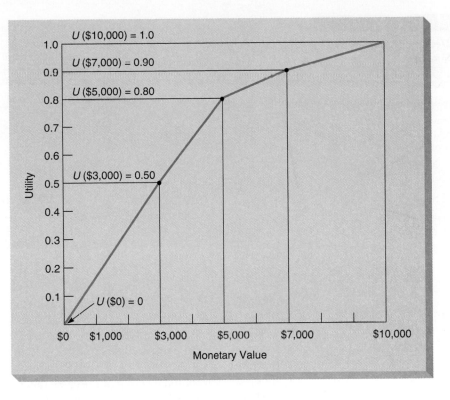

how the person feels about the future. It may well be that you have one utility curve for some situations you face and completely different curves for others.

Utility as a Decision-Making Criterion

Utility values replace monetary values.

After a utility curve has been determined, the utility values from the curve are used in making decisions. Monetary outcomes or values are replaced with the appropriate utility values and then decision analysis is performed as usual. The expected utility for each alternative is

FIGURE 3.10

Preferences for Risk

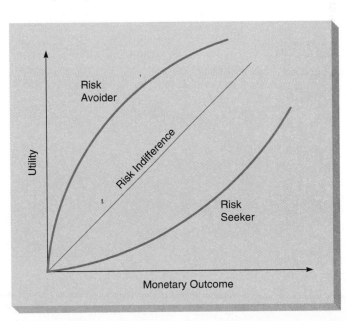

FIGURE 3.11

**Decision Facing Mark
Simkin**

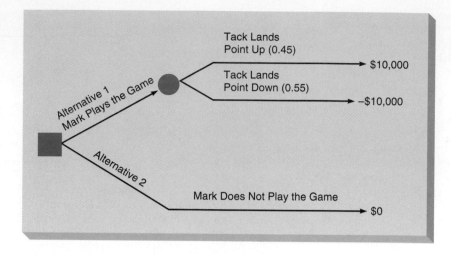

computed instead of the EMV. Let's take a look at an example in which a decision tree is used and expected utility values are computed in selecting the best alternative.

Mark Simkin loves to gamble. He decides to play a game that involves tossing thumbtacks in the air. If the point on the thumbtack is facing up after it lands, Mark wins $10,000. If the point on the thumbtack is down, Mark loses $10,000. Should Mark play the game (alternative 1) or should he not play the game (alternative 2)?

Alternatives 1 and 2 are displayed in the tree shown in Figure 3.11. As can be seen, alternative 1 is to play the game. Mark believes that there is a 45% chance of winning $10,000 and a 55% chance of suffering the $10,000 loss. Alternative 2 is not to gamble. What should Mark do? Of course, this depends on Mark's utility for money. As stated previously, he likes to gamble. Using the procedure just outlined, Mark was able to construct a utility curve showing his preference for money. Mark has a total of $20,000 to gamble, so he has constructed the utility curve based on a best payoff of $20,000 and a worst payoff of a $20,000 loss. This curve appears in Figure 3.12.

FIGURE 3.12

**Utility Curve for Mark
Simkin**

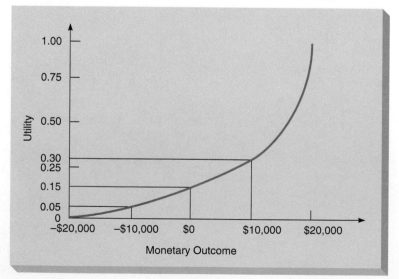

IN ACTION   Using Utility and Decision Trees in Hip Replacement

Should you or a family member undergo a somewhat dangerous surgery, or is it better to be managed medically by drugs? Should a health care firm put a new drug on its list of approved medicines? What medical procedures should the government reimburse? Individuals and institutions face medical treatment decision problems from a variety of perspectives. For example, the decision an individual patient faces is driven by the medical treatment that best describes the patient's attitudes about risk (utility) and quality of life over the rest of his or her life.

One common application of utility theory decision tree modeling in medicine is the total-hip replacement surgery for patients with severe arthritis of the hip. Over 120,000 hip replacements are performed per year in North America. Although this surgery is mostly successful, the treatment decision for an individual patient can be difficult. Although surgery offers the potential of increased quality of life, it also carries the risk of death.

A decision tree helps define all of the time-sequenced outcomes that can occur in dealing with arthritis of the hip. Conservative management by medicine is a surgical alternative, but the disease is degenerative and a worsening condition is inevitable. A successful surgery, which restores full function, is likely, but uncertainty exists even then. First, infection may cause the new prosthetic hip to fail. Or the new hip may fail over time as a result of breakage or malfunction. Both cases require a revision surgery, whose risks are greater than the first surgery. Decision trees and utility theory help patients first assess their personal risk levels and then allow the patient to compute life expectancy based on sex and race.

Source: G. Hazen, J. Pellissier, and J. Sounderpandian. "Stochastic Tree Models in Medical Decision Making," *Interfaces* (July–August, 1998): 64–80.

Mark's objective is to maximize expected utility.

We see that Mark's utility for −$10,000 is 0.05, his utility for not playing ($0) is 0.15, and his utility for $10,000 is 0.30. These values can now be used in the decision tree. Mark's objective is to maximize his expected utility, which can be done as follows:

Step 1.
$$U(-\$10,000) = 0.05$$
$$U(\$0) = 0.15$$
$$U(\$10,000) = 0.30$$

Step 2. Replace monetary values with utility values. Refer to Figure 3.13. Here are the expected utilities for alternatives 1 and 2:

$$E(\text{alternative 1: play the game}) = (0.45)(0.30) + (0.55)(0.05)$$
$$= 0.135 + 0.027 = 0.162$$

$$E(\text{alternative 2: don't play the game}) = 0.15$$

FIGURE 3.13

Using Expected Utilities in Decision Making

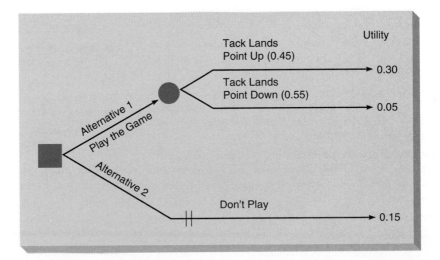

Therefore, alternative 1 is the best strategy using utility as the decision criterion. If EMV had been used, alternative 2 would have been the best strategy. The utility curve is a risk-seeker utility curve, and the choice of playing the game certainly reflects this preference for risk.

SUMMARY

Decision theory is an analytic and systematic approach to studying decision making. Six steps are usually involved in making decisions in three environments: decision making under certainty, uncertainty, and risk. In decision making under uncertainty, decision tables are constructed to compute such criteria as maximax, maximin, criterion of realism, equally likely, and minimax regret. Such methods as determining expected monetary value (EMV), expected value of perfect information (EVPI), expected opportunity loss (EOL), and sensitivity analysis are used in decision making under risk.

Decision trees are another option, particularly for larger decision problems, when one decision must be made

before other decisions can be made. For example, a decision to take a sample or to perform market research is made before we decide to construct a large plant, a small one, or no plant. In this case we can also compute the expected value of sample information (EVSI) to determine the value of the market research. Bayesian analysis can be used to revise or update probability values using both the prior probabilities and other probabilities related to the accuracy of the information source. We can, for example, determine the probability of a favorable market given that we have received positive survey results using Bayesian analysis.

GLOSSARY

Alternative. A course of action or a strategy that may be chosen by a decision maker.

Coefficient of Realism (α). A number from 0 to 1. When the coefficient is close to 1, the decision criterion is optimistic. When the coefficient is close to zero, the decision criterion is pessimistic.

Conditional Value or Payoff. A consequence, normally expressed in a monetary value, that occurs as a result of a particular alternative and state of nature.

Conditional Probability. A posterior probability.

Criterion of Realism. A decision-making criterion that uses a weighted average of the best and worst possible payoffs for each alternative.

Decision Making under Certainty. A decision-making environment in which the future outcomes or states of nature are known.

Decision Making under Risk. A decision-making environment in which several outcomes or states of nature may occur as a result of a decision or alternative. The probabilities of the outcomes or states of nature are known.

Decision Making under Uncertainty. A decision-making environment in which several outcomes or states of nature may occur. The probabilities of these outcomes, however, are not known.

Decision Node (Point). In a decision tree, this is a point where the best of the available alternatives is chosen. The branches represent the alternatives.

Decision Table. A payoff table.

Decision Theory. An analytic and systematic approach to decision making.

Decision Tree. A graphical representation of a decision making situation.

Equally Likely. A decision criterion that places an equal weight on all states of nature.

Expected Monetary Value (EMV). The average value of a decision if it can be repeated many times. This is determined by multiplying the monetary values by their respective probabilities. The results are then added to arrive at the EMV.

Expected Value of Perfect Information (EVPI). The average or expected value of information if it were completely accurate. The increase in EMV that results from having perfect information.

Expected Value of Sample Information (EVSI). The increase in EMV that results from having sample or imperfect information.

Expected Value with Perfect Information (EVwPI). The average or expected value of the decision if you knew what would happen ahead of time. You have perfect knowledge.

Hurwicz Criterion. The criterion of realism.

Laplace Criterion. The equally likely criterion.

Maximax. An optimistic decision-making criterion. This selects the alternative with the highest possible return.

Maximin. A pessimistic decision-making criterion. This alternative maximizes the minimum payoff. It selects the alternative with the best of the worst possible payoffs.

Minimax Regret. A criterion that minimizes the maximum opportunity loss.

Opportunity Loss. The amount you would lose by not picking the best alternative. For any state of nature, this is the difference between the consequences of any alternative and the best possible alternative.

Optimistic Criterion. The maximax criterion.

Payoff Table. A table that lists the alternatives, states of nature, and payoffs in a decision-making situation.

Posterior Probability. A conditional probability of a state of nature that has been adjusted based on sample information. This is found using Bayes Theorem.

Prior Probability. The initial probability of a state of nature before sample information is used with Bayes Theorem to obtain the posterior probability.

Regret. Opportunity loss.

Risk Seeker. A person who seeks risk. On the utility curve, as the monetary value increases, the utility increases at an increasing rate. This decision maker gets more pleasure for a greater risk and higher potential returns.

Risk Avoider. A person who avoids risk. On the utility curve, as the monetary value, the utility increases at a decreasing rate. This decision maker gets less utility for a greater risk and higher potential returns.

Sequential Decisions. Decisions in which the outcome of one decision influences other decisions.

State of Nature. An outcome or occurrence over which the decision maker has little or no control.

Standard Gamble. The process used to determine utility values.

State of Nature Node. In a decision tree, this is a point where the EMV is computed. The branches coming from this node represent states of nature.

Utility. The overall value or worth of a particular outcome.

Utility Assessment. The process of determining the utility of various outcomes. This is normally done using a standard gamble between any outcome for sure and a gamble between the worst and best outcomes.

Utility Curve. A graph or curve that reveals the relationship between utility and monetary values. When this curve has been constructed, utility values from the curve can be used in the decision-making process.

Utility Theory. A theory that allows decision makers to incorporate their risk preference and other factors into the decision-making process.

Weighted Average Criterion. Another name for the criterion of realism.

KEY EQUATIONS

(3-1)   EMV (Alternative i) = (payoff of first state of nature) × (its probability) + (payoff of second state of nature) × (its probability) + . . . + (payoff of last state of nature) × (its probability)

This equation computes expected monetary values.

(3-2)   Expected value *with* perfect information = (best outcome for first state of nature) × (its probability) + (best outcome for second state of nature) × (its probability) + . . . + (best outcome for last state of nature) × (its probability)

(3-3)   EVPI = expected value *with* perfect information − maximum EMV

This equation calculates the expected value of perfect information.

(3-4)   Expected value of sample information (EVSI)

$$= \begin{pmatrix} \text{expected value} \\ \textit{with} \text{ sample} \\ \text{information, assuming} \\ \text{no cost to gather it} \end{pmatrix} - \begin{pmatrix} \text{expected value} \\ \text{of the best decision} \\ \textit{without} \text{ sample} \\ \text{information} \end{pmatrix}$$

= (EV with SI + cost) − (EV without SI)

(3-5) $P(A \mid B) = \dfrac{P(B \mid A) \cdot P(A)}{P(B \mid A) \cdot P(A) + P(B \mid \overline{A}) \cdot P(\overline{A})}$

Bayes' theorem—the conditional probability of event A given that event B has occurred.

(3-6)   Utility of other outcome = $(p)(1) + (1 - p)(0) = p$

The equation determining the utility of an intermediate outcome.

SOLVED PROBLEMS

Solved Problem 3-1

Maria Rojas is considering the possibility of opening a small dress shop on Fairbanks Avenue, a few blocks from the university. She has located a good mall that attracts students. Her options are to open a small shop, a medium-sized shop, or no shop at all. The market for a dress shop can be good, average, or bad. The probabilities for these three possibilities are 0.2 for a good market, 0.5 for an average market, and 0.3 for a bad market. The net profit or loss for the medium-sized and small shops for the various market conditions are given in the following table. Building no shop at all yields no loss and no gain. What do you recommend?

ALTERNATIVE	GOOD MARKET ($)	AVERAGE MARKET ($)	BAD MARKET ($)
Small shop	75,000	25,000	−40,000
Medium-sized shop	100,000	35,000	−60,000
No shop	0	0	0

Solution

Since the decision-making environment is risk (probabilities are known), it is appropriate to use the EMV criterion. The problem can be solved by developing a payoff table that contains all alternatives, states of nature, and probability values. The EMV for each alternative is also computed, as in the following table:

ALTERNATIVE	STATE OF NATURE			EMV ($)
	GOOD MARKET ($)	AVERAGE MARKET ($)	BAD MARKET ($)	
Small shop	75,000	25,000	−40,000	15,500
Medium-sized shop	100,000	35,000	−60,000	19,500
No shop	0	0	0	0
Probabilities	0.20	0.50	0.30	

$$\text{EMV(small shop)} = (0.2)(\$75,000) + (0.5)(\$25,000)$$
$$+ (0.3)(-\$40,000) = \$15,500$$
$$\text{EMV(medium shop)} = (0.2)(\$100,000) + (0.5)(\$35,000)$$
$$+ (0.3)(-\$60,000) = \$19,500$$
$$\text{EMV(no shop)} = (0.2)(\$0) + (0.5)(\$0) + (0.3)(\$0) = \$0$$

As can be seen, the best decision is to build the medium-sized shop. The EMV for this alternative is $19,500.

Solved Problem 3-2

Cal Bender and Becky Addison have known each other since high school. Two years ago they entered the same university and today they are taking undergraduate courses in the business school. Both hope to graduate with degrees in finance. In an attempt to make extra money and to use some of the knowledge gained from their business courses, Cal and Becky have decided to look into the possibility of starting a small company that would provide word processing services to students who needed term papers or other reports prepared in a professional manner. Using a systems approach, Cal and Becky have identified three strategies. Strategy 1 is to invest in a fairly expensive microcomputer system with a high-quality laser printer. In a favorable market, they should be able to obtain a net profit of $10,000 over the next two years. If the market is unfavorable, they can lose $8,000. Strategy 2 is to purchase a less expensive system. With a favorable market, they could get a return during the next two years of $8,000. With an unfavorable market, they would incur a loss of $4,000. Their final strategy, strategy 3, is to do nothing. Cal is basically a risk taker, whereas Becky tries to avoid risk.

a. What type of decision procedure should Cal use? What would Cal's decision be?
b. What type of decision maker is Becky? What decision would Becky make?
c. If Cal and Becky were indifferent to risk, what type of decision approach should they use? What would you recommend if this were the case?

Solution

The problem is one of decision making under uncertainty. Before answering the specific questions, a decision table should be developed showing the alternatives, states of nature, and related consequences.

ALTERNATIVE	FAVORABLE MARKET ($)	UNFAVORABLE MARKET ($)
Strategy 1	10,000	−8,000
Strategy 2	8,000	−4,000
Strategy 3	0	0

a. Since Cal is a risk taker, he should use the maximax decision criteria. This approach selects the row that has the highest or maximum value. The $10,000 value, which is the maximum value from the table, is in row 1. Thus Cal's decision is to select strategy 1, which is an optimistic decision approach.

b. Becky should use the maximin decision criteria because she wants to avoid risk. The minimum or worst outcome for each row, or strategy, is identified. These outcomes are −$8,000 for strategy 1, −$4,000 for strategy 2, and $0 for strategy 3. The maximum of these values is selected. Thus, Becky would select strategy 3, which reflects a pessimistic decision approach.

c. If Cal and Becky are indifferent to risk, they could use the equally likely approach. This approach selects the alternative that maximizes the row averages. The row average for strategy 1 is $1,000[$1,000 = ($10,000 − $8,000)/2]. The row average for strategy 2 is $2,000, and the row average for strategy 3 is $0. Thus, using the equally likely approach, the decision is to select strategy 2, which maximizes the row averages.

Solved Problem 3-3

Monica Britt has enjoyed sailing small boats since she was 7 years old, when her mother started sailing with her. Today, Monica is considering the possibility of starting a company to produce small sailboats for the recreational market. Unlike other mass-produced sailboats, however, these boats will be made specifically for children between the ages of 10 and 15. The boats will be of the highest quality and extremely stable, and the sail size will be reduced to prevent problems of capsizing.

Because of the expense involved in developing the initial molds and acquiring the necessary equipment to produce fiberglass sailboats for young children, Monica has decided to conduct a pilot study to make sure that the market for the sailboats will be adequate. She estimates that the pilot study will cost her $10,000. Furthermore, the pilot study can be either successful or not successful. Her basic decision is whether to build a large manufacturing facility, a small manufacturing facility, or no facility at all. With a favorable market, Monica can expect to make $90,000 from the large facility or $60,000 from the smaller facility. If the market is unfavorable, however, Monica estimates that she would lose $30,000 with a large facility, and she would lose only $20,000 with the small facility. Monica estimates that the probability of a favorable market given a successful pilot study is 0.8. The probability of an unfavorable market given an unsuccessful pilot study result is estimated to be 0.9. Monica feels that there is a 50–50 chance that the pilot study will be successful. Of course, Monica could bypass the pilot study and simply make the decision as to whether to build a large plant, small plant, or no facility at all. Without doing any testing in a pilot study, she estimates that the probability of a successful market is 0.6. What do you recommend?

Solution

Before Monica starts to solve this problem, she should develop a decision tree that shows all alternatives, states of nature, probability values, and economic consequences. This decision tree is shown in Figure 3.14.

**Monica's Decision Tree,
Listing Alternatives, States
of Nature, Probability
Values, and Financial
Outcomes for Solved
Problem 3-3**

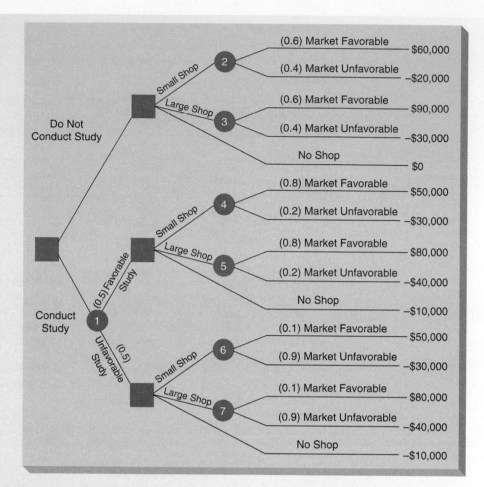

Once the decision tree has been developed, Monica can solve the problem by computing EMVs starting at the endpoints of the decision tree. The final solution is shown on the revised decision tree, Figure 3.15. The optimal solution is to *not* conduct the study but to construct the large plant directly. The expected monetary value is $42,000.

Solved Problem 3-4

Developing a small driving range for golfers of all abilities has long been a desire of John Jenkins. John, however, believes that the chance of a successful driving range is only about 40%. A friend of John's has suggested that he conduct a survey in the community to get a better feeling of the demand for such a facility. There is a 0.9 probability that the research will be favorable if the driving range facility will be successful. Furthermore, it is estimated that there is a 0.8 probability that the marketing research will be unfavorable if indeed the facility will be unsuccessful. John would like to determine the chances of a successful driving range given a favorable result from the marketing survey.

Solution

This problem requires the use of Bayes' theorem. Before we start to solve the problem, we will define the following terms:

$P(\text{UF})$ = probability of successful driving range facility

$P(\text{UF})$ = probability of unsuccessful driving range facility

$P(\text{RF} \mid \text{SF})$ = probability that the research will be favorable given a successful driving range facility

$P(\text{RU} \mid \text{SF})$ = probability that the research will be unfavorable given a successful driving range facility

$P(\text{RU} \mid \text{UF})$ = probability that the research will be unfavorable given an unsuccessful driving range facility

$P(\text{RF} \mid \text{UF})$ = probability that the research will be favorable given an unsuccessful driving range facility

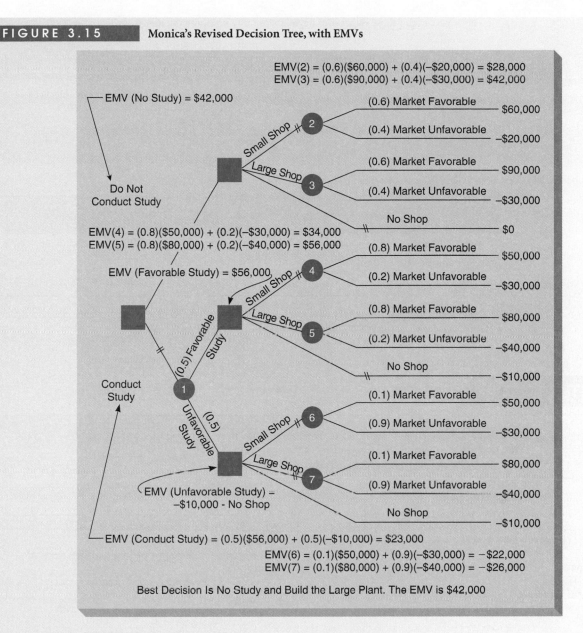

FIGURE 3.15 Monica's Revised Decision Tree, with EMVs

EMV(2) = (0.6)($60,000) + (0.4)(−$20,000) = $28,000
EMV(3) = (0.6)($90,000) + (0.4)(−$30,000) = $42,000

EMV (No Study) = $42,000

Do Not Conduct Study

(0.6) Market Favorable $60,000
(0.4) Market Unfavorable −$20,000
(0.6) Market Favorable $90,000
(0.4) Market Unfavorable −$30,000
No Shop $0

Small Shop 2
Large Shop 3

EMV(4) = (0.8)($50,000) + (0.2)(−$30,000) = $34,000
EMV(5) = (0.8)($80,000) + (0.2)(−$40,000) = $56,000

EMV (Favorable Study) = $56,000

(0.8) Market Favorable $50,000
(0.2) Market Unfavorable −$30,000
(0.8) Market Favorable $80,000
(0.2) Market Unfavorable −$40,000
No Shop −$10,000

Small Shop 4
Large Shop 5

(0.5) Favorable Study

Conduct Study

1

(0.5) Unfavorable Study

(0.1) Market Favorable $50,000
(0.9) Market Unfavorable −$30,000
(0.1) Market Favorable $80,000
(0.9) Market Unfavorable −$40,000
No Shop −$10,000

Small Shop 6
Large Shop 7

EMV (Unfavorable Study) = −$10,000 - No Shop

EMV (Conduct Study) = (0.5)($56,000) + (0.5)(−$10,000) = $23,000
EMV(6) = (0.1)($50,000) + (0.9)(−$30,000) = −$22,000
EMV(7) = (0.1)($80,000) + (0.9)(−$40,000) = −$26,000

Best Decision Is No Study and Build the Large Plant. The EMV is $42,000

Now, we can summarize what we know:

$$P(\text{SF}) = 0.4$$
$$P(\text{RF} \mid \text{SF}) = 0.9$$
$$P(\text{RU} \mid \text{UF}) = 0.8$$

From this information we can compute three additional probabilities that we need to solve the problem:

$$P(\text{UF}) = 1 - P(\text{SF}) = 1 - 0.4 = 0.6$$
$$P(\text{RU} \mid \text{SF}) = 1 - P(\text{RF} \mid \text{SF}) = 1 - 0.9 = 0.1$$
$$P(\text{RF} \mid \text{UF}) = 1 - P(\text{RU} \mid \text{UF}) = 1 - 0.8 = 0.2$$

Now we can put these values into Bayes' theorem to compute the desired probability:

$$P(SF \mid RF) = \frac{P(RF \mid SF) \cdot P(SF)}{P(RF \mid SF) \cdot P(SF) + P(RF \mid UF) \cdot P(UF)}$$

$$= \frac{(0.9)(0.4)}{(0.9)(0.4) + (0.2)(0.6)}$$

$$= \frac{0.36}{(0.36 + 0.12)} = \frac{0.36}{0.48} = 0.75$$

In addition to using formulas to solve John's problem, it is possible to perform all calculations in a table:

Revised Probabilities Given a Favorable Research Result

STATE OF NATURE	CONDITIONAL PROBABILITY		PRIOR PROBABILITY		JOINT PROBABILITY	POSTERIOR PROBABILITY
Favorable market	0.9	×	0.4	=	0.36	0.36/0.48 = 0.75
Unfavorable market	0.2	×	0.6	=	0.12	0.12/0.48 = 0.25
					0.48	

As you can see from the table, the results are the same. The probability of a successful driving range given a favorable research result is 0.36/0.48, or 0.75.

⇒ SELF-TEST

- Before taking the self-test, refer back to the learning objectives at the beginning of the chapter, the notes in the margins, and the glossary at the end of the chapter.
- Use the key at the back of the book to correct your answers.
- Restudy pages that correspond to any questions that you answered incorrectly or material you feel uncertain about.

1. In decision theory terminology, a course of action or a strategy that may be chosen by a decision maker is called a(n)
   a. payoff.
   b. alternative.
   c. state of nature.
   d. none of the above.
2. In decision theory, probabilities are associated with
   a. payoffs.
   b. alternatives.
   c. states of nature.
   d. none of the above.
3. If probabilities are available to the decision maker, then the decision-making environment is called
   a. certainty.
   b. uncertainty.
   c. risk.
   d. none of the above.
4. Which of the following is a decision-making criterion that is used for decision making under risk?
   a. expected monetary value criterion
   b. Hurwicz criterion (criterion of realism)
   c. optimistic (maximax) criterion
   d. equally likely criterion

5. The minimum expected opportunity loss
   a. is equal to the highest expected payoff.
   b. is greater than the expected value with perfect information.
   c. is equal to the expected value of perfect information.
   d. is computed when finding the minimax regret decision.
6. In using the criterion of realism (Hurwicz criterion), the coefficient of realism (α)
   a. is the probability of a good state of nature.
   b. describes the degree of optimism of the decision maker.
   c. describes the degree of pessimism of the decision maker.
   d. is usually less than zero.
7. The most that a person should pay for perfect information is
   a. the EVPI.
   b. the maximum EMV minus the minimum EMV.
   c. the maximum EOL.
   d. the maximum EMV.
8. The minimum EOL criterion will always result in the same decision as
   a. the maximax criterion.
   b. the minimax regret criterion.
   c. the maximum EMV criterion.
   d. the equally likely criterion.

9. A decision tree is preferable to a decision table when
   a. a number of sequential decisions are to be made.
   b. probabilities are available.
   c. the maximax criterion is used.
   d. the objective is to maximize regret.
10. Bayes' theorem is used to revise probabilities. The new (revised) probabilities are called
   a. prior probabilities.
   b. sample probabilities.
   c. survey probabilities.
   d. posterior probabilities.
11. On a decision tree, at each state-of-nature node,
   a. the alternative with the greatest EMV is selected.
   b. an EMV is calculated.
   c. all probabilities are added together.
   d. the branch with the highest probability is selected.
12. The EVSI
   a. is found by subtracting the EMV without sample information from the EMV with sample information.
   b. is always equal to the expected value of perfect information.
   c. equals the EMV with sample information assuming no cost for the information minus the EMV without sample information.
   d. is usually negative.

13. On a decision tree, once the tree has been drawn and the payoffs and probabilities have been placed on the tree, the analysis (computing EMVs and selecting the best alternative)
   a. is done by working backward (starting on the right and moving to the left).
   b. is done by working forward (starting on the left and moving to the right).
   c. is done by starting at the top of the tree and moving down.
   d. is done by starting at the bottom of the tree and moving up.
14. In assessing utility values,
   a. the worst outcome is given a utility of -1.
   b. the best outcome is given a utility of 0.
   c. the worst outcome is given a utility of 0.
   d. the best outcome is given a value of -1.
15. If a rational person selects an alternative that does not maximize the EMV, we would expect that this alternative
   a. minimizes the EMV.
   b. maximizes the expected utility.
   c. minimizes the expected utility.
   d. has zero utility associated with each possible payoff.

DISCUSSION QUESTIONS AND PROBLEMS

Discussion Questions

3-1 Give an example of a good decision that you made that resulted in a bad outcome. Also give an example of a bad decision that you made that had a good outcome. Why was each decision good or bad?

3-2 Describe what is involved in the decision process.

3-3 What is an alternative? What is a state of nature?

3-4 Discuss the differences among decision making under certainty, decision making under risk, and decision making under uncertainty.

3-5 What techniques are used to solve decision-making problems under uncertainty? Which technique results in an optimistic decision? Which technique results in a pessimistic decision?

3-6 Define *opportunity loss*. What decision-making criteria are used with an opportunity loss table?

3-7 What information should be placed on a decision tree?

3-8 Describe how you would determine the best decision using the EMV criterion with a decision tree.

3-9 What is the difference between prior and posterior probabilities?

3-10 What is the purpose of Bayesian analysis? Describe how you would use Bayesian analysis in the decision-making process.

3-11 What is the EVSI? How is this computed?

3-12 What is the overall purpose of utility theory?

3-13 Briefly discuss how a utility function can be assessed. What is a standard gamble, and how is it used in determining utility values?

3-14 How is a utility curve used in selecting the best decision for a particular problem?

3-15 What is a risk seeker? What is a risk avoider? How does the utility curve for these types of decision makers differ?

Problems*

3-16 Kenneth Brown is the principal owner of Brown Oil, Inc. After quitting his university teaching job, Ken has been able to increase his annual salary by a factor of over 100. At the present time, Ken is forced to consider purchasing some more equipment for Brown Oil because of competition. His alternatives are shown in the following table:

---

* Note: Ω means the problem may be solved with QM for Windows; $\times$ means the problem may be solved with Excel QM; and Ω means the problem may be solved with QM for Windows and/or Excel QM.

EQUIPMENT	FAVORABLE MARKET ($)	UNFAVORABLE MARKET ($)
Sub 100	300,000	−200,000
Oiler J	250,000	−100,000
Texan	75,000	−18,000

For example, if Ken purchases a Sub 100 and if there is a favorable market, he will realize a profit of $300,000. On the other hand, if the market is unfavorable, Ken will suffer a loss of $200,000. But Ken has always been a very optimistic decision maker.

(a) What type of decision is Ken facing?
(b) What decision criterion should he use?
(c) What alternative is best?

3-17 Although Ken Brown (discussed in Problem 3-16) is the principal owner of Brown Oil, his brother Bob is credited with making the company a financial success. Bob is vice president of finance. Bob attributes his success to his pessimistic attitude about business and the oil industry. Given the information from Problem 3-16, it is likely that Bob will arrive at a different decision. What decision criterion should Bob use, and what alternative will he select?

3-18 The *Lubricant* is an expensive oil newsletter to which many oil giants subscribe, including Ken Brown (see Problem 3-16 for details). In the last issue, the letter described how the demand for oil products would be extremely high. Apparently, the American consumer will continue to use oil products even if the price of these products doubles. Indeed, one of the articles in the *Lubricant* states that the chances of a favorable market for oil products was 70%, while the chance of an unfavorable market was only 30%. Ken would like to use these probabilities in determining the best decision.

(a) What decision model should be used?
(b) What is the optimal decision?
(c) Ken believes that the $300,000 figure for the Sub 100 with a favorable market is too high. How much lower would this figure have to be for Ken to change his decision made in part (b)?

3-19 Mickey Lawson is considering investing some money that he inherited. The following payoff table gives the profits that would be realized during the next year for each of three investment alternatives Mickey is considering:

DECISION ALTERNATIVE	STATE OF NATURE	
	GOOD ECONOMY	POOR ECONOMY
Stock market	80,000	−20,000
Bonds	30,000	20,000
CDs	23,000	23,000
Probability	0.5	0.5

(a) What decision would maximize expected profits?
(b) What is the maximum amount that should be paid for a perfect forecast of the economy?

3-20 Develop an opportunity loss table for the investment problem that Mickey Lawson faces in Problem 3-19. What decision would minimize the expected opportunity loss? What is the minimum EOL?

3-21 Allen Young has always been proud of his personal investment strategies and has done very well over the past several years. He invests primarily in the stock market. Over the past several months, however, Allen has become very concerned about the stock market as a good investment. In some cases it would have been better for Allen to have his money in a bank than in the market. During the next year, Allen must decide whether to invest $10,000 in the stock market or in a certificate of deposit (CD) at an interest rate of 9%. If the market is good, Allen believes that he could get a 14% return on his money. With a fair market, he expects to get an 8% return. If the market is bad, he will most likely get no return at all—in other words, the return would be 0%. Allen estimates that the probability of a good market is 0.4, the probability of a fair market is 0.4, and the probability of a bad market is 0.2, and he wishes to maximize his long-run average return.

(a) Develop a decision table for this problem.
(b) What is the best decision?

3-22 In Problem 3-21 you helped Allen Young determine the best investment strategy. Now, Young is thinking about paying for a stock market newsletter. A friend of Young said that these types of letters could predict very accurately whether the market would be good, fair, or poor. Then, based on these predictions, Allen could make better investment decisions.

(a) What is the most that Allen would be willing to pay for a newsletter?
(b) Young now believes that a good market will give a return of only 11% instead of 14%. Will this information change the amount that Allen would be willing to pay for the newsletter? If your answer is yes, determine the most that Allen would be willing to pay, given this new information.

3-23 Today's Electronics specializes in manufacturing modern electronic components. It also builds the equipment that produces the components. Phyllis Weinberger, who is responsible for advising the president of Today's Electronics on electronic manufacturing equipment, has developed the following table concerning a proposed facility:

	PROFIT ($)		
	STRONG MARKET	FAIR MARKET	POOR MARKET
Large facility	550,000	110,000	−310,000
Medium-sized facility	300,000	129,000	−100,000
Small facility	200,000	100,000	−32,000
No facility	0	0	0

(a) Develop an opportunity loss table.

(b) What is the minimax regret decision?

3-24 Brilliant Color is a small supplier of chemicals and equipment that are used by some photographic stores to process 35mm film. One product that Brilliant Color supplies is BC-6. John Kubick, president of Brilliant Color, normally stocks 11, 12, or 13 cases of BC-6 each week. For each case that John sells, he receives a profit of $35. Like many photographic chemicals, BC-6 has a very short shelf life, so if a case is not sold by the end of the week, John must discard it. Since each case costs John $56, he loses $56 for every case that is not sold by the end of the week. There is a probability of 0.45 of selling 11 cases, a probability of 0.35 of selling 12 cases, and a probability of 0.2 of selling 13 cases.

(a) Construct a decision table for this problem. Include all conditional values and probabilities in the table.

(b) What is your recommended course of action?

(c) If John is able to develop BC-6 with an ingredient that stabilizes it so that it no longer has to be discarded, how would this change your recommended course of action?

3-25 Megley Cheese Company is a small manufacturer of several different cheese products. One of the products is a cheese spread that is sold to retail outlets. Jason Megley must decide how many cases of cheese spread to manufacture each month. The probability that the demand will be six cases is 0.1, for 7 cases is 0.3, for 8 cases is 0.5, and for 9 cases is 0.1. The cost of every case is $45, and the price that Jason gets for each case is $95. Unfortunately, any cases not sold by the end of the month are of no value, due to spoilage. How many cases of cheese should Jason manufacture each month?

3-26 Farm Grown, Inc., produces cases of perishable food products. Each case contains an assortment of vegetables and other farm products. Each case costs $5 and sells for $15. If there are any cases not sold by the end of the day, they are sold to a large food processing company for $3 a case. The probability that daily demand will be 100 cases is 0.3, the probability that daily demand will be 200 cases is 0.4, and the probability that daily demand will be 300 cases is 0.3. Farm Grown has a policy of always satisfying customer demands. If its own supply of cases is less than the demand, it buys the necessary vegetables from a competitor. The estimated cost of doing this is $16 per case.

(a) Draw a decision table for this problem.

(b) What do you recommend?

3-27 Even though independent gasoline stations have been having a difficult time, Susan Solomon has been thinking about starting her own independent gasoline station. Susan's problem is to decide how large her station should be. The annual returns will depend on both the size of her station and a number of marketing factors related to the oil industry and demand for gasoline. After a careful analysis, Susan developed the following table:

SIZE OF FIRST STATION	GOOD MARKET ($)	FAIR MARKET ($)	POOR MARKET ($)
Small	50,000	20,000	−10,000
Medium	80,000	30,000	−20,000
Large	100,000	30,000	−40,000
Very large	300,000	25,000	−160,000

For example, if Susan constructs a small station and the market is good, she will realize a profit of $50,000.

(a) Develop a decision table for this decision.

(b) What is the maximax decision?

(c) What is the maximin decision?

(d) What is the equally likely decision?

(e) What is the criterion of realism decision? Use an α value of 0.8.

(f) Develop an opportunity loss table.

(g) What is the minimax regret decision?

3-28 A group of medical professionals is considering the construction of a private clinic. If the medical demand is high (i.e., there is a favorable market for the clinic), the physicians could realize a net profit of $100,000. If the market is not favorable, they could lose $40,000. Of course, they don't have to proceed at all, in which case there is no cost. In the absence of any market data, the best the physicians can guess is that there is a 50–50 chance the clinic will be successful. Construct a decision tree to help analyze this problem. What should the medical professionals do?

3-29 The physicians in Problem 3-28 have been approached by a market research firm that offers to perform a study of the market at a fee of $5,000. The market researchers claim their experience enables them to use Bayes' theorem to make the following statements of probability:

probability of a favorable market given
a favorable study = 0.82

probability of an unfavorable market given
a favorable study = 0.18

probability of a favorable market given
an unfavorable study = 0.11

probability of an unfavorable market given
an unfavorable study = 0.89

probability of a favorable research
study = 0.55

probability of an unfavorable research
study = 0.45

(a) Develop a new decision tree for the medical professionals to reflect the options now open with the market study.

(b) Use the EMV approach to recommend a strategy.

(c) What is the expected value of sample information? How much might the physicians be willing to pay for a market study?

3-30 Jerry Smith is thinking about opening a bicycle shop in his hometown. Jerry loves to take his own bike on 50-mile trips with his friends, but he believes that any small business should be started only if there is a good chance of making a profit. Jerry can open a small shop, a large shop, or no shop at all. Because there will be a five-year lease on the building that Jerry is thinking about using, he wants to make sure that he makes the correct decision. Jerry is also thinking about hiring his old marketing professor to conduct a marketing research study. If the study is conducted, the results could be either favorable or unfavorable. Develop a decision tree for Jerry.

3-31 Jerry Smith (of Problem 3-30) has done some analysis about the profitability of the bicycle shop. If Jerry builds the large bicycle shop, he will earn $60,000 if the market is favorable, but he will lose $40,000 if the market is unfavorable. The small shop will return a $30,000 profit in a favorable market and a $10,000 loss in an unfavorable market. At the present time, he believes that there is a 50–50 chance that the market will be favorable. His old marketing professor will charge him $5,000 for the marketing research. It is estimated that there is a 0.6 probability that the survey will be favorable. Furthermore, there is a 0.9 probability that the market will be favorable given a favorable outcome from the study. However, the marketing professor has warned Jerry that there is only a probability of 0.12 of a favorable market if the marketing research results are not favorable. Jerry is confused.

(a) Should Jerry use the marketing research?
(b) Jerry, however, is unsure the 0.6 probability of a favorable marketing research study is correct. How sensitive is Jerry's decision to this probability value? How far can this probability value deviate from 0.6 without causing Jerry to change his decision?

3-32 Bill Holliday is not sure what he should do. He can either build a quadplex (i.e., a building with four apartments), build a duplex, gather additional information, or simply do nothing. If he gathers additional information, the results could be either favorable or unfavorable, but it would cost him $3,000 to gather the information. Bill believes that there is a 50–50 chance that the information will be favorable. If the rental market is favorable, Bill will earn $15,000 with the quadplex or $5,000 with the duplex. Bill doesn't have the financial resources to do both. With an unfavorable rental market, however, Bill could lose $20,000 with the quadplex or $10,000 with the duplex. Without gathering additional information, Bill estimates that the probability of a favorable rental market is 0.7. A favorable report from the study would increase the probability of a favorable rental market to 0.9. Furthermore, an unfavorable report from the additional information would decrease the probability of a favorable rental market to 0.4. Of course, Bill could forget all of these numbers and do nothing. What is your advice to Bill?

3-33 Peter Martin is going to help his brother who wants to open a food store. Peter initially believes that there is a 50–50 chance that his brother's food store would be a success. Peter is considering doing a market research study. Based on historical data, there is a 0.8 probability that the marketing research will be favorable given a successful food store. Moreover, there is a 0.7 probability that the marketing research will be unfavorable given an unsuccessful food store.

(a) If the marketing research is favorable, what is Peter's revised probability of a successful food store for his brother?
(b) If the marketing research is unfavorable, what is Peter's revised probability of a successful food store for his brother?
(c) If the initial probability of a successful food store is 0.60 (instead of 0.50), find the probabilities in parts a and b.

3-34 Mark Martinko has been a class A racquetball player for the past five years, and one of his biggest goals is to own and operate a racquetball facility. Unfortunately, Mark thinks that the chance of a successful racquetball facility is only 30%. Mark's lawyer has recommended that he employ one of the local marketing research groups to conduct a survey concerning the success or failure of a racquetball facility. There is a 0.8 probability that the research will be favorable given a successful racquetball facility. In addition, there is a 0.7 probability that the research will be unfavorable given an unsuccessful facility. Compute revised probabilities of a successful racquetball facility given a favorable and given an unfavorable survey.

3-35 A financial advisor has recommended two possible mutual funds for investment: Fund A and Fund B. The return that will be achieved by each of these depends on whether the economy is good, fair, or poor. A payoff table has been constructed to illustrate this situation:

	STATE OF NATURE		
INVESTMENT	GOOD ECONOMY	FAIR ECONOMY	POOR ECONOMY
Fund A	$10,000	$2,000	−$5,000
Fund B	$6,000	$4,000	0
Probability	0.2	0.3	0.5

(a) Draw the decision tree to represent this situation.
(b) Perform the necessary calculations to determine which of the two mutual funds is better. Which one should you choose to maximize the expected value?
(c) Suppose there is question about the return of Fund A in a good economy. It could be higher or lower than $10,000. What value for this would cause a person to be indifferent between Fund A and Fund B (i.e., the EMVs would be the same)?

3-36 Jim Sellers is thinking about producing a new type of electric razor for men. If the market were favorable, he would get a return of $100,000, but if the market for this new type of razor were unfavorable, he would lose $60,000. Since Ron Bush is a good friend of Jim

Sellers, Jim is considering the possibility of using Bush Marketing Research to gather additional information about the market for the razor. Ron has suggested that Jim either use a survey or a pilot study to test the market. The survey would be a sophisticated questionnaire administered to a test market. It will cost $5,000. Another alternative is to run a pilot study. This would involve producing a limited number of the new razors and trying to sell them in two cities that are typical of American cities. The pilot study is more accurate but is also more expensive. It will cost $20,000. Ron Bush has suggested that it would be a good idea for Jim to conduct either the survey or the pilot before Jim makes the decision concerning whether to produce the new razor. But Jim is not sure if the value of the survey or the pilot is worth the cost.

Jim estimates that the probability of a successful market without performing a survey or pilot study is 0.5. Furthermore, the probability of a favorable survey result given a favorable market for razors is 0.7, and the probability of a favorable survey result given an unsuccessful market for razors is 0.2. In addition, the probability of an unfavorable pilot study given an unfavorable market is 0.9, and the probability of an unsuccessful pilot study result given a favorable market for razors is 0.2.

(a) Draw the decision tree for this problem without the probability values.

(b) Compute the revised probabilities needed to complete the decision, and place these values in the decision tree.

(c) What is the best decision for Jim? Use EMV as the decision criterion.

3-37 Jim Sellers has been able to estimate his utility for a number of different values. He would like to use these utility values in making the decision in Problem 3-36: $U(-\$80,000) = 0$, $U(-\$65,000) = 0.5$, $U(-\$60,000) = 0.55$, $U(-\$20,000) = 0.7$, $U(-\$5,000) = 0.8$, $U(\$0) = 0.81$, $U(\$80,000) = 0.9$, $U(\$95,000) = 0.95$, and $U(\$100,000) = 1$. Resolve Problem 3-36 using utility values. Is Jim a risk avoider?

3-38 Two states of nature exist for a particular situation: a good economy and a poor economy. An economic study may be performed to obtain more information about which of these will actually occur in the coming year. The study may forecast either a good economy or a poor economy. Currently there is a 60% chance that the economy will be good and a 40% chance that it will be poor. In the past, whenever the economy was good, the economic study predicted it would be good 80% of the time. (The other 20% of the time the prediction was wrong.) In the past, whenever the economy was poor, the economic study predicted it would be poor 90% of the time. (The other 10% of the time the prediction was wrong.)

(a) Use Bayes' theorem and find the following:
  P(good economy | prediction of good economy)
  P(poor economy | prediction of good economy)
  P(good economy | prediction of poor economy)
  P(poor economy | prediction of poor economy)

(b) Suppose the initial (prior) probability of a good economy is 70% (instead of 60%), and the probability of a poor economy is 30% (instead of 40%). Find the posterior probabilities in part a based on these new values.

3-39 The Long Island Life Insurance Company sells a term life insurance policy. If the policy holder dies during the term of the policy, the company pays $100,000. If the person does not die, the company pays out nothing and there is no further value to the policy. The company uses actuarial tables to determine the probability that a person with certain characteristics will die during the coming year. For a particular individual, it is determined that there is a 0.001 chance that the person will die in the next year and a 0.999 chance that the person will live and the company will pay out nothing. The cost of this policy is $200 per year. Based on the EMV criterion, should the individual buy this insurance policy? How would utility theory help explain why a person would buy this insurance policy?

3-40 In Problem 3-28, you helped the medical professionals analyze their decision using expected monetary value as the decision criterion. This group has also assessed their utility for money: $U(-\$45,000) = 0$, $U(-\$40,000) = 0.1$, $U(-\$5,000) = 0.7$, $U(\$0) = 0.9$, $U(\$95,000) = 0.99$, and $U(\$100,000) = 1$. Use expected utility as the decision criterion, and determine the best decision for the medical professionals. Are the medical professionals risk seekers or risk avoiders?

3-41 In this chapter a decision tree was developed for John Thompson (see Figure 3.5 for the complete decision tree analysis). After completing the analysis, John was not completely sure that he is indifferent to risk. After going through a number of standard gambles, John was able to assess his utility for money. Here are some of the utility assessments: $U(-\$190,000) = 0$, $U(-\$180,000) = 0.05$, $U(-\$30,000) = 0.10$, $U(-\$20,000) = 0.15$, $U(-\$10,000) = 0.2$, $U(\$0) = 0.3$, $U(\$90,000) = 0.5$, $U(\$100,000) = 0.6$, $U(\$190,000) = 0.95$, and $U(\$200,000) = 1.0$. If John maximizes his expected utility, does his decision change?

3-42 In the past few years, the traffic problems in Lynn McKell's hometown have gotten worse. Now, Broad Street is congested about half the time. The normal travel time to work for Lynn is only 15 minutes when Broad Street is used and there is no congestion. With congestion, however, it takes Lynn 40 minutes to get to work. If Lynn decides to take the expressway, it will take 30 minutes regardless of the traffic conditions. Lynn's utility for travel time is: $U(15 \text{ minutes}) = 0.9$, $U(30 \text{ minutes}) = 0.7$, and $U(40 \text{ minutes}) = 0.2$.

(a) Which route will minimize Lynn's expected travel time?

(b) Which route will maximize Lynn's utility?

(c) When it comes to travel time, is Lynn a risk seeker or a risk avoider?

3-43 Coren Chemical, Inc., develops industrial chemicals that are used by other manufacturers to produce photographic chemicals, preservatives, and lubricants.

One of their products, K-1000, is used by several photographic companies to make a chemical that is used in the film-developing process. To produce K-1000 efficiently, Coren Chemical uses the batch approach, in which a certain number of gallons is produced at one time. This reduces setup costs and allows Coren Chemical to produce K-1000 at a competitive price. Unfortunately, K-1000 has a very short shelf life of about one month.

Coren Chemical produces K-1000 in batches of 500 gallons, 1,000 gallons, 1,500 gallons, and 2,000 gallons. Using historical data, David Coren was able to determine that the probability of selling 500 gallons of K-1000 is 0.2. The probabilities of selling 1,000, 1,500, and 2,000 gallons are 0.3, 0.4, and 0.1, respectively. The question facing David is how many gallons to produce of K-1000 in the next batch run. K-1000 sells for $20 per gallon. Manufacturing cost is $12 per gallon, and handling costs and warehousing costs are estimated to be $1 per gallon. In the past, David has allocated advertising costs to K-1000 at $3 per gallon. If K-1000 is not sold after the batch run, the chemical loses much of its important properties as a developer. It can, however, be sold at a salvage value of $13 per gallon. Furthermore, David has guaranteed to his suppliers that there will always be an adequate supply of K-1000. If David does run out, he has agreed to purchase a comparable chemical from a competitor at $25 per gallon. David sells all of the chemical at $20 per gallon, so his shortage means that David loses the $5 to buy the more expensive chemical.

(a) Develop a decision tree of this problem.
(b) What is the best solution?
(c) Determine the expected value of perfect information.

3-44 The Jamis Corporation is involved with waste management. During the past 10 years it has become one of the largest waste disposal companies in the Midwest, serving primarily Wisconsin, Illinois, and Michigan. Bob Jamis, president of the company, is considering the possibility of establishing a waste treatment plant in Mississippi. From past experience, Bob believes that a small plant in northern Mississippi would yield a $500,000 profit regardless of the market for the facility. The success of a medium-sized waste treatment plant would depend on the market. With a low demand for waste treatment, Bob expects a $200,000 return. A medium demand would yield a $700,000 return in Bob's estimation, and a high demand would return $800,000. Although a large facility is much riskier, the potential return is much greater. With a high demand for waste treatment in Mississippi, the large facility should return a million dollars. With a medium demand, the large facility will return only $400,000. Bob estimates that the large facility would be a big loser if there were a low demand for waste treatment. He estimates that he would lose approximately $200,000 with a large treatment facility if demand were indeed low. Looking at the economic conditions for the upper part of the state of Mississippi and using his experience in the

field, Bob estimates that the probability of a low demand for treatment plants is 0.15. The probability for a medium-demand facility is approximately 0.40, and the probability of a high demand for a waste treatment facility is 0.45.

Because of the large potential investment and the possibility of a loss, Bob has decided to hire a market research team that is based in Jackson, Mississippi. This team will perform a survey to get a better feeling for the probability of a low, medium, or high demand for a waste treatment facility. The cost of the survey is $50,000. To help Bob determine whether to go ahead with the survey, the marketing research firm has provided Bob with the following information:

P(survey results | possible outcomes)

POSSIBLE OUTCOME	SURVEY RESULTS		
	LOW SURVEY RESULTS	MEDIUM SURVEY RESULTS	HIGH SURVEY RESULTS
Low demand	0.7	0.2	0.1
Medium demand	0.4	0.5	0.1
High demand	0.1	0.3	0.6

As you see, the survey could result in three possible outcomes. Low survey results mean that a low demand is likely. In a similar fashion, medium survey results or high survey results would mean a medium or a high demand, respectively. What should Bob do?

3-45 Mary is considering opening a new grocery store in town. She is evaluating three sites: downtown, the mall, and out at the busy traffic circle. Mary calculated the value of successful stores at these locations as follows: downtown, $250,000; the mall, $300,000; the circle, $400,000. Mary calculated the losses if unsuccessful to be $100,000 at either downtown or the mall and $200,000 at the circle. Mary figures her chance of success to be 50% downtown, 60% at the mall, and 75% at the traffic circle.

(a) Draw a decision tree for Mary and select her best alternative.
(b) Mary has been approached by a marketing research firm that offers to study the area to determine if another grocery store is needed. The cost of this study is $30,000. Mary believes there is a 60% chance that the survey results will be positive (show a need for another grocery store). SRP = survey results positive, SRN = survey results negative, SD = downtown, SM = success at mall, SC = success at circle, $\overline{SD}$ = don't succeed downtown, and so on. For studies of this nature: *P*(SRP | success) = 0.7; *P*(SRN | success) = 0.3; *P*(SRP | not success) = 0.2; and *P*(SRN | not success) = 0.8. Calculate the revised probabilities for success (and not success) for each location, depending on survey results.
(c) How much is the marketing research worth to Mary? Calculate the EVSI.

3-46 Sue Reynolds has to decide if she should get information (at a cost of $20,000) to invest in a retail store. If she gets the information, there is a 0.6 probability that the information will be favorable and a 0.4 probability that the information will not be favorable. If the information is favorable, there is a 0.9 probability that the store will be a success. If the information is not favorable, the probability of a successful store is only 0.2. Without any information, Sue estimates that the probability of a successful store will be 0.6. A successful store will give a return of $100,000. If the store is built but is not successful, Sue will see a loss of $80,000. Of course, she could always decide not to build the retail store.

(a) What do you recommend?
(b) What impact would a 0.7 probability of obtaining favorable information have on Sue's decision? The probability of obtaining unfavorable information would be 0.3.
(c) Sue believes that the probabilities of a successful and an unsuccessful retail store given favorable information might be 0.8 and 0.2, respectively, instead of 0.9 and 0.1, respectively. What impact, if any, would this have on Sue's decision and the best EMV?
(d) Sue had to pay $20,000 to get information. Would her decision change if the cost of the information increased to $30,000?
(e) Using the data in this problem and the following utility table, compute the expected utility. Is this the curve of a risk seeker or a risk avoider?

VALUE	MONETARY UTILITY
$100,000	1
$80,000	0.4
$0	0.2
−$20,000	0.1
−$80,000	0.05
−$100,000	0

(f) Compute the expected utility given the following utility table. Does this utility table represent a risk seeker or a risk avoider?

VALUE	MONETARY UTILITY
$100,000	1
$80,000	0.9
$0	0.8
−$20,000	0.6
−$80,000	0.4
−$100,000	0

INTERNET HOMEWORK PROBLEMS

See our Internet home page at www.prenhall.com/render for additional homework problems 3–47 to 3–60.

⇒ CASE STUDY

Starting Right Corporation

After watching a movie about a young woman who quit a successful corporate career to start her own baby food company, Julia Day decided that she wanted to do the same. In the movie, the baby food company was very successful. Julia knew, however, that it is much easier to make a movie about a successful woman starting her own company than to actually do it. The product had to be of the highest quality, and Julia had to get the best people involved to launch the new company. Julia resigned from her job and launched her new company—Starting Right.

Julia decided to target the upper end of the baby food market by producing baby food that contained no preservatives but had a great taste. Although the price would be slightly higher than for existing baby food, Julia believed that parents would be willing to pay more for a high-quality baby food. Instead of putting baby food in jars, which would require preservatives to stabilize the food, Julia decided to try a new approach. The baby food would be frozen. This would allow for natural ingredients, no preservatives, and outstanding nutrition.

Getting good people to work for the new company was also important. Julia decided to find people with experience in finance, marketing, and production to get involved with Starting Right. With her enthusiasm and charisma, Julia was able to find such a group. Their first step was to develop prototypes of the new frozen baby food and to perform a small pilot test of the new product. The pilot test received rave reviews.

The final key to getting the young company off to a good start was to raise funds. Three options were considered: corporate bonds, preferred stock, and common stock. Julia decided that each investment should be in blocks of $30,000. Furthermore, each investor should have an annual income of at least $40,000 and a net worth of $100,000 to be eligible to invest in Starting Right. Corporate bonds would return 13% per year for the next five years. Julia furthermore guaranteed that investors in the corporate bonds would get at least $20,000 back at the end of five years. Investors in preferred stock should see their initial investment increase by a factor of 4 with a good market or see the investment worth only half of the initial investment with an unfavorable market. The common stock had the greatest potential. The initial investment was expected to increase by a factor of 8 with a good market, but investors would lose everything if the market was unfavorable. During the next five years, it was expected that inflation would increase by a factor of 4.5% each year.

Discussion Questions

1. Sue Pansky, a retired grade-school teacher, is considering investing in Starting Right. She is very conservative and is a risk avoider. What do you recommend?
2. Ray Cahn, who is currently a commodities broker, is also considering an investment, although he believes that there is only an 11% chance of success. What do you recommend?
3. Lila Battle has decided to invest in Starting Right. While she believes that Julia has a good chance of being successful, Lila is a risk avoider and very conservative. What is your advice to Lila?
4. George Yates believes that there is an equally likely chance for success. What is your recommendation?
5. Peter Metarko is extremely optimistic about the market for the new baby food. What is your advice for Pete?
6. Julia Day has been told that developing the legal documents for each fund-raising alternative is expensive. Julia would like to offer alternatives for both risk-averse and risk-seeking investors. Can Julia delete one of the financial alternatives and still offer investment choices for risk seekers and risk avoiders?

⮕ CASE STUDY

Blake Electronics

In 1967, Steve Blake founded Blake Electronics in Long Beach, California, to manufacture resistors, capacitors, inductors, and other electronic components. During the Korean War, Steve was a radio operator, and it was during this time that he became proficient at repairing radios and other communications equipment. Steve viewed his four-year experience with the army with mixed feelings. He hated army life, but this experience gave him the confidence and the initiative to start his own electronics firm.

Over the years, Steve kept the business relatively unchanged. By 1980, total annual sales were in excess of $2 million. In 1984, Steve's son, Jim, joined the company after finishing high school and two years of courses in electronics at Long Beach Community College. Jim was always aggressive in high school athletics, and he became even more aggressive as general sales manager of Blake Electronics. This aggressiveness bothered Steve, who was more conservative. Jim would make deals to supply companies with electronic components before he bothered to find out if Blake Electronics had the ability or capacity to produce the components. On several occasions this behavior caused the company some embarrassing moments when Blake Electronics was unable to produce the electronic components for companies with which Jim had made deals.

In 1988, Jim started to go after government contracts for electronic components. By 1990, total annual sales had increased to more than $10 million, and the number of employees exceeded 200. Many of these employees were electronic specialists and graduates of electrical engineering programs from top colleges and universities. But Jim's tendency to stretch Blake Electronics to contracts continued as well, and by 1995 Blake Electronics had a reputation with government agencies as a company that could not deliver what it promised. Almost overnight, government contracts stopped, and Blake Electronics was left with an idle workforce and unused manufacturing equipment. This high overhead started to melt away profits, and in 1997, Blake Electronics was faced with the possibility of sustaining a loss for the first time in its history.

In 1998, Steve decided to look at the possibility of manufacturing electronic components for home use. Although this was a totally new market for Blake Electronics, Steve was convinced that this was the only way to keep Blake Electronics from dipping into the red. The research team at Blake Electronics was given the task of developing new electronic devices for home use. The first idea from the research team was the Master Control Center. The basic components for this system are shown in Figure 3.16.

The heart of the system is the master control box. This unit, which would have a retail price of $250, has two rows of five buttons. Each button controls one light or appliance and can be set as either a switch or a rheostat. When set as a switch, a light finger touch on the button either turns a light or appliance on or off. When set as a rheostat, a finger touching the button controls

FIGURE 3.16   Master Control Center

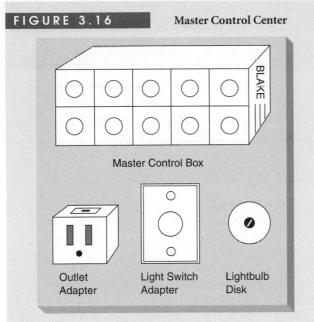

Master Control Box

Outlet Adapter   Light Switch Adapter   Lightbulb Disk

TABLE 3.14   Success Figures for MAI

OUTCOME	SURVEY RESULTS		TOTAL
	FAVORABLE	UNFAVORABLE	
Successful venture	35	20	55
Unsuccessful venture	15	30	45

the intensity of the light. Leaving your finger on the button makes the light go through a complete cycle ranging from off to bright and back to off again.

To allow for maximum flexibility, each master control box is powered by two D-sized batteries that can last up to a year, depending on usage. In addition, the research team has developed three versions of the master control box—versions A, B, and C. If a family wants to control more than 10 lights or appliances, another master control box can be purchased.

The lightbulb disk, which would have a retail price of $2.50, is controlled by the master control box and is used to control the intensity of any light. A different disk is available for each button position for all three master control boxes. By inserting the lightbulb disk between the lightbulb and the socket, the appropriate button on the master control box can completely control the intensity of the light. If a standard light switch is used, it must be on at all times for the master control box to work.

One disadvantage of using a standard light switch is that only the master control box can be used to control the particular light. To avoid this problem, the research team developed a special light switch adapter that would sell for $15. When this device is installed, either the master control box or the light switch adapter can be used to control the light.

When used to control appliances other than lights, the master control box must be used in conjunction with one or more outlet adapters. The adapters are plugged into a standard wall outlet, and the appliance is then plugged into the adapter. Each outlet adapter has a switch on top that allows the appliance to be controlled from the master control box or the outlet adapter. The price of each outlet adapter would be $25.

The research team estimated that it would cost $500,000 to develop the equipment and procedures needed to manufacture the master control box and accessories. If successful, this venture could increase sales by approximately $2 million. But will the master control boxes be a successful venture? With a 60% chance of success estimated by the research team, Steve had serious doubts about trying to market the master control boxes even though he liked the basic idea. Because of his reservations, Steve decided to send requests for proposals (RFPs) for additional marketing research to 30 marketing research companies in southern California.

The first RFP to come back was from a small company called Marketing Associates, Inc. (MAI), which would charge $100,000 for the survey. According to its proposal, MAI has been in business for about three years and has conducted about 100 marketing research projects. MAI's major strengths appeared to be individual attention to each account, experienced staff, and fast work. Steve was particularly interested in one part of the proposal, which revealed MAI's success record with previous accounts. This is shown in Table 3.14.

The only other proposal to be returned was by a branch office of Iverstine and Kinard, one of the largest marketing research firms in the country. The cost for a complete survey would be $300,000. While the proposal did not contain the same success record as MAI, the proposal from Iverstine and Kinard did contain some interesting information. The chance of getting a favorable survey result, given a successful venture, was 90%. On the other hand, the chance of getting an unfavorable survey result, given an unsuccessful venture, was 80%. Thus, it appeared to Steve that Iverstine and Kinard would be able to predict the success or failure of the master control boxes with a great amount of certainty.

Steve pondered the situation. Unfortunately, both marketing research teams gave different types of information in their proposals. Steve concluded that there would be no way that the two proposals could be compared unless he got additional information from Iverstine and Kinard. Furthermore, Steve wasn't sure what he would do with the information, and if it would be worth the expense of hiring one of the marketing research firms.

Discussion Questions

1. Does Steve need additional information from Iverstine and Kinard?
2. What would you recommend?

INTERNET CASE STUDIES

See our Internet home page at **www.prenhall.com/render** for the additional case studies:

(1) Drink-At-Home, Inc.: This case involves the development and marketing of a new beverage.

(2) Ruth Jones' Heart Bypass Operation: This case deals with a medical decision regarding surgery.

(3) Ski Right. This case involves the development and marketing of a new ski helmet.

(4) Study Time is about a student who must budget time while studying for a final exam.

BIBLIOGRAPHY

Ahlbrecht, Martin et al. "An Empirical Study on Intertemporal Decision Making under Risk," *Management Science* (June 1997): 813–826.

Bistritz, Nancy. "Rx for UK Healthcare Woes," *OR/MS Today* (April 1997): 18.

Borison, Adam. "Oglethorpe Power Corporation Decides About Investing in a Major Transmission System," *Interfaces* 25 (March–April 1995): 25–36.

Brown, Mark. "Evaluation of Vision Correction Alternatives for Myopic Adults," *Interfaces* 27, 2 (1997): 66–84.

Brown, R. "Do Managers Find Decision Theory Useful?" *Harvard Business Review* (May–June 1970): 78–89.

Brown, R. V. "The State of the Art of Decision Analysis: A Personal Perspective," *Interfaces* 22, 6 (November–December 1992): 5–14.

Congdon, Peter. *Bayesian Statistical Modeling.* New York: John Wiley & Sons, Inc., 2001.

Derfler, Frank. "Use These Decision Trees and Our Questionnaire to Find the Best Way to Reduce Your Total Cost of Ownership," *PC Magazine* (May 5, 1998): 231.

Duarte, B. P. M. "The Expected Utility Theory Applied to an Industrial Decision Problem—What Technological Alternative to Implement to Treat Industrial Solid Residuals," *Computers and Operations Research* 28, 4 (April 2001): 357–380.

Green, A. E. S. "Finding the Japanese Fleet," *Interfaces* 23, 5 (September–October 1993): 62–69.

Hammond, J. S., R. L. Kenney, and H. Raiffa. "The Hidden Traps in Decision Making," *Harvard Business Review* (September–October 1998): 47–60.

Hazen, Gordon B., James M. Pellissier, and Jayavel Sounderpandian. "Stochastic-Tree Models in Medical Decision Making," *Interfaces* 28, 4 (July–August 1998): 64–80.

Hess, S. W. "Swinging on the Branch of a Tree: Project Selection Applications," *Interfaces* 23, 6 (November–December 1993): 5–12.

Jbuedj, Coden. "Decision Making under Conditions of Uncertainty: A Wakeup Call for the Financial Planning Profession," *Journal of Financial Planning* (October 1997): 84–91.

Kirkwood, C. W. "An Overview of Methods for Applied Decision Analysis," *Interfaces* 22, 6 (November–December 1992): 28–39.

Luce, R., and H. Raiffa. *Games and Decisions.* New York: John Wiley & Sons, Inc., 1957.

McDonald, John. "Decision Trees Clarify Novel Technology Applications," *Oil and Gas Journal* (February 24, 1997): 69.

Miller, Craig. "A Systematic Approach to Tax Controversy Management," *Tax Executive* (May 15, 1998): 231.

Perdue, Robert K., William J. McAllister, Peter V. King, and Bruce G. Berkey. "Valuation of R and D Projects Using Options Pricing and Decision Analysis Models," *Interfaces* 29, 6 (November–December 1999): 57–74.

Raiffa, H. *Decision Analysis.* Reading, MA: Addison-Wesley Publishing Co., Inc., 1968.

Raiffa, Howard, John W. Pratt, and Robert Schlaifer. *Introduction to Statistical Decision Theory.* Boston: MIT Press, 1995.

Raiffa, Howard and Robert Schlaifer. *Applied Statistical Decision Theory.* New York: John Wiley & Sons, Inc., 2000.

Reilly, Terence. "Sensitivity Analysis for Dependent Variables," *Decision Sciences* 31, 3 (Summer 2000): 551–572.

Render, B., and R. M. Stair. *Cases and Readings in Management Science*, 2/e. Boston: Allyn and Bacon, Inc., 1988.

Schlaifer, R. *Analysis of Decisions under Uncertainty.* New York: McGraw-Hill Book Company, 1969.

Strait, Scott. "Decision Analysis Approach to Competitive Situations with a Pure Infinite Regress," *Decision Sciences* (September 1994): 853.

Stafira, Stanley et al. "A Methodology for Evaluating Military Systems in a Counterproliferation Role," *Management Science* (October 1997): 1420–1430.

Wallace, Stein W. "Decision Making under Uncertainty: Is Sensitivity Analysis of Any Use?" *Operations Research* 48, 1 (2000): 20–25.

APPENDIX 3.1: DECISION MODELS WITH QM FOR WINDOWS

QM for Windows can be used to solve decision theory problems discussed in this chapter. In this appendix we show you how to solve straightforward decision theory problems that involve tables.

In this chapter we solved the Thompson Lumber problem. The alternatives include constructing a large plant, a small plant, or doing nothing. The probabilities of an unfavorable and a favorable market, along with financial information, were presented in Table 3.9.

To demonstrate QM for Windows, let's use these data to solve the Thompson Lumber problem. Program 3.2 shows the results. Note that the best alternative is to construct the medium-sized plant, with an EMV of $40,000.

PROGRAM 3.2 **Computing EMV for Thompson Lumber Company Problem Using QM for Windows**

	Favorable Market	Unfavorable Market	EMV	Row Min	Row Max	Hurwicz
Probabilities	0.5	0.5				
Large Plant	200,000.	-180,000.	10,000.	-180,000.	200,000.	124,000.
Small Plant	100,000.	-20,000.	40,000.	-20,000.	100,000.	76,000.
Do Nothing	0.	0.	0.	0.	0.	0.
		maximum	40,000.	0.	200,000.	124,000.
			Best EV	maximin	maximax	Best

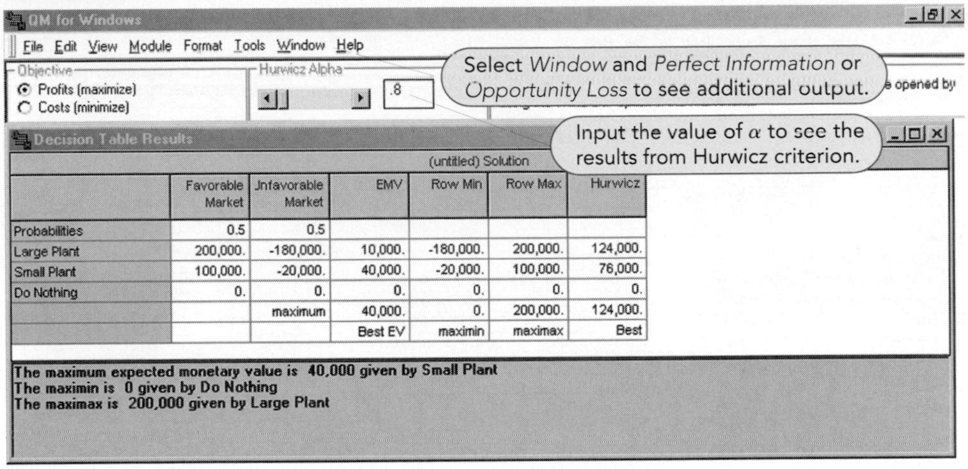

This chapter also covered decision making under uncertainty, where probability values were not available or appropriate. Solution techniques for these types of problems were presented in Section 3.4. Program 3.2 shows these results, including the maximax, maximin, and Hurwicz solutions.

Chapter 3 also covers expected opportunity loss. To demonstrate the use of QM for Windows, we can determine the EOL for the Thompson Lumber problem. The results are presented in Program 3.3. Note that this program also computes EVPI.

PROGRAM 3.3 **Opportunity Loss and EVPI for the Thompson Lumber Company Problem Using QM for Windows**

	Favorable Market Regret	Unfavorable Market Regret	Maximum Regret	Expected Regret
Probabilities	0.5	0.5		
Large Plant	0.	180,000.	180,000.	90,000.
Small Plant	100,000.	20,000.	100,000.	60,000.
Do Nothing	200,000.	0.	200,000.	100,000.
Minimax regret			100,000.	

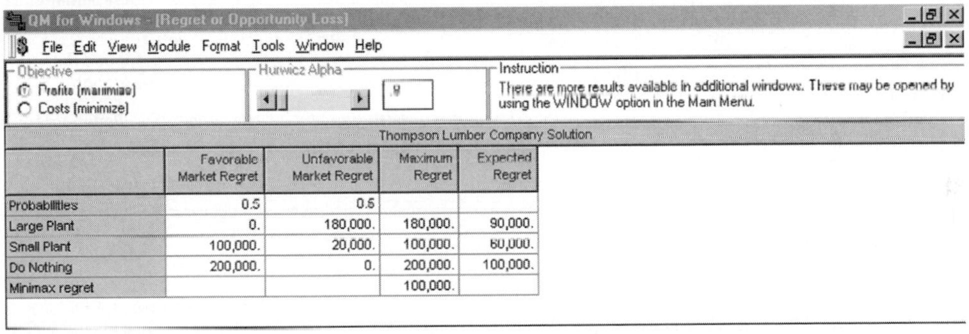

APPENDIX 3.2: DECISION TREES WITH QM FOR WINDOWS

To illustrate the use of QM for Windows for decision trees, let's use the data from Thompson Lumber example. Program 3.4 on the following page shows the output results, including the original data, intermediate results, and the best decision, which has an EMV of $106,400. Note that the nodes must be numbered, and probabilities are included for each state of nature branch while payoffs are included in the appropriate places. Program 3.4 provides only a small portion of this tree since the entire tree has 25 branches.

APPENDIX 3.3: USING EXCEL FOR BAYES' THEOREM

The following programs indicate how Excel can be used for the calculations involved with Bayes' theorem when there are only two states of nature. The Thompson Lumber example is shown here in Program 3.5A and Program 3.5B. The only inputs needed are the probabilities for cells B7, B8, and C7. Formulas have been used to compute all other values. These results correspond with the example shown in Tables 3.12 and 3.13 earlier in the chapter.

PROGRAM 3.4   **QM for Windows for Sequential Decisions**

This is the expected value given a favorable survey. The entire tree would require 25 branches.

QM for Windows - C:\My Documents\Mike\R&S\Weiss\Render_Star_7\QM

File Edit View Module Format Tools Window Help

Objective
- Profits (maximize)
- Costs (minimize)

Instruction
Other output can be viewed by using WINDOW

Thompson Lumber Solution

	Start Node	End Node	Branch Probability	Profit	Branch Use	End node	Node Type	Node Value
Start	0.	1.	0.	0.		1.	Decision	106,400.
Large	1.	2.	0.	0.	Always	2.	Chance	106,400.
Small	1.	3.	0.	0.		3.	Chance	63,600.
Do Nothing	1.	8.	0.	0.		8.	Final	0.
Favorable Market given Favorable Survey	2.	4.	0.78	190,000.		4.	Final	190,000.
Unfavorable Market given Favorable Survey	2.	5.	0.22	-190,000.		5.	Final	-190,000.
Favorable Market given Favorable Survey	3.	6.	0.78	90,000.		6.	Final	90,000.
Unfavorable Market given Favorable Survey	3.	7.	0.22	-30,000.		7.	Final	-30,000.

The ending point for each branch must be identified by a node.

These probabilities are the revised probabilities given a favorable survey.

PROGRAM 3.5A   **Formulas Used for Bayes' Calculations in Excel**

Microsoft Excel - bayes1form

File Edit View Insert Format Tools Data Window Help

A1   = Bayes Theorem for Thompson Lumber Example

	A	B	C	D	E
1	Bayes Theorem for Thompson Lumber Example				
2					
3	Fill in cells B7, B8, and C7.				
4					
5	Probability Revisions Given a Positive Survey				
6	State of Nature	P(Sur.Pos.|state of nature)	Prior Prob.	Joint Prob.	Posterior Probability
7	FM	0.7	0.5	=B7*C7	=D7/$D$9
8	UM	0.2	=1-C7	=B8*C8	=D8/$D$9
9			P(Sur.pos.)=	=SUM(D7:D8)	
10					
11	Probability Revisions Given a Negative Survey				
12	State of Nature	P(Sur.Pos.|state of nature)	Prior Prob.	Joint Prob.	Posterior Probability
13	FM	=1-B7	=C7	=B13*C13	=D13/$D$15
14	UM	=1-B8	=C8	=B14*C14	=D14/$D$15
15			P(Sur.neg.)=	=SUM(D13:D14)	
16					

Enter P(Favorable Market) in cell C7.

Enter P(Survey positive | Favorable Market) in cell B7.

Enter P(Survey positive | Unfavorable Market) in cell B8.

PROGRAM 3.5B   **Results of Bayes' Calculations in Excel**

Microsoft Excel - bayes1form

File Edit View Insert Format Tools Data Window Help

A1   = Bayes Theorem for Thompson Lumber Example

	A	B	C	D	E	F	G	H	I
1	Bayes Theorem for Thompson Lumber Example								
2									
3	Fill in cells B7, B8, and C7.								
4									
5	Probability Revisions Given a Positive Survey								
6	State of Nature	P(Sur.Pos.|state of nature)	Prior Prob.	Joint Prob.	Posterior Probability				
7	FM	0.70	0.50	0.35	0.78				
8	UM	0.20	0.50	0.10	0.22				
9			P(Sur.pos.)=	0.45					
10									
11	Probability Revisions Given a Negative Survey								
12	State of Nature	P(Sur.Pos.|state of nature)	Prior Prob.	Joint Prob.	Posterior Probability				
13	FM	0.30	0.50	0.15	0.27				
14	UM	0.80	0.50	0.40	0.73				
15			P(Sur.neg.)=	0.55					
16									

REGRESSION MODELS

After completing this chapter, students will be able to:

1. Identify variables and use them in a regression model.
2. Develop simple linear regression equations from sample data and interpret the slope and intercept.
3. Compute the coefficient of determination and the coefficient of correlation and interpret their meanings.
4. Interpret the F-test in a linear regression model.
5. List the assumptions used in regression and use residual plots to identify problems.
6. Develop a multiple regression model and use it to predict.

7. Use dummy variables to model categorical data.
8. Determine which variables should be included in a multiple regression model.
9. Transform a nonlinear function into a linear one for use in regression.
10. Understand and avoid common mistakes made in the use of regression analysis.

4.1　INTRODUCTION

Regression analysis is a very valuable tool for today's manager. Regression has been used to model such things as the relationship between level of education and income, the price of a house and the square footage, and the sales volume for a company relative to the dollars spent on advertising. When businesses are trying to decide which location is best for a new store or branch office, regression models are often used. Cost estimation models are often regression models. The applicability of regression analysis is virtually limitless.

Two purposes of regression analysis are to understand the relationship between variables and to predict the value of one based on the other.

There are generally two purposes for regression analysis. The first is to understand the relationship between variables such as advertising expenditures and sales. The second purpose is to predict the value of one variable based on the value of the other.

In this chapter, the simple linear regression model will first be developed, and then a more complex multiple regression model will be used to incorporate even more variables into our model. In any regression model, the variable to be predicted is called the *dependent variable* or *response variable*. The value of this is said to be dependent upon the value of an *independent variable*, which is sometimes called an *explanatory variable* or a *predictor variable*.

4.2　SCATTER DIAGRAMS

To investigate the relationship between variables, it is helpful to look at a graph of the data. Such a graph is often called a *scatter diagram* or a *scatter plot*. Normally the independent variable is plotted on the horizontal axis and the dependent variable is plotted on the vertical axis. The following example will illustrate this.

A scatter diagram is a graph of the data.

Triple A Construction Company renovates old homes in Albany. Over time, the company has found that its dollar volume of renovation work is dependent on the Albany area payroll. The figures for Triple A's revenues and the amount of money earned by wage earners in Albany for the past six years are presented in Table 4.1. Economists have predicted the local area payroll to be $600 million next year, and Triple A wants to plan accordingly.

Figure 4.1 provides a scatter diagram for the Triple A Construction data given in Table 4.1. This graph indicates that higher values for the local payroll seem to result in higher sales for the company. There is not a perfect relationship because not all the points lie in a straight line, but there is a relationship. A line has been drawn through the data to help show the relationship that exists between the payroll and sales. The points do not all lie on the line, so there would be some error involved if we tried to predict sales based on payroll using this or any other line. Many lines could be drawn through these points, but which one best represents the true relationship? Regression analysis provides the answer to this question.

TABLE 4.1
Triple A Construction Company Sales and Local Payroll

TRIPLE A'S SALES ($100,000s)	LOCAL PAYROLL (100,000,000s)
6	3
8	4
9	6
5	4
4.5	2
9.5	5

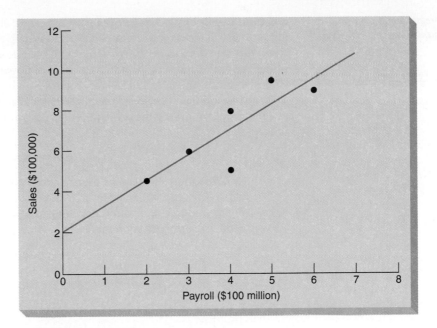

FIGURE 4.1

**Scatter Diagram of Triple A
Construction Company
Data**

4.3 SIMPLE LINEAR REGRESSION

In any regression model, there is an implicit assumption (which can be tested) that a relationship exists between the variables. There is also some random error that cannot be predicted. The underlying simple linear regression model is

$$Y = \beta_0 + \beta_1 X + \varepsilon \tag{4-1}$$

where

*The dependent variable is Y
and the independent variable
is X.*

Y = dependent variable (response variable)

X = independent variable (predictor variable or explanatory variable)

β_0 = intercept (value of Y when X = 0)

β_1 = slope of regression line

ε = random error

*Estimates of the slope and
intercept are found from
sample data.*

The true values for the intercept and slope are not known, and therefore they are estimated using sample data. The regression equation based on sample data is given as

$$\hat{Y} = b_0 + b_1 X \tag{4-2}$$

where

$$\hat{Y} = \text{predicted value of } Y$$

In the Triple A Construction example, we are trying to predict the sales, so the dependent variable (Y) would be sales. The variable we use to help predict sales is the Albany area payroll, so this is the independent variable (X). Although any number of lines can be drawn through these points to show a relationship between X and Y in Figure 4.1, the line that will be chosen is the one that in some way minimizes the errors. Error is defined as

$$\text{error} = (\text{actual value}) - (\text{predicted value})$$

$$e = Y - \hat{Y} \tag{4-3}$$

The regression line minimizes the sum of the squared errors.

Since errors may be positive or negative, the average error could be zero even though there are extremely large errors—both positive and negative. To eliminate the difficulty of negative errors canceling positive errors, the errors can be squared. The best regression line will be defined as the one with the minimum sum of the squared errors. For this reason, regression analysis is sometimes called least-squares regression.

Statisticians have developed formulas that we can use to find the equation of a straight line that would minimize the sum of the squared errors. The simple linear regression equation is

$$\hat{Y} = b_0 + b_1 X$$

The following formulas can be used to compute the intercept and the slope.

$$\bar{X} = \frac{\sum X}{n} = \text{average (mean) of X values}$$

$$\bar{Y} = \frac{\sum Y}{n} = \text{average (mean) of Y values}$$

$$b_1 = \frac{\sum (X - \bar{X})(Y - \bar{Y})}{\sum (X - \bar{X})^2} \tag{4-4}$$

$$b_0 = \bar{Y} - b_1 \bar{X} \tag{4-5}$$

The preliminary calculations are shown in Table 4.2. There are other "short-cut" formulas that are helpful when doing the computations on a calculator, and these are presented in Appendix 4.1. They will not be shown here, as computer software will be used for most of the other examples in this chapter.

Computing the slope and intercept of the regression equation for the Triple A Construction Company example, we have

$$\bar{X} = \frac{\sum X}{6} = \frac{24}{6} = 4$$

$$\bar{Y} = \frac{\sum Y}{6} = \frac{42}{6} = 7$$

$$b_1 = \frac{\sum (X - \bar{X})(Y - \bar{Y})}{\sum (X - \bar{X})^2} = \frac{12.5}{10} = 1.25$$

$$b_0 = \bar{Y} - b_1 \bar{X} = 7 - (1.25)(4) = 2$$

TABLE 4.2				
Regression Calculations for Triple A Construction	Y	X	$(X - \bar{X})^2$	$(X - \bar{X})(Y - \bar{Y})^2$
	6	3	$(3 - 4)^2 = 1$	$(3 - 4)(6 - 7) = 1$
	8	4	$(4 - 4)^2 = 0$	$(4 - 4)(8 - 7) = 0$
	9	6	$(6 - 4)^2 = 4$	$(6 - 4)(9 - 7) = 4$
	5	4	$(4 - 4)^2 = 0$	$(4 - 4)(5 - 7) = 0$
	4.5	2	$(2 - 4)^2 = 4$	$(2 - 4)(4.5 - 7) = 5$
	9.5	5	$(5 - 4)^2 = 1$	$(5 - 4)(9.5 - 7) = 2.5$
	$\sum Y = 42$	$\sum X = 24$	$\sum (X - \bar{X})^2 = 10$	$\sum (X - \bar{X})(Y - \bar{Y}) = 12.5$
	$\bar{Y} = 42/6 = 7$	$\bar{X} = 24/6 = 4$		

The estimated regression equation therefore is

$$\hat{Y} = 2 + 1.25X$$

or

$$\text{sales} = 2 + 1.25(\text{payroll})$$

If the payroll next year is \$600 million ($X = 6$), then the predicted value would be

$$\hat{Y} = 2 + 1.25(6) = 9.5$$

or \$950,000.

One of the purposes of regression is to understand the relationship among variables. This model tells us that for each \$100 million (represented by X) increase in the payroll, we would expect the sales to increase by \$125,000 since $b_1 = 1.25$ (\$100,000s). This model helps Triple A Construction see how the local economy and company sales are related.

4.4 MEASURING THE FIT OF THE REGRESSION MODEL

A regression equation can be developed for any variables X and Y, even random numbers. We certainly would not have any confidence in the ability of one random number to predict the value of another random number. How do we know that the model is actually helpful in predicting Y based on X? Should we have confidence in this model? Does the model provide better predictions (smaller errors) that simply using the average of the Y values?

Deviations (errors) may be positive or negative.

In the Triple A Construction example, sales figures (Y) varied from a low of 4.5 to a high of 9.5, and the mean was 7. If each sales value is compared with the mean, we see how far they deviate from the mean and we could compute a measure of the total variability in sales. Because Y is sometimes higher and sometimes lower than the mean, there may be both positive and negative deviations. Simply summing these values would be misleading because the negatives would cancel out the positives, making it appear that the numbers are closer to the mean than they actually are. To prevent this problem, we will use the sum of the squares total (SST) to measure the total variability in Y.

The SST measures the total variability in Y about the mean.

$$SST = \Sigma(Y - \overline{Y})^2 \tag{4-6}$$

If we did not use X to predict Y, we would simply use the mean of Y and the SST would measure the accuracy of our predictions. However, a regression line may be used to predict the value of Y, and while there are still errors involved, the sum of these squared errors will be less than the total sum of squares just computed. The sum of the squared error (SSE) is

The SSE measures the variability in Y about the regression line.

$$SSE = \Sigma e^2 = \Sigma(Y - \hat{Y})^2 \tag{4-7}$$

Table 4.3 provides the calculations for the Triple A Construction Example. The mean ($\overline{Y} = 7$) is compared to each value and we get

$$SST = 22.5$$

The prediction ($\hat{Y}$) for each observation is computed and compared to the actual value. This results in

$$SSE = 6.875$$

The SSE is much lower than the SST. Using the regression line has reduced the variability in the sum of squares by $22.5 - 6.875 = 15.625$. This is called the *sum of squares due to regression* (SSR) and indicates how much of the total variability in Y is explained by the regression model. Mathematically, this can be calculated as

$$SSR = \Sigma(\hat{Y} - \overline{Y})^2 \tag{4-8}$$

	TABLE 4.3	Sum of Squares for Triple A Construction			
Y	X	$(Y - \bar{Y})^2$	$\hat{Y}$	$(Y - \hat{Y})^2$	$(\hat{Y} - \bar{Y})^2$
6	3	$(6 - 7)^2 = 1$	$2 + 1.25(3) = 5.75$	0.0625	0.0625
8	4	$(8 - 7)^2 = 1$	$2 + 1.25(4) = 7.00$	1	1
9	6	$(9 - 7)^2 = 4$	$2 + 1.25(6) = 9.50$	0.25	0.25
5	4	$(5 - 7)^2 = 4$	$2 + 1.25(4) = 7.00$	4	4
4.5	2	$(4.5 - 7)^2 = 6.25$	$2 + 1.25(2) = 4.50$	0	0
9.5	5	$(9.5 - 7)^2 = 6.25$	$2 + 1.25(5) = 8.25$	1.5625	1.5625
		$\sum(Y - \bar{Y})^2 = 22.5$		$\sum(Y - \hat{Y})^2 = 6.875$	$\sum(\hat{Y} - \hat{Y})^2 = 15.625$
$\bar{Y} = 7$		SST = 22.5		SSE = 6.875	SSR = 15.625

Table 4.3 indicates

$$SSR = 15.625$$

There is a very important relationship between the sums of squares that we have computed.

(sum of squares total) = (sum of squares due to regression) + (sum of squares error)

$$SST = SSR + SSE \tag{4-9}$$

Figure 4.2 displays the data for Triple A Construction. The regression line is shown, as is a line representing the mean of the Y values. The errors used in computing the sums of squares are shown on this graph. Notice how the sample points are closer to the regression line than they are to the mean.

FIGURE 4.2

Deviations from the Regression Line and from the Mean

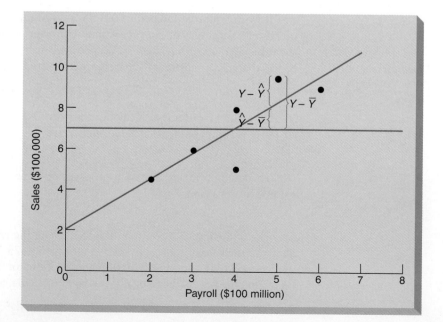

Coefficient of Determination

r^2 measures the variability in Y that is explained by the regression equation.

The SSR is sometimes called the explained variability in Y while the SSE is the unexplained variability in Y. The proportion of the variability in Y that is explained by the regression equation is called the *coefficient of determination* and is denoted by r^2. Thus,

$$r^2 = \frac{SSR}{SST} = 1 - \frac{SSE}{SST} \qquad (4\text{-}10)$$

Thus, r^2 can be found using either the SSR or the SSE. For Triple A Construction, we have

$$r^2 = \frac{15.625}{22.5} = 0.6944$$

This means that about 69% of the variability in sales (Y) is explained by the regression equation based on payroll (X).

If every point lies on the regression line, $r^2 = 1$.

If every point in the sample were on the regression line (meaning all errors are 0), then 100% of the variability in Y could be explained by the regression equation, so $r^2 = 1$ and SSE = 0. The lowest possible value of r^2 is 0, indicating that X explains 0% of the variability in Y. Thus, r^2 can range from a low of 0 to a high of 1. In developing regression equations, a good model will have an r^2 value close to 1.

Correlation Coefficient

The correlation coefficient ranges from −1 to +1.

Another measure related to the coefficient of determination is the *coefficient of correlation*. This measure also expresses the degree or strength of the linear relationship. It is usually expressed as r and can be any number between and including +1 and −1. Figure 4.3 illustrates possible scatter diagrams for different values of r. The value of r is the square root of r^2. It is negative if the slope is negative, and it is positive if the slope is positive. Thus,

$$r = \pm\sqrt{r^2} \qquad (4\text{-}11)$$

FIGURE 4.3

Four Values of the Correlation Coefficient

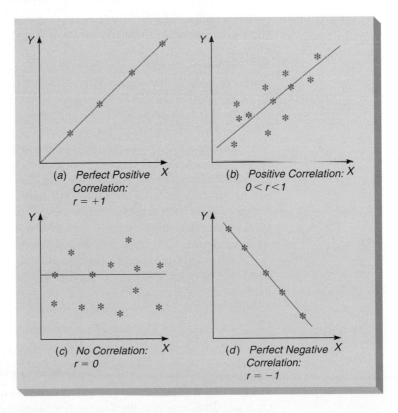

(a) *Perfect Positive Correlation:*
     $r = +1$

(b) *Positive Correlation:*
     $0 < r < 1$

(c) *No Correlation:*
     $r = 0$

(d) *Perfect Negative Correlation:*
     $r = -1$

TransAlta Utilities (TAU) is a $1.6 billion energy company operating in Canada, New Zealand, Australia, Argentina, and the United States. Headquartered in Alberta, Canada, TAU is that country's largest publicly owned utility. It serves 340,000 customers in Alberta through 57 customer-service facilities, each of which was staffed by 5 to 20 customer service linemen. The 270 linemen's jobs are to handle new connections and repairs and to patrol power lines and check substations. This existing system was not the result of some optimal central planning but was put in place incrementally as the company grew.

With help from the University of Alberta, TAU wanted to develop a causal model to decide how many linemen would be best assigned to each facility. The research team decided to build a multiple regression model with only three independent variables. The hardest part of the task was to select variables that were easy to quantify based on available data. In the end, the explanatory variables were number of urban customers, number of rural customers, and geographic size of a service area. The implicit assumptions in this model are that the time spent on customers is proportional to the number of customers; and the time spent on facilities (line patrol and substation checks) and travel are proportional to the size of the service region. By definition, the unexplained time in the model accounts for time that is not explained by the three variables (such as meetings, breaks, or unproductive time).

Not only did the results of the model please TAU managers, but the project (which included optimizing the number of facilities and their locations) saved $4 million per year.

Source: E. Erkut, T. Myroon, and K. Strangway. "TransAlta Redesigns Its Service-Delivery Network," *Interfaces* (March–April 2000): 54–69.

For the Triple A Construction example with $r^2 = 0.6944$,

$$r = \sqrt{0.6944} = 0.8333$$

We know it is positive because the slope is +1.25.

4.5 USING COMPUTER SOFTWARE FOR REGRESSION

Software such as QM for Windows (Appendix 4.2), Excel, and Excel QM is often used for these calculations. We will rely on Excel for most of the calculations in the rest of this chapter.

The Triple A Construction example will be used to show how Excel is used to develop regression models. For regression analysis in Excel, select *Tools—Data Analysis–Regression* and then input the data. In Program 4.1A, we see the drop-down menu that appears when we select *Tools*. If *Data Analysis* does not appear under *Tools*, select *Add-Ins* from the drop-down menu under *Tools*, and check the box next to *Analysis Tool Pak* and click *OK*. *Data Analysis* will now appear when you select *Tools*. A list of analysis tools will appear after we select *Data Analysis*, and we select *Regression* from this list, as shown in Program 4.1B. The Window in Program 4.1C then opens, and we input the *X* and *Y* ranges. We specify *Labels* (since the first row in our range includes the names or labels for the variables), and we specify the *Output Range* if we want the results to appear on this same spreadsheet page rather than on a new page. We press *OK*, and we get the output shown in Program 4.1D. This shows the intercept is 2 and the slope is 1.25. These are the same values we found using the formulas.

Errors are also called residuals.

Also contained in the Excel output in Program 4.1D is the information we previously computed by hand. The sums of squares are shown in the column headed by SS. Another name for *error* is *residual*. In Excel, the *sum of squares error* is shown as the sum of squares residual. The values in this output are the same values shown in Table 4.3.

$$\text{sum of squares regression} = SSR = 15.625$$

$$\text{sum of squares error (residual)} = SSE = 6.8750$$

$$\text{sum of squares total} = SST = 22.5$$

The coefficient of determination (r^2) is shown to be 0.6944. The coefficient of correlation (r) is called *Multiple R* in the Excel output, and this is 0.8333.

PROGRAM 4.1A

Select *Tools – Data Analysis* to Perform Regression in Excel

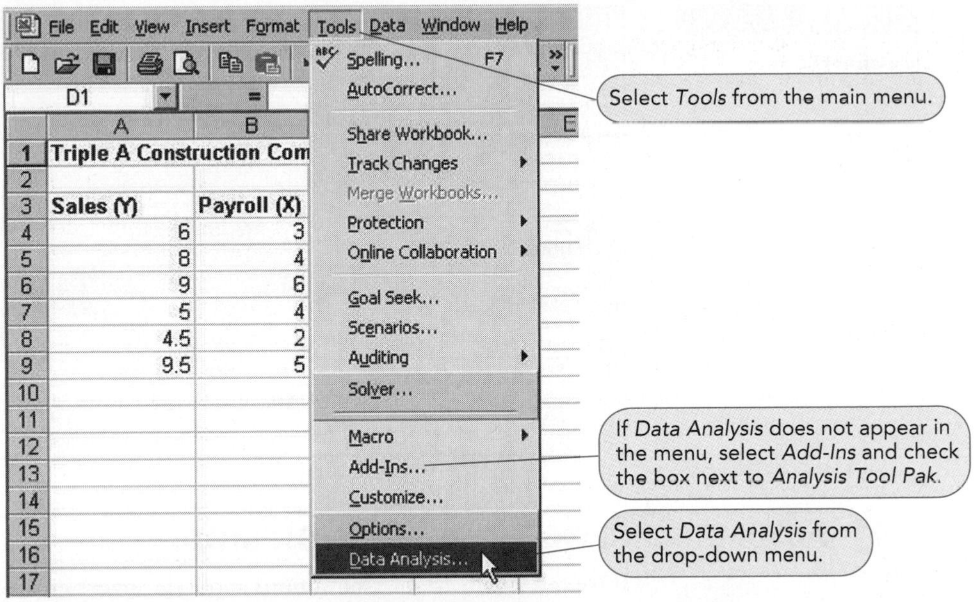

Select *Tools* from the main menu.

If *Data Analysis* does not appear in the menu, select *Add-Ins* and check the box next to *Analysis Tool Pak*.

Select *Data Analysis* from the drop-down menu.

	Sales (Y)	Payroll (X)
	6	3
	8	4
	9	6
	5	4
	4.5	2
	9.5	5

PROGRAM 4.1B

Selecting Regression as the Tool in Data Analysis

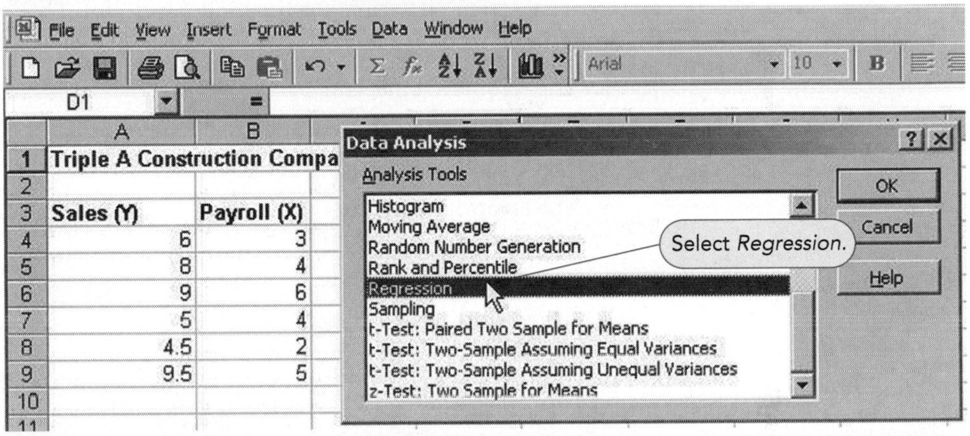

Select *Regression.*

PROGRAM 4.1C

Excel Input to Specify Location of the Data

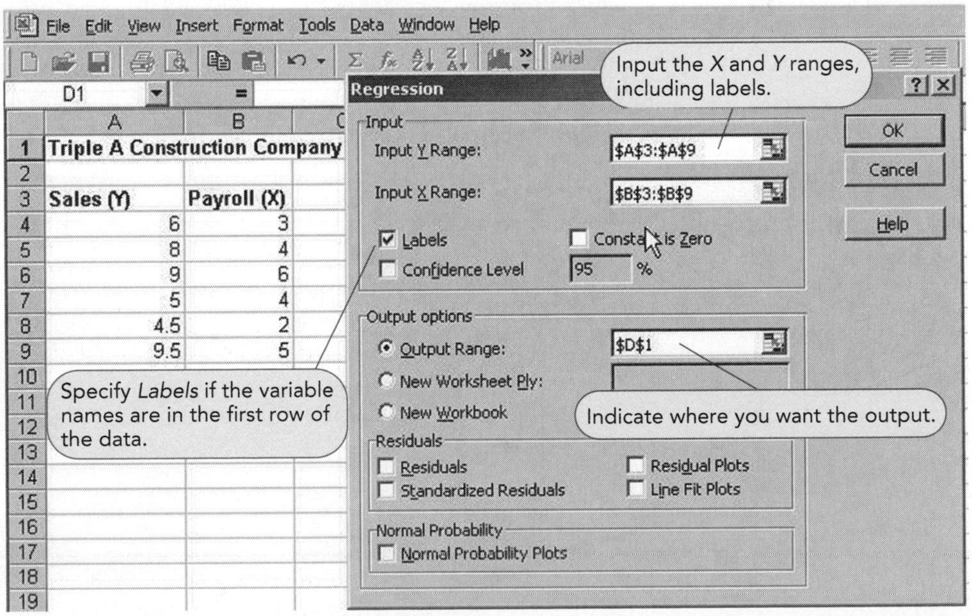

Input the *X* and *Y* ranges, including labels.

Input Y Range: $A$3:$A$9

Input X Range: $B$3:$B$9

Labels   Constant is Zero

Confidence Level 95 %

Specify *Labels* if the variable names are in the first row of the data.

Output options

Output Range: $D$1

Indicate where you want the output.

New Worksheet Ply:

New Workbook

Residuals

Residuals   Residual Plots

Standardized Residuals   Line Fit Plots

Normal Probability

Normal Probability Plots

PROGRAM 4.1D

Regression Output in Excel

	D	E	F	G	H	I	J	K	L
1	SUMMARY OUTPUT								
2									
3	*Regression Statistics*								
4	Multiple R	0.8333							
5	R Square	0.6944							
6	Adjusted R Square	0.6181							
7	Standard Error	1.3110							
8	Observations	6							
9									
10	ANOVA								
11		*df*	*SS*	*MS*	*F*	*Significance F*			
12	Regression	1	15.6250	15.6250	9.0909	0.0394			
13	Residual	4	6.8750	1.7188					
14	Total	5	22.5						
15									
16		*Coefficients*	*Standard Error*	*t Stat*	*P-value*	*Lower 95%*	*Upper 95%*	*Lower 95.0%*	*Upper 95.0%*
17	Intercept	2	1.7425	1.1477	0.3150	-2.8381	6.8381	-2.8381	6.8381
18	Payroll (X)	1.25	0.4146	3.0151	0.0394	0.0989	2.4011	0.0989	2.4011

> A high r^2 (close to 1) is desirable.

> A low significance level means the model is useful in predicting Y.

> The regression coefficients are found here.

4.6 ASSUMPTIONS OF THE REGRESSION MODEL

If we can make certain assumptions about the errors in a regression model, we can perform statistical tests to determine if the model is useful. The following assumptions are made about the errors:

1. The errors are independent.
2. The errors are normally distributed.
3. The errors have a mean of zero.
4. The errors have a constant variance (regardless of the value of X).

A plot of the errors may highlight problems with the model.

It is possible to check the data to see if these assumptions are met. Often a plot of the residuals will highlight any glaring violations of the assumptions. When the errors (residuals) are plotted against the independent variable, the pattern should appear random.

Figure 4.4 presents some typical error patterns, with Figure 4.4A displaying a pattern that is expected when the assumptions are met and the model is appropriate. The errors are random and no discernible pattern is present. Figure 4.4B demonstrates an error pattern in which the errors increase as X increases, violating the constant variance assumption. Figure 4.4C shows errors consistently increasing at first, and then consistently decreasing. A pattern such as this would indicate that the model is not linear and some other form (perhaps quadratic) should be used. In general, patterns in the plot of the errors indicate problems with the assumptions or the model specification.

FIGURE 4.4A

Pattern of Errors Indicating Randomness

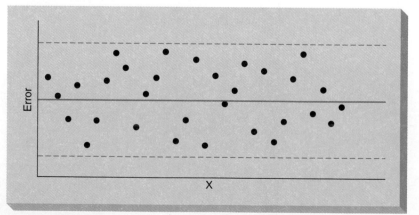

FIGURE 4.4B

Nonconstant Error
Variance

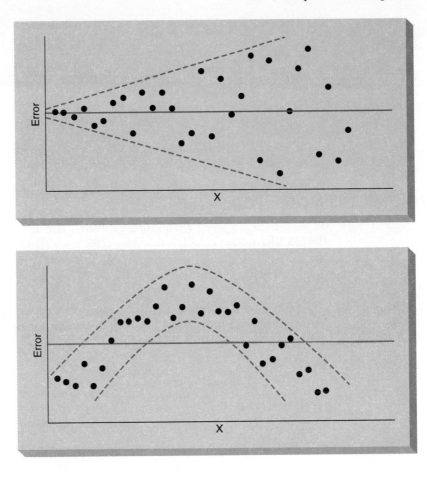

Error

X

FIGURE 4.4C

Errors Indicate
Relationship is
Not Linear

Error

X

Estimating the Variance

*The error variance is
estimated by the MSE.*

While the errors are assumed to have constant variance (σ^2), this is usually not known. It can be estimated from the sample results. The estimate of σ^2 is the *mean squared error* (MSE) and is denoted by s^2. The MSE is the sum of squares due to error divided by the degrees of freedom[1]:

$$s^2 = MSE = \frac{SSE}{n - k - 1} \qquad (4\text{-}12)$$

where

n = number of observations in the sample

k = number of independent variables

In this example, $n = 6$, and $k = 1$. So

$$s^2 = MSE = \frac{SSE}{n - k - 1} = \frac{6.8750}{6 - 1 - 1} = \frac{6.8750}{4} = 1.7188$$

---

[1] When the sample is large ($n > 30$), the prediction interval for an individual value of Y can be computed using normal tables. When the number of observations is small, the t-distribution is appropriate. See any good statistics textbook for details, such as J. E. Hanke, A. G. Reitsch and D. W. Wichern. *Business Forecasting*, 7/e. Upper Saddle River, NJ: Prentice Hall, 2001.

From this we can estimate the standard deviation as

$$s = \sqrt{MSE}$$

(4-13)

This is called the *standard error of the estimate* or the *standard deviation of the regression*. In the example shown in Program 4.1D,

$$s = \sqrt{MSE} = \sqrt{1.7188} = 1.31$$

This is used in many of the statistical tests about the model. It is also used to find interval estimates for both Y and regression coefficients[2].

4.7 TESTING THE MODEL FOR SIGNIFICANCE

To see if there is a linear relationship between X and Y, a statistical hypothesis test is performed. The null hypothesis is that there is no linear relationship between the two variables (i.e., $\beta_1 = 0$), and the alternate hypothesis is that there is a linear relationship (i.e., $\beta \neq 0$). If the null hypothesis can be rejected, then we have proven that a linear relationship does exist.

An F-test is used to determine if there is a relationship between X and Y.

An F-test is appropriate for determining whether there is a linear relationship. Excel and other software provide the results of this test. Before performing this test, we compute mean squared regression (MSR) as follows:

$$MSR = \frac{SSR}{k}$$

(4-14)

where

$$k = \text{number of independent variables in the model}$$

The F-statistic is computed from the MSR and MSE:

$$F = \frac{MSR}{MSE}$$

(4-15)

In the Triple A Construction example,

$$MSR = \frac{SSR}{k} = \frac{15.6250}{1} = 15.7650$$

$$F = \frac{MSR}{MSE} = \frac{15.625}{1.7188} = 9.0909$$

We see these same values in Program 4.1D.

If there is very little error, the denominator (MSE) of the fraction used to compute the F-statistic is very small relative to the numerator, and the F-value would be large. This would be an indication that the model is useful. A significance level related to the F-value is then found. Whenever the F-value is large, the significance level will be low, indicating that this could not have occurred by chance. When the significance level is small we can reject the null hypothesis that there is no linear relationship. Usually anything lower than 0.05 is considered small, and this will be used throughout this chapter. However, some people prefer to use a different value for the level of significance, such as 0.01 or 0.10. In this example, we have sufficient evidence to conclude that there is a linear relationship between X and Y at the 0.05 level.

If the significance level for the F-test is low, there is a relationship between X and Y.

---

[2] The MSE is a common measure of accuracy in forecasting. When used with techniques besides regression, it is common to divide the SSE by n rather than $n - k - 1$.

In Program 4.1D, the significance level for $F = 9.0909$ is given to be 0.0394. Because this value is less than 0.05, we would reject the hypothesis of no linear relationship and conclude that there is a linear relationship between X and Y. This means that X (payroll) is helpful in predicting Y (sales).

The F-test determines whether or not there is a relationship between the variables. However, just because there is a significant relationship between two variables does not necessarily mean there is a strong relationship. The best measure of the strength of the relationship is the coefficient of determination (r^2). Therefore, a good regression model should have a low significance level for the F-test and a high (close to 1) r^2. In the Triple A Construction example, we conclude that the model is useful (due to the F-test), and about 69% of the variability in sales is explained by fluctuations in the payroll. Had the F-test not indicated a significant result, then a high r^2 could simply have been due to random fluctuations and we would not have any confidence in it.

The strength of the relationship between X and Y is measured by r^2.

For linear regression, statistical tests of significance can be performed for the regression coefficients. In this example, we can test the hypothesis that the coefficient of X (payroll) is significantly different from 0. Given the assumptions about the errors, the appropriate test to use is a t-test. Program 4.1D provides this information also. The null hypothesis is that the coefficient of X (i.e., the slope of the line) is 0, meaning that X is not helpful in predicting Y. If this is rejected, then we can conclude that the slope is significantly different from 0 and X helps to predict Y. In Program 4.1D, the p-value (or *observed significance level*) is given to be 0.03935. Because this is low (less than 5%), we can conclude that the slope is not 0 and that X is useful in predicting Y. Note that the p-value for this test is the same as the significance level for the F test for the overall model. For the simple linear regression model, the test of the regression coefficient gives essentially the same information as the F-test since there is only one independent variable in the model. For multiple regression models, there will be several independent variables, and the t-tests can be used to test each coefficient individually while the F-test is for the overall model.

A statistical test can be used to determine if the slope is not 0. A low p-value indicates the coefficient is statistically significant.

The Analysis of Variance Table

When developing regression models in Excel, part of the output includes the analysis of variance (ANOVA) table. Most statistical software packages provide a table similar to this. We used this in finding the various sums of squares, which in turn were used for a variety of things. Table 4.4 provides summary information about the ANOVA table.

4.8 MULTIPLE REGRESSION ANALYSIS

A multiple regression model has more than one independent variable.

The *multiple regression model* is a practical extension of the model we just observed. It allows us to build a model with several independent variables. The underlying model is

$$Y = \beta_0 + \beta_1 X_1 + \beta_2 X_2 + \ldots + \beta_n X_n + \varepsilon \tag{4-16}$$

where

Y = dependent variable (response variable)
X_i = i^{th} independent variable (predictor variable or explanatory variable)
β_0 = intercept (value of Y when $X = 0$)
β_i = coefficient of the ith independent variable
ε = random error

TABLE 4.4

Analysis of Variance (ANOVA) Table for Regression

	DF	SS	MS	F	SIGNIFICANCE F
Regression	k	SSR	MSR = SSR/k	MSR/MSE	
Residual	n − k − 1	SSE	MSE = SSE/(n-k-1)		
Total	n − 1	SST			

To estimate the values of these coefficients, a sample is taken and the following equation is developed:

$$\hat{Y} = b_0 + b_1 X_1 + b_2 X_2 + \ldots + b_n X_n \tag{4-17}$$

where

$\hat{Y}$ = predicted value of Y

b_0 = sample intercept (and is an estimate of β_0)

b_i = sample coefficient of ith variable (and is an esimate of β_i)

Consider the case of Jenny Wilson Realty, a real estate company in Montgomery, Alabama. Jenny Wilson, owner and broker for this company, wants to develop a model to determine a suggested listing price for houses based on the size of the house and the age of the house. She selects a sample of houses that have sold recently in a particular area, and she records the selling price, the square footage of the house, the age of the house, and also the condition (good, excellent, or mint) of each house as shown in Table 4.5. Initially Jenny plans to use only the square footage and age to develop a model, although she wants to save the information on condition of the house to use later. She wants to find the coefficients for the following multiple regression model:

$$\hat{Y} = b_0 + b_1 X_1 + b_2 X_2$$

where

$\hat{Y}$ = predicted value of dependent variable (selling price)

b_0 = Y-intercept

X_1 and X_2 = value of the two independent variables (square footage and age), respectively

b_1 and b_2 = slopes for X_1 and X_2, respectively

TABLE 4.5			
Jenny Wilson Real Estate Data			

SELLING PRICE	SQUARE FOOTAGE	AGE	CONDITION
35000	1926	30	Good
47000	2069	40	Excellent
49900	1720	30	Excellent
55000	1396	15	Good
58900	1706	32	Mint
60000	1847	38	Mint
67000	1950	27	Mint
70000	2323	30	Excellent
78500	2285	26	Mint
79000	3752	35	Good
87500	2300	18	Good
93000	2525	17	Good
95000	3800	40	Excellent
97000	1740	12	Mint

PROGRAM 4.2

Multiple Regression Output in Excel for Jenny Wilson Realty Example

	A	B	C	D	E	F	G	H	I
1	SELL PRICE	SF	AGE						
2	35000	1926	30						
3	47000	2069	40						
4	49900	1720	30						
5	55000	1396	15						
6	58900	1706	32						
7	60000	1847	38						
8	67000	1950	27						
9	70000	2323	30						
10	78500	2285	26						
11	79000	3752	35						
12	87500	2300	18						
13	93000	2525	17						
14	95000	3800	40						
15	97000	1740	12						
16									
17	SUMMARY OUTPUT								
18									
19	*Regression Statistics*								
20	Multiple R	0.8197							
21	R Square	0.6719							
22	Adjusted R Sc	0.6122							
23	Standard Erro	12156.3							
24	Observations	14							
25									
26	ANOVA								
27		*df*	*SS*	*MS*	*F*	*Significance F*			
28	Regression	2	3328484242	1.66E+09	11.26195	0.0021788			
29	Residual	11	1625532901	1.48E+08					
30	Total	13	4954017143						
31									
32		*Coefficient*	*Standard Error*	*t Stat*	*P-value*	*Lower 95%*	*Upper 95%*	*Lower 95.0%*	*Upper 95.0%*
33	Intercept	60815.45	12741.0414	4.7732	0.0006	32772.5895	88858.3041	32772.5895	88858.3041
34	SF	21.91	5.1405	4.2622	0.0013	10.5956	33.2238	10.5956	33.2238
35	AGE	-1449.34	398.2825	-3.6390	0.0039	-2325.9574	-572.7289	-2325.9574	-572.7289

Callouts: *The coefficient of determination (r^2) is 0.67.* — *A low significance level for F proves a relationship exists.* — *The regression coefficients are found here.*

Excel can be used to develop multiple regression models.

The mathematics of multiple regression becomes quite complex, so we leave formulas for b_0, b_1, and b_2 to regression textbooks.[3] Excel can be used to develop a multiple regression model just as it was used for a simple linear regression model. When entering the data in Excel, it is important that all of the independent variables are in adjoining columns to facilitate the input when using *Tools—Data Analysis–Regression*. The Excel output that Jenny Wilson obtains is shown in Program 4.2, and it provides the following equation (coefficients are rounded):

$$\hat{Y} = b_0 + b_1 X_1 + b_2 X_2$$
$$= 60815 + 22X_1 - 1449X_2$$

The F-test is significant (0.002 level), indicating this model is useful, and $r^2 = 0.67$ indicating 67% of the variability in selling price is explained by these square footage and age. This means about 33% of the variability in selling price is not explained and could be due to other factors such as condition of the house, size of the lot, number of bedrooms, and size of the garage. If a new client approaches Jenny Wilson to list a house that is 1900 square feet and 10 years old, the suggested price would be

$$\hat{Y} = 60815 + 22(1900) - 1449(10)$$
$$= \$117,105$$

This figure represents the average selling price for a house of this type. Jenny may wish to adjust this based on other factors unique to this house.

---

[3] See, for example, Norman R. Draper and Harry Smith. *Applied Regression Analysis*, 3rd ed. Wiley, 1998.

4.9   BINARY OR DUMMY VARIABLES

A dummy variable is also called an indicator variable or a binary variable.

All of the variables we have used in regression examples have been quantitative variables such as sales figures, payroll numbers, square footage, and age. These have all been easily measurable and have numbers associated with them. There are many times when we believe a qualitative variable rather than a quantitative variable would be helpful in predicting the dependent variable Y. For example, regression may be used to find a relationship between annual income and certain characteristics of the employees. Years of experience at a particular job would be a quantitative variable. However, information regarding whether or not a person has a college degree might also be important. This would not be a measurable value or quantity, so a special variable called a *dummy variable* (or a *binary variable* or an *indicator variable*) would be used. A dummy variable is assigned a value of 1 if a particular condition is met (e.g., a person has a college degree), and a value of 0 otherwise.

Return to the Jenny Wilson Realty example. Jenny believes that a better model can be developed if the condition of the property is included. To incorporate the condition of the house into the model, Jenny looks at the information available (see Table 4.5), and sees that the three categories are good condition, excellent condition, and mint condition. Since these are not quantitative variables, she must use dummy variables. These are defined as

$$X_3 = 1 \text{ if house is in excellent condition}$$

$$= 0 \text{ otherwise}$$

$$X_4 = 1 \text{ if house is in mint condition}$$

$$= 0 \text{ otherwise}$$

The number of dummy variables must equal one less than the number of categories of a qualitative variable.

Notice there is no separate variable for "good" condition. If X_3 and X_4 are both 0, then the house cannot be in excellent or mint condition, so it must be in good condition. When using dummy variables, the number of variables must be 1 less than the number of categories. In this problem, there were 3 categories (good, excellent, and mint condition) so we must have 2 dummy variables. If we had mistakenly used too many variables and the number of dummy variables equaled the number of categories, then the mathematical computations could not be performed or would not give reliable values.

These dummy variables will be used with the two previous variables (X_1 — square footage, and X_2 — age) to try to predict the selling prices of houses for Jenny Wilson. Program 4.3 provides the Excel output for this new data, and this shows how the dummy variables were coded. The significance level for the F-test is 0.00017, so this model is statistically significant. The coefficient of determination (r^2) is 0.898, so this is a much better model than the previous one. The regression equation is

$$\hat{Y} = 48{,}329 + 28.2X_1 - 1{,}981X_2 + 16{,}581X_3 + 23{,}684X_4$$

This indicates that a house in excellent condition ($X_3 = 1$, $X_4 = 0$) would sell for about $16,581 more than a house in good condition ($X_3 = 0$, $X_4 = 0$). A house in mint condition ($X_3 = 0$, $X_4 = 1$) would sell for about $23,684 more than a house in good condition.

4.10   MODEL BUILDING

In developing a good regression model, possible independent variables are identified and the best ones are selected to be used in the model. The best model is a statistically significant model with a high r^2 and few variables.

PROGRAM 4.3

Excel with Dummy Variables for Jenny Wilson Realty Example

	A	B	C	D	E	F	G	H	I
1	SELL PRICE	SF	AGE	X3 (Exc)	X4 (Mint)	Condition			
2	35000	1926	30	0	0	Good			
3	47000	2069	40	1	0	Excellent			
4	49900	1720	30	1	0	Excellent			
5	55000	1396	15	0	0	Good			
6	58900	1706	32	0	1	Mint			
7	60000	1847	38	0	1	Mint			
8	67000	1950	27	0	1	Mint			
9	70000	2323	30	1	0	Excellent			
10	78500	2285	26	0	1	Mint			
11	79000	3752	35	0	0	Good			
12	87500	2300	18	0	0	Good			
13	93000	2525	17	0	0	Good			
14	95000	3800	40	1	0	Excellent			
15	97000	1740	12	0	1	Mint			
16									
17	SUMMARY OUTPUT								
18									
19	*Regression Statistics*								
20	Multiple R	0.947618							
21	R Square	0.89798							
22	Adjusted R	0.852637							
23	Standard E	7493.777							
24	Observatiol	14							
25									
26	ANOVA								
27		*df*	*SS*	*MS*	*F*	*Significance F*			
28	Regressior	4	4.45E+09	1.11E+09	19.80444	0.000174			
29	Residual	9	5.05E+08	56156698					
30	Total	13	4.95E+09						
31									
32		Coefficients	Standard E	t Stat	P-value	Lower 95%	Upper 95%	Lower 95.0%	Upper 95.0%
33	Intercept	48329.23	8713.31	5.55	0.00	28618.34	68040.11	28618.34	68040.11
34	SF	28.21	3.47	8.12	0.00	20.36	36.07	20.36	36.07
35	AGE	-1981.41	298.01	-6.65	0.00	-2655.56	-1307.26	-2655.56	-1307.26
36	X3 (Exc)	16581.32	6089.81	2.72	0.02	2805.21	30357.44	2805.21	30357.44
37	X4 (Mint)	23684.62	5324.63	4.45	0.00	11039.45	35720.70	11039.45	35729.79

The value of r^2 can never decrease when more variables are added to the model.

The adjusted r^2 may decrease when more variables are added to the model.

As more variables are added to a regression model, r^2 will usually increase, and it cannot decrease. It is tempting to keep adding variables to a model to try to increase r^2. However, if too many independent variables are included in the model, problems can arise. For this reason, the *adjusted r^2* value is often used (rather than r^2) to determine if an additional independent variable is beneficial. The adjusted r^2 takes into account the number of independent variables in the model, and it is possible for the adjusted r^2 to decrease. The formula for r^2 is

$$r^2 = \frac{SSR}{SST} = 1 - \frac{SSE}{SST}$$

The adjusted r^2 is

$$Adjusted\ r^2 = 1 - \frac{SSE/(n - k - 1)}{SST/(n - 1)}$$

Notice that as the number of variables (k) increases, $n - k - 1$ will decrease. This causes $SSE/(n - k - 1)$ to increase, and consequently the adjusted r^2 will decrease unless the extra variable in the model causes a significant decrease in the SSE. Thus, the reduction in error (and SSE) must be sufficient to offset the change in k.

A variable should not be added to the model if it causes the adjusted r^2 to decrease.

As a general rule of thumb, if the adjusted r^2 increases when a new variable is added to the model, the variable should probably remain in the model. If the adjusted r^2 decreases when a new variable is added, the variable should not remain in the model. Other factors should also be considered when trying to build the model, but they are beyond the introductory level of this chapter.

In the Jenny Wilson Realty example illustrated in Program 4.3, we saw an r^2 of about 0.90 and an adjusted r^2 of 0.85. While other variables such as the size of the lot, the number of bedrooms, and the number of bathrooms might be related to the selling price of a house, we may not want to include these in the model. It is likely that these variables would be correlated with the square footage of the house (e.g., more bedrooms usually means a larger house), which is already included in the model. Thus, the information provided by these additional variables might be duplication of information already in the model.

Multicollinearity exists when a variable is correlated to other variables.

When an independent variable is correlated with one other independent variable, the variables are said to be *collinear*. If an independent variable is correlated with a combination of other independent variables, the condition of *multicollinearity* exists. This can create problems in interpreting the coefficients of the variables as several variables are providing duplicate information. For example, if two independent variables were monthly salary expenses for a company and annual salary expenses for a company, the information provided in one is also provided in the other. Several sets of regression coefficients for these two variables would yield exactly the same results. Thus, individual interpretation of these variables would be questionable, although the model itself is still good for prediction purposes.

4.11 NONLINEAR REGRESSION

Transformations may be used to turn a nonlinear model into a linear model.

The regression models we have seen are linear models. However, at times there exist nonlinear relationships between variables. Some simple variable transformations can be used to create an apparently linear model from a nonlinear relationship. This allows us to use Excel and other linear regression programs for perform the calculations. We will demonstrate this in the following example.

On every new automobile sold in the United States, the fuel efficiency (as measured by miles per gallon of gasoline or MPG) of the automobile is prominently displayed on the window sticker. The MPG is related to several factors, one of which is the weight of the automobile. Engineers at Colonel Motors, in an attempt to improve fuel efficiency, have been asked to study the impact of weight on MPG. They have decided that a regression model should be used to do this.

A sample of twelve new automobiles was selected, and the weight and MPG rating were recorded. Table 4.6 provides this data. A scatter diagram of this data in Figure 4.5A shows the weight and MPG. A linear regression line is drawn through the points. Excel was used to develop a simple linear regression equation to relate the MPG (Y) to the weight in 1,000 lbs (X_1) in the form

$$\hat{Y} = b_0 + b_1 X_1$$

The Excel output is shown in Program 4.4. From this we get the equation

$$\hat{Y} = 47.6 - 8.2 X_1$$

or

$$MPG = 47.6 - 8.2(\text{weight in 1,000 lbs.})$$

TABLE 4.6					
Automobile Weight vs. MPG	**WEIGHT MPG**	**(1,000 LBS.)**		**WEIGHT MPG**	**(1,000 LBS.)**
	12	4.58		20	3.18
	13	4.66		23	2.68
	15	4.02		24	2.65
	18	2.53		33	1.70
	19	3.09		36	1.95
	19	3.11		42	1.92

FIGURE 4.5A

Linear Model for MPG Data

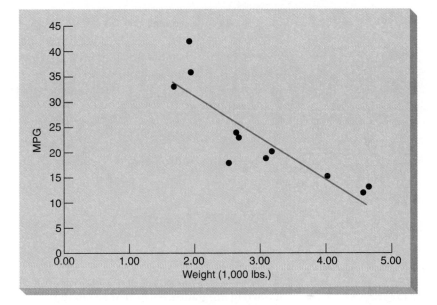

FIGURE 4.5B

Nonlinear Model for MPG Data

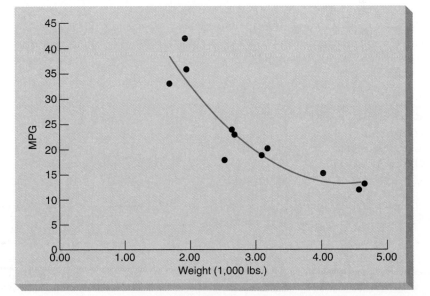

PROGRAM 4.4

Excel Output for Linear Regression Model with MPG Data

	A	B	C	D	E	F	G	H	I	J	K	L	M
1	Automobile Weight vs. MPG			SUMMARY OUTPUT									
2													
3	MPG (Y)	Weight (X1)		*Regression Statistics*									
4	12	4.58		Multiple R	0.8629								
5	13	4.66		R Square	0.7446								
6	15	4.02		Adjusted R Sc	0.7190								
7	18	2.53		Standard Erro	5.0076								
8	19	3.09		Observations	12								
9	19	3.11											
10	20	3.18		ANOVA									
11	23	2.68			df	SS	MS	F	Significance F				
12	24	2.65		Regression	1	730.9090	730.9090	29.1480	0.0003				
13	33	1.70		Residual	10	250.7577	25.0758						
14	36	1.95		Total	11	981.6667							
15	42	1.92											
16					Coefficients	Standard Err	t Stat	P-value	Lower 95%	Upper 95%	Lower 95.0	Upper 95.0%	
17				Intercept	47.6193	4.8132	9.8936	0.0000	36.8950	58.3437	36.8950	58.3437	
18				Weight	-8.2460	1.5273	-5.3989	0.0003	-11.6491	-4.8428	-11.6491	-4.8428	

The model is useful since the significance level for the F-test is small and $r^2 = 0.7446$. However, further examination of the graph in Figure 4.5A brings into question the use of a linear model. Perhaps a nonlinear relationship exists, and maybe the model should be modified to account for this. A quadratic model is illustrated in Figure 4.5B. This model would be of the form

$$MPG = b_0 + b_1(\text{weight}) + b_2(\text{weight})^2$$

The easiest way to develop this model is to define a new variable

$$X_2 = (\text{weight})^2$$

This gives us the model

$$\hat{Y} = b_0 + b_1 X_1 + b_2 X_2$$

We can create another column in Excel, and again run the regression tool. The output is shown in Program 4.5. The new equation is

$$\hat{Y} = 79.8 - 30.2 X_1 + 3.4 X_2$$

A low significance value for F and a high r^2 are indications of a good model.

The significance level for F is low (0.0002) so the model is useful, and $r^2 = 0.8478$. The adjusted r^2 increased from 0.719 to 0.814, so this new variable definitely improved the model.

PROGRAM 4.5

Excel Output for Nonlinear Regression Model with MPG Data

	A	B	C	D	E	F	G	H	I	J	K	L
1	Automobile Weight vs. MPG			SUMMARY OUTPUT								
2												
3	MPG (Y)	Weight (X1)	WeightSq. (X2)	*Regression Statistics*								
4	12	4.58	20.98	Multiple R	0.9208							
5	13	4.66	21.72	R Square	0.8478							
6	15	4.02	16.16	Adjusted R Sc	0.8140							
7	18	2.53	6.40	Standard Erro	4.0745							
8	19	3.09	9.55	Observations	12							
9	19	3.11	9.67									
10	20	3.18	10.11	ANOVA								
11	23	2.68	7.18		df	SS	MS	F	Significance F			
12	24	2.65	7.02	Regression	2	832.2557	416.1278	25.0661	0.0002			
13	33	1.70	2.89	Residual	9	149.4110	16.6012					
14	36	1.95	3.80	Total	11	981.6667						
15	42	1.92	3.69									
16					Coefficient	Standard Er	t Stat	P-value	Lower 95%	Upper 95%	Lower 95.0	Upper 95.0%
17				Intercept	79.7888	13.5962	5.8685	0.0002	49.0321	110.5454	49.0321	110.5454
18				Weight	-30.2224	8.9809	-3.3652	0.0083	-50.5386	-9.9061	-50.5386	-9.9061
19				Weight2	3.4124	1.3811	2.4708	0.0355	0.2881	6.5367	0.2881	6.5367

This model is good for prediction purposes. However, we should not try to interpret the coefficients of the variables due to the correlation between X_1 (weight) and X_2 (weight squared). Normally we would interpret the coefficient for X_1 as the change in Y that results from a 1-unit change in X_1, while holding all other variables constant. Obviously holding one variable constant while changing the other is impossible in this example since $X_2 = X_1^2$. If X_1 changes, then X_2 must change also. This is an example of a problem that exists when multicollinearity is present.

Other types of nonlinearities can be handled using a similar approach. A number of transformations exist that may help to develop a linear model from variables with nonlinear relationships.

4.12 CAUTIONS AND PITFALLS IN REGRESSION ANALYSIS

This chapter has provided a brief introduction into regression analysis, one of the most widely used quantitative techniques in business. However, some common errors are made with regression models, so caution should be observed when using this.

If the assumptions are not met, the statistical tests may not be valid. Any interval estimates are also invalid, although the model can still be used for prediction purposes.

Correlation does not necessarily mean causation. Two variables (such as the price of automobiles and your annual salary) may be highly correlated to one another, but one is not causing the other to change. They may both be changing due to other factors such as the economy in general or the inflation rate.

A high correlation does not mean one variable is causing a change in the other.

If multicollinearity is present in a multiple regression model, the model is still good for prediction, but interpretation of individual coefficients is questionable. The individual tests on the regression coefficients are not valid.

Using a regression equation beyond the range of X is very questionable. A linear relationship may exist within the range of values of X in the sample. What happens beyond this range is unknown; the linear relationship may become nonlinear at some point. For example, there is usually a linear relationship between advertising and sales within a limited range. As more money is spent on advertising, sales tend to increase even if everything else is held constant. However, at some point, increasing advertising expenditures will have less impact on sales unless the company does other things to help, such as opening new markets or expanding the product offerings. If advertising is increased and nothing else changes, the sales will probably level off at some point.

The regression equation should not be used with values of X that are below the lowest value of X or above the highest value of X found in the sample.

Related to the limitation regarding the range of X is the interpretation of the intercept (b_0). Since the lowest value for X in a sample is often much greater than 0, the intercept is a point on the regression line beyond the range of X. Therefore, we should not be concerned if the t-test for this coefficient is not significant as we should not be using the regression equation to predict a value of Y when $X = 0$. This intercept is merely used in defining the line that fits the sample points the best.

Using the F-test and concluding a linear regression model is helpful in predicting Y does not mean that this is the best relationship. While this model may explain much of the variability in Y, it is possible that a nonlinear relationship might explain even more. Similarly, if it is concluded that no linear relationship exists, another type of relationship could exist.

A significant F value may occur even when the relationship is not strong.

A statistically significant relationship does not mean it has any practical value. With large enough samples, it is possible to have a statistically significant relationship, but r^2 might be 0.01. This would normally be of little use to a manager. Similarly, a high r^2 could be found due to random chance if the sample is small. The F-test must also show significance to place any value in r^2.

SUMMARY

Regression analysis is an extremely valuable quantitative tool. Using scatter diagrams helps to see relationships between variables. The F-test is used to determine if the results can be considered useful. The coefficient of determination (r^2) is used to measure the proportion of variability in Y that is explained by the regression model. The correlation coefficient measures the relationship between two variables.

Multiple regression involves the use of more than one independent variable. Dummy variables (binary or indicator variables) are used with qualitative or categorical data. Nonlinear models can be transformed into linear models.

We saw how to use Excel to develop regression models. Interpretation of computer output was presented, and several examples were provided.

GLOSSARY

Adjusted r^2. A measure of the explanatory power of a regression model that takes into consideration the number of independent variables in the model.

Binary Variable. See Dummy Variable.

Coefficient of Correlation (r). A measure of the strength of the relationship between two variables.

Coefficient of Determination (r^2). The percent of the variability in the dependent variable (Y) that is explained by the regression equation.

Collinearity. A condition that exists when one independent variable is correlated with another independent variable.

Dependent Variable. The Y-variable in a regression model. This is what is being predicted.

Dummy Variable. A variable used to represent a qualitative factor or condition. Dummy variables have values of 0 or 1. This is also called a binary variable or an indicator variable.

Error. The difference between the actual value (Y) and the predicted value ($\hat{Y}$).

Explanatory Variable. The independent variable in a regression equation.

Independent Variable. The X-variable in a regression equation. This is used to help predict the dependent variable.

Least Squares. A reference to the criterion used to select the regression line, to minimize the squared distances between the estimated straight line and the observed values.

Mean Squared Error (MSE). An estimate of the error variance.

Multicollinearity. A condition that exists when one independent variable is correlated with other independent variables.

Multiple Regression Model. A regression model that has more than one independent variable.

Observed Significance Level. Another name for p-value.

p-value. A probability value that is used when testing a hypothesis. The hypothesis is rejected when this is low.

Predictor Variable. Another name for explanatory variable.

Regression Analysis. A forecasting procedure that uses the least squares approach on one or more independent variables to develop a forecasting model.

Residual. Another term for error.

Response Variable. The dependent variable in a regression equation.

Scatter Diagrams. Diagrams of the variable to be forecasted, plotted against another variable, such as time. Also called scatter plots.

Standard Error of the Estimate. An estimate of the standard deviation of the errors and is sometimes called the standard deviation of the regression.

Sum of Squares Error (SSE). The total sum of the squared differences between each observation (Y) and the predicted value ($\hat{Y}$).

Sum of Squares Regression (SSR). The total sum of the squared differences between each predicted value ($\hat{Y}$) and the mean ($\overline{Y}$).

Sum of Squares Total (SST). The total sum of the squared differences between each observation (Y) and the mean ($\overline{Y}$).

KEY EQUATIONS

(4-1) $Y = \beta_0 + \beta_1 X + \varepsilon$

Underlying linear model for simple linear regression.

(4-2) $\hat{Y} = b_0 + b_1 X$

Simple linear regression model computed from a sample.

(4-3) $e = Y - \hat{Y}$

Error in regression model.

(4-4) $b_1 = \dfrac{\sum(X - \overline{X})(Y - \overline{Y})}{\sum(X - \overline{X})^2}$

Slope in the regression line.

(4-5) $b_0 = \overline{Y} - b_1\overline{X}$

The intercept in the regression line.

(4-6) $SST = \sum(Y - \overline{Y})^2$

Total sums of squares.

(4-7) $SSE = \sum e^2 = \sum (Y - \hat{Y})^2$

Sum of squares due to error.

(4-8) $SSR = \sum (\hat{Y} - \bar{Y})^2$

Sum of squares due to regression.

(4-9) $SST = SSR + SSE$

Relationship among sums of squares in regression.

(4-10) $r^2 = \dfrac{SSR}{SST} = 1 - \dfrac{SSE}{SST}$

Coefficient of determination.

(4-11) $r = \pm\sqrt{r^2}$

Coefficient of correlation. This has the same sign as the slope.

(4-12) $s^2 = MSE = \dfrac{SSE}{n - k - 1}$

An estimate of the variance of the errors in regression; n is the sample size and k is the number of independent variables.

(4-13) $s = \sqrt{MSE}$

An estimate of the standard deviation of the errors. Also called the standard error of the estimate.

(4-14) $MSR = \dfrac{SSR}{k}$

Mean square regression. k is the number of independent variables.

(4-15) $F = \dfrac{MSR}{MSE}$

F-statistic used to test significance of overall regression model.

(4-16) $Y = \beta_0 + \beta_1 X_1 + \beta_2 X_2 + \ldots + \beta_n X_n + \varepsilon$

Underlying model for multiple regression model.

(4-17) $\hat{Y} = b_0 + b_1 X_1 + b_2 X_2 + \ldots + b_n X_n$

Multiple regression model computed from a sample.

(4-18) $Adjusted\ r^2 = 1 - \dfrac{SSE/(n - k - 1)}{SST/(n - 1)}$

Adjusted r^2 used in building multiple regression models.

SOLVED PROBLEMS

Solved Problem 4-1

Judith Thompson runs a florist shop on the Gulf Coast of Texas, specializing in floral arrangements for weddings and other special events. She advertises weekly in the local newspapers and is considering increasing her advertising budget. Before doing so, she decides to evaluate the past effectiveness of these ads. Five weeks are sampled, and the advertising dollars and sales volume for each of these is shown in the following table. Develop a regression equation that would help Judith evaluate her advertising. Find the coefficient of determination for this model.

SALES ($1,000)	ADVERTISING ($100)
11	5
6	3
10	7
6	2
12	8

Solution

ADVERTISING Y	SALES X	$(X - \bar{X})^2$	$(X - \bar{X})(Y - \bar{Y})$
11	5	$(5 - 5)^2 = 0$	$(5 - 5)(11 - 9) = 0$
6	3	$(3 - 5)^2 = 4$	$(3 - 5)(6 - 9) = 6$
10	7	$(7 - 5)^2 = 4$	$(7 - 5)(10 - 9) = 2$
6	2	$(2 - 5)^2 = 9$	$(2 - 5)(6 - 9) = 9$
12	8	$(8 - 5)^2 = 9$	$(8 - 5)(12 - 9) = 9$
$\sum Y = 45$	$\sum X = 25$	$\sum(X - \bar{X})^2 = 26$	$\sum(X - \bar{X})(Y - \bar{Y}) = 26$
$\bar{Y} = 45/5$	$\bar{X} = 25/5$		
$= 9$	$= 5$		

$$b_1 = \frac{\Sigma(X - \overline{X})(Y - \overline{Y})}{\Sigma(X - \overline{X})^2} = \frac{26}{26} = 1$$

$$b_0 = \overline{Y} - b_1\overline{X} = 9 - (1)(5) = 4$$

The regression equation is

$$\hat{Y} = 4 + 1X$$

To compute r^2, we use the following table:

Y	X	$\hat{Y} = 4 + 1X$	$(Y - \hat{Y})^2$	$(Y - \overline{Y})^2$
11	5	9	$(11 - 9)^2 = 4$	$(11 - 9)^2 = 4$
6	3	7	$(6 - 7)^2 = 1$	$(6 - 9)^2 = 9$
10	7	11	$(10 - 11)^2 = 1$	$(10 - 9)^2 = 1$
6	2	6	$(6 - 6)^2 = 0$	$(6 - 9)^2 = 9$
12	8	12	$(12 - 12)^2 = 0$	$(12 - 9)^2 = 9$
$\Sigma Y = 45$	$\Sigma X = 25$		$\Sigma(Y - \hat{Y})^2 = 6$	$\Sigma(Y - \overline{Y})^2 = 32$
$\overline{Y} = 9$	$\overline{X} = 5$		SSE	SST

The slope ($b_1 = 1$) tells us that for each 1 unit increase in X (or $100 in advertising), sales increase by 1 unit (or $1,000). Also, $r^2 = 0.8125$ indicating that about 81% of the variability in sales can be explained by the regression model with advertising as the independent variable.

Solved Problem 4-2

Use Excel with the data in Solved Problem 4-1 to find the regression model. What does the F-test say about this model?

Solution

Program 4.6 provides the Excel output for this problem. We see the equation is

$$\hat{Y} = 4 + 1X$$

The coefficient of determination (r^2) is shown to be 0.8125. The significance level for the F-test is 0.0366, which is less than 0.05. This indicates the model is statistically significant. Thus, there is sufficient evidence in the data to conclude that the model is useful, and there is a relationship between X (advertising) and Y (sales).

PROGRAM 4.6

Excel Output for Solved Problem 4-2

	A	B	C	D	E	F	G	H	I	J
17	SUMMARY OUTPUT									
18										
19	*Regression Statistics*									
20	Multiple R	0.9014								
21	R Square	0.8125								
22	Adjusted R Squ	0.7500								
23	Standard Error	1.4142								
24	Observations	5								
25										
26	ANOVA									
27		*df*	*SS*	*MS*	*F*	*Significance F*				
28	Regression	1	26	26	13	0.03662				
29	Residual	3	6	2						
30	Total	4	32							
31										
32		*Coefficient*	*Standard E*	*t Stat*	*P-value*	*Lower 95%*	*Upper 9!*	*Lower 95*	*Upper 95.0%*	
33	Intercept	4	1.5242	2.6244	0.0787	-0.8506	8.8506	-0.8506	8.8506	
34	Advertising ($100)	1	0.2774	3.6056	0.0366	0.1173	1.8827	0.1173	1.8827	

⟩ SELF-TEST

- Before taking the self-test, refer back to the learning objectives at the beginning of the chapter, the notes in the margins, and the glossary at the end of the chapter.
- Use the key at the back of the book to correct your answers.
- Restudy pages that correspond to any questions that you answered incorrectly or material you feel uncertain about.

1. One of the assumptions in regression analysis is that
   a. the errors have a mean of 1.
   b. the errors have a mean of 0.
   c. the observations (Y) have a mean of 1.
   d. the observations (Y) have a mean of 0.
2. A graph of the sample points that will be used to develop a regression line is called
   a. a sample graph.
   b. a regression diagram.
   c. a scatter diagram.
   d. a regression plot.
3. When using regression, an error is also called
   a. an intercept.
   b. a prediction.
   c. a coefficient.
   d. a residual.
4. In a regression model, Y is called
   a. the independent variable.
   b. the dependent variable.
   c. the regression variable.
   d. the predictor variable.
5. A quantity that provides a measure of how far each sample point is from the regression line is
   a. the SSR.
   b. the SSE.
   c. the SST.
   d. the MSR.
6. The percentage of the variation in the dependent variable that is explained by a regression equation is measured by
   a. the coefficient of correlation.
   b. the MSE.
   c. the coefficient of determination.
   d. the slope.
7. In a regression model, if every sample point is on the regression line (all errors are 0), then
   a. the correlation coefficient would be 0.
   b. the correlation coefficient would be −1 or 1.
   c. the coefficient of determination would be −1.
   d. the coefficient of determination would be 0.
8. When using dummy variables in a regression equation to model a qualitative or categorical variable, the number of dummy variables should equal to
   a. the number of categories.
   b. one more than the number of categories.
   c. one less than the number of categories.
   d. the number of other independent variables in the model.
9. A multiple regression model differs from a simple linear regression model because the multiple regression model has more than one
   a. independent variable.
   b. dependent variable.
   c. intercept.
   d. error.
10. The overall significance of a regression model is tested using an F-test. The model is significant if
    a. the F value is low.
    b. the significance level of the F-value is low.
    c. the r^2 value is low.
    d. the slope is lower than the intercept.
11. A new variable should not be added to a multiple regression model if that variable causes
    a. r^2 to decrease.
    b. the adjusted r^2 to decrease.
    c. the SST to decrease.
    d. the intercept to decrease.
12. A good regression model should have
    a. a low r^2 and a low significance level for the F-test.
    b. a high r^2 and a high significance level for the F-test.
    c. a high r^2 and a low significance level for the F-test.
    d. a low r^2 and a high significance level for the F-test.

DISCUSSION QUESTIONS AND PROBLEMS

Discussion Questions

4-1 What is the meaning of least squares in a regression model?

4-2 Discuss the use of dummy variables in regression analysis.

4-3 Discuss how the coefficient of determination and the coefficient of correlation are related and how they are used in regression analysis.

4-4 Explain how a scatter diagram can be used to identify the type of regression to use.

4-5 Explain how the adjusted r^2 value is used in developing a regression model.

4-6 Explain what information is provided by the F-test.

4-7 What is the SSE? How is this related to the SST and the SSR?

4-8 Explain how a plot of the residuals can be used in developing a regression model.

Problems

• **4-9** John Smith has developed the following forecasting model:

$$\hat{Y} = 36 + 4.3X_1$$

where

$$\hat{Y} = \text{Demand for K10 air conditioners}$$

$$X_1 = \text{the outside temperature (°F)}$$

(a) Forecast the demand for K10 when the temperature is 70°F.
(b) What is the demand for a temperature of 80°F?
(c) What is the demand for a temperature of 90°F?

4-10 The operations manager of a musical instrument distributor feels that demand for bass drums may be related to the number of television appearances by the popular rock group Green Shades during the preceding month. The manager has collected the data shown in the following table:

DEMAND FOR BASS DRUMS	GREEN SHADES TV APPEARANCE
3	3
6	4
7	7
5	6
10	8
8	5

(a) Graph these data to see whether a linear equation might describe the relationship between the group's television shows and bass drum sales.

(b) Using the equations presented in this chapter, compute the SST, SSE, and SSR. Find the least squares regression line for this data.

(c) What is your estimate for bass drum sales if the Green Shades performed on TV six times last month?

4-11 Using Excel, find the least squares regression line for the data in Problem 4-10. Based on the F-test, is there a statistically significant relationship between the demand for drums and the number of TV appearances?

4-12 Students in a management science class have just received their grades on the first test. The instructor has provided information about the first test grades in some previous classes as well as the final average for the same students. Some of these grades have been sampled and are as follows:

STUDENT	1	2	3	4	5	6	7	8	9
1st test grade	98	77	88	80	96	61	66	95	69
Final average	93	78	84	73	84	64	64	95	76

(a) Develop a regression model that could be used to predict the final average in the course based on the first test grade.

(b) Predict the final average of a student who made an 83 on the first test.

(c) Give the values of r and r^2 for this model. Interpret the value of r^2 in the context of this problem.

4-13 Using Excel, find the least squares regression line for the data in Problem 4-12. Based on the F-test, is there a statistically significant relationship between the first test grade and the final average in the course?

4-14 Steve Caples, a real estate appraiser in Lake Charles, Louisiana, has developed a regression model to help appraise residential housing in the Lake Charles area. The model was developed using recently sold homes in a particular neighborhood. The price (Y) of the house is based on the square footage (X) of the house. The model is

$$\hat{Y} = 13,473 + 37.65X$$

The coefficient of correlation for the model is 0.63.

(a) Use the model to predict the selling price of a house that is 1,860 square feet.

(b) A house with 1,860 square feet recently sold for $95,000. Explain why this is not what the model predicted.

(c) If you were going to use multiple regression to develop an appraisal model, what other quantitative variables might be included in the model?

(d) What is the coefficient of determination for this model?

---

* Note: ⬔ means the problem may be solved with QM for Windows; ✖ means the problem may be solved with Excel QM; and ⬔ means the problem may be solved with QM for Windows and/or Excel QM.

4-15 Accountants at the firm Walker and Walker believed that several traveling executives submit unusually high travel vouchers when they return from business trips. The accountants took a sample of 200 vouchers submitted from the past year; they then developed the following multiple regression equation relating expected travel cost (Y) to number of days on the road (X_1) and distance traveled (X_2) in miles:

$$\hat{Y} = \$90.00 + \$48.50X_1 + \$0.40X_2$$

The coefficient of correlation computed was 0.68.

(a) If Thomas Williams returns from a 300-mile trip that took him out of town for five days, what is the expected amount that he should claim as expenses?

(b) Williams submitted a reimbursement request for $685; what should the accountant do?

(c) Comment on the validity of this model. Should any other variables be included? Which ones? Why?

4-16 Thirteen students entered the undergraduate business program at Rollins College two years ago. The following table indicates what their grade-point averages (GPAs) were after being in the program for two years and what each student scored on one part of the SAT exam when he or she was in high school. Is there a meaningful relationship between grades and SAT scores? If a student scores a 450 on the SAT, what do you think his or her GPA will be? What about a student who scores 800?

STUDENT	SAT SCORE	GPA	STUDENT	SAT SCORE	GPA
A	421	2.90	H	481	2.53
B	377	2.93	I	729	3.22
C	585	3.00	J	501	1.99
D	690	3.45	K	613	2.75
E	608	3.66	L	709	3.90
F	390	2.88	M	366	1.60
G	415	2.15			

4-17 Bus and subway ridership in Washington, D.C., during the summer months is believed to be heavily tied to the number of tourists visiting the city. During the past 12 years, the following data have been obtained:

YEAR	NUMBER OF TOURISTS (1,000,000's)	RIDERSHIP (100,000's)
1	7	15
2	2	10
3	6	13
4	4	15
5	14	25
6	15	27

YEAR	NUMBER OF TOURISTS (1,000,000s)	RIDERSHIP (100,000s)
7	16	24
8	12	20
9	14	27
10	20	44
11	15	34
12	7	17

(a) Plot these data and determine if a linear model is reasonable.

(b) Develop a regression model.

(c) What is expected ridership if 10 million tourists visit the city?

(d) If there are no tourists at all, explain the predicted ridership.

4-18 Use Excel to develop a regression model for the data in Problem 4-17. Explain what Excel output indicates about the usefulness of this model.

4-19 The following data gives the starting salary for students who recently graduated from a local university and accepted jobs soon after graduation. The starting salary, grade point average (GPA) and major (business or other) are provided.

SALARY	$29,500	$46,000	$39,800	$36,500
GPA	3.1	3.5	3.8	2.9
Major	Other	Business	Business	Other

SALARY	$42,000	$31,500	$36,200
GPA	3.4	2.1	2.5
Major	Business	Other	Business

(a) Using a computer, develop a regression model that could be used to predict starting salary based on GPA and major.

(b) Use this model to predict the starting salary for a business major with a GPA of 3.0.

(c) What does the model say about the starting salary for a business major compared to a nonbusiness major?

(d) Do you believe this model is useful in predicting the starting salary? Justify your answer using information provided in the computer output.

4-20 The following data give the selling price, square footage, number of bedrooms, and age of houses that have sold in a neighborhood in the last 6 months. Develop three regression models to predict the selling price based upon each of the other factors individually. Which of these is best?

Selling Price	Square Footage	Bedrooms	Age
64000	1670	2	30
59000	1339	2	25
61500	1712	3	30
79000	1840	3	40
87500	2300	3	18
92500	2234	3	30
95000	2311	3	19
113000	2377	3	7
115000	2736	4	10
138000	2500	3	1
142500	2500	4	3
144000	2479	3	3
145000	2400	3	1
147500	3124	4	0
144000	2500	3	2
155500	4062	4	10
165000	2854	3	3

4-21 Use the data in Problem 4-20 and develop a regression model to predict selling price based on the square footage and number of bedrooms. Use this to predict the selling price of a 2,000 square foot house with 3 bedrooms. Compare this model with the models in 4-20. Should the number of bedrooms be included in the model? Why or why not?

4-22 Use the data in Problem 4-20 and develop a regression model to predict selling price based on the square footage, number of bedrooms, and age. Use this to predict the selling price of a 10-year-old, 2,000-square-foot house with 3 bedrooms.

4-23 Tim Cooper plans to invest money in a mutual fund that is tied to one of the major market indices, either the S&P 500 or the Dow Jones Industrial Average. To obtain even more diversification, Tim has thought about investing in both of these. To determine whether investing in two funds would help, Tim decided to take 20 weeks of data and compare the two markets. The closing price for each index is shown in the table below.

Week	1	2	3	4	5	6	7
DJIA	10226	10473	10452	10442	10471	10213	10187
S&P	1107	1141	1135	1139	1142	1108	1110

Week	8	9	10	11	12	13	14
DJIA	10240	10596	10584	10619	10628	10593	10488
S&P	1121	1157	1145	1144	1146	1143	1131

Week	15	16	17	18	19	20
DJIA	10568	10601	10459	10410	10325	10278
S&P	1142	1140	1122	1108	1096	1089

Develop a regression model that would predict the DJIA based on the S&P 500 index. Based on this model, what would you expect the DJIA to be when the S&P is 1,100? What is the correlation coefficient (r) between the two markets?

4-24 The total expenses of a hospital are related to many factors. Two of these are the number of beds in the hospital, and the number of admissions. Data was collected on 14 hospitals as shown in the table below.

Hospital	Number of Beds	Admissions (100s)	Total Expenses (Millions)
1	215	77	57
2	336	160	127
3	520	230	157
4	135	43	24
5	35	9	14
6	210	155	93
7	140	53	45
8	90	6	6
9	410	159	99
10	50	18	12
11	65	16	11
12	42	29	15
13	110	28	21
14	305	98	63

Find the best regression model to predict the total expenses of a hospital. Discuss the accuracy of this model. Should both variables be included in the model? Why or why not?

4-25 A sample of twenty automobiles was taken, and the miles per gallon (MPG), horsepower, and total weight were recorded. Develop a linear regression model to predict MPG using horsepower as the only independent variable. Develop another model with weight as the independent variable. Which of these two models is better? Explain.

MPG	Horsepower	Weight
44	67	1844
44	50	1998
40	62	1752
37	69	1980

MPG	HORSEPOWER	WEIGHT
37	66	1797
34	63	2199
35	90	2404
32	99	2611
30	63	3236
28	91	2606
26	94	2580
26	88	2507
25	124	2922
22	97	2434
20	114	3248
21	102	2812
18	114	3382
18	142	3197
16	153	4380
16	139	4036

4-26 Use the data in Problem 4-25 to develop a multiple linear regression model. How does this compare with each of the models in Problem 4-25?

4-27 Use the data in Problem 4-25 to find the best quadratic regression model (there is more than one to consider). How does this compare to the models in Problems 4-25 and 4-26?

4-28 A sample of 9 public universities and 9 private universities was taken. The total cost for the year (including room and board) and the median SAT score at each school were recorded. It was felt that schools with higher median SAT scores would have a better reputa-

tion and would charge more tuition as a result of that. The data is in the table below. Use regression to help answer the following questions based on this sample data. Do schools with higher SAT scores charge more in tuition and fees? Are private schools more expensive than public schools when SAT scores are taken into consideration? Discuss how accurate you believe these results are using information related the regression models.

CATEGORY	TOTAL COST	MEDIAN SAT
Public	14500	1330
Public	10400	1080
Public	11300	1210
Public	10300	1030
Public	15400	1030
Public	14300	1070
Public	11000	1040
Public	15700	1260
Public	13500	1080
Private	20300	1090
Private	27700	1230
Private	24100	1320
Private	28100	1290
Private	18100	1420
Private	23200	1340
Private	21400	1060
Private	21200	1150
Private	21400	1180

⫸ CASE STUDY

North–South Airline

In January 2002, Northern Airlines merged with Southeast Airlines to create the fourth largest U.S. carrier. The new North–South Airline inherited both an aging fleet of Boeing 727-300 aircraft and Stephen Ruth. Stephen was a tough former Secretary of the Navy who stepped in as new president and chairman of the board.

Stephen's first concern in creating a financially solid company was maintenance costs. It was commonly surmised in the airline industry that maintenance costs rise with the age of the aircraft. He quickly noticed that historically there had been a sig-

nificant difference in the reported B727-300 maintenance costs (from ATA Form 41's) both in the airframe and engine areas between Northern Airlines and Southeast Airlines, with Southeast having the newer fleet.

On February 12, 2001, Peg Jones, vice president for operations and maintenance, was called into Stephen's office and asked to study the issue. Specifically, Stephen wanted to know whether the average fleet age was correlated to direct airframe maintenance costs, and whether there was a relationship between average fleet age and direct engine maintenance costs. Peg was to report back by February 26 with the answer, along with quantitative and graphical descriptions of the relationship.

Peg's first step was to have her staff construct the average age of Northern and Southeast B727-300 fleets, by quarter, since the introduction of that aircraft to service by each airline in late 1993 and early 1994. The average age of each fleet was calculated by first multiplying the total number of calendar days each aircraft had been in service at the pertinent point in time by the average daily utilization of the respective fleet to total fleet hours flown. The total fleet hours flown was then divided by the number of aircraft in service at that time, giving the age of the "average" aircraft in the fleet.

The average utilization was found by taking the actual total fleet hours flown on September 30, 2001, from Northern and Southeast data, and dividing by the total days in service for all aircraft at that time. The average utilization for Southeast was 8.3 hours per day, and the average utilization for Northern was 8.7 hours per day. Because the available cost data were calculated for each yearly period ending at the end of the first quarter, average fleet age was calculated at the same points in time. The fleet data are shown in the following table. Airframe cost data and engine cost data are both shown paired with fleet average age in that table.

Discussion Question

1. Prepare Peg Jones's response to Stephen Ruth.

Note: Dates and names of airlines and individuals have been changed in this case to maintain confidentiality. The data and issues described here are real.

North–South Airline Data for Boeing 727-300 Jets

YEAR	NORTHERN AIRLINE DATA			SOUTHEAST AIRLINE DATA		
	AIRFRAME COST PER AIRCRAFT	ENGINE COST PER AIRCRAFT	AVERAGE AGE (HOURS)	AIRFRAME COST PER AIRCRAFT	ENGINE COST PER AIRCRAFT	AVERAGE AGE (HOURS)
1995	$51.80	$43.49	6,512	$13.29	$18.86	5,107
1996	54.92	38.58	8,404	25.15	31.55	8,145
1997	69.70	51.48	11,077	32.18	40.43	7,360
1998	68.90	58.72	11,717	31.78	22.10	5,773
1999	63.72	45.47	13,275	25.34	19.69	7,150
2000	84.73	50.26	15,215	32.78	32.58	9,364
2001	78.74	79.60	18,390	35.56	38.07	8,259

BIBLIOGRAPHY

Berenson, Mark L., David M. Levine, and Timothy C. Kriehbiel. *Business Statistics: Concepts and Applications*, 9th ed. Upper Saddle River, NJ: Prentice Hall, 2004.

Black, Ken. *Business Statistics: For Contemporary Decision Making*, 4th ed. John Wiley & Sons, Inc., 2003.

Draper, Norman R. and Harry Smith. *Applied Regression Analysis*, 3rd ed. Wiley, 1998.

Kunter, Michael, John Neter, Chris J. Nachtsheim, and William Wasserman. *Applied Linear Regression Models, 4th ed.*, McGraw-Hill/Irwin, 2004.

Mendenhall, William, and Terry L. Sincich. *A Second Course in Statistics: Regression Analysis, 6th ed.*, Prentice Hall, 2004.

APPENDIX 4.1: FORMULAS FOR REGRESSION CALCULATIONS

When performing regression calculations by hand, there are other formulas that can make the task easier and are mathematically equivalent to the ones presented in the chapter. These, however, make it more difficult to see the logic behind the formulas and to understand what the results actually mean.

When using these formulas, it helps to set up a table with the columns shown in Table 4.7, which has the Triple A Construction Company data that was used earlier in the chapter. The sample size (n) is 6. The totals for all columns are shown, and the averages for X and Y are calculated. Once this is done, we can use the following formulas for computations in a simple linear regression model (one independent variable). The simple linear regression equation is again given as

$$\hat{Y} = b_0 + b_1 X$$

TABLE 4.7

Preliminary Calculations for Triple A Construction

Y	X	Y^2	X^2	XY
6	3	$6^2 = 36$	$3^2 = 9$	$3(6) = 18$
8	4	$8^2 = 64$	$4^2 = 16$	$4(8) = 32$
9	6	$9^2 = 81$	$6^2 = 36$	$6(9) = 54$
5	4	$5^2 = 25$	$4^2 = 16$	$4(5) = 20$
4.5	2	$4.5^2 = 20.25$	$2^2 = 4$	$2(4.5) = 9$
9.5	5	$9.5^2 = 90.25$	$5^2 = 25$	$5(9.5) = 47.5$
$\Sigma Y = 42$	$\Sigma X = 24$	$\Sigma Y^2 = 316.5$	$\Sigma X^2 = 106$	$\Sigma XY = 180.5$
$\overline{Y} = 42/6 = 7$	$\overline{X} = 24/6 = 4$			

Slope of regression equation

$$b_1 = \frac{\Sigma XY - n\overline{X}\overline{Y}}{\Sigma X^2 - n\overline{X}^2}$$

$$b_1 = \frac{180.5 - 6(4)(7)}{106 - 6(4^2)} = 1.25$$

Intercept of regression equation

$$b_0 = \overline{Y} - b_1\overline{X}$$

$$b_0 = 7 - 1.25(4) = 2$$

Sum of squares of the error

$$SSE = \Sigma Y^2 - b_0 \Sigma Y - b_1 \Sigma XY$$

$$SSE = 316.5 - 2(42) - 1.25(180.5) = 6.875$$

Estimate of the error variance is

$$s^2 = MSE = \frac{SSE}{n-2}$$

$$s^2 = \frac{6.875}{6-2} = 1.71875$$

Estimate of the error standard deviation is

$$s = \sqrt{MSE}$$

$$s = \sqrt{1.71875} = 1.311$$

Coefficient of determination

$$r^2 = 1 - \frac{SSE}{\Sigma Y^2 - n\overline{Y}^2}$$

$$r^2 = 1 - \frac{6.875}{316.5 - 6(7^2)} = 0.6944$$

This formula for the correlation coefficient automatically determines the sign of r. This could also be found by taking the square root of r^2 and giving it the same sign as the slope.

$$r = \frac{n \sum XY - \sum X \sum Y}{\sqrt{[n \sum X^2 - (\sum X)^2][n \sum Y^2 - (\sum Y)^2]}}$$

$$r = \frac{6(180.5) - (24)(42)}{\sqrt{[6(106) - 24^2][6(316.5) - 42^2]}} = 0.833$$

APPENDIX 4.2: REGRESSION MODELS USING QM FOR WINDOWS

The use of QM for Windows to develop a regression model is very easy. We will use the Triple A Construction Company data to illustrate this. After starting QM for Windows, under *Modules* we select *Forecasting*. To enter the problem we select *New* and specify *Least Squares–Simple and Multiple Regression* as illustrated in Program 4.7A. This opens the window shown in Program 4.7B. We enter the number of observations, which is 6 in this example. There is only 1 independent (X) variable. The data is then entered, and the results are shown in Program 4.7C. The equation is given as well as other information about the model.

Recall that the MSE is an estimate of the error variance (σ^2), and the square root of this is the standard error of the estimate. The formula presented in the chapter and used in Excel is

$$MSE = SSE/(n - k - 1)$$

where n is the sample size and k is the number of independent variables. This is an unbiased estimate of σ^2. In QM for Windows, the mean squared error is computed as

$$MSE = SSE/n$$

This is simply the average error and is a biased estimate of σ^2. The standard error shown in Program 4.7C is not the square root of the MSE in the output, but rather is found using the denominator of $n - 2$. If this standard error is squared, you get the MSE we saw earlier in the Excel output.

PROGRAM 4.7A
Initial Input Screen for QM for Windows–Forecasting – Least Squares Regression

PROGRAM 4.7B

Second Input Screen for QM for Windows

QM for Windows

File Edit View Module Format Tools Window Help

Arial   9.7   **B** *I* U

Create data set for Forecasting/Least Squares - Simple and M...

Title: Triple A Construction Company   ault title

There are 6 pairs of observations in this sample.

Number of Observations   6

Number of Independent Variables   1

Row names	Column names

○ Observation 1, Observation 2, Observation 3,...
○ a, b, c, d, e, ...
○ A, B, C, D, E, ...
○ 1, 2, 3, 4, 5, ...
○ January, February, March, April, ...
  Click here to set start month
○ Other

There is only one independent variable.

Cancel   Help   OK

PROGRAM 4.7C

QM for Windows Output for Triple A Construction Data

QM for Windows

File Edit View Module Format Tools Window Help

Arial   9.7   **B** *I* U   Edit

Forecasting Results

Triple A Construction Company Summary

Measure	Value
Error Measures	
Bias (Mean Error)	0.
MAD (Mean Absolute Deviation)	0.8333
MSE (Mean Squared Error)	1.1458
Standard Error (denom=n-2-0=4)	1.311
Regression line	
Dpndnt var, Y = 2.0 + 1.25 * X1	
Statistics	
Correlation coefficient	0.8333
Coefficient of determination (r^2)	0.6944

The MSE is the SSE divided by n.

The standard error is the square root of SSE divided by n–2.

The regression equation is shown across two lines.

FORECASTING

5.1   INTRODUCTION

Every day, managers make decisions without knowing what will happen in the future. Inventory is ordered though no one knows what sales will be, new equipment is purchased though no one knows the demand for products, and investments are made though no one knows what profits will be. Managers are always trying to reduce this uncertainty and to make better estimates of what will happen in the future. Accomplishing this is the main purpose of forecasting.

There are many ways to forecast the future. In numerous firms (especially smaller ones), the entire process is subjective, involving seat-of-the-pants methods, intuition, and years of experience. There are also many *quantitative* forecasting models, such as moving averages, exponential smoothing, trend projections, and least squares regression analysis.

Regardless of the method that is used to make the forecast, the same eight overall procedures that follow are used.

Eight Steps to Forecasting

1. Determine the use of the forecast—what objective are we trying to obtain?
2. Select the items or quantities that are to be forecasted.
3. Determine the time horizon of the forecast—is it 1 to 30 days (short term), one month to one year (medium term), or more than one year (long term)?
4. Select the forecasting model or models.
5. Gather the data needed to make the forecast.
6. Validate the forecasting model.
7. Make the forecast.
8. Implement the results.

These steps present a systematic way of initiating, designing, and implementing a forecasting system. When the forecasting system is to be used to generate forecasts regularly over time, data must be collected routinely, and the actual computations or procedures used to make the forecast can be done automatically. When a computer system is used, computer forecasting files and programs are needed.

No single method is superior—whatever works best should be used.

There is seldom a single superior forecasting method. One organization may find regression effective, another firm may use several approaches, and a third may combine both quantitative and subjective techniques. Whatever tool works best for a firm is the one that should be used.

5.2   TYPES OF FORECASTS

The three categories of models are time series, causal, and qualitative.

In this chapter we consider forecasting models that can be classified into one of three categories: time-series models, causal models, and qualitative models shown in Figure 5.1.

Time-Series Models

Time-series models attempt to predict the future by using historical data. These models make the assumption that what happens in the future is a function of what has happened in the past. In other words, time-series models look at what has happened over a period of time and use a series of past data to make a forecast. Thus, if we are forecasting weekly sales for lawn mowers, we use the past weekly sales for lawn mowers in making the forecast.

The time-series models we examine in this chapter are moving average, exponential smoothing, trend projections, and decomposition. Regression analysis can be used in trend projections and in one type of decomposition model. The primary emphasis of this chapter is time series forecasting.

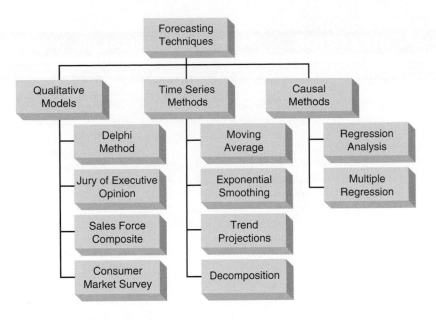

FIGURE 5.1

Forecasting Models Discussed

Causal Models

Causal models incorporate the variables or factors that might influence the quantity being forecasted into the forecasting model. For example, daily sales of a cola drink might depend on the season, the average temperature, the average humidity, whether it is a weekend or a weekday, and so on. Thus, a causal model would attempt to include factors for temperature, humidity, season, day of the week, and so on. Causal models may also include past sales data as time-series models do, but they include other factors as well.

Our job as quantitative analysts is to develop the best statistical relationship between sales or the variable being forecast and the set of independent variables. The most common quantitative causal model is regression analysis, which was presented in Chapter 4. Other causal models do exist, and many of these are based on regression analysis.

Qualitative Models

Whereas time-series and causal models rely on quantitative data, *qualitative models* attempt to incorporate judgmental or subjective factors into the forecasting model. Opinions by experts, individual experiences and judgments, and other subjective factors may be considered. Qualitative models are especially useful when subjective factors are expected to be very important or when accurate quantitative data are difficult to obtain.

Here is a brief overview of four different qualitative forecasting techniques:

Overview of four qualitative or judgmental approaches: Delphi, jury of executive opinion, sales force composite, and consumer market survey.

1. *Delphi method.* This iterative group process allows experts, who may be located in different places, to make forecasts. There are three different types of participants in the Delphi process: decision makers, staff personnel, and respondents. The *decision making group* usually consists of 5 to 10 experts who will be making the actual forecast. The staff personnel assist the decision makers by preparing, distributing, collecting, and summarizing a series of questionnaires and survey results. The respondents are a group of people whose judgments are valued and are being sought. This group provides inputs to the decision makers before the forecast is made.

2. *Jury of executive opinion.* This method takes the opinions of a small group of high-level managers, often in combination with statistical models, and results in a group estimate of demand.

IN ACTION   Forecasting Customer Demand at Taco Bell

Like most quick service restaurants, Taco Bell understands the quantitative trade-off between labor and speed of service. More than 50% of the $5 billion company's daily sales come from the 3-hour lunch period. Customers don't like to wait more than 3 minutes for services, so it is critical that proper staffing is in place at all times.

Taco Bell tested a series of forecasting models to predict demand in specific 15-minute intervals during each day of the week. The company's goal was to find the technique that minimized the average square deviation between actual and predicted data. Because company computers only stored 6 weeks of transaction data, exponential smoothing was not considered. Results indicated that a 6-week moving average was best.

Building this forecasting methodology into each of Taco Bell's 6,500 stores' computers, the model makes weekly projections of customer transactions. These in turn are used by store managers to schedule staff, who begin in 15-minute increments, not one-hour blocks as in other industries. The forecasting model has been so successful that Taco Bell has documented more than $50 million in labor cost savings, while increasing customer service, in its first four years of use.

Source: J. Hueter and W. Swart. "An Integrated Labor-Management System for Taco Bell," *Interfaces* 28, 1 (January–February 1998): 75–91.

3. *Sales force composite.* In this approach, each salesperson estimates what sales will be in his or her region; these forecasts are reviewed to ensure that they are realistic and are then combined at the district and national levels to reach an overall forecast.

4. *Consumer market survey.* This method solicits input from customers or potential customers regarding their future purchasing plans. It can help not only in preparing a forecast but also in improving product design and planning for new products.

5.3 SCATTER DIAGRAMS AND TIME SERIES

A scatter diagram helps obtain ideas about a relationship.

As with regression models, *scatter diagrams* are very helpful when forecasting time series. A scatter diagram for a time series may be plotted on a two-dimensional graph with the horizontal axis representing the time period. The variable to be forecast (such as sales) is placed on the vertical axis. Let us consider the example of a firm that needs to forecast sales for three different products.

Wacker Distributors notes that annual sales for three of its products—television sets, radios, and compact disc players—over the past ten years are as shown in Table 5.1. One

TABLE 5.1

Annual Sales of Three Products

YEAR	TELEVISION SETS	RADIOS	COMPACT DISC PLAYERS
1	250	300	110
2	250	310	100
3	250	320	120
4	250	330	140
5	250	340	170
6	250	350	150
7	250	360	160
8	250	370	190
9	250	380	200
10	250	390	190

simple way to examine these historical data, and perhaps to use them to establish a forecast, is to draw a scatter diagram for each product (Figure 5.2). This picture, showing the relationship between sales of a product and time, is useful in spotting trends or cycles. An exact mathematical model that describes the situation can then be developed if it appears reasonable to do so.

FIGURE 5.2

Scatter Diagram for Sales

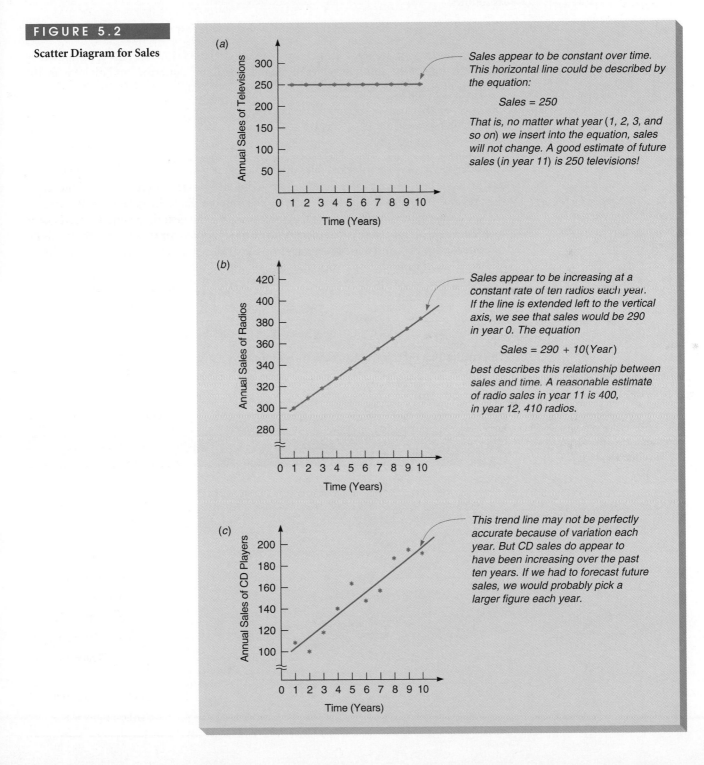

5.4   MEASURES OF FORECAST ACCURACY

We discuss several different forecasting models in this chapter. To see how well one model works, or to compare that model with other models, the forecasted values are compared with the actual or observed values. The forecast error (or deviation) is defined as follows:

$$\text{forecast error} = \text{actual value} - \text{forecast value}$$

One measure of accuracy is the *mean absolute deviation* (MAD). This is computed by taking the sum of the absolute values of the individual forecast errors and dividing by the numbers of errors (n):

$$\text{MAD} = \frac{\sum|\text{forecast error}|}{n} \tag{5-1}$$

The naïve forecast for the next period is the actual value observed in the current period.

Consider the Wacker Distributors sales of CD players seen in Table 5.1. Suppose that in the past, Wacker had forecast sales for each year to be the sales that were actually achieved in the previous year. This is sometimes called a *naïve* model. Table 5.2 gives these forecasts as well as the absolute value of the errors. In forecasting for the next time period (year 11), the forecast would be 190. Notice that there is no error computed for year 1 since there was no forecast for this year, and there is no error for year 11 since the actual value of this is not yet known. Thus, the number of errors (n) is 9.

From this, we see the following:

$$\text{MAD} = \frac{\sum|\text{forecast error}|}{n} = \frac{160}{9} = 17.8$$

This means that on the average, each forecast missed the actual value by 17.8 units.

TABLE 5.2			
Computing the Mean Absolute Deviation (MAD)			
YEAR	ACTUAL SALES OF CD PLAYERS	FORECAST SALES	ABSOLUTE VALUE OF ERRORS (DEVIATION). |ACTUAL − FORECAST|
1	110	—	—
2	100	110	|100 − 110| = 10
3	120	100	|120 − 100| = 20
4	140	120	|140 − 120| = 20
5	170	140	|170 − 140| = 30
6	150	170	|150 − 170| = 20
7	160	150	|160 − 150| = 10
8	190	160	|190 − 160| = 30
9	200	190	|200 − 190| = 10
10	190	200	|190 − 200| = 10
11	—	190	—

Sum of \|errors\| = 160

MAD = 160/9 = 17.8

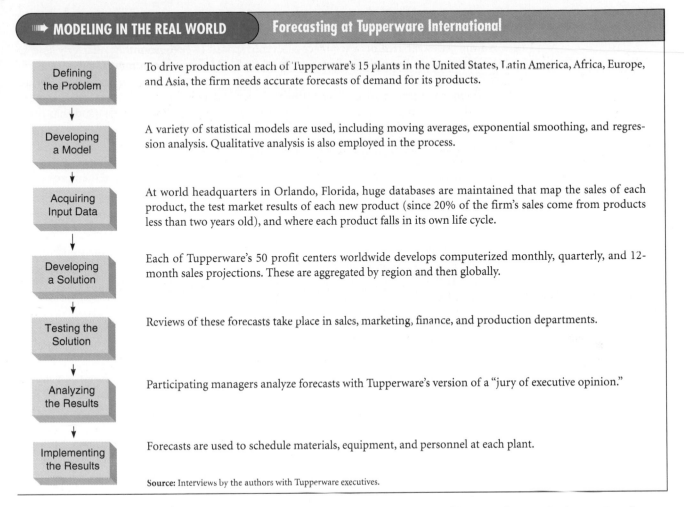

MODELING IN THE REAL WORLD   **Forecasting at Tupperware International**

Defining the Problem

To drive production at each of Tupperware's 15 plants in the United States, Latin America, Africa, Europe, and Asia, the firm needs accurate forecasts of demand for its products.

Developing a Model

A variety of statistical models are used, including moving averages, exponential smoothing, and regression analysis. Qualitative analysis is also employed in the process.

Acquiring Input Data

At world headquarters in Orlando, Florida, huge databases are maintained that map the sales of each product, the test market results of each new product (since 20% of the firm's sales come from products less than two years old), and where each product falls in its own life cycle.

Developing a Solution

Each of Tupperware's 50 profit centers worldwide develops computerized monthly, quarterly, and 12-month sales projections. These are aggregated by region and then globally.

Testing the Solution

Reviews of these forecasts take place in sales, marketing, finance, and production departments.

Analyzing the Results

Participating managers analyze forecasts with Tupperware's version of a "jury of executive opinion."

Implementing the Results

Forecasts are used to schedule materials, equipment, and personnel at each plant.

Source: Interviews by the authors with Tupperware executives.

There are other measures of the accuracy of historical errors in forecasting that are sometimes used besides the MAD. One of the most common is the *mean squared error* (MSE) which is the average of the squared errors[1]:

$$MSE = \frac{\sum (error)^2}{n} \qquad (5\text{-}2)$$

Besides the MAD and MSE, the *mean absolute percent error* (MAPE) is sometimes used. The MAPE is the average of the absolute values of the errors expressed as percentages of the actual values. This is computed as follows:

$$MAPE = \frac{\sum \left|\dfrac{error}{actual}\right|}{n} 100\% \qquad (5\text{-}3)$$

Three common measures of error are MAD, MSE, and MAPE. Bias gives the average error and may be positive or negative.

There is another common term associated with error in forecasting. *Bias* is the average error and tells whether the forecast tends to be too high or too low and by how much. Thus, bias may be negative or positive. It is not a good measure of the actual size of the errors because the negative errors can cancel out the positive errors.

---

[1] In regression analysis, the MSE formula is usually adjusted to provide an unbiased estimator of the error variance. Throughout this chapter, we will use the formula provided here.

5.5   TIME-SERIES FORECASTING MODELS

A time series is based on a sequence of evenly spaced (weekly, monthly, quarterly, and so on) data points. Examples include weekly sales of IBM personal computers, quarterly earnings reports of Microsoft Corporation, daily shipments of Eveready batteries, and annual U.S. consumer price indices. Forecasting time-series data implies that future values are predicted *only* from past values of that variable (such as we saw in Table 5.1) and that other variables, no matter how potentially valuable, are ignored.

Decomposition of a Time Series

Four components of a time series are trend, seasonality, cycles, and random variations.

Analyzing time series means breaking down past data into components and then projecting them forward. A time series typically has four components: trend, seasonality, cycles, and random variation.

1. *Trend* (*T*) is the gradual upward or downward movement of the data over time.

2. *Seasonality* (*S*) is a pattern of the demand fluctuation above or below the trend line that repeats at regular intervals.

3. *Cycles* (*C*) are patterns in annual data that occur every several years. They are usually tied into the business cycle.

4. *Random variations* (*R*) are "blips" in the data caused by chance and unusual situations; they follow no discernible pattern.

Figure 5.3 shows a time series and its components.

There are two general forms of time-series models in statistics. The first is a multiplicative model, which assumes that demand is the product of the four components. It is stated as follows:

$$\text{demand} = T \times S \times C \times R$$

An additive model adds the components together to provide an estimate. Multiple regression is often used to develop additive models. This additive relationship is stated as follows:

$$\text{demand} = T + S + C + R$$

There are other models that may be a combination of these. For example, one of the components (such as trend) might be additive while another (such as seasonality) could be multiplicative.

FIGURE 5.3

Product Demand Charted over Four Years with Trend and Seasonality Indicated

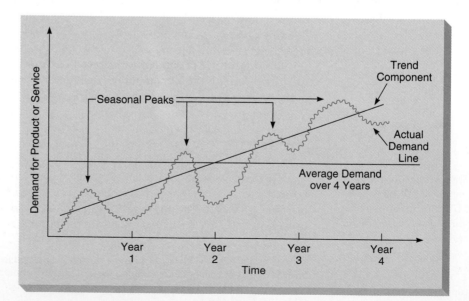

In many real-world models, forecasters assume that the random variations are averaged out over time. These random errors are often assumed to be normally distributed with a mean of zero. We will begin by looking at forecasting time series that have no trend, seasonal, or cyclical components. These models will provide ways for averaging the data to smooth out the forecasts and not be too heavily influenced by random variations. Then we will introduce forecasting models that specifically include seasonal and trend components.

Moving Averages

Moving averages smooth out variations when forecasting demands are fairly steady.

Moving averages are useful if we can assume that market demands will stay fairly steady over time. For example, a four-month moving average is found simply by summing the demand during the past four months and dividing by 4. With each passing month, the most recent month's data are added to the sum of the previous three months' data, and the earliest month is dropped. This tends to smooth out short-term irregularities in the data series.

An *n*-period moving average forecast, which serves as an estimate of the next period's demand, is expressed as follows:

$$\text{moving average forecast} = \frac{\text{sum of demands in previous } n \text{ periods}}{n} \qquad (5\text{-}4)$$

Mathematically, this is written as

$$F_t = \frac{Y_{t-1} + Y_{t-2} + \ldots + Y_{t-n}}{n} \qquad (5\text{-}5)$$

where

$$F_t = \text{forecast for time period } t$$

$$Y_t = \text{actual value in time period } t$$

$$n = \text{number of periods to average}$$

A four month moving average has $n = 4$; a five-month moving average has $n = 5$.

Wallace Garden Supply Example Storage shed sales at Wallace Garden Supply are shown in the middle column of Table 5.3. A 3-month moving average is indicated on the right. The forecast for the next January, using this technique, is 16. Were we simply asked to find a forecast for next January, we would only have to make this one calculation. The other forecasts are necessary only if we wish to compute the MAD or another measure of accuracy.

Weights can be used to put more emphasis on recent periods.

When there might be a trend or pattern emerging, weights can be used to place more emphasis on recent values. This makes the technique more responsive to changes because latter periods may be more heavily weighted. Deciding which weights to use requires some experience and a bit of luck. Choice of weights is somewhat arbitrary because there is no set formula to determine them. However, several different sets of weights may be tried, and the one with the lowest MAD should be used. One potential problem with using a weighted average is that if the latest month or period is weighted too heavily, the forecast might predict a large unusual change in the demand or sales pattern too quickly, when in fact the change is due to a random fluctuation.

A *weighted moving average* may be expressed as

$$\text{weighted moving average} = \frac{\sum (\text{weight for period } n)(\text{demand in period } n)}{\sum \text{weights}} \qquad (5\text{-}6)$$

Mathematically this is

$$F_t = \frac{w_1 Y_{t-1} + w_2 Y_{t-2} + \ldots + w_n Y_{t-n}}{w_1 + w_2 + \ldots + w_n} \qquad (5\text{-}7)$$

where

$$w_i = \text{weight for observation in time period } t\text{-}i$$

MONTH	ACTUAL SHED SALES	THREE-MONTH MOVING AVERAGE
January	10	
February	12	
March	13	
April	16	$(10 + 12 + 13)/3 = 11\frac{2}{3}$
May	19	$(12 + 13 + 16)/3 = 13\frac{2}{3}$
June	23	$(13 + 16 + 19)/3 = 16$
July	26	$(16 + 19 + 23)/3 = 19\frac{1}{3}$
August	30	$(19 + 23 + 26)/3 = 22\frac{2}{3}$
September	28	$(23 + 26 + 30)/3 = 28$
October	18	$(26 + 30 + 28)/3 = 26\frac{1}{3}$
November	16	$(30 + 28 + 18)/3 = 25\frac{1}{3}$
December	14	$(28 + 18 + 16)/3 = 20\frac{2}{3}$
January	—	$(18 + 16 + 14)/3 = 16$

TABLE 5.3

Wallace Garden Supply Shed Sales

Wallace Garden Supply decides to forecast storage shed sales by weighting the past three months as follows:

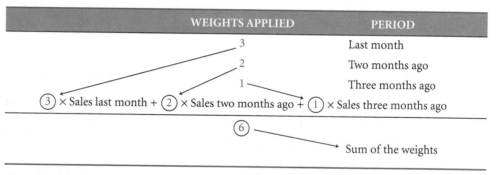

WEIGHTS APPLIED	PERIOD
3	Last month
2	Two months ago
1	Three months ago

③ × Sales last month + ② × Sales two months ago + ① × Sales three months ago

⑥ ⟶ Sum of the weights

The results of the Wallace Garden Supply weighted average forecast are shown in Table 5.4. In this particular forecasting situation, you can see that weighting the latest month more heavily provides a much more accurate projection, and calculating the MAD for each of these would verify this.

Both simple and weighted moving averages are effective in smoothing out sudden fluctuations in the demand pattern in order to provide stable estimates. Moving averages do, however, have two problems. First, increasing the size of n (the number of periods averaged) does smooth out fluctuations better, but it makes the method less sensitive to *real* changes in the data should they occur. Second, moving averages cannot pick up trends very well. Because they are averages, they will always stay within past levels and will not predict a change to either a higher or a lower level.

Moving averages have two problems: the larger number of periods may smooth out real changes, and they don't pick up trend.

Using Excel and Excel QM in Forecasting Excel and spreadsheets in general are frequently used in forecasting. Many forecasting techniques are supported by built-in Excel functions. You may also use Excel QM's forecasting module, which has six components: (1) moving averages, (2) weighted moving averages, (3) exponential smoothing, (4) regression/trend analysis, (5) decomposition, and (6) multiple regression. Programs 5.1A and 5.1B illustrate Excel QM's formulas and output, respectively, using Wallace's weighted moving average data in Table 5.4.

TABLE 5.4

Weighted Moving Average
Forecast for Wallace
Garden Supply

MONTH	ACTUAL SHED SALES	THREE-MONTH MOVING AVERAGE
January	10	
February	12	
March	13	
April	16	$[(3 \times 13) + (2 \times 12) + (10)]/6 = 12\frac{1}{6}$
May	19	$[(3 \times 16) + (2 \times 13) + (12)]/6 = 14\frac{1}{3}$
June	23	$[(3 \times 19) + (2 \times 16) + (13)]/6 = 17$
July	26	$[(3 \times 23) + (2 \times 19) + (16)]/6 = 20\frac{1}{2}$
August	30	$[(3 \times 26) + (2 \times 23) + (19)]/6 = 23\frac{5}{6}$
September	28	$[(3 \times 30) + (2 \times 26) + (23)]/6 = 27\frac{1}{2}$
October	18	$[(3 \times 28) + (2 \times 30) + (26)]/6 = 28\frac{1}{3}$
November	16	$[(3 \times 18) + (2 \times 28) + (30)]/6 = 23\frac{1}{3}$
December	14	$[(3 \times 16) + (2 \times 18) + (28)]/6 = 18\frac{2}{3}$
January	—	$[(3 \times 14) + (2 \times 16) + (18)]/6 = 15\frac{2}{3}$

PROGRAM 5.1A

Using Excel QM for Weighted Moving Average Forecasting (Showing Input Data and Formulas from Wallace Garden Supply)

Enter the weights to be placed on each of the last three periods at the top of column C: Weights must be entered from oldest to most recent.

Forecast is the weighted sum of past sales (SUMPRODUCT) divided by the sum of the weights (SUM) because weights do not sum to 1.

Error is the difference between the demand and the forecast.

The standard error is given by the square root of the total squared error divided by $n - 2$ where n is the number of periods for which forecasts exist, 9.

Calculate the total and average for each error column.

Output of Excel QM's Weighted Moving Average Program Using Data from Wallace Garden Supply

	A	B	C	D	E	F	G	H	I	J
1	**Wallace Garden Supply Shed Sales**									
2										
3	**Forecasting**			Weighted moving averages 3 period moving average						
4	Enter the data in the shaded area. Enter									
5	weights in INCREASING order from top to									
6	bottom.									
7	Data				Error analysis					
8	Period	Demand	Weights		Forecast	Error	Absolute	Squared		
9	January	10	1							
10	February	12	2							
11	March	13	3							
12	April	16			12.16667	3.833333	3.833333	14.69444		
13	May	19			14.33333	4.666667	4.666667	21.77778		
14	June	23			17	6	6	36		
15	July	26			20.5	5.5	5.5	30.25		
16	August	30			23.83333	6.166667	6.166667	38.02778		
17	September	28			27.5	0.5	0.5	0.25		
18	October	18			28.33333	-10.3333	10.33333	106.7778		
19	November	16			23.33333	-7.33333	7.333333	53.77778		
20	December	14			18.66667	-4.66667	4.666667	21.77778		
21					Total	4.333333	49	323.3333		
22					Average	0.481481	5.444444	35.92593		
23						Bias	MAD	MSE		
24							SE	6.796358		
25	**Next period**	15.3333333								

Exponential Smoothing

Exponential smoothing is a forecasting method that is easy to use and is handled efficiently by computers. Although it is a type of moving average technique, it involves little record keeping of past data. The basic exponential smoothing formula can be shown as follows:

$$\text{New forecast} = \text{last period's forecast} \tag{5-8}$$
$$+ \alpha(\text{last period's actual demand} - \text{last period's forecast})$$

where α is a weight (or *smoothing constant*) that has a value between 0 and 1, inclusive.

Equation 5-8 can also be written mathematically as

$$F_t = F_{t-1} + \alpha(Y_{t-1} - F_{t-1}) \tag{5-9}$$

where

$$F_t = \text{new forecast (for time period } t)$$
$$F_{t-1} = \text{previous forecast (for time period } t-1)$$
$$\alpha = \text{smoothing constant } (0 \le \alpha \le 1)$$
$$Y_{t-1} = \text{previous period's actual demand}$$

The concept here is not complex. The latest estimate of demand is equal to the old estimate adjusted by a fraction of the error (last period's actual demand minus the old estimate).

The smoothing constant, α, allows managers to assign weight to recent data.

The smoothing constant, α, can be changed to give more weight to recent data when the value is high or more weight to past data when it is low. For example, when $\alpha = 0.5$, it can be shown mathematically that the new forecast is based almost entirely on demand in the past three periods. When $\alpha = 0.1$, the forecast places little weight on any single period, even the most recent, and it takes many periods (about 19) of historic values into account.[2]

---

[2] The term *exponential smoothing* is used because the weight of any one period's demand in a forecast decreases exponentially over time. See an advanced forecasting book for an algebraic proof.

In January, a demand for 142 of a certain car model for February was predicted by a dealer. Actual February demand was 153 autos. Using a smoothing constant of $\alpha = 0.20$, we can forecast the March demand using the exponential smoothing model. Substituting into the formula, we obtain

$$\text{New forecast (for March demand)} = 142 + 0.2(153 - 142)$$
$$= 144.2$$

Thus, the demand forecast for the cars in March is 144.

Suppose that actual demand for the cars in March was 136. A forecast for the demand in April, using the exponential smoothing model with a constant of $\alpha = 0.20$, can be made:

$$\text{New forecast (for April demand)} = 144.2 + 0.2(136 - 144.2)$$
$$= 142.6, \text{ or } 143 \text{ autos}$$

Selecting the Smoothing Constant The exponential smoothing approach is easy to use and has been applied successfully by banks, manufacturing companies, wholesalers, and other organizations. The appropriate value of the smoothing constant, α, however, can make the difference between an accurate forecast and an inaccurate forecast. In picking a value for the smoothing constant, the objective is to obtain the most accurate forecast. Several values of the smoothing constant may be tried, and the one with the lowest MAD could be selected. This is analogous to how weights are selected for a weighted moving average forecast. Some forecasting software will automatically select the best smoothing constant. QM for Windows will display the MAD that would be obtained with values of α ranging from 0 to 1 in increments of 0.01.

Port of Baltimore Example Let us apply this concept with a trial-and-error testing of two values of α in the following example. The port of Baltimore has unloaded large quantities of grain from ships during the past eight quarters. The port's operations manager wants to test the use of exponential smoothing to see how well the technique works in predicting tonnage unloaded. He assumes that the forecast of grain unloaded in the first quarter was 175 tons. Two values of α are examined: $\alpha = 0.10$ and $\alpha = .50$. Table 5.5 shows the *detailed* calculations for $\alpha = 0.10$ only.

To evaluate the accuracy of each smoothing constant, we can compute the absolute deviations and MADs (see Table 5.6). Based on this analysis, a smoothing constant of $\alpha = 0.10$ is preferred to $\alpha = 0.50$ because its MAD is smaller.

TABLE 5.5			
Port of Baltimore Exponential Smoothing Forecasts for $\alpha = 0.10$ and $\alpha = 0.50$			

QUARTER	ACTUAL TONNAGE UNLOADED	ROUNDED FORECAST USING $\alpha = 0.10$*	ROUNDED FORECAST USING $\alpha = 0.50$*
1	180	175	175
2	168	$176 = 175.00 + 0.10(180 - 175)$	178
3	159	$175 = 175.50 + 0.10(168 - 175.50)$	173
4	175	$173 = 174.75 + 0.10(159 - 174.75)$	166
5	190	$173 = 173.18 + 0.10(175 - 173.18)$	170
6	205	$175 = 173.36 + 0.10(190 - 173.36)$	180
7	180	$178 = 175.02 + 0.10(205 - 175.02)$	193
8	182	$178 = 178.02 + 0.10(180 - 178.02)$	186
9	?	$179 = 178.22 + 0.10(182 - 178.22)$	184

Note: *Forecasts rounded to the nearest ton.

TABLE 5.6

Absolute Deviations
and MADs for Port of
Baltimore Example

QUARTER	ACTUAL TONNAGE UNLOADED	ROUNDED FORECAST WITH $\alpha = 0.10$	ABSOLUTE DEVIATIONS FOR $\alpha = 0.10$	ROUNDED FORECAST WITH $\alpha = 0.50$	ABSOLUTE DEVIATIONS FOR $\alpha = 0.50$
1	180	175	5	175	5
2	168	176	8	178	10
3	159	175	16	173	14
4	175	173	2	166	9
5	190	173	17	170	20
6	205	175	30	180	25
7	180	178	2	193	13
8	182	178	4	186	4
		Sum of absolute deviations	84		100

$$MAD = \frac{\Sigma |\text{deviations}|}{n} = 10.50 \qquad MAD = 12.50$$

Using Excel QM for Exponential Smoothing Programs 5.2A and Program 5.2B illustrate how Excel QM handles exponential smoothing. Input data and formulas appear in Program 5.2A, and output, using α of 0.1 for the port of Baltimore, are in Program 5.2B. Note that the MAD in (of 10.307) differs slightly from that in Table 5.6 because of rounding.

Exponential Smoothing with Trend Adjustment As with any averaging technique, simple exponential smoothing fails to respond to trends. A more complex exponential smoothing model that adjusts for trend can be considered. The idea is to compute a simple exponential smoothing forecast and then adjust for positive or negative lag in trend. The formula is

forecast including trend (FIT_t) = new forecast (F_t) + trend correction (T_t)

PROGRAM 5.2A

Excel QM Model of Port
of Baltimore Exponential
Smoothing Problem
Using $\alpha = .10$ (Showing
Input Data and Formulas)

PROGRAM 5.2B

Output Screen for Port of Baltimore Exponential Smoothing Excel QM Example

	A	B	C	D	E	F	G	H	I
1	**Port of Baltimore**								
2									
3	**Forecasting**			Exponential smoothing					
4	Enter alpha (between 0 and 1) then enter								
5	the past demands in the shaded area.								
6									
7	Alpha	0.1							
8	Data			Error Analysis					
9	Period	Demand		Forecast	Error	Absolute	Squared		
10	Quarter 1	180		175	5	5	25		
11	Quarter 2	168		175.5	-7.5	7.5	56.25		
12	Quarter 3	159		174.75	-15.75	15.75	248.0625		
13	Quarter 4	175		173.175	1.825	1.825	3.330625		
14	Quarter 5	190		173.3575	16.6425	16.6425	276.9728		
15	Quarter 6	205		175.0218	29.97825	29.97825	898.6955		
16	Quarter 7	180		178.0196	1.980425	1.980425	3.922083		
17	Quarter 8	182		178.2176	3.782382	3.782382	14.30642		
18				Total	35.95856	82.45856	1526.54		
19				Average	4.49482	10.30732	190.8175		
20					Bias	MAD	MSE		
21						SE	15.95065		
22	**Next period**	**178.595856**							

To smooth out the trend, the equation for the trend correction uses a smoothing constant, β, in the same way the simple exponential model uses α.

T_t is computed by

$$T_t = (1 - \beta) T_{t-1} + \beta (F_t - F_{t-1})$$
(5-10)

where

T_t = smoothed trend for period t

T_{t-1} = smoothed trend for preceding period

β = trend smooth constant that we select

F_t = simple exponential smoothed forecast for period t

F_{t-1} = forecast for previous period

β's responsiveness is like that of α—a low β gives less weight to more recent trends, and a high β gives higher weight.

The value of the trend smoothing constant, β, resembles the α constant in that a high β is more responsive to recent changes in trend. A low β value gives less weight to the most recent trends to smooth out the trend present. Values of β can be found by the trial-and-error approach, with the MAD used as a measure of comparison. Exponential smoothing with trend is one of the methods provided in the forecasting module of QM for Windows.

Simple exponential smoothing is often referred to as *first-order smoothing*. Trend-adjusted smoothing is called *second-order, double smoothing,* or *Holt's method*. Other advanced exponential smoothing models are also in use; they include seasonal-adjusted and triple smoothing, but these are beyond the scope of this book.[3]

---

[3] For more details, see E. S. Gardner, "Exponential Smoothing: The State of the Art," *Journal of Forecasting* 4, 1 (March 1985) 1–38, or John E. Hanke, Dean W. Wichern, and Arthur G. Reitsch. *Business Forecasting,* 7/e. Upper Saddle River, NJ: Prentice Hall, 2001.

Trend Projections

A trend line is a regression equation with time as the independent variable.

Another method for forecasting time series with trend is called *trend projection*. This technique fits a trend line to a series of historical data points and then projects the line into the future for medium- to long-range forecasts. There are several mathematical trend equations that can be developed (e.g., exponential and quadratic), but in this section we look at linear (straight line) trends only. A trend line is simply a linear regression equation in which the independent variable (X) is the time period. The form of this is

$$\hat{Y} = b_0 + b_1 X$$

where

$\hat{Y}$ = predicted value

b_0 = intercept

b_1 = slope of the line

X = time period (i.e., $X = 1, 2, 3, \ldots, n$)

The least squares method may be applied to find the line that minimizes the sum of the squared errors. This approach results in a straight line that minimizes the sum of the squares of the vertical distances from the line to each of the actual observations. Figure 5.4 illustrates this least squares approach. This technique also results in the trend line that minimizes the MSE.

Midwestern Manufacturing Company Example Let us consider the case of Midwestern Manufacturing Company. That firm's demand for electrical generators over the period 1996–2002 is shown in Table 5.7. A trend line to predict demand (*Y*) based on the time period can be developed using a regression model. We let 1996 be time period 1 ($X = 1$), then 1997 is time period 2 ($X = 2$), and so forth. We enter the data in Excel, and we select Tools—Data Analysis—Regression and specify the input and output ranges (see Section 4.5

FIGURE 5.4

Least Squares Method for Finding the Best-Fitting Straight Line

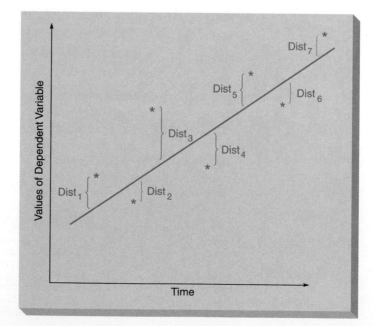

TABLE 5.7

Midwestern
Manufacturing's
Demand

YEAR	ELECTRICAL GENERATORS SOLD
1996	74
1997	79
1998	80
1999	90
2000	105
2001	142
2002	122

of the previous chapter for more details). We obtain the output in Program 5.3. From this we get

$$\hat{Y} = 56.71 + 10.54X$$

To project demand in 2003, we first denote the year 2003 in our new coding system as $X = 8$:

$$(\text{sales in 2003}) = 56.71 + 10.54(8)$$
$$= 141.03, \text{ or } 141 \text{ generators}$$

We can estimate demand for 2004 by inserting $X = 9$ in the same equation:

$$(\text{sales in 2004}) = 56.71 + 10.54(9)$$
$$= 151.57, \text{ or } 152 \text{ generators}$$

PROGRAM 5.3

Excel Output
for Midwestern
Manufacturing
Trend Line

	A	B	C	D	E	F	G	H	I
1	Midwestern Manufacturing								
2									
3	Time (X)	Demand (Y)							
4	1	74							
5	2	79							
6	3	80							
7	4	90							
8	5	105							
9	6	142							
10	7	122							
11									
12	SUMMARY OUTPUT			The next year will be time period 8.					
13									
14	Regression Statistics								
15	Multiple R	0.89491							
16	R Square	0.80086							
17	Adjusted R	0.76104		The slope of the trend line is 10.53.					
18	Standard E	12.43239							
19	Observatio	7							
20									
21	ANOVA								
22		df	SS	MS	F	Significance F			
23	Regressior	1	3108.0357	3108.0357	20.1084	0.0065			
24	Residual	5	772.8214	154.5643					
25	Total	6	3880.8571						
26									
27		Coefficients	Standard Error	t Stat	P-value	Lower 95%	Upper 95%	Lower 95.0%	Upper 95.0%
28	Intercept	56.71429	10.50729	5.39762	0.00295	29.70449	83.72408	29.70449	83.72408
29	Time (X)	10.53571	2.34950	4.48424	0.00649	4.49614	16.57529	4.49614	16.57529

FIGURE 5.5

Electrical Generators and the Computed Trend Line

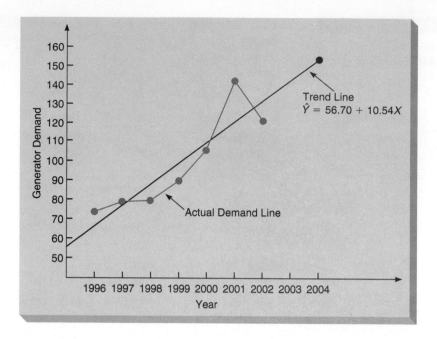

We can evaluate the effectiveness of this model just as we can any other regression model (see Chapter 4). We see the significance level for the F-test is reported in the Excel output to 0.0065, so there is a definite relationship. The strength of this relationship is measured by $r^2 = 0.80$, so this trend line explains about 80% of the variability in demand. A plot of historical demand and the trend line is provided in Figure 5.5. In this case we may wish to be cautious and try to understand the 2001–2002 swings in demand.

Using Excel QM in Trend Analysis Programs 5.4A and Program 5.4B provide the Excel QM input/formulas and results, respectively, for Midwestern Manufacturing. By changing cell C21, you can obtain forecasts for any future period.

Seasonal Variations

A seasonal index of 1 means that the season is average.

Time-series forecasting such as that in the example of Midwestern Manufacturing involves looking at the *trend* of data over a series of time observations. Sometimes, however, recurring variations at certain seasons of the year make a *seasonal* adjustment in the trend line forecast necessary. Demand for coal and fuel oil, for example, usually peaks during cold winter months. Demand for golf clubs or suntan lotion may be highest in summer. Analyzing data in monthly or quarterly terms usually makes it easy to spot seasonal patterns. A seasonal index is often used in multiplicative time series forecasting models to make an adjustment in the forecast when a seasonal component exists. An alternative is to use an additive model such as a regression model that will be introduced in a later section.

A seasonal index indicates how a particular season (e.g., month or quarter) compares with an average season. When no trend is present, the index can be found by dividing the average value for a particular season by the average of all the data. Thus, an index of 1 means the season is average. For example, if the average sales in January were 120 and the average sales in all months were 200, the seasonal index for January would be 120/200 = 0.60, so January is below average. The next example illustrates how to compute seasonal indices from historical data and to use these in forecasting future values.

PROGRAM 5.4A   **Excel QM's Trend Projection Model, Input Data, and Formulas Using Midwestern's Data**

Monthly sales of one brand of telephone answering machine at Eichler Supplies are shown in Table 5.8, for the two most recent years. The average demand in each month is computed, and these values are divided by the overall average (94) to find the seasonal index for each month. We then use the seasonal indices from Table 5.8 to adjust future forecasts. For example, suppose we expected the third year's annual demand for answering machines to be 1,200 units, which is 100 per month. We would not forecast each

PROGRAM 5.4B

Output from Excel QM Trend Projection Model

TABLE 5.8

Answering Machine Sales
and Seasonal Indices

MONTH	SALES DEMAND		AVERAGE TWO-YEAR DEMAND	MONTHLY DEMAND[a]	AVERAGE SEASONAL INDEX[b]
	YEAR 1	YEAR 2			
January	80	100	90	94	0.957
February	85	75	80	94	0.851
March	80	90	85	94	0.904
April	110	90	100	94	1.064
May	115	131	123	94	1.309
June	120	110	115	94	1.223
July	100	110	105	94	1.117
August	110	90	100	94	1.064
September	85	95	90	94	0.957
October	75	85	80	94	0.851
November	85	75	80	94	0.851
December	80	80	80	94	0.851

Total average demand = 1,128

[a] Average monthly demand = $\dfrac{1,128}{12 \text{ months}}$ = 94

[b] Seasonal index = $\dfrac{\text{average two-year demand}}{\text{average monthly demand}}$

month to have a demand of 100, but we would adjust these based on the seasonal indices as follows:

Jan. $\dfrac{1,200}{12} \times 0.957 = 96$ July $\dfrac{1,200}{12} \times 1.117 = 112$

Feb. $\dfrac{1,200}{12} \times 0.851 = 85$ Aug. $\dfrac{1,200}{12} \times 1.064 = 106$

Mar. $\dfrac{1,200}{12} \times 0.904 = 90$ Sept. $\dfrac{1,200}{12} \times 0.957 = 96$

Apr. $\dfrac{1,200}{12} \times 1.064 = 106$ Oct. $\dfrac{1,200}{12} \times 0.851 = 85$

May $\dfrac{1,200}{12} \times 1.309 = 131$ Nov. $\dfrac{1,200}{12} \times 0.851 = 85$

June $\dfrac{1,200}{12} \times 1.223 = 122$ Dec. $\dfrac{1,200}{12} \times 0.851 = 85$

Seasonal Variations with Trend

When both trend and seasonal components are present in a time series, a change from one month to the next could be due to a trend, to a seasonal variation, or simply to random fluctuations. To help with this problem, the seasonal indices should be computed using a *centered moving average* (CMA) approach whenever trend is present. Using this approach prevents a variation due to trend from being incorrectly interpreted as a variation due to the season. Consider the following example.

Centered moving averages are used to compute seasonal indices when there is trend.

TABLE 5.9

Quarterly Sales ($1,000,000s) for Turner Industries

QUARTER	YEAR 1	YEAR 2	YEAR 3	AVERAGE
1	108	116	123	115.67
2	125	134	142	133.67
3	150	159	168	159.00
4	141	152	165	152.67
Average	131.00	140.25	149.50	140.25

Quarterly sales figures for Turner Industries are shown in Table 5.9. Notice there is a definite trend as the total each year is increasing, and there is an increase for each quarter from one year to the next as well. The seasonal component is obvious as there is a definite drop from the fourth quarter of one year to the first quarter of the next. A similar pattern is observed in comparing the third quarters to the fourth quarters immediately following.

If a seasonal index for quarter 1 were computed using the overall average, the index would be too low and misleading, since this quarter has less trend than any of the others in the sample. If the first quarter of year 1 were omitted and replaced by the first quarter of year 4 (if it were available), the average for quarter 1 (and consequently the seasonal index for quarter 1) would be considerably higher. To derive an accurate seasonal index, we should use a CMA.

Consider quarter 3 of year 1 for the Turner Industries example. The actual sales in that quarter were 150. To determine the magnitude of the seasonal variation, we should compare this with an average quarter centered at that time period. Thus, we should have a total of four quarters (one year of data) with an equal number of quarters before and after quarter 3 so the trend is averaged out. Thus, we need 1.5 quarters before quarter 3 and 1.5 quarters after it. To obtain the CMA, we take quarters 2, 3, and 4 of year 1, plus one-half of quarter 1 for year 1 and one-half of quarter 1 for year 2. The average will be

$$\text{CMA (quarter 3 of year 1)} = \frac{0.5(108) + 125 + 150 + 141 + 0.5(116)}{4} = 132.00$$

TABLE 5.10

Centered Moving Averages and Seasonal Ratios for Turner Industries

YEAR	QUARTER	SALES ($1,000,000s)	CMA	SEASONAL RATIO
1	1	108		
	2	125		
	3	150	132.000	1.136
	4	141	134.125	1.051
2	1	116	136.375	0.851
	2	134	138.875	0.965
	3	159	141.125	1.127
	4	152	143.000	1.063
3	1	123	145.125	0.848
	2	142	147.875	0.960
	3	168		
	4	165		

We compare the actual sales in this quarter to the CMA and we have the following seasonal ratio:

$$\text{Seasonal ratio} = \frac{\text{Sales in quarter 3}}{\text{CMA}} = \frac{150}{132.00} = 1.136$$

Thus, sales in quarter 3 of year 1 are about 13.6% higher than an average quarter at this time. All of the CMAs and the seasonal ratios are shown in Table 5.10.

Since there are two seasonal ratios for each quarter, we average these to get the seasonal index. Thus,

$$\text{Index for Quarter 1} = I_1 = (0.851 + 0.848)/2 = 0.85$$

$$\text{Index for Quarter 2} = I_2 = (0.965 + 0.960)/2 = 0.96$$

$$\text{Index for Quarter 3} = I_3 = (1.136 + 1.127)/2 = 1.13$$

$$\text{Index for Quarter 4} = I_4 = (1.051 + 1.063)/2 = 1.06$$

The sum of these indices should be the number of seasons (4) since an average season should have an index of 1. In this example, the sum is 4. If the sum were not 4, an adjustment would be made. We would multiply each index by 4 and divide this by the sum of the indices.

Steps Used to Compute Seasonal Indices Based on CMAs

1. Compute a CMA for each observation (where possible).
2. Compute seasonal ratio = observation/CMA for each observation.
3. Average seasonal ratios to get seasonal indices.
4. If seasonal indices do not add to the number of seasons, multiply each index by (number of seasons)/(sum of the indices).

Figure 5.6 provides a scatterplot of the Turner Industries data and the CMAs. Notice that the plot of the CMAs is much smoother than the original data. A definite trend is apparent in the data.

The Decomposition Method of Forecasting with Trend and Seasonal Components

The process of isolating linear trend and seasonal factors to develop more accurate forecasts is called *decomposition*. The first step is to compute seasonal indices for each season as we have done with the Turner Industries data. Then, the data are deseasonalized by dividing each number by its seasonal index, as shown in Table 5.11.

FIGURE 5.6

Scatterplot of Turner Industries Sales and Centered Moving Average

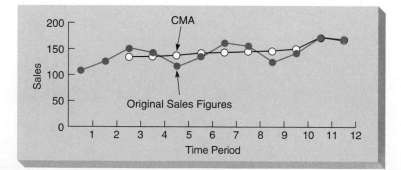

TABLE 5.11	SALES ($1,000,000s)	SEASONAL INDEX	DESEASONALIZED SALES
Deseasonalized Data for Turner Industries	108	0.85	127.059
	125	0.96	130.208
	150	1.13	132.743
	141	1.06	133.019
	116	0.85	136.471
	134	0.96	139.583
	159	1.13	140.708
	152	1.06	143.396
	123	0.85	144.706
	142	0.96	147.917
	168	1.13	148.673
	165	1.06	155.660

A trend line is then found using the deseasonalized data. Using computer software with this data, we have[4]

$$b_1 = 2.34$$
$$b_0 = 124.78$$

The trend equation is

$$\hat{Y} = 124.78 + 2.34X$$

where

$$X = \text{time}$$

This equation is used to develop the forecast based on trend, and the result is multiplied by the appropriate seasonal index to make a seasonal adjustment. For the Turner Industries data, the forecast for the first quarter of year 4 (time period $X = 13$ and seasonal index $I_1 = 0.85$) would be found as follows:

$$\hat{Y} = 124.78 + 2.34X$$
$$= 124.78 + 2.34(13)$$
$$= 155.2 \text{ (forecast before adjustment for seasonality)}$$

We multiply this by the seasonal index for quarter 1 and we get

$$\hat{Y} \times I_1 = 152.2 \times 0.85 = 131.92$$

Using this same procedure, we find the forecasts for quarters 2, 3, and 4 of the next year to be 151.24, 180.66, and 171.95, respectively.

[4] If you do the calculations by hand, the numbers may differ slightly from these due to rounding.

Steps to Develop a Forecast Using the Decomposition Method

1. Compute seasonal indices using CMAs.
2. Deseasonalize the data by dividing each number by its seasonal index.
3. Find the equation of a trend line using the deseasonalized data.
4. Forecast for future periods using the trend line.
5. Multiply the trend line forecast by the appropriate seasonal index.

Most forecasting software, including QM for Windows, includes the decomposition method as one of the available techniques. This will automatically compute the CMAs, deseasonalize the data, develop the trend line, make the forecast using the trend equation, and adjust the final forecast for seasonality.

The following example provides another application of this process. The seasonal indices and trend line have already been computed using the decomposition process.

San Diego Hospital Example A San Diego hospital used 66 months of adult inpatient hospital days to reach the following equation:

$$\hat{Y} = 8,091 + 21.5X$$

where

$$\hat{Y} = \text{forecast patient days}$$

$$X = \text{time, in months}$$

Based on this model, the hospital forecasts patient days for the next month (period 67) to be

Patient days = 8,091 + (21.5)(67) = 9,532 (trend only)

As well as this model recognized the slight upward trend line in the demand for inpatient services, it ignored the seasonality that the administration knew to be present. Table 5.12 provides seasonal indices based on the same 66 months. Such seasonal data, by the way, were found to be typical of hospitals nationwide. Note that January, March, July, and August seem to exhibit significantly higher patient days on average, while February, September, November, and December experience lower patient days.

To correct the time-series extrapolation for seasonality, the hospital multiplied the monthly forecast by the appropriate seasonality index. Thus, for period 67, which was a January,

Patient days = (9,532)(1.0436) = 9,948 (trend and seasonal)

TABLE 5.12

Seasonal Indices for Adult Inpatient Days at San Diego Hospital

MONTH	SEASONALITY INDEX	MONTH	SEASONALITY INDEX
January	1.0436	July	1.0302
February	0.9669	August	1.0405
March	1.0203	September	0.9653
April	1.0087	October	1.0048
May	0.9935	November	0.9598
June	0.9906	December	0.9805

Source: W. E. Sterk and E. G. Shryock. "Modern Methods Improve Hospital Forecasting," *Healthcare Financial Management* (March 1987): 97. Reprinted with permission of author.

PROGRAM 5.5A

QM for Windows Input
for Turner Industries
Example

PROGRAM 5.5A

QM for Windows Input for Turner Industries Example

Using this method, patient days were forecasted for January through June (periods 67 through 72) as 9,948, 9,236, 9,768, 9,678, 9,554, and 9,547. This study led to better forecasts as well as to more accurate forecast budgets.

Using QM for Windows for Decomposition Program 5.5A gives the input from QM for Windows for the Turner Industries example using the multiplicative decomposition method. The inputs involved entering a time series problem with 12 past periods of data, selecting the Multiplicative Decomposition as the Method, indicating there are 4 seasons, and selecting Centered Moving Average as the basis for smoothing. This output, shown in Program 5.5B, provides both the unadjusted forecasts found using the trend equation and

PROGRAM 5.5B   **QM for Windows Output for Turner Industries Example**

the final or adjusted forecasts found by multiplying the unadjusted forecast by the seasonal factor or index. Additional details may be seen by selecting Details and Error Analysis in the drop-down menu under Window as seen in Program 5.5B.

Using Regression with Trend and Seasonal Components

Multiple regression can be used to develop an additive decomposition model.

Multiple regression may be used to forecast with both trend and seasonal components present in a time series. One independent variable is time, and other independent variables are dummy variables to indicate the season. If we forecast quarterly data, there are four categories (quarters) so we would use three dummy variables. The basic model is an additive decomposition model and is expressed as follows:

$$\hat{Y} = a + b_1 X_1 + b_2 X_2 + b_3 X_3 + b_4 X_4$$

where

$$X_1 = \text{time period}$$
$$X_2 = 1 \text{ if quarter 2}$$
$$= 0 \text{ otherwise}$$
$$X_3 = 1 \text{ if quarter 3}$$
$$= 0 \text{ otherwise}$$
$$X_4 = 1 \text{ if quarter 4}$$
$$= 0 \text{ otherwise}$$

If $X_2 = X_3 = X_4 = 0$, then the quarter would be quarter 1. It is an arbitrary choice as to which of the quarters would not have a specific dummy variable associated with it. The forecasts will be the same regardless of which quarter does not have a specific dummy variable.

Program 5.6 provides the Excel output for the Turner Industries example. You can see how the data is input, and the regression equation (with coefficients rounded) is

$$\hat{Y} = 104.1 + 2.3X_1 + 15.7X_2 + 38.7X_3 + 30.1X_4$$

⒜⒬ IN ACTION   Forecasting Spare Parts at American Airlines

To support the operation of its fleet of more than 400 aircraft, American Airlines maintains a vast inventory of spare repairable (rotatable) aircraft parts. Its PC-based forecasting system, the Rotatables Allocation and Planning System (RAPS), provides demand forecasts for spare parts, helps allocate these parts to airports, and computes the availability of each spare part. With 5,000 different kinds of parts, ranging from landing gear to wing flaps to coffeemakers to altimeters, meeting demand for each part at each station can be extremely difficult—and expensive. The average price of a rotatable part is about $5,000, with some parts (such as avionics computers) costing well over $500,000 each.

Before developing RAPS, American used only time-series methods to forecast the demand for spare parts. The time-

series approach was slow to respond to even moderate changes in aircraft utilizations, let alone major fleet expansions. RAPS, instead, uses linear regression to establish a relationship between monthly part removals and various functions of monthly flying hours. Correlation coefficients and statistical significance tests are used to find the best regressions, which now take only one hour instead of the days that the old system needed.

The results? Using RAPS, American says that it had a one-time savings of $7 million and recurring annual savings of nearly $1 million.

Source: Mark J. Tedone. "Repairable Part Management," *Interfaces* 19, 4 (July–August 1989): 61–68.

PROGRAM 5.6

**Excel Output for Turner
Industries Example**

	A	B	C	D	E	F	G	H	I
1	Year	Quarter	Sales	X1 Time Period	X2 Qtr 2	X3 Qtr 3	X4 Qtr4		
2	1	1	108	1	0	0	0		
3		2	125	2	1	0	0		
4		3	150	3	0	1	0		
5		4	141	4	0	0	1		
6	2	1	116	5	0	0	0		
7		2	134	6	1	0	0		
8		3	159	7	0	1	0		
9		4	152	8	0	0	1		
10	3	1	123	9	0	0	0		
11		2	142	10	1	0	0		
12		3	168	11	0	1	0		
13		4	165	12	0	0	1		
14									
15	SUMMARY OUTPUT								
16									
17	*Regression Statistics*								
18	Multiple R	0.99718							
19	R Square	0.99436							
20	Adjusted R	0.99114							
21	Standard E	1.83225							
22	Observatior	12							
23									
24	ANOVA								
25		*df*	*SS*	*MS*	*F*	*Significance F*			
26	Regressior	4	4144.75	1.0362E+03	3.0865E+02	6.0284E-08			
27	Residual	7	23.5	3.3571E+00					
28	Total	11	4168.25						
29									
30		*Coefficient*	*standard Err*	*t Stat*	*P-value*	*Lower 95%*	*Upper 95%*	*ower 95.0%*	*Upper 95.0%*
31	Intercept	104.1042	1.3322	78.1449	0.0000	100.9540	107.2543	100.9540	107.2543
32	X1 Time Pe	2.3125	0.1619	14.2791	0.0000	1.9296	2.6954	1.9296	2.6954
33	X2 Qtr 2	15.6875	1.5048	10.4252	0.0000	12.1293	19.2457	12.1293	19.2457
34	X3 Qtr 3	38.7083	1.5307	25.2882	0.0000	35.0888	42.3278	35.0888	42.3278
35	X4 Qtr4	30.0625	1.5729	19.1123	0.0000	26.3431	33.7819	26.3431	33.7819

Quarter 1 is indicated by letting $X_2 = X_3 = X_4 = 0$.

If this is used to forecast sales in the first quarter of the next year, we get

$$\hat{Y} = 104.1 + 2.3(13) + 15.7(0) + 38.7(0) + 30.1(0) = 134$$

For quarter 2 of the next year we get

$$\hat{Y} = 104.1 + 2.3(14) + 15.7(1) + 38.7(0) + 30.1(0) = 152$$

Notice these are not the same values we obtained using the multiplicative decomposition method. We could compare the MAD or MSE for each method and choose the one that is better.

5.6   MONITORING AND CONTROLLING FORECASTS

After a forecast has been completed, it is important that it not be forgotten. No manager wants to be reminded when his or her forecast is horribly inaccurate, but a firm needs to determine why the actual demand (or whatever variable is being examined) differed significantly from that projected.[5]

---

[5] If the forecaster is accurate, he or she usually makes sure that everyone is aware of his or her talents. Very seldom does one read articles in *Fortune*, *Forbes*, or the *Wall Street Journal*, however, about money managers who are consistently off by 25% in their stock market forecasts.

A tracking signal measures how well predictions fit actual data.

One way to monitor forecasts to ensure that they are performing well is to employ a *tracking signal*. A tracking signal is a measurement of how well the forecast is predicting actual values. As forecasts are updated every week, month, or quarter, the newly available demand data are compared to the forecast values.

The tracking signal is computed as the *running sum of the forecast errors* (RSFE) divided by the mean absolute deviation:

$$\text{Tracking signal} = \frac{\text{RSFE}}{\text{MAD}} \tag{5-11}$$

$$= \frac{\Sigma(\text{forecast error})}{\text{MAD}}$$

where

$$\text{MAD} = \frac{\Sigma \left| \text{forecast error} \right|}{n}$$

as seen earlier in Equation 5-1.

Positive tracking signals indicate that demand is greater than the forecast. Negative signals mean that demand is less than forecast. A good tracking signal—that is, one with a low RSFE—has about as much positive error as it has negative error. In other words, small deviations are okay, but the positive and negative deviations should balance so that the tracking signal centers closely around zero.

When tracking signals are calculated, they are compared with predetermined control limits. When a tracking signal exceeds an upper or lower limit, a signal is tripped. This means that there is a problem with the forecasting method, and management may want to reevaluate the way it forecasts demand. Figure 5.7 shows the graph of a tracking signal that is exceeding the range of acceptable variation. If the model being used is exponential smoothing, perhaps the smoothing constant needs to be readjusted.

Setting tracking limits is a matter of setting reasonable values for upper and lower limits.

How do firms decide what the upper and lower tracking limits should be? There is no single answer, but they try to find reasonable values—in other words, limits not so low as to be triggered with every small forecast error and not so high as to allow bad forecasts to be regularly overlooked. George Plossl and Oliver Wight, two inventory control experts, suggested using maximums of ±4 MADs for high-volume stock items and ±8 MADs for lower-volume items.[6] Other forecasters suggest slightly lower ranges. One MAD is equivalent to

FIGURE 5.7

Plot of Tracking Signals

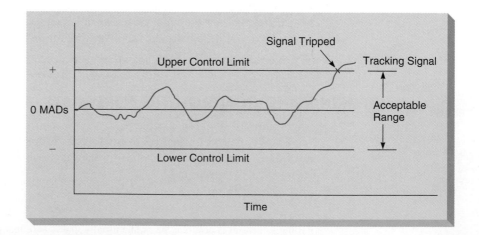

---

[6] See G. W. Plossl and O. W. Wight. *Production and Inventory Control.* Upper Saddle River, NJ: Prentice Hall, 1967.

approximately 0.8 standard deviation, so that ±2 MADs = 1.6 standard deviations, ±3 MADs = 2.4 standard deviations, and ±4 MADs = 3.2 standard deviations. This suggests that for a forecast to be "in control," 89% of the errors are expected to fall within ±2 MADs, 98% within ±3 MADs, or 99.9% within ±4 MADs whenever the errors are approximately normally distributed.[7]

Kimball's Bakery Example Here is an example that shows how the tracking signal and RSFE can be computed. Kimball's Bakery's quarterly sales of croissants (in thousands), as well as forecast demand and error computations, are in the following table. The objective is to compute the tracking signal and determine whether forecasts are performing adequately.

QUARTER	FORECAST DEMAND	ACTUAL DEMAND	ERROR	RSFE	FORECAST ERROR	CUMULATIVE ERROR	MAD	TRACKING SIGNAL
1	100	90	−10	−10	10	10	10.0	−1
2	100	95	−5	−15	5	15	7.5	−2
3	100	115	+15	0	15	30	10.0	0
4	110	100	−10	−10	10	40	10.0	−1
5	110	125	+15	+5	15	55	11.0	+0.5
5	110	140	+30	+35	30	85	14.2	+2.5

$$\text{MAD} = \frac{\sum|\text{forecast error}|}{n} = \frac{85}{6}$$

$$= 14.2$$

$$\text{tracking signal} = \frac{\text{RSFE}}{\text{MAD}} = \frac{35}{14.2}$$

$$= 2.5 \text{ MADs}$$

This tracking signal is within acceptable limits. We see that it drifted from −2.0 MADs to +2.5 MADs.

Adaptive Smoothing

A lot of research has been published on the subject of adaptive forecasting. This refers to computer monitoring of tracking signals and self-adjustment if a signal passes its preset limit. In exponential smoothing, the α and β coefficients are first selected based on values that minimize error forecasts and are then adjusted accordingly whenever the computer notes an errant tracking signal. This is called *adaptive smoothing*.

5.7   USING THE COMPUTER TO FORECAST

Appendix 5.1 illustrates QM for Windows as an alternative way of developing forecasts.

Forecast calculations are seldom performed by hand in this day of computers. Spreadsheet software can effectively manage small to medium-sized forecasting problems, as we have seen with Excel and Excel QM. Similarly, QM for Windows can be used for moderate-sized problems. Numerous general statistical programs (such as SAS, SPSS, NCSS, and Minitab)

---

[7] To prove these three percentages to yourself, just set up a normal curve for ±1.6 standard deviations (Z values). Using the normal table in Appendix A, you find that the area under that curve is 0.89. This represents ±2 MADs. Similarly, ±3 MADs = 2.4 standard deviations encompasses 98% of the area, and so on for ±4 MADs.

IN ACTION   Forecasting at Disney World

When Disney chairman Michael Eisner receives a daily report from his main theme parks in Orlando, Florida, the report contains only two numbers: the *forecast* of yesterday's attendance at the parks (Magic Kingdom, Epcot, Fort Wilderness, MGM Studios, and Blizzard Beach) and the actual attendance. An error close to zero (using MAPE as the measure) is expected. Eisner takes his forecasts very seriously.

The forecasting team at Disney World doesn't just do a daily prediction, however, and Eisner is not its only customer. It also provides daily, weekly, monthly, annual, and five-year forecasts to the labor management, maintenance, operations, finance, and park scheduling departments. It uses judgmental models, econometric models, moving average models, and regression analysis. The team's annual forecast of total volume, conducted in 1999 for the year 2000, resulted in a MAPE of 0.

With 20% of Disney World's customers coming from outside the United States, its econometric model includes such variables as consumer confidence and the gross domestic product of seven countries. Disney also surveys one million people each year to examine their future travel plans and their experiences at the parks. This helps forecast not only attendance, but behavior at each ride (how long people will wait and how many times they will ride). Inputs to the monthly forecasting model include airline specials, speeches by the Chair of the Federal Reserve, and Wall Street trends. Disney even monitors 3,000 school districts inside and out of the United States for holiday/vacation schedules.

Source: J. Newkirk and M. Haskell. "Forecasting in the Service Sector," presentation at the 12th Annual Meeting of the Production and Operations Management Society. April 1, 2001, Orlando, FL.

have forecasting modules or features and are readily available to handle time-series and causal projections. Some of these will automatically select the best parameters for a model (e.g., the smoothing constant in an exponential smoothing model) once the user has identified the type of model to use.

Dedicated forecasting software is also available, and this is sometimes completely automatic. The user simply inputs the data and the computer will determine which time series model will work best with that particular set of data.[8]

Several mainframe-oriented packages, such as General Electric's Time Series Forecasting (called FCST1 and FCST2), are oriented toward organizations that need to perform large-scale regression and exponential smoothing projections. A large number of corporations use forecasting programs that also incorporate inventory control routines. Examples are IBM's IMPACT (Inventory Management Program and Control Technique) and COGS (Consumer Goods Program).

SUMMARY

Forecasts are a critical part of a manager's function. Demand forecasts drive the production, capacity, and scheduling systems in a firm and affect the financial, marketing, and personnel planning functions.

In this chapter we introduced three types of forecasting models: time series, causal, and qualitative. Moving averages, exponential smoothing, trend projection, and decomposition time-series models were developed. Regression and multiple regression models were recognized as causal models. Four qualitative models were briefly discussed. In

addition, we explained the use of scatter diagrams and measures of forecasting accuracy. In future chapters you will see the usefulness of these techniques in determining values for the various decision-making models.

As we learned in this chapter, no forecasting method is perfect under all conditions. Even when management has found a satisfactory approach, it must still monitor and control its forecasts to make sure that errors do not get out of hand. Forecasting can often be a very challenging but rewarding part of managing.

[8] J. Yurkiewicz, "Forecasting Software Survey" *ORMS Today* (February 2003): 44-51.

GLOSSARY

Adaptive Smoothing. The process of automatically monitoring and adjusting the smoothing constants in an exponential smoothing model.

Bias. A technique for determining the accuracy of a forecasting model by measuring the average error and its direction.

Causal Models. Models that forecast using variables and factors in addition to time.

Centered Moving Average. An average of the values centered at a particular point in time. This is used to compute seasonal indices when trend is present.

Decision-Making Group. A group of experts in a Delphi technique that has the responsibility of making the forecast.

Decomposition. A forecasting model that decomposes a time series into its seasonal and trend components.

Delphi. A judgmental forecasting technique that uses decision makers, staff personnel, and respondents to determine a forecast.

Deseasonalized Data. Time series data in which each value has been divided by its seasonal index to remove the effect of the seasonal component.

Deviation. Another term used in forecasting for error.

Error. The difference between the actual value and the forecast value.

Exponential Smoothing. A forecasting method that is a combination of the last forecast and the last observed value.

Holt's Method. An exponential smoothing model that includes a trend component. This is also called a double exponential smoothing model or a second-order smoothing model.

Least Squares. A procedure used in trend projection and regression analysis to minimize the squared distances between the estimated straight line and the observed values.

Mean Absolute Deviation (MAD). A technique for determining the accuracy of a forecasting model by taking the average of the absolute deviations.

Mean Absolute Percent Error (MAPE). A technique for determining the accuracy of a forecasting model by taking the average of the absolute errors as a percentage of the observed values.

Mean Squared Error (MSE). A technique for determining the accuracy of a forecasting model by taking the average of the squared error terms for a forecasting model.

Moving Average. A forecasting technique that averages past values in computing the forecast.

Naïve Model. A time-series forecasting model in which the forecast for next period is the actual value for the current period.

Qualitative Models. Models that forecast using judgments, experience, and qualitative and subjective data.

Running Sum of Forecast Errors (RSFE). Used to develop a tracking signal for time-series forecasting models, this is a running total of the errors and may be positive or negative.

Scatter Diagrams. Diagrams of the variable to be forecasted, plotted against another variable, such as time.

Seasonal Index. An index number that indicates how a particular season compares with an average time period (with an index of 1 indicating an average season).

Smoothing Constant. A value between 0 and 1 that is used in an exponential smoothing forecast.

Time-Series Models. Models that forecast using only historical data.

Tracking Signal. A measure of how well the forecast is predicting actual values.

Trend Projection. The use of a trend line to forecast a time-series with trend present. A linear trend line is a regression line with time as the independent variable.

Weighted Moving Average. A moving average forecasting method that places different weights on past values.

KEY EQUATIONS

(5-1) $MAD = \dfrac{\Sigma |\text{forecast error}|}{n}$

A measure of overall forecast error called mean absolute deviation.

(5-2) $MSE = \dfrac{\Sigma (error)^2}{n}$

(5-3) $MAPE = \dfrac{\Sigma \left|\dfrac{error}{actual}\right|}{n} 100\%$

(5-4) $\text{Moving average} = \dfrac{\Sigma \text{ demand in previous } n \text{ periods}}{n}$

An equation for computing a moving average forecast.

(5-5) $F_t = \dfrac{Y_{t-1} + Y_{t-2} + \ldots + Y_{t-n}}{n}$

Mathematical expression for moving average forecast.

(5-6) $\text{weighted moving average} = \dfrac{\Sigma (\text{weight for period } n)(\text{demand in period } n)}{\Sigma \text{ weights}}$

An equation for computing a weighted moving average forecast.

(5-7) $F_t = \dfrac{w_1 Y_{t-1} + w_2 Y_{t-2} + \ldots + w_n Y_{t-n}}{w_1 + w_2 + \ldots + w_n}$

Mathematical expression for weighted moving average forecast.

(5-8) New forecast = last period's forecast + α(last period's actual demand − last period's forecast)

An equation for computing an exponential smoothing forecast.

(5-9) $F_t = F_{t-1} + \alpha(A_{t-1} - F_{t-1})$

Equation 5-8 rewritten mathematically.

(5-10) $T_t = (1 - \beta)T_{t-1} + \beta(F_t - F_{t-1})$

Trend component of an exponential smoothing model with trend.

(5-11)
$$\text{Tracking signal} = \frac{\text{RSFE}}{\text{MAD}}$$
$$= \frac{\Sigma(\text{forecast error})}{\text{MAD}}$$

An equation for monitoring forecasts with a tracking signal.

SOLVED PROBLEMS

Solved Problem 5-1

Demand for patient surgery at Washington General Hospital has increased steadily in the past few years, as seen in the following table.

YEAR	OUTPATIENT SURGERIES PERFORMED
1	45
2	50
3	52
4	56
5	58
6	—

The director of medical services predicted six years ago that demand in year 1 would be 42 surgeries. Using exponential smoothing with a weight of α = 0.20, develop forecasts for years 2 through 6. What is the MAD?

Solution

YEAR	ACTUAL	FORECAST (SMOOTHED)	ERROR	|ERROR|
1	45	42	+3	3
2	50	42.6 = 42 + 0.2(45 − 42)	+7.4	7.4
3	52	44.1 = 42.6 + 0.2(50 − 42.6)	+7.9	7.9
4	56	45.7 = 44.1 + 0.2(52 − 44.1)	+10.3	10.3
5	58	47.7 = 45.7 + 0.2(56 − 45.7)	+10.3	10.3
6	—	49.8 = 47.7 + 0.2(58 − 47.7)	—	—

$$\text{MAD} = \frac{\Sigma|\text{errors}|}{n} = \frac{38.9}{5} = 7.78 \qquad 38.9$$

Solved Problem 5-2

Quarterly demand for Jaguar XJ8's at a New York auto dealership is forecast with the equation

$$\dot{Y} = 10 + 3X$$

where

X = time period (quarter): quarter 1 of last year = 0

quarter 2 of last year = 1

quarter 3 of last year = 2

quarter 4 of last year = 3

quarter 1 of this year = 4, and so on

and

$$\hat{Y} = \text{predicted quarterly demand}$$

The demand for luxury sedans is seasonal, and the indices for quarters 1, 2, 3, and 4 are 0.80, 1.00, 1.30, and 0.90, respectively. Using the trend equation, forecast the demand for each quarter of next year. Then adjust each forecast to adjust for seasonal (quarterly) variations.

Solution

Quarter 2 of this year is coded $x = 5$; quarter 3 of this year, $x = 6$; and quarter 4 of this year, $x = 7$. Hence, quarter 1 of next year is coded $x = 8$; quarter 2, $x = 9$; and so on.

$\hat{Y}$ (next year quarter 1) = 10 + (3)(8) = 34   Adjusted forecast = (0.80)(34) = 27.2

$\hat{Y}$ (next year quarter 2) = 10 + (3)(9) = 37   Adjusted forecast = (1.00)(37) = 37

$\hat{Y}$ (next year quarter 3) = 10 + (3)(10) = 40   Adjusted forecast = (1.30)(40) = 52

$\hat{Y}$ (next year quarter 4) = 10 + (3)(11) = 43   Adjusted forecast = (0.90)(43) = 38.7

- ■ Before taking the self-test, refer back to the learning objectives at the beginning of the chapter, the notes in the margins, and the glossary at the end of the chapter.
- ■ Use the key at the back of the book to correct your answers.
- ■ Restudy pages that correspond to any questions that you answered incorrectly or material you feel uncertain about.

1. Qualitative forecasting models include
   a. regression analysis.
   b. Delphi.
   c. time-series models.
   d. trend lines.
2. A forecasting model that only uses historical data for the variable being forecast is called a
   a. time-series model.
   b. causal model.
   c. Delphi model.
   d. variable model.
3. One example of a causal model is
   a. exponential smoothing.
   b. trend projections.
   c. moving averages.
   d. regression analysis.
4. Which of the following is a time-series model?
   a. the Delphi model
   b. regression analysis
   c. exponential smoothing
   d. multiple regression
5. Which of the following is not a component of a time-series?
   a. seasonality
   b. causal variations
   c. trend
   d. random variations
6. Which of the following may be negative?
   a. MAD
   b. bias
   c. MAPE
   d. MSE
7. When comparing several forecasting models to determine which one best fits a particular set of data, the model that should be selected is the one
   a. with the highest MSE.
   b. with the MAD closest to 1.
   c. with a bias of 0.
   d. with the lowest MAD.
8. In exponential smoothing, if you wish to give a significant weight to the most recent observations, then the smoothing constant should be
   a. close to 0.
   b. close to 1.
   c. close to 0.5.
   d. less than the error.
9. A trend equation is a regression equation in which
   a. there are multiple independent variables.
   b. the intercept and the slope are the same.
   c. the dependent variable is time.
   d. the independent variable is time.
10. Sales for a company are typically higher in the summer months than in the winter months. This variation would be called a
    a. trend.
    b. seasonal factor.
    c. random factor.
    d. cyclical factor.
11. A naïve forecast for monthly sales is equivalent to
    a. a one-month moving average model.
    b. an exponential smoothing model with $\alpha = 0$.
    c. a seasonal model in which the seasonal index is 1.
    d. none of the above.
12. If the seasonal index for January is 0.80, then
    a. January sales tend to be 80% higher than an average month.
    b. January sales tend to be 20% higher than an average month.
    c. January sales tend to be 80% lower than an average month.
    d. January sales tend to be 20% lower than an average month.
13. If both trend and seasonal components are present in a time-series, then the seasonal indices
    a. should be computed based on an overall average.
    b. should be computed based on CMAs.
    c. will all be greater than 1.
    d. should be ignored in developing the forecast.
14. Which of the following is used to alert the user of a forecasting model that a significant error occurred in one of the periods?
    a. a seasonal index
    b. a smoothing constant
    c. a tracking signal
    d. a regression coefficient

DISCUSSION QUESTIONS AND PROBLEMS

Discussion Questions

5-1 Describe briefly the steps used to develop a forecasting system.

5-2 What is a time-series forecasting model?

5-3 What is the difference between a causal model and a time-series model?

5-4 What is a qualitative forecasting model, and when is it appropriate?

5-5 What are some of the problems and drawbacks of the moving average forecasting model?

5-6 What effect does the value of the smoothing constant have on the weight given to the past forecast and the past observed value?

5-7 Describe briefly the Delphi technique.

5-8 What is MAD, and why is it important in the selection and use of forecasting models?

5-9 A seasonal index may be less than one, equal to one, or greater than one. Explain what each of these values would mean.

5-10 Explain what would happen if the smoothing constant in an exponential smoothing model was equal to zero. Explain what would happen if the smoothing constant was equal to one.

5-11 Explain when a CMA (rather than an overall average) should be used in computing a seasonal index. Explain why this is necessary.

Problems*

5-12 Develop a four-month moving average forecast for Wallace Garden Supply and compute the MAD. A three-month moving average forecast was developed in the section on moving averages in Table 5.3.

5-13 Using MAD, determine whether the forecast in Problem 5-12 or the forecast in the section concerning Wallace Garden Supply is more accurate.

5-14 Data collected on the yearly demand for 50-pound bags of fertilizer at Wallace Garden Supply are shown in the following table. Develop a three-year moving average to forecast sales. Then estimate demand again with a weighted moving average in which sales in the most recent year are given a weight of 2 and sales in the other two years are each given a weight of 1. Which method do you think is best?

YEAR	DEMAND FOR FERTILIZER (1,000s OF BAGS)
1	4
2	6
3	4

YEAR	DEMAND FOR FERTILIZER (1,000s OF BAGS)
4	5
5	10
6	8
7	7
8	9
9	12
10	14
11	15

5-15 Develop a trend line for the demand for fertilizer in Problem 5-14 using any computer software.

5-16 In Problems 5-14 and 5-15, three different forecasts were developed for the demand for fertilizer. These three forecasts are a three-year moving average, a weighted moving average, and a trend line. Which one would you use? Explain your answer.

5-17 Use exponential smoothing with a smoothing constant of 0.3 to forecast the demand for fertilizer given in Problem 5-14. Assume that last period's forecast for year 1 is 5,000 bags to begin the procedure. Would you prefer to use the exponential smoothing model or the weighted average model developed in Problem 5-14? Explain your answer.

5-18 Sales of Cool-Man air conditioners have grown steadily during the past five years.

YEAR	SALES
1	450
2	495
3	518
4	563
5	584
6	?

The sales manager had predicted, before the business started, that year 1's sales would be 410 air conditioners. Using exponential smoothing with a weight of $\alpha = 0.30$, develop forecasts for years 2 through 6.

5-19 Using smoothing constants of 0.6 and 0.9, develop forecasts for the sales of Cool-Man air conditioners (see Problem 5-18).

---

* Note: ⚕ means the problem may be solved with QM for Windows; ✖ means the problem may be solved with Excel QM; and ⚕✖ means the problem may be solved with QM for Windows and/or Excel QM.

5-20 What effect did the smoothing constant have on the forecast for Cool-Man air conditioners? (See Problems 5-18 and 5-19). Which smoothing constant gives the most accurate forecast?

5-21 Use a three-year moving average forecasting model to forecast the sales of Cool-Man air conditioners (see Problem 5-18).

5-22 Using the trend projection method, develop a forecasting model for the sales of Cool-Man air conditioners (see Problem 5-18).

5-23 Would you use exponential smoothing with a smoothing constant of 0.3, a three-year moving average, or a trend to predict the sales of Cool-Man air conditioners? Refer to Problems 5-18, 5-21, and 5-22.

5-24 Sales of industrial vacuum cleaners at R. Lowenthal Supply Co. over the past 13 months are as follows:

SALES (1,000s)	MONTH	SALES (1,000s)	MONTH
11	January	14	August
14	February	17	September
16	March	12	October
10	April	14	November
15	May	16	December
17	June	11	January
11	July		

(a) Using a moving average with three periods, determine the demand for vacuum cleaners for next February.

(b) Using a weighted moving average with three periods, determine the demand for vacuum cleaners for February. Use 3, 2, and 1 for the weights of the most recent, second most recent, and third most recent periods, respectively. For example, if you were forecasting the demand for February, November would have a weight of 1, December would have a weight of 2, and January would have a weight of 3.

(c) Evaluate the accuracy of each of these methods.

(d) What other factors might R. Lowenthal consider in forecasting sales?

5-25 Passenger miles flown on Northeast Airlines, a commuter firm serving the Boston hub, are as follows for the past 12 weeks:

WEEK	ACTUAL PASSENGER MILES (1,000s)	WEEK	ACTUAL PASSENGER MILES (1,000s)
1	17	7	20
2	21	8	18
3	19	9	22
4	23	10	20
5	18	11	15
6	16	12	22

(a) Assuming an initial forecast for week 1 of 17,000 miles, use exponential smoothing to compute miles for weeks 2 through 12. Use $\alpha = 0.2$.

(b) What is the MAD for this model?

(c) Compute the RSFE and tracking signals. Are they within acceptable limits?

5-26 Emergency calls to Winter Park, Florida's 911 system, for the past 24 weeks are as follows:

WEEK	CALLS	WEEK	CALLS	WEEK	CALLS
1	50	9	35	17	55
2	35	10	20	18	40
3	25	11	15	19	35
4	40	12	40	20	60
5	45	13	55	21	75
6	35	14	35	22	50
7	20	15	25	23	40
8	30	16	55	24	65

(a) Compute the exponentially smoothed forecast of calls for each week. Assume an initial forecast of 50 calls in the first week and use $\alpha = 0.1$. What is the forecast for the 25th week?

(b) Reforecast each period using $\alpha = 0.6$.

(c) Actual calls during the 25th week were 85. Which smoothing constant provides a superior forecast?

5-27 Using the 911 call data in Problem 5-26, forecast calls for weeks 2 through 25 using $\alpha = 0.9$. Which is best? (Again, assume that actual calls in week 25 were 85 and use an initial forecast of 50 calls.)

5-28 Consulting income at Kate Walsh Associates for the period February–July has been as follows:

MONTH	INCOME ($1,000s)
February	70.0
March	68.5
April	64.8
May	71.7
June	71.3
July	72.8

Use exponential smoothing to forecast August's income. Assume that the initial forecast for February is $65,000. The smoothing constant selected is $\alpha = 0.1$.

5-29 Resolve Problem 5-28 with $\alpha = 0.3$. Using MAD, which smoothing constant provides a better forecast?

5-30 A major source of revenue in Texas is a state sales tax on certain types of goods and services. Data are compiled and the state comptroller uses them to project future revenues for the state budget. One particular category of goods is classified as Retail Trade. Four years of quarterly data for one particular area of southeast Texas follow:

Quarter	Year 1	Year 2	Year 3	Year 4
1	218	225	234	250
2	247	254	265	283
3	243	255	264	289
4	292	299	327	356

(a) Compute seasonal indices for each quarter based on a CMA.
(b) Deseasonalize the data and develop a trend line on the deseasonalized data.
(c) Use the trend line to forecast the sales for each quarter of year 5.
(d) Use the seasonal indices to adjust the forecasts found in part (c) to obtain the final forecasts.

5-31 Using the data in problem 5-30, develop a multiple regression model to predict sales (both trend and seasonal components), using dummy variables to incorporate the seasonal factor into the model. Use this model to predict sales for each quarter of the next year. Comment on the accuracy of this model.

5-32 The unemployment rates in the United States during a ten-year period are given in the following table. Use exponential smoothing to find the best forecast for next year. Use smoothing constants of 0.2, 0.4, 0.6, and 0.8. Which one had the lowest MAD?

Year	1	2	3	4	5	6	7	8	9	10
Unemployment rate (%)	7.2	7.0	6.2	5.5	5.3	5.5	6.7	7.4	6.8	6.1

5-33 Management of Davis's Department Store has used time-series extrapolation to forecast retail sales for the next four quarters. The sales estimates are $100,000, $120,000, $140,000, and $160,000 for the respective quarters before adjusting for seasonality. Seasonal indices for the four quarters have been found to be 1.30, 0.90, 0.70, and 1.10, respectively. Compute a seasonalized or adjusted sales forecast.

5-34 In the past, Judy Holmes's tire dealership sold an average of 1,000 radials each year. In the past two years, 200 and 250, respectively, were sold in fall, 300 and 350 in winter, 150 and 165 in spring, and 300 and 285 in summer. With a major expansion planned, Judy projects sales next year to increase to 1,200 radials. What will the demand be each season?

INTERNET HOMEWORK PROBLEMS

See our Internet home page at **www.prenhall.com/render** for additional homework problems 5-35 to 5-43.

⟶ CASE STUDY

Forecasting Attendance at SWU Football Games

Southwestern University (SWU), a large state college in Stephenville, Texas, 30 miles southwest of the Dallas/Fort Worth metroplex, enrolls close to 20,000 students. In a typical town–gown relationship, the school is a dominant force in the small city, with more students during fall and spring than permanent residents.

A longtime football powerhouse, SWU is a member of the Big Eleven conference and is usually in the top 20 in college football rankings. To bolster its chances of reaching the elusive and long-desired number-one ranking, in 1997 SWU hired the legendary Bo Pitterno as its head coach. Although the number-one ranking remained out of reach, attendance at the five Saturday home games each year increased. Prior to Pitterno's arrival, attendance generally averaged 25,000 to 29,000 per game. Season ticket sales bumped up by 10,000 just with the announcement of the new coach's arrival. Stephenville and SWU were ready to move to the big time!

The immediate issue facing SWU, however, was not NCAA ranking. It was capacity. The existing SWU stadium, built in 1953, has seating for 54,000 fans. The following table indicates attendance at each game for the past six years.

One of Pitterno's demands upon joining SWU had been a stadium expansion, or possibly even a new stadium. With attendance increasing, SWU administrators began to face the issue head-on. Pitterno had wanted dormitories solely for his athletes in the stadium as an additional feature of any expansion.

SWU's president, Dr. Marty Starr, decided it was time for his vice president of development to forecast when the existing stadium would "max out." He also sought a revenue projection, assuming an average ticket price of $20 in 2003 and a 5% increase each year in future prices.

Discussion Questions

1. Develop a forecasting model, justifying its selection over other techniques, and project attendance through 2004.
2. What revenues are to be expected in 2003 and 2004?
3. Discuss the school's options.

Southwestern University Football Game Attendance, 1997–2002

GAME	1997 ATTENDEES	OPPONENT	1998 ATTENDEES	OPPONENT	1999 ATTENDEES	OPPONENT
1	34,200	Baylor	36,100	Oklahoma	35,900	TCU
2*	39,800	Texas	40,200	Nebraska	46,500	Texas Tech
3	38,200	LSU	39,100	UCLA	43,100	Alaska
4**	26,900	Arkansas	25,300	Nevada	27,900	Arizona
5	35,100	USC	36,200	Ohio State	39,200	Rice

GAME	2000 ATTENDEES	OPPONENT	2001 ATTENDEES	OPPONENT	2002 ATTENDEES	OPPONENT
1	41,900	Arkansas	42,500	Indiana	46,900	LSU
2*	46,100	Missouri	48,200	North Texas	50,100	Texas
3	43,900	Florida	44,200	Texas A&M	45,900	Prairie View A&M
4**	30,100	Miami	33,900	Southern	36,300	Montana
5	40,500	Duke	47,800	Oklahoma	49,900	Arizona State

*Homecoming games
**During the fourth week of each season, Stephenville hosted a hugely popular southwestern crafts festival. This event brought tens of thousands of tourists to the town, especially on weekends, and had an obvious negative impact on game attendance.

Source: J. Heizer and B. Render. *Operations Management*, 6/e. Upper Saddle River, N.J.: Prentice Hall, 2001, p. 126.

INTERNET CASE STUDY

See our Internet home page at **www.prenhall.com/render** for this additional case study:

(1) Akron Zoological Park. This case involves forecasting attendance at Akron's zoo.

BIBLIOGRAPHY

Berenson, Mark L., David M. Levine, and Timothy C. Kriehbiel. *Business Statistics: Concepts and Applications*, 9th ed. Upper Saddle River, NJ: Prentice Hall, 2004.

Black, Ken. *Business Statistics: For Contemporary Decision Making*, 4th ed. John Wiley & Sons, Inc., 2003.

Chambers, J. C., C. Satinder, S. K. Mullick, and D. D. Smith. "How to Choose the Right Forecasting Technique," *Harvard Business Review* 49, 4 (July–August 1971): 45–74.

Clements, Dale W. and Richard A. Reid. "Analytical MS/OR Tools Applied to a Plant Closure," *Interfaces* 24, 2 (March–April 1994): 1–43.

De Lurgio, S. A. *Forecasting Principles and Applications*. New York: Irwin-McGraw-Hill, 1998.

Diebold, F. X. *Elements of Forecasting*, 2/e. Cincinnati: South-Western College Publishing, 2001.

Duran, Jorge A. and Benito E. Flores. "Forecasting Practices in Mexican Companies," *Interfaces* 28, 6 (November–December 1998): 56–62.

Gardner, E. S. "Exponential Smoothing: The State of the Art," *Journal of Forecasting* 4, 1 (March 1985). 1–38.

Georgoff, D. M., and R. G. Murdick. "Manager's Guide to Forecasting," *Harvard Business Review* 64, 1 (January–February 1986): 110–120.

Granger, Clive W. and J. M. Hashem Pesaran. "Economic and Statistical Measures of Forecast Accuracy," *Journal of Forecasting*, 19, 7 (December 2000): 537–560.

Hanke, J. E., A. G. Reitsch, and D. W. Wichern. *Business Forecasting*, 7/e. Upper Saddle River, NJ: Prentice Hall, 2001.

Heizer, J., and B. Render. *Operations Management, 7/e*. Upper Saddle River, NJ: Prentice Hall, 2004.

Hueter, Jackie and William Swart. "An Integrated Labor-Management System for Taco Bell," *Interfaces* 28, 1 (January–February 1998): 75–91.

Li, X. "An Intelligent Business Forecaster for Strategic Business Planning," *Journal of Forecasting* 18, 3 (May 1999): 181–205.

Meade, Nigel. "Evidence for the Selection of Forecasting Methods," *Journal of Forecasting* 19, 6 (November 2000): 515–535.

Snyder, Ralph D. and Roland G. Shami. "Exponential Smoothing of Seasonal Data: A Comparison," *Journal of Forecasting* 20, 3 (April 2001): 197–202.

Yurkiewicz, J. "Forecasting Software Survey," *OR/MS Today*, 30, 1 (February 2003): 44–51.

APPENDIX 5.1: FORECASTING WITH QM FOR WINDOWS

In this section we look at our other forecasting software package, QM for Windows. QM for Windows can project moving averages (both simple and weighted), do simple and trend-adjusted exponential smoothing, handle least squares trend projection, and solve regression problems.

To illustrate QM for Windows, let's use the following data, shown earlier as Table 5.7.

YEAR	ELECTRICAL GENERATORS SOLD AT MIDWESTERN MANUFACTURING
1996	74
1997	79
1998	80
1999	90
2000	105
2001	142
2002	122

Program 5.7A shows the input for a three-year simple moving average analysis with QM for Windows. The method and the number of periods to average are selected by dragging your mouse or clicking on those respective screen areas. Output results, in Program 5.7B, include error terms as well as the ability to select a graph (through an icon on the bottom of the screen).

Similarly, Program 5.8 illustrates QM for Windows analysis of the same data using exponential smoothing with $\alpha = 0.3$. Program 5.9 illustrates the use of trend projection in QM for Windows and produces the model

$$\text{sales} = 56.71 + 10.54(\text{year})$$

If year = 8, the sales forecast is shown to be $56.71 + 10.54(8) = 141$ generators.

PROGRAM 5.7A

QM for Windows Input for Moving Averages

PROGRAM 5.7B

QM for Windows Output for Moving Averages

File Edit View Module Format Tools Window Help	
Method	#
Moving Averages ▼	

Window menu:
- Cascade
- Tile
- Edit data
- 1 Forecasting Results
- 2 Details and Error Analysis
- 3 Graph

Instruction: There are more results available in additional windows. These may be opened by using the WINDOW option in the Main Menu.

Select Window to see a graph and additional information.

Forecasting Results

Measure	
Error Measures	
Bias (Mean Error)	23.5833
MAD (Mean Absolute Deviation)	23.5833
MSE (Mean Squared Error)	815.7501
Standard Error (denom=n-2=2)	40.3918
Forecast	
next period	123.

The forecast for 2003 (the next time period) is 123.

PROGRAM 5.8

QM for Windows Output Using Exponential Smoothing and $\alpha = 0.3$ for Midwestern Manufacturing

QM for Windows - C:\Prentice\Data\RenderStair7\midwestern.FOR

| Method | Alpha for smoothing | | Note |
| Exponential Smoothing ▼ | ◄ ▶ | .3 | Error analysis begins in period 2. |

Forecasting Results

Midwestern Manufacturing Summary	
Measure	Value
Error Measures	
Bias (Mean Error)	19.7598
MAD (Mean Absolute Deviation)	19.7598
MSE (Mean Squared Error)	671.565
Standard Error (denom=n-2=4)	31.7387
Forecast	
next period	109.5677

Forecasting/Time series analysis   Solution Screen   Ernest Lisa Student

PROGRAM 5.9

QM for Windows Output Using Trend Analysis for Midwestern Manufacturing

QM for Windows - C:\Prentice\Data\RenderStair7\midwestern.FOR

| Method |
| Trend Analysis (regress over time) ▼ |

Forecasting Results

Midwestern Manufacturing Summary			
Measure	Value	Future Period	Forecast
Error Measures		8.	141.
Bias (Mean Error)	0.	9.	151.5357
MAD (Mean Absolute Deviation)	8.5816	10.	162.0714
MSE (Mean Squared Error)	110.4031	11.	172.6072
Standard Error (denom=n-2=5)	12.4324	12.	183.1429
Regression line		13.	193.6786
Demand(y) = 56.71427		14.	204.2143
+ 10.5357 * Time(x)		15.	214.75
Statistics		16.	225.2858
Correlation coefficient	0.8949	17.	235.8215
Coefficient of determination (r^2)	0.8009	18.	246.3572
		19.	256.8929
		20.	267.4286

INVENTORY CONTROL MODELS

After completing this chapter, students will be able to:

1. Understand the importance of inventory control and ABC analysis.

2. Use the economic order quantity (EOQ) to determine how much to order.

3. Compute the reorder point (ROP) in determining when to order more inventory.

4. Handle inventory problems that allow quantity discounts or noninstantaneous receipt.

5. Understand the use of safety stock with known and unknown stockout costs.

6. Describe the use of material requirements planning in solving dependent-demand inventory problems.

7. Discuss just-in-time inventory concepts to reduce inventory levels and costs.

8. Discuss enterprise resource planning systems.

Summary • CD-ROM Inventory Topics • Glossary • Key Equations • Solved Problems • Self-Test • Discussion Questions and Problems • Internet Homework Problems • Case Study: Sturdivant Sound Systems • Case Study: Martin-Pullin Bicycle Corporation • Internet Case Studies • Bibliography

Appendix 6.1: Inventory Control with QM for Windows

6.1 INTRODUCTION

Inventory is one of the most expensive and important assets to many companies, representing as much as 50% of total invested capital. Managers have long recognized that good inventory control is crucial. On one hand, a firm can try to reduce costs by reducing on-hand inventory levels. On the other hand, customers become dissatisfied when frequent inventory outages, called *stockouts*, occur. Thus, companies must make the balance between low and high inventory levels. As you would expect, cost minimization is the major factor in obtaining this delicate balance.

Inventory is any stored resource that is used to satisfy a current or future need.

Inventory is any stored resource that is used to satisfy a current or a future need. Raw materials, work-in-process, and finished goods are examples of inventory. Inventory levels for finished goods are a direct function of demand. When we determine the demand for completed clothes dryers, for example, it is possible to use this information to determine how much sheet metal, paint, electric motors, switches, and other raw materials and work-in-process are needed to produce the finished product.

All organizations have some type of inventory planning and control system. A bank has methods to control its inventory of cash. A hospital has methods to control blood supplies and other important items. State and federal governments, schools, and virtually every manufacturing and production organization are concerned with inventory planning and control. Studying how organizations control their inventory is equivalent to studying how they achieve their objectives by supplying goods and services to their customers. Inventory is the common thread that ties all the functions and departments of the organization together.

Figure 6.1 illustrates the basic components of an inventory planning and control system. The *planning* phase is concerned primarily with what inventory is to be stocked and how it is to be acquired (whether it is to be manufactured or purchased). This information is then used in *forecasting* demand for the inventory and in *controlling* inventory levels. The feedback loop in Figure 6.1 provides a way of revising the plan and forecast based on experiences and observation.

Through inventory planning, an organization determines what goods and/or services are to be produced. In cases of physical products, the organization must also determine whether to produce these goods or to purchase them from another manufacturer. When this has been determined, the next step is to forecast the demand. As discussed in Chapter 5, there are many mathematical techniques that can be used in forecasting demand for a particular product. The emphasis in this chapter is on inventory control, that is, how to maintain adequate inventory levels within an organization.

FIGURE 6.1

Inventory Planning and Control

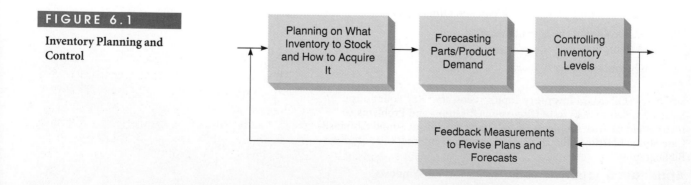

6.2 IMPORTANCE OF INVENTORY CONTROL

Inventory control serves several important functions and adds a great deal of flexibility to the operation of the firm. Consider the following five uses of inventory:

1. The decoupling function
2. Storing resources
3. Irregular supply and demand
4. Quantity discounts
5. Avoiding stockouts and shortages

Decoupling Function

One of the major functions of inventory is to decouple manufacturing processes within the organization. If you did not store inventory, there could be many delays and inefficiencies. For example, when one manufacturing activity has to be completed before a second activity can be started, it could stop the entire process. If, however, you have some stored inventory between processes, it could act as a buffer.

Inventory can act as a buffer.

Storing Resources

Agricultural and seafood products often have definite seasons over which they can be harvested or caught, but the demand for these products is somewhat constant during the year. In these and similar cases, inventory can be used to store these resources.

Resources can be stored in work-in-process.

In a manufacturing process, raw materials can be stored by themselves, in work-in-process, or in the finished product. Thus, if your company makes lawn mowers, you might obtain lawn mower tires from another manufacturer. If you have 400 finished lawn mowers and 300 tires in inventory, you actually have 1,900 tires stored in inventory. Three hundred tires are stored by themselves, and 1,600 (1,600 = 4 tires per lawn mower × 400 lawn mowers) tires are stored in the finished lawn mowers. In the same sense, *labor* can be stored in inventory. If you have 500 subassemblies and it takes 50 hours of labor to produce each assembly, you actually have 25,000 labor hours stored in inventory in the subassemblies. In general, any resource, physical or otherwise, can be stored in inventory.

Irregular Supply and Demand

When the supply or demand for an inventory item is irregular, storing certain amounts in inventory can be important. If the greatest demand for Diet-Delight beverage is during the summer, you will have to make sure that there is enough supply to meet this irregular demand. This might require that you produce more of the soft drink in the winter than is actually needed to meet the winter demand. The inventory levels of Diet-Delight will gradually build up over the winter, but this inventory will be needed in the summer. The same is true for irregular *supplies.*

Quantity Discounts

Another use of inventory is to take advantage of quantity discounts. Many suppliers offer discounts for large orders. For example, an electric jigsaw might normally cost $20 per unit. If you order 300 or more saws in one order, your supplier may lower the cost to $18.75. Purchasing in larger quantities can substantially reduce the cost of products. There are, however, some disadvantages of buying in larger quantities. You will have higher storage costs and higher costs due to spoilage, damaged stock, theft, insurance, and so on. Furthermore, by investing in more inventory, you will have less cash to invest elsewhere.

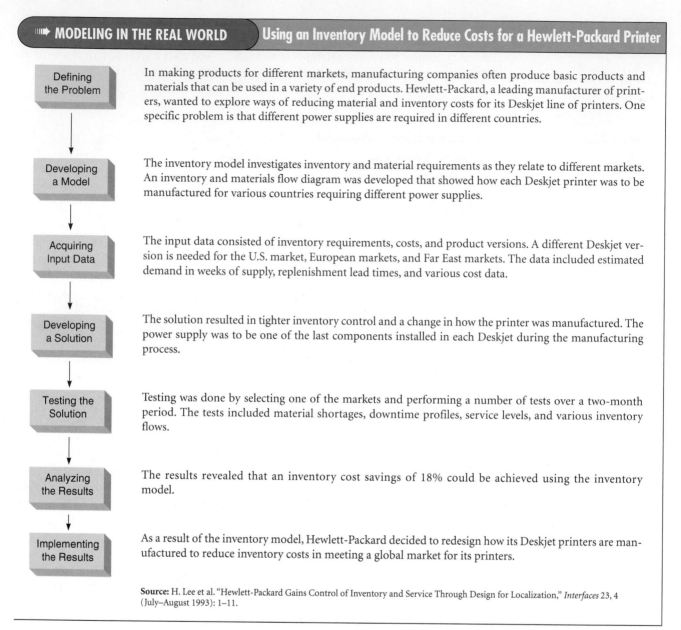

MODELING IN THE REAL WORLD   Using an Inventory Model to Reduce Costs for a Hewlett-Packard Printer

Defining the Problem

In making products for different markets, manufacturing companies often produce basic products and materials that can be used in a variety of end products. Hewlett-Packard, a leading manufacturer of printers, wanted to explore ways of reducing material and inventory costs for its Deskjet line of printers. One specific problem is that different power supplies are required in different countries.

Developing a Model

The inventory model investigates inventory and material requirements as they relate to different markets. An inventory and materials flow diagram was developed that showed how each Deskjet printer was to be manufactured for various countries requiring different power supplies.

Acquiring Input Data

The input data consisted of inventory requirements, costs, and product versions. A different Deskjet version is needed for the U.S. market, European markets, and Far East markets. The data included estimated demand in weeks of supply, replenishment lead times, and various cost data.

Developing a Solution

The solution resulted in tighter inventory control and a change in how the printer was manufactured. The power supply was to be one of the last components installed in each Deskjet during the manufacturing process.

Testing the Solution

Testing was done by selecting one of the markets and performing a number of tests over a two-month period. The tests included material shortages, downtime profiles, service levels, and various inventory flows.

Analyzing the Results

The results revealed that an inventory cost savings of 18% could be achieved using the inventory model.

Implementing the Results

As a result of the inventory model, Hewlett-Packard decided to redesign how its Deskjet printers are manufactured to reduce inventory costs in meeting a global market for its printers.

Source: H. Lee et al. "Hewlett-Packard Gains Control of Inventory and Service Through Design for Localization," *Interfaces* 23, 4 (July–August 1993): 1–11.

Avoiding Stockouts and Shortages

Another important function of inventory is to avoid shortages or stockouts. If you are repeatedly out of stock, customers are likely to go elsewhere to satisfy their needs. Lost goodwill can be an expensive price to pay for not having the right item at the right time.

6.3   INVENTORY DECISIONS

Even though there are literally millions of different types of products produced in our society, there are only two fundamental decisions that you have to make when controlling inventory:

1. How much to order
2. When to order

TABLE 6.1	Inventory Cost Factors
ORDERING COST FACTORS	**CARRYING COST FACTORS**
Developing and sending purchase orders	Cost of capital
Processing and inspecting incoming inventory	Taxes
Bill paying	Insurance
Inventory inquiries	Spoilage
Utilities, phone bills, and so on, for the purchasing department	Theft
Salaries and wages for purchasing department employees	Obsolescence
Supplies such as forms and paper for the purchasing department	Salaries and wages for warehouse employees
	Utilities and building costs for the warehouse
	Supplies such as forms and paper for the warehouse

A major objective of all inventory models is to minimize inventory costs.

The purpose of all inventory models and techniques is to determine rationally how much to order and when to order. As you know, inventory fulfills many important functions within an organization. But as the inventory levels go up to provide these functions, the cost of storing and holding inventory also increases. Thus, you must reach a fine balance in establishing inventory levels. A major objective in controlling inventory is to minimize total inventory costs. Some of the most significant inventory costs follow:

1. Cost of the items (purchase cost or material cost)
2. Cost of ordering
3. Cost of carrying, or holding, inventory
4. Cost of stockouts

The most common factors associated with ordering costs and holding costs are shown in Table 6.1. Notice that the ordering costs are generally independent of the size of the order, and many of these involve personnel time. An ordering cost is incurred each time an order is placed, whether the order is for 1 unit or 1,000 units. The time to process the paperwork, pay the bill, and so forth does not depend on the number of units ordered.

On the other hand, the holding cost varies as the size of the inventory varies. If 1,000 units are placed into inventory, the taxes, insurance, cost of capital, and other holding costs will be higher than if only 1 unit was put into inventory. Similarly, if the inventory level is low, there is little chance of spoilage and obsolescence.

The cost of the items, or the purchase cost, is what is paid to acquire the inventory. The stockout cost indicates the lost sales and goodwill (future sales) that result from not having the items available for the customers. This is discussed later in the chapter.

6.4 ECONOMIC ORDER QUANTITY: DETERMINING HOW MUCH TO ORDER

The *economic order quantity* (EOQ) is one of the oldest and most commonly known inventory control techniques. Research on its use dates back to a 1915 publication by Ford W. Harris. This technique is still used by a large number of organizations today. It is relatively easy to use, but it does make a number of assumptions. Some of the more important assumptions follow:

1. Demand is known and constant.
2. The lead time, that is, the time between the placement of the order and the receipt of the order, is known and constant.

IN ACTION Keeping Inventory Modeling Simple at Teradyne

Teradyne, a huge manufacturer of electronic testing equipment for semiconductor plants worldwide, recently asked Wharton Business School to evaluate its global inventory parts system. Teradyne's system is complex because it stocks over 10,000 parts of a wide variety in price (from a few dollars to $10,000), because its customers are dispersed all over the world, and because customers demand immediate response when a part is needed.

The professors considered a variety of very sophisticated inventory models that are beyond the scope of this textbook, but in the end, they selected two very basic models they felt could be used to improve the current inventory system. An important consideration in using basic models is their simplicity, which improved the professors' communication with Teradyne executives. In the field of modeling, it is very important for managers who depend on the models to thoroughly understand the underlying processes and the model's limitations.

Input data to the inventory models included actual planned inventory levels, holding costs, observed demand rates, and estimated lead times. The outputs included service levels and a prediction of the expected number of late part shipments. The first inventory model showed that Teradyne could reduce late shipments by over 90% with just a 3% increase in inventory investment. The second model showed that the company could reduce inventory by 37%, while improving customer service levels by 4%.

Source: M. A. Cohen, Y. Zheng, and Y. Wang. "Identifying Opportunities for Improving Teradyne's Service Parts Logistics System," *Interfaces* 29, 4 (July–August 1999): 1–18.

3. The receipt of inventory is instantaneous. In other words, the inventory from an order arrives in one batch, at one point in time.

4. Quantity discounts are not possible.

5. The only variable costs are the cost of placing an order, *ordering cost*, and the cost of holding or storing inventory over time, *holding* or *carrying cost*.

6. Orders are placed so that stockouts or shortages are avoided completely.

When these assumptions are *not* met, adjustments must be made to the EOQ model. These are discussed later in this chapter.

The inventory usage curve has a sawtooth shape.

With these assumptions, inventory usage has a sawtooth shape, as in Figure 6.2. In Figure 6.2, Q represents the amount that is ordered. If this amount is 500 dresses, all 500 dresses arrive at one time when an order is received. Thus, the inventory level jumps from 0 to 500 dresses. In general, an inventory level increases from 0 to Q units when an order arrives.

FIGURE 6.2

Inventory Usage over Time

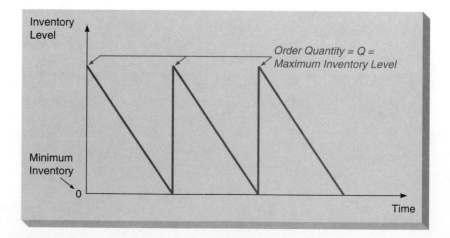

Because demand is constant over time, inventory drops at a uniform rate over time. (Refer to the sloped line in Figure 6.2.) Another order is placed such that when the inventory level reaches 0, the new order is received and the inventory level again jumps to Q units, represented by the vertical lines. This process continues indefinitely over time.

Inventory Costs in the EOQ Situation

The objective of the simple EOQ model is to minimize total inventory cost. The relevant costs are the ordering and holding costs.

The objective of most inventory models is to minimize the total costs. With the assumptions just given, the relevant costs are the ordering cost and the carrying, or holding cost. All other costs, such as the cost of the inventory itself (the purchase cost), are constant. Thus, if we minimize the sum of the ordering and carrying costs, we are also minimizing the total costs.

The annual ordering cost is simply the number of orders per year times the cost of placing each order. Since the inventory level changes daily, it is appropriate to use the average inventory level to determine annual holding or carrying cost. The annual carrying cost will equal the average inventory times the inventory carrying cost per unit per year. Again looking at Figure 6.2, we see that the maximum inventory is the order quantity (Q), and the average inventory will be one-half of that. Table 6.2 provides a numerical example to illustrate this. Notice that for this situation, if the order quantity is 10, the average inventory will be 5, or one-half of Q. Thus:

The average inventory level is one-half the maximum level.

$$\text{average inventory level} = \frac{Q}{2} \tag{6-1}$$

Using the following variables, we can develop mathematical expressions for the annual ordering and carrying costs:

$$Q = \text{number of pieces to order}$$

$$\text{EOQ} = Q^* = \text{optimal number of pieces to order}$$

$$D = \text{annual demand in units for the inventory item}$$

$$C_o = \text{ordering cost of each order}$$

$$C_h = \text{holding or carrying cost per unit per year}$$

TABLE 6.2

Computing Average Inventory

DAY	INVENTORY LEVEL		
	BEGINNING	ENDING	AVERAGE
April 1 (order received)	10	8	9
April 2	8	6	7
April 3	6	4	5
April 4	4	2	3
April 5	2	0	1

Maximum level April 1 = 10 units
Total of daily averages = 9 + 7 + 5 + 3 + 1 = 25
Number of days = 5
Average inventory level = 25/5 = 5 units

Total Cost as a Function of Order Quantity

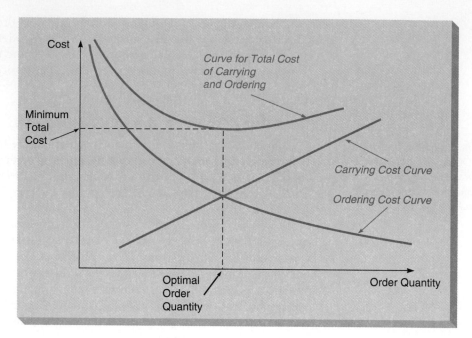

Annual ordering cost = (number of orders placed per year) × (ordering cost per order)

$$= \frac{\text{annual demand}}{\text{number of units in each order}} \times (\text{ordering cost per order})$$

$$= \frac{D}{Q} C_o$$

Annual holding or carrying cost = (average inventory) × (carrying cost per unit per year)

$$= \frac{\text{order quantity}}{2} \times (\text{carrying cost per unit per year})$$

$$= \frac{Q}{2} C_h$$

A graph of the holding cost, the ordering cost, and the total of these two is shown in Figure 6.3. The lowest point on the total cost curves occurs where the ordering cost is equal to the carrying cost. Thus, to minimize total costs given this situation, the order quantity should occur where these two costs are equal.

Finding the EOQ

We derive the EOQ equation by setting ordering cost equal to carrying cost.

When the EOQ assumptions are met, costs are minimized when annual ordering cost = annual holding cost:

$$\frac{D}{Q} C_o = \frac{Q}{2} C_h$$

Solving this for Q gives the optimal order quantity:

$$2DC_o = Q^2 C_h$$

$$\frac{2DC_o}{C_h} = Q^2$$

$$\sqrt{\frac{2DC_o}{C_h}} = Q$$

This optimal order quantity is often denoted by Q^*. Thus, the economic order quantity is given by the following formula:

$$EOQ = Q^* = \sqrt{\frac{2DC_o}{C_h}}$$

This EOQ is the basis for many more advanced models, and some of these are discussed later in this chapter.

Economic Order Quantity (EOQ) Model

$$\text{Annual ordering cost} = \frac{D}{Q} C_o \tag{6-2}$$

$$\text{Annual holding cost} = \frac{Q}{2} C_h \tag{6-3}$$

$$EOQ = Q^* = \sqrt{\frac{2DC_o}{C_h}} \tag{6-4}$$

Sumco Pump Company Example

Sumco, a company that sells pump housings to other manufacturers, would like to reduce its inventory cost by determining the optimal number of pump housings to obtain per order. The annual demand is 1,000 units, the ordering cost is $10 per order, and the average carrying cost per unit per year is $0.50. Using these figures, if the EOQ assumptions are met, we can calculate the optimal number of units per order:

$$Q^* = \sqrt{\frac{2DC_o}{C_h}}$$

$$= \sqrt{\frac{2(1,000)(10)}{0.50}}$$

$$= \sqrt{40,000}$$

$$= 200 \text{ units}$$

The relevant total annual inventory cost is the sum of the ordering costs and the carrying costs.

$$\text{total annual cost} = \text{order cost} + \text{holding cost}$$

The total annual inventory cost is equal to ordering plus holding costs for the simple EOQ model.

In terms of the variables in the model, the total cost (TC) can now be expressed as

$$TC = \frac{D}{Q} C_o + \frac{Q}{2} C_h \tag{6-5}$$

PROGRAM 6.1A

Input Data and Excel QM Formulas for the Sumco Pump Company Example

	Microsoft Excel - formulas.xls

File Edit View Insert Format Tools Data QM Window Help

	A	B	C	D	E	F
1	**Sumco Pump Company**					
2						
3	Inventory	Economic Order Quantity Model				
4	Enter the data in the shaded area					
5						
6						
7	Data					
8	Demand rate, D	1000				
9	Setup cost, S	10				
10	Holding cost, H	0.5 (fixed amount)				
11	Unit Price, P	0				
12						
13	Results					
14	Optimal Order Quantity, Q*	=SQRT(2*B8*B9/B10)				
15	Maximum Inventory	=B14				
16	Average Inventory	=B14/2				
17	Number of Setups	=B8/B14				
18						
19	Holding cost	=B16*B10				
20	Setup cost	=B17*B9				
21						
22	Unit costs	=B11*B8				
23	Total cost, T_c	=B19+B20+B22				

Callouts: Enter demand rate, setup cost, holding cost, and unit price. — No unit price is entered in this example, but if available, it should be. — Compute optimal order quantity, maximum inventory, average inventory, and number of setups. — Compute total holding, setup, and unit cost. — Compute total costs.

The total annual inventory cost for Sumco is computed as follows:

$$TC = \frac{D}{Q} C_o + \frac{Q}{2} C_h$$

$$= \frac{1,000}{200}(10) + \frac{200}{2}(0.5)$$

$$= \$50 + \$50 = \$100$$

The number of orders per year (D/Q) is 5, and the average inventory ($Q/2$) is 100.

As you might expect, the ordering cost is equal to the carrying cost. You may wish to try different values for Q, such as 100 or 300 pumps. You will find that the minimum total cost occurs when Q is 200 units. The EOQ, Q^*, is 200 pumps.

Using Excel QM for Basic EOQ Inventory Problems The Sumco Pump Company example, and a variety of other inventory problems we address in this chapter, can be easily solved using Excel QM. Program 6.1A shows the input data for Sumco and the Excel formulas needed for the EOQ model. Program 6.1B contains the solution for this example, including the optimal order quantity, maximum inventory level, average inventory level, and the number of setups or orders.

Purchase Cost of Inventory Items

Sometimes the total inventory cost expression is written to include the actual cost of the material purchased. With the EOQ assumptions, the purchase cost does not depend on the particular order policy found to be optimal, because regardless of how many orders are

PROGRAM 6.1B

Excel QM Solution for the Sumco Pump Company Example

	A	B	C	D	E	F	G	H
1	**Sumco Pump Company**							
2								
3	Inventory	Economic Order Quantity Model						
4	Enter the data in the shaded area							
5								
6								
7	Data							
8	Demand rate, D	1000						
9	Setup cost, S	10						
10	Holding cost, H	0.5	(fixed amount)					
11	Unit Price, P	0						
12								
13	Results							
14	Optimal Order Quantity, Q*	200						
15	Maximum Inventory	200						
16	Average Inventory	100						
17	Number of Setups	5						
18								
19	Holding cost	$50.00						
20	Setup cost	$50.00						
21								
22	Unit costs	$0.00						
23	Total cost, T_c	$100.00						

placed each year, we still incur the same annual purchase cost of $D \times C$, where C is the purchase cost per unit and D is the annual demand in units.[1]

It is useful to know how to calculate the average inventory level in dollar terms when the price per unit is given. This can be done as follows. With the variable Q representing the quantity of units ordered, and assuming a unit cost of C, we can determine the average dollar value of inventory:

$$\text{average dollar level} = \frac{(CQ)}{2} \tag{6-6}$$

This formula is analogous to Equation 6-1.

Inventory carrying costs for many businesses and industries are also often expressed as an annual percentage of the unit cost or price. When this is the case, a new variable is introduced. Let I be the annual inventory holding charge as a percent of unit price or cost. Then the cost of storing one unit of inventory for the year, C_h, is given by $C_h = IC$, where C is the unit price or cost of an inventory item. Q^* can be expressed, in this case, as

I is the annual carrying cost as a percentage of the cost per unit.

$$Q^* = \sqrt{\frac{2DC_o}{IC}} \tag{6-7}$$

Sensitivity Analysis with the EOQ Model

The EOQ model assumes that all input values are fixed and known with certainty. However, since these values are often estimated or may change over time, it is important to understand how the order quantity might change if different input values are used. Determining the effects of these changes is called *sensitivity analysis*.

---

[1] Later in this chapter, we discuss the case in which price can affect order policy, that is, when quantity discounts are offered.

The EOQ formula is given as follows:

$$EOQ = \sqrt{\frac{2DC_o}{C_h}}$$

Because of the square root in the formula, any changes in the inputs (D, C_o, C_h) will result in relatively minor changes in the optimal order quantity. For example, if C_o were to increase by a factor of 4, the EOQ would only increase by a factor of 2. Consider the Sumco example just presented. The EOQ for this company is as follows:

$$EOQ = \sqrt{\frac{2(1,000)(10)}{0.50}} = 200$$

If we increased C_o from \$10 to \$40,

$$EOQ = \sqrt{\frac{2(1,000)(40)}{0.50}} = 400$$

In general, the EOQ changes by the square root of a change in any of the inputs.

6.5 REORDER POINT: DETERMINING WHEN TO ORDER

Now that we have decided how much to order, we look at the second inventory question: when to order. The time between the placing and receipt of an order, called the lead time or delivery time, is often a few days or even a few weeks. Inventory must be available to meet the demand during this time. Thus, the *when to order* decision is usually expressed in terms of a *reorder point* (ROP), the inventory level at which an order should be placed. The ROP is given as

The reorder point (ROP) determines when to order inventory. It is found by multiplying the daily demand times the lead time in days.

$$ROP = (\text{demand per day}) \times (\text{lead time for a new order in days})$$
$$= d \times L \tag{6-8}$$

Figure 6.4 shows the ROP graphically. The slope of the graph is the daily inventory usage. This is expressed in units demanded per day, d. The *lead time, L,* is the time that it takes to

FIGURE 6.4

Reorder Point Curve

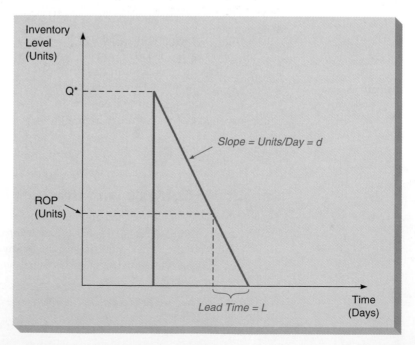

receive an order. Thus, if an order is placed when the inventory level reaches the ROP, the new inventory arrives at the same instant the inventory is reaching 0. Let's take a look at an example.

Procomp's Computer Chip Example Procomp's demand for computer chips is 8,000 per year. The firm has a daily demand of 40 units. Delivery of an order takes three working days. The reorder point for chips is calculated as follows:

$$\text{ROP} = d \times L = 40 \text{ units per day} \times 3 \text{ days}$$

$$= 120 \text{ units}$$

Hence, when the inventory stock of chips drops to 120, an order should be placed. The order will arrive three days later, just as the firm's stock is depleted to 0. It should be mentioned that this calculation assumes that all of the assumptions listed previously are correct. When demand is not known with complete certainty, these calculations have to be modified. This is discussed later in this chapter.

6.6 EOQ WITHOUT THE INSTANTANEOUS RECEIPT ASSUMPTION

When a firm receives its inventory over a period of time, a new model is needed that does not require the *instantaneous inventory receipt* assumption. This new model is applicable when inventory continuously flows or builds up over a period of time after an order has been placed or when units are produced and sold simultaneously. Under these circumstances, the daily demand rate must be taken into account. Figure 6.5 shows inventory levels as a function of time. Because this model is especially suited to the production environment, it is commonly called the *production run model*.

The production run model eliminates the instantaneous receipt assumption.

In the production process, instead of having an ordering cost, there will be a *setup cost*. This is the cost of setting up the production facility to manufacture the desired product. It normally includes the salaries and wages of employees who are responsible for setting up the equipment, engineering and design costs of making the setup, paperwork, supplies, utilities, and so on. The carrying cost per unit is composed of the same factors as the traditional EOQ model, although the annual carrying cost equation changes due to a change in average inventory.

Solving the production run model involves setting setup costs equal to holding costs and solving for Q.

The optimal production quantity can be derived by setting setup costs equal to holding or carrying costs and solving for the order quantity. Let's start by developing the expression for carrying cost. You should note, however, that making setup cost equal to carrying cost does not always guarantee optimal solutions for models more complex than the production run model.

FIGURE 6.5

Inventory Control and the Production Process

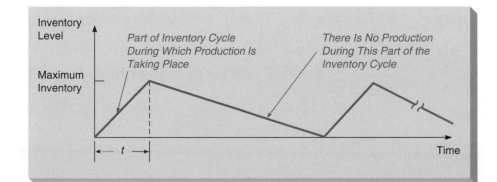

Annual Carrying Cost for Production Run Model

As with the EOQ model, the carrying costs of the production run model are based on the average inventory, and the average inventory is one-half the maximum inventory level. However, since the replenishment of inventory occurs over a period of time and demand continues during this time, the maximum inventory will be less than the order quantity Q. We can develop the annual carrying, or holding, cost expression using the following variables:

$$Q = \text{number of pieces per order, or production run}$$

$$C_s = \text{setup cost}$$

$$C_h = \text{holding or carrying cost per unit per year}$$

$$p = \text{daily production rate}$$

$$d = \text{daily demand rate}$$

$$t = \text{length of production run in days}$$

The maximum inventory level is as follows:

(total produced during the production run) − (total used during production run)

$$= (\text{daily production rate})(\text{number of days of production})$$
$$- (\text{daily demand})(\text{number of days of production})$$

$$= (pt) - (dt)$$

Since

$$\text{total produced} = Q = pt,$$

we know that

$$t = \frac{Q}{p}$$

$$\text{Maximum inventory level} = pt - dt = p\frac{Q}{p} - d\frac{Q}{p} = Q\left(1 - \frac{d}{p}\right)$$

Since the average inventory is one-half of the maximum, we have

$$\text{average inventory} = \frac{Q}{2}\left(1 - \frac{d}{p}\right) \tag{6-9}$$

and

$$\text{annual holding cost} = \frac{Q}{2}\left(1 - \frac{d}{p}\right)C_h \tag{6-10}$$

Annual Setup Cost of Annual Ordering Cost

When a product is produced over time, setup cost replaces ordering cost. Both of these are independent of the size of the order and the size of the production run. This cost is simply the number of orders (or production runs) times the ordering cost (setup cost). Thus,

$$\text{annual setup cost} = \frac{D}{Q}C_s \tag{6-11}$$

and

$$\text{annual ordering cost} = \frac{D}{Q}C_o \tag{6-12}$$

Determining the Optimal Production Quantity

When the assumptions of the production run model are met, costs are minimized when the setup cost equals the holding cost. We can find the optimal quantity by setting these costs equal and solving for Q. Thus,

$$\text{annual holding cost} = \text{annual setup cost}$$

$$\frac{Q}{2}\left(1 - \frac{d}{p}\right)C_h = \frac{D}{Q}C_s$$

Here is the formula for the optimal production quantity. Notice the similarity to the basic EOQ model.

Solving this for Q, we get the optimal production quantity (Q^*):

$$Q^* = \sqrt{\frac{2DC_s}{C_h\left(1 - \dfrac{d}{p}\right)}} \tag{6-13}$$

It should be noted that if the situation does not involve production but rather involves the receipt of inventory over a period of time, this same model is appropriate, but C_o replaces C_s in the formula.

Production Run Model

$$\text{Annual holding cost} = \frac{Q}{2}\left(1 - \frac{d}{p}\right)C_h$$

$$\text{Annual setup cost} = \frac{D}{Q}C_s$$

$$\text{Optimal production quantity } Q^* = \sqrt{\frac{2DC_s}{C_h\left(1 - \dfrac{d}{p}\right)}}$$

Brown Manufacturing

Brown Manufacturing produces commercial refrigeration units in batches. The firm's estimated demand for the year is 10,000 units. It costs about $100 to set up the manufacturing process, and the carrying cost is about 50 cents per unit per year. When the production process has been set up, 80 refrigeration units can be manufactured daily. The demand during the production period has traditionally been 60 units each day. Brown operates its refrigeration unit production area 167 days per year. How many refrigeration units should Brown Manufacturing produce in each batch? How long should the production part of the cycle shown in Figure 6.5 last? Here is the solution:

$$\text{Annual demand} = D = 10,000 \text{ units}$$

$$\text{Setup cost} = C_s = \$100$$

$$\text{Carrying cost} = C_h = \$0.50 \text{ per unit per year}$$

$$\text{Daily production rate} = p = 80 \text{ units daily}$$

$$\text{Daily demand rate} = d = 60 \text{ units daily}$$

$$1. \quad Q^* = \sqrt{\frac{2DC_s}{C_h\left(1 - \dfrac{d}{p}\right)}}$$

$$2. \quad Q^* = \sqrt{\frac{2 \times 10,000 \times 100}{0.5\left(1 - \dfrac{60}{80}\right)}}$$

$$= \sqrt{\frac{2,000,000}{0.5\left(\frac{1}{4}\right)}} = \sqrt{16,000,000}$$

$$= 4,000 \text{ units}$$

If $Q^* = 4,000$ units and we know that 80 units can be produced daily, the length of each production cycle will be $Q/p = 4,000/80 = 50$ days. Thus, when Brown decides to produce refrigeration units, the equipment will be set up to manufacture the units for a 50-day time span.

Using Excel QM for Production Run Models The Brown Manufacturing production run model can also be solved using Excel QM. Program 6.2A contains the input data and the Excel formulas for this problem. Program 6.2B provides the solution results, including the optimal production quantity, maximum inventory level, average inventory level, and the number of setups.

IN ACTION   Implementing Speed and Quality in the Production Run at Milton Bradley

Milton Bradley, a division of Hasbro, Inc., has been manufacturing toys for more than 100 years. Founded by Milton Bradley in 1860, the company started by making a lithograph of Abraham Lincoln. Using his printing skills, Bradley developed games, including the Checkered Game of Life, the Game of Life, Chutes and Ladders, Candy Land, Scrabble, and Lite Brite. Today, the company produces hundreds of games, requiring billions of plastic parts.

When Milton Bradley has determined the optimal quantities for its production run, it must implement these quantities. Some games require literally hundreds of plastic parts, including spinners, hotels, people, animals, cars, and so on. Getting the correct number of parts into each toy is critical. According to Garry Brennan, director of manufacturing at Hasbro, getting the right number of pieces to the right production line is the most important issue for the credibility of the company. Some companies, including Wal-Mart, can require 20,000 or more perfectly assembled games delivered to their warehouses and stores in a matter of days.

Not getting the correct number of parts or pieces is very frustrating for customers. It can also be time consuming, expensive, and frustrating for Milton Bradley to supply the extra parts or get returned toys and games. If shortages are found during the assembly stage, the entire production run can be stopped until the problem is corrected. Counting parts by hand or machine was problematic and not always accurate. As a result, Milton Bradley decided to weigh the pieces and complete games to determine if the correct number of parts have been included. If the weight is not exactly correct, there is a problem that needs to be resolved before the game or toy is packaged and shipped. Using highly accurate digital scales, Milton Bradley has been able to get the right parts to the right production line at the right time. Without this simple implementation approach, the most sophisticated production run results would be meaningless.

Source: Doug Smock. "Games Tip the Scale at Milton Bradley," *Plastics World* (March 1997): 22–26.

PROGRAM 6.2A   **Excel QM Formulas and Input Data for the Brown Manufacturing Problem**

X Microsoft Excel - formulas.xls

File Edit View Insert Format Tools Data QM Window Help

	A	B	C	D	F
1	**Brown Manufacturing**				
2					
3	Inventory	Production Order Quantity Model			
4	Enter the data in the shaded area. You may have to do some work to enter the daily				
5					
6	Data				
7	Demand rate, D	10000			
8	Setup cost, S	100			
9	Holding cost, H	0.5	(fixed amount)		
10	Daily production rate, p	80			
11	Daily demand rate, d	60			
12	Unit price, P	0			
13					
14	**Results**				
15	Optimal production quantity, Q*	=SQRT(2*B7*B8/B9)*SQRT(B10/(B10-B11))			
16	Maximum Inventory	=B15*(B10-B11)/B10			
17	Average Inventory	=B16/2			
18	Number of Setups	=B7/B15			
19					
20	Holding cost	=B17*B9			
21	Setup cost	=B18*B8			
22					
23	Unit costs	=B12*B7			
24					
25	Total cost, T$_o$	=B20+B21+B23			

Callouts:
- Enter the demand rate, setup cost, and holding cost. Notice that the holding cost is a fixed dollar amount rather than a percentage of the unit price.
- Enter daily production rate and daily demand rate.
- Calculate the optimal production quantity.
- Calculate the maximum inventory.
- Calculate the average number of setups.
- Calculate the annual holding costs based on average inventory and the annual setup cost based on the number of setups.

PROGRAM 6.2B

The Solution Results for the Brown Manufacturing Problem Using Excel QM

X Microsoft Excel - captures.xls

File Edit View Insert Format Tools Data Accounting QM Window Help

	A	B	C	D	E	F	G	H
1	**Brown Manufacturing**							
2								
3	Inventory	Production Order Quantity Model						
4	Enter the data in the shaded area. You may have to do some work to enter the daily production rate.							
5								
6	Data							
7	Demand rate, D	10000						
8	Setup cost, S	100						
9	Holding cost, H	0.5	(fixed amount)					
10	Daily production rate, p	80						
11	Daily demand rate, d	60						
12	Unit price, P	0						
13								
14	**Results**							
15	Optimal production quantity, Q*	4000						
16	Maximum Inventory	1000						
17	Average Inventory	500						
18	Number of Setups	2.5						
19								
20	Holding cost	250						
21	Setup cost	250						
22								
23	Unit costs	0						
24								
25	Total cost, T$_o$	500						

Chart: Inventory: Cost vs Quantity

Cost ($) vs Order Quantity (Q), with y-axis 0 to 1200, x-axis values 1000, 2667, 4333, 6000, 7667.

Legend: Setup cost, Holding cost, Total cost

6.7   QUANTITY DISCOUNT MODELS

In developing the EOQ model, we assumed that quantity discounts were not available. However, many companies do offer quantity discounts. If such a discount is possible, but all of the other EOQ assumptions are met, it is possible to find the quantity that minimizes the total inventory cost by using the EOQ model and making some adjustments.

When quantity discounts are available, the material cost becomes a relevant cost, as it changes based on the order quantity. The total relevant costs are as follows:

$$\text{total cost} = \text{material cost} + \text{ordering cost} + \text{carrying cost}$$

$$\text{total cost} = DC + \frac{D}{Q}C_o + \frac{Q}{2}C_h \tag{6-14}$$

where

$$D = \text{annual demand in units}$$

$$C_o = \text{ordering cost of each order}$$

$$C = \text{cost per unit}$$

$$C_h = \text{holding or carrying cost per unit per year}$$

Since holding cost per unit per year is based on the cost of the items, it is convenient to express this as

$$C_h = IC$$

where

$$I = \text{holding cost as a percentage of the unit cost } (C)$$

For a specific purchase cost (C), given the assumptions we have made, ordering the EOQ will minimize total inventory costs. However, in the discount situation, this quantity may not be large enough to qualify for the discount, so we must also consider ordering this minimum quantity for the discount. A typical quantity discount schedule is shown in Table 6.3.

As can be seen in the table, the normal cost for the item is $5. When 1,000 to 1,999 units are ordered at one time, the cost per unit drops to $4.80, and when the quantity ordered at one time is 2,000 units or more, the cost is $4.75 per unit. As always, management must decide when and how much to order. But with quantity discounts, how does the manager make these decisions?

The overall objective of the quantity discount model is to minimize total inventory costs, which now include actual material costs.

As with other inventory models discussed so far, the overall objective will be to minimize the total cost. Because the unit cost for the third discount in Table 6.3 is lowest, you might be tempted to order 2,000 units or more to take advantage of the lower material cost. Placing an order for that quantity with the greatest discount cost, however, might not min-

TABLE 6.3			
Quantity Discount Schedule	DISCOUNT NUMBER	DISCOUNT QUANTITY	DISCOUNT (%)	DISCOUNT COST ($)
	1	0 to 999	0	5.00
	2	1,000 to 1,999	4	4.80
	3	2,000 and over	5	4.75

imize the total inventory cost. As the discount quantity goes up, the material cost goes down, but the carrying cost increases because the orders are large. Thus, the major trade-off when considering quantity discounts is between the reduced material cost and the increased carrying cost.

Figure 6.6 provides a graphical representation of the total cost for this situation. Notice the cost curve drops considerably when the order quantity reaches the minimum for each discount. With the specific costs in this example, we see that the EOQ for the second price category $(1,000 \leq Q \leq 1,999)$ is less than 1,000 units. Although the total cost for this EOQ is less than the total cost for the EOQ with the cost in category 1, the EOQ is not large enough to obtain this discount. Therefore, the lowest possible total cost for this discount price occurs at the minimum quantity required to obtain the discount $(Q = 1,000)$. The process for determining the minimum cost quantity in this situation is summarized in the following box.

Quantity Discount Model

1. For each discount price (C), compute $EOQ = \sqrt{\dfrac{2DC_o}{IC}}$.

2. If EOQ < minimum for discount, adjust the quantity to Q = minimum for discount.

3. For each EOQ or adjusted Q, compute total cost $= DC + \dfrac{D}{Q}C_o + \dfrac{Q}{2}C_h$.

4. Choose the lowest cost quantity.

Brass Department Store Example Let's see how this procedure can be applied by showing an example. Brass Department Store stocks toy race cars. Recently, the store was given a quantity discount schedule for the cars; this quantity discount schedule is shown in

FIGURE 6.6

Total Cost Curve for the Quantity Discount Model

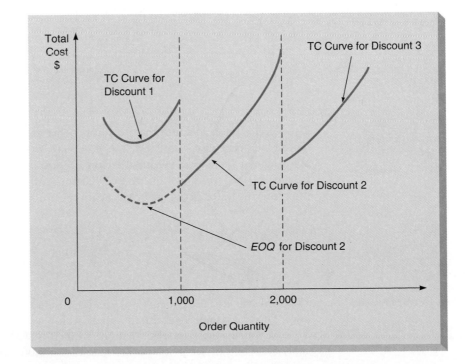

Table 6.3. Thus, the normal cost for the toy race cars is $5. For orders between 1,000 and 1,999 units, the unit cost is $4.80, and for orders of 2,000 or more units, the unit cost is $4.75. Furthermore, the ordering cost is $49 per order, the annual demand is 5,000 race cars, and the inventory carrying charge as a percentage of cost, I, is 20% or 0.2. What order quantity will minimize the total inventory cost?

The first step is to compute EOQ for every discount in Table 6.3. This is done as follows:

$$EOQ_1 = \sqrt{\frac{(2)(5,000)(49)}{(0.2)(5.00)}} = 700 \text{ cars per order}$$

EOQ values are computed.

$$EOQ_2 = \sqrt{\frac{(2)(5,000)(49)}{(0.2)(4.80)}} = 714 \text{ cars per order}$$

$$EOQ_3 = \sqrt{\frac{(2)(5,000)(49)}{(0.2)(4.75)}} = 718 \text{ cars per order}$$

EOQ values are adjusted.

The second step is to adjust those quantities that are below the allowable discount range. Since EOQ_1 is between 0 and 999, it does not have to be adjusted. EOQ_2 is below the allowable range of 1,000 to 1,999, and therefore, it must be adjusted to 1,000 units. The same is true for EOQ_3; it must be adjusted to 2,000 units. After this step, the following order quantities must be tested in the total cost equation:

$$Q_1 = 700$$
$$Q_2 = 1,000$$
$$Q_3 = 2,000$$

The total cost is computed.

The third step is to use Equation 6-14 and compute a total cost for each of the order quantities. This is accomplished with the aid of Table 6.4.

The fourth step is to select that order quantity with the lowest total cost. Looking at Table 6.4, you can see that an order quantity of 1,000 toy race cars minimizes the total

| TABLE 6.4 | | | Total Cost Computations for Brass Department Store | | | |

DISCOUNT NUMBER	UNIT PRICE (C)	ORDER QUANTITY (Q)	ANNUAL MATERIAL COST ($) = DC	ANNUAL ORDERING COST ($) = $\frac{D}{Q}C_o$	ANNUAL CARRYING COST ($) = $\frac{Q}{2}C_h$	TOTAL ($)
1	$5.00	700	25,000	350.00	350.00	25,700.00
2	4.80	1,000	24,000	245.00	480.00	24,725.00
3	4.75	2,000	23,750	122.50	950.00	24,822.50

Q* is selected.

cost. It should be recognized, however, that the total cost for ordering 2,000 cars is only slightly greater than the total cost for ordering 1,000 cars. Thus, if the third discount cost is lowered to $4.65, for example, this order quantity might be the one that minimizes the total inventory cost.

Using Excel QM for Quantity Discount Problems As seen in the previous analysis, the quantity discount model is more complex than the inventory models discussed so far in this chapter. Fortunately, we can use the computer to simplify the calculations. Program 6.3A shows the Excel formulas and input data needed for Excel QM for the Brass Department Store problem. Program 6.3B provides the solution to this problem, including adjusted order quantities and total costs for each price break.

| PROGRAM 6.3A | Excel QM's Formulas and the Input Data for the Brass Department Store Quantity Discount Problem |

PROGRAM 6.3B

Excel QM's Solution to the Brass Department Store Problem

Microsoft Excel - captures.xls

File Edit View Insert Format Tools Data Window Help

Brass Department Store

	A	B	C	D	E	F	G	H
3	Inventory	Quantity Discount Model						
5	Data							
6	Demand rate, D	5000						
7	Setup cost, S	49						
8	Holding cost %, I	20%						
10		Range 1	Range 2	Range 3				
11	Minimum quantity	0	1000	2000				
12	Unit Price, P	5	4.8	4.75				
14	Results							
15		Range 1	Range 2	Range 3				
16	Q* (Square root formula)	700	714.434508	718.184846				
17	Order Quantity	700	1000	2000	=			
19	Holding cost	$350.00	$480.00	$950.00				
20	Setup cost	$350.00	$245.00	$122.50				
22	Unit costs	$25,000.00	$24,000.00	$23,750.00				
24	Total cost, T_o	$25,700.00	$24,725.00	$24,822.50	minimum	$24,725.00		
25	Optimal Order Quantity		1000					

6.8   USE OF SAFETY STOCK

Safety stock helps in avoiding stockouts. It is extra stock kept on hand.

When the EOQ assumptions are met, it is possible to schedule orders to arrive so that stockouts are completely avoided. However, if the demand or the lead time is uncertain, the exact demand during the lead time (which is the ROP in the EOQ situation) will not be known with certainty. Therefore, to prevent stockouts, it is necessary to carry additional inventory called *safety stock*.

When demand is unusually high during the lead time, you dip into the safety stock instead of encountering a *stockout*. Thus, the main purpose of safety stock is to avoid stockouts when the demand is higher than expected. Its use is shown in Figure 6.7. Note that although stockouts can often be avoided by using safety stock, there is still a chance that they may occur. The demand may be so high that all the safety stock is used up, and thus there is still a stockout.

One of the best ways to implement a safety stock policy is to adjust the ROP. This can be accomplished by adding the number of units of safety stock as a buffer to the ROP. As you recall, when demand and lead time are constant,

$$ROP = d \times L$$

$$d = \text{daily demand (or average daily demand)}$$

$$L = \text{order lead time or the number of working days it takes to deliver an order (or average lead time)}$$

Safety stock is included in the ROP.

When demand during the lead time is uncertain and safety stock is necessary, the ROP becomes

$$ROP = d \times L + SS \qquad (6\text{-}15)$$

where

$$SS = \text{safety stock}$$

FIGURE 6.7

Use of Safety Stock

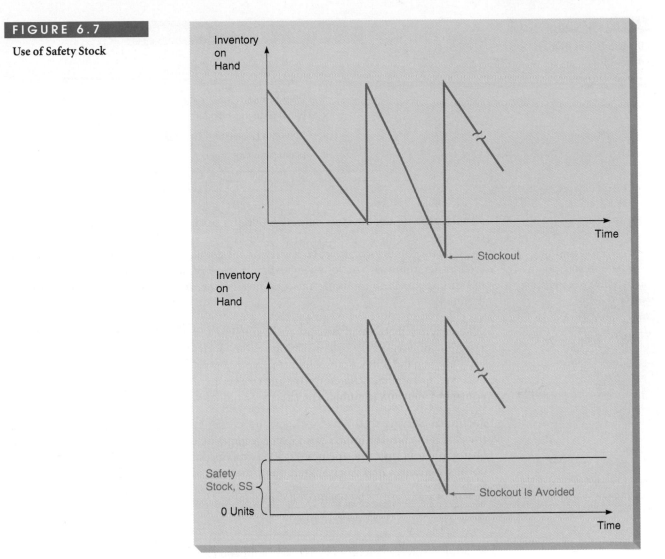

How to determine the correct amount of safety stock is the only remaining question. If cost data are available, the objective is to minimize total cost, which includes the stockout cost. If cost data are not available, it is necessary to establish a service level or policy.

ROP with Known Stockout Costs

When the EOQ is fixed and the ROP is used to place orders, the only time that a stockout can occur is during the lead time. As you recall, the lead time is the time between when the order is placed and when it is received.

It is necessary to know the probability of demand.

We use a stockout cost per unit.

The objective is to find the safety stock quantity that will minimize the total of the expected stockout cost plus the expected holding cost. To compute these costs, it is necessary to know the stockout cost per unit as well as the probability distribution describing the demand during the lead time. The stockout cost should normally include the lost sales resulting from customers being unable to purchase the item due to the current stockout, as well as the loss of future sales due to loss of goodwill. If too many stockouts occur, customers will eventually go to the competition first. In general, stockout costs should include

TABLE 6.5	NUMBER OF UNITS	PROBABILITY
Probability of Demand for ABCO, Inc.	30	0.2
	40	0.2
ROP ⟶	50	0.3
	60	0.2
	70	0.1
		1.0

all costs that are the direct or indirect result of a stockout. Estimating this value is sometimes very difficult.

The probability distribution describing the demand over the lead time could be discrete or continuous. The following example provides an illustration of how we might use this approach to minimize the total inventory costs with a discrete probability distribution.

The objective is minimizing total cost.

ABCO Example ABCO, Inc., has determined that its ROP is 50 ($= d \times L$) units. Its carrying cost per unit per year is $5 and stockout cost is $40 per unit. ABCO has experienced the probability distribution for inventory demand during the reorder period shown in Table 6.5. The optimal number of orders per year is 6.[2]

The objective of ABCO is to find the ROP, including safety stock, that will minimize total expected cost. Total expected cost is the sum of expected stockout cost plus expected additional carrying cost. When we know the stockout cost and the probability of demand over the lead time, the inventory problem becomes a decision making under risk problem. (Refer to Chapter 3 for a discussion of decision making under risk.) For ABCO, the alternatives are to use an ROP of 30 (alternative 1), 40 (alternative 2), 50 (alternative 3), 60 (alternative 4), or 70 units (alternative 5). The states of nature are demand values 30 (state of nature 1), 40 (state of nature 2), 50 (state of nature 3), 60 (state of nature 4), or 70 units (state of nature 5) over the lead time.

Determining the economic consequences for any alternative and state of nature combination involves a careful analysis of stockout and additional carrying cost. Consider a situation where the reorder point is 30 units. This means that we will place an order for additional units when the inventory on hand reaches 30 units. If the demand over lead time is also 30 units, there will be no stockouts and no extra units on hand when the new order arrives. Thus, stockouts and additional carrying costs will be 0. When the ROP equals the demand over lead time, total cost will be 0.

Stockout and additional carrying costs will be zero when ROP = demand over lead time.

Consider what happens when the ROP is 30 units but the demand is 40 units. In this case we will be 10 units short. The cost of this stockout situation is $2,400 ($2,400 = 10 units short × $40 per stockout × 6 orders per year). Note that we have to multiply the stockout cost per unit and the number of units short times the number of orders per year (6 in this case) to determine *annual* expected stockout cost. If the reorder point is 30 units and the demand over lead time is 50 units, the stockout cost will be $4,800 ($4,800 = 20 units short × $40 × 6). When the demand over lead time is 60 units, the stockout cost will be $7,200, and it will be $9,600 when demand over lead time is 70

[2] We have assumed that we already know Q^* and ROP. If this assumption is not made, the values of Q^*, ROP, and safety stock would have to be determined simultaneously. This requires a more complex solution.

TABLE 6.6

ABCO's Stockout Costs: The Economic Consequences of Every Alternative and State of Nature

PROBABILITY	0.20	0.20	0.30	0.20	0.10	
STATE OF NATURE	DEMAND DURING LEAD TIME					
ALTERNATIVE	30	40	50	60	70	EMV
ROP 30	$ 0	$2,400	$4,800	$7,200	$9,600	$4,320
40	50	0	2,400	4,800	7,200	$2,410
50	100	50	0	2,400	4,800	$990
60	150	100	50	0	2,400	$305
70	200	150	100	50	0	$110

units. In general, when the ROP is less than demand over lead time, total cost is equal to stockout cost.

> Total cost = stockout cost = number of units short × stockout cost per unit
> × number of orders per year (when the ROP *is less than* demand over lead time)

Now consider a reorder point of 70 units. As before, if demand over lead time is also 70, the total cost is 0. If the demand over lead time is 60 units, we will have 10 additional units on hand when the new inventory is received. If this situation continues during the year, we will have 10 additional units on hand on average. The additional carrying cost is $50 ($50 = 10 additional units × $5 carrying cost per unit per year). If the demand over lead time is 50 units, we will have 20 additional units on hand when the new inventory arrives (20 = 70 − 50). If this situation continues during the year, the additional carrying cost will be $100 ($100 = 20 additional units × $5 per unit per year). When the ROP is greater than the demand over lead time, total costs will be equal to total additional carrying costs.

> Total cost = total additional carrying cost = number of surplus units × the carrying
> cost (when the ROP *is greater than* the expected demand over the lead time)

Using the procedures described previously, we can compute the economic consequence for every alternative state of nature combination. The results are presented in Table 6.6.

Figure 6.8 graphically shows that the best alternative is a reorder point of 70 units with an expected monetary value (EMV) of $110. While in this example the optimal solution is to use the highest ROP, this does not always occur. If the cost of a stockout relative to the holding cost were changed, or if the probabilities were changed, other quantities less than the highest ROP could be optimal.

FIGURE 6.8

EMVs for Each Reorder Point

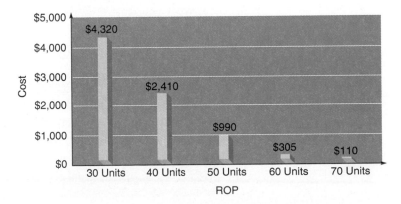

Safety Stock with Unknown Stockout Costs

Determining stockout costs may be difficult or impossible.

When stockout costs are not available or if they do not apply, the preceding type of analysis cannot be used. Actually, there are many situations when stockout costs are unknown or extremely difficult to determine. For example, let's assume that you run a small bicycle shop that sells mopeds and bicycles with a one-year service warranty. Any adjustments made within the year are done at no charge to the customer. If the customer comes in for maintenance under the warranty, and you do not have the necessary part, what is the stockout cost? It cannot be lost profit because the maintenance is done free of charge. Thus, the major stockout cost is the loss of goodwill. The customer may not buy another bicycle from your shop if you have a poor service record. In this situation, it could be very difficult to determine the stockout cost. In other cases, a stockout cost may simply not apply. What is the stockout cost for lifesaving drugs in a hospital? The drug may only cost $10 per bottle. Is the stockout cost $10? Is it $100 or $10,000? Perhaps the stockout cost should be $1 million. What is the cost when a life may be lost as a result of not having the drug?

An alternative to determining safety stock is to use service level and the normal distribution.

An alternative approach to determining safety stock levels is to use a *service level*. In general, a service level is the percent of the time that you will not be out of stock of a particular item. Stated in other terms, the chance or probability of having a stockout is 1 minus the service level. This relationship is expressed as

$$\text{service level} = 1 - \text{probability of a stockout}$$

or

$$\text{probability of a stockout} = 1 - \text{service level}$$

To determine the safety stock level, it is only necessary to know the probability of demand during the lead time and the desired service level. Here is an example of how the safety stock level can be determined when the probability of demand over the lead time follows a normal curve.

Hinsdale Company Example The Hinsdale Company carries an inventory item that has a normally distributed demand during the reorder period. The mean (average) demand is 350 units and the standard deviation is 10. Hinsdale wants to follow a policy that results in stockouts occurring only 5% of the time. How much safety stock should be maintained? Figure 6.9 may help you to visualize the example.

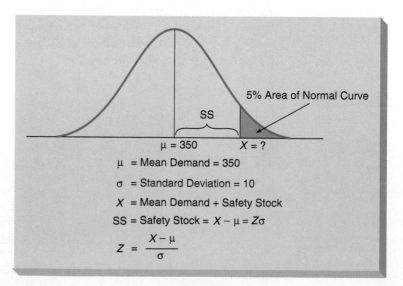

We use the properties of a standardized normal curve to get a Z value for an area under the normal curve of $0.95 = (1 - 0.05)$. Using a normal table (see Appendix A), we find a Z value of 1.65.

$$Z = 1.65$$

Z is also equal to

$$\frac{X - \mu}{\sigma} = \frac{SS}{\sigma}$$

$$Z = 1.65 = \frac{SS}{\sigma}$$

Solving for safety stock gives the following (because stock is usually in integer amounts):

$$SS = 1.65(10) = 16.5 \text{ units, or } 17 \text{ units}$$

Different safety stock levels will be generated for different *service levels*. The relationship between service levels and safety stock, however, is not linear. As the service level increases, the safety stock increases at an increasing rate. Indeed, at service levels greater than 97%, the safety stock becomes very large. Of course, high levels of safety stock mean higher carrying costs. If you are using a service level, you should be aware of how much your service level is costing you in terms of carrying the safety stock in inventory. Let's assume that Hinsdale has a carrying cost of $1 per unit per year. What is the carrying cost for service levels that range from 90% to 99.99%? This cost information is summarized in Table 6.7.

A safety stock level is determined for each service level.

Table 6.7 is developed by looking in the normal curve table for every service level. Finding the service level in the body of the table, we can obtain the Z value from the table in the standard way. Next, the Z values must be converted into the safety stock units. Recall the standard deviation of sales during lead time for Hinsdale is 10. Therefore, the relationship between Z and the safety stock can be developed as follows:

1. We know that $Z = \dfrac{X - \mu}{\sigma}$

2. We also know that $SS = X - \mu$.

TABLE 6.7	SERVICE LEVEL (%)	Z VALUE FROM NORMAL CURVE TABLE	SAFETY STOCK (UNITS)	CARRYING COST ($)
Cost of Different Service Levels	90	1.28	12.8	12.80
	91	1.34	13.4	13.40
	92	1.41	14.1	14.10
	93	1.48	14.8	14.80
	94	1.55	15.5	15.50
	95	1.65	16.5	16.50
	96	1.75	17.5	17.50
	97	1.88	18.8	18.80
	98	2.05	20.5	20.50
	99	2.33	23.3	23.20
	99.99	3.72	37.2	37.20

FIGURE 6.10

Service Level versus
Annual Carrying Costs

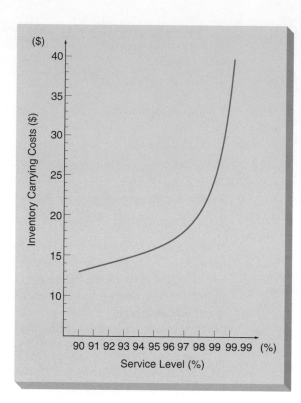

3. Thus, we can rewrite Z as $Z = \dfrac{\text{SS}}{\sigma}$.

4. By transposing terms, we have

$$SS = Z\sigma \qquad\qquad (6\text{-}16)$$

$$= Z(10)$$

Thus, the safety stock can be determined by multiplying the Z values by 10. Since the carrying cost is $1 per unit per year, the carrying cost is the same numerically as the safety stock. A graph of the carrying cost as a function of service level is given in Figure 6.10.

As you can see from Figure 6.10, the carrying cost is increasing at an increasing rate. Moreover, the carrying cost gets extremely large when the service level is greater than 98%. Therefore, as you are setting service levels, you should be aware of the additional carrying cost that you will encounter. Although Figure 6.10 was developed for a specific case, the general shape of the curve is the same for all service-level problems.

Carrying cost increases at an increasing rate as the service level increases.

6.9   ABC ANALYSIS

Earlier, we showed how to develop inventory policies using quantitative techniques. There are also some very practical considerations that should be incorporated into the implementation of inventory decisions, such as *ABC analysis*.

The purpose of ABC analysis is to divide all of a company's inventory items into three groups (group A, group B, and group C) based on the overall inventory value of the items. A prudent manager should spend more time managing those items representing the greatest dollar inventory cost because this is where the greatest potential savings are. A brief description of each group follows, with general guidelines as to how to categorize items.

TABLE 6.8	INVENTORY GROUP	DOLLAR USAGE (%)	INVENTORY ITEMS (%)	ARE QUANTITATIVE CONTROL TECHNIQUES USED?
Summary of ABC Analysis	A	70	10	Yes
	B	20	20	In some cases
	C	10	70	No

The inventory items in the A group account for a major portion of the inventory costs of the organization. As a result, their inventory levels must be monitored carefully. These items typically make up more than 70% of the company's business in dollars, but may consist of only 10% of all inventory items. In other words, a few inventory items are very costly to the company. Thus, great care should be taken in forecasting the demand and developing good inventory management policies for this group of items (refer to Table 6.8). Since there are relatively few of these, the time involved would not be excessive.

The items in the B group are typically moderately priced items and represent much less investment than the A items. Thus, it may not be appropriate to spend as much time developing optimal inventory policies for this group as with the A group since these inventory costs are much lower. Typically, the group B items represent about 20% of the company's business in dollars, and about 20% of the items in inventory.

The items in the C group are the very low-cost items that represent very little in terms of the total dollars invested in inventory. These items may constitute only 10% of the company's business in dollars, but they may consist of 70% of the items in inventory. From a cost-benefit perspective, it would not be good to spend as much time managing these items as the A and B items.

For the group C items, the company should develop a very simple inventory policy, and this may include a relatively large safety stock. Since the items cost very little, the holding cost associated with a large safety stock will also be very low. More care should be taken in determining the safety stock with the higher priced group B items. For the very expensive group A items, the cost of carrying the inventory is so high, it is beneficial to carefully analyze the demand for these so that safety stock is at an appropriate level. Otherwise, the company may have exceedingly high holding costs for the group A items.

IN ACTION   Inventory Modeling at the Philippines San Miguel Corporation

In a typical manufacturing firm, inventories compose a big part of assets. At the San Miguel Corporation (SMC), which produces and distributes more than 300 products to every corner of the Philippine archipelago, raw material accounts for about 10% of total assets. The significant amount of money tied up in inventory encouraged the company's Operations Research Department to develop a series of cost-minimizing inventory models.

One major SMC product, ice cream, uses dairy and cheese curd imported from Australia, New Zealand, and Europe. The normal mode of delivery is sea, and delivery frequencies are limited by supplier schedules. Stockouts, however, are avoidable through airfreight expediting. SMC's inventory model for ice cream balances ordering, carrying, and stockout costs while considering delivery frequency constraints and minimum order quantities. Results showed that current safety stocks of 30 to 51 days could be cut in half for dairy and cheese curd. Even with the increased use of expensive airfreight, SMC saved $170,000 per year through the new policy.

Another SMC product, beer, consists of three major ingredients: malt, hops, and chemicals. Since these ingredients are characterized by low expediting costs and high unit costs, inventory modeling pointed to optimal policies that reduced safety stock levels, saving another $180,000 per year.

Source: E. Del Rosario. "Logistical Nightmare," *OR/MS Today* (April 1999): 44–45.

6.10   DEPENDENT DEMAND: THE CASE FOR MATERIAL REQUIREMENTS PLANNING

In all the inventory models discussed earlier, we assume that the demand for one item is independent of the demand for other items. For example, the demand for refrigerators is usually independent of the demand for toaster ovens. Many inventory problems, however, are interrelated; the demand for one item is dependent on the demand for another item. Consider a manufacturer of small power lawn mowers. The demand for lawn mower wheels and spark plugs is dependent on the demand for lawn mowers. Four wheels and one spark plug are needed for each finished lawn mower. Usually when the demand for different items is dependent, the relationship between the items is known and constant. Thus, you should forecast the demand for the final products and compute the requirements for component parts.

As with the inventory models discussed previously, the major questions that must be answered are *how much to order* and *when to order*. But with dependent demand, inventory scheduling and planning can be very complex indeed. In these situations, MRP can be employed effectively. Some of the benefits of MRP follow:

1. Increased customer service and satisfaction
2. Reduced inventory costs
3. Better inventory planning and scheduling
4. Higher total sales
5. Faster response to market changes and shifts
6. Reduced inventory levels without reduced customer service

Although most MRP systems are computerized, the analysis is straightforward and similar from one computerized system to the next. Here is the typical procedure.

Material Structure Tree

We begin by developing a *bill of materials* (BOM). The BOM identifies the components, their descriptions, and the number required in the production of one unit of the final product. From the BOM, we develop a material structure tree. Let's say that demand for product A is 50 units. Each unit of A requires 2 units of B and 3 units of C. Now, each unit of B requires 2 units of D and 3 units of E. Furthermore, each unit of C requires 1 unit of E and 2 units of F. Thus, the demand for B, C, D, E, and F is completely dependent on the demand for A. Given this information, a material structure tree can be developed for the related inventory items (see Figure 6.11).

Parents and components are identified in the material structure tree.

The structure tree has three levels: 0, 1, and 2. Items above any level are called *parents*, and items below any level are called *components*. There are three parents: A, B, and C. Each parent item has at least one level below it. Items B, C, D, E, and F are components because each item has at least one level above it. In this structure tree, B and C are both parents and components.

The material structure tree shows how many units are needed at every level of production.

Note that the number in the parentheses in Figure 6.11 indicates how many units of that particular item are needed to make the item immediately above it. Thus B(2) means that it takes 2 units of B for every unit of A, and F(2) means that it takes 2 units of F for every unit of C.

After the material structure tree has been developed, the number of units of each item required to satisfy demand can be determined. This information can be displayed as follows:

FIGURE 6.11

Material Structure Tree for
Item A

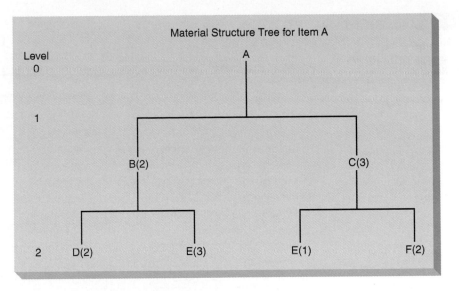

Part B: 2 × number of A's = 2 × 50 = 100
Part C: 3 × number of A's = 3 × 50 = 150
Part D: 2 × number of B's = 2 × 100 = 200
Part E: 3 × number of B's + 1 × number of C's = 3 × 100 + 1 × 150 = 450
Part F: 2 × number of C's = 2 × 150 = 300

Thus, for 50 units of A we need 100 units of B, 150 units of C, 200 units of D, 450 units of E, and 300 units of F. Of course, the numbers in this table could have been determined directly from the material structure tree by multiplying the numbers along the branches times the demand for A, which is 50 units for this problem. For example, the number of units of D needed is simply 2 × 2 × 50 = 200 units.

Gross and Net Material Requirements Plan

Once the materials structure tree has been developed, we construct a gross material requirements plan. This is a time schedule that shows when an item must be ordered from suppliers when there is no inventory on hand, or when the production of an item must be started in order to satisfy the demand for the finished product at a particular date. Let's assume that all of the items are produced or manufactured by the same company. It takes one week to make A, two weeks to make B, one week to make C, one week to make D, two weeks to make E, and three weeks to make F. With this information, the gross material requirements plan can be constructed to reveal the production schedule needed to satisfy the demand of 50 units of A at a future date. (Refer to Figure 6.12.)

The interpretation of the material in Figure 6.12 is as follows: If you want 50 units of A at week 6, you must start the manufacturing process in week 5. Thus, in week 5 you need 100 units of B and 150 units of C. These two items take 2 weeks and 1 week to produce. (See the lead times.) Production of B should be started in week 3, and C should be started in week 4. (See the order release for these items.) Working backward, the same computations can be made for all the other items. The material requirements plan graphically reveals when each item should be started and completed in order to have 50 units of A at week 6.

FIGURE 6.12

Gross Material Requirements Plan for 50 Units of A

		Week	1	2	3	4	5	6	
A	Required Date						50		Lead Time = 1 Week
	Order Release					50			
B	Required Date					100			Lead Time = 2 Weeks
	Order Release			100					
C	Required Date					150			Lead Time = 1 Week
	Order Release				150				
D	Required Date			200					Lead Time = 1 Week
	Order Release		200						
E	Required Date			300	150				Lead Time = 2 Weeks
	Order Release	300	150						
F	Required Date				300				Lead Time = 3 Weeks
	Order Release	300							

Now, a net requirements plan can be developed given the on-hand inventory in Table 6.9; here is how it is done.

Using on-hand inventory to compute net requirements.

Using these data, we can develop a net material requirements plan that includes gross requirements, on-hand inventory, net requirements, planned-order receipts, and planned-order releases for each item. It is developed by beginning with A and working backward through the other items. Figure 6.13 shows a net material requirements plan for product A.

The net requirements plan is constructed like the gross requirements plan. Starting with item A, we work backward determining net requirements for all items. These computations are done by referring constantly to the structure tree and lead times. The gross requirements for A are 50 units in week 6. Ten items are on hand, and thus the net requirements and planned-order receipt are both 40 items in week 6. Because of the one-week lead

TABLE 6.9

On-Hand Inventory

ITEM	ON-HAND INVENTORY
A	10
B	15
C	20
D	10
E	10
F	5

FIGURE 6.13

Net Material Requirements
Plan for 50 units of A.

Item		Week						Lead Time
		1	2	3	4	5	6	
A	Gross						50	1
	On-Hand 10						10	
	Net						40	
	Order Receipt						40	
	Order Release					40		
B	Gross					80 ^{A}		2
	On-Hand 15					15		
	Net					65		
	Order Receipt					65		
	Order Release			65				
C	Gross					120 ^{A}		1
	On-Hand 20					10		
	Net					100		
	Order Receipt					100		
	Order Release				100			
D	Gross			130 ^{B}				1
	On-Hand 10			10				
	Net			120				
	Order Receipt			120				
	Order Release		120					
E	Gross			195 ^{B}	100 ^{C}			2
	On-Hand 10			10	0			
	Net			185	100			
	Order Receipt			185	100			
	Order Release	185	100					
F	Gross				200 ^{C}			3
	On-Hand 5				5			
	Net				195			
	Order Receipt				195			
	Order Release	195						

time, the planned-order release is 40 items in week 5. (See the arrow connecting the order receipt and order release.) Look down column 5 and refer to the structure tree in Figure 6.12. Eighty (2×40) items of B and $120 = 3 \times 40$ items of C are required in week 5 in order to have a total of 50 items of A in week 6. The letter A in the upper-right corner for items B and C means that this demand for B and C was generated as a result of the demand for the parent, A. Now the same type of analysis is done for B and C to determine the net requirements for D, E, and F.

Two or More End Products

So far, we have considered only one end product. For most manufacturing companies, there are normally two or more end products that use some of the same parts or components. All of the end products must be incorporated into a single net material requirements plan.

In the MRP example just discussed, we developed a net material requirements plan for product A. Now, we show how to modify the net material requirements plan when a second end product is introduced. Let's call the second end product AA. The material structure tree for product AA is as follows.

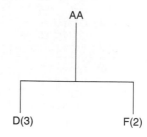

Let's assume that we need 10 units of AA. With this information we can compute the gross requirements for AA:

Part D: $3 \times$ number of AA's = $3 \times 10 = 30$
Part F: $2 \times$ number of AA's = $2 \times 10 = 20$

To develop a net material requirements plan, we need to know the lead time for AA. Let's assume that it is one week. We also assume that we need 10 units of AA in week 6 and that we have no units of AA on hand.

Now, we are in a position to modify the net material requirements plan for product A to include AA. This is done in Figure 6.14.

Look at the top row of the figure. As you can see, we have a gross requirement of 10 units of AA in week 6. We don't have any units of AA on hand, so the net requirement is also 10 units of AA. Because it takes one week to make AA, the order release of 10 units of AA is in week 5. This means that we start making AA in week 5 and have the finished units in week 6.

Because we start making AA in week 5, we must have 30 units of D and 20 units of F in week 5. See the rows for D and F in Figure 6.14. The lead time for D is one week. Thus, we must give the order release in week 4 to have the finished units of D in week 5. Note that there was no inventory on hand for D in week 5. The original 10 units of inventory of D were used in week 5 to make B, which was subsequently used to make A. We also need to have 20 units of F in week 5 to produce 10 units of AA by week 6. Again, we have no on-hand inventory of F in week 5. The original 5 units were used in week 4 to make C, which

---

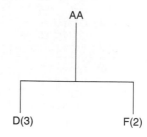

IN ACTION   MRP Builds Profits at Compaq

Cal Monteith, Compaq's manager of master planning and production control in Houston, was in the process of phasing out one of Compaq's personal computer models when he was told that Compaq had underestimated demand. The new schedule suggested that he build 10,000 more PCs. Could he do it? Monteith faced these questions: What parts were on hand and on order? What labor was available? Could the plant handle the capacity? Did vendors have the capacity? What product lines could be rescheduled?

Traditionally, amassing such information required not only MRP reports but a variety of additional reports. Even then a response was based on partial information.

New software, including a combination of spreadsheets, inquiry languages, and report writers, allowed Monteith to search huge databases, isolate the relevant data (customer orders, forecasts, inventory, and capacity), and do some quick calculations. One such piece of software is FastMRP, which is based in Ottawa, Canada. Another is Carp Systems International of Kanata, Ontario. The result: Compaq was able to make schedule adjustments that added millions of dollars to the bottom line.

Source: "Carp System International and FastMRP," *New York Times* (October 18, 1992): F9.

FIGURE 6.14

Net Material Requirements Plan, Including AA

Item	Inventory	Week 1	2	3	4	5	6	Lead Time
AA	Gross On-Hand: 0 Net Order Receipt Order Release					10	10 0 10 10	1 Week
A	Gross On-Hand: 10 Net Order Receipt Order Release					40	50 10 40 40	1 Week
B	Gross On-Hand: 15 Net Order Receipt Order Release			65		80 A 15 65 65		2 Weeks
C	Gross On-Hand: 20 Net Order Receipt Order Release				100	120 A 20 100 100		1 Week
D	Gross On-Hand: 10 Net Order Receipt Order Release		120	130 B 10 120 120	30	30 AA 0 30 30		1 Week
E	Gross On-Hand: 10 Net Order Receipt Order Release	185	100	195 B 10 185 185	100 C 0 100 100			2 Weeks
F	Gross On-Hand: 5 Net Order Receipt Order Release	195	20		200 C 5 195 195	20 AA 0 20 20		3 Weeks

was subsequently used to make A. The lead time for F is three weeks. Thus, the order release for 20 units of F must be in week 2. (See the F row in Figure 6.14.)

This example shows how the inventory requirements of two products can be reflected in the same net material requirements plan. Some manufacturing companies can have more than 100 end products that must be coordinated in the same net material requirements plan. Although such a situation can be very complicated, the same principles we used in this example are employed. Remember that computer programs have been developed to handle large and complex manufacturing operations.

In addition to using MRP to handle end products and finished goods, MRP can also be used to handle spare parts and components. This is important because most manufacturing companies sell spare parts and components for maintenance. A net material requirements plan should also reflect these spare parts and components.

6.11 JUST-IN-TIME INVENTORY CONTROL

With JIT, inventory arrives just before it is needed.

During the past two decades, there has been a trend to make the manufacturing process more efficient. One objective is to have less in-process inventory on hand. This is known as JIT inventory. With this approach, inventory arrives just in time to be used during the manufacturing process to produce subparts, assemblies, or finished goods. One technique of implementing JIT is a manual procedure called *kanban*. *Kanban* in Japanese means "card." With a dual-card kanban system, there is a conveyance kanban, or C-kanban, and a production kanban, or P-kanban. The kanban system is very simple. Here is how it works:

Four Steps of Kanban

1. A user takes a container of parts or inventory along with its accompanying C-kanban to his or her work area. When there are no more parts or the container is empty, the user returns the empty container along with the C-kanban to the producer area.

2. At the producer area, there is a full container of parts along with a P-kanban. The user detaches the P-kanban from the full container of parts. Then the user takes the full container of parts along with the original C-kanban back to his or her area for immediate use.

3. The detached P-kanban goes back to the producer area along with the empty container. The P-kanban is a signal that new parts are to be manufactured or that new parts are to be placed into the container. When the container is filled, the P-kanban is attached to the container.

4. This process repeats itself during the typical workday. The dual-card kanban system is shown in Figure 6.15.

As seen in Figure 6.15, full containers along with their C-kanban go from the storage area to a user area, typically on a manufacturing line. During the production process, parts in the container are used up. When the container is empty, the empty container along with the same C-kanban goes back to the storage area. Here, the user picks up a new full container. The P-kanban from the full container is removed and sent back to the production area along with the empty container to be refilled.

At a minimum, two containers are required using the kanban system. One container is used at the user area, and another container is being refilled for future use. In reality, there are usually more than two containers. This is how inventory control is accomplished. Inventory managers can introduce additional containers and their associated P-kanbans into the system. In a similar fashion, the inventory manager can remove containers and the P-kanbans to have tighter control over inventory buildups.

In addition to being a simple, easy-to-implement system, the kanban system can also be very effective in controlling inventory costs and in uncovering production bottlenecks. Inventory arrives at the user area or on the manufacturing line just when it is needed. Inventory does not build up unnecessarily, cluttering the production line or adding to unnecessary inventory expense. The kanban system reduces inventory levels and makes for a more

FIGURE 6.15

The Kanban System

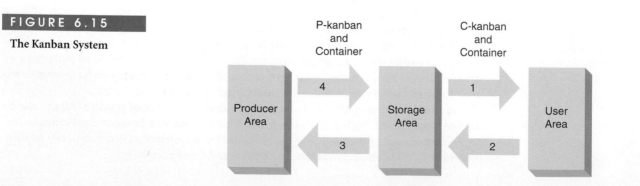

IN ACTION   MRP and JIT at Welpac, Westair, and Rio Bravo Electronics

Peter Antonioni, the purchasing manager for Welpac, a large hardware company, packages thousands of general hardware items for builders and other customers. About 10,000 raw materials are placed in about 5,000 end products. The company uses MRP to help it with its purchasing effort. The results have been better inventory control and lower costs.

As a result of the use of MRP, the British firm Westair has been able to increase inventory turnover by 60%. In addition, MRP has helped the company reduce inventory lead times from four to six weeks to days.

Rio Bravo Electronics, located in Juarez, Mexico, uses JIT to make sure that products are shipped on time. Every two hours or so, the supply of parts on the floor is replenished from the main materials storage area using a JIT delivery system. The company is involved with the "*maquiladora* concept," which allows Rio Bravo to receive materials in Mexico duty-free and then ship the finished components back to the United States. Rio Bravo assembles wiring harnesses for the U.S. company Delphi Packard Electric Systems.

Source: Holder Roy, *Works Management* 48, 3 (March 1995): 18–21; *Works Management* 48, 3 (March 1995): 7; and Jeffrey L. Funk, *International Journal of Operations & Production Management* 15, 5 (1995): 60–71.

effective operation. It is like putting the production line on an inventory diet. Like any diet, the inventory diet imposed by the kanban system makes the production operation more streamlined. Furthermore, production bottlenecks and problems can be uncovered. Many production managers remove containers and their associated P-kanban from the kanban system in order to "starve" the production line to uncover bottlenecks and potential problems.

In implementing a kanban system, a number of work rules or kanban rules are normally implemented. One typical kanban rule is that no containers are filled without the appropriate P-kanban. Another rule is that each container must hold exactly the specified number of parts or inventory items. These and similar rules make the production process more efficient. Only those parts that are actually needed are produced. The production department does not produce inventory just to keep busy. It produces inventory or parts only when they are needed in the user area or on an actual manufacturing line.

6.12   ENTERPRISE RESOURCE PLANNING

Over the years, MRP has evolved to include not only the materials required in production, but also the labor hours, material cost, and other resources related to production. When approached in this fashion, the term MRP II is often used, and the word *resource* replaces the word *requirements*. As this concept evolved and sophisticated computer software programs were developed, these systems were called *enterprise resource planning* (ERP) systems.

The objective of an ERP system is to reduce costs by integrating all of the operations of a firm. This starts with the supplier of the materials needed and flows through the organization to include invoicing the customer of the final product. Data are entered once into a database, and then these data can be quickly and easily accessed by anyone in the organization. This benefits not only the functions related to planning and managing inventory, but also other business processes such as accounting, finance, and human resources.

The benefits of a well-developed ERP system are reduced transaction costs and increased speed and accuracy of information. However, there are drawbacks as well. The software is expensive to buy and costly to customize. The implementation of an ERP system may require a company to change its normal operations, and employees are often resistant to change. Also, training employees on the use of the new software can be expensive.

There are many ERP systems available. The most common ones are from the firms SAP, Oracle, People Soft, Baan, and JD Edwards. Even small systems can cost hundreds of thousands of dollars. The larger systems can cost hundreds of millions of dollars.

SUMMARY

This chapter introduces the fundamentals of inventory control theory. We show that the two most important problems are (1) how much to order and (2) when to order.

We investigate the economic order quantity, which determines how much to order, and the reorder point, which determines when to order. In addition, we explore the use of sensitivity analysis to determine what happens to computations when one or more of the values used in one of the equations changes.

The basic EOQ inventory model presented in this chapter makes a number of assumptions: (1) known and constant demand and lead times, (2) instantaneous receipt of inventory, (3) no quantity discounts, (4) no stockouts or shortages, and (5) the only variable costs are ordering costs and carrying costs. If these assumptions are valid, the EOQ inventory model provides optimal solutions. On the other hand, if these assumptions do not hold, the basic EOQ

model does not apply. In these cases, more complex models are needed, including the production run, quantity discount, and safety stock models. We also present ABC analysis to determine what inventory to control.

When the demand for inventory is not independent of the demand for another product, a technique such as MRP is needed. MRP can be used to determine the gross and net material requirements for products. Computer software is necessary to implement major inventory systems including MRP systems successfully. Today, many companies are using ERP software to integrate all of the operations within a firm, including inventory, accounting, finance, and human resources.

JIT can lower inventory levels, reduce costs, and make a manufacturing process more efficient. Kanban, a Japanese word meaning "card," is one way to implement the JIT approach.

GLOSSARY

ABC Analysis. An analysis that divides inventory into three groups. Group A is more important than group B, which is more important than group C.

Annual Setup Cost. The cost to set up the manufacturing or production process for the production run model.

Average Inventory. The average inventory on hand. In this chapter the average inventory is $Q/2$ for the EOQ model.

Bill of Materials (BOM). A list of the components in a product, with a description and the quantity required to make one unit of that product.

Economic Order Quantity (EOQ). The amount of inventory ordered that will minimize the total inventory cost. It is also called the optimal order quantity, or Q^*.

Enterprise Resource Planning (ERP). A computerized information system that integrates and coordinates the operations of a firm.

Instantaneous Inventory Receipt. A system in which inventory is received or obtained at one point in time and not over a period of time.

Just-in-Time (JIT) Inventory. An approach whereby inventory arrives just in time to be used in the manufacturing process.

Kanban. A manual JIT system developed by the Japanese. Kanban means "card" in Japanese.

Lead Time. The time it takes to receive an order after it is placed (called L in the chapter).

Material Requirements Planning (MRP). An inventory model that can handle dependent demand.

Production Run Model An inventory model in which inventory is produced or manufactured instead of being ordered or purchased. This model eliminates the instantaneous receipt assumption.

Quantity Discount. The cost per unit when large orders of an inventory item are placed.

Reorder Point (ROP). The number of units on hand when an order for more inventory is placed.

Safety Stock. Extra inventory that is used to help avoid stockouts.

Safety Stock with Known Stockout Costs. An inventory model in which the probability of demand during lead time and the stockout cost per unit are known.

Safety Stock with Unknown Stockout Costs. An inventory model in which the probability of demand during lead time is known. The stockout cost is not known.

Sensitivity Analysis. The process of determining how sensitive the optimal solution is to changes in the values used in the equations.

Service Level. The chance, expressed as a percent, that there will not be a stockout. Service level = 1 − probability of a stockout.

Stockout. A situation that occurs when there is no inventory on hand.

KEY EQUATIONS

Equations 6-1 through 6-6 are associated with the economic order quantity (EOQ).

(6-1)   Average inventory level $= \dfrac{Q}{2}$

(6-2)   Annual ordering cost $= \dfrac{D}{Q} C_o$

(6-3)   Annual holding cost $= \dfrac{Q}{2} C_h$

(6-4) $\text{EOQ} = Q^* = \sqrt{\dfrac{2DC_o}{C_h}}$

(6-5) $TC = \dfrac{D}{Q}C_o + \dfrac{Q}{2}C_h$

Total relevant inventory cost.

(6-6) Average dollar level $= C\dfrac{Q}{2}$

(6-7) $\text{EOQ} = \sqrt{\dfrac{2DC_o}{IC}}$

EOQ with C_h expressed as percentage of unit cost.

(6-8) $\text{ROP} = d \times L$

Reorder point: d is the daily demand and L is the lead time in days.

Equations 6-9 through 6-13 are associated with the production run model.

(6-9) average inventory $= \dfrac{Q}{2}\left(1 - \dfrac{d}{p}\right)$

(6-10) annual holding cost $= \dfrac{Q}{2}\left(1 - \dfrac{d}{p}\right)C_h$

(6-11) annual setup cost $= \dfrac{D}{Q}C_s$

(6-12) annual ordering cost $= \dfrac{D}{Q}C_o$

(6-13) $Q^* = \sqrt{\dfrac{2DC_s}{C_h\left(1 - \dfrac{d}{p}\right)}}$

Optimal production quantity.

Equation 6-14 is used for the quantity discount model.

(6-14) Total cost $= DC + \dfrac{D}{Q}C_o + \dfrac{Q}{2}C_h$

Total inventory cost (including purchase cost).

Equations 6-15 and 6-16 are used when safety stock is required.

(6-15) $\text{ROP} = d \times L + SS$

where d is the average demand during the lead time, L is the average lead time, and SS is the amount of safety stock.

(6-16) $SS = Z\sigma$

Safety stock using the normal distribution.

SOLVED PROBLEMS

Solved Problem 6-1

Patterson Electronics supplies microcomputer circuitry to a company that incorporates microprocessors into refrigerators and other home appliances. One of the components has an annual demand of 250 units, and this is constant throughout the year. Carrying cost is estimated to be $1 per unit per year, and the ordering cost is $20 per order.

a. To minimize cost, how many units should be ordered each time an order is placed?
b. How many orders per year are needed with the optimal policy?
c. What is the average inventory if costs are minimized?
d. Suppose the ordering cost is not $20, and Patterson has been ordering 150 units each time an order is placed. For this order policy to be optimal, what would the ordering cost have to be?

Solutions

a. The EOQ assumptions are met, so the optimal order quantity is

$$\text{EOQ} = Q^* = \sqrt{\dfrac{2DC_o}{C_h}} = \sqrt{\dfrac{2(250)20}{1}} = 100 \text{ units}$$

b. Number of orders per year $= \dfrac{D}{Q} = \dfrac{250}{100} = 2.5$ orders per year

Note that this would mean in one year the company places 3 orders and in the next year it would only need 2 orders, since some inventory would be carried over from the previous year. It averages 2.5 orders per year.

c. Average Inventory $= \dfrac{Q}{2} = \dfrac{100}{2} = 50$ units

d. Given an annual demand of 250, a carrying cost of $1, and an order quantity of 150, Patterson Electronics must determine what the ordering cost would have to be for the order policy of 150 units to be optimal. To find the answer to this problem, we must solve the traditional EOQ equation for the ordering cost. As you can see in the calculations that follow, an ordering cost of $45 is needed for the order quantity of 150 units to be optimal.

$$Q = \sqrt{\dfrac{2DC_o}{C_h}}$$

$$C_o = Q^2 \dfrac{C_h}{2D}$$

$$= \dfrac{(150)^2(1)}{2(250)}$$

$$= \dfrac{22,500}{500} = \$45$$

Solved Problem 6-2

Flemming Accessories produces paper slicers used in offices and in art stores. The minislicer has been one of its most popular items: Annual demand is 6,750 units and is constant throughout the year. Kristen Flemming, owner of the firm, produces the minislicers in batches. On average, Kristen can manufacture 125 minislicers per day. Demand for these slicers during the production process is 30 per day. The setup cost for the equipment necessary to produce the minislicers is $150. Carrying costs are $1 per minislicer per year. How many minislicers should Kristen manufacture in each batch?

Solution

The data for Flemming Accessories are summarized as follows:

$$D = 6{,}750 \text{ units}$$

$$C_s = \$150$$

$$C_h = \$1$$

$$d = 30 \text{ units}$$

$$p = 125 \text{ units}$$

This is a production run problem that involves a daily production rate and a daily demand rate. The appropriate calculations are shown here:

$$Q^* = \sqrt{\dfrac{2DC_s}{C_h(1 - d/p)}}$$

$$= \sqrt{\dfrac{2(6{,}750)(150)}{1(1 - 30/125)}}$$

$$= 1{,}632$$

Solved Problem 6-3

Dorsey Distributors has an annual demand for a metal detector of 1,400. The cost of a typical detector to Dorsey is $400. Carrying cost is estimated to be 20% of the unit cost, and the ordering cost is $25 per order. If Dorsey orders in quantities of 300 or more, it can get a 5% discount on the cost of the detectors. Should Dorsey take the quantity discount? Assume the demand is constant.

Solution

The solution to any quantity discount model involves determining the total cost of each alternative after quantities have been computed and adjusted for the original problem and every discount. We start the analysis with no discount:

$$\text{EOQ (no discount)} = \sqrt{\frac{2(1,400)(25)}{0.2(400)}}$$

$$= 29.6 \text{ units}$$

$$\text{Total cost (no discount)} = \text{material cost} + \text{ordering cost} + \text{carrying cost}$$

$$= \$400(1,400) + \frac{1,400(\$25)}{29.6} + \frac{29.6(\$400)(0.2)}{2}$$

$$= \$560,000 + \$1,183 + \$1,183 = \$562,366$$

The next step is to compute the total cost for the discount:

$$\text{EOQ (with discount)} = \sqrt{\frac{2(1,400)(25)}{0.2(\$380)}}$$

$$= 30.3 \text{ units}$$

$$Q \text{ (adjusted)} = 300 \text{ units}$$

Because this last economic order quantity is below the discounted price, we must adjust the order quantity to 300 units. The next step is to compute total cost.

$$\text{Total cost (with discount)} = \text{material cost} + \text{ordering cost} + \text{carrying cost}$$

$$= \$380(1,400) + \frac{1,400(25)}{300} + \frac{300(\$380)(0.2)}{2}$$

$$= \$532,000 + \$117 + \$11,400 = \$543,517$$

The optimal strategy is to order 300 units at a total cost of $543,517.

⟶ SELF-TEST

- Before taking the self-test, refer back to the learning objectives at the beginning of the chapter, the notes in the margins, and the glossary at the end of the chapter.
- Use the key at the back of the book to correct your answers.
- Restudy pages that correspond to any questions that you answered incorrectly or material you feel uncertain about.

1. Which of the following is a basic component of an inventory control system?
   a. planning what inventory to stock and how to acquire it
   b. forecasting the demand for parts and products
   c. controlling inventory levels
   d. developing and implementing feedback measurements for revising plans and forecasts
   e. all of the above are components of an inventory control system

2. Which of the following is a valid use of inventory?
   a. the decoupling function
   b. to take advantage of quantity discounts
   c. to avoid shortages and stockouts
   d. to smooth out irregular supply and demand
   e. all of the above are valid uses of inventory

3. One assumption necessary for the EOQ model is instantaneous replenishment. This means
   a. the lead time is zero.
   b. the production time is assumed to be zero.
   c. the entire order is delivered at one time.
   d. replenishment cannot occur until the on-hand inventory is zero.

4. If the EOQ assumptions are met and a company orders the EOQ each time an order is placed, then the
   a. total annual holding costs are minimized.
   b. total annual ordering costs are minimized.
   c. total of all inventory costs are minimized.
   d. order quantity will always be less than the average inventory.

5. If the EOQ assumptions are met and a company orders more than the economic order quantity, then
   a. total annual holding cost will be greater than the total annual ordering cost.
   b. total annual holding cost will be less than the total annual ordering cost.
   c. total annual holding cost will be equal to the total annual ordering cost.
   d. total annual holding cost will be equal to the total annual purchase cost.

6. The reorder point is
   a. the quantity that is reordered each time an order is placed.
   b. the amount of inventory that would be needed to meet demand during the lead time.
   c. equal to the average inventory when the EOQ assumptions are met.
   d. assumed to be zero if there is instantaneous replenishment.

7. If the EOQ assumptions are met, then
   a. annual stockout cost will be zero.
   b. total annual holding cost will equal total annual ordering cost.
   c. average inventory will be one-half the order quantity.
   d. all of the above are true.

8. In the production run model, the maximum inventory level will be
   a. greater than the production quantity.
   b. equal to the production quantity.
   c. less than the production quantity.
   d. equal to the daily production rate plus the daily demand.

9. Why is the annual purchase (material) cost not considered to be a relevant inventory cost if the EOQ assumptions are met?
   a. This cost will be zero.
   b. This cost is constant and not affected by the order quantity.
   c. This cost is insignificant compared with the other inventory costs.
   d. This cost is never considered to be an inventory cost.

10. A JIT system will usually result in
    a. a low annual holding cost.
    b. very few orders per year.
    c. frequent shutdowns in an assembly line.
    d. high levels of safety stock

11. Manufacturers use MRP when
    a. the demand for one product is dependent on the demand for other products
    b. the demand for each product is independent of the demand for other products.
    c. demand is totally unpredictable.
    d. purchase cost is extremely high.

DISCUSSION QUESTIONS AND PROBLEMS

Discussion Questions

6-1 Why is inventory an important consideration for managers?

6-2 What is the purpose of inventory control?

6-3 Under what circumstances can inventory be used as a hedge against inflation?

6-4 Why wouldn't a company always store large quantities of inventory to eliminate shortages and stockouts?

6-5 What are some of the assumptions made in using the EOQ?

6-6 Discuss the major inventory costs that are used in determining the EOQ.

6-7 What is the ROP? How is it determined?

6-8 What is the purpose of sensitivity analysis?

6-9 What assumptions are made in the production run model?

6-10 What happens to the production run model when the daily production rate becomes very large?

6-11 Briefly describe what is involved in solving a quantity discount model.

6-12 Discuss the methods that are used in determining safety stock when the stockout cost is known and when the stockout cost is unknown.

6-13 Briefly describe what is meant by ABC analysis. What is the purpose of this inventory technique?

6-14 What is the overall purpose of MRP?

6-15 What is the difference between the gross and net material requirements plan?

6-16 What is the objective of JIT?

Problems*

6-17 Lila Battle has determined that the annual demand for number 6 screws is 100,000 screws. Lila, who works in her brother's hardware store, is in charge of purchasing. She estimates that it costs $10 every time an order is placed. This cost includes her wages, the cost of the forms used in placing the order, and so on. Furthermore, she estimates that the cost of carrying one screw in inventory for a year is one-half of 1 cent. Assume that the demand is constant throughout the year.

(a) How many number 6 screws should Lila order at a time if she wishes to minimize total inventory cost?

(b) How many orders per year would be placed? What would the annual ordering cost be?

(c) What would the average inventory be? What would the annual holding cost be?

6-18 It takes approximately 8 working days for an order of number 6 screws to arrive once the order has been placed. (Refer to Problem 6-17.) The demand for number 6 screws is fairly constant, and on the average, Lila has observed that her brother's hardware store sells 500 of these screws each day. Because the demand is fairly constant, Lila believes that she can avoid stockouts completely if she only orders the number 6 screws at the correct time. What is the ROP?

6-19 Lila's brother believes that she places too many orders for screws per year. He believes that an order should be placed only twice per year. If Lila follows her brother's policy, how much more would this cost every year over the ordering policy that she developed in Problem 6-17? If only two orders were placed each year, what effect would this have on the ROP?

6-20 Barbara Bright is the purchasing agent for West Valve Company. West Valve sells industrial valves and fluid control devices. One of the most popular valves is the Western, which has an annual demand of 4,000 units. The cost of each valve is $90, and the inventory carrying cost is estimated to be 10% of the cost of each valve. Barbara has made a study of the costs involved in placing an order for any of the valves that West Valve stocks, and she has concluded that the average ordering cost is $25 per order. Furthermore, it takes about two weeks for an order to arrive from the supplier, and during this time the demand per week for West valves is approximately 80.

(a) What is the EOQ?

(b) What is the ROP?

(c) What is the average inventory? What is the annual holding cost?

(d) How many orders per year would be placed? What is the annual ordering cost?

6-21 Ken Ramsing has been in the lumber business for most of his life. Ken's biggest competitor is Pacific Woods. Through many years of experience, Ken knows that the ordering cost for an order of plywood is $25 and that the carrying cost is 25% of the unit cost. Both Ken and Pacific Woods receive plywood in loads that cost $100 per load. Furthermore, Ken and Pacific Woods use the same supplier of plywood, and Ken was able to find out that Pacific Woods orders in quantities of 4,000 loads at a time. Ken also knows that 4,000 loads is the EOQ for Pacific Woods. What is the annual demand in loads of plywood for Pacific Woods?

6-22 Shoe Shine is a local retail shoe store located on the north side of Centerville. Annual demand for a popular sandal is 500 pairs, and John Dirk, the owner of Shoe Shine, has been in the habit of ordering 100 pairs at a time. John estimates that the ordering cost is $10 per order. The cost of the sandal is $5 per pair. For John's ordering policy to be correct, what would the carrying cost as a percentage of the unit cost have to be? If the carrying cost were 10% of the cost, what would the optimal order quantity be?

6-23 In Problem 6-17 you helped Lila Battle determine the optimal order quantity for number 6 screws. She had estimated that the ordering cost was $10 per order. At this time, though, she believes that this estimate was too low. Although she does not know the exact ordering cost, she believes that it could be as high as $40 per order. How would the optimal order quantity change if the ordering cost were $20, $30, and $40?

6-24 Ross White's machine shop uses 2,500 brackets during the course of a year, and this usage is relatively constant throughout the year. These brackets are purchased from a supplier 100 miles away for $15 each, and the lead time is 2 days. The holding cost per bracket per year is $1.50 (or 10% of the unit cost) and the ordering cost per order is $18.75. There are 250 working days per year.

(a) What is the EOQ?

(b) Given the EOQ, what is the average inventory? What is the annual inventory holding cost?

(c) In minimizing cost, how many orders would be made each year? What would be the annual ordering cost?

(d) Given the EOQ, what is the total annual inventory cost (including purchase cost)?

(e) What is the time between orders?

(f) What is the ROP?

6-25 Ross White (see Problem 6-24) wants to reconsider his decision of buying the brackets and is considering making the brackets in-house. He has determined that setup costs would be $25 in machinist time and lost production time, and 50 brackets could be produced in a day once the machine has been set up. Ross estimates

---

* Note: ⚲ means the problem may be solved with QM for Windows; ✄ means the problem may be solved with Excel QM; and ⚲ means the problem may be solved with QM for Windows and/or Excel QM.

that the cost (including labor time and materials) of producing one bracket would be $14.80. The holding cost would be 10% of this cost.

(a) What is the daily demand rate?
(b) What is the optimal production quantity?
(c) How long will it take to produce the optimal quantity? How much inventory is sold during this time?
(d) If Ross uses the optimal production quantity, what would be the maximum inventory level? What would be the average inventory level? What is the annual holding cost?
(e) How many production runs would there be each year? What would be the annual setup cost?
(f) Given the optimal production run size, what is the total annual inventory cost?
(g) If the lead time is one-half day, what is the ROP?

6-26 Upon hearing that Ross White (see Problems 6-24 and 6-25) is considering producing the brackets in-house, the vendor has notified Ross that the purchase price would drop from $15 per bracket to $14.50 per bracket if Ross will purchase the brackets in lots of 1,000. Lead times, however would increase to 3 days for this larger quantity.

(a) What is the total annual inventory cost plus purchase cost if Ross buys the brackets in lots of 1,000 at $14.50 each?
(b) If Ross does buy in lots of 1,000 brackets, what is the new ROP?
(c) Given the options of purchasing the brackets at $15 each, producing them in-house at $14.80, and taking advantage of the discount, what is your recommendation to Ross White?

6-27 After analyzing the costs of various options for obtaining brackets, Ross White (see Problems 6-24, 6-25, and 6-26) recognizes that although he knows that lead time is 2 days and demand per day averages 10 units, the demand during the lead time often varies. Ross has kept very careful records and has determined lead time demand is normally distributed with a standard deviation of 1.5 units.

(a) What Z value would be appropriate for a 98% service level?
(b) What safety stock should Ross maintain if he wants a 98% service level?
(c) What is the adjusted ROP for the brackets?
(d) What is the annual holding cost for the safety stock if the annual holding cost per unit is $1.50?

6-28 Douglas Boats is a supplier of boating equipment for the states of Oregon and Washington. It sells 5,000 White Marine WM-4 diesel engines every year. These engines are shipped to Douglas in a shipping container of 100 cubic feet, and Douglas Boats keeps the warehouse full of these WM-4 motors. The warehouse can hold 5,000 cubic feet of boating supplies. Douglas estimates that the ordering cost is $10 per order, and the carrying cost is estimated to be $10 per motor per year. Douglas Boats is considering the possibility of expanding the warehouse for the WM-4 motors. How much should Douglas Boats expand, and how much would it be worth for the company to make the expansion? Assume demand is constant throughout the year.

6-29 Northern Distributors is a wholesale organization that supplies retail stores with lawn care and household products. One building is used to store Neverfail lawn mowers. The building is 25 feet wide by 40 feet deep by 8 feet high. Anna Oldham, manager of the warehouse, estimates that about 60% of the warehouse can be used to store the Neverfail lawn mowers. The remaining 40% is used for walkways and a small office. Each Neverfail lawn mower comes in a box that is 5 feet by 4 feet by 2 feet high. The annual demand for these lawn mowers is 12,000, and the ordering cost for Northern Distributors is $30 per order. It is estimated that it costs Northern $2 per lawn mower per year for storage. Northern Distributors is thinking about increasing the size of the warehouse. The company can only do this by making the warehouse deeper. At the present time, the warehouse is 40 feet deep. How many feet of depth should be added on to the warehouse to minimize the annual inventory costs? How much should the company be willing to pay for this addition? Remember that only 60% of the total area can be used to store Neverfail lawn mowers. Assume all EOQ conditions are met.

6-30 Lisa Surowsky was asked to help in determining the best ordering policy for a new product. Currently, the demand for the new product has been projected to be about 1,000 units annually. To get a handle on the carrying and ordering costs, Lisa prepared a series of average inventory costs. Lisa thought that these costs would be appropriate for the new product. The results are summarized in the following table. These data were compiled for 10,000 inventory items that were carried or held during the year and were ordered 100 times during the past year. Help Lisa determine the EOQ.

Cost Factor	Cost ($)
Taxes	2,000
Processing and inspection	1,500
New product development	2,500
Bill paying	500
Ordering supplies	50
Inventory insurance	600
Product advertising	800
Spoilage	750
Sending purchasing orders	800
Inventory inquiries	450
Warehouse supplies	280
Research and development	2,750
Purchasing salaries	3,000
Warehouse salaries	2,800
Inventory theft	800
Purchase order supplies	500
Inventory obsolescence	300

6-31 Jan Gentry is the owner of a small company that produces electric scissors used to cut fabric. The annual demand is for 8,000 scissors, and Jan produces the scissors in batches. On the average, Jan can produce 150 scissors per day, and during the production process, demand for scissors has been about 40 scissors per day. The cost to set up the production process is $100, and it costs Jan 30 cents to carry one pair of scissors for one year. How many scissors should Jan produce in each batch?

6-32 Jim Overstreet, inventory control manager for Itex, receives wheel bearings from Wheel-Rite, a small producer of metal parts. Unfortunately, Wheel-Rite can only produce 500 wheel bearings per day. Itex receives 10,000 wheel bearings from Wheel-Rite each year. Since Itex operates 200 working days each year, its average daily demand for wheel bearings is 50. The ordering cost for Itex is $40 per order, and the carrying cost is 60 cents per wheel bearing per year. How many wheel bearings should Itex order from Wheel-Rite at one time? Wheel-Rite has agreed to ship the maximum number of wheel bearings that it produces each day to Itex when an order has been received.

6-33 North Manufacturing has a demand for 1,000 pumps each year. The cost of a pump is $50. It costs North Manufacturing $40 to place an order, and the carrying cost is 25% of the unit cost. If pumps are ordered in quantities of 200, North Manufacturing can get a 3% discount on the cost of the pumps. Should North Manufacturing order 200 pumps at a time and take the 3% discount?

6-34 Mr. Beautiful, an organization that sells weight training sets, has an ordering cost of $40 for the BB-1 set. (BB-1 stands for Body Beautiful Number 1.) The carrying cost for BB-1 is $5 per set per year. To meet demand, Mr. Beautiful orders large quantities of BB-1 seven times a year. The stockout cost for BB-1 is estimated to be $50 per set. Over the past several years, Mr. Beautiful has observed the following demand during the lead time for BB-1:

DEMAND DURING LEAD TIME	PROBABILITY
40	0.1
50	0.2
60	0.2
70	0.2
80	0.2
90	0.1

The ROP for BB-1 is 60 units. What level of safety stock should be maintained for BB-1?

6-35 Linda Lechner is in charge of maintaining hospital supplies at General Hospital. During the past year, the mean lead time demand for bandage BX-5 was 60. Furthermore, the standard deviation for BX-5 was 7. Linda would like to maintain a 90% service level. What safety stock level do you recommend for BX-5?

6-36 Ralph Janaro simply does not have time to analyze all of the items in his company's inventory. As a young manager, he has more important things to do. The following is a table of six items in inventory along with the unit cost and the demand in units.

IDENTIFICATION CODE	UNIT COST ($)	DEMAND IN UNITS
XX1	5.84	1,200
B66	5.40	1,110
3CPO	1.12	896
33CP	74.54	1,104
R2D2	2.00	1,110
RMS	2.08	961

(a) Find the total amount spent on each item during the year. What is the total investment for all of these?
(b) Find the percentage of the total investment in inventory that is spent on each item.
(c) Based on the percentages in part (b), which item(s) would be classified in categories A, B, and C using ABC analysis?
(d) Which item(s) should Ralph most carefully control using quantitative techniques?

6-37 The demand for barbecue grills has been fairly large in the past several years, and Home Supplies, Inc., usually orders new barbecue grills five times a year. It is estimated that the ordering cost is $60 per order. The carrying cost is $10 per grill per year. Furthermore, Home Supplies, Inc., has estimated that the stockout cost is $50 per unit. The ROP is 650 units. Although the demand each year is high, it varies considerably. The demand during the lead time is shown in the following table:

DEMAND DURING LEAD TIME	PROBABILITY
600	0.3
650	0.2
700	0.1
750	0.1
800	0.05
850	0.05
900	0.05
950	0.05
1,000	0.05
1,050	0.03
1,100	0.02
	Total 1.00

The lead time is 12 working days. How much safety stock should Home Supplies, Inc., maintain?

6-38 Dillard Travey receives 5,000 tripods annually from Quality Suppliers to meet his annual demand. Dillard runs a large photographic outlet, and the tripods are used primarily with 35-mm cameras. The ordering cost is $15 per order, and the carrying cost is 50 cents per unit per year. Quality is starting a new option for its customers. When an order is placed, Quality will ship one-third of the order every week for three weeks instead of shipping the entire order at one time. Weekly demand over the lead time is 100 tripods.

(a) What is the order quantity if Dillard has the entire order shipped at one time?

(b) What is the order quantity if Dillard has the order shipped over three weeks using the new option from Quality Suppliers, Inc.? To simplify your calculations, assume that the average inventory is equal to one-half of the maximum inventory level for Quality's new option.

(c) Calculate the total cost for each option. What do you recommend?

6-39 Linda Lechner has just been severely chastised for her inventory policy. (See Problem 6-35.) Sue Surrowski, her boss, believes that the service level should be either 95% or 98%. Compute the safety stock levels for a 95% and a 98% service level. Linda knows that the carrying cost of BX-5 is 50 cents per unit per year. Compute the carrying cost that is associated with a 90%, a 95%, and a 98% service level.

6-40 Quality Suppliers, Inc., has decided to extend its shipping option. (Refer to Problem 6-38 for details.) Now, Quality Suppliers is offering to ship the amount ordered in five equal shipments, one each week. It will take five weeks for this entire order to be received. What are the order quantity and total cost for this new shipping option?

6-41 Xemex has collected the following inventory data for the six items that it stocks:

ITEM CODE	UNIT COST ($)	ANNUAL DEMAND (UNITS)	ORDERING COST ($)	CARRYING COST AS A PERCENTAGE OF UNIT COST
1	10.60	600	40	20
2	11.00	450	30	25
3	2.25	500	50	15
4	150.00	560	40	15
5	4.00	540	35	16
6	4.10	490	40	17

Lynn Robinson, Xemex's inventory manager, does not feel that all of the items can be controlled. What ordered quantities do you recommend for which inventory product(s)?

6-42 Georgia Products offers the following discount schedule for its 4- by 8-foot sheets of good-quality plywood:

ORDER	UNIT COST ($)
9 sheets or less	18.00
10 to 50 sheets	17.50
More than 50 sheets	17.25

Home Sweet Home Company orders plywood from Georgia Products. Home Sweet Home has an ordering cost of $45. The carrying cost is 20%, and the annual demand is 100 sheets. What do you recommend?

6-43 Sunbright Citrus Products produces orange juice, grapefruit juice, and other citrus-related items. Sunbright obtains fruit concentrate from a cooperative in Orlando consisting of approximately 50 citrus growers. The cooperative will sell a minimum of 100 cans of fruit concentrate to citrus processors such as Sunbright. The cost per can is $9.90.

Last year, the cooperative developed the Incentive Bonus Program to give an incentive to their large customers to buy in quantity. It works like this: If 200 cans of concentrate are purchased, 10 cans of free concentrate are included in the deal. In addition, the names of the companies purchasing the concentrate are added to a drawing for a new personal computer. The personal computer has a value of about $3,000, and currently about 1,000 companies are eligible for this drawing. At 300 cans of concentrate, the cooperative will give away 30 free cans and will also place the company name in the drawing for the personal computer. When the quantity goes up to 400 cans of concentrate, 40 cans of concentrate will be given away free with the order. In addition, the company is also placed in a drawing for the personal computer and a free trip for two. The value of the trip for two is approximately $5,000. About 800 companies are expected to qualify and to be in the running for this trip.

Sunbright estimates that its annual demand for fruit concentrate is 1,000 cans. In addition, the ordering cost is estimated to be $10, while the carrying cost is estimated to be 10%, or about $1 per unit. The firm is intrigued with the incentive bonus plan. If the company decides that it will keep the car, the trip, or the computer if they are won, what should it do?

6-44 George Grim used to be an accounting professor at a state university. Several years ago, he started to develop seminars and programs for a CPA review course, which helps accounting students and others interested in passing the CPA exam. To develop an effective seminar, George developed a number of books and other related materials to help. The main product was the CPA review manual developed by George. The manual was an instant success for his seminars and other seminars and courses across the country. Today, George spends most of his time refining and distributing this CPA review manual. The price of the manual is $45.95. George's total cost to manufacture and produce the manual is $32.90. George wants to avoid stockouts or to develop a stockout policy that would be cost-effective. If there is a stockout on the CPA review manual, George loses the profit from the sale of the manual.

George has determined from past experience that the reorder point from his printer is 400 units, assuming no safety stock. The question that George must answer is how much safety stock he should have as a buffer. On average, George places one order per year for the CPA review manual. The frequency of demand for the CPA review manuals during lead time is as follows:

DEMAND	FREQUENCY	DEMAND	FREQUENCY
300	1	600	4
350	2	650	4
400	2	700	3
450	3	750	2
500	4	800	2
550	5		

George estimates that his carrying cost per unit per year is $7. What level of safety stock should George carry to minimize total inventory costs?

 6-45 John Lindsay sells disks that contain 25 software packages that perform a variety of financial functions, including net present value, internal rate of return, and other financial programs typically used by business students majoring in finance. Depending on the quantity ordered, John offers the following price discounts. The annual demand is 2,000 units on average. His setup cost to produce the disks is $250. He estimates holding costs to be 10% of the price, or about $1 per unit per year.

PRICE RANGES	QUANTITY ORDERED		
	FROM	TO	PRICE
	1	500	$10.00
	501	1,000	9.95
	1,001	1,500	9.90
	1,500	2,000	9.85

(a) What is the optimal number of disks to produce at a time?
(b) What is the impact of the following quantity-price schedule on the optimal order quantity?

PRICE RANGES	QUANTITY ORDERED		
	FROM	TO	PRICE
	1	500	$10.00
	501	1,000	9.99
	1,001	1,500	9.98
	1,501	2,000	9.97

6-46 Emarpy Appliance produces all kinds of major appliances. Richard Feehan, the president of Emarpy, is concerned about the production policy for the company's best selling refrigerator. The demand for this has been relatively constant at about 8,000 units each year. The production capacity for this product is 200 units per day. Each time production starts, it costs the company $120 to move materials into place, reset the assembly line, and clean the equipment. The holding cost of a refrigerator is $50 per year. The current production plan calls for 400 refrigerators to be produced in each production run. Assume there are 250 working days per year.

(a) What is the daily demand of this product?
(b) If the company were to continue to produce 400 units each time production starts, how many days would production continue?
(c) Under the current policy, how many production runs per year would be required? What would the annual setup cost be?
(d) If the current policy continues, how many refrigerators would be in inventory when production stops? What would the average inventory level be?
(e) If the company produces 400 refrigerators at a time, what would the total annual setup cost and holding cost be?

6-47 Consider the Emarpy Appliance situation in Problem 6-46. If Richard Feehan wants to minimize the total annual inventory cost, how many refrigerators should be produced in each production run? How much would this save the company in inventory costs compared with the current policy of producing 400 in each production run?

6-48 This chapter presents a material structure tree for item A in Figure 6.11. Assume that it now takes 1 unit of item B to make every unit of item A. What impact does this have on the material structure tree and the number of items of D and E that are needed?

6-49 Given the information in Problem 6-48, develop a gross material requirements plan for 50 units of item A.

6-50 Using the data from Figures 6.11–6.13, develop a net material requirements plan for 50 units of item A assuming that it only takes 1 unit of item B for each unit of item A.

6-51 The demand for product S is 100 units. Each unit of S requires 1 unit of T and 1/2 unit of U. Each unit of T requires 1 unit of V, 2 units of W, and 1 unit of X. Finally, each unit of U requires 1/2 unit of Y and 3 units of Z. All items are manufactuured by the same firm. It takes two weeks to make S, one week to make T, two weeks to make U, two weeks to make V, three weeks to make W, one week to make X, two weeks to make Y, and one week to make Z.

(a) Construct a material structure tree and a gross material requirements plan for the dependent inventory items.
(b) Identify all levels, parents, and components.
(c) Construct a net material requirements plan using the following on-hand inventory data:

Item	S	T	U	V	W	X	Y	Z
On-Hand Inventory	20	20	10	30	30	25	15	10

6-52 The Webster Manufacturing Company prooduces a popular type of serving cart. This product, the SL72, is made from the following parts: 1 unit of Part A, 1 unit of Part B, and 1 unit of Subassembly C. Each subassembly C is made up of 2 units of Part D, 4 units of Part E, and 2 units of Part F. Develop a material structure tree for this.

6-53 The lead time for each of the parts in the SL72 (Problem 6-52) is one week, except for Part B, which has a lead time of two weeks. Develop a net materials requirements plan for an order of 800 SL72s. Assume that currently there are no parts in inventory.

6-54 Refer to Problem 6-53. Develop a net material requirements plan assuming that there are currently 150 units of Part A, 40 units of Part B, 50 units of Subassembly C, and 100 units of Part F currently in inventory.

INTERNET HOMEWORK PROBLEMS

See our Internet home page at www.prehall.com/render for additional homework problems 6-55 to 6-62.

➤ CASE STUDY

Sturdivant Sound Systems

Sturdivant Sound Systems manufactures and sells stereo and compact disc (CD) sound systems in both console and component styles. All parts of the sound systems, with the exception of speakers, are produced in the Rochester, New York, plant. Speakers used in the assembly of Sturdivant's systems are purchased from Morris Electronics of Concord, New Hampshire.

Jason Pierce, purchasing agent for Sturdivant Sound Systems, submits a purchase requisition for the speakers once every four weeks. The company's annual requirements total 5,000 units (20 per working day), and the cost per unit is $60. (Sturdivant does not purchase in greater quantities because Morris Electronics, the supplier, does not offer quantity discounts.) Rarely does a shortage of speakers occur because Morris promises delivery within one week following receipt of a purchase requisition. (Total time between date of order and date of receipt is 10 days.)

Associated with the purchase of each shipment are procurement costs. These costs, which amount to $20 per order, include the costs of preparing the requisition, inspecting and storing the delivered goods, updating inventory records, and issuing a voucher and a check for payment. In addition to procurement costs, Sturdivant Sound Systems incurs inventory carrying costs, which include insurance, storage, handling, taxes, and so on. These costs equal $6 per unit per year.

Beginning in August of this year, management of Sturdivant Sound Systems will embark on a companywide cost control program in an attempt to improve its profits. One of the areas to be scrutinized closely for possible cost savings is inventory procurement.

Discussion Questions

1. Compute the optimal order quantity.
2. Determine the appropriate ROP (in units).
3. Compute the cost savings that the company will realize if it implements the optimal inventory procurement decision.
4. Should procurement costs be considered a linear function of the number of orders?

Source: Professor Jerry Kinard, Western Carolina University.

⊪➡ CASE STUDY

Martin-Pullin Bicycle Corporation

Martin-Pullin Bicycle Corp. (MPBC), located in Dallas, is a wholesale distributor of bicycles and bicycle parts. Formed in 1981 by cousins Ray Martin and Jim Pullin, the firm's primary retail outlets are located within a 400-mile radius of the distribution center. These retail outlets receive the order from Martin-Pullin within two days after notifying the distribution center, provided that the stock is available. However, if an order is not fulfilled by the company, no backorder is placed; the retailers arrange to get their shipment from other distributors, and MPBC loses that amount of business.

The company distributes a wide variety of bicycles. The most popular model, and the major source of revenue to the company, is the AirWing. MPBC receives all the models from a single manufacturer overseas, and shipment takes as long as four weeks from the time an order is placed. With the cost of communication, paperwork, and customs clearance included, MPBC estimates that each time an order is placed, it incurs a cost of $65. The purchase price paid by MPBC, per bicycle, is roughly 60% of the suggested retail price for all the styles available, and the inventory carrying cost is 1% per month (12% per year) of the purchase price paid by MPBC. The retail price (paid by the customers) for the AirWing is $170 per bicycle.

MPBC is interested in making an inventory plan for 2002. The firm wants to maintain a 95% service level with its customers to minimize the losses on the lost orders. The data collected for the past two years are summarized in the following table. A forecast for AirWing model sales in the upcoming year 2002 has been developed and will be used to make an inventory plan for MPBC.

Demands for AirWing Model

MONTH	2000	2001	FORECAST FOR 2002
January	6	7	8
February	12	14	15
March	24	27	31
April	46	53	59
May	75	86	97
June	47	54	60
July	30	34	39
August	18	21	24
September	13	15	16
October	12	13	15
November	22	25	28
December	38	42	47
Total	343	391	439

Discussion Questions

1. Develop an inventory plan to help MPBC.
2. Discuss ROPs and total costs.
3. How can you address demand that is not at the level of the planning horizon?

Source: Professor Kala Chand Seal, Loyola Marymount University.

INTERNET CASE STUDIES

See our Internet home page at **www.prenhall.com/render** for these additional case studies:

(1) LaPlace Power and Light: This case involves a public utility in Louisiana and its use of electric cables for connecting houses to power lines.

(2) Western Ranchman Outfitters: This case involves managing the inventory of a popular style of jeans when the delivery date is sometimes unpredictable.

(3) Professional Video Management: This case involves a videotape system in which discounts from suppliers are possible.

(4) Drake Radio: This case involves ordering FM tuners.

BIBLIOGRAPHY

Allnoch, Allen. "Manufacturing Software Plays Key Role," *IIE Solutions* (November 1997): 58–60.

Andersson, Jonas and Johan Marklund. "Decentralized Inventory Control in a Two-Level Distribution System," *European Journal of Operational Research* 127, 3 (2000): 483–506.

Brown, Alexander O., Hau L. Lee, and Raja Petrakian. "Xilinx Improves Its Semiconductor Supply Chain Using Product and Process Postponement," *Interfaces* 30, 4 (July–August 2000): 65–80.

Brucker, H. D., G. A. Flowers, and R. D. Peck. "MRP Shop-Floor Control in a Job Shop: Definitely Works," *Production and Inventory Management Journal* 33, 2 (Second Quarter 1992): 43.

Chen, Fangruo. "Sales-Force Incentives and Inventory Management," *Manufacturing and Service Operations Management* 2, 2 (2000): 186–202.

Ding, F. and M. Yuen. "A Modified MRP for a Production System with the Coexistence of MRP and Kanbans," *Journal of Operations Management* 10, 2 (April 1991): 267–277. "Fully Automated System Achieves True JIT," *Modern Materials Handling* (April 1998): 22–27.

Emmons, Hamilton et al. "The Role of Return Policies in Pricing and Decisions." *Management Science* (February 1998): 276–283.

Funk, Jeffrey L. "Just-in-Time Manufacturing and Logistical Complexity: A Contingency Model," *International Journal of Operations & Production Management* 15, 5 (1995): 60–71.

Gould, Eppen et al. "Backup Agreements in Fashion Buying." *Management Science* (November 1997): 1469–1484.

Greis, Noel. "Assessing Service Level Targets in Production and Inventory Planning," *Decision Sciences* 25, 1 (January–February 1994): 15–40.

Hill, Roger M. "On Optimal Two-Stage Lot Sizing and Inventory Batching Policies," *International Journal of Production Economics* 66, 2 (2000): 149–158.

Holder, Roy. "MRP Helps Welpac Win Through Effective Purchasing," *Works Management* 48, 3 (March 1995): 18–21.

Imai, Masakki. "Will America's Corporate Theme Song Be 'Just-in-Time'?" *Journal for Quality & Participation* (March 1998): 26–29.

Jacobs, F. R. and D. C. Whybark. "A Comparison of Reorder Point and Material Requirements Planning Inventory Control Logic," *Decision Sciences* 23, 2 (March–April 1992): 332–342.

Jayaraman, Vaidyanathan, Cindy Burnett, and Derek Frank. "Separating Inventory Flows in the Materials Management Department of Hancock Medical Center," *Interfaces* 30, 4 (July–August 2000): 56–64.

Karabakal, Nejat, Ali Gunal, and Warren Witchie. "Supply-Chain Analysis at Volkswagen of America," *Interfaces* 30, 4 (July–August, 2000): 46–55.

Millet, Ido. "How to Find Inventory by Not Looking," *Interfaces* (March 1994): 69–75.

Ramesesh, Ranga V. and Ram Rachmadugu. "Lot-Sizing Decision Under Limited-Time Price Reduction," *Decision Sciences* 32, 1 (Winter 2001): 125–143.

Ramdas, Kamalini and Robert E. Spekman. "Chain or Shackles: Understanding What Drives Supply-Chain Performance," *Interfaces* 30, 4 (July–August 2000): 3–21.

Sox, Charles et al. "Coordinating Production and Inventory to Improve Service," *Management Science* (September 1997): 1189–1197.

van der Duyn Schouten, Frank et al. "The Value of Supplier Information to Improve Management of a Retailer's Inventory," *Decision Sciences* 25, 1 (January–February 1994): 1–14.

APPENDIX 6.1: INVENTORY CONTROL WITH QM FOR WINDOWS

A variety of inventory control models are covered in this chapter. Each model makes different assumptions and uses slightly different approaches. The use of QM for Windows is similar for these different types of inventory problems. As you can see in the inventory menu for QM for Windows, most of the inventory problems discussed in this chapter can be solved using your computer.

To demonstrate QM for Windows, we start with the basic EOQ model. Sumco, a manufacturing company discussed in the chapter, has an annual demand of 1,000 units, an ordering cost of $10 per unit, and a carrying cost of $0.50 per unit per year. With these data, we can use QM for Windows to determine the economic order quantity. The results are shown in Program 6.4.

PROGRAM 6.4

QM for Windows Results for EOQ Model

Parameter	Value		Parameter	Value
Demand rate(D)	1000		Optimal order quantity (Q*)	200.
Setup/Ordering cost(S)	10		Maximum Inventory Level (Imax)	200.
Holding cost(H)	0.5		Average inventory	100.
Unit cost	0		Orders per period(year)	5.
			Annual Setup cost	50.
			Annual Holding cost	50.
			Unit costs (PD)	0.
			Total Cost	100.

The production run inventory problem, which requires the daily production and demand rate in addition to the annual demand, the ordering cost per order, and the carrying cost per unit per year, is also covered in this chapter. Brown's Manufacturing example is used in this chapter to show how the calculations can be made manually. We can use QM for Windows on these data. Program 6.5 shows the results.

PROGRAM 6.5

QM for Windows Results for the Production Run Model

The quantity discount model allows the material cost to vary with the quantity ordered. In this case the model must consider and minimize material, ordering, and carrying costs by examining each price discount. Program 6.6 shows how QM for Windows can be used to solve the quantity discount model discussed in the chapter. Note that the program output shows the input data in addition to the results.

PROGRAM 6.6

QM for Windows Results for the Quantity Discount Model

When an organization has a large number of inventory items, ABC analysis is often used. As discussed in this chapter, total dollar volume for an inventory item is one way to determine if quantitative control techniques should be used. Performing the necessary calculations is done in Program 6.7, which shows how QM for Windows can be used to compute dollar volume and determine if quantitative control techniques are justified for each inventory item with this new example.

PROGRAM 6.7

QM for Windows Results for ABC Analysis

QM for Windows - C:\My Documents\Mike\R&S\Weiss\Render.Stair.7\QM for Windows files\abc1.inv

File Edit View Module Format Tools Window Help

Percent of items that are A items: 15

Percent of items that are B items: 30

Instruction
Click on Edit to return to data.

Inventory Results

(untitled) Solution

Item name	Demand	Price	Dollar Volume	Percent of $-Vol	Cumultv $-vol %	Category
Item 1	7,000.	10.	70,000.	56.59	56.59	A
Item 2	2,000.	10.	20,000.	16.17	72.76	B
Item 3	1,000.	10.	10,000.	8.08	80.84	B
Item 4	2,000.	5.	10,000.	8.08	88.92	C
Item 5	2,500.	3.	7,500.	6.06	94.99	C
Item 6	800.	4.	3,200.	2.59	97.57	C
Item 7	600.	5.	3,000.	2.43	100.	C
TOTAL	15,900.		123,700.			

CHAPTER 7

LINEAR PROGRAMMING MODELS: GRAPHICAL AND COMPUTER METHODS

LEARNING OBJECTIVES

After completing this chapter, students will be able to:

1. Understand the basic assumptions and properties of linear programming (LP).
2. Graphically solve any LP problem that has only two variables by both the corner point and isoprofit line methods.
3. Understand special issues in LP such as infeasibility, unboundedness, redundancy, and alternative optimal solutions.
4. Understand the role of sensitivity analysis.
5. Use Excel spreadsheets to solve LP problems.

CHAPTER OUTLINE

Summary • Glossary • Solved Problems • Self-Test • Discussion Questions and Problems • Internet Homework Problems • Case Study: Mexicana Wire Works • Internet Case Study • Bibliography

7.1   INTRODUCTION

Linear programming is a technique that helps in resource allocation decisions.

Many management decisions involve trying to make the most effective use of an organization's resources. Resources typically include machinery, labor, money, time, warehouse space, and raw materials. These resources may be used to make products (such as machinery, furniture, food, or clothing) or services (such as schedules for airlines or production, advertising policies, or investment decisions). *Linear programming* (LP) is a widely used mathematical modeling technique designed to help managers in planning and decision making relative to resource allocation. We devote this and the next two chapters to illustrating how and why linear programming works.

Despite its name, LP and the more general category of techniques called *"mathematical" programming* have very little to do with computer programming. In the world of management science, *programming* refers to modeling and solving a problem mathematically. Computer programming has, of course, played an important role in the advancement and use of LP. Real-life LP problems are too cumbersome to solve by hand or with a calculator. So throughout the chapters on LP we give examples of how valuable a computer program can be in solving an LP problem.

7.2   REQUIREMENTS OF A LINEAR PROGRAMMING PROBLEM

In the past 50 years, LP has been applied extensively to military, industrial, financial, marketing, accounting, and agricultural problems. Even though these applications are diverse, all LP problems have four properties in common.

First LP property: Problems seek to maximize or minimize an objective.

All problems seek to *maximize* or *minimize* some quantity, usually profit or cost. We refer to this property as the *objective function* of an LP problem. The major objective of a typical manufacturer is to maximize dollar profits. In the case of a trucking or railroad distribution system, the objective might be to minimize shipping costs. In any event, this objective must be stated clearly and defined mathematically. It does not matter, by the way, whether profits and costs are measured in cents, dollars, or millions of dollars.

Second LP property: Constraints limit the degree to which the objective can be obtained.

The second property that LP problems have in common is the presence of restrictions, or *constraints*, that limit the degree to which we can pursue our objective. For example, deciding how many units of each product in a firm's product line to manufacture is restricted by available personnel and machinery. Selection of an advertising policy or a financial portfolio is limited by the amount of money available to be spent or invested. We want, therefore, to maximize or minimize a quantity (the objective function) subject to limited resources (the constraints).

Third LP property: There must be alternatives available.

There must be alternative courses of action to choose from. For example, if a company produces three different products, management may use LP to decide how to allocate among them its limited production resources (of personnel, machinery, and so on). Should it devote all manufacturing capacity to make only the first product, should it produce equal amounts of each product, or should it allocate the resources in some other ratio? If there were no alternatives to select from, we would not need LP.

Fourth LP property: Mathematical relationships are linear.

The objective and constraints in LP problems must be expressed in terms of *linear* equations or inequalities. Linear mathematical relationships just mean that all terms used in the objective function and constraints are of the first degree (i.e., not squared, or to the third or higher power, or appearing more than once). Hence, the equation $2A + 5B = 10$ is an acceptable linear function, while the equation $2A^2 + 5B^3 + 3AB = 10$ is not linear because the variable A is squared, the variable B is cubed, and the two variables appear again as a product of each other.

You will see the term *inequality* quite often when we discuss LP problems. By inequalities we mean that not all LP constraints need be of the form $A + B = C$. This particular

TABLE 7.1	PROPERTIES OF LINEAR PROGRAMS
LP Properties and Assumptions	1. One objective function
	2. One or more constraints
	3. Alternative courses of action
	4. Objective function and constraints are linear

	ASSUMPTIONS OF LP
	1. Certainty
	2. Proportionality
	3. Additivity
	4. Divisibility
	5. Nonnegative variables

An inequality has a ≤ or ≥ sign.

relationship, called an *equation*, implies that the term A plus the term B are together exactly equal to the term C. In most LP problems, we see inequalities of the form $A + B \leq C$ or $A + B \geq C$. The first of these means that A plus B is less than or equal to C. The second means that A plus B is greater than or equal to C. This concept provides a lot of flexibility in defining problem limitations. A summary of these properties and the assumptions is given in Table 7.1.

Basic Assumptions of LP

Technically, there are five additional requirements of an LP problem of which you should be aware:

Five technical requirements are (1) certainty, (2) proportionality, (3) additivity, (4) divisibility, and (5) nonnegativity.

We assume that conditions of *certainty* exist; that is, numbers in the objective and constraints are known with certainty and do not change during the period being studied.

We also assume that *proportionality* exists in the objective and constraints. This means that if production of 1 unit of a product uses 3 hours of a particular scarce resource, then making 10 units of that product uses 30 hours of the resource.

The third technical assumption deals with *additivity*, meaning that the total of all activities equals the sum of the individual activities. For example, if an objective is to maximize profit = $8 per unit of first product made plus $3 per unit of second product made, and if 1 unit of each product is actually produced, the profit contributions of $8 and $3 must add up to produce a sum of $11.

HISTORY   How Linear Programming Started

Linear programming was conceptually developed before World War II by the outstanding Soviet mathematician A. N. Kolmogorov. Another Russian, Leonid Kantorovich, won the Nobel Prize in Economics for advancing the concepts of optimal planning. An early application of LP, by Stigler in 1945, was in the area we today call "diet problems."

Major progress in the field, however, took place in 1947 and later when George D. Dantzig developed the solution procedure known as the *simplex algorithm*. Dantzig, then an Air Force mathematician, was assigned to work on logistics problems. He noticed that many problems involving limited resources and more than one demand could be set up in terms of a series of equations and inequalities. Although early LP applications were military in nature, industrial applications rapidly became apparent with the spread of business computers. In 1984, N. Karmarkar developed an algorithm that appears to be superior to the simplex method for many very large applications.

We make the *divisibility* assumption that solutions need not be in whole numbers (integers). Instead, they are divisible and may take any fractional value. In production problems, we often define variables as the number of units produced per week or per month, and a fractional value (e.g., 0.3 chairs) would simply mean that there is work in process. Something that was started in one week can be finished in the next. However, in other types of problems, fractional values do not make sense. If a fraction of a product cannot be purchased (for example, one-third of a submarine), an integer programming problem exists. Integer programming is discussed in more detail in Chapter 11.

Finally, we assume that all answers or variables are *nonnegative*. Negative values of physical quantities are impossible; you simply cannot produce a negative number of chairs, shirts, lamps, or computers.

7.3 FORMULATING LP PROBLEMS

Formulating a linear program involves developing a mathematical model to represent the managerial problem. Thus, in order to formulate a linear program, it is necessary to completely understand the managerial problem being faced. Once this is understood, we can begin to develop the mathematical statement of the problem. The steps in formulating a linear program follow:

1. Completely understand the managerial problem being faced.

2. Identify the objective and the constraints.

3. Define the decision variables.

4. Use the decision variables to write mathematical expressions for the objective function and the constraints.

Product mix problems use LP to decide how much of each product to make, given a series of resource restrictions.

One of the most common LP applications is the *product mix problem*. Two or more products are usually produced using limited resources such as personnel, machines, raw materials, and so on. The profit that the firm seeks to maximize is based on the profit contribution per unit of each product. (Profit contribution, you may recall, is just the selling price per unit minus the variable cost per unit.[1]) The company would like to determine how many units of each product it should produce so as to maximize overall profit given its limited resources. A problem of this type is formulated in the following example.

Flair Furniture Company

The Flair Furniture Company produces inexpensive tables and chairs. The production process for each is similar in that both require a certain number of hours of carpentry work and a certain number of labor hours in the painting and varnishing department. Each table takes 4 hours of carpentry and 2 hours in the painting and varnishing shop. Each chair requires 3 hours in carpentry and 1 hour in painting and varnishing. During the current production period, 240 hours of carpentry time are available and 100 hours in painting and varnishing time are available. Each table sold yields a profit of $7; each chair produced is sold for a $5 profit.

Flair Furniture's problem is to determine the best possible combination of tables and chairs to manufacture in order to reach the maximum profit. The firm would like this production mix situation formulated as an LP problem.

---

[1] Technically, we maximize total contribution margin, which is the difference between unit selling price and costs that vary in proportion to the quantity of the item produced. Depreciation, fixed general expense, and advertising are excluded from calculations. Problem 7-40 deals with these issues.

	HOURS REQUIRED TO PRODUCE 1 UNIT		
DEPARTMENT	(T) TABLES	(C) CHAIRS	AVAILABLE HOURS THIS WEEK
Carpentry	4	3	240
Painting and varnishing	2	1	100
Profit per unit	$7	$5	

TABLE 7.2

Flair Furniture Company Data

We begin by summarizing the information needed to formulate and solve this problem (see Table 7.2). This helps us understand the problem being faced. Next we identify the objective and the constraints. The objective is

Maximize profit

The constraints are

1. The hours of carpentry time used cannot exceed 240 hours per week.
2. The hours of painting and varnishing time used cannot exceed 100 hours per week.

The decision variables that represent the actual decisions we will make are defined as

T = number of tables to be produced per week

C = number of chairs to be produced per week

Now we can create the LP objective function in terms of T and C. The objective function is maximize profit = $7T + $5C.

Our next step is to develop mathematical relationships to describe the two constraints in this problem. One general relationship is that the amount of a resource used is to be less than or equal to ($\leq$) the amount of resource *available*.

In the case of the carpentry department, the total time used is

(4 hours per table)(number of tables produced)
+ (3 hours per chair)(number of chairs produced)

The resource constraints put limits on the carpentry labor resource and the painting labor resource mathematically.

So the first constraint may be stated as follows:

Carpentry time used is $\leq$ carpentry time available.

$4T + 3C \leq 240$ (hours of carpentry time)

Similarly, the second constraint is as follows:

Painting and varnishing time used is $\leq$ painting and varnishing time available.

②$T + 1C \leq 100$ (hours of painting and varnishing time)

(This means that each table produced takes two hours of the painting and varnishing resource.)

Both of these constraints represent production capacity restrictions and, of course, affect the total profit. For example, Flair Furniture cannot produce 70 tables during the production period because if $T = 70$, both constraints will be violated. It also cannot make $T = 50$ tables and $C = 10$ chairs. Why? Because this would violate the second constraint that no more than 100 hours of painting and varnishing time be allocated.

To obtain meaningful solutions, the values for T and C must be nonnegative numbers. That is, all potential solutions must represent real tables and real chairs. Mathematically, this means that

$T \geq 0$ (number of tables produced is greater than or equal to 0)

$C \geq 0$ (number of chairs produced is greater than or equal to 0)

The complete problem may now be restated mathematically as

$$\text{maximize profit} = \$7T + \$5C$$

subject to the constraints

Here is a complete mathematical statement of the LP problem.

$4T + 3C \leq 240$	(carpentry constraint)
$2T + 1C \leq 100$	(painting and varnishing constraint)
$T \geq 0$	(first nonnegativity constraint)
$C \geq 0$	(second nonnegativity constraint)

While the nonnegativity constraints are technically separate constraints, they are often written on a single line with the variables separated by commas. In this example, this would be written as

$$T, C \geq 0$$

7.4 GRAPHICAL SOLUTION TO AN LP PROBLEM

The easiest way to solve a small LP problem such as that of the Flair Furniture Company is with the graphical solution approach. The graphical procedure is useful only when there are two decision variables (such as number of tables to produce, T, and number of chairs to produce, C) in the problem. When there are more than two variables, it is not possible to plot the solution on a two-dimensional graph and we must turn to more complex approaches, the topic of Chapter 9. But the graphical method is invaluable in providing us with insights into how other approaches work. For that reason alone, it is worthwhile to spend the rest of this chapter exploring graphical solutions as an intuitive basis for the chapters on mathematical programming that follow.

The graphical method works only when there are two decision variables, but it provides valuable insight into how larger problems are structured.

Graphical Representation of Constraints

To find the optimal solution to an LP problem, we must first identify a set, or region, of feasible solutions. The first step in doing so is to plot each of the problem's constraints on a graph. The variable T (tables) is plotted as the horizontal axis of the graph and the variable C (chairs) is plotted as the vertical axis. The *nonnegativity constraints* mean that we are always working in the first (or northeast) quadrant of a graph (see Figure 7.1).

Nonnegativity constraints mean we are always in the graphical area when $T \geq 0$ and $C \geq 0$.

To represent the first constraint graphically, $4T + 3C \leq 240$, we must first graph the equality portion of this, which is:

$$4T + 3C = 240$$

As you may recall from elementary algebra, a linear equation in two variables is a straight line. The easiest way to plot the line is to find any two points that satisfy the equation, then draw a straight line through them.

Plotting the first constraint involves finding points at which the line intersects the T and C axes.

The two easiest points to find are generally the points at which the line intersects the T and C axes.

FIGURE 7.1

Quadrant Containing All Positive Values

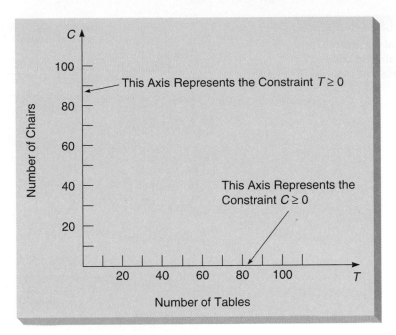

When Flair Furniture produces no tables, namely $T = 0$, it implies that

$$4(0) + 3C = 240$$

or

$$3C = 240$$

or

$$C = 80$$

In other words, if *all* of the carpentry time available is used to produce chairs, 80 chairs *could* be made. Thus, this constraint equation crosses the vertical axis at 80.

To find the point at which the line crosses the horizontal axis, we assume that the firm makes no chairs, that is, $C = 0$. Then

$$4T + 3(0) = 240$$

or

$$4T = 240$$

or

$$T = 60$$

Hence, when $C = 0$, we see that $4T = 240$ and that $T = 60$.

The carpentry constraint is illustrated in Figure 7.2. It is bounded by the line running from point ($T = 0$, $C = 80$) to point ($T = 60$, $C = 0$).

Recall, however, that the actual carpentry constraint was the *inequality* $4T + 3C \leq 240$. How can we identify all of the solution points that satisfy this constraint? It turns out that there are three possibilities. First, we know that any point that lies on the line $4T +$

**Graph of Carpentry
Constraint Equation**
$4T + 3C = 240$

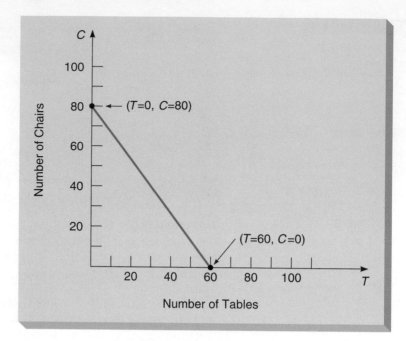

3C = 240 satisfies the constraint. Any combination of tables and chairs on the line will use up all 240 hours of carpentry time.[2] We see this by picking a point such as $T = 30$ tables and $C = 40$ chairs (see Figure 7.3). You should be able to see how exactly 240 hours of the carpentry resource are used.

**Region That Satisfies the
Carpentry Constraint**

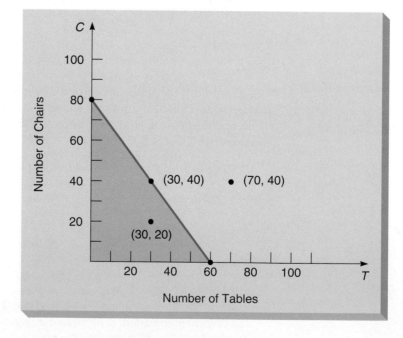

[2] Thus, what we have done is to plot the constraint equation in its most binding position, that is, using all of the carpentry resource.

The real question is: Where are the problem points satisfying $4T + 3C \leq 240$? We can answer this question by checking two possible solution points, let's say ($T = 30$, $C = 20$) and ($T = 70$, $C = 40$). You see in Figure 7.3 that the first point is below the constraint line and the second point lies above it. Let us examine the first solution more carefully. If we substitute the (T, C) values into the carpentry constraint, the result is

$$4(T = 30) + 3(C = 20) = (4)(30) + (3)(20) = 120 + 60 = 180$$

Since 180 is less than the 240 hours available, the point (30, 20) satisfies the constraint. For the second solution point, we follow the same procedure:

$$4(T = 70) + 3(C = 40) = (4)(70) + (3)(40) = 280 + 120 = 400$$

Four hundred exceeds the carpentry time available and hence violates the constraint. So we now know that the point (70, 40) is an unacceptable production level. As a matter of fact, any point *above* the constraint line violates that restriction. (This is something you may wish to test for yourself with a few other points.) Any point *below* the line does not violate the constraint. In Figure 7.3 the shaded region represents all points that satisfy the original inequality constraint.

Next, let us identify the solution corresponding to the second constraint, which limits the time available in the painting and varnishing department. That constraint was given as $2T + 1C \leq 100$. As before, we start by graphing the equality portion of this constraint, which is:

$$2T + 1C = 100$$

The line from ($T = 0$, $C = 100$) to ($T = 50$, $C = 0$) in Figure 7.4 represents all combinations of tables and chairs that use exactly 100 hours of painting and varnishing department time. It is constructed in a fashion similar to the first constraint. When $T = 0$, then

$$2(0) + 1C = 100$$

FIGURE 7.4

Region That Satisfies the Painting and Varnishing Constraint

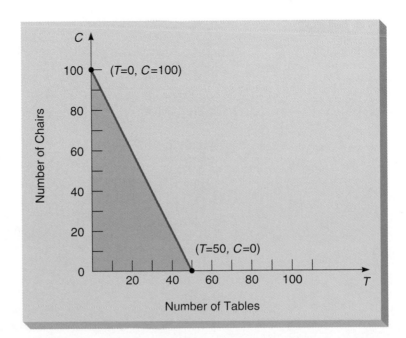

or

$$C = 100$$

When $C = 0$, then

$$2T + 1(0) = 100$$

or

$$2T = 100$$

or

$$T = 50$$

The constraint is bounded by the line between ($T = 0$, $C = 100$) to ($T = 50$, $C = 0$) and the shaded area again contains all possible combinations that do not exceed 100 hours. Thus, the shaded area represents the original inequality $2T + 1C \leq 100$.

Now that each individual constraint has been plotted on a graph, it is time to move on to the next step. We recognize that to produce a chair or a table, both the carpentry and painting and varnishing departments must be used. In an LP problem we need to find that set of solution points that satisfies all of the constraints *simultaneously*. Hence, the constraints should be redrawn on one graph (or superimposed one upon the other). This is shown in Figure 7.5.

The shaded region now represents the area of solutions that does not exceed either of the two Flair Furniture constraints. It is known by the term *area of feasible solutions* or, more simply, the *feasible region*. The feasible region in an LP problem must satisfy *all* conditions specified by the problem's constraints, and is thus the region where all constraints overlap. Any point in the region would be a *feasible solution* to the Flair Furniture problem; any point outside the shaded area would represent an *infeasible solution*. Hence, it would be

In LP problems we are interested in satisfying all constraints at the same time.

The feasible region is the overlapping area of constraints that satisfies all of the restrictions on resources.

FIGURE 7.5

Feasible Solution Region for the Flair Furniture Company Problem

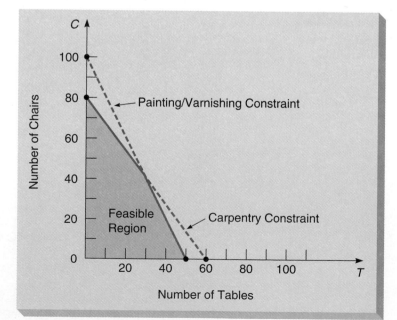

feasible to manufacture 30 tables and 20 chairs ($T = 30$, $C = 20$) during a production period because both constraints are observed.

Carpentry constraint	$4T + 3C \leq 240$ hours available
	$(4)(30) + (3)(20) = 180$ hours used ⊘
Painting constraint	$2T + 1C \leq 100$ hours available
	$(2)(30) + (1)(20) = 80$ hours used ⊘

But it would violate both of the constraints to produce 70 tables and 40 chairs, as we see here mathematically:

Carpentry constraint	$4T + 3C \leq 240$ hours available
	$(4)(70) + (3)(40) = 400$ hours used ⊗
Painting constraint	$2T + 1C \leq 100$ hours available
	$(2)(70) + (1)(40) = 180$ hours used ⊗

Furthermore, it would also be infeasible to manufacture 50 tables and 5 chairs ($T = 50$, $C = 5$). Can you see why?

Carpentry constraint	$4T + 3C \leq 240$ hours available
	$(4)(50) + (3)(5) = 215$ hours used ⊘
Painting constraint	$2T + 1C \leq 100$ hours available
	$(2)(50) + (1)(5) = 105$ hours used ⊗

This possible solution falls within the time available in carpentry but exceeds the time available in painting and varnishing and thus falls outside the feasible region.

Isoprofit Line Solution Method

Now that the feasible region has been graphed, we may proceed to find the optimal solution to the problem. The optimal solution is the point lying in the feasible region that produces the highest profit. Yet there are many, many possible solution points in the region. How do we go about selecting the best one, the one yielding the highest profit?

The isoprofit method is the first method we introduce for finding the optimal solution.

There are a few different approaches that can be taken in solving for the optimal solution when the feasible region has been established graphically. The speediest one to apply is called the *isoprofit line method*.

We start the technique by letting profits equal some arbitrary but small dollar amount. For the Flair Furniture problem we may choose a profit of $210. This is a profit level that can be obtained easily without violating either of the two constraints. The objective function can be written as $210 = 7T + 5C$.

This expression is just the equation of a line; we call it an *isoprofit line*. It represents all combinations of (T, C) that would yield a total profit of $210. To plot the profit line, we proceed exactly as we did to plot a constraint line. First, let $T = 0$ and solve for the point at which the line crosses the C axis.

$$\$210 = \$7(0) + \$5C$$

$$C = 42 \text{ chairs}$$

Then, let $C = 0$ and solve for T.

$$\$210 = \$7T + \$5(0)$$

$$T = 30 \text{ tables}$$

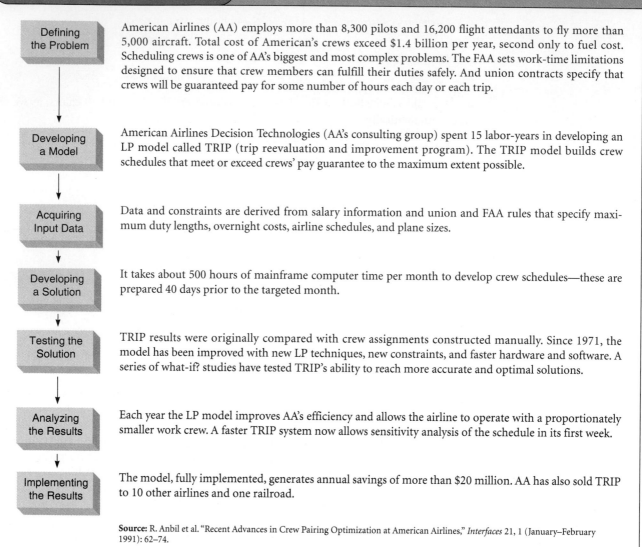

MODELING IN THE REAL WORLD   **Setting Crew Schedules at American Airlines**

Defining the Problem

American Airlines (AA) employs more than 8,300 pilots and 16,200 flight attendants to fly more than 5,000 aircraft. Total cost of American's crews exceed $1.4 billion per year, second only to fuel cost. Scheduling crews is one of AA's biggest and most complex problems. The FAA sets work-time limitations designed to ensure that crew members can fulfill their duties safely. And union contracts specify that crews will be guaranteed pay for some number of hours each day or each trip.

Developing a Model

American Airlines Decision Technologies (AA's consulting group) spent 15 labor-years in developing an LP model called TRIP (trip reevaluation and improvement program). The TRIP model builds crew schedules that meet or exceed crews' pay guarantee to the maximum extent possible.

Acquiring Input Data

Data and constraints are derived from salary information and union and FAA rules that specify maximum duty lengths, overnight costs, airline schedules, and plane sizes.

Developing a Solution

It takes about 500 hours of mainframe computer time per month to develop crew schedules—these are prepared 40 days prior to the targeted month.

Testing the Solution

TRIP results were originally compared with crew assignments constructed manually. Since 1971, the model has been improved with new LP techniques, new constraints, and faster hardware and software. A series of what-if? studies have tested TRIP's ability to reach more accurate and optimal solutions.

Analyzing the Results

Each year the LP model improves AA's efficiency and allows the airline to operate with a proportionately smaller work crew. A faster TRIP system now allows sensitivity analysis of the schedule in its first week.

Implementing the Results

The model, fully implemented, generates annual savings of more than $20 million. AA has also sold TRIP to 10 other airlines and one railroad.

Source: R. Anbil et al. "Recent Advances in Crew Pairing Optimization at American Airlines," *Interfaces* 21, 1 (January–February 1991): 62–74.

Isoprofit involves graphing parallel profit lines.

We can now connect these two points with a straight line. This profit line is illustrated in Figure 7.6. All points on the line represent feasible solutions that produce a profit of $210.[3]

Now, obviously, the isoprofit line for $210 does not produce the highest possible profit to the firm. In Figure 7.7 we try graphing two more lines, each yielding a higher profit. The middle equation, $280 = $7T + $5C, was plotted in the same fashion as the lower line. When $T = 0$,

$$\$280 = \$7(0) + \$5C$$

$$C = 56$$

---

[3] *Iso* means "equal" or "similar." Thus, an isoprofit line represents a line with all profits the same, in this case $210.

FIGURE 7.6

Profit Line of $210 Plotted for the Flair Furniture Company

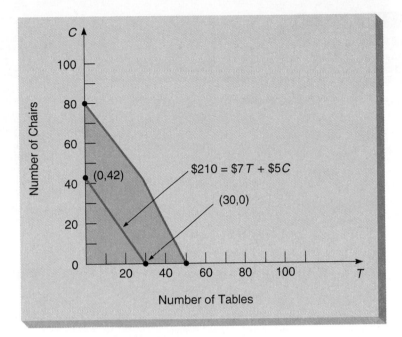

When $C = 0$,

$$\$280 = \$7T + \$5(0)$$

$$T = 40$$

Again, any combination of tables (T) and chairs (C) on this isoprofit line produces a total profit of $280.

Note that the third line generates a profit of $350, even more of an improvement. The farther we move from the 0 origin, the higher our profit will be. Another important point is that these isoprofit lines are parallel. We now have two clues as to how to find the optimal

FIGURE 7.7

Four Isoprofit Lines Plotted for the Flair Furniture Company

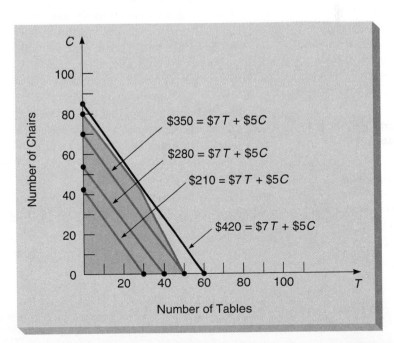

FIGURE 7.8

Optimal Solution to the
Flair Furniture Problem

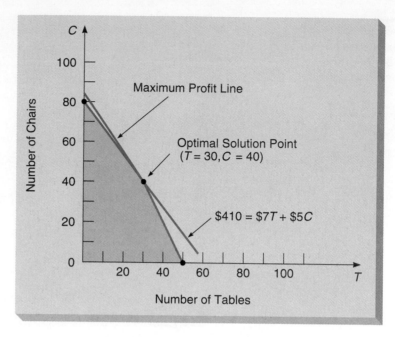

We draw a series of parallel isoprofit lines until we find the highest isoprofit line, that is, the one with the optimal solution.

solution to the original problem. We can draw a series of parallel lines (by carefully moving our ruler in a plane parallel to the first profit line). The highest profit line that still touches some point of the feasible region pinpoints the optimal solution. Notice that the fourth line ($420) is too high to be considered.

The highest possible isoprofit line is illustrated in Figure 7.8. It touches the tip of the feasible region at the corner point ($T = 30$, $C = 40$) and yields a profit of $410.

Corner Point Solution Method

A second approach to solving LP problems employs the *corner point method*. This technique is simpler conceptually than the isoprofit line approach, but it involves looking at the profit at every corner point of the feasible region.

The mathematical theory behind LP is that the optimal solution must lie at one of the corner points in the feasible region.

The mathematical theory behind LP states that an optimal solution to any problem (that is, the values of T, C that yield the maximum profit) will lie at a *corner point*, or *extreme point*, of the feasible region. Hence, it is only necessary to find the values of the variables at each corner; the maximum profit or optimal solution will lie at one (or more) of them.

Once again we can see that the feasible region for the Flair Furniture Company problem is a four-sided polygon with four corner, or extreme, points (Figure 7.9). These points are labeled ①, ②, ③, and ④ on the graph. To find the (T, C) values producing the maximum profit, we find the coordinates of each corner point and test their profit levels.

Testing corner points ①, ②, and ④ is easy because their T, C coordinates are quickly identified.

Point ①: ($T = 0$, $C = 0$)   profit = $7(0) + $5(0) = $0
Point ②: ($T = 0$, $C = 80$)   profit = $7(0) + $5(80) = $400
Point ④: ($T = 50$, $C = 0$)   profit = $7(50) + $5(0) = $350

We skipped corner point ③ momentarily because, to find its coordinates *accurately*, we have to solve for the intersection of the two constraint lines.[4] As you may recall from

---

[4] Of course, if a graph is perfectly drawn, you can always find point ③ by careful examination of the intersection's coordinates. Otherwise, the algebraic method shown here provides more precision.

FIGURE 7.9

Four Corner Points of the Feasible Region

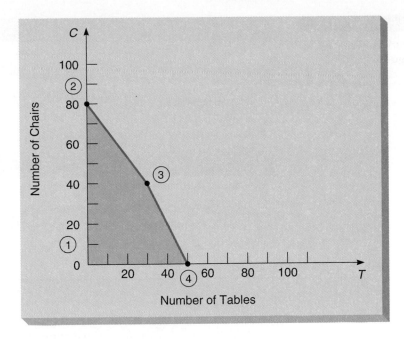

Solving for corner point ③ requires the use of simultaneous equations, an algebraic technique.

your last course in algebra, we can apply the *simultaneous equations method* to the two constraint equations:

$$4T + 3C = 240 \quad \text{(carpentry line)}$$
$$2T + 1C = 100 \quad \text{(painting line)}$$

To solve these equations simultaneously, we multiply the second equation by -2:

$$-2(2T + 1C = 100) = -4T - 2C = -200$$

and then add it to the first equation:

$$\begin{array}{r} +4T + 3C = 240 \\ \hline + 1C = 40 \end{array}$$

or

$$C = 40$$

Doing this has enabled us to eliminate one variable, T, and to solve for C. We can now substitute 40 for C in either of the original equations and solve for T. Let's use the first equation. When $C = 40$, then

$$4T + (3)(40) = 240$$
$$4T + 120 = 240$$

or

$$4T = 120$$
$$T = 30$$

Thus point ③ has the coordinates ($T = 30$, $C = 40$); we can compute its profit level to complete the analysis.

$$\text{Point ③ } (T = 30, C = 40) \text{ profit } = \$7(30) + \$5(40) = \$410$$

TABLE 7.3	ISOPROFIT METHOD

Summaries of Graphical Solution Methods

ISOPROFIT METHOD

1. Graph all constraints and find the feasible region.

2. Select a specific profit (or cost) line and graph it to find the slope.

3. Move the objective function line in the direction of increasing profit (or decreasing cost) while maintaining the slope. The last point it touches in the feasible region is the optimal solution.

4. Find the values of the decision variables at this last point and compute the profit (or cost).

CORNER POINT METHOD

1. Graph all constraints and find the feasible region.

2. Find the corner points of the feasible region.

3. Compute the profit (or cost) at each of the feasible corner points.

4. Select the corner point with the best value of the objective function found in step 3. This is the optimal solution.

Because point ③ produces the highest profit of any corner point, the product mix of $T = 30$ tables and $C = 40$ chairs is the optimal solution to Flair Furniture's problem. This solution yields a profit of $410 per production period, which is the figure that we obtained using the isoprofit line method.

Table 7.3 provides a summary of both the isoprofit method and the corner point method. Either of these can be used when there are two decision variables. If a problem has more than two decision variables, we must rely on the computer software or use the simplex algorithm discussed in Chapter 9.

7.5   SOLVING FLAIR FURNITURE'S LP PROBLEM USING QM FOR WINDOWS AND EXCEL

Almost every organization has access to computer programs that are capable of solving enormous LP problems. Although each computer program is slightly different, the approach each takes toward handling LP problems is basically the same. The format of the input data and the level of detail provided in output results may differ from program to program and computer to computer, but once you are experienced in dealing with computerized LP algorithms, you can easily adjust to minor changes.

Using QM for Windows

Let us begin by demonstrating QM for Windows on the Flair Furniture Company problem. To use QM for Windows, select the Linear Programming module. Then specify the number of constraints (other than the nonnegativity constraints, as it is assumed that the variables must be nonnegative), the number of variables, and whether the objective is to be maximized or minimized. For the Flair Furniture Company problem, there are two constraints and two variables. Once these numbers are specified, the input window opens as shown in Program 7.1A. Then you can enter the coefficients for the objective function and the constraints. Placing the cursor over the X1 or X2 and typing a new name such as Tables and Chairs will change the variable names. The constraint names can be similarly modified. When you select the Solve button, you get the output shown in Program 7.1B. Modify the problem by selecting the Edit button and returning to the input screen to make any desired changes.

PROGRAM 7.1A

QM for Windows Linear Programming Computer Screen for Input of Flair Furniture Company Example

Once the problem has been solved, a graph may be displayed by selecting Window—Graph from the menu bar in QM for Windows. Program 7.1C shows the output for the graphical solution. Notice that in addition to the graph, the corner points and the original problem are also shown. Later we return to see additional information related to sensitivity analysis that is provided by QM for Windows.

Using Excel's Solver Command to Solve LP Problems

Excel and other spreadsheets offer their users the ability to analyze LP problems using built-in problem solving tools. Excel uses a tool named Solver to find the solutions to linear programming related problems (which we use in Chapters 7–9), and integer and noninteger programming problems (the topic of Chapter 11). Excel QM does not contain an LP module, because Solver is part of the basic Excel program. Software add-ins for Excel (such as *What'sBest!* From Lindo Systems, Inc.) expand the normal Excel capabilities. These will improve the speed and expand the size limitations of Solver.

What Are the Limitations of Solver in Solving LP Problems? Solver depends on an algorithmic approach to the optimal solution set, that is, it operates using a series of rules and computations to search for and approximate the optimal solution. Occasionally, Solver may require the user to adjust the rules it uses. Additionally, Solver may be sensitive to the initial values it uses to search for the final solution. In practice, these limitations are rarely encountered.

Solver is limited to 200 changing cells (variables) each with two constraints and up to 100 additional constraints. These capabilities make Solver suitable for the solution of small, real-world problems.

Using Solver to Solve the Flair Furniture Problem As you recall, this is the formulation for Flair Furniture:

Objective Function: maximize profit = $\$7T + \$5C$

subject to:

$$4T + 3C \le 240$$
$$2T + 1C \le 100$$

PROGRAM 7.1B

Sample Linear Programming Computer Run Using QM for Windows Software on the Flair Furniture Company Data

PROGRAM 7.1C

**QM for Windows'
Graphical Output for the
Flair Furniture Company
Problem**

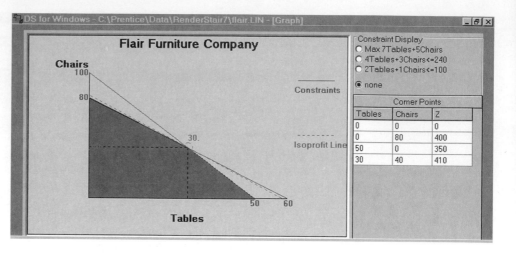

In using the Solver tool in Excel to solve linear programs, the problem should be entered as shown in Program 7.2A. Column A in the spreadsheet is usually reserved for identifying what is in each row. The steps in this process are as follows:

1. Enter the variable names and the coefficients for the objective function and constraints as shown in Program 7.2A (cells B3:C6 in example).

PROGRAM 7.2A

Setting up the Flair Furniture Company LP Problem Using Excel and Solver. This Spreadsheet Shows the Formulas Developed by the User

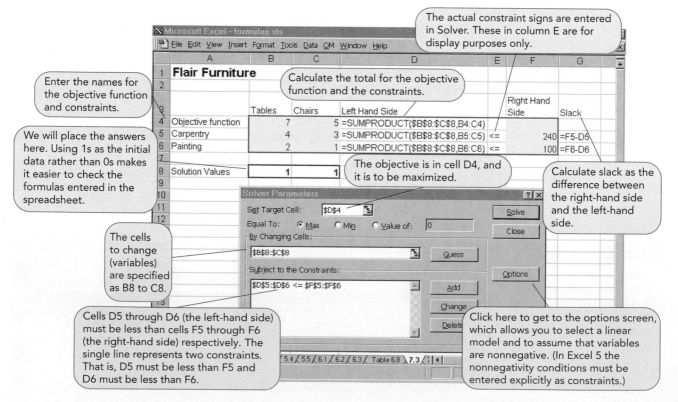

2. Specify cells where the values of the variables will be located (cells B8:C8). Solver will put the solution here.

3. Write a formula to compute the value of the objective function (cell D4). Note that the SUMPRODUCT function is helpful with this.

4. Write formulas to compute the left-hand sides of the constraints (cells D5:D6). The formula in D4 may be copied and pasted to these cells.

5. Indicate constraint signs ($\leq$, =, and $\geq$) for display purposes only (cells E5:E6). The actual signs must be entered into Solver later, but having these displayed in the spreadsheet is helpful.

6. Input the right-hand side values for each constraint (cells F5:F6).

7. If desired, write a formula for the slack of each constraint (cells G5:G6). Solver also has an option that allows you to see the slack, so it is not essential that this be presented here. Now the spreadsheet is ready for the Solver tool.

Although the input does not have to be exactly in these positions, it must be included somewhere on the spreadsheet. Once this has been done, this portion of the spreadsheet provides a model of the problem. If desired, you can manually change the values for the variables (cells B8 and C8), and the objective function and slack values for the constraints will be computed automatically. Putting a 1 in each of these positions helps you to see if the formulas were entered correctly.

Once the problem is entered in an Excel spreadsheet, follow these steps to use Solver:

1. In Excel, select Tools—Solver. If Solver does not appear on the menu under Tools, select Tools—Add-ins and then check the box next to Solver Add-in. Solver then will display in the Tools drop-down menu.

2. Once Solver has been selected, a window will open for the input of the Solver Parameters as shown in Program 7.2A. Move the cursor to the Set Target Cell box and fill in the cell that is used to calculate the value of the objective function (D4).

3. Move the cursor to the By Changing Cells box and input the cells that will contain the values for the variables (cells B8:C8).

4. Move the cursor to the Subject to the Constraints box, and then select Add. This opens the window shown in Program 7.2B.

5. The Cell Reference box is for the range of cells that contain the left-hand sides of the constraints (Cells D5:D6).

6. Select the $\leq$ to change the type of constraint if necessary. Since these are both $\leq$, no change is necessary. (Note that if there had been some $\geq$ or = constraints in addition to the $\leq$ constraints, you would have to input all of one type [e.g., $\leq$] first, and then select Add to input the other type of constraint.)

PROGRAM 7.2B

Window Used to Enter Constraints in Solver

PROGRAM 7.2C

Solver Window for Selecting Linear Model and Nonnegative Variables

7. Move the cursor to the Constraint box to input the right-hand sides of the constraints (F5:F6). Select Add to finish this set of constraints and begin inputting another set, or select OK if there are no other constraints to add.

8. From the Solver Parameters window in Program 7.2A, select Options and check Assume Linear Model and check Assume Non-negative as illustrated in Program 7.2C. Then click OK.

9. Review the information in the Solver window to make sure it is correct, and click Solve.

10. The Solver Solutions window in Program 7.2D is displayed and indicates that a solution was found and the values for the variables are shown in cells B8 and C8, and the

PROGRAM 7.2D   **Solution to Flair Furniture Company Problem Using Excel's Solver**

PROGRAM 7.2E

Excel's Answer Report for
Flair Furniture Company
Problem

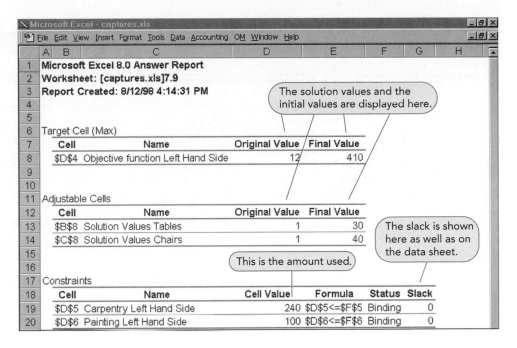

objective function value (cell D4) and slacks (cells G5:G6) are shown also. Select Keep Solver Solution and the values in the spreadsheet will be kept at the optimal solution. You may select what sort of additional information (Answer, Sensitivity, Limits) is to be presented from the reports Window. (These are discussed later in this chapter.) You may select any of these and select OK to have these automatically generated.

Note that the optimal solution is now shown in the *changing cells* (Cells B8 and C8, which served as the variables). The reports selection in Program 7.2E performs more extensive analysis of this solution. The Answer Report shows that the two constraints were binding in the solution (no slack).

7.6 SOLVING MINIMIZATION PROBLEMS

Many LP problems involve minimizing an objective such as cost instead of maximizing a profit function. A restaurant, for example, may wish to develop a work schedule to meet staffing needs while minimizing the total number of employees. A manufacturer may seek to distribute its products from several factories to its many regional warehouses in such a way as to minimize total shipping costs. A hospital may want to provide a daily meal plan for its patients that meets certain nutritional standards while minimizing food purchase costs.

Minimization problems can be solved graphically by first setting up the feasible solution region and then using either the corner point method or an isocost line approach (which is analogous to the isoprofit approach in maximization problems) to find the values of the decision variables (e.g., X_1 and X_2) that yield the minimum cost. Let's take a look at a common LP problem referred to as the diet problem. This situation is similar to the one that the hospital faces in feeding its patients at the least cost.

Holiday Meal Turkey Ranch

The Holiday Meal Turkey Ranch is considering buying two different brands of turkey feed and blending them to provide a good, low-cost diet for its turkeys. Each feed contains, in varying proportions, some or all of the three nutritional ingredients essential for fattening turkeys. Each pound of brand 1 purchased, for example, contains 5 ounces of ingredient A,

4 ounces of ingredient B, and $\frac{1}{2}$ ounce of ingredient C. Each pound of brand 2 contains 10 ounces of ingredient A, 3 ounces of ingredient B, but no ingredient C. The brand 1 feed costs the ranch 2 cents a pound, while the brand 2 feed costs 3 cents a pound. The owner of the ranch would like to use LP to determine the lowest-cost diet that meets the minimum monthly intake requirement for each nutritional ingredient.

Table 7.4 summarizes the relevant information. If we let

$$X_1 = \text{number of pounds of brand 1 feed purchased}$$

$$X_2 = \text{number of pounds of brand 2 feed purchased}$$

then we may proceed to formulate this linear programming problem as follows:

$$\text{minimize cost (in cents)} = 2X_1 + 3X_2$$

subject to these constraints: 0

$5X_1 + 10X_2 \geq 90$ ounces	(ingredient A constraint)
$4X_1 + 3X_2 \geq 48$ ounces	(ingredient B constraint)
$\frac{1}{2} X_1 \geq 1 \frac{1}{2}$ ounces	(ingredient C constraint)
$X_1 \geq 0$	(nonnegativity constraint)
$X_2 \geq 0$	(nonnegativity constraint)

Before solving this problem, we want to be sure to note three features that affect its solution. First, you should be aware that the third constraint implies that the farmer *must* pur-

TABLE 7.4			
Holiday Meal Turkey Ranch Data		**COMPOSITION OF EACH POUND OF FEED (OZ.)**		**MINIMUM MONTHLY REQUIREMENT PER TURKEY (OZ.)**
	INGREDIENT	BRAND 1 FEED	BRAND 2 FEED	
	A	5	10	90
	B	4	3	48
	C	$\frac{1}{2}$	0	$1\frac{1}{2}$
	Cost per pound	2 cents	3 cents	

chase enough brand 1 feed to meet the minimum standards for the C nutritional ingredient. Buying only brand 2 would not be feasible because it lacks C. Second, as the problem is formulated, we will be solving for the best blend of brands 1 and 2 to buy per turkey per month. If the ranch houses 5,000 turkeys in a given month, it need simply multiply the X_1 and X_2 quantities by 5,000 to decide how much feed to order overall. Third, we are now dealing with a series of greater-than-or-equal-to constraints. These cause the feasible solution area to be above the constraint lines in this example.

We plot the three constraints to develop a feasible solution region for the minimization problem.

Note that minimization problems are often unbounded (i.e., open outward).

Using the Corner Point Method on a Minimization Problem   To solve the Holiday Meal Turkey Ranch problem, we first construct the feasible solution region. This is done by plotting each of the three constraint equations as in Figure 7.10. Note that the third constraint, $\frac{1}{2} X_1 \geq 1 \frac{1}{2}$, can be rewritten and plotted as $X_1 \geq 3$. (This involves multiplying both sides of the inequality by 2 but does not change the position of the constraint line in any way.) Minimization problems are often unbounded outward (i.e., on the right side and on top), but this causes no difficulty in solving them. As long as they are bounded inward (on the left side and the bottom), corner points may be established. The optimal solution will lie at one of the corners as it would in a maximization problem.

In this case, there are three corner points: *a*, *b*, and *c*. For point *a*, we find the coordinates at the intersection of the ingredient C and B constraints, that is, where the line $X_1 = 3$ crosses the line $4X_1 + 3X_2 = 48$. If we substitute $X_1 = 3$ into the B constraint equation, we get

$$4(3) + 3X_2 = 48$$

or

$$X_2 = 12$$

Thus, point *a* has the coordinates ($X_1 = 3, X_2 = 12$).

To find the coordinates of point *b* algebraically, we solve the equations $4X_1 + 3X_2 = 48$ and $5X_1 + 10X_2 = 90$ simultaneously. This yields ($X_1 = 8.4, X_2 = 4.8$).

FIGURE 7.10

Feasible Region for the Holiday Meal Turkey Ranch Problem

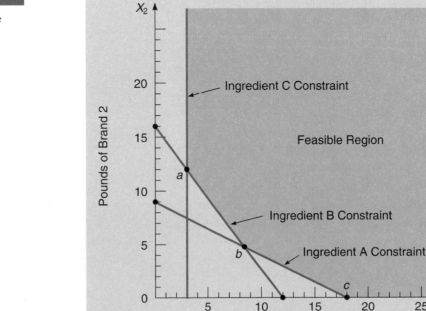

The coordinates at point c are seen by inspection to be ($X_1 = 18$, $X_2 = 0$). We now evaluate the objective function at each corner point and we get:

$$\text{Cost} = 2X_1 + 3X_2$$
$$\text{Cost at point } a = 2(3) + 3(12) = 42$$
$$\text{Cost at point } b = 2(8.4) + 3(4.8) = 31.2$$
$$\text{Cost at point } c = 2(18) + 3(0) = 36$$

Hence, the minimum cost solution is to purchase 8.4 pounds of brand 1 feed and 4.8 pounds of brand 2 feed per turkey per month. This will yield a cost of 31.2 cents per turkey.

The isocost line method is analogous to the isoprofit line method we used on maximization problems.

Isocost Line Approach As mentioned before, the *isocost line* approach may also be used to solve LP minimization problems such as that of the Holiday Meal Turkey Ranch. As with isoprofit lines, we need not compute the cost at each corner point, but instead draw a series of parallel cost lines. The lowest cost line (that is, the one closest in toward the origin) to touch the feasible region provides us with the optimal solution corner.

For example, we start in Figure 7.11 by drawing a 54-cent cost line, namely $54 = 2X_1 + 3X_2$. Obviously, there are many points in the feasible region that would yield a lower total cost. We proceed to move our isocost line toward the lower left, in a plane parallel to the 54-cent solution line. The last point we touch while still in contact with the feasible region is the same as corner point b of Figure 7.10. It has the coordinates ($X_1 = 8.4$, $X_2 = 4.8$) and an associated cost of 31.2 cents.

Computer Approach For the sake of completeness, we also solve the Holiday Meal Turkey Ranch problem using the QM for Windows software package (see Program 7.3) and with Excel's Solver function (see Programs 7.4A and 7.4B).

FIGURE 7.11

Graphical Solution to the Holiday Meal Turkey Ranch Problem Using the Isocost Line

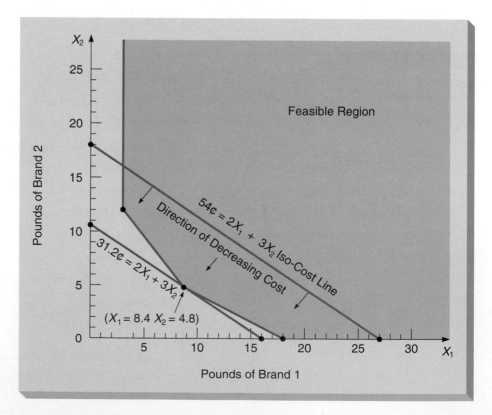

PROGRAM 7.3

Solving the Holiday Meal
Turkey Ranch Problem
Using QM for Windows
Software

QM for Windows – C:\Prentice\Data\RenderStair7\HolidayMeal.LIN

Objective
○ Maximize
◉ Minimize

Linear Programming Results

Holiday Meal Turkey Ranch Solution					
	Brand 1	Brand 2		RHS	Dual
Minimize	2.	3.			
Ingredient A	5.	10.	>=	90.	-0.24
Ingredient B	4.	3.	>=	48.	-0.2
Ingredient C	0.5	0.	>=	1.5	0.
Solution->	8.4	4.8		31.2	

7.7 FOUR SPECIAL CASES IN LP

Four special cases and difficulties arise at times when using the graphical approach to solving LP problems: (1) infeasibility, (2) unboundedness, (3) redundancy, and (4) alternate optimal solutions.

No Feasible Solution

Lack of a feasible solution region can occur if constraints conflict with one another.

When there is no solution to an LP problem that satisfies all of the constraints given, then no feasible solution exists. Graphically, it means that no feasible solution region exists—a situation that might occur if the problem was formulated with conflicting constraints. This, by the way, is a frequent occurrence in real-life, large-scale LP problems that involve hundreds of constraints. For example, if one constraint is supplied by the marketing manager who states that at least 300 tables must be produced (namely, $X_1 \geq 300$) to meet sales demand, and a second restriction is supplied by the production manager, who insists that no more than 220 tables be produced (namely, $X_1 \leq 220$) because of a lumber shortage, no

PROGRAM 7.4A   Setting Up the Holiday Meal Turkey Ranch LP Problem Using Excel and Solver

Microsoft Excel – formulas.xls

File Edit View Insert Format Tools Data Window Help

	A	B	C	D	E	F	G
1	**Holiday Meal Turkey Ranch**						

Enter the names for the objective function and constraints.

Enter the data, including the decision variable names, in columns B, C, and F.

		Brand 1	Brand 2	Left Hand Side		Right Hand Side	Surplus
4	Objective function	2	3	=SUMPRODUCT($B$9:$C$9,B4:C4)			
5	Ingredient A	5	10	=SUMPRODUCT($B$9:$C$9,B5:C5)	>=	90	
6	Ingredient B	4	3	=SUMPRODUCT($B$9:$C$9,B6:C6)	>=	48	=D6-F6
7	Ingredient C	0.5	0	=SUMPRODUCT($B$9:$C$9,B7:C7)	>=	1.5	=D7-F7
8							
9	Solution Values	1	1				

We will place the answers here.

Calculate surplus as the difference between the left-hand side and the right-hand side.

The objective is in cell D4. The cells to change are specified as B9 to C9. Cells D5 through D7 (the left-hand side) must be less than cells F5 through F7 (the right-hand side) respectively.

Solver Parameters

Set Target Cell: $D$4

Equal To: ○ Max ◉ Min ○ Value of: 0

By Changing Cells:
$B$9:$C$9

Subject to the Constraints:
$D$5:$D$7 >= $F$5:$F$7

Solve
Close
Guess
Options
Add
Change
Reset All
Delete
Help

This problem is a cost minimization problem.

18							
19							
20							
21							
22							
23							

Ready   NUM

PROGRAM 7.4B

Solution to the Holiday Meal Turkey Ranch Using Excel's Solver

	A	B	C			
1	**Holiday Meal Turkey Ranch**					
2						
3		Brand 1	Brand 2	Left Hand Side		Right Hand Side	Surplus
4	Objective function	2	3	31.2			
5	Ingredient A	5	10	90	>=	90	
6	Ingredient B	4	3	48	>=	48	0
7	Ingredient C	0.5	0	4.2	>=	1.5	2.7
8							
9	Solution Values	**8.4**	**4.8**				

Solver has found that we should produce 8.4 lbs. of Brand 1 feed and 4.8 lbs. of Brand 2 feed. The minimum cost is 31.2¢, shown in cell D4.

The surplus is displayed in this column.

Solver Results

Solver found a solution. All constraints and optimality conditions are satisfied.

Reports
Answer
Sensitivity
Limits

○ Keep Solver Solution
○ Restore Original Values

OK   Cancel   Save Scenario...   Help

feasible solution region results. When the operations research analyst coordinating the LP problem points out this conflict, one manager or the other must revise his or her inputs. Perhaps more raw materials could be procured from a new source, or perhaps sales demand could be lowered by substituting a different model table to customers.

As a further graphic illustration of this, let us consider the following three constraints:

$$X_1 + 2X_2 \le 6$$
$$2X_1 + X_2 \le 8$$
$$X_1 \ge 7$$

As seen in Figure 7.12, there is no feasible solution region for this LP problem because of the presence of conflicting constraints.

FIGURE 7.12

A Problem with No Feasible Solution

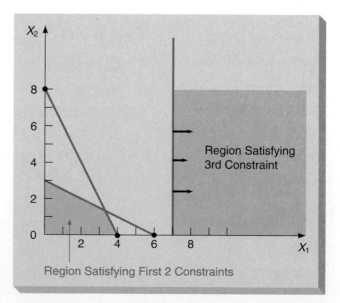

Region Satisfying 3rd Constraint

Region Satisfying First 2 Constraints

Unboundedness

When the profit in a maximization problem can be infinitely large, the problem is unbounded and is missing one or more constraints.

Sometimes a linear program will not have a finite solution. This means that in a maximization problem, for example, one or more solution variables, and the profit, can be made infinitely large without violating any constraints. If we try to solve such a problem graphically, we will note that the feasible region is open-ended.

Let us consider a simple example to illustrate the situation. A firm has formulated the following LP problem:

$$\text{maximize profit } = \quad \$3X_1 + \$5X_2$$
$$\text{subject to:} \qquad X_1 \qquad\qquad \geq 5$$
$$X_2 \leq 10$$
$$X_1 + 2X_2 \geq 10$$
$$X_1, X_2 \geq 0$$

As you see in Figure 7.13, because this is a maximization problem and the feasible region extends infinitely to the right, there is *unboundedness*, or an unbounded solution. This implies that the problem has been formulated improperly. It would indeed be wonderful for the company to be able to produce an infinite number of units of X_1 (at a profit of \$3 each!), but obviously no firm has infinite resources available or infinite product demand.

Redundancy

A redundant constraint is one that does not affect the feasible solution region.

The presence of redundant constraints is another common situation that occurs in large LP formulations. *Redundancy* causes no major difficulties in solving LP problems graphically, but you should be able to identify its occurrence. A redundant constraint is simply one that does not affect the feasible solution region. In other words, one constraint may be more binding or restrictive than another and thereby negate its need to be considered.

A Solution Region That Is Unbounded to the Right

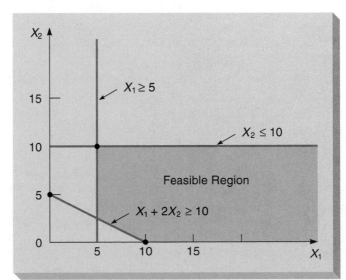

Let's look at the following example of an LP problem with three constraints:

$$\text{maximize profit} = \$1X_1 + \$2X_2$$

subject to:

$$X_1 + X_2 \leq 20$$
$$2X_1 + X_2 \leq 30$$
$$X_1 \leq 25$$
$$X_1, X_2 \geq 0$$

The third constraint, $X_1 \leq 25$, is redundant and unnecessary in the formulation and solution of the problem because it has no effect on the feasible region set from the first two more restrictive constraints (see Figure 7.14).

Alternate Optimal Solutions

Multiple optimal solutions are possible in LP problems.

An LP problem may, on occasion, have two or more *alternate optimal solutions*. Graphically, this is the case when the objective function's isoprofit or isocost line runs perfectly parallel to one of the problem's constraints—in other words, when they have the same slope.

Management of a firm noticed the presence of more than one optimal solution when they formulated this simple LP problem:

$$\text{maximize profit} = \$3X_1 + \$2X_2$$

subject to:

$$6X_1 + 4X_2 \leq 24$$
$$X_1 \leq 3$$
$$X_1, X_2 \geq 0$$

As we see in Figure 7.15, our first isoprofit line of $8 runs parallel to the constraint equation. At a profit level of $12, the isoprofit line will rest directly on top of the

FIGURE 7.14

Problem with a Redundant Constraint

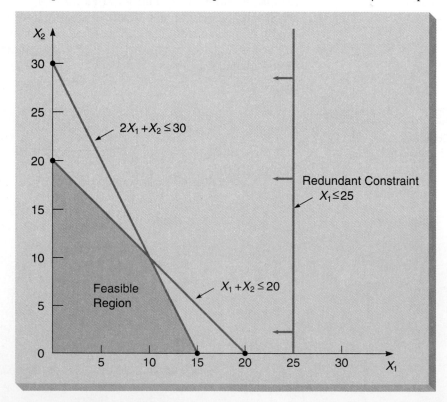

**Example of Alternate
Optimal Solutions**

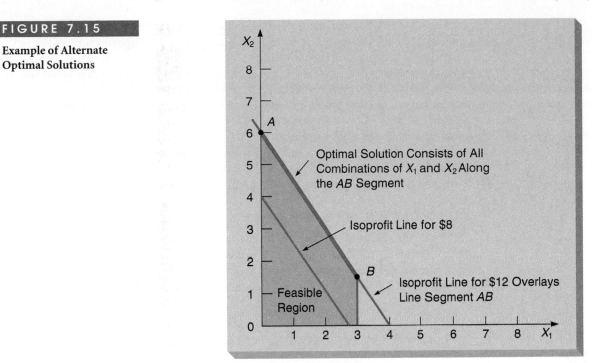

segment of the first constraint line. This means that any point along the line between *A* and *B* provides an optimal X_1 and X_2 combination. Far from causing problems, the existence of more than one optimal solution allows management great flexibility in deciding which combination to select. The profit remains the same at each alternate solution.

7.8 SENSITIVITY ANALYSIS

Optimal solutions to LP problems have thus far been found under what are called *deterministic assumptions*. This means that we assume complete certainty in the data and relationships of a problem—namely, prices are fixed, resources known, time needed to produce a unit exactly set. But in the real world, conditions are dynamic and changing. How can we handle this apparent discrepancy?

How sensitive is the optimal solution to changes in profits, resources, or other input parameters?

One way we can do so is by continuing to treat each particular LP problem as a deterministic situation. However, when an optimal solution is found, we recognize the importance of seeing just how *sensitive* that solution is to model assumptions and data. For example, if a firm realizes that profit per unit is not $5 as estimated but instead is closer to $5.50, how will the final solution mix and total profit change? If additional resources, such as 10 labor hours or 3 hours of machine time, should become available, will this change the problem's answer? Such analyses are used to examine the effects of changes in three areas: (1) contribution rates for each variable, (2) technological coefficients (the numbers in the constraint equations), and (3) available resources (the right-hand-side quantities in each constraint). This task is alternatively called *sensitivity analysis, postoptimality analysis, parametric programming,* or *optimality analysis.*

An important function of sensitivity analysis is to allow managers to experiment with values of the input parameters.

Sensitivity analysis also often involves a series of what-if? questions. What if the profit on product 1 increases by 10%? What if less money is available in the advertising budget constraint? What if workers each stay one hour longer every day at $1\frac{1}{2}$-time pay to provide increased production capacity? What if new technology will allow a product to be wired in one-third the time it used to take? So we see that sensitivity analysis can be used to deal not only with errors in estimating input parameters to the LP model but also with management's experiments with possible future changes in the firm that may affect profits.

There are two approaches to determining just how sensitive an optimal solution is to changes. The first is simply a trial-and-error approach. This approach usually involves resolving the entire problem, preferably by computer, each time one input data item or parameter is changed. It can take a long time to test a series of possible changes in this way.

The approach we prefer is the analytic postoptimality method. After an LP problem has been solved, we attempt to determine a range of changes in problem parameters that will not affect the optimal solution or change the variables in the solution. This is done without resolving the whole problem.

Postoptimality analysis means examining changes after the optimal solution has been reached.

Let's investigate sensitivity analysis by developing a small production mix problem. Our goal will be to demonstrate graphically and through the simplex tableau how sensitivity analysis can be used to make linear programming concepts more realistic and insightful.

High Note Sound Company

The High Note Sound Company manufactures quality compact disc (CD) players and stereo receivers. Each of these products requires a certain amount of skilled artisanship, of which there is a limited weekly supply. The firm formulates the following LP problem in order to determine the best production mix of CD players (X_1) and receivers (X_2):

$$\text{maximize profit } = \$50X_1 + \$120X_2$$

$$\text{subject to: } \quad 2X_1 + 4X_2 \leq 80 \quad \text{(hours of available electricians' time)}$$

$$3X_1 + 1X_2 \leq 60 \quad \text{(hours of audio technicians' time available)}$$

$$X_1, X_2 \geq 0$$

The solution to this problem is illustrated graphically in Figure 7.16. Given this information and deterministic assumptions, the firm should produce only stereo receivers (20 of them) for a weekly profit of $2,400.

FIGURE 7.16

High Note Sound Company Graphical Solution

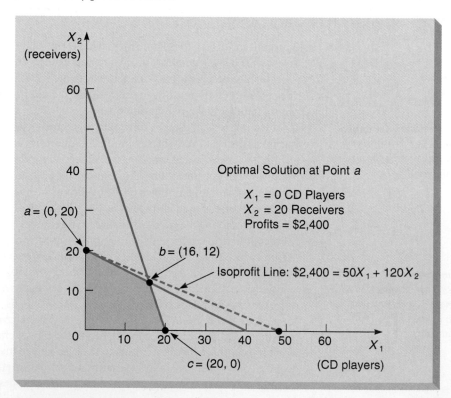

Changes in the Objective Function Coefficient

Changes in contribution rates are examined first.

In real-life problems, contribution rates (usually profit or cost) in the objective functions fluctuate periodically, as do most of a firm's expenses. Graphically, this means that although the feasible solution region remains exactly the same, the slope of the isoprofit or isocost line will change. It is easy to see in Figure 7.17 that the High Note Sound Company's profit line is optimal at point *a*. But what if a technical breakthrough just occurred that raised the profit per stereo receiver (X_2) from $120 to $150? Is the solution still optimal? The answer is definitely yes, for in this case the slope of the profit line accentuates the profitability at point *a*. The new profit is $3,000 = 0($50) + 20($150).

On the other hand, if X_2's profit coefficient was overestimated and should only have been $80, the slope of the profit line changes enough to cause a new corner point (*b*) to become optimal. Here the profit is $1,760 = 16($50) + 12($80).

A new corner point becomes optimal if an objective function coefficient is decreased or increased too much.

This example illustrates a very important concept about changes in objective function coefficients. We can increase or decrease the objective function coefficient (profit) of any variable, and the current corner point may remain optimal if the change is not too large. However, if we increase or decrease this coefficient by too much, then the optimal solution would be at a different corner point. How much can the objective function coefficient change before another corner point becomes optimal? Both QM for Windows and Excel provide the answer.

FIGURE 7.17   **Changes in the Receiver Contribution Coefficients**

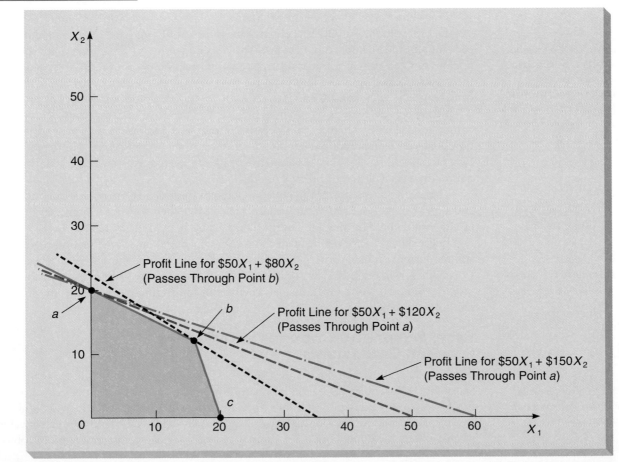

QM for Windows and Changes in Objective Function Coefficients

The QM for Windows input for the High Note Sound Company example is shown in Program 7.5A. When the solution has been found, selecting Window and Ranging allows us to see additional information on sensitivity analysis. Program 7.5B provides the output related to sensitivity analysis.

PROGRAM 7.5A

Input to QM for Windows for High Note Sound Company Data

QM for Windows - C:\Prentice\Data\RenderStair7\HighNote.LIN

Objective
● Maximize
○ Minimize

High Note Sound

	CD players	Receivers		RHS
Maximize	50	120		
Electrician hrs	2	4	<=	80
Audio tech hrs	3	1	<=	60

PROGRAM 7.5B

High Note Sound Company's LP Sensitivity Analysis Output Using Input from Program 7.5A

QM for Windows - C:\Prentice\Data\RenderStair7\HighNote.LIN

◇ Ranging

High Note Sound Solution

Variable	Value	Reduced Cost	Original Val	Lower Bound	Upper Bound
CD players	0.	10.	50.	-Infinity	60.
Receivers	20.	0.	120.	100.	Infinity
Constraint	Dual Value	Slack/Surplus	Original Val	Lower Bound	Upper Bound
Electrician hrs	30.	0.	80.	0.	240.
Audio tech hrs	0.	40.	60.	20.	Infinity

The current solution remains optimal unless an objective function coefficient is increased to a value above the upper bound or decreased to a value below the lower bound.

From Program 7.5B, we see the profit on CD players was $50, which is indicated as the Original Value in the output. This objective function coefficient has a lower bound of negative infinity and an upper bound of $60. This means that the current corner point solution remains optimal as long as the profit on CD players does not go above $60. If it equals $60, there would be two optimal solutions as the objective function would be parallel to the first constraint. The points (0, 20) and (16, 12) would both give a profit of $2400. The profit on CD players may decrease any amount as indicated by the negative infinity, and the optimal corner point does not change. This negative infinity is logical because currently there are no CD players being produced because the profit is too low. Any decrease in the profit on CD players would make them less attractive relative to the receivers, and we certainly would not produce any CD players because of this.

The profit on receivers has an upper bound of infinity (it may increase by any amount) and a lower bound of $100. If this profit equaled $100, then the corner points (0, 20) and (16, 12) would both be optimal. The profit at each of these would be $2000.

The upper and lower bounds relate to changing only one coefficient at a time.

In general, a change can be made to one (and only one) objective function coefficient, and the current optimal corner point remains optimal as long as the change is between the Upper and Lower Bounds. If two or more coefficients are changed simultaneously, then the problem should be solved with the new coefficients to determine whether or not this current solution remains optimal.

Excel Solver and Changes in Objective Function Coefficients

Excel Solver gives allowable increases and decreases rather than upper and lower bounds.

Program 7.6A illustrates how Solver in Excel could be used with this example. The Sensitivity Report output is seen in Program 7.6B. Notice that Excel does not provide lower bounds and upper bounds for the objective function coefficients. Instead, it gives the allowable increases and decreases for these. By adding the allowable increase to the current value, we may obtain the upper bound. For example, the Allowable Increase on the profit (objec-

PROGRAM 7.6A **Excel Spreadsheet Analysis of High Note Sound Company**

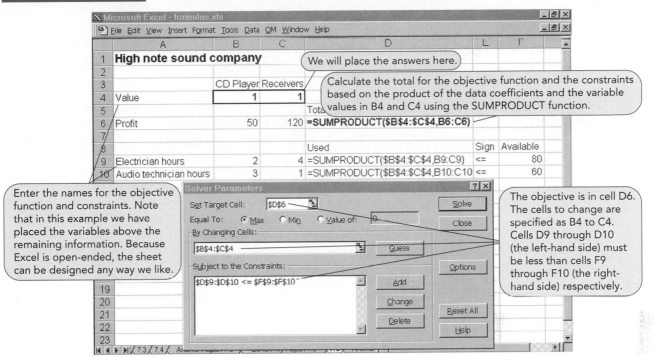

PROGRAM 7.6B

Excel's Sensitivity Analysis Output for High Note Sound Company

tive coefficient) for CD players is 10, which means that the upper bound on this profit is $50 + $10 = $60. Similarly, we may subtract the allowable decrease from the current value to obtain the lower bound.

Changes in the Technological Coefficients

Changes in technological coefficients affect the shape of the feasible solution region.

Changes in what are called the *technological coefficients* often reflect changes in the state of technology. If fewer or more resources are needed to produce a product such as a CD player or stereo receiver, coefficients in the constraint equations will change. These changes will have no effect on the objective function of an LP problem, but they can produce a significant change in the shape of the feasible solution region, and hence in the optimal profit or cost.

Figure 7.18 illustrates the original High Note Sound Company graphical solution as well as two separate changes in technological coefficients. In Figure 7.18, Part (a), we see that the optimal solution lies at point a, which represents $X_1 = 0$, $X_2 = 20$. You should be able to prove to yourself that point a remains optimal in Figure 7.18, Part (b) despite a constraint change from $3X_1 + 1X_2 \leq 60$ to $2X_1 + 1X_2 \leq 60$. Such a change might take place when the firm discovers that it no longer demands three hours of audio technicians' time to produce a CD player, but only two hours.

In Figure 7.18, Part (c), however, a change in the other constraint changes the shape of the feasible region enough to cause a new corner point (g) to become optimal. Before moving on, see if you reach an objective function value of $1,954 profit at point g (versus a profit of $1,920 at point f).[5]

FIGURE 7.18   **Change in the Technological Coefficients for the High Note Sound Company**

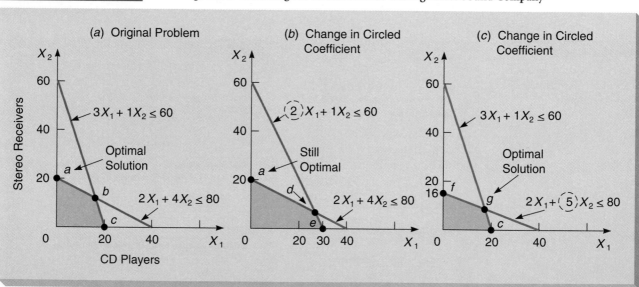

---

[5] Note that the values of X_1 and X_2 at point g are fractions. Although the High Note Sound Company cannot produce $\frac{2}{3}$, $\frac{3}{4}$ or $\frac{9}{10}$ of a CD player or stereo, we can assume that the firm can *begin* a unit one week and complete it the next. As long as the production process is fairly stable from week to week, this raises no major problems. If solutions *must* be whole numbers each period, refer to our discussion of integer programming in Chapter 11 to handle the situation.

IN ACTION   Using LP to Assist AIDS Patients in Italy

Home care for AIDS patients, in the form of nurses, doctors, and social workers, was introduced by law in Italy in 1990. Organizations that provide home-care work with a limited budget must provide a minimum standard of service. A lack of balance between patient needs and available resources can lead to a low level of service, an excessive workload for the medical and social workers, or both.

To produce an optimal schedule for admitting new patients into the home health care system, Italian researchers turned to LP. Using available quantities of each resource as constraints, the objective is to maximize the sum of the number of patients that can be admitted each week. The LP model produces an optimal admissions schedule for a given 12-week planning period.

But to complicate the problem, patients fell into various categories of "dependency," ranging from "self-sufficient" to "permanently in bed" to "hospitalized" to "dead." Patients move with predicted probabilities from one category to another, and different classes are given different weights to express priority. This practical and flexible LP tool for public health has also been extended to support centralized decision making by evaluating the impact of different budget assignments.

Source: V. DeAngelis, "Planning Home Assistance for AIDS Patients in the City of Rome, Italy," *Interfaces* 28, 3 (May–June, 1998): 75–83.

Changes in the Resources or Right-Hand-Side Values

The right-hand-side values of the constraints often represent resources available to the firm. The resources could be labor hours or machine time or perhaps money or production materials available. In the High Note Sound Company example, the two resources are hours available of electricians' time and hours of audio technicians' time. If additional hours were available, a higher total profit could be realized. How much should the company be willing to pay for additional hours? Is it profitable to have some electricians work overtime? Should we be willing to pay for more audio technician time? Sensitivity analysis about these resources will help us answer these questions.

If the right-hand side of a constraint is changed, the feasible region will change (unless the constraint is redundant), and often the optimal solution will change. In the High Note Sound Company example, there were 80 hours of electrician time available each week and the maximum possible profit was $2,400. If the available electricians' hours are increased to 100 hours, the new optimal solution seen in Figure 7.19, Part (a) is (0, 25) and the profit is $3,000. Thus, the extra 20 hours of time resulted in an increase in profit of $600 or $30 per hour. If the hours were decreased to 60 hours as shown in Figure 7.19, Part (b), the new optimal solution is (0, 15) and the profit is $1,800. Thus, reducing the hours by 20 results in a decrease in profit of $600 or $30 per hour. This $30 per hour change in profit that resulted from a change in the hours available is called the dual price or dual value. The *dual price* for a constraint is the improvement in the objective function value that results from a one-unit increase in the right-hand side of the constraint.

The dual price is the value of one additional unit of a scarce resource.

The dual price of $30 per hour of electrician time tells us we can increase profit if we have more electrician hours. However, there is a limit to this as there is limited audio technician time. If the total hours of electrician time were 240 hours, the optimal solution would be (0, 60) as shown in Figure 7.19, Part (c) and the profit would be $7,200. Again, this is an increase of $30 profit per hour (the dual price) for each of the 160 hours that were added to the original amount. If the number of hours increased beyond 240, then profit would no longer increase and the optimal solution would still be (0, 60) as shown in Figure 7.19, Part (c). There would simply be excess (slack) hours of electrician time and all of the audio technician time would be used. Thus, the dual price is relevant only within limits. Both QM for Windows and Excel Solver provide these limits.

FIGURE 7.19

Changes in the Electricians' Time Resource for the High Note Sound Company

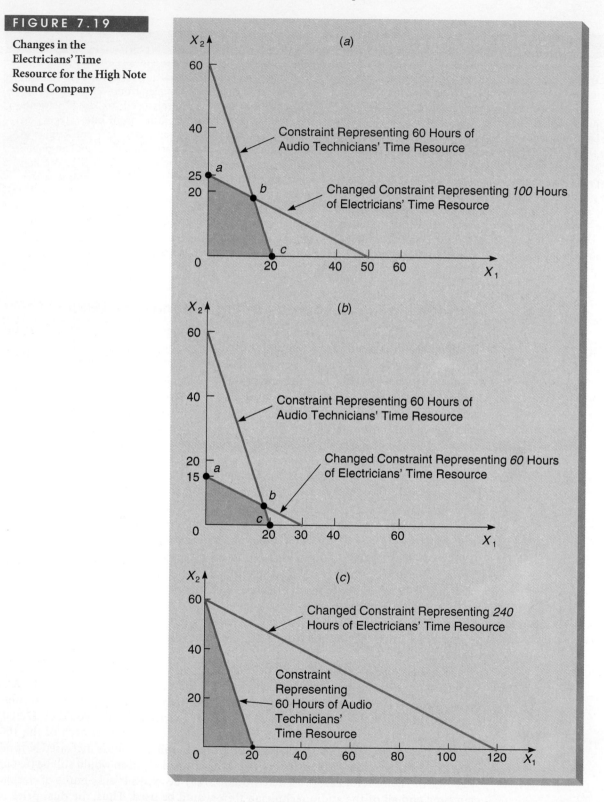

QM For Windows and Changes in Right-Hand-Side Values

Dual prices will change if the amount of the resource (the right-hand side of the constraint) goes above the upper bound or below the lower bound given in the Ranging section of the QM for Windows output.

The QM for Windows sensitivity analysis output was shown in Program 7.5B. The dual value for the electrician hours constraint is given as 30, and the lower bound is zero while the upper bound is 240. This means that each additional hour of electrician time, up to a total of 240 hours, will increase the maximum possible profit by $30. Similarly, if the available electrician time is decreased, the maximum possible profit will decrease by $30 per hour until the available time is decreased to the lower bound of 0. If the amount of electrician time (the right-hand-side value for this constraint) is outside this range (0 to 240), then the dual value is no longer relevant and the problem should be resolved with the new right-hand-side value.

In Program 7.5B, the dual value for audio technician hours is shown to be $0 and the slack is 40. There are 40 hours of audio technician time that are not being used despite the fact that they are currently available. If additional hours were made available they would not increase profit but would simply increase the amount of slack. This dual value of zero is relevant as long as the right-hand side does not go below the lower bound of 20. The upper limit is infinity indicating that adding more hours would simply increase the amount of slack.

Excel Solver and Changes in Right-Hand-Side Values

The shadow price gives the value of one additional unit of a scarce resource.

The Sensitivity report from Excel Solver was shown in Program 7.6B. Notice that Solver gives the shadow price instead of the dual price. The shadow price in the Excel output is the equivalent to the dual price for this maximization problem. A shadow price is the increase in the objective function value (e.g., profit or cost) that results from a one-unit increase in the right-hand-side of a constraint.

The Allowable Increase and Allowable Decrease for the right-hand side of each constraint is provided, and the shadow price is relevant for changes within these limits. For the electrician hours, the right-hand-side value of 80 may be increased by 160 (for a total of 240) or decreased by 80 (for a total of 0) and the shadow price remains relevant. If a change is made that exceeds these limits, then the problem should be resolved to find the impact of the change.

SUMMARY

In this chapter we introduce a mathematical modeling technique called linear programming (LP). It is used in reaching an optimum solution to problems that have a series of constraints binding the objective. We use both the corner point method and the isoprofit/isocost approaches for graphically solving problems with only two decision variables.

The graphical solution approaches of this chapter provide a conceptual basis for tackling larger, more complex problems, some of which are addressed in Chapter 8. To solve real-life LP problems with numerous variables and constraints, we need a solution procedure such as the simplex algorithm, the subject of Chapter 9. The simplex algorithm is the method that QM for Windows and Excel use to tackle LP problems.

In this chapter we also present the important concept of sensitivity analysis. Sometimes referred to as postoptimality analysis, sensitivity analysis is used by management to answer a series of what-if? questions about LP model parameters. It also tests just how sensitive the optimal solution is to changes in profit or cost coefficients, technological coefficients, and right-hand-side resources. We explored sensitivity analysis graphically (i.e., for problems with only two decision variables) and with computer output, but we will return to the topic again in Chapter 9 as we see how to conduct sensitivity analysis algebraically through the simplex algorithm.

GLOSSARY

Alternate Optimal Solution. A situation in which more than one optimal solution is possible. It arises when the slope of the objective function is the same as the slope of a constraint.

Constraint. A restriction on the resources available to a firm (stated in the form of an inequality or an equation).

Corner Point or Extreme Point. A point that lies on one of the corners of the feasible region. This means that it falls at the intersection of two constraint lines.

Corner Point Method. The method of finding the optimal solution to an LP problem by testing the profit or cost level at each corner point of the feasible region. The theory of LP states that the optimal solution must lie at one of the corner points.

Dual Price (value). The improvement in the objective function value that results from a one-unit increase in the right-hand side of that constraint.

Feasible Region. The area satisfying all of the problem's resource restrictions; that is, the region where all constraints overlap. All possible solutions to the problem lie in the feasible region.

Feasible Solution. A point lying in the feasible region. Basically, it is any point that satisfies all of the problem's constraints.

Inequality. A mathematical expression containing a greater-than-or-equal-to relation ($\geq$) or a less-than-or-equal-to relation ($\leq$) used to indicate that the total consumption of a resource must be $\geq$ or $\leq$ some limiting value.

Infeasible Solution. Any point lying outside the feasible region. It violates one or more of the stated constraints.

Isocost Line. A straight line representing all combinations of X_1 and X_2 for a particular cost level.

Isoprofit Line. A straight line representing all nonnegative combinations of X_1 and X_2 for a particular profit level.

Linear Programming (LP). A mathematical technique used to help management decide how to make the most effective use of an organization's resources.

Mathematical Programming. The general category of mathematical modeling and solution techniques used to allocate resources while optimizing a measurable goal. LP is one type of programming model.

Nonnegativity Constraints. A set of constraints that requires each decision variable to be nonnegative; that is, each X_i must be greater than or equal to 0.

Objective Function. A mathematical statement of the goal of an organization, stated as an intent to maximize or to minimize some important quantity such as profits or costs.

Product Mix Problem. A common LP problem involving a decision as to which products a firm should produce given that it faces limited resources.

Redundancy. The presence of one or more constraints that do not affect the feasible solution region.

Sensitivity Analysis. The study of how sensitive an optimal solution is to model assumptions and to data changes. It is often referred to as postoptimality analysis.

Shadow Price. The increase in the objective function value that results from a one-unit increase in the right-hand side of that constraint.

Simultaneous Equation Method. The algebraic means of solving for the intersection point of two or more linear constraint equations.

Technological Coefficients. Coefficients of the variables in the constraint equations. The coefficients represent the amount of resources needed to produce one unit of the variable.

Unboundedness. A condition that exists when a solution variable and the profit can be made infinitely large without violating any of the problem's constraints in a maximization process.

SOLVED PROBLEMS

Solved Problem 7-1

Personal Mini Warehouses is planning to expand its successful Orlando business into Tampa. In doing so, the company must determine how many storage rooms of each size to build. Its objective and constraints follow:

$$\text{maximize monthly earnings} = 50X_1 + 20X_2$$

$$\text{subject to:} \quad 2X_1 + 4X_2 \leq 400 \quad \text{(advertising budget available)}$$

$$100X_1 + 50X_2 \leq 8{,}000 \quad \text{(square footage required)}$$

$$X_1 \leq 60 \quad \text{(rental limit expected)}$$

$$X_1, X_2 \geq 0$$

where

$$X_1 = \text{number of large spaces developed}$$

$$X_2 = \text{number of small spaces developed}$$

Solution

An evaluation of the five corner points of the accompanying graph indicates that corner point C produces the greatest earnings. Refer to the graph and table.

CORNER POINT	VALUES OF X_1, X_2	OBJECTIVE FUNCTION VALUE ($)
A	(0, 0)	0
B	(60, 0)	3,000
C	(60, 40)	3,800
D	(40, 80)	3,600
E	(0, 100)	2,000

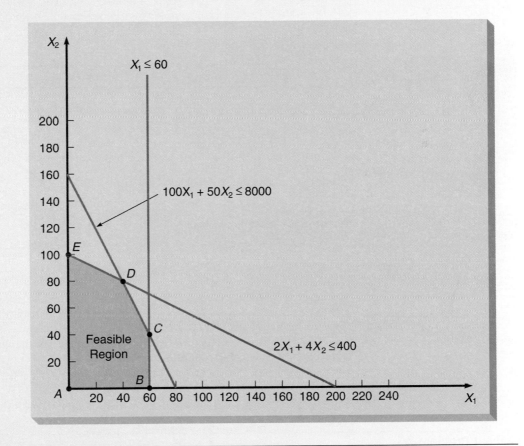

Solved Problem 7-2

The solution obtained with QM for Windows for Solved Problem 7-1 is given in the following program. Use this to answer the following questions.

a. For the optimal solution, how much of the advertising budget is spent?
b. For the optimal solution, how much square footage will be used?
c. Would the solution change if the budget were only $300 instead of $400?
d. What would the optimal solution be if the profit on the large spaces were reduced from $50 to $45?
e. How much would earnings increase if the square footage requirement were increased from 8,000 to 9,000?

Linear Programming Results   _ |□| x|

		Solved Problem 7-2 Solution			
	X1	X2		RHS	Dual
Maximize	50.	20.			
Constraint 1	2.	4.	<=	400.	0.
Constraint 2	100.	50.	<=	8,000.	0.4
Constraint 3	1.	0.	<=	60.	10.
Solution->	60.	40.		3,800.	

Ranging   _ |□| x|

		Solved Problem 7-2 Solution			
Variable	Value	Reduced Cost	Original Val	Lower Bound	Upper Bound
X1	60.	0.	50.	40.	Infinity
X2	40.	0.	20.	0.	25.
Constraint	Dual Value	Slack/Surplus	Original Val	Lower Bound	Upper Bound
Constraint 1	0.	120.	400.	280.	Infinity
Constraint 2	0.4	0.	8,000.	6,000.	9,500.
Constraint 3	10.	0.	60.	40.	80.

Solution

a. In the optimal solution, $X_1 = 60$ and $X_2 = 40$. Using these values in the first constraint gives us

$$2X_1 + 4X_2 = 2(60) + 4(40) = 280$$

Another way to find this is by looking at the slack:

Slack for constraint 1 = 120 so the amount used is $400 - 120 = 280$

b. For the second constraint we have

$$100X_1 + 50X_2 = 100(60) + 50(40) = 8,000 \text{ square feet}$$

Instead of computing this, you may simply observe that the slack is 0, so all of the 8,000 square feet will be used.

c. No, the solution would not change. The dual price is 0 and there is slack available. The value 300 is between the lower bound of 280 and the upper bound of infinity. Only the slack for this constraint would change.

d. Since the new coefficient for X_1 is between the lower bound (40) and the upper bound (infinity), the current corner point remains optimal. So $X_1 = 60$ and $X_2 = 40$, and only the monthly earnings change.

$$\text{Earnings} = 45(60) + 20(40) = \$3,500$$

e. The dual price for this constraint is 0.4, and the upper bound is 9,500. The increase of 1,000 units will result in an increase in earnings of $1,000(0.4 \text{ per unit}) = \$400$.

Solved Problem 7-3

Solve the following LP formulation graphically, using the isocost line approach:

$$\text{minimize costs} = 24X_1 + 28X_2$$

$$\text{subject to: } 5X_1 + 4X_2 \leq 2,000$$

$$X_1 \qquad \geq 80$$

$$X_1 + X_2 \geq 300$$

$$X_2 \geq 100$$

$$X_1, X_2 \geq 0$$

Solution

A graph of the four constraints follows. The arrows indicate the direction of feasibility for each constraint. The next graph illustrates the feasible solution region and plots of two possible objective function cost lines. The first, $10,000, was selected arbitrarily as a starting point. To find the optimal corner point, we need to move the cost line in the direction of lower cost, that is, down and to the left. The last point where a cost line touches the feasible region as it moves toward the origin is corner point D. Thus D, which represents $X_1 = 200$, $X_2 = 100$, and a cost of $7,600, is optimal.

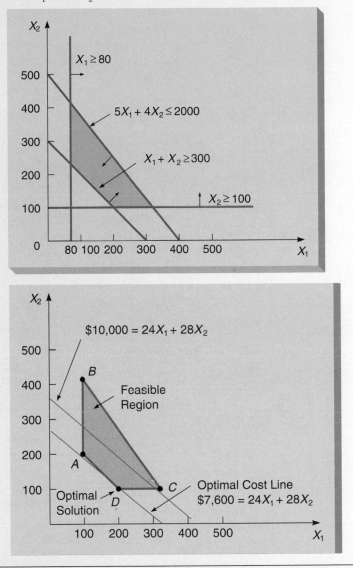

Solve the following problems, using the corner point method.

$$\text{maximize profit} = 30X_1 + 40X_2$$

$$\text{subject to:} \quad 4X_1 + 2X_2 \leq 16$$

$$2X_1 - X_2 \geq 2$$

$$X_2 \leq 2$$

$$X_1, X_2 \geq 0$$

Solution

The graph appears next with the feasible region shaded.

CORNER POINT	COORDINATES	PROFIT ($)
A	$X_1 = 1, X_2 = 0$	30
B	$X_1 = 4, X_2 = 0$	120
C	$X_1 = 3, X_2 = 2$	170
D	$X_1 = 2, X_2 = 2$	140

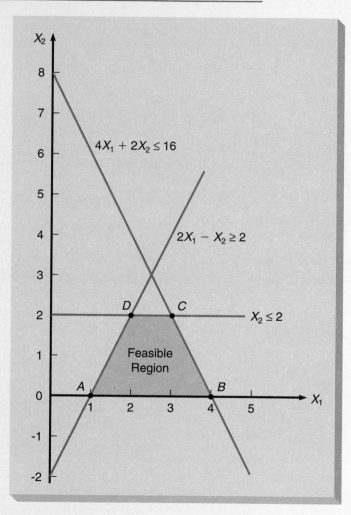

The optimal profit of $170 is at corner point C.

⟩⟩⟩⟩ SELF-TEST

- ■ Before taking the self-test, refer back to the learning objectives at the beginning of the chapter, the notes in the margins, and the glossary at the end of the chapter.
- ■ Use the key at the back of the book to correct your answers.
- ■ Restudy pages that correspond to any questions that you answered incorrectly or material you feel uncertain about.

1. When using a graphical solution procedure, the region bounded by the set of constraints is called the
   a. solution.   b. feasible region.
   c. infeasible region.   d. maximum profit region.
   e. none of the above.

2. In an LP problem, at least one corner point must be an optimal solution if an optimal solution exists.
   a. True   b. False

3. An LP problem has a bounded feasible region. If this problem has an equality (=) constraint, then
   a. this must be a minimization problem.
   b. the feasible region must consist of a line segment.
   c. the problem must be degenerate.
   d. the problem must have more than one optimal solution.

4. Which of the following would cause a change in the feasible region?
   a. increasing an objective function coefficient in a maximization problem
   b. adding a redundant constraint
   c. changing the right-hand side of a nonredundant constraint
   d. increasing an objective function coefficient in a minimization problem

5. If a nonredundant constraint is removed from an LP problem, then
   a. the feasible region will get larger.
   b. the feasible region will get smaller.
   c. the problem would become nonlinear.
   d. the problem would become infeasible.

6. In the optimal solution to a linear program, there are 20 units of slack for a constraint. From this we know
   a. the dual price for this constraint is 20.
   b. the dual price for this constraint is 0.
   c. this constraint must be redundant.
   d. the problem must be a maximization problem.

7. A linear program has been solved and sensitivity analysis has been performed. The ranges for the objective function coefficients have been found. For the profit on X_1, the upper bound is 80, the lower bound is 60, and the current value is 75. Which of the following must be true if the profit on this variable is lowered to 70 and the optimal solution is found?
   a. a new corner point will become optimal
   b. the maximum possible total profit may increase
   c. the values for all the decision variables will remain the same
   d. all of the above are possible

8. A graphical method should only be used to solve an LP problem when
   a. there are only two constraints.
   b. there are more than two constraints.
   c. there are only two variables.
   d. there are more than two variables.

9. In LP, variables do not have to be integer valued and may take on any fractional value. This assumption is called
   a. proportionality.   b. divisibility.
   c. additivity.   d. certainty.

10. In solving a linear program, no feasible solution exists. To resolve this problem we might
    a. add another variable.
    b. add another constraint.
    c. remove or relax a constraint.
    d. try a different computer program.

11. If the feasible region gets larger due to a change in one of the constraints, the optimal value of the objective function
    a. must increase or remain the same for a maximization problem.
    b. must decrease or remain the same for a maximization problem.
    c. must increase or remain the same for a minimization problem.
    d. cannot change.

12. When alternate optimal solutions exist in an LP problem, then
    a. the objective function will be parallel to one of the constraints.
    b. one of the constraints will be redundant.
    c. two constraints will be parallel.
    d. the problem will also be unbounded.

13. If a linear program is unbounded, the problem probably has not been formulated correctly. Which of the following would most likely cause this?
    a. a constraint was inadvertently omitted
    b. an unnecessary constraint was added to the problem
    c. the objective function coefficients are too large
    d. the objective function coefficients are too small

14. A feasible solution to an LP problem
    a. must satisfy all of the problem's constraints simultaneously.
    b. need not satisfy all of the constraints, only some of them.
    c. must be a corner point of the feasible region.
    d. must give the maximum possible profit.

DISCUSSION QUESTIONS AND PROBLEMS

Discussion Questions

7-1 Discuss the similarities and differences between minimization and maximization problems using the graphical solution approaches of LP.

7-2 It is important to understand the assumptions underlying the use of any quantitative analysis model. What are the assumptions and requirements for an LP model to be formulated and used?

7-3 It has been said that each LP problem that has a feasible region has an infinite number of solutions. Explain.

7-4 You have just formulated a maximization LP problem and are preparing to solve it graphically. What criteria should you consider in deciding whether it would be easier to solve the problem by the corner point method or the isoprofit line approach?

7-5 Under what condition is it possible for an LP problem to have more than one optimal solution?

7-6 Develop your own set of constraint equations and inequalities and use them to illustrate graphically each of the following conditions:
  (a) an unbounded problem
  (b) an infeasible problem
  (c) a problem containing redundant constraints

7-7 The production manager of a large Cincinnati manufacturing firm once made the statement, "I would like to use LP, but it's a technique that operates under conditions of certainty. My plant doesn't have that certainty; it's a world of uncertainty. So LP can't be used here." Do you think this statement has any merit? Explain why the manager may have said it.

7-8 The mathematical relationships that follow were formulated by an operations research analyst at the Smith–Lawton Chemical Company. Which ones are invalid for use in an LP problem, and why?

$$\text{maximize profit} = 4X_1 + 3X_1X_2 + 8X_2 + 5X_3$$

$$\text{subject to:} \quad 2X_1 + X_2 + 2X_3 \le 50$$

$$X_1 - 4X_2 \ge 6$$

$$1.5X_1^2 + 6X_2 + 3X_3 \ge 21$$

$$19X_2 - \tfrac{1}{3}X_3 = 17$$

$$5X_1 + 4X_2 + 3\sqrt{X_3} \le 80$$

$$-X_1 - X_2 + X_3 = 5$$

7-9 Discuss the role of sensitivity analysis in LP. Under what circumstances is it needed, and under what conditions do you think it is not necessary?

7-10 A linear program has the objective of maximizing profit = $12X + 8Y$. The maximum profit is $8,000. Using a computer we find the upper bound for profit on X is 20 and the lower bound is 9. Discuss the changes to the optimal solution (the values of the variables and the profit) that would occur if the profit on X were increased to $15. How would the optimal solution change if the profit on X were increased to $25?

7-11 A linear program has a maximum profit of $600. One constraint in this problem is $4X + 2Y \le 80$. Using a computer we find the dual price for this constraint is 3, and there is a lower bound of 75 and an upper bound of 100. Explain what this means.

7-12 Develop your own original LP problem with two constraints and two real variables.
  (a) Explain the meaning of the numbers on the right-hand side of each of your constraints.
  (b) Explain the significance of the technological coefficients.

  (c) Solve your problem graphically to find the optimal solution.
  (d) Illustrate graphically the effect of increasing the contribution rate of your first variable (X_1) by 50% over the value you first assigned it. Does this change the optimal solution?

7-13 Explain how a change in a technological coefficient can affect a problem's optimal solution. How can a change in resource availability affect a solution?

Problems*

7-14 The Electrocomp Corporation manufactures two electrical products: air conditioners and large fans. The assembly process for each is similar in that both require a certain amount of wiring and drilling. Each air conditioner takes 3 hours of wiring and 2 hours of drilling. Each fan must go through 2 hours of wiring and 1 hour of drilling. During the next production period, 240 hours of wiring time are available and up to 140 hours of drilling time may be used. Each air conditioner sold yields a profit of $25. Each fan assembled may be sold for a $15 profit. Formulate and solve this LP production mix situation to find the best combination of air conditioners and fans that yields the highest profit. Use the corner point graphical approach.

7-15 Electrocomp's management realizes that it forgot to include two critical constraints (see Problem 7-14). In particular, management decides that to ensure an adequate supply of air conditioners for a contract, at least 20 air conditioners should be manufactured. Because Electrocomp incurred an oversupply of fans in the preceding period, management also insists that no more than 80 fans be produced during this production period. Resolve this product mix problem to find the new optimal solution.

7-16 A candidate for mayor in a small town has allocated $40,000 for last-minute advertising in the days preceding the election. Two types of ads will be used: radio and television. Each radio ad costs $200 and reaches an estimated 3,000 people. Each television ad costs $500 and reaches an estimated 7,000 people. In planning the advertising campaign, the campaign manager would like to reach as many people as possible, but she has stipulated that at least 10 ads of each type must be used. Also, the number of radio ads must be at least as great as the number of television ads. How many ads of each type should be used? How many people will this reach?

7-17 The Outdoor Furniture Corporation manufactures two products, benches and picnic tables, for use in yards and parks. The firm has two main resources: its carpenters (labor force) and a supply of redwood for use in the furniture. During the next production

---

* Note: means the problem may be solved with QM for Windows; means the problem may be solved with Excel; and means the problem may be solved with QM for Windows and/or Excel.

cycle, 1,200 hours of labor are available under a union agreement. The firm also has a stock of 3,500 feet of good-quality redwood. Each bench that Outdoor Furniture produces requires 4 labor hours and 10 feet of redwood; each picnic table takes 6 labor hours and 35 feet of redwood. Completed benches will yield a profit of $9 each, and tables will result in a profit of $20 each. How many benches and tables should Outdoor Furniture produce to obtain the largest possible profit? Use the graphical LP approach.

7-18 The dean of the Western College of Business must plan the school's course offerings for the fall semester. Student demands make it necessary to offer at least 30 undergraduate and 20 graduate courses in the term. Faculty contracts also dictate that at least 60 courses be offered in total. Each undergraduate course taught costs the college an average of $2,500 in faculty wages, and each graduate course costs $3,000. How many undergraduate and graduate courses should be taught in the fall so that total faculty salaries are kept to a minimum?

7-19 MSA Computer Corporation manufactures two models of minicomputers, the Alpha 4 and the Beta 5. The firm employs five technicians, working 160 hours each per month, on its assembly line. Management insists that full employment (i.e., *all* 160 hours of time) be maintained for each worker during next month's operations. It requires 20 labor hours to assemble each Alpha 4 computer and 25 labor hours to assemble each Beta 5 model. MSA wants to see at least 10 Alpha 4s and at least 15 Beta 5s produced during the production period. Alpha 4s generate $1,200 profit per unit, and Beta 5s yield $1,800 each. Determine the most profitable number of each model of minicomputer to produce during the coming month.

7-20 A winner of the Texas Lotto has decided to invest $50,000 per year in the stock market. Under consideration are stocks for a petrochemical firm and a public utility. Although a long-range goal is to get the highest possible return, some consideration is given to the risk involved with the stocks. A risk index on a scale of 1–10 (with 10 being the most risky) is assigned to each of the two stocks. The total risk of the portfolio is found by multiplying the risk of each stock by the dollars invested in that stock.

The following table provides a summary of the return and risk:

STOCK	ESTIMATED RETURN	RISK INDEX
Petrochemical	12%	9
Utility	6%	4

The investor would like to maximize the return on the investment, but the average risk index of the investment should not be higher than 6. How much should be invested in each stock? What is the average risk for this investment? What is the estimated return for this investment?

7-21 Referring to the Texas Lotto situation in Problem 7-20, suppose the investor has changed his attitude about the investment and wishes to give greater emphasis to the risk of the investment. Now the investor wishes to minimize the risk of the investment as long as a return of at least 8% is generated. Formulate this as an LP problem and find the optimal solution. How much should be invested in each stock? What is the average risk for this investment? What is the estimated return for this investment?

7-22 Solve the following LP problem using the corner point graphical method:

$$\text{maximize profit} = 4X + 4Y$$
$$\text{subject to:} \quad 3X + 5Y \leq 150$$
$$X - 2Y \leq 10$$
$$5X + 3Y \leq 150$$
$$X, Y \geq 0$$

7-23 Consider this LP formulation:

$$\text{minimize cost} = \$X + 2Y$$
$$\text{subject to:} \quad X + 3Y \geq 90$$
$$8X + 2Y \geq 160$$
$$3X + 2Y \geq 120$$
$$Y \leq 70$$
$$X, Y \geq 0$$

Graphically illustrate the feasible region and apply the isocost line procedure to indicate which corner point produces the optimal solution. What is the cost of this solution?

7-24 The stock brokerage firm of Blank, Leibowitz, and Weinberger has analyzed and recommended two stocks to an investors' club of college professors. The professors were interested in factors such as short-term growth, intermediate growth, and dividend rates. These data on each stock are as follows:

| | STOCK ($) | |
FACTOR	LOUISIANA GAS AND POWER	TRIMEX INSULATION COMPANY
Short-term growth potential, per dollar invested	.36	.24
Intermediate growth potential (over next three years), per dollar invested	1.67	1.50
Dividend rate potential	4%	8%

Each member of the club has an investment goal of (1) an appreciation of no less than $720 in the short term, (2) an appreciation of at least $5,000 in the next three years, and (3) a dividend income of at least $200 per year. What is the smallest investment that a professor can make to meet these three goals?

7-25 Woofer Pet Foods produces a low-calorie dog food for overweight dogs. This product is made from beef products and grain. Each pound of beef costs $0.90, and each pound of grain costs $0.60. A pound of the dog food must contain at least 9 units of Vitamin 1 and 10 units of Vitamin 2. A pound of beef contains 10 units of Vitamin 1 and 12 units of Vitamin 2. A pound of grain contains 6 units of Vitamin 1 and 9 units of Vitamin 2. Formulate this as an LP problem to minimize the cost of the dog food. How many pounds of beef and grain should be included in each pound of dog food? What is the cost and vitamin content of the final product?

7-26 The seasonal yield of olives in a Piraeus, Greece, vineyard is greatly influenced by a process of branch pruning. If olive trees are pruned every two weeks, output is increased. The pruning process, however, requires considerably more labor than permitting the olives to grow on their own and results in a smaller size olive. It also, though, permits olive trees to be spaced closer together. The yield of 1 barrel of olives by pruning requires 5 hours of labor and 1 acre of land. The production of a barrel of olives by the normal process requires only 2 labor hours but takes 2 acres of land. An olive grower has 250 hours of labor available and a total of 150 acres for growing. Because of the olive size difference, a barrel of olives produced on pruned trees sells for $20, whereas a barrel of regular olives has a market price of $30. The grower has determined that because of uncertain demand, no more than 40 barrels of pruned olives should be produced. Use graphical LP to find

(a) the maximum possible profit.
(b) the best combination of barrels of pruned and regular olives.
(c) the number of acres that the olive grower should devote to each growing process.

7-27 Consider the following four LP formulations. Using a graphical approach, determine

(a) which formulation has more than one optimal solution.
(b) which formulation is unbounded.
(c) which formulation has no feasible solution.
(d) which formulation is correct as is.

Formulation 1

maximize $10X_1 + 10X_2$
subject to: $2X_1 \leq 10$
$\qquad 2X_1 + 4X_2 \leq 16$
$\qquad 4X_2 \leq 8$
$\qquad X_1 \geq 6$

Formulation 3

maximize $3X_1 + 2X_2$
subject to: $X_1 + X_2 \geq 5$
$\qquad X_1 \geq 2$
$\qquad 2X_2 \geq 8$

Formulation 2

maximize $X_1 + 2X_2$
subject to: $X_1 \leq 1$
$\qquad 2X_2 \leq 2$
$\qquad X_1 + 2X_2 \leq 2$

Formulation 4

maximize $3X_1 + 3X_2$
subject to: $4X_1 + 6X_2 \leq 48$
$\qquad 4X_1 + 2X_2 \leq 12$
$\qquad 3X_2 \geq 3$
$\qquad 2X_1 \geq 2$

7-28 Graph the following LP problem and indicate the optimal solution point:

$$\text{maximize profit} = \$3X + \$2Y$$

subject to:
$$2X + Y \leq 150$$
$$2X + 3Y \leq 300$$

(a) Does the optimal solution change if the profit per unit of X changes to $4.50?
(b) What happens if the profit function should have been $3X + $3Y?

7-29 Graphically analyze the following problem:

$$\text{maximize profit} = \$4X + \$6Y$$

subject to:
$$X + 2Y \leq 8 \text{ hours}$$
$$6X + 4Y \leq 24 \text{ hours}$$

(a) What is the optimal solution?
(b) If the first constraint is altered to $X + 3Y \leq 8$, does the feasible region or optimal solution change?

7-30 Examine the LP formulation in Problem 7-29. The problem's second constraint reads

$$6X + 4Y \leq 24 \text{ hours} \quad \text{(time available on machine 2)}$$

If the firm decides that 36 hours of time can be made available on machine 2 (namely, an additional 12 hours) at an additional cost of $10, should it add the hours?

7-31 Consider the following LP problem:

$$\text{maximize profit} = 5X + 6Y$$

subject to:
$$2X + Y \leq 120$$
$$2X + 3Y \leq 240$$
$$X, Y \leq 0$$

(a) What is the optimal solution to this problem? Solve it graphically.
(b) If a technical breakthrough occurred that raised the profit per unit of X to $8, would this affect the optimal solution?
(c) Instead of an increase in the profit coefficient X to $8, suppose that profit was overestimated and should only have been $3. Does this change the optimal solution?

7-32 Consider the LP formulation given in Problem 7-31. If the second constraint is changed from $2X + 3Y \leq 240$ to $2X + 4Y \leq 240$, what effect will this have on the optimal solution?

Output for Problem 7-33

Linear Programming Results

Problem 7-33 Solution

	X	Y		RHS	Dual
Maximize	5.	6.			
Constraint 1	2.	1.	<=	120	0.75
Constraint 2	2.	3.	<=	240.	1.75
Solution->	30.	60.		510.	

Ranging

Problem 7-33 Solution

Variable	Value	Reduced Cost	Original Val	Lower Bound	Upper Bound
X	30.	0.	5.	4.	12.
Y	60.	0.	6.	2.5	7.5
Constraint	Dual Value	Slack/Surplus	Original Val	Lower Bound	Upper Bound
Constraint 1	0.75	0.	120.	80.	240.
Constraint 2	1.75	0.	240.	120.	360.

7-33 The computer output given above is for Problem 7-31. Use this to answer the following questions.

(a) How much could the profit on X increase or decrease without changing the values of X and Y in the optimal solution?
(b) If the right-hand side of constraint 1 were increased by 1 unit, how much would the profit increase?
(c) If the right-hand side of constraint 1 were increased by 10 units, how much would the profit increase?

7-34 The computer output below is for a product mix problem in which there are two products and three resource constraints. Use the output to help you answer the following questions. Assume that you wish to maximize profit in each case.

(a) How many units of product 1 and product 2 should be produced?
(b) How much of each of the three resources is being used?
(c) What are the dual prices for each resource?
(d) If you could obtain more of one of the resources, which one should you obtain? How much should you be willing to pay for this?
(e) What would happen to profit if, with the original output, management decided to produce one more unit of product 2?

Output for Problem 7-34

Linear Programming Results

Problem 734 Solution

	X1	X2		RHS	Dual
Maximize	50.	20.			
Constraint 1	1.	2.	<=	45.	0.
Constraint 2	3.	3.	<=	87.	0.
Constraint 3	2.	1.	<=	50.	25.
Solution->	25.	0.		1,250.	

Ranging

Problem 734 Solution

Variable	Value	Reduced Cost	Original Val	Lower Bound	Upper Bound
X1	25.	0.	50.	40.	Infinity
X2	0.	5.	20.	-Infinity	25.
Constraint	Dual Value	Slack/Surplus	Original Val	Lower Bound	Upper Bound
Constraint 1	0.	20.	45.	25.	Infinity
Constraint 2	0.	12.	87.	75.	Infinity
Constraint 3	25.	0.	50.	0.	58.

Output for Problem 7-35

Linear Programming Results   _ □ ×

Problem 7-35 Solution					
	X1	X2		RHS	Dual
Maximize	8.	5.			
Constraint 1	1.	1.	<=	10.	5.
Constraint 2	1.	0.	<=	6.	3.
Solution->	6.	4.		68.	

Ranging   _ □ ×

Problem 7-35 Solution					
Variable	Value	Reduced Cost	Original Val	Lower Bound	Upper Bound
X1	6.	0.	8.	5.	Infinity
X2	4.	0.	5.	0.	8.
Constraint	Dual Value	Slack/Surplus	Original Val	Lower Bound	Upper Bound
Constraint 1	5.	0.	10.	6.	Infinity
Constraint 2	3.	0.	6.	0.	10.

7-35 Graphically solve the following problem.

$$\text{Maximize profit} = 8X_1 + 5X_2$$

$$\text{subject to:}\quad X_1 + X_2 \le 10$$

$$X_1 \le 6$$

$$X_1, X_2 \ge 0$$

(a) What is the optimal solution?
(b) Change the right-hand side of constraint 1 to 11 (instead of 10) and resolve the problem. How much did the profit increase as a result of this?
(c) Change the right-hand side of constraint 1 to 6 (instead of 10) and resolve the problem. How much did the profit decrease as a result of this? Looking at the graph, what would happen if the right-hand-side value were to go below 6?
(d) Change the right-hand-side value of constraint 1 to 5 (instead of 10) and resolve the problem. How much did the profit decrease from the original profit as a result of this?
(e) Using the computer output on this page, what is the dual price of constraint 1? What is the lower bound on this?
(f) What conclusions can you draw from this regarding the bounds of the right-hand-side values and the dual price?

7-36 Serendipity[6]

The three princes of Serendip
Went on a little trip.

They could not carry too much weight;
More than 300 pounds made them hesitate.
They planned to the ounce. When they returned to Ceylon
They discovered that their supplies were just about gone
When, what to their joy, Prince William found
A pile of coconuts on the ground.
"Each will bring 60 rupees," said Prince Richard with a grin
As he almost tripped over a lion skin.
"Look out!" cried Prince Robert with glee
As he spied some more lion skins under a tree.
"These are worth even more—300 rupees each
If we can just carry them all down to the beach."
Each skin weighed fifteen pounds and each coconut, five,
But they carried them all and made it alive.
The boat back to the island was very small
15 cubic feet baggage capacity—that was all.
Each lion skin took up one cubic foot
While eight coconuts the same space took.
With everything stowed they headed to sea
And on the way calculated what their new wealth might be.
"Eureka!" cried Prince Robert, "Our worth is so great

---

[6] The word *serendipity* was coined by the English writer Horace Walpole after a fairy tale titled *The Three Princes of Serendip*. Source of problem is unknown.

That there's no other way we could return in this state.
Any other skins or nut that we might have brought
Would now have us poorer. And now I know what—
I'll write my friend Horace in England, for surely
Only he can appreciate our serendipity."

Formulate and solve **Serendipity** by graphical LP in order to calculate "what their new wealth might be."

Problems 7-37, 7-38, 7-39, and 7-41 test your ability to formulate LP problems that have more than two variables. They cannot be solved graphically but will give you a chance to set up a larger problem.

7-37 The Feed 'N Ship Ranch fattens cattle for local farmers and ships them to meat markets in Kansas City and Omaha. The owners of the ranch seek to determine the amounts of cattle feed to buy so that minimum nutritional standards are satisfied, and at the same time total feed costs are minimized. The feed mix can be made up of the three grains that contain the following ingredients per pound of feed:

INGREDIENT	FEED (OZ.)		
	STOCK X	STOCK Y	STOCK Z
A	3	2	4
B	2	3	1
C	1	0	2
D	6	8	4

The cost per pound of stocks X, Y, and Z are $2, $4, and $2.50, respectively. The minimum requirement per cow per month is 4 pounds of ingredient A, 5 pounds of ingredient B, 1 pound of ingredient C, and 8 pounds of ingredient D.

The ranch faces one additional restriction: it can only obtain 500 pounds of stock Z per month from the feed supplier regardless of its need. Because there are usually 100 cows at the Feed 'N Ship Ranch at any given time, this means that no more than 5 pounds of stock Z can be counted on for use in the feed of each cow per month.

(a) Formulate this as an LP problem.
(b) Solve using LP software.

7-38 The Weinberger Electronics Corporation manufactures four highly technical products that it supplies to aerospace firms that hold NASA contracts. Each of the products must pass through the following departments before they are shipped: wiring, drilling, assembly, and inspection. The time requirement in hours for each unit produced and its corresponding profit value are summarized in the following table:

PRODUCT	DEPARTMENT				UNIT PROFIT ($)
	WIRING	DRILLING	ASSEMBLY	INSPECTION	
XJ201	0.5	0.3	0.2	0.5	9
XM897	1.5	1	4	1	12
TR29	1.5	2	1	0.5	15
BR788	1	3	2	0.5	11

The production available in each department each month, and the minimum monthly production requirement to fulfill contracts, are as follows:

DEPARTMENT	CAPACITY (HOURS)	PRODUCT	MINIMUM PRODUCTION LEVEL
Wiring	15,000	XJ201	150
Drilling	17,000	XM897	100
Assembly	26,000	TR29	300
Inspection	12,000	BR788	400

The production manager has the responsibility of specifying production levels for each product for the coming month. Help him by formulating (that is, setting up the constraints and objective function) Weinberger's problem using LP.

7-39 A sporting goods manufacturer is developing a production schedule for two types of racquetball racquets. An order has been received for 180 of the standard model and 90 of the professional model. These are to be delivered at the end of this month. Another order has been received for 200 of the standard model and 120 of the professional model, but these are not to be delivered until the end of next month. Production in each of the two months may be in normal time or overtime. In the current month, a standard racquet may be produced at a cost of $40 on normal time, and a professional model may be produced at a cost of $60 on regular time. Overtime raises the cost of these to $50 and $70. Due to a new labor contract for next month, all costs will increase by 10% at the end of this month.

The total number of racquets that may be produced in a month on regular time is 230, and an additional 80 racquets may be produced using overtime each month. Given the large order for delivery at the end of next month, the company is considering producing some extra racquets this month and keeping them in storage until the end of next month. The cost for keeping these in inventory for one month is estimated to be $2 per racquet. Formulate this as an LP problem to minimize cost.

7-40 Modem Corporation of America (MCA) is the world's largest producer of modem communication devices for microcomputers. MCA sold 9,000 of the regular model and 10,400 of the smart ("intelligent") model this September. Its income statement for the month is shown in the table on the next page. Costs presented are typical of prior months and are expected to remain at the same levels in the near future.

The firm is facing several constraints as it prepares its November production plan. First, it has experienced a tremendous demand and has been unable to keep any significant inventory in stock. This situation is not expected to change. Second, the firm is located in a small Iowa town from which additional labor is not readily available. Workers can be shifted from production of one modem to another, however. To produce the 9,000 regular modems in September required 5,000 direct labor hours. The 10,400 intelligent modems absorbed 10,400 direct labor hours.

Table for Problem 7-40
MCA Income Statement Month Ended September 30

	REGULAR MODEMS	INTELLIGENT MODEMS
Sales	$450,000	$640,000
Less: Discounts	10,000	15,000
Returns	12,000	9,500
Warranty replacements	4,000	2,500
Net sales	$424,000	$613,000
Sales costs		
Direct labor	60,000	76,800
Indirect labor	9,000	11,520
Materials cost	90,000	128,000
Depreciation	40,000	50,800
Cost of sales	$199,000	$267,120
Gross profit	$225,000	$345,880
Selling and general expenses		
General expenses—variable	30,000	35,000
General expenses—fixed	36,000	40,000
Advertising	28,000	25,000
Sales commissions	31,000	60,000
Total operating cost	$125,000	$160,000
Pretax income	$100,000	$185,880
Income taxes (25%)	25,000	46,470
Net income	$ 75,000	$139,410

Third, MCA is experiencing a problem affecting the intelligent modems model. Its component supplier is able to guarantee only 8,000 microprocessors for November delivery. Each intelligent modem requires one of these specially made microprocessors. Alternative suppliers are not available on short notice.

MCA wants to plan the optimal mix of the two modem models to produce in November to maximize profits for MCA.

(a) Formulate, using September's data, MCA's problem as a linear program.
(b) Solve the problem graphically.
(c) Discuss the implications of your recommended solution.

7-41 Working with chemists at Virginia Tech and George Washington Universities, landscape contractor Kenneth Golding blended his own fertilizer, called "Golding-Grow." It consists of four chemical compounds, C-30, C-92, D-21, and E-11. The cost per pound for each compound is indicated as follows:

CHEMICAL COMPOUND	COST PER POUND ($)
C-30	0.12
C-92	0.09
D-21	0.11
E-11	0.04

The specifications for Golding-Grow are as follows: (1) E-11 must constitute at least 15% of the blend; (2) C-92 and C-30 must together constitute at least 45% of the blend; (3) D-21 and C-92 can together constitute no more than 30% of the blend; and (4) Golding-Grow is packaged and sold in 50-pound bags.

(a) Formulate an LP problem to determine what blend of the four chemicals will allow Golding to minimize the cost of a 50-pound bag of the fertilizer.
(b) Solve by computer to find the best solution.

INTERNET HOMEWORK PROBLEMS

See our Internet home page at **www.prenhall.com/render** for additional homework problems 7-42 to 7-46.

⫸ CASE STUDY

Mexicana Wire Works

Ron Garcia felt good about his first week as a management trainee at Mexicana Wire Winding, Inc. He had not yet developed any technical knowledge about the manufacturing process, but he had toured the entire facility, located in the suburbs of Mexico City, and had met many people in various areas of the operation.

FIGURE 7.20

Mexicana Wire Winding, Inc.

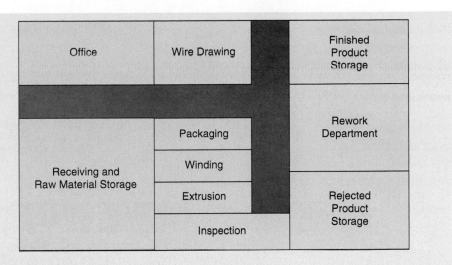

Mexicana, a subsidiary of Westover Wire Works, a Texas firm, is a medium-sized producer of wire windings used in making electrical transformers. Carlos Alverez, the production control manager, described the windings to Garcia as being of standardized design. Garcia's tour of the plant, laid out by process type (see Figure 7.20), followed the manufacturing sequence for the windings: drawing, extrusion, winding, inspection, and packaging. After inspection, good product is packaged and sent to finished product storage; defective product is stored separately until it can be reworked.

On March 8, Vivian Espania, Mexicana's general manager, stopped by Garcia's office and asked him to attend a staff meeting at 1:00 P.M.

"Let's get started with the business at hand," Vivian said, opening the meeting. "You all have met Ron Garcia, our new management trainee. Ron studied operations management in his MBA program in southern California, so I think he is competent to help us with a problem we have been discussing for a long time without resolution. I'm sure that each of you on my staff will give Ron your full cooperation."

Vivian turned to José Arroyo, production control manager. "José, why don't you describe the problem we are facing?"

"Well," José said, "business is very good right now. We are booking more orders than we can fill. We will have some new equipment on line within the next several months, which will take care of our capacity problems, but that won't help us in April. I have located some retired employees who used to work in the drawing department, and I am planning to bring them in as temporary employees in April to increase capacity there. Because we are planning to refinance some of our long-term debt, Vivian wants our profits to look as good as possible in April. I'm having a hard time figuring out which orders to run and which to back-order so that I can make the bottom line look as good as possible. Can you help me with this?"

Garcia was surprised and apprehensive to receive such an important, high-profile assignment so early in his career. Recovering quickly, he said, "Give me your data and let me work with it for a day or two."

April Orders

Product W0075C	1,400 units
Product W0033C	250 units
Product W0005X	1,510 units
Product W0007X	1,116 units

Note: Vivian Espania has given her word to a key customer that we will manufacture 600 units of product W0007X and 150 units of product W0075C for him during April.

Standard Cost

PRODUCT	MATERIAL	LABOR	OVERHEAD	SELLING PRICE
W0075C	$33.00	$ 9.90	$23.10	$100.00
W0033C	25.00	7.50	17.50	80.00
W0005X	35.00	10.50	24.50	130.00
W0007X	75.00	11.25	63.75	175.00

Selected Operating Data

Average output per month = 2,400 units

Average machine utilization = 63%

Average percentage of production set to rework department = 5% (mostly from Winding Department)

Average no. of rejected units awaiting rework = 850 (mostly from Winding Department)

Plant Capacity (Hours)

DRAWING	EXTRUSION	WINDING	PACKAGING
4,000	4,200	2,000	2,300

Note: Inspection capacity is not a problem; we can work overtime as necessary to accommodate any schedule.

Bill of Labor (Hours/Unit)

PRODUCT	DRAWING	EXTRUSION	WINDING	PACKAGING
W0075C	1.0	1.0	1.0	1.0
W0033C	2.0	1.0	3.0	0.0
W0005X	0.0	4.0	0.0	3.0
W0007X	1.0	1.0	0.0	2.0

Discussion Questions

1. What recommendations should Ron Garcia make, with what justification? Provide a detailed analysis with charts, graphs, and computer printouts included.
2. Discuss the need for temporary workers in the drawing department.
3. Discuss the plant layout.

Source: Professor Victor E. Sower, Sam Houston State University. This case material is based on an actual situation, with names and data altered for confidentiality.

INTERNET CASE STUDY

See our Internet home page at **www.prenhall.com/render** for this additional case study: Agri Chem Corporation. This case involves a company's response to an energy shortage.

BIBLIOGRAPHY

Bodington, C. E. and T. E. Baker. "A History of Mathematical Programming in the Petroleum Industry," *Interfaces* 20, 4 (July–August 1990): 117–132.

Bretthauer, Kurt M., and Murray J. Cote. "A Model for Planning Resource Requirements in Health Care Organizations," *Decision Sciences*, 29, 1 (Winter 1998): 243–270.

Butler, John C. and James S. Dyer. "Optimizing Natural Gas Flows with Linear Programming and Scenarios," *Decision Sciences*, 30, 2 (Spring 1999): 563–577.

Chakravarti, N. "Tea Company Steeped in OR," *OR/MS Today*, 27, 2 (April 2000): 32–34.

Dell, Robert F. "Optimizing Army Base Realignment and Closure," *Interfaces* 28, 6 (November–December 1998): 1–18.

Desroisers, Jacques. "Air Transat Uses ALTITUDE to Manage Its Aircraft Routing, Crew Pairing, and Work Assignment," *Interfaces* 30, 2 (March–April 2000): 41–53.

Eliman, A. A., M. Girgis, and S. Kotob. "A Solution to Post-Crash Debt Entanglements in Kuwait's al-Manakh Stock Market," *Interfaces* 27, (January–February 1997): 89–106.

Farley, A. A. "Planning the Cutting of Photographic Color Paper Rolls for Kodak (Australasia) Pty. Ltd.," *Interfaces* 21, 1 (January–February 1991): 92–106.

Greenberg, H. J. "How to Analyze the Results of Linear Programs— Part 1: Preliminaries," *Interfaces* 23, 4 (July–August 1993): 56–68.

Greenberg, H. J. "How to Analyze the Results of Linear Programs—Part 3: Infeasibility Diagnosis," *Interfaces* 23, 6 (November–December 1993): 120–139.

Hueter, Jackie and William Swart. "An Integrated Labor-Management System for Taco Bell," *Interfaces* 28, 1 (January–February 1998): 75–91.

Kontogiorgis, S. and S. Acharya. "US Airways Automates Its Weekend Fleet Assignment," *Interfaces* 29, 3 (May–June 1999): 52–62.

LeBlanc, Larry J., Dale Randels, Jr., and T. K. Swann. "Heery International's Spreadsheet Optimization Model for Assigning Managers to Construction Projects," *Interfaces* 30, 6 (November–December 2000): 95–106.

Orden, A. "LP from the '40s to the '90s," *Interfaces* 23, 5 (September–October 1993): 2–12.

Pate-Cornell, M. E. and T. L. Dillon. "The Right Stuff," *OR/MS Today*, 27, 1 (February 2000): 36–39.

Quinn, P., B. Andrews, and H. Parsons. "Allocating Telecommunications Resources at L. L. Bean, Inc.," *Interfaces* 21, 1 (January–February 1991): 75–91.

Rubin, D. S. and H. M. Wagner. "Shadow Prices: Tips and Traps for Managers and Instructors," *Interfaces* 20, 4 (July–August 1990): 150–157.

Ryan, David M. "Optimization Earns Its Wings," *OR/MS Today*, 27, 2 (April 2000): 26–30.

Saltzman, M. J. "Survey: Mixed Integer Programming," *OR/MS Today* 21, 2 (April 1994): 42–51.

Schuster, Edmund W. and Stuart J. Allen. "Raw Material Management at Welch's Inc." *Interfaces* 28, 5 (September–October 1998): 13–24.

Sexton, T. R., S. Sleeper, and R. E. Taggart, Jr. "Improving Pupil Transportation in North Carolina," *Interfaces* 24, 1 (January–February 1994): 87–104.

Summerour, J. "Chilean Forestry Firm: A Model of Success," *OR/MS Today*, 26, 2 (April 1999): 22–23.

Zappe, C., W. Webster, and I. Horowitz. "Using Linear Programming to Determine Post-Facto Consistency in Performance Evaluations of Major League Baseball Players," *Interfaces* 23, 6 (November–December 1993): 107–119.

CHAPTER 8

LINEAR PROGRAMMING MODELING APPLICATIONS: WITH COMPUTER ANALYSES IN EXCEL AND QM FOR WINDOWS

LEARNING OBJECTIVES

After completing this chapter, students will be able to:

1. Model a wide variety of medium to large LP problems.
2. Understand major application areas, including marketing, production, labor scheduling, fuel blending, transportation, and finance.
3. Gain experience in solving LP problems with QM for Windows and Excel Solver Software.

CHAPTER OUTLINE

Summary • Self-Test • Problems • Internet Homework Problems • Case Study: Red Brand Canners • Case Study: Chase Manhattan Bank • Bibliography

8.1   INTRODUCTION

The graphical method of linear programming (LP) discussed in Chapter 7 is useful for understanding how to formulate and solve small LP problems. The purpose of this chapter is to go one step further and show how a large number of real-life problems can be modeled using LP. We do this by presenting examples of models in the areas of production mix, labor scheduling, job assignment, production scheduling, marketing research, media selection, shipping and transportation, transshipment ingredient mix, and financial portfolio selection. We will solve many of these LP problems using Excel's Solver and QM for Windows.

Although some of these models are relatively small numerically, the principles developed here are definitely applicable to larger problems. Moreover, this practice in "paraphrasing" LP model formulations should help develop your skills in applying the technique to other, less common applications.

8.2   MARKETING APPLICATIONS

Media Selection

Media selection problems can be approached with LP from two perspectives. The objective can be to maximize audience exposure or to minimize advertising costs.

Linear programming models have been used in the advertising field as a decision aid in selecting an effective media mix. Sometimes the technique is employed in allocating a fixed or limited budget across various media, which might include radio or television commercials, newspaper ads, direct mailings, magazine ads, and so on. In other applications, the objective is the maximization of audience exposure. Restrictions on the allowable media mix might arise through contract requirements, limited media availability, or company policy. An example follows.

The Win Big Gambling Club promotes gambling junkets from a large Midwestern city to casinos in the Bahamas. The club has budgeted up to $8,000 per week for local advertising. The money is to be allocated among four promotional media: TV spots, newspaper ads, and two types of radio advertisements. Win Big's goal is to reach the largest possible high-potential audience through the various media. The following table presents the number of potential gamblers reached by making use of an advertisement in each of the four media. It also provides the cost per advertisement placed and the maximum number of ads that can be purchased per week.

MEDIUM	AUDIENCE REACHED PER AD	COST PER AD ($)	MAXIMUM ADS PER WEEK
TV spot (1 minute)	5,000	800	12
Daily newspaper (full-page ad)	8,500	925	5
Radio spot (30 seconds, prime time)	2,400	290	25
Radio spot (1 minute, afternoon)	2,800	380	20

Win Big's contractual arrangements require that at least five radio spots be placed each week. To ensure a broad-scoped promotional campaign, management also insists that no more than $1,800 be spent on radio advertising every week.

The problem can now be stated mathematically as follows. Let

X_1 = number of 1-minute TV spots taken each week

X_2 = number of full-page daily newspaper ads taken each week

X_3 = number of 30-second prime-time radio spots taken each week

X_4 = number of 1-minute afternoon radio spots taken each week

Objective:

$$\text{maximize audience coverage} = 5{,}000X_1 + 8{,}500X_2 + 2{,}400X_3 + 2{,}800X_4$$

subject to:

$$X_1 < 12 \quad \text{(maximum TV spots/week)}$$
$$X_2 \le 5 \quad \text{(maximum newspaper ads/week)}$$
$$X_3 \le 25 \quad \text{(maximum 30-second radio spots/week)}$$
$$X_4 \le 20 \quad \text{(maximum 1-minute radio spots/week)}$$
$$800X_1 + 925X_2 + 290X_3 + 380X_4 \le \$8{,}000 \quad \text{(weekly advertising budget)}$$
$$X_3 + X_4 \ge 5 \quad \text{(minimum radio spots contracted)}$$
$$290X_3 + 380X_4 \le \$1{,}800 \quad \text{(maximum dollars spent on radio)}$$
$$X_1, X_2, X_3, X_4, X_5, \ge 0$$

PROGRAM 8.1A   **Excel Formulation of Win Big's LP Problem, Using the Solver Command**

PROGRAM 8.1B

Solution to the Win Big Gambling Club LP Model Using Input from Program 8.1A

The solution to this LP formulation, using Excel's Solver (see Programs 8.1A and 8.1B), is found to be

$X_1 = 1.97$ TV spots
$X_2 = 5$ newspaper ads
$X_3 = 6.2$ 30-second radio spots
$X_4 = 0$ one-minute radio spots

This produces an audience exposure of 67,240 contacts. Because X_1 and X_3 are fractional, Win Big would probably round them to 2 and 6, respectively. Problems that demand all-integer solutions are discussed in detail in Chapter 11.

Marketing Research

Linear programming has also been applied to marketing research problems and the area of consumer research. The next example illustrates how statistical pollsters can reach strategy decisions with LP.

Management Sciences Associates (MSA) is a marketing and computer research firm based in Washington, D.C., that handles consumer surveys. One of its clients is a national press service that periodically conducts political polls on issues of widespread interest. In a survey for the press service, MSA determines that it must fulfill several requirements in order to draw statistically valid conclusions on the sensitive issue of new U.S. immigration laws:

1. Survey at least 2,300 U.S. households in total.
2. Survey at least 1,000 households whose heads are 30 years of age or younger.
3. Survey at least 600 households whose heads are between 31 and 50 years of age.
4. Ensure that at least 15% of those surveyed live in a state that borders on Mexico.
5. Ensure that no more than 20% of those surveyed who are 51 years of age or over live in a state that borders on Mexico.

MSA decides that all surveys should be conducted in person. It estimates that the costs of reaching people in each age and region category are as follows:

REGION	COST PER PERSON SURVEYED ($)		
	AGE ≤ 30	AGE 31–50	AGE ≥ 51
State bordering Mexico	$7.50	$6.80	$5.50
State not bordering Mexico	$6.90	$7.25	$6.10

MSA's goal is to meet the five sampling requirements at the least possible cost. We let

X_1 = number surveyed who are 30 or younger and live in a border state

X_2 = number surveyed who are 31–50 and live in a border state

X_3 = number surveyed who are 51 or older and live in a border state

X_4 = number surveyed who are 30 or younger and do not live in a border state

X_5 = number surveyed who are 31–50 and do not live in a border state

X_6 = number surveyed who are 51 or older and do not live in a border state

Objective function:

$$\text{minimize total interview costs} = \$7.50X_1 + \$6.80X_2 + \$5.50X_3 \\ + \$6.90X_4 + \$7.25X_5 + \$6.10X_6$$

IN ACTION   Scheduling Planes at Delta Airlines With Coldstart

It has been said that an airline seat is the most perishable commodity in the world. Each time an airliner takes off with an empty seat, a revenue opportunity is lost forever. For Delta Airlines, which flies more than 2,500 domestic flight legs per day using about 450 aircraft of 10 different models, its schedule is the very heartbeat of the airline.

One flight leg for Delta might consist of a Boeing 757 jet assigned to fly at 6:21 A.M. from Atlanta to arrive in Boston at 8:45 A.M. Delta's problem, the same as that of every competitor, is to match airplanes such as 747s, 757s, or 767s, to flight legs such as Atlanta–Boston, and fill seats with paying passengers. Recent advances in LP algorithms and computer hardware have made it possible to solve optimization problems of this scope for the first time. Delta calls its huge LP model Coldstart and runs the model every day. Delta is the first airline to solve a problem of this scope.

The typical size of a daily Coldstart model is about 40,000 constraints and 60,000 variables. The constraints are aircraft availability, balancing arrivals and departures at airports, aircraft maintenance needs, and so on. Coldstart's objective is to minimize a combination of operating costs and lost passenger revenue, called spill costs.

The savings from the model so far have been phenomenal, estimated at $220,000 per day over Delta's earlier schedule planning tool, which was nicknamed "Warmstart." Delta expects to save $300 million over the next three years through this use of LP.

Sources: R. Subramanian, et al. *Interfaces* 24, 1 (January–February, 1994): 104–120; Peter R. Horner. *OR/MS Today* 22, 4 (August 1995): 14–15.

subject to:

$$X_1 + X_2 + X_3 + X_4 + X_5 + X_6 \geq 2{,}300 \quad \text{(total households)}$$
$$X_1 + \qquad\qquad X_4 \qquad\qquad\quad \geq 1{,}000 \quad \text{(households 30 or younger)}$$
$$\qquad X_2 + \qquad\qquad X_5 \quad \geq \ \ 600 \quad \text{(households 31–50 in age)}$$
$$X_1 + X_2 + X_3 \geq 0.15(X_1 + X_2 + X_3 + X_4 + X_5 + X_6) \quad \text{(border states)}$$
$$X_3 \leq 0.2(X_3 + X_6) \ \text{(limit on age group 51+ who can live in border state)}$$
$$X_1, X_2, X_3, X_4, X_5, X_6 \geq 0$$

The computer solution to MSA's problem costs $15,166 and is presented in the following table and in Program 8.2, which illustrates the input and output from QM for Windows. Note that the variables in the constraints are moved to the left-hand-side of the inequality.

REGION	AGE ≤ 30	AGE 31–50	AGE ≥ 51
State bordering Mexico	0	600	140
State not bordering Mexico	1,000	0	560

PROGRAM 8.2

Using QM for Windows to Solve MSA's LP Problem

QM for Windows - C:\Prentice\Data\Renstair\Mansc393.lin

Objective
○ Maximize
● Minimize

Linear Programming Results

Management Science Associates Solution									
	X1	X2	X3	X4	X5	X6		RHS	Dual
Minimize	7.5	6.8	5.5	6.9	7.25	6.1			
Constraint 1	1.	1.	1.	1.	1.	1.	>=	2,300.	-5.98
Constraint 2	1.	0.	0.	1.	0.	0.	>=	1,000.	-0.92
Constraint 3	0.	1.	0.	0.	1.	0.	>=	600.	-0.82
Constraint 4	0.85	0.85	0.85	-0.15	-0.15	-0.15	>=	0.	0.
Constraint 5	0.	0.	0.8	0.	0.	-0.2	<-	0.	0.6
Solution->	0.	600.	140.	1,000.	0.	559.9999		15,166.	

8.3 **MANUFACTURING APPLICATIONS**

Production Mix

A fertile field for the use of LP is in planning for the optimal mix of products to manufacture. A company must meet a myriad of constraints, ranging from financial concerns to sales demand to material contracts to union labor demands. Its primary goal is to generate the largest profit possible.

Fifth Avenue Industries, a nationally known manufacturer of menswear, produces four varieties of ties. One is an expensive, all-silk tie, one is an all-polyester tie, and two are blends of polyester and cotton. The following table illustrates the cost and availability (per monthly production planning period) of the three materials used in the production process:

MATERIAL	COST PER YARD ($)	MATERIAL AVAILABLE PER MONTH (YARDS)
Silk	21	800
Polyester	6	3,000
Cotton	9	1,600

The firm has fixed contracts with several major department store chains to supply ties. The contracts require that Fifth Avenue Industries supply a minimum quantity of each tie but allow for a larger demand if Fifth Avenue chooses to meet that demand. (Most of the ties are not shipped with the name Fifth Avenue on their label, incidentally, but with "private stock" labels supplied by the stores.) Table 8.1 summarizes the contract demand for each of the four styles of ties, the selling price per tie, and the fabric requirements of each variety.

Fifth Avenue's goal is to maximize its monthly profit. It must decide upon a policy for product mix. Let

$$X_1 = \text{number of all-silk ties produced per month}$$

$$X_2 = \text{number of polyester ties}$$

$$X_3 = \text{number of blend 1 poly–cotton ties}$$

$$X_4 = \text{number of blend 2 poly–cotton ties}$$

But first the firm must establish the profit per tie.

1. For all-silk ties (X_1), each requires 0.125 yard of silk, at a cost of $21 per yard. Therefore, the cost per tie is $2.62. The selling price per silk tie is $6.70, leaving a net profit of ($6.70 − $2.62 =) $4.08 per unit of X_1.

2. For all-polyester ties (X_2), each requires 0.08 yard of polyester at a cost of $6 per yard. The cost per tie is, therefore, $0.48. The net profit per unit of X_2 is ($3.55 − $0.48 =) $3.07.

3. For poly-cotton blend 1 (X_3), each tie requires 0.05 yard of polyester at $6 per yard and 0.05 yard of cotton at $9 per yard, for a cost of $0.30 + $0.45 = $0.75 per tie. The profit is $3.56.

4. Try to compute the net profit for blend 2. You should calculate a cost of $0.81 per tie and a net profit of $4.

VARIETY OF TIE	SELLING PRICE PER TIE ($)	MONTHLY CONTRACT MINIMUM	MONTHLY DEMAND	MATERIAL REQUIRED PER TIE (YARDS)	MATERIAL REQUIREMENTS
All silk	6.70	6,000	7,000	0.125	100% silk
All polyester	3.55	10,000	14,000	0.08	100% polyester
Poly–cotton blend 1	4.31	13,000	16,000	0.10	50% polyester–50% cotton
Poly–cotton blend 2	4.81	6,000	8,500	0.10	30% polyester–70% cotton

TABLE 8.1   Data for Fifth Avenue Industries

The objective function may now be stated as

$$\text{maximize profit} = \$4.08X_1 + \$3.07X_2 + \$3.56X_3 + \$4.00X_4$$

subject to:

$$
\begin{aligned}
0.125X_1 &\leq 800 && \text{(yards of silk)} \\
0.08X_2 + 0.05X_3 + 0.03X_4 &\leq 3,000 && \text{(yards of polyester)} \\
0.05X_3 + 0.07X_4 &\leq 1,600 && \text{(yards of cotton)} \\
X_1 &\geq 6,000 && \text{(contract minimum for all silk)} \\
X_1 &\leq 7,000 && \text{(contract maximum)} \\
X_2 &\geq 10,000 && \text{(contract minimum for all polyester)} \\
X_2 &\leq 14,000 && \text{(contract maximum)} \\
X_3 &\geq 13,000 && \text{(contract minimum for blend 1)} \\
X_3 &\leq 16,000 && \text{(contract maximum)} \\
X_4 &\geq 6,000 && \text{(contract minimum for blend 2)} \\
X_4 &\leq 8,500 && \text{(contract maximum)} \\
X_1, X_2, X_3, X_4 &\geq 0
\end{aligned}
$$

Using Excel and its Solver command, the computer-generated solution is to produce 6,400 all-silk ties each month; 14,000 all-polyester ties; 16,000 poly–cotton blend 1 ties; and 8,500 poly–cotton blend 2 ties. This produces a profit of $160,020 per production period. See Programs 8.3A and 8.3B on the next page for details.

Production Scheduling

Setting a low-cost production schedule over a period of weeks or months is a difficult and important management problem in most plants. The production manager has to consider many factors: labor capacity, inventory and storage costs, space limitations, product demand, and labor relations. Because most companies produce more than one product, the scheduling process is often quite complex.

Basically, the problem resembles the product mix model for each period in the future. The objective is either to maximize profit or to minimize the total cost (production plus inventory) of carrying out the task.

Production scheduling is amenable to solution by LP because it is a problem that must be solved on a regular basis. When the objective function and constraints for a firm are established, the inputs can easily be changed each month to provide an updated schedule.

PROGRAM 8.3A

Excel Formulation for Fifth Avenue Industries LP Problem Using Solver

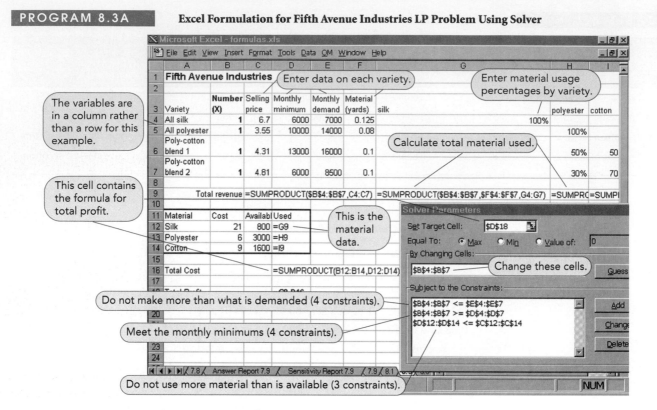

PROGRAM 8.3B

Output from Program 8.3A with Solution to Fifth Avenue's LP Problem

	A	B	C	D	E	F	G	H	I
1	**Fifth Avenue Industries**								
2									
3	Variety	**Number (X)**	Selling price	Monthly minimum	Monthly demand	Material (yards)	silk	polyester	cotton
4	All silk	**6400**	6.7	6000	7000	0.125	100%		
5	All polyester	**14000**	3.55	10000	14000	0.08		100%	
6	Poly-cotton blend 1	**16000**	4.31	13000	16000	0.1		50%	50%
7	Poly-cotton blend 2	**8500**	4.81	6000	8500	0.1		30%	70%
8									
9		Total revenue	202425				800	2175	1395
10									
11	Material	Cost	Available	Used					
12	Silk	21	800	800					
13	Polyester	6	3000	2175					
14	Cotton	9	1600	1395					
15									
16	Total Cost			42405					
17									
18	Total Profit			**160020**					

An example of production scheduling: Greenberg Motors

Greenberg Motors, Inc., manufactures two different electrical motors for sale under contract to Drexel Corp., a well-known producer of small kitchen appliances. Its model GM3A is found in many Drexel food processors, and its model GM3B is used in the assembly of blenders.

Three times each year, the procurement officer at Drexel contracts Irwin Greenberg, the founder of Greenberg Motors, to place a monthly order for each of the coming four months. Drexel's demand for motors varies each month based on its own sales forecasts, production capacity, and financial position. Greenberg has just received the January–April order and must begin his own four-month production plan. The demand for motors is shown in Table 8.2.

Production planning at Greenberg Motors must consider four factors:

1. The desirability of producing the same number of each motor each month. This simplifies planning and the scheduling of workers and machines.

2. The necessity to keep down inventory carrying, or holding, costs. This suggests producing in each month only what is needed in that month.

3. Warehouse limitations that cannot be exceeded without great additional storage costs.

4. The company's no-layoff policy, which has been effective in preventing a unionization of the shop. This suggests a minimum production capacity that should be used each month.

Although these four factors often conflict, Greenberg has found that LP is an effective tool in setting up a production schedule that will minimize his total costs of per unit production and monthly holding.

Double-subscripted variables are often used in LP. Greenberg Motors is more easily formulated with this approach, as is the next example in this chapter.

Double-subscripted variables can be used here to develop the LP model. We let

$$X_{A,i} = \text{number of model GM3A motors produced in month } i$$
$$(i = 1, 2, 3, 4 \text{ for January–April})$$

$$X_{B,i} = \text{number of model GM3B motors produced in month } i$$

Production costs are currently $10 per GM3A motor produced and $6 per GM3B unit. A labor agreement going into effect on March 1 will raise each figure by 10%, however. We can write the part of the objective function that deals with production cost as

$$\text{cost of production} = \$10X_{A1} + \$10X_{A2} + \$11X_{A3} + \$11X_{A4}$$
$$+ \$6X_{B1} + \$6X_{B2} + \$6.60X_{B3} + \$6.60X_{B4}$$

To include the inventory carrying costs in the model, we can introduce a second variable. Let

$$I_{A,i} = \text{level of on-hand inventory for GM3A motors at end of month } i$$
$$(i = 1, 2, 3, 4)$$

$$I_{B,i} = \text{level of on-hand inventory for GM3B motors at end of month } i$$

Each GM3A motor held in stock costs $0.18 per month, and each GM3B has a carrying cost of $0.13 per month. Greenberg's accountants allow monthly ending inventories as an

TABLE 8.2				
Four-Month Order Schedule for Electrical Motors	MODEL	JANUARY	FEBRUARY	MARCH	APRIL
	GM3A	800	700	1,000	1,100
	GM3B	1,000	1,200	1,400	1,400

acceptable approximation to the average inventory levels during the month. So the carrying cost part of the LP objective function is

$$\text{cost of carrying inventory} = \$0.18I_{A1} + 0.18I_{A2} + 0.18I_{A3} + 0.18I_{A4}$$
$$+ 0.13I_{B1} + 0.13I_{B2} + 0.13I_{B3} + 0.13I_{B4}$$

The total objective function becomes

$$\text{minimize total costs} = 10X_{A1} + 10X_{A2} + 11X_{A3} + 11X_{A4} + 6X_{B1} + 6X_{B2}$$
$$+ 6.6X_{B3} + 6.6X_{B4} + 0.18I_{A1} + 0.18I_{A2} + 0.18I_{A3} + 0.18I_{A4}$$
$$+ 0.13I_{B1} + 0.13I_{B2} + 0.13I_{B3} + 0.13I_{B4}$$

Inventory constraints set the relationship between closing inventory this month, closing inventory last month, this month's production, and sales this month.

In setting up the constraints, we must recognize the relationship between last month's ending inventory, the current month's production, and the sales to Drexel this month. The inventory at the end of a month is

$$\begin{pmatrix} \text{inventory} \\ \text{at the} \\ \text{end of} \\ \text{this month} \end{pmatrix} = \begin{pmatrix} \text{inventory} \\ \text{at the} \\ \text{end of} \\ \text{last month} \end{pmatrix} + \begin{pmatrix} \text{current} \\ \text{month's} \\ \text{production} \end{pmatrix} - \begin{pmatrix} \text{sales} \\ \text{to Drexel} \\ \text{this month} \end{pmatrix}$$

Suppose that Greenberg is starting the new four-month production cycle with a change in design specifications that left no old motors in stock on January 1. Then, recalling that January's demand for GM3As is 800 and for GM3Bs is 1,000, we can write

$$I_{A1} = 0 + X_{A1} - 800$$
$$I_{B1} = 0 + X_{B1} - 1,000$$

Transposing all unknown variables to the left of the equal sign and multiplying all terms by -1, these January constraints can be rewritten as

$$X_{A1} - I_{A1} = 800$$
$$X_{B1} - I_{B1} = 1,000$$

The constraints on demand in February, March, and April follow:

$$\begin{array}{ll} X_{A2} + I_{A1} - I_{A2} = 700 & \text{February GM3A demand} \\ X_{B2} + I_{B1} - I_{B2} = 1,200 & \text{February GM3B demand} \\ X_{A3} + I_{A2} - I_{A3} = 1,000 & \text{March GM3A demand} \\ X_{B3} + I_{B2} - I_{B3} = 1,400 & \text{March GM3B demand} \\ X_{A4} + I_{A3} - I_{A4} = 1,100 & \text{April GM3A demand} \\ X_{B4} + I_{B3} - I_{B4} = 1,400 & \text{April GM3B demand} \end{array}$$

If Greenberg also wants to have on hand an additional 450 GM3As and 300 GM3Bs at the end of April, we add the constraints

$$I_{A4} = 450$$
$$I_{B4} = 300$$

The constraints discussed address demand; they do not, however, consider warehouse space of labor requirements. First, we note that the storage area for Greenberg Motors can hold a maximum of 3,300 motors of either type (they are similar in size) at any one time. Then

$$I_{A1} + I_{B1} \leq 3,300$$
$$I_{A2} + I_{B2} \leq 3,300$$
$$I_{A3} + I_{B3} \leq 3,300$$
$$I_{A4} + I_{B4} \leq 3,300$$

Second, we return to the issue of employment. So that no worker is ever laid off, Greenberg has a base employment level of 2,240 labor hours per month. In a busy period, though, the company can bring two skilled former employees on board (they are now retired) to increase capacity to 2,560 hours per month. Each GM3A motor produced requires 1.3 hours of labor, and each GM3B takes a worker 0.9 hour to assemble.

Employment constraints are set for each month.

$1.3X_{A1} + 0.9X_{B1} \geq 2,240$	(January minimum worker hours/month)
$1.3X_{A1} + 0.9X_{B1} \leq 2,560$	(January maximum labor available/month)
$1.3X_{A2} + 0.9X_{B2} \geq 2,240$	(February labor minimum)
$1.3X_{A2} + 0.9X_{B2} \leq 2,560$	(February labor maximum)
$1.3X_{A3} + 0.9X_{B3} \geq 2,240$	(March labor minimum)
$1.3X_{A3} + 0.9X_{B3} \leq 2,560$	(March labor maximum)
$1.3X_{A4} + 0.9X_{B4} \geq 2,240$	(April labor minimum)
$1.3X_{A4} + 0.9X_{B4} \leq 2,560$	(April labor maximum)
All variables ≥ 0	Nonnegativity constraints

The solution to the Greenberg Motors problem was found by computer and is shown in Table 8.3. The four-month total cost is $76,301.61.

TABLE 8.3

Solution to Greenberg Motor Problem

PRODUCTION SCHEDULE	JANUARY	FEBRUARY	MARCH	APRIL
Units of GM3A produced	1,277	1,138	842	792
Units of GM3B produced	1,000	1,200	1,400	1,700
Inventory of GM3A carried	477	915	758	450
Inventory of GM3B carried	0	0	0	300
Labor hours required	2,560	2,560	2,355	2,560

This example illustrates a relatively simple production planning problem in that there were only two products being considered. The 16 variables and 22 constraints may not seem trivial, but the technique can also be applied successfully with dozens of products and hundreds of constraints.

8.4 EMPLOYEE SCHEDULING APPLICATIONS

Assignment Problems

We can assign people to jobs using LP or use a special assignment algorithm discussed in Chapter 10.

Assignment problems involve determining the most efficient assignment of people to jobs, machines to tasks, police cars to city sectors, salespeople to territories, and so on. The objective might be to minimize travel times or costs or to maximize assignment effectiveness. Assignments can be handled with their own special solution procedures (see Chapter 10). Assignment problems are unique because they not only have a coefficient of 1 associated with each variable in the LP constraints; the right-hand side of each constraint is also always equal to 1. The use of LP in solving assignment problems, as illustrated by the following case, yields solutions of either 0 or 1 for each variable in the formulation.

The law firm of Ivan and Ivan maintains a large staff of young attorneys who hold the title of junior partner. Ivan, concerned with the effective utilization of his personnel resources, seeks some objective means of making lawyer-to-client assignments.

On March 1, four new clients seeking legal assistance came to Ivan. Although the current staff is overloaded, Ivan would like to accommodate the new clients. He reviews current case loads and identifies four junior partners who, although busy, could possibly be assigned to the cases. Each young lawyer can handle at most one new client. Furthermore, each lawyer differs in skills and specialty interests.

Seeking to maximize the overall effectiveness of the new client assignments, Ivan draws up the following table, in which he rates the estimated effectiveness (on a scale of 1 to 9) of each lawyer on each new case.

Ivan's Effectiveness Ratings

	CLIENT'S CASE			
LAWYER	DIVORCE	CORPORATE MERGER	EMBEZZLEMENT	EXHIBITIONISM
Adams	6	2	8	5
Brooks	9	3	5	8
Carter	4	8	3	4
Darwin	6	7	6	4

Here is another example of double-subscripted variables.

To solve using LP, we again employ double-subscripted variables. Let

$$X_{ij} = \begin{cases} 1 \text{ if attorney } i \text{ is assigned to case } j \\ 0 \text{ otherwise} \end{cases}$$

where

$i = 1, 2, 3, 4$ stands for Adams, Brooks, Carter, and Darwin, respectively

$j = 1, 2, 3, 4$ stands for divorce, merger, embezzlement, and exhibitionism, respectively

The LP formulation follows:

$$\text{maximize effectiveness} = 6X_{11} + 2X_{12} + 8X_{13} + 5X_{14} + 9X_{21} + 3X_{22}$$
$$+ 5X_{23} + 8X_{24} + 4X_{31} + 8X_{32} + 3X_{33} + 4X_{34}$$
$$+ 6X_{41} + 7X_{42} + 6X_{43} + 4X_{44}$$

$$\begin{aligned}
\text{subject to: } & X_{11} + X_{21} + X_{31} + X_{41} = 1 && \text{(divorce case)} \\
& X_{12} + X_{22} + X_{32} + X_{42} = 1 && \text{(merger)} \\
& X_{13} + X_{23} + X_{33} + X_{43} = 1 && \text{(embezzlement)} \\
& X_{14} + X_{24} + X_{34} + X_{44} = 1 && \text{(exhibitionism)} \\
& X_{11} + X_{12} + X_{13} + X_{14} = 1 && \text{(Adams)} \\
& X_{21} + X_{22} + X_{23} + X_{24} = 1 && \text{(Brooks)} \\
& X_{31} + X_{32} + X_{33} + X_{34} = 1 && \text{(Carter)} \\
& X_{41} + X_{42} + X_{43} + X_{44} = 1 && \text{(Darwin)}
\end{aligned}$$

PROGRAM 8.4

Solving Ivan and Ivan's Assignment Scheduling LP Problem Using QM for Windows

QM for Windows - C:\Prentice\Data\RenderStair7\Ivan.LIN

Objective
● Maximize
○ Minimize

Linear Programming Results

Ivan and Ivan Solution

	x11	x12	x13	x14	x21	x22	x23	x24	x31	x32	x33	x34	x41	x42	x43	x44		RHS	Dual
Maximize	6.	2.	8.	5.	9.	3.	5.	8.	4.	8.	3.	4.	6.	7.	6.	4.			
Divorce	1.	1.	1.	1.													=	1.	5.
Merger					1.	1.	1.	1.									=	1.	8.
Embezzlement									1.	1.	1.	1.					=	1.	4.
Exhibitionism													1.	1.	1.	1.	=	1.	5.
Adams	1.				1.				1.				1.				=	1.	1.
Brooks		1.				1.				1.				1.			=	1.	4.
Carter			1.				1.				1.				1.		=	1.	3.
Darwin				1.				1.				1.				1.	=	1.	0.
Solution->	0.	0.	1.	0.	0.	0.	0.	1.	0.	1.	0.	0.	1.	0.	0.	0.		30.	

The law firm's problem is solved in Program 8.4 using QM for Windows. There is a total effectiveness rating of 30 by letting $X_{13} = 1$, $X_{24} = 1$, $X_{32} = 1$, and $X_{41} = 1$. All other variables are therefore equal to zero.

Labor Planning

Labor planning problems address staffing needs over a specific time period. They are especially useful when managers have some flexibility in assigning workers to jobs that require overlapping or interchangeable talents. Large banks frequently use LP to tackle their labor scheduling.

Hong Kong Bank of Commerce and Industry is a busy bank that has requirements for between 10 and 18 tellers, depending on the time of day. The lunch time, from noon to 2 P.M., is usually heaviest. Table 8.4 indicates the workers needed at various hours that the bank is open.

The bank now employs 12 full-time tellers, but many people are on its roster of available part-time employees. A part-time employee must put in exactly four hours per day but can start anytime between 9 A.M. and 1 P.M. Part-timers are a fairly inexpensive labor pool, since no retirement or lunch benefits are provided for them. Full-timers, on the other hand, work from 9 A.M. to 5 P.M. but are allowed 1 hour for lunch. (Half of the full-timers eat at 11 A.M., the other half at noon.) Full-timers thus provide 35 hours per week of productive labor time.

TABLE 8.4

Hong Kong Bank of Commerce and Industry

TIME PERIOD	NUMBER OF TELLERS REQUIRED
9 A.M.–10 A.M.	10
10 A.M.–11 A.M.	12
11 A.M.–Noon	14
Noon–1 P.M.	16
1 P.M.–2 P.M.	18
2 P.M.–3 P.M.	17
3 P.M.–4 P.M.	15
4 P.M.–5 P.M.	10

By corporate policy, the bank limits part-time hours to a maximum of 50% of the day's total requirement. Part-timers earn $8 per hour (or $32 per day) on average, and full-timers earn $100 per day in salary and benefits, on average. The bank would like to set a schedule that would minimize its total personnel costs. It will release one or more of its full-time tellers if it is profitable to do so.

We can let

$$F = \text{full-time tellers}$$

$$P_1 = \text{part-timers starting at 9 A.M. (leaving at 1 P.M.)}$$

$$P_2 = \text{part-timers starting at 10 A.M. (leaving at 2 P.M.)}$$

$$P_3 = \text{part-timers starting at 11 A.M. (leaving at 3 P.M.)}$$

$$P_4 = \text{part-timers starting at noon (leaving at 4 P.M.)}$$

$$P_5 = \text{part-timers starting at 1 P.M. (leaving at 5 P.M.)}$$

Objective function:

$$\text{minimize total daily personnel cost} = \$100F + \$32(P_1 + P_2 + P_3 + P_4 + P_5)$$

Constraints:

For each hour, the available labor hours must be at least equal to the required labor hours.

$$
\begin{array}{lll}
F + P_1 & \geq 10 & \text{(9 A.M.–10 A.M. needs)} \\
F + P_1 + P_2 & \geq 12 & \text{(10 A.M.–11 A.M. needs)} \\
\tfrac{1}{2}F + P_1 + P_2 + P_3 & \geq 14 & \text{(11 A.M.–noon needs)} \\
\tfrac{1}{2}F + P_1 + P_2 + P_3 + P_4 & \geq 16 & \text{(noon–1 P.M. needs)} \\
F \quad\quad + P_2 + P_3 + P_4 + P_5 & \geq 18 & \text{(1 P.M.–2 P.M. needs)} \\
F \quad\quad\quad\quad + P_3 + P_4 + P_5 & \geq 17 & \text{(2 P.M.–3 P.M. needs)} \\
F \quad\quad\quad\quad\quad\quad + P_4 + P_5 & \geq 15 & \text{(3 P.M.–4 P.M. needs)} \\
F \quad\quad\quad\quad\quad\quad\quad\quad + P_5 & \geq 10 & \text{(4 P.M.–5 P.M. needs)}
\end{array}
$$

Only 12 full-time tellers are available, so

$$F \leq 12$$

Part-time worker hours cannot exceed 50% of total hours required each day, which is the sum of the tellers needed each hour.

$$4(P_1 + P_2 + P_3 + P_4 + P_5) \leq 0.50(10 + 12 + 14 + 16 + 18 + 17 + 15 + 10)$$

or

$$4P_1 + 4P_2 + 4P_3 + 4P_4 + 4P_5 \leq 0.50(112)$$

$$F, P_1, P_2, P_3, P_4, P_5 \geq 0$$

Alternate optimal solutions are common in many LP problems. The sequence in which you enter the constraints into QM for Windows can affect the solution found.

There are several alternate optimal schedules that Hong Kong Bank can follow. The first is to employ only 10 full-time tellers ($F = 10$) and to start two part-timers at 10 A.M. ($P_2 = 2$), 7 part-timers at 11 A.M. ($P_3 = 7$), and 5 part-timers at noon ($P_4 = 5$). No part-timers would begin at 9 A.M. or 1 P.M.

The second solution also employs 10 full-time tellers, but starts 6 part-timers at 9 A.M. ($P_1 = 6$), 1 part-timer at 10 A.M. ($P_2 = 1$), 2 part-timers at 11 A.M. and 5 at noon ($P_3 = 2$ and $P_4 = 5$), and 0 part-timers at 1 P.M. ($P_5 = 0$). The cost of either of these two policies is $1448 per day.

8.5   FINANCIAL APPLICATIONS

Portfolio Selection

A problem frequently encountered by managers of banks, mutual funds, investment services, and insurance companies is the selection of specific investments from among a wide variety of alternatives. The manager's overall objective is usually to maximize expected return on investment, given a set of legal, policy, or risk restraints.

Maximizing return on investment subject to a set of risk constraints is a popular financial application of LP.

For example, the International City Trust (ICT) invests in short-term trade credits, corporate bonds, gold stocks, and construction loans. To encourage a diversified portfolio, the board of directors has placed limits on the amount that can be committed to any one type of investment. ICT has $5 million available for immediate investment and wishes to do two things: (1) maximize the interest earned on the investments made over the next six months, and (2) satisfy the diversification requirements as set by the board of directors.

The specifics of the investment possibilities are as follows:

INVESTMENT	INTEREST EARNED (%)	MAXIMUM INVESTMENT ($ MILLIONS)
Trade credit	7	1.0
Corporate bonds	11	2.5
Gold stocks	19	1.5
Construction loans	15	1.8

In addition, the board specifies that at least 55% of the funds invested must be in gold stocks and construction loans, and that no less than 15% be invested in trade credit.

To formulate ICT's investment decision as an LP problem, we let

$$X_1 = \text{dollars invested in trade credit}$$

$$X_2 = \text{dollars invested in corporate bonds}$$

$$X_3 = \text{dollars invested in gold stocks}$$

$$X_4 = \text{dollars invested in construction loans}$$

Objective:

$$\text{maximize dollars of interest earned} = 0.07X_1 + 0.11X_2 + 0.19X_3 + 0.15X_4$$

$$
\begin{aligned}
\text{subject to:} \quad & X_1 && \le 1{,}000{,}000 \\
& X_2 && \le 2{,}500{,}000 \\
& X_3 && \le 1{,}500{,}000 \\
& X_4 \le 1{,}800{,}000 \\
& X_3 + X_4 \ge 0.55(X_1 + X_2 + X_3 + X_4) \\
& X_1 && \ge 0.15(X_1 + X_2 + X_3 + X_4) \\
& X_1 + X_2 + X_3 + X_4 \le 5{,}000{,}000 \\
& X_1, X_2, X_3, X_4 \ge 0
\end{aligned}
$$

Few financial markets in recent years have experienced the rapid growth and innovations of the secondary mortgage market. This growth has been spurred by federal agencies whose mandate is to make home ownership easier and more affordable by increasing the flow of funds available. Prudential Securities has entered this $1 trillion market for mortgage-backed securities (MBSs) in a huge way, typically trading $5 billion of MBSs per week. These securities, which are mortgage loans pooled by government agencies, are traded in a somewhat complex market by a network of dealers like Prudential.

To reduce investment risk and to value securities properly and quickly for its investors, Prudential has developed and implemented a number of quantitative analysis models. Its LP

model, run hundreds of times per day by Prudential traders, salespeople, and clients, designs an optimal securities portfolio to meet investors' criteria under different interest rate environments. Constraints include the minimum and maximum percentages of a portfolio to invest in any security, the duration of the MBS, and the total amount to be invested. The model helps managers decide how much to invest in each available MBS in order to meet clients' goals.

Source: Yosi Ben-Dov, Lakhbir Hayre, and Vincent Pica. "Mortgage Valuation Models at Prudential Securities," *Interfaces*, 22, 1 (January–February 1992): 55–71.

ICT maximizes its interest earned by making the following investment: $X_1 = \$750,000$, $X_2 = \$950,000$, $X_3 = \$1,500,000$, and $X_4 = \$1,800,000$, and the total interest earned is $712,000.

8.6   TRANSPORTATION APPLICATIONS

Shipping Problem

The transportation or shipping problem involves determining the amount of goods or items to be transported from a number of origins to a number of destinations. The objective usually is to minimize total shipping costs or distances. Constraints in this type of problem deal with capacities at each origin and requirements at each destination. The transportation problem is a very specific case of LP, and in fact, a special algorithm has been developed to solve it. That solution procedure is one of the topics of Chapter 10.

Transporting goods from several origins to several destinations efficiently is called the "transportation problem." It can be solved with LP, as we see here, or with a special algorithm introduced in Chapter 10.

The Top Speed Bicycle Co. manufactures and markets a line of 10-speed bicycles nationwide. The firm has final assembly plants in two cities in which labor costs are low, New Orleans and Omaha. Its three major warehouses are located near the large market areas of New York, Chicago, and Los Angeles.

The sales requirements for the next year at the New York warehouse are 10,000 bicycles, at the Chicago warehouse 8,000 bicycles, and at the Los Angeles warehouse 15,000 bicycles. The factory capacity at each location is limited. New Orleans can assemble and ship 20,000 bicycles; the Omaha plant can produce 15,000 bicycles per year. The cost of shipping one bicycle from each factory to each warehouse differs, and these unit shipping costs are as follows:

FROM \ TO	NEW YORK	CHICAGO	LOS ANGELES
New Orleans	$2	$3	$5
Omaha	3	1	4

The company wishes to develop a shipping schedule that will minimize its total annual transportation costs.

Double-subscripted variables are again employed in this example.

To formulate this problem using LP, we again employ the concept of double-subscripted variables. We let the first subscript represent the origin (factory) and the second subscript the destination (warehouse). Thus, in general, X_{ij} refers to the number of bicycles shipped from origin i to destination j. We could instead denote X_6 as the variable for origin 2 to destination 3, but generally most find the double subscripts more descriptive and easier to use. So let

$$X_{11} = \text{number of bicycles shipped from New Orleans to New York}$$

$$X_{12} = \text{number of bicycles shipped form New Orleans to Chicago}$$

$$X_{13} = \text{number of bicycles shipped from New Orleans to Los Angeles}$$

$$X_{21} = \text{number of bicycles shipped from Omaha to New York}$$

$$X_{22} = \text{number of bicycles shipped from Omaha to Chicago}$$

$$X_{23} = \text{number of bicycles shipped from Omaha to Los Angeles}$$

This problem can be formulated as follows:

In a transportation problem, there will be one constraint for each demand source and one constraint for each supply destination.

$$\text{Minimize total shipping costs} = 2X_{11} + 3X_{12} + 5X_{13} + 3X_{21} + 1X_{22} + 4X_{23}$$

subject to:

$$X_{11} + X_{21} = 10,000 \quad \text{(New York demand)}$$
$$X_{12} + X_{22} = 8,000 \quad \text{(Chicago demand)}$$
$$X_{13} + X_{23} = 15,000 \quad \text{(Los Angeles demand)}$$
$$X_{11} + X_{12} + X_{13} \le 20,000 \quad \text{(New Orleans factory supply)}$$
$$X_{21} + X_{22} + X_{23} \le 15,000 \quad \text{(Omaha factory supply)}$$
$$\text{All variables} \ge 0$$

Why are transportation problems a special class of LP problems? The answer is that every coefficient in front of a variable in the constraint equations is always equal to 1. This special trait is also seen in another special category of LP problems, the assignment problem discussed earlier. (The assignment problem can be viewed as a special case of the transportation problem in which the supply at each source and the demand at each destination is one.)

Using Excel and its Solver command, the computer-generated solution to Top Speed's problem is shown in the table that follows and in Programs 8.5A and 8.5B on page 310. The total shipping cost is $96,000.

FROM \ TO	NEW YORK	CHICAGO	LOS ANGELES
New Orleans	10,000	0	8,000
Omaha	0	8,000	7,000

Truck Loading Problem

The truck loading problem involves deciding which items to load on a truck so as to maximize the value of a load shipped. As an example, we consider Goodman Shipping, an

PROGRAM 8.5A   **Excel Solver Formulation of the Top Speed Bicycle LP Problem**

Enter the origin and destination names, the shipping costs, and the total supply and demand figures.

Our target cell is the total cost cell (B21), which we wish to minimize by changing the shipment cells (B17 through D18).

These guarantee that we meet the demand exactly (3 constraints).

These guarantee that we do not exceed the supply (2 constraints).

Solver will place the shipments in these cells.

Solver Parameters
Set Target Cell: $B$21
Equal To: ○ Max ● Min ○ Value of:
By Changing Cells:
$B$17:$D$18
Subject to the Constraints:
$B$12:$D$12 = $B$19:$D$19
$E$17:$E$18 <= $E$10:$E$11

The total shipments to and from each location are calculated here.

	A	B	C	D	E
1	**Top Spee**				
2					
3	**Transportatic**				
4	Enter the transportation costs, supplies and demands in				
5	SOLVER, SOLVE on the menu bar at the top.				
6	If SOLVER is not a menu option in the Tools menu then g				
7					
8	Data				
9	COSTS	New York	Chicago	Los Angele	Supply
10	New Orleans	2	3	5	200
11	Omaha	3	1	4	15000
12	Demand	10000	8000	15000	=CONCATENATE(SUM(B12:D12)," \ ",SUM(B
13					
14					
15	**Shipments**				
16	Shipments	=B9	=C9	=D9	Row Total
17	=A10	1	1	1	=SUM(B17:D17)
18	=A11	1	1	1	=SUM(B18:D18)
19	Column Total	=SUM(B17:B18)	=SUM(C17	=SUM(D17	=CONCATENATE(INT(SUM(B19:D19)+0.5)," \ ",INT(SUM(E
20					
21	Total Cost	**=SUMPRODUCT(B10:D11,B17:D18)**			
22					
23					
24					

Answer
Ready
NUM

The total cost is computed here by multiplying the unit shipping costs in the data table by the shipments in the shipment table using the SUMPRODUCT function. We are multiplying corresponding elements in tables this time rather than just rows or columns.

PROGRAM 8.5B

Solution to Top Speed's LP Problem Output from Excel Formulation in Program 8.5A

Microsoft Excel - captures.xls
File Edit View Insert Format Tools Data Accounting OM Window Help

	A	B	C	D	E	F	G	H
1	**Top Speed Bicycle Company**							
2								
3	**Transportation**							
4	Enter the transportation costs, supplies and demands in the shaded area. Then go to							
5	TOOLS, SOLVER, SOLVE on the menu bar at the top.							
6	If SOLVER is not a menu option in the Tools menu then go to TOOLS, ADD-INS.							
7								
8	Data							
9	COSTS	New York	Chicago	Los Angele	Supply			
10	New Orleans	2	3	5	20000			
11	Omaha	3	1	4	15000			
12	Demand	10000	8000	15000	33000 \ 35000			
13								
14								
15	**Shipments**							
16	Shipments	New York	Chicago	Los Angele	Row Total			
17	New Orleans	**10000**	0	8000	18000			
18	Omaha	0	8000	7000	15000			
19	Column Total	10000	8000	15000	33000 \ 33000			
20								
21	Total Cost	**96000**						

Orlando firm owned by Steven Goodman. One of his trucks, with a capacity of 10,000 pounds, is about to be loaded.[1] Awaiting shipment are the following items:

ITEM	VALUE ($)	WEIGHT (POUNDS)
1	22,500	7,500
2	24,000	7,500
3	8,000	3,000
4	9,500	3,500
5	11,500	4,000
6	9,750	3,500

Each of these six items, we see, has an associated dollar value and weight.

The objective is to maximize the total value of the items loaded onto the truck without exceeding the truck's weight capacity. We let X_i be the proportion of each item i loaded on the truck:

$$\text{Maximize load value} = \$22{,}500X_1 + \$24{,}000X_2 + \$8{,}000X_3 + \$9{,}500X_4$$
$$+ \$11{,}500X_5 + \$9{,}750X_6$$

$$\text{subject to:} \quad 7{,}500X_1 + 7{,}500X_2 + 3{,}000X_3 + 3{,}500X_4 + 4{,}000X_5$$
$$+ 3{,}500X_6 \leq 10{,}000 \text{ lb capacity}$$
$$X_1 \leq 1$$
$$X_2 \leq 1$$
$$X_3 \leq 1$$
$$X_4 \leq 1$$
$$X_5 \leq 1$$
$$X_6 \leq 1$$
$$X_1, X_2, X_3, X_4, X_5, X_6 \geq 0$$

These final six constraints reflect the fact that at most one "unit" of an item can be loaded onto the truck. In effect, if Goodman can load a *portion* of an item (say, item 1 is a batch of 1,000 folding chairs, not all of which need be shipped together), the X_is will all be proportions ranging from 0 (nothing) to 1 (all of that item loaded).

To solve this LP problem, we turn to Excel's Solver. Program 8.6A shows Goodman's Excel formulation and input data and Program 8.6B shows the solution, which yields a total load value of $31,500.

The answer leads us to an interesting issue that we deal with in detail in Chapter 11. What does Goodman do if fractional values of items cannot be loaded? For example, if luxury cars were the items being loaded, we clearly cannot ship one-third of a Maserati.

If the proportion of item 1 was rounded up to 1.00, the weight of the load would increase to 15,000 pounds. This would violate the 10,000 pounds maximum weight constraint. Therefore, the fraction of item 1 must be rounded down to zero. This would drop the value of the load to 7,500 pounds, leaving 2,500 pounds of the load capacity unused. Because no other item weighs less than 2,500 pounds, the truck cannot be filled up further.

---

[1] Adapted from an example in S. L. Savage. *What's Best!* Oakland, CA: General Optimization, Inc., and Holden-Day, 1985.

PROGRAM 8.6A   **Using an Excel Spreadsheet and Solver to Structure Goodman's LP Problem**

Thus we see that by using regular LP and rounding the fractional weights, the truck would carry only item 2, for a load weight of 7,500 pounds and a load value of $24,000.

QM for Windows and spreadsheet optimizers such as Excel's Solver are capable of dealing with *integer programming* problems as well; that is, LP problems requiring integer solutions. Using Excel, the integer solution to Goodman's problem is to load items 3, 4, and 6, for a total weight of 10,000 pounds and load value of $27,250.

PROGRAM 8.6B

Excel Solution to Goodman's Problem, Using Data Input from Program 8.6A

Item	Percent Loaded	Max Percent Loaded	Value ($)	Weight (lbs)
1	0.333333	1	22500	7500
2	1	1	24000	7500
3	0	1	8000	3000
4	0	1	9500	3500
5	0	1	11500	4000
6	0	1	9750	3500
	Total		$ 31,500	10000
			Weight Capacity	10000

8.7 TRANSSHIPMENT APPLICATIONS

When goods are shipped to an intermediate point, a transportation problem becomes a transshipment problem.

The transportation problem is actually a special case of the transshipment problem. If items are being transported from the source through an intermediate point (called a *transshipment point*) before reaching a final destination, then the problem is called a *transshipment problem*. For example, a company might be manufacturing a product at several factories to be shipped to a set of regional distribution centers. From these centers the items are shipped to retail outlets that are the final destinations. An example follows.

Distribution Centers

Frosty Machines manufactures snowblowers in factories located in Toronto and Detroit. These are shipped to regional distribution centers in Chicago and Buffalo, where they are delivered to the supply houses in New York, Philadelphia, and St. Louis. Figure 8.1 illustrates the basic network representation of this situation. The shipping costs vary, as shown in the following table. Forecasted demands for New York, Philadelphia, and St. Louis are also seen in this table, as are the available supplies of snowblowers at the two factories. Notice that snowblowers may not be shipped directly from Toronto or Detroit to any of the final destinations. This is why Chicago and Buffalo are listed not only as destinations but also as sources.

			TO			
FROM	CHICAGO	BUFFALO	NEW YORK CITY	PHILADELPHIA	ST. LOUIS	SUPPLY
Toronto	$4	$7	—	—	—	800
Detroit	$5	$7	—	—	—	700
Chicago	—	—	$6	$4	$5	—
Buffalo	—	—	$2	$3	$4	—
Demand	—	—	450	350	300	

Frosty would like to minimize the transportation costs associated with shipping sufficient snowblowers to meet the demands at the three destinations while not exceeding the supply of each factory. Thus, we have supply and demand constraints similar to the transportation problem. Since there are no units being produced in Chicago or Buffalo, anything shipped

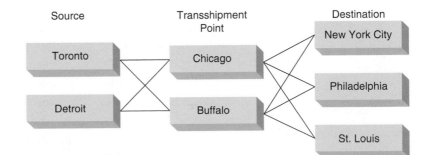

from these transshipment points must have arrived from either Toronto or Detroit. Therefore, Chicago and Buffalo will each have a constraint indicating this. The verbal statement of this problem would be as follows:

Minimize cost
subject to:

1. the number of units shipped from Toronto is not more than 800
2. the number of units shipped from Detroit is not more than 700
3. the number of units shipped to New York is 450
4. the number of units shipped to Philadelphia is 350
5. the number of units shipped to St. Louis is 300
6. the number of units shipped out of Chicago is equal to the number of units shipped into Chicago
7. the number of units shipped out of Buffalo is equal to the number of units shipped into Buffalo

The decision variables should represent the number of units shipped from each source to each transshipment point and the number of units shipped from each transshipment point to each final destination, as these are the decisions management must make. The decision variables are

$$T_1 = \text{the number of units shipped from Toronto to Chicago}$$

$$T_2 = \text{the number of units shipped from Toronto to Buffalo}$$

$$D_1 = \text{the number of units shipped from Detroit to Chicago}$$

$$D_2 = \text{the number of units shipped from Detroit to Buffalo}$$

$$C_1 = \text{the number of units shipped from Chicago to New York}$$

$$C_2 = \text{the number of units shipped from Chicago to Philadelphia}$$

$$C_3 = \text{the number of units shipped from Chicago to St. Louis}$$

$$B_1 = \text{the number of units shipped from Buffalo to New York}$$

$$B_2 = \text{the number of units shipped from Buffalo to Philadelphia}$$

$$B_3 = \text{the number of units shipped from Buffalo to St. Louis}$$

The linear program is
Minimize cost =

$$4T_1 + 7T_2 + 5D_1 + 7D_2 + 6C_1 + 4C_2 + 5C_3 + 2B_1 + 3B_2 + 4B_3$$

subject to:

$$
\begin{array}{lll}
T_1 + T_2 \le 800 & & \text{supply at Toronto} \\
D_1 + D_2 \le 700 & & \text{supply at Detroit} \\
C_1 + B_1 = 450 & & \text{demand at New York} \\
C_2 + B_2 = 350 & & \text{demand at Philadelphia} \\
C_3 + B_3 = 300 & & \text{demand at St. Louis} \\
T_1 + D_1 = C_1 + C_2 + C_3 & & \text{shipping through Chicago} \\
T_2 + D_2 = B_1 + B_2 + B_3 & & \text{shipping through Buffalo} \\
T_1, T_2, D_1, D_2, C_1, C_2, C_3, B_1, B_2, B_3 \ge 0 & & \text{nonnegativity constraints}
\end{array}
$$

To solve this on the computer, we must move all the decision variables in the last two constraints to the left-hand sides of the equations. Thus,

$$T_1 + D_1 = C_1 + C_2 + C_3$$

becomes

$$T_1 + D_1 - C_1 - C_2 - C_3 = 0$$

and

$$T_2 + D_2 = B_1 + B_2 + B_3$$

becomes

$$T_2 + D_2 - B_1 - B_2 - B_3 = 0$$

Solving this with QM for Windows yields the output in Program 8.7. From this we see that we should ship 650 units from Toronto to Chicago, 150 units from Toronto to Buffalo, and 300 units from Detroit to Buffalo. A total of 350 units will be shipped from Chicago to Philadelphia, 300 from Chicago to St. Louis, and 450 from Buffalo to New York. The total cost will be $9,550.

PROGRAM 8.7

Solving Frosty Machines Transshipment Problem Using QM for Windows

QM for Windows - C:\My Documents\Mike\R&S\Weiss\Render.Stair.7\QM for Windows files\FROSTY2.lin

Linear Programming Results

Frosty Machines Transshipment Problem Solution												
	T1	T2	D1	D2	C1	C2	C3	B1	B2	B3	RHS	Dual
Minimize	4.	7.	5.	7.	6.	4.	5.	2.	3.	4.		
Toronto supply	1.	1.	0.	0.	0.	0.	0.	0.	0.	0.	<= 800.	0.
Detroit supply	0.	0.	1.	1.	0.	0.	0.	0.	0.	0.	<= 700.	0.
NY demand	0.	0.	0.	0.	1.	0.	0.	1.	0.	0.	= 450.	-9.
Philadelphia demand	0.	0.	0.	0.	0.	1.	0.	0.	1.	0.	= 350.	-8.
St. Louis demand	0.	0.	0.	0.	0.	0.	1.	0.	0.	1.	= 300.	-9.
Chicago	1.	0.	1.	0.	-1.	-1.	-1.	0.	0.	0.	= 0.	-4.
Buffalo	0.	1.	0.	1.	0.	0.	0.	-1.	-1.	-1.	= 0.	-7.
Solution->	650.	150.	0.	300.	0.	350.	300.	450.	0.	0.	9,550.	

8.8 INGREDIENT BLENDING APPLICATIONS

Diet Problems

The diet problem, one of the earliest applications of LP, was originally used by hospitals to determine the most economical diet for patients. Known in agricultural applications as the feed mix problem, the diet problem involves specifying a food or feed ingredient combination that satisfies stated nutritional requirements at a minimum cost level.

The Whole Food Nutrition Center uses three bulk grains to blend a natural cereal that it sells by the pound. The store advertises that each 2-ounce serving of the cereal, when taken with $\frac{1}{2}$ cup of whole milk, meets an average adult's minimum daily requirement for protein, riboflavin, phosphorus, and magnesium. The cost of each bulk grain and the protein, riboflavin, phosphorus, and magnesium units per pound of each are shown in Table 8.5.

TABLE 8.5		Whole Food's Natural Cereal Requirements			
GRAIN	COST PER POUND (CENTS)	PROTEIN (UNITS/LB)	RIBOFLAVIN (UNITS/LB)	PHOSPHORUS (UNITS/LB)	MAGNESIUM (UNITS/LB)
A	33	22	16	8	5
B	47	28	14	7	0
C	38	21	25	9	6

The minimum adult daily requirement (called the U.S. Recommended Daily Allowance, or USRDA) for protein is 3 units; for riboflavin, 2 units; for phosphorus, 1 unit; and for magnesium, 0.425 unit. Whole Food wants to select the blend of grains that will meet the USRDA at a minimum cost.

We let

$$X_A = \text{pounds of grain A in one 2-ounce serving of cereal}$$

$$X_B = \text{pounds of grain B in one 2-ounce serving of cereal}$$

$$X_C = \text{pounds of grain C in one 2-ounce serving of cereal}$$

Objective function:

$$\text{minimize total cost of mixing a 2-ounce serving} = \$0.33X_A + \$0.47X_B + \$0.38X_C$$

subject to:

$$22X_A + 28X_B + 21X_C \geq 3 \qquad \text{(protein units)}$$
$$16X_A + 14X_B + 25X_C \geq 2 \qquad \text{(riboflavin units)}$$
$$8X_A + 7X_B + 9X_C \geq 1 \qquad \text{(phosphorus units)}$$
$$5X_A + 0X_B + 6X_C \geq 0.425 \qquad \text{(magnesium units)}$$
$$X_A + X_B + X_C = 0.125 \qquad \text{(total mix is 2 ounces or 0.125 pound)}$$
$$X_A, X_B, X_C \geq 0$$

The solution to this problem requires mixing together 0.025 lb of grain A, 0.050 lb of grain B, and 0.050 lb of grain C. Another way of stating the solution is in terms of the proportion of the 2-ounce serving of each grain, namely, 0.4 ounce of grain A, 0.8 ounce of grain B, and 0.8 ounce of grain C in each serving. The cost per serving is $0.05. Program 8.8 illustrates this solution using the QM for Windows software package.

Ingredient Mix and Blending Problems

Diet and feed mix problems are actually special cases of a more general class of LP problems known as *ingredient* or *blending problems*. Blending problems arise when a decision must be made regarding the blending of two or more resources to produce one or more products. Resources, in this case, contain one or more essential ingredients that must be blended so that each final product contains specific percentages of each ingredient. The following example deals with an application frequently seen in the petroleum industry, the blending of crude oils to produce refinable gasoline.

PROGRAM 8.8

Solving Whole Food's LP Problem with QM for Windows

QM for Windows – C:\Prentice\Data\RenderStair7\Whole417.lin

Objective
○ Maximize
● Minimize

Linear Programming Results

Whole Food Nutrition Center Solution

	X1	X2	X3		RHS	Dual
Minimize	0.33	0.47	0.38			
Constraint 1	22.	28.	21.	>=	3.	-0.038
Constraint 2	16.	14.	25.	>=	2.	0.
Constraint 3	8.	7.	9.	>=	1.	-0.088
Constraint 4	5.	0.	6.	>=	0.425	0.
Constraint 5	1.	1.	1.	=	0.125	1.21
Solution->	0.025	0.05	0.05		0.05	

Major oil refineries all use LP for blending crude oils to produce gasoline grades.

The Low Knock Oil Company produces two grades of cut-rate gasoline for industrial distribution. The grades, regular and economy, are produced by refining a blend of two types of crude oil, type X100 and type X220. Each crude oil differs not only in cost per barrel, but in composition as well. The following table indicates the percentage of crucial ingredients found in each of the crude oils and the cost per barrel for each:

CRUDE OIL TYPE	INGREDIENT A (%)	INGREDIENT B (%)	COST/BARREL ($)
X100	35	55	30.00
X220	60	25	34.80

Weekly demand for the regular grade of Low Knock gasoline is at least 25,000 barrels, and demand for the economy is at least 32,000 barrels per week. *At least* 45% of each barrel of regular must be ingredient A. *At most* 50% of each barrel of economy should contain ingredient B.

The Low Knock management must decide how many barrels of each type of crude oil to buy each week for blending to satisfy demand at minimum cost. To solve this as an LP problem, the firm lets

X_1 = barrels of crude X100 blended to produce the refined regular

X_2 = barrels of crude X100 blended to produce the refined economy

X_3 = barrels of crude X220 blended to produce the refined regular

X_4 = barrels of crude X220 blended to produce the refined economy

This problem can be formulated as follows:

Objective:

$$\text{minimize cost} = \$30X_1 + \$30X_2 + \$34.80X_3 + \$34.80X_4$$

subject to:

$$X_1 + X_3 \geq 25{,}000 \quad \text{(demand for regular)}$$
$$X_2 + X_4 \geq 32{,}000 \quad \text{(demand for economy)}$$

At least 45% of each barrel of regular must be ingredient A.

$$(X_1 + X_3) = \text{total amount of crude blended to produce the refined regular}$$
$$\text{gasoline demand}$$

Thus,

$$0.45(X_1 + X_3) = \text{minimum amount of ingredient A required}$$

But

$$0.35X_1 + 0.60X_3 = \text{amount of ingredient A in refined regular gas}$$

So

$$0.35X_1 + 0.60X_3 \geq 0.45X_1 + 0.45X_3$$

or

$$-0.10X_1 + 0.15X_3 \geq 0 \qquad \text{(ingredient A in regular constraint)}$$

Similarly, at most 50% of each barrel of economy should be ingredient B.

$$X_2 + X_4 = \text{total amount of crude blended to produce the refined economy}$$
$$\text{gasoline demanded}$$

Thus,

$$0.50(X_2 + X_4) = \text{maximum amount of ingredient B allowed}$$

But

$$0.55X_2 + 0.25X_4 = \text{amount of ingredient B in refined economy gas}$$

So

$$0.55X_2 + 0.25X_4 \leq 0.50X_2 + 0.50X_4$$

or

$$0.05X_2 - 0.25X_4 \leq 0 \text{ (ingredient B in economy constraint)}$$

Here is the entire LP formulation:

$$\text{minimize cost} = 30X_1 + 30X_2 + 34.80X_3 + 34.80X_4$$
$$\text{subject to:} \quad X_1 \qquad + \quad X_3 \qquad\qquad \geq 25,000$$
$$X_2 + \qquad\qquad X_4 \geq 32,000$$
$$-0.10X_1 \qquad + \ 0.15X_3 \qquad\qquad \geq 0$$
$$0.05X_2 \qquad\qquad - \quad 0.25X_4 \leq 0$$
$$X_1, X_2, X_3, X_4 \geq 0$$

Using QM for Windows, the solution to Low Knock Oil's formulation was found to be

$$X_1 = 15,000 \text{ barrels of X100 into regular}$$
$$X_2 = 26,666.67 \text{ barrels of X100 into economy}$$
$$X_3 = 10,000 \text{ barrels of X220 into regular}$$
$$X_4 = 5,333.33 \text{ barrels of X220 into economy}$$

The cost of this mix is $1,783,600. Refer to Program 8.9 for details.

PROGRAM 8.9

Using QM for Windows to Solve Low Knock Oil's LP Problem

QM for Windows

File Edit View Module Format Tools Window Help

Objective
○ Maximize
● Minimize

Instruction
There are more results available in additional windows. These may be opened by using the WINDOW option in the Main Menu.

Linear Programming Results

Low Knock Oil Company Solution

	X1	X2	X3	X4		RHS	Dual
Minimize	30.	30.	34.8	34.8			
Constraint 1	1.	0.	1.	0.	>=	25,000.	-31.92
Constraint 2	0.	1.	0.	1.	>=	32,000.	-30.8
Constraint 3	-0.1	0.	0.15	0.	>=	0.	-19.2
Constraint 4	0.	0.05	0.	-0.25	<=	0.	16.
Solution->	15,000.	26,666.67	10,000.	5,333.333		1,783,599.99	

SUMMARY

In this chapter, we continued our discussion of LP models. To gain more experience in formulating problems from a variety of disciplines, we examined applications from marketing, production, scheduling, finance, transportation, transshipment, and ingredient blending. We also solved most of these problems with two computer programs for LP: QM for Windows and Excel's Solver.

⟡➡ SELF-TEST

■ Before taking the self-test, refer back to the learning objectives at the beginning of the chapter, the notes in the margins, and the glossary at the end of the chapter.

■ Use the key at the back of the book to correct your answers.

■ Restudy pages that correspond to any questions that you answered incorrectly or material you feel uncertain about.

1. Linear programming can be used to select effective media mixes, allocate fixed or limited budgets across media, and maximize audience exposure.
   a. True　　　　　b. False

2. Blending problems arise when one must decide which of two or more ingredients is to be chosen to produce a product.
   a. True　　　　　b. False

3. Using LP to maximize audience exposure in an advertising campaign is an example of the type of LP application known as
   a. marketing research.
   b. media selection.
   c. portfolio assessment.
   d. media budgeting.
   e. all of the above.

4. The following *does not* represent a factor a manager might consider when employing LP for a production scheduling:
   a. labor capacity
   b. space limitations
   c. product demand
   d. risk assessment
   e. inventory costs

5. A typical transportation problem has 4 sources and 3 destinations. How many decision variables would there be in the linear program for this?
   a. 3　　　　　b. 4
   c. 7　　　　　d. 12

6. A typical transportation problem has 4 sources and 3 destinations. How many constraints would there be in the linear program for this?
   a. 3　　　　　b. 4
   c. 7　　　　　d. 12

7. When applying LP to diet problems, the objective function is usually designed to
   a. maximize profits from blends of nutrients.
   b. maximize ingredient blends.

   c. minimize production losses.
   d. maximize the number of products to be produced.
   e. minimize the costs of nutrient blends.

8. The diet problem is
   a. also called the feed mix problem in agriculture.
   b. a special case of the ingredient mix problem.
   c. a special case of the blending problem.
   d. all of the above.

9. The following problem type is such a special case of LP that a special algorithm has been developed to solve it:
   a. the transportation problem
   b. the diet problem
   c. the ingredient mix problem
   d. the production mix problem
   e. none of the above

10. Which of the following would have a 1 as the right-hand-side value of each constraint?
    a. a transportation problem
    b. an assignment problem
    c. a portfolio selection problem
    d. a diet problem

11. The selection of specific investments from among a wide variety of alternatives is the type of LP problem known as
    a. the product mix problem.
    b. the investment banker problem.
    c. the portfolio selection problem.
    d. the Wall Street problem.
    e. none of the above.

12. A transshipment problem has 2 sources, 3 transshipment points, and 5 final destinations. How many constraints would this linear program have?
    a. 7　　　　　b. 10
    c. 21　　　　　d. 30

PROBLEMS*

⚕⚡• 8-1　(Production problem) Winkler Furniture manufactures two different types of china cabinets: a French Provincial model and a Danish Modern model. Each

cabinet produced must go through three departments: carpentry, painting, and finishing. The table on page 321 contains all relevant information concerning pro-

---

* Note: ⚕ means the problem may be solved with QM for Windows: ⚡ means the problem may be solved with Excel; and ⚕⚡ means the problem may be solved with QM for Windows and/or Excel.

Data for Problem 8-1

CABINET STYLE	CARPENTRY (HOURS/ CABINET)	PAINTING (HOURS/ CABINET)	FINISHING (HOURS/ CABINET)	NET REVENUE/ CABINET ($)
French Provincial	3	$1\frac{1}{2}$	$\frac{3}{4}$	28
Danish Modern	2	1	$\frac{3}{4}$	25
Department capacity (hours)	360	200	125	

duction times per cabinet produced and production capacities for each operation per day, along with net revenue per unit produced. The firm has a contract with an Indiana distributor to produce a minimum of 300 of each cabinet per week (or 60 cabinets per day). Owner Bob Winkler would like to determine a product mix to maximize his daily revenue.

(a) Formulate as an LP problem.
(b) Solve using an LP software program or spreadsheet.

8-2 *(Investment decision problem)* The Heinlein and Krampf Brokerage firm has just been instructed by one of its clients to invest $250,000 for her money obtained recently through the sale of land holdings in Ohio. The client has a good deal of trust in the investment house, but she also has her own ideas about the distribution of the funds being invested. In particular, she requests that the firm select whatever stocks and bonds they believe are well rated, but within the following guidelines:

(a) Municipal bonds should constitute at least 20% of the investment.
(b) At least 40% of the funds should be placed in a combination of electronic firms, aerospace firms, and drug manufacturers.
(c) No more than 50% of the amount invested in municipal bonds should be placed in a high-risk, high-yield nursing home stock.

Subject to these restraints, the client's goal is to maximize projected return on investments. The analysts at Heinlein and Krampf, aware of these guidelines, prepare a list of high-quality stocks and bonds and their corresponding rates of return.

INVESTMENT	PROJECTED RATE OF RETURN (%)
Los Angeles municipal bonds	5.3
Thompson Electronics, Inc.	6.8
United Aerospace Corp.	4.9
Palmer Drugs	8.4
Happy Days Nursing Homes	11.8

(a) Formulate this portfolio selection problem using LP.
(b) Solve this problem.

8-3 *(Restaurant work scheduling problem).* The famous Y. S. Chang Restaurant is open 24 hours a day. Waiters and busboys report for duty at 3 A.M., 7 A.M., 11 A.M., 3 P.M., 7 P.M., or 11 P.M., and each works an 8-hour shift. The following table shows the minimum number of workers needed during the six periods into which the day is divided. Chang's scheduling problem is to determine how many waiters and busboys should report for work at the start of each time period to minimize the total staff required for one day's operation. (*Hint:* Let X_i equal the number of waiters and busboys beginning work in time period i, where $i = 1, 2, 3, 4, 5, 6$.)

PERIOD	TIME	NUMBER OF WAITERS AND BUSBOYS REQUIRED
1	3 A.M.–7 A.M.	3
2	7 A.M.–11 A.M.	12
3	11 A.M.–3 P.M.	16
4	3 P.M.–7 P.M.	9
5	7 P.M.–11 P.M.	11
6	11 P.M.–3 A.M.	4

8-4 *(Animal feed mix problem)* The Battery Park Stable feeds and houses the horses used to pull tourist-filled carriages through the streets of Charleston's historic waterfront area. The stable owner, an ex-racehorse trainer, recognizes the need to set a nutritional diet for the horses in his care. At the same time, he would like to keep the overall daily cost of feed to a minimum.

The feed mixes available for the horses' diet are an oat product, a highly enriched grain, and a mineral product. Each of these mixes contains a certain amount of five ingredients needed daily to keep the average horse healthy. The table on page 322 shows these minimum requirements, units of each ingredient per pound of feed mix, and costs for the three mixes.

In addition, the stable owner is aware that an overfed horse is a sluggish worker. Consequently, he determines that 6 pounds of feed per day are the most that any horse needs to function properly. Formulate this problem and solve for the optimal daily mix of the three feeds.

Data for Problem 8-4

Diet Requirement (Ingredients)	Oat Product (Units/LB)	Enriched Grain (Units/LB)	Mineral Product (Units/LB)	Minimum Daily Requirement (Units)
		FEED MIX		
A	2	3	1	6
B	$\frac{1}{2}$	1	$\frac{1}{2}$	2
C	3	5	6	9
D	1	$1\frac{1}{2}$	2	8
E	$\frac{1}{2}$	$\frac{1}{2}$	$1\frac{1}{2}$	5
Cost/lb	$0.09	$0.14	$0.17	

8-5   (*Ballplayer selection problem*) The Dubuque Sackers, a class D baseball team, face a tough four-game road trip against league rivals in Des Moines, Davenport, Omaha, and Peoria. Manager "Red" Revelle faces the task of scheduling his four starting pitchers for appropriate games. Because the games are to be played back to back in less than one week, Revelle cannot count on any pitcher to start in more than one game.

Revelle knows the strengths and weaknesses not only of his pitchers, but also of his opponents. He has developed a performance rating for each of his starting pitchers against each of these teams. The ratings are listed in the table on this page. What pitching rotation should manager Revelle set to provide the highest total of the performance ratings?

(a) Formulate this problem using LP.
(b) Solve the problem.

8-6   (*Media selection problem*) The advertising director for Diversey Paint and Supply, a chain of four retail stores on Chicago's North Side, is considering two media possibilities. One plan is for a series of half-page ads in the Sunday *Chicago Tribune* newspaper, and the other is for advertising time on Chicago TV. The stores are expanding their lines of do-it-yourself tools, and the advertising director is interested in an exposure level of at least 40% within the city's neighborhoods and 60% in northwest suburban areas.

The TV viewing time under consideration has an exposure rating per spot of 5% in city homes and 3% in the northwest suburbs. The Sunday newspaper has corresponding exposure rates of 4% and 3% per ad. The cost of a half-page *Tribune* advertisement is $925; a television spot costs $2,000.

Diversey Paint would like to select the least costly advertising strategy that would meet desired exposure levels.

(a) Formulate using LP.
(b) Solve the problem.

8-7   (*Automobile leasing problem*) Sundown Rent-a-Car, a large automobile rental agency operating in the Midwest, is preparing a leasing strategy for the next six months. Sundown leases cars from an automobile manufacturer and then rents them to the public on a daily basis. A forecast of the demand for Sundown's cars in the next six months follows:

Month	March	April	May	June	July	August
Demand	420	400	430	460	470	440

Cars may be leased from the manufacturer for either three, four, or five months. These are leased on the first day of the month and are returned on the last day of the month. Every six months the automobile manufacturer is notified by Sundown about the number of cars needed during the next six months. The automobile manufacturer has stipulated that at least 50% of the cars leased during a six-month period must be on the five-month lease. The cost per month on each of the three types of leases are $420 for the three-month lease, $400 for the four-month lease, and $370 for the five-month lease.

Currently, Sundown has 390 cars. The lease on 120 cars expires at the end of March. The lease on another 140 cars expires at the end of April, and the lease on the rest of these expires at the end of May.

Data for Problem 8-5

Starting Pitcher	Des Moines	Davenport	Omaha	Peoria
		OPPONENT		
"Dead-Arm" Jones	0.60	0.80	0.50	0.40
"Spitball" Baker	0.70	0.40	0.80	0.30
"Ace" Parker	0.90	0.80	0.70	0.80
"Gutter" Wilson	0.50	0.30	0.40	0.20

Use LP to determine how many cars should be leased in each month on each type of lease to minimize the cost of leasing over the six-month period. How many cars are left at the end of August?

8-8 Management of Sundown Rent-a-Car (see Problem 8-7) has decided that perhaps the cost during the six-month period is not the appropriate cost to minimize because the agency may still be obligated to additional months on some leases after that time. For example, if Sundown had some cars delivered at the beginning of the sixth month, Sundown would still be obligated for two additional months on a three-month lease. Use LP to determine how many cars should be leased in each month on each type of lease to minimize the cost of leasing over the entire life of these leases.

8-9 *(High school busing problem)* The Arden County, Maryland, superintendent of education is responsible for assigning students to the *three* high schools in his county. He recognizes the need to bus a certain number of students, for several sectors of the county are beyond walking distance to a school. The superintendent partitions the county into *five* geographic sectors as he attempts to establish a plan that will minimize the total number of student miles traveled by bus. He also recognizes that if a student happens to live in a certain sector and is assigned to the high school in that sector, there is no need to bus that student because he or she can walk to school. The three schools are located in sectors B, C, and E.

The accompanying table reflects the number of high-school-age students living in each sector and the distance in miles from each sector to each school.

	DISTANCE TO SCHOOL			
SECTOR	SCHOOL IN SECTOR B	SCHOOL IN SECTOR C	SCHOOL IN SECTOR E	NUMBER OF STUDENTS
A	5	8	6	700
B	0	4	12	500
C	4	0	7	100
D	7	2	5	800
E	12	7	0	400
				2,500

Each high school has a capacity of 900 students. Set up the objective function and constraints of this problem using LP so that the total number of student miles traveled by bus is minimized. (Note the resemblance to the transportation problem illustrated earlier in this chapter.) Then solve the problem.

8-10 *(Pricing and marketing strategy problem)* The I. Kruger Paint and Wallpaper Store is a large retail distributor of the Supertrex brand of vinyl wallcoverings. Kruger will enhance its citywide image in Miami if it can outsell other local stores in total number of rolls of Supertrex next year. It is able to estimate the demand function as follows:

Number of rolls of Supertrex sold = 20 × dollars spent on advertising + 6.8 × dollars spent on in-store displays + 12 × dollars invested in on-hand wallpaper inventory – 65,000 × percentage markup taken above wholesale cost of a roll

The store budgets a total of $17,000 for advertising, in-store displays, and on-hand inventory of Supertrex for next year. It decides it must spend at least $3,000 on advertising; in addition, at least 5% of the amount invested in on-hand inventory should be devoted to displays. Markups on Supertrex seen at other local stores range from 20% to 45%. Kruger decides that its markup had best be in this range as well.

(a) Formulate as an LP problem.
(b) Solve the problem.
(c) What is the difficulty with the answer?
(d) What constraint would you add?

8-11 *(College meal selection problem)* Kathy Roniger, campus dietician for a small Idaho college, is responsible for formulating a nutritious meal plan for students. For an evening meal, she feels that the following five meal-content requirements should be met: (1) between 900 and 1,500 calories; (2) at least 4 milligrams of iron; (3) no more than 50 grams of fat; (4) at least 26 grams of protein; and (5) no more than 50 grams of carbohydrates. On a particular day, Roniger's food stock includes seven items that can be prepared and served for supper to meet these requirements. The cost per pound for each food item and the contribution to each of the five nutritional requirements are given in the accompanying table:

Data for Problem 8-11

	TABLE OF FOOD VALUES* AND COSTS					
FOOD ITEM	CALORIES/ POUND	IRON (MG/LB)	FAT (GM/LB)	PROTEIN (GM/LB)	CARBOHYDRATES (GM/LB)	COST/ POUND ($)
Milk	295	0.2	16	16	22	0.60
Ground meat	1216	0.2	96	81	0	2.35
Chicken	394	4.3	9	74	0	1.15
Fish	358	3.2	0.5	83	0	2.25
Beans	128	3.2	0.8	7	28	0.58
Spinach	118	14.1	1.4	14	19	1.17
Potatoes	279	2.2	0.5	8	63	0.33

Source: Pennington, Jean A. T. and Judith S. Douglas. *Bowes and Church's Food Values of Portions Commonly Used,* 18th Ed., Philadelphia, Lippincott Williams & Wilkins, 2004, pp. 100–130.

What combination and amounts of food items will provide the nutrition Roniger requires at the least total food cost?

(a) Formulate as an LP problem.
(b) What is the cost per meal?
(c) Is this a well-balanced diet?

8-12 *(High tech production problem)* Quitmeyer Electronics Incorporated manufactures the following six microcomputer peripheral devices: internal modems, external modems, graphics circuit boards, CD drives, hard disk drives, and memory expansion boards. Each of these technical products requires time, in minutes, on three types of electronic testing equipment, as shown in the table at the bottom of the page.

The first two test devices are available 120 hours per week. The third (device 3) requires more preventive maintenance and may be used only 100 hours each week. The market for all six computer components is vast, and Quitmeyer Electronics believes that it can sell as many units of each product as it can manufacture. The table that follows summarizes the revenues and material costs for each product:

DEVICE	REVENUE PER UNIT SOLD ($)	MATERIAL COST PER UNIT ($)
Internal modem	200	35
External modem	120	25
Graphics circuit board	180	40
CD drive	130	45
Hard disk drive	430	170
Memory expansion board	260	60

In addition, variable labor costs are $15 per hour for test device 1, $12 per hour for test device 2, and $18 per hour for test device 3. Quitmeyer Electronics wants to maximize its profits.

(a) Formulate this problem as an LP model.
(b) Solve the problem by computer. What is the best product mix?
(c) What is the value of an additional minute of time per week on test device 1? Test device 2? Test device 3? Should Quitmeyer Electronics add more test device time? If so, on which equipment?

8-13 *(Nuclear plant staffing problem)* South Central Utilities has just announced the August 1 opening of its second nuclear generator at its Baton Rouge, Louisiana, nuclear power plant. Its personnel department has been directed to determine how many nuclear technicians need to be hired and trained over the remainder of the year.

The plant currently employs 350 fully trained technicians and projects the following personnel needs:

MONTH	PERSONNEL HOURS NEEDED
August	40,000
September	45,000
October	35,000
November	50,000
December	45,000

By Louisiana law, a reactor employee can actually work no more than 130 hours per month. (Slightly over one hour per day is used for check-in and check-out, recordkeeping, and for daily radiation health scans.) Policy at South Central Utilities also dictates that layoffs are not acceptable in those months when the nuclear plant is overstaffed. So, if more trained employees are available than are needed in any month, each worker is still fully paid, even though he or she is not required to work the 130 hours.

Training new employees is an important and costly procedure. It takes one month of one-on-one classroom instruction before a new technician is permitted to work alone in the reactor facility. Therefore, South Central must hire trainees one month before they are actually needed. Each trainee teams up with a skilled nuclear technician and requires 90 hours of that employee's time, meaning that 90 hours less of the technician's time are available that month for actual reactor work.

Personnel department records indicate a turnover rate of trained technicians at 5% per month. In other words, about 5% of the skilled employees at the start of any month resign by the end of that month. A trained technician earns an average monthly salary of $2,000 (regardless of the number of hours worked, as noted earlier). Trainees are paid $900 during their one month of instruction.

(a) Formulate this staffing problem using LP.
(b) Solve the problem. How many trainees must begin each month?

Data for Problem 8-12

	INTERNAL MODEM	EXTERNAL MODEM	CIRCUIT BOARD	CD DRIVES	HARD DRIVES	MEMORY BOARDS
Test device 1	7	3	12	6	18	17
Test device 2	2	5	3	2	15	17
Test device 3	5	1	3	2	9	2

8-14 (*Agricultural production planning problem*) Margaret Black's family owns five parcels of farmland broken into a southeast sector, north sector, northwest sector, west sector, and southwest sector. Margaret is involved primarily in growing wheat, alfalfa, and barley crops and is currently preparing her production plan for next year. The Pennsylvania Water Authority has just announced its yearly water allotment, with the Black farm receiving 7,400 acre-feet. Each parcel can only tolerate a specified amount of irrigation per growing season, as specified in the following table:

Parcel	Area (Acres)	Water Irrigation Limit (Acre-Feet)
Southeast	2,000	3,200
North	2,300	3,400
Northwest	600	800
West	1,100	500
Southwest	500	600

Each of Margaret's crops needs a minimum amount of water per acre, and there is a projected limit on sales of each crop. Crop data follow:

Crop	Maximum Sales	Water Needed Per Acre (Acre-Feet)
Wheat	110,000 bushels	1.6
Alfalfa	1,800 tons	2.9
Barley	2,200 tons	3.5

Margaret's best estimate is that she can sell wheat at a net profit of $2 per bushel, alfalfa at $40 per ton, and barley at $50 per ton. One acre of land yields an average of 1.5 tons of alfalfa and 2.2 tons of barley. The wheat yield is approximately 50 bushels per acre.

(a) Formulate Margaret's production plan.
(b) What should the crop plan be, and what profit will it yield?

(c) The Water Authority informs Margaret that for a special fee of $6,000 this year, her farm will qualify for an additional allotment of 600 acre-feet of water. How should she respond?

8-15 (*Material blending problem*) Amalgamated Products has just received a contract to construct steel body frames for automobiles that are to be produced at the new Japanese factory in Tennessee. The Japanese auto manufacturer has strict quality control standards for all of its component subcontractors and has informed Amalgamated that each frame must have the following steel content:

Material	Minimum Percent	Maximum Percent
Manganese	2.1	2.3
Silicon	4.3	4.6
Carbon	5.05	5.35

Amalgamated mixes batches of eight different available materials to produce one ton of steel used in the body frames. The table on this page details these materials.

Formulate and solve the LP model that will indicate how much each of the eight materials should be blended into a 1-ton load of steel so that Amalgamated meets its requirements while minimizing costs.

8-16 Refer to Problem 8-15. Find the cause of the difficulty and recommend how to adjust it. Then solve the problem again.

8-17 (*Hospital expansion problem*) Mt. Sinai Hospital in New Orleans is a large, private, 600-bed facility complete with laboratories, operating rooms, and x-ray equipment. In seeking to increase revenues, Mt. Sinai's administration has decided to make a 90 bed addition on a portion of adjacent land currently used for staff parking. The administrators feel that the labs, operating rooms, and x-ray department are not being fully utilized at present and do not need to be expanded to handle additional patients. The addition of 90 beds, however, involves deciding how many beds should be

Data for Problem 8-15

Material Available	Manganese (%)	Silicon (%)	Carbon (%)	Pounds Available	Cost Per Pound
Alloy 1	70.0	15.0	3.0	No limit	$0.12
Alloy 2	55.0	30.0	1.0	300	0.13
Alloy 3	12.0	26.0	0	No limit	0.15
Iron 1	1.0	10.0	3.0	No limit	0.09
Iron 2	5.0	2.5	0	No limit	0.07
Carbide 1	0	24.0	18.0	50	0.10
Carbide 2	0	25.0	20.0	200	0.12
Carbide 3	0	23.0	25.0	100	0.09

allocated to the medical staff for medical patients and how many to the surgical staff for surgical patients.

The hospital's accounting and medical records departments have provided the following pertinent information. The average hospital stay for a medical patient is 8 days, and the average medical patient generates $2,280 in revenues. The average surgical patient is in the hospital 5 days and receives a $1,515 bill. The laboratory is capable of handling 15,000 tests per year more than it was handling. The average medical patient requires 3.1 lab tests and the average surgical patient takes 2.6 lab tests. Furthermore, the average medical patient uses one x-ray, whereas the average surgical patient requires two x-rays. If the hospital was expanded by 90 beds, the x-ray department could handle up to 7,000 x-rays without significant additional cost. Finally, the administration estimates that up to 2,800 additional operations could be performed in existing operating room facilities. Medical patients, of course, do not require surgery, whereas each surgical patient generally has one surgery performed.

Formulate this problem so as to determine how many medical beds and how many surgical beds should be added to maximize revenues. Assume that the hospital is open 365 days a year. Then solve the problem.

8-18 Prepare a written report to the CEO of Mt. Sinai Hospital in Problem 8-17 on the expansion of the hospital. Round off your answers to the nearest *integer*. The format of presentation of results is important. The CEO is a busy person and wants to be able to find your optimal solution quickly in your report. Cover all the areas given in the following sections, but do not mention any X's, slack or surplus variables, or shadow prices.

(a) What is the maximum revenue per year, how many medical patients/year are there, and how many surgical patients/year are there? How many medical beds and how many surgical beds of the 90-bed addition should be added?

(b) Are there any empty beds with this optimal solution? If so, how many empty beds are there? Discuss the effect of acquiring more beds if needed.

(c) Are the laboratories being used to their capacity? Is it possible to perform more lab tests/year? If so, how many more? Discuss the effect of acquiring more lab space if needed.

(d) Is the x-ray facility being used to its maximum? Is it possible to do more x-rays/year? If so, how many more? Discuss the effect of acquiring more x-ray facilities if needed.

(e) Is the operating room being used to capacity? Is it possible to do more operations/year? If so, how many more? Discuss the effect of acquiring more operating room facilities if needed. (**Source:** Professor Chris Vertullo.)

8-19 *(Rock transshipment problem)* Bamm Mining Company is currently extracting rock from two mines. Once it is taken from the ground and loaded

on a truck, it is sent to one of two plants for processing. The processed rock is then shipped to one of three builders' supply stores, where it is sold for landscaping purposes. The cost of transportation, the supply available at each mine, and the processing capacity of each plant are given in the following table:

Cost per Ton for Shipping

	TO PROCESSING PLANT		
FROM MINE	#1	#2	DAILY SUPPLY
A	$6	$ 8	320 tons
B	$7	$10	450 tons
Processing capacity (per day)	500 tons	500 tons	

The cost of shipping from each processing plant to each store and the daily demand are as follows:

Cost per Ton for Shipping

	TO		
FROM PLANT	BUILDERS' HOME	HOMEOWNERS' HEADQUARTERS	HARDWARE CITY
#1	$13	$17	$20
#2	$19	$22	$21
Daily demand	200	240	330

(a) Formulate a linear program that can be used to determine how to meet the demands of the three stores at the least cost.

(b) Solve this by computer. How many tons should be shipped from each mine to each plant? How many tons should go from each plant to each store?

8-20 In the Bamm Mining Company (Problem 8-19) situation, the cost of processing the rock is $22 per ton at Plant 1 and $18 per ton at Plant 2.

(a) Formulate a linear program to minimize to the total processing and transportation cost.

(b) Solve this by computer. What is the optimal solution?

8-21 *(Hospital food transportation problem)* Northeast General, a large hospital in Providence, Rhode Island, has initiated a new procedure to ensure that patients receive their meals while the food is still as hot as possible. The hospital will continue to prepare the food in its kitchen but will now deliver it in bulk (not individual servings) to one of three new serving stations in the building. From there, the food will be reheated and meals will be placed on individual trays, loaded onto a cart, and distributed to the various floors and wings of the hospital.

The three new serving stations are as efficiently located as possible to reach the various hallways in the hospital. The number of trays that each station can serve are on the table on the next page:

Location	Capacity (Meals)
Station 5A	200
Station 3G	225
Station 1S	275

There are six wings to Northeast General that must be served. The number of patients in each follows:

Wing	1	2	3	4	5	6
Patients	80	120	150	210	60	80

The purpose of the new procedure is to increase the temperature of the hot meals that the patient receives. Therefore, the amount of time needed to deliver a tray from a serving station will determine the proper distribution of food from serving station to wing. The following table summarizes the time (minutes) associated with each possible distribution channel.

What is your recommendation for handling the distribution of trays from the three serving stations?

From \ To	Wing 1	Wing 2	Wing 3	Wing 4	Wing 5	Wing 6
Station 5A	12	11	8	9	6	6
Station 3G	6	12	7	7	5	8
Station 1S	8	9	6	6	7	9

8-22 (*Portfolio selection problem*) Daniel Grady is the financial advisor for a number of professional athletes. An analysis of the long-term goals for many of these athletes has resulted in a recommendation to purchase stocks with some of their income that is set aside for investments. Five stocks have been identified as having very favorable expectations for future performance. Although the expected return is important in these investments, the risk, as measured by the beta of the stock, is also important. (A high value of beta indicates that the stock has a relatively high risk.) The expected return and the betas for five stocks are as follows:

Stock	1	2	3	4	5
Expected return (%)	11.0	9.0	6.5	15.0	13.0
Beta	1.20	0.85	0.55	1.40	1.25

Daniel would like to minimize the beta of the stock portfolio (calculated using a weighted average of the amounts put into the different stocks) while maintaining an expected return of at least 11%. Since future conditions may change, Daniel has decided that no more than 35% of the portfolio should be invested in any one stock.

(a) Formulate this as a linear program. (*Hint*: Define the variables to be the proportion of the total investment that would be put in each stock. Include a constraint that restricts the sum of these variables to be 1.)
(b) Solve this problem. What are the expected return and beta for this portfolio?

8-23 (*Airline fuel problem*) Coast-to-Coast Airlines is investigating the possibility of reducing the cost of fuel purchases by taking advantage of lower fuel costs in certain cities. Since fuel purchases represent a substantial portion of operating expenses for an airline, it is important that these costs be carefully monitored. However, fuel adds weight to an airplane, and consequently, excess fuel raises the cost of getting from one city to another. In evaluating one particular flight rotation, a plane begins in Atlanta, flies from Atlanta to Los Angeles, from Los Angeles to Houston, from Houston to New Orleans, and from New Orleans to Atlanta. When the plane arrives in Atlanta, the flight rotation is said to have been completed, and then it starts again. Thus, the fuel on board when the flight arrived in Atlanta must be taken into consideration when the flight begins. Along each leg of this route, there is a minimum and a maximum amount of fuel that may be carried. This and additional information is provided in the table on this page.

The regular fuel consumption is based on the plane carrying the minimum amount of fuel. If more than this is carried, the amount of fuel consumed is higher. Specifically, for each 1,000 gallons of fuel above the minimum, 5% (or 50 gallons per 1,000 gallons of extra fuel) is lost due to excess fuel consumption. For example, if 25,000 gallons of fuel were on board when the plane takes off from Atlanta, the fuel consumed on this route would be 12 + 0.05 = 12.05 thousand gallons. If 26 thousand gallons were on board, the fuel consumed would be increased by another 0.05 thousand, for a total of 12.1 thousand gallons.

Formulate this as an LP problem to minimize the cost. How many gallons should be purchased in each city? What is the total cost of this?

Data for Problem 8-23	Leg	Minimum Fuel Required (1,000 gal.)	Maximum Fuel Allowed (1,000 gal.)	Regular Fuel Consumption (1,000 gal.)	Fuel Price Per Gallon
	Atlanta–Los Angeles	24	36	12	$1.15
	Los Angeles–Houston	15	23	7	$1.25
	Houston–New Orleans	9	17	3	$1.10
	New Orleans–Atlanta	11	20	5	$1.18

INTERNET HOMEWORK PROBLEMS

See our Internet home page at **www.prenhall.com/render** for additional
homework problems 8-24 to 8-28.

CASE STUDY

Red Brand Canners

On Monday, September 13, 1999, Mitchell Gordon, vice president of operations at Red Brand Canners, asked the controller, the sales manager, and the production manager to meet with him to discuss the amount of tomato products to pack that season. The tomato crop, which had been purchased at planting, was beginning to arrive at the cannery, and packing operations would have to be started by the following Monday. Red Brand Canners is a medium-sized company that cans and distributes a variety of fruit and vegetable products under private brands in the western states.

William Cooper, the controller, and Charles Myers, the sales manager, were the first to arrive in Gordon's office. Dan Tucker, the production manager, came in a few minutes later and said that he had picked up Produce Inspection's latest estimate of the quality of the incoming tomatoes. According to the report, about 20% of the crop was grade A quality and the remaining portion of the 3-million-pound crop was grade B.

Gordon asked Myers about the demand for tomato products for the coming year. Myers replied that they could sell all of the whole canned tomatoes they could produce. The expected demand for tomato juice and tomato paste, on the other hand, was limited. The sales manager then passed around the latest demand forecast, which is shown in Table 8.6. He reminded the group that the selling prices had been set in light of the long-term marketing strategy of the company and that the potential sales had been forecast at these prices.

Bill Cooper, after looking at Myers's estimates of demand, said that it looked like the company "should do quite well [on

the tomato crop] this year." With the new accounting system that had been set up, he had been able to compute the contribution for each product, and according to his analysis, the incremental profit on whole tomatoes was greater than the incremental profit on any other tomato product. In May, after Red Brand had signed contracts agreeing to purchase the grower's production at an average delivered price of 6 cents per pound, Cooper had computed the tomato products' contributions (see Table 8.7).

Dan Tucker brought to Cooper's attention that although there was ample production capacity, it was impossible to produce all whole tomatoes because too small a portion of the tomato crop was grade A quality. Red Brand used a numerical scale to record the quality of both raw produce and prepared products. This scale ran from 0 to 10, the higher number representing better quality. According to this scale, grade A tomatoes averaged nine points per pound and grade B tomatoes averaged five points per pound. Tucker noted that the minimum average input quality was eight points per pound for canned whole tomatoes and six points per pound for juice. Paste could be made entirely from grade B tomatoes. This meant that whole-tomato production was limited to 800,000 pounds.

Gordon stated that this was not a real limitation. He had been recently solicited to purchase 80,000 pounds of grade A tomatoes at $8 \frac{1}{2}$ cents per pound and at that time had turned down the offer. He felt, however, that the tomatoes were still available.

Myers, who had been doing some calculations, said that although he agreed that the company "should do quite well this

TABLE 8.6			
Demand Forecasts	PRODUCT	SELLING PRICE PER CASE ($)	DEMAND FORECAST (CASES)
	24–2 $\frac{1}{2}$ whole tomatoes	4.00	800,000
	24–2 $\frac{1}{2}$ choice peach halves	5.40	10,000
	24–2 $\frac{1}{2}$ peach nectar	4.60	5,000
	24–2 $\frac{1}{2}$ tomato juice	4.50	50,000
	24–2 $\frac{1}{2}$ cooking apples	4.90	15,000
	24–2 $\frac{1}{2}$ tomato paste	3.80	80,000

TABLE 8.7   Product Item Profitability

PRODUCT	24–2½ WHOLE TOMATOES	24–2½ CHOICE PEACH HALVES	24–2½ PEACH NECTAR	24–2½ TOMATO JUICE	24–2½ COOKING APPLES	24–2½ TOMATO PASTE
Selling price	$4.00	$5.40	$4.60	$4.50	$4.90	$3.80
Variable cost Direct labor	1.18	1.40	1.27	1.32	0.70	0.54
Variable overhead	0.24	0.32	0.23	0.36	0.22	0.26
Variable selling	0.40	0.30	0.40	0.85	0.28	0.38
Packaging material	0.70	0.56	0.60	0.65	0.70	0.77
Fruit*	1.08	1.80	1.70	1.20	0.90	1.50
Total variable costs	3.60	4.38	4.20	4.38	2.80	3.45
Contribution	0.40	1.02	0.40	0.12	1.10	0.35
Less allocated overhead	0.28	0.70	0.52	0.21	0.75	0.23
Net profit	0.12	0.32	(0.12)	(0.09)	0.35	0.12

* Product usage is as follows:

Product	Pounds per Case
Whole tomatoes	18
Peach halves	18
Peach nectar	17
Tomato juice	20
Cooking apples	27
Tomato paste	25

TABLE 8.8

Marginal Analysis of Tomato Products

Z = cost per pound of grade A tomatoes in cents

Y = cost per pound of grade B tomatoes in cents

$$(600{,}000 \text{ lb} \times Z) + (2{,}400{,}000 \text{ lb} \times Y) = (3{,}000{,}000 \text{ lb} \times 6) \quad (1)$$

$$\frac{Z}{9} = \frac{Y}{5} \quad (2)$$

Z = 9.32 cents per pound

Y = 5.18 cents per pound

PRODUCT	CANNED WHOLE TOMATOES	TOMATO JUICE	TOMATO PASTE
Selling price	$4.00	$4.50	$3.80
Variable cost (excluding tomato cost)	2.52	3.18	1.95
	$1.48	$1.32	$1.85
Tomato cost	1.49	1.24	1.30
Marginal profit	($0.01)	$0.08	$0.55

year," it would not be by canning whole tomatoes. It seemed to him that the tomato cost should be allocated on the basis of quality and quantity rather than by quantity only, as Cooper had done. Therefore, he had recomputed the marginal profit on this basis (see Table 8.8), and from his results had concluded that Red Brand should use 2 million pounds of the grade B tomatoes for paste, and the remaining 400,000 pounds of grade B tomatoes and all of the grade A tomatoes for juice. If the demand expectations were realized, a contribution of $48,000 would be made on this year's tomato crop.

Discussion Questions

1. Structure this problem verbally, including a written description of the constraints and objective. What are the decision variables?
2. Develop a *mathematical* formulation for Red Brand's objective function and constraints.
3. Solve the problem and discuss the results.

Source: "Red Brand Canners" revised with permission of Stanford University, Graduate School of Business, Copyright © 1969 and 1977 by the Board of Trustees of the Leland Stanford Junior University.

⇒ CASE STUDY

Chase Manhattan Bank

The workload in many areas of bank operations has the characteristics of a nonuniform distribution with respect to time of day. For example, at Chase Manhattan Bank in New York, the number of domestic money transfer requests received from customers, if plotted against time of day, would appear to have the shape of an inverted U curve with the peak around 1 P.M. For efficient use of resources, the personnel available should, therefore, vary correspondingly. Figure 8.2 shows a typical workload curve and corresponding personnel requirements at different hours of the day.

A variable capacity can be achieved effectively by employing part-time personnel. Because part-timers are not entitled to all the fringe benefits, they are often more economical than full-time employees. Other considerations, however, may limit the extent to which part-time people can be hired in a given department. The problem is to find an optimum workforce schedule that would meet personnel requirements at any given time and also be economical.

Some of the factors affecting personnel assignment are listed here:

1. By corporate policy, part-time personnel hours are limited to a maximum of 40% of the day's total requirement.

2. Full-time employees work for 8 hours (1 hour for lunch included) per day. Thus, a full-timer's productive time is 35 hours per week.
3. Part-timers work for at least 4 hours per day but less than 8 hours and are not allowed a lunch break.
4. Fifty percent of the full-timers go to lunch between 11 A.M. and noon, and the remaining 50% go between noon and 1 P.M.
5. The shift starts at 9 A.M. and ends at 7 P.M. (i.e., overtime is limited to 2 hours). Any work left over at 7 P.M. is considered holdover for the next day.
6. A full-time employee is not allowed to work more than 5 hours overtime per week. He or she is paid at the normal rate for overtime hours—*not* at one-and-a-half times the normal rate applicable to hours in excess of 40 per week. Fringe benefits are not applied to overtime hours.

In addition, the following costs are pertinent:

1. The average cost per full-time personnel hour (fringe benefits included) is $10.11.

TABLE 8.9 **Workforce Requirements**

TIME PERIOD	NUMBER OF PERSONNEL REQUIRED
9–10 A.M.	14
10–11	25
11–12	26
12–1 P.M.	38
1–2	55
2–3	60
3–4	51
4–5	29
5–6	14
6–7	9

FIGURE 8.2

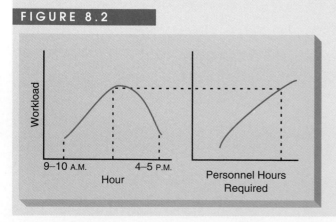

2. The average cost per overtime personnel hour for full-timers (straight rate excluding fringe benefits) is $8.08.
3. The average cost per part-time personnel hour is $7.82.

The personnel hours required, by hour of day, are given in Table 8.9.

The bank's goal is to achieve the minimum possible personnel cost subject to meeting or exceeding the hourly workforce requirements as well as the constraints on the workers listed earlier.

Discussion Questions

1. What is the minimum-cost schedule for the bank?
2. What are the limitations of the model used to answer question 1?
3. Costs might be reduced by relaxing the constraint that no more than 40% of the day's requirement be met by part-timers. Would changing the 40% to a higher value significantly reduce costs?

Source: Adapted from Shyam L. Moondra. "An L. P. Model for Work Force Scheduling for Banks," *Journal of Bank Research* (Winter 1976).

BIBLIOGRAPHY

See the Bibliography at the end of Chapter 7.

CHAPTER 9

LINEAR PROGRAMMING: THE SIMPLEX METHOD

LEARNING OBJECTIVES

After completing this chapter, students will be able to:

1. Convert LP constraints to equalities with slack, surplus, and artificial variables.
2. Set up and solve LP problems with simplex tableaus.
3. Interpret the meaning of every number in a simplex tableau.
4. Recognize special cases such as infeasibility, unboundedness and degeneracy.
5. Use the simplex tables to conduct sensitivity analysis.
6. Construct the dual problem from the primal problem.

CHAPTER OUTLINE

Summary • Glossary • Key Equation • Solved Problems • Self-Test • Discussion Questions and Problems • Internet Homework Problems • Case Study: Coastal States Chemicals and Fertilizers • Bibliography

9.1 INTRODUCTION

In Chapter 7 we looked at examples of linear programming (LP) problems that contained two decision variables. With only two variables it is possible to use a graphical approach. We plotted the feasible region and then searched for the optimal corner point and corresponding profit or cost. This approach provides a good way to understand the basic concepts of LP. Most real-life LP problems, however, have more than two variables and are thus too large for the simple graphical solution procedure. Problems faced in business and government can have dozens, hundreds, or even thousands of variables. We need a more powerful method than graphing, so in this chapter we turn to a procedure called the *simplex method*.

Recall that the theory of LP states the optimal solution will lie at a corner point of the feasible region. In large LP problems, the feasible region cannot be graphed because it has many dimensions, but the concept is the same.

How does the simplex method work? The concept is simple, and similar to graphical LP in one important respect. In graphical LP we examine each of the corner points; LP theory tells us that the optimal solution lies at one of them. In LP problems containing several variables, we may not be able to graph the feasible region, but the optimal solution will still lie at a corner point of the many-sided, many-dimensional figure (called an *n*-dimensional polyhedron) that represents the area of feasible solutions. The simplex method examines the corner points in a systematic fashion, using basic algebraic concepts. It does so in an *iterative* manner, that is, repeating the same set of procedures time after time until an optimal solution is reached. Each iteration brings a higher value for the objective function so that we are always moving closer to the optimal solution.

The simplex method systematically examines corner points, using algebraic steps, until an optimal solution is found.

Why should we study the simplex method? It is important to understand the ideas used to produce solutions. The simplex approach yields not only the optimal solution to the X_i variables and the maximum profit (or minimum cost), but valuable economic information as well. To be able to use computers successfully and to interpret LP computer printouts, we need to know what the simplex method is doing and why.

We begin by solving a maximization problem using the simplex method. We then tackle a minimization problem and look at a few technical issues that are faced when employing the simplex procedure. From there we examine how to conduct sensitivity analysis using the simplex tables. The chapter concludes with a discussion of the *dual*, which is an alternative way of looking at any LP problem.

9.2 HOW TO SET UP THE INITIAL SIMPLEX SOLUTION

Let us consider the case of the Flair Furniture Company from Chapter 7. Instead of the graphical solution we used in that chapter, we now demonstrate the simplex method. You may recall that we let

$$T = \text{number of tables produced}$$

$$C = \text{number of chairs produced}$$

and that the problem was formulated as

maximize profit	$= \$7T + \$5C$	(objective function)
subject to:	$2T + 1C \leq 100$	(painting hours constraint)
	$4T + 3C \leq 240$	(carpentry hours constraint)
	$T, C \geq 0$	(nonnegativity constraints)

Converting the Constraints to Equations

Slack variables are added to each less-than-or-equal-to constraint. Each slack variable represents an unused resource.

The first step of the simplex method requires that we convert each inequality constraint (except nonnegativity constraints) in an LP formulation into an equation.[1] Less-than-or-equal-to constraints ($\leq$) such as in the Flair problem are converted to equations by adding a *slack variable* to each constraint. Slack variables represent unused resources; these may be in the form of time on a machine, labor hours, money, warehouse space, or any number of such resources in various business problems.

In our case at hand, we can let

S_1 = slack variable representing unused hours in the painting department

S_2 = slack variable representing unused hours in the carpentry department

The constraints to the problem may now be written as

$$2T + 1C + S_1 = 100$$

and

$$4T + 3C + S_2 = 240$$

Thus, if the production of tables (T) and chairs (C) uses less than 100 hours of painting time available, the unused time is the value of the slack variable, S_1. For example, if $T = 0$ and $C = 0$ (in other words, if nothing is produced), we have $S_1 = 100$ hours of slack time in the painting department. If Flair produces $T = 40$ tables and $C = 10$ chairs, then

$$2T + 1C + S_1 = 100$$
$$2(40) + 1(10) + S_1 = 100$$
$$S_1 = 10$$

and there will be 10 hours of slack, or unused, painting time available.

To include all variables in each equation, which is a requirement of the next simplex step, slack variables not appearing in an equation are added with a coefficient of 0. This means, in effect, that they have no influence on the equations in which they are inserted; but it does allow us to keep tabs on all variables at all times. The equations now appear as follows:

$$2T + 1C + 1S_1 + 0S_2 = 100$$
$$4T + 3C + 0S_1 + 1S_2 = 240$$
$$T, C, S_1, S_2 \geq 0$$

Because slack variables yield no profit, they are added to the original objective function with 0 profit coefficients. The objective function becomes

$$\text{maximize profit} = \$7T + \$5C + \$0S_1 + \$0S_2$$

Finding an Initial Solution Algebraically

Let's take another look at the new constraint equations. We see that there are two equations and four variables. Think back to your last algebra course. When you have the same number of unknown variables as you have equations, it is possible to solve for unique values of the variables. But when there are four unknowns (T, C, S_1, and S_2, in this case) and only

---

[1] This is because the simplex is a matrix algebra method that requires all mathematical relationships to be equations, with each equation containing all of the variables.

FIGURE 9.1

Corner Points of the Flair Furniture Company Problem

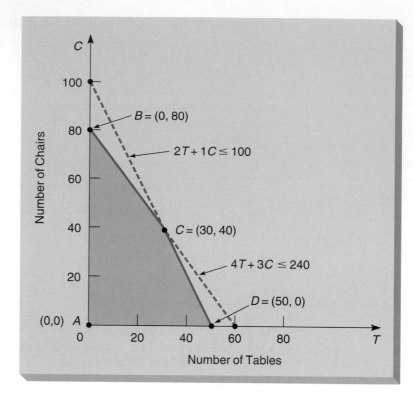

A basic feasible solution to a system of n equations is found by setting all but n variables equal to 0 and solving for the other variables.

two equations, you can let two of the variables equal 0 and then solve for the other two. For example, if $T = C = 0$, then $S_1 = 100$ and $S_2 = 240$. A solution found in this manner is called a *basic feasible solution*.

The simplex method begins with an initial feasible solution in which all real variables (such as T and C) are set equal to 0. This trivial solution always produces a profit of $0, as well as slack variables equal to the constant (right-hand-side) terms in the constraint equations. It's not a very exciting solution in terms of economic returns, but it is one of the original corner point solutions (see Figure 9.1). As mentioned, the simplex method will start at this corner point (A) and then move up or over to the corner point that yields the most improved profit (B or D). Finally, the technique will move to a new corner point (C), which happens to be the optimal solution to the Flair Furniture problem. The simplex method considers only feasible solutions and hence will touch no possible combinations other than the corner points of the shaded region in Figure 9.1.

Simplex considers only corner points as it seeks the best solution.

The First Simplex Tableau

To simplify handling the equations and objective function in an LP problem, we place all of the coefficients into tabular form. The first *simplex tableau* is shown in Table 9.1. An explanation of its parts and how the tableau is derived follows.

Constraint Equations We see that Flair Furniture's two constraint equations can be expressed as follows:

Here are the constraints in tabular form.

SOLUTION MIX	T	C	S_1	S_2	QUANTITY (RIGHT-HAND SIDE)
S_1	2	1	1	0	100
S_2	4	3	0	1	240

TABLE 9.1   Flair Furniture's Initial Simplex Tableau

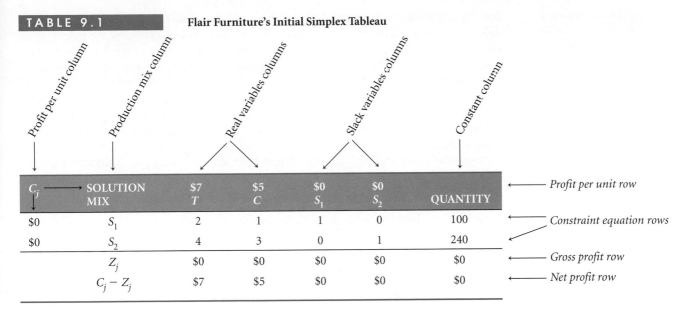

C_j	SOLUTION MIX	$7 T	$5 C	$0 S_1	$0 S_2	QUANTITY	
$0	S_1	2	1	1	0	100	← Constraint equation rows
$0	S_2	4	3	0	1	240	
	Z_j	$0	$0	$0	$0	$0	← Gross profit row
	$C_j - Z_j$	$7	$5	$0	$0	$0	← Net profit row

The numbers (2, 1, 1, 0) in the first row represent the coefficients of the first equation, namely, $2T + 1C + 1S_1 + 0S_2$. The numbers (4, 3, 0, 1) in the second row are the algebraic equivalent of the constraint $4T + 3C + 0S_1 + 1S_2$.

The initial solution mix begins with real, or decision, variables set equal to zero.

As suggested earlier, we begin the initial solution procedure at the origin, where $T = 0$ and $C = 0$. The values of the other two variables must then be nonzero, so $S_1 = 100$ and $S_2 = 240$. These two slack variables constitute the *initial solution mix*; their values are found in the *quantity* (or right-hand-side [RHS]) *column*. Because T and C are not in the solution mix, their initial values are automatically equal to 0.

This initial solution is a *basic feasible solution* and is described in vector, or column, form as

Here is the basic feasible solution in column form.

$$\begin{bmatrix} T \\ C \\ S_1 \\ S_2 \end{bmatrix} = \begin{bmatrix} 0 \\ 0 \\ 100 \\ 240 \end{bmatrix}$$

Variables in the solution mix are called basic. Those not in the solution are called nonbasic.

Variables in the solution mix, which is called the *basis* in LP terminology, are referred to as basic variables. In this example, the basic variables are S_1 and S_2. Variables not in the solution mix or basis and that have been set equal to zero (T and C in this case), are called *nonbasic variables*. Of course, if the optimal solution to this LP problem turned out to be $T = 30$, $C = 40$, $S_1 = 0$, and $S_2 = 0$, or

$$\begin{bmatrix} T \\ C \\ S_1 \\ S_2 \end{bmatrix} = \begin{bmatrix} 30 \\ 40 \\ 0 \\ 0 \end{bmatrix} \text{ (in vector form)}$$

then T and C would be the final basic variables, and S_1 and S_2 would be the *nonbasic variables*. Notice that for any corner point, exactly two of the four variables will equal zero.

Substitution Rates   Many students are unsure as to the actual meaning of the numbers in the columns under each variable. We know that the entries are the coefficients for that variable. Under T are the coefficients $\binom{2}{4}$, under C are $\binom{1}{3}$, under S_1 are $\binom{1}{0}$, and under S_2 are $\binom{0}{1}$.

Substitution rates are numbers in the body of the table. This paragraph explains how to interpret their meaning.

But what is their interpretation? The numbers in the body of the simplex tableau (see Table 9.1) can be thought of as *substitution rates*. For example, suppose we now wish to make T larger than 0, that is, produce some tables. For every unit of the T product introduced into the current solution, 2 units of S_1 and 4 units of S_2 must be removed from the solution. This is so because each table requires 2 hours of the currently unused painting department slack time, S_1. It also takes 4 hours of carpentry time; hence 4 units of variable S_2 must be removed from the solution for every unit of T that enters. Similarly, the substitution rates for each unit of C that enters the current solution are 1 unit of S_1 and 3 units of S_2.

Another point that you are reminded of throughout this chapter is that for any variable ever to appear in the solution mix column, it must have the number 1 someplace in its column and 0s in every other place in that column. We see that column S_1 contains $\begin{pmatrix} 1 \\ 0 \end{pmatrix}$, so variable S_1 is in the solution. Similarly, the S_2 column is $\begin{pmatrix} 0 \\ 1 \end{pmatrix}$, so S_2 is also in the solution.[2]

Adding the Objective Function We now continue to the next step in establishing the first simplex tableau. We add a row to reflect the objective function values for each variable. These contribution rates, called C_j, appear just above each respective variable, as shown in the following table:

$C_j \longrightarrow$		$\$7$	$\$5$	$\$0$	$\$0$	
	SOLUTION MIX	T	C	S_1	S_2	QUANTITY
$\$0$	S_1	2	1	1	0	100
$\$0$	S_2	4	3	0	1	240

The unit profit rates are not just found in the top C_j row: in the leftmost column, C_j indicates the unit profit for each variable *currently* in the solution mix. If S_1 were removed from the solution and replaced, for example, by C, $\$5$ would appear in the C_j column just to the left of the term C.

The Z_j and $C_j - Z_j$ Rows We can complete the initial Flair Furniture simplex tableau by adding two final rows. These last two rows provide us with important economic information, including the total profit and the answer as to whether the current solution is optimal.

We compute the Z_j value for each column of the initial solution in Table 9.1 by multiplying the 0 contribution value of each number in the C_j column by each number in that

---

[2] If there had been *three* less-than-or-equal-to constraints in the Flair Furniture problem, there would be three slack variables, S_1, S_2, and S_3. The 1s and 0s would appear like this:

SOLUTION MIX	S_1	S_2	S_3
S_1	1	0	0
S_2	0	1	0
S_3	0	0	1

IN ACTION — Resource Allocation at Pantex

Companies often use optimization techniques such as LP to allocate limited resources to maximize profits or minimize costs. One of the most important resource allocation problems faced by the United States is dismantling old nuclear weapons and maintaining the safety, security, and reliability of the remaining systems. This is the problem faced by Pantex, a $300 million corporation.

Pantex is responsible for disarming, evaluating, and maintaining the U.S. nuclear stockpile. The company is also responsible for storing critical weapon components that relate to U.S.–Russian nonproliferation agreements. Pantex constantly makes trade-offs in meeting the requirements of disarming some nuclear weapons versus maintaining existing nuclear weapon systems, while effectively allocating limited resources. Like many manufacturers, Pantex must allocate scarce resources among competing demands, all of which are important.

The team charged with solving the resource allocation problem at Pantex developed the Pantex Process Model (PPM). PPM is a sophisticated optimization system capable of analyzing nuclear needs over different time horizons. Since its development, PPM has become the primary tool for analyzing, planning, and scheduling issues at Pantex. PPM also helps to determine future resources. For example, it was used to gain government support for $17 million to modify an existing plant with new buildings and $70 million to construct a new plant.

Source: Kjeldgaard, Edwin et al. "Swords into Plowshares: Nuclear Weapon Dismantlement, Evaluation, and Maintenance at Pantex." Interfaces, 30, 1 (January–February 2000): 57–82.

The Z-row entry in the quantity column provides the gross profit.

row and the jth column, and summing. The Z_j value for the quantity column provides the total contribution (gross profit in this case) of the given solution.

$$Z_j \text{ (for gross profit)} = \text{(profit per unit of } S_1\text{)} \times \text{(number of units of } S_1\text{)}$$
$$+ \text{(profit per unit of } S_2\text{)} \times \text{(number of units of } S_2\text{)}$$
$$= \$0 \times 100 \text{ units} + \$0 \times 240 \text{ units}$$
$$= \$0 \text{ profit}$$

The Z_j values for the other columns (under the variables T, C, S_1, and S_2) represent the gross profit *given up* by adding one unit of this variable into the current solution. Their calculations are as follows:

$$Z_j = \text{(profit per unit of } S_1\text{)} \times \text{(substitution rate in row 1)}$$
$$+ \text{(profit per unit of } S_2\text{)} \times \text{(substitution rate in row 2)}$$

Thus,

$$Z_j \text{ (for column } T\text{)} = (\$0)(2) + (\$0)(4) = \$0$$
$$Z_j \text{ (for column } C\text{)} = (\$0)(1) + (\$0)(3) = \$0$$
$$Z_j \text{ (for column } S_1\text{)} = (\$0)(1) + (\$0)(0) = \$0$$
$$Z_j \text{ (for column } S_2\text{)} = (\$0)(0) + (\$0)(1) = \$0$$

We see that there is no profit *lost* by adding one unit of either T (tables), C (chairs), S_1, or S_2.

The $C_j - Z_j$ row gives the net profit from introducing one unit of each variable into the solution.

The $C_j - Z_j$ number in each column represents the net profit, that is, the profit gained minus the profit given up, that will result from introducing 1 unit of each product or variable into the solution. It is not calculated for the quantity column. To compute these numbers, simply subtract the Z_j total for each column from the C_j value at the very top of that variable's column. The calculations for the net profit per unit (the $C_j - Z_j$ row) in this example follow:

		COLUMN		
	T	C	S_1	S_2
C_j for column	$7	$5	$0	$0
Z_j for column	0	0	0	0
$C_j - Z_j$ for column	$7	$5	$0	$0

It is obvious to us when we compute a profit of $0 that the initial solution is not optimal. By examining the numbers in the $C_j - Z_j$ row of Table 9.1, we see that the total profit can be increased by $7 for each unit of T (tables) and by $5 for each unit of C (chairs) added to the solution mix. A negative number in the $C_j - Z_j$ row would tell us that profits would *decrease* if the corresponding variable were added to the solution mix. An optimal solution is reached in the simplex method when the $C_j - Z_j$ row contains no positive numbers. Such is not the case in our initial tableau.

We reach an optimal solution when the $C_j - Z_j$ row has no positive numbers in it.

9.3 SIMPLEX SOLUTION PROCEDURES

After an initial tableau has been completed, we proceed through a series of five steps to compute all the numbers needed in the next tableau. The calculations are not difficult, but they are complex enough that even the smallest arithmetic error can produce a wrong answer.

Here are the five simplex steps.

We first list the five steps and then carefully explain and apply them in completing the second and third tableaus for the Flair Furniture Company data.

Five Steps of the Simplex Method for Maximization Problems

1. Variable entering the solution has the largest positive $C_j - Z_j$.

1. Determine which variable to enter into the solution mix next. One way of doing this is by identifying the column, and hence the variable, with the largest positive number in the $C_j - Z_j$ row of the preceding tableau. This means that we will now be producing some of the product contributing the greatest additional profit per unit. The column identified in this step is called the *pivot column*.

2. Variable leaving the solution is determined by a ratio we must compute.

2. Determine which variable to replace. Because we have just chosen a new variable to enter the solution mix, we must decide which basic variable currently in the solution will have to leave to make room for it. Step 2 is accomplished by dividing each amount in the *quantity* column by the corresponding number in the column selected in step 1. The row with the *smallest nonnegative number* calculated in this fashion will be replaced in the next tableau. (This smallest number, by the way, gives the maximum number of units of the variable that may be placed in the solution.) This row is often referred to as the *pivot row*. The number at the intersection of the pivot row and pivot column is referred to as the *pivot number*.

3. New pivot-row calculations are done next.

3. Compute new values for the pivot row. To do this, we simply divide every number in the row by the pivot number.

4. Other new rows are calculated with formula (9-1).

4. Compute the new values for each remaining row. (In our Flair Furniture problem there are only two rows in the LP tableau, but most larger problems have many more rows.) All remaining row(s) are calculated as follows:

(new row numbers) = (numbers in old row)

$$- \left[\begin{pmatrix} \text{number above} \\ \text{or below} \\ \text{pivot number} \end{pmatrix} \times \begin{pmatrix} \text{corresponding number in} \\ \text{the new row, that is, the} \\ \text{row replaced in step 3} \end{pmatrix} \right] \quad (9\text{-}1)$$

5. Finally Z_j and $C_j - Z_j$ rows are recomputed.

5. Compute the Z_j and $C_j - Z_j$ rows, as demonstrated in the initial tableau. If all numbers in the $C_j - Z_j$ row are 0 or negative, an optimal solution has been reached. If this is not the case, return to step 1.

9.4   THE SECOND SIMPLEX TABLEAU

Here we apply the five steps to Flair Furniture.

Now that we have listed the five steps needed to move from an initial solution to an improved solution, we apply them to the Flair Furniture problem. Our goal is to add a new variable to the solution mix, or basis, to raise the profit from its current tableau value of $0.

First, T (tables) enters the solution mix because its $C_j - Z_j$ value of $7 is largest.

Step 1. To decide which of the variables will enter the solution next (it must be either T or C, since they are the only two nonbasic variables at this point), we select the one with the largest positive $C_j - Z_j$ value. Variable T, tables, has a $C_j - Z_j$ value of $7, implying that each unit of T added into the solution mix will contribute $7 to the overall profit. Variable C, chairs, has a $C_j - Z_j$ value of only $5. The other two variables, S_1 and S_2, have 0 values and can add nothing more to profit. Hence, we select T as the variable to enter the solution mix and identify its column (with an arrow) as the pivot column. This is shown in Table 9.2.

Step 2. Since T is about to enter the solution mix, we must decide which variable is to be replaced. There can only be as many basic variables as there are constraints in any LP problem, so either S_1 or S_2 will have to leave to make room for the introduction of T, tables, into the basis. To identify the pivot row, each number in the quantity column is divided by the corresponding number in the T column.

For the S_1 row:

$$\frac{100 \text{ (hours of painting time available)}}{2 \text{ (hours required per table)}} = 50 \text{ tables}$$

For the S_2 row:

$$\frac{240 \text{ (hours of carpentry time available)}}{4 \text{ (hours required per table)}} = 60 \text{ tables}$$

S_1 leaves the solution mix because the smaller of the two ratios indicates that the next pivot row will be the first row.

The smaller of these two ratios, 50, indicates the maximum number of units of T that can be produced without violating either of the original constraints. This corresponds to point D in Figure 9.2. The other ratio (60) corresponds to point E on this graph. Thus, the smallest ratio is chosen so that the next solution is feasible. Also, when $T = 50$, there is no slack in constraint 1, so $S_1 = 0$. This means that S_1 will be the next variable to be replaced at this iteration of the simplex method. The row with the smallest ratio (row 1) is the pivot row. The pivot row and the pivot number (the number at the intersection of the pivot row and pivot column) are identified in Table 9.3.

Step 3. Now that we have decided which variable is to enter the solution mix (T) and which is to leave (S_1), we begin to develop the second, improved simplex tableau. Step 3

TABLE 9.2

Pivot Column Identified in the Initial Simplex Tableau

C_j		$7	$5	$0	$0	
	SOLUTION MIX	T	C	S_1	S_2	QUANTITY (RHS)
$0	S_1	2	1	1	0	100
$0	S_2	4	3	0	1	240
	Z_j	$0	$0	$0	$0	$0
	$C_j - Z_j$	$7	$5	$0	$0	total profit

Pivot column

FIGURE 9.2

Graph of the Flair
Furniture Company
Problem

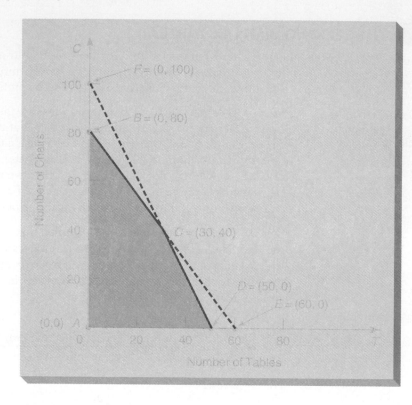

The new pivot row is computed by dividing every number in the pivot row by the pivot number.

involves computing a replacement for the pivot row. This is done by dividing every number in the pivot row by the pivot number:

$$\frac{2}{2} = 1 \qquad \frac{1}{2} = \frac{1}{2} \qquad \frac{1}{2} = \frac{1}{2} \qquad \frac{0}{2} = 0 \qquad \frac{100}{2} = 50$$

The new version of the entire pivot row appears in the accompanying table. Note that T is now in the solution mix and that 50 units of T are being produced. The C_j value is listed as a $7 contribution per unit of T in the solution. This will definitely provide Flair Furniture with a more profitable solution than the $0 generated in the initial tableau.

C_j	SOLUTION MIX	T	C	S_1	S_2	QUANTITY
$7	T	1	½	½	0	50

TABLE 9.3

Pivot Row and Pivot
Number Identified in the
Initial Simplex Tableau

C_j		$7	$5	$0	$0	
	SOLUTION MIX	T	C	S_1	S_2	QUANTITY
$0	S_1	2	1	1	0	100 ← Pivot row
$0	S_2	4	3	0	1	240
	Z_j	$0	$0	$0	$0	$0
	$C_j - Z_j$	$7	$5	$0	$0	

Pivot number

Pivot column

Step 4. This step is intended to help us compute new values for the other row in the body of the tableau, that is, the S_2 row. It is slightly more complex than replacing the pivot row and uses the formula (Equation 9.1) shown earlier. The expression on the right side of the following equation is used to calculate the left side.

We can now recompute the S_2 row.

$\begin{pmatrix} \text{Number in} \\ \text{New } S_2 \text{ Row} \end{pmatrix}$	$=$	$\begin{pmatrix} \text{Number in} \\ \text{Old } S_2 \text{ Row} \end{pmatrix}$	$-$	$\begin{bmatrix} \begin{pmatrix} \text{Number Below} \\ \text{Pivot Number} \end{pmatrix}$	$\times$	$\begin{pmatrix} \text{Corresponding Number} \\ \text{in the New } T \text{ Row} \end{pmatrix} \end{bmatrix}$
0	=	4	−	(4)	×	(1)
1	=	3	−	(4)	×	$(\frac{1}{2})$
−2	=	0	−	(4)	×	$(\frac{1}{2})$
1	=	1	−	(4)	×	(0)
40	=	240	−	(4)	×	(50)

This new S_2 row will appear in the second tableau in the following format:

C_j	SOLUTION MIX	T	C	S_1	S_2	QUANTITY
$7	T	1	$\frac{1}{2}$	$\frac{1}{2}$	0	50
$0	S_2	0	1	−2	1	40

We note that the T column contains $\begin{pmatrix} 1 \\ 0 \end{pmatrix}$ and the S_2 column contains $\begin{pmatrix} 0 \\ 1 \end{pmatrix}$. These 0s and 1s indicate that T and S_2 are in the basis (the solution mix).

Now that T and S_2 are in the solution mix, take a look at the values of the coefficients in their respective columns. The T column contains $\begin{pmatrix} 1 \\ 0 \end{pmatrix}$, a condition necessary for that variable to be in the solution. Similarly, the S_2 column has $\begin{pmatrix} 0 \\ 1 \end{pmatrix}$, that is, it contains a 1 and a 0. Basically, the algebraic manipulations we just went through in steps 3 and 4 were simply directed at producing 0s and 1s in the appropriate positions. In step 3 we divided every number in the pivot row by the pivot number; this guaranteed that there would be a 1 in the T column's top row. To derive the new second row, we multiplied the first row (each row is really an equation) by a constant (the number 4 here) and subtracted it from the second equation. The result was the new S_2 row with a 0 in the T column.

Step 5. The final step of the second iteration is to introduce the effect of the objective function. This involves computing the Z_j and $C_j - Z_j$ rows. Recall that the Z_j entry for the quantity column gives us the gross profit for the current solution. The other Z_j values represent the gross profit given up by adding one unit of each variable into this new solution. The Z_j values are calculated as follows:

We find the new profit in the Z row.

$$Z_j(\text{for } T \text{ column}) = (\$7)(1) + (\$0)(0) = \$7$$
$$Z_j(\text{for } C \text{ column}) = (\$7)(\tfrac{1}{2}) + (\$0)(1) = \$\tfrac{7}{2}$$
$$Z_j(\text{for } S_1 \text{ column}) = (\$7)(\tfrac{1}{2}) + (\$0)(-2) = \$\tfrac{7}{2}$$
$$Z_j(\text{for } S_2 \text{ column}) = (\$7)(0) + (\$0)(1) = \$0$$
$$Z_j(\text{for total profit}) = (\$7)(50) + (\$0)(40) = \$350$$

Note that the current profit is $350.

TABLE 9.4

Completed Second Simplex Tableau for Flair Furniture

C_j	SOLUTION MIX	$7	$5	$0	$0	
		T	C	S_1	S_2	QUANTITY
$7	T	1	$\frac{1}{2}$	$\frac{1}{2}$	0	50
$0	S_2	0	1	-2	1	40
	Z_j	$7	$\frac{7}{2}$	$\frac{7}{2}$	$0	$350
	$C_j - Z_j$	$0	$\frac{3}{2}$	$-\$\frac{7}{2}$	$0	

The $C_j - Z_j$ row indicates the net profit, given the current solution, of one more unit of each variable. For example, C has a profit of $1.50 per unit.

The $C_j - Z_j$ numbers represent the net profit that will result, given our present production mix, if we add one unit of each variable into the solution.

	COLUMN			
	T	C	S_1	S_2
C_j for column	$7	$5	$0	$0
Z_j for column	$7	$\frac{7}{2}$	$\frac{7}{2}$	$0
$C_j - Z_j$ for column	$0	$\frac{3}{2}$	$-\$\frac{7}{2}$	$0

The Z_j and $C_j - Z_j$ rows are inserted into the complete second tableau as shown in Table 9.4.

Interpreting the Second Tableau

Table 9.4 summarizes all of the information for the Flair Furniture Company's production mix decision as of the second iteration of the simplex method. Let's briefly look over a few important items.

We can look at the current solution as a corner point in the graphical method.

Current Solution At this point, the solution point of 50 tables and 0 chairs ($T = 50$, $C = 0$) generates a profit of $350. T is a basic variable; C is a nonbasic variable. Using a graphical LP approach, this corresponds to corner point D, as shown earlier in Figure 9.2.

Resource Information We also see in Table 9.4 that slack variable S_2, representing the amount of unused time in the carpentry department, is in the basis. It has a value of 40, implying that 40 hours of carpentry time remain available. Slack variable S_1 is nonbasic and has a value of 0 hours. There is no slack time in the painting department.

Here is an explanation of the meaning of substitution rates.

Substitution Rates We mentioned earlier that the substitution rates are the coefficients in the heart of the tableau. Look at the C column. If 1 unit of C (1 chair) is added to the current solution, $\frac{1}{2}$ units of T and 1 unit of S_2 must be given up. This is because the solution $T = 50$ tables uses up all 100 hours of time in the painting department. (The original constraint, you may recall, was $2T + 1C + S_1 = 100$.) To capture the 1 painting hour needed to make 1 chair, $\frac{1}{2}$ of a table *less* must be produced. This frees up 1 hour to be used in making 1 chair.

But why must 1 unit of S_2 (i.e., 1 hour of carpentry time) be given up to produce 1 chair? The original constraint was $4T + 3C + S_2 = 240$ hours of carpentry time. Doesn't this indicate that 3 hours of carpentry time are required to produce 1 unit of C? The answer is that we are looking at *marginal* rates of substitution. Adding 1 chair replaced $\frac{1}{2}$ table. Because $\frac{1}{2}$ table required ($\frac{1}{2} \times 4$ hours per table) = 2 hours of carpentry time, 2 units of S_2 are freed. Thus only 1 *more* unit of S_2 is needed to produce 1 chair.

Just to be sure you have this concept down pat, let's look at one more column, S_1, as well. The coefficients are $\begin{pmatrix} \frac{1}{2} \\ -2 \end{pmatrix}$. These substitution rate values mean that if 1 hour of slack painting time is added to the current solution, $\frac{1}{2}$ of a table (T) *less* will be produced. However, note that if 1 unit of S_1 is added into the solution, 2 hours of carpentry time (S_2) will no longer be used. These will be *added* to the current 40 slack hours of carpentry time. Hence, a *negative* substitution rate means that if 1 unit of a column variable is added to the solution, the value of the corresponding solution (or row) variable will be increased. A *positive* substitution rate tells us that if 1 unit of the column variable is added to the solution, the row variable will decrease by the rate.

Can you interpret the rates in the T and S_2 columns now?

The $C_j - Z_j$ row tells us (1) whether the current solution is optimal and (2) if it is not, which variable should enter the solution mix next.

Net Profit Row The $C_j - Z_j$ row is important to us for two reasons. First, it indicates whether the current solution is optimal. When there are no positive numbers in the bottom row, an optimum solution to an LP maximization problem has been reached. In the case of Table 9.4, we see that $C_j - Z_j$ values for T, S_1, and S_2 are 0 or negative. The value for $C\left(\frac{3}{2}\right)$ means that the net profit can be increased by \$1.50 $\left(= \frac{3}{2}\right)$ for each chair added into the current solution.

Because the $C_j - Z_j$ value for T is 0, for every unit of T added the total profit will remain unchanged, because we are already producing as many tables as possible. A negative number, such as the $-\frac{7}{2}$ in the S_1 column, implies that total profit will *decrease* by \$3.50 if 1 unit of S_1 is added to the solution. In other words, making one slack hour available in the painting department ($S_1 = 0$ currently) means that we would have to produce one-half table less. Since each table results in a \$7 contribution, we would be losing $\frac{1}{2} \times \$7 = \$\frac{7}{2}$, for a net loss of \$3.50.

Later in this chapter we discuss in detail the subject of *shadow prices*. These relate to $C_j - Z_j$ values in the slack variable columns. Shadow prices are simply another way of interpreting negative $C_j - Z_j$ values; they may be viewed as the potential increase in profit if one more hour of the scarce resource (such as painting or carpentry time) could be made *available*.

We mentioned previously that there are two reasons to consider the $C_j - Z_j$ row carefully. The second reason, of course, is that we use the row to determine which variable will enter the solution next. Since an optimal solution has not been reached yet, let's proceed to the third simplex tableau.

9.5 DEVELOPING THE THIRD TABLEAU

Since not all numbers in the $C_j - Z_j$ row of the latest tableau are 0 or negative, the previous solution is not optimal, and we must repeat the five simplex steps.

C (chairs) will be the next solution mix variable because it has the only positive value in the $C_j - Z_j$ row.

Step 1. Variable C will enter the solution next by virtue of the fact that its $C_j - Z_j$ value of $\frac{3}{2}$ is the largest (and only) positive number in the row. This means that for every unit of C (chairs) we start to produce, the objective function will increase in value by \$ $\frac{3}{2}$, or \$1.50. The C column is the new pivot column.

Step 2. The next step involves identifying the pivot row. The question is, which variable currently in the solution (T or S_2) will have to leave to make room for C to enter? Again, each number in the quantity column is divided by its corresponding substitution rate in the C column.

$$\text{For the } T \text{ row: } \quad \frac{50}{\frac{1}{2}} = 100 \text{ chairs}$$

$$\text{For the } S_2 \text{ row: } \quad \frac{40}{1} = 40 \text{ chairs}$$

TABLE 9.5

Pivot Row, Pivot Column, and Pivot Number Identified in the Second Simplex Tableau

C_j		$7	$5	$0	$0	
	SOLUTION MIX	T	C	S_1	S_2	QUANTITY
$7	T	1	$\frac{1}{2}$	$\frac{1}{2}$	0	50
$0	S_2	0	①	−2	1	40 ← Pivot row
			Pivot number			
	Z_j	$7	$$\frac{7}{2}$$	$$\frac{7}{2}$$	$0	$350
	$C_j - Z_j$	$0	$$\frac{3}{2}$$	−$$\frac{7}{2}$$	$0	(total profit)
		Pivot column ↑				

We replace the variable S_2 because it is in the pivot row.

These ratios correspond to the values of C (the variable entering the solution mix) at points F and C in Figure 9.2 on page 342. The S_2 row has the smallest ratio, so variable S_2 will leave the basis (and will become a nonbasic variable equal to zero) and will be replaced by C (which will have a value of 40). The new pivot row, pivot column, and pivot number are all shown in Table 9.5.

The pivot row for the third tableau is replaced here.

Step 3. The pivot row is replaced by dividing every number in it by the (circled) pivot number. Since every number is divided by 1, there is no change.

$$\frac{0}{1} = 0 \quad \frac{1}{1} = 1 \quad \frac{-2}{1} = -2 \quad \frac{1}{1} = 1 \quad \frac{40}{1} = 40$$

The entire new C row looks like this:

C_j	SOLUTION MIX	T	C	S_1	S_2	QUANTITY
$5	C	0	1	−2	1	40

It will be placed in the new simplex tableau in the same row position that S_2 was in before (see Table 9.5).

Step 4. The new values for the T row may now be computed

$$\begin{pmatrix} \text{number} \\ \text{in new} \\ T \text{ row} \end{pmatrix} = \begin{pmatrix} \text{number} \\ \text{in old} \\ T \text{ row} \end{pmatrix} - \left[\begin{pmatrix} \text{number} \\ \text{above pivot} \\ \text{number} \end{pmatrix} \times \begin{pmatrix} \text{corresponding} \\ \text{number in new} \\ C \text{ row} \end{pmatrix} \right]$$

The new T row is computed here.

$$
\begin{array}{ccccccc}
1 & = & 1 & - & (\frac{1}{2}) & \times & (0) \\
0 & = & \frac{1}{2} & - & (\frac{1}{2}) & \times & (1) \\
\frac{3}{2} & = & \frac{1}{2} & - & (\frac{1}{2}) & \times & (-2) \\
-\frac{1}{2} & = & 0 & - & (\frac{1}{2}) & \times & (1) \\
30 & = & 50 & - & (\frac{1}{2}) & \times & (40)
\end{array}
$$

Hence, the new T row will appear in the third tableau in the following position:

C_j	SOLUTION MIX	T	C	S_1	S_2	QUANTITY
$7	T	1	0	$\frac{1}{2}$	$-\frac{1}{2}$	30
$5	C	0	1	-2	1	40

The final step is again computing the Z_j and $C_j - Z_j$ values.

Step 5. Finally, the Z_j and $C_j - Z_j$ rows are calculated for the third tableau:

$$Z_j \text{ (for } T \text{ column)} = (\$7)(1) + (\$5)(0) = \$7$$

$$Z_j \text{ (for } C \text{ column)} = (\$7)(0) + (\$5)(1) = \$5$$

$$Z_j \text{ (for } S_1 \text{ column)} = (\$7)(\tfrac{1}{2}) + (\$5)(-2) = \$\tfrac{1}{2}$$

$$Z_j \text{ (for } S_2 \text{ column)} = (\$7)(-\tfrac{1}{2}) + (\$5)(1) = \$\tfrac{3}{2}$$

$$Z_j \text{ (for total profit)} = (\$7)(30) + (\$5)(40) = \$410$$

The net profit per-unit row appears as follows:

	COLUMN			
	T	C	S_1	S_2
C_j for column	$7	$5	$0	$0
Z_j for column	$7	$5	$\frac{1}{2}$	$\frac{3}{2}$
$C_j - Z_j$ for column	$0	$0	$-\frac{1}{2}$	$-\frac{3}{2}$

An optimal solution is reached because all $C_j - Z_j$ values are zero or negative.

All results for the third iteration of the simplex method are summarized in Table 9.6. Note that since every number in the table's $C_j - Z_j$ row is 0 or negative, an optimal solution has been reached.

That solution is

The final solution is to make 30 tables and 40 chairs at a profit of $410. This is the same as the graphical solution presented earlier.

$T = 30$ tables

$C = 40$ chairs

$S_1 = 0$ slack hours in the painting department

$S_2 = 0$ slack hours in the carpentry department

profit = $410 for the optimal solution

TABLE 9.6

Final Simplex Tableau for the Flair Furniture Problem

C_j		$7	$5	$0	$0	
	SOLUTION MIX	T	C	S_1	S_2	QUANTITY
$7	T	1	0	$\frac{1}{2}$	$-\frac{1}{2}$	30
$5	C	0	1	-2	1	40
	Z_j	$7	$5	$\frac{1}{2}$	$\frac{3}{2}$	$410
	$C_j - Z_j$	$0	$0	$-\frac{1}{2}$	$-\frac{3}{2}$	

T and C are the final basic variables, and S_1 and S_2 are nonbasic (and thus automatically equal to 0). This solution corresponds to corner point C in Figure 9.2.

It's always possible to make an arithmetic error when you are going through the numerous simplex steps and iterations, so it is a good idea to verify your final solution. This can be done in part by looking at the original Flair Furniture Company constraints and objective function.

Verifying that the solution does not violate any of the original constraints is a good way to check that no mathematical errors were made.

$$\text{First constraint: } 2T + 1C \leq 100 \text{ painting department hours}$$
$$2(30) + 1(40) \leq 100$$
$$100 \leq 100 \checkmark$$
$$\text{Second constraint: } 4T + 3C \leq 240 \text{ carpentry department hours}$$
$$4(30) + 3(40) \leq 240$$
$$240 \leq 240 \checkmark$$
$$\text{Objective function: profit } = \$7T + \$5C$$
$$= \$7(30) + \$5(40)$$
$$= \$410$$

9.6 REVIEW OF PROCEDURES FOR SOLVING LP MAXIMIZATION PROBLEMS

Before moving on to other issues concerning the simplex method, let's review briefly what we've learned so far for LP maximization problems.

I. Formulate the LP problem's objective function and constraints.

II. Add slack variables to each less-than-or-equal-to constraint and to the problem's objective function.

III. Develop an initial simplex tableau with slack variables in the basis and the decision variables set equal to 0. Compute the Z_j and $C_j - Z_j$ values for this tableau.

IV. Follow these five steps until an optimal solution has been reached:

Here is a review of the five simplex steps.

1. Choose the variable with the greatest positive $C_j - Z_j$ to enter the solution. This is the pivot column.
2. Determine the solution mix variable to be replaced and the pivot row by selecting the row with the smallest (nonnegative) ratio of the quantity-to-pivot column substitution rate. This row is the pivot row.
3. Calculate the new values for the pivot row.
4. Calculate the new values for the other row(s).
5. Calculate the Z_j and $C_j - Z_j$ values for this tableau. If there are any $C_j - Z_j$ numbers greater than 0, return to step 1. If there are no $C_j - Z_j$ numbers that are greater than 0, an optimal solution has been reached.

9.7 SURPLUS AND ARTIFICIAL VARIABLES

To handle $\geq$ and $=$ constraints, the simplex method makes a conversion like it made to $\leq$ constraints.

Up to this point in the chapter, all of the LP constraints you have seen were of the less-than-or-equal-to ($\leq$) variety. Just as common in real-life problems—especially in LP minimization problems—are greater-than-or-equal-to ($\geq$) constraints and equalities. To use the simplex method, each of these must be converted to a special form also. If they are not, the simplex technique is unable to set up an initial solution in the first tableau.

Before moving on to the next section of this chapter, which deals with solving LP minimization problems with the simplex method, we take a look at how to convert a few typical constraints:

Constraint 1: $5X_1 + 10X_2 + 8X_3 \geq 210$
Constraint 2: $25X_1 + 30X_2 \quad\quad = 900$

Surplus Variables

We subtract a surplus variable to form an equality when dealing with a ≥ constraint.

Greater-than-or-equal-to ($\geq$) constraints, such as constraint 1 as just described, require a different approach than do the less-than-or-equal-to ($\leq$) constraints we saw in the Flair Furniture problem. They involve the subtraction of a *surplus variable* rather than the addition of a slack variable. The surplus variable tells us how much the solution exceeds the constraint amount. Because of its analogy to a slack variable, surplus is sometimes simply called *negative slack*. To convert the first constraint, we begin by subtracting a surplus variable, S_1, to create an equality.

Constraint 1 rewritten: $5X_1 + 10X_2 + 8X_3 - S_1 = 210$

If, for example, a solution to an LP problem involving this constraint is $X_1 = 20$, $X_2 = 8$, $X_3 = 5$, the amount of surplus could be computed as follows:

$$5X_1 + 10X_2 + 8X_3 - S_1 = 210$$
$$5(20) + 10(8) + 8(5) - S_1 = 210$$
$$100 + 80 + 40 - S_1 = 210$$
$$-S_1 = 210 - 220$$
$$S_1 = 10 \text{ surplus units}$$

There is one more step, however, in preparing a $\geq$ constraint for the simplex method.

Artificial Variables

There is one small problem in trying to use the first constraint (as it has just been rewritten) in setting up an initial simplex solution. Since all "real" variables such as X_1, X_2, and X_3 are set to 0 in the initial tableau, S_1 takes on a negative value.

$$5(0) + 10(0) + 8(0) - S_1 = 210$$
$$0 - S_1 = 210$$
$$S_1 = -210$$

All variables in LP problems, be they real, slack, or surplus, *must* be nonnegative at all times. If $S_1 = -210$, this important condition is violated.

Artificial variables are needed in ≥ and = constraints.

To resolve the situation, we introduce one last kind of variable, called an *artificial variable*. We simply add the artificial variable, A_1, to the constraint as follows:

Constraint 1 completed: $5X_1 + 10X_2 + 8X_3 - S_1 + A_1 = 210$

Now, not only the X_1, X_2, and X_3 variables may be set to 0 in the initial simplex solution, but the S_1 surplus variable as well. This leaves us with $A_1 = 210$.

Let's turn our attention to constraint 2 for a moment. This constraint is already an equality, so why worry about it? To be included in the initial simplex solution, it turns out, even an equality must have an artificial variable added to it.

Constraint 2 rewritten: $25X_1 + 30X_2 + A_2 = 900$

The reason for inserting an artificial variable into an equality constraint deals with the usual problem of finding an initial LP solution. In a simple constraint such as number 2, it's easy to guess that $X_1 = 0$, $X_2 = 30$ would yield an initial feasible solution. But what if our problem had 10 equality constraints, each containing seven variables? It would be *extremely* difficult to sit down and "eyeball" a set of initial solutions. By adding artificial variables, such as A_2, we can provide an automatic initial solution. In this case, when X_1 and X_2 are set equal to 0, $A_2 = 900$.

Artificial variables have no physical meaning and drop out of the solution mix before the final tableau.

Artificial variables have no meaning in a physical sense and are nothing more than computational tools for generating initial LP solutions. If an artificial variable has a positive (nonzero) value, then the original constraint where this artificial variable was added has not been satisfied. A feasible solution has been found when all artificial variables are equal to zero, indicating all constraints have been met. Before the final simplex solution has been reached, all artificial variables must be gone from the solution mix. This matter is handled through the problem's objective function.

Surplus and Artificial Variables in the Objective Function

Whenever an artificial or surplus variable is added to one of the constraints, it must also be included in the other equations and in the problem's objective function, just as was done for slack variables. Since artificial variables must be forced out of the solution, we can assign a very high C_i cost to each. In minimization problems, variables with *low* costs are the most desirable ones and the first to enter the solution. Variables with *high* costs leave the solution quickly, or never enter it at all. Rather than set an actual dollar figure of $10,000 or $1 million for each artificial variable, however, we simply use the letter $M to represent a very large number.[3] Surplus variables, like slack variables, carry a zero cost. In maximization problems, we use negative M.

To make sure that an artificial variable is forced out before the final solution is reached, it is assigned a very high cost (M).

If a problem had an objective function that read

$$\text{minimize cost} = \$5X_1 + \$9X_2 + \$7X_3$$

and constraints such as the two mentioned previously, the completed objective function and constraints would appear as follows:

$$\text{minimize cost} = \$5X_1 + \$9X_2 + \$7X_3 + \$0S_1 + \$MA_1 + \$MA_2$$

$$\text{subject to:} \quad 5X_1 + 10X_2 + 8X_3 - 1S_1 + 1A_1 + 0A_2 = 210$$

$$25X_1 + 30X_2 + 0X_3 + 0S_1 + 0A_1 + 1A_2 = 900$$

9.8 SOLVING MINIMIZATION PROBLEMS

Now that we have discussed how to deal with objective functions and constraints associated with minimization problems, let's see how to use the simplex method to solve a typical problem.

The Muddy River Chemical Company Example The Muddy River Chemical Corporation must produce exactly 1,000 pounds of a special mixture of phosphate and potassium for a customer. Phosphate costs $5 per pound and potassium costs $6 per pound. No more than 300 pounds of phosphate can be used, and at least 150 pounds of potassium must be used. The problem is to determine the least-cost blend of the two ingredients.

---

[3] A technical point: if an artificial variable is ever used in a *maximization* problem (an occasional event), it is assigned an objective function value of $-\$M$ to force it from the basis.

IN ACTION   Linear Programming Modeling in the Forests of Chile

Faced with a series of challenges in making short-term harvesting decisions, Forestal Arauco, a Chilean forestry firm, turned to professors at the University of Chile for LP modeling help. One of the problems in short-term harvesting of trees is to match demand of products—defined by length and diameter—with the supply of standing timber.

The manual system used at the time by foresters led to a significant amount of waste of timber, where higher diameter logs, suited for export or sawmills, ended up being used for pulp, with a considerable loss in value. An LP model, labeled OPTICORT by the professors, was the logical way to get better schedules.

"The system not only optimized the operational decisions in harvesting, but also changed the way managers looked at the problem," says Professor Andres Weintraub. "The model and its concepts became the natural language to discuss the operations. They had to negotiate the parameters, and the model would do the dirty work. The system had to run in a few minutes to allow discussion and negotiation; that was a critical feature for the success of this tool," he adds.

The LP program took about two years to develop, and the researchers were careful to observe two cardinal rules: (1) The solution approach had to be comfortable and clear to the user, and (2) the system had to provide answers to the user in a fast development, so the user could see quick improvements.

Source: J. Summerour. "Chilean Forestry Firm a 'Model' of Success," *OR/MS Today* (April 1999): 22–23.

Here is the mathematical formulation of the minimization problem for Muddy River Chemical Corp.

This problem may be restated mathematically as

$$\text{minimize cost} = \$5X_1 + \$6X_2$$
$$\text{subject to:} \quad X_1 + X_2 = 1{,}000 \text{ lb}$$
$$X_1 \leq 300 \text{ lb}$$
$$X_2 \geq 150 \text{ lb}$$
$$X_1, X_2 \geq 0$$

where

$$X_1 = \text{number of pounds of phosphate}$$
$$X_2 = \text{number of pounds of potassium}$$

Note that there are three constraints, not counting the nonnegativity constraints; the first is an equality, the second a less-than-or-equal-to, and the third a greater-than-or-equal-to constraint.

Graphical Analysis

Looking at a graphical solution first will help us understand the steps in the simplex method.

To have a better understanding of the problem, a brief graphical analysis may prove useful. There are only two decision variables, X_1 and X_2, so we are able to plot the constraints and feasible region. Because the first constraint, $X_1 + X_2 = 1{,}000$, is an equality, the solution must lie somewhere on the line *ABC* (see Figure 9.3). It must also lie between points *A* and *B* because of the constraint $X_1 \leq 300$. The third constraint, $X_2 \geq 150$, is actually redundant and nonbinding since X_2 will automatically be greater than 150 pounds if the first two constraints are observed. Hence, the feasible region consists of all points on the line segment *AB*. As you recall from Chapter 7, however, an optimal solution will always lie at a corner point of the feasible region (even if the region is only a straight line). The solution must therefore be either at point *A* or point *B*. A quick analysis reveals that the least-cost solution lies at corner *B*, namely $X_1 = 300$ pounds of phosphate, $X_2 = 700$ pounds of potassium. The total cost is $5,700.

FIGURE 9.3

Muddy River Chemical
Corporation's Feasible
Region Graph

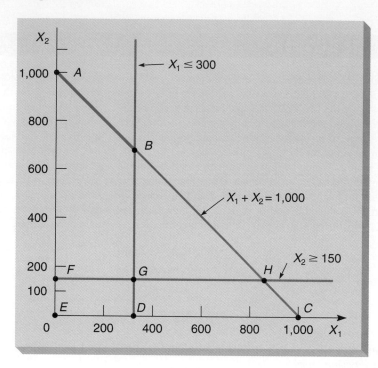

You don't need the simplex method to solve the Muddy River Chemical problem, of course. But we can guarantee you that few problems will be this simple. In general, you can expect to see several variables and many constraints. The purpose of this section is to illustrate the straightforward application of the simplex method to minimization problems. When the simplex procedure is used to solve this, it will methodically move from corner point to corner point until the optimal solution is reached. In Figure 9.3, the simplex method will begin at point E, then move to point F, then to point G, and finally to point B, which is the optimal solution.

Converting the Constraints and Objective Function

First, insert slack, surplus, and artificial variables. This makes it easier to set up the initial simplex tableau in Table 9.7.

The first step is to apply what we learned in the preceding section to convert the constraints and objective function into the proper form for the simplex method. The equality constraint, $X_1 + X_2 = 1,000$, just involves adding an artificial variable, A_1.

$$X_1 + X_2 + A_1 = 1,000$$

The second constraint, $X_1 \leq 300$, requires the insertion of a slack variable—let's call it S_1.

$$X_1 + S_1 = 300$$

The last constraint is $X_2 \geq 150$, which is converted to an equality by subtracting a surplus variable, S_2, and adding an artificial variable, A_2.

$$X_2 - S_2 + A_2 = 150$$

Finally, the objective function, cost $= \$5X_1 + \$6X_2$, is rewritten as

$$\text{minimize cost} = \$5X_1 + \$6X_2 + \$0S_1 + \$0S_2 + \$MA_1 + \$MA_2$$

The complete set of constraints can now be expressed as follows:

$$1X_1 + 1X_2 + 0S_1 + 0S_2 + 1A_1 + 0A_2 = 1,000$$
$$1X_1 + 0X_2 + 1S_1 + 0S_2 + 0A_1 + 0A_2 = 300$$
$$0X_1 + 1X_2 + 0S_1 - 1S_2 + 0A_1 + 1A_2 = 150$$
$$X_1, X_2, S_1, S_2, A_1, A_2 \geq 0$$

Rules of the Simplex Method for Minimization Problems

The minimization simplex rules are slightly different. Now, the new variable to enter the solution mix will be in the column with the negative $C_j - Z_j$ value indicating the greatest improvement.

Minimization problems are quite similar to the maximization problems tackled earlier in this chapter. The significant difference involves the $C_j - Z_j$ row. Our objective is to minimize cost, and a negative $C_j - Z_j$ value indicates that the total cost will decrease if that variable is selected to enter the solution. Thus, the new variable to enter the solution in each tableau (the pivot column variable) will be the one with a negative $C_j - Z_j$ that gives the largest improvement. We choose the variable that decreases costs the most. In minimization problems, an optimal solution is reached when all the numbers in the $C_j - Z_j$ row are 0 or *positive*—just the opposite from the maximization case.[4] All other simplex steps, as seen in the following, remain the same.

Steps for Simplex Minimization Problems

1. Choose the variable with a negative $C_j - Z_j$ that indicates the largest decrease in cost to enter the solution. The corresponding column is the pivot column.
2. Determine the row to be replaced by selecting the one with the smallest (nonnegative) quantity-to-pivot column substitution rate ratio. This is the pivot row.
3. Calculate new values for the pivot row.
4. Calculate new values for the other rows.
5. Calculate the Z_j and $C_j - Z_j$ values for this tableau. If there are any $C_j - Z_j$ numbers less than 0, return to step 1.

First Simplex Tableau for the Muddy River Chemical Corporation Problem

Now we solve Muddy River Chemical Corporation's LP formulation using the simplex method. The initial tableau is set up just as in the earlier maximization example. Its first three rows are shown in the accompanying table. We note the presence of the M costs associated with artificial variables A_1 and A_2, but we treat them as if they were any large

---

[4] We should note that there is a second way to solve minimization problems with the simplex method: It involves a simple mathematical trick. It happens that minimizing the cost objective is the same as *maximizing* the negative of the cost objective function. This means that instead of writing the Muddy River objective function as

$$\text{minimize cost} = 5X_1 + 6X_2$$

we can instead write

$$\text{maximize } (-\text{cost}) = -5X_1 - 6X_2$$

The solution that maximizes $(-\text{cost})$ also minimizes cost. It also means that the same simplex procedure shown earlier for maximization problems can be used if this trick is employed. The only change is that the objective function must be multiplied by (-1).

number. As noted earlier, they have the effect of forcing the artificial variables out of the solution quickly because of their large costs.

C_j	SOLUTION MIX	X_1	X_2	S_1	S_2	A_1	A_2	QUANTITY
$\$M$	A_1	1	1	0	0	1	0	1,000
$\$0$	S_1	1	0	1	0	0	0	300
$\$M$	A_2	0	1	0	-1	0	1	150

The numbers in the Z_j row are computed by multiplying the C_j column on the far left of the tableau times the corresponding numbers in each other column. They are then entered in Table 9.7.

$$Z_j(\text{for } X_1 \text{ column}) = \$M(1) \quad + \$0(1) \quad + M(0) \quad = \$M$$

$$Z_j(\text{for } X_2 \text{ column}) = \$M(1) \quad + \$0(0) \quad + \$M(1) = \$2M$$

$$Z_j(\text{for } S_1 \text{ column}) = \$M(0) \quad + \$0(1) \quad + \$M(0) = \$0$$

$$Z_j(\text{for } S_2 \text{ column}) = \$M(0) \quad + \$0(0) \quad + \$M(-1) = \$-M$$

$$Z_j(\text{for } A_1 \text{ column}) = \$M(1) \quad + \$0(0) \quad + \$M(0) = \$M$$

$$Z_j(\text{for } A_2 \text{ column}) = \$M(0) \quad + \$0(0) \quad + \$M(1) = \$M$$

$$Z_j(\text{for total cost}) = \$M(1,000) + \$0(300) + \$M(150) = \$1,150M$$

The $C_j - Z_j$ entries are determined as follows:

	COLUMN					
	X_1	X_2	S_1	S_2	A_1	A_2
C_j for column	$\$5$	$\$6$	$\$0$	$\$0$	$\$M$	$\$M$
Z_j for column	$\$M$	$\$2M$	$\$0$	$-\$M$	$\$M$	$\$M$
$C_j - Z_j$ for column	$-\$M + \$5$	$-\$2M + \$6$	$\$0$	$\$M$	$\$0$	$\$0$

TABLE 9.7

Initial Simplex Tableau for
the Muddy River Chemical
Corporation Problem

C_j		$\$5$	$\$6$	$\$0$	$\$0$	$\$M$	$\$M$	
	SOLUTION MIX	X_1	X_2	S_1	S_2	A_1	A_2	QUANTITY
$\$M$	A_1	1	1	0	0	1	0	1,000
$\$0$	S_1	1	0	1	0	0	0	300
$\$M$	A_2	0	①	0	-1	0	1	150 ←Pivot row
	Z_j	$\$M$	$\$2M$	0	$-\$M$	$\$M$	$\$M$	$\$1,150M$
	$C_j - Z_j$	$-\$M + 5$	$-\$2M + 6$	$\$0$	$\$M$	$\$0$	0	(total cost)

Pivot number

Pivot column

Here is the initial simplex solution.

This initial solution was obtained by letting each of the variables X_1, X_2, and S_2 assume a value of 0. The current basic variables are $A_1 = 1,000$, $S_1 = 300$, and $A_2 = 150$. This complete solution could be expressed in vector, or column, form as

$$
\begin{bmatrix} X_1 \\ X_2 \\ S_1 \\ S_2 \\ A_1 \\ A_2 \end{bmatrix} = \begin{bmatrix} 0 \\ 0 \\ 300 \\ 0 \\ 1,000 \\ 150 \end{bmatrix}
$$

An extremely high cost, $1,150M from page 354, is associated with this answer. We know that this can be reduced significantly and now move on to the solution procedures.

Developing a Second Tableau

We examine whether the current solution is optimal by looking at the $C_j - Z_j$ row.

In the $C_j - Z_j$ row of Table 9.7, we see that there are two entries with negative values, X_1 and X_2. In the simplex rules for minimization problems, this means that an optimal solution does not yet exist. The pivot column is the one with the *negative* entry in the $C_j - Z_j$ row that indicates the largest improvement—shown in Table 9.7 as the X_2 column, which means that X_2 will enter the solution next.

Which variable will leave the solution to make room for the new variable, X_2? To find out, we divide the elements of the quantity column by the respective pivot column substitution rates.

For the A_1 row $= \dfrac{1,000}{1} = 1,000$

For the S_1 row $= \dfrac{300}{0}$ (this is an undefined ratio, so we ignore it)

A_2 is the pivot row because 150 is the smallest quotient.

For the A_2 row $= \dfrac{150}{1} = 150$ (smallest quotient, indicating pivot row)

Hence, the pivot row is the A_2 row, and the pivot number (circled) is at the intersection of the X_2 column and the A_2 row.

The entering row for the next simplex tableau is found by dividing each element in the pivot row by the pivot number, 1. This leaves the old pivot row unchanged, except that it now represents the solution variable X_2. The other two rows are altered one at a time by again applying the formula shown earlier in step 4.

(new row numbers) = (numbers in old row)

$$
-\left[\left(\frac{\text{number above or below}}{\text{pivot number}} \right) \times \left(\frac{\text{corresponding number}}{\text{in newly replaced row}} \right) \right]
$$

A_1 Row	S_1 Row
$1 = 1 - (1)(0)$	$1 = 1 - (0)(0)$
$0 = 1 - (1)(1)$	$0 = 0 - (0)(1)$
$0 = 0 - (1)(0)$	$1 = 1 - (0)(0)$
$1 = 0 - (1)(-1)$	$0 = 0 - (0)(-1)$
$1 = 1 - (1)(0)$	$0 = 0 - (0)(0)$
$-1 = 0 - (1)(1)$	$0 = 0 - (0)(1)$
$850 = 1,000 - (1)(150)$	$300 = 300 - (0)(150)$

TABLE 9.8		

Second Simplex Tableau for the Muddy River Chemical Corporation Problem

C_j →		$5	$6	$0	$0	$M	$M	
	SOLUTION MIX	X_1	X_2	S_1	S_2	A_1	A_2	QUANTITY
$M	A_1	1	0	0	1	1	−1	850
$0	S_1	①	0	1	0	0	0	300 ← Pivot row
				Pivot number				
$6	X_2	0	1	0	−1	0	1	150
	Z_j	$M	$6	$0	$M − 6	$M	−$M + 6	$850M + $900
	$C_j − Z_j$	−$M + 5	$0	$0	−$M + 6	$0	$2M − 6	
		Pivot column						

The Z_j and $C_j − Z_j$ rows are computed next.

$$Z_j(\text{for } X_1) \quad = \$M(1) \quad + \$0(1) \quad + \$6(0) \quad = \$M$$

$$Z_j(\text{for } X_2) \quad = \$M(0) \quad + \$0(0) \quad + \$6(1) \quad = \$6$$

$$Z_j(\text{for } S_1) \quad = \$M(0) \quad + \$0(1) \quad + \$6(0) \quad = \$0$$

$$Z_j(\text{for } S_2) \quad = \$M(1) \quad + \$0(0) \quad + \$6(-1) \quad = \$M − 6$$

$$Z_j(\text{for } A_1) \quad = \$M(1) \quad + \$0(0) \quad + \$6(0) \quad = \$M$$

$$Z_j(\text{for } A_2) \quad = \$M(-1) \quad + \$0(0) \quad + \$6(1) \quad = −\$M + 6$$

$$Z_j(\text{for total cost}) = \$M(850) \ + \$0(300) \ + \$6(150) = \$850M + 900$$

	COLUMN					
	X_1	X_2	S_1	S_2	A_1	A_2
C_j for column	$5	$6	$0	$0	$M	$M
Z_j for column	$M	$6	$0	$M − 6	$M	−$M + 6
$C_j − Z_j$ for column	−$M + 5	$0	$0	−$M + 6	$0	$2M − 6

All of these computational results are presented in Table 9.8.

The solution after the second tableau is still not optimal.

The solution at the end of the second tableau (point *F* in Figure 9.3) is $A_1 = 850$, $S_1 = 300$, $X_2 = 150$. X_1, S_2, and A_2 are currently the nonbasic variables and have zero value. The cost at this point is still quite high, $850M + 900. This answer is not optimal because not every number in the $C_j − Z_j$ row is zero or positive.

Developing a Third Tableau

The new pivot column is the X_1 column. To determine which variable will leave the basis to make room for X_1, we check the *quantity column–to–pivot column* ratios again.

The third tableau is developed in this section.

$$\text{For the } A_1 \text{ row} = \frac{850}{1} = 850$$

$$\text{For the } S_1 \text{ row} = \frac{300}{1} = 300 \qquad \text{smallest ratio}$$

$$\text{For the } X_2 \text{ row} = \frac{150}{0} = \text{undefined}$$

TABLE 9.9

Third Simplex Tableau for the Muddy River Chemical Corporation Problem

C_j →		$5	$6	$0	$0	$M	$M	
	SOLUTION MIX	X_1	X_2	S_1	S_2	A_1	A_2	QUANTITY
$M	A_1	0	0	−1	①	1	−1	550 ←Pivot row
$5	X_1	1	0	1	0	0	0	300 ↖Pivot number
$6	X_2	0	1	0	−1	0	1	150
	Z_j	$5	$6	−$M + 5	$M − 6	$M	−$M + 6	$550M + 2,400
	$C_j − Z_j$	$0	$0	$M − 5	−$M + 6	$0	$2M − 6	

Pivot column ┘

Hence, variable S_1 will be replaced by X_1.[5] The pivot number, row, and column are labeled in Table 9.8.

To replace the pivot row, we divide each number in the S_1 row by 1 (the circled pivot number), leaving the row unchanged. The new X_1 row is shown in Table 9.9. The other computations for this third simplex tableau follow:

Here are the computations for the third tableau.

A_1 Row	S_1 Row
$0 = 1 − (1)(1)$	$0 = 0 − (0)(1)$
$0 = 0 − (1)(0)$	$1 = 1 − (0)(0)$
$-1 = 0 − (1)(1)$	$0 = 0 − (0)(1)$
$1 = 1 − (1)(0)$	$-1 = -1 − (0)(0)$
$1 = 1 − (1)(0)$	$0 = 0 − (0)(0)$
$-1 = -1 − (1)(0)$	$1 = 1 − (0)(0)$
$550 = 850 − (1)(300)$	$150 = 150 − (0)(300)$

The Z_j and $C_j − Z_j$ rows are computed next.

$$Z_j(\text{for } X_1) = \$M(0) + \$5(1) + \$6(0) = \$5$$
$$Z_j(\text{for } X_2) = \$M(0) + \$5(0) + \$6(1) = \$6$$
$$Z_j(\text{for } S_1) = \$M(-1) + \$5(1) + \$6(0) = -\$M + 5$$
$$Z_j(\text{for } S_2) = \$M(1) + \$5(0) + \$6(-1) = \$M - 6$$
$$Z_j(\text{for } A_1) = \$M(1) + \$5(0) + \$6(0) = \$M$$
$$Z_j(\text{for } A_2) = \$M(-1) + \$5(0) + \$6(1) = -\$M + 6$$
$$Z_j(\text{for total cost}) = \$M(550) + \$5(300) + \$6(150) = \$550M + 2,400$$

	COLUMN					
	X_1	X_2	S_1	S_2	A_1	A_2
C_j for column	$5	$6	$0	$0	$M	$M
Z_j for column	$5	$6	−$M + 5	$M − 6	$M	−$M + 6
$C_j − Z_j$ for column	$0	$0	$M − 5	−$M + 6	$0	$2M − 6

[5] At this point, it might appear to be more cost-effective to replace the A_1 row instead of the S_1 row. This would remove the last artificial variable, and its large M cost, from the basis. The simplex method, however, does not always pick the most direct route to reaching the final solution. You may be assured, though, that it *will* lead us to the correct answer. In Figure 9.3, this would involve moving to point H instead of point G.

The third solution is still not optimal.

The solution at the end of the three iterations (Point G in Figure 9.3) is still not optimal because the S_2 column contains a $C_j - Z_j$ value that is negative. Note that the current total cost is nonetheless lower than at the end of the second tableau, which in turn is lower than the initial solution cost. We are headed in the right direction but have one more tableau to go!

Fourth Tableau for the Muddy River Chemical Corporation Problem

The pivot column is now the S_2 column. The ratios that determine the row and variable to be replaced are computed as follows:

$$\text{For the } A_1 \text{ row: } \frac{550}{1} = 550 \qquad \text{row to be replaced}$$

$$\text{For the } X_1 \text{ row: } \frac{300}{0} \qquad \text{undefined}$$

$$\text{For the } X_2 \text{ row: } \frac{150}{-1} \qquad \text{not considered because it is negative}$$

Here are the computations for the fourth solution.

Each number in the pivot row is divided by the pivot number (again 1, by coincidence). The other two rows are computed as follows and are shown in Table 9.10.

X_1 Row	X_2 Row
$1 = 1 - (0)(0)$	$0 = 0 - (-1)(0)$
$0 = 0 - (0)(0)$	$1 = 1 - (-1)(0)$
$1 = 1 - (0)(-1)$	$-1 = 0 - (-1)(-1)$
$0 = 0 - (0)(1)$	$0 = -1 - (-1)(1)$
$0 = 0 - (0)(1)$	$1 = 0 - (-1)(1)$
$0 = 0 - (0)(-1)$	$0 = 1 - (-1)(-1)$
$300 = 300 - (0)(550)$	$700 = 150 - (-1)(550)$

$$Z_j (\text{for } X_1) \quad = \$0(0) \quad + \$5(1) \quad + \$6(0) \quad = \$5$$

$$Z_j (\text{for } X_2) \quad = \$0(0) \quad + \$5(0) \quad + \$6(1) \quad = \$6$$

$$Z_j (\text{for } S_1) \quad = \$0(-1) \quad + \$5(1) \quad + \$6(-1) \quad = -\$1$$

$$Z_j (\text{for } S_2) \quad = \$0(1) \quad + \$5(0) \quad + \$6(0) \quad = \$0$$

$$Z_j (\text{for } A_1) \quad = \$0(1) \quad + \$5(0) \quad + \$6(1) \quad = \$6$$

$$Z_j (\text{for } A_2) \quad = \$0(-1) \quad + \$5(0) \quad + \$6(0) \quad = \$0$$

$$Z_j (\text{for total cost}) = \$0(550) + \$5(300) + \$6(700) = \$5,700$$

	COLUMN					
	X_1	X_2	S_1	S_2	A_1	A_2
C_j for column	\$5	\$6	\$0	\$0	\$M	\$M
Z_j for column	\$5	\$6	-\$1	\$0	\$6	\$0
$C_j - Z_j$ for column	\$0	\$0	\$1	\$0	\$M - 6	\$M

TABLE 9.10

Fourth and Optimal Solution to the Muddy River Chemical Corporation Problem

C_j		$5	$6	$0	$0	$M	$M	
	SOLUTION MIX	X_1	X_2	S_1	S_2	A_1	A_2	QUANTITY
$0	S_2	0	0	−1	1	1	−1	550
$5	X_1	1	0	1	0	0	0	300
$6	X_2	0	1	−1	0	1	0	700
	Z_j	$5	$6	−$1	$0	$6	$0	$5,700
	$C_j - Z_j$	$0	$0	$1	$0	$M − 6	$M	

The optimal solution has been reached because only positive or zero values appear in the $C_j - Z_j$ row.

On examining the $C_j - Z_j$ row in Table 9.10, only positive or 0 values are found. The fourth tableau therefore contains the optimum solution. That solution is $X_1 = 300$, $X_2 = 700$, $S_2 = 550$. The artificial variables are both equal to 0, as is S_1. Translated into management terms, the chemical company's decision should be to blend 300 pounds of phosphate (X_1) with 700 pounds of potassium (X_2). This provides a surplus (S_2) of 550 pounds of potassium more than required by the constraint $X_2 \geq 150$. The cost of this solution is $5,700. If you look back to Figure 9.3, you can see that this is identical to the answer found by the graphical approach.

Although small problems such as this can be solved graphically, more realistic product blending problems demand use of the simplex method, usually in computerized form.

9.9 REVIEW OF PROCEDURES FOR SOLVING LP MINIMIZATION PROBLEMS

Just as we summarized the steps for solving LP maximization problems with the simplex method in Section 9.6, let us do so for minimization problems here:

I. Formulate the LP problem's objective function and constraints.

II. Include slack variables in each less-than-or-equal-to constraint, artificial variables in each equality constraint, and both surplus and artificial variables in each greater-than-or-equal-to constraint. Then add all of these variables to the problem's objective function.

III. Develop an initial simplex tableau with artificial and slack variables in the basis and the other variables set equal to 0. Compute the Z_j and $C_j - Z_j$ values for this tableau.

IV. Follow these five steps until an optimal solution has been reached:

1. Choose the variable with the negative $C_j - Z_j$ indicating the greatest improvement to enter the solution. This is the pivot column.
2. Determine the row to be replaced by selecting the one with the smallest (nonnegative) quantity-to-pivot column substitution rate ratio. This is the pivot row.
3. Calculate the new values for the pivot row.
4. Calculate the new values for the other row(s).
5. Calculate the Z_j and $C_j - Z_j$ values for the tableau. If there are any $C_j - Z_j$ numbers less than 0, return to step 1. If there are no $C_j - Z_j$ numbers that are less than 0, an optimal solution has been reached.

9.10 SPECIAL CASES

In Chapter 7 we addressed some special cases that may arise when solving LP problems graphically (see Section 8 of Chapter 7). Here we describe these cases again, this time as they refer to the simplex method.

Infeasibility

A situation with no feasible solution may exist if the problem was formulated improperly.

Infeasibility, you may recall, comes about when there is no solution that satisfies all of the problem's constraints. In the simplex method, an infeasible solution is indicated by looking at the final tableau. In it, all $C_j - Z_j$ row entries will be of the proper sign to imply optimality, but an artificial variable (A_1) will still be in the solution mix.

Table 9.11 illustrates the final simplex tableau for a hypothetical minimization type of LP problem. The table provides an example of an improperly formulated problem, probably containing conflicting constraints. No feasible solution is possible because an artificial variable, A_2, remains in the solution mix, even though all $C_j - Z_j$ are positive or 0 (the criterion for an optimal solution in a minimization case).

Unbounded Solutions

No finite solution may exist in problems that are not bounded. This means that a variable can be infinitely large without violating a constraint.

Unboundedness describes linear programs that do not have finite solutions. It occurs in maximization problems, for example, when a solution variable can be made infinitely large without violating a constraint (refer back to Figure 7.13). In the simplex method, the condition of unboundedness will be discovered prior to reaching the final tableau. We will note the problem when trying to decide which variable to remove from the solution mix. As seen earlier in this chapter, the procedure is to divide each quantity column number by the corresponding pivot column number. The row with the smallest positive ratio is replaced. But if all the ratios turn out to be negative or undefined, it indicates that the problem is unbounded.

Table 9.12 illustrates the second tableau calculated for a particular LP maximization problem by the simplex method. It also points to the condition of unboundedness. The solution is not optimal because not all $C_j - Z_j$ entries are 0 or negative, as required in a maximization problem. The next variable to enter the solution should be X_1. To determine which variable will leave the solution, we examine the ratios of the quantity column numbers to their corresponding numbers in the X_1, or pivot, column.

Ratio for the X_2 row: $\dfrac{30}{-1}$

Ratio for the S_2 row: $\dfrac{10}{-2}$

Negative ratios unacceptable

Since both pivot column numbers are negative, an unbounded solution is indicated.

TABLE 9.11

Illustration of Infeasibility

C_j		$5	$8	$0	$0	$M	$M	
	SOLUTION MIX	X_1	X_2	S_1	S_2	A_1	A_2	QUANTITY
$5	X_1	1	0	−2	3	−1	0	200
$8	X_2	0	1	1	2	−2	0	100
$M	A_2	0	0	0	−1	−1	1	20
	Z_j	$5	$8	−$2	$31 − M	−$21 − M	$M	$1,800 + 20M
	$C_j − Z_j$	$0	$0	$2	$M − 31	$2M + 21	$0	

TABLE 9.12

Problem with an Unbounded Solution

C_j	SOLUTION MIX	$6 X_1	$9 X_2	$0 S_1	$0 S_2	QUANTITY
$9	X_2	−1	1	2	0	30
$0	S_2	−2	0	−1	1	10
	Z_j	−$9	$9	$18	$0	$270
	$C_j − Z_j$	$15	$0	−$18	$0	

$\llcorner$ Pivot column

Degeneracy

Degeneracy is another situation that can occur when solving an LP problem using the simplex method. It develops when three constraints pass through a single point. For example, suppose a problem has only these three constraints $X_1 \le 10$, $X_2 \le 10$, and $X_1 + X_2 < 20$. All three constraint lines will pass through the point (10, 10). Degeneracy is first recognized *Tied ratios in the simplex calculations signal degeneracy.* when the ratio calculations are made. If there is a *tie* for the smallest ratio, this is a signal that degeneracy exists. As a result of this, when the next tableau is developed, one of the variables in the solution mix will have a value of zero.

Table 9.13 provides an example of a degenerate problem. At this iteration of the given maximization LP problem, the next variable to enter the solution will be X_1, since it has the only positive $C_j − Z_j$ number. The ratios are computed as follows:

For the X_2 row: $\dfrac{10}{\frac{1}{4}} = 40$

For the S_2 row: $\dfrac{20}{4} = 5$ ⟵ tie for the smallest ratio indicates degeneracy

For the S_3 row: $\dfrac{10}{2} = 5$

Cycling may result from degeneracy. Theoretically, degeneracy could lead to a situation known as *cycling*, in which the simplex algorithm alternates back and forth between the same nonoptimal solutions; that is, it puts a new variable in, then takes it out in the next tableau, puts it back in, and so on. One simple way of dealing with the issue is to select either row (S_2 or S_3 in this case) arbitrarily. If we are unlucky and cycling does occur, we simply go back and select the other row.

TABLE 9.13

Problem Illustrating Degeneracy

C_j	SOLUTION MIX	$5 X_1	$8 X_2	$2 X_3	$0 S_1	$0 S_2	$0 S_3	QUANTITY
$8	X_2	$\frac{1}{4}$	1	1	−2	0	0	10
$0	S_2	4	0	$\frac{1}{3}$	−1	1	0	20
$0	S_3	2	0	2	$\frac{2}{5}$	0	1	10
	Z_j	$2	$8	$8	$16	$0	$0	$80
	$C_j − Z_j$	$3	$0	−$6	−$16	$0	$0	

$\llcorner$ Pivot column

TABLE 9.14	$C_j \rightarrow$	$3	$2	$0	$0	
Problem with Alternate Optimal Solutions	SOLUTION MIX	X_1	X_2	S_1	S_2	QUANTITY
$2	X_2	$3/2$	1	1	0	6
$0	S_2	1	0	$1/2$	1	3
	Z_j	$3	$2	$2	$0	$12
	$C_j - Z_j$	$0	$0	$-$2	$0	

More Than One Optimal Solution

Alternate optimal solutions may exist if the $C_j - Z_j$ value = 0 for a variable not in the solution mix.

Multiple, or alternate, optimal solutions can be spotted when the simplex method is being used by looking at the final tableau. If the $C_j - Z_j$ value is equal to 0 for a variable that is not in the solution mix, more than one optimal solution exists.

Let's take Table 9.14 as an example. Here is the last tableau of a maximization problem; each entry in the $C_j - Z_j$ row is 0 or negative, indicating that an optimal solution has been reached. That solution is read as $X_2 = 6$, $S_2 = 3$, profit = $12. Note, however, that variable X_1 can be brought into the solution mix without increasing or decreasing profit. The new solution, with X_1 in the basis, would become $X_1 = 3$, $X_2 = 3/2$, with profit still at $12. Can you modify Table 9.14 to prove this? You might note, by the way, that this example of an alternate optimal solution corresponds to the graphical solution shown in Figure 7.15.

9.11 SENSITIVITY ANALYSIS WITH THE SIMPLEX TABLEAU

In Chapter 7 we introduce the topic of sensitivity analysis as it applies to LP problems that we have solved graphically. This valuable concept shows how the optimal solution and the value of its objective function change, given changes in various inputs to the problem. Graphical analysis is useful in understanding intuitively and visually how feasible regions and the slopes of objective functions can change as model coefficients change. Computer programs handling LP problems of all sizes provide sensitivity analysis as an important output feature. Those programs use the information provided in the final simplex tableau to compute ranges for the objective function coefficients and ranges for the RHS values. They also provide "shadow prices," a concept that we introduce in this section.

High Note Sound Company Revisited

In Section 7.9 we use the High Note Sound Company to illustrate sensitivity analysis graphically. High Note is a firm that makes compact disk (CD) players (called X_1) and stereo receivers (called X_2). Its LP formulation is repeated here:

$$\text{maximize profit} = \$50X_1 + \$120X_2$$

subject to: $\quad 2X_1 + 4X_2 \leq 80 \quad$ (hours of electricians' time available)
$\quad\quad\quad\quad\quad 3X_1 + 1X_2 \leq 60 \quad$ (hours of audio technicians' time available)

High Note's graphical solution is also repeated, as we see in Figure 9.4.

High Note Sound
Company Graphical
Solution

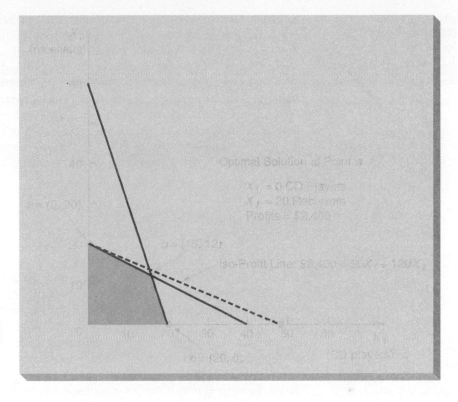

Optimal Solution at Point a

$X_1 = 0$ CD players
$X_2 = 20$ Receivers
Profits = $2,400

iso-Profit Line: $2,400 = 50X_1 + 120X_2$

Changes in the Objective Function Coefficients

In Chapter 7 we saw how to use graphical LP to examine the objective function coefficients. A second way of illustrating the sensitivity analysis of objective function coefficients is to consider the results in a final simplex tableau. For the High Note Sound Company, this tableau was shown in Table 9.15. The optimal solution is seen to be as follows:

$X_2 = 20$ stereo receivers
$S_2 = 40$ hours of slack time of audio technicians
$X_1 = 0$ CD players
$S_1 = 0$ hours of slack time of electricians

Basic variables

Nonbasic variables

Basic variables (those in the solution mix) and *nonbasic variables* (those set equal to 0) must be handled differently using sensitivity analysis. Let us first consider the case of a nonbasic variable.

Optimal Solution by the
Simplex Method

C_j		$50	$120	$0	$0	
	SOLUTION MIX	X_1	X_2	S_1	S_2	QUANTITY
$120	X_2	½	1	¼	0	20
$0	S_2	3⁄2	0	-¼	1	40
	Z_j	$60	$120	$30	$0	$2,400
	$C_j - Z_j$	$10	$0	-$30	$0	

Nonbasic Objective Function Coefficient Our goal here is to find out how sensitive the problem's optimal solution is to changes in the contribution rates of variables not currently in the basis (X_1 and S_1). Just how much would the objective function coefficients have to change before X_1 or S_1 would enter the solution mix and replace one of the basic variables?

The answer lies in the $C_j - Z_j$ row of the final simplex tableau (as in Table 9.15). Since this is a maximization problem, the basis will not change unless the $C_j - Z_j$ value of one of the nonbasic variables becomes positive. That is, the current solution will be optimal as long as all numbers in the bottom row are less than or equal to 0. It will not be optimal if X_1's $C_j - Z_j$ value is positive, or if S_1's $C_j - Z_j$ value is greater than 0. Therefore, the values of C_j for X_1 and S_1 that do not bring about any change in the optimal solution are given by

The solution is optimal as long as all $C_j - Z_j \leq 0$.

$$C_j - Z_j \leq 0$$

This is the same as writing

$$C_j \leq Z_j$$

Since X_1's C_j value is \$50 and its Z_j value is \$60, the current solution is optimal as long as the profit per CD player does not exceed \$60, or correspondingly, does not increase by more than \$10. Similarly, the contribution rate per unit of S_1 (or per hour of electrician's time) may increase from \$0 up to \$30 without changing the current solution mix.

In both cases, when you are maximizing an objective function, you may increase the value of C_j up to the value of Z_j. You may also *decrease* the value of C_j for a nonbasic variable to negative infinity ($-\infty$) without affecting the solution. This range of C_j values is called the *range of insignificance* for nonbasic variables.

The range over which C_j rates for nonbasic variables can vary without causing a change in the optimal solution mix is called the range of insignificance.

$$-\infty \leq C_j (\text{for } X_1) \leq \$60$$
$$-\infty \leq C_j (\text{for } S_1) \leq \$30$$

Basic Objective Function Coefficient Sensitivity analysis on objective function coefficients of variables that are in the basis or solution mix is slightly more complex. We saw that a change in the objective function coefficient for a nonbasic variable affects only the $C_j - Z_j$ value for that variable. But a change in the profit or cost of a basic variable can affect the $C_j - Z_j$ values of *all* nonbasic variables because this C_j is not only in the C_j row but also in the C_j column. This then impacts the Z_j row.

Testing basic variables involves reworking the final simplex tableau.

Let us consider changing the profit contribution of stereo receivers in the High Note Sound Company problem. Currently, the objective function coefficient is \$120. The change in this value can be denoted by the Greek capital letter delta (Δ). We rework the final simplex tableau (first shown in Table 9.15) and see our results in Table 9.16.

Notice the new $C_j - Z_j$ values for nonbasic variables X_1 and S_1. These were determined in exactly the same way as we did earlier in this chapter. But wherever the C_j value for X_2 of \$120 was seen in Table 9.15, a new value of \$120 + Δ is used in Table 9.16.

Once again, we recognize that the current optimal solution will change only if one or more of the $C_j - Z_j$ row values becomes greater than 0. The question is, how may the value of Δ vary so that all $C_j - Z_j$ entries remain negative? To find out, we solve for Δ in each column. From the X_1 column:

$$-10 - \tfrac{1}{2}\Delta \leq 0$$
$$-10 \leq \tfrac{1}{2}\Delta$$
$$-20 \leq \Delta \text{ or } \Delta \geq -20$$

TABLE 9.16

Change in the Profit
Contribution of Stereo
Receivers

C_j →	SOLUTION MIX	$50 X_1	$120 + \Delta$ X_2	$0 S_1	$0 S_2	QUANTITY
$120 + \Delta$	X_2	$\frac{1}{2}$	1	$\frac{1}{4}$	0	20
$0	S_2	$\frac{5}{2}$	0	$-\frac{1}{4}$	1	40
	Z_j	$60 + \frac{1}{2}\Delta$	$120 + \Delta$	$30 + \frac{1}{4}\Delta$	$0	$2,400 + 20\Delta$
	$C_j - Z_j$	$-$10 $-\frac{1}{2}\Delta$	$0	$-$30 $-\frac{1}{4}\Delta$	$0	

This inequality means that the optimal solution will not change unless X_2's profit coefficient decreases by at least $20, which is a change of $\Delta = -$20$. Hence, variable X_1 will not enter the basis unless the profit per stereo receiver drops from $120 to $100 or less. This, interestingly, is exactly what we noticed graphically in Figure 7.17. When the profit per stereo receiver dropped to $80, the optimal solution changed from corner point a to corner point b.

Now we examine the S_1 column:

$$-30 - \tfrac{1}{4}\Delta \leq 0$$

$$-30 \leq \tfrac{1}{4}\Delta$$

$$-120 \leq \Delta \text{ or } \Delta \geq -120$$

This inequality implies that S_1 is less sensitive to change than X_1. S_1 will not enter the basis unless the profit per unit of X_2 drops from $120 all the way down to $0.

Since the first inequality is more binding, we can say that the *range of optimality* for X_2's profit coefficient is

The range of optimality is the range of values over which a basic variable's coefficient can change without causing a change in the optimal solution mix.

$$\$100 \leq C_j (\text{for } X_2) \leq \infty$$

As long as the profit per stereo receiver is greater than or equal to $100, the current production mix of $X_2 = 20$ receivers and $X_1 = 0$ CD players will be optimal.

In analyzing larger problems, we would use this procedure to test for the range of optimality of every real decision variable in the final solution mix. The procedure helps us avoid the time-consuming process of reformulating and resolving the entire LP problem each time a small change occurs. Within the bounds set, changes in profit coefficients would not force a firm to alter its product mix decision or change the number of units produced. Overall profits, of course, will change if a profit coefficient increases or decreases, but such computations are quick and easy to perform.

Changes in Resources or RHS Values

Making changes in the RHS values (the resources of electricians' and audio technicians' time) result in changes in the feasible region and often the optimal solution.

The shadow price is the value of one additional unit of a scarce resource. Shadow pricing provides an important piece of economic information.

Shadow Prices This leads us to the important subject of *shadow prices*. Exactly how much should a firm be willing to pay to make additional resources available? Is one more hour of machine time worth $1 or $5 or $20? Is it worthwhile to pay workers an overtime rate to stay one extra hour each night to increase production output? Valuable management information could be provided if the worth of additional resources were known.

Fortunately, this information is available to us by looking at the final simplex tableau of an LP problem. An important property of the $C_j - Z_j$ row is that the negatives of the numbers in its slack variable (S_i) columns provide us with what we call shadow prices. A *shadow price* is the change in value of the objective function from an increase of one unit of a scarce resource (e.g., by making one more hour of machine time or labor time or other resource available).

The final simplex tableau for the High Note Sound Company problem is repeated as Table 9.17 (it was first shown as Table 9.15). The tableau indicates that the optimal solution is $X_1 = 0$, $X_2 = 20$, $S_1 = 0$, and $S_2 = 40$ and that profit = $2,400. Recall that S_1 represents slack availability of the electricians' resource and S_2 the unused time in the audio technicians' department.

The firm is considering hiring an extra electrician on a part-time basis. Let's say that it will cost $22 per hour in wages and benefits to bring the part-timer on board. Should the firm do this? The answer is yes; the shadow price of the electrician time resource is $30. Thus, the firm will *net* $8 (= $30 − $22) for every hour the new worker helps in the production process.

Should High Note also hire a part-time audio technician at a rate of $14 per hour? The answer is no: The shadow price is $0, implying no increase in the objective function by making more of this second resource available. Why? Because not all of the resource is currently being used—40 hours are still available. It would hardly pay to buy more of the resource.

Right-Hand-Side Ranging Obviously, we can't add an unlimited number of units of resource without eventually violating one of the problem's constraints. When we understand and compute the shadow price for an additional hour of electricians' time ($30), we will want to determine how many hours we can actually use to increase profits. Should the new resource be added 1 hour per week, 2 hours, or 200 hours? In LP terms, this process involves finding the range over which shadow prices will stay valid. *Right-hand-side ranging* tells us the number of hours High Note can add or remove from the electrician department and still have a shadow price of $30.

Ranging is simple in that it resembles the simplex process we used earlier in this chapter to find the minimum ratio for a new variable. The S_1 column and quantity column from Table 9.17 are repeated in the following table; the ratios, both positive and negative, are also shown.

QUANTITY	S_1	RATIO
20	$\frac{1}{4}$	$20 / \left(\frac{1}{4} \right) = 80$
40	$-\frac{1}{4}$	$40 / \left(-\frac{1}{4} \right) = -160$

TABLE 9.17

Final Tableau for the High Note Sound Company

C_j		$50	$120	$0	$50	
	SOLUTION MIX	X_1	X_2	S_1	S_2	QUANTITY
$120 X_2		$\frac{1}{2}$	1	$\frac{1}{4}$	0	20
$0 S_2		$\frac{5}{2}$	0	$-\frac{1}{4}$	1	40
	Z_j	$60	$120	$30	$0	$2,400
	$C_j - Z_j$	−$10	$0	−$30	$0	

Objective function increases by $30 if 1 additional hour of electricians' time is made available

The smallest positive ratio (80 in this example) tells us by how many hours the electricians' time resource can be *reduced* without altering the current solution mix. Hence, we can decrease the RHS resource by as much as 80 hours—basically from the current 80 hours all the way down to 0 hours—without causing a basic variable to be pivoted out of the solution.

The smallest negative ratio (−160) tells us the number of hours that can be added to the resource before the solution mix changes. In this case, we can increase electricians' time by 160 hours, up to 240 (= 80 currently + 160 may be added) hours. We have now established the range of electricians' time over which the shadow price of $30 is valid. That range is from 0 to 240 hours.

The audio technician resource is slightly different in that all 60 hours of time originally available have not been used. (Note that $S_2 = 40$ hours in Table 9.17.) If we apply the ratio test, we see that we can reduce the number of audio technicians' hours by only 40 (the smallest positive ratio = 40/1) before a shortage occurs. But since we are not using all the hours currently available, we can increase them indefinitely without altering the problem's solution. Note that there are no negative substitution rates in the S_2 column, so there are no negative ratios. Hence, the valid range for *this* shadow price would be from 20 (= 60 − 40) hours to an unbounded upper limit.

Changes in the RHS values of constraints may change the optimal quantity values of the solution mix variables.

The substitution rates in the slack variable column can also be used to determine the actual values of the solution mix variables if the right-hand side of a constraint is changed. The following relationship is used to find these values.

New quantity = original quantity + (substitution rate)(change in right hand side)

For example, if 12 more electrician hours were made available, the new values in the quantity column of the simplex tableau are found as follows:

ORIGINAL QUANTITY	S_1	NEW QUANTITY
20	$\frac{1}{4}$	$20 + \left(\frac{1}{4}\right)(12) = 23$
40	$-\frac{1}{4}$	$40 + \left(-\frac{1}{4}\right)(12) = 37$

Thus, if 12 hours are added, $X_2 = 23$ and $S_2 = 37$. All other variables are nonbasic and remain zero. This yields a total profit of $50(0) + 120(23) = \$2,760$, which is an increase of $360 (or the shadow price of $30 per hour for 12 hours of electrician time). A similar analysis with the other constraint and the S_2 column would show that if any additional audio technician hours were added, only the slack for that constraint would increase.

Sensitivity Analysis by Computer

To confirm our calculations of High Note Sound Company's sensitivity analysis, let us turn to Program 9.1, an Excel computer run of the problem. Note that we previously used QM for Windows and Excel to analyze High Note in Chapter 7 when we treated the topic graphically. Program 9.1A repeats the Excel solution and formulation, and Program 9.1B illustrates sensitivity analysis.

PROGRAM 9.1A

Excel Solution to the High Note LP Problem

	A	B	C	D	E	F	G	H
1	**High note sound company**							
2								
3		CD Player	Receivers					
4	**Value**	**0**	**20**					
5				Total				
6	Profit	50	120	2400				
7								
8				Used	Sign	Available		
9	Electrician hours	2	4	80	<=	80		
10	Audio technician hours	3	1	20	<=	60		
11								

Here is the solution: Profit = $2,400.

By selecting Sensitivity, we can produce Program 9.1b.

This formulation is shown in detail as Program 7.6a.

Solver Results

Solver found a solution. All constraints and optimality conditions are satisfied.

Reports
Answer
Sensitivity
Limits

⊙ Keep Solver Solution
○ Restore Original Values

OK   Cancel   Save Scenario...   Help

PROGRAM 9.1B

Excel's Sensitivity Analysis Output for High Note Sound Company

1 **Microsoft Excel 8.0 Sensitivity Report**
2 **Worksheet: [captures.xls]7.8**
3 **Report Created: 8/13/98 10:54:59 AM**

We will use 80 hours of electrician time and 20 hours of audio technician time.

6 Adjustable Cells

Cell	Name	Final Value	Reduced Cost	Objective Coefficient	Allowable Increase	Allowable Decrease
$B$4	Value CD Players	0	-10	50	10	1E+30
$C$4	Value Receivers	20	0	120	1E+30	20

12 Constraints

Cell	Name	Final Value	Shadow Price	Constraint R.H. Side	Allowable Increase	Allowable Decrease
$D$9	Electrician hours Used	80	30	80	160	80
$D$10	Audio technician hours Used	20	0	60	1E+30	40

9.12 THE DUAL

Every LP primal has a dual. The dual provides useful economic information.

Every LP problem has another LP problem associated with it, which is called its *dual*. The first way of stating a linear problem is called the *primal* of the problem; we can view all of the problems formulated thus far as primals. The second way of stating the same problem is called the *dual*. The optimal solutions for the primal and the dual are equivalent, but they are derived through alternative procedures.

The dual contains economic information useful to management, and it may also be easier to solve, in terms of less computation, than the primal problem. Generally, if the LP primal involves maximizing a profit function subject to less-than-or-equal-to resource constraints, the dual will involve minimizing total opportunity costs subject to greater-than-or-equal-to product profit constraints. Formulating the dual problem from a given primal is not terribly complex, and once it is formulated, the solution procedure is exactly the same as for any LP problem.

Let's illustrate the *primal–dual relationship* with the High Note Sound Company data. As you recall, the primal problem is to determine the best production mix of CD players (X_1) and stereo receivers (X_2) to maximize profit.

$$\text{maximize profit} = \$50X_1 + \$120X_2$$

$$\text{subject to:} \quad 2X_1 + 4X_2 \leq 80 \quad \text{(hours of available electrician time)}$$
$$3X_1 + 1X_2 \leq 60 \quad \text{(hours of audio technician time available)}$$

The dual variables represent the potential value of resources.

The dual of this problem has the objective of minimizing the opportunity cost of not using the resources in an optimal manner. Let's call the variables that it will attempt to solve for U_1 and U_2. U_1 represents the potential hourly contribution or worth of electrician time; in other words, the dual value of 1 hour of the electricians' resource. U_2 stands for the imputed worth of the audio technicians' time, or the dual technician resource. Thus, each constraint in the primal problem will have a corresponding variable in the dual problem. Also, each decision variable in the primal problem will have a corresponding constraint in the dual problem.

The RHS quantities of the primal *constraints* become the dual's *objective function* coefficients. The total opportunity cost that is to be minimized will be represented by the function $80U_1 + 60U_2$, namely,

$$\text{minimize opportunity cost} = 80U_1 + 60U_2$$

The corresponding dual constraints are formed from the transpose[6] of the primal constraints coefficients. Note that if the primal constraints are $\leq$, the dual constraints are $\geq$.

$$2U_1 + 3U_2 \geq 50 \longrightarrow \text{Primal profit coefficients}$$
$$4U_1 + 1U_2 \geq 120 \longrightarrow \text{Coefficients from the second primal constraint}$$
$$\longrightarrow \text{Coefficients from the first primal constraint}$$

Let's look at the meaning of these dual constraints. In the first inequality, the RHS constant ($\$50$) is the income from one CD player. The coefficients of U_1 and U_2 are the amounts of each scarce resource (electrician time and audio technician time) that are required to produce a CD player. That is, 2 hours of electricians' time and 3 hours of audio technicians' time are used up in making one CD player. Each CD player produced yields $\$50$ of revenue to High Note Sound Company. This inequality states that the total imputed value or potential worth of the scarce resources needed to produce a CD player must be at least equal to the profit derived from the product. The second constraint makes an analogous statement for the stereo receiver product.

---

[6] For example, the transpose of the set of numbers $\begin{pmatrix} a & b \\ c & d \end{pmatrix}$ is $\begin{pmatrix} a & c \\ b & d \end{pmatrix}$. In the case of the transpose of the primal coefficients $\begin{pmatrix} 2 & 4 \\ 3 & 1 \end{pmatrix}$, the result is $\begin{pmatrix} 2 & 3 \\ 4 & 1 \end{pmatrix}$. Refer to CD Module 5, dealing with matrices and determinants, for a review of the transpose concept.

Dual Formulation Procedures

The mechanics of formulating a dual from the primal problem are summarized in the following list.

These are the five steps for formulating a dual.

Steps to Form a Dual

1. If the primal is a maximization, the dual is a minimization, and vice versa.
2. The RHS values of the primal constraints become the dual's objective function coefficients.
3. The primal objective function coefficients become the RHS values of the dual constraints.
4. The transpose of the primal constraint coefficients become the dual constraint coefficients.
5. Constraint inequality signs are reversed.[7]

Solving the Dual of the High Note Sound Company Problem

The simplex algorithm is applied to solve the preceding dual problem. With appropriate surplus and artificial variables, it can be restated as follows:

$$\text{minimize opportunity cost} = 80U_1 + 60U_2 + 0S_1 + 0S_2 + MA_1 + MA_2$$

$$\text{subject to:} \qquad 2U_1 + 3U_2 - 1S_1 + 1A_1 = 50$$

$$4U_1 + 1U_2 - 1S_2 + 1A_2 = 120$$

The first and second tableaus are shown in Table 9.18. The third tableau, containing the optimal solution of $U_1 = 30$, $U_2 = 0$, $S_1 = 10$, $S_2 = 0$, opportunity cost = \$2,400, appears in Figure 9.5 along with the final tableau of the primal problem.

TABLE 9.18   **First and Second Tableaus of the High Note Dual Problem**

		$C_j \longrightarrow$	80	60	0	0	M	M	
		SOLUTION MIX	U_1	U_2	S_1	S_2	A_1	A_2	QUANTITY
First tableau	M	A_1	2	3	-1	0	1	0	50
	M	A_2	4	1	0	-1	0	1	120
		Z_j	$\$6M$	$\$4M$	$-\$M$	$-\$M$	$\$M$	$\$M$	$\$170M$
		$C_j - Z_j$	$80 - 6M$	$60 - 4M$	M	M	0	0	
Second tableau	$80	U_1	1	$\tfrac{3}{2}$	$-\tfrac{1}{2}$	0	$\tfrac{1}{2}$	0	25
	M	A_2	0	-5	2	-1	-2	1	20
		Z_j	$\$80$	$\$120 - 5M$	$-\$40 + 2M$	$-\$M$	$\$40 - 2M$	$\$M$	$\$2,000 + 20M$
		$C_j - Z_j$	0	$5M - 60$	$-2M + 40$	M	$3M - 40$	0	

---

[7] If the jth primal constraint should be an equality, the ith dual variable is unrestricted in sign. This technical issue is discussed in L. Cooper and D. Steinberg. *Methods and Applications of Linear Programming*. Philadelphia: W. B. Saunders, 1974, p. 170.

FIGURE 9.5   Comparison of the Primal and Dual Optimal Tableaus

Primal's Optimal Solution

$C_j \rightarrow$	Solution Mix	Quantity	$50 X_1	$120 X_2	$0 S_1	$0 S_2
$120	X_2	20	$\frac{1}{2}$	1	$\frac{1}{4}$	0
$0	S_2	40	$\frac{5}{2}$	0	$-\frac{1}{4}$	1
	Z_j	$2,400	60	120	30	0
	$C_j - Z_j$		−10	0	−30	0

Dual's Optimal Solution

$C_j \rightarrow$	Solution Mix	Quantity	80 U_1	60 U_2	0 S_1	0 S_2	M A_1	M A_2
80	U_1	30	1	$\frac{1}{4}$	0	$-\frac{1}{4}$	0	$\frac{1}{2}$
0	S_1	10	0	$-\frac{5}{2}$	1	$-\frac{1}{2}$	−1	$\frac{1}{2}$
	Z_j	$2,400	80	20	0	−20	0	40
	$C_j - Z_j$		0	40	0	20	M	M − 40

The solution to the dual yields shadow prices.

We mentioned earlier that the primal and dual lead to the same solution even though they are formulated differently. How can this be?

It turns out that in the final simplex tableau of a primal problem, the absolute values of the numbers in the $C_j - Z_j$ row under the slack variables represent the solutions to the dual problem, that is, the optimal U_is (see Figure 9.5). In the earlier section on sensitivity analysis we termed these numbers in the columns of the slack variables *shadow prices*. Thus, the solution to the dual problem presents the marginal profits of each additional unit of resource.

It also happens that the absolute value of the $C_j - Z_j$ values of the slack variables in the optimal *dual* solution represent the optimal values of the *primal* X_1 and X_2 variables. The minimum opportunity cost derived in the dual must always equal the maximum profit derived in the primal.

Also note the other relationships between the primal and the dual that are indicated in Figure 9.5 by arrows. Columns A_1 and A_2 in the optimal dual tableau may be ignored because, as you recall, artificial variables have no physical meaning.

9.13　KARMARKAR'S ALGORITHM

The biggest change to take place in the field of LP solution techniques in four decades was the 1984 arrival of an alternative to the simplex algorithm. Developed by Narendra Karmarkar, the new method, called Karmarkar's algorithm, often takes significantly less computer time to solve very large-scale LP problems. [8]

As we saw, the simplex algorithm finds a solution by moving from one adjacent corner point to the next, following the outside edges of the feasible region. In contrast, Karmarkar's method follows a path of points on the *inside* of the feasible region. Karmarkar's method is also unique in its ability to handle an *extremely* large number of constraints and variables, thereby giving LP users the capacity to solve previously unsolvable problems.

Although it is likely that the simplex method will continue to be used for many LP problems, a new generation of LP software built around Karmarkar's algorithm is already becoming popular. Delta Air Lines became the first commercial airline to use the Karmarkar program, called KORBX, which was developed and is sold by AT&T. Delta found that the program streamlined the monthly scheduling of 7,000 pilots who fly more than 400 airplanes to 166 cities worldwide. With increased efficiency in allocating limited resources, Delta saves millions of dollars in crew time and related costs.

SUMMARY

In Chapter 7 we examined the use of graphical methods to solve LP problems that contained only two decision variables. This chapter moves us one giant step further by introducing the simplex method. The simplex method is an iterative procedure for reaching the optimal solution to LP problems of any dimension. It consists of a series of rules that, in effect, algebraically examine corner points in a systematic way. Each step moves us closer to the optimal solution by increasing profit or decreasing cost, while maintaining feasibility.

This chapter explains the procedure for converting less-than-or-equal-to, greater-than-or-equal-to, and equality constraints into the simplex format. These conversions employed the inclusion of slack, surplus, and artificial variables. An initial simplex tableau is developed that portrays the problem's original data formulations. It also contains a row providing profit or cost information and a net evaluation row. The latter, identified as the $C_j - Z_j$ row, is examined in determining whether an optimal solution had yet been reached. It also points out which variable would next enter the solution mix, or basis, if the current solution was nonoptimal.

The simplex method consists of five steps: (1) identifying the pivot column, (2) identifying the pivot row and number, (3) replacing the pivot row, (4) computing new values for each remaining row, and (5) computing the Z_j and $C_j - Z_j$ rows and examining for optimality. Each tableau of this iterative procedure is displayed and explained for a sample maximization and minimization problem.

A few special issues in LP that arise in using the simplex method are also discussed in this chapter. Examples of infeasibility, unbounded solutions, degeneracy, and multiple optimal solutions are presented.

Although large LP problems are seldom, if ever, solved by hand, the purpose of this chapter is to help you gain an understanding of how the simplex method works. Understanding the underlying principles help you to interpret and analyze computerized LP solutions.

Chapter 9 also provides a foundation for another issue: answering questions about the problem after an optimal solution has been found, which is called postoptimality analysis, or sensitivity analysis. Included in this discussion is the analysis of the value of additional resources, called shadow pricing. Finally, the relationship between a primal LP problem and its dual is explored. We illustrate how to derive the dual from a primal and how the solutions to the dual variables are actually the shadow prices.

GLOSSARY

Artificial Variable. A variable that has no meaning in a physical sense but acts as a tool to help generate an initial LP solution.

Basic Feasible Solution. A solution to an LP problem that corresponds to a corner point of the feasible region.

---

[8] For details, see Narendra Karmarkar. "A New Polynomial Time Algorithm for Linear Programming," *Combinatorica* 4, 4 (1984): 373–395, or J. N. Hooker. "Karmarkar's Linear Programming Algorithm," *Interfaces* 16, 4 (July–August 1986): 75–90.

Basis. The set of variables that are in the solution, have positive, nonzero values, and are listed in the solution mix column. They are also called **basic variables**.

$C_j - Z_j$ **Row.** The row containing the net profit or loss that will result from introducing one unit of the variable indicated in that column into the solution.

Current Solution. The basic feasible solution that is the set of variables presently in the solution. It corresponds to a corner point of the feasible region.

Degeneracy. A condition that arises when there is a tie in the values used to determine which variable will enter the solution next. It can lead to cycling back and forth between two nonoptimal solutions.

Infeasibility. The situation in which there is no solution that satisfies all of a problem's constraints.

Iterative Procedure. A process (algorithm) that repeats the same steps over and over.

Nonbasic Variables. Variables not in the solution mix or basis. Nonbasic variables are equal to zero.

Pivot Number. The number at the intersection of the pivot row and pivot column.

Pivot Column. The column with the largest positive number in the $C_j - Z_j$ row of a maximization problem, or the largest negative $C_j - Z_j$ improvement value in a minimization problem. It indicates which variable will enter the solution next.

Pivot Row. The row corresponding to the variable that will leave the basis in order to make room for the variable entering (as indicated by the new pivot column). This is the smallest positive ratio found by dividing the quantity column values by the pivot column values for each row.

Primal–Dual Relationship. Alternative ways of stating an LP problem.

Quantity Column. A column in the simplex tableau that gives the numeric value of each variable in the solution mix column.

Range of Insignificance. The range of values over which a nonbasic variable's coefficient can vary without causing a change in the optimal solution mix.

Range of Optimality. The range of values over which a basic variable's coefficient can change without causing a change in the optimal solution mix.

Right-Hand-Side Ranging. A method used to find the range over which shadow prices remain valid.

Shadow Prices. The coefficients of slack variables in the $C_j - Z_j$ row. They represent the value of one additional unit of a resource.

Simplex Method. A matrix algebra method for solving LP problems.

Simplex Tableau. A table for keeping track of calculations at each iteration of the simplex method.

Slack Variable. A variable added to less-than-or-equal-to constraints in order to create an equality for a simplex method. It represents a quantity of unused resource.

Solution Mix. A column in the simplex tableau that contains all the basic variables in the solution.

Substitution Rates. The coefficients in the central body of each simplex table. They indicate the number of units of each basic variable that must be removed from the solution if a new variable (as represented at any column head) is entered.

Surplus Variable. A variable inserted in a greater-than-or-equal-to constraint to create an equality. It represents the amount of resource usage above the minimum required usage.

Unboundedness. A condition describing LP maximization problems having solutions that can become infinitely large without violating any stated constraints.

Z_j **Row.** The row containing the figures for gross profit or loss given up by adding one unit of a variable into the solution.

KEY EQUATION

(9-1)   (New row numbers) = (numbers in old row)

$$-\left[\left(\frac{\text{number above or below}}{\text{pivot number}}\right) \times \left(\begin{array}{c}\text{corresponding number} \\ \text{in newly replaced row}\end{array}\right)\right]$$

Formula for computing new values for nonpivot rows in the simplex tableau (step 4 of the simplex procedure).

SOLVED PROBLEMS

Solved Problem 9-1

Convert the following constraints and objective function into the proper form for use in the simplex method:

$$\text{minimize cost} = 4X_1 + 1X_2$$

subject to:

$$3X_1 + X_2 = 3$$

$$4X_1 + 3X_2 \geq 6$$

$$X_1 + 2X_2 \leq 3$$

Solution

$$\text{minimize cost} = 4X_1 + 1X_2 + 0S_1 + 0S_2 + MA_1 + MA_2$$

$$
\begin{aligned}
\text{subject to:} \quad & 3X_1 + 1X_2 && + 1A_1 && = 3 \\
& 4X_1 + 3X_2 - 1S_1 && + 1A_2 && = 6 \\
& 1X_1 + 2X_2 && + 1S_2 && = 3
\end{aligned}
$$

Solved Problem 9-2

Solve the following LP problem:

$$\text{maximize profit} = \$9X_1 + \$7X_2$$

$$
\begin{aligned}
\text{subject to:} \quad & 2X_1 + 1X_2 \le 40 \\
& X_1 + 3X_2 \le 30
\end{aligned}
$$

Solution

We begin by adding slack variables and converting inequalities into equalities.

$$\text{maximize profit} = 9X_1 + 7X_2 + 0S_1 + 0S_2$$

$$
\begin{aligned}
\text{subject to:} \quad & 2X_1 + 1X_2 + 1S_1 + 0S_2 = 40 \\
& 1X_1 + 3X_2 + 0S_1 + 1S_2 = 30
\end{aligned}
$$

The initial tableau is then as follows:

C_j		$\$9$	$\$7$	$\$0$	$\$0$	
	SOLUTION MIX	X_1	X_2	S_1	S_2	QUANTITY
$\$0$	S_1	②	1	1	0	40
$\$0$	S_2	1	3	0	1	30
	Z_j	$\$0$	$\$0$	$\$0$	$\$0$	$\$0$
	$C_j - Z_j$	9	7	0	0	

The correct second tableau and third tableau and some of their calculations follow. The optimal solutions, given in the third tableau, are $X_1 = 18$, $X_2 = 4$, $S_1 = 0$, $S_2 = 0$, and profit = $190.

Steps 1 and 2 To go from the first to the second tableau, we note that the pivot column (in the first tableau) is X_1, which has the highest $C_j - Z_j$ value, $9. The pivot row is S_1 since 40/2 is less than 30/1, and the pivot number is 2.

Step 3 The new X_1 row is found by dividing each number in the old S_1 row by the pivot number, namely, 2/2 = 1, 1/2 = 1/2, 1/2 = 1/2, 0/2 = 0, and 40/2 = 20.

Step 4 The new values for the S_2 row are computed as follows:

$$
\begin{pmatrix} \text{number in} \\ \text{new } S_2 \text{ row} \end{pmatrix} = \begin{pmatrix} \text{number in} \\ \text{old } S_2 \text{ row} \end{pmatrix} - \left[\begin{pmatrix} \text{number below} \\ \text{pivot number} \end{pmatrix} \times \begin{pmatrix} \text{corresponding} \\ \text{number in} \\ \text{new } X_1 \text{ row} \end{pmatrix} \right]
$$

$$
\begin{aligned}
0 &= 1 - [(1) \times (1)] \\
\tfrac{5}{2} &= 3 - [(1) \times (\tfrac{1}{2})] \\
-\tfrac{1}{2} &= 0 - [(1) \times (\tfrac{1}{2})] \\
1 &= 1 - [(1) \times (0)] \\
10 &= 30 - [(1) \times (20)]
\end{aligned}
$$

Step 5 The following new Z_j and $C_j - Z_j$ rows are formed:

$$Z_j(\text{for } X_1) = \$9(1) + 0(0) = \$9 \qquad\qquad C_j - Z_j = \$9 - \$9 = 0$$

$$Z_j(\text{for } X_2) = \$9(\tfrac{1}{2}) + 0(\tfrac{5}{2}) = \$\tfrac{9}{2} \qquad\qquad C_j - Z_j = \$7 - \tfrac{9}{2} = \$\tfrac{5}{2}$$

$$Z_j(\text{for } S_1) = \$9(\tfrac{1}{2}) + 0(-\tfrac{1}{2}) = \$\tfrac{9}{2} \qquad\qquad C_j - Z_j = 0 - \tfrac{9}{2} = -\$\tfrac{9}{2}$$

$$Z_j(\text{for } S_2) = \$9(0) + 0(1) = \$0 \qquad\qquad C_j - Z_j = 0 - 0 = 0$$

$$Z_j(\text{profit}) = \$9(20) + 0(10) = \$180$$

C_j		$\$9$	$\$7$	$\$0$	$\$0$	
	SOLUTION MIX	X_1	X_2	S_1	S_2	QUANTITY
$\$9$	X_1	1	$\tfrac{1}{2}$	$\tfrac{1}{2}$	0	20
0	S_2	0	$\tfrac{5}{2}$	$-\tfrac{1}{2}$	1	10 ⟵ Pivot row
	Z_j	$\$9$	$\$\tfrac{9}{2}$	$\$\tfrac{9}{2}$	$\$0$	$\$180$
	$C_j - Z_j$	0	$\tfrac{5}{2}$	$-\tfrac{9}{2}$	0	

Pivot column (under X_2)

The solution above is not optimal, and you must perform steps 1 to 5 again. The new pivot column is X_2, the new pivot row is S_2, and $\tfrac{5}{2}$ (circled in the second tableau) is the new pivot number.

C_j		$\$9$	$\$7$	$\$0$	$\$0$	
	SOLUTION MIX	X_1	X_2	S_1	S_2	QUANTITY
$\$9$	X_1	1	0	$\tfrac{3}{5}$	$-\tfrac{1}{5}$	18
7	X_2	0	1	$-\tfrac{1}{5}$	$\tfrac{2}{5}$	4
	Z_j	$\$9$	$\$7$	$\$4$	$\$1$	$\$190$
	$C_j - Z_j$	0	0	-4	-1	

The final solution is $X_1 = 18$, $X_2 = 4$, profit = $\$190$.

Solved Problem 9-3

Use the final simplex tableau in Solved Problem 9-2 to answer the following questions.

a. What are the shadow prices for the two constraints?
b. Perform RHS ranging for constraint 1.
c. If the right-hand side of constraint 1 were increased by 10, what would the maximum possible profit be? Give the values for all the variables.
d. Find the range of optimality for the profit on X_1.

Solution

a. Shadow price $= -(C_j - Z_j)$
   For constraint 1, shadow price $= -(-4) = 4$.
   For constraint 2, shadow price $= -(-1) = 1$.
b. For constraint 1, we use the S_1 column.

QUANTITY	S_1	RATIO
18	$\tfrac{3}{5}$	$18/\left(\tfrac{3}{5}\right) = 30$
4	$-\tfrac{1}{5}$	$4/\left(-\tfrac{1}{5}\right) = -20$

The smallest positive ratio is 30, so we may reduce the right-hand side of constraint 1 by 30 units (for a lower bound of $40 - 30 = 10$). Similarly, the negative ratio of -20 tells us that we may increase the right-hand side of constraint 1 by 20 units (for an upper bound of $40 + 20 = 60$).

c. The maximum possible profit = original profit + 10(shadow price)

$$= 190 + 10(4) = 230$$

The values for the basic variables are found using the original quantities and the substitution rates.

ORIGINAL QUANTITY	S_1	NEW QUANTITY
18	$\tfrac{3}{5}$	$18 + \left(\tfrac{3}{5}\right)(10) = 24$
4	$-\tfrac{1}{5}$	$4 + \left(-\tfrac{1}{5}\right)(10) = 2$

$X_1 = 24$, $X_2 = 2$, $S_1 = 0$, $S_2 = 0$ (both slack variables remain nonbasic variables)

profit $= 9(24) + 7(2) = 230$ (which was also found using the shadow price)

d. Let Δ = change in profit for X_1.

C_j →		$9 + \Delta$	7	0	0	
	SOLUTION MIX	X_1	X_2	S_1	S_2	QUANTITY
$9 + \Delta$	X_1	1	0	$\tfrac{3}{5}$	$-\tfrac{1}{5}$	18
7	X_2	0	1	$-\tfrac{1}{5}$	$\tfrac{2}{5}$	4
	Z_j	$9 + \Delta$	7	$4 + \left(\tfrac{3}{5}\right)\Delta$	$1 - \left(\tfrac{1}{5}\right)\Delta$	$190 + 18\Delta$
	$C_j - Z_j$	0	0	$-4 - \left(\tfrac{3}{5}\right)\Delta$	$-1 + \left(\tfrac{1}{5}\right)\Delta$	

For this solution to remain optimal, the $C_j - Z_j$ values must remain negative or zero.

$$-4 - \left(\tfrac{3}{5}\right)\Delta \leq 0$$

$$-4 \leq \left(\tfrac{3}{5}\right)\Delta$$

$$-20/3 \leq \Delta$$

and

$$-1 + \left(\tfrac{1}{5}\right)\Delta \leq 0$$

$$\left(\tfrac{1}{5}\right)\Delta \leq 1$$

$$\Delta \leq 5$$

So the change in profit (Δ) must be between $-20/3$ and 5. The original profit was 9, so this solution remains optimal as long as the profit on X_1 is between $2.33 = 9 - 20/3$ and $14 = 9 + 5$.

Solved Problem 9-4

Solve the following LP problem using Excel and answer the questions regarding a firm that manufactures both lawn mowers and snowblowers:

$$\text{maximize profit} = \$30 \text{ mowers} + \$80 \text{ blowers}$$

subject to:
$$2 \text{ mowers} + 4 \text{ blowers} \leq 1,000 \text{ labor hours available}$$
$$6 \text{ mowers} + 2 \text{ blowers} \leq 1,200 \text{ lb of steel available}$$
$$1 \text{ blower} \leq 200 \text{ snowblower engines available}$$

a. What is the best product mix? What is the optimal profit?
b. What are the shadow prices? When the optimal solution has been reached, which resource has the highest marginal value?
c. Over what range in each of the RHS values are these shadows valid?
d. What are the ranges over which the objective function coefficients can vary for each of the two decision variables?
e. State the dual to this problem. What is its solution?

Solution

a. The best product mix is 100 lawn mowers and 200 snowblowers, yielding a profit of $19,000. This is found by formulating the model in Program 9.2A and solving using Excel's Solver in Program 9.2B.
b. The shadow prices are seen in Program 9.2C. Each constraint has one shadow price associated with it. For labor, the value of one additional hour over the existing 1,000 is $15. There is zero value to an additional pound of steel since the row 3 slack variable currently has a value of 200 pounds. In other words, with 200 unused pounds of steel, there is no point in paying for addi-

---

PROGRAM 9.2A

Excel Formulation for Solved Problem 9-4

PROGRAM 9.2B

Excel Solution to Solved Problem 9-4

	A	B	C	D	E	F	G	H
1	**Manufacturing Example**							
2								
3		mower	blower					
4	**variable->**	100	200					
5				Total profit				
6	profit	30	80	19000				
7								
8				used		available		
9	labor hours	2	4	1000	<	1000		
10	steel (lbs)	6	2	1000	<	1200		
11	snowblower engines		1	200	<	200		

Produce 100 mowers and 200 blowers for a total profit of 19,000.

Select the Answer and Sensitivity Reports.

Solver Results

Solver found a solution. All constraints and optimality conditions are satisfied.

Reports
Answer
Sensitivity
Limits

- Keep Solver Solution
- Restore Original Values

OK   Cancel   Save Scenario...   Help

tional steel. Finally, there is a value of $20 for each additional snowblower engine made available. So snowblower engines have the highest marginal value at the optimal solution.

c. The shadow price of labor hours is valid from 800 hours to 1,066.66 hours; that is, it can increase by 66 ⅔ (or 67) hours or decrease by as much as 200 hours. The shadow price for pounds of steel is valid from 1,000 pounds up to an infinite number of pounds. The shadow price for snowblower engines ranges from 180 engines up to 250 engines.

d. Without changing the current solution mix, the profit coefficient for the mowers can range from $0 to $40, and the coefficient for the blowers can range from $60 to infinity.

PROGRAM 9.2C

Excel Sensitivity Analysis for Solved Problem 9-4

	A	B	C	D	E	F	G	H	I
1	Microsoft Excel 8.0 Sensitivity Report								
2	Worksheet: [captures.xls]9.2								
3	Report Created: 9/8/98 1:24:23 PM								
4									
5									
6	Adjustable Cells								
7				Final	Reduced	Objective	Allowable	Allowable	
8		Cell	Name	Value	Cost	Coefficient	Increase	Decrease	
9		$B$4	variable-> mower	100	0	30	10	30	
10		$C$4	variable-> blower	200	0	80	1E+30	20	
11									
12	Constraints								
13				Final	Shadow	Constraint	Allowable	Allowable	
14		Cell	Name	Value	Price	R.H. Side	Increase	Decrease	
15		$D$9	labor hours used	1000	15	1000	66.66666667	200	
16		$D$10	steel (lbs) used	1000	0	1200	1E+30	200	
17		$D$11	snowblower engines used	200	20	200	50	20	

The number of blowers and mowers should remain the same even if the per-unit profit on mowers rises by up to 10 or falls by up to 30.

Each additional labor hour would yield an additional $15 in profit for up to 66.67 more units.

e. The dual can be written as

$$\text{minimize } 1,000U_1 + 1,200U_2 + 200U_3$$

$$\text{subject to:} \quad 2U_1 + \quad 6U_2 + \quad 0U_3 \geq 30$$

$$4U_1 + \quad 2U_2 + \quad 1U_3 \geq 80$$

The solution to the dual will be the shadow prices in the primal. So $U_1 = 15$, $U_2 = 0$, and $U_3 = 20$. The dual solution provides the marginal profits of each additional unit of resource.

⇒ SELF-TEST

■ Before taking the self-test, refer back to the learning objectives at the beginning of the chapter, the notes in the margins, and the glossary at the end of the chapter.

■ Use the key at the back of the book to correct your answers.

■ Restudy pages that correspond to any questions that you answered incorrectly or material you feel uncertain about.

1. A basic feasible solution is a solution to an LP problem that corresponds to a corner point of the feasible region.
   a. True
   b. False

2. In preparing a $\geq$ constraint for an initial simplex tableau, we would
   a. add a slack variable.
   b. add a surplus variable.
   c. subtract an artificial variable.
   d. subtract a surplus variable and add an artificial variable.

3. In the initial simplex tableau, the solution mix variables can be
   a. only slack variables.
   b. slack and surplus variables.
   c. artificial and surplus variables.
   d. slack and artificial variables.

4. Even if an LP problem involves many variables, an optimal solution will always be found at a corner point of the n-dimensional polyhedron forming the feasible region.
   a. True
   b. False

5. Which of the following in a simplex tableau indicates that an optimal solution for a maximization problem has been found?
   a. all the $C_j - Z_j$ values are negative or zero
   b. all the $C_j - Z_j$ values are positive or zero
   c. all the substitution rates in the pivot column are negative or zero
   d. there are no more slack variables in the solution mix

6. To formulate a problem for solution by the simplex method, we must add slack variables to
   a. all inequality constraints.
   b. only equality constraints.
   c. only "greater than" constraints.
   d. only "less than" constraints.

7. If in the optimal tableau of an LP problem an artificial variable is present in the solution mix, this implies
   a. infeasibility.
   b. unboundedness.
   c. degeneracy.
   d. alternate optimal solutions.

8. If in the final optimal simplex tableau the $C_j - Z_j$ value for a nonbasic variable is zero, this implies
   a. feasibility.
   b. unboundedness.
   c. degeneracy.
   d. alternate optimal solutions.

9. In a simplex tableau, all of the substitution rates in the pivot column are negative. This indicates
   a. there is no feasible solution to this problem.
   b. the solution is unbounded.

   c. there is more than one optimal solution.
   d. the solution is degenerate.

10. The pivot column in a maximization problem is the column with
    a. the greatest positive $C_j - Z_j$.
    b. the greatest negative $C_j - Z_j$.
    c. the greatest positive Z_j.
    d. the greatest negative Z_j.

11. A change in the objective function coefficient (C_j) for a basic variable can affect
    a. the $C_j - Z_j$ values of all the nonbasic variables.
    b. the $C_j - Z_j$ values of all the basic variables.
    c. only the $C_j - Z_j$ value of that variable.
    d. the C_j values of other basic variables.

12. Linear programming has few applications in the real world due to the assumption of certainty in the data and relationships of a problem.
    a. True
    b. False

13. In a simplex tableau, one variable will leave the basis and be replaced by another variable. The leaving variable is
    a. the basic variable with the largest C_j.
    b. the basic variable with the smallest C_j.
    c. the basic variable in the pivot row.
    d. the basic variable in the pivot column.

14. Which of the following must equal 0?
    a. basic variables
    b. solution mix variables
    c. nonbasic variables
    d. objective function coefficients for artificial variables

15. The shadow price for a constraint
    a. is the value of an additional unit of that resource.
    b. is always equal to zero if there is positive slack for that constraint.
    c. is found from the $C_j - Z_j$ value in the slack variable column.
    d. all of the above.

16. The solution to the dual LP problem
    a. presents the marginal profits of each additional unit of resource.
    b. can always be derived by examining the Z_j row of the primal's optimal simplex tableau.
    c. is better than the solution to the primal.
    d. all of the above.

17. The number of constraints in a dual problem will equal the number of
    a. constraints in the primal problem.
    b. variables in the primal problem.
    c. variables plus the number of constraints in the primal problem.
    d. variables in the dual problem.

DISCUSSION QUESTIONS AND PROBLEMS

Discussion Questions

9-1 Explain the purpose and procedures of the simplex method.

9-2 How do the graphical and simplex methods of solving LP problems differ? In what ways are they the same? Under what circumstances would you prefer to use the graphical approach?

9-3 What are slack, surplus, and artificial variables? When is each used, and why? What value does each carry in the objective function?

9-4 You have just formulated an LP problem with 12 decision variables and eight constraints. How many basic variables will there always be? What is the difference between a basic and a nonbasic variable?

9-5 What are the simplex rules for selecting the pivot column? The pivot row? The pivot number?

9-6 How do maximization and minimization problems differ when applying the simplex method?

9-7 Explain what the Z_j value indicates in the simplex tableau.

9-8 Explain what the $C_j - Z_j$ value indicates in the simplex tableau.

9-9 What is the reason behind the use of the minimum ratio test in selecting the pivot row? What might happen without it?

9-10 A particular LP problem has the following objective function:

$$\text{maximize profit} = \$8X_1 + \$6X_2 + \$12X_3 - \$2X_4$$

Which variable should enter at the second simplex tableau? If the objective function were

$$\text{minimize cost} = \$2.5X_1 + \$2.9X_2 + \$4.0X_3 + \$7.9X_4$$

which variable would be the best candidate to enter the second tableau?

9-11 What happens if an artificial variable is in the final optimal solution? What should the manager who formulated the LP problem do?

9-12 The great Romanian operations researcher, Dr. Ima Student, proposes that instead of selecting the variable with the largest positive $C_j - Z_j$ value (in a maximization LP problem) to enter the solution mix next, a different approach be used. She suggests that any variable with a positive $C_j - Z_j$ can be chosen, even if it isn't the largest. What will happen if we adopt this new rule for the simplex procedure? Will an optimal solution still be reached?

9-13 What is a shadow price? How does the concept relate to the dual of an LP problem? How does it relate to the primal?

9-14 If a primal problem has 12 constraints and eight variables, how many constraints and variables will its corresponding dual have?

9-15 Explain the relationship between each number in a primal and corresponding numbers in the dual.

9-16 Create your own original LP maximization problem with two variables and three less-than-or-equal-to constraints. Now form the dual for this primal problem.

Problems*

• **9-17** The first constraint in the High Note example in this chapter is

$$2X_1 + 4X_2 \leq 80 \text{ (hours of electrician time available)}$$

Table 9.17 gives the final simplex tableau for this example on page 366. From the tableau, it was determined that the maximum increase in electrician hours was 160 (for a total of 240 hours).

(a) Change the right-hand side of that constraint to 240 and graph the new feasible region.
(b) Find the new optimal corner point. How much did the profit increase as a result of this?
(c) What is the shadow price?
(d) Increase the electrician hours available by one unit more (to 241) and find the optimal solution. How much did the profit increase as a result of this one extra hour? Explain why the shadow price from the simplex tableau is no longer relevant.

• **9-18** The Dreskin Development Company is building two apartment complexes. It must decide how many units to construct in each complex subject to labor and material constraints. The profit generated for each apartment in the first complex is estimated at $900, for each apartment in the second complex, $1,500. A partial initial simplex tableau for Dreskin is given in the following table:

C_j		$900	$1,500	$0	$0	
	SOLUTION MIX	X_1	X_2	S_1	S_2	QUANTITY
		14	4	1	0	3,360
		10	12	0	1	9,600
	Z_j					
	$C_j - Z_j$					

(a) Complete the initial tableau.
(b) Reconstruct the problem's original constraints (excluding slack variables).

---

* Note: ♒ means the problem may be solved with QM for Windows; ✖ means the problem may be solved with Excel; and ♒✖ means the problem may be solved with QM for Windows and/or Excel.

(c) Write the problem's original objective function.

(d) What is the basis for the initial solution?

(e) Which variable should enter the solution at the next iteration?

(f) Which variable will leave the solution at the next iteration?

(g) How many units of the variable entering the solution next will be in the basis in the second tableau?

(h) How much will profit increase in the next solution?

9-19 Consider the following LP problem:

maximize earnings $= \$0.80X_1 + \$0.40X_2 + \$1.20X_3 - \$0.10X_4$

subject to: $X_1 + 2X_2 + X_3 + 5X_4 \leq 150$

$$X_2 - 4X_3 + 8X_4 = 70$$

$$6X_1 + 7X_2 + 2X_3 - X_4 \geq 120$$

$$X_1, X_2, X_3, X_4 \geq 0$$

(a) Convert these constraints to equalities by adding the appropriate slack, surplus, or artificial variables. Also, add the new variables into the problem's objective function.

(b) Set up the complete initial simplex tableau for this problem. Do not attempt to solve.

(c) Give the values for all variables in this initial solution.

9-20 Solve the following LP problem graphically. Then set up a simplex tableau and solve the problem using the simplex method. Indicate the corner points generated at each iteration by the simplex method on your graph.

maximize profit $= \$3X_1 + \$5X_2$

subject to: $X_2 \leq 6$

$$3X_1 + 2X_2 \leq 18$$

$$X_1, X_2 \geq 0$$

9-21 Consider the following LP problem:

maximize $10X_1 + 8X_2$

subject to: $4X_1 + 2X_2 \leq 80$

$$X_1 + 2X_2 \leq 50$$

$$X_1, X_2 \geq 0$$

(a) Solve this problem graphically.

(b) Set up the initial simplex tableau. On the graph, identify the corner point represented by this tableau.

(c) Select the pivot column. Which variable is the entering variable?

(d) Compute the ratio of the quantity-to-pivot column substitution rate for each row. Identify the points on the graph related to these ratios.

(e) How many units of the entering variable will be brought into the solution in the second tableau? What would happen if the largest ratio rather than the smallest ratio were selected to determine this (see the graph)?

(f) Which variable is the leaving variable? What will the value of this variable be in the next tableau?

(g) Finish solving this problem using the simplex algorithm.

(h) The solution in each simplex tableau is a corner point on the graph. Identify the corner point associated with each tableau.

9-22 Solve the following LP problem first graphically and then by the simplex algorithm:

minimize cost $= 4X_1 + 5X_2$

subject to: $X_1 + 2X_2 \geq 80$

$$3X_1 + X_2 \geq 75$$

$$X_1, X_2 \geq 0$$

What are the values of the basic variables at each iteration? Which are the nonbasic variables at each iteration?

9-23 The final simplex tableau for an LP maximization problem is shown in the table at the bottom of this page. Describe the situation encountered here.

9-24 Solve the following problem by the simplex method. What condition exists that prevents you from reaching an optimal solution?

maximize profit $= 6X_1 + 3X_2$

subject to: $2X_1 - 2X_2 \leq 2$

$$-X_1 + X_2 \leq 1$$

$$X_1, X_2 \geq 0$$

Tableau for Problem 9-23

C_j		3	5	0	0	$-M$	
	SOLUTION MIX	X_1	X_2	S_1	S_2	A_1	QUANTITY
$\$5$	X_2	1	1	2	0	0	6
$-M$	A_1	-1	0	-2	-1	1	2
	Z_j	$\$5 + M$	$\$5$	$\$10 + 2M$	$\$M$	$-\$M$	$\$30 - 2M$
	$C_j - Z_j$	$-2 - M$	0	$-10 - 2M$	$-M$	0	

9-25 Consider the following financial problem:

$$\text{maximize return on investment} = \$2X_1 + \$3X_2$$

$$\text{subject to:} \quad 6X_1 + 9X_2 \leq 18$$

$$9X_1 + 3X_2 \geq 9$$

$$X_1, X_2 \geq 0$$

(a) Find the optimal solution using the simplex method.
(b) What evidence indicates that an alternate optimal solution exists?
(c) Find the alternate optimal solution.
(d) Solve this problem graphically as well, and illustrate the alternate optimal corner points.

9-26 At the third iteration of a particular LP maximization problem, the tableau at the bottom of this page is established:

What special condition exists as you improve the profit and move to the next iteration? Proceed to solve the problem for the optimal solution.

9-27 A pharmaceutical firm is about to begin production of three new drugs. An objective function designed to minimize ingredient costs and three production constraints are as follows:

$$\text{minimize cost} = 50X_1 + 10X_2 + 75X_3$$

$$\text{subject to:} \quad X_1 - X_2 \qquad = 1,000$$

$$2X_2 + 2X_3 = 2,000$$

$$X_1 \qquad \leq 1,500$$

$$X_1, X_2, X_3 \geq 0$$

(a) Convert these constraints and objective function to the proper form for use in the simplex tableau.
(b) Solve the problem by the simplex method. What is the optimal solution and cost?

9-28 The Bitz-Karan Corporation faces a blending decision in developing a new cat food called Yum-Mix. Two basic ingredients have been combined and tested, and the firm has determined that to each can of Yum-Mix at least 30 units of protein and at least 80 units of riboflavin must be added. These two nutrients are available in two competing brands of animal food supplements. The cost per kilogram of the brand A supplement is $9, and the cost per kilogram of brand B supplement is $15. A kilogram of brand A added to each production batch of Yum-Mix provides a supplement of 1 unit of protein and 1 unit of riboflavin to each can. A kilogram of brand B provides 2 units of protein and 4 units of riboflavin in each can. Bitz-Karan must satisfy these minimum nutrient standards while keeping costs of supplements to a minimum.

(a) Formulate this problem to find the best combination of the two supplements to meet the minimum requirements at the least cost.
(b) Solve for the optimal solution by the simplex method.

9-29 The Roniger Company produces two products: bed mattresses and box springs. A prior contract requires that the firm produce at least 30 mattresses or box springs, in any combination. In addition, union labor agreements demand that stitching machines be kept running at least 40 hours per week, which is one production period. Each box spring takes 2 hours of stitching time, and each mattress takes 1 hour on the machine. Each mattress produced costs $20; each box spring costs $24.

(a) Formulate this problem so as to minimize total production costs.
(b) Solve using the simplex method.

9-30 Each coffee table produced by Meising Designers nets the firm a profit of $9. Each bookcase yields a $12 profit. Meising's firm is small, and its resources are limited. During any given production period of one week, 10 gallons of varnish and 12 lengths of high-quality redwood are available. Each coffee table requires approximately 1 gallon of varnish and 1 length of redwood. Each bookcase takes 1 gallon of varnish and 2 lengths of wood. Formulate Meising's production mix decision as an LP problem, and solve using the simplex method. How many tables and bookcases should be produced each week? What will the maximum profit be?

9-31 Bagwell Distributors packages and distributes industrial supplies. A standard shipment can be packaged in a class A container, a class K container,

Tableau for Problem 9-26

C_j		$\$6$	$\$3$	$\$5$	0	0	0	
	SOLUTION MIX	X_1	X_2	X_3	S_1	S_2	S_3	QUANTITY
$\$5$	X_3	0	1	1	1	0	3	5
$\$6$	X_1	1	−3	0	0	0	1	12
$\$0$	S_2	0	2	0	1	1	−1	10
	Z_j	$\$6$	−$\$13$	$\$5$	$\$5$	$\$0$	$\$21$	$\$97$
	$C_j - Z_j$	$\$0$	$\$16$	$\$0$	−$\$5$	$\$0$	−$\$21$	

or a class T container. A single class A container yields a profit of $8; a class K container, a profit of $6; and a class T container, a profit of $14. Each shipment prepared requires a certain amount of packing material and a certain amount of time, as seen in the following table:

CLASS OF CONTAINER	PACKING MATERIAL (POUNDS)	PACKING TIME (HOURS)
A	2	2
K	1	6
T	3	4
Total amount of resource available each week	120 pounds	240 hours

Bill Bagwell, head of the firm, must decide the optimal number of each class of container to pack each week. He is bound by the previously mentioned resource restrictions, but he also decides that he must keep his six full-time packers employed all 240 hours (6 workers, 40 hours) each week. Formulate and solve this problem using the simplex method.

9-32 The Foggy Bottom Development Corporation has just purchased a small hotel for conversion to condominium apartments. The building, in a popular area of Washington, DC, near the U.S. State Department, will be highly marketable, and each condominium sale is expected to yield a good profit. The conversion process, however, includes several options. Basically, four types of condominiums can be designed out of the former hotel rooms. They are deluxe one-bedroom apartments, regular one-bedroom apartments, deluxe studios, and efficiency apartments. Each will yield a different profit, but each type also requires a different level of investment in carpeting, painting, appliances, and carpentry work. Bank loans dictate a limited budget that may be allocated to each of these needs. Profit and cost data, and cost of conversion requirements, for each apartment are shown in the accompanying table.

Thus, we see that the cost of carpeting a deluxe one-bedroom unit will be $1,100, the cost of carpeting a regular one-bedroom unit is $1,000, and so on. A total of $35,000 is budgeted for all new carpeting in the building.

Zoning regulations dictate that the building contain no more than 50 condominiums when the conversion is completed—and no less than 25 units. The development company also decides that to have a good blend of owners, at least 40% but no more than 70% of the units should be one-bedroom apartments. Not all money budgeted in each category need be spent, although profit is not affected by cost savings. But since the money represents a bank loan, under no circumstances may it be exceeded or even shifted from one area, such as carpeting, to another, such as painting.

(a) Formulate Foggy Bottom Development Corporation's decision as a linear program to maximize profits.
(b) Convert your objective function and constraints to a form containing the appropriate slack, surplus, and artificial variables.

9-33 The initial simplex tableau on page 385 was developed by Tommy Gibbs, vice president of a large cotton spinning mill. Unfortunately, Gibbs quit before completing this important LP application. Stephanie Robbins, the newly hired replacement, was immediately given the task of using LP to determine what different kinds of yarn the mill should use to minimize costs. Her first need was to be certain that Gibbs correctly formulated the objective function and constraints. She could find no statement of the problem in the files, so she decided to reconstruct the problem from the initial tableau.

(a) What is the correct formulation, using real decision variables (that is, X_i's) only?
(b) Which variable will enter this current solution mix in the second tableau? Which basic variable will leave?

Tableau for Problem 9-32

	TYPE OF APARTMENT				
RENOVATION REQUIREMENT	DELUXE ONE-BEDROOM ($)	REGULAR ONE-BEDROOM ($)	DELUXE STUDIO ($)	EFFICIENCY ($)	TOTAL BUDGETED ($)
New carpeting	1,100	1,000	600	500	35,000
Painting	700	600	400	300	28,000
New appliances	2,000	1,600	1,200	900	45,000
Carpentry work	1,000	400	900	200	19,000
Profit per unit	8,000	6,000	5,000	3,500	

Simplex Tableau for Problem 9-33

C_j		$12	$18	$10	$20	$7	$8	$0	$0	$0	$0	$0	M	M	M	M	
	SOLUTION MIX	X_1	X_2	X_3	X_4	X_5	X_6	S_1	S_2	S_3	S_4	S_5	A_1	A_2	A_3	A_4	QUANTITY
$M	A_1	1	0	-3	0	0	0	0	0	0	0	0	1	0	0	0	100
0	S_1	0	25	1	2	8	0	1	0	0	0	0	0	0	0	0	900
M	A_2	2	1	0	4	0	1	0	-1	0	0	0	0	1	0	0	250
M	A_3	18	-15	-2	-1	15	0	0	0	-1	0	0	0	0	1	0	150
0	S_4	0	0	0	0	0	25	0	0	0	1	0	0	0	0	0	300
M	A_4	0	0	0	2	6	0	0	0	0	0	-1	0	0	0	1	70
	Z_j	$21M	-$14M	-$5M	$5M	$21M	$M	$0	$0	-$M	$0	-$M	$M	$M	$M	$M	$570M
	$C_j - Z_j$	$12-21M$	$18+14M$	$10+5M$	$20-5M$	$7-21M$	$8-M$	0	0	M	0	M	0	0	0	0	

9-34 Consider the following optimal tableau, where S_1 and S_2 are slack variables added to the original problem:

C_j		$10	$30	$0	$0	
	SOLUTION MIX	X_1	X_2	S_1	S_2	QUANTITY
$10	X_1	1	4	2	0	160
$ 0	S_2	0	6	-7	1	200
	Z_j	$10	$40	$20	$0	$1,600
	$C_j - Z_j$	0	-10	-20	0	

(a) What is the range of optimality for the contribution rate of the variable X_1?

(b) What is the range of insignificance of the contribution rate of the variable X_2?

(c) How much would you be willing to pay for one more unit of the first resource, which is represented by slack variable S_1?

(d) What is the value of one more unit of the second resource? Why?

(e) What would the optimal solution be if the profit on X_2 were changed to $35 instead of $30?

(f) What would the optimal solution be if the profit on X_1 were changed to $12 instead of $10? How much would the maximum profit change?

(g) How much could the right-hand side in constraint number 2 be decreased before profit would be affected?

9-35 A linear program has been formulated and solved. The optimal simplex tableau for this is given at the bottom of this page.

(a) What are the shadow prices for the three constraints? What does a zero shadow price mean? How can this occur?

(b) How much could the right-hand side of the first constraint be changed without changing the solution mix (i.e., perform RHS ranging for this constraint)?

(c) How much could the right-hand side of the third constraint be changed without changing the solution mix?

9-36 Clapper Electronics produces two models of telephone-answering devices, model 102 (X_1) and model H23 (X_2). Jim Clapper, vice president for production, formulates their constraints as follows:

$$2X_1 + 1X_2 \leq 40 \text{ (hours of time available on soldering machine)}$$

$$1X_1 + 3X_2 \leq 30 \text{ (hours of time available in inspection department)}$$

Clapper's objective function is
$$\text{maximize profit} = \$9X_1 + \$7X_2$$

Tableau for Problem 9-35

C_j		80	120	90	0	0	0	
	SOLUTION MIX	X_1	X_2	X_3	S_1	S_2	S_3	QUANTITY
120	X_2	-1.5	1	0	0.125	-0.75	0	37.5
90	X_3	3.5	0	1	-0.125	1.25	0	12.5
0	S_3	-1.0	0	0	0	-0.5	1	10.0
	Z_j	135	120	90	3.75	22.5	0	5,625
	$C_j - Z_j$	-55	0	0	-3.75	-22.5	0	

Solving the problem using the simplex method, he produces the following final tableau:

C_j		$9	$7	$0	$0	
	SOLUTION MIX	X_1	X_2	S_1	S_2	QUANTITY
$9	X_1	1	0	$3/5$	$-1/5$	18
7	X_2	0	1	$-1/5$	$2/5$	4
	Z_j	$9	$7	$4	$1	$190
	$C_j - Z_j$	0	0	-4	-1	

(a) What is the optimal mix of models 102 and H23 to produce?
(b) What do variables S_1 and S_2 represent?
(c) Clapper is considering renting a second soldering machine at a cost to the firm of $2.50 per hour. Should he do so?
(d) Clapper computes that he can hire a part-time inspector for only $1.75 per hour. Should he do so?

9-37 Refer to Table 9.6 on page 347, which is the optimal tableau for the Flair Furniture Company problem.
(a) What are the values of the shadow prices?
(b) Interpret the physical meaning of each shadow price in the context of the furniture problem.
(c) What is the range over which the profit per table can vary without changing the optimal basis (solution mix)?
(d) What is the range of optimality for C (number of chairs produced)?
(e) How many hours can Flair Furniture add to or remove from the first resource (painting department time) without changing the basis?
(f) Conduct RHS ranging on the carpentry department resource to determine the range over which the shadow price remains valid.

9-38 Consider the optimal solution to the Muddy River Chemical Corporation problem in Table 9.10.
(a) For each of the two chemical ingredients, phosphate and potassium, determine the range over which their cost may vary without affecting the basis.
(b) If the original constraint that "no more than 300 pounds of phosphate can be used" ($X_1 \le 300$) were changed to $X_1 \le 400$, would the basis change? Would the values of X_1, X_2, and S_2 change?

9-39 Formulate the dual of this LP problem.

$$\text{maximize profit} = 80X_1 + 75X_2$$
$$1X_1 + 3X_2 \le 4$$
$$2X_1 + 5X_2 \le 8$$

Find the dual of the problem's dual.

9-40 What is the dual of the following LP problem?

Primal: $\text{minimize cost} = 120X_1 + 250X_2$

subject to: $12X_1 + 20X_2 \ge 50$
$$X_1 + 3X_2 \ge 4$$

9-41 The third, and final, simplex tableau for the LP problem stated here follows:

$$\text{maximize profit} = 200X_1 + 200X_2$$

subject to: $2X_1 + X_2 \le 8$
$$X_1 + 3X_2 \le 9$$

What are the solutions to the dual variables, U_1 and U_2? What is the optimal dual cost?

C_j		$200	$200	$0	$0	
	SOLUTION MIX	X_1	X_2	S_1	S_2	QUANTITY
$200	X_1	1	0	$3/5$	$-1/5$	3
200	X_2	0	1	$-1/5$	$2/5$	2
	Z_j	$200	$200	$80	$40	$1,000
	$C_j - Z_j$	0	0	-80	-40	

9-42 The accompanying tableau provides the optimal solution to this dual:

$$\text{minimize cost} = 120U_1 + 240U_2$$

subject to: $2U_1 + 2U_2 \ge 0.5$
$$U_1 + 3U_2 \ge 0.4$$

What does the corresponding primal problem look like, and what is its optimal solution?

Tableau for Problem 9-42

C_j		120	240	0	0	M	M	
	SOLUTION MIX	U_1	U_2	S_1	S_2	A_1	A_2	QUANTITY
$120	U_1	1	0	$-3/4$	$1/2$	$3/4$	$-1/2$	0.175
240	U_2	0	1	$1/4$	$-1/2$	$-1/4$	$1/2$	0.075
	Z_j	$120	$240	$-$30	$-$60	$30	$60	$39
	$C_j - Z_j$	0	0	30	60	$M - 30$	$M - 60$	

9-43 Given the following dual formulation, reconstruct the original primal problem:

minimize cost $= 28U_1 + 53U_2 + 70U_3 + 18U_4$

subject to:
$$U_1 + \qquad\qquad U_4 \geq 10$$
$$U_1 + 2U_2 + U_3 \qquad \geq 5$$
$$- 2U_2 + \qquad 5U_4 \geq 31$$
$$5U_3 \qquad \geq 28$$
$$12U_1 + \qquad 2U_3 - U_4 \geq 17$$
$$U_1, U_2, U_3, U_4 \geq 0$$

9-44 A firm that makes three products, and has three machines available as resources, constructs the following LP problem:

maximize profit $= 4X_1 + 4X_2 + 7X_3$

subject to:
$$1X_1 + 7X_2 + 4X_3 \leq 100 \text{ (hours on machine 1)}$$
$$2X_1 + 1X_2 + 7X_3 \leq 110 \text{ (hours on machine 2)}$$
$$8X_1 + 4X_2 + 1X_3 \leq 100 \text{ (hours on machine 3)}$$

Solve this problem by computer and answer these questions:

(a) Before the third iteration of the simplex method, which machine still has unused time available?
(b) When the final solution is reached, is there any unused time available on any of the three machines?
(c) What would it be worth to the firm to make an additional hour of time available on the third machine?
(d) How much would the firm's profit increase if an extra 10 hours of time were made available on the second machine at not extra cost?

9-45 Management analysts at a Fresno laboratory have developed the following LP primal problem:

minimize cost $= 23X_1 + 18X_2$

subject to:
$$8X_1 + 4X_2 \geq 120$$
$$4X_1 + 6X_2 \geq 115$$
$$9X_1 + 4X_2 \geq 116$$

This model represents a decision concerning number of hours spent by biochemists on certain laboratory experiments (X_1) and number of hours spent by biophysicists on the same series of experiments (X_2). A biochemist costs $23 per hour, while a biophysicist's salary averages $18 per hour. Both types of scientists can be used on three needed laboratory operations: test 1, test 2, and test 3. The experiments and their times are as follows:

LAB EXPERIMENT	SCIENTIST TYPE		MINIMUM TEST TIME NEEDED PER DAY
	BIOPHYSICIST	BIOCHEMIST	
Test 1	8	4	120
Test 2	4	6	115
Test 3	9	4	116

This means that a biophysicist can complete 8, 4, and 9 of tests 1, 2, and 3 per hour. Similarly, a biochemist can perform 4 of test 1, 6 of test 2, and 4 of test 3 per hour. The optimal solution to the lab's primal problem is

$$X_1 = 8.12 \text{ hours and } X_2 = 13.75 \text{ hours}$$

total cost $= \$434.37$ per day

The optimal solution to the dual problem is

$$U_1 = 2.07, \quad U_2 = 1.63, \quad U_3 = 0$$

(a) What is the dual of the primal LP problem?
(b) Interpret the meaning of the dual and its solution.

9-46 Refer to Problem 9-45.
(a) If this is solved with the simplex algorithm, how many constraints and how many variables (including slack, surplus, and artificial variables) would be used?
(b) If the dual of this problem were formulated and solved with the simplex algorithm, how many constraints and how many variables (including slack, surplus, and artificial variables) would be used?
(c) If the simplex algorithm were used, would it be easier to solve the primal problem or the dual problem?

9-47 The Flair Furniture Company first described in Chapter 7, and again in this chapter, manufactures inexpensive tables (T) and chairs (C). The firm's daily LP formulation is given as

maximize profits $= \$7T + 5C$

subject to:
$$4T + 3C \leq 240 \text{ hours of carpentry time available}$$
$$2T + 1C \leq 100 \text{ hours of painting time available}$$

In addition, Flair finds that three more constraints are in order. First, each table and chair must be inspected and may need reworking. The following constraint describes the time required on the average for each:

$$\tfrac{1}{2}T + \tfrac{3}{5}C \leq 36 \text{ hours of inspection/rework time available}$$

Second, Flair faces a resource constraint relating to the lumber needed for each table or chair and the amount available each day:

$$32T + 10C \leq 1{,}248 \text{ linear feet of lumber available for production}$$

Finally, the demand for tables is found to be a maximum of 40 daily. There are no similar constraints regarding chairs.

$T \leq 40$ maximum table production daily

These data have been entered in the QM for Windows software that is available with this book. The inputs and results are shown in the accompanying printout. Refer to the computer output in Programs 9.3, 9.4, and 9.5 in answering these questions.

(a) How many tables and chairs should Flair Furniture produce daily? What is the profit generated by this solution?

(b) Will Flair use all of its resources to their limits each day? Be specific in explaining your answer.

(c) Explain the physical meaning of each shadow price.

(d) Should Flair purchase more lumber if it is available at $0.07 per linear foot? Should it hire more carpenters at $12.75 per hour?

(e) Flair's owner has been approached by a friend whose company would like to use several hours in the painting facility every day. Should Flair sell time to the other firm? If so, how much? Explain.

(f) What is the range within which the carpentry hours, painting hours, and inspection/rework hours can fluctuate before the optimal solution changes?

(g) Within what range for the current solution can the profit contribution of tables and chairs change?

PROGRAM 9.3

QM for Windows Input Data for Flair Furniture's Revised Problem for Problem 9-47

QM for Windows - C:\My Documents\Mike\R&S\Weiss\Render Stair 7\QM for Windows files\Flair.revised.lin

File Edit View Module Format Tools Window Help

Objective
- ● Maximize
- ○ Minimize

Revised Flair Furniture

	Tables	Chairs		RHS	
Maximize	7.	5.			
Carpentry hours	4.	3.	<=	240	
Painting hours	2.	1.	<=	100	
Inspection hours	0.5	0.6	<=	36	
Lumber (linear ft)	32.	10.	<=	1,248	
Demand	1.	0.	<=	40	

PROGRAM 9.4

Solution Results for Flair Furniture's Problem 9-47

QM for Windows - C:\Prentice\Data\RenderStair7\Flair.revised.lin

Objective
- ● Maximize
- ○ Minimize

Linear Programming Results

Simplex Iteration 3

Cj	Basic Variables	7 Tables	5 Chairs	0 slack 1	0 slack 2	0 slack 3	0 slack 4	0 slack 5	Quantity
0	slack 1	0.	0.	1.	0.	-3.9437	-0.0634	0.	18.9296
0	slack 2	0.	0.	0.	1.	-0.8451	-0.0493	0.	8.0563
5	Chairs	0.	1.	0.	0.	2.2535	-0.0352	0.	37.1831
7	Tables	1.	0.	0.	0.	-0.7042	0.0423	0.	27.3803
0	slack 5	0.	0.	0.	0.	0.7042	-0.0423	1.	12.6197
	zj	7.	5.	0.	0.	6.338	0.1197	0.	377.5775
	cj-zj	0.	0.	0.	0.	-6.338	-0.1197	0.	

PROGRAM 9.5

Sensitivity Analysis for Problem 9-47

QM for Windows - C:\Prentice\Data\RenderStair7\Flair.revised.lin

Objective
- ● Maximize
- ○ Minimize

Ranging

Revised Flair Furniture Solution

Variable	Value	Reduced Cost	Original Val	Lower Bound	Upper Bound
Tables	27.38	0.	7.	4.17	16.
Chairs	37.18	0.	5.	2.19	8.4
Constraint	Dual Value	Slack/Surplus	Original Val	Lower Bound	Upper Bound
Carpentry hours	0.	18.9296	240.	221.07	Infinity
Painting hours	0.	8.0563	100.	91.94	Infinity
Inspection hours	6.338	0.	36.	19.5	40.8
Lumber (linear ft)	0.1197	0.	1.248.	600.	1,411.43
Demand	0.	12.6197	40.	27.38	Infinity

9-48 A Chicago manufacturer of office equipment is desperately attempting to control its profit and loss statement. The company currently manufactures 15 different products, each coded with a one-letter and three-digit designation.

(a) How many of each of the 15 products should be produced each month?
(b) Clearly explain the meaning of each shadow price.
(c) A number of workers interested in saving money for the holidays have offered to work overtime next month at a rate of $12.50 per hour. What should the response of management be?

(d) Two tons of steel alloy are available from an overstocked supplier at a total cost of $8,000. Should the steel be purchased? All or part of the supply?
(e) The accountants have just discovered that an error was made in the contribution to profit for product N150. The correct value is actually $8.88. What are the implications of this error?
(f) Management is considering the abandonment of five product lines (those beginning with the letters A through E). If no minimum monthly demand is established, what are the implications? Note that there already is no minimum for two of these products. Use the corrected value for N150.

PRODUCT	STEEL ALLOY REQUIRED (LB)	PLASTIC REQUIRED (SQ FT)	WOOD REQUIRED (BD FT)	ALUMINUM REQUIRED (LB)	FORMICA REQUIRED (BD FT)	LABOR REQUIRED (HOURS)	MINIMUM MONTHLY DEMAND (UNITS)	CONTRIBUTION TO PROFIT
A158	—	0.4	0.7	5.8	10.9	3.1	—	$18.79
B179	4	0.5	1.8	10.3	2.0	1.0	20	6.31
C023	6	—	1.5	1.1	2.3	1.2	10	8.19
D045	10	0.4	2.0	—	—	4.8	10	45.88
E388	12	1.2	1.2	8.1	4.9	5.5	—	63.00
F422	—	1.4	1.5	7.1	10.0	0.8	20	4.10
G366	10	1.4	7.0	6.2	11.1	9.1	10	81.15
H600	5	1.0	5.0	7.3	12.4	4.8	20	50.06
I701	1	0.4	—	10.0	5.2	1.9	50	12.79
J802	1	0.3	—	11.0	6.1	1.4	20	15.88
K900	—	0.2	—	12.5	7.7	1.0	20	17.91
L901	2	1.8	1.5	13.1	5.0	5.1	10	49.99
M050	—	2.7	5.0	—	2.1	3.1	20	24.00
N150	10	1.1	5.8	—	—	7.7	10	88.88
P259	10	—	6.2	15.0	1.0	6.6	10	77.01
Availability per month	980	400	600	2,500	1,800	1,000		

INTERNET HOMEWORK PROBLEMS

See our Internet home page at **www.prenhall.com/render** for additional homework problems 9-49 to 9-53.

⇒ CASE STUDY

Coastal States Chemicals and Fertilizers

In December 2001, Bill Stock, general manager for the Louisiana Division of Coastal States Chemicals and Fertilizers, received a letter from Fred McNair of the Cajan Pipeline Company, which notified Coastal States that priorities had been established for the allocation of natural gas. The letter stated that Cajan Pipeline, the primary supplier of natural gas to Coastal States, might be instructed to curtail natural gas supplies to its industrial and commercial customers by as much as 40% during the ensuing winter months. Moreover, Cajan Pipeline had the approval of the Federal Power Commission (FPC) to curtail such supplies.

Possible curtailment was attributed to the priorities established for the use of natural gas:

First priority: residential and commercial heating
Second priority: commercial and industrial users that use natural gas as a source of raw material
Third priority: commercial and industrial users whereby natural gas is used as boiler fuel

Almost all of Coastal States' uses of natural gas were in the second and third priorities. Hence, its plants were certainly subject to brownouts, or natural gas curtailments. The occurrence and severity of the brownouts depended on a number of complex factors. First, Cajan Pipeline was part of an interstate transmission network that delivered natural gas to residential and commercial buildings on the Atlantic coast and in northeastern regions of the United States. Hence, the severity of the forthcoming winter in these regions would have a direct impact on the use of natural gas.

Second, the demand for natural gas was soaring because it was the cleanest and most efficient fuel. There were almost no environmental problems in burning natural gas. Moreover, maintenance problems due to fuel-fouling in fireboxes and boilers were negligible with natural gas systems. Also, burners were much easier to operate with natural gas than with oil or coal.

Finally, the supply of natural gas was dwindling. The traditionally depressed price of natural gas had discouraged new exploration for gas wells; hence, shortages appeared imminent.

Stock and his staff at Coastal States had been aware of the possibility of shortages of natural gas and had been investigating ways of converting to fuel oil or coal as a substitute for natural gas. Their plans, however, were still in the developmental stages. Coastal States required an immediate contingency plan to minimize the effect of a natural gas curtailment on its multiplant operations. The obvious question was, what operations should be curtailed, and to what extent could the adverse effect upon profits be minimized? Coastal States had approval from the FPC and Cajan Pipeline to specify which of its plants would bear the burden of the curtailment if such cutbacks were necessary. McNair, of Cajan Pipeline, replied, "It's your 'pie': we don't care how you divide it if we make it smaller."

The Model

Six plants of Coastal States Louisiana Division were to share in the "pie." They were all located in the massive Baton Rouge–Geismar–Gramercy industrial complex along the Mississippi River between Baton Rouge and New Orleans. Products manufactured at those plants that required significant amounts of natural gas were phosphoric acid, urea, ammonium phosphate,

TABLE 9.19		**Contribution to Profit and Overhead**		
PRODUCT	CONTRIBUTION PER TON ($)	CAPACITY (TONS PER DAY)	MAXIMUM PRODUCTION RATE (PERCENT OF CAPACITY)	NATURAL GAS CONSUMPTION (1,000 CU FT PER TON)
Phosphoric acid	60	400	80	5.5
Urea	80	250	80	7.0
Ammonium phosphate	90	300	90	8.0
Ammonium nitrate	100	300	100	10.0
Chlorine	50	800	60	15.0
Caustic soda	50	1,000	60	16.0
Vinyl chloride monomer	65	500	60	12.0
Hydrofluoric acid	70	400	80	11.0

ammonium nitrate, chlorine, caustic soda, vinyl chloride monomer, and hydrofluoric acid.

Stock called a meeting of members of his technical staff to discuss a contingency plan for allocation of natural gas among the products if a curtailment developed. The objective was to minimize the impact on profits. After detailed discussion, the meeting was adjourned. Two weeks later, the meeting reconvened. At this session, the data in Table 9.19 were presented.

Coastal States' contract with Cajan Pipeline specified a maximum natural gas consumption of 36,000 cu ft $\times 10^3$ per day for all six member plants. With these data, the technical staff proceeded to develop a model that would specify changes in production rates in response to a natural gas curtailment. (Curtailments are based on contracted consumption and not current consumption.)

Discussion Questions

1. Develop a contingency model and specify the production rates for each product for
   (a) a 20% natural gas curtailment.
   (b) a 40% natural gas curtailment.
2. Explain which of the products in the table should require the most emphasis with regard to energy conservation.
3. What problems do you foresee if production rates are not reduced in a planned and orderly manner?
4. What impact will the natural gas shortage have on company profits?

Source: Professor Jerry Kinard, Western Carolina University.

BIBLIOGRAPHY

See the Bibliography at the end of Chapter 7.

CHAPTER 10

TRANSPORTATION AND ASSIGNMENT MODELS

After completing this chapter, students will be able to:

1. Structure special LP problems using the transportation and assignment models.

2. Use the northwest corner, VAM, MODI, and stepping-stone methods.

3. Solve facility location and other application problems with transportation models.

4. Solve assignment problems with the Hungarian (matrix reduction) method.

CHAPTER OUTLINE

Summary • Glossary • Key Equations • Solved Problems • Self-Test • Discussion Questions and Problems • Internet Homework Problems • Case Study: Andrew–Carter, Inc. • Case Study: Old Oregon Wood Store • Internet Case Studies • Bibliography

Appendix 10.1: Using QM for Windows

Appendix 10.2: Comparison of Simplex Algorithm and Transportation Algorithm

10.1   INTRODUCTION

In this chapter we explore two special linear programming (LP) models. Because of their structure, these models—called the transportation and assignment models—can be solved using more efficient computational procedures than the simplex method.

Both transportation and assignment problems are members of a category of LP techniques called *network flow problems*. Networks, described in detail in Chapter 12, consist of nodes (or points) and arcs (or lines) that join the modes together. Roadways, telephone systems, and citywide water systems are all examples of networks.

Transportation Model

The first model we examine, the *transportation problem*, deals with the distribution of goods from several points of supply (*sources*) to a number of points of demand (*destinations*). Usually, we have a given capacity of goods at each source and a given requirement for the goods at each destination. An example of this is shown in Figure 10.1. The objective of such a problem is to schedule shipments from sources to destinations so that total transportation and production costs are minimized.

Transportation models can also be used when a firm is trying to decide where to locate a new facility. Before opening a new warehouse, factory, or sales office, it is good practice to consider a number of alternative sites. Good financial decisions concerning facility location also attempt to minimize total transportation and production costs for the entire system.

Assignment Model

The assignment problem refers to the class of LP problems that involve determining the most efficient assignment of people to projects, salespeople to territories, contracts to bidders, jobs to machines, and so on. The objective is most often to minimize total costs or total time of performing the tasks at hand. One important characteristic of assignment problems is that only one job or worker is assigned to one machine or project.

Special-Purpose Algorithms

The special-purpose transportation and assignment algorithms are more efficient than using LP's simplex method.

Although LP can be used to solve these types of problems (as seen in Chapter 8), more efficient special-purpose algorithms have been developed for the transportation and assignment applications. As in the simplex algorithm, they involve finding an initial solution, testing this solution to see if it is optimal, and developing an improved solution. This process continues until an optimal solution is reached. Unlike the simplex method, the transportation and assignment methods are fairly simple in terms of computation.

FIGURE 10.1

Example of a Transportation Problem in a Network Format

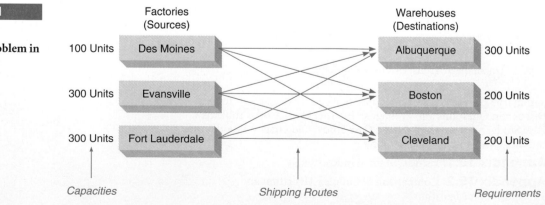

Streamlined versions of the simplex method are important for two reasons:

1. Their computation times are generally 100 times faster than the simplex algorithm.
2. They require less computer memory (and hence can permit larger problems to be solved).

In the first half of this chapter we take a look at the makeup of a typical transportation problem. We explain two common techniques for developing initial solutions: the northwest corner method and Vogel's approximation method. After an initial solution is developed, it must be evaluated by either the stepping-stone method or the modified distribution (MODI) method, both of which are to be presented. Complications that commonly arise, such as the situation in which demand is not exactly equal to supply and the case of a degenerate solution, are also examined.

In the second half of the chapter, we introduce a solution procedure for assignment problems alternatively called the *Hungarian method*, *Flood's technique*, or the *reduced matrix method*.

10.2   SETTING UP A TRANSPORTATION PROBLEM

Let us begin with an example dealing with the Executive Furniture Corporation, which manufactures office desks at three locations: Des Moines, Evansville, and Fort Lauderdale. The firm distributes the desks through regional warehouses located in Albuquerque, Boston, and Cleveland (see Figure 10.2). An estimate of the monthly production capacity at each factory and an estimate of the number of desks that are needed each month at each of the three warehouses is shown as Figure 10.1.

The firm has found that production costs per desk are identical at each factory, and hence the only relevant costs are those of shipping from each *source* to each *destination*. These costs are shown in Table 10.1. They are assumed to be constant regardless of the volume shipped.[1] The transportation problem may now be described as *how to select the shipping routes to be used and the number of desks shipped on each route so as to minimize total transportation cost*. This, of course, must be done while observing the restrictions regarding factory capacities and warehouse requirements.

Our goal is to select the shipping routes and units to be shipped to minimize total transportation cost.

The first step at this point is setting up a *transportation table*; its purpose is to summarize conveniently and concisely all relevant data and to keep track of algorithm computations. (In this respect, it serves the same role that the simplex tableau did for LP problems.) Using the information for the Executive Furniture Corporation displayed in Figure 10.1

The transportation table is a convenient means of summarizing all the data.

---

[1] The other assumptions that hold for LP problems (see Chapter 7) are still applicable to transportation problems.

**Geographical Locations of
Executive Furniture's
Factories and Warehouses**

Key:

Factory

Warehouse

and Table 10.1, we proceed to construct a transportation table and to label its various components in Table 10.2.

We see in Table 10.2 that the total factory supply available is exactly equal to the total warehouse demand. When this situation of equal demand and supply occurs (something that is rather unusual in real life), a *balanced problem* is said to exist. Later in this chapter we take a look at how to deal with unbalanced problems, namely, those in which destination requirements may be greater than or less than origin capacities.

*Balanced supply and demand
occurs when total demand
equals total supply.*

10.3   DEVELOPING AN INITIAL SOLUTION: NORTHWEST CORNER RULE

When the data have been arranged in tabular form, we must establish an initial feasible solution to the problem. One systematic procedure, known as the *northwest corner rule*, requires that we start in the upper left-hand cell (or northwest corner) of the table and allocate units to shipping routes as follows:

1. Exhaust the supply (factory capacity) at each row before moving down to the next row.

2. Exhaust the (warehouse) requirements of each column before moving to the right to the next column.

3. Check that all supply and demands are met.

**Transportation Costs per
Desk for Executive
Furniture Corp.**

TO FROM	ALBUQUERQUE	BOSTON	CLEVELAND
DES MOINES	$5	$4	$3
EVANSVILLE	$8	$4	$3
FORT LAUDERDALE	$9	$7	$5

TABLE 10.2

Transportation Table for Executive Furniture Corporation

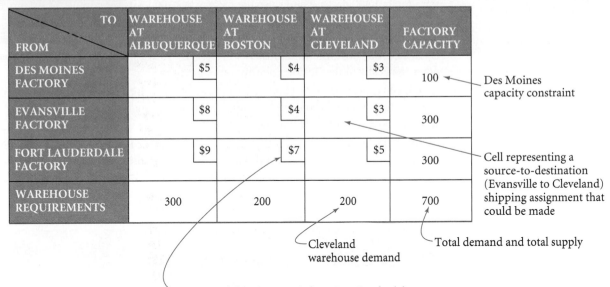

Des Moines capacity constraint

Cell representing a source-to-destination (Evansville to Cleveland) shipping assignment that could be made

Cleveland warehouse demand

Total demand and total supply

Cost of shipping 1 unit from Fort Lauderdale factory to Boston warehouse

We can now use the northwest corner rule to find an initial feasible solution to the Executive Furniture Corporation problem shown in Table 10.2.

It takes five steps in this example to make the initial shipping assignments (see Table 10.3):

Here is an explanation of the five steps needed to make an initial shipping assignment for Executive Furniture.

1. Beginning in the upper left-hand corner, we assign 100 units from Des Moines to Albuquerque. This exhausts the capacity or supply at the Des Moines factory. But it still leaves the warehouse at Albuquerque 200 desks short. Move down to the second row in the same column.

TABLE 10.3

Initial Solution to Executive Furniture Problem Using the Northwest Corner Method

FROM \ TO	ALBUQUERQUE (A)		BOSTON (B)		CLEVELAND (C)		FACTORY CAPACITY
DES MOINES (D)	100	$5		$4		$3	100
EVANSVILLE (E)	200	$8	100	$4		$3	300
FORT LAUDERDALE (F)		$9	100	$7	200	$5	300
WAREHOUSE REQUIREMENTS	300		200		200		700

Means that the firm is shipping 100 units along the Fort Lauderdale–Boston route

2. Assign 200 units from Evansville to Albuquerque. This meets Albuquerque's demand for a total of 300 desks. The Evansville factory has 100 units remaining, so we move to the right to the next column of the second row.

3. Assign 100 units from Evansville to Boston. The Evansville supply has now been exhausted, but Boston's warehouse is still short by 100 desks. At this point, we move down vertically in the Boston column to the next row.

4. Assign 100 units from Fort Lauderdale to Boston. This shipment will fulfill Boston's demand for a total of 200 units. We note, though, that the Fort Lauderdale factory still has 200 units available that have not been shipped.

5. Assign 200 units from Fort Lauderdale to Cleveland. This final move exhausts Cleveland's demand *and* Fort Lauderdale's supply. This always happens with a balanced problem. The initial shipment schedule is now complete.

We can easily compute the cost of this shipping assignment.

| ROUTE | | UNITS | | PER UNIT | | TOTAL |
FROM	TO	SHIPPED	×	COST ($)	=	COST ($)
D	A	100		5		500
E	A	200		8		1,600
E	B	100		4		400
F	B	100		7		700
F	C	200		5		1,000
						Total 4,200

A feasible solution is reached when all demand and supply constraints are met.

This solution is feasible since demand and supply constraints are all satisfied. It was also very quick and easy to reach. However, we would be very lucky if this solution yielded the optimal transportation cost for the problem, because this route-loading method totally ignored the costs of shipping over each of the routes.

After the initial solution has been found, it must be evaluated to see if it is optimal. We compute an improvement index for each empty cell using either the stepping-stone method or the MODI method. If this indicates a better solution is possible, we use the stepping-stone path to move from this solution to improved solutions until we find an optimal solution.

10.4 STEPPING-STONE METHOD: FINDING A LEAST-COST SOLUTION

The *stepping-stone method* is an iterative technique for moving from an initial feasible solution to an optimal feasible solution. This process has two distinct parts: The first involves testing the current solution to determine if improvement is possible, and the second part involves making changes to the current solution in order to obtain an improved solution. This process continues until the optimal solution is reached.

For the stepping-stone method to be applied to a transportation problem, one rule about the number of shipping routes being used must first be observed: *The number of occupied routes (or squares) must always be equal to one less than the sum of the number of rows plus the number of columns.* In the Executive Furniture problem, this means that the initial solution must have $3 + 3 - 1 = 5$ squares used. Thus

occupied shipping routes (squares) = number of rows + number of columns − 1

$$5 = 3 + 3 - 1$$

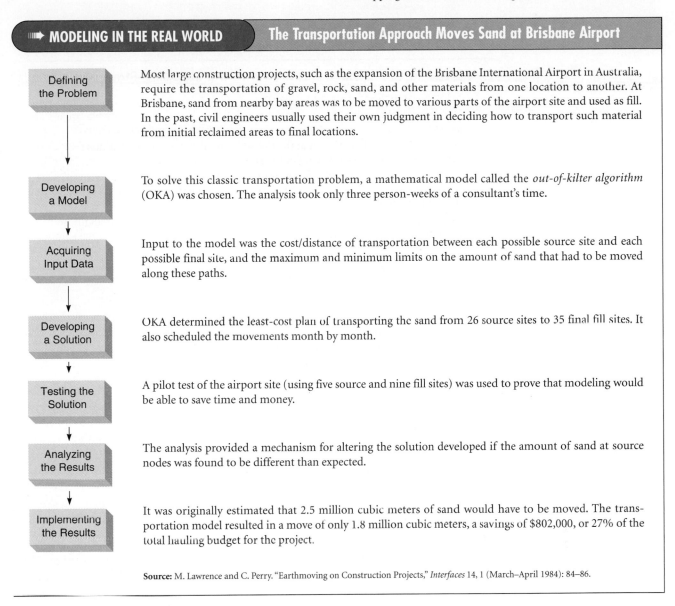

⫸ MODELING IN THE REAL WORLD   *The Transportation Approach Moves Sand at Brisbane Airport*

Defining the Problem

Most large construction projects, such as the expansion of the Brisbane International Airport in Australia, require the transportation of gravel, rock, sand, and other materials from one location to another. At Brisbane, sand from nearby bay areas was to be moved to various parts of the airport site and used as fill. In the past, civil engineers usually used their own judgment in deciding how to transport such material from initial reclaimed areas to final locations.

Developing a Model

To solve this classic transportation problem, a mathematical model called the *out-of-kilter algorithm* (OKA) was chosen. The analysis took only three person-weeks of a consultant's time.

Acquiring Input Data

Input to the model was the cost/distance of transportation between each possible source site and each possible final site, and the maximum and minimum limits on the amount of sand that had to be moved along these paths.

Developing a Solution

OKA determined the least-cost plan of transporting the sand from 26 source sites to 35 final fill sites. It also scheduled the movements month by month.

Testing the Solution

A pilot test of the airport site (using five source and nine fill sites) was used to prove that modeling would be able to save time and money.

Analyzing the Results

The analysis provided a mechanism for altering the solution developed if the amount of sand at source nodes was found to be different than expected.

Implementing the Results

It was originally estimated that 2.5 million cubic meters of sand would have to be moved. The transportation model resulted in a move of only 1.8 million cubic meters, a savings of $802,000, or 27% of the total hauling budget for the project.

Source: M. Lawrence and C. Perry. "Earthmoving on Construction Projects," *Interfaces* 14, 1 (March–April 1984): 84–86.

When the number of occupied routes is less than this, the solution is called *degenerate*. Later in this chapter we talk about what to do if the number of used squares is less than the number of rows plus the number of columns minus 1.

Testing the Solution for Possible Improvement

The stepping-stone method involves testing each unused route to see if shipping one unit on that route would increase or decrease total costs.

How does the stepping-stone method work? Its approach is to evaluate the cost-effectiveness of shipping goods via transportation routes not currently in the solution. Each unused shipping route (or square) in the transportation table is tested by asking the following question: "What would happen to total shipping costs if one unit of our product (in our example, one desk) were tentatively shipped on an unused route?"

This testing of each unused square is conducted using the following five steps:

Five Steps to Test Unused Squares with the Stepping-Stone Method

1. Select an unused square to be evaluated.
2. Beginning at this square, trace a closed path back to the original square via squares that are currently being used and moving with only horizontal and vertical moves.
3. Beginning with a plus (+) sign at the unused square, place alternate minus (−) signs and plus signs on each corner square of the closed path just traced.
4. Calculate an *improvement index* by adding together the unit cost figures found in each square containing a plus sign and then subtracting the unit costs in each square containing a minus sign.
5. Repeat steps 1 to 4 until an improvement index has been calculated for all unused squares. If all indices computed are greater than or equal to zero, an optimal solution has been reached. If not, it is possible to improve the current solution and decrease total shipping costs.

To see how the stepping-stone method works, let us apply these steps to the Executive Furniture Corporation data in Table 10.3 to evaluate unused shipping routes. The four currently unassigned routes are Des Moines to Boston, Des Moines to Cleveland, Evansville to Cleveland, and Fort Lauderdale to Albuquerque.

Closed paths are used to trace alternate plus and minus signs.

Steps 1 and 2. Beginning with the Des Moines–Boston route, we first trace a closed path using only currently occupied squares (see Table 10.4) and then place alternate plus signs and minus signs in the corners of this path. To indicate more clearly the meaning of a *closed path*, we see that only squares currently used for shipping can be used in turning the corners of the route being traced. Hence the path Des Moines–Boston to Des Moines–Albuquerque to Fort Lauderdale–Albuquerque to Fort Lauderdale–Boston to Des Moines–Boston would not be acceptable since the Fort Lauderdale–Albuquerque square is currently empty. It turns out that *only one* closed route is possible for each square we wish to test.

How to assign + and − signs.

Step 3. How do we decide which squares are given plus signs and which minus signs? The answer is simple. Since we are testing the cost-effectiveness of the Des Moines–Boston shipping route, we pretend we are shipping one desk from Des Moines to Boston. This is one more unit than we *were* sending between the two cities, so we place a plus sign in the box. But if we ship one *more* unit than before from Des Moines to Boston, we end up sending 101 desks out of the Des Moines factory.

That factory's capacity is only 100 units; hence we must ship one desk *less* from Des Moines–Albuquerque—this change is made to avoid violating the factory capacity constraint. To indicate that the Des Moines–Albuquerque shipment has been reduced, we place a minus sign in its box. Continuing along the closed path, we notice that we are no longer meeting the Albuquerque warehouse requirement for 300 units. In fact, if the Des Moines–Albuquerque shipment is reduced to 99 units, the Evansville–Albuquerque load has to be increased by 1 unit, to 201 desks. Therefore, we place a plus sign in that box to indicate the increase. Finally, we note that if the Evansville–Albuquerque route is assigned 201 desks, the Evansville–Boston route must be reduced by 1 unit, to 99 desks, to maintain the Evansville factory capacity constraint of 300 units. Thus, a minus sign is placed in the Evansville–Boston box. We observe in Table 10.4 that all four routes on the closed path are thereby balanced in terms of demand-and-supply limitations.

TABLE 10.4   **Evaluating the Unused Des Moines–Boston Shipping Route**

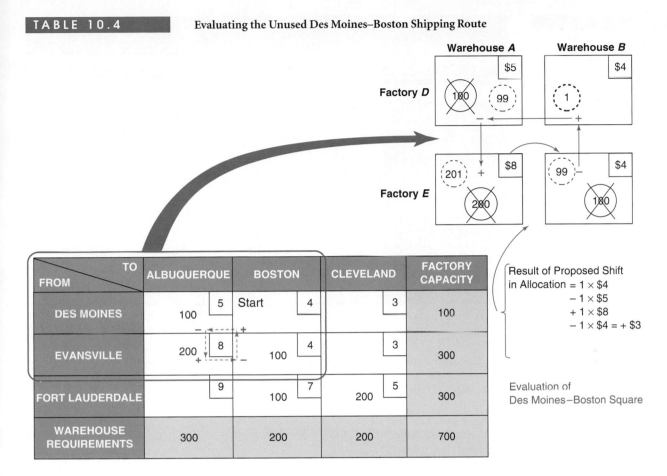

FROM \ TO	ALBUQUERQUE	BOSTON	CLEVELAND	FACTORY CAPACITY
DES MOINES	100 5	Start 4	3	100
EVANSVILLE	200 8	100 4	3	300
FORT LAUDERDALE	9	100 7	200 5	300
WAREHOUSE REQUIREMENTS	300	200	200	700

Result of Proposed Shift
in Allocation = 1 × $4
− 1 × $5
+ 1 × $8
− 1 × $4 = + $3

Evaluation of
Des Moines–Boston Square

Improvement index computation involves adding costs in squares with plus signs and subtracting costs in squares with minus signs. I_{ij} is the improvement index on the route from source i to destination j.

Step 4. An *improvement index* (I_{ij}) for the Des Moines–Boston route is now computed by adding unit costs in squares with plus signs and subtracting costs in squares with minus signs. Hence

$$\text{Des Moines–Boston index} = I_{DB} = +\$4 - \$5 + \$8 - \$4 = +\$3$$

This means that for every desk shipped via the Des Moines–Boston route, total transportation costs will *increase* by $3 over their current level.

Step 5. Let us now examine the Des Moines–Cleveland unused route, which is slightly more difficult to trace with a closed path. Again, you will notice that we turn each corner along the path only at squares that represent existing routes. The path can go *through* the Evansville–Cleveland box but cannot turn a corner or place a + or − sign there. Only an occupied square may be used as a stepping stone (Table 10.5).

The closed path we use is $+ DC - DA + EA - EB + FB - FC$.

$$\text{Des Moines–Cleveland improvement index} = I_{DC}$$
$$= +\$3 - \$5 + \$8 - \$4 + \$7 - \$5$$
$$= +\$4$$

A path can go through any box but can only turn at a box or cell that is occupied.

Thus, opening this route will also not lower our total shipping costs.

TABLE 10.5

Evaluating the Des
Moines–Cleveland (*D-C*)
Shipping Route

TO FROM	(A) ALBUQUERQUE	(B) BOSTON	(C) CLEVELAND	FACTORY CAPACITY
(D) DES MOINES	$5 — 100 ◄- - - - - - -	$4	$3 Start - - -+	100 100
(E) EVANSVILLE	$8 + - - - - - - ► 200	$4 — 100	$3 +	300
(F) FORT LAUDERDALE	$9 + 100	$7 100 200	$5 — 300	300
WAREHOUSE REQUIREMENTS	300	200	200	700

The other two routes may be evaluated in a similar fashion:

$$\text{Evansville–Cleveland index} = I_{EC} = +\$3 - \$4 + \$7 - \$5$$
$$= +\$1$$

(closed path: $+EC - EB + FB - FC$)

$$\text{Fort Lauderdale–Albuquerque index} = I_{FA} = +\$9 - \$7 + \$4 - \$8$$
$$= -\$2$$

(closed path: $+FA - FB + EB - EA$)

Because this last improvement index (I_{FA}) is negative, a cost savings may be attained by making use of the (currently unused) Fort Lauderdale–Albuquerque route.

Obtaining an Improved Solution

To reduce our overall costs, we want to select the route with the negative index indicating the largest improvement.

Each negative index computed by the stepping-stone method represents the amount by which total transportation costs could be decreased if 1 unit or product were shipped on that route. We found only one negative index in the Executive Furniture problem, that being −$2 on the Fort Lauderdale factory–Albuquerque warehouse route. If, however, there were more than one negative improvement index, our strategy would be to choose the route (unused square) with the negative index indicating the largest improvement.

The maximum we can ship on the new route is found by looking at the closed path's minus signs. We select the smallest number found in the squares with minus signs.

The next step, then, is to ship the maximum allowable number of units (or desks, in our case) on the new route (Fort Lauderdale to Albuquerque). What is the maximum quantity that can be shipped on the money-saving route? That quantity is found by referring to the closed path of plus signs and minus signs drawn for the route and selecting the *smallest number* found in those squares containing *minus signs*. To obtain a new solution, that number is added to all squares on the closed path with plus signs and subtracted from all squares on the path assigned minus signs. All other squares are unchanged.

TABLE 10.6

Stepping-Stone Path Used
to Evaluate Route *F–A*

FROM \ TO	A	B	C	FACTORY CAPACITY
D	$5 / 100	$4	$3	100
E	$8 / −200	$4 / +100	$3	300
F	$9 / +	$7 / −100	$5 / 200	300
WAREHOUSE REQUIREMENTS	300	200	200	700

Let us see how this process can help improve Executive Furniture's solution. We repeat the transportation table (Table 10.6) for the problem. Note that the stepping-stone route for Fort Lauderdale to Albuquerque (*F–A*) is drawn in. The maximum quantity that can be shipped on the newly opened route (*F–A*) is the smallest number found in squares containing minus signs—in this case, 100 units. Why 100 units? Since the total cost decreases by $2 per unit shipped, we know we would like to ship the maximum possible number of units. Table 10.6 indicates that each unit shipped over the *F–A* route results in an increase of 1 unit shipped from *E* to *B* and a decrease of 1 unit in both the amounts shipped from *F* to *B* (now 100 units) and from *E* to *A* (now 200 units). Hence the maximum we can ship over the *F–A* route is 100. This results in 0 units being shipped from *F* to *B*.

Changing the shipping route involves adding to squares on the closed path with plus signs and subtracting from squares with minus signs.

We add 100 units to the 0 now being shipped on route *F–A*; then proceed to subtract 100 from route *F–B*, leaving 0 in that square (but still balancing the row total for *F*); then add 100 to route *E–B*, yielding 200; and finally, subtract 100 from route *E–A*, leaving 100 units shipped. Note that the new numbers still produce the correct row and column totals as required.

The new solution is shown in Table 10.7.

Total shipping cost has been reduced by (100 units) × ($2 saved per unit) = $200, and is now $4,000. This cost figure can, of course, also be derived by multiplying each unit shipping cost times the number of units transported on its route, namely, (100 × $5) + (100 × $8) + (200 × $4) + (100 × $9) + (200 × $5) = $4,000.

TABLE 10.7

Second Solution to the
Executive Furniture
Problem

FROM \ TO	A	B	C	FACTORY CAPACITY
D	$5 / 100	$4	$3	100
E	$8 / 100	$4 / 200	$3	300
F	$9 / 100	$7	$5 / 200	300
WAREHOUSE REQUIREMENTS	300	200	200	700

The solution shown in Table 10.7 may or may not be optimal. To determine whether further improvement is possible, we return to the first five steps given earlier to test each square that is *now* unused. The four improvement indices—each representing an available shipping route—are as follows:

Improvement indices for each of the four unused shipping routes must now be tested to see if any are negative.

$$D \text{ to } B = I_{DB} = +\$4 - \$5 + \$8 - \$4 = +\$3$$

$$(\text{closed path:} +DB - DA + EA - EB)$$

$$D \text{ to } C = I_{DC} = +\$3 - \$5 + \$9 - \$5 = +\$2$$

$$(\text{closed path:} +DC - DA + FA - FC)$$

$$E \text{ to } C = I_{EC} = +\$3 - \$8 + \$9 - \$5 = -\$1$$

$$(\text{closed path:} +EC - EA + FA - FC)$$

$$F \text{ to } B = I_{FB} = +\$7 - \$4 + \$8 - \$9 = +\$2$$

$$(\text{closed path:} +FB - EB + EA - FA)$$

Hence, an improvement can be made by shipping the maximum allowable number of units from *E* to *C* (see Table 10.8). Only the squares *E–A* and *F–C* have minus signs in the closed path; because the smallest number in these two squares is 100, we add 100 units to *E–C* and *F–A* and subtract 100 units from *E–A* and *F–C*. The new cost for this third solution, $3,900, is computed in the following table:

Total Cost of Third Solution

ROUTE		DESKS		PER UNIT		TOTAL
FROM	TO	SHIPPED	×	COST ($)	=	COST ($)
D	A	100		5		500
E	B	200		4		800
E	C	100		3		300
F	A	200		9		1,800
F	C	100		5		500
						Total 3,900

TABLE 10.8

Path to Evaluate the E–C Route

FROM \ TO	A	B	C	FACTORY CAPACITY
D	$5 \quad 100	$4	$3	100
E	$8 \quad 100 −	$4 \quad 200	$3 \quad Start +	300
F	$9 \quad 100 +	$7	$5 \quad 200 −	300
WAREHOUSE REQUIREMENTS	300	200	200	700

TABLE 10.9

Third and Optimal Solution

FROM \ TO	A	B	C	FACTORY CAPACITY
D	$5 \newline 100	$4	$3	100
E	$8	$4 \newline 200	$3 \newline 100	300
F	$9 \newline 200	$7	$5 \newline 100	300
WAREHOUSE REQUIREMENTS	300	200	200	700

Table 10.9 contains the optimal shipping assignments because each improvement index that can be computed at this point is greater than or equal to zero, as shown in the following equations. Improvement indices for the table are

Since all four of these improvement indices are greater than or equal to zero, we have reached an optimal solution.

$$D \text{ to } B = I_{DB} = +\$4 - \$5 + \$9 - \$5 + \$3 - \$4$$

$$= +\$2 \text{ (path: } +DB - DA + FA - FC + EC - EB)$$

$$D \text{ to } C = I_{DC} = +\$3 - \$5 + \$9 - \$5 = +\$2 \text{ (path: } +DC - DA + FA - FC)$$

$$E \text{ to } A = I_{EA} = +\$8 - \$9 + \$5 - \$3 = +\$1 \text{ (path: } +EA - FA + FC - EC)$$

$$F \text{ to } B = I_{FB} = +\$7 - \$5 + \$3 - \$4 = +\$1 \text{ (path: } +FB - FC + EC - EB)$$

The hardest part in solving problems like this is identifying every stepping-stone path so that we can compute the improvement indices. In Section 10.5, we introduce an easier way to evaluate empty cells in transportation problems, especially larger ones with more sources and destinations, called the MODI method. We also demonstrate another way to develop an initial solution to a transportation problem: Vogel's approximation method. Before investigating these, let us summarize the steps in the transportation algorithm:

Summary of Steps in Transportation Algorithm (Minimization)

The transportation algorithm has four basic steps.

1. Set up a balanced transportation table.
2. Develop initial solution using either the northwest corner method or Vogel's approximation method.
3. Calculate an improvement index for each empty cell using either the stepping-stone method or the MODI method. If improvement indices are all nonnegative, stop; the optimal solution has been found. If any index is negative, continue to step 4.
4. Select the cell with the improvement index indicating the greatest decrease in cost. Fill this cell using a stepping-stone path and go to step 3.

Using Excel QM to Solve Transportation Problems Excel QM's Transportation module uses Excel's built-in Solver routine to find optimal solutions to transportation problems such as Executive Furniture. Program 10.1A illustrates the input data and total cost formulas. To reach an optimal solution, we must go to Excel's Tools bar, select Solver, and then select Solve. The output is shown in Program 10.1B.

PROGRAM 10.1A   **Excel QM Input Screen and Formulas, Using Executive Furniture Data**

Enter the origin and destination names, the shipping costs, and the total supply and demand figures.

The target cell is the total cost cell (B22), which we wish to minimize by changing the shipment cells (B17 through D19).

Set Target Cell: $B$22

Equal To: ○ Max

By Changing Cells:

$B$17:$D$19

Subject to the Constraints:

$B$12:$D$12 = $B$20:$D$20
$E$17:$E$19 <= $E$9:$E$11

Guarantee that we meet the demand exactly (3 constraints).

Guarantee that we do not exceed the supply (3 constraints).

Microsoft Excel

File Edit View

	A	B	C	D	E
1	**Executive Furniture Company**				
2					
3	Transportation		Enter the transportation costs, supplies and demand		
4			SOLVE on the menu bar at the top.		
5			If SOLVER is not a menu option in the Tools menu t		
6					
7	Data				
8	COSTS	Albuquerque	Boston	Cleveland	Supply
9	Des Moines	5	4	3	
10	Evansville	8	4	3	
11	Fort Lauderdale	9	7	5	
12	Demand	300	200	200	=CONCATENATE(SUM(B12:D12)," \ ",SUM(E9:E11))
13					
14					
15	Shipments				
16	Shipments	=B8	=C8	=D8	Row Total
17	=A9	1	1	1	=SUM(B17:D17)
18	=A10	1	1	1	=SUM(B18:D18)
19	=A11	1	1	1	=SUM(B19:D19)
20	Column Total	=SUM(B17:B19)	=SUM(C17:C19)	=SUM(D17:D19)	=CONCATENATE(INT(SUM(B20:D20)+0.5)," \ ",INT(SUM(E1
21					
22	Total Cost	=SUMPRODUCT(B9:D11,B17:D19)			
23					
24					
25					

Solver will place the shipments in this cell.

The total shipments to and from each location are calculated here.

The total cost is created here by multiplying the unit shipping costs in the data table by the shipments in the shipment table using the SUMPRODUCT function.

PROGRAM 10.1B

Output from Excel QM with Optimal Solution to Executive Furniture Problem

Microsoft Excel - captures.xls

File Edit View Insert Format Tools Data

Solver Results

Solver found a solution. All constraints and optimality conditions are satisfied.

● Keep Solver Solution
○ Restore Original Values

Reports
Answer
Sensitivity
Limits

OK   Cancel   Save Scenario...   Help

	A	B	C	D	
1	**Executive Furniture Com**				
2					
3	Transportation		Enter the tran		
4			Then go to T		
5			If SOLVER is		
6			INS.		
7	Data				
8	COSTS	Albuquerq	Boston	Cleveland	Supply
9	Des Moines	5	4	3	100
10	Evansville	8	4	3	300
11	Fort Lauderdale	9	7	5	300
12	Demand	300	200	200	700 \ 700
13					
14					
15	Shipments				
16	Shipments	Albuquerq	Boston	Cleveland	Row Total
17	Des Moines	100	0	0	100
18	Evansville	0	200	100	300
19	Fort Lauderdale	200	0	100	300
20	Column Total	300	200	200	700 \ 700
21					
22	Total Cost	3900			

10.5 MODI METHOD

MODI has some advantages over the stepping-stone method.

The MODI (*modified distribution*) method allows us to compute improvement indices quickly for each unused square without drawing all of the closed paths. Because of this, it can often provide considerable time savings over the stepping-stone method for solving transportation problems.

If there is a negative improvement index indicating an improvement can be made, then only one stepping-stone path must be found. This is used as it was before to determine what changes should be made to obtain the improved solution.

How to Use the MODI Approach

In applying the MODI method, we begin with an initial solution obtained by using the northwest corner rule.[2] But now we must compute a value for each row (call the values R_1, R_2, R_3 if there are three rows) and for each column (K_1, K_2, K_3) in the transportation table. In general, we let

$$R_i = \text{value assigned to row } i$$

$$K_j = \text{value assigned to column } j$$

$$C_{ij} = \text{cost in square } ij \text{ (cost of shipping from source } i \text{ to destination } j)$$

The MODI method then requires five steps:

Here are the five MODI steps.

Five Steps in the MODI Method to Test Unused Squares

1. To compute the values for each row and column, set

$$R_i + K_j = C_{ij} \tag{10-1}$$

   but *only for those squares that are currently used or occupied.* For example, if the square at the intersection of row 2 and column 1 is occupied, we set $R_2 + K_1 = C_{21}$.

2. After all equations have been written, set $R_1 = 0$.
3. Solve the system of equations for all R and K values.
4. Compute the improvement index for each unused square by the formula

$$\text{improvement index } (I_{ij}) = C_{ij} - R_i - K_j \tag{10-2}$$

5. Select the best negative index and proceed to solve the problem as you did using the stepping-stone method.

---

[2] Note that any initial feasible solution will do: northwest corner rule, Vogel's approximation method solution, or any arbitrary assignment.

The San Miguel Corporation, based in the Philippines, faces unique distribution challenges. With more than 300 products, including beer, alcoholic drinks, juices, bottled water, feeds, poultry, and meats to be distributed to every corner of the Philippine archipelago, shipping and warehousing costs make up a large part of total product cost.

The company grappled with these questions:

- Which products should be produced in each plant and in which warehouse should they be stored?
- Which warehouses should be maintained and where should new ones be located?
- When should warehouses be closed or opened?
- Which demand centers should each warehouse serve?

Turning to the transportation model of LP, San Miguel is able to answer these questions. The firm uses these types of warehouses: company owned and staffed, rented but company staffed, and contracted out (i.e., not company owned or staffed).

San Miguel's Operations Research Department computed that the firm saves $7.5 million annually with optimal beer warehouse configurations over the existing national configurations. In addition, analysis of warehousing for ice cream and other frozen products indicated that the optimal configuration of warehouses, compared with existing setups, produced a $2.17 million savings.

Source: Elise del Rosario. "Logistical Nightmare," *OR/MS Today* (April 1999): 44–46.

Solving the Executive Furniture Corporation Problem with MODI

Let us try out these rules on the Executive Furniture Corporation problem. The initial northwest corner solution is repeated in Table 10.10. MODI will be used to compute an improvement index for each unused square. Note that the only change in the transportation table is the border labeling the R_is (rows) and K_js (columns).

We first set up an equation for each occupied square:

Solving for R and K values.

$$\textbf{(1)} \quad R_1 + K_1 = 5$$

$$\textbf{(2)} \quad R_2 + K_1 = 8$$

$$\textbf{(3)} \quad R_2 + K_2 = 4$$

$$\textbf{(4)} \quad R_3 + K_2 = 7$$

$$\textbf{(5)} \quad R_3 + K_3 = 5$$

TABLE 10.10

Initial Solution to Executive Furniture Problem in the MODI Format

R_i \ K_j		K_1 ALBUQUERQUE	K_2 BOSTON	K_3 CLEVELAND	FACTORY CAPACITY
	FROM \ TO				
R_1	DES MOINES	5 100	4	3	100
R_2	EVANSVILLE	8 200	4 100	3	300
R_3	FORT LAUDERDALE	9	7 100	5 200	300
	WAREHOUSE REQUIREMENTS	300	200	200	700

Letting $R_1 = 0$, we can easily solve, step by step, for K_1, R_2, K_2, R_3, and K_3.

$$(1)\quad R_1 + K_1 = 5$$
$$0 + K_1 = 5 \quad K_1 = 5$$
$$(2)\quad R_2 + K_1 = 8$$
$$R_2 + 5 = 8 \quad R_2 = 3$$
$$(3)\quad R_2 + K_2 = 4$$
$$3 + K_2 = 4 \quad K_2 = 1$$
$$(4)\quad R_3 + K_2 = 7$$
$$R_3 + 1 = 7 \quad R_3 = 6$$
$$(5)\quad R_3 + K_3 = 5$$
$$6 + K_3 = 5 \quad K_3 = -1$$

You can observe that these R and K values will not always be positive; it is common for zero and negative values to occur as well. Also, after solving for the R's and K's in a few practice problems, you may become so proficient that the calculations can be done in your head instead of by writing the equations out.

The next step is to compute the improvement index for each unused cell. That formula, again, is

$$\text{improvement index } I_{ij} = C_{ij} - R_i - K_j$$

These are the same indices calculated by the stepping-stone method, but now we have to trace only one closed path.

We have:

Des Moines–Boston index $I_{DB} = C_{12} - R_1 - K_2 = 4 - 0 - 1$
$$= +\$3$$

Des Moines–Cleveland index $I_{DC} = C_{13} - R_1 - K_3 = 3 - 0 - (-1)$
$$= +\$4$$

Evansville–Cleveland index $I_{EC} = C_{23} - R_2 - K_3 = 3 - 3 - (-1)$
$$= +\$1$$

Fort Lauderdale–Albuquerque index $I_{FA} = C_{31} - R_3 - K_1 = 9 - 6 - 5$
$$= -\$2$$

Note that these indices are exactly the same as the ones calculated when we used the stepping-stone approach (see Tables 10.4 and 10.5). Since one of the indices is negative, the current solution is not optimal. But now it is necessary to trace only one closed path, for Fort Lauderdale–Albuquerque, in order to proceed with the solution procedures as used in the stepping-stone method.

To improve the solution we follow these four steps.

For your convenience, the steps we follow to develop an improved solution after the improvement indices have been computed are outlined briefly:

1. Beginning at the square with the best improvement index (Fort Lauderdale–Albuquerque), trace a closed path (a stepping-stone path) back to the original square via squares that are currently being used.

2. Beginning with a plus (+) sign at the unused square, place alternate minus (−) signs and plus signs on each corner square of the closed path just traced.

3. Select the smallest quantity found in those squares containing minus signs. *Add* that number to all squares on the closed path with plus signs; *subtract* the number from all squares assigned minus signs.

4. Compute new improvement indices for this new solution using the MODI method. Note that new R_i and K_j values must be calculated.

Following this procedure, the second and third solutions to the Executive Furniture Corporation problem can be found. In tabular form, the result of your MODI computations will look identical to Tables 10.7 (second solution using stepping-stone) and 10.9 (optimal solution). With each new MODI solution, we must recalculate the R and K values. These values then are used to compute new improvement indices in order to determine whether further shipping cost reduction is possible.

10.6 VOGEL'S APPROXIMATION METHOD: ANOTHER WAY TO FIND AN INITIAL SOLUTION

In addition to the northwest corner method of setting an initial solution to transportation problems, we talk about one other important technique—*Vogel's approximation method* (VAM). VAM is not quite as simple as the northwest corner approach, but it facilitates a very good initial solution—as a matter of fact, one that is often the *optimal* solution.

Vogel's approximation method tackles the problem of finding a good initial solution by taking into account the costs associated with each route alternative. This is something that the northwest corner rule does not do. To apply VAM, we first compute for each row and column the penalty faced if we should ship over the *second best* route instead of the *least-cost* route.

The six steps involved in determining an initial VAM solution are illustrated on our now familiar Executive Furniture Corporation data. (We begin with the same layout originally shown in Table 10.2.)

Here are the six steps of VAM.

VAM Step 1. For each row and column of the transportation table, find the difference between the two lowest unit shipping costs. These numbers represent the difference between the distribution cost on the *best* route in the row or column and the *second best* route in the row or column. (This is the *opportunity cost* of not using the best route.)

Step 1 has been done in Table 10.11. The numbers at the heads of the columns and to the right of the rows represent these differences. For example, in row *E* the three transportation costs are $8, $4, and $3. The two lowest costs are $4 and $3, so their difference is $1.

VAM Step 2. Identify the row or column with the greatest opportunity cost, or difference. In the case of Table 10.11, the row or column selected is column *A*, with a difference of 3.

Assignments in VAM are based on penalty costs.

VAM Step 3. Assign as many units as possible to the lowest-cost square in the row or column selected.

Step 3 has been done in Table 10.12. Under column *A*, the lowest-cost route is *D–A* (with a cost of $5) and 100 units have been assigned to that square. No more were placed in the square because doing so would exceed *D*'s availability.

TABLE 10.11

Transportation Table with
VAM Row and Column
Differences Shown

		ALBUQUERQUE *A*	BOSTON *B*	CLEVELAND *C*	TOTAL AVAILABLE	
		3	0	0	OPPORTUNITY ← COSTS	
DES MOINES *D*		5	4	3	100	1
EVANSVILLE *E*		8	4	3	300	1
FORT LAUDERDALE *F*		9	7	5	300	2
TOTAL REQUIRED		300	200	200	700	

VAM Step 4. Eliminate any row or column that has just been completely satisfied by the assignment just made. This can be done by placing *X*s in each appropriate square.

Step 4 has been done in Table 10.12's *D* row. No future assignments will be made to the *D–B* or *D–C* routes.

VAM Step 5. Recompute the cost differences for the transportation table, omitting rows or columns eliminated in the preceding step.

This is also shown in Table 10.12. *A*'s, *B*'s, and *C*'s differences each change. *D*'s row is eliminated, and *E*'s and *F*'s differences remain the same as in Table 10.11.

VAM Step 6. Return to step 2 for the rows and columns remaining and repeat the steps until an initial feasible solution has been obtained.

In our case, column *B* now has the greatest difference, which is 3. We assign 200 units to the lowest-cost square in column *B* that has not been crossed out. This is seen to be *E–B*. Since *B*'s requirements have now been met, we place an *X* in the *F–B* square to eliminate it. Differences are once again recomputed. This process is summarized in Table 10.13.

TABLE 10.12

VAM Assignment with *D*'s
Requirements Satisfied

		A	*B*	*C*	TOTAL AVAILABLE	
		3̸ 1	0̸ 3	0̸ 2	OPPORTUNITY ← COSTS	
D		5 / 100	4 / *X*	3 / *X*	100	1
E		8	4	3	300	1
F		9	7	5	300	2
TOTAL REQUIRED		300	200	200	700	

TABLE 10.13

Second VAM Assignment with *B*'s Requirements Satisfied

TO FROM	A $\cancel{3}\,1$	B $\cancel{0}\,3$	C $\cancel{0}\,2$	TOTAL AVAILABLE	OPPORTUNITY COSTS
D	100 5	X 4	X 3	100	$\cancel{1}$
E	8	200 4	3	300	$\cancel{1}5$
F	9	X 7	5	300	$\cancel{2}4$
TOTAL REQUIRED	300	200	200	700	

The greatest difference is now in row *E*. Hence, we shall assign as many units as possible to the lowest-cost square in row *E*, that is, *E–C* with a cost of $3. The maximum assignment of 100 units depletes the remaining availability at *E*. The square *E–A* may therefore be crossed out. This is illustrated in Table 10.14.

The final two allocations, at *F–A* and *F–C*, may be made by inspecting supply restrictions (in the rows) and demand requirements (in the columns). We see that an assignment of 200 units to *F–A* and 100 units to *F–C* completes the table (see Table 10.15).

The cost of this VAM assignment is = (100 units × $5) + (200 units × $4) + (100 units × $3) + (200 units × $9) + (100 units × $5) = $3,900.

VAM may yield an optimal solution with its initial solution, meaning fewer computations than other techniques.

After this initial solution has been found, you should evaluate it with either the stepping-stone method or the MODI method. In this example, the improvement indices will show that the initial solution found with Vogel's approximation method is the optimal solution to the Executive Furniture Corporation problem. Although Vogel's approximation initial solution is not always the optimal solution, it is usually a lower-cost initial solution than that found with the northwest corner method. Thus, though it requires more calculations to develop the initial solution, VAM tends to minimize the total number of computations required to reach an optimal solution.

TABLE 10.14

Third VAM Assignment with *E*'s Requirements Satisfied

TO FROM	A	B	C	TOTAL AVAILABLE
D	100 5	X 4	X 3	100
E	X 8	200 4	100 3	300
F	9	X 7	5	300
TOTAL REQUIRED	300	200	200	700

TABLE 10.15

Final Assignments to
Balance Column and Row
Requirements

FROM \ TO	A	B	C	TOTAL AVAILABLE
D	5	4	3	
	100	X	X	100
E	8	4	3	
	X	200	100	300
F	9	7	5	
	200	X	100	300
TOTAL REQUIRED	300	200	200	700

10.7 UNBALANCED TRANSPORTATION PROBLEMS

Dummy sources or destinations are used to balance problems in which demand is not equal to supply.

A situation occurring quite frequently in real-life problems is the case in which total demand is not equal to total supply. These *unbalanced problems* can be handled easily by the preceding solution procedures if we first introduce *dummy sources* or *dummy destinations*. In the event that total supply is greater than total demand, a dummy destination (warehouse), with demand exactly equal to the surplus, is created. If total demand is greater than total supply, we introduce a dummy source (factory) with a supply equal to the excess of demand over supply. In either case, shipping cost coefficients of zero are assigned to each dummy location or route because no shipments will actually be made from a dummy factory or to a dummy warehouse. Any units assigned to a dummy destination represent excess capacity, and units assigned to a dummy source represent unmet demand.

Demand Less Than Supply

Considering the original Executive Furniture Corporation problem, suppose that the Des Moines factory increases its rate of production to 250 desks. (That factory's capacity used to be 100 desks per production period.) The firm is now able to supply a total of 850 desks each period. Warehouse requirements, however, remain the same (at 700 desks), so the row and column totals do not balance.

To balance this type of problem, we simply add a dummy column that will represent a fake warehouse requiring 150 desks. This is somewhat analogous to adding a slack variable in solving an LP problem. Just as slack variables were assigned a value of zero dollars in the LP objective function, the shipping costs to this dummy warehouse are all set equal to zero.

The northwest corner rule is used once again, in Table 10.16, to find an initial solution to this modified Executive Furniture problem. To complete this task and find an optimal solution, you would employ either the stepping-stone or MODI method.

Note that the 150 units from Fort Lauderdale to the dummy warehouse represent 150 units that are *not* shipped from Fort Lauderdale.

Demand Greater Than Supply

The second type of unbalanced condition occurs when total demand is greater than total supply. This means that customers or warehouses require more of a product than the firm's factories can provide. In this case we need to add a dummy row representing a fake factory.

TABLE 10.16   **Initial Solution to an Unbalanced Problem Where Demand is Less Than Supply**

FROM \ TO	ALBUQUERQUE (A)	BOSTON (B)	CLEVELAND (C)	DUMMY WAREHOUSE	FACTORY CAPACITY
DES MOINES (D)	5 — 250	4	3	0	250 ← New Des Moines capacity
EVANSVILLE (E)	8 — 50	4 — 200	3 — 50	0	300
FORT LAUDERDALE (F)	9	7	5 — 150	0 — 150	300
WAREHOUSE REQUIREMENTS	300	200	200	150	850

Total cost = 250($5) + 50($8) + 200($4) + 50($3) + 150($5) + 150($0) = $3,350

The new factory will have a supply exactly equal to the difference between total demand and total real supply. The shipping costs from the dummy factory to each destination will be zero.

Let us set up such an unbalanced problem for the Happy Sound Stereo Company. Happy Sound assembles high-fidelity stereophonic systems at three plants and distributes through three regional warehouses. The production capacities at each plant, demand at each warehouse, and unit shipping costs are presented in Table 10.17.

As can be seen in Table 10.18, a dummy plant adds an extra row, balances the problem, and allows us to apply the northwest corner rule to find the initial solution shown. This initial solution shows 50 units being shipped from the dummy plant to warehouse *C*. This means that warehouse *C* will be 50 units short of its requirements. In general, any units shipped from a dummy source represent unmet demand at the respective destination.

TABLE 10.17

Unbalanced Transportation Table for Happy Sound Stereo Company

FROM \ TO	WAREHOUSE A	WAREHOUSE B	WAREHOUSE C	PLANT SUPPLY
PLANT W	$6	$4	$9	200
PLANT X	$10	$5	$8	175
PLANT Y	$12	$7	$6	75
WAREHOUSE DEMAND	250	100	150	450 / 500

Totals do not balance

TABLE 10.18				

Initial Solution to an Unbalanced Problem in which Demand Is Greater Than Supply

FROM \ TO	WAREHOUSE A	WAREHOUSE B	WAREHOUSE C	PLANT SUPPLY
PLANT W	6 200	4	9	200
PLANT X	10 50	5 100	8 25	175
PLANT Y	12	7	6 75	75
DUMMY PLANT	0	0	0 50	50
WAREHOUSE DEMAND	250	100	150	500

Total cost of initial solution = 200($6) + 50($10) + 100($5) + 25($8) + 75($6) + 50($0) = $2,850

10.8 DEGENERACY IN TRANSPORTATION PROBLEMS

We briefly mentioned the subject of *degeneracy* earlier in this chapter. Degeneracy occurs when the number of occupied squares or routes in a transportation table solution is less than the number of rows plus the number of columns minus 1. Such a situation may arise in the initial solution or in any subsequent solution. Degeneracy requires a special procedure to correct the problem. Without enough occupied squares to trace a closed path for each unused route, it would be impossible to apply the stepping-stone method or to calculate the R and K values needed for the MODI technique. You might recall that no problem discussed in the chapter thus far has been degenerate.

Degeneracy arises when the number of occupied squares is less than the number of rows + columns − 1.

To handle degenerate problems, we create an artificially occupied cell—that is, we place a zero (representing a fake shipment) in one of the unused squares and then treat that square as if it were occupied. The square chosen must be in such a position as to allow *all* stepping-stone paths to be closed, although there is usually a good deal of flexibility in selecting the unused square that will receive the zero.

Degeneracy in an Initial Solution

Degeneracy can occur in our application of the northwest corner rule to find an initial solution, as we see in the case of the Martin Shipping Company. Martin has three warehouses from which to supply its three major retail customers in San Jose. Martin's shipping costs, warehouse supplies, and customer demands are presented in Table 10.19. Note that origins in this problem are warehouses and destinations are retail stores. Initial shipping assignments are made in the table by application of the northwest corner rule.

This initial solution is degenerate because it violates the rule that the number of used squares must be equal to the number of rows plus the number of columns minus 1 (i.e., 3 + 3 − 1 = 5 is greater than the number of occupied boxes). In this particular problem, degeneracy arose because both a column and a row requirement (that being column 1 and row 1) were satisfied simultaneously. This broke the stair-step pattern that we usually see with northwest corner solutions.

To correct the problem, we can place a zero in an unused square. With the northwest corner method, this zero should be placed in one of the cells that is adjacent to the last filled cell so the stair-step pattern continues. In this case, those squares representing either the

TO / FROM	CUSTOMER 1	CUSTOMER 2	CUSTOMER 3	WAREHOUSE SUPPLY
WAREHOUSE 1	8 100	2	6	100
WAREHOUSE 2	10	9 100	9 20	120
WAREHOUSE 3	7	10	7 80	80
CUSTOMER DEMAND	100	100	100	300

shipping route from warehouse 1 to customer 2 or from warehouse 2 to customer 1 will do. If you treat the new zero square just like any other occupied square, any of the regular solution methods can be used.

Degeneracy During Later Solution Stages

A transportation problem can become degenerate after the initial solution stage if the filling of an empty square results in two (or more) filled cells becoming empty simultaneously instead of just one cell becoming empty. Such a problem occurs when two or more squares assigned minus signs on a closed path tie for the lowest quantity. To correct this problem, a zero should be put in one (or more) of the previously filled squares so that only one previously filled square becomes empty.

Bagwell Paint Example After one iteration of the stepping-stone method, cost analysts at Bagwell Paint produced the transportation table shown as Table 10.20. We observe that the solution in Table 10.20 is not degenerate, but it is also not optimal. The improvement indices for the four currently unused squares are

$$\text{factory } A - \text{warehouse 2 index} = +2$$

$$\text{factory } A - \text{warehouse 3 index} = +1$$

$$\text{factory } B - \text{warehouse 3 index} = -15 \longleftarrow \text{Only route with a negative index}$$

$$\text{factory } C - \text{warehouse 2 index} = +11$$

TO / FROM	WAREHOUSE 1	WAREHOUSE 2	WAREHOUSE 3	FACTORY CAPACITY
FACTORY A	8 70	5	16	70
FACTORY B	15 50	10 80	7	130
FACTORY C	3 30	9	10 50	80
WAREHOUSE REQUIREMENT	150	80	50	280

Total shipping cost = $2,700

TABLE 10.21

Tracing a Closed Path for
the Factory B–Warehouse
3 Route

TO FROM	WAREHOUSE 1	WAREHOUSE 3
FACTORY B	15 50 — ← - - - - - - - +	7
FACTORY C	3 30 + - - - - - - → — 50	10

Hence, an improved solution can be obtained by opening the route from factory B to warehouse 3. Let us go through the stepping-stone procedure for finding the next solution to Bagwell Paint's problem. We begin by drawing a closed path for the unused square representing factory B–warehouse 3. This is shown in Table 10.21, which is an abbreviated version of Table 10.20 and contains only the factories and warehouses necessary to close the path.

The smallest quantity in a square containing a minus sign is 50, so we add 50 units to the factory B–warehouse 3 and factory C–warehouse 1 routes, and subtract 50 units from the two squares containing minus signs. However, this act causes two formerly occupied squares to drop to 0. It also means that there are not enough occupied squares in the new solution and that it will be degenerate. We will have to place an artificial zero in one of the previously filled squares (generally, the one with the lowest shipping cost) to handle the degeneracy problem.

10.9 MORE THAN ONE OPTIMAL SOLUTION

Multiple solutions are possible when one or more improvement indices in the optimal solution stages are equal to zero.

Just as with LP problems, it is possible for a transportation problem to have multiple optimal solutions. Such a situation is indicated when one or more of the improvement indices that we calculate for each unused square is zero in the optimal solution. This means that it is possible to design alternative shipping routes with the same total shipping cost. The alternate optimal solution can be found by shipping the most to this unused square using a stepping-stone path. Practically speaking, multiple optimal solutions provide management with greater flexibility in selecting and using resources.

10.10 MAXIMIZATION TRANSPORTATION PROBLEMS

The optimal solution to a maximization problem has been found when all improvement indices are negative or zero.

If the objective in a transportation problem is to maximize profit, a minor change is required in the transportation algorithm. Since the improvement index for an empty cell indicates how the objective function value will change if one unit is placed in that empty cell, the optimal solution is reached when all the improvement indices are negative or zero. If any index is positive, the cell with the largest positive improvement index is selected to be filled using a stepping-stone path. This new solution is evaluated and the process continues until there are no positive improvement indices.

10.11 UNACCEPTABLE OR PROHIBITED ROUTES

A prohibited route is assigned a very high cost to prevent it from being used.

At times there are transportation problems in which one of the sources is unable to ship to one or more of the destinations. When this occurs, the problem is said to have an *unacceptable* or *prohibited route*. In a minimization problem, such a prohibited route is assigned a very high cost to prevent this route from ever being used in the optimal solution. After this high cost is placed in the transportation table, the problem is solved using the techniques previously discussed. In a maximization problem, the very high cost used in minimization problems is given a negative sign, turning it into a very bad profit. The procedure described in Section 10.10 is then used.

10.12 FACILITY LOCATION ANALYSIS

Locating a new facility within one overall distribution system is aided by the transportation method.

The transportation method has proved to be especially useful in helping a firm decide where to locate a new factory or warehouse. Since a new location is an issue of major financial importance to a company, several alternative locations must ordinarily be considered and evaluated. Even though a wide variety of subjective factors are considered, including quality of labor supply, presence of labor unions, community attitude and appearance, utilities, and recreational and educational facilities for employees, a final decision also involves minimizing total shipping and production costs. This means that each alternative facility location should be analyzed within the framework of one *overall* distribution system. The new location that will yield the minimum cost for the *entire system* will be the one recommended. Let us consider the case of the Hardgrave Machine Company.

Locating a New Factory for Hardgrave Machine Company

The Hardgrave Machine Company produces computer components at its plants in Cincinnati, Salt Lake City, and Pittsburgh. These plants have not been able to keep up with demand for orders at Hardgrave's four warehouses in Detroit, Dallas, New York, and Los Angeles. As a result, the firm has decided to build a new plant to expand its productive capacity. The two sites being considered are Seattle and Birmingham; both cities are attractive in terms of labor supply, municipal services, and ease of factory financing.

Table 10.22 presents the production costs and output requirements for each of the three existing plants, demand at each of the four warehouses, and estimated production

TABLE 10.22

Hardgrave's Demand and Supply Data

WAREHOUSE	MONTHLY DEMAND (UNITS)	PRODUCTION PLANT	MONTHLY SUPPLY	COST TO PRODUCE ONE UNIT ($)
Detroit	10,000	Cincinnati	15,000	48
Dallas	12,000	Salt Lake	6,000	50
New York	15,000	Pittsburgh	14,000	52
Los Angeles	9,000		35,000	
	46,000			

Supply needed from new plant = 46,000 − 35,000 = 11,000 units per month

ESTIMATED PRODUCTION COST PER UNIT AT PROPOSED PLANTS	
Seattle	$53
Birmingham	$49

TABLE 10.23

Hardgrave's Shipping Costs

TO FROM	DETROIT	DALLAS	NEW YORK	LOS ANGELES
CINCINNATI	$25	$55	$40	$60
SALT LAKE	35	30	50	40
PITTSBURGH	36	45	26	66
SEATTLE	60	38	65	27
BIRMINGHAM	35	30	41	50

costs of the new proposed plants. Transportation costs from each plant to each warehouse are summarized in Table 10.23.

The important question that Hardgrave now faces is this: Which of the new locations will yield the lowest cost for the firm in combination with the existing plants and warehouses? Note that the cost of each individual plant-to-warehouse route is found by adding the shipping costs (in the body of Table 10.23) to the respective unit production costs (from Table 10.22). Thus, the total production plus shipping cost of one computer component from Cincinnati to Detroit is $73 ($25 for shipping plus $48 for production).

We solve two transportation problems to find the new plant with lowest system cost.

To determine which new plant (Seattle or Birmingham) shows the lowest total systemwide cost of distribution and production, we solve two transportation problems—one for each of the two possible combinations. Tables 10.24 and 10.25 show the resulting two optimum solutions with the total cost for each. It appears that Seattle should be selected as the new plant site: Its total cost of $3,704,000 is less than the $3,741,000 cost at Birmingham.

Using Excel QM as a Solution Tool We can use Excel QM to solve each of the two Hardgrave Machine Company problems. To illustrate, Program 10.2A reflects the Birmingham computer analysis. As we saw earlier in this chapter, the Transportation module of Excel QM uses Solver. The output appears in Program 10.2B.

TABLE 10.24

Birmingham Plant Optimal Solution: Total Hardgrave Cost Is $3,741,000

TO FROM	DETROIT	DALLAS	NEW YORK	LOS ANGELES	MONTHLY SUPPLY
CINCINNATI	73 10,000	103	88 1,000	108 4,000	15,000
SALT LAKE	85	80 1,000	100	90 5,000	6,000
PITTSBURGH	88	97	78 14,000	118	14,000
BIRMINGHAM	84	79 11,000	90	99	11,000
MONTHLY DEMAND	10,000	12,000	15,000	9,000	46,000

TABLE 10.25

Seattle Plant Optimal
Solution: Total Hardgrave
Cost Is $3,704,000

FROM \ TO	DETROIT	DALLAS	NEW YORK	LOS ANGELES	MONTHLY SUPPLY
CINCINNATI	73	103	88	108	
	10,000	4,000	1,000		15,000
SALT LAKE	85	80	100	90	
		6,000			6,000
PITTSBURGH	88	97	78	118	
			14,000		14,000
SEATTLE	113	91	118	80	
		2,000		9,000	11,000
MONTHLY DEMAND	10,000	12,000	15,000	9,000	46,000

PROGRAM 10.2A   **Excel QM Input Screen, Showing Formulas**

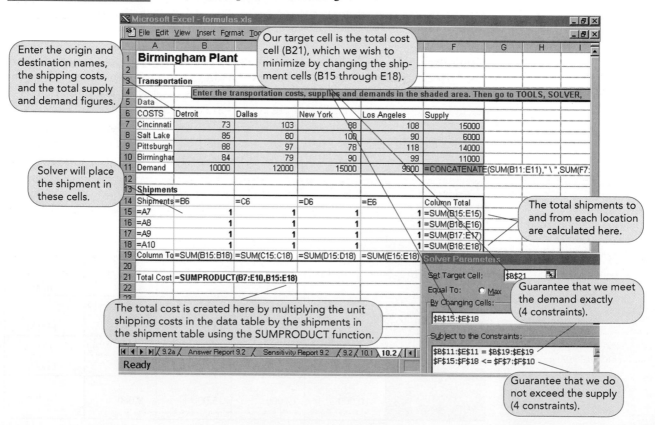

Enter the origin and destination names, the shipping costs, and the total supply and demand figures.

Our target cell is the total cost cell (B21), which we wish to minimize by changing the shipment cells (B15 through E18).

Solver will place the shipment in these cells.

The total shipments to and from each location are calculated here.

The total cost is created here by multiplying the unit shipping costs in the data table by the shipments in the shipment table using the SUMPRODUCT function.

Guarantee that we meet the demand exactly (4 constraints).

Guarantee that we do not exceed the supply (4 constraints).

PROGRAM 10.2B

Output from Excel QM Analysis in Program 10.2A with Optimal Solution to Hardgrave Machine Problem for Birmingham

	A	B	C	D		
1	**Birmingham Plant**					
2						
3	**Transportation**					
4		Enter the transportati				
5	Data					
6	COSTS	Detroit	Dallas	New York	Los Angel	Supply
7	Cincinnati	73	103	88	108	15000
8	Salt Lake	85	80	100	90	6000
9	Pittsburgh	88	97	78	118	14000
10	Birmingha	84	79	90	99	11000
11	Demand	10000	12000	15000	9000	46000 \ 46000
12						
13	**Shipments**					
14	Shipments	Detroit	Dallas	New York	Los Angel	Column To
15	Cincinnati	**10000**	**0**	**1000**	**4000**	15000
16	Salt Lake	**0**	**1000**	**0**	**5000**	6000
17	Pittsburgh	**0**	**0**	**14000**	**0**	14000
18	Birmingha	**0**	**11000**	**0**	**0**	11000
19	Column To	10000	12000	15000	9000	46000 \ 46000
20						
21	Total Cost	**3741000**				

Solver Results

Solver found a solution. All constraints and optimality conditions are satisfied.

Reports: Answer, Sensitivity, Limits

○ Keep Solver Solution
○ Restore Original Values

[OK] [Cancel] [Save Scenario...] [Help]

10.13   APPROACH OF THE ASSIGNMENT MODEL

The second special-purpose LP algorithm discussed in this chapter is the assignment method. Each assignment problem has associated with it a table, or matrix. Generally, the rows contain the objects or people we wish to assign, and the columns comprise the tasks or things we want them assigned to. The numbers in the table are the costs associated with each particular assignment.

An assignment problem can be viewed as a transportation problem in which the capacity from each source (or person to be assigned) is 1 and the demand at each destination (or job to be done) is 1. Such a formulation could be solved using the transportation algorithm, but it would have a severe degeneracy problem. However, this type of problem is very easy to solve using the assignment method.

As an illustration of the assignment method, let us consider the case of the Fix-It Shop, which has just received three new rush projects to repair: (1) a radio, (2) a toaster oven, and (3) a broken coffee table. Three repair persons, each with different talents and abilities, are available to do the jobs. The Fix-It Shop owner estimates what it will cost in wages to assign each of the workers to each of the three projects. The costs, which are shown in Table 10.26, differ because the owner believes that each worker will differ in speed and skill on these quite varied jobs.

The goal is to assign projects to people (one project to one person) so that the total costs are minimized.

The owner's objective is to assign the three projects to the workers in a way that will result in the lowest total cost to the shop. Note that the assignment of people to projects must be on a one-to-one basis; each project will be assigned exclusively to one worker only.

TABLE 10.26

Estimated Project Repair Costs for the Fix-It Shop Assignment Problem

	PROJECT		
PERSON	**1**	**2**	**3**
Adams	$11	$14	$ 6
Brown	8	10	11
Cooper	9	12	7

Summary of Fix-It Shop Assignment Alternatives and Costs

PROJECT ASSIGNMENT				
1	2	3	LABOR COSTS ($)	TOTAL COSTS ($)
Adams	Brown	Cooper	11 + 10 + 7	28
Adams	Cooper	Brown	11 + 12 + 11	34
Brown	Adams	Cooper	8 + 14 + 7	29
Brown	Cooper	Adams	8 + 12 + 6	26
Cooper	Adams	Brown	9 + 14 + 11	34
Cooper	Brown	Adams	9 + 10 + 6	25

One way to solve (small) problems is to enumerate all possible outcomes.

Hence the number of rows must always equal the number of columns in an assignment problem's cost table.

Because the Fix-It Shop problem only consists of three workers and three projects, one easy way to find the best solution is to list all possible assignments and their respective costs. For example, if Adams is assigned to project 1, Brown to project 2, and Cooper to project 3, the total cost will be $11 + $10 + $7 = $28. Table 10.27 summarizes all six assignment options. The table also shows that the least-cost solution would be to assign Cooper to project 1, Brown to project 2, and Adams to project 3, at a total cost of $25.

Obtaining solutions by enumeration works well for small problems but quickly becomes inefficient as assignment problems become larger. For example, a problem involving the assignment of four workers to four projects requires that we consider 4! ($= 4 \times 3 \times 2 \times 1$) or 24 alternatives. A problem with eight workers and eight tasks, which actually is not that large in a realistic situation, yields 8! ($= 8 \times 7 \times 6 \times 5 \times 4 \times 3 \times 2 \times 1$) or 40,320 possible solutions! Since it would clearly be impractical to compare so many alternatives, a more efficient solution method is needed.

The Hungarian Method (Flood's Technique)

Matrix reduction reduces the table to a set of opportunity costs. These show the penalty of not making the least-cost (or best) assignment.

The *Hungarian method* of assignment provides us with an efficient means of finding the optimal solution without having to make a direct comparison of every option. It operates on a principle of *matrix reduction*, which means that by subtracting and adding appropriate numbers in the cost table or matrix, we can reduce the problem to a matrix of *opportunity costs*. Opportunity costs show the relative penalties associated with assigning *any* person to a project as opposed to making the *best* or least-cost assignment. We would like to make assignments such that the opportunity cost for each assignment is zero. The Hungarian method will indicate when it is possible to make such assignments.

There are basically three steps in the assignment method[3]:

Three Steps of the Assignment Method

Here are the three steps of the assignment method.

1. *Find the opportunity cost table by*
   (a) Subtracting the smallest number in each row of the original cost table or matrix from every number in that row.
   (b) Then subtracting the smallest number in each column of the table obtained in part (a) from every number in that column.

---

[3] The steps apply if we can assume that the matrix is balanced, that is, the number of rows in the matrix equals the number of columns. In Section 10.14 we discuss how to handle unbalanced problems.

2. *Test the table resulting from step 1 to see whether an optimal assignment can be made.* The procedure is to draw the minimum number of vertical and horizontal straight lines necessary to cover all zeros in the table. If the number of lines equals either the number of rows or columns in the table, an optimal assignment can be made. If the number of lines is less than the number of rows or columns, we proceed to step 3.

3. *Revise the present opportunity cost table.* This is done by subtracting the smallest number not covered by a line from every other uncovered number. This same smallest number is also added to any number(s) lying at the intersection of horizontal and vertical lines. We then return to step 2 and continue the cycle until an optimal assignment is possible.

The assignment method is much easier than using LP.

This assignment "algorithm" is not nearly as difficult to apply as the LP algorithm we discussed in Chapters 7 to 9, or even as complex as the transportation procedures we saw earlier in this chapter. All it requires is some careful addition and subtraction and close attention to the three preceding steps. These steps are charted in Figure 10.3. Let us now apply them.

FIGURE 10.3   **Steps in the Assignment Method**

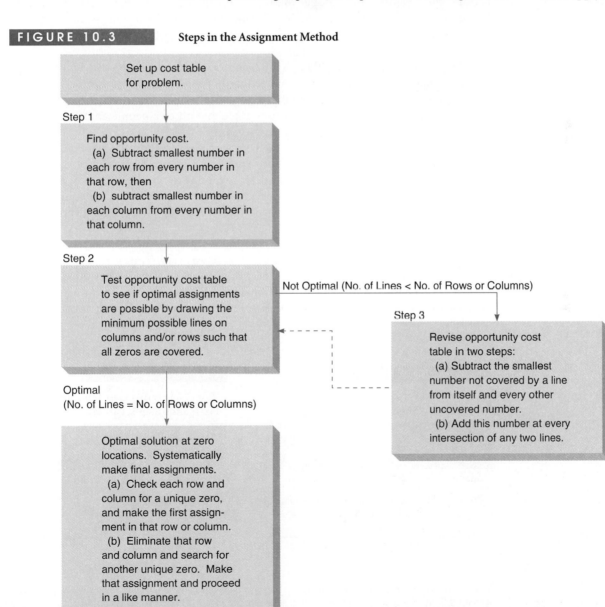

Row and column opportunity costs reflect the cost we are sacrificing by not making the least-cost selection.

Step 1: Find the Opportunity Cost Table. As mentioned earlier, the opportunity cost of any decision we make in life consists of the opportunities that are sacrificed in making that decision. For example, the opportunity cost of the unpaid time a person spends starting a new business is the salary that person would earn for those hours that he or she could have worked on another job. This important concept in the assignment method is best illustrated by applying it to a problem. For your convenience, the original cost table for the Fix-It Shop problem is repeated in Table 10.28.

Suppose that we decide to assign Cooper to project 2. The table shows that the cost of this assignment is $12. Based on the concept of opportunity costs, this is not the best decision, since Cooper could perform project 3 for only $7. The assignment of Cooper to project 2 then involves an opportunity cost of $5 (= $12 − $7), the amount we are sacrificing by making this assignment instead of the least-cost one. Similarly, an assignment of Cooper to project 1 represents an opportunity cost of $9 − $7 = $2. Finally, because the assignment of Cooper to project 3 is the best assignment, we can say that the opportunity cost of this assignment is zero ($7 − $7). The results of this operation for each of the rows in Table 10.28 are called the row opportunity costs and are shown in Table 10.29.

We note at this point that although the assignment of Cooper to project 3 is the cheapest way to make use of Cooper, it is not necessarily the least-expensive approach to completing project 3. Adams can perform the same task for only $6. In other words, if we look at this assignment problem from a project angle instead of a people angle, the *column* opportunity costs may be completely different.

Total opportunity costs reflect the row and column opportunity cost analyses.

What we need to complete step 1 of the assignment method is a *total* opportunity cost table, that is, one that reflects both row and column opportunity costs. This involves following part (b) of step 1 to derive column opportunity costs.[4] We simply take the costs in Table 10.29 and subtract the smallest number in each column from each number in that column. The resulting total opportunity costs are given in Table 10.30.

You might note that the numbers in columns 1 and 3 are the same as those in Table 10.29, since the smallest column entry in each case was zero. Thus it may turn out that the assignment of Cooper to project 3 is part of the optimal solution because of the relative nature of opportunity costs. What we are trying to measure are the relative efficiencies for the entire cost table and to find what assignments are best for the overall solution.

TABLE 10.28

Cost of Each Person-Project Assignment for the Fix-It Shop Problem

PERSON	PROJECT		
	1	2	3
Adams	$11	$14	$ 6
Brown	8	10	11
Cooper	9	12	7

TABLE 10.29

Row Opportunity Cost Table for the Fix-It Shop Step 1, Part (a)

PERSON	PROJECT		
	1	2	3
Adams	$5	$8	$0
Brown	0	2	3
Cooper	2	5	0

---

[4] Can you think of a situation in which part (b) of step 1 would not be required? See if you can design a cost table in which an optimal solution is possible after part (a) of step 1 is completed.

Step 2: Test for an Optimal Assignment. The objective of the Fix-It Shop owner is to assign the three workers to the repair projects in such a way that total labor costs are kept at a minimum. When translated to making assignments using our total opportunity cost table, this means that we would like to have a total assigned opportunity cost of 0. In other words, an optimal solution has zero opportunity costs for all of the assignments.

When a zero opportunity cost is found for all of the assignments, an optimal assignment can be made.

Looking at Table 10.30, we see that there are four possible zero opportunity cost assignments. We could assign Adams to project 3 and Brown to either project 1 or project 2. But this leaves Cooper without a zero opportunity cost assignment. Recall that two workers cannot be given the same task; each must do one and only one repair project, and each project must be assigned to only one person. Hence, even though four zeros appear in this cost table, it is not yet possible to make an assignment yielding a total opportunity cost of zero.

This line test is used to see if a solution is optimal.

A simple test has been designed to help us determine whether an optimal assignment can be made. The method consists of finding the *minimum* number of straight lines (vertical and horizontal) necessary to cover all zeros in the cost table. (Each line is drawn so that it covers as many zeros as possible at one time.) If the number of lines equals the number of rows or columns in the table, then an optimal assignment can be made. If, on the other hand, the number of lines is less than the number of rows or columns, an optimal assignment cannot be made. In the latter case, we must proceed to step 3 and develop a new total opportunity cost table.

Table 10.31 illustrates that it is possible to cover all four zero entries in Table 10.30 with only two lines. Because there are three rows, an optimal assignment may not yet be made.

Step 3: Revise the Opportunity-Cost Table. An optimal solution is seldom obtained from the initial opportunity cost table. Often, we need to revise the table in order to shift one (or more) of the zero costs from its present location (covered by lines) to a new uncovered location in the table. Intuitively, we would want this uncovered location to emerge with a new zero opportunity cost.

This is accomplished by *subtracting* the smallest number not covered by a line from all numbers not covered by a straight line. This same smallest number is then added to every number (including zeros) lying at the intersection of any two lines.

The smallest uncovered number in Table 10.31 is 2, so this value is subtracted from each of the four uncovered numbers. A 2 is also added to the number that is covered by the intersecting horizontal and vertical lines. The results of step 3 are shown in Table 10.32.

To test now for an optimal assignment, we return to step 2 and find the minimum number of lines necessary to cover all zeros in the revised opportunity cost table. Because it requires three lines to cover the zeros (see Table 10.33), an optimal assignment can be made.

Total Opportunity Cost Table for the Fix-It Shop Step 1, Part (b)

PERSON	PROJECT		
	1	2	3
Adams	$5	$6	$0
Brown	0	0	3
Cooper	2	3	0

Test for Optimal Solution to Fix-It Shop Problem

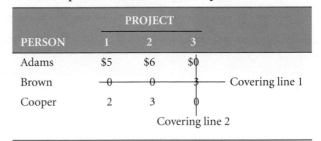

PERSON	PROJECT		
	1	2	3
Adams	$5	$6	$0
Brown	0	0	3
Cooper	2	3	0

Covering line 1

Covering line 2

TABLE 10.32

Revised Opportunity Cost Table for the Fix-It Shop Problem

	PROJECT		
PERSON	1	2	3
Adams	$3	$4	$0
Brown	0	0	5
Cooper	0	1	0

TABLE 10.33

Optimality Test on the Revised Fix-It Shop Opportunity Cost Table

	PROJECT		
PERSON	1	2	3
Adams	$3	$4	$0
Brown	0	0	5 — Covering line 2
Cooper	0	1	0

Covering line 1   Covering line 3

Making the Final Assignment

Making an optimal assignment involves first checking the rows and columns where there is only one zero cell.

It is apparent that the Fix-It Shop problem's optimal assignment is Adams to project 3, Brown to project 2, and Cooper to project 1. In solving larger problems, however, it is best to rely on a more systematic approach to making valid assignments. One such way is first to select a row or column that contains only one zero cell. Such a situation is found in the first row, Adams's row, in which the only zero is in the project 3 column. An assignment can be made to that cell, and then lines drawn through its row and column (see Table 10.34). From the uncovered rows and columns, we again choose a row or column in which there is only one zero cell. We make that assignment and continue the procedure until each person is assigned to one task.

The total labor costs of this assignment are computed from the original cost table (see Table 10.28). They are as follows:

ASSIGNMENT	COST ($)
Adams to project 3	6
Brown to project 2	10
Cooper to project 1	9
Total cost	25

Using Excel QM for the Fix-It Shop Assignment Problem Excel QM's Assignment module can be used to solve the Fix-It problem. The input screen, using data from Table 10.28 is shown first, as Program 10.3A. The constraints are also shown in Program 10.3A. When the data are all entered, we choose the Tools command, followed by the Solver command. Excel's Solver uses LP to optimize assignment problems. We then select the Solve command. The solution is shown in Program 10.3B.

TABLE 10.34   Making the Final Fix-It Shop Assignments

	(A) FIRST ASSIGNMENT				(B) SECOND ASSIGNMENT				(C) THIRD ASSIGNMENT		
	1	2	3		1	2	3		1	2	3
Adams	3	4	[0]	Adams	3	4	[0]	Adams	3	4	[0]
Brown	0	0	5	Brown	0	0	5	Brown	0	[0]	5
Cooper	0	1	0	Cooper	[0]	1	0	Cooper	[0]	1	0

PROGRAM 10.3A   Excel QM's Assignment Module

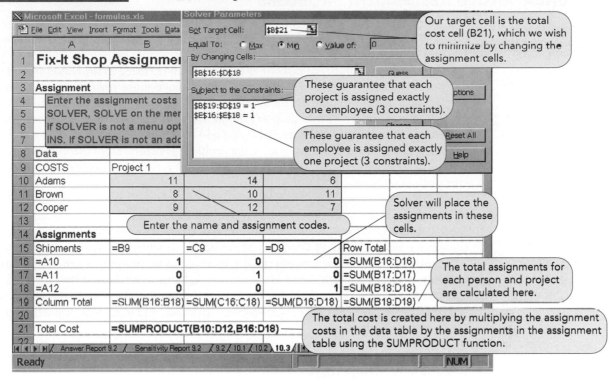

PROGRAM 10.3B   Excel QM Output Screen for the Fix-It Shop Problem

10.14 UNBALANCED ASSIGNMENT PROBLEMS

A balanced assignment problem is one in which the number of rows equals the number of columns.

The solution procedure to assignment problems just discussed requires that the number of rows in the table equal the number of columns. Such a problem is called a *balanced assignment problem*. Often, however, the number of people or objects to be assigned does not equal the number of tasks or clients or machines listed in the columns, and the problem is *unbalanced*. When this occurs, and we have more rows than columns, we simply add a *dummy column* or task (similar to how we handled unbalanced transportation problems earlier in this chapter). If the number of tasks that need to be done exceeds the number of people available, we add a *dummy row*. This creates a table of equal dimensions and allows us to solve the problem as before. Since the dummy task or person is really nonexistent, it is reasonable to enter zeros in its row or column as the cost or time estimate.

Suppose the owner of the Fix-It Shop realizes that a fourth worker, Davis, is also available to work on one of the three rush jobs that just came in. Davis can do the first project for $10, the second for $13, and the third project for $8. The shop's owner still faces the same basic problem, that is, which worker to assign to which project to minimize total labor costs. We do not have a fourth project, however, so we simply add a dummy column or dummy project. The initial cost table is shown in Table 10.35. One of the four workers, you should realize, will be assigned to the dummy project; in other words, the worker will not really be assigned any of the tasks. Problem 10-35 asks you to find the optimal solution for the data in Table 10.35.

10.15 MAXIMIZATION ASSIGNMENT PROBLEMS

Maximization problems can easily be converted to minimization problems. This is done by subtracting each rating from the largest rating in the table.

Some assignment problems are phrased in terms of maximizing the payoff, profit, or effectiveness of an assignment instead of minimizing costs. It is easy to obtain an equivalent minimization problem by converting all numbers in the table to opportunity costs. This is brought about by subtracting every number in the original payoff table from the largest single number in that table. The transformed entries represent opportunity costs; it turns out that minimizing opportunity costs produces the same assignment as the original maximization problem. Once the optimal assignment for this transformed problem has been computed, the total payoff or profit is found by adding the original payoffs of those cells that are in the optimal assignment.

Let us consider the following example. The British navy wishes to assign four ships to patrol four sectors of the North Sea. In some areas ships are to be on the outlook for illegal fishing boats, and in other sectors to watch for enemy submarines, so the commander rates each ship in terms of its probable efficiency in each sector. These relative efficiencies are illustrated in Table 10.36. On the basis of the ratings shown, the commander wants to determine the patrol assignments producing the greatest overall efficiencies.

TABLE 10.35
Estimated Project Repair Costs for Fix-It Shop with Davis Included

	PROJECT			
PERSON	1	2	3	DUMMY
Adams	$11	$14	$6	$0
Brown	8	10	11	0
Cooper	9	12	7	0
Davis	10	13	8	0

TABLE 10.36

Efficiencies of British Ships in Patrol Sectors

SHIP	SECTOR			
	A	B	C	D
1	20	60	50	55
2	60	30	80	75
3	80	100	90	80
4	65	80	75	70

TABLE 10.37

Opportunity Costs of British Ships

SHIP	SECTOR			
	A	B	C	D
1	80	40	50	45
2	40	70	20	25
3	20	0	10	20
4	35	20	25	30

Row subtractions: the smallest number in each row is subtracted from every number in that row.

Column subtractions: the smallest number in each column is subtracted from every number in that column.

Step by step, the solution procedure is as follows. We first convert the maximizing efficiency table into a minimizing opportunity cost table. This is done by subtracting each rating from 100, the largest rating in the whole table. The resulting opportunity costs are given in Table 10.37.

We now follow steps 1 and 2 of the assignment algorithm. The smallest number in each row is subtracted from every number in that row (see Table 10.38); and then the smallest number in each column is subtracted from every number in that column (as shown in Table 10.39).

The minimum number of straight lines needed to cover all zeros in this total opportunity cost table is four. Hence an optimal assignment can be made already. You should be able by now to spot the best solution, namely, ship 1 to sector *D*, ship 2 to sector *C*, ship 3 to sector *B*, and ship 4 to sector *A*.

The overall efficiency, computed from the original efficiency data in Table 10.36, can now be shown:

ASSIGNMENT	EFFICIENCY
Ship 1 to sector *D*	55
Ship 2 to sector *C*	80
Ship 3 to sector *B*	100
Ship 4 to sector *A*	65
Total efficiency	300

TABLE 10.38

Row Opportunity Costs for the British Navy Problem

SHIP	SECTOR			
	A	B	C	D
1	40	0	10	5
2	20	50	0	5
3	20	0	10	20
4	15	0	5	10

TABLE 10.39

Total Opportunity Costs for the British Navy Problem

SHIP	SECTOR			
	A	B	C	D
1	25	0	10	0
2	5	50	0	0
3	5	0	10	15
4	0	0	5	5

IN ACTION Scheduling American League Umpires with the Assignment Model

Scheduling umpires in professional baseball is a complex problem that must include a number of criteria. In assigning officials to games, one objective typically is to minimize total travel cost while satisfying a set of frequency-oriented constraints such as limiting the number of times an official or crew is exposed to each team, balancing home and away game exposures, balancing exposures to teams over the course of a season, and so on. These constraints complicate the problem to such an extent that except for the most trivial cases, the use of a computer-based system is essential.

The American League is composed of 14 professional baseball teams organized into three divisions. The game schedule, constructed each winter prior to the start of the baseball season, is a difficult scheduling problem in itself. Consideration must be given to such factors as the number of games played against other teams both within and outside a division, the split between home games and road trips, travel time, and possible conflicts in cities that have teams in the National League.

The objectives of balancing crew assignments relatively evenly and minimizing travel costs are by nature conflicting. Attempting to balance crew assignments necessitates considerable airline travel and equipment moves, and hence increased travel costs.

Using an assignment model as part of a microcomputer-based decision support system, the American League was able to reduce travel mileage by about 4% during the first year of use. This not only saved the league $30,000 but improved the crew exposure balance.

Source: J. Evans. "Scheduling American League Umpires," *Interfaces* (November–December 1988): 42–51.

SUMMARY

In this chapter we explored the transportation model and the assignment model. We saw how to develop an initial solution to the transportation problem with the northwest corner method and with Vogel's approximation method. Both the stepping-stone path method and the MODI method were used to calculate improvement indices for the empty cells. Improved solutions were developed using a stepping-stone path. The special cases of the transportation problem included degeneracy, unbalanced problems, and multiple optimal solutions. We demonstrated how to use the transportation model for facility location analysis.

We saw how the assignment problem may be viewed as a special case of the transportation problem. The Hungarian method for solving assignment problems was presented. When assignment problems are unbalanced, dummy rows or columns are used to balance the problem. Assignment problems with maximization objectives were also presented.

GLOSSARY

Balanced Assignment Problem. An assignment problem in which the number of rows is equal to the number of columns.

Balanced Transportation Problem. The condition under which total demand (at all destinations) is equal to total supply (at all sources).

Degeneracy. A condition that occurs when the number of occupied squares in any solution is less than the number of rows plus the number of columns minus 1 in a transportation table.

Destination. A demand location in a transportation problem.

Dummy Destination. An artificial destination added to a transportation table when total supply is greater than total demand. The demand at the dummy destination is set so that total supply and demand are equal. The transportation cost for dummy destination cells is zero.

Dummy Rows or Columns. Extra rows or columns added in order to "balance" an assignment problem so that the number of rows equals the number of columns.

Dummy Source. An artificial source added to a transportation table when total demand is greater than total supply. The supply at the dummy source is set so that total demand and supply are equal. The transportation cost for dummy source cells is zero.

Facility Location Analysis. An application of the transportation method to help a firm decide where to locate a new factory, warehouse, or other facility.

Flood's Technique. Another name for the Hungarian Method.

Hungarian Method. A matrix reduction approach to solving the assignment problem.

Improvement Index. The net cost of shipping one unit on a route not used in the current transportation problem solution.

Matrix Reduction. The approach of the assignment method that reduces the original assignment costs to a table of opportunity costs.

Modified Distribution (MODI) Method. A technique that is used to evaluate the empty cells in a transportation problem.

Northwest Corner Rule. A systematic procedure for establishing an initial feasible solution to the transportation problem.

Opportunity Costs. In an assignment problem, this is the additional cost incurred when the assignment with the lowest possible cost in a row or column is not selected.

Source. An origin or supply location in a transportation problem.

Stepping-Stone Method. An iterative technique for moving from an initial feasible solution to an optimal solution in transportation problems.

Transportation Problems. A specific case of LP concerned with scheduling shipments from sources to destinations so that total transportation costs are minimized.

Transportation Table. A table summarizing all transportation data to help keep track of all algorithm computations. It stores information on demands, supplies, shipping costs, units shipped, origins, and destinations.

Vogel's Approximation Method (VAM). An algorithm used to find a relatively efficient initial feasible solution to a transportation problem. This initial solution is often the optimal solution.

KEY EQUATIONS

(10-1) $R_i + K_j = C_{ij}$

An equation used to compute the MODI cost values (R_i, K_j) for each column and row intersection for squares used in the solution.

(10-2) Improvement index $(I_{ij}) = C_{ij} - R_i - K_j$

The equation used to compute the improvement index for each unused square by the MODI method. If all improvement indices are greater than or equal to zero, an optimal solution has been reached.

SOLVED PROBLEMS

Solved Problem 10-1

Don Yale, president of Hardrock Concrete Company, has plants in three locations and is currently working on three major construction projects, located at different sites. The shipping cost per truckload of concrete, plant capacities, and project requirements are provided in the accompanying table.

a. Formulate an initial feasible solution to Hardrock's transportation problem using the northwest corner rule.
b. Then evaluate each unused shipping route (each empty cell) by applying the stepping-stone method and computing all improvement indices. Remember to do the following:

1. Check that supply and demand are equal.

2. Load the table via the northwest corner method.

3. Check that there are the proper number of occupied cells for a "normal" solution, namely, number of rows + number of columns − 1 = number of occupied cells.

4. Find a closed path to each empty cell.

5. Determine the improvement index for each unused cell.

6. Move as many units as possible to the cell that provides the most improvement (if there is one).

7. Repeat steps 3 through 6 until no further improvement can be found.

FROM \ TO	PROJECT A	PROJECT B	PROJECT C	PLANT CAPACITIES
PLANT 1	$10	$4	$11	70
PLANT 2	$12	$5	$8	50
PLANT 3	$9	$7	$6	30
PROJECT REQUIREMENTS	40	50	60	150

Solution

a. Northwest corner solution

Initial cost = 40($10) + 30($4) + 20($5) + 30($8) + 30($6) = $1,040

FROM \ TO	PROJECT A	PROJECT B	PROJECT C	PLANT CAPACITIES
PLANT 1	$10 40	$4 30	$11	70
PLANT 2	$12	$5 20	$8 30	50
PLANT 3	$9	$7	$6 30	30
PROJECT REQUIREMENTS	40	50	60	150

b. Using the stepping-stone method, the following improvement indices are computed:

Path: plant 1 to project C = $11 − $4 + $5 − $8 = +$4

(closed path: 1C to 1B to 2B to 2C)

FROM \ TO	PROJECT A	PROJECT B	PROJECT C	PLANT CAPACITIES
PLANT 1	10 40	4 30 −	11 +	70
PLANT 2	12	5 20 +	8 30 −	50
PLANT 3	9	7	6 30	30
PROJECT REQUIREMENTS	40	50	60	150

Path: plant 1 to project C

Path: plant 2 to project $A = \$12 - \$5 + \$4 - \$10 = +\$1$

(closed path: $2A$ to $2B$ to $1B$ to $1A$)

FROM \ TO	PROJECT A	PROJECT B	PROJECT C	PLANT CAPACITIES
PLANT 1	40 ⟶ 10	30 ⟶ 4	11	70
PLANT 2	12	20 ⟶ 5	30 ⟶ 8	50
PLANT 3	9	7	30 ⟶ 6	30
PROJECT REQUIREMENTS	40	50	60	150

Path: plant 2 to project A

Path: plant 3 to project $A = \$9 - \$6 + \$8 - \$5 + \$4 - \$10 = \$0$

(closed path: $3A$ to $3C$ to $2C$ to $2B$ to $1B$ to $1A$)

FROM \ TO	PROJECT A	PROJECT B	PROJECT C	PLANT CAPACITIES
PLANT 1	40 ⟶ 10	30 ⟶ 4	11	70
PLANT 2	12	20 ⟶ 5	30 ⟶ 8	50
PLANT 3	9	7	30 ⟶ 6	30
PROJECT REQUIREMENTS	40	50	60	150

Path: plant 3 to project A

Path: plant 3 to project B = $7 − $6 + $8 − $5 = +$4

(closed path: $3B$ to $3C$ to $2C$ to $2B$)

FROM \ TO	PROJECT A	PROJECT B	PROJECT C	PLANT CAPACITIES
PLANT 1	10 40	4 30	11	70
PLANT 2	12	5 20	8 30	50
PLANT 3	9	7	6 30	30
PROJECT REQUIREMENTS	40	50	60	150

Path: plant 3 to project B

Since all indices are greater than or equal to zero (all are positive or zero), this initial solution provides the optimal transportation schedule, namely, 40 units from 1 to A, 30 units from 1 to B, 20 units from 2 to B, 30 units from 2 to C, and 30 units from 3 to C.

Had we found a path that allowed improvement, we would move all units possible to that cell and then check every empty cell again. Because the plant 3 to project A improvement index was equal to zero, we note that multiple optimal solutions exist.

Solved Problem 10-2

The initial solution found in Solved Problem 10-1 was optimal, but the improvement index for one of the empty cells was zero, indicating another optimal solution. Use a stepping-stone path to develop this other optimal solution.

Solution

Using the stepping-stone path, we see that the lowest number of units in a cell where a subtraction is to be made is 20 units from plant 2 to project B. Therefore, 20 units will be subtracted from each cell with a minus sign and added to each cell with a plus sign. The result is shown here.

FROM \ TO	PROJECT A	PROJECT B	PROJECT C	PLANT CAPACITIES
PLANT 1	10 20	4 50	11	70
PLANT 2	12	5	8 50	50
PLANT 3	9 20	7	6 10	30
PROJECT REQUIREMENTS	40	50	60	150

Solved Problem 10-3

Solve the Hardgrave Machine Company facility location problem shown in Table 10.25 on page 420 with an LP formulation.

Solution

First we shall formulate this transportation problem as an LP model by introducing double-subscripted decision variables. We let X_{11} denote the number of units shipped from origin 1 (Cincinnati) to destination 1 (Detroit), X_{12} denote shipments from origin 1 (Cincinnati) to destination 2 (Dallas), and so on. In general, the decision variables for a transportation problem having m origins and n destinations are written as

$$X_{ij} = \text{number of units shipped from origin } i \text{ to destination } j$$

where

$$i = 1, 2, \ldots, m \quad \text{and} \quad j = 1, 2, \ldots, n$$

Because the objective of the transportation model is to minimize total transportation costs, we develop the following cost expression:

$$\text{minimize} = 73X_{11} + 103X_{12} + 88X_{13} + 108X_{14}$$
$$+\ 85X_{21} + 80X_{22} + 100X_{23} + 90X_{24}$$
$$+\ 88X_{31} + 97X_{32} + 78X_{33} + 118X_{34}$$
$$+\ 113X_{41} + 91X_{42} + 118X_{43} + 80X_{44}$$

Now we establish supply constraints for each of the four plants:

$$X_{11} + X_{12} + X_{13} + X_{14} \leq 15{,}000 \text{ (Cincinnati supply)}$$
$$X_{21} + X_{22} + X_{23} + X_{24} \leq\ 6{,}000 \text{ (Salt Lake supply)}$$
$$X_{31} + X_{32} + X_{33} + X_{34} \leq 14{,}000 \text{ (Pittsburgh supply)}$$
$$X_{41} + X_{42} + X_{43} + X_{44} \leq 11{,}000 \text{ (Seattle supply)}$$

With four warehouses as the destinations, we need the following four demand constraints:

$$X_{11} + X_{21} + X_{31} + X_{41} = 10{,}000 \text{ (Detroit demand)}$$
$$X_{12} + X_{22} + X_{32} + X_{42} = 12{,}000 \text{ (Dallas demand)}$$
$$X_{13} + X_{23} + X_{33} + X_{43} = 15{,}000 \text{ (New York demand)}$$
$$X_{14} + X_{24} + X_{34} + X_{44} =\ 9{,}000 \text{ (Los Angeles demand)}$$

In Chapters 7, 8 and 9, we saw how QM for Windows and Excel spreadsheets can be used to solve LP problems. A computer solution will confirm that total shipping costs will be $3,704,000.

Although LP codes can indeed be used on transportation problems, the special transportation module for Excel QM (shown earlier) and QM for Windows (shown in Appendix 10.1) tend to be easier to input, run, and interpret.

Solved Problem 10-4

Prentice Hall, Inc., a publisher headquartered in New Jersey, wants to assign three recently hired college graduates, Jones, Smith, and Wilson to regional sales districts in Omaha, Dallas, and Miami. But the firm also has an opening in New York and would send one of the three there if it were more economical than a move to Omaha, Dallas, or Miami. It will cost $1,000 to relocate Jones to New York, $800 to relocate Smith there, and $1,500 to move Wilson. What is the optimal assignment of personnel to offices?

HIREE \ OFFICE	OMAHA	MIAMI	DALLAS
JONES	$800	$1,100	$1,200
SMITH	$500	$1,600	$1,300
WILSON	$500	$1,000	$2,300

Solution

a. The cost table has a fourth column to represent New York. To balance the problem, we add a dummy row (person) with a zero relocation cost to each city.

HIREE \ OFFICE	OMAHA	MIAMI	DALLAS	NEW YORK
JONES	$800	$1,100	$1,200	$1,000
SMITH	$500	$1,600	$1,300	$800
WILSON	$500	$1,000	$2,300	$1,500
DUMMY	0	0	0	0

b. Subtract smallest number in each row and cover zeros (column subtraction will give the same numbers and therefore is not necessary).

HIREE \ OFFICE	OMAHA	MIAMI	DALLAS	NEW YORK
JONES	0	300	400	200
SMITH	0	1,100	800	300
WILSON	0	500	1,800	1,000
DUMMY	0	0	0	0

c. Subtract smallest uncovered number (200), add it to each square where two lines intersect, and cover all zeros.

HIREE \ OFFICE	OMAHA	MIAMI	DALLAS	NEW YORK
JONES	0	100	200	0
SMITH	0	900	600	100
WILSON	0	300	1,600	800
DUMMY	200	0	0	0

d. Subtract smallest uncovered number (100), add it to each square where two lines intersect, and cover all zeros.

OFFICE HIREE	OMAHA	MIAMI	DALLAS	NEW YORK
JONES	0	0	100	0
SMITH	0	800	500	100
WILSON	0	200	1,500	800
DUMMY	300	0	0	100

e. Subtract smallest uncovered number (100), add it to squares where two lines intersect, and cover all zeros.

OFFICE HIREE	OMAHA	MIAMI	DALLAS	NEW YORK
JONES	100	0	100	0
SMITH	0	700	400	0
WILSON	0	100	1,400	700
DUMMY	400	0	0	100

f. Since it takes four lines to cover all zeros, an optimal assignment can be made at zero squares. We assign

Dummy (no one) to Dallas

Wilson to Omaha

Smith to New York

Jones to Miami

Cost = \$0 + \$500 + \$800 + \$1,100 = \$2,400

⟫ SELF-TEST

- Before taking the self-test, refer back to the learning objectives at the beginning of the chapter, the notes in the margins, and the glossary at the end of the chapter.
- Use the key at the back of the book to correct your answers.
- Restudy pages that correspond to any questions that you answered incorrectly or material you feel uncertain about.

1. If the total demand equals the total supply in a transportation problem, the problem is
   a. degenerate.
   b. balanced.
   c. unbalanced.
   d. infeasible.

2. Which of the following is used to evaluate a solution to a transportation problem to determine if it is optimal?
   a. northwest corner method
   b. Vogel's approximation method (VAM)
   c. the modified distribution (MODI) method
   d. all of the above

3. In a transportation problem, what indicates that the minimum cost solution has been found?
   a. all improvement indices are negative or zero
   b. all improvement indices are positive or zero
   c. all improvement indices are equal to zero
   d. all cells in the dummy row are empty

4. Vogel's approximation method always provides a lower cost initial solution than the northwest corner method.
   a. True
   b. False

5. If the number of filled cells in a transportation table does not equal the number of rows plus the number of columns minus 1, then the problem is said to be
   a. unbalanced.
   b. degenerate.
   c. optimal.
   d. a maximization problem.

6. If a solution to a transportation problem is degenerate, then
   a. it will be impossible to evaluate all empty cells without removing the degeneracy.
   b. a dummy row or column must be added.
   c. there will be more than one optimal solution.
   d. the problem has no feasible solution.

7. If the total demand is greater than the total capacity in a transportation problem, then
   a. the optimal solution will be degenerate.
   b. a dummy source must be added.

   c. a dummy destination must be added.
   d. both a dummy source and a dummy destination must be added.

8. In solving a facility location problem in which there are two possible locations being considered, the transportation algorithm may be used. In doing this,
   a. two rows (sources) would be added to the existing rows and the enlarged problem would be solved.
   b. two separate transportation problems would be solved.
   c. costs of zero would be used for each of the new facilities.
   d. the MODI method must be used to evaluate the empty cells.

9. The Hungarian method is
   a. a way to develop an initial solution to a transportation problem.
   b. used to solve assignment problems.
   c. also called Vogel's approximation method.
   d. only used for problems in which the objective is to maximize profit.

10. In an assignment problem, it may be necessary to add more than one row to the table.
    a. True
    b. False

11. When using the Hungarian method, an optimal assignment can always be made when every row and every column has at least one zero.
    a. True
    b. False

12. An assignment problem can be viewed as a special type of transportation problem with which of the following features?
    a. the capacity for each source and the demand for each destination is equal to one
    b. the number of rows is equal to the number of columns
    c. the cost for each shipping route is equal to one
    d. all of the above

DISCUSSION QUESTIONS AND PROBLEMS

Discussion Questions

10-1 Is the transportation model an example of decision making under certainty or decision making under uncertainty? Why?

10-2 Why does VAM provide a good initial feasible solution? Could the northwest corner rule ever provide an initial solution with as low a cost?

10-3 What is a *balanced* transportation problem? Describe the approach you would use to solve an *unbalanced* problem.

10-4 The stepping-stone method is being used to solve a transportation problem. The smallest quantity in a cell with a minus sign is 35, but two different cells with minus signs have 35 units in them. What problem will this cause, and how should this difficulty be resolved?

10-5 The stepping-stone method is being used to solve a transportation problem. There is only one empty cell having a negative improvement index, and this index is −2. The stepping-stone path for this cell indicates that the smallest quantity for the cells with minus signs is 80 units. If the total cost for the current solution is $900, what will the total cost be for the improved solution? What can you conclude about how much the total cost will decrease when developing each new solution for any transportation problem?

10-6 Explain what happens when the solution to a transportation problem does not have $m + n - 1$ occupied squares (where m = number of rows in the table and n = number of columns in the table).

10-7 What is the enumeration approach to solving assignment problems? Is it a practical way to solve a 5 row × 5 column problem? A 7 × 7 problem? Why?

10-8 Think back to the transportation problem at the beginning of this chapter. How could an assignment problem be solved using the transportation approach? Set up the Fix-It Shop problem (shown in Table 10.26) using the transportation approach. What condition will make the solution of this problem difficult?

10-9 You are the plant supervisor and are responsible for scheduling workers to jobs on hand. After estimating the cost of assigning each of five available workers in your plant to five projects that must be completed immediately, you solve the problem using the Hungarian method. The following solution is reached and you post these job assignments:

Jones to project *A*

Smith to project *B*

Thomas to project *C*

Gibbs to project *D*

Heldman to project *E*

The optimal cost was found to be $492 for these assignments. The plant general manager inspects your original cost estimates and informs you that increased employee benefits mean that each of the 25 numbers in your cost table is too low by $5. He suggests that you immediately rework the problem and post the new assignments.

Is this necessary? Why? What will the new optimal cost be?

10-10 Sue Simmons' marketing research firm has local representatives in all but five states. She decides to expand to cover the whole United States by transferring five experienced volunteers from their current locations to new offices in each of the five states. Simmons's goal is to relocate the five representatives at the least total cost. Consequently, she sets up a 5 × 5 relocation cost table and prepares to solve it for the best assignments by use of the Hungarian method. At the last moment, Simmons recalls that although the first four volunteers did not pose any objections to being placed in any of the five new cities, the fifth volunteer *did* make one restriction. That person absolutely refused to be assigned to the new office in Tallahassee, Florida—fear of southern roaches, the representative claimed! How should Sue alter the cost matrix to ensure that this assignment is not included in the optimal solution?

Problems*

· 10-11 The management of the Executive Furniture Corporation decided to expand the production capacity at its Des Moines factory and to cut back production at its other factories. It also recognizes a shifting market for its desks and revises the requirements at its three warehouses.

(a) Use the northwest corner rule to establish an initial feasible shipping schedule and calculate its cost.

(b) Use the stepping-stone method to test whether an improved solution is possible.

(c) Explain the meaning and implications of an improvement index that is equal to 0. What decisions might management make with this information? Exactly how is the final solution affected?

Data for Problem 10-11

NEW WAREHOUSE REQUIREMENTS		NEW FACTORY CAPACITIES	
Albuquerque (*A*)	200 desks	Des Moines (*D*)	300 desks
Boston (*B*)	200 desks	Evansville (*E*)	150 desks
Cleveland (*C*)	300 desks	Fort Lauderdale (*F*)	250 desks

Table for Problem 10-11

FROM \ TO	ALBUQUERQUE	BOSTON	CLEVELAND
DES MOINES	5	4	3
EVANSVILLE	8	4	3
FORT LAUDERDALE	9	7	5

* Note: 🔍 means the problem may be solved with QM for Windows; ✘ means the problem may be solved with Excel QM; and 🔍✘ means the problem may be solved with QM for Windows and/or Excel QM.

Data for Problem 10-13

From \ To	Project A	Project B	Project C	Plant Capacities
Plant 1	$10	$4	$11	70
Plant 2	12	5	8	50
Plant 3	9	7	6	30
Project Requirements	40	50	60	150

: 10-12 Using the expanded production capacity given in Problem 10-11, use VAM and the stepping-stone method to find the optimal solution to this problem.

: 10-13 The Hardrock Concrete Company has plants in three locations and is currently working on three major construction projects, each located at a different site. The shipping cost per truckload of concrete, daily plant capacities, and daily project requirements are provided in the table above.

(a) Formulate an initial feasible solution to Hardrock's transportation problem using the northwest corner rule. Then evaluate each unused shipping route by computing all improvement indices. Is this solution optimal? Why?

(b) Is there more than one optimal solution to this problem? Why?

: 10-14 Hardrock Concrete's owner has decided to increase the capacity at his smallest plant (see Problem 10-13). Instead of producing 30 loads of concrete per day at plant 3, that plant's capacity is doubled to 60 loads. Find the new optimal solution using the northwest corner rule and stepping-stone method. How has changing the third plant's capacity altered the optimal shipping assignment? Discuss the concepts of degeneracy and multiple optimal solutions with regard to this problem.

• 10-15 The Saussy Lumber Company ships pine flooring to three building supply houses from its mills in Pineville, Oak Ridge, and Mapletown. Determine the best transportation schedule for the data given in the

table. Use the northwest corner rule and the stepping-stone method.

• 10-16 Using the same Saussy Lumber Company data and the same initial solution you found with the northwest corner rule, resolve Problem 10-15 using the MODI method.

: 10-17 The Krampf Lines Railway Company specializes in coal handling. On Friday, April 13, Krampf had empty cars at the following towns in the quantities indicated:

TOWN	SUPPLY OF CARS
Morgantown	35
Youngstown	60
Pittsburgh	25

By Monday, April 16, the following towns will need coal cars as follows:

TOWN	DEMAND FOR CARS
Coal Valley	30
Coaltown	45
Coal Junction	25
Coalsburg	20

Table for Problem 10-15

From \ To	Supply House 1	Supply House 2	Supply House 3	Mill Capacity (Tons)
PINEVILLE	$3	$3	$2	25
OAK RIDGE	4	2	3	40
MAPLETOWN	3	2	3	30
SUPPLY HOUSE DEMAND (TONS)	30	30	35	95

Table for Problem 10-17

FROM \ TO	COAL VALLEY	COALTOWN	COAL JUNCTION	COALSBURG
MORGANTOWN	50	30	60	70
YOUNGSTOWN	20	80	10	90
PITTSBURGH	100	40	80	30

Using a railway city-to-city distance chart, the dispatcher constructs a mileage table for the preceding towns. The result is shown in the table.

Minimizing total miles over which cars are moved to new locations, compute the best shipment of coal cars. Use the northwest corner rule and the MODI method.

10-18 An air conditioning manufacturer produces room air conditioners at plants in Houston, Phoenix, and Memphis. These are sent to regional distributors in Dallas, Atlanta, and Denver. The shipping costs vary, and the company would like to find the least-cost way to meet the demands at each of the distribution centers. Dallas needs to receive 800 air conditioners per month, Atlanta needs 600, and Denver needs 200. Houston has 850 air conditioners available each month, Phoenix has 650, and Memphis has 300. The shipping cost per unit from Houston to Dallas is $8, to Atlanta is $12, and to Denver is $10. The cost per unit from Phoenix to Dallas is $10, to Atlanta is $14, and to Denver is $9. The cost per unit from Memphis to Dallas is $11, to Atlanta is $8, and to Denver is $12. How many units should be shipped from each plant to each regional distribution center? What is the total cost for this?

10-19 The state of Missouri has three major power-generating companies (A, B, and C). During the months of peak demand, the Missouri Power Authority authorizes these companies to pool their excess supply and to distribute it to smaller independent power companies that do not have generators large enough to handle the demand. Excess supply is distributed on the basis of cost per kilowatt hour transmitted. The following table shows the demand and supply in millions of kilowatt hours and the cost per kilowatt hour of transmitting electric power to four small companies in cities W, X, Y, and Z:

FROM \ TO	W	X	Y	Z	EXCESS SUPPLY
A	12¢	4¢	9¢	5¢	55
B	8¢	1¢	6¢	6¢	45
C	1¢	12¢	4¢	7¢	30
UNFILLED POWER DEMAND	40	20	50	20	

Use VAM to find an initial transmission assignment of the excess power supply. Then apply the MODI technique to find the least-cost distribution system.

10-20 Consider the transportation table given below.

Find an initial solution using the northwest corner rule. What special condition exists? Explain how you will proceed to solve the problem.

10-21 The three blood banks in Franklin County are coordinated through a central office that facilitates blood delivery to four hospitals in the region. The cost to ship a standard container of blood from each bank to

Table for Problem 10-20

FROM \ TO	DESTINATION A	DESTINATION B	DESTINATION C	SUPPLY
SOURCE 1	$8	$9	$4	72
SOURCE 2	5	6	8	38
SOURCE 3	7	9	6	46
SOURCE 4	5	3	7	19
DEMAND	110	34	31	175

Table for Problem 10-21

To From	HOSPITAL 1	HOSPITAL 2	HOSPITAL 3	HOSPITAL 4	SUPPLY
BANK 1	$8	$9	$11	$16	50
BANK 2	12	7	5	8	80
BANK 3	14	10	6	7	120
DEMAND	90	70	40	50	250

each hospital is shown in the table above. Also given are the biweekly number of containers available at each bank and the biweekly number of containers of blood needed at each hospital. How many shipments should be made biweekly from each blood bank to each hospital so that total shipment costs are minimized?

10-22 The B. Hall Real Estate Investment Corporation has identified four small apartment buildings in which it would like to invest. Mrs. Hall has approached three savings and loan companies regarding financing. Because Hall has been a good client in the past and has maintained a high credit rating in the community, each savings and loan company is willing to consider providing all or part of the mortgage loan needed on each property. Each loan officer has set differing interest rates on each property (rates are affected by the neighborhood of the apartment building, condition of the property, and desire by the individual savings and loan to finance various-size buildings), *and* each loan company has placed a maximum credit ceiling on how much it will lend Hall in total. This information is summarized in the table on this page.

Each apartment building is equally attractive as an investment to Hall, so she has decided to purchase all buildings possible at the lowest total payment of interest. From which savings and loan companies should she borrow to purchase which buildings? More than one savings and loan can finance the same property.

10-23 The J. Mehta Company's production manager is planning for a series of one-month production periods for

stainless steel sinks. The demand for the next four months is as follows:

MONTH	DEMAND FOR STAINLESS STEEL SINKS
1	120
2	160
3	240
4	100

The Mehta firm can normally produce 100 stainless steel sinks in a month. This is done during regular production hours at a cost of $100 per sink. If demand in any one month cannot be satisfied by regular production, the production manager has three other choices: (1) he can produce up to 50 more sinks per month in overtime but at a cost of $130 per sink; (2) he can purchase a limited number of sinks from a friendly competitor for resale (the maximum number of outside purchases over the four-month period is 450 sinks, at a cost of $150 each); or (3) he can fill the demand from his on-hand inventory. The inventory carrying cost is $10 per sink per month. Back orders are not permitted. Inventory on hand at the beginning of month 1 is 40 sinks. Set up this "production smoothing" problem as a transportation problem to minimize cost. Use the northwest corner rule to find an initial level for production and outside purchases over the four-month period.

Table for Problem 10-22

SAVINGS AND LOAN COMPANY	PROPERTY (INTEREST RATES) (%)				MAXIMUM CREDIT LINE ($)
	HILL ST.	BANKS ST.	PARK AVE.	DRURY LANE	
First Homestead	8	8	10	11	80,000
Commonwealth	9	10	12	10	100,000
Washington Federal	9	11	10	9	120,000
Loan required to purchase building	$60,000	$40,000	$130,000	$70,000	

Data for Problem 10-24

TO DISTRIBUTION CENTERS / FROM PLANTS	LOS ANGELES	NEW YORK	NORMAL PRODUCTION	UNIT PRODUCTION COST ($)
ATLANTA	$8	$5	600	6
TULSA	$4	$7	900	5
NEW ORLEANS	$5	$6	500	4 (anticipated)
HOUSTON	$4	$6	500	3 (anticipated)
FORECAST DEMAND	800	1,200	2,000	

Existing plants → ATLANTA, TULSA

Proposed locations → NEW ORLEANS, HOUSTON

Indicates distribution cost (shipping, handling, storage) will be $6 per carrier if sent from Houston to New York

10-24 Ashley's Auto Top Carriers currently maintains plants in Atlanta and Tulsa that supply major distribution centers in Los Angeles and New York. Because of an expanding demand, Ashley has decided to open a third plant and has narrowed the choice to one of two cities—New Orleans or Houston. The pertinent production and distribution costs, as well as the plant capacities and distribution demands, are shown in the table above.

Which of the new possible plants should be opened?

10-25 Marc Smith, vice-president for operations of HHN, Inc., a manufacturer of cabinets for telephone switches, is constrained from meeting the five-year forecast by limited capacity at the existing three plants.

These three plants are Waterloo, Pusan, and Bogota. You, as his able assistant, have been told that because of existing capacity constraints and the expanding world market for HHN cabinets, a new plant is to be added to the existing three plants. The real estate department has advised Marc that two sites seem particularly good because of a stable political situation and tolerable exchange rate: Dublin, Ireland, and Fontainebleau, France. Marc suggests that you should be able to take the following data and determine where the fourth plant should be located on the basis of production costs and transportation costs. *Note:* This problem is degenerate with the data for both locations.

Data for Problem 10-25

MARKET AREA	WATERLOO	PUSAN	BOGOTA	FONTAINEBLEAU	DUBLIN
Canada					
Demand 4,000					
Production cost	$50	$30	$40	$50	$45
Transportation cost	10	25	20	25	25
South America					
Demand 5,000					
Production cost	50	30	40	50	45
Transportation cost	20	25	10	30	30
Pacific Rim					
Demand 10,000					
Production cost	50	30	40	50	45
Transportation cost	25	10	25	40	40
Europe					
Demand 5,000					
Production cost	50	30	40	50	45
Transportation cost	25	40	30	10	20
Capacity	8,000	2,000	5,000	9,000	9,000

10-26 Don Levine Corporation is considering adding an additional plant to its three existing facilities in Decatur, Minneapolis, and Carbondale. Both St. Louis and East St. Louis are being considered. Evaluating only the transportation costs per unit as shown in the table, which site is best?

To	FROM EXISTING PLANTS			
	DECATUR	MINNEAPOLIS	CARBONDALE	DEMAND
Blue Earth	$20	$17	$21	250
Ciro	25	27	20	200
Des Moines	22	25	22	350
Capacity	300	200	150	

To	FROM PROPOSED PLANTS	
	EAST ST. LOUIS	ST. LOUIS
Blue Earth	$29	$27
Ciro	30	28
Des Moines	30	31
Capacity	150	150

10-27 Using the data from Problem 10-26 plus the unit production costs shown in the following table, which locations yield the lowest cost?

LOCATION	PRODUCTION COSTS
Decatur	$50
Minneapolis	60
Carbondale	70
East St. Louis	40
St. Louis	50

10-28 In a job shop operation, four jobs may be performed on any of four machines. The hours required for each job on each machine are presented in the following table. The plant supervisor would like to assign jobs so that total time is minimized. Use the assignment method to find the best solution.

JOB	MACHINE			
	W	X	Y	Z
A12	10	14	16	13
A15	12	13	15	12
B2	9	12	12	11
B9	14	16	18	16

10-29 Four automobiles have entered Bubba's Repair Shop for various types of work, ranging from a transmission overhaul to a brake job. The experience level of the mechanics is quite varied, and Bubba would like to minimize the time required to complete all of the jobs. He has estimated the time in minutes for each mechanic to complete each job. Billy can complete job 1 in 400 minutes, job 2 in 90 minutes, job 3 in 60 minutes, and job 4 in 120 minutes. Taylor will finish job 1 in 650 minutes, job 2 in 120 minutes, job 3 in 90 minutes, and job 4 in 180 minutes. Mark will finish job 1 in 480 minutes, job 2 in 120 minutes, job 3 in 80 minutes, and job 4 in 180 minutes. John will complete job 1 in 500 minutes, job 2 in 110 minutes, job 3 in 90 minutes, and job 4 in 150 minutes. Each mechanic should be assigned to just one of these jobs. What is the minimum total time required to finish the four jobs? Who should be assigned to each job?

10-30 Baseball umpiring crews are currently in four cities where three-game series are beginning. When these are finished, the crews are needed to work games in four different cities. The distances (miles) from each of the cities where the crews are currently working to the cities where the new games will begin are shown in the following table:

FROM	TO			
	KANSAS CITY	CHICAGO	DETROIT	TORONTO
Seattle	1,500	1,730	1,940	2,070
Arlington	460	810	1,020	1,270
Oakland	1,500	1,850	2,080	X
Baltimore	960	610	400	330

The X indicates that the crew in Oakland cannot be sent to Toronto. Determine which crew should be sent to each city to minimize the total distance traveled. How many miles will be traveled if these assignments are made?

10-31 In Problem 10-30, the minimum travel distance was found. To see how much better this solution is than the assignments that might have been made without using the Hungarian method, find the assignments that would give the maximum distance traveled. Compare this total distance with the distance found in Problem 10-30.

10-32 Roscoe Davis, chairman of a college's business department, has decided to apply the Hungarian method in assigning professors to courses next semester. As a criterion for judging who should teach each course, Professor Davis reviews the past two years' teaching evaluations (which were filled out by students). Since each of the four professors taught each of the four courses at one time or another during the two-year period, Davis is able to record a course rating for each instructor. These ratings are shown in the table. Find the best assignment of professors to courses to maximize the overall teaching rating.

	COURSE			
PROFESSOR	STATISTICS	MANAGEMENT	FINANCE	ECONOMICS
Anderson	90	65	95	40
Sweeney	70	60	80	75
Williams	85	40	80	60
McKinney	55	80	65	55

10-33 The hospital administrator at St. Charles General must appoint head nurses to four newly established departments: urology, cardiology, orthopedics, and obstetrics. In anticipation of this staffing problem, she had hired four nurses: Hawkins, Condriac, Bardot, and Hoolihan. Believing in the quantitative analysis approach to problem solving, the administrator has interviewed each nurse, considered his or her background, personality, and talents, and developed a cost scale ranging from 0 to 100 to be used in the assignment. A 0 for Nurse Bardot being assigned to the cardiology unit implies that she would be perfectly suited to that task. A value close to 100, on the other hand, would imply that she is not at all suited to head that unit. The accompanying table gives the complete set of cost figures that the hospital administrator felt represented all possible assignments. Which nurse should be assigned to which unit?

	DEPARTMENT			
NURSE	UROLOGY	CARDIOLOGY	ORTHOPEDICS	OBSTETRICS
Hawkins	28	18	15	75
Condriac	32	48	23	38
Bardot	51	36	24	36
Hoolihan	25	38	55	12

10-34 The Gleaming Company has just developed a new dishwashing liquid and is preparing for a national television promotional campaign. The firm has decided to schedule a series of 1-minute commercials during the peak homemaker audience viewing hours of 1 to 5 P.M. To reach the widest possible audience, Gleaming wants to schedule one commercial on each of four networks and to have one commercial appear during each of the four 1-hour time blocks. The exposure ratings for each hour, which represent the number of viewers per $1,000 spent, are presented in the following table. Which network should be scheduled each hour to provide the maximum audience exposure?

	NETWORK			
VIEWING HOURS	A	B	C	INDEPENDENT
1–2 P.M.	27.1	18.1	11.3	9.5
2–3 P.M.	18.9	15.5	17.1	10.6
3–4 P.M.	19.2	18.5	9.9	7.7
4–5 P.M.	11.5	21.4	16.8	12.8

10-35 As mentioned in Section 10.14, the Fix-It Shop has added a fourth repairman, Davis. Solve the accompanying cost table for the new optimal assignment of workers to projects. Why did this solution occur?

	PROJECT		
WORKER	1	2	3
Adams	$11	$14	$6
Brown	8	10	11
Cooper	9	12	7
Davis	10	13	8

10-36 The Patricia Garcia Company is producing seven new medical products. Each of Garcia's eight plants can add one more product to its current line of medical devices. The unit manufacturing costs for producing the different parts at the eight plants are shown in the following table. How should Garcia assign the new products to the plants to minimize manufacturing costs?

Data for Problem 10-36

ELECTRONIC COMPONENT	PLANT							
	1	2	3	4	5	6	7	8
C53	$0.10	$0.12	$0.13	$0.11	$0.10	$0.06	$0.16	$0.12
C81	0.05	0.06	0.04	0.08	0.04	0.09	0.06	0.06
D5	0.32	0.40	0.31	0.30	0.42	0.35	0.36	0.49
D44	0.17	0.14	0.19	0.15	0.10	0.16	0.19	0.12
E2	0.06	0.07	0.10	0.05	0.08	0.10	0.11	0.05
E35	0.08	0.10	0.12	0.08	0.09	0.10	0.09	0.06
G99	0.55	0.62	0.61	0.70	0.62	0.63	0.65	0.59

Data for Problem 10-37

CAPACITY SOURCE	JAN.	FEB.	MAR.	APR.	MAY	JUNE	JULY	AUG.
Labor								
Regular time	235	255	290	300	300	290	300	290
Overtime	20	24	26	24	30	28	30	30
Subcontract	12	15	15	17	17	19	19	20
Demand	255	294	321	301	330	320	345	340

10-37 Haifa Instruments, an Israeli producer of portable kidney dialysis units and other medical products, develops an eight-month aggregate plan. Demand and capacity (in units) are forecast as shown in the table.

The cost of producing each dialysis unit is $1,000 on regular time, $1,300 on overtime, and $1,500 on a subcontract. Inventory carrying cost is $100 per unit per month. There is no beginning or ending inventory in stock.

(a) Set up a production plan, using the transportation model, that minimizes cost. What is this plan's cost?

(b) Through better planning, regular time production can be set at exactly the same value, 275 per month. Does this alter the solution?

(c) If overtime costs rise from $1,300 to $1,400, does this change your answer to part (a)? What if they fall to $1,200?

10-38 NASA's astronaut crew currently includes 10 mission specialists who hold a doctoral degree in either astrophysics or astromedicine. One of these specialists will be assigned to each of the 10 flights scheduled for the upcoming nine months. Mission specialists are responsible for carrying out scientific and medical experiments in space or for launching, retrieving, or repairing satellites. The chief of astronaut personnel,

himself a former crew member with three missions under his belt, must decide who should be assigned and trained for each of the very different missions. Clearly, astronauts with medical educations are more suited to missions involving biological or medical experiments, whereas those with engineering- or physics-oriented degrees are best suited to other types of missions. The chief assigns each astronaut a rating on a scale of 1 to 10 for each possible mission, with a 10 being a perfect match for the task at hand and a 1 being a mismatch. Only one specialist is assigned to each flight, and none is reassigned until all others have flown at least once.

(a) Who should be assigned to which flight?

(b) NASA has just been notified that Anderson is getting married in February and has been granted a highly sought publicity tour in Europe that month. (He intends to take his wife and let the trip double as a honeymoon.) How does this change the final schedule?

(c) Certo has complained that he was misrated on his January missions. Both ratings should be 10s, he claims to the chief, who agrees and recomputes the schedule. Do any changes occur over the schedule set in part (b)?

(d) What are the strengths and weaknesses of this approach to scheduling?

Data for Problem 10-38

	MISSION									
ASTRONAUT	JAN. 12	JAN. 27	FEB. 5	FEB. 26	MAR. 26	APR. 12	MAY 1	JUN. 9	AUG. 20	SEP. 19
Vincze	9	7	2	1	10	9	8	9	2	6
Veit	8	8	3	4	7	9	7	7	4	4
Anderson	2	1	10	10	1	4	7	6	6	7
Herbert	4	4	10	9	9	9	1	2	3	4
Schatz	10	10	9	9	8	9	1	1	1	1
Plane	1	3	5	7	9	7	10	10	9	2
Certo	9	9	8	8	9	1	1	2	2	9
Moses	3	2	7	6	4	3	9	7	7	9
Brandon	5	4	5	9	10	10	5	4	9	8
Drtina	10	10	9	7	6	7	5	4	8	8

INTERNET HOMEWORK PROBLEMS

See our Internet home page at **www.prenhall.com/render** for additional problems 10-39 through 10-45.

⭢ CASE STUDY

Andrew–Carter, Inc.

Andrew–Carter, Inc. (A–C), is a major Canadian producer and distributor of outdoor lighting fixtures. Its fixture is distributed throughout North America and has been in high demand for several years. The company operates three plants that manufacture the fixture and distribute it to five distribution centers (warehouses).

During the present recession, A–C has seen a major drop in demand for its fixture as the housing market has declined. Based on the forecast of interest rates, the head of operations feels that demand for housing and thus for its product will remain depressed for the foreseeable future. A–C is considering closing one of its plants, as it is now operating with a forecasted excess capacity of 34,000 units per week. The forecasted weekly demands for the coming year are

Warehouse 1	9,000 units
Warehouse 2	13,000 units
Warehouse 3	11,000 units
Warehouse 4	15,000 units
Warehouse 5	8,000 units

The plant capacities in units per week are

Plant 1, regular time	27,000 units
Plant 1, on overtime	7,000 units
Plant 2, regular time	20,000 units
Plant 2, on overtime	5,000 units
Plant 3, regular time	25,000 units
Plant 3, on overtime	6,000 units

If A–C shuts down any plants, its weekly costs will change, as fixed costs are lower for a nonoperating plant. Table 10.40 shows production costs at each plant, both variable at regular time and overtime, and fixed when operating and shut down. Table 10.41 shows distribution costs from each plant to each warehouse (distribution center).

Discussion Questions

1. Evaluate the various configurations of operating and closed plants that will meet weekly demand. Determine which configuration minimizes total costs.
2. Discuss the implications of closing a plant.

Source: Professor Michael Ballot, University of the Pacific.

			FIXED COST PER WEEK	
PLANT	**VARIABLE COST**	**OPERATING**		**NOT OPERATING**
No. 1, regular time	$2.80/unit	$14,000		$6,000
No. 1, overtime	3.52			
No. 2, regular time	2.78	12,000		5,000
No. 2, overtime	3.48			
No. 3, regular time	2.72	15,000		7,500
No. 3, overtime	3.42			

TABLE 10.40 Andrew–Carter, Inc., Variable Costs and Fixed Production Costs per Week

	TO DISTRIBUTION CENTER				
FROM PLANT	**W1**	**W2**	**W3**	**W4**	**W5**
No. 1	$0.50	$0.44	$0.49	$0.46	$0.56
No. 2	0.40	0.52	0.50	0.56	0.57
No. 3	0.56	0.53	0.51	0.54	0.35

TABLE 10.41 Andrew–Carter, Inc., Distribution Costs per Unit

⇒ CASE STUDY

Old Oregon Wood Store

In 1992, George Brown started the Old Oregon Wood Store to manufacture Old Oregon tables. Each table is carefully constructed by hand using the highest-quality oak. Old Oregon tables can support more than 500 pounds, and since the start of the Old Oregon Wood Store, not one table has been returned because of faulty workmanship or structural problems. In addition to being rugged, each table is beautifully finished using a urethane varnish that George developed over 20 years of working with wood-finishing materials.

The manufacturing process consists of four steps: preparation, assembly, finishing, and packaging. Each step is performed by one person. In addition to overseeing the entire operation, George does all of the finishing. Tom Surowski performs the preparation step, which involves cutting and forming the basic components of the tables. Leon Davis is in charge of the assembly, and Cathy Stark performs the packaging.

Although each person is responsible for only one step in the manufacturing process, everyone can perform any one of the steps. It is George's policy that occasionally everyone should complete several tables on his or her own without any help or assistance. A small competition is used to see who can complete an entire table in the least amount of time. George maintains average total and intermediate completion times. The data are shown in Figure 10.4.

It takes Cathy longer than the other employees to construct an Old Oregon table. In addition to being slower than the other employees, Cathy is also unhappy about her current responsibility of packaging, which leaves her idle most of the day. Her first preference is finishing, and her second preference is preparation.

In addition to quality, George is concerned with costs and efficiency. When one of the employees misses a day, it causes major scheduling problems. In some cases, George assigns another employee overtime to complete the necessary work. At other times, George simply waits until the employee returns to work to complete his or her step in the manufacturing process. Both solutions cause problems. Overtime is expensive, and waiting causes delays and sometimes stops the entire manufacturing process.

To overcome some of these problems, Randy Lane was hired. Randy's major duties are to perform miscellaneous jobs and to help out if one of the employees is absent. George has given Randy training in all phases of the manufacturing process, and he is pleased with the speed at which Randy has been able to learn how to completely assemble Old Oregon tables. Total and intermediate completion times are given in Figure 10.5.

FIGURE 10.4

Manufacturing Time in Minutes

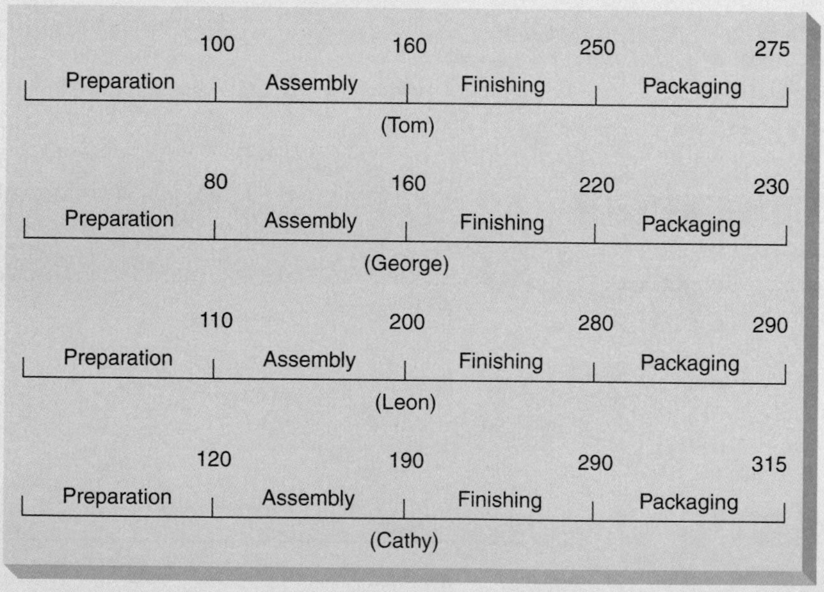

100	160	250	275
Preparation	Assembly	Finishing	Packaging

(Tom)

80	160	220	230
Preparation	Assembly	Finishing	Packaging

(George)

110	200	280	290
Preparation	Assembly	Finishing	Packaging

(Leon)

120	190	290	315
Preparation	Assembly	Finishing	Packaging

(Cathy)

FIGURE 10.5

Randy's Completion Times in Minutes

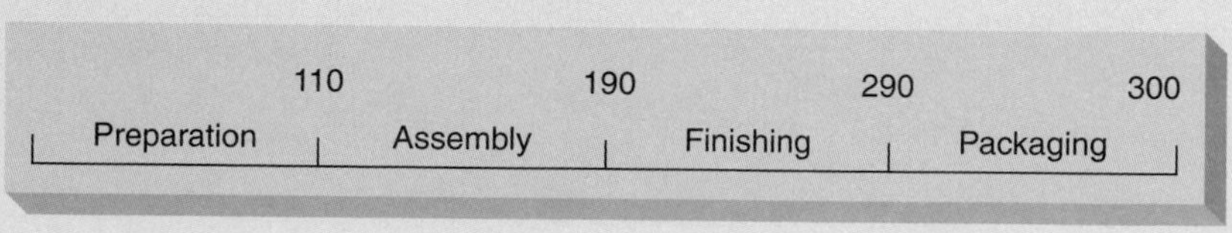

110	190	290	300
Preparation	Assembly	Finishing	Packaging

Discussion Questions

1. What is the fastest way to manufacture Old Oregon tables using the original crew? How many could be made per day?
2. Would production rates and quantities change significantly if George would allow Randy to perform one of the four functions and make one of the original crew the backup person?
3. What is the fastest time to manufacture a table with the original crew if Cathy is moved to either preparation or finishing?
4. Whoever performs the packaging function is severely underutilized. Can you find a better way of utilizing the four- or five-person crew than either giving each a single job or allowing each to manufacture an entire table? How many tables could be manufactured per day with this scheme?

INTERNET CASE STUDIES

See our Internet home page at www.prenhall.com/render for these additional case studies:
(1) Northwest General Hospital. This case involves improving the food distribution system in a hospital to reduce the chances of food getting cold before it is delivered to the patients.
(2) Custom Vans, Inc. This case involves finding the best location for a plant that will manufacture showers used in customized vans.

BIBLIOGRAPHY

Awad, Rania M. and John W. Chinneck. "Proctor Assignment at Carleton University," *Interfaces* 28, 2 (March–April 1998): 58–71.

Bowman, E. "Production Scheduling by the Transportation Method of Linear Programming," *Operations Research* 4 (1956).

Dawid, Herbert, Johannes Konig, and Christine Strauss. "An Enhanced Rostering Model for Airline Crews," *Computers and Operations Research* 28, 7 (June 2001): 671–688.

Domich, P. D., K. L. Hoffman, R. H. F. Jackson, and M. A. McClain. "Locating Tax Facilities: A Graphics-Based Microcomputer Optimization Model," *Management Science* 37 (August 1991): 960–979.

Koksalan, Murat and Haldun Sural. "Efes Beverage Group Makes Location and Distribution Decisions for Its Malt Plants," *Interfaces* 29, 2 (March–April, 1999): 89–103.

McKeown, P. and B. Workman. "A Study in Using Linear Programming to Assign Students to Schools," *Interfaces* 6, 4 (August 1976).

Pooley, J. "Integrated Production and Distribution Facility Planning at Ault Foods," *Interfaces* 24, 4 (July–August 1994): 113–121.

Render, B. and R. M. Stair. *Introduction to Management Science*. Boston: Allyn and Bacon, Inc. 1992.

APPENDIX 10.1: USING QM FOR WINDOWS

QM for Windows has both a transportation module and an assignment module in its menu. Both are easy to use in terms of data entry and easy to interpret in terms of output. Program 10.4 uses the sample transportation data of Table 10.42 on the next page as input. Program 10.5 shows the output screens for the Fix-It Shop assignment example presented earlier in this chapter.

PROGRAM 10.4

QM for Windows Input and Results for the Transportation Data in Table 10.42

Transportation

Objective
○ Maximize
● Minimize

Starting method
Any starting method

Original Problem

Sample Transportation Run Solution

	Destination 1	Destination 2	Destination 3	SUPPLY
Source 1	200.	600.	300.	8.
Source 2	400.	200.	700.	11.
Source 3	500.	800.	300.	12.
DEMAND	10.	12.	9.	31.

Transportation Shipments

Sample Transportation Run Solution

	Destination 1	Destination 2	Destination 3
Optimal cost = 8,300.00			
Source 1	8.		
Source 2		11.	
Source 3	2.	1.	9.

Sample Data for QM for Windows Transportation Program

FROM \ TO	WAREHOUSE 1	WAREHOUSE 2	WAREHOUSE 3	AMOUNT AVAILABLE
FACTORY 1	200	600	300	8
FACTORY 2	400	200	700	11
FACTORY 3	500	800	300	12
AMOUNT NEEDED	10	12	9	31

QM for Windows Output for Fix-It Shop Example

QM for Windows - C:\My Documents\Mike\R&S\Weiss\Render.Stair.7\QM for Windows files\prog105.ass

File Edit View Module Format Tools Window Help

Objective
○ Maximize
◉ Minimize

Assignments

Fix-It Shop Solution

Optimal cost = $25	Project 1	Project 2	Project 3
Adams	11.	14.	Assign 6
Brown	8.	Assign 10	11.
Cooper	Assign 9	12.	7.

APPENDIX 10.2: COMPARISON OF SIMPLEX ALGORITHM AND TRANSPORTATION ALGORITHM

Since the transportation algorithm is used for solving a special type of linear program, it provides the same type of information that is provided by the simplex algorithm. A list of related features in these two algorithms is provided in Table 10.43.

Comparison of Simplex Algorithm and Transportation Algorithm

SIMPLEX ALGORITHM	TRANSPORTATION ALGORITHM
Constraints ⟷	Rows and columns
Decision variables ⟷	Cells in the table
Basic variables ⟷	Filled cells
Nonbasic variables ⟷	Empty cells
Slack variables ⟷	Cells in dummy destination
Artificial variables ⟷	Cells in dummy source
$C_j - Z_j$ ⟷	Improvement index
Smallest ratio of quantity to pivot column coefficients to find leaving variable ⟷	Smallest number of units in stepping-stone path cells with minus signs
Variable leaving the basis ⟷	Cell that becomes empty
Entering (pivot column) variable ⟷	Empty cell to become filled
Degenerate solution—zero in quantity column ⟷	Degenerate solution—zero is placed in empty cell

CHAPTER 11

INTEGER PROGRAMMING, GOAL PROGRAMMING, AND NONLINEAR PROGRAMMING

LEARNING OBJECTIVES

After completing this chapter, students will be able to:

1. Understand the difference between LP and integer programming.
2. Understand and solve the three types of integer programming problems.
3. Apply the branch and bound method to solve integer programming problems.
4. Solve goal programming problems graphically and using a modified simplex technique.
5. Formulate nonlinear programming problems and solve using Excel.

CHAPTER OUTLINE

11.1   INTRODUCTION

Integer programming is the extension of LP that solves problems requiring integer solutions.

We have just seen two special types of linear programming (LP) models—the transportation and assignment models—that were handled by making certain modifications to the general LP approach. This chapter presents a series of other important mathematical programming models that arise when some of the basic assumptions of LP are made more or less restrictive.

For example, one assumption of LP is that decision variables can take on fractional values such as $X_1 = 0.33$, $X_2 = 1.57$, or $X_3 = 109.4$. Yet a large number of business problems can be solved only if variables have *integer* values. When an airline decides how many Boeing 757's or Boeing 777's to purchase, it can't place an order for 5.38 aircraft; it must order 4, 5, 6, 7, or some other integer amount. In Section 11.2 we present the subject of integer programming. We show you how to solve integer programming problems both graphically and by use of an algorithm called the branch and bound method.

Goal programming is the extension of LP that permits more than one objective to be stated.

A major limitation of LP is that it forces the decision maker to state one objective only. But what if a business has several objectives? Management may indeed want to maximize profit, but it might also want to maximize market share, maintain full employment, and minimize costs. Many of these goals can be conflicting and difficult to quantify. South States Power and Light, for example, wants to build a nuclear power plant in Taft, Louisiana. Its objectives are to maximize power generated, reliability, and safety, and to minimize cost of operating the system and the environmental effects on the community. Goal programming is an extension to LP that can permit multiple objectives such as these.

Nonlinear programming is the case in which objectives or constraints are nonlinear.

Linear programming can, of course, be applied only to cases in which the constraints and objective function are linear. Yet in many situations this is not the case. The price of various products, for example, may be a function of the number of units produced. As more are made, the price per unit decreases. Hence an objective function may read as follows:

$$\text{maximize profit} = 25X_1 - 0.4X_1{}^2 + 30X_2 - 0.5X_2{}^2$$

Because of the squared terms, this is a nonlinear programming problem.

Let's examine each of these extensions of LP—integer, goal, and nonlinear programming—one at a time.

11.2   INTEGER PROGRAMMING

Solution values must be whole numbers in integer programming.

An *integer programming* model is a model that has constraints and an objective function identical to that formulated by LP. The only difference is that one or more of the decision variables has to take on an integer value in the final solution. There are three types of integer programming problems:

There are three types of integer programs: pure integer programming; mixed-integer programming; and 0–1 integer programming.

1. Pure integer programming problems are cases in which all variables are required to have integer values.

2. Mixed-integer programming problems are cases in which some, but not all, of the decision variables are required to have integer values.

3. Zero–one integer programming problems are special cases in which all the decision variables must have integer solution values of 0 or 1.

Solving an integer programming problem is much more difficult than solving an LP problem. The solution time required to solve some of these may be excessive even on the fastest computer. The most common algorithm for solving integer programming problems is the branch and bound method. We demonstrate how this can be used on the following example of a pure integer problem.

Harrison Electric Company Example of Integer Programming

The Harrison Electric Company, located in Chicago's Old Town area, produces two products popular with home renovators: old-fashioned chandeliers and ceiling fans. Both the chandeliers and fans require a two-step production process involving wiring and assembly. It takes about 2 hours to wire each chandelier and 3 hours to wire a ceiling fan. Final assembly of the chandeliers and fans requires 6 and 5 hours, respectively. The production capability is such that only 12 hours of wiring time and 30 hours of assembly time are available. If each chandelier produced nets the firm $7 and each fan $6, Harrison's production mix decision can be formulated using LP as follows:

$$\text{maximize profit} = \$7X_1 + \$6X_2$$

$$\text{subject to:} \quad 2X_1 + 3X_2 \leq 12 \text{ (wiring hours)}$$

$$6X_1 + 5X_2 \leq 30 \text{ (assembly hours)}$$

$$X_1, X_2 \geq 0$$

where

$$X_1 = \text{number of chandeliers produced}$$

$$X_2 = \text{number of ceiling fans produced}$$

With only two variables and two constraints, Harrison's production planner, Wes Wallace, employed the graphical LP approach (see Figure 11.1) to generate the optimal solution of

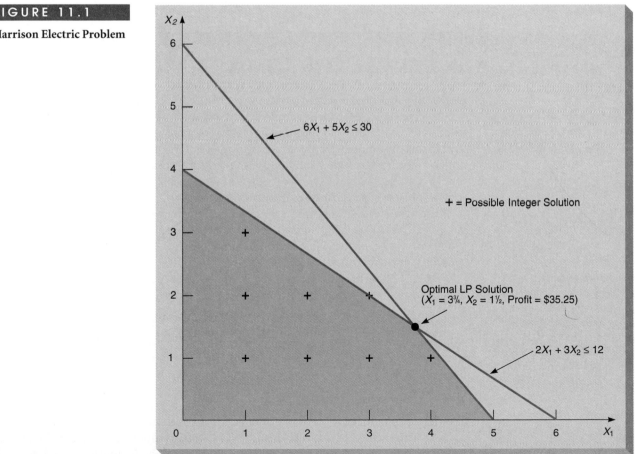

FIGURE 11.1

Harrison Electric Problem

TABLE 11.1	CHANDELIERS (X_1)	CEILING FANS (X_2)	PROFIT $(\$7X_1 + \$6X_2)$	
Integer Solutions to the Harrison Electric Company Problem	0	0	$0	
	1	0	7	
	2	0	14	
Although enumeration is feasible for some small integer programming problems, it can be difficult or impossible for large ones.	3	0	21	
	4	0	28	
	5	0	35	← *Optimal solution to integer programming problem*
	0	1	6	
	1	1	13	
	2	1	20	
	3	1	27	
	4	1	34	← *Solution if rounding off is used*
	0	2	12	
	1	2	19	
	2	2	26	
	3	2	33	
	0	3	18	
	1	3	25	
	0	4	24	

$X_1 = 3.75$ chandeliers and $X_2 = 1.5$ ceiling fans during the production cycle. Recognizing that the company could not produce and sell a fraction of a product, Wes decided that he was dealing with an integer programming problem.

Rounding off is one way to reach integer solution values, but it often does not yield the best solution.

It seemed to Wes that the simplest approach was to round off the optimal fractional solutions for X_1 and X_2 to integer values of $X_1 = 4$ chandeliers and $X_2 = 2$ ceiling fans. Unfortunately, rounding can produce two problems. First, the new integer solution may not be in the feasible region and thus is not a practical answer. This is the case if we round to $X_1 = 4$, $X_2 = 2$. Second, even if we round off to a feasible solution, such as $X_1 = 4$, $X_2 = 1$, it may not be the *optimal* feasible integer solution.

Listing all feasible solutions and selecting the one with the best objective function value is called the *enumeration* method. Obviously this can be quite tedious for even small problems, and it is virtually impossible for large problems as the number of feasible integer solutions is extremely large.

An important concept to understand is that an integer programming solution can never be better than the solution to the same LP problem. The integer problem is usually worse in terms of higher cost or lower profit.

Table 11.1 lists the entire set of integer-valued solutions to the Harrison Electric problem. By inspecting the right-hand column, we see that the optimal *integer* solution is

$$X_1 = 5 \text{ chandeliers}, \ X_2 = 0 \text{ ceiling fans}, \text{ with a profit} = \$35$$

Note that this integer restriction results in a lower profit level than the original optimal LP solution. As a matter of fact, an integer programming solution can *never* produce a greater profit than the LP solution to the same problem; *usually*, it means a lesser value.

Branch and Bound Method

The most common algorithm for solving linear programs is called the *branch and bound* method. This method begins with the solution to the relaxation of the integer LP problem to allow continuous (non-integer) solutions. If the variables are integer valued, this solution must also be the solution to the integer problem. If these variables are not integer valued, the feasible region is divided by adding constraints restricting the value of one of the variables that was not integer valued. The divided feasible region results in subproblems that are then solved. Bounds on the value of the objective function are found and used to help determine which subproblems can be eliminated from consideration and when the optimal solution has been found. If the solution to a subproblem does not yield an optimal solution, a new subproblem is selected and branching continues. The specific steps involved when dealing with a maximization problem are as follows:

Branch and bound breaks the feasible solution region into subproblems until an optimal solution is found.

Six Steps in Solving Integer Programming Maximization Problems by Branch and Bound[2]

1. Solve the original problem using LP. If the answer satisfies the integer constraints, we are done. If not, this value provides an initial upper bound.

2. Find any feasible solution that meets the integer constraints for use as a lower bound. Usually, rounding down each variable will accomplish this.

3. Branch on one variable from step 1 that does not have an integer value. Split the problem into two subproblems based on integer values that are immediately above and below the noninteger value. For example, if $X_2 = 3.75$ was in the final LP solution, introduce the constraint $X_2 \geq 4$ in the first subproblem and $X_2 \leq 3$ in the second subproblem.

4. Create nodes at the top of these new branches by solving the new problems.

5. (a) If a branch yields a solution to the LP problem that is *not feasible*, terminate the branch.

   (b) If a branch yields a solution to the LP problem that is feasible, but not an integer solution, go to step 6.

   (c) If the branch yields a *feasible integer* solution, examine the value of the objective function. If this value equals the upper bound, an optimal solution has been reached. If it is not equal to the upper bound, but exceeds the lower bound, set it as the new lower bound and go to step 6. Finally, if it is less than the lower bound, terminate this branch.

6. Examine both branches again and set the upper bound equal to the maximum value of the objective function at all final nodes. If the upper bound equals the lower bound, stop. If not, go back to step 3.

Harrison Electric Company Revisited

Recall that the Harrison Electric Company's integer programming formulation is

$$\text{maximize profit} = \$7X_1 + \$6X_2$$

$$\text{subject to:} \quad 2X_1 + 3X_2 \leq 12$$

$$6X_1 + 5X_2 \leq 30$$

and both X_1 and X_2 must be nonnegative integers, where

$$X_1 = \text{number of chandeliers produced}$$

$$X_2 = \text{number of ceiling fans produced}$$

Recall that Figure 11.1 illustrates graphically that the optimal, noninteger solution is

$$X_1 = 3.75 \text{ chandeliers}$$

$$X_2 = 1.5 \text{ ceiling fans}$$

$$\text{profit} = \$35.25$$

---

[2] Minimization problems involve reversing the roles of the upper and lower bounds.

Since X_1 and X_2 are not integers, this solution is not valid. The profit value of $35.25 will serve as an initial *upper bound*. We note that rounding down gives $X_1 = 3$, $X_2 = 1$, profit = $27, which is feasible and can be used as a *lower bound*.

We divide the problem into subproblems A and B.

The problem is now divided into two subproblems, A and B. We can consider branching on either variable that does not have an integer solution; let us pick X_1 this time.

Subproblem A			Subproblem B		
maximize profit = $7X_1 + $6X_2$			maximize profit = $7X_1 + $6X_2$		
subject to:	$2X_1 + 3X_2$	≤ 12	subject to:	$2X_1 + 3X_2$	≤ 12
	$6X_1 + 5X_2$	≤ 30		$6X_1 + 5X_2$	≤ 30
	X_1	≥ 4		X_1	≤ 3

If you solve both subproblems graphically, you will observe the solutions:

subproblem A's optimal solution $[X_1 = 4, X_2 = 1.2,$ profit = $35.20]$

subproblem B's optimal solution $[X_1 = 3, X_2 = 2,$ profit = $33.00]$

This information is presented in branch form in Figure 11.2. We have completed steps 1 to 4 of the branch and bound method.

We can stop the search of the subproblem B branch because it has an all-integer feasible solution (see step 5(c)). The profit value of $33 becomes the new *lower bound*. Subproblem A's branch is searched further since it has a noninteger solution. The second *upper bound* takes on the value $35.20, replacing $35.25 from the first node.

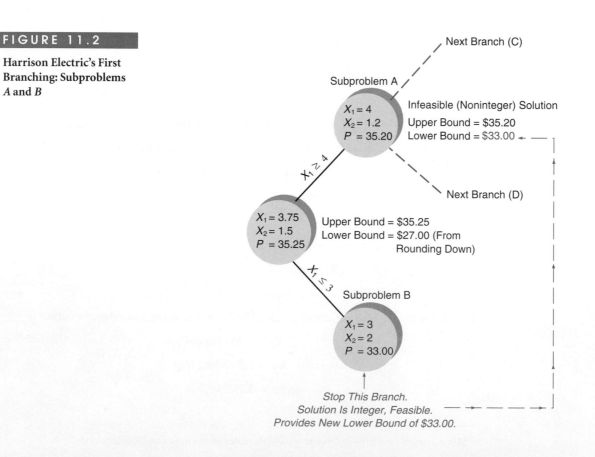

FIGURE 11.2

Harrison Electric's First Branching: Subproblems A and B

Next Branch (C)

Subproblem A

$X_1 = 4$
$X_2 = 1.2$
$P = 35.20$

Infeasible (Noninteger) Solution
Upper Bound = $35.20
Lower Bound = $33.00

$X_1 \geq 4$

$X_1 = 3.75$
$X_2 = 1.5$
$P = 35.25$

Upper Bound = $35.25
Lower Bound = $27.00 (From Rounding Down)

Next Branch (D)

$X_1 \leq 3$

Subproblem B

$X_1 = 3$
$X_2 = 2$
$P = 33.00$

Stop This Branch.
Solution Is Integer, Feasible.
Provides New Lower Bound of $33.00.

Subproblem A's branching yields subproblems C and D.

Subproblem *A* is now branched into two new subproblems: *C* and *D*. Subproblem *C* has the additional constraint of $X_2 \geq 2$. Subproblem *D* adds the constraint $X_2 \leq 1$. The logic for developing these subproblems is that since subproblems *A*'s optimal solution of $X_2 = 1.2$ is not feasible, the integer feasible answer must lie either in the region $X_2 \geq 2$ or in the region $X_2 \leq 1$.

Subproblem C		Subproblem D	
maximize profit = $7X_1 + 6X_2$		maximize profit = $7X_1 + 6X_2$	
subject to:	$2X_1 + 3X_2 \leq 12$	subject to:	$2X_1 + 3X_2 \leq 12$
	$6X_1 + 5X_2 \leq 30$		$6X_1 + 5X_2 \leq 30$
	$X_1 \qquad \geq 4$		$X_1 \qquad \geq 4$
	$X_2 \geq 2$		$X_2 \leq 1$

Subproblem *C* has no feasible solution whatsoever because the first two constraints are violated if the $X_1 \geq 4$ and $X_2 \geq 2$ constraints are observed. We terminate this branch and do not consider its solution.

Subproblem *D*'s optimal solution is $X_1 = 4\frac{1}{6}$, $X_2 = 1$, profit = $35.16. This noninteger solution yields a *new upper bound* of $35.16, replacing $35.20. Subproblems *C* and *D*, as well as the final branches for the problem, are shown in Figure 11.3.

Harrison Electric's Full Branch and Bound Solution

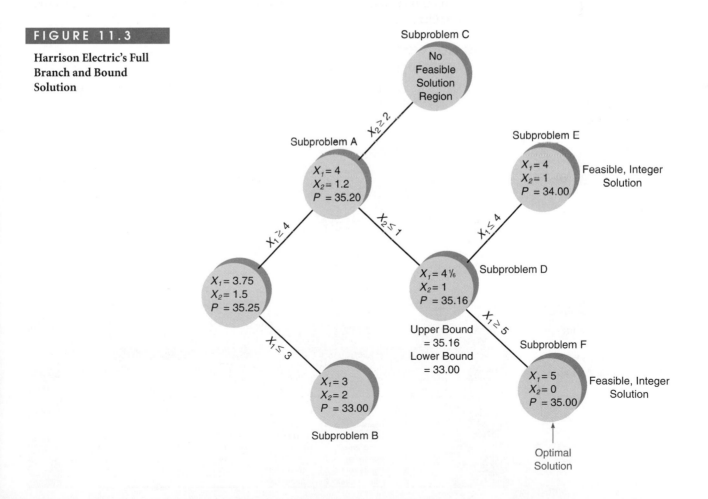

Finally, we create subproblems E and F and solve for X_1 and X_2 with the added constraints $X_1 \leq 4$ and $X_1 \geq 5$. The subproblems and their solutions are

	Subproblem E		Subproblem F
maximize profit = $7X_1 + $6X_2$		maximize profit = $7X_1 + $6X_2$	

Subproblem E

maximize profit = $\$7X_1 + \$6X_2$

subject to:
$$2X_1 + 3X_2 \leq 12$$
$$6X_1 + 5X_2 \leq 30$$
$$X_1 \geq 4$$
$$X_1 \leq 4$$
$$X_2 \leq 1$$

Optimal solution to E:

$X_1 = 4$, $X_2 = 1$, profit = $34

Subproblem F

maximize profit = $\$7X_1 + \$6X_2$

subject to:
$$2X_1 + 3X_2 \leq 12$$
$$6X_1 + 5X_2 \leq 30$$
$$X_1 \geq 4$$
$$X_1 \geq 5$$
$$X_2 \leq 1$$

Optimal solution to F:

$X_1 = 5$, $X_2 = 0$, profit = $35

The stopping rule for the branching process is that we continue until the new upper bound is less than or equal to the lower bound *or* no further branching is possible. The latter is the case here since both branches yielded feasible integer solutions. The optimal solution is at subproblem F's node: $X_1 = 5$, $X_2 = 0$, profit = $35. You can, of course, confirm this by looking back to Table 11.1.

The branch and bound method has been computerized and does a good job of solving problems with a small to medium number of integer variables. On especially large problems, the analyst must sometimes settle for a near-optimal answer. Much research has been conducted on this subject, and new algorithms that increase the computer's efficiency are constantly under study.

Using Software to Solve the Harrison Integer Programming Problem

QM for Windows and Excel spreadsheets are capable of handling integer programming problems such as the Harrison Electric case. Program 11.1A illustrates the input data to QM for Windows, and Program 11.1B provides the results.

PROGRAM 11.1A

QM for Windows Analysis of Harrison Electric's Problem Using Integer Programming: Input Screen

QM for Windows - C:\Prentice\Data\Hrrsn587.int

Objective
● Maximize
○ Minimize

Harrison Electric

	Chandeliers	Ceiling Fans		RHS
Maximize	7	6		
Wiring hours	2	3	<=	12
Assembly hours	6	5	<=	30

PROGRAM 11.1B

Output Screen Using QM for Windows on Harrison Electric's Integer Programming Problem

QM for Windows - C:\Prentice\Data\Hrrsn587.int

Objective
● Maximize
○ Minimize

Iteration Results

Harrison Electric Solution

Iteration	Level	Added constraint	Solution type	Solution Value	Chandeliers	Ceiling Fans
			Optimal	35.	5.	0.
1	0.		NONinteger	35.25	3.75	1.5
2	1.	Chandeliers<= 3	INTEGER	33.	3.	2.
3	1.	Chandeliers>= 4	NONinteger	35.2	4.	1.2
4	2.	Ceiling Fans<= 1	NONinteger	35.1667	4.1667	1.
5	3.	Chandeliers<= 4	INTEGER	34.	4.	1.
6	3.	Chandeliers>= 5	INTEGER	35.	5.	0.
7	2.	Ceiling Fans>= 2	Infeasible			

PROGRAM 11.2A   Using Excel's Solver Command to Formulate Harrison's Integer Programming Model

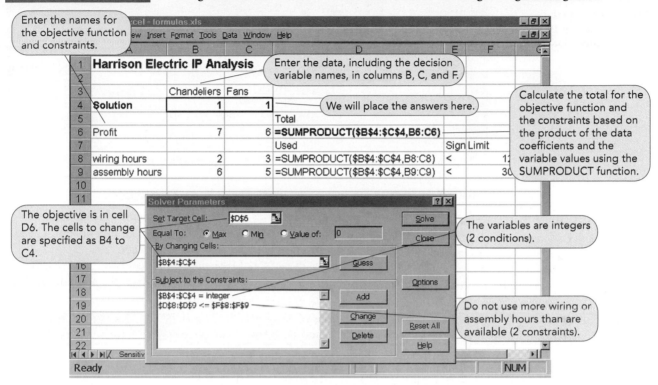

Enter the names for the objective function and constraints.

Enter the data, including the decision variable names, in columns B, C, and F.

We will place the answers here.

Calculate the total for the objective function and the constraints based on the product of the data coefficients and the variable values using the SUMPRODUCT function.

The objective is in cell D6. The cells to change are specified as B4 to C4.

The variables are integers (2 conditions).

Do not use more wiring or assembly hours than are available (2 constraints).

The solutions to the branch and bound subproblems identified in the previous section are presented in the output. The optimal, continuous (noninteger) solution is identified as level 0 (iteration 1) in the output. The solutions to subproblems *A* and *B* correspond to level 1 (iterations 2 and 3) in the output. Level 2 in the output gives the solutions to subproblems *C* and *D*; and level 3 in the output gives the solutions to subproblems *E* and *F*.

Programs 11.2A, B, and C illustrate an Excel spreadsheet approach to the same problem. Program 11.2A formulates the problem for Solver, Program 11.2B shows how to specify that the variables are integers, and Program 11.2C shows the solution. Both QM for Windows and Excel produce the same solution of 5 chandeliers and 0 ceiling fans.

PROGRAM 11.2B

Integer Variables Are Specified with Drop-down Menu in Solver

PROGRAM 11.2C

Excel Solution to the Harrison Electric Integer Programming Model

	A	B	C	D	E	F	G	H	I
1	**Harrison Electric IP Analysis**								
2									
3		Chandeliers	Fans						
4	**Solution**	5	0						
5				Total					
6	Profit	7	6	**35**					
7				Used	Sign	Limit			
8	wiring hours	2	3	10	<	12			
9	assembly hours	6	5	30	<	30			
10									

Mixed-Integer Programming Problem Example

Although the Harrison Electric example was a pure integer problem, there are many situations in which some of the variables are restricted to be integers and others are not. The following is an example of such a mixed-integer programming problem.

Bagwell Chemical Company, in Jackson, Mississippi, produces two industrial chemicals. The first product, xyline, must be produced in 50-pound bags; the second, hexall, is

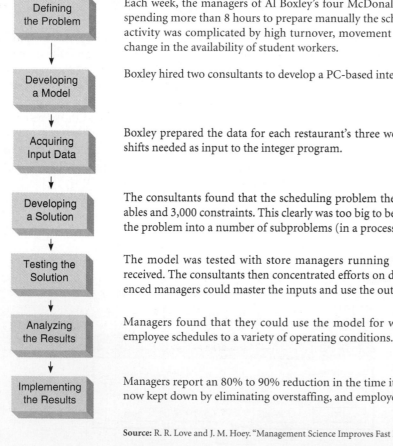

⯈ MODELING IN THE REAL WORLD   **Scheduling Employees at McDonald's**

Defining the Problem

Each week, the managers of Al Boxley's four McDonald's restaurants in Cumberland, Maryland, were spending more than 8 hours to prepare manually the schedules for 150 employees. This time-consuming activity was complicated by high turnover, movement of employees among restaurants, and constant change in the availability of student workers.

Developing a Model

Boxley hired two consultants to develop a PC-based integer programming model.

Acquiring Input Data

Boxley prepared the data for each restaurant's three work areas, 150 employees, and 30 possible work shifts needed as input to the integer program.

Developing a Solution

The consultants found that the scheduling problem they formulated resulted in 100,000 decision variables and 3,000 constraints. This clearly was too big to be solved very quickly on a PC. So they subdivided the problem into a number of subproblems (in a process called "decomposition into network flows").

Testing the Solution

The model was tested with store managers running the program. Initial schedules were favorably received. The consultants then concentrated efforts on developing user-friendly screens so that inexperienced managers could master the inputs and use the outputs successfully.

Analyzing the Results

Managers found that they could use the model for what-if? analysis, to measure the sensitivity of employee schedules to a variety of operating conditions.

Implementing the Results

Managers report an 80% to 90% reduction in the time it takes to generate employee schedules. Costs are now kept down by eliminating overstaffing, and employee morale and efficiency are improved.

Source: R. R. Love and J. M. Hoey. "Management Science Improves Fast Food Operations," *Interfaces* 20, 2 (March–April 1990): 21–29.

sold by the pound in dry bulk and hence can be produced in any quantity. Both xyline and hexall are composed of three ingredients—A, B, and C—as follows:

AMOUNT PER 50-POUND BAG OF XYLINE (LB)	AMOUNT PER POUND OF HEXALL (LB)	AMOUNT OF INGREDIENTS AVAILABLE
30	0.5	2,000 lb—ingredient A
18	0.4	800 lb—ingredient B
2	0.1	200 lb—ingredient C

Bagwell sells 50-pound bags of xyline for $85 and hexall in any weight for $1.50 per pound.

If we let X = number of 50-pound bags of xyline produced and Y = number of pounds of hexall (in dry bulk) mixed, Bagwell's problem can be described with mixed-integer programming:

$$\text{maximize profit} = \$85X + \$1.50Y$$

$$\text{subject to:} \quad 30X + 0.5Y \leq 2{,}000$$

$$18X + 0.4Y \leq 800$$

$$2X + 0.1Y \leq 200$$

$$X, Y \geq 0 \text{ and } X \text{ integer.}$$

Note that Y represents bulk weight of hexall and is not required to be integer valued.

Using QM for Windows and Excel to Solve Bagwell's Integer Programming Model The solution to Bagwell's problem is to produce 44 bags of xyline and 20 pounds of hexall, yielding a profit of $3,770. (The optimal linear solution, by the way, is to produce 44.444 bags of xyline and 0 pounds of hexall, yielding a profit of $3,777.78.) This is first illustrated in Program 11.3, which uses the Mixed Integer Programming module in QM for Windows. Note that variable X is identified as Integer, while Y is Real in Program 11.3.

In Programs 11.4A and 11.4B we use Excel to provide an alternative solution method.

IN ACTION   Selling Seats at American Airlines Using Integer Programming

American Airlines (AA) describes *yield management* as "selling the right seats to the right customers at the right prices." The role of yield management is to determine how much of each product to put on the shelf (make available for sale). American's storefront is the computerized reservations system called SABRE.

The AA yield-management problem is a mixed-integer program that requires data such as passenger demand, cancellations, and other estimates of passenger behavior that are subject to frequent changes. To solve the system-wide yield-management problem would require approximately 250 million decision variables.

To bring this problem down to a manageable size, AA's integer programming model creates three smaller and easier subproblems. The airline looks at the following:

1. Overbooking, which is the practice of intentionally selling more reservations for a flight than there are actual seats on the aircraft.

2. Discount allocation, which is the process of determining the number of discount fares to offer on a flight.
3. Traffic management, which is the process of controlling reservations by passenger origin and destination to provide the mix of markets that maximizes revenue.

Yield management, much disliked by airline passengers who view it as a way of squeezing the most money out of travelers as possible, has been a big winner for AA and other airlines. In one year, American increased profits by about $1 billion using this approach.

Sources: T. Cook. "SABRE Soars," *OR/MS Today* (June 1998): 26–31 and B. Smith, J. Leimkuhler, and R. Darrow. "Yield Management at American Airlines," *Interfaces* 22, 1 (January–February 1992): 8–31.

PROGRAM 11.3

Bagwell's Mixed Integer Program Using QM for Windows

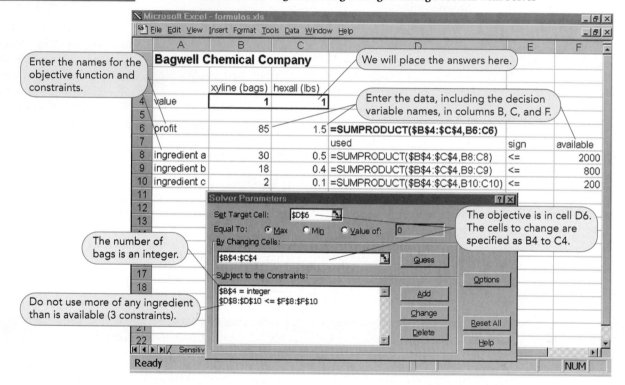

PROGRAM 11.4A

Excel Formulation of Bagwell's Integer Programming Problem with Solver

PROGRAM 11.4B

Excel Solution to the Bagwell Chemical Analysis Problem

11.3 MODELING WITH 0-1 (BINARY) VARIABLES

In this section we demonstrate how 0–1 variables can be used to model several diverse situations. Typically a 0–1 variable is assigned a value of 0 if a certain condition is not met and 1 if the condition is met. Another name for a 0–1 variable is a *binary variable*. A common problem of this type, the assignment problem, involves deciding which individuals to assign to a set of jobs. (This is discussed in Chapter 10.) In this assignment problem, a value of 1 indicates a person is assigned to a specific job, and a value of 0 indicates the assignment was not made. We present other types of 0–1 problems to show the wide applicability of this modeling technique.

Capital Budgeting Example

A common capital budgeting decision involves selecting from a set of possible projects when budget limitations make it impossible to select all of these. A separate 0–1 variable can be defined for each project. We will see this in the following example.

Quemo Chemical Company is considering three possible improvement projects for its plant: a new catalytic converter, a new software program for controlling operations, and expanding the warehouse used for storage. Capital requirements and budget limitations in the next two years prevent the firm from undertaking all of these at this time. The net present value (the future value of the project discounted back to the present time) of each of the projects, the capital requirements, and the available funds for the next two years are given in Table 11.2.

To formulate this as an integer programming problem, we identify the objective function and the constraints as follows:

maximize net present value of projects undertaken

subject to: Total funds used in year 1 ≤ $20,000

Total funds used in year 2 ≤ $16,000

We define the decision variables as

$$X_1 = \begin{cases} 1 \text{ if catalytic converter project is funded} \\ 0 \text{ otherwise} \end{cases}$$

$$X_2 = \begin{cases} 1 \text{ if software project is funded} \\ 0 \text{ otherwise} \end{cases}$$

$$X_3 = \begin{cases} 1 \text{ if warehouse expansion project is funded} \\ 0 \text{ otherwise} \end{cases}$$

The mathematical statement of the integer programming problem becomes

maximize $25{,}000X_1 + 18{,}000X_2 + 32{,}000X_3$

subject to: $8{,}000X_1 + 6{,}000X_2 + 12{,}000X_3 \le 20{,}000$

$7{,}000X_1 + 4{,}000X_2 + 8{,}000X_3 \le 16{,}000$

$X_1, X_2, X_3 = 0 \text{ or } 1$

TABLE 11.2				
Quemo Chemical Company Information	PROJECT	NET PRESENT VALUE	YEAR 1	YEAR 2
	Catalytic Converter	$25,000	$8,000	$7,000
	Software	$18,000	$6,000	$4,000
	Warehouse Expansion	$32,000	$12,000	$8,000
	Available Funds		$20,000	$16,000

If this were solved with computer software, we would see that the optimal solution is $X_1 = 1$, $X_2 = 0$, $X_3 = 1$ with an objective function value of 57,000. This means that Quemo should fund the catalytic converter project and the warehouse expansion project but not the new software project. The net present value of these investments will be $57,000.

Limiting the Number of Alternatives Selected

One common use of 0–1 variables involves limiting the number of projects or items that are selected from a group. Suppose that in the Quemo Chemical Company example, the company is required to select no more than 2 of the 3 projects *regardless* of the funds available. This could be modeled by adding the following constraint to the problem:

$$X_1 + X_2 + X_3 \leq 2$$

If we wished to force the selection of *exactly* 2 of the 3 projects for funding, the following constraint should be used:

$$X_1 + X_2 + X_3 = 2$$

This forces exactly two of the variables to have values of 1, whereas the other variable must have a value of 0.

Dependent Selections

At times the selection of one project depends in some way upon the selection of another project. This situation can be modeled with the use of 0–1 variables. Now suppose in the Quemo Chemical problem that the new catalytic converter could be purchased only if the software was purchased also. The following constraint would force this to occur:

$$X_1 \leq X_2$$

or equivalently

$$X_1 - X_2 \leq 0$$

Thus, if the software is not purchased, the value of X_2 is 0, and the value of X_1 must be 0 also because of this constraint. However, if the software is purchased ($X_2 = 1$), then it is possible that the catalytic converter could be purchased ($X_1 = 1$) also, although this is not required.

If we wished for the catalytic converter and the software projects to either both be selected or both not be selected, we should use the following constraint:

$$X_1 = X_2$$

or equivalently

$$X_1 - X_2 = 0$$

Thus, if either of these variables is equal to 0, the other must be 0 also. If either of these is equal to 1, the other must be 1 also.

Fixed Charge Problem Example

Often businesses are faced with decisions involving a fixed charge that will affect the cost of future operations. Building a new factory or entering into a long-term lease on an existing facility would involve a fixed cost that might vary depending upon the size of the facility and the location. Once a factory is built, the variable production costs will be affected by the labor cost in the particular city where it is located. An example follows.

		ANNUAL	VARIABLE COST	ANNUAL
TABLE 11.3	SITE	FIXED COST	PER UNIT	CAPACITY
	Baytown, TX	$340,000	$32	21,000
Fixed and Variable Costs	Lake Charles, LA	$270,000	$33	20,000
for Sitka Manufacturing	Mobile, AL	$290,000	$30	19,000

Sitka Manufacturing is planning to build at least one new plant, and three cities are being considered: Baytown, Texas; Lake Charles, Louisiana; and Mobile, Alabama. Once the plant or plants have been constructed, the company wishes to have sufficient capacity to produce at least 38,000 units each year. The costs associated with the possible locations are given in Table 11.3.

In modeling this as an integer program, the objective function is to minimize the total of the fixed cost and the variable cost. The constraints are: (1) total production capacity is at least 38,000; (2) number of units produced at the Baytown plant is 0 if the plant is not built, and it is no more than 21,000 if the plant is built; (3) number of units produced at the Lake Charles plant is 0 if the plant is not built, and it is no more than 20,000 if the plant is built; (4) number of units produced at the Mobile plant is 0 if the plant is not built, and it is no more than 19,000 if the plant is built.

Then we define the decision variables as

$$X_1 = \begin{cases} 1 \text{ if factory is built in Baytown} \\ 0 \text{ otherwise} \end{cases}$$

$$X_2 = \begin{cases} 1 \text{ if factory is built in Lake Charles} \\ 0 \text{ otherwise} \end{cases}$$

$$X_3 = \begin{cases} 1 \text{ if factory is built in Mobile} \\ 0 \text{ otherwise} \end{cases}$$

$$X_4 = \text{number of units produced at Baytown plant}$$

$$X_5 = \text{number of units produced at Lake Charles plant}$$

$$X_6 = \text{number of units produced at Mobile plant}$$

The integer programming problem formulation becomes

$$\text{minimize cost} = 340{,}000X_1 + 270{,}000X_2 + 290{,}000X_3 + 32X_4 + 33X_5 + 30X_6$$

The number of units produced must be 0 if the plant is not built.

subject to:
$$X_4 + X_5 + X_6 \geq 38{,}000$$
$$X_4 \leq 21{,}000X_1$$
$$X_5 \leq 20{,}000X_2$$
$$X_6 \leq 19{,}000X_3$$
$$X_1, X_2, X_3 = 0 \text{ or } 1; \ X_4, X_5, X_6 \geq 0 \text{ and integer}$$

Notice that if $X_1 = 0$ (meaning Baytown plant is not built), then X_4 (number of units produced at Baytown plant) must equal zero also due to the second constraint. If $X_1 = 1$, then X_4 may be any integer value less than or equal to the limit of 21,000. The third and fourth constraints are similarly used to guarantee that no units are produced at the other locations if the plants are not built. The optimal solution is

$$X_1 = 0, \qquad X_2 = 1, \qquad X_3 = 1, \qquad X_4 = 0, \qquad X_5 = 19,000, \qquad X_6 = 19,000$$

objective function value = 1,757,000

This means that factories will be built at Lake Charles and Mobile. Each of these will produce 19,000 units each year, and the total annual cost will be $1,757,000.

Financial Investment Example

Numerous financial applications exist with 0–1 variables. A very common type of problem involves selecting from a group of investment opportunities. The following example illustrates this application.

Here is an example of stock portfolio analysis with 0–1 programming.

The Houston-based investment firm of Simkin, Simkin, and Steinberg specializes in recommending oil stock portfolios for wealthy clients. One such client has made the following specifications: (1) at least two Texas oil firms must be in the portfolio, (2) no more than one investment can be made in foreign oil companies, (3) one of the two California oil stocks must be purchased. The client has up to $3 million available for investments and insists on purchasing large blocks of shares of each company that he invests in. Table 11.4 describes various stocks that Simkin considers. The objective is to maximize annual return on investment subject to the constraints.

To formulate this as a 0–1 integer programming problem, Simkin lets X_i be a 0–1 integer variable, where $X_i = 1$ if stock i is purchased and $X_i = 0$ if stock i is not purchased.

$$\text{maximize return} = 50X_1 + 80X_2 + 90X_3 + 120X_4 + 110X_5 + 40X_6 + 75X_7$$

subject to: $\qquad X_1 + X_4 + X_5 \geq 2$ (Texas constraint)

$$X_2 + X_3 \leq 1 \quad \text{(foreign oil constraint)}$$

$$X_6 + X_7 = 1 \quad \text{(California constraint)}$$

$$480X_1 + 540X_2 + 680X_3 + 1,000X_4 + 700X_5 + 510X_6 + 900X_7 \leq 3,000$$
$$(\$3 \text{ million limit})$$

All variables must be 0 or 1 in value.

TABLE 11.4			EXPECTED ANNUAL	COST FOR BLOCK OF
Oil Investment Opportunities	STOCK	COMPANY NAME	RETURN ($1,000s)	SHARES ($1,000s)
	1	Trans-Texas Oil	50	480
	2	British Petroleum	80	540
	3	Dutch Shell	90	680
	4	Houston Drilling	120	1,000
	5	Texas Petroleum	110	700
	6	San Diego Oil	40	510
	7	California Petro	75	900

PROGRAM 11.5A   **Excel Formulation for Solving Simkin's 0–1 Integer Programming Problem**

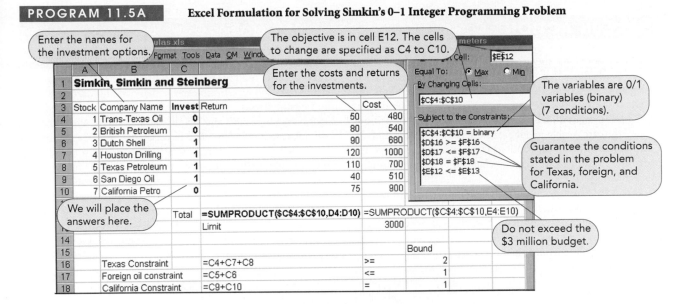

Using Excel to Solve the Simkin Example To solve this problem by computer, you can use Excel and its Solver function. Programs 11.5A and 11.5B show this approach. As we see in the output screen (Program 11.5B), X_3, X_4, X_5, and X_6 are all equal to 1 in the all-integer solution, and X_1, X_2, and X_7 are 0. This means that Simkin should invest in Dutch Shell, Houston Drilling, Texas Petroleum, and San Diego Oil, and not in the other three oil firms. The expected return is $360,000.

You might also recall that assignment problems solved by LP, in Chapter 8, are also actually 0–1 integer programs. All assignments of people to jobs, for example, are presented by either a 1 (person gets job) or a 0 (person not assigned to particular job).

PROGRAM 11.5B   **Excel Solution to Simkin's 0–1 Integer Programming Problem**

Microsoft Excel - captures.xls

File Edit View Insert Format Tools Data Accounting OM Window Help

	A	B	C	D	E	F	G	H	I
1	**Simkin, Simkin and Steinberg**								
2									
3	Stock	Company Name	**Invest**	Return	Cost				
4		1 Trans-Texas Oil	**0**	50	480				
5		2 British Petroleum	**0**	80	540				
6		3 Dutch Shell	**1**	90	680				
7		4 Houston Drilling	**1**	120	1000				
8		5 Texas Petroleum	**1**	110	700				
9		6 San Diego Oil	**1**	40	510				
10		7 California Petro	**0**	75	900				
11									
12			Total	**360**	2890				
13				Limit	3000				
14									
15						Bound			
16		Texas Constraint		2	>=	2			
17		Foreign oil constraint		1	<=	1			
18		California Constraint		1	=	1			

IN ACTION Continental Airlines Saves $40 Million Using CrewSolver

Airlines use state-of-the-art processes and automated tools to develop schedules that maximize profit. These schedules will assign aircraft to specific routes, and then schedule pilots and flight attendant crews to each of these aircraft. When disruptions occur, planes and personnel are often left in positions where they are unable to adhere to the next day's assignments. Airlines face schedule disruptions from a variety of unexpected reasons such as bad weather, mechanical problems, and crew unavailability.

In 1993, Continental Airlines began an effort to develop a system of dealing with disruptions in real time. Working with CALEB Technologies, Continental developed the CrewSolver and OptSolver systems (based on 0–1 integer programming models) to produce comprehensive recovery solutions for both aircraft and crews. These solutions retain revenue and promote customer satisfaction by reducing flight cancellations and minimizing delays. These crew recovery solutions are low cost while maintaining a high quality of life for pilots and flight attendants.

In late 2000 and throughout 2001, Continental and other airlines experienced four major disruptions. The first two were due to severe snowstorms in early January and in March 2001. The Houston floods caused by Tropical Storm Allison closed a major hub in June 2001 and left aircraft in locations where they were not scheduled to be. The terrorist attacks of September 11, 2001 left aircraft and crews scattered about and totally disrupted the flight schedules. The CrewSolver system provided a faster and more efficient recovery than had been possible in the past. It is estimated that the CrewSolver system saved approximately $40 million for these major disruptions in 2001. This system also saved additional money and made recovery much easier when there were minor disruptions due to local weather problems at other times throughout the year.

Source: "A New Era for Crew Recovery at Continental Airlines," Gang Yu, Michael Arguello, Gao Song, Sandra M. McCowan, Anna White, *Interfaces* Vol. 33, No. 1, January–February 2003, pp. 5–22.

11.4 GOAL PROGRAMMING

Firms usually have more than one goal.

In today's business environment, profit maximization or cost minimization are not always the only objectives that a firm sets forth. Often, maximizing total profit is just one of several goals, including such contradictory objectives as maximizing market share, maintaining full employment, providing quality ecological management, minimizing noise level in the neighborhood, and meeting numerous other noneconomic goals.

Goal programming permits multiple goals.

The shortcoming of mathematical programming techniques such as linear and integer programming is that their objective function is measured in one dimension only. It's not possible for LP to have *multiple goals* unless they are all measured in the same units (such as dollars), a highly unusual situation. An important technique that has been developed to supplement LP is called *goal programming*.

Goal programming is capable of handling decision problems involving multiple goals. A four-decade old concept, it began with the work of Charnes and Cooper in 1961 and has been refined and extended by Lee and Ignizio in the 1970s (see the Bibliography).

Goal programming "satisfices," as opposed to LP, which tries to "optimize." This means coming as close as possible to reaching goals.

In typical decision-making situations, the goals set by management can be achieved only at the expense of other goals. It is necessary to establish a hierarchy of importance among these goals so that lower-priority goals are tackled only after higher-priority goals are satisfied. Since it is not always possible to achieve every goal to the extent the decision maker desires, goal programming attempts to reach a satisfactory level of multiple objectives. This, of course, differs from LP, which tries to find the best possible outcome for a *single* objective. Nobel laureate Herbert A. Simon, of Carnegie-Mellon University, states that modern managers may not be able to optimize, but may instead have to "*satisfice*" or "come as close as possible" to reaching goals. This is the case with models such as goal programming.

The objective function is the main difference between goal programming and LP.

How, specifically, does goal programming differ from LP? The objective function is the main difference. Instead of trying to maximize or minimize the objective function directly, with goal programming we try to minimize *deviations* between set goals and what we can actually achieve within the given constraints. In the LP simplex approach, such deviations are called slack and surplus variables. Because the coefficient for each of these in the objective function is zero, slack and surplus variables do not have an impact on the optimal solution. In goal programming, the deviational variables are typically the only variables in the objective function, and the objective is to minimize the total of these *deviational variables*.

In goal programming we want to minimize deviational variables, which are the only terms in the objective function.

When the goal programming model is formulated, the computational algorithm is almost the same as a minimization problem solved by the simplex method.

Example of Goal Programming: Harrison Electric Company Revisited

To illustrate the formulation of a goal programming problem, let's look back at the Harrison Electric Company case presented earlier in this chapter as an integer programming problem. That problem's LP formulation, you recall, is

$$\text{maximize profit} = \$7X_1 + \$6X_2$$

$$\text{subject to:} \quad 2X_1 + 3X_2 \leq 12 \text{ (wiring hours)}$$

$$6X_1 + 5X_2 \leq 30 \text{ (assembly hours)}$$

$$X_1, X_2 \geq 0$$

where

$$X_1 = \text{number of chandeliers produced}$$

$$X_2 = \text{number of ceiling fans produced}$$

We saw that if Harrison's management had a single goal, say profit, LP could be used to find the optimal solution. But let's assume that the firm is moving to a new location during a particular production period and feels that maximizing profit is not a realistic goal. Management sets a profit level, which would be satisfactory during the adjustment period, of $30. We now have a goal programming problem in which we want to find the production mix that achieves this goal as closely as possible, given the production time constraints. This simple case will provide a good starting point for tackling more complicated goal programs.

We first define two deviational variables:

$$d_1^- = \text{underachievement of the profit target}$$

$$d_1^+ = \text{overachievement of the profit target}$$

Now we can state the Harrison Electric problem as a *single-goal* programming model:

$$\text{minimize under or overachievement of profit target} = d_1^- + d_1^+$$

$$\text{subject to:} \quad \$7X_1 + \$6X_2 + d_1^- - d_1^+ = \$30 \quad \text{(profit goal constraint)}$$

$$2X_1 + 3X_2 \qquad\qquad \leq 12 \quad \text{(wiring hours constraint)}$$

$$6X_1 + 5X_2 \qquad\qquad \leq 30 \quad \text{(assembly hours constraint)}$$

$$X_1, X_2, d_1^-, d_1^+ \geq 0$$

Note that the first constraint states that the profit made, $\$7X_1 + \$6X_2$, plus any underachievement of profit minus any overachievement of profit has to equal the target of $30. For example, if $X_1 = 3$ chandeliers and $X_2 = 2$ ceiling fans, then $33 profit has been made. This exceeds $30 by $3, so d_1^+ must be equal to 3. Since the profit goal constraint was *overachieved*, Harrison did not underachieve and d_1^- will clearly be equal to zero. This problem is now ready for solution by a goal programming algorithm.

Deviational variables are zero if a goal is completely obtained.

If the target profit of $30 is exactly achieved, we see that both d_1^+ and d_1^- are equal to zero. The objective function will also be minimized at zero. If Harrison's management was only concerned with *underachievement* of the target goal, how would the objective function change? It would be as follows: minimize underachievement = d_1^-. This is also a reasonable goal since the firm would probably not be upset with an overachievement of its target.

In general, once all goals and constraints are identified in a problem, management should analyze each goal to see if underachievement or overachievement of that goal is an acceptable situation. If overachievement is acceptable, the appropriate d^+ variable can be eliminated from the objective function. If underachievement is okay, the d^- variable should be dropped. If management seeks to attain a goal exactly, both d^- and d^+ must appear in the objective function.

Extension to Equally Important Multiple Goals

Let's now look at the situation in which Harrison's management wants to achieve several goals, each equal in priority.

Goal 1: to produce profit of $30 if possible during the production period

Goal 2: to fully utilize the available wiring department hours

Goal 3: to avoid overtime in the assembly department

Goal 4: to meet a contract requirement to produce at least seven ceiling fans

We need a clear definition of deviational variables, such as these.

The deviational variables can be defined as follows:

d_1^- = underachievement of the profit target

d_1^+ = overachievement of the profit target

d_2^- = idle time in the wiring department (underutilization)

d_2^+ = overtime in the wiring department (overutilization)

d_3^- = idle time in the assembly department (underutilization)

d_3^+ = overtime in the assembly department (overutilization)

d_4^- = underachievement of the ceiling fan goal

d_4^+ = overachievement of the ceiling fan goal

Management is unconcerned about whether there is overachievement of the profit goal, overtime in the wiring department, idle time in the assembly department, or more than seven ceiling fans are produced: hence, d_1^+, d_2^+, d_3^-, and d_4^+ may be omitted from the objective function. The new objective function and constraints are

$$\text{minimize total deviation} = d_1^- + d_2^- + d_3^+ + d_4^-$$

$$\text{subject to:} \quad 7X_1 + 6X_2 + d_1^- - d_1^+ = 30 \quad \text{(profit constraint)}$$

$$2X_1 + 3X_2 + d_2^- - d_2^+ = 12 \quad \text{(wiring hours constraint)}$$

$$6X_1 + 5X_2 + d_3^- - d_3^+ = 30 \quad \text{(assembly constraint)}$$

$$X_2 + d_4^- - d_4^+ = 7 \quad \text{(ceiling fan constraint)}$$

$$\text{All } X_i, d_i \text{ variables} \geq 0.$$

Ranking Goals with Priority Levels

A key idea in goal programming is that one goal is more important than another. Priorities are assigned to each deviational variable.

In most goal programming problems, one goal will be more important than another, which in turn will be more important than a third. The idea is that goals can be ranked with respect to their importance in management's eyes. Lower-order goals are considered only after higher-order goals are met. Priorities (P_i's) are assigned to each deviational variable— with the ranking that P_1 is the most important goal, P_2 the next most important, then P_3, and so on.

Let's say Harrison Electric sets the priorities shown in the accompanying table.

GOAL	PRIORITY
Reach a profit as much above $30 as possible	P_1
Fully use wiring department hours available	P_2
Avoid assembly department overtime	P_3
Produce at least seven ceiling fans	P_4

Priority 1 is infinitely more important than Priority 2, which is infinitely more important than the next goal, and so on.

This means, in effect, that the priority of meeting the profit goal (P_1) is infinitely more important than the wiring goal (P_2), which is, in turn, infinitely more important than the assembly goal (P_3), which is infinitely more important than producing at least seven ceiling fans (P_4).

With ranking of goals considered, the new objective function becomes

$$\text{minimize total deviation} = P_1 d_1^- + P_2 d_2^- + P_3 d_3^+ + P_4 d_4^-$$

The constraints remain identical to the previous ones.

IN ACTION   The Use of Goal Programming for Tuberculosis Drug Allocation in Manila

Allocation of resources is critical when applied to the health industry. It is a matter of life and death when neither the right supply nor the correct quantity is available to meet patient demand. This was the case faced by the Manila (Philippines) Health Center, whose drug supply to patients afflicted with Category I tuberculosis (TB) was not being efficiently allocated to its 45 regional health centers. When the TB drug supply does not reach patients on time, the disease becomes worse and can result in death. Only 74% of TB patients were being cured in Manila, 11% short of the 85% target cure rate set by the government. Unlike other diseases, TB can only be treated with four medicines and cannot be cured by alternative drugs.

Researchers at the Mapka Institute of Technology set out to create a model, using goal programming, to optimize the allocation of resources for TB treatment while considering supply constraints. The objective function of the model was to meet the target cure rate of 85% (which is the equivalent of minimizing the

underachievement in the allocation of anti-TB drugs to the 45 centers). Four goal constraints considered the interrelationships among variables in the distribution system. Goal 1 was to satisfy the medication requirement (a six-month regimen) for each patient. Goal 2 was to supply each health center with the proper allocation. Goal 3 was to satisfy the cure rate of 85%. Goal 4 was to satisfy the drug requirements of each health center.

The goal programming model successfully dealt with all of these goals and raised the TB cure rate to 88%, a 13% improvement in drug allocation over the previous distribution approach. This means that 335 lives per year were saved through this thoughtful use of goal programming.

Source: G. J. C. Esmeria. "An Application of Goal Programming in the Allocation of Anti-TB Drugs in Rural Health Centers in the Philippines," *Proceedings of the 12th Annual Conference of the Production and Operations Management Society* (March 2001), Orlando, FL: 50.

Solving Goal Programming Problems Graphically

Just as we solved LP problems graphically in Chapter 7, we can analyze goal programming problems graphically. First, we must be aware of three characteristics of goal programming problems: (1) goal programming models are all minimization problems; (2) there is no single objective, but multiple goals to be attained; and (3) the deviation from a high-priority goal must be minimized to the greatest extent possible before the next-highest-priority goal is considered.

Let us use the Harrison Electric Company goal programming problem as an example. The model is formulated as

$$\text{minimize total deviation} = P_1d_1^- + P_2d_2^- + P_3d_3^+ + P_4d_4^-$$

$$\text{subject to:}\quad 7X_1 + 6X_2 + d_1^- - d_1^+ = 30 \text{ (profit)}$$

$$2X_1 + 3X_2 + d_2^- - d_2^+ = 12 \text{ (wiring)}$$

$$6X_1 + 5X_2 + d_3^- - d_3^+ = 30 \text{ (assembly)}$$

$$X_2 + d_4^- - d_4^+ = 7 \text{ (ceiling fans)}$$

$$X_1, X_2, d_i^-, d_i^+ \geq 0 \text{ (nonnegativity)}$$

where

$$X_1 = \text{number of chandeliers produced}$$

$$X_2 = \text{number of ceiling fans produced}$$

Graphical constraints are drawn, one at a time.

To solve this problem, we graph one constraint at a time, starting with the one that has the highest-priority deviational variables. This is the profit constraint, since d_1^- has priority P_1 in the objective function. Figure 11.4 shows the profit constraint line. Note that in graphing the line, the deviational variables d_1^- and d_1^+ are ignored. To minimize d_1^- (the underachievement of $30 profit), the feasible area is the shaded region. Any point in the shaded region satisfies the first goal because profit exceeds $30.

Figure 11.5 includes the second priority goal of minimizing d_2^-. The region below the constraint line $2X_1 + 3X_2 = 12$ represents the values for d_2^-, while the region above the line stands for d_2^+. To avoid underutilizing wiring department hours, the area below the line is eliminated. But this goal must be attained within the feasible area already defined by satisfying the first goal.

The third goal is to avoid overtime in the assembly department, which means we want d_3^+ to be as close to zero as possible. As we can see in Figure 11.6, this goal can also be fully attained. The area that contains solution points that will satisfy the first three priority goals is bounded by the points *A, B, C, D*. Inside this narrow strip, any solution will meet the three most critical goals.

The fourth goal is to produce at least seven ceiling fans, and hence to minimize d_4^-. To achieve this final goal, the area below the constraint line $X_2 = 7$ must be eliminated. But we cannot do this without violating one of the higher-priority goals. We want, then, to find a solution point that still satisfies the first three goals, and also comes as close as possible to achieving the fourth goal. Do you see which point this would be?

The solution is found at corner point A, which satisfies the first three goals and comes close to achieving the fourth goal.

Corner point *A* appears to be the optimal solution. We easily see that its coordinates are $X_1 = 0$ chandeliers and $X_2 = 6$ ceiling fans. Substituting these values into the goal constraints, we find that the other variables are

$$d_1^- = \$0, \qquad d_1^+ = \$6, \qquad d_2^- = 0 \text{ hours}, \qquad d_2^+ = 6 \text{ hours}$$

$$d_3^- = \$0 \text{ hours}, \qquad d_3^+ = 0 \text{ hours}, \qquad d_4^- = 1 \text{ ceiling fan}$$

$$d_4^+ = 0 \text{ ceiling fans}$$

FIGURE 11.4

Analysis of First Goal

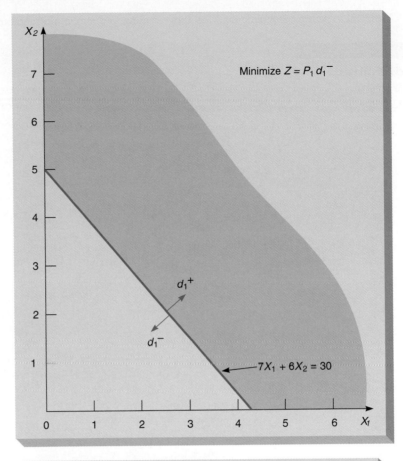

FIGURE 11.5

Analysis of First and Second Goals

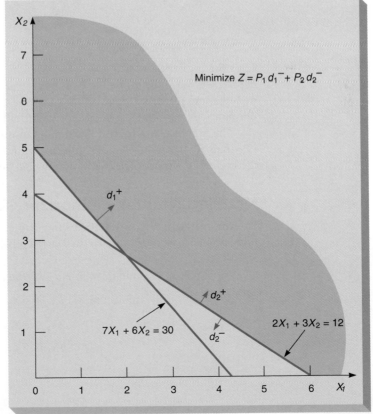

FIGURE 11.6

Analysis of All Four Priority Goals

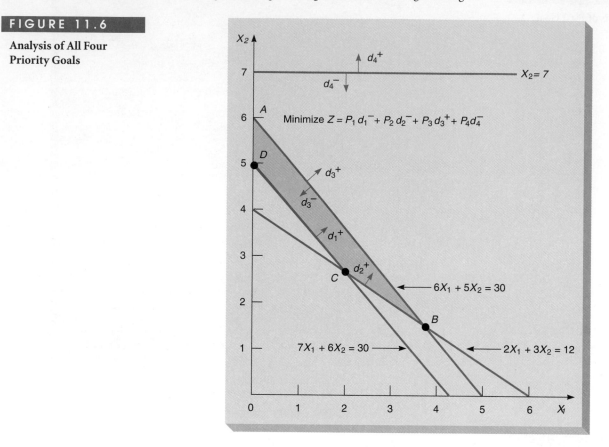

Thus the profit goal was met and exceeded by $6 (a $36 profit was attained), the wiring department was fully utilized as 6 hours of overtime were used there, the assembly department had no idle time (or overtime), and the ceiling fan goal was underachieved by only one fan. This was the most satisfactory solution to the problem.

The graphical approach to goal programming has the same drawbacks as it did with LP—namely, it can only handle problems with two real variables. By modifying the simplex method of LP, a more general solution to goal programming problems can be found.

Modified Simplex Method for Goal Programming

To demonstrate how the modified simplex method can be used to solve a goal programming problem, we again turn to the Harrison Electric Company example.

$$\text{minimize} = P_1 d_1^- + P_2 d_2^- + P_3 d_3^+ + P_4 d_4^-$$

$$\text{subject to:} \quad 7X_1 + 6X_2 + d_1^- - d_1^+ = 30$$

$$2X_1 + 3X_2 + d_2^- - d_2^+ = 12$$

$$6X_1 + 5X_2 + d_3^- - d_3^+ = 30$$

$$X_2 + d_4^- - d_4^+ = 7$$

$$X_1, X_2, d_i^-, d_i^+ \geq 0$$

Table 11.5 presents the initial simplex tableau for this problem. We should point out four features of this tableau that differ from the simplex tableaus we saw in Chapter 9:

Here are four differences between LP simplex tableau and goal programming tableau.

1. The variables in the problem are listed at the top, with the decision variables (X_1 and X_2) first, then the negative deviational variables, and finally, the positive deviational variables. The priority level of each variable is assigned on the very top row.

2. The negative deviational variables for each constraint provide the initial basic feasible solution. This is analogous to the LP simplex tableau, in which slack variables provide the initial solution. (Thus we see that $d_1^- = 30$, $d_2^- = 12$, $d_3^- = 30$, and $d_4^- = 7$.) The priority level of each variable in the current solution mix is entered in the C_j column on the far left. Note that the coefficients in the body of the tableau are set up exactly as they were in the regular simplex approach.

3. There is a separate Z_j and $C_j - Z_j$ row for each of the P_i priorities. Since profit goals, department hour goals, and production goals are each measured in different units, the four separate priority rows are needed. In goal programming, the bottom row of the simplex tableau contains the highest ranked (P_1) goal, the next row has the P_2 goal, and so on. The rows are computed exactly as in the regular simplex method, but they are done for each priority level. In Table 11.5, the $C_j - Z_j$ value for column X_1, for example, is read as $-7P_1 - 2P_2 + 0P_3 + 0P_4$.

Each P_i priority has a separate Z_j and $C_j - Z_j$ row.

Selecting the variable to enter the solution mix next.

4. In selecting the variable to enter the solution mix, we start with the highest-priority row, P_1, and select the most negative $C_j - Z_j$ value in it. (The pivot column is X_1 in Table 11.5.) If there was no negative number in the $C_j - Z_j$ row for P_1, we would move up to priority P_2's $C_j - Z_j$ row and select the largest negative number there. A negative $C_j - Z_j$ that has a positive number in a P row underneath it, however, is ignored. This means that deviations from a more important goal (one in a lower row) would be *increased* if that variable were brought into the solution.

After we set up the initial modified simplex tableau, we move toward the optimal solution just as with the regular minimization simplex procedures described in detail in Chapter 9. Keeping in mind the four features just listed, the next step in moving from Table

TABLE 11.5

Initial Goal Programming Tableau

C_j	SOLUTION MIX	0 X_1	0 X_2	P_1 d_1^-	P_2 d_2^-	0 d_3^-	P_4 d_4^-	0 d_1^+	0 d_2^+	P_3 d_3^+	0 d_4^+	QUANTITY
P_1	d_1^-	7	6	1	0	0	0	−1	0	0	0	30
P_2	d_2^-	2	3	0	1	0	0	0	−1	0	0	12
0	d_3^-	6	5	0	0	1	0	0	0	−1	0	30
P_4	d_4^-	0	1	0	0	0	1	0	0	0	−1	7
	P_4	0	1	0	0	0	1	0	0	0	−1	7
Z_j	P_3	0	0	0	0	0	0	0	0	0	0	0
	P_2	2	3	0	1	0	0	0	−1	0	0	12
	P_1	7	6	1	0	0	0	−1	0	0	0	30
	P_4	0	−1	0	0	0	0	0	0	0	1	
$C_j - Z_j$	P_3	0	0	0	0	0	0	0	0	1	0	
	P_2	−2	−3	0	0	0	0	0	1	0	0	
	P_1	−7	−6	0	0	0	0	1	0	0	0	

Pivot column

TABLE 11.6

Second Goal Programming Tableau

C_j		0	0	P_1	P_2	0	P_4	0	0	P_3	0	
	SOLUTION MIX	X_1	X_2	d_1^-	d_2^-	d_3^-	d_4^-	d_1^+	d_2^+	d_3^+	d_4^+	QUANTITY
0	X_1	1	$6/7$	$1/7$	0	0	0	$-1/7$	0	0	0	$30/7$
P_2	d_2^-	0	$9/7$	$-2/7$	1	0	0	$2/7$	-1	0	0	$24/7$
0	d_3^-	0	$-1/7$	$-6/7$	0	1	0	$6/7$	0	-1	0	$30/7$
P_4	d_4^-	0	1	0	0	0	1	0	0	0	-1	7
Z_j	P_4	0	1	0	0	0	1	0	0	0	-1	7
	P_3	0	0	0	0	0	0	0	0	0	0	0
	P_2	0	$9/7$	$-2/7$	1	0	0	$2/7$	-1	0	0	$24/7$
	P_1	0	0	0	0	0	0	0	0	0	0	0
$C_j - Z_j$	P_4	0	-1	0	0	0	0	0	0	0	1	
	P_3	0	0	0	0	0	0	0	0	1	0	
	P_2	0	$-9/7$	$2/7$	0	0	0	$-2/7$	1	0	0	
	P_1	0	0	1	0	0	0	0	0	0	0	

└─Pivot column

11.5 to Table 11.6 is to find the pivot row. We do this by dividing the quantity values by their corresponding pivot column (X_1) values and picking the one with the smallest positive ratio. Thus d_1^- leaves the basis in the second tableau and is replaced by X_1.

The new rows of the tableau are computed exactly as they are in the regular simplex method. You may recall that this means first computing a new pivot row and then using the formula in Section 9.3 to find the other new rows.

We see in the new $C_j - Z_j$ row for priority P_1, in Table 11.6, that there are no negative values. Thus, the first priority's goal has been reached. Priority 2 is the next objective, and we find two negative entries in its $C_j - Z_j$ row. Again, the largest one is selected as the pivot column and X_2 will become the next variable to enter the solution mix.

Let us skip two tableaus and go directly to Table 11.7, which contains the most satisfactory solution to the problem. (One of the homework problems gives you the chance to work through to this final tableau.)

Notice in the final solution that the first, second, and third goals have been totally achieved: there are no negative $C_j - Z_j$ entries in their rows. A negative value appears (in the d_3^+ column) in the priority 4 row, however, indicating that it has not been fully attained. Indeed, d_4^- is equal to 1, meaning that we have underachieved the ceiling fan goal by one fan. But there is a positive number (see the shaded "1") in the d_3^+ column at the P_3 priority level, and thus at a higher-priority level. If we try to force d_3^+ into the solution mix to attain the P_4 goal, it will be at the expense of a more important goal (P_3) which has already been satisfied. We do not want to sacrifice the P_3 goal, so this will be the best possible goal programming solution. The answer is

$$X_1 = 0 \text{ chandeliers produced}$$

$$X_2 = 6 \text{ ceiling fans produced}$$

$$d_1^+ = \$6 \text{ over the profit goal}$$

$$d_2^+ = 6 \text{ wiring hours over the minimum set}$$

$$d_4^- = 1 \text{ fan less than desired}$$

TABLE 11.7

Final Solution to Harrison Electric's Goal Program

C_j	SOLUTION MIX	0 X_1	0 X_2	P_1 d_1^-	P_2 d_2^-	0 d_3^-	P_4 d_4^-	0 d_1^+	0 d_2^+	P_3 d_3^+	0 d_4^+	QUANTITY
0	d_2^+	$8/5$	0	0	-1	$3/5$	0	0	1	$-3/5$	0	6
0	X_2	$6/5$	1	0	0	$1/5$	0	0	0	$-1/5$	0	6
0	d_1^+	$1/5$	0	-1	0	$6/5$	0	1	0	$-6/5$	0	6
P_4	d_4^-	$-6/5$	0	0	0	$-1/5$	1	0	0	$1/5$	-1	1
Z_j	P_4	$-6/5$	0	0	0	$-1/5$	1	0	0	$1/5$	-1	1
	P_3	0	0	0	0	0	0	0	0	0	0	0
	P_2	0	0	0	0	0	0	0	0	0	0	0
	P_1	0	0	0	0	0	0	0	0	1	0	0
$C_j - Z_j$	P_4	$6/5$	0	0	0	$1/5$	0	0	0	$-1/5$	1	
	P_3	0	0	0	0	0	0	0	0	**1**	0	
	P_2	0	0	0	1	0	0	0	0	0	0	
	P_1	0	0	1	0	0	0	0	0	0	0	

Goal Programming with Weighted Goals

When priority levels are used in goal programming, any goal in the top priority level is infinitely more important than the goals in lower priority levels. However, there may be times when one goal is more important than another goal, but it may be only two or three times as important. Instead of placing these goals in different priority levels, they would be placed in the same priority level but with different weights. When using weighted goal programming, the coefficients in the objective function for the deviational variables include both the priority level and the weight. If all goals are in the same priority level, then simply using the weights as objective function coefficients is sufficient.

Consider the Harrison Electric example, in which the least important goal is goal 4 (produce at least seven ceiling fans). Suppose Harrison decides to add another goal of producing at least two chandeliers. The goal of seven ceiling fans is considered twice as important as this goal, so both of these should be in the same priority level. The goal of 2 chandeliers is assigned a weight of 1, while the 7 ceiling fan goal will be given a weight of 2. Both of these will be in priority level 4. A new constraint (goal) would be added:

$$X_1 + d_5^- - d_5^+ = 2 \quad \text{(chandeliers)}$$

The new objective function value would be

$$\text{Minimize total deviation} = P_1 d_1^- + P_2 d_2^- + P_3 d_3^+ + P_4 (2d_4^-) + P_4 d_5^-$$

Note that the ceiling fan goal has a weight of 2. The weight for the chandelier goal is 1. Technically all of the goals in the other priority levels are assigned weights of 1 also.

Using QM for Windows to Solve Harrison's Problem QM for Windows goal programming module is illustrated in Programs 11.6A, 11.6B, and 11.6C. The input screen is shown first, in Program 11.6A. Note in this first screen that there are two priority level columns for each constraint. For this example, the priority for either the positive or the negative deviation will be zero since the objective function does not contain both types of deviational

PROGRAM 11.6A

Harrison Electric's Goal Programming Analysis Using QM for Windows: Inputs

QM for Windows – C:\Prentice\Data\Renstair\Hrrsn617.goa

Harrison Electric Company

	Wt(d+)	Prty(d+)	Wt(d-)	Prty(d-)	X1	X2		RHS
Constraint 1	0	0	1	1	7	6	=	30
Constraint 2	0	0	1	2	2	3	=	12
Constraint 3	1	3	0	0	6	5	=	30
Constraint 4	0	0	1	4	0	1	=	7

PROGRAM 11.6B

Final Tableau for Harrison Electric Using QM for Windows

QM for Windows – C:\Prentice\Data\Renstair\Hrrsn617.goa

Final Tableau

Harrison Electric Company Solution

	X1	X2	d- 1	d- 2	d- 3	d- 4	d+ 1	d+ 2	d+ 3	d+ 4	RHS
Constraint 1	1.6	0.	0.	-1.	0.6	0.	0.	1.	-0.6	0.	6.
Constraint 2	1.2	1.	0.	0.	0.2	0.	0.	0.	-0.2	0.	6.
Constraint 3	0.2	0.	-1.	0.	1.2	0.	1.	0.	-1.2	0.	6.
Constraint 4	-1.2	0.	0.	0.	-0.2	1.	0.	0.	0.2	-1.	1.
Priority 4	-1.2	0.	0.	0.	-0.2	0.	0.	0.	0.2	-1.	1.
Priority 3	0.	0.	0.	0.	0.	0.	0.	0.	-1.	0.	0.
Priority 2	0.	0.	0.	-1.	0.	0.	0.	0.	0.	0.	0.
Priority 1	0.	0.	-1.	0.	0.	0.	0.	0.	0.	0.	0.

PROGRAM 11.6C

Summary Solution Screen for Harrison Electric's Goal Programming Problem Using QM for Windows

QM for Windows – C:\Prentice\Data\Renstair\Hrrsn617.goa

Summary

Harrison Electric Company Solution

Item			
Decision variable analysis	Value		
X1	0.		
X2	6.		
Priority analysis	Nonachievement		
Priority 1	0.		
Priority 2	0.		
Priority 3	0.		
Priority 4	1.		
Constraint Analysis	RHS	d+ (row i)	d- (row i)
Constraint 1	30.	6.	0.
Constraint 2	12.	6.	0.
Constraint 3	30.	0.	0.
Constraint 4	7.	0.	1.

variables for any of these goals. If a problem had a goal with both deviational variables in the objective function, both priority level columns for this goal (constraint) would contain values other than zero. Also, the weight for each deviational variable contained in the objective function is listed as 1. (It is 0 if the variable is not appearing in the objective function.) If different weights are used, they would be placed in the appropriate weight column within one priority level.

The final tableau is shown in Program 11.6B, and this is identical in content to Table 11.7. The solution with an analysis of deviations and goal achievement is shown in Program 11.6C. We see that the first two constraints have negative deviational variables equal to 0, indicating full achievement of those goals. In fact, the positive deviational variables both have values of 6, indicating overachievement of these goals by 6 units each. Goal (constraint) 3 has both deviational variables equal to 0, indicating complete achievement of that goal, whereas goal 4 has a negative deviational variable equal to 1, indicating under-achievement by 1 unit.

11.5   NONLINEAR PROGRAMMING

Linear, integer, and goal programming all assume that a problem's objective function and constraints are linear. That means that they contain no nonlinear terms such as X_1^3, $1/X_2$, $\log X_3$, or $5X_1X_2$. Yet in many mathematical programming problems, the objective function and/or one or more of the constraints are nonlinear.

In this section, we examine three categories of nonlinear programming (NLP) problems and illustrate how Excel can often be used to solve such problems.

Nonlinear Objective Function and Linear Constraints

Here is an example of a nonlinear objective function.

The Great Western Appliance Company sells two models of toaster ovens, the Microtoaster (X_1) and the Self-Clean Toaster Oven (X_2). The firm earns a profit of $28 for each Microtoaster regardless of the number sold. Profits for the Self-Clean model, however, increase as more units are sold because of fixed overhead. Profit on this model may be expressed as $21X_2 + 0.25X_2^2$.

Hence the firm's objective function is nonlinear:

$$\text{maximize profit} = 28X_1 + 21X_2 + 0.25X_2^2$$

Great Western's profit is subject to two linear constraints on production capacity and sales time available.

$$X_1 + X_2 \leq 1{,}000 \text{ (units of production capacity)}$$
$$0.5X_1 + 0.4X_2 \leq 500 \text{ (hours of sales time available)}$$
$$X_1, X_2 \geq 0$$

Quadratic programming contains squared terms in the objective function.

When an objective function contains squared terms (such as $0.25X_2^2$) and the problem's constraints are linear, it is called a *quadratic programming* problem. A number of useful problems in the field of portfolio selection fall into this category. Quadratic programs can be solved by a modified method of the simplex method. Such work is outside the scope of this book but can be found in sources listed in the Bibliography.

 IN ACTION   Goal Programming Model for Prison Expenditures in Virginia

Prisons across the United States are overcrowded, and there is need for immediate expansion of their capacity and replacement or renovation of obsolete facilities. This study demonstrates how goal programming was used on the capital allocation problem faced by the Department of Corrections of Virginia.

The expenditure items considered by the Virginia corrections department included new and renovated maximum, medium, and minimum security facilities; community diversion programs; and personnel increases. The goal programming technique forced all prison projects to be completely accepted or rejected.

Model variables defined the construction, renovation, or establishment of a particular type of correctional facility for a specific location or purpose and indicated the people required by the facilities. The goal constraints fell into five categories: additional inmate capacity created by new and renovated correctional facilities; operating and personnel costs associated

with each expenditure item; the impact of facility construction and renovation on imprisonment, sentence length, and early releases and parole; the mix of different facility types required by the system; and the personnel requirements resulting from the various capital expenditures for correctional facilities.

The solution results for Virginia were one new maximum security facility for drug, alcohol, and psychiatric treatment activities; one new minimum security facility for youthful offenders; two new regular minimum security facilities; two new community diversion programs in urban areas, renovation of one existing medium security and one minimum security facility; 250 new correctional officers; four new administrators; 46 new treatment specialist/counselors; and six new medical personnel.

Source: R. Russell, B. Taylor, and A. Keown. *Computer Environmental Urban Systems* 11, 4 (1986): 135–146.

PROGRAM 11.7A   **An Excel Formulation of Great Western Appliance's Nonlinear Programming Problem**

For purposes of illustration, we can turn to Excel's powerful Solver command to solve Great Western's model. Programs 11.7A and 11.7B provide the input and outputs, respectively.

Both Nonlinear Objective Function and Nonlinear Constraints

An example in which the objective and constraints are both nonlinear.

The annual profit at a medium-sized (200–400 beds) Hospicare Corporation–owned hospital depends on the number of medical patients admitted (X_1) and the number of surgical patients admitted (X_2). The nonlinear objective function for Hospicare is

$$\$13X_1 + \$6X_1X_2 + \$5X_2 + \$1/X_2$$

PROGRAM 11.7B

Solution to Great Western Appliance's NLP Problem Using Excel Solver Command Shown in Program 11.7A

PROGRAM 11.8A

An Excel Formulation of Hospicare Corp.'s NLP Problem

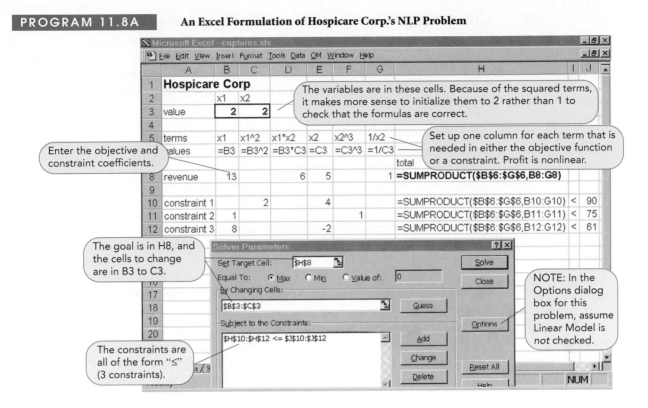

The corporation identifies three constraints, two of which are also nonlinear, that affect operations. They are

An example of nonlinear constraints.

$$2X_1^2 + 4X_2 \leq 90 \text{ (nursing capacity, in thousands of labor-days)}$$

$$X_1 + X_2^3 \leq 75 \text{ (x-ray capacity, in thousands)}$$

$$8X_1 - 2X_2 \leq 61 \text{ (marketing budget required, in thousands of \$)}$$

Excel's Solver is capable of formulating such a problem (see Program 11.8A). The optimal solution is provided in Program 11.8B.

PROGRAM 11.8B

Excel Solution to the Hospicare Corp.'s NLP Problem, Using Solver

	A	B	C	D	E	F	G	H	I	J
1	**Hospicare Corp**									
2		x1	x2							
3	value	6.066259	4.100253							
4										
5	terms	x1	x1^2	x1*x2	x2	x2^3	1/x2			
6	values	6.066259	36.79949	24.87319	4.100253	68.93374	0.243887			
7								total		
8	revenue	13			6	5	1	**248.85**		
9										
10	constraint 1		2		4			90	<	90
11	constraint 2	1				1		75	<	75
12	constraint 3	8			-2			40.33	<	61

Linear Objective Function with Nonlinear Constraints

Thermlock Corp. produces massive rubber washers and gaskets like the type used to seal joints on the NASA Space Shuttles. To do so, it combines two ingredients: rubber (X_1) and oil (X_2). The cost of the industrial quality rubber used is $5 per pound and the cost of the high viscosity oil is $7 per pound. Two of the three constraints Thermlock faces are nonlinear. The firm's objective function and constraints are

$$\text{minimize costs} = \$5X_1 + \$7X_2$$

$$\text{subject to:} \qquad 3X_1 + 0.25X_1^2 + 4X_2 + 0.3X_2^2 \geq 125 \text{ (hardness constraint)}$$

$$13X_1 + X_1^3 \geq \ 80 \text{ (tensile strength)}$$

$$0.7X_1 + X_2 \ \geq \ 17 \text{ (elasticity)}$$

To solve this nonlinear programming, we turn again to Excel. Program 11.9A illustrates how to formulate the constraints and how to set up the Solver parameters. The output is provided in Program 11.9B.

Computational Procedures for Nonlinear Programming

We cannot always find an optimal solution to nonlinear programs.

Unlike LP methods, computational procedures to solve many nonlinear problems do not always yield an optimal solution in a finite number of steps. In addition, there is no general method for solving all nonlinear problems. *Classical optimization* techniques, based on calculus, can handle some special cases, usually simpler types of problems. The *gradient method*, sometimes called the *steepest ascent method*, is an iterative procedure that moves from one feasible solution to the next in improving the value of the objective

---

PROGRAM 11.9A   **Excel Formulation of Thermlock's NLP Problem**

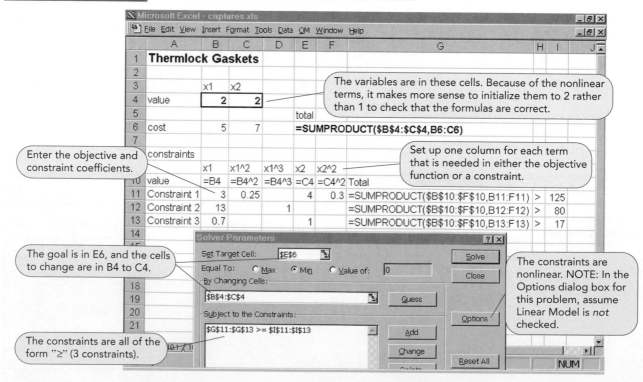

PROGRAM 11.9B

Solution to Thermlock's NLP Problem Using the Excel Solver

	A	B	C	D	E	F	G	H	I
1	**Thermlock Gaskets**								
2									
3		x1	x2						
4	value	**3.325326**	**14.67227**						
5					total				
6	cost	5	7		**119.3325**				
7									
8	constraints								
9		x1	x1^2	x1^3	x2	x2^2			
10	value	3.325326	11.05779	36.77076	14.67227	215.2756	Total		
11	Constraint 1	3	0.25		4	0.3	136.0122	>	125
12	Constraint 2	13		1			80	>	80
13	Constraint 3	0.7			1		17	>	17

function. It has been computerized and can handle problems with both nonlinear constraints and objectives. But perhaps the best way to deal with nonlinear problems is to try to reduce them into a form that is linear or almost linear. *Separable programming* deals with a class of problems in which the objective and constraints are approximated by linear functions. In this way, the powerful simplex algorithm may again be applied. In general, work in the area of NLP is the least charted and most difficult of all the quantitative analysis models.

SUMMARY

This chapter addresses three special types of LP problems. The first, integer programming, examines LP problems that cannot have fractional answers. We also note that there are three types of integer programming problems: (1) pure or all-integer programs, (2) mixed problems, in which *some* solution variables need not be integer, and (3) 0–1 problems, in which all solutions are either 0 or 1. We also demonstrate how 0–1 variables can be used to model special situations such as fixed charge problems. QM for Windows and Excel are used to illustrate computer approaches to these problems. The branch and bound method, a popular algorithm for solving all-integer and mixed-integer linear problems, is also described.

The latter part of the chapter deals with goal programming. This extension of LP allows problems to have multiple goals. We discuss how to solve such a problem both graphically and by using a modified method of the simplex algorithm. Again, software such as QM for Windows is a powerful tool in solving this offshoot of LP. Finally, the advanced topic of NLP is introduced as a special mathematical programming problem. Excel is seen to be a useful tool in solving simple NLP models.

GLOSSARY

Branch and Bound Method. An algorithm for solving all-integer and mixed-integer linear programs and assignment problems. It divides the set of feasible solutions into subsets that are examined systematically.

Deviational Variables. Terms that are minimized in a goal programming problem. Like slack variables in LP, they are real. They are the only terms in the objective function.

Goal Programming. A mathematical programming technique that permits decision makers to set and prioritize multiple objectives.

Integer Programming. A mathematical programming technique that produces integer solutions to linear programming problems.

Nonlinear Programming. A category of mathematical programming techniques that allows the objective function and/or constraints to be nonlinear.

Satisficing. The process of coming as close as possible to reaching your set of objectives.

0–1 Integer Programming. Problems in which all decision variables must have integer values of 0 or 1. This is also called a binary variable

SOLVED PROBLEMS

Solved Problem 11-1

Consider the 0–1 integer programming problem that follows:

$$\text{maximize} \quad 50X_1 + 45X_2 + 48X_3$$

$$\text{subject to:} \quad 19X_1 + 27X_2 + 34X_3 \leq 80$$

$$22X_1 + 13X_2 + 12X_3 \leq 40$$

$$X_1, X_2, X_3 \text{ must be either 0 or 1}$$

Now reformulate this problem with additional constraints so that no more than two of the three variables can take on a value equal to 1 in the solution. Further, make sure that if $X_1 = 1$, then $X_2 = 1$ also. Then solve the new problem using Excel.

Solution

Excel can handle all-integer, mixed-integer, and 0–1 integer problems. Program 11.10A below shows two new constraints to handle the reformulated problem. These constraints are

$$X_1 + X_2 + X_3 \leq 2$$

and

$$X_1 - X_2 \quad \leq 0$$

The output is shown in Program 11.10B on page 485. The optimal solution is $X_1 = 1$, $X_2 = 1$, $X_3 = 0$, with an objective function value of 95.

PROGRAM 11.10A   **Excel Formulation for Solved Problem 11-1's 0–1 Integer Program**

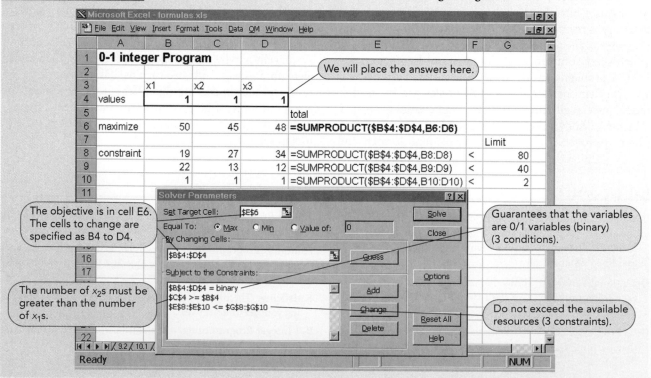

PROGRAM 11.10B

Output from Excel Formulation in Program 11.10A with Solution to Solved Problem 11-1's 0–1 IP Problem

X Microsoft Excel – captures.xls

File Edit View Insert Format Tools Data Accounting OM Window Help

	A	B	C	D	E	F	G	H	I
1	**0-1 integer Program**								
2									
3		x1	x2	x3					
4	values	1	1	0					
5					total				
6	maximize	50	45	48	**95**				
7							Limit		
8	constraint	19	27	34	46	<	80		
9		22	13	12	35	<	40		
10		1	1	1	2	<	2		
11									
12									
13									

Solver Results

Solver found a solution. All constraints and optimality conditions are satisfied.

Reports
Answer
Sensitivity
Limits

○ Keep Solver Solution
○ Restore Original Values

OK   Cancel   Save Scenario...   Help

Solved Problem 11-2

Recall the Harrison Electric Company goal programming problem seen in Section 11.4. Its LP formulation was

$$\text{maximize profit} = \$7X_1 + \$6X_2$$

$$\text{subject to:} \qquad 2X_1 + 3X_2 \leq 12 \text{ (wiring hours)}$$

$$6X_1 + 5X_2 \leq 30 \text{ (assembly hours)}$$

$$X_1, X_2 \geq 0$$

where

$$X_1 = \text{number of chandeliers produced}$$

$$X_2 = \text{number of ceiling fans produced}$$

Reformulate Harrison Electrical as a goal programming model with the following goals:

Priority 1: Produce at least 4 chandeliers and 3 ceiling fans.

Priority 2: Limit overtime in the assembly department to 10 hours and in the wiring department to 6 hours.

Priority 3: Maximize profit.

Solution

$$\text{minimize} \quad P_1(d_1^- + d_2^-) + P_2(d_3^+ + d_4^+) + P_3 d_5^-$$

$$\text{subject to:} \quad X_1 + \qquad\qquad d_1^- - d_1^+ = 4 \left.\right\} \text{Priority 1}$$
$$X_2 + d_2^- - d_2^+ = 3$$

$$2X_1 + 3X_2 + d_3^- - d_3^+ = 18 \left.\right\} \text{Priority 2}$$
$$6X_1 + 5X_2 + d_4^- - d_4^+ = 40$$

$$7X_1 + 6X_2 + d_5^- - d_5^+ = 99{,}999\} \text{ Priority 3}$$

In the priority 3 goal constraint, the 99,999 represents an unrealistically high profit. It is just a mathematical trick to use as a target so that we can get as close as possible to the maximum profit.

⫸ **SELF-TEST**

- ■ Before taking the self-test, refer back to the learning objectives at the beginning of the chapter, the notes in the margins, and the glossary at the end of the chapter.
- ■ Use the key at the back of the book to correct your answers.
- ■ Restudy pages that correspond to any questions that you answered incorrectly or material you feel uncertain about.

1. If all of the decision variables require integer solutions, the problem is
   a. a pure integer programming type of problem.
   b. a simplex method type of problem.
   c. a mixed-integer programming type of problem.
   d. a Gorsky type of problem.

2. In a mixed-integer programming problem
   a. some integers must be even and others must be odd.
   b. some decision variables must require integer results only and some variables must allow for continuous results.
   c. different objectives are mixed together even though they sometimes have relative priorities established.

3. A model containing a linear objective function and linear constraints but requiring that one or more of the decision variables take on an integer value in the final solution is called
   a. an integer programming problem.
   b. a goal programming problem.
   c. a nonlinear programming problem.
   d. a multiple objective LP problem.

4. An integer programming solution can never produce a greater profit than the LP solution to the same problem.
   a. True
   b. False

5. In goal programming, if all the goals are achieved, the value of the objective function will always be zero.
   a. True
   b. False

6. The objective in a goal programming problem with one priority level is to maximize the sum of the deviational variables.
   a. True
   b. False

7. Nobel laureate Herbert A. Simon of Carnegie-Mellon University says that modern managers should always optimize, not satisfice.
   a. True
   b. False

8. The fixed charge problem is typically classified as
   a. a goal programming problem.
   b. a 0–1 integer problem.
   c. a quadratic programming problem.
   d. an assignment problem.

9. The 0–1 integer programming problem
   a. requires the decision variables to have values between 0 and 1.
   b. requires that the constraints all have coefficients between 0 and 1.
   c. requires that the decision variables have coefficients between 0 and 1.
   d. requires the decision variables to be equal to 0 or 1.

10. Goal programming
    a. requires only that you know whether the goal is direct profit maximization or cost minimization.
    b. allows you to have multiple goals.
    c. is an algorithm with the goal of a quicker solution to the pure integer programming problem.
    d. is an algorithm with the goal of a quicker solution to the mixed-integer programming problem.

11. Nonlinear programming includes problems
    a. in which the objective function is linear but some constraints are not linear.
    b. in which the constraints are linear but the objective function is not linear.
    c. in which both the objective function and all of the constraints are not linear.
    d. solvable by quadratic programming.
    e. all of the above.

DISCUSSION QUESTIONS AND PROBLEMS

Discussion Questions

11-1 Compare the similarities and differences of linear and goal programming.

11-2 When the branch and bound algorithm is used to solve a pure integer problem, a variable whose value is not integer is selected, and branching on this variable results in two new LP subproblems. Explain why the solutions to the LP subproblems cannot have an objective function value better than the previous upper bound.

11-3 List the advantages and disadvantages of solving integer programming problems by (a) rounding off, (b) enumeration, and (c) the branch and bound method.

11-4 What is the difference between the three types of integer programming problems? Which do you think is most common, and why?

11-5 What are the meaning and role of the lower bound and upper bound in the branch and bound method?

11-6 What is meant by "satisficing," and why is the term often used in conjunction with goal programming?

11-7 What are deviational variables? How do they differ from decision variables in traditional LP problems?

11-8 If you were the president of the college you are attending and were employing goal programming to assist in decision making, what might your goals be? What kinds of constraints would you include in your model?

11-9 What does it mean to rank goals in goal programming? How does this affect the problem's solution?

11-10 How does the solution of goal programming problems with the modified simplex method differ from the use of the regular simplex approach for LP problems?

11-11 Which of the following are NLP problems, and why?

(a) maximize profit $= 3X_1 + 5X_2 + 99X_3$
    subject to: $X_1 \geq 10$
                  $X_2 \leq 5$
                  $X_3 \geq 18$

(b) minimize cost $= 25X_1 + 30X_2 + 8X_1X_2$
    subject to: $X_1 \qquad\quad \geq 8$
                  $X_1 + \quad X_2 \geq 12$
                  $0.0005X_1 - \quad X_2 = 11$

(c) minimize $Z = P_1d_1^- + P_2d_2^+ + P_3d_3^+$
    subject to: $X_1 + X_2 + d_1^- - d_1^+ = 300$
                  $X_2 + d_2^- - d_2^+ = 200$
                  $X_1 + \qquad\quad d_3^- - d_3^+ = 100$

(d) maximize profit $= 3X_1 + 4X_2$
    subject to: $X_1^2 - 5X_2 \geq 8$
                  $3X_1 + 4X_2 \geq 12$

(e) minimize cost $= 18X_1 + 5X_2 + X_2^2$
    subject to: $4X_1 - 3X_2 \geq 8$
                  $X_1 + \quad X_2 \geq 18$

Are any of these quadratic programming problems?

Problems*

• **11-12** Elizabeth Bailey is the owner and general manager of Princess Brides, which provides a wedding planning service in Southwest Louisiana. She uses radio advertising to market her business. Two types of ads are available—those during prime time hours and those at other times. Each prime time ad costs $390 and reaches 8,200 people, while the offpeak ads each cost $240 and reach 5,100 people. Bailey has budgeted $1,800 per week for advertising. Based on comments from her customers, Bailey wants to have at least 2 prime time ads and no more than 6 off peak ads.

(a) Formulate this as a linear program and solve using a computer.

(b) Find a good or optimal integer solution part (a) by rounding off or making an educated guess at the answer.

(c) Solve this as an integer programming problem using the branch and bound method.

‡ **11-13** A group of college students is planning a camping trip during the upcoming break. The group must hike several miles through the woods to get to the campsite, and anything that is needed on this trip must be packed in a knapsack and carried to the campsite. One particular student, Tina Shawl, has identified eight items that she would like to take on the trip, but the combined weight is too great to take all of them. She has decided to rate the utility of each item on a scale of 1 to 100, with 100 being the most beneficial. The item weights in pounds and their utility values are given below.

ITEM	1	2	3	4	5	6	7	8
Weight	8	1	7	6	3	12	5	14
Utility	80	20	50	55	50	75	30	70

Recognizing that the hike to the campsite is a long one, a limit of 35 pounds has been set as the maximum total weight of the items to be carried.

(a) Formulate this as a 0–1 programming problem to maximize the total utility of the items carried. Solve this knapsack problem using a computer.

(b) Suppose item number 3 is an extra battery pack, which may be used with several of the other items. Tina has decided that she will only take item number 5, a CD player, if she also takes item number 3. On the other hand, if she takes item number 3, she may or may not take item number 5. Modify this problem to reflect this and solve the new problem.

11-14 Student Enterprises sells two sizes of wall posters, a large 3- by 4-foot poster and a smaller 2- by 3-foot poster. The profit earned from the sale of each large poster is $3; each smaller poster earns $2. The firm, although profitable, is not large; it consists of one art student, Jan Meising, at the University of Kentucky. Because of her classroom schedule, Jan has the following weekly constraints: (1) up to three large posters can be sold, (2) up to five smaller posters can be sold, (3) up to 10 hours can be spent on posters during the week, with each large poster requiring 2 hours of work and each small one taking 1 hour. With the semester almost over, Jan plans on taking a three-month summer vacation to England and doesn't want to leave any unfinished posters behind. Find the integer solution that will maximize her profit.

11-15 An airline owns an aging fleet of Boeing 737 jet airplanes. It is considering a major purchase of up to 17 new Boeing model 757 and 767 jets. The decision must take into account numerous cost and capability factors, including the following: (1) the airline can finance up to $1.6 billion in purchases; (2) each Boeing 757 will cost $80 million, and each Boeing 767 will cost $110 million; (3) at least one-third of the planes purchased should be the longer-range 757; (4) the annual maintenance budget is to be no more than $8 million; (5) the annual maintenance cost per 757 is estimated to be $800,000, and it is $500,000 for each 767 purchased; and (6) each 757 can carry 125,000 passengers per year, whereas each 767 can fly 81,000 passengers annually. Formulate this as an integer programming problem to maximize the annual passenger-carrying capability. What category of integer programming problem is this? Solve this problem.

11-16 Trapeze Investments is a venture capital firm that is currently evaluating six different investment opportunities. There is not sufficient capital to invest in all of these, but more than one will be selected. A 0–1 integer programming model is planned to help determine which of the six opportunities to choose. Variables X_1, X_2, X_3, X_4, X_5, and X_6 represent the six choices. For each of the following situations, write a constraint (or several constraints) that would be used.

(a) At least 3 of these choices are to be selected.
(b) Either investment 1 or investment 4 must be undertaken, but not both.
(c) If investment 4 is selected, then investment 6 must also be selected. However, if investment 4 is not selected, it is still possible to select number 6.

(d) Investment 5 cannot be selected unless both investments 2 and 3 are also selected.
(e) Investment 5 must be selected if both investments 2 and 3 are also selected.

11-17 Horizon Wireless, a cellular telephone company, is expanding into a new era. Relay towers are necessary to provide wireless telephone coverage to the different areas of the city. A grid is superimposed on a map of the city to help determine where the towers should be located. The grid consists of 8 areas labeled A through H. Six possible tower locations (numbered 1–6) have been identified, and each location could serve several areas. The table below indicates the areas served by each of the towers.

TOWER LOCATION	1	2	3	4	5	6
Areas served	A, B, D	B, C, G	C, D, E, F	E, F, H	E, G, H	A, D, F

Formulate this as a 0–1 programming model to minimize the total number of towers required to cover all the areas. Solve this using a computer.

11-18 Innis Construction Company specializes in building moderately priced homes in Cincinnati, Ohio. Tom Innis has identified eight potential locations to construct new single-family dwellings, but he cannot put up homes on all of the sites because he has only $300,000 to invest in all projects. The accompanying table shows the cost of constructing homes in each area and the expected profit to be made from the sale of each home. Note that the home-building costs differ considerably due to lot costs, site preparation, and differences in the models to be built. Note also that a fraction of a home cannot be built.

LOCATION	COST OF BUILDING AT THIS SITE ($)	EXPECTED PROFIT ($)
Clifton	60,000	5,000
Mt. Auburn	50,000	6,000
Mt. Adams	82,000	10,000
Amberly	103,000	12,000
Norwood	50,000	8,000
Covington	41,000	3,000
Roselawn	80,000	9,000
Eden Park	69,000	10,000

(a) Formulate Innis's problem using 0–1 integer programming.
(b) Solve with QM for Windows or Excel.

11-19 A real estate developer is considering three possible projects: a small apartment complex, a small shopping center, and a mini-warehouse. Each of these requires different funding over the next two years, and the net present value of the investments also varies. The following table provides the required investment amounts (in $1,000's) and the net present value (NPV) of each (also expressed in $1,000's):

	NPV	INVESTMENT	
		YEAR 1	YEAR 2
Apartment	18	40	30
Shopping center	15	30	20
Mini-warehouse	14	20	20

The company has $80,000 to invest in year 1 and $50,000 to invest in year 2.

(a) Develop an integer programming model to maximize the NPV in this situation.

(b) Solve the problem in part (a) using computer software. Which of the three projects would be undertaken if NPV is maximized? How much money would be used each year?

11-20 Refer to the real estate investment situation in Problem 11-19.

(a) Suppose that the shopping center and the apartment would be on adjacent properties, and the shopping center would only be considered if the apartment were also built. Formulate the constraint that would stipulate this.

(b) Formulate a constraint that would force exactly two of the three projects to be undertaken.

11-21 Triangle Utilities provides electricity for three cities. The company has four electric generators that are used to provide electricity. The main generator operates 24 hours per day, with an occasional shutdown for routine maintenance. Three other generators (1, 2, and 3) are available to provide additional power when needed. A startup cost is incurred each time one of these generators is started. The startup costs are $6,000 for 1, $5,000 for 2, and $4,000 for 3. These generators are used in the following ways: A generator may be started at 6:00 A.M. and run for either 8 hours or 16 hours, or it may be started at 2:00 P.M. and run for 8 hours (until 10:00 P.M.). All generators except the main generator are shut down at 10:00 P.M. Forecasts indicate the need for 3,200 megawatts more than provided by the main generator before 2:00 P.M., and this need goes up to 5,700 megawatts between 2:00 and 10:00 P.M. Generator 1 may provide up to 2,400 megawatts, generator 2 may provide up to 2,100 megawatts, and generator 3 may provide up to 3,300 megawatts. The cost per megawatt used per eight hour period is $8 for 1, $9 for 2, and $7 for 3.

(a) Formulate this problem as an integer programming problem to determine the least-cost way to meet the needs of the area.

(b) Solve using computer software.

11-22 The campaign manager for a politician who is running for reelection to a political office is planning the campaign. Four ways to advertise have been selected: TV ads, radio ads, billboards, and newspaper ads. The cost of these are $900 for each TV ad, $500 for each radio ad, $600 for a billboard for one month, and $180 for each newspaper ad. The audience reached by each type of advertising has been estimated to be 40,000 for each TV ad, 32,000 for each radio ad, 34,000 for each billboard, and 17,000 for each newspaper ad. The total monthly advertising budget is $16,000. The following goals have been established and ranked:

1. The number of people reached should be at least 1,500,000.
2. The total monthly advertising budget should not be exceeded.
3. Together, the number of ads on either TV or radio should be at least 6.
4. No more than 10 ads of any one type of advertising should be used.

(a) Formulate this as a goal programming problem.

(b) Solve this using computer software.

(c) Which goals are completely met and which of them are not?

11-23 Solve the following integer programming problem using the branch and bound approach.

$$\text{maximize profit} = \$2X_1 + \$3X_2$$

$$\text{subject to:} \quad X_1 + 3X_2 \le 9$$

$$3X_1 + X_2 \le 7$$

$$X_1 - X_2 \le 1$$

where both X_1 and X_2 must be nonnegative integer values.

11-24 Geraldine Shawhan is president of Shawhan File Works, a firm that manufactures two types of metal file cabinets. The demand for her two-drawer model is up to 600 cabinets per week; demand for a three-drawer cabinet is limited to 400 per week. Shawhan File Works has a weekly operating capacity of 1,300 hours, with the two-drawer cabinet taking 1 hour to produce and the three drawer cabinet requiring 2 hours. Each two-drawer model sold yields a $10 profit, and the profit for the large model is $15. Shawhan has listed the following goals in order of importance:

1. Attain a profit as close to $11,000 as possible each week.
2. Avoid underutilization of the firm's production capacity.
3. Sell as many two- and three-drawer cabinets as the demand indicates.

Set this up as a goal programming problem.

11-25 Solve Problem 11-24 graphically. Are any goals unachieved in this solution? Explain.

11-26 Hilliard Electronics produces specially coded computer chips for laser surgery in 64MB, 256MB, and 512MB sizes. (1MB means that the chip holds 1 million bytes of information.) To produce a 64MB chip requires 8 hours of labor, a 256MB chip takes 13 hours, and a 512MB chip requires 16 hours. Hilliard's monthly production capacity is 1,200 hours. Mr. Blank, the firm's sales manager, estimates that the maximum monthly sales of the 64MB, 256MB, and 512MB chips are 40, 50, and 60, respectively. The company has the following goals (ranked in order from most important to least important):

1. Fill an order from the best customer for thirty 64MB chips and thirty-five 256MB chips.
2. Provide sufficient chips to at least equal the sales estimates set by Mr. Blank.
3. Avoid underutilization of the production capacity.

Formulate this problem using goal programming.

11-27 The modified simplex method is presented for the Harrison Electric Company example in Tables 11.5, 11.6, and 11.7 on pages 475–477. Two iterations of the method were skipped between the second tableau in Table 11.6 and the final tableau in Table 11.7. Apply the method to provide the missing third and fourth tableaus. To which corner point (A, B, C, or D) in Figure 11.6 does each of these tableaus correspond?

11-28 An Oklahoma manufacturer makes two products: speaker telephones (X_1) and pushbutton telephones (X_2). The following goal programming model has been formulated to find the number of each to produce each day to meet the firm's goals:

minimize $P_1d_1^- + P_2d_2^- + P_3d_3^+ + P_4d_1^+$

subject to: $2X_1 + 4X_2 + d_1^- - d_1^+ = 80$

$8X_1 + 10X_2 + d_2^- - d_2^+ = 320$

$8X_1 + 6X_2 + d_3^- - d_3^+ = 240$

all $X_i, d_i \geq 0$

(a) Set up the complete initial goal programming tableau for this problem.
(b) Find the optimal solution using the modified simplex method.

11-29 Major Bill Bligh, director of the Army War College's new six-month attaché training program, is concerned about how the 20 officers taking the course spend their precious time while in his charge. Major Bligh recognizes that there are 168 hours per week and thinks that his students have been using them rather inefficiently. Bligh lets

X_1 = number of hours of sleep needed per week

X_2 = number of personal hours (eating, personal hygiene, handling laundry, and so on)

X_3 = number of hours of class and studying

X_4 = number of hours of social time off base (dating, sports, family visits, and so on)

He thinks that students should study 30 hours a week to have time to absorb material. This is his most important goal. Bligh feels that students need at most 7 hours sleep per night on average and that this goal is number 2. He believes that goal number 3 is to

provide at least 20 hours per week of social time.
(a) Formulate this as a goal programming problem.
(b) Solve the problem using computer software.

11-30 Hinkel Rotary Engine, Ltd., produces four- and six-cylinder models of automobile engines. The firm's profit for each four-cylinder engine sold during its quarterly production cycle is $1,800 − $50X_1$, where X_1 is the number sold. Hinkel makes $2,400 − $70X_2$ for each of the larger engines sold, with X_2 equal to the number of six-cylinder engines sold. There are 5,000 hours of production time available during each production cycle. A four-cylinder engine requires 100 hours of production time, whereas six-cylinder engines take 130 hours to manufacture. Formulate this production planning problem for Hinkel.

11-31 Motorcross of Wisconsin produces two models of snowmobiles, the XJ6 and the XJ8. In any given production-planning week Motorcross has 40 hours available in its final testing bay. Each XJ6 requires 1 hour to test and each XJ8 takes 2 hours. The revenue (in $1,000s) for the firm is nonlinear and is stated as (number of XJ6s)(4 − 0.1 number of XJ6s) + (number of XJ8s)(5 − 0.2 number of XJ8s).

(a) Formulate this problem.
(b) Solve using Excel.

11-32 During the busiest season of the year, Green-Gro Fertilizer produces two types of fertilizers. The standard type (X) is just fertilizer, and the other type (Y) is a special fertilizer and weed-killer combination. The following model has been developed to determine how much of each type should be produced to maximize profit subject to a labor constraint:

maximize profit = $12X - 0.04X^2 + 15Y - 0.06Y^2$

subject to: $2X + 4Y \leq 160$ hours

$X, Y \geq 0$

Find the optimal solution to this problem.

11-33 Pat McCormack, a financial advisor for Investors R Us, is evaluating two stocks in a particular industry. He wants to minimize the variance of a portfolio consisting of these two stocks, but he wants to have an expected return of at least 9%. After obtaining historical data on the variance and returns, he develops the following nonlinear program:

minimize portfolio variance = $0.16X^2 + 0.2XY + 0.09Y^2$

subject to: $X + Y = 1$ all funds must be invested

$0.11X + 0.08Y \geq 0.09$ return on the investment

$X, Y \geq 0$

where

X = proportion of money invested in stock 1

Y = proportion of money invested in stock 2

Solve this using Excel and determine how much to invest in each of the two stocks. What is the return for this portfolio? What is the variance of this portfolio?

11-34 Summertime Tees sells two very popular styles of embroidered shirts in southern Florida: a tank top and a regular T-shirt. The cost of the tank top is $6, and the cost of the T-shirt is $8. The demand for these is sensitive to the price, and historical data indicate that the weekly demands are given by

$$X_1 = 500 - 12P_1$$

$$X_2 = 400 - 15P_2$$

where

X_1 = demand for tank top; P_1 = price for tank top

X_2 = demand for regular T-shirt; P_2 = price for regular T-shirt

(a) Develop an equation for the total profit.
(b) Use Excel to find the optimal solution to the following nonlinear program. Use the profit function developed in part (a).

maximize profit

subject to: $X_1 = 500 - 12P_1$

$X_2 = 400 - 15P_2$

$P_1 \leq 20$

$P_2 \leq 25$

$X_1, P_1, X_2, P_2 \geq 0$

11-35 The integer programming problem in the box below has been developed to help First National Bank decide where, out of 10 possible sites, to locate four new branch offices:

where X_i represents Winter Park, Maitland, Osceola, Downtown, South Orlando, Airport, Winter Garden, Apopka, Lake Mary, Cocoa Beach, for i equals 1 to 10, respectively.

(a) Where should the four new sites be located, and what will be the expected return?
(b) If at least one new branch *must* be opened in Maitland or Osceola, will this change the answers? Add the new constraint and rerun.
(c) The expected return at Apopka was overestimated. The correct value is $160,000 per year (that is, 160). Using the original assumptions (namely, ignoring (b)), does your answer to part (a) change?

IP for Problem 11-35

maximize expected returns $= 120X_1 + 100X_2 + 110X_3 + 140X_4 + 155X_5 + 128X_6 + 145X_7 + 190X_8 + 170X_9 + 150X_{10}$

subject to:

$20X_1 + 30X_2 + 20X_3 + 25X_4 + 30X_5 + 30X_6 + 25X_7 + 20X_8 + 25X_9 + 30X_{10} \leq 110$

$15X_1 + 5X_2 + 20X_3 + 20X_4 + 5X_5 + 5X_6 + 10X_7 + 20X_8 + 5X_9 + 20X_{10} \leq 50$

$X_2 + X_6 + X_7 + X_9 + X_{10} \leq 3$

$X_2 + X_3 + X_5 + X_8 + X_9 \geq 2$

$X_1 + X_3 + X_{10} \geq 1$

$X_1 + X_2 + X_3 + X_4 + X_5 + X_6 + X_7 + X_8 + X_9 + X_{10} \leq 4$

all $X_i = 0$ or 1

INTERNET HOMEWORK PROBLEMS

See our Internet home page at **www.prenhall.com/render** for additional
homework problems 11-36 to 11-41.

⟫ CASE STUDY

Schank Marketing Research

Schank Marketing Research has just signed contracts to conduct studies for four clients. At present, three project managers are free for assignment to the tasks. Although all are capable of handling each assignment, the times and costs to complete the studies depend on the experience and knowledge of each manager. Using his judgment, John Schank, the president, has been able to establish a cost for each possible assignment. These costs, which are really the salaries each manager would draw on each task, are summarized in the following table.

Schank is very hesitant about neglecting NASA, which has been an important customer in the past. (NASA has employed the firm to study the public's attitude toward the Space Shuttle and proposed Space Station.) In addition, Schank has promised to try to provide Ruth a salary of at least $3,000 on his next assignment. From previous contracts, Schank also knows that Gardener does not get along well with the management at CBT Television, so he hopes to avoid assigning her to CBT. Finally, as

Hines Corporation is also an old and valued client, Schank feels that it is twice as important to assign a project manager immediately to Hines's task as it is to provide one to General Foundry, a brand-new client. Schank wants to minimize the total costs of all projects while considering each of these goals. He feels that all of these goals are important, but if he had to rank them, he would put his concern about NASA first, his worry about Gardener second, his need to keep Hines Corporation happy third, his promise to Ruth fourth, and his concern about minimizing all costs last.

Each project manager can handle, at most, one new client.

Discussion Questions

1. If Schank were not concerned about noncost goals, how would he formulate this problem so that it could be solved quantitatively?
2. Develop a formulation that will incorporate all five objectives.

PROJECT MANAGER	CLIENT			
	HINES CORP.	NASA	GENERAL FOUNDRY	CBT TELEVISION
Gardener	$3,200	$3,000	$2,800	$2,900
Ruth	2,700	3,200	3,000	3,100
Hardgraves	1,900	2,100	3,300	2,100

⟫ CASE STUDY

Oakton River Bridge

The Oakton River had long been considered an impediment to the development of a certain medium-sized metropolitan area in the southeast. Lying to the east of the city, the river made it difficult for people living on its eastern bank to commute to jobs in and around the city and to take advantage of the shopping and cultural attractions that the city had to offer. Similarly, the river inhibited those on its western bank from access to the ocean resorts lying one hour to the east. The bridge over the Oakton

River had been built prior to World War II and was grossly inadequate to handle the existing traffic, much less the increased traffic that would accompany the forecasted growth in the area. A congressional delegation from the state prevailed upon the federal government to fund a major portion of a new toll bridge over the Oakton River and the state legislature appropriated the rest of the needed monies for the project.

Progress in construction of the bridge has been in accordance with what was anticipated at the start of construction. The state highway commission, which will have operational jurisdiction over the bridge, has concluded that the opening of the bridge for traffic is likely to take place at the beginning of the next summer, as scheduled. A personnel task force has been established to recruit, train, and schedule the workers needed to operate the toll facility.

The personnel task force is well aware of the budgetary problems facing the state. They have taken as part of their mandate the requirement that personnel costs be kept as low as possible. One particular area of concern is the number of toll collectors that will be needed. The bridge is scheduling three shifts of collectors: shift A from midnight to 8 A.M., shift B from 8 A.M. to 4 P.M., and shift C from 4 P.M. to midnight. Recently, the state employees union negotiated a contract with the state which requires that all toll collectors be permanent, full-time employees. In addition, all collectors must work a five-on, two-off schedule on the same shift. Thus, for example, a worker could be assigned to work Tuesday, Wednesday, Thursday, Friday, and Saturday on shift A, followed by Sunday and Monday off. An employee could not be scheduled to work, say, Tuesday on shift A followed by Wednesday, Thursday, Friday, and Saturday on shift B or on any other mixture of shifts during a five-day block. The employees would choose their assignments in order of their seniority.

The task force has received projections of traffic flow on the bridge by day and hour. These projections are based on extrapolations of existing traffic patterns—the pattern of commuting, shopping, and beach traffic currently experienced with growth projections factored in. Standards data from other state-operated toll facilities have allowed the task force to convert these traffic flows into toll collector requirements, that is, the minimum number of collectors required per shift, per day, to handle the anticipated traffic load. These toll collector requirements are summarized in the following table:

Minimum Number of Toll Collectors Required per Shift

SHIFT	SUN.	MON.	TUE.	WED.	THU.	FRI.	SAT.
A	8	13	12	12	13	13	15
B	10	10	10	10	10	13	15
C	15	13	13	12	12	13	8

The numbers in the table include one or two extra collectors per shift to fill in for collectors who call in sick and to provide relief for collectors on their scheduled breaks. Note that each of the eight collectors needed for shift A on Sunday, for example, could have come from any of the A shifts scheduled to begin on Wednesday, Thursday, Friday, Saturday, or Sunday.

Discussion Questions

1. Determine the minimum number of toll collectors that would have to be hired to meet the requirements expressed in the table.
2. The union had indicated that it might lift its opposition to the mixing of shifts in a five-day block in exchange for additional compensation and benefits. By how much could the number of toll collectors required be reduced if this is done?

Source: B. Render, R. M. Stair, and I. Greenberg. *Cases and Readings in Management Science*, 2/e, 1990, pp. 55–56. Reprinted by permission of Prentice Hall, Upper Saddle River, New Jersey.

⮞ CASE STUDY

Puyallup Mall

Jane Rodney, president of the Rodney Development Company, was trying to decide what types of stores to include in her new shopping center at Puyallup Mall. She had already contracted for a supermarket, a drugstore, and a few other stores that she considered essential. However, she had available an additional 16,000 square feet of floor space yet to allocate. She drew up a list of the 15 types of stores she might consider (see Table 11.8) including the floor space required by each. Jane did not think she would have any trouble finding occupants for any type of store.

The lease agreements Jane used in her developments included two types of payment. The store had to pay a certain annual rent, depending on the size and type of store. In addition, Jane was to receive a small percentage of the store's sales if the sales exceeded a specified minimum amount. The amount of annual rent from each store is shown in the second column of the table. To estimate the profitability of each type of store, Jane calculated the present value of all future rent and sales percentage payments. These are given in the third column. Jane wants to achieve the highest total *present value* over the set of stores she selects. However, she could not simply pick those stores with the highest present values, for there were several restrictions. The first, of course, was that she has available only 16,000 square feet.

In addition, a condition on the financing of the project required that the total annual rent should be at least as much as the annual fixed costs (taxes, management fees, debt service, and so forth). These annual costs were $130,000 for this part of the project. Finally, the total funds available for construction of this part of the project were $700,000, and each type of store required different construction costs depending on the size and type of store (fourth column in the table).

TABLE 11.8 **Characteristics of Possible Leases, Puyallup Mall Shopping Center**

TYPE OF STORE	SIZE OF STORE (1,000s OF SQ FT)	ANNUAL RENT ($1,000s)	PRESENT VALUE ($1,000s)	CONSTRUCTION COST ($1000s)
Clothing				
1. Men's	1.0	$4.4	$28.1	$24.6
2. Women's	1.6	6.1	34.6	32.0
3. Variety (both)	2.0	8.3	50.0	41.4
Restaurants				
4. Fancy restaurant	3.2	24.0	162.0	124.4
5. Lunchroom	1.8	19.5	77.8	64.8
6. Cocktail lounge	2.1	20.7	100.4	79.8
7. Candy and ice cream shop	1.2	7.7	45.2	38.6
Hard Goods				
8. Hardware store	2.4	19.4	80.2	66.8
9. Cutlery and variety	1.6	11.7	51.4	45.1
10. Luggage and leather	2.0	15.2	62.5	54.3
Miscellaneous				
11. Travel agency	0.6	3.9	18.0	15.0
12. Tobacco shop	0.5	3.2	11.6	13.4
13. Camera store	1.4	11.3	50.4	42.0
14. Toys	2.0	16.0	73.6	63.7
15. Beauty parlor	1.0	9.6	51.2	40.0

In addition, Jane had certain requirements in terms of the mix of stores that she considered best. She wanted at least one store from each of the clothing, hard goods, and miscellaneous groups, and at least two from the restaurant category. She wanted no more than two from the clothing group. Furthermore, the number of stores in the miscellaneous group should not exceed the total number of stores in the clothing and hard goods groups combined.

Discussion Question

1. Which tenants should be selected for the mall?

Source: Adapted from H. Bierman, C. P. Bonini, and W. H. Hausman. *Quantitative Analysis*, 7/e. Homewood, IL: Richard D. Irwin, Inc., pp. 467–468, copyright © 1986.

BIBLIOGRAPHY

Arntzen, Bruce C. et al. "Global Supply Chain Management at Digital Equipment Corporation," *Interfaces* 25, 1 (January–February 1995): 69–93.

Bean, James C., Charles E. Noon, Sarah M. Ryan, and Gary J. Salton. "Selecting Tenants in a Shopping Mall," *Interfaces* 18, 2 (March–April 1988): 1–9.

Bertsimas, Dimitris, Christopher Darnell, and Robert Soucy. "Portfolio Construction Through Mixed-Integer Programming at Grantham, Mayo, Van Otterloo and Company," *Interfaces* 29, 1 (January 1999): 49–66.

Bohl, Alan H. "Computer Aided Formulation of Silicon Defoamers for the Paper Industry," *Interfaces* 24, 5 (September–October 1994): 41–48.

Charnes, A. and W. W. Cooper. *Management Models and Industrial Applications of Linear Programming*, Vols. I and II. New York: John Wiley and Sons, 1961.

Dawid, Herbert, Johannes Konig, and Christine Strauss. "An Enhanced Rostering Model for Airline Crews," *Computers and Operations Research* 28, 7 (June 2001): 671–688.

Drees, Lawrence David and Wilbert E. Wilhelm. "Scheduling Experiments on a Nuclear Reactor Using Mixed Integer Programming," *Computers and Operations Research* 28, 10 (September 2001): 1013–1037.

Hueter, Jackie and William Swart. "An Integrated Labor-Management System for Taco Bell," *Interfaces* 28, 1 (January–February 1998): 75–91.

Ignizio, J. P. *Goal Programming and Extensions.* Lexington, MA: D.C. Heath and Company, 1976.

Katok, Elena and Dennis Ott. "Using Mixed-Integer Programming to Reduce Label Changes in the Coors Aluminum Can Plant," *Interfaces* 30, 2 (March 2000): 1–12.

Kuby, Michael et al. "Planning China's Coal and Electricity Delivery System," *Interfaces* 25, 1 (January–February 1995): 41–68.

Lee, Sang M. and Marc J. Schniederjans. "A Multicriterial Assignment Problem: A Goal Programming Approach,"*Interfaces* 13, 4 (August 1983): 75–79.

Stowe, J. D. "An Integer Programming Solution for the Optimal Credit Investigation/Credit Granting Sequence." *Financial Management* 14 (Summer 1985): 66–76.

Subramanian, R. et al. "Coldstart: Fleet Assignment at Delta Airlines," *Interfaces* 24, 1 (January–February 1994): 104–120.

Tingley, Kim M., and Judith S. Liebmen. "A Goal Programming Example in Public Health Resource Allocation," *Management Science* 30, 3 (March 1984): 279–289.

Wang, Hongbo. "A Branch and Bound Approach for Sequencing Expansion Projects," *Production and Operations Management* 4, 1 (Winter 1995): 57–75.

Zangwill, W. I. *Nonlinear Programming: A Unified Approach.* Upper Saddle River, NJ: Prentice Hall, 1969.

NETWORK MODELS

12.1 INTRODUCTION

Three network models are covered in this chapter.

This chapter covers three network models that can be used to solve a variety of problems: the minimal-spanning tree technique, the maximal-flow technique, and the shortest-route technique. The *minimal-spanning tree technique* determines the path through the network that connects all the points while minimizing total distance. When the points represent houses in a subdivision, the minimal-spanning tree technique can be used to determine the best way to connect all of the houses to electrical power, water systems, and so on, in a way that minimizes the total distance or length of power lines or water pipes. The *maximal-flow technique* finds the maximum flow of any quantity or substance through a network. This technique can determine, for example, the maximum number of vehicles (cars, trucks, and so forth) that can go through a network of roads from one location to another. Finally, the *shortest-route technique* can find the shortest path through a network. For example, this technique can find the shortest route from one city to another through a network of roads.

All of the examples used to describe the various network techniques in this chapter are small and simple compared to real problems. This is done to make it easier for you to understand the techniques. In many cases, these smaller network problems can be solved by inspection or intuition. For larger problems, however, finding a solution can be very difficult and requires the use of these powerful network techniques. Larger problems may require hundreds, or even thousands, of iterations. To computerize these techniques, it is necessary to use the systematic approach we present.

The circles in the networks are called nodes. *The lines connecting them are called* arcs.

You will see several types of networks in this chapter. Although they represent many different things, some terminology is common to all of them. The points on the network are referred to as *nodes*. Typically these are presented as circles, although sometimes squares or rectangles are used for the nodes. The lines connecting the nodes are called *arcs*.

12.2 MINIMAL-SPANNING TREE TECHNIQUE

This minimal-spanning tree technique connects nodes at a minimum distance.

The minimal-spanning tree technique involves connecting all the points of a network together while minimizing the distance between them. It has been applied, for example, by telephone companies to connect a number of phones together while minimizing the total length of telephone cable.

Let us consider the Lauderdale Construction Company, which is currently developing a luxurious housing project in Panama City Beach, Florida. Melvin Lauderdale, owner and president of Lauderdale Construction, must determine the least expensive way to provide water and power to each house. The network of houses is shown in Figure 12.1.

As seen in Figure 12.1, there are eight houses on the gulf. The distance between each house in hundreds of feet is shown on the network. The distance between houses 1 and 2, for example, is 300 feet. (The number 3 is between nodes 1 and 2.) Now, the minimal-spanning tree technique is used to determine the minimal distance that can be used to connect all of the nodes. The approach is outlined as follows:

There are four steps for the minimal-spanning tree problem.

Steps for the Minimal-Spanning Tree Technique

1. Select any node in the network.
2. Connect this node to the nearest node that minimizes the total distance.
3. Considering all of the nodes that are now connected, find and connect the nearest node that is not connected. If there is a tie for the nearest node, select one arbitrarily. A tie suggests there may be more than one optimal solution.
4. Repeat the third step until all nodes are connected.

FIGURE 12.1

Network for Lauderdale
Construction

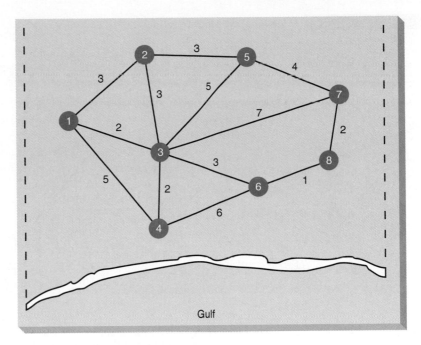

Step 1: We select node 1.
Step 2: We connect node 1 to
node 3.

Now, we solve the network in Figure 12.1 for Melvin Lauderdale. We start by arbitrarily selecting node 1. Since the nearest node is the third node at a distance of 2 (200 feet), we connect node 1 to node 3. This is shown in Figure 12.2.

Considering nodes 1 and 3, we look for the next-nearest node. This is node 4, which is the closest to node 3. The distance is 2 (200 feet). Again, we connect these nodes (see Figure 12.3, part (a)).

FIGURE 12.2

First Iteration for
Lauderdale Construction

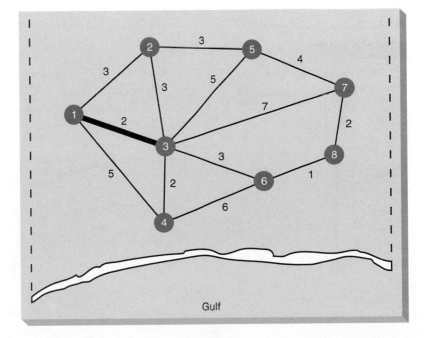

FIGURE 12.3   Second and Third Iterations

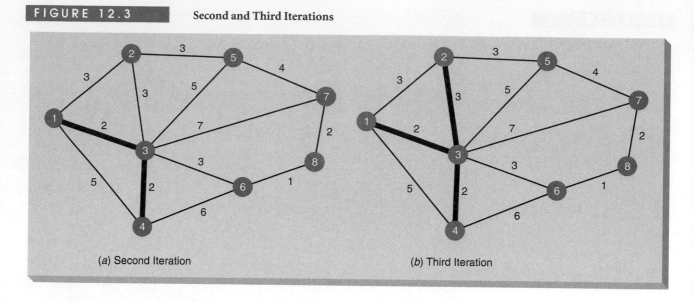

(a) Second Iteration

(b) Third Iteration

Step 3: We connect the next nearest node.

Step 4: We repeat the process.

We continue, looking for the nearest unconnected node to nodes 1, 3, and 4. This is node 2 or node 6, both at a distance of 3 from node 3. We will pick node 2 and connect it to node 3 (see Figure 12.3, part (b)).

We continue the process. There is another tie for the next iteration with a minimum distance of 3 (node 2–node 5 and node 3–node 6). You should note that we do not consider node 1–node 2 with a distance of 3 because both nodes 1 and 2 are already connected. We arbitrarily select node 5 and connect it to node 2 (see Figure 12.4, part (a)). The next nearest node is node 6, and we connect it to node 3 (see Figure 12.4, part (b)).

At this stage, we have only two unconnected nodes left. Node 8 is the nearest to node 6, with a distance of 1 and we connect it (see Figure 12.5, part (a)). Then the remaining node 7 is connected to node 8 (see Figure 12.5, part (b)).

FIGURE 12.4   Fourth and Fifth Iterations

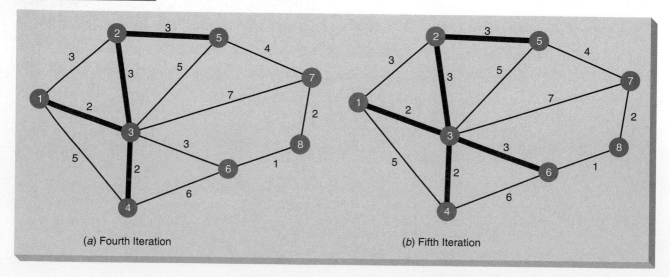

(a) Fourth Iteration

(b) Fifth Iteration

FIGURE 12.5   Sixth and Seventh (Final) Iterations

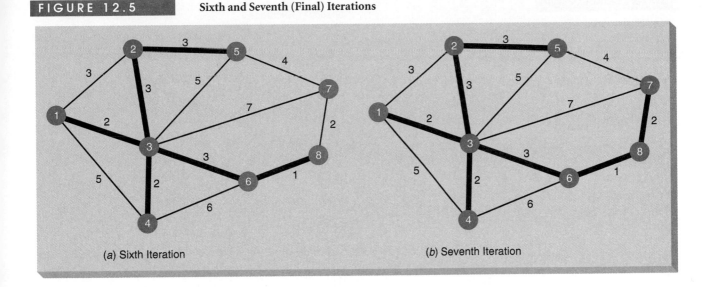

(a) Sixth Iteration

(b) Seventh Iteration

The final solution can be seen in the seventh and final iteration (see Figure 12.5, part (b)). Nodes 1, 2, 4, and 6 are all connected to node 3. Node 2 is connected to node 5. Node 6 is connected to node 8, and node 8 is connected to node 7. All of the nodes are now connected. The total distance is found by adding the distances for the arcs used in the spanning tree. In this example, the distance is 2 + 2 + 3 + 3 + 3 + 1 + 2 = 16 (or 1,600 feet).

12.3 MAXIMAL-FLOW TECHNIQUE

The maximal-flow technique finds the most that can flow through a network.

The *maximal-flow technique* allows us to determine the maximum amount of a material that can flow through a network. It has been used, for example, to find the maximum number of automobiles that can flow through a state highway system.

IN ACTION   Spanning Tree Analysis of a Telecommunications Network

Network models have been used to solve a variety of problems for many different companies. In telecommunications, there is always a need to connect computer systems and devices together in an efficient and effective manner. Digital Equipment Corporation (DEC) for example, was concerned about how computer systems and devices were connected to a local area network (LAN) using a technology called Ethernet. The DECnet routing department was responsible for this and other network and telecommunications solutions.

Because of a number of technical difficulties, it was important to have an effective way to transport packets of information throughout the LAN. The solution was to use a spanning tree algorithm. The success of this approach can be seen in a poem written by one of the developers:

"I think I shall never see a graph more lovely than a tree.

A tree whose critical property is loop-free connectivity.

A tree that must be sure to span, so packets can reach every LAN.

First the route must be selected, by ID it is elected.

Least-cost paths from the root are traced.

In the tree these paths are placed.

A mesh is made for folks by me, then bridges find a spanning tree."

Source: Radia Perlman et al. "Spanning the LAN," *Data Communications* (October 21, 1997): 68–70.

FIGURE 12.6

**Road Network for
Waukesha**

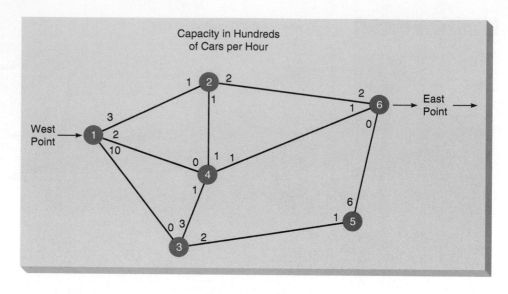

Capacity in Hundreds
of Cars per Hour

Waukesha, a small town in Wisconsin, is in the process of developing a road system for the downtown area. Bill Blackstone, one of the city planners, would like to determine the maximum number of cars that can flow through the town from west to east. The road network is shown in Figure 12.6.

The streets are indicated by their respective nodes. Look at the street between nodes 1 and 2. The numbers by the nodes indicate the maximum number of cars (in hundreds of cars per hour) that can flow *from* the various nodes. The number 3 by node 1 indicates that 300 cars per hour can flow *from* node 1 to node 2. Look at the numbers 1, 1, and 2 by node 2. These numbers indicate the maximum flow *from* node 2 to nodes 1, 4, and 6, respectively. As you can see, the maximum flow from node 2 back to node 1 is 100 cars per hour (1). One hundred cars per hour (1) can flow from node 2 to node 4, and 200 cars (2) can flow to node 6. Note that traffic can flow in both directions down a street. A zero (0) means no flow or a one-way street.

*Traffic can flow in both
directions.*

The maximal-flow technique is not difficult. It involves the following steps:

*The four maximal-flow
technique steps.*

Four Steps of the Maximal-Flow Technique

1. Pick any path from the start (source) to the finish (sink) with some flow. If no path with flow exists, then the optimal solution has been found.
2. Find the arc on this path with the smallest flow capacity available. Call this capacity *C*. This represents the maximum additional capacity that can be allocated to this route.
3. For each node on this path, decrease the flow capacity in the direction of flow by the amount *C*. For each node on this path, increase the flow capacity in the reverse direction by the amount *C*.
4. Repeat these steps until an increase in flow is no longer possible.

*We start by arbitrarily picking
a path and adjusting the flow.*

We start by arbitrarily picking the path 1–2–6, which is at the top of the network. What is the maximum flow from west to east? It is 2 because only 2 units (200 cars) can flow from node 2 to node 6. Now we adjust the flow capacities (see Figure 12.7). As you can see, we subtracted the maximum flow of 2 along the path 1–2–6 in the direction of the flow (west to east) and added 2 to the path in the direction against the flow (east to west). The result is the new path in Figure 12.7.

FIGURE 12.7

Capacity Adjustment for
Path 1–2–6 Iteration 1

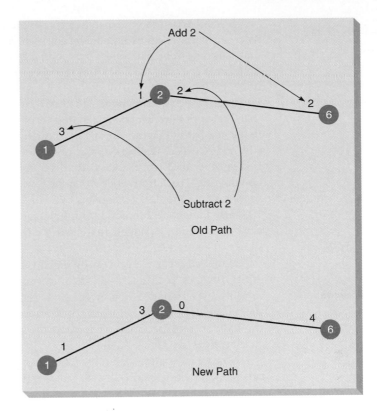

IN ACTION   Traffic-Control System on the Hanshin Expressway

The Hanshin expressway started with a 2.3-kilometer section of road in Osaka City, Japan, in the 1960s. This small stretch of highway was the first urban toll expressway in Osaka City. The traffic flow was approximately 5,000 cars per day. Today, the expressway includes about 200 kilometers of roadway in a system that connects Osaka and Kobe, Japan. The traffic flow in the early 1990s was more than 800,000 vehicles per day, with peak traffic flows that exceeded 1 million cars per day.

As discussed in this chapter, maximizing the flow of traffic through a network involves an investigation of current and future capacity of the various branches in the network. In addition to capacity analysis, Hanshin decided to use an automated traffic control system to maximize the flow of traffic through the existing expressway and to reduce congestion and bottlenecks caused by accidents, and by road maintenance or disabled cars. It was hoped that the control system would also increase income from the expressway.

Hanshin's management investigated the number of accidents and breakdowns on the expressway to help reduce

problems and further increase traffic flow. The traffic control system provides both direct and indirect control. Direct control includes controlling the number of vehicles entering the expressway at the various on-ramps. Indirect control involves providing comprehensive and up-to-the-minute information concerning traffic flows and the general traffic conditions on the expressway. Information on general traffic conditions is obtained using vehicle detectors, TV cameras, ultrasonic detectors, and automatic vehicle identifiers that read information on license plates. The data gathered from these devices gives people at home and driving the information they need to determine if they will use the Hanshin expressway.

This application reveals that a solution to a problem involves a variety of components, including quantitative analysis, equipment, and other elements, such as providing information to riders.

Source: T. Yoshino et al. "The Traffic-Control System on the Hanshin Expressway," *Interfaces* 25 (January–February 1995): 94–108.

It is important to note that the new path in Figure 12.7 reflects the new relative capacity at this stage. The flow number by any node represents two factors. One factor is the flow that can come *from* that node. The second factor is flow that can be *reduced* coming *into* the node. First consider the flow from west to east. Look at the path that goes from node 1 to node 2. The number 1 by node 1 tells us that 100 cars can flow *from* node 1 to node 2. Looking at the path from node 2 to node 6, we can see that the number 0 by node 2 tells us that 0 cars can flow *from* node 2 to node 6. Now consider the flow from east to west shown in the new path in Figure 12.7. First, consider the path from node 6 to node 2. The number 4 by node 6 tells us that we can reduce the flow *into* node 6 by 2 (or 200 cars) and that there is a capacity of 2 (or 200 cars) that can come *from* node 6. These two factors total 4. Looking at the path from node 2 to node 1, we see the number 3 by node 2. This tells us that we can reduce the flow *into* node 2 by 2 (or 200 cars) and that we have a capacity of 1 (or 100 cars) *from* node 2 to node 1. At this stage, we have a flow of 200 cars through the network from node 1 to node 2 to node 6. We have also reflected the new relative capacity, as shown in Figure 12.7.

The process is repeated.

Now we repeat the process by picking another path with existing capacity. We will arbitrarily pick path 1–2–4–6. The maximum capacity along this path is 1. In fact, the capacity at every node along this path (1–2–4–6) going from west to east is 1. Remember, the capacity of branch 1–2 is now 1 because 2 units (200 cars per hour) are now flowing through the network. Thus, we increase the flow along path 1–2–4–6 by 1 and adjust the capacity flow (see Figure 12.8).

Now we have a flow of 3 units (300 cars): 200 cars per hour along path 1–2–6 plus 100 cars per hour along path 1–2–4–6. Can we still increase the flow? Yes, along path 1–3–5–6. This is the bottom path. The maximum flow is 2 because this is the maximum from node 3 to node 5. The increased flow along this path is shown in Figure 12.9.

We continue until there are no more paths with unused capacity.

Again we repeat the process, trying to find a path with any unused capacity through the network. If you carefully check the last iteration in Figure 12.9, you will see that there are no more paths from node 1 to node 6 with unused capacity, even though several other

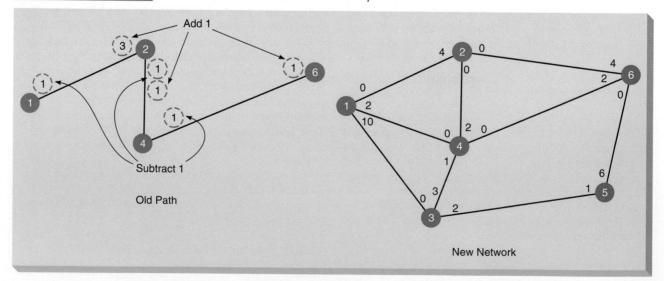

FIGURE 12.8　　**Second Iteration for Waukesha Road System**

FIGURE 12.9

Third and Final Iteration
for Waukesha Road System

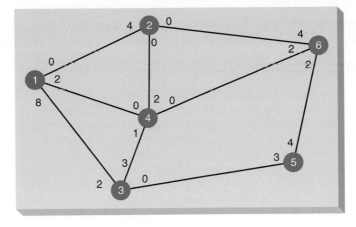

branches in the network do have unused capacity. The maximum flow of 500 cars per hour is summarized in the following table:

PATH	FLOW (CARS PER HOUR)
1–2–6	200
1–2–4–6	100
1–3–5–6	200
	Total 500

You can also compare the original network to the final network to see the flow between any of the nodes.

12.4 SHORTEST-ROUTE TECHNIQUE

The shortest-route technique minimizes the distance through a network.

The *shortest-route technique* finds how a person or item can travel from one location to another while minimizing the total distance traveled. In other words, it finds the shortest route to a series of destinations.

Every day, Ray Design, Inc., must transport beds, chairs, and other furniture items from the factory to the warehouse. This involves going through several cities. Ray would like to find the route with the shortest distance. The road network is shown in Figure 12.10.

FIGURE 12.10

Roads from Ray's Plant to
Warehouse

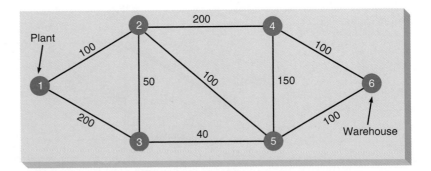

In the early 1990s, North Carolina was spending almost $150 million on transporting students to schools. The state's student transportation system involved some 13,000 buses, 100 school districts, and 700,000 students. In 1989, the General Assembly of the state decided to investigate ways that could be used to save money by developing a better way of transporting students. The General Assembly was committed to funding school districts that transported students efficiently, while only reimbursing justifiable expenses for those districts that were not efficient in terms of how they transported students to and from public schools.

The input data to North Carolina's network model included the number of buses used and the total operating expenses. Total operating expenses included driver salaries, salaries to other transportation personnel, payments to local governments, fuel costs, parts and repair costs, and other

related costs. These input values were used to compute an efficiency score for the various districts. These efficiency scores were then used to help in allocating funds to the districts. Those districts with an efficiency score of 0.9 or higher received full funding. Converting efficiency scores to funding was originally received with skepticism. After several years, however, more state officials realized the usefulness of the approach. In 1994–1995, the efficiency-based funding approach was used alone to determine funding.

The use of efficiency-based funding resulted in the elimination of hundreds of school buses, with savings over a three-year period greater than $25 million.

Source: T. Sexton et al. "Improving Pupil Transportation in North Carolina," *Interfaces* 24 (January–February 1994): 87–103.

The shortest-route technique can be used to minimize total distance from any starting node to a final node. The technique is summarized in the following steps:

The steps of the shortest-route technique.

Steps of the Shortest-Route Technique

1. Find the nearest node to the origin (plant). Put the distance in a box by the node.
2. Find the next-nearest node to the origin (plant), and put the distance in a box by the node. In some cases, several paths will have to be checked to find the nearest node.
3. Repeat this process until you have gone through the entire network. The last distance at the ending node will be the distance of the shortest route. You should note that the distance placed in the box by each node is the shortest route to this node. These distances are used as intermediate results in finding the next-nearest node.

Looking at Figure 12.10, we can see that the nearest node to the plant is node 2, with a distance of 100 miles. Thus we will connect these two nodes. This first iteration is shown in Figure 12.11.

We look for the nearest node to the origin.

Now we look for the next-nearest node to the origin. We check nodes 3, 4, and 5. Node 3 is the nearest, but there are two possible paths. Path 1–2–3 is nearest to the origin, with a total distance of 150 miles (see Figure 12.12).

FIGURE 12.11

First Iteration for Ray Design

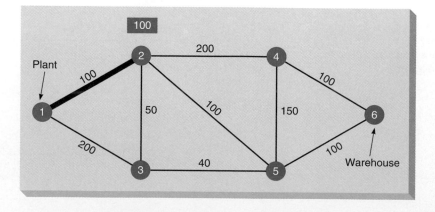

Second Iteration for Ray Design

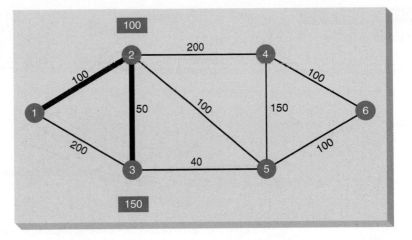

MODELING IN THE REAL WORLD   AT&T Solves Network Problems

Defining the Problem

Serving over 80 million customers in the United States and requiring over 40 thousand miles of cable, AT&T's fiber-optic network is the largest in the industry. Handling about 80 billion calls each year, AT&T defined maintaining network reliability, while maximizing network flow and minimizing network resources, as one of its most important problems.

Developing a Model

AT&T developed several comprehensive models to analyze reliability issues. These models investigated two important aspects of network reliability: (1) preventing failures, and (2) responding quickly when failures occur. The models included real time network routing (RTNR), fast automatic restoration (FASTAR), and synchronous optical network (SONET).

Acquiring Input Data

Over 10 months was spent on collecting data for the models. Because of the vast amount of data, AT&T used data aggregation to reduce the size of the network problem to make the solution easier.

Developing a Solution

The solution used an optimization routine to find the best way to route voice and data traffic through the network to minimize the number of message failures and network resources required. Because of the huge amount of data and the large size of the problem, an optimization solution was generated for each set of possible traffic demand and failure possibilities.

Testing the Solution

AT&T performed testing by comparing the solutions obtained by the new optimization approach to the solutions obtained by older planning tools. Improvement expectations of 5% to 10% were established. The company also used computer simulation to test the solution over varying conditions.

Analyzing the Results

To analyze the results, AT&T had to reverse the aggregation steps performed during data collection. Once the disaggregation process was completed, AT&T was able to determine the best routing approach through the vast network. The analysis of the results included an investigation of embedded capacity and spare capacity provided by the solution.

Implementing the Results

When implemented, the new approach was able to reduce network resources by more than 30%, while maintaining high network reliability. During the study, 99.98% of all calls were successfully completed on the first attempt. The successful implementation also resulted in ideas for changes and improvements, including a full optimization approach that could identify unused capacity and place it into operation.

Source: Ken Ambs et al. "Optimizing Restoration Capacity at the AT&T Network," *Interfaces* 30, 1 (January–February 2000): 26–44.

FIGURE 12.13

Third Iteration for Ray Design

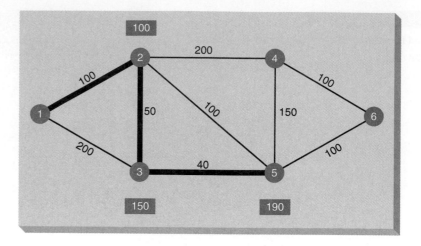

The process is repeated.

We repeat the process. The next-nearest node is either node 4 or node 5. Node 4 is 200 miles from node 2, and node 2 is 100 miles from node 1. Thus, node 4 is 300 miles from the origin. There are two paths for node 5, 2–5 and 3–5, to the origin. Note that we don't have to go all the way back to the origin because we already know the shortest route from node 2 and node 3 to the origin. The minimum distances are placed in boxes by these nodes. Path 2–5 is 100 miles, and node 2 is 100 miles from the origin. Thus, the total distance is 200 miles. In a similar fashion, we can determine that the path from node 5 to the origin through node 3 is 190 (40 miles between node 5 and 3 plus 150 miles from node 3 to the origin). Thus, we pick node 5 going through node 3 to the origin (see Figure 12.13).

The next-nearest node will be either node 4 or node 6, as the last remaining nodes. Node 4 is 300 miles from the origin (300 = 200 from node 4 to node 2 plus 100 from node 2 to the origin). Node 6 is 290 miles from the origin (290 = 100 + 190). Node 6 has the minimum distance, and because it is the ending node, we are done (refer to Figure 12.14). The shortest route is path 1–2–3–5–6, with a minimum distance of 290 miles.

FIGURE 12.14

Fourth and Final Iteration for Ray Design

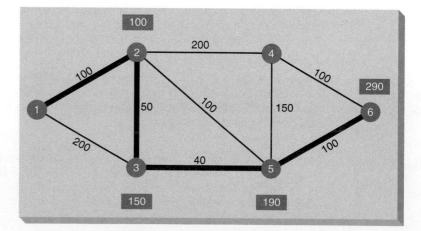

SUMMARY

We presented three important network techniques in this chapter. First, we discussed the minimal-spanning tree technique, which determines the path through the network that connects all of the nodes while minimizing total distance. Then the maximal-flow technique was discussed, which finds the maximum flow of any quantity or substance that can go through a network. Finally, the shortest-route technique, which finds the shortest path through a network, was examined.

GLOSSARY

Maximal-Flow Technique. Finds the maximum flow of any quantity or substance through a network.

Minimal-Spanning Tree Technique. Determines the path through the network that connects all of the nodes while minimizing total distance.

Shortest-Route Technique. Determines the shortest path through a network.

SOLVED PROBLEMS

Solved Problem 12-1

Roxie LaMothe, owner of a large horse breeding farm near Orlando, is planning to install a complete water system connecting all of the various stables and barns. The location of the facilities and the distances between them is given in the network shown in Figure 12.15. Roxie must determine the least expensive way to provide water to each facility. What do you recommend?

FIGURE 12.15

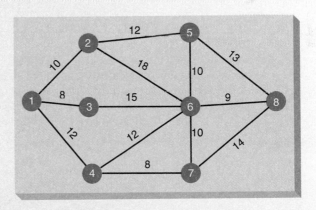

Solution

This is a typical minimum-spanning tree problem that can be solved by hand. We begin by selecting node 1 and connecting it to the nearest node, which is node 3. Nodes 1 and 2 are the next to be connected, followed by nodes 1 and 4. Now we connect node 4 to node 7 and node 7 to node 6. At this point, the only remaining points to be connected are node 6 to node 8 and node 6 to node 5. The final solution can be seen in Figure 12.16.

FIGURE 12.16

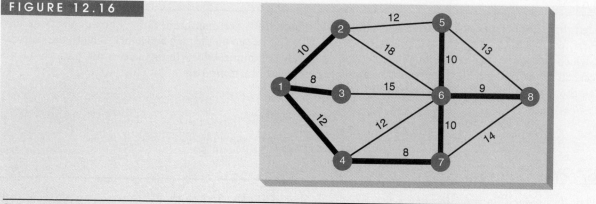

Solved Problem 12-2

PetroChem, an oil refinery located on the Mississippi River south of Baton Rouge, Louisiana, is designing a new plant to produce diesel fuel. Figure 12.17 shows the network of the main processing centers along with the existing rate of flow (in thousands of gallons of fuel). The management at PetroChem would like to determine the maximum amount of fuel that can flow through the plant, from node 1 to node 7.

FIGURE 12.17

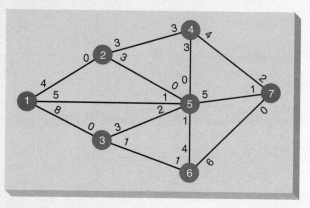

Solution

This problem can be solved using the steps outlined in the chapter on the maximal-flow technique. We start by arbitrarily picking path 1–2–5–7. The maximum flow is 3 along this path. The next path we choose is 1–2–4–7. The maximum flow possible, considering the 1–2–5–7 flow, is 1. The 1–7 flow is 4, and the 1–5–6–7 flow is 1. Finally, the 1–3–6–7 flow is 1. The total flow is 10 (10 = 3 + 1 + 4 + 1 + 1). The network of Figure 12.18, showing only the flow in thousands of gallons, details the by-hand solution.

FIGURE 12.18

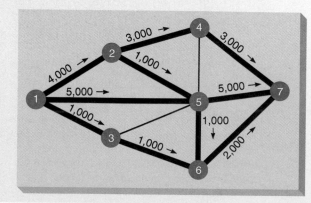

Solved Problem 12-3

The network of Figure 12.19 shows the highways and cities surrounding Leadville, Colorado. Leadville Tom, a bicycle helmet manufacturer, must transport his helmets to a distributor based in Dillon, Colorado. To do this, he must go through several cities. Tom would like to find the shortest way to get from Leadville to Dillon. What do you recommend?

FIGURE 12.19

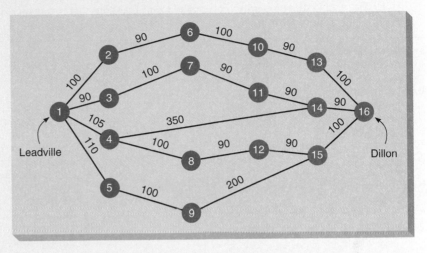

Solution

This problem can be solved using the shortest-route technique discussed in the chapter. The nearest node to the origin (Leadville) is node 3, with a distance of 90 miles. Thus, we put 90 in a box by node 3. The next-nearest node to the origin is node 7 at 190 miles. Again, we put 190 in a box by node 7. Next is node 11 at 280 miles and then node 14 at 370 miles. Finally, we see that the next-nearest (and final) node is node 16 at 460 miles. See Figure 12.20 for the solution.

FIGURE 12.20

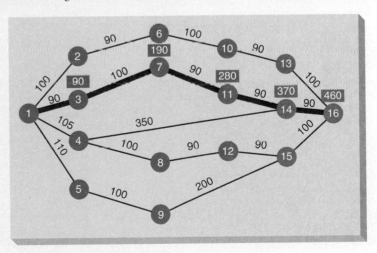

⟶ SELF-TEST

- Before taking the self-test, refer back to the learning objectives at the beginning of the chapter, the notes in the margins, and the glossary at the end of the chapter.
- Use the key at the back of the book to correct your answers.
- Restudy pages that correspond to any questions that you answered incorrectly or material you feel uncertain about.

1. Which technique is used to connect all points of a network together while minimizing the distance between them?
   a. maximal flow
   b. minimal flow
   c. minimal-spanning tree
   d. shortest route
   e. longest span
2. The first step of the minimal-spanning tree technique is to
   a. select the node with the highest distance between it and any other node.
   b. select the node with the lowest distance between it and any other node.
   c. select the node that is closest to the origin.
   d. select any arc that connects two nodes.
   e. select any node.
3. The first step of the maximal-flow technique is to
   a. select any node.
   b. pick any path from the start to the finish with some flow.
   c. pick the path with the maximum flow.
   d. pick the path with the minimal flow.
   e. pick a path where the flow going into each node is greater than the flow coming out of each node.
4. In which technique do you connect the nearest node to the existing solution that is not currently connected?
   a. maximal tree
   b. shortest route
   c. minimal-spanning tree
   d. maximal flow
   e. minimal flow
5. In the shortest-route technique, the objective is to determine the route from an origin to a destination that passes through the fewest number of other nodes.
   a. True
   b. False
6. Adjusting the flow capacity numbers on a path is an important step in which technique?
   a. maximal flow
   b. minimal flow
   c. maximal-spanning tree
   d. minimal-spanning tree
   e. shortest route

7. When the optimal solution has been reached with the maximal-flow technique, every node will be connected with at least one other node.
   a. True
   b. False
8. A large city is planning for delays during rush hour when roads are closed for maintenance. On a normal weekday, 160,000 vehicles travel on a freeway from downtown to a point 15 miles to the west. Which of the techniques discussed in this chapter would help the city planners determine if alternate routes provide sufficient capacity for all the traffic?
   a. minimal spanning tree technique
   b. maximal-flow technique
   c. shortest-route technique
9. The computing center at a major university is installing new fiber optic cables for a campuswide computer network. Which of the techniques in this chapter could be used to determine the least amount of cable needed to connect the 20 buildings on campus?
   a. minimal spanning tree technique
   b. maximal-flow technique
   c. shortest-route technique
10. In a minimal spanning tree problem, the optimal solution has been found when
    a. the start node and the finish node are connected by a continuous path.
    b. the flow from the start node is equal to the flow into the finish node.
    c. all arcs have been selected to be a part of the tree.
    d. all nodes have been connected and are a part of the tree.
11. _____ is a technique that is used to find how a person or item can travel from one location to another while minimizing the total distance traveled.
12. The technique that allows us to determine the maximum amount of a material that can flow through a network is called _____.
13. The _____ technique can be used to connect all of the points of a network together while minimizing the distance between them.

DISCUSSION QUESTIONS AND PROBLEMS

Discussion Questions

12-1 What is the minimal-spanning tree technique? What types of problems can be solved using this quantitative analysis technique?

12-2 Describe the steps of the maximal-flow technique.

12-3 Give several examples of problems that can be solved using the maximal-flow technique.

12-4 What are the steps of the shortest-route technique?

12-5 Describe a problem that can be solved by the shortest-route technique.

12-6 Is it possible to get alternate optimal solutions with the shortest-route technique? Is there an automatic way of knowing if you have an alternate optimal solution?

Problems*

12-7 Bechtold Construction is in the process of installing power lines to a large housing development. Steve Bechtold wants to minimize the total length of wire used, which will minimize his costs. The housing development is shown as a network in Figure 12.21.

Each house has been numbered, and the distances between houses are given in hundreds of feet. What do you recommend?

12-8 The city of New Berlin is considering making several of its streets one-way. What is the maximum number of cars per hour that can travel from east to west? The network is shown in Figure 12.22.

12-9 Transworld Moving has been hired to move the office furniture and equipment of Cohen Properties to their new headquarters. What route do you recommend? The network of roads is shown in Figure 12.23.

12-10 Because of a sluggish economy, Bechtold Construction has been forced to modify its plans for the housing development in Problem 12-7. The result is that the path from node 6 to 7 now has a distance of 7. What impact does this have on the total length of wire needed to install the power lines?

12-11 Due to increased property taxes and an aggressive road development plan, the city of New Berlin has been able to increase the road capacity of two of its roads (see Problem 12-8). The capacity along the road

FIGURE 12.21

Network for Problem 12-7

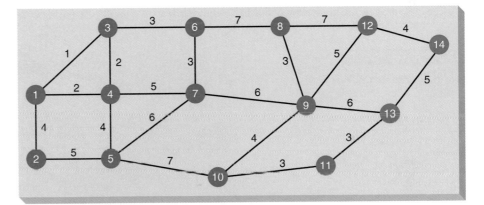

FIGURE 12.22

Network for Problem 12-8

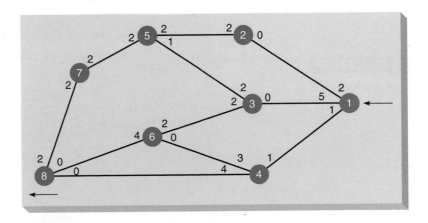

* Note: 𝒬 means the problem may be solved with QM for Windows.

FIGURE 12.23

Network for Problem 12-9

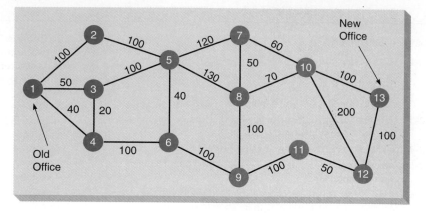

represented by the path from node 1–2 has been increased from 2 to 5. In addition, the capacity from node 1–4 has been increased from 1 to 3. What impact do these changes have on the number of cars per hour that can travel from east to west?

12-12 The director of security wants to connect security video cameras to the main control site from five potential trouble locations. Ordinarily, cable would simply be run from each location to the main control site. However, because the environment is potentially explosive, the cable must be run in a special conduit that is continually air purged. This conduit is very expensive but large

enough to handle five cables (the maximum that might be needed). Use the minimal-spanning tree technique to find a minimum distance route for the conduit between the locations noted in Figure 12.24. (Note that it makes no difference which one is the main control site.)

12-13 One of our best customers has had a major plant breakdown and wants us to make as many widgets for him as possible during the next few days, until he gets the necessary repairs done. With our general-purpose equipment there are several ways to make widgets (ignoring costs). Any sequence of activities that takes one from node 1 to node 6 in Figure 12.25 will

FIGURE 12.24

Network for Problem 12-12

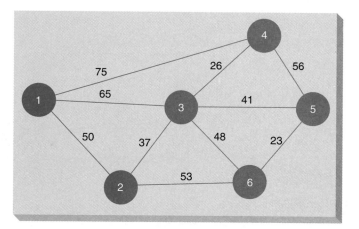

FIGURE 12.25

Network for Problem 12-13

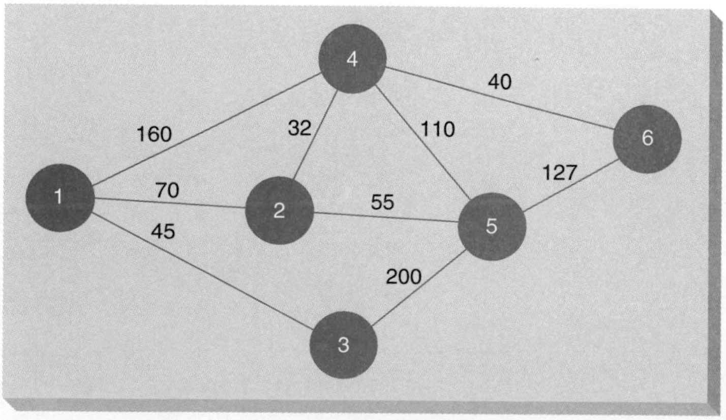

produce a widget. How many widgets can we produce per day? Quantities given are number of widgets per day.

12-14 Transworld Moving, like other moving companies, closely follows the impact of road construction to make sure that its routes remain the most efficient. Unfortunately, there has been unexpected road construction due to a lack of planning for road repair around the town of New Haven, represented by node 9 in the network. (See Problem 12-9.) All roads leading to node 9, except the road from node 9 to node 11, can no longer be traveled. Does this have any impact on the route that should be used to ship the office furniture and equipment of Cohen Properties to their new headquarters?

12-15 Solve the minimal-spanning tree problem in the network shown in Figure 12.26. Assume that the numbers in the network represent distance in hundreds of yards.

12-16 Refer to Problem 12-15. What impact would changing the value for path 6–7 to 500 yards have on the solution to the problem and the total distance?

12-17 The road system around the hotel complex on International Drive (node 1) to Disney World (node 11) in Orlando, Florida, is shown in the network of Figure 12.27. The numbers by the nodes represent the traffic flow in hundreds of cars per hour. What is the maximum flow of cars from the hotel complex to Disney World?

12-18 A road construction project would increase the road capacity around the outside roads from International Drive to Disney World by 200 cars per hour (see Problem 12-17). The two paths affected would be 1–2–6–9–11 and 1–5–8–10–11. What impact would this have on the total flow of cars? Would the total flow of cars increase by 400 cars per hour?

12-19 Solve the maximal-flow problem presented in the network of Figure 12.28 on the next page. The numbers in the network represent thousands of gallons per hour as they flow through a chemical processing plant.

12-20 Two terminals in the chemical processing plant, represented by nodes 6 and 7, require emergency repair (see Problem 12-19). No material can flow into or out of these nodes. What impact does this have on the capacity of the network?

12-21 Solve the shortest-route problem presented in the network of Figure 12.29 on the next page, going from node 1 to node 16. All numbers represent kilometers between German towns near the Black Forest.

12-22 Due to bad weather, the roads represented by nodes 7 and 8 have been closed (see Problem 12-21). No traffic can get onto or off of these roads. Describe the impact that this will have (if any) on the shortest route through this network.

12-23 Grey Construction would like to determine the least expensive way of connecting houses it is building with

Network for Problem 12-15

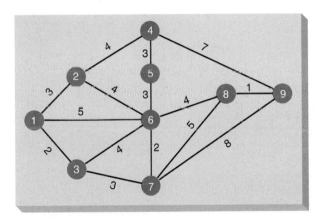

Network for Problem 12-17

FIGURE 12.28

Network for Problem 12-19

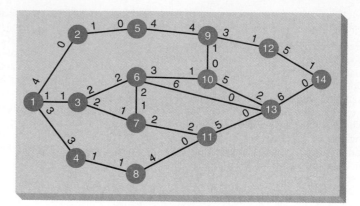

FIGURE 12.29

Network for Problem 12-21

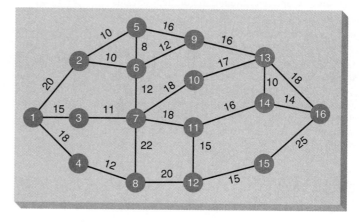

cable TV. It has identified 11 possible branches or routes that could be used to connect the houses. The cost in hundreds of dollars and the branches are summarized in the following table.

(a) What is the least expensive way to run cable to the houses?

Branch	Start Node	End Node	Cost ($100)
Branch 1	1	2	5
Branch 2	1	3	6
Branch 3	1	4	6
Branch 4	1	5	5
Branch 5	2	6	7
Branch 6	3	7	5
Branch 7	4	7	7
Branch 8	5	8	4
Branch 9	6	7	1
Branch 10	7	9	6
Branch 11	8	9	2

(b) After reviewing cable and installation costs, Grey Construction would like to alter the costs for installing cable TV between its houses. The first branches need to be changed. The changes are summarized in the following table. What is the impact on total costs?

Branch	Start Node	End Node	Cost ($100)
Branch 1	1	2	5
Branch 2	1	3	1
Branch 3	1	4	1
Branch 4	1	5	1
Branch 5	2	6	7
Branch 6	3	7	5
Branch 7	4	7	7
Branch 8	5	8	4
Branch 9	6	7	1
Branch 10	7	9	6
Branch 11	8	9	2

12-24 In going from Quincy to Old Bainbridge, there are 10 possible roads that George Olin can take. Each road can be considered a branch in the shortest-route problem.

(a) Determine the best way to get from Quincy (node 1) to Old Bainbridge (node 8) that will minimize total distance traveled. All distances are in hundreds of miles.

BRANCH	START NODE	END NODE	DISTANCE (IN HUNDREDS OF MILES)
Branch 1	1	2	3
Branch 2	1	3	2
Branch 3	2	4	3
Branch 4	3	5	3
Branch 5	4	5	1
Branch 6	4	6	4
Branch 7	5	7	2
Branch 8	6	7	2
Branch 9	6	8	3
Branch 10	7	8	6

(b) George Olin made a mistake in estimating the distances from Quincy to Old Bainbridge. The new distances are in the following table. What impact does this have on the shortest route from Quincy to Old Bainbridge?

BRANCH	START NODE	END NODE	DISTANCE (IN HUNDREDS OF MILES)
Branch 1	1	2	3
Branch 2	1	3	2
Branch 3	2	4	3
Branch 4	3	5	1
Branch 5	4	5	1
Branch 6	4	6	4
Branch 7	5	7	2
Branch 8	6	7	2
Branch 9	6	8	3
Branch 10	7	8	6

12-25 South Side Oil and Gas, a new venture in Texas, has developed an oil pipeline network to transport oil from exploration fields to the refinery and other locations. There are 10 pipelines (branches) in the network. The oil flow in hundreds of gallons and the network of pipelines is given in the following table.

(a) What is the maximum that can flow through the network?

BRANCH	START NODE	END NODE	CAPACITY	REVERSE CAPACITY	FLOW
Branch 1	1	2	10	4	10
Branch 2	1	3	8	2	5
Branch 3	2	4	12	1	10
Branch 4	2	5	6	6	0
Branch 5	3	5	8	1	5
Branch 6	4	6	10	2	10
Branch 7	5	6	10	10	0
Branch 8	5	7	5	5	5
Branch 9	6	8	10	1	10
Branch 10	7	8	10	1	5

(b) South Side Oil and Gas needs to modify its pipeline network flow patterns. The new data is in the following table. What impact does this have on the maximum flow through the network?

BRANCH	START NODE	END NODE	CAPACITY	REVERSE CAPACITY	FLOW
Branch 1	1	2	10	4	10
Branch 2	1	3	8	2	5
Branch 3	2	4	12	1	10
Branch 4	2	5	0	0	0
Branch 5	3	5	8	1	5
Branch 6	4	6	10	2	10
Branch 7	5	6	10	10	0
Branch 8	5	7	5	5	5
Branch 9	6	8	10	1	10
Branch 10	7	8	10	1	5

12-26 The following table represents a network with the arcs identified by their starting and ending nodes. Draw the network and use the minimal spanning tree to find the minimum distance required to connect these nodes.

ARC	DISTANCE
1–2	12
1–3	8
2–3	7
2–4	10
3–4	9
3–5	8
4–5	8
4–6	11
5–6	9

12-27 The network in Figure 12.30 represents streets of a city with the indicated number of cars per hour that can travel these streets. Find the maximum number of cars that could travel per hour through this system. How many cars would travel on each street (arc) to allow this maximum flow?

12-28 Refer to Problem 12-27. How would the maximum number of cars be affected if the street from node 3 to node 6 were temporarily closed?

12-29 Use the shortest route algorithm to determine the minimum distance from node 1 to node 7 in Figure 12.31. Which nodes are included in this route?

12-30 Northwest University is in the process of completing a computer bus network that will connect computer facilities throughout the university. The prime objective is to string a main cable from one end of the campus to the other (nodes 1–25) through underground conduits. These conduits are shown in the network of Figure 12.32; the distance between them is in hundreds of feet. Fortunately, these underground conduits have remaining capacity through which the bus cable can be placed.

(a) Given the network for this problem, how far (in hundreds of feet) is the shortest route from node 1 to node 25?

(b) In addition to the computer bus network, a new phone system is also being planned. The phone system would use the same underground conduits. If the phone system were installed, the following paths along the conduit would be at capacity and would not be available for the computer bus network: 6–11, 7–12, and 17–20. What changes (if any) would you have to make to the path used for the computer bus if the phone system were installed?

(c) The university *did* decide to install the new phone system before the cable for the computer network. Because of unexpected demand for computer networking facilities, an additional cable is needed for node 1 to node 25. Unfortunately, the cable for the first or original network has completely used up the capacity along its path. Given this situation, what is the best path for the second network cable?

FIGURE 12.30

Network for Problem 12-27

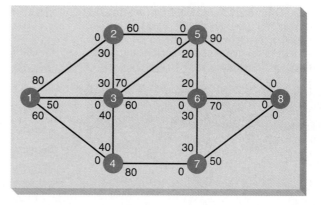

FIGURE 12.31

Network for Problem 12-29

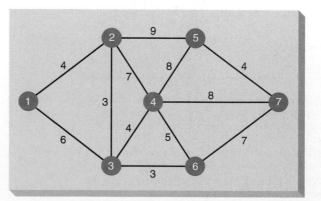

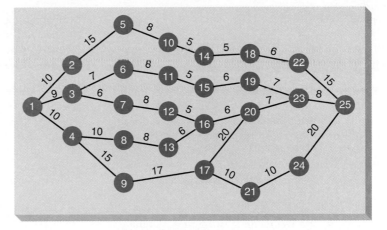

INTERNET HOMEWORK PROBLEMS

See our Internet home page at **www.prenhall.com/render** for additional homework problems 12-31 through 12-35.

➤ CASE STUDY

Binder's Beverage

Bill Binder's business nearly went under when Colorado almost passed the bottle bill. Binder's Beverage produced soft drinks for many of the large grocery stores in the area. After the bottle bill failed, Binder's Beverage flourished. In a few short years, the company had a major plant in Denver with a warehouse in east Denver. The problem was getting the fin-

ished product to the warehouse. Although Bill was not good with distances, he was good with times. Denver is a big city with numerous roads that could be taken from the plant to the warehouse, as shown in Figure 12.33.

The soft drink plant is located at the corner of North Street and Columbine Street. High Street also intersects North and Columbine Street at the plant. Twenty minutes due north of the

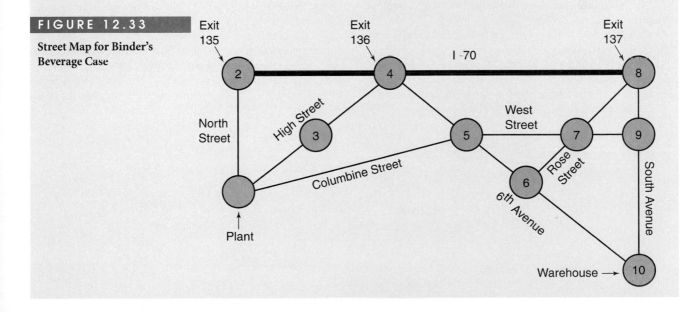

plant on North Street is I-70, the major east–west highway in Denver.

North Street intersects I-70 at Exit 135. It takes five minutes driving east on I-70 to reach Exit 136. This exit connects I-70 with High Street and 6th Avenue. Ten minutes east on I-70 is Exit 137. This exit connects I-70 with Rose Street and South Avenue.

From the plant, it takes 20 minutes on High Street, which goes in a northeast direction, to reach West Street. It takes another 20 minutes on High Street to reach I-70 and Exit 136.

It takes 30 minutes on Columbine Street to reach West Street from the plant. Columbine Street travels east and slightly north.

West Street travels east and west. From High Street, it takes 15 minutes to get to 6th Avenue on West Street. Columbine Street also comes into this intersection. From this intersection, it

takes an additional 20 minutes on West Street to get to Rose Street, and another 15 minutes to get to South Avenue.

From Exit 136 on 6th Avenue, it takes 5 minutes to get to West Street. Sixth Avenue continues to Rose Street, requiring 25 minutes. Sixth Avenue then goes directly to the warehouse. From Rose Street, it takes 40 minutes to get to the warehouse on 6th Avenue.

At Exit 137, Rose Street travels southwest. It takes 20 minutes to intersect with West Street, and another 20 minutes to get to 6th Avenue. From Exit 137, South Avenue goes due south. It takes 10 minutes to get to West Street and another 15 minutes to get to the Warehouse.

Discussion Question

1. What route do you recommend?

⇢ CASE STUDY

Southwestern University Traffic Problems

Southwestern University (SWU), located in the small town of Stephenville, Texas, is experiencing increased interest in its football program now that a big-name coach has been hired. The increase in season ticket sales for the upcoming season means additional revenues, but it also means increased complaints due to the traffic problems associated with the football games. When a new stadium is built, this will only get worse. Marty Starr, SWU's president, has asked the University Planning Committee to look into this problem.

Based on traffic projections, Dr. Starr would like to have sufficient capacity so that 35,000 cars per hour could travel from the stadium to the interstate highway. To alleviate the anticipated traffic problems, some of the current streets leading from the university to the interstate highway are being considered for

widening to increase the capacity. The current street capacities with the number of cars (in 1,000s) per hour are shown in Figure 12.34. Since the major problem will be after the game, only the flows away from the stadium are indicated. These flows include some streets closest to the stadium being transformed into one-way streets for a short period after each game with police officers directing traffic.

Alexander Lee, a member of the University Planning Committee, has said that a quick check of the road capacities in the diagram in Figure 12.33 indicates that the total number of cars per hour that may leave the stadium (node 1) is 33,000. The number of cars that may pass through nodes 2, 3, and 4 is 35,000 per hour, and the number of cars that may pass through nodes 5, 6, and 7 is even greater. Therefore, Dr. Lee has suggested that the current capacity is 33,000 cars per hour. He has also suggested

FIGURE 12.34

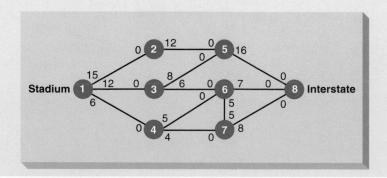

that a recommendation be made to the city manager for expansion of one of the routes from the stadium to the highway to permit an additional 2,000 cars per hour. He recommends expanding whichever route is cheapest. If the city chooses not to expand the roads, it is felt that the traffic problem would be a nuisance but would be manageable.

Based on past experience, it is believed that as long as the street capacity is within 2,500 cars per hour of the number that leave the stadium, the problem is not too severe. However, the severity of the problem grows dramatically for each additional 1,000 cars that are added to the streets.

Discussion Questions

1. If there is no expansion, what is the maximum number of cars that may actually travel from the stadium to the interstate per hour? Why is this number not equal to 33,000, as Dr. Lee suggested?
2. If the cost for expanding a street were the same for each street, which street(s) would you recommend expanding to increase the capacity to 33,000? Which streets would you recommend expanding to get the total capacity of the system to 35,000 per hour?

INTERNET CASE STUDY

See our Internet home page at **www.prenhall.com/render** for
this additional case study:
Ranch Development Project. This case involves finding the least-cost way to
provide water and sewer services to homes in a new housing development.

BIBLIOGRAPHY

Ahuja, R. K., T. L. Magnanti, and J. B. Orlin. *Network Flows: Theory, Algorithms, and Applications.* Upper Saddle River, NJ: Prentice Hall, 1993.

Bazlamacci, Cuneyt F. and Khalil S. Hindi. "Minimum-Weight Spanning Tree Algorithms: A Survey and Empirical Study," *Computers and Operations Research* 28, 8 (July 2001): 767–785.

Bentley, Jon. "Faster and Faster and Faster," *UNIX Review* (June 1997): 59.

Cipra, Barry. "Taking Hard Problems to the Limit: Mathematics," *Science* (March 4, 1997): 1570.

Current, J. "The Minimum-Covering/Shortest Path Problem," *Decision Sciences* 19 (Summer 1988): 490–503.

Erel, Erdal and Hadi Gokcen. "Shortest-Route Formulation of Mixed-Model Assembly Line Balancing Problem," *European Journal of Operational Research* 116, 1 (1999): 194–204.

Jain, A., and J. W. Mamer. "Approximations for the Random Minimal Spanning Tree with Application to Network Provisioning," *Operations Research* 36 (July–August 1988): 575–584.

Johnsonbaugh, Richard. *Discrete Mathematics*, 5/e. Upper Saddle River, NJ: Prentice Hall, 2001.

Kawatra, R. and D. Bricker. "A Multiperiod Planning Model for the Capacitated Minimal Spanning Tree Problem," *European Journal of Operational Research* 121, 2 (2000): 412–419.

Onal, Hayri et al. "Two Formulations of the Vehicle Routing Problem," *The Logistics and Transportation Review* (June 1996): 177–191.

Perlman, Radia et al. "Spanning the LAN," *Data Communications* (October 21, 1997): 68–70.

Sancho, N. G. F. "On the Maximum Expected Flow in a Network," *Journal of Operational Research Society* 39 (May 1988): 481–485.

Williams, Martyn. "When Does the Shortest Route Between Tokyo and Singapore Include a Stop in New York?" *Data Communications* (December 19, 1997): 45.

APPENDIX 12.1: NETWORK MODELS WITH QM FOR WINDOWS

Network models, including the minimal-spanning tree, maximal-flow, and shortest-route techniques are covered in this chapter. QM for Windows can be used to solve each of these network problems. The branches (arcs) are identified by the starting and ending nodes for each of these techniques, so the network must be drawn before inputting the problem. With the minimal spanning tree problem, the cost or distance is input for each branch. For the maximal-flow technique, the flow capacity and the reverse flow capacity is given for each branch. For the shortest-route technique, the distance associated with each branch is given.

The minimal-spanning technique connects nodes on a network while minimizing distance or costs. The Lauderdale Construction Company example is used to describe the overall procedure (see Section 12.2). Program 12.1 shows the output from QM for Windows for this problem. Note that all input data are also displayed. The Include column shows which branches are included as part of the solution. The solution shows that the minimum distance is 16 (16 hundred feet).

PROGRAM 12.1

QM for Windows for the Minimum-Spanning Tree Method

QM for Windows – C:\Prentice\Data\RenderStair7\Ldrdl765.net

Starting node for iterations: 1

Note
Multiple optimal solutions exist

Networks Results

Branch name	Start node	End node	Cost	Include	Cost
Lauderdale Construction Solution					
Branch 1	1.	2.	3.	Y	3.
Branch 2	1.	3.	2.	Y	2.
Branch 3	1.	4.	5.		
Branch 4	2.	3.	3.		
Branch 5	2.	5.	3.	Y	3.
Branch 6	3.	4.	2.	Y	2.
Branch 7	3.	5.	5.		
Branch 8	3.	6.	3.	Y	3.
Branch 9	3.	7.	7.		
Branch 10	4.	6.	6.		
Branch 11	5.	7.	4.		
Branch 12	6.	8.	1.	Y	1.
Branch 13	7.	8.	2.	Y	2.
Total					16.

The maximal-flow problem determines the maximum flow of cars, chemicals, or other items through an existing network. The Waukesha Road example was explained in Section 12.3. Program 12.2 shows the input data for this problem. Program 12.3 shows how QM for Windows can be used to solve this problem.

PROGRAM 12.2

QM for Windows for the Maximal-Flow Model

QM for Windows – C:\Prentice\Data\RenderStair7\Wksh766.net

Source: 1   Sink: 6

Branch name	Start node	End node	Capacity	Reverse capacity
Waukesha				
Branch 1	1	2	3	1
Branch 2	1	3	10	0
Branch 3	1	4	2	0
Branch 4	2	4	1	1
Branch 5	2	6	2	2
Branch 6	3	4	3	1
Branch 7	3	5	2	1
Branch 8	4	6	1	1
Branch 9	5	6	6	0

PROGRAM 12.3

Output from the Maximal-Flow Model

QM for Windows – C:\Prentice\Data\RenderStair7\Wksh766.net

Source: 1   Sink: 6

Iterations

Iteration	Path	Flow	Cumulative Flow
Waukesha Solution			
1	1-> 2-> 6	2.	2.
2	1-> 3-> 5-> 6	2.	4.
3	1-> 2-> 4-> 6	1.	5.

The shortest-route problem determines how a person or item can travel from one location to another while minimizing total distance traveled. In this chapter we explore the Ray Design problem (see Section 12.4). To illustrate the use of QM for Windows, let's use these data to solve a typical shortest-route problem. The input data are shown in Program 12.4. The output results are shown in Program 12.5.

PROGRAM 12.4

QM for Windows Input for the Shortest-Route Model

PROGRAM 12.5

QM for Windows Results for the Shortest-Route Model

PROJECT MANAGEMENT

After completing this chapter, students will be able to:

1. Understand how to plan, monitor, and control projects with the use of PERT.

2. Determine earliest start, earliest finish, latest start, latest finish, and slack times for each activity, along with the total project completion time.

3. Reduce total project time at the least total cost by crashing the network using manual or linear programming techniques.

4. Understand the important role of software in project management.

13.1 Introduction
13.2 PERT
13.3 PERT/Cost
13.4 Critical Path Method
13.5 Other Topics in Project Management

Summary • Glossary • Key Equations • Solved Problems • Self-Test • Discussion Questions and Problems • Internet Homework Problems • Case Study: Southwestern University Stadium Construction • Case Study: Family Planning Research Center of Nigeria • Internet Case Studies • Bibliography

Appendix 13.1: Project Management with QM for Windows

13.1 INTRODUCTION

Project management can be used to manage complex projects.

Most realistic projects that organizations like Microsoft, General Motors, or the U.S. Defense Department undertake are large and complex. A builder putting up an office building, for example, must complete thousands of activities costing millions of dollars. NASA must inspect countless components before it launches a rocket. Avondale Shipyards in New Orleans requires tens of thousands of steps in constructing an ocean-going tugboat. Almost every industry worries about how to manage similar large-scale, complicated projects effectively. It is a difficult problem, and the stakes are high. Millions of dollars in cost overruns have been wasted due to poor planning of projects. Unnecessary delays have occurred due to poor scheduling. How can such problems be solved?

The first step in planning and scheduling a project is to develop the *work breakdown structure*. This involves identifying the activities that must be performed in the project. There may be varying levels of detail, and each activity may be broken into its most basic components. The time, cost, resource requirements, predecessors, and person(s) responsible are identified for each activity. When this has been done, a schedule for the project can be developed.

The *program evaluation and review technique* (PERT) and the *critical path method* (CPM) are two popular quantitative analysis techniques that help managers plan, schedule, monitor, and control large and complex projects. They were developed because there was a critical need for a better way to manage (see the History box).

Framework of PERT and CPM

There are six steps common to both PERT and CPM. The procedure follows:

Six Steps of PERT and CPM

1. Define the project and all of its significant activities or tasks.
2. Develop the relationships among the activities. Decide which activities must precede others.
3. Draw the network connecting all of the activities.
4. Assign time and/or cost estimates to each activity.
5. Compute the longest time path through the network; this is called the *critical path*.
6. Use the network to help plan, schedule, monitor, and control the project.

The critical path is important because activities on the critical path can delay the entire project.

Finding the critical path is a major part of controlling a project. The activities on the critical path represent tasks that will delay the entire project if they are delayed. Managers derive flexibility by identifying noncritical activities and replanning, rescheduling, and reallocating resources such as personnel and finances.

PERT is probabilistic, whereas CPM is deterministic.

Although PERT and CPM are similar in their basic approach, they do differ in the way activity times are estimated. For every PERT activity, three time estimates are combined to determine the expected activity completion time and its variance. Thus, PERT is a *probabilistic* technique; it allows us to find the probability that the entire project will be completed by any given date. On the other hand, CPM is called a *deterministic* approach. It uses two time estimates, the *normal time* and the *crash time*, for each activity. The normal completion time is the time we estimate it will take under normal conditions to complete the activity. The crash completion time is the shortest time it would take to finish an activity if additional funds and resources were allocated to the task.

In this chapter we investigate not only PERT and CPM, but also a technique called PERT/Cost that combines the benefits of both PERT and CPM.

HISTORY   How PERT and CPM Started

Managers have been planning, scheduling, monitoring, and controlling large-scale projects for hundreds of years, but it has only been in the past 50 years that QA techniques have been applied to major projects. One of the earliest techniques was the *Gantt chart*. This type of chart shows the start and finish times of one or more activities, as shown in the accompanying chart.

In 1958, the Special Projects Office of the U.S. Navy developed the program evaluation and review technique (PERT) to plan and control the Polaris missile program. This project involved the coordination of thousands of contractors. Today PERT is still used to monitor countless government contract schedules. At about the same time (1957), the critical path method (CPM) was developed by J. E. Kelly of Remington Rand and M. R. Walker of du Pont. Originally, CPM was used to assist in the building and maintenance of chemical plants at du Pont.

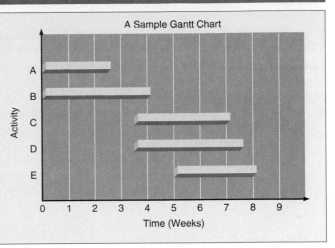

13.2 PERT

Almost any large project can be subdivided into a series of smaller activities or tasks that can be analyzed with PERT. When you recognize that projects can have thousands of specific activities, you see why it is important to be able to answer such questions as the following:

Questions answered by PERT.

1. When will the entire project be completed?
2. What are the *critical* activities or tasks in the project, that is, the ones that will delay the entire project if they are late?
3. Which are the *noncritical* activities, that is, the ones that can run late without delaying the entire project's completion?
4. What is the probability that the project will be completed by a specific date?
5. At any particular date, is the project on schedule, behind schedule, or ahead of schedule?
6. On any given date, is the money spent equal to, less than, or greater than the budgeted amount?
7. Are there enough resources available to finish the project on time?
8. If the project is to be finished in a shorter amount of time, what is the best way to accomplish this at the least cost?

PERT (or PERT/Cost) can help answer each of these questions.

General Foundry Example of PERT

General Foundry, Inc., a metalworks plant in Milwaukee, has long been trying to avoid the expense of installing air pollution control equipment. The local environmental protection group has recently given the foundry 16 weeks to install a complex air filter system on its main smokestack. General Foundry was warned that it will be forced to close unless the device is installed in the allotted period. Lester Harky, the managing partner, wants to make sure that installation of the filtering system progresses smoothly and on time.

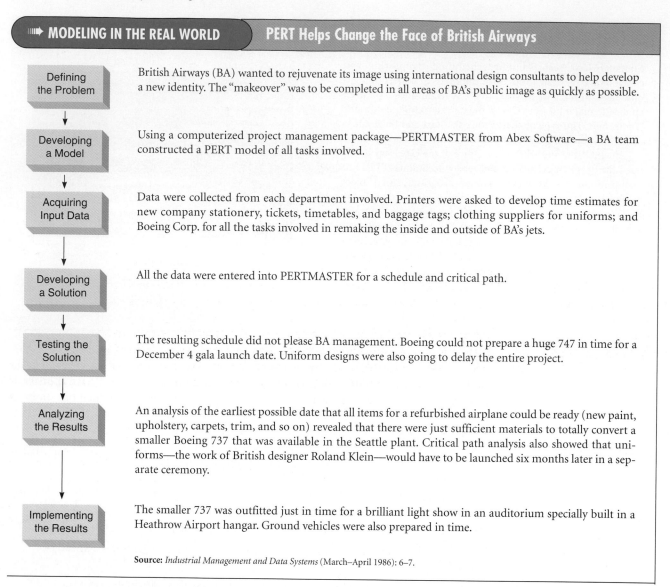

Defining the Problem

British Airways (BA) wanted to rejuvenate its image using international design consultants to help develop a new identity. The "makeover" was to be completed in all areas of BA's public image as quickly as possible.

Developing a Model

Using a computerized project management package—PERTMASTER from Abex Software—a BA team constructed a PERT model of all tasks involved.

Acquiring Input Data

Data were collected from each department involved. Printers were asked to develop time estimates for new company stationery, tickets, timetables, and baggage tags; clothing suppliers for uniforms; and Boeing Corp. for all the tasks involved in remaking the inside and outside of BA's jets.

Developing a Solution

All the data were entered into PERTMASTER for a schedule and critical path.

Testing the Solution

The resulting schedule did not please BA management. Boeing could not prepare a huge 747 in time for a December 4 gala launch date. Uniform designs were also going to delay the entire project.

Analyzing the Results

An analysis of the earliest possible date that all items for a refurbished airplane could be ready (new paint, upholstery, carpets, trim, and so on) revealed that there were just sufficient materials to totally convert a smaller Boeing 737 that was available in the Seattle plant. Critical path analysis also showed that uniforms—the work of British designer Roland Klein—would have to be launched six months later in a separate ceremony.

Implementing the Results

The smaller 737 was outfitted just in time for a brilliant light show in an auditorium specially built in a Heathrow Airport hangar. Ground vehicles were also prepared in time.

Source: *Industrial Management and Data Systems* (March–April 1986): 6–7.

The first step is to define the project and all project activities.

When the project begins, the building of the internal components for the device (activity *A*) and the modifications that are necessary for the floor and roof (activity *B*) can be started. The construction of the collection stack (activity *C*) can begin once the internal components are completed, and pouring of the new concrete floor and installation of the frame (activity *D*) can be completed as soon as the roof and floor have been modified. After the collection stack has been constructed, the high-temperature burner can be built (activity *E*), and the installation of the pollution control system (activity *F*) can begin. The air pollution device can be installed (activity *G*) after the high-temperature burner has been built, the concrete floor has been poured, and the frame has been installed. Finally, after the control system and pollution device have been installed, the system can be inspected and tested (activity *H*).

All of these activities seem rather confusing and complex until they are placed in a network. First, all of the activities must be listed. This information is shown in Table 13.1. We see in the table that before the collection stack can be constructed (activity *C*), the internal components must be built (activity *A*). Thus, activity *A* is the immediate predecessor of activity *C*. Similarly, both activities *D* and *E* must be performed just prior to installation of the air pollution device (activity *G*).

Immediate predecessors are determined in the second step.

TABLE 13.1			
Activities and Immediate Predecessors for General Foundry, Inc.	ACTIVITY	DESCRIPTION	IMMEDIATE PREDECESSORS
	A	Build internal components	—
	B	Modify roof and floor	—
	C	Construct collection stack	*A*
	D	Pour concrete and install frame	*B*
	E	Build high-temperature burner	*C*
	F	Install control system	*C*
	G	Install air pollution device	*D, E*
	H	Inspect and test	*F, G*

Drawing the PERT Network

Activities and events are drawn and connected in the third step.

Once the activities have all been specified (step 1 of the PERT procedure) and management has decided which activities must precede others (step 2), the network can be drawn (step 3).

There are two common techniques for drawing PERT networks. The first is called activity-on-node (AON) because the nodes represent the activities. The second is called activity-on-arc (AOA) because the arcs are used to represent the activities. In this book, we present the AON technique, as this is easier and is often used in commercial software.

In constructing an AON network, there should be one node representing the start of the project and one node representing the finish of the project. There will be one node (represented as a rectangle in this chapter) for each activity. Figure 13.1 gives the entire network for General Foundry. The arcs (arrows) are used to show the predecessors for the activities. For example, the arrows leading into activity *G* indicate that both *D* and *E* are immediate predecessors for *G*.

FIGURE 13.1	Network for General Foundry, Inc.

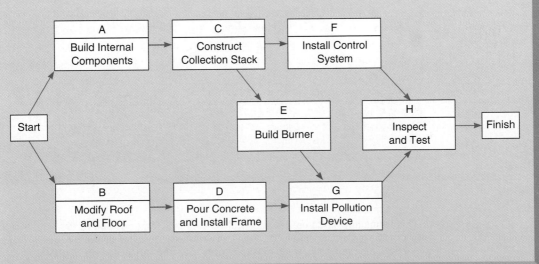

Activity Times

The fourth step is to assign activity times.

The next step in the PERT procedure is to assign estimates of the time required to complete each activity. Time is usually given in units of weeks. For one-of-a-kind projects or for new jobs, providing *activity time estimates* is not always an easy task. Without solid historical data, managers are often uncertain as to activity times. For this reason, the developers of PERT employed a probability distribution based on three time estimates for each activity:

Optimistic time (*a*) = time an activity will take if everything goes as well as possible. There should be only a small probability (say, $\frac{1}{100}$) of this occurring.

Pessimistic time (*b*) = time an activity would take assuming very unfavorable conditions. There should also be only a small probability that the activity will really take this long.

Most likely time (*m*) = most realistic time estimate to complete the activity.

The beta probability distribution is often used.

PERT often assumes that time estimates follow the *beta probability distribution* (see Figure 13.2). This continuous distribution has been found to be appropriate, in many cases, for determining an expected value and variance for activity completion times.

To find the *expected activity time* (*t*), the beta distribution weights the estimates as follows:

$$t = \frac{a + 4m + b}{6}$$

(13-1)

To compute the dispersion or *variance of activity completion time*, we use this formula[1]:

$$\text{variance} = \left(\frac{b - a}{6}\right)^2$$

(13-2)

FIGURE 13.2   Beta Probability Distribution with Three Time Estimates

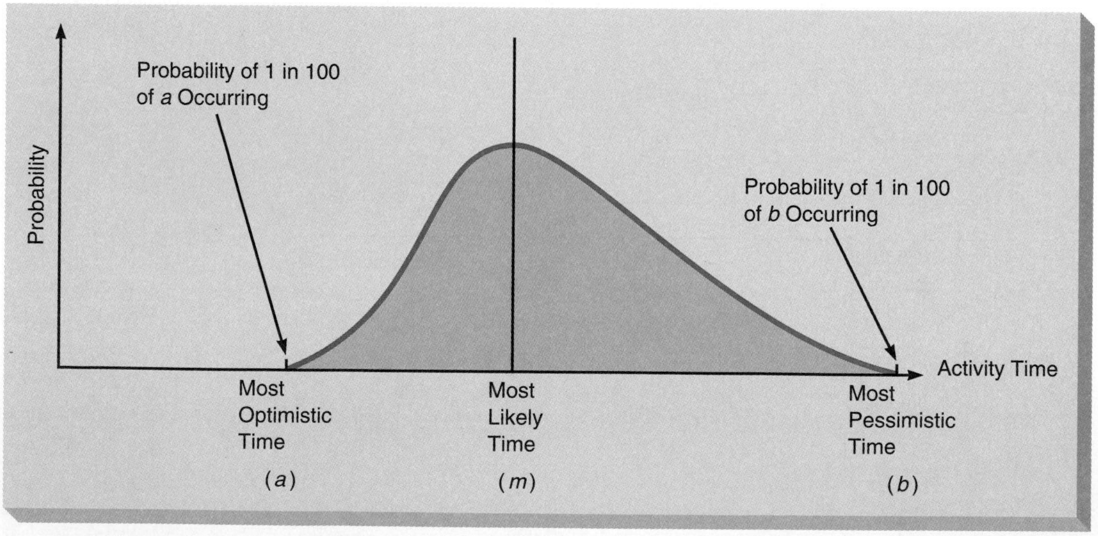

---

[1] This formula is based on the statistical concept that from one end of the beta distribution to the other are 6 standard deviations (±3 standard deviations from the mean). Because $b - a$ is 6 standard deviations, one standard deviation is $(b - a)/6$. Thus the variance is $[(b - a)/6]^2$.

TABLE 13.2   Time Estimates (Weeks) for General Foundry, Inc.

ACTIVITY	OPTIMISTIC, a	MOST PROBABLE, m	PESSIMISTIC, b	EXPECTED TIME, $t = [(a + 4m + b)/6]$	VARIANCE, $[(b - a)/6]^2$
A	1	2	3	2	$\left(\dfrac{3-1}{6}\right)^2 = \dfrac{4}{36}$
B	2	3	4	3	$\left(\dfrac{4-2}{6}\right)^2 = \dfrac{4}{36}$
C	1	2	3	2	$\left(\dfrac{3-1}{6}\right)^2 = \dfrac{4}{36}$
D	2	4	6	4	$\left(\dfrac{6-2}{6}\right)^2 = \dfrac{16}{36}$
E	1	4	7	4	$\left(\dfrac{7-1}{6}\right)^2 = \dfrac{36}{36}$
F	1	2	9	3	$\left(\dfrac{9-1}{6}\right)^2 = \dfrac{64}{36}$
G	3	4	11	5	$\left(\dfrac{11-3}{6}\right)^2 = \dfrac{64}{36}$
H	1	2	3	$\underline{2}$	$\left(\dfrac{3-1}{6}\right)^2 = \dfrac{4}{36}$
				25	

Table 13.2 shows General Foundry's optimistic, most likely, and pessimistic time estimates for each activity. It also reveals the expected time (t) and variance for each of the activities, as computed with Equations 13-1 and 13-2.

How to Find the Critical Path

Once the expected completion time for each activity has been determined, we accept it as the actual time of that task. Variability in times will be considered later.

Although Table 13.2 indicates that the total expected time for all eight of General Foundry's activities is 25 weeks, it is obvious in Figure 13.3 that several of the tasks can be taking place simultaneously. To find out just how long the project will take, we perform the critical path analysis for the network.

The fifth step is to compute the longest path through the network—the critical path.

The *critical path* is the longest time path route through the network. If Lester Harky wants to reduce the total project time for General Foundry, he will have to reduce the length of some activity on the critical path. Conversely, any delay of an activity on the critical path will delay completion of the entire project.

FIGURE 13.3   General Foundry's Network with Expected Activity Times

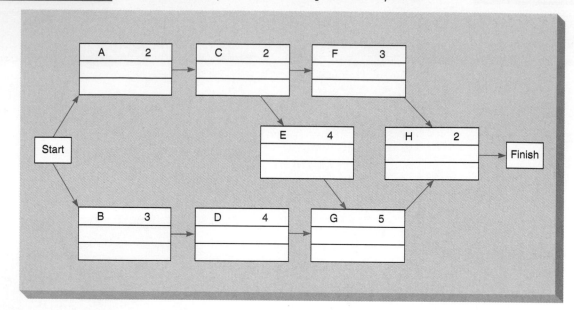

To find the critical path, we need to determine the following quantities for each activity in the network:

1. *Earliest start time* (ES): the earliest time an activity can begin without violation of immediate predecessor requirements
2. *Earliest finish time* (EF): the earliest time at which an activity can end
3. *Latest start time* (LS): the latest time an activity can begin without delaying the entire project
4. *Latest finish time* (LF): the latest time an activity can end without delaying the entire project

In the network, we represent these times as well as the activity times (t) in the nodes, as seen here:

ACTIVITY	t
ES	EF
LS	LF

We first show how to determine the earliest times. When we find these, the latest times can be computed.

Earliest Times   There are two basic rules to follow when computing ES and EF times. The first rule is for the earliest finish time, which is computed as follows:

$$\text{earliest finish time} = \text{earliest start time} + \text{expected activity time}$$

$$EF = ES + t \tag{13-3}$$

Also, before any activity can be started, all of its predecessor activities must be completed. In other words, we search for the largest EF for all of the immediate predecessors in determining ES. The second rule is for the earliest start time, which is computed as follows:

The ES is the largest EF of the immediate predecessors.

earliest start = largest of the earliest finish times of immediate predecessors

ES = largest EF of immediate predecessors

The start of the whole project will be set at time zero. Therefore, any activity that has no predecessors will have an earliest start time of zero. So ES = 0 for both *A* and *B* in the General Foundry problem, as seen here:

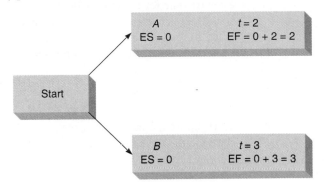

The earliest times are found by beginning at the start of the project and making a forward pass through the network.

The rest of the earliest times for General Foundry are shown in Figure 13.4. These are found using a *forward pass* through the network. At each step, EF = ES + *t*, and ES is the largest EF of the predecessors. Notice that activity *G* has an earliest start time of 8, since both *D* (with EF = 7) and *E* (with EF = 8) are immediate predecessors. Activity *G* cannot start until both predecessors are finished, and so we choose the larger of the earliest finish times for these. Thus, *G* has ES = 8. The finish time for the project will be 15 weeks, which is the EF for activity *H*.

FIGURE 13.4   **General Foundry's Earliest Start (ES) and Earliest Finish (EF) Times**

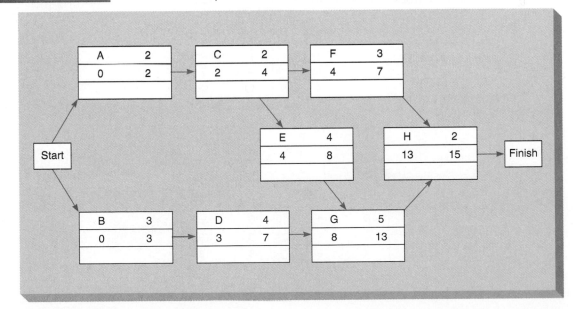

Latest Times The next step in finding the critical path is to compute the latest start time (LS) and the latest finish time (LF) for each activity. We do this by making a *backward pass* through the network, that is, starting at the finish and working backward.

There are two basic rules to follow when computing the latest times. The first rule involves the latest start time, which is computed as

The latest times are found by beginning at the finish of the project and making a backward pass through the network.

$$\text{latest start time} = \text{latest finish time} - \text{activity time}$$

$$LS = LF - t \tag{13-4}$$

Also, since all immediate predecessors must be finished before an activity can begin, the latest start time for an activity determines the latest finish time for its immediate predecessors. If an activity is the immediate predecessor for two or more activities, it must be finished so that all following activities can begin by their latest start times. Thus, the second rule involves the latest finish time, which is computed as

The LF is the smallest LS of the activities that immediately follow.

$$\text{latest finish time} = \text{smallest of latest start times for following activities, or}$$

$$LF = \text{smallest LS of following activities}$$

To compute the latest times, we start at the finish and work backwards. Since the finish time for the General Foundry project is 15, activity H has $LF = 15$. The latest start for activity H is

$$LS = LF - t = 15 - 2 = 13 \text{ weeks}$$

Continuing to work backward, this latest start time of 13 becomes the latest finish time for immediate predecessors F and G. All of the latest times are shown in Figure 13.5. Notice that for activity C, which is the immediate predecessor for two activities (E and F), the latest finish time is the smaller of the latest start times (4 and 10) for activities E and F.

Slack time is free time for an activity.

Concept of Slack in Critical Path Computations When ES, LS, EF, and LF have been determined, it is a simple matter to find the amount of *slack time*, or free time, that each

FIGURE 13.5   General Foundry's Latest Start (LS) and Latest Finish (LF) Times

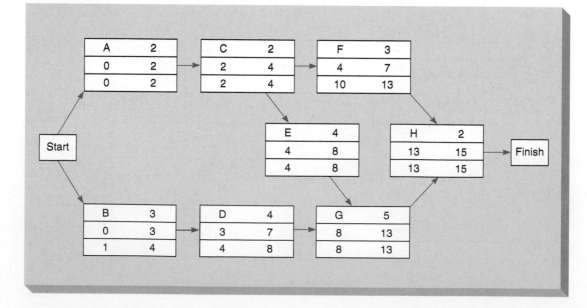

Flight 199's three engines screech its arrival as the wide-bodied jet lumbers down Orlando's taxiway with 200 passengers arriving from San Juan. In an hour, the plane is to be airborne again.

But before this jet can depart, there is business to attend to: hundreds of passengers and tons of luggage and cargo to unload and load; hundreds of meals, thousands of gallons of jet fuel, countless soft drinks and bottles of liquor to restock; cabin and restrooms to clean; toilet holding tanks to drain; and engines, wings, and landing gear to inspect.

The 12-person ground crew knows that a miscue anywhere—a broken cargo loader, lost baggage, misdirected passengers—can mean a late departure and trigger a chain reaction of headaches from Orlando to Dallas to every destination of a connecting flight.

Dennis Dettro, the operations manager for Delta's Orlando International Airport, likes to call the turnaround operation "a well-orchestrated symphony." Like a pit crew awaiting a race car, trained crews are in place for Flight 199 with baggage carts and tractors, hydraulic cargo loaders, a truck to load food and drinks, another to lift the cleanup crew, another to put fuel on, and a fourth to take water off. The "orchestra" usually performs so smoothly that most passengers never suspect the proportions of the effort. PERT and Gantt charts aid Delta and other airlines with the staffing and scheduling that are necessary for this symphony to perform.

Sources: *New York Times* (January 21, 1997): C1, C20; and *Wall Street Journal* (August 1994): B1.

activity has. Slack is the length of time an activity can be delayed without delaying the whole project. Mathematically,

$$\text{slack} = \text{LS} - \text{ES} \quad \text{or} \quad \text{slack} = \text{LF} - \text{EF} \tag{13-5}$$

Table 13.3 summarizes the ES, EF, LS, LF, and slack times for all of General Foundry's activities. Activity *B*, for example, has 1 week of slack time since LS − ES = 1 − 0 = 1 (or, similarly, LF − EF = 4 − 3 = 1). This means that it can be delayed up to 1 week without causing the project to run any longer than expected.

Critical activities have no slack time.

On the other hand, activities *A, C, E, G,* and *H* have no slack time; this means that none of them can be delayed without delaying the entire project. Because of this, they are called *critical activities* and are said to be on the *critical path*. Lester Harky's critical path is shown in network form in Figure 13.6. The total project completion time, 15 weeks, is seen as the largest number in the EF or LF columns of Table 13.3. Industrial managers call this a boundary timetable.

TABLE 13.3 **General Foundry's Schedule and Slack Times**	**ACTIVITY**	**EARLIEST START, ES**	**EARLIEST FINISH, EF**	**LATEST START, LS**	**LATEST FINISH, LF**	**SLACK, LS − ES**	**ON CRITICAL PATH?**
	A	0	2	0	2	0	Yes
	B	0	3	1	4	1	No
	C	2	4	2	4	0	Yes
	D	3	7	4	8	1	No
	E	4	8	4	8	0	Yes
	F	4	7	10	13	6	No
	G	8	13	8	13	0	Yes
	H	13	15	13	15	0	Yes

FIGURE 13.6   **General Foundry's Critical Path (A–C–E–G–H)**

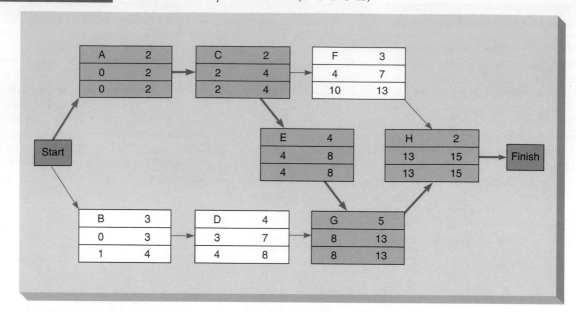

Probability of Project Completion

The *critical path analysis* helped us determine that the foundry's expected project completion time is 15 weeks. Harky knows, however, that if the project is not completed in 16 weeks, General Foundry will be forced to close by environmental controllers. He is also aware that there is significant variation in the time estimates for several activities. Variation in activities that are on the critical path can affect overall project completion—possibly delaying it. This is one occurrence that worries Harky considerably.

Computing project variance is done by summing activity variances along the critical path.

PERT uses the variance of critical path activities to help determine the variance of the overall project. If the activity times are statistically independent, the project variance is computed by summing the variances of the critical activities:

$$\text{project variance} = \Sigma \text{ variances of activities on the critical path} \tag{13-6}$$

From Table 13.2 we know that

CRITICAL ACTIVITY	VARIANCE
A	$\frac{4}{36}$
C	$\frac{4}{36}$
E	$\frac{36}{36}$
G	$\frac{64}{36}$
H	$\frac{4}{36}$

Hence, the project variance is

$$\text{project variance} = \tfrac{4}{36} + \tfrac{4}{36} + \tfrac{36}{36} + \tfrac{64}{36} + \tfrac{4}{36} = \tfrac{112}{36} = 3.111$$

FIGURE 13.7

Probability Distribution for Project Completion Times

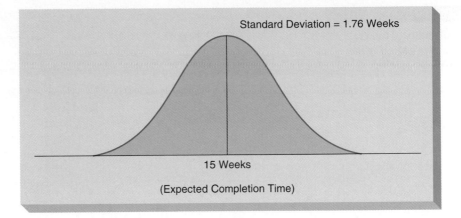

Computing the standard deviation.

We know that the standard deviation is just the square root of the variance, so

$$\text{project standard deviation} = \sigma_T = \sqrt{\text{project variance}}$$
$$= \sqrt{3.11} = 1.76 \text{ weeks}$$

PERT has two assumptions.

How can this information be used to help answer questions regarding the probability of finishing the project on time? In addition to assuming that the activity times are independent, we also assume that total project completion time follows a normal probability distribution. With these assumptions, the bell-shaped curve shown in Figure 13.7 can be used to represent project completion dates. It also means that there is a 50% chance that the entire project will be completed in less than the expected 15 weeks and a 50% chance that it will exceed 15 weeks.[2]

For Harky to find the probability that his project will be finished on or before the 16-week deadline, he needs to determine the appropriate area under the normal curve. The standard normal equation can be applied as follows:

Computing the probability of project completion.

$$Z = \frac{\text{due date} - \text{expected date of completion}}{\sigma_T}$$

$$= \frac{16 \text{ weeks} - 15 \text{ weeks}}{1.76 \text{ weeks}} = 0.57$$

(13-7)

where

Z is the number of standard deviations the due date or target date lies from the mean or expected date.

Referring to the normal table in Appendix A, we find a probability of 0.71566. Thus, there is a 71.6% chance that the pollution control equipment can be put in place in 16 weeks or less. This is shown in Figure 13.8.

---

[2] You should be aware that noncritical activities also have variability (as seen in Table 13.2). In fact, a different critical path can evolve because of the probabilistic situation. This may also cause the probability estimates to be unreliable. In such instances, it is better to use simulation to determine the probabilities.

FIGURE 13.8

Probability of General Foundry's Meeting the 16-Week Deadline

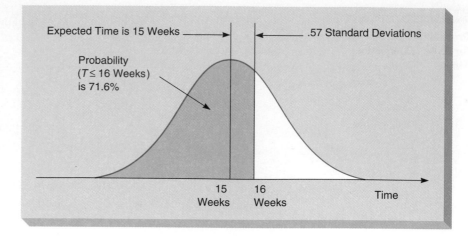

The sixth and final step is to monitor and control the project using the information provided by PERT.

What PERT Was Able to Provide

PERT has thus far been able to provide Lester Harky with several valuable pieces of management information:

1. The project's expected completion date is 15 weeks.

2. There is a 71.6% chance that the equipment will be in place within the 16-week deadline. PERT can easily find the probability of finishing by any date Harky is interested in.

3. Five activities (*A, C, E, G, H*) are on the critical path. If any one of them is delayed for any reason, the entire project will be delayed.

4. Three activities (*B, D, F*) are not critical but have some slack time built in. This means that Harky can borrow from their resources, if needed, possibly to speed up the entire project.

5. A detailed schedule of activity starting and ending dates has been made available (see Table 13.3).

Sensitivity Analysis and Project Management

During any project, the time required to complete an activity can vary from the projected or expected time. If the activity is on the critical path, the total project completion time will change, as discussed previously. In addition to having an impact on the total project completion time, there is also an impact on the earliest start, earliest finish, latest start, latest finish, and slack times for other activities. The exact impact depends on the relationship between the various activities.

In previous sections we define an immediate predecessor activity as an activity that comes immediately before a given activity. In general, a *predecessor activity* is one that must be completed before the given activity can be started. Consider activity *G* (install pollution device) for the General Foundry example. As seen previously, this activity is on the critical path. Predecessor activities are *A, B, C, D,* and *E*. All of these activities must be completed before activity *G* can be started. A *successor activity* is an activity that can be started only after the given activity is finished. Activity *H* is the only successor activity for activity *G*. A *parallel activity* is an activity that does not directly depend on the given activity. Again consider activity *G*. Are there any parallel activities for this activity? Looking at the network for General Foundry, it can be seen that activity *F* is a parallel activity of activity *G*.

After predecessor, successor, and parallel activities have been defined, we can explore the impact that an increase (decrease) in an activity time for a critical path activity would

TABLE 13.4

Impact of an Increase (Decrease) in an Activity Time for a Critical Path Activity

ACTIVITY TIME	SUCCESSOR ACTIVITY	PARALLEL ACTIVITY	PREDECESSOR ACTIVITY
Earliest start	Increase (decrease)	No change	No change
Earliest finish	Increase (decrease)	No change	No change
Latest start	Increase (decrease)	Increase (decrease)	No change
Latest finish	Increase (decrease)	Increase (decrease)	No change
Slack	No change	Increase (decrease)	No change

have on other activities in the network. The results are summarized in Table 13.4. If the time it takes to complete activity G increases, there will be an increase in the earliest start, earliest finish, latest start, and latest finish times for all successor activities. Because these activities follow activity G, these times will also increase. Because slack time is equal to latest finish time minus the earliest finish time (or the latest start time minus earliest start time; LF − EF or LS − ES), there will be no change in the slack for successor activities. Because activity G is on the critical path, an increase in activity time will increase the total project competition time. This would mean that the latest finish, latest start, and slack time will also increase for all parallel activities. You can prove this to yourself by completing a backward pass through the network using a higher total project competition time. There are no changes for predecessor activities.

13.3 PERT/COST

Using PERT/Cost to plan, schedule, monitor, and control project cost helps accomplish the sixth and final step of PERT.

Although PERT is an excellent method of monitoring and controlling project length, it does not consider another very important factor, project *cost*. *PERT/Cost* is a modification of PERT that allows a manager to plan, schedule, monitor, and control cost as well as time.

We begin this section by investigating how costs can be planned and scheduled. Then we see how costs can be monitored and controlled.

IN ACTION   Costing Projects at Nortel

Many companies, including Nortel, a large telecommunications company, are benefiting from project management. With more than 20,000 active projects worth a total of more than $2 billion, effectively managing projects at Nortel has been challenging. Getting the needed input data, including times and costs, can be difficult.

Like most companies, Nortel used standard accounting practices to monitor and control costs. This typically involves allocating costs to each department. Most projects, however, span multiple departments. This can make it very difficult to get timely cost information. Project managers often get project cost data later than they want. Because the cost data are allocated to departments, the data are often not detailed enough to help manage projects and get an accurate picture of true project costs.

To get more accurate cost data for project management, Nortel adopted an activity-based-costing (ABC) method often

used in manufacturing operations. In addition to standard cost data, each project activity was coded with a project identification number and a regional research and development location number. This greatly improved the ability of project managers to control costs. Because some of the month-end costing processes were simplified, the approach also lowered project costs in most cases. Project managers also were able to get more detailed costing information. Because the cost data were coded for each project, getting timely feedback was also possible. In this case, getting good input data reduced project costs, reduced the time needed to get critical project feedback, and made project management more accurate.

Source: Chris Dorey. "The ABCs of R&D at Nortel," *CMA Magazine* (March 1998): 19–23.

Planning and Scheduling Project Costs: Budgeting Process

The overall approach in the budgeting process of a project is to determine how much is to be spent every week or month. This is accomplished as follows:

Four Steps of the Budgeting Process

1. Identify all costs associated with each of the activities. Then add these costs together to get one estimated cost or budget for each activity.

2. If you are dealing with a large project, several activities can be combined into larger work packages. A *work package* is simply a logical collection of activities. Since the General Foundry project we have been discussing is small, one activity will be a work package.

3. Convert the budgeted cost per activity into a cost per time period. To do this, we assume that the cost of completing any activity is spent at a uniform rate over time. Thus, if the budgeted cost for a given activity is $48,000 and the activity's expected time is four weeks, the budgeted cost per week is $12,000 (= $48,000/4 weeks).

4. Using the earliest and latest start times, find out how much money should be spent during each week or month to finish the project by the date desired.

Budgeting for General Foundry Let us apply this budgeting process to the General Foundry problem. The Gantt chart for this problem, shown in Figure 13.9, illustrates this process. In this chart, a horizontal bar shows when each activity will be performed based on the earliest times. To develop a budget schedule, we will determine how much will be spent on each activity during each week and fill these amounts into the chart in place of the bars. Lester Harky has carefully computed the costs associated with each of his eight activities. He has also divided the total budget for each activity by the activity's expected completion time to determine the weekly budget for the activity. The budget for activity A, for example, is $22,000 (see Table 13.5). Since its expected time (t) is 2 weeks, $11,000 is spent each week to complete the activity. Table 13.5 also provides two pieces of data we found earlier using PERT: the earliest start time (ES) and latest start time (LS) for each activity.

Looking at the total of the budgeted activity costs, we see that the entire project will cost $308,000. Finding the weekly budget will help Harky determine how the project is progressing on a week-to-week basis.

FIGURE 13.9

Gantt Chart for General Foundry Example

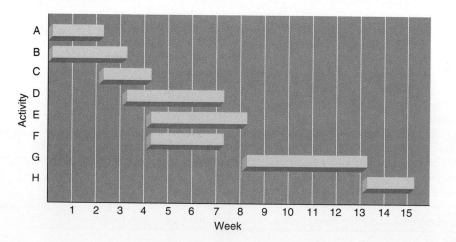

TABLE 13.5   Activity Cost for General Foundry, Inc.

ACTIVITY	EARLIEST START TIME, ES	LATEST START TIME, LS	EXPECTED TIME, t	TOTAL BUDGETED COST ($)	BUDGETED COST PER WEEK ($)
A	0	0	2	22,000	11,000
B	0	1	3	30,000	10,000
C	2	2	2	26,000	13,000
D	3	4	4	48,000	12,000
E	4	4	4	56,000	14,000
F	4	10	3	30,000	10,000
G	8	8	5	80,000	16,000
H	13	13	2	16,000	8,000
				Total 308,000	

A budget is computed using ES.

The weekly budget for the project is developed from the data in Table 13.5. The earliest start time for activity A, for example, is 0. Because A takes 2 weeks to complete, its weekly budget of $11,000 should be spent in weeks 1 and 2. For activity B, the earliest start time is 0, the expected completion time is 3 weeks, and the budgeted cost per week is $10,000. Thus, $10,000 should be spent for activity B in each of weeks 1, 2, and 3. Using the earliest start time, we can find the exact weeks during which the budget for each activity should be spent. These weekly amounts can be summed for all activities to arrive at the weekly budget for the entire project. This is shown in Table 13.6. Notice the similarities between this chart and the Gantt chart shown in Figure 13.9.

Do you see how the weekly budget for the project (total per week) is determined in Table 13.6? The only two activities that can be performed during the first week are activities

TABLE 13.6   Budgeted Cost (Thousands of Dollars) for General Foundry, Inc., Using Earliest Start Times

ACTIVITY	WEEK 1	2	3	4	5	6	7	8	9	10	11	12	13	14	15	TOTAL
A	11	11														22
B	10	10	10													30
C			13	13												26
D				12	12	12	12									48
E					14	14	14	14								56
F					10	10	10									30
G									16	16	16	16	16			80
H														8	8	16
																308
Total per week	21	21	23	25	36	36	36	14	16	16	16	16	16	8	8	
Total to date	21	42	65	90	126	162	198	212	228	244	260	276	292	300	308	

A and *B* because their earliest start times are 0. Thus, during the first week, a total of $21,000 should be spent. Because activities *A* and *B* are still being performed in the second week, a total of $21,000 should also be spent during that period. The earliest start time for activity *C* is at the end of week 2 (ES = 2 for activity *C*). Thus, $13,000 is spent on activity *C* in both weeks 3 and 4. Because activity *B* is also being performed during week 3, the total budget in week 3 is $23,000. Similar computations are done for all activities to determine the total budget for the entire project for each week. Then these weekly totals can be added to determine the total amount that should be spent to date (total to date). This information is displayed in the bottom row of the table.

Another budget is computed using LS.

Those activities along the critical path must spend their budgets at the times shown in Table 13.6. The activities that are *not* on the critical path, however, can be started at a later date. This concept is embodied in the latest starting time, LS, for each activity. Thus, if *latest starting times* are used, another budget can be obtained. This budget will delay the expenditure of funds until the last possible moment. The procedures for computing the budget when LS is used are the same as when ES is used. The results of the new computations are shown in Table 13.7.

Compare the budgets given in Tables 13.6 and 13.7. The amount that should be spent to date (total to date) for the budget in Table 13.7 uses fewer financial resources in the first few weeks. This is because this budget is prepared using the latest start times. Thus the budget in Table 13.7 shows the *latest* possible time that funds can be expended and still finish the project on time. The budget in Table 13.6 reveals the *earliest* possible time that funds can be expended. Therefore, a manager can choose any budget that falls between the budgets presented in these two tables. These two tables form feasible budget ranges. This concept is illustrated in Figure 13.10.

The budget ranges for General Foundry were established by plotting the total-to-date budgets for ES and LS. Lester Harky can use any budget between these feasible ranges and still complete the air pollution project on time. Budgets like the ones shown in Figure 13.10 are normally developed before the project is started. Then, as the project is being completed, funds expended should be monitored and controlled.

Although there are cash flow and money management advantages to delaying activities until their latest start times, such delays can create problems with finishing the project on

TABLE 13.7　Budgeted Cost (Thousands of Dollars) for General Foundry, Inc., Using Latest Start Times

ACTIVITY	1	2	3	4	5	6	7	8	9	10	11	12	13	14	15	TOTAL
A	11	11														22
B		10	10	10												30
C			13	13												26
D					12	12	12	12								48
E					14	14	14	14								56
F											10	10	10			30
G									16	16	16	16	16			80
H														8	8	16
																308
Total per week	11	21	23	23	26	26	26	26	16	16	26	26	26	8	8	
Total to date	11	32	55	78	104	130	156	182	198	214	240	266	292	300	308	

FIGURE 13.10   **Budget Ranges for General Foundry**

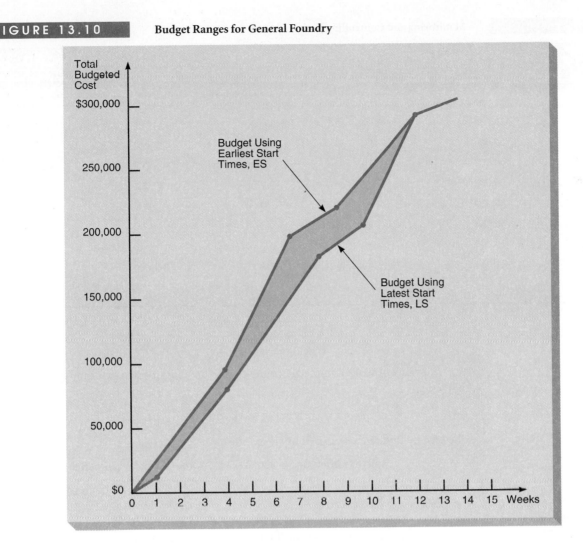

schedule. If an activity is not started until its latest start time, there is no slack remaining. Any subsequent delays in this activity will delay the project. For this reason, it may not be desirable to schedule all activities to start at the latest start time.

Monitoring and Controlling Project Costs

Is the project on schedule and within its budget?

The purpose of monitoring and controlling project costs is to ensure that the project is progressing on schedule and that cost overruns are kept to a minimum. The status of the entire project should be checked periodically.

Lester Harky wants to know how his air pollution project is going. It is now the sixth week of the 15-week project. Activities *A, B,* and *C* have been finished. These activities incurred costs of $20,000, $36,000, and $26,000 respectively. Activity *D* is only 10% completed and so far the cost expended has been $6,000. Activity *E* is 20% completed with an incurred cost of $20,000, and activity *F* is 20% completed with an incurred cost of $4,000. Activities *G* and *H* have not been started. Is the air pollution project on schedule? What is the value of work completed? Are there any cost overruns?

TABLE 13.8			Monitoring and Controlling Budgeted Cost		
ACTIVITY	TOTAL BUDGETED COST ($)	PERCENT OF COMPLETION	VALUE OF WORK COMPLETED ($)	ACTUAL COST ($)	ACTIVITY DIFFERENCE ($)
A	22,000	100	22,000	20,000	−2,000
B	30,000	100	30,000	36,000	6,000
C	26,000	100	26,000	26,000	0
D	48,000	10	4,800	6,000	1,200
E	56,000	20	11,200	20,000	8,800
F	30,000	20	6,000	4,000	−2,000
G	80,000	0	0	0	0
H	16,000	0	0	0	0
Total	100,000			112,000	12,000

Overrun ↗

The value of work completed, or the cost to date for any activity, can be computed as follows:

value of work completed = (percent of work completed) × (total activity budget)   (13-8)

The activity difference is also of interest:

activity difference = actual cost − value of work completed   (13-9)

If an activity difference is negative, there is a cost underrun, but if the number is positive, there has been a cost overrun.

Compute the value of work completed by multiplying budgeted cost times percent of completion.

Table 13.8 provides this information for General Foundry. The second column contains the total budgeted cost (from Table 13.6), and the third column contains the percent of completion. With these data and the actual cost expended for each activity, we can compute the value of work completed and the overruns or underruns for every activity.

One way to measure the value of the work completed is to multiply the total budgeted cost times the percent of completion for every activity.[3] Activity D, for example, has a value of work completed of $4,800 (= $48,000 times 10%). To determine the amount of overrun or underrun for any activity, the value of work completed is subtracted from the actual cost. These differences can be added to determine the overrun or underrun for the project. As you see, at week 6 there is a $12,000 cost overrun. Furthermore, the value of work completed is only $100,000, and the actual cost of the project to date is $112,000. How do these costs compare with the budgeted costs for week 6? If Harky had decided to use the budget for earliest start times (see Table 13.6) we can see that $162,000 should have been spent. Thus the project is behind schedule and there are cost overruns. Harky needs to move faster on this project to finish on time, and he must control future costs carefully to try to eliminate the current cost overrun of $12,000. To monitor and control

---

[3] The percent of completion for each activity can be measured in other ways as well. For example, one might examine the ratio of labor hours expended to total labor hours estimated.

IN ACTION   Project Management and Software Development

Although computers have revolutionized how companies conduct business and allowed some organizations to achieve a long-term competitive advantage in the marketplace, the software that controls these computers is often more expensive than intended and takes longer to develop than expected. In some cases, large software projects are never fully completed. The London Stock Exchange, for example, had an ambitious software project called TAURUS that was intended to improve computer operations at the exchange. The TAURUS project, which cost hundreds of millions of dollars, was never completed. After numerous delays and cost overruns, the project was finally halted. The FLORIDA system, an ambitious software development project for the Department of Health and Rehabilitative Services (HRS) for the state of Florida, was also delayed, cost more than expected, and didn't operate as every-

one had hoped. Although not all software development projects are delayed or over budget, it has been estimated that more than half of all software projects cost more than 189% of their original projections.

To control large software projects, many companies are now using project management techniques. Ryder Systems, Inc., American Express Financial Advisors, and United Airlines have all created project management departments for their software and information systems projects. These departments have the authority to monitor large software projects and make changes to deadlines, budgets, and resources used to complete software development efforts.

Source: Julia King. "Tough Love Reins in IS Projects," *Computerworld* (June 19, 1995): 1–2.

costs, the budgeted amount, the value of work completed, and the actual costs should be computed periodically.

In the next section we see how a project can be shortened by spending additional money. The technique is called the critical path method (CPM).

13.4 CRITICAL PATH METHOD

CPM is deterministic.

As mentioned earlier, CPM is a *deterministic* network model. This means it assumes that both the time to complete each activity and the cost of doing so are known with certainty. Unlike PERT, it does not employ probability concepts. Instead, CPM uses two sets of time and cost estimates for activities: a normal time and cost and a crash time and cost. The *normal time* estimate is like PERT's expected time. The *normal cost* is an estimate of how much money it will take to complete an activity in its normal time. The *crash time* is the shortest possible activity time. *Crash cost* is the price of completing the activity on a crash or deadline basis. The critical path calculations for a CPM network follow the same steps as used in PERT; you just find the early start times (ES), late start times (LS), early finish (EF), late finish (LF), and slack as shown earlier.

Project Crashing with CPM

Shortening a project is called crashing.

Suppose that General Foundry had been given 14 weeks instead of 16 weeks to install the new pollution control equipment or face a court-ordered shutdown. As you recall, the length of Lester Harky's critical path was 15 weeks. What can he do? We see that Harky cannot possibly meet the deadline unless he is able to shorten some of the activity times. This process of shortening a project, called *crashing*, is usually achieved by adding extra resources (such as equipment or people) to an activity. Naturally, crashing costs more money, and managers are usually interested in speeding up a project at the *least additional cost*.

Project crashing with CPM involves four steps:

Four Steps of Project Crashing

1. Find the normal critical path and identify the critical activities.
2. Compute the crash cost per week (or other time period) for all activities in the network. This process uses the following formula[4]:

$$\text{crash cost/time period} = \frac{\text{crash cost} - \text{normal cost}}{\text{normal time} - \text{crash time}} \tag{13-10}$$

3. Select the activity on the critical path with the smallest crash cost per week. Crash this activity to the maximum extent possible or to the point at which your desired deadline has been reached.
4. Check to be sure that the critical path you were crashing is still critical. Often, a reduction in activity time along the critical path causes a noncritical path or paths to become critical. If the critical path is still the longest path through the network, return to step 3. If not, find the new critical path and return to step 3.

General Foundry's normal and crash times and normal and crash costs are shown in Table 13.9. Note, for example, that activity B's normal time is 3 weeks (this estimate was also used for PERT) and its crash time is 1 week. This means that the activity can be shortened by 2 weeks if extra resources are provided. The normal cost is $30,000, and the crash cost is $34,000. This implies that crashing activity B will cost General Foundry an additional $4,000. CPM assumes that crashing costs are linear. As shown in Figure 13.11, activity B's crash cost per week is $2,000. Crash costs for all other activities can be computed in a similar fashion. Then steps 3 and 4 can be applied to reduce the project's completion time.

Activities A, C, and E are on the critical path, and each have a minimum crash cost per week of $1,000. Harky can crash activity A by 1 week to reduce the project completion time to 14 weeks. The cost is an additional $1,000.

There are now two critical paths.

At this stage, there are two critical paths. The original critical path consists of activities A, C, E, G, and H, with a total completion time of 14 weeks. The new critical path consists of activities B, D, G, and H, also with a total completion time of 14 weeks. Any further crashing must be done to both critical paths. For example, if Harky wants to reduce the

---

TABLE 13.9			Normal and Crash Data for General Foundry, Inc.			
	TIME (WEEKS)		**COST ($)**		**CRASH COST PER WEEK ($)**	**CRITICAL PATH?**
ACTIVITY	**NORMAL**	**CRASH**	**NORMAL**	**CRASH**		
A	2	1	22,000	23,000	1,000	Yes
B	3	1	30,000	34,000	2,000	No
C	2	1	26,000	27,000	1,000	Yes
D	4	3	48,000	49,000	1,000	No
E	4	2	56,000	58,000	1,000	Yes
F	3	2	30,000	30,500	500	No
G	5	2	80,000	86,000	2,000	Yes
H	2	1	16,000	19,000	3,000	Yes

---

[4] This formula assumes that crash costs are linear. If they are not, adjustments must be made.

FIGURE 13.11

Crash and Normal Times and Costs for Activity B

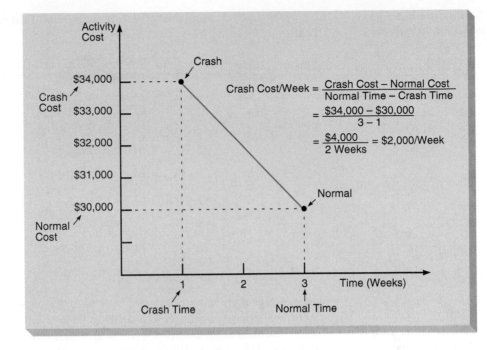

project completion time by an additional 2 weeks, both paths must be reduced. This can be done by reducing activity G, which is on both critical paths, by two weeks for an additional cost of $2,000 per week. The total completion time would be 12 weeks, and total crashing cost would be $5,000 ($1,000 to reduce activity A by one week and $4,000 to reduce activity G by two weeks).

For small networks, such as General Foundry's, it is possible to use the four-step procedure to find the least cost of reducing the project completion dates. For larger networks, however, this approach is difficult and impractical, and more sophisticated techniques, such as linear programming, must be employed.

Project Crashing with Linear Programming

Linear programming (see Chapters 7 to 9) is another approach to finding the best project crashing schedule. We illustrate its use on General Foundry's network. The data needed are derived from Table 13.9 and Figure 13.12.

FIGURE 13.12   **General Foundry's Network with Activity Times**

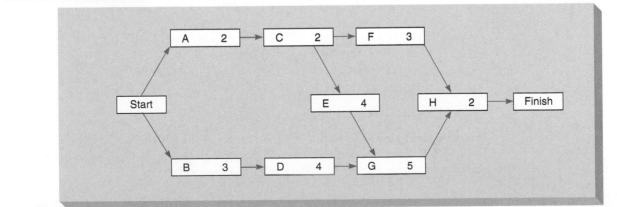

The first step is to define decision variables for the linear program.

We begin by defining the decision variables. If X is the earliest finish time for an activity, then

$$X_A = \text{EF for activity } A$$
$$X_B = \text{EF for activity } B$$
$$X_C = \text{EF for activity } C$$
$$X_D = \text{EF for activity } D$$
$$X_E = \text{EF for activity } E$$
$$X_F = \text{EF for activity } F$$
$$X_G = \text{EF for activity } G$$
$$X_H = \text{EF for activity } H$$
$$X_{\text{start}} = \text{start time for project (usually 0)}$$
$$X_{\text{finish}} = \text{earliest finish time for the project}$$

Although the starting node has a variable (X_{start}) associated with it, this is not necessary since it will be given a value of 0, and this could be used instead of the variable.

Y is defined as the number of weeks that each activity is crashed. Y_A is the number of weeks we decide to crash activity A, Y_B the amount of crash time used for activity B, and so on, up to Y_H.

The next step is to determine the objective function.

Objective Function Since the objective is to minimize the cost of crashing the total project, our LP objective function is

$$\text{minimize crash cost} = 1{,}000Y_A + 2{,}000Y_B + 1{,}000Y_C + 1{,}000Y_D + 1{,}000Y_E$$
$$+ 500Y_F + 2{,}000Y_G + 3{,}000Y_H$$

(These cost coefficients were drawn from the sixth column of Table 13.9.)

Crash constraints are determined next.

Crash Time Constraints Constraints are required to ensure that each activity is not crashed more than its maximum allowable crash time. The maximum for each Y variable is the difference between the normal time and the crash time (from Table 13.9):

$$Y_A \leq 1$$
$$Y_B \leq 2$$
$$Y_C \leq 1$$
$$Y_D \leq 1$$
$$Y_E \leq 2$$
$$Y_F \leq 1$$
$$Y_G \leq 3$$
$$Y_H \leq 1$$

Project Completion Constraint This constraint specifies that the last event must take place before the project deadline date. If Harky's project must be crashed down to 12 weeks, then

$$X_{\text{finish}} \leq 12$$

The final step is to determine event constraints.

Constraints Describing the Network The final set of constraints describes the structure of the network. Every activity will have one constraint for each of its predecessors. The form of these constraints is

$$\text{earliest finish time} \geq \text{earliest finish time for predecessor} + \text{activity time}$$
$$\text{EF} \geq \text{EF}_{predecessor} + (t - Y)$$

or

$$X \geq X_{predecessor} + (t - Y)$$

The activity time is given as $t - Y$, or the normal activity time minus the time saved by crashing. We know $\text{EF} = \text{ES} + \text{activity time}$, and $\text{ES} = \text{largest EF of predecessors}$.

We begin by setting the start of the project to time zero: $X_{start} = 0$.

For activity A,

$$X_A \geq X_{start} + (2 - Y_A)$$

or

$$X_A - X_{start} + Y_A \geq 2$$

For activity B,

$$X_B \geq X_{start} + (3 - Y_B)$$

or

$$X_B - X_{start} + Y_B \geq 3$$

For activity C,

$$X_C \geq X_A + (2 - Y_C)$$

or

$$X_C - X_A + Y_C \geq 2$$

For activity D,

$$X_D \geq X_B + (4 - Y_D)$$

or

$$X_D - X_B + Y_D \geq 4$$

For activity E,

$$X_E \geq X_C + (4 - Y_E)$$

or

$$X_E - X_C + Y_E \geq 4$$

For activity F,

$$X_F \geq X_C + (3 - Y_F)$$

or

$$X_F - X_C + Y_F \geq 3$$

For activity G, we need two constraints since there are two predecessors. The first constraint for activity G is

$$X_G \geq X_D + (5 - Y_G)$$

or

$$X_G - X_D + Y_G \geq 5$$

The second constraint for activity G is

$$X_G \geq X_E + (5 - Y_G)$$

or

$$X_G - X_E + Y_G \geq 5$$

PROGRAM 13.1   **Solution to Crashing Problem Using Solver in Excel**

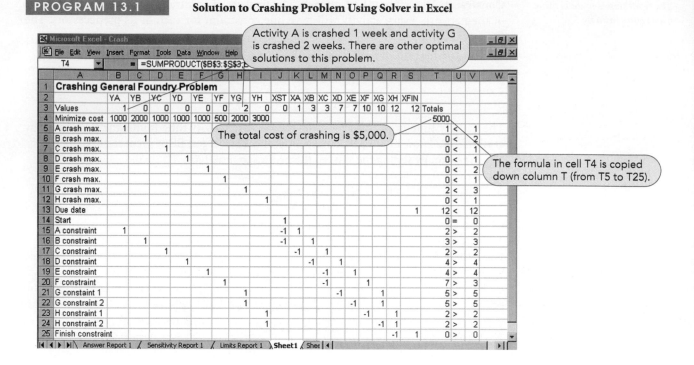

> Activity A is crashed 1 week and activity G is crashed 2 weeks. There are other optimal solutions to this problem.

> The total cost of crashing is $5,000.

> The formula in cell T4 is copied down column T (from T5 to T25).

For activity H we need two constraints since there are two predecessors. The first constraint for activity H is

$$X_H \geq X_F + (2 - Y_H)$$

or

$$X_H - X_F + Y_H \geq 2$$

The second constraint for activity H is

$$X_H \geq X_G + (2 - Y_H)$$

or

$$X_H - X_G + Y_H \geq 2$$

To indicate the project is finished when activity H is finished, we have

$$X_{\text{finish}} \geq X_H$$

After adding nonnegativity constraints, this LP problem can be solved for the optimal Y values. This can be done with QM for Windows or Excel. Program 13.1 provides the Excel solution to this problem.

13.5   OTHER TOPICS IN PROJECT MANAGEMENT

We have seen how to schedule a project and develop budget schedules. However, there are other things that are important and helpful to a project manager. We now briefly introduce these to you.

Subprojects

For extremely large projects, an activity may be made of several smaller subactivities. Each activity might be viewed as a smaller project or a subproject of the original project. The person in charge of the activity might wish to create a PERT/CPM chart for managing this subproject. Many software packages have the ability to include several levels of subprojects.

Milestones

Major events in a project are often referred to as *milestones*. These are often reflected in *Gantt charts* and PERT charts to highlight the importance of reaching these events.

Resource Leveling

In addition to managing the time and costs involved in a project, a manager must also be concerned with the resources used in a project. These resources might be equipment or people. In planning a project (and often as part of the work breakdown structure), a manager must identify which resources are needed with each activity. For example, in a construction project there may be several activities requiring the use of heavy equipment such as a crane. If the construction company has only one such crane, then conflicts will occur if two activities requiring the use of this crane are scheduled for the same day. To alleviate problems such as this, *resource leveling* is employed. This means that one or more activities are moved from the earliest start time to another time (no later than the latest start time) so that the resource utilization is more evenly distributed over time. If the resources are construction crews, this is very beneficial in that the crews are kept busy and overtime is minimized.

Software

There are numerous project management software packages on the market for both mainframe computers and personal computers. Some of these are Microsoft Project®, Harvard Project Manager, MacProject, Timeline, Primavera Project Planner, Artemis, and Open Plan. Most of this software will draw PERT charts as well as *Gantt charts*. They can be used to develop budget schedules, automatically adjust future start times based on the actual start times for prior activities, and level the resource utilization.

Good software for personal computers ranges in price from a few hundred dollars to several thousand dollars. For mainframe computers, software may cost considerably more. Companies have paid several hundred thousand dollars for project management software and support because it helps management make better decisions and keep track of things that would otherwise be unmanageable.

SUMMARY

The fundamentals of PERT and CPM are presented in this chapter. Both of these techniques are excellent for controlling large and complex projects.

PERT is probabilistic and allows three time estimates for each activity. These estimates are used to compute the project's expected completion time, variance, and the probability that the project will be completed by a given date. PERT/Cost, an extension of standard PERT, can be used to plan, schedule, monitor, and control project costs.

Using PERT/Cost, it is possible to determine if there are cost overruns or underruns at any point in time. It is also possible to determine whether the project is on schedule.

CPM, although similar to PERT, has the ability to crash projects by reducing their completion time through additional resource expenditures. Finally, we see that linear programming can also be used to crash a network by a desired amount at a minimum cost.

GLOSSARY

Activity. A time-consuming job or task that is a key subpart of the total project.

Activity-on-Arc (AOA). A network in which the activities are represented by arcs.

Activity-on-Node (AON). A network in which the activities are represented by nodes. This is the model illustrated in our book.

Activity Time Estimates. Three time estimates that are used in determining the expected completion time and variance for an activity in a PERT network.

Backward Pass. A procedure that moves from the end of the network to the beginning of the network. It is used in determining the latest finish and start times.

Beta Probability Distribution. A probability distribution that is often used in computing the expected activity completion times and variances in networks.

CPM. Critical path method. A deterministic network technique that is similar to PERT but allows for project crashing.

Crashing. The process of reducing the total time that it takes to complete a project by expending additional funds.

Critical Path. The series of activities that have zero slack. It is the longest time path through the network. A delay for any activity that is on the critical path will delay the completion of the entire project.

Critical Path Analysis. An analysis that determines the total project completion time, the critical path for the project, slack, ES, EF, LS, and LF for every activity.

Earliest Finish Time (EF). The earliest time that an activity can be finished without violation of precedence requirements.

Earliest Start Time (ES). The earliest time that an activity can start without violation of precedence requirements.

Event A point in time that marks the beginning or ending of an activity.

Expected Activity Time. The average time that it should take to complete an activity. $t = (a + 4m + b)/6$.

Forward Pass. A procedure that moves from the beginning of a network to the end of the network. It is used in determining earliest activity start times and earliest finish times.

Gantt Chart. A bar chart indicating when the activities (represented by bars) in a project will be performed.

Immediate Predecessor. An activity that must be completed before another activity can be started.

Latest Finish Time (LF). The latest time that an activity can be finished without delaying the entire project.

Latest Start Time (LS). The latest time that an activity can be started without delaying the entire project.

Milestone A major event in a project.

Most Likely Time (m). The amount of time that you would expect it would take to complete the activity.

Network A graphical display of a project that contains both activities and events.

Optimistic Time (a). The shortest amount of time that could be required to complete the activity.

PERT Program evaluation and review technique. A network technique that allows three time estimates for each activity in a project.

PERT/Cost. A technique that allows a decision maker to plan, schedule, monitor, and control project *cost* as well as project time.

Pessimistic Time (b). The greatest amount of time that could be required to complete the activity.

Resource Leveling The process of smoothing out the utilization of resources in a project.

Slack Time. The amount of time that an activity can be delayed without delaying the entire project. Slack is equal to the latest start time minus the earliest start time, or the latest finish time minus the earliest finish time.

Variance of Activity Completion Time A measure of dispersion of the activity completion time. Variance $= [(b - a)/6]^2$.

Work Breakdown Structure (WBS). A list of the activities that must be performed in a project.

KEY EQUATIONS

(13-1) $t = \dfrac{a + 4m + b}{6}$

Expected activity completion time for activity.

(13-2) $\text{Variance} = \left(\dfrac{b - a}{6}\right)^2$

Activity variance.

(13-3) $\text{EF} = \text{ES} + t$

Earliest finish time.

(13-4) $\text{LS} = \text{LF} - t$

Latest start time.

(13-5) $\text{Slack} = \text{LS} - \text{ES}$ *or* $\text{slack} = \text{LF} - \text{EF}$

Slack time in an activity.

(13-6) Project variance = $\sum$ variances of activities on critical path.

(13-7) $Z = \dfrac{\text{due date} - \text{expected date of completion}}{\sigma_T}$

Number of standard deviations the target date lies from the expected date, using the normal distribution.

(13-8) Value of work completed = (percent of work completed) × (total activity budget)

(13-9) Activity difference = actual cost − value of work completed

(13-10) crash cost/time period = $\dfrac{\text{crash cost} - \text{normal cost}}{\text{normal time} - \text{crash time}}$

The cost in CPM of reducing an activity's length per time period.

SOLVED PROBLEMS

Solved Problem 13-1

To complete the wing assembly for an experimental aircraft, Scott DeWitte has laid out the major steps and seven activities involved. These activities have been labeled *A* through *G* in the following table, which also shows their estimated completion times (in weeks) and immediate predecessors. Determine the expected time and variance for each activity.

ACTIVITY	a	m	b	IMMEDIATE PREDECESSORS
A	1	2	3	—
B	2	3	4	—
C	4	5	6	A
D	8	9	10	B
E	2	5	8	C, D
F	4	5	6	B
G	1	2	3	E

Solution

Although not required for this problem, a diagram of all the activities can be useful. A PERT diagram for the wing assembly is shown in Figure 13.13.

 **FIGURE 13.13** **PERT Diagram for Scott DeWitte (Solved Problem 13-1)**

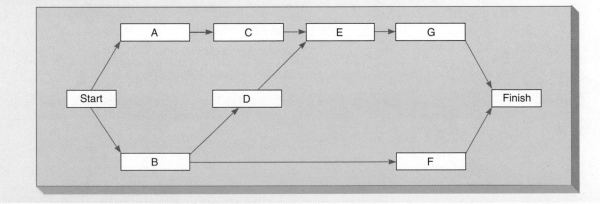

Expected times and variances can be computed using the formulas presented in the chapter. The results are summarized in the following table:

ACTIVITY	EXPECTED TIME (IN WEEKS)	VARIANCE
A	2	$\frac{1}{9}$
B	3	$\frac{1}{9}$
C	5	$\frac{1}{9}$
D	9	$\frac{1}{9}$
E	5	1
F	5	$\frac{1}{9}$
G	2	$\frac{1}{9}$

Solved Problem 13-2

Referring to Solved Problem 13-1, now Scott would like to determine the critical path for the entire wing assembly project as well as the expected completion time for the total project. In addition, he would like to determine the earliest and latest start and finish times for all activities.

Solution

The critical path, earliest start times, earliest finish times, latest start times, and latest finish times can be determined using the procedures outlined in the chapter. The results are summarized in the following table:

ACTIVITY	ACTIVITY TIME				SLACK
	ES	EF	LS	LF	
A	0	2	5	7	5
B	0	3	0	3	0
C	2	7	7	12	5
D	3	12	3	12	0
E	12	17	12	17	0
F	3	8	14	19	11
G	17	19	17	19	0

Expected project length = 19 weeks

Variance of the critical path = 1.333

Standard deviation of the critical path = 1.155 weeks

The activities along the critical path are B, D, E, and G. These activities have zero slack, as shown in the table. The expected project completion time is 19. The earliest and latest start and finish times are shown in the table.

SELF-TEST

- Before taking the self-test, refer back to the learning objectives at the beginning of the chapter, the notes in the margins, and the glossary at the end of the chapter.
- Use the key at the back of the book to correct your answers.
- Restudy pages that correspond to any questions that you answered incorrectly or material you feel uncertain about.

1. Network models such as PERT and CPM are used to
   a. plan large and complex projects.
   b. schedule large and complex projects.
   c. monitor large and complex projects.
   d. control large and complex projects.
   e. all of the above.
2. The primary difference between PERT and CPM is that
   a. PERT uses one time estimate.
   b. CPM has three time estimates.
   c. PERT has three time estimates.
   d. with CPM, it is assumed that all activities can be performed at the same time.
3. The earliest start time for an activity is equal to
   a. the largest EF of the immediate predecessors.
   b. the smallest EF of the immediate predecessors.
   c. the largest ES of the immediate predecessors.
   d. the smallest ES of the immediate predecessors.
4. The latest finish time for an activity is found during the backward pass through the network. The latest finish time is equal to
   a. the largest LF of the activities for which it is an immediate predecessor.
   b. the smallest LF of the activities for which it is an immediate predecessor.
   c. the largest LS of the activities for which it is an immediate predecessor.
   d. the smallest LS of the activities for which it is an immediate predecessor.
5. When PERT is used and probabilities are found, one of the assumptions that is made is that
   a. all activities are on the critical path.
   b. activity times are independent.
   c. all activities have the same variance.
   d. the project variance is equal to the sum of the variances of all activities in the project.
   e. all of the above.
6. In PERT, the time estimate b represents
   a. the most optimistic time.
   b. the most likely time.
   c. the most pessimistic time.
   d. the expected time.
   e. none of the above.
7. In PERT, slack time equals
   a. $ES + t$.
   b. $LS - ES$.
   c. 0.
   d. $EF - ES$.
   e. none of the above.

8. The standard deviation for the PERT project is approximately
   a. the square root of the sum of the variances along the critical path.
   b. the sum of the critical path activity standard deviations.
   c. the square root of the sum of the variances of the project activities.
   d. all of the above.
   e. none of the above.
9. The critical path is the
   a. shortest path in a network.
   b. longest path in a network.
   c. path with the smallest variance.
   d. path with the largest variance.
   e. none of the above.
10. If the project completion time is normally distributed and the due date for the project is greater than the expected completion time, then the probability that the project will be finished by the due date is
    a. less than 0.50.
    b. greater than 0.50.
    c. equal to 0.50.
    d. undeterminable without more information.
11. If activity A is on the critical path, then the slack for A will equal
    a. $LF - EF$.
    b. $LS - ES$.
    c. 0.
    d. all of the above.
12. If a project is to be crashed at the minimum possible additional cost, then the first activity to be crashed must be
    a. on the critical path.
    b. the one with the shortest activity time.
    c. the one with the longest activity time.
    d. the one with the lowest cost.
13. _____ activities are ones that will delay the entire project if they are late or delayed.
14. PERT stands for _____.
15. Project crashing can be performed using a _____.
16. PERT can use three estimates for activity time. These three estimates are _____, _____, and _____.
17. The latest start time minus the earliest start time is called the _____ time for any activity.
18. The percent of project completion, value of work completed, and actual activity costs are used to _____ projects.

DISCUSSION QUESTIONS AND PROBLEMS

Discussion Questions

13-1 What are some of the questions that can be answered with PERT and CPM?

13-2 What are the major differences between PERT and CPM?

13-3 What is an activity? What is an event? What is an immediate predecessor?

13-4 Describe how expected activity times and variances can be computed in a PERT network.

13-5 Briefly discuss what is meant by critical path analysis. What are critical path activities, and why are they important?

13-6 What are the earliest activity start time and latest activity start time? How are they computed?

13-7 Describe the meaning of slack and discuss how it can be determined.

13-8 How can we determine the probability that a project will be completed by a certain date? What assumptions are made in this computation?

13-9 Briefly describe PERT/Cost and how it is used.

13-10 What is crashing, and how is it done by hand?

13-11 Why is linear programming useful in CPM crashing?

Problems*

‡ 13-12 Sid Davidson is the personnel director of Babson and Willcount, a company that specializes in consulting and research. One of the training programs that Sid is considering for the middle-level managers of Babson and Willcount is leadership training. Sid has listed a number of activities that must be completed before a training program of this nature could be conducted. The activities and immediate predecessors appear in the following table:

ACTIVITY	IMMEDIATE PREDECESSORS
A	—
B	—
C	—
D	B
E	A, D
F	C
G	E, F

Develop a network for this problem.

Ǫ • 13-13 Sid Davidson was able to determine the activity times for the leadership training program. He would like to determine the total project completion time and the

critical path. The activity times appear in the following table (see Problem 13-12):

ACTIVITY	TIME (DAYS)
A	2
B	5
C	1
D	10
E	3
F	6
G	8
	35

• 13-14 Jean Walker is making plans for spring break at the beaches in Florida. In applying techniques she learned in her quantitative methods class, she has identified the activities that are necessary to prepare for her trip. The following table lists the activities and the immediate predecessors. Draw the network for this project.

ACTIVITY	IMMEDIATE PREDECESSOR
A	—
B	—
C	A
D	B
E	C, D
F	A
G	E, F

Ǫ ‡ 13-15 The following are the activity times for the project in Problem 13-14. Find the earliest, latest, and slack times for each activity. Then find the critical path.

ACTIVITY	TIME (DAYS)
A	3
B	7
C	4
D	2
E	5
F	6
G	3

---

* Note: Ǫ means the problem may be solved with QM for Windows; ✗ means the problem may be solved with Excel; and Ǫ̲ₓ means the problem may be solved with QM for Windows and/or Excel.

• **13-16** Monohan Machinery specializes in developing weed-harvesting equipment that is used to clear small lakes of weeds. George Monohan, president of Monohan Machinery, is convinced that harvesting weeds is far better than using chemicals to kill weeds. Chemicals cause pollution, and the weeds seem to grow faster after chemicals have been used. George is contemplating the construction of a machine that would harvest weeds on narrow rivers and waterways. The activities that are necessary to build one of these experimental weed-harvesting machines are listed in the following table. Construct a network for these activities.

ACTIVITIES	IMMEDIATE PREDECESSORS
A	—
B	—
C	A
D	A
E	B
F	B
G	C, E
H	D, F

13-17 After consulting with Butch Radner, George Monohan was able to determine the activity times for constructing the weed-harvesting machine to be used on narrow rivers. George would like to determine ES, EF, LS, LF, and slack for each activity. The total project completion time and the critical path should also be determined. (See Problem 13-16 for details.) The activity times are shown in the following table:

ACTIVITY	TIME (WEEKS)
A	6
B	5
C	3
D	2
E	4
F	6
G	10
H	7

13-18 A project was planned using PERT with three time estimates. The expected completion time of the project was determined to be 40 weeks. The variance of the critical path is 9.

(a) What is the probability that the project will be finished in 40 weeks or less?

(b) What is the probability that the project takes longer than 40 weeks?

(c) What is the probability that the project will be finished in 46 weeks or less?

(d) What is the probability that the project will take longer than 46 weeks?

(e) The project manager wishes to set the due date for the completion of the project so that there is a 90% chance of finishing on schedule. Thus, there would only be a 10% chance the project would take longer than this due date. What should this due date be?

13-19 Tom Schriber, a director of personnel of Management Resources, Inc., is in the process of designing a program that its customers can use in the job-finding process. Some of the activities include preparing resumés, writing letters, making appointments to see prospective employers, researching companies and industries, and so on. Some of the information on the activities is shown in the following table:

ACTIVITY	DAYS a	DAYS m	DAYS b	IMMEDIATE PREDECESSORS
A	8	10	12	—
B	6	7	9	—
C	3	3	4	—
D	10	20	30	A
E	6	7	8	C
F	9	10	11	B, D, E
G	6	7	10	B, D, E
H	14	15	16	F
I	10	11	13	F
J	6	7	8	G, H
K	4	7	8	I, J
L	1	2	4	G, H

(a) Construct a network for this problem.

(b) Determine the expected time and variance for each activity.

(c) Determine ES, EF, LS, LF, and slack for each activity.

(d) Determine the critical path and project completion time.

(e) Determine the probability that the project will be finished in 70 days or less.

(f) Determine the probability that the project will be finished in 80 days or less.

(g) Determine the probability that the project will be finished in 90 days or less.

13-20 Using PERT, Ed Rose was able to determine that the expected project completion time for the construction of a pleasure yacht is 21 months and the project variance is 4.

(a) What is the probability that the project will be completed in 17 months or less?

(b) What is the probability that the project will be completed in 20 months or less?

(c) What is the probability that the project will be completed in 23 months or less?

(d) What is the probability that the project will be completed in 25 months or less?

: 13-21 The air pollution project discussed in the chapter has progressed over the past several weeks, and it is now the end of week 8. Lester Harky would like to know the value of the work completed, the amount of any cost overruns or underruns for the project, and the extent to which the project is ahead of or behind schedule by developing a table like Table 13.8 on page 544. The revised cost figures are shown in the following table:

ACTIVITY	PERCENT OF COMPLETION	ACTUAL COST ($)
A	100	20,000
B	100	36,000
C	100	26,000
D	100	44,000
E	50	25,000
F	60	15,000
G	10	5,000
H	10	1,000

: 13-22 Fred Ridgeway has been given the responsibility of managing a training and development program. He knows the earliest start time, the latest start time, and the total costs for each activity. This information is given in the following table:

ACTIVITY	ES	LS	t	TOTAL COST ($1,000s)
A	0	0	6	10
B	1	4	2	14
C	3	3	7	5
D	4	9	3	6
E	6	6	10	14
F	14	15	11	13
G	12	18	2	4
H	14	14	11	6
I	18	21	6	18
J	18	19	4	12
K	22	22	14	10
L	22	23	8	16
M	18	24	6	18

(a) Using earliest start times, determine Fred's total monthly budget.

(b) Using latest start times, determine Fred's total monthly budget.

: 13-23 General Foundry's project crashing data are shown in Table 13.9 on page 546. Crash this project to 13 weeks using CPM. What are the final times for each activity after crashing?

: 13-24 Bowman Builders manufactures steel storage sheds for commercial use. Joe Bowman, president of Bowman Builders, is contemplating producing sheds for home use. The activities necessary to build an experimental model and related data are given in the accompanying table.

(a) What is the project completion date?

(b) Formulate an LP problem to crash this project to 10 weeks.

ACTIVITY	NORMAL TIME	CRASH TIME	NORMAL COST ($)	CRASH COST ($)	IMMEDIATE PREDECESSORS
A	3	2	1,000	1,600	—
B	2	1	2,000	2,700	—
C	1	1	300	300	—
D	7	3	1,300	1,600	A
E	6	3	850	1,000	B
F	2	1	4,000	5,000	C
G	4	2	1,500	2,000	D, E

: 13-25 The Bender Construction Co. is involved in constructing municipal buildings and other structures that are used primarily by city and state municipalities. This requires developing legal documents, drafting feasibility studies, obtaining bond ratings, and so forth. Recently, Bender was given a request to submit a proposal for the construction of a municipal building. The first step is to develop legal documents and to perform all steps necessary before the construction contract is signed. This requires more than 20 separate activities that must be completed. These activities, their immediate predecessors, and time requirements are given in Table 13.10 on the next page.

As you can see, optimistic (a), most likely (m), and pessimistic (b) time estimates have been given for all of the activities described in the table. Using the data, determine the total project completion time for this preliminary step, the critical path, and slack time for all activities involved.

: 13-26 Getting a degree from a college or university can be a long and difficult task. Certain courses must be completed before other courses may be taken.

TABLE 13.10				Data for Problem 13-25, Bender Construction Company	
	TIME REQUIRED (WEEKS)				
ACTIVITY	a	m	b	DESCRIPTION OF ACTIVITY	IMMEDIATE PREDECESSORS
1	1	4	5	Draft of legal documents	—
2	2	3	4	Preparation of financial statements	—
3	3	4	5	Draft of history	—
4	7	8	9	Draft demand portion of feasibility study	—
5	4	4	5	Review and approval of legal documents	1
6	1	2	4	Review and approval of history	3
7	4	5	6	Review of feasibility study	4
8	1	2	4	Draft final financial portion of feasibility study	7
9	3	4	4	Draft facts relevant to the bond transaction	5
10	1	1	2	Review and approval of financial statements	2
11	18	20	26	Receive firm price of project	—
12	1	2	3	Review and completion of financial portion of feasibility study	8
13	1	1	2	Completion of draft statement	6, 9, 10, 11, 12
14	.10	.14	.16	All material sent to bond rating services	13
15	.2	.3	.4	Statement printed and distributed to all interested parties	14
16	1	1	2	Presentation to bond rating services	14
17	1	2	3	Bond rating received	16
18	3	5	7	Marketing of bonds	15, 17
19	.1	.1	.2	Purchase contract executed	18
20	.1	.14	.16	Final statement authorized and completed	19
21	2	3	6	Purchase contract	19
22	.1	.1	.2	Bond proceeds available	20
23	0	.2	.2	Sign construction contract	21, 22

Develop a network diagram, in which every activity is a particular course that must be taken for a given degree program. The immediate predecessors will be course prerequisites. Don't forget to include all university, college, and departmental course requirements. Then try to group these courses into semesters or quarters for your particular school. How long do you think it will take you to graduate? Which courses, if not taken in the proper sequence, could delay your graduation?

13-27 Dream Team Productions was in the final design phases of its new film, *Killer Worms*, to be released next summer. Market Wise, the firm hired to coordinate the release of *Killer Worm* toys, identified 16 critical tasks (see page 560) to be completed before the release of the film.

(a) How many weeks in advance of the film release should Market Wise start its marketing campaign? What are the critical path activities? The tasks are as follows:

ACTIVITY	IMMEDIATE PREDECESSOR	OPTIMISTIC TIME	MOST LIKELY TIME	PESSIMISTIC TIME
Task 1	—	1	2	4
Task 2	—	3	3.5	4
Task 3	—	10	12	13
Task 4	—	4	5	7
Task 5	—	2	4	5
Task 6	Task 1	6	7	8
Task 7	Task 2	2	4	5.5
Task 8	Task 3	5	7.7	9
Task 9	Task 3	9.9	10	12
Task 10	Task 3	2	4	5
Task 11	Task 4	2	4	6
Task 12	Task 5	2	4	6
Task 13	Tasks 6, 7, 8	5	6	6.5
Task 14	Tasks 10, 11, 12	1	1.1	2
Task 15	Tasks 9, 13	5	7	8
Task 16	Task 14	5	7	9

(b) If Tasks 9 and 10 were not necessary, what impact would this have on the critical path and the number of weeks needed to complete the marketing campaign?

 13-28 The estimated times (in weeks) and immediate predecessors for the activities in a project are given in the following table. Assume that the activity times are independent.

ACTIVITY	IMMEDIATE PREDECESSOR	a	m	b
A	—	9	10	11
B	—	4	10	16
C	A	9	10	11
D	B	5	8	11

(a) Calculate the expected time and variance for each activity.
(b) What is the expected completion time of the critical path? What is the expected completion time of the other path in the network?
(c) What is the variance of the critical path? What is the variance of the other path in the network?
(d) If the time to complete path A–C is normally distributed, what is the probability that this path will be finished in 22 weeks or less?
(e) If the time to complete path B–D is normally distributed, what is the probability that this path will be finished in 22 weeks or less?
(f) Explain why the probability that the critical path will be finished in 22 weeks or less is not necessarily the probability that the project will be finished in 22 weeks or less.

13-29 The following costs have been estimated for the activities in a project.

ACTIVITY	IMMEDIATE PREDECESSORS	TIME	COST ($)
A	—	8	8,000
B	—	4	12,000
C	A	3	6,000
D	B	5	15,000
E	C, D	6	9,000
F	C, D	5	10,000
G	F	3	6,000

(a) Develop a cost schedule based on earliest start times.
(b) Develop a cost schedule based on latest start times.
(c) Suppose that it has been determined that the $6,000 for activity G is not evenly spread over the three weeks. Instead, the cost for the first week is $4,000, and the cost is $1,000 per week for each of the last two weeks. Modify the cost schedule based on earliest start times to reflect this situation.

INTERNET HOMEWORK PROBLEMS

See our Internet home page at **www.prenhall.com/render** for additional homework problems 13-30 to 13-37.

CASE STUDY

Southwestern University Stadium Construction

After six months of study, much political arm wrestling, and some serious financial analysis, Dr. Martin Starr, president of Southwestern University, had reached a decision. To the delight of its students, and to the disappointment of its athletic boosters, SWU would not be relocating to a new football site but would expand the capacity at its on-campus stadium.

Adding 21,000 seats, including dozens of luxury skyboxes, would not please everyone. The influential football coach, Bo Pitterno, had long argued the need for a first-class stadium, one with built-in dormitory rooms for his players and a palatial office appropriate for the coach of a future NCAA champion team. But the decision was made, and *everyone*, including the coach, would learn to live with it.

The job now was to get construction going immediately after the 2002 season ended. This would allow exactly 270 days until the 2003 season opening game. The contractor, Hill Construction (Bob Hill being an alumnus, of course), signed the contract. Bob Hill looked at the tasks his engineers had outlined and looked President Starr in the eye. "I guarantee the team will be able to take the field

on schedule next year," he said with a sense of confidence. "I sure hope so," replied Starr. "The contract penalty of $10,000 per day for running late is nothing compared to what Coach Pitterno will do to you if our opening game with Penn State is delayed or cancelled." Hill, sweating slightly, did not respond. In football-crazy Texas, Hill Construction would be *mud* if the 270-day target were missed.

Back in his office, Hill again reviewed the data. (See Table 13.11 and note that optimistic time estimates can be used as crash times.) He then gathered his foremen. "People, if we're not 75% sure we'll finish this stadium in less than 270 days, I want this project crashed! Give me the cost figures for a target date of 250 days—also for 240 days. I want to be *early*, not just on time!"

Discussion Questions

1. Develop a network drawing for Hill Construction and determine the critical path. How long is the project expected to take?
2. What is the probability of finishing in 270 days?
3. If it were necessary to crash to 250 or 240 days, how would Hill do so, and at what costs? As noted in the case, assume that optimistic time estimates can be used as crash times.

TABLE 13.11   **Southwestern University Stadium Project**

| | | | TIME ESTIMATES (DAYS) | | | |
ACTIVITY	DESCRIPTION	PREDECESSORS	OPTIMISTIC	MOST LIKELY	PESSIMISTIC	CRASH COST/DAY
A	Bonding, insurance, tax structuring	—	20	30	40	$1,500
B	Foundation, concrete footings for boxes	A	20	65	80	$3,500
C	Upgrading skyboxes, stadium seating	A	50	60	100	$4,000
D	Upgrading walkways, stairwells, elevators	C	30	50	100	$1,900
E	Interior wiring, lathes	B	25	30	35	$9,500
F	Inspection approvals	E	1	1	1	0
G	Plumbing	D, E	25	30	35	$2,500
H	Painting	G	10	20	30	$2,000
I	Hardware/air conditioning/metal workings	H	20	25	60	$2,000
J	Tile/carpeting/windows	H	8	10	12	$6,000
K	Inspection	J	1	1	1	0
L	Final detail work/cleanup	I, K	20	25	60	$4,500

Source: Adapted from J. Heizer and B. Render. *Operations Management*, 6/e. Upper Saddle River, NJ: Prentice Hall, 2000: 693–694.

⇒ CASE STUDY

Family Planning Research Center of Nigeria

Dr. Adinombe Watage, deputy director of the Family Planning Research Center in Nigeria's Over-the-River Province, was assigned the task of organizing and training five teams of field workers to perform educational and outreach activities as part of a large project to demonstrate acceptance of a new method of birth control. These workers already had training in family planning education but must receive specific training regarding the new method of contraception. Two types of materials must also be prepared: (1) those for use in training the workers, and (2) those for distribution in the field. Training faculty must be brought in and arrangements made for transportation and accommodations for the participants.

Dr. Watage first called a meeting of his office staff. Together they identified the activities that must be carried out, their necessary sequences, and the time that they would require. Their results are displayed in Table 13.12.

Louis Odaga, the chief clerk, noted that the project had to be completed in 60 days. Whipping out his solar-powered calculator, he added up the time needed. It came to 94 days. "An impossible task, then," he noted. "No," Dr. Watage replied, "some of these tasks can go forward in parallel." "Be careful, though," warned Mr. Oglagadu, the chief nurse, "there aren't that many of us to go around. There are only 10 of us in this office."

"I can check whether we have enough heads and hands once I have tentatively scheduled the activities," Dr. Watage responded. "If the schedule is too tight, I have permission from the Pathminder Fund to spend some funds to speed it up, just so long as I can prove that it can be done at the least cost necessary. Can you help me prove that? Here are the costs for the activities with the elapsed time that we planned and the costs and times if we shorten them to an absolute minimum." Those data are given in Table 13.13.

Discussion Questions

1. Some of the tasks in this project can be done in parallel. Prepare a diagram showing the required network of tasks and define the critical path. What is the length of the project without crashing?
2. At this point, can the project be done given the personnel constraint of 10 persons?
3. If the critical path is longer than 60 days, what is the least amount that Dr. Watage can spend and still achieve this schedule objective? How can he prove to Pathminder Foundation that this is the minimum-cost alternative?

Source: Professor Curtis P. McLaughlin, Kenan-Flagler Business School, University of North Carolina at Chapel Hill.

TABLE 13.12   Family Planning Research Center Activities

ACTIVITY	MUST FOLLOW	TIME (DAYS)	STAFFING NEEDED
A. Identify faculty and their schedules	—	5	2
B. Arrange transport to base	—	7	3
C. Identify and collect training materials	—	5	2
D. Arrange accommodations	A	3	1
E. Identify team	A	7	4
F. Bring in team	B, E	2	1
G. Transport faculty to base	A, B	3	2
H. Print program material	C	10	6
I. Have program materials delivered	H	7	3
J. Conduct training program	D, F, G, I	15	0
K. Perform fieldwork training	J	30	0

TABLE 13.13	Family Planning Research Center Costs				
	NORMAL		MINIMUM		AVERAGE COST
ACTIVITY	TIME	COST ($)	TIME	COST ($)	PER DAY SAVED ($)
A. Identify faculty	5	400	2	700	100
B. Arrange transport	7	1,000	4	1,450	150
C. Identify materials	5	400	3	500	50
D. Make accommodations	3	2,500	1	3,000	250
E. Identify team	7	400	4	850	150
F. Bring team in	2	1,000	1	2,000	1,000
G. Transport faculty	3	1,500	2	2,000	500
H. Print materials	10	3,000	5	4,000	200
I. Deliver materials	7	200	2	600	80
J. Train team	15	5,000	10	7,000	400
K. Do fieldwork	30	10,000	20	14,000	400

INTERNET CASE STUDIES

See our Internet home page at **www.prenhall.com/render** for these additional case studies:

(1) Alpha Beta Gamma Record. This case involves publishing a monthly magazine for a fraternity.

(2) Bay Community Hospital. This case involves the acquisition and installation of equipment to be used in a new medical procedure.

(3) Cranston Construction Company. This case involves the construction of a new building at a university.

(4) Haygood Brothers Construction Company. This case involves planning the construction of a house.

(5) Shale Oil Company. This case involves planning the shutdown of a petrochemical plant for routine maintenance.

BIBLIOGRAPHY

Charoenngam, Chotchai et al. "Cost/Schedule Information System," *Cost Engineering* (September 1997): 29–36.

Dorey, Chris. "The ABCs of R&D at Nortel," *CMA Magazine* (March 1998): 19–23.

Graham, Robert et al. "Creating an Environment for Successful Projects," *Research Technology Management* (February 1998): 60–65.

Jorgensen, Trond and Stein W. Wallace. "Improving Project Cost Estimation by Taking into Account Managerial Flexibility," *European Journal of Operational Research* 127, 2 (2000): 239–251.

Kolisch, Rainer. "Resource Allocation Capabilities of Commercial Project Management Software Packages," *Interfaces* 29, 4 (July–August, 1999): 19–31.

Mantel, Samuel J., Jack R. Meredith, Scott M. Shafer, and Margaret M. Sutton. *Project Management in Practice.* New York: John Wiley & Sons, Inc., 2001.

Premachandra, I. M. "An Approximation of the Activity Duration Distribution in PERT," *Computers and Operations Research*, 28, 5 (April 2001): 443–452.

Roe, Justin. "Bringing Discipline to Project Management," *Harvard Business Review* (April 1998): 153–160.

Sander, Wayne. "The Project Manager's Guide," *Quality Progress* (January 1998): 109

Sivathanu, Pillai. "Enhanced PERT for Program Analysis, Control, and Evaluation," *International Journal of Project Management* (February 1993): 39.

APPENDIX 13.1: PROJECT MANAGEMENT WITH QM FOR WINDOWS

PERT is one of the most popular project management techniques. In this chapter we explore the General Foundry, Inc., example. When expected times and variances have been computed for each activity, we can use the data to determine slack, the critical path, and the total project completion time. Program 13.2A shows the QM for Windows input screen for the General Foundry problem. By selecting the precedence list as the type of network, the data can be input without ever constructing the network. The method indicated is for three time estimates, although this can be changed to a single time estimate, crashing, or cost budgeting. Program 13.2B provides the output for the General Foundry problem. The critical path consists of the activities with zero slack.

PROGRAM 13.2A

QM for Windows Input Screen for General Foundry, Inc.

	Optimistic time	Most Likely time	Pessimistic time	Prec 1	Prec 2	Prec 3	Prec 4	Prec 5	Pr
A	1	2	3						
B	2	3	4						
C	1	2	3	A					
D	2	4	6	B					
E	1	4	7	C					
F	1	2	9	C					
G	3	4	11	D	E				
H	1	2	3	F	G				

PROGRAM 13.2B

QM for Windows Solution Screen for General Foundry, Inc.

General Foundry Solution

	Activity time	Early Start	Early Finish	Late Start	Late Finish	Slack	Standard Deviation
Project	15.						1.7638
A	2.	0.	2.	0.	2.	0.	0.3333
B	3.	0.	3.	1.	4.	1.	0.3333
C	2.	2.	4.	2.	4.	0.	0.3333
D	4.	3.	7.	4.	8.	1.	0.6667
E	4.	4.	8.	4.	8.	0.	1.
F	3.	4.	7.	10.	13.	6.	1.3333
G	5.	8.	13.	8.	13.	0.	1.3333
H	2.	13.	15.	13.	15.	0.	0.3333

In addition to basic project management, QM for Windows also allows for project crashing, in which additional resources are used to reduce project completion time. Program 13.3A shows the input screen for the General Foundry data from Table 13.9. The output is shown in Program 13.3B. This indicates that the normal time is 15 weeks, but the project may be finished in 7 weeks if necessary; it may be finished in any number of weeks between 7 and 15. Selecting Windows—Crash Schedule provides additional information regarding these other times.

PROGRAM 13.3A

QM for Windows Input Screen for Crashing General Foundry Example

	Normal time	Crash time	Normal Cost	Crash Cost	Prec 1	Prec 2	Prec 3	Prec 4
A	2	1	22,000	23,000				
B	3	1	30,000	34,000				
C	2	1	26,000	27,000	A			
D	4	3	48,000	49,000	B			
E	4	2	56,000	58,000	C			
F	3	2	30,000	30,500	C			
G	5	2	80,000	86,000	D	E		
H	2	1	16,000	19,000	F	G		

PROGRAM 13.3B

QM for Windows Output Screen for Crashing General Foundry Example

General Foundry Solution

	Normal time	Crash time	Normal Cost	Crash Cost	Crash cost/pd	Crash by	Crashing cost
Project	15.	7.					
A	2.	1.	22,000.	23,000.	1,000.	1.	1,000.
B	3.	1.	30,000.	34,000.	2,000.	2.	4,000.
C	2.	1.	26,000.	27,000.	1,000.	1.	1,000.
D	4.	3.	48,000.	49,000.	1,000.	1.	1,000.
E	4.	2.	56,000.	58,000.	1,000.	2.	2,000.
F	3.	2.	30,000.	30,500.	500.	0.	0.
G	5.	2.	80,000.	86,000.	2,000.	3.	6,000.
H	2.	1.	16,000.	19,000.	3,000.	1.	3,000.
TOTALS			308,000.				18,000.

Monitoring and controlling projects is always an important aspect of project management. In this chapter we demonstrate how to construct budgets using the earliest and latest start times. Programs 13.4 and 13.5 show how QM for Windows can be used to develop budgets using earliest and latest starting times for a project. The data come from the General Foundry example in Tables 13.6 and 13.7.

PROGRAM 13.4

QM for Windows for Budgeting with Earliest Start Times for General Foundry

General Foundry Solution

	Period 1	Period 2	Period 3	Period 4	Period 5	Period 6	Period 7	Period 8	Period 9	Period 10	Period 11	Period 12	Period 13	Period 14	Period 15
A	11.	11.													
B	10.	10.	10.												
C			13.	13.											
D				12.	12.	12.	12.								
E					14.	14.	14.	14.							
F					10.	10.	10.								
G									16.	16.	16.	16.	16.		
H														8.	8.
Total in	21.	21.	23.	25.	36.	36.	36.	14.	16.	16.	16.	16.	16.	8.	8.
Cumulative	21.	42.	65.	90.	126.	162.	198.	212.	228.	244.	260.	276.	292.	300.	308.

PROGRAM 13.5

QM for Windows for Budgeting with Latest Start Times for General Foundry

QM for Windows - C:\Program Files\QMwin32\crash.pro - [Late Start Budget]

File Edit View Module Format Tools Window Help

Network type
- (•) Precedence list
- ( ) Start/end node numbers

Method
Cost Budgeting

General Foundry Solution

	Period 1	Period 2	Period 3	Period 4	Period 5	Period 6	Period 7	Period 8	Period 9	Period 10	Period 11	Period 12	Period 13	Period 14	Period 15
A	11.	11.													
B		10.	10.	10.											
C			13.	13.											
D					12.	12.	12.	12.							
E					14.	14.	14.	14.							
F											10.	10.	10.		
G									16.	16.	16.	16.	16.		
H														8.	8.
Total in	11.	21.	23.	23.	26.	26.	26.	26.	16.	16.	26.	26.	26.	8.	8.
Cumulative	11.	32.	55.	78.	104.	130.	156.	182.	198.	214.	240.	266.	292.	300.	308.

WAITING LINES AND QUEUING THEORY MODELS

After completing this chapter, students will be able to:

1. Describe the trade-off curves for cost-of-waiting time and cost of service.

2. Understand the three parts of a queuing system: the calling population, the queue itself, and the service facility.

3. Describe the basic queuing system configurations.

4. Understand the assumptions of the common models dealt with in this chapter.

5. Analyze a variety of operating characteristics of waiting lines.

Summary • Glossary • Key Equations • Solved Problems • Self-Test • Discussion Questions and Problems • Internet Homework Problems • Case Study: New England Foundry • Case Study: Winter Park Hotel • Internet Case Study • Bibliography

Appendix 14.1: Using QM for Windows

14.1 INTRODUCTION

The study of *waiting lines*, called *queuing theory*, is one of the oldest and most widely used quantitative analysis techniques. Waiting lines are an everyday occurrence, affecting people shopping for groceries, buying gasoline, making a bank deposit, or waiting on the telephone for the first available airline reservationist to answer. Queues,[1] another term for waiting lines, may also take the form of machines waiting to be repaired, trucks in line to be unloaded, or airplanes lined up on a runway waiting for permission to take off. The three basic components of a queuing process are arrivals, service facilities, and the actual waiting line.

In this chapter we discuss how analytical models of waiting lines can help managers evaluate the cost and effectiveness of service systems. We begin with a look at waiting line costs and then describe the characteristics of waiting lines and the underlying mathematical assumptions used to develop queuing models. We also provide the equations needed to compute the operating characteristics of a service system and show examples of how they are used. Later in the chapter, you will see how to save computational time by applying queuing tables and by running waiting line computer programs.

14.2 WAITING LINE COSTS

One of the goals of queuing analysis is finding the best level of service for an organization.

Most waiting line problems are centered on the question of finding the ideal level of services that a firm should provide. Supermarkets must decide how many cash register checkout positions should be opened. Gasoline stations must decide how many pumps should be opened and how many attendants should be on duty. Manufacturing plants must determine the optimal number of mechanics to have on duty each shift to repair machines that break down. Banks must decide how many teller windows to keep open to serve customers during various hours of the day. In most cases, this level of service is an option over which management has control. An extra teller, for example, can be borrowed from another chore or can be hired and trained quickly if demand warrants it. This may not always be the case, though. A plant may not be able to locate or hire skilled mechanics to repair sophisticated electronic machinery.

When an organization *does* have control, its objective is usually to find a happy medium between two extremes. On the one hand, a firm can retain a large staff and provide *many* service facilities. This may result in excellent customer service, with seldom more than one or two customers in a queue. Customers are kept happy with the quick response and appreciate the convenience. This, however, can become expensive.

The other extreme is to have the *minimum* possible number of checkout lines, gas pumps, or teller windows open. This keeps the *service cost* down but may result in customer dissatisfaction. How many times would you return to a large discount department store that had only one cash register open during the day you shop? As the average length of the queue increases and poor service results, customers and goodwill may be lost.

Managers must deal with the trade-off between the cost of providing good service and the cost of customer waiting time. The latter may be hard to quantify.

Most managers recognize the trade-off that must take place between the cost of providing good service and the cost of customer waiting time. They want queues that are short enough so that customers don't become unhappy and either storm out without buying or buy but never return. But they are willing to allow some waiting in line if it is balanced by a significant savings in service costs.

---

[1] The word *queue* is pronounced like the letter *Q*, that is, "kew."

Total expected cost is the sum of service plus waiting costs.

One means of evaluating a service facility is thus to look at a *total expected cost*, a concept illustrated in Figure 14.1. Total expected cost is the sum of expected *service costs* plus expected *waiting costs*.

Service costs are seen to increase as a firm attempts to raise its level of service. For example, if three teams of stevedores, instead of two, are employed to unload a cargo ship, service costs are increased by the additional price of wages. As service improves in speed, however, the cost of time spent waiting in lines decreases. This waiting cost may reflect lost productivity of workers while their tools or machines are awaiting repairs or may simply be an estimate of the costs of customers lost because of poor service and long queues.

Three Rivers Shipping Company Example As an illustration, let's look at the case of the Three Rivers Shipping Company. Three Rivers runs a huge docking facility located on the Ohio River near Pittsburgh. Approximately five ships arrive to unload their cargoes of steel and ore during every 12-hour work shift. Each hour that a ship sits idle in line waiting to be unloaded costs the firm a great deal of money, about $1,000 per hour. From experience, management estimates that if one team of stevedores is on duty to handle the unloading work, each ship will wait an average of 7 hours to be unloaded. If two teams are working, the average waiting time drops to 4 hours; for three teams, it's 3 hours; and for four teams of stevedores, only 2 hours. But each additional team of stevedores is also an expensive proposition, due to union contracts.

The goal is to find the service level that minimizes total expected cost.

Three Rivers' superintendent would like to determine the optimal number of teams of stevedores to have on duty each shift. The objective is to minimize total expected costs. This analysis is summarized in Table 14.1. To minimize the sum of service costs and waiting costs, the firm makes the decision to employ two teams of stevedores each shift.

FIGURE 14.1

Queuing Costs and Service Levels

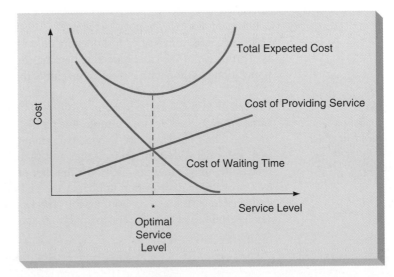

TABLE 14.1   Three Rivers Shipping Company Waiting Line Cost Analysis

	NUMBER OF TEAMS OF STEVEDORES WORKING			
	1	2	3	4
(a) Average number of ships arriving per shift	5	5	5	5
(b) Average time each ship waits to be unloaded (hours)	7	4	3	2
(c) Total ship hours lost per shift $(a \times b)$	35	20	15	10
(d) Estimated cost per hour of idle ship time	$1,000	$1,000	$1,000	$1,000
(e) Value of ship's lost time or waiting cost $(c \times d)$	$35,000	$20,000	$15,000	$10,000
(f) Stevedore team salary,* or service cost	$6,000	$12,000	$18,000	$24,000
(g) Total expected cost $(e + f)$	$41,000	$32,000 (Optimal cost)	$33,000	$34,000

*Stevedore team salaries are computed as the number of people in a typical team (assumed to be 50), times the number of hours each person works per day (12 hours), times an hourly salary of $10 per hour. If two teams are employed, the rate is just doubled.

14.3 CHARACTERISTICS OF A QUEUING SYSTEM

In this section we take a look at the three parts of a queuing system: (1) the arrivals or inputs to the system (sometimes referred to as the *calling population*), (2) the queue or the waiting line itself, and (3) the service facility. These three components have certain characteristics that must be examined before mathematical queuing models can be developed.

Arrival Characteristics

The input source that generates arrivals or customers for the service system has three major characteristics. It is important to consider the *size* of the calling population, the *pattern* of arrivals at the queuing system, and the *behavior* of the arrivals.

Unlimited (or infinite) calling populations are assumed for most queuing models.

Size of the Calling Population   Population sizes are considered to be either *unlimited* (essentially *infinite*) or *limited* (*finite*). When the number of customers or arrivals on hand at any given moment is just a small portion of potential arrivals, the calling population is considered unlimited. For practical purposes, examples of unlimited populations include cars arriving at a highway tollbooth, shoppers arriving at a supermarket, or students arriving to register for classes at a large university. Most queuing models assume such an infinite calling population. When this is not the case, modeling becomes much more complex. An example of a finite population is a shop with only eight machines that might break down and require service.

Arrivals are random when they are independent of one another and cannot be predicted exactly.

Pattern of Arrivals at the System   Customers either arrive at a service facility according to some known schedule (for example, one patient every 15 minutes or one student for advising every half hour) or else they arrive *randomly*. Arrivals are considered random when they are independent of one another and their occurrence cannot be predicted exactly. Frequently in queuing problems, the number of arrivals per unit of time can be estimated by a probability distribution known as the *Poisson distribution*. For any given arrival rate, such as two customers per hour, or four trucks per minute, a discrete Poisson distribution can be established by using the formula

$$P(X) = \frac{e^{-\lambda}\lambda^X}{X!} \quad \text{for} \quad X = 0, 1, 2, 3, 4, \ldots \tag{14-1}$$

where

$$P(X) = \text{probability of } X \text{ arrivals}$$

$$X = \text{number of arrivals per unit of time}$$

$$\lambda = \text{average arrival rate}$$

$$e = 2.7183$$

The Poisson probability distribution is used in many queuing models to represent arrival patterns.

With the help of the table in Appendix C, the values of $e^{-\lambda}$ are easy to find. We can use these in the formula to find probabilities. For example, if $\lambda = 2$, from Appendix C we find $e^{-2} = 0.1353$. The Poisson probabilities that X is 0, 1, and 2 when $\lambda = 2$ are as follows:

$$P(X) = \frac{e^{-\lambda}\lambda^X}{X!}$$

$$P(0) = \frac{e^{-2}2^0}{0!} = \frac{(0.1353)1}{1} = 0.1353 \approx 14\%$$

$$P(1) = \frac{e^{-2}2^1}{1!} = \frac{e^{-2}2}{1} = \frac{0.1353(2)}{1} = 0.2706 \approx 27\%$$

$$P(2) = \frac{e^{-2}2^2}{2!} = \frac{e^{-2}4}{2(1)} = \frac{0.1353(4)}{2} = 0.2706 \approx 27\%$$

These probabilities, as well as others for $\lambda = 2$ and $\lambda = 4$, are shown in Figure 14.2. Notice that the chances that 9 or more customers will arrive in a particular time period are virtually nil. Arrivals, of course, are not always Poisson (they may follow some other distribution) and should be examined to make certain that they are well approximated by Poisson before that distribution is applied. This usually involves observing arrivals, plotting the data, and applying statistical measures of goodness of fit, a topic discussed in more advanced texts.

FIGURE 14.2   **Two Examples of the Poisson Distribution for Arrival Times**

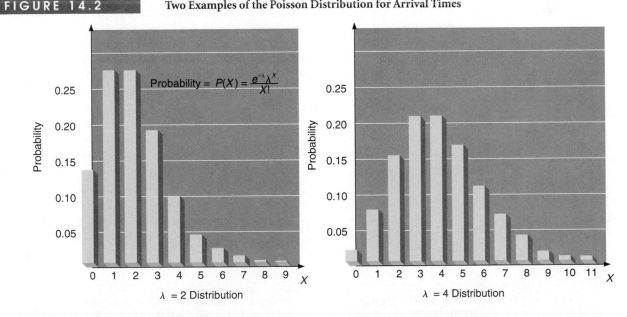

Probability $= P(X) = \frac{e^{-\lambda}\lambda^x}{X!}$

$\lambda = 2$ Distribution

$\lambda = 4$ Distribution

The concepts of balking and reneging.

Behavior of the Arrivals Most queuing models assume that an arriving customer is a patient customer. Patient customers are people or machines that wait in the queue until they are served and do not switch between lines. Unfortunately, life and quantitative analysis are complicated by the fact that people have been known to balk or renege. *Balking* refers to customers who refuse to join the waiting line because it is too long to suit their needs or interests. *Reneging* customers are those who enter the queue but then become impatient and leave without completing their transaction. Actually, both of these situations just serve to accentuate the need for queuing theory and waiting line analysis. How many times have you seen a shopper with a basket full of groceries, including perishables such as milk, frozen food, or meats, simply abandon the shopping cart before checking out because the line was too long? This expensive occurrence for the store makes managers acutely aware of the importance of service-level decisions.

Waiting Line Characteristics

The models in this chapter assume unlimited queue length.

The waiting line itself is the second component of a queuing system. The length of a line can be either *limited* or *unlimited*. A queue is limited when it cannot, by law of physical restrictions, increase to an infinite length. This may be the case in a small restaurant that has only 10 tables and can serve no more than 50 diners an evening. Analytic queuing models are treated in this chapter under an assumption of *unlimited queue* length. A queue is unlimited when its size is unrestricted, as in the case of the tollbooth serving arriving automobiles.

Most queuing models use the FIFO rule. This is obviously not appropriate in all service systems, especially those dealing with emergencies.

A second waiting line characteristic deals with *queue discipline*. This refers to the rule by which customers in the line are to receive service. Most systems use a queue discipline known as the *first-in, first-out rule* (FIFO). In a hospital emergency room or an express checkout line at a supermarket, however, various assigned priorities may preempt FIFO. Patients who are critically injured will move ahead in treatment priority over patients with broken fingers or noses. Shoppers with fewer than 10 items may be allowed to enter the express checkout queue but are *then* treated as first-come, first-served. Computer programming runs are another example of queuing systems that operate under priority scheduling. In most large companies, when computer-produced paychecks are due out on a specific date, the payroll program has highest priority over other runs.[2]

Service Facility Characteristics

The third part of any queuing system is the service facility. It is important to examine two basic properties: (1) the configuration of the service system and (2) the pattern of service times.

Number of service channels in a queuing system is the number of servers.

Basic Queuing System Configurations Service systems are usually classified in terms of their number of channels, or number of servers, and number of phases, or number of service stops, that must be made. A *single-channel system*, with one server, is typified by the drive-in bank that has only one open teller, or by the type of drive-through fast-food restaurant that has become so popular in the United States. If, on the other hand, the bank had several tellers on duty and each customer waited in one common line for the first available teller, we would have a *multi-channel system* at work. Many banks today are multi-channel service systems, as are most large barber shops and many airline ticket counters.

Single-phase *means the customer receives service at only one station before leaving the system.* Multiphase *implies two or more stops before leaving the system.*

A *single-phase system* is one in which the customer receives service from only one station and then exits the system. A fast-food restaurant in which the person who takes your order also brings you the food and takes your money is a single-phase system. So is a driver's license agency in which the person taking your application also grades your test and collects the license fee. But if the restaurant requires you to place your order at one station, pay at a

---

[2] The term *FIFS* (*f*irst *i*n, *f*irst *s*erved) is often used in place of FIFO. Another discipline, LIFS (*l*ast *i*n, *f*irst *s*erved), is common when material is stacked or piled and the items on top are used first.

second, and pick up the food at a third service stop, it becomes a *multiphase system*. Similarly, if the driver's license agency is large or busy, you will probably have to wait in a line to complete the application (the first service stop), then queue again to have the test graded (the second service stop), and finally go to a third service counter to pay the fee. To help you relate the concepts of channels and phases, Figure 14.3 presents four possible configurations.

FIGURE 14.3   **Four Basic Queuing System Configurations**

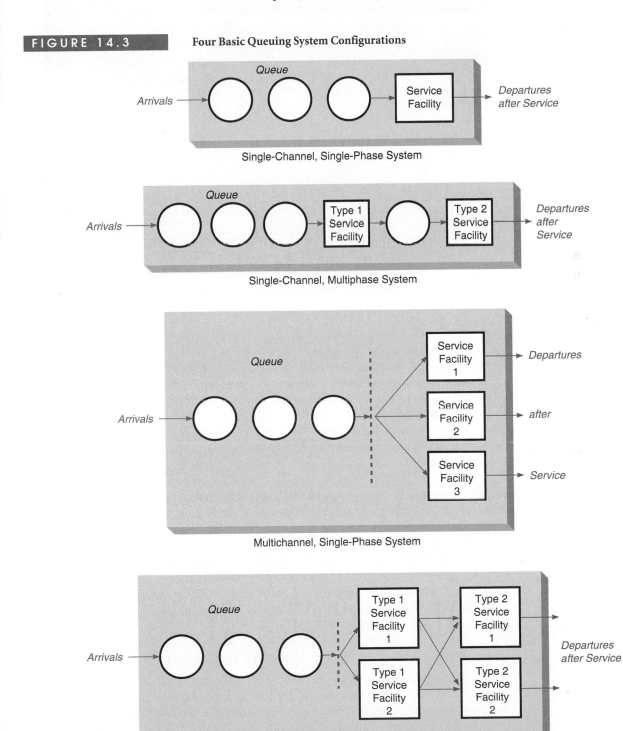

Single-Channel, Single-Phase System

Single-Channel, Multiphase System

Multichannel, Single-Phase System

Multichannel, Multiphase System

FIGURE 14.4

Two Examples of the Exponential Distribution for Service Times (see Section 2.12 for discussion of this)

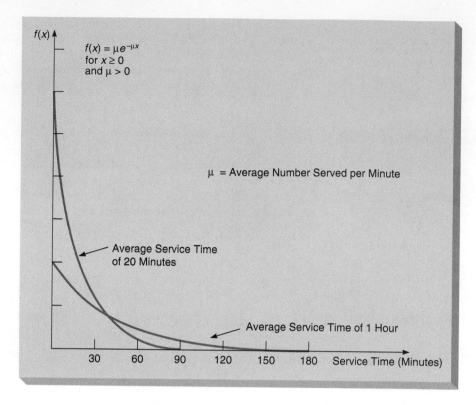

$$f(x) = \mu e^{-\mu x}$$ for $x \geq 0$ and $\mu > 0$

μ = Average Number Served per Minute

Average Service Time of 20 Minutes

Average Service Time of 1 Hour

Service Time (Minutes)

Service times often follow the negative exponential distribution.

Service Time Distribution Service patterns are like arrival patterns in that they can be either constant or random. If service time is constant, it takes the same amount of time to take care of each customer. This is the case in a machine-performed service operation such as an automatic car wash. More often, service times are randomly distributed. In many cases it can be assumed that random service times are described by the *negative exponential probability distribution*. This is a mathematically convenient assumption if arrival rates are Poisson distributed.

Figure 14.4 illustrates that if service times follow an exponential distribution, the probability of any very long service time is low. For example, when an average service time is 20 minutes, seldom if ever will a customer require more than 90 minutes in the service facility. If the mean service time is one hour, the probability of spending more than 180 minutes in service is virtually zero.

It is important to confirm that the queuing assumptions of Poisson arrivals and exponential services are valid before applying the model.

The exponential distribution is important to the process of building mathematical queuing models because many of the models' theoretical underpinnings are based on the assumption of Poisson arrivals and exponential services. Before they are applied, however, the quantitative analyst can and should observe, collect, and plot service time data to determine if they fit the exponential distribution.

Identifying Models Using Kendall Notation

D. G. Kendall developed a notation that has been widely accepted for specifying the pattern of arrivals, the service time distribution, and the number of channels in a queuing model. This notation is often seen in software for queuing models. The basic three-symbol Kendall notation is in the form

arrival distribution/service time distribution/number of service channels open

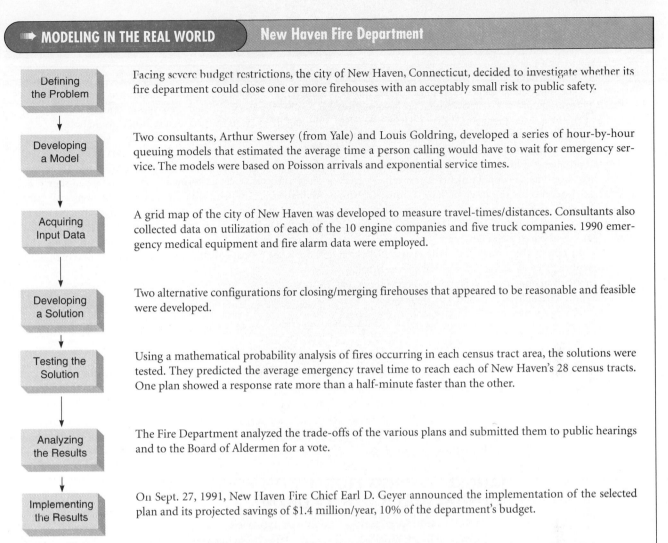

Source: A. J. Swersey, L. Goldring, and E. D. Geyer, "Improving Fire Department Productivity," *Interfaces* 23, 1 (January–February 1993): 109–129.

where specific letters are used to represent probability distributions. The following letters are commonly used in Kendall notation:

M = Poisson distribution for number of occurrences (or exponential times)

D = Constant (deterministic) rate

G = General distribution with mean and variance known

Thus, a single channel model with Poisson arrivals and exponential service times would be represented by

$$M/M/1$$

An M/M/2 model has Poisson arrivals, exponential service times, and two channels.

When a second channel is added, we would have

$$M/M/2$$

If there are m distinct service channels in the queuing system with Poisson arrivals and exponential service times, the Kendall notation would be $M/M/m$. A three-channel system

The hospital outpatient eye clinic at the United Kingdom's Royal Preston Hospital is not unlike clinics at hospitals throughout the world. It is regularly overbooked, overrun, and has excessive patient waiting times. Even though its Patient Charter states that no one should wait to be seen for more than 30 minutes past their appointment time, patients, on average, waited over 50 minutes.

Many problems in hospital clinics can be explained as a vicious circle of events: (1) appointments staff overbook every clinic session because of the large patient volume; (2) this means patients wait in long queues; (3) doctors are overburdened; and (4) when a doctor is ill, the staff spends much time canceling and rescheduling appointments.

To break out of this circle, the clinic at Royal Preston needed to reduce patient waiting times. This was done by applying computer-driven queuing models and attempting to reduce the patient time variability. The hospital used the queuing software to specifically address the 30-minute statistic in the Patient

Charter. Researchers assumed that (1) each patient arrived on time, (2) the service distribution was known from past history, (3) 12% of patients missed their appointments, and (4) one-third of the patients queued for a second consultation.

Making a list of 13 recommendations (many nonquantitative) to the clinic, researchers returned two years later to find that most of their suggestions were followed (or at least seriously attempted), yet performance of the clinic had shown no dramatic improvement. Patient waiting times were still quite long, the clinic was still overbooked, and appointments sometimes had to be canceled. The conclusion: Even though models can often help *understand* a problem, some problems, like those in the outpatient clinic, are messy and hard to fix.

Source: J. C. Bennett and D. J. Worthington. "An Example of Good but Partially Successful OR Engagement: Improving Outpatient Clinic Operations," *Interfaces* (September–October 1998): 56–69.

with Poisson arrivals and constant service time would be identified as $M/D/3$. A four-channel system with Poisson arrivals and service times that are normally distributed would be identified as $M/G/4$.

There is a more detailed notation with additional terms that indicate the maximum number in the system and the population size. When these are omitted, it is assumed there is no limit to the queue length or the population size. Most of the models we study here will have those properties.

14.4   SINGLE-CHANNEL QUEUING MODEL WITH POISSON ARRIVALS AND EXPONENTIAL SERVICE TIMES ($M/M/1$)

In this section we present an analytical approach to determine important measures of performance in a typical service system. After these numeric measures have been computed, it will be possible to add in cost data and begin to make decisions that balance desirable service levels with waiting line service costs.

Assumptions of the Model

The single-channel, single-phase model considered here is one of the most widely used and simplest queuing models. It involves assuming that seven conditions exist:

These seven assumptions must be met if the single-channel, single-phase model is to be applied.

1. Arrivals are served on a FIFO basis.

2. Every arrival waits to be served regardless of the length of the line; that is, there is no balking or reneging.

3. Arrivals are independent of preceding arrivals, but the average number of arrivals (the arrival rate) does not change over time.

4. Arrivals are described by a Poisson probability distribution and come from an infinite or very large population.

5. Service times also vary from one customer to the next and are independent of one another, but their average rate is known.

6. Service times occur according to the negative exponential probability distribution.

7. The average service rate is greater than the average arrival rate.

When these seven conditions are met, we can develop a series of equations that define the queue's *operating characteristics*. The mathematics used to derive each equation is rather complex and outside the scope of this book, so we will just present the resulting formulas here.

Queuing Equations

We let

$$\lambda = \text{mean number of arrivals per time period (for example, per hour)}$$

$$\mu = \text{mean number of people or items served per time period}$$

When determining the arrival rate (λ) and the service rate (μ), the same time period must be used. For example, if the λ is the average number of arrivals per hour, then μ must indicate the average number that could be served per hour.

The queuing equations follow.

These seven queuing equations for the single-channel, single-phase model describe the important operating characteristics of the service system.

1. The average number of customers or units in the system, L, that is, the number in line plus the number being served:

$$L = \frac{\lambda}{\mu - \lambda} \tag{14-2}$$

2. The average time a customer spends in the system, W, that is, the time spent in line plus the time spent being served:

$$W = \frac{1}{\mu - \lambda} \tag{14-3}$$

3. The average number of customers in the queue, L_q:

$$L_q = \frac{\lambda^2}{\mu(\mu - \lambda)} \tag{14-4}$$

4. The average time a customer spends waiting in the queue, W_q:

$$W_q = \frac{\lambda}{\mu(\mu - \lambda)} \tag{14-5}$$

5. The *utilization factor* for the system, ρ (the Greek lowercase letter rho), that is, the probability that the service facility is being used:

$$\rho = \frac{\lambda}{\mu} \tag{14-6}$$

6. The percent idle time, P_0, that is, the probability that no one is in the system:

$$P_0 = 1 - \frac{\lambda}{\mu} \tag{14-7}$$

7. The probability that the number of customers in the system is greater than k, $P_{n>k}$:

$$P_{n>k} = \left(\frac{\lambda}{\mu}\right)^{k+1} \tag{14-8}$$

Arnold's Muffler Shop Case

We now apply these formulas to the case of Arnold's Muffler Shop in New Orleans. Arnold's mechanic, Reid Blank, is able to install new mufflers at an average rate of 3 per hour, or about 1 every 20 minutes. Customers needing this service arrive at the shop on the average of 2 per hour. Larry Arnold, the shop owner, studied queuing models in an MBA program and feels that all seven of the conditions for a single-channel model are met. He proceeds to calculate the numerical values of the preceding operating characteristics.

λ = 2 cars arriving per hour

μ = 3 cars serviced per hour

$L = \dfrac{\lambda}{\mu - \lambda} = \dfrac{2}{3 - 2} = \dfrac{2}{1}$ = 2 cars in the system on the average

$W = \dfrac{1}{\mu - \lambda} = \dfrac{1}{3 - 2}$ = 1 hour that an average car spends in the system

$L_q = \dfrac{\lambda^2}{\mu(\mu - \lambda)} = \dfrac{2^2}{3(3 - 2)} = \dfrac{4}{3(1)} = \dfrac{4}{3}$ = 1.33 cars waiting on line on the average

$W_q = \dfrac{\lambda}{\mu(\mu - \lambda)} = \dfrac{2}{3(3 - 2)} = \dfrac{2}{3}$ hour = 40 minutes = average waiting time per car

Note that W and W_q are in *hours*, since λ was defined as the number of arrivals per *hour*.

$\rho = \dfrac{\lambda}{\mu} = \dfrac{2}{3}$ = 0.67   = percent of time mechanic is busy, or the probability that the server is busy

$P_0 = 1 - \dfrac{\lambda}{\mu} = 1 - \dfrac{2}{3}$ = 0.33 = probability that there are 0 cars in the system

Probability of More Than k Cars in the System

k	$P_{n>k} = \left(\frac{2}{3}\right)^{k+1}$	
0	(0.667)	← *Note that this is equal to $1 - P_0 = 1 - 0.33 = 0.667$.*
1	0.444	
2	0.296	
3	(0.198)	← *Implies that there is a 19.8% chance that more than 3 cars are in the system.*
4	0.132	
5	0.088	
6	0.058	
7	0.039	

Using Excel QM on the Arnold's Muffler Shop Queue Excel QM easily handles Arnold's single-channel, single-phase model. Using the equations shown in Program 14.1A, Excel QM provides the results in Program 14.1B.

PROGRAM 14.1A

Input Data and Formulas Using Excel QM for Arnold's Muffler Shop Queuing Problem

PROGRAM 14.1B

Output from Excel QM Analysis in Program 14.1A

Conducting an economic analysis is the next step. It permits cost factors to be included.

Introducing Costs into the Model Now that the characteristics of the queuing system have been computed, Arnold decides to do an economic analysis of their impact. The waiting line model was valuable in predicting potential waiting times, queue lengths, idle times, and so on. But it did not identify optimal decisions or consider cost factors. As stated earlier, the solution to a queuing problem may require management to make a trade-off between the increased cost of providing better service and the decreased waiting costs derived from providing that service. These two costs are called the waiting cost and the service cost.

The total service cost is

$$\text{total service cost} = (\text{number of channels})(\text{cost per channel})$$

$$\text{total service cost} = mC_s \tag{14-9}$$

where

$$m = \text{number of channels}$$

$$C_s = \text{service cost (labor cost) of each channel}$$

The waiting cost when the waiting time cost is based on time in the system is

$$\text{total waiting cost} = (\text{total time spent waiting by all arrivals})(\text{cost of waiting})$$

$$= (\text{number of arrivals})(\text{average wait per arrival})C_w$$

so,

$$\text{total waiting cost} = (\lambda W)C_w \tag{14-10}$$

If the waiting time cost is based on time in the queue, this becomes

$$\text{total waiting cost} = (\lambda W_q)C_w \tag{14-11}$$

These costs are based on whatever time units (often hours) are used in determining λ. Adding the total service cost to the total waiting cost, we have the total cost of the queuing system. When the waiting cost is based on the time in the system, this is

$$\text{total cost} = \text{total service cost} + \text{total waiting cost}$$

$$\text{total cost} = mC_s + \lambda W C_w \tag{14-12}$$

When the waiting cost is based on time in the queue, the total cost is

$$\text{total cost} = mC_s + \lambda W_q C_w \tag{14-13}$$

Customer waiting time is often considered the most important factor.

At times we may wish to determine the daily cost, and then we simply find the total number of arrivals per day. Let us consider the situation for Arnold's Muffler Shop.

Arnold estimates that the cost of customer waiting time, in terms of customer dissatisfaction and lost goodwill, is $10 per hour of time spent *waiting* in line. (After customers' cars are actually being serviced on the rack, customers don't seem to mind waiting.) Because on the average a car has a $\frac{2}{3}$ hour wait and there are approximately 16 cars serviced per day (2 per hour times 8 working hours per day), the total number of hours that customers spend waiting for mufflers to be installed each day is $\frac{2}{3} \times 16 = \frac{32}{3}$, or $10\frac{2}{3}$ hours. Hence, in this case,

$$\text{total daily waiting cost} = (8 \text{ hours per day})\lambda W_q C_w = (8)(2)(\tfrac{2}{3})(\$10) = \$106.67$$

The only other cost that Larry Arnold can identify in this queuing situation is the pay rate of Reid Blank, the mechanic. Blank is paid $7 per hour.

$$\text{total daily service cost} = (8 \text{ hours per day})mC_s = 8(1)(\$7) = \$56$$

Waiting costs plus service costs equal total cost.

The total daily cost of the system as it is currently configured is the total of the waiting cost and the service cost, which gives us

$$\text{total daily cost of the queuing system} = \$106.67 + \$56 = \$162.67$$

Now comes a decision. Arnold finds out through the muffler business grapevine that the Rusty Muffler, a cross-town competitor, employs a mechanic named Jimmy Smith who can efficiently install new mufflers at the rate of 4 per hour. Larry Arnold contacts Smith and inquires as to his interest in switching employers. Smith says that he would consider leaving the Rusty Muffler but only if he were paid a \$9 per hour salary. Arnold, being a crafty businessman, decides that it may be worthwhile to fire Blank and replace him with the speedier but more expensive Smith.

He first recomputes all the operating characteristics using a new service rate of 4 mufflers per hour.

$\lambda = 2$ cars arriving per hour

$\mu = 4$ cars serviced per hour

$$L = \frac{\lambda}{\mu - \lambda} = \frac{2}{4 - 2} = 1 \text{ car in the system on the average}$$

$$W = \frac{1}{\mu - \lambda} = \frac{1}{4 - 2} = \frac{1}{2} \text{ hour in the system on the average}$$

$$L_q = \frac{\lambda^2}{\mu(\mu - \lambda)} = \frac{2^2}{4(4 - 2)} = \frac{4}{8} = \frac{1}{2} \text{ cars waiting in line on the average}$$

$$W_q = \frac{\lambda}{\mu(\mu - \lambda)} = \frac{2}{4(4 - 2)} = \frac{2}{8} = \frac{1}{4} \text{ hour} = 15 \text{ minutes average waiting time per car in the queue}$$

$$\rho = \frac{\lambda}{\mu} = \frac{2}{4} = 0.5 = \text{percent of time mechanic is busy}$$

$$P_0 = 1 - \frac{\lambda}{\mu} = 1 - 0.5 = 0.5 = \text{probability that there are 0 cars in the system}$$

Probability of More Than k Cars in the System

k	$P_{n>k} = \left(\frac{2}{4}\right)^{k+1}$
0	0.5
1	0.25
2	0.125
3	0.062
4	0.031
5	0.016
6	0.008
7	0.004

It is quite evident that Smith's speed will result in considerably shorter queues and waiting times. For example, a customer would now spend an average of $\frac{1}{2}$ hour in the system and

$\frac{1}{4}$ hour waiting in the queue, as opposed to 1 hour in the system and $\frac{2}{3}$ hour in the queue with Blank as mechanic. The total daily waiting time cost with Smith as the mechanic will be

$$\text{total daily waiting cost} = (8 \text{ hours per day})\lambda W_q C_w = (8)(2)(\tfrac{1}{4})(\$10) = \$40.00 \text{ per day}$$

Notice that the total time spent waiting for the 16 customers per day is now

$$(16 \text{ cars per day}) \times (\tfrac{1}{4} \text{ hour per car}) = 4 \text{ hours}$$

instead of 10.67 hours with Blank. Thus, the waiting is much less than half of what it was, even though the service rate only changed from 3 per hour to 4 per hour.

Here is a comparison for total costs using the two different mechanics.

The service cost will go up due to the higher salary, but the overall cost will decrease, as we see here:

$$\text{service cost of Smith} = 8 \text{ hours/day} \times \$9/\text{hour} = \$72 \text{ per day}$$

$$\text{total expected cost} = \text{waiting cost} + \text{service cost} = \$40 + \$72$$

$$= \$112 \text{ per day}$$

Because the total daily expected cost with Blank as mechanic was \$162, Arnold may very well decide to hire Smith and reduce costs by \$162 − \$112 = \$50 per day.

Enhancing the Queuing Environment

Although reducing the waiting time is an important factor in reducing the waiting time cost of a queuing system, a manager might find other ways to reduce this cost. The total waiting time cost is based on the total amount of time spent waiting (based on W or W_q) and the cost of waiting (C_w). Reducing either of these will reduce the overall cost of waiting. Enhancing the queuing environment by making the wait less unpleasant may reduce C_w as customers will not be as upset by having to wait. There are magazines in the waiting room of doctors' offices for patients to read while waiting. There are tabloids on display by the checkout lines in grocery stores, and customers read the headlines to pass time while waiting. Music is often played while telephone callers are placed on hold. At major amusement parks there are video screens and televisions in some of the queue lines to make the wait more interesting. For some of these, the waiting line is so entertaining that it is almost an attraction itself.

All of these things are designed to keep the customer busy and to enhance the conditions surrounding the waiting so that it appears that time is passing more quickly than it actually is. Consequently, the cost of waiting (C_w) becomes lower and the total cost of the queuing system is reduced. Sometimes, reducing the total cost in this way is easier than reducing the total cost by lowering W or W_q. In the case of Arnold's Muffler Shop, Arnold might consider putting a television in the waiting room and remodeling this room so customers feel more comfortable while waiting for their cars to be serviced.

14.5 MULTIPLE-CHANNEL QUEUING MODEL WITH POISSON ARRIVALS AND EXPONENTIAL SERVICE TIMES (*M/M/m*)

The next logical step is to look at a multiple-channel queuing system, in which two or more servers or channels are available to handle arriving customers. Let us still assume that customers awaiting service form one single line and then proceed to the first available server.

An example of such a multichannel, single-phase waiting line is found in many banks today. A common line is formed and the customer at the head of the line proceeds to the first free teller (Refer back to Figure 14.3 for a typical multichannel configuration.)

The multichannel model also assumes Poisson arrivals and exponential services.

The multiple-channel system presented here again assumes that arrivals follow a Poisson probability distribution and that service times are distributed exponentially. Service is first come, first served, and all servers are assumed to perform at the same rate. Other assumptions listed earlier for the single-channel model apply as well.

Equations for the Multichannel Queuing Model

If we let

$$m = \text{number of channels open,}$$

$$\lambda = \text{average arrival rate, and}$$

$$\mu = \text{average service rate at each channel}$$

the following formulas may be used in the waiting line analysis.

1. The probability that there are zero customers or units in the system:

$$P_0 = \frac{1}{\left[\sum_{n=0}^{n=m-1} \frac{1}{n!}\left(\frac{\lambda}{\mu}\right)^n\right] + \frac{1}{m!}\left(\frac{\lambda}{\mu}\right)^m \frac{m\mu}{m\mu - \lambda}} \quad \text{for} \quad m\mu > \lambda \qquad (14\text{-}14)$$

2. The average number of customers or units in the system:

$$L = \frac{\lambda\mu(\lambda/\mu)^m}{(m-1)!(m\mu - \lambda)^2} P_0 + \frac{\lambda}{\mu} \qquad (14\text{-}15)$$

3. The average time a unit spends in the waiting line or being serviced (namely, in the system):

$$W = \frac{\mu(\lambda/\mu)^m}{(m-1)!(m\mu - \lambda)^2} P_0 + \frac{1}{\mu} = \frac{L}{\lambda} \qquad (14\text{-}16)$$

4. The average number of customers or units in line waiting for service:

$$L_q = L - \frac{\lambda}{\mu} \qquad (14\text{-}17)$$

5. The average time a customer or unit spends in the queue waiting for service:

$$W_q = W - \frac{1}{\mu} = \frac{L_q}{\lambda} \qquad (14\text{-}18)$$

6. Utilization rate:

$$\rho = \frac{\lambda}{m\mu} \qquad (14\text{-}19)$$

These equations are obviously more complex than the ones used in the single-channel model, yet they are used in exactly the same fashion and provide the same type of information as did the simpler model.

Arnold's Muffler Shop Revisited

For an application of the multichannel queuing model, let's return to the case of Arnold's Muffler Shop. Earlier, Larry Arnold examined two options. He could retain his current mechanic, Reid Blank, at a total expected cost of $162 per day; or he could fire Blank and hire a slightly more expensive but faster worker named Jimmy Smith. With Smith on board, service system costs could be reduced to $112 per day.

The muffler shop considers opening a second muffler service channel that operates at the same speed as the first one.

A third option is now explored. Arnold finds that at minimal after-tax cost he can open a *second* garage bay in which mufflers can be installed. Instead of firing his first mechanic, Blank, he would hire a second worker. The new mechanic would be expected to install mufflers at the same rate as Blank—about $\mu = 3$ per hour. Customers, who would still arrive at the rate of $\lambda = 2$ per hour, would wait in a single line until one of the two mechanics is free. To find out how this option compares with the old single-channel waiting line system, Arnold computes several operating characteristics for the $m = 2$ channel system.

$$P_0 = \frac{1}{\left[\sum_{n=0}^{1} \frac{1}{n!}\left(\frac{2}{3}\right)^n\right] + \frac{1}{2!}\left(\frac{2}{3}\right)^2\left(\frac{2(3)}{2(3)-2}\right)}$$

$$= \frac{1}{1 + \frac{2}{3} + \frac{1}{2}\left(\frac{4}{9}\right)\left(\frac{6}{6-2}\right)} = \frac{1}{1 + \frac{2}{3} + \frac{1}{3}} = \frac{1}{2} = 0.5$$

= probability of 0 cars in the system

$$L = \left(\frac{(2)(3)(\frac{2}{3})^2}{1![2(3)-2]^2}\right)\left(\frac{1}{2}\right) + \frac{2}{3} = \frac{\frac{8}{3}}{16}\left(\frac{1}{2}\right) + \frac{2}{3} = \frac{3}{4} = 0.75$$

= average number of cars in the system

$$W = \frac{L}{\lambda} = \frac{\frac{3}{4}}{2} = \frac{3}{8} \text{ hours} = 22\frac{1}{2} \text{ minutes}$$

= average time a car spends in the system

$$L_q = L - \frac{\lambda}{\mu} = \frac{3}{4} - \frac{2}{3} = \frac{1}{12} = 0.083$$

= average number of cars in the queue

$$W_q = \frac{L_q}{\lambda} = \frac{0.083}{2} = 0.0415 \text{ hour} = 2\frac{1}{2} \text{ minutes}$$

= average time a car spends in the queue

Dramatically lower waiting time results from opening the second service bay.

These data are compared with earlier operating characteristics in Table 14.2. The increased service from opening a second channel has a dramatic effect on almost all characteristics. In particular, time spent waiting in line drops from 40 minutes with one mechanic (Blank) or 15 minutes with Smith down to only $2\frac{1}{2}$ minutes! Similarly, the average number of cars

TABLE 14.2	Effect of Service Level on Arnold's Operating Characteristics		
		LEVEL OF SERVICE	
OPERATING CHARACTERISTIC	ONE MECHANIC (REID BLANK) $\mu = 3$	TWO MECHANICS $\mu = 3$ FOR EACH	ONE FAST MECHANIC (JIMMY SMITH) $\mu = 4$
Probability that the system is empty (P_0)	0.33	0.50	0.50
Average number of cars in the system (L)	2 cars	0.75 car	1 car
Average time spent in the system (W)	60 minutes	22.5 minutes	30 minutes
Average number of cars in the queue (L_q)	1.33 cars	0.083 car	0.50 car
Average time spent in the queue (W_q)	40 minutes	2.5 minutes	15 minutes

in the queue falls to 0.083 (about $\frac{1}{12}$ of a car).[3] But does this mean that a second bay should be opened?

To complete his economic analysis, Arnold assumes that the second mechanic would be paid the same as the current one, Blank, namely, $7 per hour. The daily waiting cost now will be

$$\text{total daily waiting cost} = (8 \text{ hours per day})\lambda W_q C_w = (8)(2)(0.0415)(\$10) = \$6.64$$

Notice that the total waiting time for the 16 cars per day is $(16 \text{ cars/day}) \times (0.0415 \text{ hour/car}) = 0.664$ hours per day instead of the 10.67 hours with only one mechanic.

The service cost is doubled, as there are two mechanics, so this is

$$\text{total daily service cost} = (8 \text{ hours per day})mC_s = (8)2(\$7) = \$112$$

The total daily cost of the system as it is currently configured is the total of the waiting cost and the service cost, which is

$$\text{total daily cost of the queuing system} = \$6.64 + \$112 = \$118.64$$

As you recall, total cost with just Blank as mechanic was found to be $162 per day. Cost with just Smith was just $112. Although opening a second channel would be likely to have a positive effect on customer goodwill and hence lower the cost of waiting time, it means an increase in the cost of providing service. Look back to Figure 14.1 and you will see that such trade-offs are the basis of queuing theory. Arnold's decision is to replace his present worker with the speedier Smith and *not* to open a second service bay.

Using Excel QM for Analysis of Arnold's Multichannel Queuing Model Just as we used Excel QM to model Arnold's single-channel queue (in Program 14.1), we can model the multichannel case with Excel as well. Programs 14.2A and 14.2B provide the input/ formulas and output, respectively.

---

[3] You might note that adding a second mechanic does not cut queue waiting time and length just in half, but makes it even smaller. This is because of the *random* arrival and service processes. When there is only one mechanic and two customers arrive within a minute of each other, the second will have a long wait. The fact that the mechanic may have been idle for 30 to 40 minutes before they both arrive does not change this average waiting time. Thus, single-channel models often have high wait times relative to multichannel models.

PROGRAM 14.2A   **Input Data and Formulas for Arnold's Multichannel Queuing Decision Using Excel QM**

PROGRAM 14.2B

Output from Excel QM Analysis in Program 14.2A

IN ACTION   Shortening the Arrest-to-Arraignment Time in New York City's Police Department

On March 23, 1990, the *New York Times* ran a front-page story on a woman who spent 45 hours in prearraignment detention in that city under the headline "Trapped in the terror of New York's holding pens." Indeed, people arrested in New York City at that time averaged a 40-hour wait (some more than 70 hours) prior to arraignment. These people were held in crowded, noisy, stressful, unhealthy, and often dangerous holding facilities, and in effect, denied a speedy court appearance. That same year, the New York Supreme Court ruled that the city was to attempt to arraign in 24 hours or to release the prisoner.

The arrest-to-arraignment (ATA) process, which has the general characteristics of a large queuing system, involves these steps: arrest of suspected criminal, transport to a police precinct, search/fingerprinting, paperwork for arrest, transport to a central booking facility, additional paperwork, processing of fingerprints, a bail interview, transport to either the courthouse or an outlying precinct, checks for a criminal record, and finally, an assistant district attorney drawing up a complaint document.

To solve the very complex problem of improving this system, the city hired Queues Enforth Development, Inc., a Massachusetts consulting firm. Their Monte Carlo simulation of the ATA process included single- and multiple-server queuing models. The modeling approach successfully reduced the average ATA time to 24 hours and resulted in an annual cost savings of $9.5 million for the city and state.

Source: R. C. Larson, M. F. Colan, and M. C. Shell. "Improving the New York Arrest-to-Arraignment System," *Interfaces* 23, 1 (January–February 1993): 76–96.

14.6 CONSTANT SERVICE TIME MODEL ($M/D/1$)

Some service systems have constant service times instead of exponentially distributed times. When customers or equipment are processed according to a fixed cycle, as in the case of an automatic car wash or an amusement park ride, constant service rates are appropriate. Because constant rates are certain, the values for L_q, W_q, L, and W are always less than they would be in the models we have just discussed, which have variable service times. As a matter of fact, both the average queue length and the average waiting time in the queue are *halved* with the constant service rate model.

Constant service rates speed the process compared to exponentially distributed service times with the same value of μ.

Equations for the Constant Service Time Model

Constant service model formulas follow:

1. Average length of the queue:

$$L_q = \frac{\lambda^2}{2\mu(\mu - \lambda)} \tag{14-20}$$

2. Average waiting time in the queue:

$$W_q = \frac{\lambda}{2\mu(\mu - \lambda)} \tag{14-21}$$

3. Average number of customers in the system:

$$L = L_q + \frac{\lambda}{\mu} \tag{14-22}$$

4. Average time in the system:

$$W = W_q + \frac{1}{\mu} \tag{14-23}$$

Garcia-Golding Recycling, Inc.

Garcia-Golding Recycling, Inc., collects and compacts aluminum cans and glass bottles in New York City. Its truck drivers, who arrive to unload these materials for recycling, currently wait an average of 15 minutes before emptying their loads. The cost of the driver and truck time wasted while in queue is valued at $60 per hour. A new automated compactor can be purchased that will process truck loads at a constant rate of 12 trucks per hour (i.e., 5 minutes per truck). Trucks arrive according to a Poisson distribution at an average rate of 8 per hour. If the new compactor is put in use, its cost will be amortized at a rate of $3 per truck unloaded. A summer intern from a local college did the following analysis to evaluate the costs versus benefits of the purchase.

$$\textit{Current} \text{ waiting cost/trip} = (\tfrac{1}{4} \text{ hour waiting now})(\$60/\text{hour cost})$$

$$= \$15/\text{trip}$$

$$\textit{New} \text{ system: } \lambda = 8 \text{ trucks/hour arriving,}$$

$$\mu = 12 \text{ trucks/hour served}$$

Cost analysis for the recycling example.

$$\text{Average waiting time in queue} = W_q = \frac{\lambda}{2\mu(\mu - \lambda)} = \frac{8}{2(12)(12 - 8)}$$

$$= \frac{1}{12} \text{ hour}$$

$$\text{Waiting cost/trip with new compactor} = (\tfrac{1}{12} \text{ hour wait})(\$60/\text{hour cost}) = \$5/\text{trip}$$

$$\text{Savings with new equipment} = \$15 \text{ (current system)} - \$5 \text{ (new system)}$$

$$= \$10/\text{trip}$$

$$\text{Cost of new equipment amortized} = \$3/\text{trip}$$

$$\text{Net savings} = \$7/\text{trip}$$

Using Excel QM for Garcia-Golding's Constant Service Time Model To help solve this constant service time model with Excel QM, we refer to Programs 14.3A and 14.3B. The former provides an input screen and Excel formulas, and the latter contains the computed model parameters, including W_q.

PROGRAM 14.3A
Input Data and Formulas for Excel QM's Constant Service Time Queuing Model Applied to Garcia-Golding Recycling, Inc.

PROGRAM 14.3B

Output from Excel QM Constant Service Time Model in Program 14.3A

	A	B	C	D	E	F
1	**Garcia-Golding Recycling**					
2						
3	Waiting Lines	M/D/1 (Constant Service Times)				
4	The arrival RATE and service RATE both must be rates and use the same time unit.					
5	Given a time such as 10 minutes, convert it to a rate such as 6 per hour.					
6	Data			Results		
7	Arrival rate (λ)	8		Average server utilization(ρ)	0.666667	
8	Service rate (μ)	12		Average number of customers in the queue(L_q)	0.666667	
9				Average number of customers in the system(L)	1.333333	
10				Average waiting time in the queue(W_q)	0.083333	
11				Average time in the system(W)	0.166667	
12				Probability (% of time) system is empty (P_0)	0.333333	
13						
14	Waiting cost/hour	$ 60.00				
15	Waiting cost/trip	$ 5.00				

14.7   FINITE POPULATION MODEL (*M/M/1* WITH FINITE SOURCE)

When there is a limited population of potential customers for a service facility, we need to consider a different queuing model. This model would be used, for example, if you were considering equipment repairs in a factory that has five machines, if you were in charge of maintenance for a fleet of 10 commuter airplanes, or if you ran a hospital ward that has 20 beds. The limited population model permits any number of repair people (servers) to be considered.

The reason this model differs from the three earlier queuing models is that there is now a *dependent* relationship between the length of the queue and the arrival rate. To illustrate the extreme situation, if your factory had five machines and all were broken and awaiting repair, the arrival rate would drop to zero. In general, as the waiting line becomes longer in the limited population model, the arrival rate of customers or machines drops lower.

In this section we describe a finite calling population model that has the following assumptions:

1. There is only one server.
2. The population of units seeking service is finite.[4]
3. Arrivals follow a Poisson distribution, and service times are exponentially distributed.
4. Customers are served on a first-come, first-served basis.

Equations for the Finite Population Model

Using

$$\lambda = \text{mean arrival rate}, \quad \mu = \text{mean service rate}, \quad N = \text{size of the population}$$

the operating characteristics for the finite population model with a single channel or server on duty are as follows:

---

[4] Although there is no definite number that we can use to divide finite from infinite populations, the general rule of thumb is this: If the number in the queue is a significant proportion of the calling population, use a finite queuing model. *Finite Queuing Tables*, by L. G. Peck and R. N. Hazelwood (New York: John Wiley & Sons, Inc. 1958), eliminates much of the mathematics involved in computing the operating characteristics for such a model.

1. Probability that the system is empty:

$$P_0 = \frac{1}{\sum\limits_{n=0}^{N} \frac{N!}{(N-n)!} \left(\frac{\lambda}{\mu}\right)^n} \tag{14-24}$$

2. Average length of the queue:

$$L_q = N - \left(\frac{\lambda + \mu}{\lambda}\right)(1 - P_0) \tag{14-25}$$

3. Average number of customers (units) in the system:

$$L = L_q + (1 - P_0) \tag{14-26}$$

4. Average waiting time in the queue:

$$W_q = \frac{L_q}{(N-L)\lambda} \tag{14-27}$$

5. Average time in the system:

$$W = W_q + \frac{1}{\mu} \tag{14-28}$$

6. Probability of n units in the system:

$$P_n = \frac{N!}{(N-n)!}\left(\frac{\lambda}{\mu}\right)^n P_0 \quad \text{for } n = 0, 1, \dots, N \tag{14-29}$$

Department of Commerce Example

Past records indicate that each of the five high-speed "page" printers at the U.S. Department of Commerce, in Washington, DC, needs repair after about 20 hours of use. Breakdowns have been determined to be Poisson distributed. The one technician on duty can service a printer in an average of 2 hours, following an exponential distribution.

To compute the system's operation characteristics we first note that the mean arrival rate is $\lambda = \frac{1}{20} = 0.05$ printer/hour. The mean service rate is $\mu = \frac{1}{2} = 0.50$ printer/hour. Then

1. $P_0 = \dfrac{1}{\sum\limits_{n=0}^{5} \dfrac{5!}{(5-n)!}\left(\dfrac{0.05}{0.5}\right)^n} = 0.564$ (we leave these calculations for you to confirm)

2. $L_q = 5 - \left(\dfrac{0.05 + 0.5}{0.05}\right)(1 - P_0) = 5 - (11)(1 - 0.564) = 5 - 4.8$

   $= 0.2$ printer

3. $L = 0.2 + (1 - 0.564) = 0.64$ printer

4. $W_q = \dfrac{0.2}{(5 - 0.64)(0.05)} = \dfrac{0.2}{0.22} = 0.91$ hour

5. $W = 0.91 + \dfrac{1}{0.50} = 2.91$ hours

If printer downtime costs \$120 per hour and the technician is paid \$25 per hour, we can also compute the total cost per hour:

$$\text{total hourly cost} = \text{(average number of printers down)(cost per downtime hour)} + \text{cost per technician hour}$$

$$= (0.64)(\$120) + \$25 = \$76.80 + \$25.00 = \$101.80$$

Solving the Department of Commerce Finite Population Model with Excel QM
Program 14.4A shows the input data and formulas used to help solve this problem using Excel QM. The results are provided in Program14.4B. Note that the computer calculations

PROGRAM 14.4A

Excel QM Input Data and Formulas for Solving the Department of Commerce Finite Population Queuing Model

PROGRAM 14.4B

Output from Excel QM's Program 14.4A

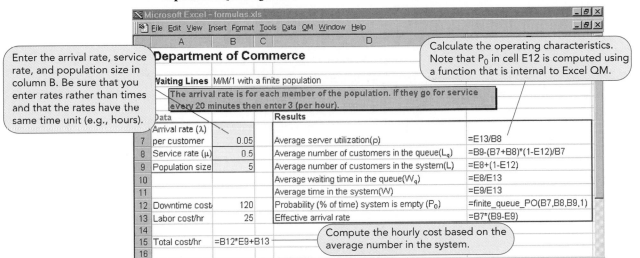

are slightly more accurate because there is less rounding than we did in our calculations in the preceding section.

14.8   SOME GENERAL OPERATING CHARACTERISTIC RELATIONSHIPS

A steady state is the normal operating condition of the queuing system.

A queuing system is in a transient state before the steady state is reached.

Certain relationships exist among specific operating characteristics for any queuing system in a *steady state*. A steady state condition exists when a queuing system is in its normal stabilized operating condition, usually after an initial or *transient state* that may occur (e.g., having customers waiting at the door when a business opens in the morning). Both the arrival rate and the service rate should be stable in this state. John D. C. Little is credited with the first two of these relationships, and hence they are called *Little's Flow Equations*:

$$L = \lambda W \quad (\text{or } W = L/\lambda) \tag{14-30}$$

$$L_q = \lambda W_q \quad (\text{or } W_q = L_q/\lambda) \tag{14-31}$$

A third condition that must always be met is

Average time in system = average time in queue + average time receiving service

$$W = W_q + 1/\mu \tag{14-32}$$

The advantage of these formulas is that once one of these four characteristics is known, the other characteristics can easily be found. This is important because for certain queuing models, one of these may be much easier to determine than the others. These are applicable to all of the queuing systems discussed in this chapter except the finite population model.

14.9   MORE COMPLEX QUEUING MODELS AND THE USE OF SIMULATION

Many practical waiting line problems that occur in production and operations service systems have characteristics like those of Arnold's Muffler Shop, Garcia-Golding Recycling Inc., or the Department of Commerce. This is true when the situation calls for single- or multichannel waiting lines, with Poisson arrivals and exponential or constant service times, an infinite calling population, and FIFO service.

More sophisticated models exist to handle variations of basic assumptions, but when even these do not apply we can turn to computer simulation, the topic of Chapter 15.

Often, however, *variations* of this specific case are present in an analysis. Service times in an automobile repair shop, for example, tend to follow the normal probability distribution instead of the exponential. A college registration system in which seniors have first choice of courses and hours over all other students is an example of a first-come, first-served model with a preemptive priority queue discipline. A physical examination for military recruits is an example of a multiphase system—one that differs from the single-phase models discussed in this chapter. A recruit first lines up to have blood drawn at one station, then waits to take an eye exam at the next station, talks to a psychiatrist at the third, and is examined by a doctor for medical problems at the fourth. At each phase, the recruit must enter another queue and wait his or her turn.

Models to handle these cases have been developed by operations researchers. The computations for the resulting mathematical formulations are somewhat more complex than the ones covered in this chapter,[5] and many real-world queuing applications are too complex to be modeled analytically at all. When this happens, quantitative analysts usually turn to *computer simulation*.

Simulation, the topic of Chapter 15, is a technique in which random numbers are used to draw inferences about probability distributions (such as arrivals and services). Using this

---

[5] Often, the *qualitative* results of queuing models are as useful as the quantitative results. Results show that it is inherently more efficient to pool resources, use central dispatching, and provide single multiple-server systems rather than multiple single-server systems.

approach, many hours, days, or months of data can be developed by a computer in a few seconds. This allows analysis of controllable factors, such as adding another service channel, without actually doing so physically. Basically, whenever a standard analytical queuing model provides only a poor approximation of the actual service system, it is wise to develop a simulation model instead.

SUMMARY

Waiting lines and service systems are important parts of the business world. In this chapter we describe several common queuing situations and present mathematical models for analyzing waiting lines following certain assumptions. Those assumptions are that (1) arrivals come from an infinite or very large population, (2) arrivals are Poisson distributed, (3) arrivals are treated on a FIFO basis and do not balk or renege, (4) service times follow the negative exponential distribution or are constant, and (5) the average service rate is faster than the average arrival rate.

The models illustrated in this chapter are for single-channel, single-phase and multichannel, single-phase problems. After a series of operating characteristics are computed, total expected costs are studied. As shown graphically in Figure 14.1, total cost is the sum of the cost of providing service plus the cost of waiting time.

Key operating characteristics for a system are shown to be (1) utilization rate, (2) percent idle time, (3) average time spent waiting in the system and in the queue, (4) average number of customers in the system and in the queue, and (5) probabilities of various numbers of customers in the system.

The chapter emphasizes that a variety of queuing models exist that do not meet all of the assumptions of the traditional models. In these cases we use more complex mathematical models or turn to a technique called computer simulation. The application of simulation to problems of queuing systems, inventory control, machine breakdown, and other quantitative analysis situations is the topic discussed in Chapter 15.

GLOSSARY

Balking. The case in which arriving customers refuse to join the waiting line.

Calling Population. The population of items from which arrivals at the queuing system come.

FIFO. A queue discipline (meaning first-in, first-out) in which the customers are served in the strict order of arrival.

Kendall Notation. A method of classifying queuing systems based on the distribution of arrivals, the distribution of service times, and the number of service channels.

Limited or Finite Population. A case in which the number of customers in the system is a significant proportion of the calling population.

Limited Queue Length. A waiting line that cannot increase beyond a specific size.

Little's Equations. A set of relationships that exist for any queuing system in a steady state.

$M/D/1$. Kendall notation for the constant service time model.

$M/M/m$. Kendall notation for the multichannel queuing model (with m servers) and Poisson arrivals and exponential service times.

$M/M/1$. Kendall notation for the single-channel model with Poisson arrivals and exponential service times.

Multichannel Queuing System. A system that has more than one service facility, all fed by the same single queue.

Multiphase System. A system in which service is received from more than one station, one after the other.

Negative Exponential Probability Distribution. A probability distribution that is often used to describe random service times in a service system.

Operating Characteristics. Descriptive characteristics of a queuing system, including the average number of customers in a line and in the system, the average waiting times in a line and in the system, and percent idle time.

Poisson Distribution. A probability distribution that is often used to describe random arrivals in a queue.

Queue Discipline. The rule by which customers in a line receive service.

Queuing Theory. The mathematical study of waiting lines or queues.

Reneging. The case in which customers enter a queue but then leave before being serviced.

Service Cost. The cost of providing a particular level of service.

Single-Channel Queuing System. A system with one service facility fed by one queue.

Single-Phase System. A queuing system in which service is received at only one station.

Steady State. The normal, stabilized operating condition of a queuing system.

Transient State. The initial condition of a queuing system before a steady state is reached.

Unlimited or Infinite Population. A calling population that is very large relative to the number of customers currently in the system.

Unlimited Queue Length. A queue that can increase to an infinite size.

Utilization Factor (ρ). The proportion of the time that service facilities are in use.

Waiting Cost. The cost to the firm of having customers or objects waiting to be serviced.

Waiting Line (Queue). One or more customers or objects waiting to be served.

KEY EQUATIONS

λ = mean number of arrivals per time period

μ = mean number of people or items served per time period

(14-1) $P(X) = \dfrac{e^{-\lambda}\lambda^X}{X!}$

Poisson probability distribution used in describing arrivals.

Equations 14-2 through 14-8 describe operating characteristics in the single-channel model that has Poisson arrival and exponential service rates.

(14-2)　L = average number of units (customers) in the system

$\quad = \dfrac{\lambda}{\mu - \lambda}$

(14-3)　$W =$ average time a unit spends in the system (waiting time + service time)

$\quad = \dfrac{1}{\mu - \lambda}$

(14-4)　$L_q =$ average number of units in the queue $= \dfrac{\lambda^2}{\mu(\mu - \lambda)}$

(14-5)　$W_q =$ average time a unit spends waiting in the queue

$\quad = \dfrac{\lambda}{\mu(\mu - \lambda)}$

(14-6)　$\rho =$ utilization factor for the system $= \dfrac{\lambda}{\mu}$

(14-7)　$P_0 =$ probability of 0 units in the system (that is, the service unit is idle)

$\quad = 1 - \dfrac{\lambda}{\mu}$

(14-8) $P_{n>k} =$ probability of more than k units in the system

$\quad = \left(\dfrac{\lambda}{\mu}\right)^{k+1}$

Equations 14-9 through 14-13 are used for finding the costs of a queuing system.

(14-9) Total hourly service cost $= mC_s$

where

m = number of channels

C_s = service cost (labor cost) of each channel

(14-10) Total waiting cost per time period $= (\lambda W)C_w$

C_w = cost of waiting

Waiting time cost based on time in the system.

(14-11) Total waiting cost per time period $= (\lambda W_q)C_w$

Waiting time cost based on time in the queue.

(14-12) Total cost $= mC_s + \lambda W C_w$

Waiting time cost based on time in the system.

(14-13) Total cost $= mC_s + \lambda W_q C_w$

Waiting time cost based on time in the queue.

Equations 14-14 through 14-19 describe operating characteristics in multichannel models that have Poisson arrival and exponential service rates, where m = the number of open channels.

(14-14)
$$P_0 = \dfrac{1}{\left[\displaystyle\sum_{n=0}^{n=m-1} \dfrac{1}{n!}\left(\dfrac{\lambda}{\mu}\right)^n\right] + \dfrac{1}{m!}\left(\dfrac{\lambda}{\mu}\right)^m \dfrac{m\mu}{m\mu - \lambda}}$$

for　$m\mu > \lambda$

The probability that there are no people or units in the system.

(14-15) $L = \dfrac{\lambda\mu(\lambda/\mu)^m}{(m-1)!(m\mu - \lambda)^2}P_0 + \dfrac{\lambda}{\mu}$

The average number of people or units in the system.

(14-16) $W = \dfrac{\mu(\lambda/\mu)^m}{(m-1)!(m\mu - \lambda)^2}P_0 + \dfrac{1}{\mu} = \dfrac{L}{\lambda}$

The average time a unit spends in the waiting line or being serviced (namely, in the system).

(14-17) $L_q = L - \dfrac{\lambda}{\mu}$

The average number of people or units in line waiting for service.

(14-18) $W_q = W - \dfrac{1}{\mu} = \dfrac{L_q}{\lambda}$

The average time a person or unit spends in the queue waiting for service.

(14-19) $\rho = \dfrac{\lambda}{m\mu}$

Utilization rate.

Equations 14-20 through 14-23 describe operating characteristics in single-channel models that have Poisson arrivals and constant service rates.

(14-20) $L_q = \dfrac{\lambda^2}{2\mu(\mu - \lambda)}$

The average length of the queue.

(14-21) $W_q = \dfrac{\lambda}{2\mu(\mu - \lambda)}$

The average waiting time in the queue.

(14-22) $L = L_q + \dfrac{\lambda}{\mu}$

The average number of customers in the system.

(14-23) $W = W_q + \dfrac{1}{\mu}$

The average waiting time in the system.

Equations 14-24 through 14-29 describe operating characteristics in single-channel models that have Poisson arrivals and exponential service rates and a finite calling population.

(14-24) $P_0 = \dfrac{1}{\displaystyle\sum_{n=0}^{N} \dfrac{N!}{(N-n)!}\left(\dfrac{\lambda}{\mu}\right)^n}$

The probability that the system is empty.

(14-25) $L_q = N - \left(\dfrac{\lambda + \mu}{\lambda}\right)(1 - P_0)$

Average length of the queue.

(14-26) $L = L_q + (1 - P_0)$

Average number of units in the system.

(14-27) $W_q = \dfrac{L_q}{(N - L)\lambda}$

Average time in the queue.

(14-28) $W = W_q + \dfrac{1}{\mu}$

Average time in the system.

(14-29) $P_n = \dfrac{N!}{(N - n)!}\left(\dfrac{\lambda}{\mu}\right)^n P_0$ for $n = 0, 1..., N$

Probability of n units in the system.

Equations 14-30 to 14-32 are Little's Flow Equations, which can be used when a steady state condition exists.

(14-30) $L = \lambda W$

(14-31) $L_q = \lambda W_q$

(14-32) $W = W_q + 1/\mu$

SOLVED PROBLEMS

Solved Problem 14-1

The Maitland Furniture store gets an average of 50 customers per shift. The manager of Maitland wants to calculate whether she should hire 1, 2, 3, or 4 salespeople. She has determined that average waiting times will be 7 minutes with one salesperson, 4 minutes with two salespeople, 3 minutes with three salespeople, and 2 minutes with four salespeople. She has estimated the cost per minute that customers wait at $1. The cost per salesperson per shift (including fringe benefits) is $70.

How many salespeople should be hired?

Solution

The manager's calculations are as follows:

	NUMBER OF SALESPEOPLE			
	1	2	3	4
(a) Average number of customers per shift	50	50	50	50
(b) Average waiting time per customer (minutes)	7	4	3	2
(c) Total waiting time per shift ($a \times b$) (minutes)	350	200	150	100
(d) Cost per minute of waiting time (estimated)	$1.00	$1.00	$1.00	$1.00
(e) Value of lost time ($c \times d$) per shift	$350	$200	$150	$100
(f) Salary cost per shift	$70	$140	$210	$280
(g) Total cost per shift	$420	$340	$360	$380

Because the minimum total cost per shift relates to two salespeople, the manager's optimum strategy is to hire two salespeople.

Solved Problem 14-2

Marty Schatz owns and manages a chili dog and soft drink store near the campus. Although Marty can service 30 customers per hour on the average (μ), he only gets 20 customers per hour (λ). Because Marty could wait on 50% more customers than actually visit his store, it doesn't make sense to him that he should have any waiting lines.

Marty hires you to examine the situation and to determine some characteristics of his queue. After looking into the problem, you make the seven assumptions listed in Section 14.4 on page 576. What are your findings?

Solution

$$L = \frac{\lambda}{\mu - \lambda} = \frac{20}{30 - 20} = 2 \text{ customers in the system on the average}$$

$$W = \frac{1}{\mu - \lambda} = \frac{1}{30 - 20} = 0.1 \text{ hour (6 minutes) that the average customer spends in the total system}$$

$$L_q = \frac{\lambda^2}{\mu(\mu - \lambda)} = \frac{20^2}{30(30 - 20)} = 1.33 \text{ customers waiting for service in line on the average}$$

$$w_q = \frac{\lambda}{\mu(\mu - \lambda)} = \frac{20}{30(30 - 20)} = \frac{1}{15} \text{ hour} = (4 \text{ minutes}) = \text{average waiting time of a customer in the queue awaiting service}$$

$$\rho = \frac{\lambda}{\mu} = \frac{20}{30} = 0.67 = \text{percent of the time that Marty is busy waiting on customers}$$

$$P_0 = 1 - \frac{\lambda}{\mu} = 1 - \rho = 0.33 = \text{probability that there are no customers in the system (being waited on or waiting in the queue) at any given time}$$

Probability of *k* or More Customers Waiting in Line and/or Being Waited On

k	$P_{n>k} = \left(\frac{\lambda}{\mu}\right)^{k+1}$
0	0.667
1	0.444
2	0.296
3	0.198

Solved Problem 14-3

Refer to Solved Problem 14-2. Marty agreed that these figures seemed to represent his approximate business situation. You are quite surprised at the length of the lines and elicit from him an estimated value of the customer's waiting time (in the queue, not being waited on) at 10 cents per minute. During the 12 hours that he is open he gets $(12 \times 20) = 240$ customers. The average customer is in a queue 4 minutes, so the total customer waiting time is $(240 \times 4 \text{ minutes}) = 960$ minutes. The value of 960 minutes is $(\$0.10)(960 \text{ minutes}) = \$96$. You tell Marty that not only is 10 cents per minute quite conservative, but he could probably save most of that $96 of customer ill will if he hired another salesclerk. After much haggling, Marty agrees to provide you with all the chili dogs you can eat during a week-long period in exchange for your analysis of the results of having two clerks wait on the customers.

Assuming that Marty hires one additional salesclerk whose service rate equals Marty's rate, complete the analysis.

Solution

With two cash registers open, the system becomes two-channel, or $m = 2$. The computations yield

$$P_0 = \cfrac{1}{\left[\displaystyle\sum_{n=0}^{n=m-1} \frac{1}{n!}\left[\frac{20}{30}\right]^n\right] + \frac{1}{2!}\left[\frac{20}{30}\right]^2\left[\frac{2(30)}{2(30)-20}\right]}$$

$$= \frac{1}{(1)(2/3)^0 + (1)(2/3)^1 + (1/2)(4/9)(6/4)} = 0.5$$

= probability of no customers in the system

$$L = \left[\frac{(20)(30)(20/30)^2}{(2-1)![(2)(30-20)]^2}\right]0.5 + \frac{20}{30} = 0.75 \text{ customer in the system on the average}$$

$$W = \frac{L}{\lambda} = \frac{3/4}{20} = \frac{3}{80} \text{ hours} = 2.25 \text{ minutes that the average customer spends in the total system}$$

$$L_q = L - \frac{\lambda}{\mu} = \frac{3}{4} - \frac{20}{30} = \frac{1}{12} = 0.083 \text{ customer waiting for service in line on the average}$$

$$W_q = \frac{L_q}{\lambda} = \frac{\raise2pt\hbox{1}\!\!/\!\lower2pt\hbox{12}}{20} = \frac{1}{240} \text{ hour} = \frac{1}{4}\text{ minute} = \text{average waiting time of a customer in the queue} \\ \text{itself (not being serviced)}$$

$$\rho = \frac{\lambda}{m\mu} = \frac{20}{2(30)} = \frac{1}{3} = 0.33 = \text{utilization rate}$$

You now have (240 customers) × (1/240 hour) = 1 hour total customer waiting time per day.

Total cost of 60 minutes of customer waiting time is (60 minutes)($0.10 per minute) = $6.

Now you are ready to point out to Marty that the hiring of one additional clerk will save $96 − $6 = $90 of customer ill will per 12-hour shift. Marty responds that the hiring should also reduce the number of people who look at the line and leave as well as those who get tired of waiting in line and leave. You tell Marty that you are ready for two chili dogs, extra hot.

Solved Problem 14-4

Vacation Inns is a chain of hotels operating in the southwestern part of the United States. The company uses a toll-free telephone number to take reservations for any of its hotels. The average time to handle each call is 3 minutes, and an average of 12 calls are received per hour. The probability distribution that describes the arrivals is unknown. Over a period of time it is determined that the average caller spends 6 minutes either on hold or receiving service. Find the average time in the queue, the average time in the system, the average number in the queue, and the average number in the system.

Solution

The probability distributions are unknown, but we are given the average time in the system (6 minutes). Thus, we can use Little's equations:

$$W = 6 \text{ minutes} = 6/60 \text{ hours} = 0.1 \text{ hours}$$

$$\lambda = 12 \text{ per hour}$$

$$\mu = 60/3 = 20 \text{ per hour}$$

$$\text{Average time in queue} = W_q = W - 1/\mu = 0.1 - 1/20 = 0.1 - 0.05 = 0.05 \text{ hours}$$

$$\text{Average number in system} = L = \lambda W = 12(0.1) = 1.2 \text{ callers}$$

$$\text{Average number in queue} = L_q = \lambda W_q = 12(0.05) = 0.6 \text{ callers}$$

SELF-TEST

- Before taking the self-test, refer back to the learning objectives at the beginning of the chapter, the notes in the margins, and the glossary at the end of the chapter.
- Use the key at the back of the book to correct your answers.
- Restudy pages that correspond to any questions that you answered incorrectly or material you feel uncertain about.

1. Most systems use the queue discipline known as the FIFO rule.
   a. True
   b. False

2. Before using exponential distributions to build queuing models, the quantitative analyst should determine if the service-time data fit the distribution.
   a. True
   b. False

3. In a multichannel, single-phase queuing system, the arrival will pass through at least two different service facilities.
   a. True
   b. False

4. Which of the following is *not* an assumption in $M/M/1$ models?
   a. arrivals come from an infinite or very large population
   b. arrivals are Poisson distributed
   c. arrivals are treated on a FIFO basis and do not balk or renege
   d. service times follow the exponential distribution
   e. the average arrival rate is faster than the average service rate

5. A queuing system described as $M/D/2$ would have
   a. exponential service times.
   b. two queues.
   c. constant service times.
   d. constant arrival rates.

6. Cars enter the drive-through of a fast-food restaurant to place an order, and then they proceed to pay for the food and pick up the order. This is an example of
   a. a multichannel system.
   b. a multiphase system.
   c. a multiqueue system.
   d. none of the above.

7. The utilization factor for a system is defined as
   a. mean number of people served divided by the mean number of arrivals per time period.
   b. the average time a customer spends waiting in a queue.
   c. proportion of the time the service facilities are in use.
   d. the percent idle time.
   e. none of the above.

8. Which of the following would not have a FIFO queue discipline?
   a. fast-food restaurant
   b. post office
   c. checkout line at grocery store
   d. emergency room at a hospital

9. A company has one computer technician who is responsible for repairs on the company's 20 computers. As a computer breaks, the technician is called to make the repair. If the repairperson is busy, the machine must wait to be repaired. This is an example of
   a. a multichannel system.
   b. a finite population system.
   c. a constant service rate system.
   d. a multiphase system.

10. In performing a cost analysis of a queuing system, the waiting time cost (C_w) is sometimes based on the time in the queue and sometimes based on the time in the system. The waiting cost should be based on time in the system for which of the following situations?
    a. waiting in line to ride an amusement park ride
    b. waiting to discuss a medical problem with a doctor
    c. waiting for a picture and an autograph from a rock star
    d. waiting for a computer to be fixed so it can be placed back in service

11. Customers enter the waiting line at a cafeteria on a first-come, first-served basis. The arrival rate follows a Poisson distribution, and service times follow an exponential distribution. If the average number of arrivals is 6 per minute and the average service rate of a single server is 10 per minute, what is the average number of customers in the system?
    a. 0.6
    b. 0.9
    c. 1.5
    d. 0.25
    e. none of the above

12. In the standard queuing model, we assume that the queue discipline is _____.

13. The service *time* in the $M/M/1$ queuing model is assumed to be _____.

14. When managers find standard queuing formulas inadequate or the mathematics unsolvable, they often resort to _____ to obtain their solutions.

DISCUSSION QUESTIONS AND PROBLEMS

Discussion Questions

14-1 What is the waiting line problem? What are the components in a waiting line system?

14-2 What are the assumptions underlying common queuing models?

14-3 Describe the important operating characteristics of a queuing system.

14-4 Why must the service rate be greater than the arrival rate in a single-channel queuing system?

14-5 Briefly describe three situations in which the FIFO discipline rule is not applicable in queuing analysis.

14-6 Provide examples of four situations in which there is a limited, or finite, population.

14-7 What are the components of the following systems? Draw and explain the configuration of each.

(a) barbershop
(b) car wash
(c) laundromat
(d) small grocery store

14-8 Give an example of a situation in which the waiting time cost would be based on waiting time in the queue. Give an example of a situation in which the waiting time cost would be based on waiting time in the system.

14-9 Do you think the Poisson distribution, which assumes independent arrivals, is a good estimation of arrival rates in the following queuing systems? Defend your position in each case.

(a) cafeteria in your school
(b) barbershop
(c) hardware store
(d) dentist's office
(e) college class
(f) movie theater

Problems*

14-10 The Schmedley Discount Department Store has approximately 300 customers shopping in its store between 9 A.M. and 5 P.M. on Saturdays. In deciding how many cash registers to keep open each Saturday, Schmedley's manager considers two factors: customer waiting time (and the associated waiting cost) and the service costs of employing additional checkout clerks. Checkout clerks are paid an average of $8 per hour. When only one is on duty, the waiting time per customer is about 10 minutes (or $\frac{1}{6}$ of an hour); when two clerks are on duty, the average checkout time is 6 minutes per person; 4 minutes when three clerks are working; and 3 minutes when four clerks are on duty.

Schmedley's management has conducted customer satisfaction surveys and has been able to estimate that the store suffers approximately $10 in lost sales and goodwill for every *hour* of customer time spent waiting in checkout lines. Using the information provided, determine the optimal number of clerks to have on duty each Saturday to minimize the store's total expected cost.

14-11 The Rockwell Electronics Corporation retains a service crew to repair machine breakdowns that occur on an average of $\lambda = 3$ per day (approximately Poisson in nature).

The crew can service an average of $\mu = 8$ machines per day, with a repair time distribution that resembles the exponential distribution.

(a) What is the utilization rate of this service system?
(b) What is the average downtime for a machine that is broken?
(c) How many machines are waiting to be serviced at any given time?
(d) What is the probability that more than one machine is in the system? Probability that more than two are broken and waiting to be repaired or being serviced? More than three? More than four?

14-12 From historical data, Harry's Car Wash estimates that dirty cars arrive at the rate of 10 per hour all day Saturday. With a crew working the wash line, Harry figures that cars can be cleaned at the rate of one every 5 minutes. One car at a time is cleaned in this example of a single-channel waiting line.

Assuming Poisson arrivals and exponential service times, find the

(a) average number of cars in line.
(b) average time a car waits before it is washed.
(c) average time a car spends in the service system.
(d) utilization rate of the car wash.
(e) probability that no cars are in the system.

14-13 Mike Dreskin manages a large Los Angeles movie theater complex called Cinema I, II, III, and IV. Each of the four auditoriums plays a different film; the schedule is set so that starting times are staggered to avoid the large crowds that would occur if all four movies started at the same time. The theater has a single ticket booth and a cashier who can maintain an average service rate of 280 movie patrons per hour. Service times are assumed to follow an exponential distribution. Arrivals on a typically active day are Poisson distributed and average 210 per hour.

---
* Note: means the problem may be solved with QM for Windows; ✗ means the problem may be solved with Excel QM; and means the problem may be solved with QM for Windows and/or Excel QM.

To determine the efficiency of the current ticket operation, Mike wishes to examine several queue operating characteristics.

(a) Find the average number of moviegoers waiting in line to purchase a ticket.

(b) What percentage of the time is the cashier busy?

(c) What is the average time that a customer spends in the system?

(d) What is the average time spent waiting in line to get to the ticket window?

(e) What is the probability that there are more than two people in the system? More than three people? More than four?

14-14 A university cafeteria line in the student center is a self-serve facility in which students select the food items they want and then form a single line to pay the cashier. Students arrive at a rate of about four per minute according to a Poisson distribution. The single cashier ringing up sales takes about 12 seconds per customer, following an exponential distribution.

(a) What is the probability that there are more than two students in the system? More than three students? More than four?

(b) What is the probability that the system is empty?

(c) How long will the average student have to wait before reaching the cashier?

(d) What is the expected number of students in the queue?

(e) What is the average number in the system?

(f) If a second cashier is added (who works at the same pace), how will the operating characteristics computed in parts (b), (c), (d), and (e) change? Assume that customers wait in a single line and go to the first available cashier.

14-15 The wheat harvesting season in the American Midwest is short, and most farmers deliver their truckloads of wheat to a giant central storage bin within a two-week span. Because of this, wheat-filled trucks waiting to unload and return to the fields have been known to back up for a block at the receiving bin. The central bin is owned cooperatively, and it is to every farmer's benefit to make the unloading/storage process as efficient as possible. The cost of grain deterioration caused by unloading delays, the cost of truck rental, and idle driver time are significant concerns to the cooperative members. Although farmers have difficulty quantifying crop damage, it is easy to assign a waiting and unloading cost for truck and driver of $18 per hour. The storage bin is open and operated 16 hours per day, 7 days per week, during the harvest season and is capable of unloading 35 trucks per hour according to an exponential distribution. Full trucks arrive all day long (during the hours the bin is open) at a rate of about 30 per hour, following a Poisson pattern.

To help the cooperative get a handle on the problem of lost time while trucks are waiting in line or unloading at the bin, find the

(a) average number of trucks in the unloading system.

(b) average time per truck in the system.

(c) utilization rate for the bin area.

(d) probability that there are more than three trucks in the system at any given time.

(e) total daily cost to the farmers of having their trucks tied up in the unloading process.

The cooperative, as mentioned, uses the storage bin only two weeks per year. Farmers estimate that enlarging the bin would cut unloading costs by 50% next year. It will cost $9,000 to do so during the off-season. Would it be worth the cooperative's while to enlarge the storage area?

14-16 Ashley's Department Store in Kansas City maintains a successful catalog sales department in which a clerk takes orders by telephone. If the clerk is occupied on one line, incoming phone calls to the catalog department are answered automatically by a recording machine and asked to wait. As soon as the clerk is free, the party that has waited the longest is transferred and answered first. Calls come in at a rate of about 12 per hour. The clerk is capable of taking an order in an average of 4 minutes. Calls tend to follow a Poisson distribution, and service times tend to be exponential. The clerk is paid $10 per hour, but because of lost goodwill and sales, Ashley's loses about $50 per hour of customer time spent waiting for the clerk to take an order.

(a) What is the average time that catalog customers must wait before their calls are transferred to the order clerk?

(b) What is the average number of callers waiting to place an order?

(c) Ashley's is considering adding a second clerk to take calls. The store would pay that person the same $10 per hour. Should it hire another clerk? Explain.

14-17 Automobiles arrive at the drive-through window at a post office at the rate of 4 every 10 minutes. The average service time is 2 minutes. The Poisson distribution is appropriate for the arrival rate and service times are exponentially distributed.

(a) What is the average time a car is in the system?

(b) What is the average number of cars in the system?

(c) What is the average time cars spend waiting to receive service?

(d) What is the average number of cars in line *behind* the customer receiving service?

(e) What is the probability that there are no cars at the window?

(f) What percentage of the time is the postal clerk busy?

(g) What is the probability that there are exactly 2 cars in the system?

14-18 For the post office in Problem 14-17, a second drive-through window is being considered. A single line would be formed and as a car reached the front of the line it would go to the next available clerk. The clerk at the new window works at the same rate as the current one.

(a) What is the average time a car is in the system?

(b) What is the average number of cars in the system?

(c) What is the average time cars spend waiting to receive service?

(d) What is the average number of cars in line *behind* the customer receiving service?

(e) What is the probability that there are no cars in the system?

(f) What percentage of the time are the clerks busy?

(g) What is the probability that there are exactly 2 cars in the system?

14-19 Juhn and Sons Wholesale Fruit Distributors employ one worker whose job is to load fruit on outgoing company trucks. Trucks arrive at the loading gate at an average of 24 per day, or 3 per hour, according to a Poisson distribution. The worker loads them at a rate of 4 per hour, following approximately the exponential distribution in service times.

Determine the operating characteristics of this loading gate problem. What is the probability that there will be more than three trucks either being loaded or waiting? Discuss the results of your queuing model computation.

14-20 Juhn believes that adding a second fruit loader will substantially improve the firm's efficiency. He estimates that a two-person crew, still acting like a single-server system, at the loading gate will double the loading rate from 4 trucks per hour to 8 trucks per hour. Analyze the effect on the queue of such a change and compare the results with those found in Problem 14-19.

14-21 Truck drivers working for Juhn and Sons (see Problems 14-19 and 14-20) are paid a salary of $10 per hour on average. Fruit loaders receive about $6 per hour. Truck drivers waiting in the queue or at the loading gate are drawing a salary but are productively idle and unable to generate revenue during that time. What would be the *hourly* cost savings to the firm associated with employing two loaders instead of one?

14-22 Juhn and Sons Wholesale Fruit Distributors (of Problem 14-19) are considering building a second platform or gate to speed the process of loading their fruit trucks. This, they think, will be even more efficient than simply hiring another loader to help out the first platform (as in Problem 14-20).

Assume that workers at each platform will be able to load 4 trucks per hour each and that trucks will continue to arrive at the rate of 3 per hour. Find the waiting line's new operating conditions. Is this new approach indeed speedier than the other two considered?

14-23 Bill First, general manager of Worthmore Department Store, has estimated that every hour of customer time spent waiting in line for the sales clerk to become available costs the store $100 in lost sales and goodwill. Customers arrive at the checkout counter at the rate of 30 per hour, and the average service time is 3 minutes. The Poisson distribution describes the arrivals and the service times are exponentially distributed. The number of sales clerks can be 2, 3, or 4, with each one working at the same rate.

Bill estimates the salary and benefits for each clerk to be $10 per hour. The store is open 10 hours per day.

(a) Find the average time in the line if 2, 3, and 4 clerks are used.

(b) What is the total time spent waiting in line each day if 2, 3, and 4 clerks are used?

(c) Calculate the total of the daily waiting cost and the service cost if 2, 3, and 4 clerks are used. What is the minimum total daily cost?

14-24 Billy's Bank is the only bank in a small town in Arkansas. On a typical Friday, an average of 10 customers per hour arrive at the bank to transact business. There is one single teller at the bank, and the average time required to transact business is 4 minutes. It is assumed that service times can be described by the exponential distribution. Although this is the only bank in town, some people in the town have begun using the bank in a neighboring town about 20 miles away. A single line would be used, and the customer at the front of the line would go to the first available bank teller. If a single teller at Billy's is used, find

(a) the average time in the line.

(b) the average number in the line.

(c) the average time in the system.

(d) the average number in the system.

(e) the probability that the bank is empty.

14-25 Refer to the Billy's Bank situation in Problem 14-24. Billy is considering adding a second teller (who would work at the same rate as the first) to reduce the waiting time for customers, and he assumes that this will cut the waiting time in half. If a second teller is added, find

(a) the average time in the line.

(b) the average number in the line.

(c) the average time in the system.

(d) the average number in the system.

(e) the probability that the bank is empty.

14-26 For the Billy's Bank situation in Problems 14-24 and 14-25, the salary and benefits for a teller would be $12 per hour. The bank is open 8 hours each day. It has been estimated that the waiting time cost per hour is $25 per hour in the line.

(a) How many customers would enter the bank on a typical day?

(b) How much total time would the customers spend waiting in line during the entire day if one teller were used? What is the total daily waiting time cost?

(c) How much total time would the customers spend waiting in line during the entire day if two tellers were used? What is the total waiting time cost?

(d) If Billy wishes to minimize the total waiting time and personnel cost, how many tellers should be used?

14-27 Customers arrive at an automated coffee vending machine at a rate of 4 per minute, following a Poisson distribution. The coffee machine dispenses a cup of coffee in exactly 10 seconds.

(a) What is the average number of people waiting in line?

(b) What is the average number in the system?

(c) How long does the average person wait in line before receiving service?

14-28 The average number of customers in the system in the single-channel, single-phase model described in Section 14.4 is

$$L = \frac{\lambda}{\mu - \lambda}$$

Show that for $m = 1$ server, the multichannel queuing model in Section 14.5,

$$L = \frac{\lambda\mu \left(\dfrac{\lambda}{\mu}\right)^m}{(m-1)!(m\mu - \lambda)^2} P_0 + \frac{\lambda}{\mu}$$

is identical to the single-channel system. Note that the formula for P_0 (Equation 14-12) must be utilized in this highly algebraic exercise.

14-29 One mechanic services 5 drilling machines for a steel plate manufacturer. Machines break down on an average of once every 6 working days, and breakdowns tend to follow a Poisson distribution. The mechanic can handle an average of one repair job per day. Repairs follow an exponential distribution.

(a) How many machines are waiting for service, on average?

(b) How many are in the system, on average?

(c) How many drills are in running order, on average?

(d) What is the average waiting time in the queue?

(e) What is the average wait in the system?

14-30 A technician monitors a group of five computers that run an automated manufacturing facility. It takes an average of 15 minutes (exponentially distributed) to adjust a computer that develops a problem. The computers run for an average of 85 minutes (Poisson distributed) without requiring adjustments. What is the

(a) average number of computers waiting for adjustment?

(b) average number of computers not in working order?

(c) probability the system is empty?

(d) average time in the queue?

(e) average time in the system?

14-31 The typical subway station in Washington, DC, has 6 turnstiles, each of which can be controlled by the station manager to be used for either entrance or exit control—but never for both. The manager must decide at different times of the day just how many turnstiles to use for entering passengers and how many to be set up to allow exiting passengers.

At the Washington College Station, passengers enter the station at a rate of about 84 per minute between the hours of 7 and 9 A.M. Passengers exiting trains at the stop reach the exit turnstile area at a rate of about 48 per minute during the same morning rush hours. Each turnstile can allow an average of 30 passengers per minute to enter or exit. Arrival and service times have been thought to follow Poisson and exponential distributions, respectively. Assume riders form a common queue at both entry and exit turnstile areas and proceed to the first empty turnstile.

The Washington College Station manager does not want the average passenger at his station to have to wait in a turnstile line for more than 6 seconds, nor does he want more than 8 people in any queue at any average time.

(a) How many turnstiles should be opened in each direction every morning?

(b) Discuss the assumptions underlying the solution of this problem using queuing theory.

INTERNET HOMEWORK PROBLEMS

See our Internet home page at **www.prenhall.com/render** for additional homework problems 14-32 to 14-36.

▌▶ CASE STUDY

New England Foundry

For more than 75 years, New England Foundry, Inc., has manufactured wood stoves for home use. In recent years, with increasing energy prices, George Mathison, president of New England Foundry, has seen sales triple. This dramatic increase in sales has made it even more difficult for George to maintain quality in all the wood stoves and related products.

Unlike other companies manufacturing wood stoves, New England Foundry is *only* in the business of making stoves and stove-related products. Their major products are the Warmglo I, the Warmglo II, the Warmglo III, and the Warmglo IV. The Warmglo I is the smallest wood stove, with a heat output of 30,000 Btu, and the Warmglo IV is the largest, with a heat output of 60,000 Btu. In addition, New England Foundry, Inc., produces a large array of products that have been designed to be used with one of their four stoves, including warming shelves, surface thermometers, stovepipes, adaptors, stove gloves, trivets, mitten racks, andirons, chimneys, and heat shields. New England Foundry also publishes a newsletter and several paperback books on stove installation, stove operation, stove maintenance, and wood sources. It is George's belief that its wide assortment of products was a major contributor to the sales increases.

The Warmglo III outsells all the other stoves by a wide margin. The heat output and available accessories are ideal for the typical home. The Warmglo III also has a number of outstanding features that make it one of the most attractive and heat-efficient stoves on the market. Each Warmglo III has a thermostatically controlled primary air intake valve that allows the stove to adjust itself automatically to produce the correct heat output for varying weather conditions. A secondary air opening is used to increase the heat output in case of very cold weather. The internal stove parts produce a horizontal flame path for more efficient burning, and the output gases are forced to take an S-shaped path through the stove. The S-shaped path allows more complete combustion of the gases and better heat transfer from the fire and gases through the cast iron to the area to be heated. These features, along with the accessories, resulted in expanding sales and prompted George to build a new factory to manufacture Warmglo III stoves. An overview diagram of the factory is shown in Figure 14.5.

The new foundry uses the latest equipment, including a new Disamatic that helps in manufacturing stove parts. Regardless of new equipment or procedures, casting operations have remained basically unchanged for hundreds of years. To begin with, a wooden pattern is made for every cast-iron piece in the stove. The wooden pattern is an exact duplication of the cast-iron piece that is to be manufactured. New England Foundry has all of its patterns made by Precision Patterns, Inc., and these patterns are stored in the pattern shop and maintenance room. Then a specially formulated sand is molded around the wooden pattern. There can be two or more sand molds for each pattern. Mixing the sand and making the molds are done in the molding room. When the wooden pattern is removed, the resulting sand molds form a negative image of the desired casting. Next, the molds are transported to the casting room, where molten iron is poured into the molds and allowed to cool. When the iron has solidified, the molds are moved into the cleaning, grinding, and preparation room. The molds are dumped into large vibrators that shake most of the sand from the casting. The rough castings are then subjected to both sandblasting to remove the rest of the sand and grinding to finish some of the surfaces of the castings. The castings are then painted with a special heat-resistant paint, assembled into workable stoves, and inspected for manufacturing defects that may have gone undetected thus far. Finally, the finished stoves are moved to storage and shipping, where they are packaged and shipped to the appropriate locations.

At present, the pattern shop and the maintenance department are located in the same room. One large counter is used by both maintenance personnel to get tools and parts and by sand molders that need various patterns for the molding operation. Peter Nawler and Bob Bryan, who work behind the counter, are able to service a total of 10 people per hour (or about 5 per hour each). On the average, 4 people from maintenance and 3 people from the molding department arrive at the counter per hour. People from the molding department and from maintenance arrive randomly, and to be served they form a single line. Pete and Bob have always had a policy of first-come, first-served. Because of the location of the pattern shop and maintenance department, it takes about 3 minutes for a person from the maintenance department to walk to the pattern and maintenance room, and it

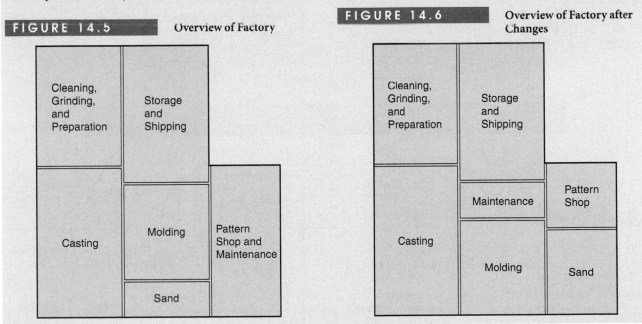

FIGURE 14.5   Overview of Factory

FIGURE 14.6   Overview of Factory after Changes

takes about 1 minute for a person to walk from the molding department to the pattern and maintenance room.

After observing the operation of the pattern shop and maintenance room for several weeks, George decided to make some changes to the layout of the factory. An overview of these changes is shown in Figure 14.6.

Separating the maintenance shop from the pattern shop had a number of advantages. It would take people from the maintenance department only 1 minute instead of 3 to get to the new maintenance department. Using time and motion studies, George was also able to determine that improving the layout of the maintenance department would allow Bob to serve 6 people from the maintenance department per hour, and improving the layout of the pattern department would allow Pete to serve 7 people from the molding shop per hour.

Discussion Questions

1. How much time would the new layout save?
2. If maintenance personnel were paid $9.50 per hour and molding personnel were paid $11.75 per hour, how much could be saved per hour with the new factory layout?

⇒ CASE STUDY

Winter Park Hotel

Donna Shader, manager of the Winter Park Hotel, is considering how to restructure the front desk to reach an optimum level of staff efficiency and guest service. At present, the hotel has five clerks on duty, each with a separate waiting line, during the peak check-in time of 3:00 P.M. to 5:00 P.M. Observation of arrivals during this time show that an average of 90 guests arrive each hour (although there is no upward limit on the number that could arrive at any given time). It takes an average of 3 minutes for the front-desk clerk to register each guest.

Donna is considering three plans for improving guest service by reducing the length of time guests spend waiting in line. The first proposal would designate one employee as a quick-service clerk for guests registering under corporate accounts, a market segment that fills about 30% of all occupied rooms. Because corporate guests are preregistered, their registration takes just 2 minutes. With these guests separated from the rest of the clientele, the average time for registering a typical guest would climb to 3.4 minutes. Under plan 1, noncorporate guests would choose any of the remaining four lines.

The second plan is to implement a single-line system. All guests could form a single waiting line to be served by whichever of five clerks became available. This option would require sufficient lobby space for what could be a substantial queue.

The third proposal involves using an automatic teller machine (ATM) for check-ins. This ATM would provide approximately the same service rate as a clerk would. Given that initial use of this technology might be minimal, Shader estimated that 20% of customers, primarily frequent guests, would be willing to use the machines. (This might be a conservative estimate if the guests perceive direct benefits from using the ATM, as bank customers do. Citibank reports that some 95% of its Manhattan customers use its ATMs.) Donna would set up a single queue for customers who prefer human check-in clerks. This would be served by the five clerks, although Donna is hopeful that the machine will allow a reduction to four.

Discussion Questions

1. Determine the average amount of time that a guest spends checking in. How would this change under each of the stated options?
2. Which option do you recommend?

INTERNET CASE STUDY

See our Internet home page at **www.prenhall.com/render** for this additional case study: Pantry Shopper. This case involves providing better service in a grocery store.

BIBLIOGRAPHY

Barron, K. "Hurry Up and Wait," *Forbes* (October 16, 2000): 158–164.

Cooper, R. B. *Introduction to Queuing Theory*, 2/e. New York: Elsevier— North Holland, 1980.

Dessouky, M. M. "Using Queuing Network Models to Set Lot-Sizing Policies for Printed Circuit Board Assembly Operations," *Production and Inventory Management Journal* (3rd Quarter 1998): 38–42.

Grassmann, Winfried, K. "Finding the Right Number of Servers in Real-World Queuing Systems," *Interfaces* 18, 2 (March–April 1988): 94–104.

Katz, K., B. Larson, and R. Larson. "Prescription for the Waiting-in-Line Blues," *Sloan Management Review* (Winter 1991): 44–53.

Larson, Richard C. "Perspectives on Queues: Social Justice and the Psychology of Queuing," *Operations Research* 35, 6 (November–December 1987): 895–905.

Panico, J. A. *Queuing Theory: A Study of Waiting Lines for Business, Economics and Sciences.* Upper Saddle River, NJ: Prentice Hall, 1969.

Prabhu, N. U. *Foundations of Queuing Theory.* Norwell, MA: Kluewer Academic Publishers, 1997.

Quinn, Phil, Bruce Andrews, and Henry Parsons. "Allocating Telecommunications Resources at L.L. Bean, Inc.," *Interfaces* 21, 1 (January–February 1991): 75–91.

Samuelson, Douglas A. "Predictive Dialing for Outbound Telephone Call Centers," *Interfaces* 29, 5 (September 1999): 66–81.

Swersey, Arthur J. et al. "Improving Fire Department Productivity," *Interfaces* 23, 1 (January–February 1993): 109–129.

Tarko, A. P. "Random Queues in Signalized Road Networks," *Transportation Science* 34, 4 (November 2000): 415–425.

APPENDIX 14.1: USING QM FOR WINDOWS

This appendix illustrates the ease of use of the QM for Windows in solving queuing problems. Program 14.5 represents the Arnold's Muffler Shop analysis, with 2 servers. The only required inputs are selection of the proper model, a title, whether to include costs, the time units being used for arrival and service rates (hours in this example), the arrival rate (2 cars per hour), the service rate (3 cars per hour), and the number of servers (2). Because the time units are specified as hours, W and W_q are given in hours, but they are also converted into minutes and seconds, as seen in Program 14.5.

Program 14.6 reflects a constant service time model, illustrated in the chapter by Garcia-Golding Recycling, Inc. The other queuing models can also be solved by QM for Windows, which additionally provides cost/economic analysis.

PROGRAM 14.5

Using QM for Windows to Solve a Multichannel Queuing Model (Arnold Muffler Shop Data)

QM for Windows

File Edit View Module Format Tools Window Help

Cost analysis: ● No costs ○ Use Costs
Time unit (arrival, service rate): hours

Waiting Lines Results

(untitled) Solution

Parameter	Value	Parameter	Value	Minutes	Seconds
M/M/s		Average server utilization	0.3333		
Arrival rate(lambda)	2.	Average number in the queue(Lq)	0.0833		
Service rate(mu)	3.	Average number in the system(Ls)	0.75		
Number of servers	2.	Average time in the queue(Wq)	0.0417	2.5	150.
		Average time in the system(Ws)	0.375	22.5	1,350.

PROGRAM 14.6

Using QM for Windows to Solve a Constant Service Time Model (Garcia-Golding Data)

QM for Windows

File Edit View Module Format Tools Window Help

Cost analysis: ● No costs ○ Use Costs
Time unit (arrival, service rate): hours

Waiting Lines Results

Garcia-Golding Recycling, Inc. Solution

Parameter	Value	Parameter	Value	Minutes	Seconds
Constant service times		Average server utilization	0.6667		
Arrival rate(lambda)	8.	Average number in the queue(Lq)	0.6667		
Service rate(mu)	12.	Average number in the system(Ls)	1.3333		
Number of servers	1.	Average time in the queue(Wq)	0.0833	5.	300.
		Average time in the system(Ws)	0.1667	10.	600.

SIMULATION MODELING

After completing this chapter, students will be able to:

1. Tackle a wide variety of problems by simulation.
2. Understand the seven steps of conducting a simulation.
3. Explain the advantages and disadvantages of simulation.
4. Develop random number intervals and use them to generate outcomes.
5. Understand alternative computer simulation packages available.

CHAPTER OUTLINE

Summary • Glossary • Solved Problems • Self-Test • Discussion Questions and Problems • Internet Homework Problems • Case Study: Alabama Airlines • Case Study: Statewide Development Corporation • Internet Case Studies • Bibliography

15.1 INTRODUCTION

We are all aware to some extent of the importance of simulation models in our world. Boeing Corporation and Airbus Industries, for example, commonly build *simulation* models of their proposed jet aircraft and then test the aerodynamic properties of the models. Your local civil defense organization may carry out rescue and evacuation practices as it simulates the natural disaster conditions of a hurricane or tornado. The U.S. Army simulates enemy attacks and defense strategies in war games played on a computer. Business students take courses that use management games to simulate realistic competitive business situations. And thousands of business, government, and service organizations develop simulation models to assist in making decisions concerning inventory control, maintenance scheduling, plant layout, investments, and sales forecasting.

As a matter of fact, simulation is one of the most widely used quantitative analysis tools. Various surveys of the largest U.S. corporations reveal that over half use simulation in corporate planning.

Simulation sounds like it may be the solution to all management problems. This is, unfortunately, by no means true. Yet we think you may find it one of the most flexible and fascinating of the quantitative techniques in your studies. Let's begin our discussion of simulation with a simple definition.

To *simulate* is to try to duplicate the features, appearance, and characteristics of a real system. In this chapter we show how to simulate a business or management system by building a *mathematical model* that comes as close as possible to representing the reality of the system. We won't build any *physical* models, as might be used in airplane wind tunnel simulation tests. But just as physical model airplanes are tested and modified under experimental conditions, our mathematical models are used to experiment and to estimate the effects of various actions. The idea behind simulation is to imitate a real-world situation mathematically, then to study its properties and operating characteristics, and, finally, to draw conclusions and make action decisions based on the results of the simulation. In this way, the real-life system is not touched until the advantages and disadvantages of what may be a major policy decision are first measured on the system's model.

The idea behind simulation is to imitate a real-world situation with a mathematical model that does not affect operations. The seven steps of simulation are illustrated in Figure 15.1.

Using simulation, a manager should (1) define a problem, (2) introduce the variables associated with the problem, (3) construct a numerical model, (4) set up possible courses of action for testing, (5) run the experiment, (6) consider the results (possibly deciding to modify the model or change data inputs), and (7) decide what course of action to take. These steps are illustrated in Figure 15.1.

The problems tackled by simulation can range from very simple to extremely complex, from bank teller lines to an analysis of the U.S. economy. Although very small simulations can be conducted by hand, effective use of this technique requires some automated means of calculation, namely, a computer. Even large-scale models, simulating perhaps years of business decisions, can be handled in a reasonable amount of time by computer. Though simulation is one of the oldest quantitative analysis tools (see the History box on page 640), it was not until the introduction of computers in the mid-1940s and early 1950s that it became a practical means of solving management and military problems.

The explosion of personal computers has created a wealth of computer simulation languages and broadened the use of simulation. Now, even spreadsheet software can be used to conduct fairly complex simulations.

We begin this chapter with a presentation of the advantages and disadvantages of simulation. An explanation of the Monte Carlo method of simulation follows. Three sample simulations, in the areas of inventory control, queuing, and maintenance planning, are presented. Other simulation models besides the Monte Carlo approach are also discussed briefly. Finally, the important role of computers in simulation is illustrated.

FIGURE 15.1

Process of Simulation

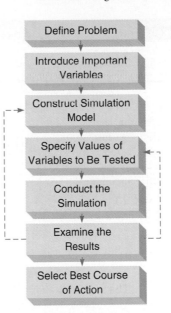

FIGURE 15.1

Process of Simulation

15.2   ADVANTAGES AND DISADVANTAGES OF SIMULATION

Simulation is a tool that has become widely accepted by managers for several reasons:

These eight advantages of simulation make it one of the most widely used quantitative analysis techniques in corporate America.

1. It is relatively straightforward and flexible.

2. Recent advances in software make some simulation models very easy to develop.

3. It can be used to analyze large and complex real-world situations that cannot be solved by conventional quantitative analysis models. For example, it may not be possible to build and solve a mathematical model of a city government system that incorporates important economic, social, environmental, and political factors. Simulation has been used successfully to model urban systems, hospitals, educational systems, national and state economies, and even world food systems.

4. Simulation allows what-if? types of questions. Managers like to know in advance what options are attractive. With a computer, a manager can try out several policy decisions within a matter of minutes.

5. Simulations do not interfere with the real-world system. It may be too disruptive, for example, to experiment with new policies or ideas in a hospital, school, or manufacturing plant. With simulation, experiments are done with the model, not on the system itself.

6. Simulation allows us to study the interactive effect of individual components or variables to determine which ones are important.

7. "Time compression" is possible with simulation. The effect of ordering, advertising, or other policies over many months or years can be obtained by computer simulation in a short time.

8. Simulation allows for the inclusion of real-world complications that most quantitative analysis models cannot permit. For example, some queuing models require exponential or Poisson distributions; some inventory and network models require normality. But simulation can use *any* probability distribution that the user defines; it does not require standard distributions.

HISTORY   Simulation

The history of simulation goes back 5,000 years to Chinese war games, called *weich'i*, and continues through 1780, when the Prussians used the games to help train their army. Since then, all major military powers have used war games to test out military strategies under simulated environments.

From military or operational gaming, a new concept, *Monte Carlo simulation*, was developed as a quantitative technique by the great mathematician John von Neumann during World War II. Working with neutrons at the Los Alamos Scientific Laboratory, von Neumann used simulation to solve physics problems that were too complex or expensive to ana- lyze by hand or by physical model. The random nature of the neutrons suggested the use of a roulette wheel in dealing with probabilities. Because of the gaming nature, von Neumann called it the Monte Carlo model of studying laws of chance.

With the advent and common use of business computers in the 1950s, simulation grew as a management tool. Specialized computer languages were developed in the 1960s (GPSS and SIMSCRIPT) to handle large-scale problems more effectively. In the 1980s, prewritten simulation programs to handle situations ranging from queuing to inventory were developed. They have such names as Xcell, SLAM, Witness, and MAP/1.

The main disadvantages of simulation are:

The four disadvantages of simulation are cost, its trial-and-error nature, the need to generate answers to tests, and uniqueness.

1. Good simulation models for complex situations can be very expensive. It is often a long, complicated process to develop a model. A corporate planning model, for example, may take months or even years to develop.

2. Simulation does not generate optimal solutions to problems as do other quantitative analysis techniques such as economic order quantity, linear programming, or PERT. It is a trial-and-error approach that can produce different solutions in repeated runs.

3. Managers must generate all of the conditions and constraints for solutions that they want to examine. The simulation model does not produce answers by itself.

4. Each simulation model is unique. Its solutions and inferences are not usually transferable to other problems.

15.3 MONTE CARLO SIMULATION

When a system contains elements that exhibit chance in their behavior, the *Monte Carlo method* of simulation can be applied.

The basic idea in Monte Carlo simulation is to generate values for the variables making up the model being studied. There are a lot of variables in real-world systems that are probabilistic in nature and that we might want to simulate. A few examples of these variables follow:

Variables we may want to simulate abound in business problems because very little in life is certain.

1. Inventory demand on a daily or weekly basis

2. Lead time for inventory orders to arrive

3. Times between machine breakdowns

4. Times between arrivals at a service facility

5. Service times

6. Times to complete project activities

7. Number of employees absent from work each day

The basis of Monte Carlo simulation is experimentation on the chance (or *probabilistic*) elements through random sampling. The technique breaks down into five simple steps:

Five Steps of Monte Carlo Simulation

1. Setting up a probability distribution for important variables
2. Building a cumulative probability distribution for each variable in step 1
3. Establishing an interval of random numbers for each variable
4. Generating random numbers
5. Actually simulating a series of trials

The Monte Carlo method can be used with variables that are probabilistic.

We will examine each of these steps and illustrate them with the following example.

Harry's Auto Tire Example Harry's Auto Tire sells all types of tires, but a popular radial tire accounts for a large portion of Harry's overall sales. Recognizing that inventory costs can be quite significant with this product, Harry wishes to determine a policy for managing this inventory. To see what the demand would look like over a period of time, he wishes to simulate the daily demand for a number of days.

To establish a probability distribution for tires we assume that historical demand is a good indicator of future outcomes.

Step 1: Establishing Probability Distributions. One common way to establish a *probability distribution* for a given variable is to examine historical outcomes. The probability, or relative frequency, for each possible outcome of a variable is found by dividing the frequency of observation by the total number of observations. The daily demand for radial tires at Harry's Auto Tire over the past 200 days is shown in Table 15.1. We can convert these data to a probability distribution, if we assume that past demand rates will hold in the future, by dividing each demand frequency by the total demand, 200. This is illustrated in Table 15.2.

Probability distributions, we should note, need not be based solely on historical observations. Often, managerial estimates based on judgment and experience are used to create a distribution. Sometimes, a sample of sales, machine breakdowns, or service rates is used to create probabilities for those variables. And the distributions themselves can be either empirical, as in Table 15.1, or based on the commonly known normal, binomial, Poisson, or exponential patterns.

Step 2: Building a Cumulative Probability Distribution for Each Variable. The conversion from a regular probability distribution, such as in the right-hand column of Table 15.2, to a *cumulative distribution* is an easy job. A cumulative probability is the probability that a variable (demand) will be less than or equal to a particular value. A cumulative dis-

TABLE 15.1		
Historical Daily Demand for Radial Tires at Harry's Auto Tire	**DEMAND FOR TIRES**	**FREQUENCY (DAYS)**
	0	10
	1	20
	2	40
	3	60
	4	40
	5	30
		200

TABLE 15.2

Probability of Demand for Radial Tires

DEMAND VARIABLE	PROBABILITY OF OCCURRENCE
0	10/200 = 0.05
1	20/200 = 0.10
2	40/200 = 0.20
3	60/200 = 0.30
4	40/200 = 0.20
5	30/200 = 0.15
	200/200 = 1.00

tribution lists all of the possible values and the probabilities. In Table 15.3 we see that the cumulative probability for each level of demand is the sum of the number in the probability column (middle column) added to the previous cumulative probability (rightmost column). The cumulative probability, graphed in Figure 15.2, is used in step 3 to help assign random numbers.

Step 3: Setting Random Number Intervals. After we have established a cumulative probability distribution for each variable included in the simulation, we must assign a set of numbers to represent each possible value or outcome. These are referred to as *random number intervals*. Random numbers are discussed in detail in step 4. Basically, a *random number* is a series of digits (say, two digits from 01, 02, . . . , 98, 99, 00) that have been selected by a totally random process.

If there is a 5% chance that demand for a product (such as Harry's radial tires) is 0 units per day, we want 5% of the random numbers available to correspond to a demand of 0 units. If a total of 100 two-digit numbers is used in the simulation (think of them as being numbered chips in a bowl), we could assign a demand of 0 units to the first five random numbers: 01, 02, 03, 04, and 05.[1] Then a simulated demand for 0 units would be created every time one of the numbers 01 to 05 was drawn. If there is also a 10% chance that demand for the same product is 1 unit per day, we could let the next 10 random numbers (06, 07, 08, 09, 10, 11, 12, 13, 14, and 15) represent that demand—and so on for other demand levels.

Random numbers can actually be assigned in many different ways—as long as they represent the correct proportion of the outcomes.

TABLE 15.3

Cumulative Probabilities for Radial Tires

DAILY DEMAND	PROBABILITY	CUMULATIVE PROBABILITY
0	0.05	0.05
1	0.10	0.15
2	0.20	0.35
3	0.30	0.65
4	0.20	0.85
5	0.15	1.00

Cumulative probabilities are found by summing all the previous probabilities up to the current demand.

---

[1] Alternatively, we could have assigned the random numbers 00, 01, 02, 03, 04 to represent a demand of 0 units. The two digits 00 can be thought of as either 0 or 100. As long as 5 numbers out of 100 are assigned to the 0 demand, it doesn't make any difference which 5 they are.

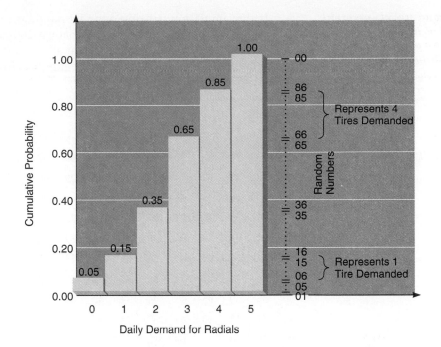

FIGURE 15.2

Graphical Representation of the Cumulative Probability Distribution for Radial Tires

The relation between intervals and cumulative probability is that the top end of each interval is equal to the cumulative probability percentage.

In general, using the cumulative probability distribution computed and graphed in step 2, we can set the interval of random numbers for each level of demand in a very simple fashion. You will note in Table 15.4 that the interval selected to represent each possible daily demand is very closely related to the cumulative probability on its left. The top end of each interval is always equal to the cumulative probability percentage.

Similarly, we can see in Figure 15.2 and in Table 15.4 that the length of each interval on the right corresponds to the probability of one of each of the possible daily demands. Hence, in assigning random numbers to the daily demand for three radial tires, the range of the random number interval (36 to 65) corresponds *exactly* to the probability (or proportion) of that outcome. A daily demand for three radial tires occurs 30% of the time. Any of the 30 random numbers greater than 35 up to and including 65 are assigned to that event.

Step 4: Generating Random Numbers. Random numbers may be generated for simulation problems in several ways. If the problem is very large and the process being studied involves thousands of simulation trials, computer programs are available to generate the random numbers needed.

TABLE 15.4

Assignment of Random Number Intervals for Harry's Auto Tire

DAILY DEMAND	PROBABILITY	CUMULATIVE PROBABILITY	INTERVAL OF RANDOM NUMBERS
0	0.05	0.05	01 to 05
1	0.10	0.15	06 to 15
2	0.20	0.35	16 to 35
3	0.30	0.65	36 to 65
4	0.20	0.85	66 to 85
5	0.15	1.00	86 to 00

There are several ways to pick random numbers—random number generators (which are a built-in feature in spreadsheets and many computer languages), tables (such as Table 15.5), a roulette wheel, and so on.

If the simulation is being done by hand, as in this book, the numbers may be selected by the spin of a roulette wheel that has 100 slots, by blindly grabbing numbered chips out of a hat, or by any method that allows you to make a random selection.[2] The most commonly used means is to choose numbers from a table of random digits such as Table 15.5.

TABLE 15.5

Table of Random Numbers

52	06	50	88	53	30	10	47	99	37	66	91	35	32	00	84	57	07
37	63	28	02	74	35	24	03	29	60	74	85	90	73	59	55	17	60
82	57	68	28	05	94	03	11	27	79	90	87	92	41	09	25	36	77
69	02	36	49	71	99	32	10	75	21	95	90	94	38	97	71	72	49
98	94	90	36	06	78	23	67	89	85	29	21	25	73	69	34	85	76
96	52	62	87	49	56	59	23	78	71	72	90	57	01	98	57	31	95
33	69	27	21	11	60	95	89	68	48	17	89	34	09	93	50	44	51
50	33	50	95	13	44	34	62	64	39	55	29	30	64	49	44	30	16
88	32	18	50	62	57	34	56	62	31	15	40	90	34	51	95	26	14
90	30	36	24	69	82	51	74	30	35	36	85	01	55	92	64	09	85
50	48	61	18	85	23	08	54	17	12	80	69	24	84	92	16	49	59
27	88	21	62	69	64	48	31	12	73	02	68	00	16	16	46	13	85
45	14	46	32	13	49	66	62	74	41	86	98	92	98	84	54	33	40
81	02	01	78	82	74	97	37	45	31	94	99	42	49	27	64	89	42
66	83	14	74	27	76	03	33	11	97	59	81	72	00	64	61	13	52
74	05	81	82	93	09	96	33	52	78	13	06	28	30	94	23	37	39
30	34	87	01	74	11	46	82	59	94	25	34	32	23	17	01	58	73
59	55	72	33	62	13	74	68	22	44	42	09	32	46	71	79	45	89
67	09	80	98	99	25	77	50	03	32	36	63	65	75	94	19	95	88
60	77	46	63	71	69	44	22	03	85	14	48	69	13	30	50	33	24
60	08	19	29	36	72	30	27	50	64	85	72	75	29	87	05	75	01
80	45	86	99	02	34	87	08	86	84	49	76	24	08	01	86	29	11
53	84	49	63	26	65	72	84	85	63	26	02	75	26	92	62	40	67
69	84	12	94	51	36	17	02	15	29	16	52	56	43	26	22	08	62
37	77	13	10	02	18	31	19	32	85	31	94	81	43	31	58	33	51

Source: Excerpted from *A Million Random Digits with 100,000 Normal Deviates* (New York: Free Press, 1955), p. 7, with permission of the Rand Corporation.

---

[2] One more method of generating random numbers is called the von Neumann midsquare method, developed in the 1940s. Here's how it works: (1) select any arbitrary number with n digits (for example, $n = 4$ digits), (2) square the number, (3) extract the middle n digits as the next random number. As an example of a four-digit arbitrary number, use 3,614. The square of 3,614 is 13,060,996. The middle four digits of this new number are 0609. Thus 0609 is the next random number and steps 2 and 3 are repeated. The midsquare method is simple and easily programmed, but sometimes the numbers repeat quickly and are *not* random. For example, try using the method starting with 6,100 as your first arbitrary number!

IN ACTION   Simulating GM's OnStar System to Evaluate Strategic Alternatives

General Motors (GM) has a two-way vehicle communication system, OnStar, that is the leader in the telematics business of providing communications services to automobiles. Communication can be by an automated system (a virtual advisor) or with a human advisor via a cell-phone connection. This is used for such things as crash notification, navigation, Internet access, and traffic information. OnStar answers thousands of emergency calls each month, and many lives have been saved by providing a rapid emergency response.

In developing the new business model for OnStar, GM used an integrated simulation model to analyze the new telematics industry. Six factors were considered in this model—customer acquisition, customer choice, alliances, customer service, financial dynamics, and societal results. The team responsible for this model reported that an aggressive strategy would be the best way to approach this new industry. This included installation of OnStar in every GM vehicle and free first year subscription service. This eliminated the high cost of dealer installation, but it carried with it a cost that was not recoverable if the buyer chose not to purchase the OnStar subscription.

The implementation of this business strategy and subsequent growth progressed as indicated by the model. As of fall 2001, OnStar had an 80% market share with more than two million subscribers, and this number was growing rapidly. The OnStar business is valued at between $4 and $10 billion.

Source: "A Multimethod Approach for Creating New Business Models: The General Motors OnStar Project," *Interfaces*, Vol. 32, No. 1, Jan.–Feb. 2002, pp. 20–34.

Table 15.5 was itself generated by a computer program. It has the characteristic that every digit or number in it has an equal chance of occurring. In a very large random number table, 10% of digits would be 1s, 10% 2s, 10% 3s, and so on. Because *everything* is random, we can select numbers from anywhere in the table to use in our simulation procedures in step 5.

Step 5: Simulating the Experiment. We can simulate outcomes of an experiment by simply selecting random numbers from Table 15.5. Beginning anywhere in the table, we note the interval in Table 15.4 or Figure 15.2 into which each number falls. For example, if the random number chosen is 81 and the interval 66 to 85 represents a daily demand for four tires, we select a demand of four tires.

We now illustrate the concept further by simulating 10 days of demand for radial tires at Harry's Auto Tire (see Table 15.6). We select the random numbers needed from Table 15.5, starting in the upper left-hand corner and continuing down the first column.

TABLE 15.6	DAY	RANDOM NUMBER	SIMULATED DAILY DEMAND
Ten-Day Simulation of Demand for Radial Tires	1	52	3
	2	37	3
	3	82	4
	4	69	4
	5	98	5
	6	96	5
	7	33	2
	8	50	3
	9	88	5
	10	90	5

39 = total 10-day demand

3.9 = average daily demand for tires

Simulated results can differ from analytical results in a short simulation.

It is interesting to note that the average demand of 3.9 tires in this 10-day simulation differs significantly from the *expected* daily demand, which we can compute from the data in Table 15.2.

$$\text{Expected daily demand} = \sum_{i=0}^{5} (\text{probability of } i \text{ tires}) \times (\text{demand of } i \text{ tires})$$

$$= (0.05)(0) + (0.10)(1) + (0.20)(2) + (0.30)(3) + (0.20)(4) + (0.15)(5)$$

$$= 2.95 \text{ tires}$$

If this simulation were repeated hundreds or thousands of times, it is much more likely that the average *simulated* demand would be nearly the same as the *expected* demand.

Naturally, it would be risky to draw any hard and fast conclusions regarding the operation of a firm from only a short simulation. However, this simulation by hand demonstrates the important principles involved. It helps us to understand the process of Monte Carlo simulation that is used in computerized simulation models.

The simulation for Harry's Auto Tire involved only one variable. The true power of simulation is seen when several random variables are involved and the situation is more complex. In Section 15.4 we see a simulation of an inventory problem in which both the demand and the lead time may vary.

As you might expect, the computer can be a very helpful tool in carrying out the tedious work in larger simulation undertakings. In the next two sections, we demonstrate how QM for Windows and Excel can both be used for simulation.

Using QM for Windows for Simulation

Program 15.1 is a Monte Carlo simulation using the QM for Windows software. Inputs to this model are the possible values for the variable, the number of trials to be generated, and either the associated frequency or the probability for each value. If frequencies are input, QM for Windows will compute the probabilities as well as the cumulative probability distribution. We see that the expected value (2.95) is computed mathematically, and we can compare the actual sample average (2.908) with this. If another simulation is performed, the sample average may change.

PROGRAM 15.1   **Monte Carlo Computer Simulation of Harry's Auto Tire Using QM for Windows**

Category name	Value	Frequency	Probability	Value * Frequency	Occurrences	Percentage	Occurences * Value
Category 1	0.	10.	0.05	0.05	0.	11.	0.044	0.
Category 2	1.	20.	0.1	0.15	0.1	29.	0.116	29.
Category 3	2.	40.	0.2	0.35	0.4	55.	0.22	110.
Category 4	3.	60.	0.3	0.65	0.9	75.	0.3	225.
Category 5	4.	40.	0.2	0.85	0.8	37.	0.148	148.
Category 6	5.	30.	0.15	1.	0.75	43.	0.172	215.
Total		200.	1.	Expected	2.95	250.	1.	727.
							Average	2.908

Find the result of each individual day by selecting Window, then Individual Runs.

When you enter the frequencies, QM for Windows automatically computes the probabilities.

The expected value is computed mathematically.

This is the average value for this simulation run.

Simulation with Excel Spreadsheets

The ability to generate random numbers and then "look up" these numbers in a table in order to associate them with a specific event makes spreadsheets excellent tools for conducting simulations. Excel QM does not have a simulation module, because we are able to model all simulation problems directly in Excel. Program 15.2A illustrates an Excel simulation for Harry's Auto Tire.

Notice that the cumulative probabilities are calculated in column D of Program 15.2A. This procedure reduces the chance of error and is useful in larger simulations involving more levels of demand.

The RAND() function in column H is used to generate a random number between 0 and 1. The VLOOKUP function in column I looks up the random number (generated in column H) in the leftmost column of the defined lookup table ($C$3:$E$8). It moves downward through this column until it finds a cell that is bigger than the random number. It then goes to the previous row and gets the value from column E of the table.

In the output screen of Program 15.2B, for example, the first random number shown is .585. Excel looked down the left-hand column of the lookup table ($C$3:$E$8) of Program 15.2B until it found .65. From the previous row it retrieved the value in column E, which is 3. Pressing the [**F9**] function key recalculates the random numbers and the simulation.

The FREQUENCY function in Excel (column C in Program 15.2A) is used to tabulate how often a value occurs in a set of data. This is an array function, so special procedures are required to enter it. First, highlight the entire range where this is to be located (C16:C21 in this example). Then enter the function, as illustrated in cell C16, and press CTRL + SHIFT + ENTER. This causes the formula to be entered as an array into all the cells that were highlighted (cells C16:C21).

A function (NORMINV) in Excel makes generating normal random numbers very easy, as seen in Program 15.3A. The mean is 40 and the standard deviation is 5. The format is

$$=\text{NORMINV (probability, mean, standard\_deviation)}$$

The results are shown in Program 15.3B.

PROGRAM 15.2A   **Using Excel to Simulate Tire Demand for Harry's Auto Tire Shop**

PROGRAM 15.2B

Excel Simulation Results for Harry's Auto Tire Shop Showing a Simulated Average of 2.8 Tires per Day

Microsoft Excel - captures.xls

File　Edit　View　Insert　Format　Tools　Data　OM　Window　Help

Harry's Tire Shop

	Probability	Probability Range (Lower)	Cumulative Probability	Tires Demand		Day	Random Number	Simulated Demand
	0.05	0	0.05	0		1	0.585179	3
	0.1	0.05	0.15	1		2	0.25655	2
	0.2	0.15	0.35	2		3	0.784846	4
	0.3	0.35	0.65	3		4	0.187033	2
	0.2	0.65	0.85	4		5	0.059602	1
	0.15	0.85	1	5		6	0.567122	3
						7	0.918419	5
						8	0.009024	0
						9	0.834601	4
						10	0.823247	4
							Average	2.8

> The spreadsheet output shows a simulated average of 2.8 tires per day.

Results (Frequency table)

Tires Demanded	Frequency	Percentage	Cum %
0	1	10%	10%
1	1	10%	20%
2	2	20%	40%
3	2	20%	60%
4	3	30%	90%
5	1	10%	100%
	10		

14.1 / 14.2 / 14.3 / 14.4 / 15.1 / 15.3 / 15.4 / 15.5 / CD 1.1 / Notes /

PROGRAM 15.3A

Generating Normal Random Numbers in Excel

> The mean is 40 and the standard deviation is 5. Use RAND ( ) to generate random numbers.

> Excel develops frequency distribution for the 200 random numbers.

Microsoft Excel - Book2

File　Edit　View　Insert　Format　Tools　Data　Window　Help

A4　=　=NORMINV(RAND(),40,5)

Generating Normal Rando

	A	B	C	D	E	F
3	Random number		Value	Frequency	Percentage	
4	=NORMINV(RAND(),40,5)		26	=FREQUENCY(A4:A203,C4:C19)	=D4/$D$20	
5	=NORMINV(RAND(),40,5)		28	=FREQUENCY(A4:A203,C4:C19)	=D5/$D$20	
6	=NORMINV(RAND(),40,5)		30	=FREQUENCY(A4:A203,C4:C19)	=D6/$D$20	
7	=NORMINV(RAND(),40,5)		32	=FREQUENCY(A4:A203,C4:C19)	=D7/$D$20	
8	=NORMINV(RAND(),40,5)		34	=FREQUENCY(A4:A203,C4:C19)	=D8/$D$20	
9	=NORMINV(RAND(),40,5)		36	=FREQUENCY(A4:A203,C4:C19)	=D9/$D$20	
10	=NORMINV(RAND(),40,5)		38	=FREQUENCY(A4:A203,C4:C19)	=D10/$D$20	
11	=NORMINV(RAND(),40,5)		40	=FREQUENCY(A4:A203,C4:C19)	=D11/$D$20	
12	=NORMINV(RAND(),40,5)		42	=FREQUENCY(A4:A203,C4:C19)	=D12/$D$20	
13	=NORMINV(RAND(),40,5)		44	=FREQUENCY(A4:A203,C4:C19)	=D13/$D$20	
14	=NORMINV(RAND(),40,5)		46	=FREQUENCY(A4:A203,C4:C19)	=D14/$D$20	
15	=NORMINV(RAND(),40,5)		48	=FREQUENCY(A4:A203,C4:C19)	=D15/$D$20	
16	=NORMINV(RAND(),40,5)		50	=FREQUENCY(A4:A203,C4:C19)	=D16/$D$20	
17	=NORMINV(RAND(),40,5)		52	=FREQUENCY(A4:A203,C4:C19)	=D17/$D$20	
18	=NORMINV(RAND(),40,5)		54	=FREQUENCY(A4:A203,C4:C19)	=D18/$D$20	
19	=NORMINV(RAND(),40,5)		56	=FREQUENCY(A4:A203,C4:C19)	=D19/$D$20	
20	=NORMINV(RAND(),40,5)			=SUM(D4:D19)		
201	=NORMINV(RAND(),40,5)					
202	=NORMINV(RAND(),40,5)					
203	=NORMINV(RAND(),40,5)					
204						

> Rows 21 to 200 are hidden.

PROGRAM 15.3B

Excel Output with Normal Random Numbers

	A	B	C	D	E	F	G	H	I	J	K	L
1	Generating Normal Random Numbers											
2												
3	Random number	Value	Frequency		Percentage							
4	43.10718633		26	0	0.0%							
5	39.6860879		28	0	0.0%							
6	46.10070856		30	3	1.5%							
7	32.34896677		32	8	4.0%							
8	43.64412927		34	11	5.5%							
9	38.54037469		36	23	11.5%							
10	50.87755663		38	23	11.5%							
11	46.41630322		40	27	13.5%							
12	31.92909854		42	29	14.5%							
13	34.12232228		44	31	15.5%							
14	41.98593852		46	20	10.0%							
15	47.43525561		48	15	7.5%							
16	39.5438543		50	6	3.0%							
17	43.64799462		52	3	1.5%							
18	42.73882961		54	1	0.5%							
19	35.80549002		56	0	0.0%							
20	46.36633786			200								
201	50.21517164											
202	39.52233338											
203	33.27219484											
204												

15.4 SIMULATION AND INVENTORY ANALYSIS

In Chapter 6 we introduced the subject of "deterministic" inventory models. These commonly used models are based on the assumption that both product demand and reorder lead time are known, constant values. In many real-world inventory situations, though, demand and lead time are variables, and accurate analysis becomes extremely difficult to handle by any means other than simulation.

Simulation is useful when demand and lead time are probabilistic—in this case the inventory models like economic order quantity (of Chapter 6) can't be used.

In this section we present an inventory problem with two decision variables and two probabilistic components. The owner of the hardware store described in the next section would like to establish *order quantity* and *reorder point* decisions for a particular product that has probabilistic (uncertain) daily demand and reorder lead time. He wants to make a series of simulation runs, trying out various order quantities and reorder points, to minimize his total inventory cost for the item. Inventory costs in this case include an ordering, holding, and stockout cost.

Simkin's Hardware Store

Mark Simkin, owner and general manager of Simkin's Hardware, wants to find a good, low-cost inventory policy for one particular product: the Ace model electric drill. Due to the complexity of this situation, he has decided to use simulation to help with this. The first step in the simulation process seen in Figure 15.1 is to define the problem. Simkin specifies this to be finding a good inventory policy for the Ace electric drill.

In the second step of this process, Simkin identifies two types of variables: the controllable and uncontrollable inputs. The controllable inputs (or decision variables) are the order quantity and the reorder point. Simkin must specify the values that he wishes to consider. The other important variables are the uncontrollable inputs: the fluctuating daily demand and the variable lead time. Monte Carlo simulation is used to simulate the values for both of these.

Daily demand for the Ace model drill is relatively low but subject to some variability. Over the past 300 days, Simkin has observed the sales shown in column 2 of Table 15.7. He converts this historical frequency data into a probability distribution for the variable daily

⫸ MODELING IN THE REAL WORLD · U.S. Postal Service Simulates Automation

Defining the Problem

The U.S. Postal Service (USPS) recognizes that automation technology is the only way to handle increases in mail volume, stay price competitive, and satisfy service goals. To do so, it needs to evaluate automation options: (1) on other automated or semiautomated equipment, (2) on the workforce, (3) on facilities, and (4) on other costs of operation.

Developing a Model

Kenan Systems Corporation was hired to develop a national simulation model called META (model for evaluating technology alternatives) to quantify the effects of different automation strategies. The initial version of META took three months to develop.

Acquiring Input Data

Data needed were collected from the USPS technology resource and delivery services departments. They included a nationwide survey that measured 3,200 of the 150,000 city carrier routes.

Developing a Solution

Users specify inputs for the quantity and type of mail to be processed, the people/equipment used to sort the mail, the flow of mail, and unit costs. META models how the entire nationwide mail system will function with these scenarios or inputs. META is not an optimization model; rather, it allows users to examine changes in output that result from modifying inputs.

Testing the Solution

META's simulations were submitted to a three-month period of testing and validation to ensure that scenarios run produced reliable outputs. Hundreds of META scenarios were run.

Analyzing the Results

USPS uses META to analyze the effect of rate discounts, technology changes or advances, and changes to current processing operations.

Implementing the Results

The U.S. Postal Service estimates savings starting in 1995 at 100,000 work years annually, which translates into more than $4 billion. The simulation model also ensures that future technologies will be implemented in a timely and cost-effective manner.

Sources: M. E. Debry, A. H. DeSilva, and F. J. DiLisio. "Management Science in Automating Postal Operations: Facility and Equipment Planning in the United States Postal Service," *Interfaces* 22, 1 (January–February 1992): 110–130 and M. D. Lasky and C. T. Balbach. "Special Delivery: New, Sophisticated Software Helps United States Postal Service Sort Out Complex Problems While Identifying $2 Billion per Year in Potential Savings," *OR/MS Today* 23, 6 (December 1996): 38–41.

TABLE 15.7

Probabilities and Random Number Intervals for Daily Ace Drill Demand

(1) DEMAND FOR ACE DRILL	(2) FREQUENCY (DAYS)	(3) PROBABILITY	(4) CUMULATIVE PROBABILITY	(5) INTERVAL OF RANDOM NUMBERS
0	15	0.05	0.05	01 to 05
1	30	0.10	0.15	06 to 15
2	60	0.20	0.35	16 to 35
3	120	0.40	0.75	36 to 75
4	45	0.15	0.90	76 to 90
5	30	0.10	1.00	91 to 00
	300	1.00		

TABLE 15.8

Probabilities and Random Number Intervals for Reorder Lead Time

(1) LEAD TIME (DAYS)	(2) FREQUENCY (ORDERS)	(3) PROBABILITY	(4) CUMULATIVE PROBABILITY	(5) RANDOM NUMBER INTERVAL
1	10	0.20	0.20	01 to 20
2	25	0.50	0.70	21 to 70
3	15	0.30	1.00	71 to 00
	50	1.00		

demand (column 3). A cumulative probability distribution is formed in column 4. Finally, Simkin establishes an interval of random numbers to represent each possible daily demand (column 5).

When Simkin places an order to replenish his inventory of Ace electric drills, there is a delivery lag of one to three days. This means that lead time can also be considered a probabilistic variable. The number of days it took to receive the past 50 orders is presented in Table 15.8. In a fashion similar to that for the demand variable, Simkin establishes a probability distribution for the lead time variable (column 3 of Table 15.8), computes the cumulative distribution (column 4), and assigns random number intervals for each possible time (column 5).

The third step in the simulation process is to develop the simulation model. A *flow diagram* or *flowchart* is helpful in the logical coding procedures for programming this simulation process (see Figure 15.3).

In flowcharts, special symbols are used to represent different parts of a simulation. The rectangular boxes represent actions that must be taken. The diamond shaped figures represent branching points where the next step depends on the answer to the question in the diamond. The beginning and ending points of the simulation are represented as ovals or rounded rectangles.

The fourth step of this simulation is to specify the values of the variables that we wish to test.

A delivery lag is the lead time in receiving an order—the time it was placed until it was received.

The first inventory policy that Simkin's Hardware wants to simulate is an order quantity of 10 with a reorder point of 5. That is, every time the on-hand inventory level at the end of the day is 5 or less, Simkin will call his supplier and place an order for 10 more drills. If the lead time is one day, by the way, the order will not arrive the next morning but at the beginning of the following working day.

The fifth step of the simulation process is to actually conduct the simulation, and the Monte Carlo method is used for this. The entire process is simulated for a 10-day period in Table 15.9. We can assume that beginning inventory is 10 units on day 1. (Actually, it makes little difference in a long simulation what the initial inventory level is. Since we would tend in real life to simulate hundreds or thousands of days, the beginning values will tend to be averaged out.) Random numbers for Simkin's inventory problem are selected from the second column of Table 15.5.

Table 15.9 is filled in by proceeding one day (or line) at a time, working from left to right. It is a four-step process:

Here is how we simulated the Simkin Hardware example.

1. Begin each simulated day by checking whether any ordered inventory has just arrived (column 2). If it has, increase the current inventory (in column 3) by the quantity ordered (10 units, in this case).

2. Generate a daily demand from the demand probability distribution in Table 15.7 by selecting a random number. This random number is recorded in column 4. The demand simulated is recorded in column 5.

FIGURE 15.3   **Flow Diagram for Simkin's Inventory Example**

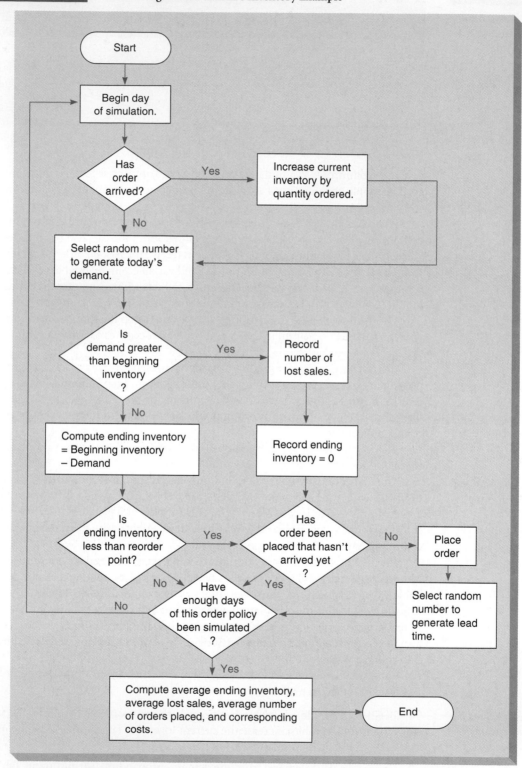

TABLE 15.9			Simkin Hardware's First Inventory Simulation						

ORDER QUANTITY = 10 UNITS			REORDER POINT = 5 UNITS						
(1) **DAY**	**(2)** **UNITS** **RECEIVED**	**(3)** **BEGINNING** **INVENTORY**	**(4)** **RANDOM** **NUMBER**	**(5)** **DEMAND**	**(6)** **ENDING** **INVENTORY**	**(7)** **LOST** **SALES**	**(8)** **ORDER?**	**(9)** **RANDOM** **NUMBER**	**(10)** **LEAD** **TIME**
1	...	10	06	1	9	0	No		
2	0	9	63	3	6	0	No		
3	0	6	57	3	③[a]	0	Yes	⑫[b]	1
4	0	3	㉔[c]	5	0	2	No[d]		
5	⑩[e]	10	52	3	7	0	No		
6	0	7	69	3	4	0	Yes	33	2
7	0	4	32	2	2	0	No		
8	0	2	30	2	0	0	No		
9	⑩[f]	10	48	3	7	0	No		
10	0	7	88	4	3	0	Yes	14	1
					Total 41	2			

[a]This is the first time inventory dropped to the reorder point of 5 drills. Because no prior order was outstanding, an order is placed.

[b]The random number 02 is generated to represent the first lead time. It was drawn from column 2 of Table 15.5 as the next number in the list being used. A separate column could have been used to draw lead time random numbers from if we had wanted to do so, but in this example we did not do so.

[c]Again, notice that the random digits 02 were used for lead time (see footnote b). So the next number in the column is 94.

[d]No order is placed on day 4 because there is one outstanding from the previous day that has not yet arrived.

[e]The lead time for the first order placed is one day, but as noted in the text, an order does not arrive the next morning but at the beginning of the following working day. Thus the first order arrives at the start of day 5.

[f]This is the arrival of the order placed at the close of business on day 6. Fortunately for Simkin, no lost sales occurred during the two-day lead time until the order arrived.

3. Compute the ending inventory every day and record it in column 6. Ending inventory equals beginning inventory minus demand. If on-hand inventory is insufficient to meet the day's demand, satisfy as much as possible and note the number of lost sales (in column 7).

4. Determine whether the day's ending inventory has reached the reorder point (5 units). If it has and if there are no outstanding orders, place an order (column 8). Lead time for a new order is simulated by first choosing a random number from Table 15.5 and recording it in column 9. (We can continue down the same string of the random number table that we were using to generate numbers for the demand variable). Finally, we convert this random number into a lead time by using the distribution set in Table 15.8.

Analyzing Simkin's Inventory Costs

Now that the simulation results have been generated, Simkin is ready to proceed to step 6 of this process—examining the results. Since the objective is to find a low-cost solution, Simkin must determine, given these results, what the costs would be. In doing this, Simkin finds some interesting results. The average daily ending inventory is

$$\text{average ending inventory} = \frac{41 \text{ total units}}{10 \text{ days}} = 4.1 \text{ units per day}$$

We also note the average lost sales and number of orders placed per day:

$$\text{average lost sales} = \frac{2 \text{ sales lost}}{10 \text{ days}} = 0.2 \text{ unit per day}$$

$$\text{average number of orders placed} = \frac{3 \text{ orders}}{10 \text{ days}} = 0.3 \text{ order per day}$$

These data are useful in studying the inventory costs of the policy being simulated.

Simkin's store is open for business 200 days per year. He estimates that the cost of placing each order for Ace drills is $10. The cost of holding a drill in stock is $6 per drill per year, which can also be viewed as 3 cents per drill per day (over a 200-day year). Finally, Simkin estimates that the cost of each shortage, or lost sale, is $8. What is Simkin's total daily inventory cost for the ordering policy of order quantity, $Q = 10$ and reorder point, ROP = 5?

Let us examine the three cost components:

$$\text{daily order cost} = (\text{cost of placing one order})$$
$$\times \ (\text{number of orders placed per day})$$
$$= \$10 \text{ per order} \times 0.3 \text{ order per day} = \$3$$

$$\text{daily holding cost} = (\text{cost of holding one unit for one day})$$
$$\times \ (\text{average ending inventory})$$
$$= \$0.03 \text{ per unit per day} \times 4.1 \text{ units per day}$$
$$= \$0.12$$

$$\text{daily stockout cost} = (\text{cost per lost sale})$$
$$\times \ (\text{average number of lost sales per day})$$
$$= \$8 \text{ per lost sale} \times 0.2 \text{ lost sales per day}$$
$$= \$1.60$$

$$\text{total daily inventory cost} = \text{daily order cost} \ + \ \text{daily holding cost}$$
$$+ \ \text{daily stockout cost} \ = \$4.72$$

Thus the total daily inventory cost for this simulation is $4.72. Annualizing this daily figure to a 200-day working year suggests that this inventory policy's cost is approximately $944.

Now once again we want to emphasize something very important. This simulation should be extended many more days before we draw any conclusions as to the cost of the inventory policy being tested. If a hand simulation is being conducted, 100 days would provide a better representation. If a computer is doing the calculations, 1,000 days would be helpful in reaching accurate cost estimates.

It is important to remember that the simulation should be conducted for many, many days before it is legitimate to draw any solid conclusions.

Let's say that Simkin *does* complete a 1,000-day simulation of the policy that order quantity = 10 drills, reorder point = 5 drills. Does this complete his analysis? The answer is *no*—this is just the beginning! We should now verify that the model is correct and validate that the model truly represents the situation on which it is based. As indicated in Figure 15.1, once the results of the model are examined, we may want to go back and modify the model that we have developed. If we are satisfied that the model performed as we expected, then we can specify other values of the variables. Simkin must now compare *this* potential strategy to other possibilities. For example, what about $Q = 10$, ROP = 4; or $Q = 12$, ROP = 6; or $Q = 14$, ROP = 5? Perhaps every combination of values of Q from 6 to 20 drills and ROP from 3 to 10 should be simulated. After simulating all reasonable combinations of order quantities and reorder points, Simkin would go to step 7 of the simulation process and probably select the pair yielding the lowest total inventory cost.

Volkswagen (VW) of America imports, markets, and distributes VWs and Audis in the United States from its parent company in Germany. As part of a reengineering effort, VW developed a computer simulation model, using PROMODEL software, to analyze how to save money in its huge supply chain.

Since the early 1900s, vehicle distribution in the United States has followed the system introduced by Ford Motor. This structure, in which manufacturers view auto dealers as their primary customers, is so old that its original performance intentions are rarely examined. Dealers and auto manufacturers are loosely coupled, with each managing its own inventory costs. Like other manufacturers, VW encourages dealers to carry as much stock as possible but understands that too much inventory could force a dealer out of business. Dealers recognize the threatening inventory costs but know that if they don't purchase enough cars, VW may restrict

supply or appoint additional dealers. The average VW dealer sells 30 cars per month and stocks fewer than 100 in inventory.

To better the chances of a customer getting his or her first choice of car, to be able to deliver that car in 48 hours, and to be able to reduce total system (dealers *and* VW) costs for transportation, financing and storage, VW considered a *new* strategy: pooling vehicles in regional depots. Rather than opening these centers and observing how well the concept worked, VW focused on simulating the flow of cars from plants to dealers. The model showed that there would be significant savings by opening its distribution centers. VW managers also learned that supply-chain performance must be viewed from the system level.

Source: N. Karabakal, A. Gunal, and W. Ritchie, "Supply-Chain Analysis at Volkswagen of America," *Interfaces* (July–August 2000): 46–55.

15.5 SIMULATION OF A QUEUING PROBLEM

An important area of simulation application has been in the analysis of waiting line problems. As mentioned earlier, the assumptions required for solving queuing problems analytically are quite restrictive. For most realistic queuing systems, simulation may actually be the only approach available.

This section illustrates the simulation at a large unloading dock and its associated queue. Arrivals of barges at the dock are not Poisson distributed, and unloading rates (service times) are not exponential or constant. As such, the mathematical waiting line models of Chapter 14 cannot be used.

Port of New Orleans

Barge arrivals and unloading rates are both probabilistic variables. Unless they follow the queuing probability distributions of Chapter 14, we must turn to a simulation approach.

Fully loaded barges arrive at night in New Orleans following their long trips down the Mississippi River from industrial midwestern cities. The number of barges docking on any given night ranges from 0 to 5. The probability of 0, 1, 2, 3, 4, or 5 arrivals is displayed in Table 15.10. In the same table, we establish cumulative probabilities and corresponding random number intervals for each possible value.

A study by the dock superintendent reveals that because of the nature of their cargo, the number of barges unloaded also tends to vary from day to day. The superintendent provides information from which we can create a probability distribution for the variable *daily unloading rate* (see Table 15.11). As we just did for the arrival variable, we can set up an interval of random numbers for the unloading rates.

TABLE 15.10

Overnight Barge Arrival Rates and Random Number Intervals

NUMBER OF ARRIVALS	PROBABILITY	CUMULATIVE PROBABILITY	RANDOM NUMBER INTERVAL
0	0.13	0.13	01 to 13
1	0.17	0.30	14 to 30
2	0.15	0.45	31 to 45
3	0.25	0.70	46 to 70
4	0.20	0.90	71 to 90
5	0.10	1.00	91 to 00

TABLE 15.11	DAILY UNLOADING RATE	PROBABILITY	CUMULATIVE PROBABILITY	RANDOM NUMBER INTERVAL
Unloading Rates and Random Number Intervals	1	0.05	0.05	01 to 05
	2	0.15	0.20	06 to 20
	3	0.50	0.70	21 to 70
	4	0.20	0.90	71 to 90
	5	0.10	1.00	91 to 00
		1.00		

Barges are unloaded on a first-in, first-out basis. Any barges that are not unloaded the day of arrival must wait until the following day. Tying up a barge in dock is an expensive proposition, and the superintendent cannot ignore the angry phone calls from barge line owners reminding him that "time is money!" He decides that before going to the Port of New Orleans's controller to request additional unloading crews, a simulation study of arrivals, unloadings, and delays should be conducted. A 100-day simulation would be ideal, but for purposes of illustration, the superintendent begins with a shorter 15-day analysis. Random numbers are drawn from the top row of Table 15.5 to generate daily arrival rates. They are drawn from the second row of Table 15.5 to create daily unloading rates. Table 15.12 shows the day-by-day port simulation.

TABLE 15.12			Queuing Simulation of Port of New Orleans Barge Unloadings			
(1) DAY	(2) NUMBER DELAYED FROM PREVIOUS DAY	(3) RANDOM NUMBER	(4) NUMBER NIGHTLY ARRIVALS	(5) TOTAL TO BE UNLOADED	(6) RANDOM NUMBER	(7) NUMBER UNLOADED
1	⊖[a]	52	3	3	37	3
2	0	06	0	0	63	⓪[b]
3	0	50	3	3	28	3
4	0	88	4	4	02	1
5	3	53	3	6	74	4
6	2	30	1	3	35	3
7	0	10	0	0	24	⓪[c]
8	0	47	3	3	03	1
9	2	99	5	7	29	3
10	4	37	2	6	60	3
11	3	66	3	6	74	4
12	2	91	5	7	85	4
13	3	35	2	5	90	4
14	1	32	2	3	73	③[d]
15	0	00	5	5	59	3
	20		41			39
	Total delays		Total arrivals			Total unloadings

[a]We can begin with no delays from the previous day. In a long simulation, even if we started with 5 overnight delays, that initial condition would be averaged out.

[b]Three barges *could* have been unloaded on day 2. But because there were no arrivals and no backlog existed, zero unloadings took place.

[c]The same situation as noted in footnote b takes place.

[d]This time 4 barges could have been unloaded, but since only 3 were in the queue, the number unloaded is recorded as 3.

The superintendent will probably be interested in at least three useful and important pieces of information:

Here are the simulation results regarding average barge delays, average nightly arrivals, and average unloadings.

$$\text{average number of barges delayed to the next day} = \frac{20 \text{ delays}}{15 \text{ days}}$$

$$= 1.33 \text{ barges delayed per day}$$

$$\text{average number of nightly arrivals} = \frac{41 \text{ arrivals}}{15 \text{ days}} = 2.73 \text{ arrivals}$$

$$\text{average number of barges unloaded each day} = \frac{39 \text{ unloadings}}{15 \text{ days}} = 2.60 \text{ unloadings}$$

When these data are analyzed in the context of delay costs, idle labor costs, and the cost of hiring extra unloading crews, it will be possible for the dock superintendent and port controller to make a better staffing decision. They may even elect to resimulate the process assuming different unloading rates that would correspond to increased crew sizes. Although simulation is a tool that cannot guarantee an optimal solution to problems such as this, it can be helpful in recreating a process and identifying good decision alternatives.

Using Excel to Simulate the Port of New Orleans Queuing Problem

As we saw earlier in this chapter, simulation problems can be modeled in Excel directly (Excel QM does not contain a simulation module.) To illustrate the Port of New Orleans problem, Program 15.4A provides the formulas needed. For a review of the VLOOKUP

PROGRAM 15.4A   **An Excel Model for the Port of New Orleans Queuing Simulation**

PROGRAM 15.4B

Output from the Excel
Formulas in Program
15.4A

Day	Previously delayed	Random number	Arrivals	Total to be unloaded	Random Number	Possibly unloaded	Unloaded
1	0	0.990073	5	5	0.715591	4	4
2	1	0.02753	0	1	0.581144	3	1
3	0	0.624446	3	3	0.897867	4	3
4	0	0.166571	1	1	0.104936	2	1
5	0	0.784053	4	4	0.392847	3	3
6	1	0.361456	2	3	0.072112	2	2
7	1	0.422756	2	3	0.101345	2	2
8	1	0.522196	3	4	0.694828	3	3
9	1	0.113926	0	1	0.074691	2	1
10	0	0.753562	4	4	0.944656	5	4

Barge Arrivals

Demand	Probability	Lower	Cumulative	Demand
0	0.13	0	0.13	0
1	0.17	0.13	0.3	1
2	0.15	0.3	0.45	2
3	0.25	0.45	0.7	3
4	0.2	0.7	0.9	4
5	0.1	0.9	1	5

Unloading rates

Number	Probability	Lower	Cumulative	Unloading
1	0.05	0	0.05	1
2	0.15	0.05	0.2	2
3	0.5	0.2	0.7	3
4	0.2	0.7	0.9	4
5	0.1	0.9	1	5

function, refer back to Program 15.2A. The results of the Excel simulation are shown in Program 15.4B.

15.6 FIXED TIME INCREMENT AND NEXT EVENT INCREMENT SIMULATION MODELS

Simulation models are classified as fixed time increment or next event increment models according to when the system is updated and information is recorded.

Simulation models are often classified into two categories: *fixed time increment models* and *next event increment models*. These terms refer to the frequency in which the system status is updated. With a fixed time increment model, we update the status of the system at fixed time intervals (e.g., every week or every day). We use next event increment models when it is necessary to record information each time the system status changes. For example, if we need to determine the average time a customer must wait in line, we need to know when each customer arrives and when each customer leaves.

All of the examples we have seen so far are classified as fixed time increment models. These involved the status of the system (the number of units inventory or the number of barges arriving) at the beginning or end of a day. We were able to compute all of the pertinent information from these data. Randomly generating the number of events that occurred each day and updating the status of the system obtained these results.

In a next event increment model, rather than generate the number of events each time period, we randomly generate the time that elapses until the next event occurs. Whenever an event occurs, the system status is updated and recorded. This allows us to compute the necessary performance measures such as the average time in the queue or the average time in the system. The example in the following section illustrates this.

15.7 SIMULATION MODEL FOR A MAINTENANCE POLICY

Maintenance problems are an area in which simulation is widely used.

Simulation is a valuable technique for analyzing various maintenance policies before actually implementing them. A firm can decide whether to add more maintenance staff based on machine downtime costs and costs of additional labor. It can simulate replacing parts that have not yet failed in exploring ways to prevent future breakdowns. Many companies use computerized simulation models to decide if and when to shut down an entire plant for maintenance activities. This section provides an example of the value of simulation in setting maintenance policy.

Three Hills Power Company

The Three Hills Power Company provides electricity to a large metropolitan area through a series of almost 200 hydroelectric generators. Management recognizes that even a well-maintained generator will have periodic failures or breakdowns. Energy demands over the past three years have been consistently high, and the company is concerned over downtime of generators. It currently employs four highly skilled and highly paid ($30 per hour) repairpersons. Each works every fourth 8-hour shift. In this way there is a repairperson on duty 24 hours a day, seven days a week.

As expensive as the maintenance staff salaries are, breakdown expenses are even more costly. For each hour that one of its generators is down, Three Hills loses approximately $75. This amount is the charge for reserve power that Three Hills must "borrow" from the neighboring utility company.

Stephanie Robbins has been assigned to conduct a management analysis of the breakdown problem. She determines that simulation is a workable tool because of the probabilistic nature of this problem. Stephanie decides her objective is to determine (1) the service maintenance cost, (2) the simulated machine breakdown cost, and (3) the total of these breakdown and maintenance costs (which gives the total cost of this system). Since the total downtime of the machines is needed to compute the breakdown cost, Stephanie must know when each machine breaks and when each machine returns to service. Therefore, a next event step simulation model must be used. In planning for this simulation, a flowchart, as seen in Figure 15.4, is developed.

Stephanie identifies two important maintenance system components. First, the time between successive generator breakdowns varies historically from as little as one-half hour to as much as three hours. For the past 100 breakdowns Stephanie tabulates the frequency of various times between machine failures (see Table 15.13). She also creates a probability distribution and assigns random number intervals to each expected time range.

Robbins then notes that the people who do repairs log their maintenance time in one-hour time blocks. Because of the time it takes to reach a broken generator, repair times are generally rounded to one, two, or three hours. In Table 15.14 she performs a statistical analysis of past repair times, similar to that conducted for breakdown times.

Robbins begins conducting the simulation by selecting a series of random numbers to generate simulated times between generator breakdowns and a second series to simulate

TABLE 15.13	TIME BETWEEN RECORDED MACHINE FAILURES (HOURS)	NUMBER OF TIMES OBSERVED	PROBABILITY	CUMULATIVE PROBABILITY	RANDOM NUMBER INTERVAL
Time Between Generator Breakdown at Three Hills Power	0.5	5	0.05	0.05	01 to 05
	1.0	6	0.06	0.11	06 to 11
	1.5	16	0.16	0.27	12 to 27
	2.0	33	0.33	0.60	28 to 60
	2.5	21	0.21	0.81	61 to 81
	3.0	19	0.19	1.00	82 to 00
	Total	100	1.00		

FIGURE 15.4   **Three Hills Flow Diagram**

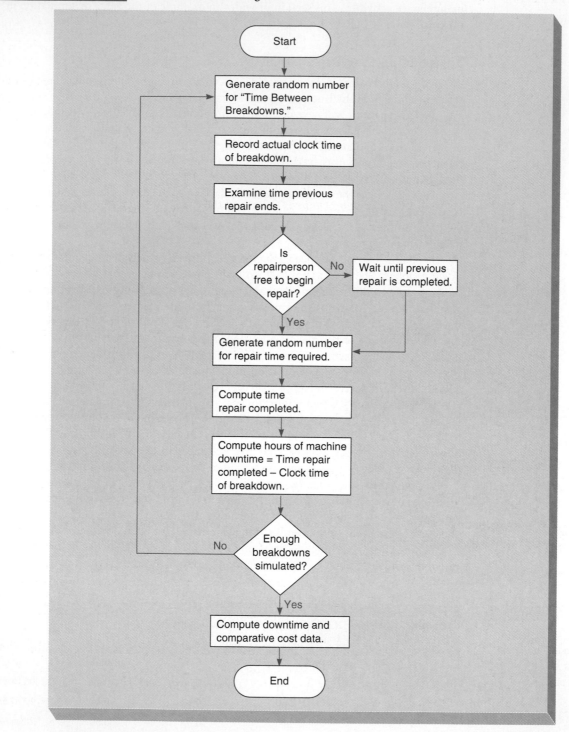

TABLE 15.14	REPAIR TIME REQUIRED (HOURS)	NUMBER OF TIMES OBSERVED	PROBABILITY	CUMULATIVE PROBABILITY	RANDOM NUMBER INTERVAL
Generator Repair Times Required	1	28	0.28	0.28	01 to 28
	2	52	0.52	0.80	29 to 80
	3	20	0.20	1.00	81 to 00
	Total	100	1.00		

repair times required. A simulation of 15 machine failures is presented in Table 15.15 on the next page. We now examine the elements in the table, one column at a time.

Column 1: Breakdown Number. This is just the count of breakdowns as they occur, going from 1 to 15.

Column 2: Random Number for Breakdowns. This is a number used to simulate time between breakdowns. The numbers in this column have been selected from Table 15.5, from the second column from the right-hand side of the table.

Column 3: Time Between Breakdowns. This number is generated from column 2 random numbers and the random number intervals defined in Table 15.13. The first random number, 57, falls in the interval 28 to 60, implying a time of 2 hours since the prior breakdown.

Column 4: Time of Breakdown. This converts the data in column 3 into an actual time of day for each breakdown. This simulation assumes that the first day begins at midnight (00:00 hours). Since the time between zero breakdowns and the first breakdown is 2 hours, the first recorded machine failure is at 02:00 on the clock. The second breakdown, you note, occurs 1.5 hours later, at a calculated clock time of 03:30 (or 3:30 A.M.).

Column 5: Time Repairperson Is Free to Begin Repair. This is 02:00 hours for the first breakdown if we assume that the repairperson began work at 00:00 hours and was not tied

---

IN ACTION Simulating Jackson Memorial Hospital's Operating Rooms

Miami's Jackson Memorial Hospital, Florida's largest with 1,576 inpatient beds, is also one of the United States' finest. In June 1996, it received the highest accreditation score of any public sector hospital in the country. Jackson's Department of Management Systems Engineering is constantly seeking ways of increasing hospital efficiency, and the construction of new operating rooms (ORs) prompted the development of a simulation of the existing 31 ORs.

The OR boundary includes the Holding Area and the Recovery Area, all of which were experiencing problems due to ineffective scheduling of OR services. A simulation study, modeled using the ARENA software package, sought to maximize the current use of OR rooms and staff. Inputs to the model included (1) the amount of time a patient waits in holding, (2) the specific process the patient undergoes, (3) the staff schedule, (4) room availability, and (5) time of day.

The first hurdle that the research team had to deal with at Jackson was the vast amount of records to scour so as to extract information for the probabilistic simulation model. The second hurdle was the *quality* of the data. A thorough analysis of the records determined which were good and which had to be discarded. In the end, Jackson's carefully screened databases led to a good set of model inputs. The simulation model then successfully developed five measures of OR performance: (1) number of procedures a day, (2) average case time, (3) staff utilization, (4) room utilization, and (5) average waiting time in the holding area.

Source: M. A. Centeno et al. "Challenges of Simulating Hospital Facilities," *Proceedings of the 12th Annual Conference of the Production and Operations Management Society*, Orlando, FL (March 2001): 50.

TABLE 15.15   Simulation of Generator Breakdowns and Repairs

(1) BREAKDOWN NUMBER	(2) RANDOM NUMBER FOR BREAKDOWNS	(3) TIME BETWEEN BREAKDOWNS	(4) TIME OF BREAKDOWN	(5) TIME REPAIRPERSON IS FREE TO BEGIN THIS REPAIR	(6) RANDOM NUMBER FOR REPAIR TIME	(7) REPAIR TIME REQUIRED	(8) TIME REPAIR ENDS	(9) NUMBER OF HOURS MACHINE DOWN
1	57	2	02:00	02:00	07	1	03:00	1
2	17	1.5	03:30	03:30	60	2	05:30	2
3	36	2	05:30	05:30	77	2	07:30	2
4	72	2.5	08:00	08:00	49	2	10:00	2
5	85	3	11:00	11:00	76	2	13:00	2
6	31	2	13:00	13:00	95	3	16:00	3
7	44	2	15:00	16:00	51	2	18:00	3
8	30	2	17:00	18:00	16	1	19:00	2
9	26	1.5	18:30	19:00	14	1	20:00	1.5
10	09	1	19:30	20:00	85	3	23:00	3.5
11	49	2	21:30	23:00	59	2	01:00	3.5
12	13	1.5	23:00	01:00	85	3	04:00	5
13	33	2	01:00	04:00	40	2	06:00	5
14	89	3	04:00	06:00	42	2	08:00	4
15	13	1.5	05:30	08:00	52	2	10:00	4.5
								Total 44

up from a previous generator failure. Before recording this time on the second and all subsequent lines, however, we must check column 8 to see what time the repairperson finishes the previous job. Look, for example, at the seventh breakdown. The breakdown occurs at 15:00 hours (or 3:00 P.M.). But the repairperson does not complete the previous job, the sixth breakdown, until 16:00 hours. Hence the entry in column 5 is 16:00 hours.

One further assumption is made to handle the fact that each repairperson works only an 8-hour shift: When each person is replaced by the next shift, he or she simply hands the tools over to the new worker. The new repairperson continues working on the same broken generator until the job is completed. There is no lost time and no overlap of workers. Hence, labor costs for each 24-hour day are exactly 24 hours × $30 per hour = $720.

Column 6: Random Number for Repair Time. This is a number selected from the rightmost column of Table 15.5. It helps simulate repair times.

Column 7: Repair Time Required. This is generated from column 6's random numbers and Table 15.14's repair time distribution. The first random number, 07, represents a repair time of 1 hour since it falls in the random number interval 01 to 28.

Column 8: Time Repair Ends. This is the sum of the entry in column 5 (time repairperson is free to begin) plus the required repair time from column 7. Since the first repair begins at 02:00 and takes one hour to complete, the time repair ends is recorded in column 8 as 03:00.

Column 9: Number of Hours the Machine Is Down. This is the difference between column 4 (time of breakdown) and column 8 (time repair ends). In the case of the first breakdown, that difference is 1 hour (03:00 minus 02:00). In the case of the tenth breakdown, the difference is 23:00 hours minus 19:30 hours, or 3.5 hours.

Cost Analysis of the Simulation

The simulation of 15 generator breakdowns in Table 15.15 spans a time of 34 hours of operation. The clock began at 00:00 hours of day 1 and ran until the final repair at 10:00 hours of day 2.

The critical factor that interests Robbins is the total number of hours that generators are out of service (from column 9). This is computed to be 44 hours. She also notes that toward the end of the simulation period, a backlog is beginning to appear. The thirteenth breakdown occurred at 01:00 hours but could not be worked on until 04:00 hours. The fourteenth and fifteenth breakdowns experienced similar delays. Robbins is determined to write a computer program to carry out a few hundred more simulated breakdowns but first wants to analyze the data she has collected thus far.

She measures her objectives as follows:

service maintenance cost = 34 hours of worker service time × $30 per hour

= $1,020

simulated machine breakdown cost = 44 total hours of breakdown
× $75 lost per hour of downtime

= $3,300

total simulated maintenance
cost of the current system = service cost + breakdown cost

= $1,020 + $3,300

= $4,320

A total cost of $4,320 is reasonable only when compared with other more attractive or less attractive maintenance options. Should, for example, the Three Hills Power Company add a second full-time repairperson to each shift? Should it add just one more worker and let him or her come on duty every fourth shift to help catch up on any backlogs? These are two alternatives that Robbins may choose to consider through simulation. You can help by solving Problem 15-25 at the end of the chapter.

Preventive maintenance policies can also be simulated.

As mentioned at the outset of this section, simulation can also be used in other maintenance problems, including the analysis of *preventive maintenance*. Perhaps the Three Hills Power Company should consider strategies for replacing generator motors, valves, wiring, switches, and other miscellaneous parts that typically fail. It could (1) replace all parts after a certain type when one fails on any generator, or (2) repair or replace all parts after a certain length of service based on an estimated average service life. This would again be done by setting probability distributions for failure rates, selecting random numbers, and simulating past failures and their associated costs.

Building an Excel Simulation Model for Three Hills Power Company

Programs 15.5A and 15.5B provide an Excel spreadsheet approach to simulating the Three Hills Power maintenance problem. Formulas are shown in Program 15.5A and the results in Program 15.5B.

15.8 TWO OTHER TYPES OF SIMULATION MODELS

Simulation models are often broken into three categories. The first, the Monte Carlo method just discussed, uses the concepts of probability distribution and random numbers to evaluate system responses to various policies. The other two categories are operational gaming and systems simulation. Although in theory the three methods are distinctly different, the growth of computerized simulation has tended to create a common basis in procedures and blur these differences.[3]

Operational Gaming

Operational gaming refers to simulation involving two or more competing players. The best examples are military games and business games. Both allow participants to match their management and decision-making skills in hypothetical situations of conflict.

Military games are used worldwide to train a nation's top military officers, to test offensive and defensive strategies, and to examine the effectiveness of equipment and armies. Business games, first developed by the firm Booz, Allen and Hamilton in the 1950s, are popular with both executives and business students. They provide an opportunity to test business skills and decision-making ability in a competitive environment. The person or team that performs best in the simulated environment is rewarded by knowing that his or her company has been most successful in earning the largest profit, grabbing a high market share, or perhaps increasing the firm's trading value on the stock exchange.

During each period of competition, be it a week, month, or quarter, teams respond to market conditions by coding their latest management decisions with respect to inventory,

---

[3] Theoretically, random numbers are used only in Monte Carlo simulation. However, in some complex gaming or systems simulation problems in which all relationships cannot be defined exactly, it may be necessary to use the probability concepts of the Monte Carlo method.

PROGRAM 15.5A   **An Excel Spreadsheet Model for Simulating Three Hills Power Company Maintenance Problem**

Use the RAND function to generate random numbers between 0 and 1.

The repairperson is free no earlier than when finished with the previous repair.

Use the VLOOKUP function to determine the time between breakdowns based on the random number generated and the probability table in A17 to E22.

Use the RAND function to generate random numbers between 0 and 1.

Use the VLOOKUP function to determine the repair time based on the random number generated and the probability table in G17 to I19.

	A	B	C		F	G	H	
1	Three Hills Power							
2								
3	Breakdown number	Random number	Time between breakdowns		Time of breakdown	Time repairperson is free	Random Number	Repair time	Repair ends
4	1	=RAND()	=VLOOKUP(B4,$C$17:$E$22,3,TRUE)	=C4	=D4	=RAND	=VLOOKU	=E4+G4
5	2	=RAND()	=VLOOKUP(B5,$C$17:$E$22,3,TRUE)	=D4+C5	=MAX(D5,H4)	=RAND	=VLOOKU	=E5+G5
6	3	=RAND()	=VLOOKUP(B6,$C$17:$E$22,3,TRUE)	=D5+C6	=MAX(D6,H5)	=RAND	=VLOOKU	=E6+G6
7	4	=RAND()	=VLOOKUP(B7,$C$17:$E$22,3,TRUE)	=D6+C7	=MAX(D7,H6)	=RAND	=VLOOKU	=E7+G7
8	5	=RAND()	=VLOOKUP(B8,$C$17:$E$22,3,TRUE)	=D7+C8	=MAX(D8,H7)	=RAND	=VLOOKU	=E8+G8
9	6	=RAND()	=VLOOKUP(B9,$C$17:$E$22,3,TRUE)	=D8+C9	=MAX(D9,H8)	=RAND	=VLOOKU	=E9+G9
10	7	=RAND()	=VLOOKUP(B10,$C$17:$E$22,3,TRUE)	=D9+C10	=MAX(D10,H9)	=RAND	=VLOOKU	=E10+G10
11	8	=RAND()	=VLOOKUP(B11,$C$17:$E$22,3,TRUE)	=D10+C11	=MAX(D11,H10)	=RAND	=VLOOKU	=E11+G11
12	9	=RAND()	=VLOOKUP(B12,$C$17:$E$22,3,TRUE)	=D11+C12	=MAX(D12,H11)	=RAND	=VLOOKU	=E12+G12
13	10	=RAND()	=VLOOKUP(B13,$C$17:$E$22,3,TRUE)	=D12+C13	=MAX(D13,H12)	=RAND	=VLOOKU	=E13+G13
14								
15	**Demand Table**						**Repair times**	
16	Time between	Probability	Lower		Cumulative	Demand	Time	Probability	Lower
17	0.5	0.05	=0		=B17	=A17	1	0.28	=0
18	1	0.06	=C17+B17		=D17+B18	=A18	2	0.52	=I17+
19	1.5	0.16	=C18+B18		=D18+B19	=A19	3	0.2	=I18+
20	2	0.33	=C19+B19		=D19+B20	=A20			
21	2.5	0.21	=C20+B20		=D20+B21	=A21			
22	3	0.19	=C21+B21		=D21+B22	=A22			

Except for the first time, the breakdown time is the time of the previous breakdown plus the random time generated.

PROGRAM 15.5B

Output from Excel Spreadsheet in Program 15.5A

Three Hills Power Company

	A	B	C	D	E	F	G	H	I	J	K
1	**Three Hills Power Company**										
2											
3	Breakdown number	Random number	Time between breakdowns	Time of breakdown	Time repairperson is free	Random Number	Repair time	Repair ends			
4	1	0.238655	1.5	1.5	1.5	0.105438	1	2.5			
5	2	0.038649	0.5	2	2.5	0.721456	2	4.5			
6	3	0.779849	2.5	4.5	4.5	0.893948	3	7.5			
7	4	0.631268	2.5	7	7.5	0.495521	2	9.5			
8	5	0.673484	2.5	9.5	9.5	0.837798	3	12.5			
9	6	0.720866	2.5	12	12.5	0.596008	2	14.5			
10	7	0.224151	1.5	13.5	14.5	0.938882	3	17.5			
11	8	0.609992	2.5	16	17.5	0.577619	2	19.5			
12	9	0.96837	3	19	19.5	0.400685	2	21.5			
13	10	0.003379	0.5	19.5	21.5	0.338775	2	23.5			
14											
15	**Demand Table**						**Repair times**				
16	Time between	Probability	Lower		Cumulative	Demand	Time	Probability	Lower	Cumulative	Lead time
17	0.5	0.05	0		0.05	0.5	1	0.28	0	0.28	1
18	1	0.06	0.05		0.11	1	2	0.52	0.28	0.8	2
19	1.5	0.16	0.11		0.27	1.5	3	0.2	0.8	1	3
20	2	0.33	0.27		0.6	2					
21	2.5	0.21	0.6		0.81	2.5					
22	3	0.19	0.81		1	3					

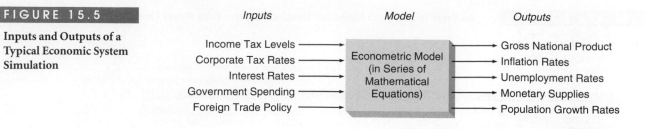

FIGURE 15.5

Inputs and Outputs of a Typical Economic System Simulation

production, financing, investment, marketing, and research. The competitive business environment is simulated by computer, and a new printout summarizing current market conditions is presented to players. This allows teams to simulate years of operating conditions in a matter of days, weeks, or a semester.

Systems Simulation

Systems simulation is similar to business gaming in that it allows users to test various managerial policies and decisions to evaluate their effect on the operating environment. This variation of simulation models the dynamics of large *systems*. Such systems include corporate operations,[4] the national economy, a hospital, or a city government system.

In a *corporate operating system*, sales, production levels, marketing policies, investments, union contracts, utility rates, financing, and other factors are all related in a series of mathematical equations that are examined by simulation. In a simulation of an *urban government*, systems simulation can be employed to evaluate the impact of tax increases, capital expenditures for roads and buildings, housing availability, new garbage routes, immigration and out-migration, locations of new schools or senior citizen centers, birth and death rates, and many more vital issues. Simulations of *economic systems*, often called econometric models, are used by government agencies, bankers, and large organizations to predict inflation rates, domestic and foreign money supplies, and unemployment levels. Inputs and outputs of a typical economic system simulation are illustrated in Figure 15.5.

The value of systems simulation lies in its allowance of what-if? questions to test the effects of various policies. A corporate planning group, for example, can change the value of any input, such as an advertising budget, and examine the impact on sales, market share, or short-term costs. Simulation can also be used to evaluate different research and development projects or to determine long-range planning horizons.

Econometric models are huge simulations involving thousands of regression equations tied together by economic factors. They use what-if? questions to test out various policies.

15.9 VERIFICATION AND VALIDATION

In the development of a simulation model, it is important that the model be checked to see that it is working properly and providing a good representation of the real world situation. The *verification* process involves determining that the computer model is internally consistent and following the logic of the conceptual model.

Validation is the process of comparing a model to the real system that it represents to make sure that it is accurate. The assumptions of the model should be checked to see that the appropriate probability distribution is being used. An analysis of the inputs and outputs should be made to see that the results are reasonable. If we know what the actual out-

---

[4] This is sometimes referred to as *industrial dynamics*, a term coined by Jay Forrester. Forrester's goal was to find a way "to show how policies, decisions, structure, and delays are interrelated to influence growth and stability" in industrial systems. See J. W. Forrester. *Industrial Dynamics* (Cambridge, MA: The MIT Press, 1961).

IN ACTION   Simulating Taco Bell's Restaurant Operation

Determining how many employees to schedule each 15 minutes to perform each function in a Taco Bell restaurant is a complex and vexing problem. So Taco Bell, the $5 billion giant with 6,500 U.S. and foreign locations, decided to build a simulation model. It selected MOSDIM as its software to develop a new labor-management system called LMS.

To develop and use a simulation model, Taco Bell had to collect quite a bit of data. Almost everything that takes place in a restaurant, from customer arrival patterns to the time it takes to wrap a taco, had to be translated into reliable, accurate data. Just as an example, analysts had to conduct time studies and data analysis for every task that is part of preparing every item on the menu. To the researcher's surprise, the hours devoted to collecting data greatly exceeded those it took to actually build the LMS model.

Inputs to LMS include staffing, such as number of people and positions. Outputs are performance measures, such as mean time in the system, mean time at the counter, people utilization and equipment utilization. The model paid off. More than $53 million in labor costs were saved in LMS's first four years of use.

Sources: J. Hueter and W. Swart. "An Integrated Labor-Management System for Taco Bell," *Interfaces* 28, 1 (January–February 1998): 75–91, and L. Pringle. "The Productivity Engine," *OR/MS Today*, 27, (June 2000): 30.

Verification relates to building the model right. Validation relates to building the right model.

puts are for a specific set of inputs, we could use those inputs in the computer model to see that the outputs of the simulation are consistent with the real world system.

It has been said that verification answers the question "Did we build the model right?" On the other hand, validation answers the question "Did we build the right model?" Only after we are convinced that the model is good should we feel comfortable in using the results.

15.10   ROLE OF COMPUTERS IN SIMULATION

We recognize that computers are critical in simulating complex tasks. They can generate random numbers, simulate thousands of time periods in a matter of seconds or minutes, and provide management with reports that make decision making easier. As a matter of fact, a computer approach is almost a necessity for us to draw valid conclusions from a simulation. Because we require a very large number of simulations, it would be a real burden to rely on pencil and paper alone.

Three types of computer programming languages are available to help the simulation process. The first type, *general-purpose languages*, includes Visual Basic, C++, and Java. The second type, *special-purpose simulation languages*, have three advantages: (1) they require less programming time for large simulations, (2) they are usually more efficient and easier to check for errors, and (3) they have random number generators already built in as subroutines. Three of the major special-purpose languages are GPSS/H, SLAM II, and SIMSCRIPT II.5.

Special-purpose simulation languages have several advantages over general-purpose languages like BASIC.

Simulation has proven so popular that a third type, commercial, easy-to-use *prewritten simulation programs*, are also available. Some are generalized to handle a wide variety of situations, ranging from queuing to inventory. These include Extend, AutoMod, ALPHA/Sim, SIMUL8, STELLA, Arena, AweSim!, SLX, and numerous others.[5] These programs run on personal computers and often have animated graphic capabilities. Many of these packages have tools for testing to see if the appropriate probability distribution is being used and for statistically analyzing the output.

---

[5] For a list of simulation software products, see James J. Swain, "Simulation Reloaded," *OR/MS Today* 30, 4 (August 2003): 46–57.

As shown in Programs 15.2, 15.3, 15.4, and 15.5, spreadsheet software such as Excel can be used to develop simulations quickly and easily. There are many Excel add-ins, such as @Risk, Crystal Ball, RiskSim, and XLSim, which can be used for basic simulation.

SUMMARY

The purpose of this chapter is to discuss the concept and approach of simulation as a problem-solving tool. Simulation involves building a mathematical model that attempts to describe a real-world situation. The model's goal is to incorporate important variables and their interrelationships in such a way that we can study the impact of managerial changes on the total system. The approach has many advantages over other quantitative analysis techniques and is especially useful when a problem is too complex or difficult to solve by other means.

The Monte Carlo method of simulation is developed through the use of probability distributions and random numbers. Random number intervals are established to represent possible outcomes for each probabilistic variable in the model. Random numbers are then either selected from a random number table or generated by computer to simulate variable outcomes. The simulation procedure is conducted for many time periods to evaluate the long-term impact of each policy value being studied. Monte Carlo simulation by hand is illustrated on problems of inventory control, queuing, and machine maintenance. We illustrate both fixed time step models and next event step models. Finally, we note the importance of verification and validation in the simulation process.

Operational gaming and systems simulation, two other categories of simulation, are also presented in this chapter. The chapter concludes with a discussion of the important role of the computer in the simulation process.

GLOSSARY

Fixed Time Increment Model. A simulation model in which the system status is updated at specific intervals of time.

Flow Diagram or Flowchart. A graphical means of presenting the logic of a simulation model. It is a tool that helps in writing a simulation computer program.

General-Purpose Languages. Computer programming languages, such as Visual Basic, C++, or Java, that are used to simulate a problem.

Monte Carlo Simulation. Simulations that experiment with probabilistic elements of a system by generating random numbers to create values for those elements.

Next Event Time Increment Model. A simulation model in which the system status is updated whenever the next event occurs.

Operational Gaming. The use of simulation in competitive situations such as military games and business or management games.

Prewritten Simulation Programs. These graphical programs are prestructured to handle a variety of situations.

Random Number. A number whose digits are selected completely at random.

Random Number Interval. A range of random numbers assigned to represent a possible simulation outcome.

Simulation. A quantitative analysis technique that involves building a mathematical model that represents a real-world situation. The model is then experimented with to estimate the effects of various actions and decisions.

Special-Purpose Simulation Languages. Programming languages especially designed to be efficient in handling simulation problems. The category includes GPSS/H, SIMSCRIPT II.5, and SLAM II.

Systems Simulation. Simulation models dealing with the dynamics of large organizational or governmental systems.

Validation. The process of comparing a model to the real system that it represents to make sure that it is accurate.

Verification. The process of determining that the computer model is internally consistent and following the logic of the conceptual model.

SOLVED PROBLEMS

Solved Problem 15-1

Higgins Plumbing and Heating maintains a stock of 30-gallon hot water heaters that it sells to homeowners and installs for them. Owner Jerry Higgins likes the idea of having a large supply on hand to meet customer demand, but he also recognizes that it is expensive to do so. He examines hot water heater sales over the past 50 weeks and notes the following:

HOT WATER HEATER SALES PER WEEK	NUMBER OF WEEKS THIS NUMBER WAS SOLD
4	6
5	5
6	9
7	12
8	8
9	7
10	3
	Total 50

a. If Higgins maintains a constant supply of 8 hot water heaters in any given week, how many times will he be out of stock during a 20-week simulation? We use random numbers from the seventh column of Table 15.5, beginning with the random digits 10.

b. What is the average number of sales per week (including stockouts) over the 20-week period?

c. Using an analytic nonsimulation technique, what is the expected number of sales per week? How does this compare with the answer in part (b)?

Solution

Because the variable of interest is the number of sales per week, a fixed time increment model should be used.

HEATER SALES	PROBABILITY	RANDOM NUMBER INTERVALS
4	0.12	01 to 12
5	0.10	13 to 22
6	0.18	23 to 40
7	0.24	41 to 64
8	0.16	65 to 80
9	0.14	81 to 94
10	0.06	95 to 00
	1.00	

a.

WEEK	RANDOM NUMBER	SIMULATED SALES	WEEK	RANDOM NUMBER	SIMULATED SALES
1	10	4	11	08	4
2	24	6	12	48	7
3	03	4	13	66	8
4	32	6	14	97	10
5	23	6	15	03	4
6	59	7	16	96	10
7	95	10	17	46	7
8	34	6	18	74	8
9	34	6	19	77	8
10	51	7	20	44	7

With a supply of 8 heaters, Higgins will be out of stock three times during the 20-week period (in weeks 7, 14, and 16).

b. Average sales by simulation = $\dfrac{\text{total sales}}{\text{20 weeks}} = \dfrac{135}{20} = 6.75$ per week.

c. Using expected values,

$$E(\text{sales}) = 0.12(4 \text{ heaters}) + 0.10(5) + 0.18(6) + 0.24(7)$$
$$+ 0.16(8) + 0.14(9) + 0.06(10)$$
$$= 6.88 \text{ heaters}$$

With a longer simulation, these two approaches will lead to even closer values.

Solved Problem 15-2

The manager of Denton Savings and Loan is attempting to determine how many tellers are needed at the drive-in window during peak times. As a general policy, the manager wishes to offer service such that average customer waiting time does not exceed 2 minutes. Given the existing service level, as shown in the following data, does the drive-in window meet this criterion?

DATA FOR SERVICE TIME			
SERVICE TIME (MINUTES)	PROBABILITY (FREQUENCY)	CUMULATIVE PROBABILITY	RANDOM NUMBER INTERVAL
0	0.00	0.00	(impossible)
1.0	0.25	0.25	01 to 25
2.0	0.20	0.45	26 to 45
3.0	0.40	0.85	46 to 85
4.0	0.15	1.00	86 to 00

DATA FOR CUSTOMER ARRIVALS			
TIME BETWEEN SUCCESSIVE CUSTOMER ARRIVALS	PROBABILITY (FREQUENCY)	CUMULATIVE PROBABILITY	RANDOM NUMBER INTERVAL
0	0.10	0.10	01 to 10
1.0	0.35	0.45	11 to 45
2.0	0.25	0.70	46 to 70
3.0	0.15	0.85	71 to 85
4.0	0.10	0.95	86 to 95
5.0	0.05	1.00	96 to 00

Solution

Since average waiting time is a variable of concern, a next event time increment model should be used.

(1) CUSTOMER NUMBER	(2) RANDOM NUMBER	(3) INTERVAL TO ARRIVAL	(4) TIME OF ARRIVAL	(5) RANDOM NUMBER	(6) SERVICE TIME	(7) START SERVICE	(8) END SERVICE	(9) WAIT TIME	(10) IDLE TIME
1	50	2	9:02	52	3	9:02	9:05	0	2
2	28	1	9:03	37	2	9:05	9:07	2	0
3	68	2	9:05	82	3	9:07	9:10	2	0
4	36	1	9:06	69	3	9:10	9:13	4	0
5	90	4	9:10	98	4	9:13	9:17	3	0
6	62	2	9:12	96	4	9:17	9:21	5	0
7	27	1	9:13	33	2	9:21	9:23	8	0
8	50	2	9:15	50	3	9:23	9:26	8	0
9	18	1	9:16	88	4	9:26	9:30	10	0
10	36	1	9:17	90	4	9:30	9:34	13	0
11	61	2	9:19	50	3	9:34	9:37	15	0
12	21	1	9:20	27	2	9:37	9:39	17	0
13	46	2	9:22	45	2	9:39	9:41	17	0
14	01	0	9:22	81	3	9:41	9:44	19	0
15	14	1	9:23	66	3	9:44	9:47	21	0

Read the data as in the following example for the first row:

Column 1: Number of customer.
Column 2: From third column of random number Table 15.5.
Column 3: Time interval corresponding to random number (random number of 50 implies a 2-minute interval).
Column 4: Starting at 9 A.M. the first arrival is at 9:02.
Column 5: From the first column of the random number Table 15.5.
Column 6: Teller time corresponding to random number 52 is 3 minutes.
Column 7: Teller is available and can start at 9:02.
Column 8: Teller completes work at 9:05 (9:02 + 0:03).
Column 9: Wait time for customer is 0 as the teller was available.
Column 10: Idle time for the teller was 2 minutes (9:00 to 9:02).

The drive-in window clearly does not meet the manager's criteria for an average wait time of 2 minutes. As a matter of fact, we can observe an increasing queue buildup after only a few customer simulations. This observation can be confirmed by expected value calculations on both arrival and service rates.

⇢ SELF-TEST

- Before taking the self-test, refer back to the learning objectives at the beginning of the chapter, the notes in the margins, and the glossary at the end of the chapter.
- Use the key at the back of the book to correct your answers.
- Restudy pages that correspond to any questions that you answered incorrectly or material you feel uncertain about.

1. Simulation is a technique usually reserved for studying only the simplest and most straightforward of problems.
   a. True   **b.** False
2. A simulation model is designed to arrive at a single specific numerical answer to a given problem.
   a. True   **b.** False
3. Simulation typically requires a familiarity with statistics to evaluate the results.
   a. True   **b.** False
4. A next event time increment simulation model would be warranted if the variable of concern is
   a. the daily sales of newspapers.
   b. the amount of rainfall on a particular day.
   c. the average time each customer spends waiting in line.
   d. the number of 911 calls placed in a day.
5. The verification process involves making sure that
   a. the model adequately represents the real world system.
   b. the model is internally consistent and logical.
   c. the correct random numbers are used.
   d. enough trial runs are simulated.
6. The validation process involves making sure that
   a. the model adequately represents the real world system.
   b. the model is internally consistent and logical.
   c. the correct random numbers are used.
   d. enough trial runs are simulated.
7. Which of the following is an *advantage* of simulation?
   a. It allows time compression.
   b. It is always relatively simple and inexpensive.
   c. The results are usually transferable to other problems.
   d. It will always find the optimal solution to a problem.
8. Which of the following is a *disadvantage* of simulation?
   a. It is inexpensive even for the most complex problem.
   b. It always generates the optimal solution to a problem.
   c. The results are usually transferable to other problems.
   d. Managers must generate all of the conditions and constraints for solutions that they wish to examine.
9. A meteorologist was simulating the number of days that rain would occur in a month. The random number interval from 01 to 30 was used to indicate that rain occurred on a particular day, and the interval 31–00 indicated that rain did not occur. What is the probability that rain did occur?
   a. 0.30   **b.** 0.31
   c. 1.00   **d.** 0.70
10. Simulation is best thought of as a technique to
    a. give concrete numerical answers.
    b. increase understanding of a problem.
    c. provide rapid solutions to relatively simple problems.
    d. provide optimal solutions to complex problems.
11. Specialized computer languages have been developed that allow one to readily simulate specific types of problems.
    a. True   **b.** False
12. When simulating the Monte Carlo experiment, the average simulated demand over the long run should approximate the
    a. real demand.   **b.** expected demand.
    c. sampled demand.   **d.** daily demand.
13. The idea behind simulation is to
    a. imitate a real-world situation.
    b. study the properties and operating characteristics of a real-world situation.
    c. draw conclusions and make action decisions based on simulation results.
    d. all of the above.
14. Using simulation for a queuing problem would be appropriate if
    a. the arrival rate follows a Poisson distribution.
    b. the service rate is constant.
    c. the FIFO queue discipline is assumed.
    d. there is a 10% chance an arrival would leave before receiving service.
15. Special-purpose simulation languages include
    a. C++.
    b. BASIC.
    c. GPSS.
    d. Java.
    e. all of the above.
16. A probability distribution has been developed, and the probability of 2 arrivals in the next hour is 0.20. A random number interval is to be assigned to this. Which of the following would *not* be an appropriate interval?
    a. 01–20
    b. 21–40
    c. 00–20
    d. 00–19
    e. all of the above would be appropriate
17. In a Monte Carlo simulation, a variable that we might want to simulate is
    a. lead time for inventory orders to arrive.
    b. times between machine breakdowns.
    c. time between arrivals at a service facility.
    d. number of employees absent from work each day.
    e. all of the above.
18. Use the following random numbers to simulate *yes* and *no* answers to 10 questions by starting in the first *row* and letting
    a. the double-digit number 00–49 represent *yes* and 50–99 represent *no*.
    b. the double-digit even numbers represent *yes* and the odd numbers represent *no*.
    c. Random Numbers: 52 06 50 88 53 30 10 47 99 37 66 91 35 32 00 84 57 00

DISCUSSION QUESTIONS AND PROBLEMS

Discussion Questions

15-1 What are the advantages and limitations of simulation models?

15-2 Why might a manager be forced to use simulation instead of an analytical model in dealing with a problem of
(a) Inventory ordering policy?
(b) Ships docking in a port to unload?
(c) Bank teller service windows?
(d) The U.S. economy?

15-3 What types of management problems can be solved more easily by quantitative analysis techniques other than simulation?

15-4 What are the major steps in the simulation process?

15-5 What is Monte Carlo simulation? What principles underlie its use, and what steps are followed in applying it?

15-6 List three ways in which random numbers may be generated for use in a simulation.

15-7 Discuss the concepts of verification and validation in simulation.

15-8 When is it appropriate to use a next event time increment simulation model?

15-9 In the simulation of an order policy for drills at Simkin's Hardware, would the results (Table 15.9) change significantly if a longer period were simulated? Why is the 10-day simulation valid or invalid?

15-10 Why is a computer necessary in conducting a real-world simulation?

15-11 What is operational gaming? What is systems simulation? Give examples of how each may be applied.

15-12 Do you think the application of simulation will increase strongly in the next 10 years? Why or why not?

15-13 Why would an analyst ever prefer a general-purpose language such as BASIC in a simulation when there are advantages to using special-purpose languages such as GPSS/H, SIMSCRIPT II.5, and SLAM II?

Problems*

The problems that follow involve simulations that are to be done by hand. You are aware that to obtain accurate and meaningful results, long periods must be simulated. This is usually handled by computer. If you are able to program some of the problems using a spreadsheet (see Programs 15.2, 15.3, 15.4, and 15.5), or QM for Windows (see Program 15.1) we suggest that you try to do so. If not, the hand simulations will still help you in understanding the simulation process.

15-14 Clark Property Management is responsible for the maintenance, rental, and day-to-day operation of a large apartment complex on the east side of New Orleans. George Clark is especially concerned about the cost projections for replacing air conditioner compressors. He would like to simulate the number of compressor failures each year over the next 20 years. Using data from a similar apartment building he manages in a New Orleans suburb, Clark establishes a table of relative frequency of failures during a year as shown in the following table:

NUMBER OF A.C. COMPRESSOR FAILURES	PROBABILITY (RELATIVE FREQUENCY)
0	0.06
1	0.13
2	0.25
3	0.28
4	0.20
5	0.07
6	0.01

He decides to simulate the 20-year period by selecting two-digit random numbers from the third column of Table 15.5, starting with the random number 50.

Conduct the simulation for Clark. Is it common to have three or more consecutive years of operation with two or fewer compressor failures per year?

15-15 The number of cars arriving per hour at Lundberg's Car Wash during the past 200 hours of operation is observed to be the following:

NUMBER OF CARS ARRIVING	FREQUENCY
3 or less	0
4	20
5	30
6	50
7	60
8	40
9 or more	0
	Total 200

---

* Note: Ⓠ means the problem may be solved with QM for Windows; ✖ means the problem may be solved with Excel; and Ⓠ✖ means the problem may be solved with QM for Windows and/or Excel.

(a) Set up a probability and cumulative probability distribution for the variable of car arrivals.
(b) Establish random number intervals for the variable.
(c) Simulate 15 hours of car arrivals and compute the average number of arrivals per hour. Select the random numbers needed from the first column of Table 15.5, beginning with the digits 52.

• **15-16** Compute the expected number of cars arriving in Problem 15-15 using the expected value formula. Compare this with the results obtained in the simulation.

• **15-17** Refer to the data in Solved Problem 15-1, which deals with Higgins Plumbing and Heating. Higgins has now collected 100 weeks of data and finds the following distribution for sales:

Hot Water Heater Sales per Week	Number of Weeks This Number Was Sold
3	2
4	9
5	10
6	15
7	25
8	12
9	12
10	10
11	5

(a) Resimulate the number of stockouts incurred over a 20-week period (assuming Higgins maintains a constant supply of 8 heaters).
(b) Conduct this 20-week simulation two more times and compare your answers with those in part (a). Did they change significantly? Why or why not?
(c) What is the new expected number of sales per week?

• **15-18** An increase in the size of the barge unloading crew at the Port of New Orleans (see Section 15.5) has resulted in a new probability distribution for daily unloading rates. In particular, Table 15.11 may be revised as shown here:

Daily Unloading Rate	Probability
1	0.03
2	0.12
3	0.40
4	0.28
5	0.12
6	0.05

(a) Resimulate 15 days of barge unloadings and compute the average number of barges delayed, average number of nightly arrivals, and average number of barges unloaded each day. Draw random

numbers from the bottom row of Table 15.5 to generate daily arrivals and from the second-from-the-bottom row to generate daily unloading rates.
(b) How do these simulated results compare with those in the chapter?

15-19 Every home football game for the past eight years at Eastern State University has been sold out. The revenues from ticket sales are significant, but the sale of food, beverages, and souvenirs has contributed greatly to the overall profitability of the football program. One particular souvenir is the football program for each game. The number of programs sold at each game is described by the following probability distribution:

Number (in 100s) of Programs Sold	Probability
23	0.15
24	0.22
25	0.24
26	0.21
27	0.18

Historically, Eastern has never sold less than 2,300 programs or more than 2,700 programs at one game. Each program costs $0.80 to produce and sells for $2.00. Any programs that are not sold are donated to a recycling center and do not produce any revenue.

(a) Simulate the sales of programs at 10 football games. Use the last column in the random number table (Table 15.5) and begin at the top of the column.
(b) If the university decided to print 2,500 programs for each game, what would the average profits be for the 10 games simulated in part (a)?
(c) If the university decided to print 2,600 programs for each game, what would the average profits be for the 10 games simulated in part (a)?

15-20 Refer to Problem 15-19. Suppose the sale of football programs described by the probability distribution in that problem only applies to days when the weather is good. When poor weather occurs on the day of a football game, the crowd that attends the game is only half of capacity. When this occurs, the sales of programs decreases, and the total sales are given in the following table:

Number (in 100s) of Programs Sold	Probability
12	0.25
13	0.24
14	0.19
15	0.17
16	0.15

Programs must be printed two days prior to game day. The university is trying to establish a policy for determining the number of programs to print based on the weather forecast.

(a) If the forecast is for a 20% chance of bad weather, simulate the weather for ten games with this forecast. Use column 4 of Table 15.5.

(b) Simulate the demand for programs at 10 games in which the weather is bad. Use column 5 of the random number table (Table 15.5) and begin with the first number in the column.

(c) Beginning with a 20% chance of bad weather and an 80% chance of good weather, develop a flowchart that would be used to prepare a simulation of the demand for football programs for 10 games.

(d) Suppose there is a 20% chance of bad weather, and the university has decided to print 2,500 programs. Simulate the total profits that would be achieved for 10 football games.

15-21 Dumoor Appliance Center sells and services several brands of major appliances. Past sales for a particular model of refrigerator have resulted in the following probability distribution for demand:

DEMAND PER WEEK:	0	1	2	3	4
Probability:	0.20	0.40	0.20	0.15	0.05

The lead-time in weeks is described by the following distribution:

LEAD TIME (WEEKS):	1	2	3
Probability:	0.15	0.35	0.50

Based on cost considerations as well as storage space, the company has decided to order 10 of these each time an order is placed. The holding cost is $1 per week for each unit that is left in inventory at the end of the week. The stockout cost has been set at $40 per stockout. The company has decided to place an order whenever there are only two refrigerators left at the end of the week. Simulate 10 weeks of operation for Dumoor Appliance assuming there are currently 5 units in inventory. Determine what the weekly stockout cost and weekly holding cost would be for the problem.

15-22 Repeat the simulation in Problem 15-21 assuming that the reorder point is 4 units rather than 2. Compare the costs for these two situations.

15-23 Simkin's Hardware Store simulated an inventory ordering policy for Ace electric drills that involved an order quantity of 10 drills with a reorder point of 5. The first attempt to develop a cost-effective ordering strategy is illustrated in Table 15.9. The brief simulation resulted in a total daily inventory cost of $4.72. Simkin would now like to compare this strategy with one in which he orders 12 drills, with a reorder point of 6. Conduct a 10-day simulation for him and discuss the cost implications.

15-24 Draw a flow diagram to represent the logic and steps of simulating barge arrivals and unloadings at the Port of New Orleans (see Section 15.5). For a refresher in flowcharts, see Figure 15.3.

15-25 Stephanie Robbins is the Three Hills Power Company management analyst assigned to simulate maintenance costs. In Section 15.7 we describe the simulation of 15 generator breakdowns and the repair times required when one repairperson is on duty per shift. The total simulated maintenance cost of the current system is $4,320.

Robbins would now like to examine the relative cost-effectiveness of adding one more worker per shift. The new repairperson would be paid $30 per hour, the same rate as the first is paid. The cost per breakdown hour is still $75. Robbins makes one vital assumption as she begins—that repair times with two workers will be exactly one-half the times required with only one repairperson on duty per shift. Table 15.14 can then be restated as follows:

REPAIR TIME REQUIRED (HOURS)	PROBABILITY
$\frac{1}{2}$	0.28
1	0.52
$1\frac{1}{2}$	0.20
	1.00

(a) Simulate this proposed maintenance system change over a 15-generator breakdown period. Select the random numbers needed for time between breakdowns from the second-from-the-bottom row of Table 15.5 (beginning with the digits 69). Select random numbers for generator repair times from the last row of the table (beginning with 37).

(b) Should Three Hills add a second repairperson each shift?

15-26 The Brennan Aircraft Division of TLN Enterprises operates a large number of computerized plotting machines. For the most part, the plotting devices are used to create line drawings of complex wing airfoils and fuselage part dimensions. The engineers operating the automated plotters are called loft lines engineers.

The computerized plotters consist of a minicomputer system connected to a 4- by 5-foot flat table with a series of ink pens suspended above it. When a sheet of clear plastic or paper is properly placed on the table, the computer directs a series of horizontal and vertical pen movements until the desired figure is drawn.

The plotting machines are highly reliable, with the exception of the four sophisticated ink pens that are built in. The pens constantly clog and jam in a raised or lowered position. When this occurs, the plotter is unusable.

Currently, Brennan Aircraft replaces each pen as it fails. The service manager has, however, proposed replacing all four pens every time one fails. This should cut down the frequency of plotter failures. At present, it takes one hour to replace one pen. All four pens could be replaced in two hours. The total cost of a plotter being unusable is $50 per hour. Each pen costs $8.

If only one pen is replaced each time a clog or jam occurs, the following breakdown data are thought to be valid:

HOURS BETWEEN PLOTTER FAILURES IF ONE PEN IS REPLACED DURING A REPAIR	PROBABILITY
10	0.05
20	0.15
30	0.15
40	0.20
50	0.20
60	0.15
70	0.10

Based on the service manager's estimates, if all four pens are replaced each time one pen fails, the probability distribution between failures is as follows:

HOURS BETWEEN PLOTTER FAILURES IF ALL FOUR PENS ARE REPLACED DURING A REPAIR	PROBABILITY
100	0.15
110	0.25
120	0.35
130	0.20
140	0.05

(a) Simulate Brennan Aircraft's problem and determine the best policy. Should the firm replace one pen or all four pens on a plotter each time a failure occurs?

(b) Develop a second approach to solving this problem, this time without simulation. Compare the results. How does it affect Brennan's policy decision using simulation?

✄ː 15-27 Dr. Mark Greenberg practices dentistry in Topeka, Kansas. Greenberg tries hard to schedule appointments so that patients do not have to wait beyond their appointment time. His October 20 schedule is shown in the following table.

SCHEDULED APPOINTMENT AND TIME		EXPECTED TIME NEEDED
Adams	9:30 A.M.	15
Brown	9:45 A.M.	20
Crawford	10:15 A.M.	15
Dannon	10:30 A.M.	10
Erving	10:45 A.M.	30
Fink	11:15 A.M.	15
Graham	11:30 A.M.	20
Hinkel	11:45 A.M.	15

Unfortunately, not every patient arrives exactly on schedule, and expected times to examine patients are just that—*expected*. Some examinations take longer than expected, and some take less time.

Greenberg's experience dictates the following:

(a) 20% of the patients will be 20 minutes early.
(b) 10% of the patients will be 10 minutes early.
(c) 40% of the patients will be on time.
(d) 25% of the patients will be 10 minutes late.
(e) 5% of the patients will be 20 minutes late.

He further estimates that

(a) 15% of the time he will finish in 20% less time than expected.
(b) 50% of the time he will finish in the expected time.
(c) 25% of the time he will finish in 20% more time than expected.
(d) 10% of the time he will finish in 40% more time than expected.

Dr. Greenberg has to leave at 12:15 P.M. on October 20 to catch a flight to a dental convention in New York. Assuming that he is ready to start his workday at 9:30 A.M. and that patients are treated in order of their scheduled exam (even if one late patient arrives after an early one), will he be able to make the flight? Comment on this simulation.

✄ː 15-28 The Pelnor Corporation is the nation's largest manufacturer of industrial-size washing machines. A main ingredient in the production process is 8- by 10-foot sheets of stainless steel. The steel is used for both interior washer drums and outer casings.

Steel is purchased weekly on a contractual basis from the Smith-Layton Foundry, which, because of limited availability and lot sizing, can ship either 8,000 or 11,000 square feet of stainless steel each week. When Pelnor's weekly order is placed, there is a 45% chance that 8,000 square feet will arrive and a 55% chance of receiving the larger size order.

Pelnor uses the stainless steel on a stochastic (nonconstant) basis. The probabilities of demand each week follow:

Steel Needed per Week (Sq Ft)	Probability
6,000	0.05
7,000	0.15
8,000	0.20
9,000	0.30
10,000	0.20
11,000	0.10

Pelnor has a capacity to store no more than 25,000 square feet of steel at any time. Because of the contract, orders *must* be placed each week regardless of the on-hand supply.

(a) Simulate stainless steel order arrivals and use for 20 weeks. (Begin the first week with a starting inventory of 0 stainless steel.) If an end-of-week inventory is ever negative, assume that back orders are permitted and fill the demand from the next arriving order.

(b) Should Pelnor add more storage area? If so, how much? If not, comment on the system.

15-29 Milwaukee's General Hospital has an emergency room that is divided into six departments: (1) the initial exam station, to treat minor problems or make diagnoses; (2) an x-ray department; (3) an operating room; (4) a cast-fitting room; (5) an observation room for recovery and general observation before final diagnoses or release; and (6) an out-processing department where clerks check patients out and arrange for payment or insurance forms.

The probabilities that a patient will go from one department to another are presented in the table below:

(a) Simulate the trail followed by 10 emergency room patients. Proceed one patient at a time from each one's entry at the initial exam station until he or she leaves through out-processing. You should be aware that a patient can enter the same department more than once.

(b) Using your simulation data, what are the chances that a patient enters the x-ray department twice?

15-30 Management of the First Syracuse Bank is concerned over a loss of customers at its main office downtown. One solution that has been proposed is to add one or more drive-through teller stations to make it easier for customers in cars to obtain quick service without parking. Chris Carlson, the bank president, thinks the bank should only risk the cost of installing one drive-through. He is informed by his staff that the cost (amortized over a 20-year period) of building a drive-through is $12,000 per year. It also costs $16,000 per year in wages and benefits to staff each new teller window.

The director of management analysis, Beth Shader, believes that the following two factors encourage the immediate construction of two drive-through stations, however. According to a recent article in *Banking Research* magazine, customers who wait in long lines for drive-through teller service will cost banks an average of $1 per minute in loss of goodwill. Also, adding a second drive-through will cost an additional $16,000 in staffing, but amortized construction costs can be cut to a total of $20,000 per year if two drive-throughs are installed together instead of one at a time. To complete her analysis, Shader collected one month's arrival and service rates at a competing downtown bank's drive-through

Table for Problem 15-29

From	To	Probability
Initial exam at emergency room entrance	X-ray department	0.45
	Operating room	0.15
	Observation room	0.10
	Out-processing clerk	0.30
X-ray department	Operating room	0.10
	Cast-fitting room	0.25
	Observation room	0.35
	Out-processing clerk	0.30
Operating room	Cast-fitting room	0.25
	Observation room	0.70
	Out-processing clerk	0.05
Cast-fitting room	Observation room	0.55
	X-ray department	0.05
	Out-processing clerk	0.40
Observation room	Operating room	0.15
	X-ray department	0.15
	Out-processing clerk	0.70

stations. These data are shown as observation analyses 1 and 2 in the following tables.

(a) Simulate a one-hour time period, from 1 to 2 P.M., for a single-teller drive-through.
(b) Simulate a one-hour time period, from 1 to 2 P.M., for a two-teller system.
(c) Conduct a cost analysis of the two options. Assume that the bank is open 7 hours per day and 200 days per year.

OBSERVATION ANALYSIS 1: INTERARRIVAL TIMES FOR 1,000 OBSERVATIONS	
TIME BETWEEN ARRIVALS (MINUTES)	NUMBER OF OCCURRENCES
1	200
2	250
3	300
4	150
5	100

OBSERVATION ANALYSIS 2: CUSTOMER SERVICE TIME FOR 1,000 CUSTOMERS	
SERVICE TIME (MINUTES)	NUMBER OF OCCURRENCES
1	100
2	150
3	350
4	150
5	150
6	100

INTERNET HOMEWORK PROBLEMS

See our Internet home page at **www.prenhall.com/render** for additional homework problems 15-31 to 15-37.

⇒ CASE STUDY

Alabama Airlines

Alabama Airlines opened its doors in June 1995 as a commuter service with its headquarters and only hub located in Birmingham. A product of airline deregulation, Alabama Air joined the growing number of successful short-haul, point-to-point airlines, including Lone Star, Comair, Atlantic Southeast, Skywest, and Business Express.

Alabama Air was started and managed by two former pilots, David Douglas (who had been with the defunct Eastern Airlines) and Savas Ozatalay (formerly with Pan Am). It acquired a fleet of 12 used prop-jet planes and the airport gates vacated by Delta Airlines' 1994 downsizing.

With business growing quickly, Douglas turned his attention to Alabama Air's toll-free reservations system. Between midnight and 6:00 A.M., only one telephone reservations agent had been on duty. The time between incoming calls during this period is distributed as shown in Table 15.16. Douglas carefully observed and timed the agent and estimated that the time taken to process passenger inquiries is distributed as shown in Table 15.17.

TABLE 15.16	Incoming Call Distribution
TIME BETWEEN CALLS (MINUTES)	PROBABILITY
1	0.11
2	0.21
3	0.22
4	0.20
5	0.16
6	0.10

TABLE 15.17	Service Time Distribution
TIME TO PROCESS CUSTOMER ENQUIRIES (MINUTES)	PROBABILITY
1	0.20
2	0.19
3	0.18
4	0.17
5	0.13
6	0.10
7	0.03

TABLE 15.18	Incoming Call Distribution

TIME BETWEEN CALLS (MINUTES)	PROBABILITY
1	0.22
2	0.25
3	0.19
4	0.15
5	0.12
6	0.07

All customers calling Alabama Air go on hold and are served in the order of the calls unless the reservations agent is available for immediate service. Douglas is deciding whether a second agent should be on duty to cope with customer demand. To maintain customer satisfaction, Alabama Air does not want a customer on hold for more than 3 to 4 minutes and also wants to maintain a "high" operator utilization.

Further, the airline is planning a new TV advertising campaign. As a result, it expects an increase in toll-free line phone inquiries. Based on similar campaigns in the past, the incoming call distribution from midnight to 6 A.M. is expected to be as shown in Table 15.18. (The same service time distribution will apply.)

Discussion Questions

1. What would you advise Alabama Air to do for the current reservation system based on the original call distribution? Create a simulation model to investigate the scenario. Describe the model carefully and justify the duration of the simulation, assumptions, and measures of performance.
2. What are your recommendations regarding operator utilization and customer satisfaction if the airline proceeds with the advertising campaign?

Source: Professor Zbigniew H. Przasnyski, Loyola Marymount University.

⇒ CASE STUDY

Statewide Development Corporation

Statewide Development Corporation has built a very large apartment complex in Gainesville, Florida. As part of the student-oriented marketing strategy that has been developed, it is stated that if any problems with plumbing or air conditioning are experienced, a maintenance person will begin working on the problem within one hour. If a tenant must wait more than one hour for the repair person to arrive, a $10 deduction from the monthly rent will be made for each additional hour of time waiting. An answering machine will take the calls and record the time of the call if the maintenance person is busy. Past experience at other complexes has shown that during the week when most occupants are at school, there is little difficulty in meeting the one hour guarantee. However, it is observed that weekends have been particularly troublesome during the summer months.

A study of the number of calls to the office on weekends concerning air conditioning and plumbing problems has resulted in the following distribution:

TIME BETWEEN CALLS (MINUTES)	PROBABILITY
30	0.15
60	0.30
90	0.30
120	0.25

The time required to complete a service call varies according to the difficulty of the problem. Parts needed for most repairs are kept in a storage room at the complex. However, for certain types of unusual problems, a trip to a local supply house is necessary. If a part is available on site, the maintenance person finishes one job before checking on the next complaint. If the part is not available on site and any other calls have been received, the maintenance person will stop by the other apartment(s) before going to the supply house. It takes approximately one hour to drive to the supply house, pick up a part, and return to the apartment complex. Past records indicate that, on approximately 10% of all calls, a trip must be made to the supply house.

The time required to resolve a problem if the part is available on site varies according to the following:

TIME FOR REPAIR (MINUTES)	PROBABILITY
30	0.45
60	0.30
90	0.20
120	0.05

It takes approximately 30 minutes to diagnose difficult problems for which parts are not on site. Once the part has been obtained from a supply house, it takes approximately one hour to install the new part. If any new calls have been recorded while the maintenance person has been away picking up a new part, these new calls will wait until the new part has been installed.

The cost of salary and benefits for a maintenance person is $20 per hour. Management would like to determine whether two maintenance people should be working on weekends instead of just one. It can be assumed that each person works at the same rate.

Discussion Questions

1. Use simulation to help you analyze this problem. State any assumptions that you are making about this situation to help clarify the problem.
2. On a typical weekend day, how many tenants would have to wait more than an hour, and how much money would the company have to credit these tenants?

INTERNET CASE STUDIES

See our Internet home page at **www.prenhall.com/render** for these additional case studies:

(1) Abjar Transport Company. This case involves a trucking company in Saudi Arabia.

(2) Biales Waste Disposal. Simulation is used to help a German company evaluate the profitability of a customer in Italy.

(3) Buffalo Alkali and Plastics. This case involves determining a good maintenance policy for a soda ash plant.

BIBLIOGRAPHY

Abdou, G. and S. P. Dutta. "A Systematic Simulation Approach for the Design of JIT Manufacturing Systems," *Journal of Operations Management* 11, 3 (September 1993): 25–38.

Banks, Jerry, John S. Carson, Barry L. Nelson, David M. Nicol. *Discrete-Event System Simulation,* 3/e. Upper Saddle River, NJ: Prentice Hall, 2001.

Banks, J. and V. Norman. "Justifying Simulation in Today's Manufacturing Environment," *IIE Solutions* (November 1995).

———. "Second Look at Simulation Software," *OR/MS Today* 23, 4 (August 1996): 55–57.

Brennan, J. E., B. L. Golden, and H. K. Rappoport. "Go with the Flow: Improving Red Cross Bloodmobiles Using Simulation Analysis," *Interfaces* 22, 5 (September–October 1992): 1–13.

Evans, J. R. and D. L. Olson. *Introduction to Simulation and Risk Analysis,* 2/e. Upper Saddle River, NJ: Prentice Hall, 2002.

Fishman, George S. *Monte Carlo: Concepts, Algorithms, and Applications.* New York: Springer-Verlag, 1996.

Fishman, G. S. and V. G. Kulkarni. "Improving Monte Carlo Efficiency by Increasing Variance," *Management Science* 38, 10 (October 1992): 1432–1444.

Hartvigsen, David. *SimQuick: Process Simulation with Excel—Updated Version,* 1/e. Upper Saddle River, NJ: Prentice Hall, 2001.

Hutchinson, J., G. K. Leong, and P. T. Ward. "Improving Delivery Performance in Gear Manufacturing at Jeffrey Division of Dresser Industries," *Interfaces* 23, 2 (March–April 1993): 69–79.

Pegden, C. D., R. E. Shannon, and R. P. Sadowski. *Introduction to Simulation Using SIMAN.* New York: McGraw-Hill, 1995.

Premachandra, I. M. and Liliana Gonzalez. "A Simulation Model Solved the Problem of Scheduling Drilling Rigs at Clyde Dam," *Interfaces* 26, 2 (March 1996): 80–91.

Samuelson, Douglas A. "Predictive Dialing for Outbound Telephone Call Centers," *Interfaces* 29, 5 (September 1999): 66–81.

Winston, Wayne L. *Simulation Modeling Using @Risk.* Pacific Grove, CA: Duxbury, 2001.

CHAPTER 16

MARKOV ANALYSIS

LEARNING OBJECTIVES

After completing this chapter, students will be able to:

1. Determine future states or conditions using Markov analysis.

2. Compute long-term or steady-state conditions using only the matrix of transition probabilities.

3. Understand the use of absorbing state analysis in predicting future conditions.

CHAPTER OUTLINE

16.1 INTRODUCTION

Markov analysis is a technique that deals with the probabilities of future occurrences by analyzing presently known probabilities.[1] The technique has numerous applications in business, including market share analysis, bad debt prediction, university enrollment predictions, and determining whether a machine will break down in the future.

Markov analysis makes the assumption that the system starts in an initial state or condition. For example, two competing manufacturers might have 40% and 60% of the market sales, respectively, as initial states. Perhaps in two months the market shares for the two companies will change to 45% and 55% of the market, respectively. Predicting these future states involves knowing the system's likelihood or probability of changing from one state to another. For a particular problem, these probabilities can be collected and placed in a matrix or table. This *matrix of transition probabilities* shows the likelihood that the system will change from one time period to the next. This is the Markov process, and it enables us to predict future states or conditions.

The matrix of transition probabilities shows the likelihood of change.

Like many other quantitative techniques, Markov analysis can be studied at any level of depth and sophistication. Fortunately, the major mathematical requirements are just that you know how to perform basic matrix manipulations and solve several equations with several unknowns. If you are not familiar with these techniques, you may wish to review Module 5 on the CD that accompanies this book, which covers matrices and other useful mathematical tools, before you begin this chapter.

Because the level of this course prohibits a detailed study of Markov mathematics, we limit our discussion to Markov processes that follow four assumptions:

There are four assumptions of Markov analysis.

1. There are a limited or finite number of possible states.
2. The probability of changing states remains the same over time.
3. We can predict any future state from the previous state and the matrix of transition probabilities.
4. The size and makeup of the system (e.g., the total number of manufacturers and customers) do not change during the analysis.

16.2 STATES AND STATE PROBABILITIES

States are used to identify all possible conditions of a process or a system. For example, a machine can be in one of two states at any point in time. It can be either functioning correctly or not functioning correctly. We can call the proper operation of the machine the first state, and we can call the incorrect functioning the second state. Indeed, it is possible to identify specific states for many processes or systems. If there are only three grocery stores in a small town, a resident can be a customer of any one of the three at any point in time. Therefore, there are three states corresponding to the three grocery stores. If students can take one of three specialties in the management area (let's say management science, management information systems, or general management), each of these areas can be considered a state.

In Markov analysis we also assume that the states are both *collectively exhaustive* and *mutually exclusive*. Collectively exhaustive means that we can list all of the possible states of a system or process. Our discussion of Markov analysis assumes that there is a finite number of states for any system. Mutually exclusive means that a system can be in only one state at any point in time. A student can be in only one of the three management specialty areas

Collectively exhaustive and mutually exclusive states are two additional assumptions of Markov analysis.

---

[1] The founder of the concept was A. A. Markov, whose 1905 studies of the sequence of experiments connected in a chain were used to describe the principle of Brownian motion.

and *not* in two or more areas at the same time. It also means that a person can only be a customer of *one* of the three grocery stores at any point in time.

After the states have been identified, the next step is to determine the probability that the system is in this state. Such information is then placed into a *vector of state probabilities*.

$$\pi(i) = \text{vector of state probabilities for period } i$$

$$= (\pi_1, \pi_2, \pi_3, \ldots, \pi_n) \tag{16-1}$$

where

$$n = \text{number of states}$$

$$\pi_1, \pi_2, \ldots, \pi_n = \text{probability of being in state 1, state 2,} \ldots, \text{ state } n$$

In some cases, in which we are only dealing with one item, such as one machine, it is possible to know with complete certainty what state this item is in. For example, if we are investigating only one machine, we may know that at this point in time the machine is functioning correctly. Then the vector of states can be represented as follows:

$$\pi(1) = (1, 0)$$

where

$$\pi(1) = \text{vector of states for the machine in period 1}$$

$$\pi_1 = 1 = \text{probability of being in the first state}$$

$$\pi_2 = 0 = \text{probability of being in the second state}$$

This shows that the probability the machine is functioning correctly, state 1, is 1, and the probability that the machine is functioning incorrectly, state 2, is 0 for the first period. In most cases, however, we are dealing with more than one item.

The Vector of State Probabilities for Three Grocery Stores Example

Let's look at the vector of states for people in the small town with the three grocery stores. There could be a total of 100,000 people that shop at the three grocery stores during any given month. Forty thousand people may be shopping at American Food Store, which will be called state 1. Thirty thousand people may be shopping at Food Mart, which will be called state 2, and 30,000 people may be shopping at Atlas Foods, which will be called state 3. The probability that a person will be shopping at one of these three grocery stores is as follows:

State 1—American Food Store:	$40,000/100,000 = 0.40 = 40\%$
State 2—Food Mart:	$30,000/100,000 = 0.30 = 30\%$
State 3—Atlas Foods:	$30,000/100,000 = 0.30 = 30\%$

These probabilities can be placed in the vector of state probabilities shown as follows:

$$\pi(1) = (0.4, 0.3, 0.3)$$

where

$$\pi(1) = \text{vector of state probabilities for the three grocery stores for period 1}$$

$$\pi_1 = 0.4 = \text{probability that a person will shop at American Food, state 1}$$

$$\pi_2 = 0.3 = \text{probability that a person will shop at Food Mart, state 2}$$

$$\pi_3 = 0.3 = \text{probability that a person will shop at Atlas Foods, state 3}$$

The vector of state probabilities represents market shares.

You should also notice that the probabilities in the vector of states for the three grocery stores represent the *market shares* for these three stores for the first period. Thus American Food has 40% of the market, Food Mart has 30%, and Atlas Foods has 30% of the market in period 1. When we are dealing with market shares, the market shares can be used in place of probability values.

Management of these three groceries should be interested in how their market shares change over time. Customers do not always remain with one store, but they may go to a different store for their next purchase. In this example, a study has been performed to determine how loyal the customers have been. It is determined that 80% of the customers who shop at American Food Store one month will return to that store next month. However, of the other 20% of American's customers, 10% will switch to Food Mart and the other 10% will switch to Atlas Foods for their next purchase. For customers who shop this month at Food Mart, 70% will return, 10% will switch to American Food Store, and 20% will switch to Atlas Foods. Of the customers who shop this month at Atlas Foods, 60% will return, but 20% will go to American Food Store and 20% will switch to Food Mart.

Figure 16.1 provides a tree diagram to illustrate this situation. Notice that of the 40% market share for American Food Store this month, 32% ($0.40 \times 0.80 = 0.32$) will return, 4% will shop at Food Mart, and 4% will shop at Atlas Foods. To find the market share for American next month, we can add this 32% of returning customers to the 3% that leave Food Mart to come to American and the 6% that leave Atlas Foods to come to American. Thus, American Food Store will have a 41% market share next month.

Although a tree diagram and the calculations just illustrated could be used to find the state probabilities for the next month and the month after that, the tree would soon get very large. Rather than use a tree diagram, it is easier to use a matrix of transition probabilities. This matrix is used along with the current state probabilities to predict the future conditions.

FIGURE 16.1

Tree Diagram for Three Grocery Store Example

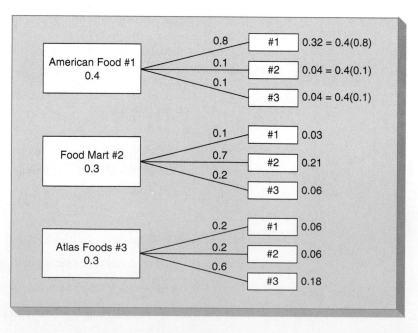

16.3 MATRIX OF TRANSITION PROBABILITIES

The matrix of transition probabilities allows us to get from a current state to a future state.

The concept that allows us to get from a current state, such as market shares, to a future state is the *matrix of transition probabilities*. This is a matrix of conditional probabilities of being in a future state given a current state. The following definition is helpful:

Let P_{ij} = conditional probability of being in state j in the future given the current state of i

For example, P_{12} is the probability of being in state 2 in the future given the event was in state 1 in the period before.

Let P = matrix of transition probabilities

$$P = \begin{bmatrix} P_{11} & P_{12} & P_{13} & \cdots & P_{1n} \\ P_{21} & P_{22} & P_{23} & \cdots & P_{2n} \\ \vdots & & & & \vdots \\ P_{m1} & & \cdots & & P_{mn} \end{bmatrix} \qquad (16\text{-}2)$$

Individual P_{ij} values are usually determined empirically. For example, if we have observed over time that 10% of the people currently shopping at store 1 (or state 1) will be shopping at store 2 (state 2) next period, then we know that $P_{12} = 0.1$ or 10%.

Transition Probabilities for the Three Grocery Stores

We used historical data with the three grocery stores to determine what percentage of the customers would switch each month. We put these transitional probabilities into the following matrix:

$$P = \begin{bmatrix} 0.8 & 0.1 & 0.1 \\ 0.1 & 0.7 & 0.2 \\ 0.2 & 0.2 & 0.6 \end{bmatrix}$$

Recall that American Food represents state 1, Food Mart is state 2, and Atlas Foods is state 3. The meaning of these probabilities can be expressed in terms of the various states, as follows:

Row 1

$0.8 = P_{11}$ = probability of being in state 1 after being in state 1 the preceding period

$0.1 = P_{12}$ = probability of being in state 2 after being in state 1 the preceding period

$0.1 = P_{13}$ = probability of being in state 3 after being in state 1 the preceding period

Row 2

$0.1 = P_{21}$ = probability of being in state 1 after being in state 2 the preceding period

$0.7 = P_{22}$ = probability of being in state 2 after being in state 2 the preceding period

$0.2 = P_{23}$ = probability of being in state 3 after being in state 2 the preceding period

Row 3

$0.2 = P_{31}$ = probability of being in state 1 after being in state 3 the preceding period

$0.2 = P_{32}$ = probability of being in state 2 after being in state 3 the preceding period

$0.6 = P_{33}$ = probability of being in state 3 after being in state 3 the preceding period

The probability values for any row must sum to 1.

Note that the three probabilities in the top row sum to 1. The probabilities for any row in a matrix of transition probabilities will also sum to 1.

After the state probabilities have been determined along with the matrix of transition probabilities, it is possible to predict future state probabilities.

16.4 PREDICTING FUTURE MARKET SHARES

One of the purposes of Markov analysis is to predict the future. Given the vector of state probabilities and the matrix of transition probabilities, it is not very difficult to determine the state probabilities at a future date. With this type of analysis, we are able to compute the probability that a person will be shopping at one of the grocery stores in the future. Because this probability is equivalent to market share, it is possible to determine future market shares for American Food, Food Mart, and Atlas Foods. When the current period is 0, calculating the state probabilities for the next period (period 1) can be accomplished as follows:

Computing future market shares.

$$\pi(1) = \pi(0)P \tag{16-3}$$

Furthermore, if we are in any period n, we can compute the state probabilities for period $n + 1$ as follows:

$$\pi(n + 1) = \pi(n)P \tag{16-4}$$

Equation 16-3 can be used to answer the question of next period's market shares for the grocery stores. The computations are

$$\pi(1) = \pi(0)P$$

$$= (0.4, 0.3, 0.3) \begin{bmatrix} 0.8 & 0.1 & 0.1 \\ 0.1 & 0.7 & 0.2 \\ 0.2 & 0.2 & 0.6 \end{bmatrix}$$

$$= [(0.4)(0.8) + (0.3)(0.1) + (0.3)(0.2), \ (0.4)(0.1) \\ + (0.3)(0.7) + (0.3)(0.2), \ (0.4)(0.1) + (0.3)(0.2) + (0.3)(0.6)]$$

$$= (0.41, 0.31, 0.28)$$

As you can see, the market share for American Food and Food Mart has increased while the market share for Atlas Foods has decreased. Will this trend continue in the next period and the one after that? From Equation 16-4, we can derive a model that will tell us what the state probabilities will be in any time period in the future. Consider two time periods from now:

$$\pi(2) = \pi(1)P$$

Since we know that

$$\pi(1) = \pi(0)P$$

we have

$$\pi(2) = [\pi(1)]P = [\pi(0)P]P = \pi(0)PP = \pi(0)P^2$$

In general,

$$\pi(n) = \pi(0)P^n \tag{16-5}$$

Thus, the state probabilities n periods in the future can be obtained from the current state probabilities and the matrix of transition probabilities.

In the three grocery store examples, we saw that American Food and Food Mart had increased market shares in the next period, while Atlas Food lost market share. Will Atlas eventually lose its entire market share? Or will a stable condition be reached by all three groceries? Although Equation 16-5 provides some help in determining this, it is better to discuss this in terms of equilibrium or steady state conditions. To help introduce the concept of equilibrium, we present a second application of Markov analysis: machine breakdowns.

16.5 MARKOV ANALYSIS OF MACHINE OPERATIONS

Paul Tolsky, owner of Tolsky Works, has recorded the operation of his milling machine for several years. Over the past two years, 80% of the time the milling machine functioned correctly during the current month if it had functioned correctly in the preceding month. This also means that only 20% of the time did the machine not function correctly for a given month when it was functioning correctly during the preceding month. In addition, it has been observed that 90% of the time the machine remained incorrectly adjusted for any given month if it was incorrectly adjusted the preceding month. Only 10% of the time did the machine operate correctly in a given month when it did *not* operate correctly during the preceding month. In other words, this machine *can* correct itself when it has not been functioning correctly in the past, and this happens 10% of the time. These values can now be used to construct the matrix of transition probabilities. Again, state 1 is a situation in which the machine is functioning correctly, and state 2 is a situation in which the machine is not functioning correctly. The matrix of transition probabilities for this machine is

$$P = \begin{bmatrix} 0.8 & 0.2 \\ 0.1 & 0.9 \end{bmatrix}$$

where

$P_{11} = 0.8 =$ probability that the machine will be *correctly* functioning this month given it was *correctly* functioning last month

$P_{12} = 0.2 =$ probability that the machine will *not* be correctly functioning this month given it was *correctly* functioning last month

$P_{21} = 0.1 =$ probability that the machine will be functioning *correctly* this month given it was *not* correctly functioning last month

$P_{22} = 0.9 =$ probability that the machine will *not* be correctly functioning this month given that it was *not* correctly functioning last month

The row probabilities must sum to 1 because the events are mutually exclusive and collectively exhaustive.

Look at this matrix for the machine. The two probabilities in the top row are the probabilities of functioning correctly and not functioning correctly given that the machine was functioning correctly in the last period. Because these are mutually exclusive and collectively exhaustive, the row probabilities again sum to 1.

What is the probability that Tolsky's machine will be functioning correctly one month from now? What is the probability that the machine will be functioning correctly in two months? To answer these questions, we again apply Equation 16-3:

$$\pi(1) = \pi(0)P$$

$$= (1, 0) \begin{bmatrix} 0.8 & 0.2 \\ 0.1 & 0.9 \end{bmatrix}$$

$$= [(1)(0.8) + (0)(0.1), \ (1)(0.2) + (0)(0.9)]$$

$$= (0.8, 0.2)$$

Therefore, the probability that the machine will be functioning correctly one month from now, given that it is now functioning correctly, is 0.80. The probability that it will *not* be functioning correctly in one month is 0.20. Now we can use these results to determine the probability that the machine will be functioning correctly two months from now. The analysis is exactly the same:

$$\pi(2) = \pi(1)P$$

$$= (0.8, 0.2)\begin{bmatrix} 0.8 & 0.2 \\ 0.1 & 0.9 \end{bmatrix}$$

$$= [(0.8)(0.8) + (0.2)(0.1), \ (0.8)(0.2) + (0.2)(0.9)]$$

$$= (0.66, 0.34)$$

This means that two months from now there is a probability of 0.66 that the machine will still be functioning correctly. The probability that the machine will not be functioning correctly is 0.34. Of course, we could continue this analysis as many times as we want in computing state probabilities for future months.

16.6 EQUILIBRIUM CONDITIONS

Looking at the Tolsky machine example, it is easy to think that eventually all market shares or state probabilities will be either 0 or 1. This is usually not the case. *Equilibrium share* of the market values or probabilities are normally encountered.

One way to compute the equilibrium share of the market, or equilibrium state probabilities, is to use Markov analysis for a large number of periods. It is possible to see if the future values are approaching a stable value. For example, it is possible to repeat Markov analysis for 15 periods for Tolsky's machine. This is not too difficult to do by hand. The results for this computation appear in Table 16.1.

The machine starts off functioning correctly (in state 1) in the first period. In period 5, there is only a 0.4934 probability that the machine is still functioning correctly, and by

TABLE 16.1

State Probabilities for the Machine Example for 15 Periods

PERIOD	STATE 1	STATE 2
1	1.0	0.0
2	0.8	0.2
3	0.66	0.34
4	0.562	0.438
5	0.4934	0.5066
6	0.44538	0.55462
7	0.411766	0.588234
8	0.388236	0.611763
9	0.371765	0.628234
10	0.360235	0.639754
11	0.352165	0.647834
12	0.346515	0.653484
13	0.342560	0.657439
14	0.339792	0.660207
15	0.337854	0.662145

period 10, this probability is only 0.360235. In period 15, the probability that the machine is still functioning correctly is about 0.34. The probability that the machine will be functioning correctly at a future period is decreasing—but it is decreasing at a decreasing rate. What would you expect in the long run? If we made these calculations for 100 periods, what would happen? Would there be an equilibrium in this case? If the answer is *yes*, what would it be? Looking at Table 16.1, it appears that there will be an equilibrium at 0.333333 or $\frac{1}{3}$. But how can we be sure?

Equilibrium conditions exist if state probabilities do not change after a large number of periods.

By definition, an *equilibrium condition* exists if the state probabilities or market shares do not change after a large number of periods. Thus, at equilibrium, the state probabilities for a future period must be the same as the state probabilities for the current period. This fact is the key to solving for the equilibrium state probabilities. This relationship can be expressed as follows:

From Equation 16-4 it is always true that

$$\pi(\text{next period}) = \pi(\text{this period})P$$

or

$$\pi(n + 1) = \pi(n)P$$

At equilibrium, we know that

$$\pi(n + 1) = \pi(n)$$

Therefore, at equilibrium

$$\pi(n + 1) = \pi(n)P = \pi(n)$$

So

$$\pi(n) = \pi(n)P$$

or, dropping the *n* term,

$$\pi = \pi P \qquad (16\text{-}6)$$

At equilibrium, state probabilities for the next period equal the state probabilities for this period.

Equation 16-6 states that at equilibrium, the state probabilities for the *next* period are the same as the state probabilities for the *current* period. For Tolsky's machine, this can be expressed as follows:

$$\pi = \pi P$$

$$(\pi_1, \pi_2) = (\pi_1, \pi_2) \begin{bmatrix} 0.8 & 0.2 \\ 0.1 & 0.9 \end{bmatrix}$$

Using matrix multiplication, we get

$$(\pi_1, \pi_2) = [(\pi_1)(0.8) + (\pi_2)(0.1), (\pi_1)(0.2) + (\pi_2)(0.9)]$$

The *first term* on the left-hand side, π_1, is equal to the *first term* on the right-hand side $(\pi_1)(0.8) + (\pi_2)(0.1)$. In addition, the *second term* on the left-hand side, π_2, is equal to the *second term* on the right-hand side $(\pi_1)(0.2) + (\pi_2)(0.9)$. This gives us the following:

$$\pi_1 = 0.8\pi_1 + 0.1\pi_2 \qquad (a)$$

$$\pi_2 = 0.2\pi_1 + 0.9\pi_2 \qquad (b)$$

We also know that the state probabilities, π_1 and π_2 in this case, must sum to 1. (Looking at Table 16.1, you note that π_1 and π_2 sum to 1 for all 15 periods.) We can express this property as follows:

$$\pi_1 + \pi_2 + \cdots + \pi_n = 1 \qquad (c)$$

For Tolsky's machine, we have

$$\pi_1 + \pi_2 = 1 \tag{d}$$

Now, we have three equations for the machine (**a**, **b**, and **d**). We know that Equation **d** must hold. Thus, we can drop either Equation **a** or **b** and solve the remaining two equations for π_1 and π_2. It is necessary to drop one of the equations so that we end up with two unknowns and two equations. If we were solving for equilibrium conditions that involved three states, we would end up with four equations. Again, it would be necessary to drop one of the equations so that we end up with three equations and three unknowns. In general, when solving for equilibrium conditions, it will always be necessary to drop one of the equations such that the total number of equations is the same as the total number of variables for which we are solving. The reason that we can drop one of the equations is that they are interrelated mathematically. In other words, one of the equations is redundant in specifying the relationships between the various equilibrium equations.

Let us arbitrarily drop Equation **a**. Thus we will be solving the following two equations:

$$\pi_2 = 0.2\pi_1 + 0.9\pi_2$$

$$\pi_1 + \pi_2 = 1$$

Rearranging the first equation, we get

$$0.1\pi_2 = 0.2\pi_1$$

or

$$\pi_2 = 2\pi_1$$

Substituting this into Equation **d**, we have

$$\pi_1 + \pi_2 = 1$$

or

$$\pi_1 + 2\pi_1 = 1$$

or

$$3\pi_1 = 1$$
$$\pi_1 = \tfrac{1}{3} = 0.33333333$$

Thus

$$\pi_2 = \tfrac{2}{3} = 0.66666667$$

Compare these results with Table 16.1. As you can see, the equilibrium state probability for state 1 is 0.33333333, and the equilibrium state probability for state 2 is 0.66666667. These values are what you would expect by looking at the tabled results. This analysis indicates that it is only necessary to know the matrix of transition in determining the equilibrium market shares. The initial values for the state probabilities or the market shares do not influence the equilibrium state probabilities. The analysis for determining equilibrium state probabilities or market shares is the same when there are more states. If there are three states (as in the grocery store example), we have to solve three equations for the three equilibrium states; if there are four states, we have to solve four simultaneous equations for the four unknown equilibrium values, and so on.

You may wish to prove to yourself that the equilibrium states we have just computed are, in fact, equilibrium states. This can be done by multiplying the equilibrium states times

Defining the Problem

For more than two decades, the AIDS epidemic has caused great pain to individuals, families, and society in general. When it comes to federal funding, one problem is predicting the patterns of Medicaid enrollment among people with AIDS.

Developing a Model

A Markov model was developed to trace people with AIDS as they move between assistance categories in Medicaid.

Acquiring Input Data

To use the Markov model, data on how patients flowed between care categories were obtained. In addition, beginning states or conditions provided the needed data for the vector of state probabilities.

Developing a Solution

It was found that most Medicaid-eligible people with AIDS were Medicaid recipients prior to their AIDS diagnosis. These people shifted significantly between various Medicaid eligibility categories in distinct and predictable ways.

Testing the Solution

The model was tested by comparing the Markov analysis with actual patterns and trends. One result was that the number of people with AIDS enrolling in Medicaid is increasing by about 4% annually.

Analyzing the Results

Knowing how AIDS-infected persons are likely to move from one assistance category to another through the use of Markov analysis can help health agencies plan for the resources they need to provide adequate care.

Implementing the Results

The Medicaid program in Maryland was able to predict funding requirements for persons with AIDS as they moved through the Medicaid program.

Source: Linda M. Bartnyska. "Patterns in Maryland Medicaid Enrollment among Persons with AIDS," *Inquiry* 32, 2 (Summer 1995): 184–195.

---

the original matrix of transition. The results will be the same equilibrium states. Performing this analysis is also an excellent way to check your answers to end-of-chapter problems or examination questions.

16.7   ABSORBING STATES AND THE FUNDAMENTAL MATRIX: ACCOUNTS RECEIVABLE APPLICATION

In the examples discussed thus far, we assume that it is possible for the process or system to go from one state to any other state between any two periods. In some cases, however, if you are in a state, you cannot go to another state in the future. In other words, when you are in a given state, you are "absorbed" by it, and you will remain in that state. Any state that has this property is called an *absorbing state*. An example of this is the accounts receivable application.

If you are in an absorbing state, you cannot go to another state in the future.

An accounts receivable system normally places debts or receivables from its customers into one of several categories or states depending on how overdue the oldest unpaid bill is.

Of course, the exact categories or states depend on the policy set by each company. Four typical states or categories for an accounts receivable application follow:

State 1 (π_1): paid, all bills

State 2 (π_2): bad debt, overdue more than three months

State 3 (π_3): overdue less than one month

State 4 (π_4): overdue between one and three months

At any given period, in this case one month, a customer can be in one of these four states.[2] For this example it will be assumed that if the oldest unpaid bill is over three months due, it is automatically placed in the bad debt category. Therefore, a customer can be paid in full (state 1), have the oldest unpaid bill overdue less than one month (state 3), have the oldest unpaid bill overdue between one and three months inclusive (state 4), or have the oldest unpaid bill overdue more than three months, which is a bad debt (state 2).

Like any other Markov process, we can set up a matrix of transition probabilities for these four states. This matrix will reflect the propensity of customers to move among the four accounts receivable categories from one month to the next. The probability of being in the paid category for any item or bill in a future month, given that a customer is in the paid category for a purchased item this month, is 100% or 1. It is impossible for a customer to completely pay for a product one month and to owe money on it in a future month. Another absorbing state is the bad debts state. If a bill is not paid in three months, we are assuming that the company will completely write it off and not try to collect it in the future. Thus, once a person is in the bad debt category, that person will remain in that category forever. For any absorbing state, the probability that a customer will be in this state in the future is 1, and the probability that a customer will be in any other state is 0.

If a person is in an absorbing state now, the probability of being in an absorbing state in the future is 100%.

These values will be placed in the matrix of transition probabilities. But before we construct this matrix, we need to know the probabilities for the other two states—a debt of less than one month and a debt that is between one and three months old. For a person in the less than one month category, there is a 0.60 probability of being in the paid category, a 0 probability of being in the bad debt category, a 0.20 probability of remaining in the less than one month category, and a probability of 0.20 of being in the one to three month category in the next month. Note that there is a 0 probability of being in the bad debt category the next month because it is impossible to get from state 3, less than one month, to state 2, more than three months overdue, in just one month. For a person in the one to three month category, there is a 0.40 probability of being in the paid category, a 0.10 probability of being in the bad debt category, a 0.30 probability of being in the less than one month category, and a 0.20 probability of remaining in the one to three month category in the next month.

How can we get a probability of 0.30 of being in the one to three month category for one month, and in the one month or less category in the next month? Because these categories are determined by the oldest unpaid bill, it is possible to pay one bill that is one to

---

[2] You should also be aware that the four states can be placed in any order you choose. For example, it might seem more natural to order this problem with the states:

1. Paid
2. Overdue less than one month
3. Overdue one to three months
4. Overdue more than three months; bad debt

This is perfectly legitimate, and the only reason this ordering is not used is to facilitate some matrix manipulations you will see shortly.

three months old and still have another bill that is one month or less old. In other words, any customer may have more than one outstanding bill at any point in time. With this information, it is possible to construct the matrix of transition probabilities of the problem.

THIS MONTH	NEXT MONTH			
	PAID	BAD DEBT	<1 MONTH	1 TO 3 MONTHS
Paid	1	0	0	0
Bad debt	0	1	0	0
Less than 1 month	0.6	0	0.2	0.2
1 to 3 months	0.4	0.1	0.3	0.2

Thus

$$P = \begin{bmatrix} 1 & 0 & 0 & 0 \\ 0 & 1 & 0 & 0 \\ 0.6 & 0 & 0.2 & 0.2 \\ 0.4 & 0.1 & 0.3 & 0.2 \end{bmatrix}$$

If we know the fraction of the people in each of the four categories or states for any given period, we can determine the fraction of the people in these four states or categories for any future period. These fractions are placed in a vector of state probabilities and multiplied times the matrix of transition probabilities. This procedure was described in Section 16.5.

In the long run, everyone will be either in the paid or bad debt category.

Even more interesting are the equilibrium conditions. Of course, in the long run, everyone will be either in the paid or bad debt category. This is because the categories are absorbing states. But how many people, or how much money, will be in each of these categories? Knowing the total amount of money that will be in either the paid or bad debt category will help a company manage its bad debts and cash flow. This analysis requires the use of the *fundamental matrix.*

To obtain the fundamental matrix, it is necessary to *partition* the matrix of transition probabilities, *P*. This can be done as follows:

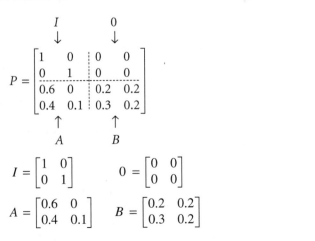

$$
\begin{array}{cc}
I & 0 \\
\downarrow & \downarrow \\
\end{array}
$$

$$P = \left[\begin{array}{cc|cc} 1 & 0 & 0 & 0 \\ 0 & 1 & 0 & 0 \\ \hline 0.6 & 0 & 0.2 & 0.2 \\ 0.4 & 0.1 & 0.3 & 0.2 \end{array}\right] \qquad (16\text{-}7)$$

$$
\begin{array}{cc}
\uparrow & \uparrow \\
A & B \\
\end{array}
$$

$$I = \begin{bmatrix} 1 & 0 \\ 0 & 1 \end{bmatrix} \qquad 0 = \begin{bmatrix} 0 & 0 \\ 0 & 0 \end{bmatrix}$$

$$A = \begin{bmatrix} 0.6 & 0 \\ 0.4 & 0.1 \end{bmatrix} \qquad B = \begin{bmatrix} 0.2 & 0.2 \\ 0.3 & 0.2 \end{bmatrix}$$

where

I = an identity matrix (i.e., a matrix with 1s on the diagonal and 0s everyplace else)

0 = a matrix with all 0s

The fundamental matrix can be computed as follows:

$$F = (I - B)^{-1} \tag{16-8}$$

F is the fundamental matrix.   In Equation 16-8, $(I - B)$ means that we subtract matrix B from matrix I. The superscript -1 means that we take the inverse of the result of $(I - B)$. Here is how we can compute the fundamental matrix for the accounts receivable application:

$$F = (I - B)^{-1}$$

or

$$F = \left(\begin{bmatrix} 1 & 0 \\ 0 & 1 \end{bmatrix} - \begin{bmatrix} 0.2 & 0.2 \\ 0.3 & 0.2 \end{bmatrix} \right)^{-1}$$

Subtracting B from I, we get

$$F = \begin{bmatrix} 0.8 & -0.2 \\ -0.3 & 0.8 \end{bmatrix}^{-1}$$

Taking the inverse of a large matrix involves several steps, as described in Module 5 on the CD that accompanies your textbook. Appendix 16.2 shows how this inverse can be found using Excel. However, for a matrix with two rows and two columns, the computations are relatively simple, as shown here.

The inverse of the matrix $\begin{bmatrix} a & b \\ c & d \end{bmatrix}$ is

$$\begin{bmatrix} a & b \\ c & d \end{bmatrix}^{-1} = \begin{bmatrix} \dfrac{d}{r} & \dfrac{-b}{r} \\ \dfrac{-c}{r} & \dfrac{a}{r} \end{bmatrix} \tag{16-9}$$

where

$$r = ad - bc$$

To find the matrix F in the accounts receivable example, we first compute

$$r = ad - bc = (0.8)(0.8) - (-0.3)(-0.2) = 0.64 - 0.06 = 0.58$$

With this we have

$$F = \begin{bmatrix} 0.8 & -0.2 \\ -0.3 & 0.8 \end{bmatrix}^{-1} = \begin{bmatrix} \dfrac{0.8}{0.58} & \dfrac{-(-0.2)}{0.58} \\ \dfrac{-(-0.3)}{0.58} & \dfrac{0.8}{0.58} \end{bmatrix} = \begin{bmatrix} 1.38 & 0.34 \\ 0.52 & 1.38 \end{bmatrix}$$

Now we are in a position to use the fundamental matrix in computing the amount of bad debt money that we could expect in the long run. First we need to multiply the fundamental matrix, F, times the matrix A. This is accomplished as follows:

$$FA = \begin{bmatrix} 1.38 & 0.34 \\ 0.52 & 1.38 \end{bmatrix} \times \begin{bmatrix} 0.6 & 0 \\ 0.4 & 0.1 \end{bmatrix}$$

or

$$FA = \begin{bmatrix} 0.97 & 0.03 \\ 0.86 & 0.14 \end{bmatrix}$$

The FA matrix indicates the probability that an amount will end up in an absorbing state.

The new *FA* matrix has an important meaning. It indicates the probability that an amount in one of the nonabsorbing states will end up in one of the absorbing states. The top row of this matrix indicates the probabilities that an amount in the less than one month category will end up in the paid and the bad debt category. The probability that an amount that is less than one month overdue will be paid is 0.97, and the probability that an amount that is less than one month overdue will end up as a bad debt is 0.03. The second row has a similar interpretation for the other nonabsorbing state, which is the one to three month category. Therefore, 0.86 is the probability that an amount that is one to three months overdue will eventually be paid, and 0.14 is the probability that an amount that is one to three months overdue will never be paid but will become a bad debt.

The matrix M represents the money in the absorbing states—paid or bad debt.

This matrix can be used in a number of ways. If we know the amount of the less than one month category and the one to three month category, we can determine the amount of money that will be paid and the amount of money that will become bad debts. We let the matrix *M* represent the amount of money that is in each of the nonabsorbing states as follows:

$$M = (M_1, M_2, M_3, \ldots, M_n)$$

where

$$n = \text{number of nonabsorbing states}$$

$$M_1 = \text{amount in the first state or category}$$

$$M_2 = \text{amount in the second state or category}$$

$$M_n = \text{amount in the } n\text{th state or category}$$

Assume that there is \$2,000 in the less than one month category and \$5,000 in the one to three month category. Then *M* would be represented as follows:

$$M = (2,000, 5,000)$$

Ⓐ IN ACTION   Using Markov Analysis in the Sport of Curling

Markov analysis has been widely applied to the field of sports, including baseball, jai alai, and now the relatively unknown but growing sport of curling. Essentially, curling resembles shuffleboard on ice. The game is played indoors on sheets of ice 14 feet wide and 146 feet long. At each end is a "house," which is four concentric circles into which teams try to position their 45-pound circular, polished granite "rocks."

The strategic advantage in curling is known as "having the hammer" (similar to having the final at-bat in baseball). The only difference in the start of each game is which team wins the toss and starts with the hammer. Thus, an initial Markov state will be either [0, 0] or [0, 1]. The likelihood of reaching different states at the end of the game is determined by transition probability matrices (which were obtained from 13 recent years of statistical data recorded at the Canadian Men's Curling Championship). Researchers developed a Markov model to determine the expected value of winning the toss in curling. They also studied which strategies are better during a game.

Remarkably, curling was the focus of a recent scene during an episode of NBC's TV series *ER*. As the camera panned the hospital hallway, a group of ER personnel scurried down the hallway curling. Curling's first *real* appearance was the 2002 Winter Olympics in Salt Lake City, Utah. Now you can closely follow this event in future competitions to observe the value of winning the toss!

Source: K. J. Kostak and K. A. Willoughby. "OR/MS 'Rocks' the House," *OR/MS Today* (December 1999): 36–39.

The amount of money that will end up as being paid and the amount that will end up as bad debts can be computed by multiplying the matrix M times the FA matrix that was computed previously. Here are the computations:

$$\text{amount paid and amount in bad debts} = MFA$$

$$= (2{,}000, \ 5{,}000) \begin{bmatrix} 0.97 & 0.03 \\ 0.86 & 0.14 \end{bmatrix}$$

$$= (6{,}240, \ 760)$$

Thus, out of the total of \$7,000 (\$2,000 in the less than one month category and \$5,000 in the one to three month category), \$6,240 will be eventually paid, and \$760 will end up as bad debts.

SUMMARY

With the assumptions discussed in this chapter, it is possible to use Markov analysis to predict future states and to determine equilibrium conditions. We also explore a special case of Markov analysis in which there is one or more absorbing states. This involves using the fundamental matrix to determine equilibrium conditions.

In this chapter only three applications of Markov analysis are explored. We investigate Tolsky's machine, the market shares for three grocery stores, and an accounts receivable system. The applications of the method are far reaching, and any dynamic system that meets the model's assumptions can be analyzed by the Markov approach.

GLOSSARY

Absorbing State. A state that, when entered, cannot be left. The probability of going from an absorbing state to any other state is 0.

Equilibrium Condition. A condition that exists when the state probabilities for a future period are the same as the state probabilities for a previous period.

Fundamental Matrix. A matrix that is the inverse of the I minus B matrix. It is needed to compute equilibrium conditions when absorbing states are involved.

Market Share. The fraction of the population that shops at a particular store or market. When expressed as a fraction, market shares can be used in place of state probabilities.

Markov Analysis. A type of analysis that allows us to predict the future by using the state probabilities and the matrix of transition probabilities.

Matrix of Transition Probabilities. A matrix containing all transition probabilities for a certain process or system.

State Probability. The probability of an event occurring at a point in time. Examples include the probability that a person will be shopping at a given grocery store during a given month.

Transition Probability. The conditional probability that we will be in a future state given a current or existing state.

Vector of State Probabilities. A collection or vector of all state probabilities for a given system or process. The vector of state probabilities could be the initial state or future state.

KEY EQUATIONS

(16-1) $\pi(i) = (\pi_1, \pi_2, \pi_3, \ldots, \pi_n)$

The vector of state probabilities for period i.

(16-2) $P = \begin{bmatrix} P_{11} & P_{12} & P_{13} & \cdots & P_{1n} \\ P_{21} & P_{22} & P_{23} & \cdots & P_{2n} \\ \vdots & & & & \vdots \\ P_{m1} & P_{m2} & P_{m3} & & P_{mn} \end{bmatrix}$

The matrix of transition probabilities, that is, the probability of going from one state into another.

(16-3) $\pi(1) = \pi(0)P$

Formula for calculating the state 1 probabilities given state 0 data.

(16-4) $\pi(n + 1) = \pi(n)P$

Formula for calculating the state probabilities for the period $n + 1$ if we are in period n.

(16-5) $\pi(n) = \pi(0)P^n$

Formula for computing the state probabilities for period n if we are in period 0.

(16-6) $\pi = \pi P$ at equilibrium

The equilibrium state equation used to derive equilibrium probabilities.

(16-7) $P = \left[\begin{array}{c|c} I & 0 \\ \hline A & B \end{array}\right]$

The partition of the matrix of transition for absorbing state analysis.

(16-8) $F = (I - B)^{-1}$

The fundamental matrix, used in computing probabilities of ending up in an absorbing state.

(16-9) $\begin{bmatrix} a & b \\ c & d \end{bmatrix}^{-1} = \begin{bmatrix} \dfrac{d}{r} & \dfrac{-b}{r} \\ \dfrac{-c}{r} & \dfrac{a}{r} \end{bmatrix}$ where $r = ad - bc$

The inverse of a matrix with 2 rows and 2 columns.

SOLVED PROBLEMS

Solved Problem 16-1

George Walls, president of Bradley School, is concerned about declining enrollments. Bradley School is a technical college that specializes in training computer programmers and computer operators. Over the years, there has been a lot of competition among Bradley School, International Technology, and Career Academy. The three schools compete in providing education in the areas of programming, computer operations, and basic secretarial skills.

To gain a better understanding of which of these schools is emerging as a leader, George decided to conduct a survey. His survey looked at the number of students who transferred from one school to the other during their academic careers. On the average, Bradley School was able to retain 65% of those students it originally enrolled. Twenty percent of the students originally enrolled transferred to Career Academy and 15% transferred to International Technology. Career Academy had the highest retention rate: 90% of its students remained at Career Academy for their full academic program. George estimated that about half the students who left Career Academy went to Bradley School, and the other half went to International Technology. International Technology was able to retain 80% of its students after they enrolled. Ten percent of the originally enrolled students transferred to Career Academy, and the other 10% percent enrolled in Bradley School.

Currently, Bradley School has 40% of the market. Career Academy, a much newer school, has 35% of the market. The remaining market share—25%—consists of students attending International Technology. George would like to determine the market share for Bradley for the next year. What are the equilibrium market shares for Bradley School, International Technology, and Career Academy?

Solution

The data for this problem are summarized as follows:

State 1 initial share = 0.40—Bradley School

State 2 initial share = 0.35—Career Academy

State 3 initial share = 0.25—International Technology

The transition matrix values are

FROM	TO		
	1 BRADLEY	2 CAREER	3 INTERNATIONAL
1 BRADLEY	0.65	0.20	0.15
2 CAREER	0.05	0.90	0.05
3 INTERNATIONAL	0.10	0.10	0.80

For George to determine market share for Bradley School for next year, he has to multiply the current market shares times the matrix of transition probability. Here is the overall structure of these calculations:

$$(0.40 \ 0.35 \ 0.25) \begin{bmatrix} 0.65 & 0.20 & 0.15 \\ 0.05 & 0.90 & 0.05 \\ 0.10 & 0.10 & 0.80 \end{bmatrix}$$

Thus, the market shares for Bradley School, International Technology, and Career Academy can be computed by multiplying the current market shares times the matrix of transition probabilities as shown. The result will be a new matrix with three numbers, each representing the market share for one of the schools. The detailed matrix computations follow:

$$\text{market share for Bradley School} = (0.40)(0.65) + (0.35)(0.05) + (0.25)(0.10)$$
$$= 0.303$$

$$\text{market share for Career Academy} = (0.40)(0.20) + (0.35)(0.90) + (0.25)(0.10)$$
$$= 0.420$$

$$\text{market share for International Technology} = (0.40)(0.15) + (0.35)(0.05) + (0.25)(0.80)$$
$$= 0.278$$

Now George would like to compute the equilibrium market shares for the three schools. At equilibrium conditions, the future market share is equal to the existing or current market share times the matrix of transition probabilities. By letting the variable X represent various market shares for these three schools, it is possible to develop a general relationship that will allow us to compute equilibrium market shares.

Let

$$X_1 = \text{market share for Bradley School}$$

$$X_2 = \text{market share for Career Academy}$$

$$X_3 = \text{market share for International Technology}$$

At equilibrium,

$$(X_1, X_2, X_3) = (X_1, X_2, X_3) \begin{bmatrix} 0.65 & 0.20 & 0.15 \\ 0.05 & 0.90 & 0.05 \\ 0.10 & 0.10 & 0.80 \end{bmatrix}$$

The next step is to make the appropriate multiplications on the right-hand side of the equation. Doing this will allow us to obtain three equations with the three unknown X values. In addition, we know that the sum of the market shares for any particular period must equal 1. Thus we are able to generate four equations, which are now summarized:

$$X_1 = 0.65X_1 + 0.05X_2 + 0.10X_3$$

$$X_2 = 0.20X_1 + 0.90X_2 + 0.10X_3$$

$$X_3 = 0.15X_1 + 0.05X_2 + 0.80X_3$$

$$X_1 + X_2 + X_3 = 1$$

Because we have four equations and only three unknowns, we are able to delete one of the top three equations, which will give us three equations and three unknowns. These equations can then be solved using standard algebraic procedures to obtain the equilibrium market share values for Bradley School, International Technology, and Career Academy. The results of these calculations are shown in the following table:

SCHOOL	MARKET SHARE
X_1 (Bradley)	0.158
X_2 (Career)	0.579
X_3 (International)	0.263

Solved Problem 16-2

Central State University administers computer competency examinations every year. These exams allow students to "test out" of the introductory computer class held at the university. Results of the exams can be placed in one of the following four states:

State 1: pass all of the computer exams and be exempt from the course

State 2: do not pass all of the computer exams on the third attempt and be required to take the course

State 3: fail the computer exams on the first attempt

State 4: fail the computer exams on the second attempt

The course coordinator for the exams has noticed the following matrix of transition probabilities:

$$\begin{bmatrix} 1 & 0 & 0 & 0 \\ 0 & 1 & 0 & 0 \\ 0.8 & 0 & 0.1 & 0.1 \\ 0.2 & 0.2 & 0.4 & 0.2 \end{bmatrix}$$

Currently, there are 200 students who did not pass all of the exams on the first attempt. In addition, there are 50 students who did not pass on the second attempt. In the long run, how many students will be exempted from the course by passing the exams? How many of the 250 students will be required to take the computer course?

Solution

The transition matrix values are summarized as follows:

FROM	TO			
	1	2	3	4
1	1	0	0	0
2	0	1	0	0
3	0.8	0	0.1	0.1
4	0.2	0.2	0.4	0.2

The first step in determining how many students will be required to take the course and how many will be exempt from it is to partition the transition matrix into four matrices. These are the I, 0, A, and B matrices:

$$I = \begin{bmatrix} 1 & 0 \\ 0 & 1 \end{bmatrix}$$

$$0 = \begin{bmatrix} 0 & 0 \\ 0 & 0 \end{bmatrix}$$

$$A = \begin{bmatrix} 0.8 & 0 \\ 0.2 & 0.2 \end{bmatrix}$$

$$B = \begin{bmatrix} 0.1 & 0.1 \\ 0.4 & 0.2 \end{bmatrix}$$

The next step is to compute the fundamental matrix, which is represented by the letter F. This matrix is determined by subtracting the B matrix from the I matrix and taking the inverse of the result:

$$F = (I - B)^{-1} = \begin{bmatrix} 0.9 & -0.1 \\ -0.4 & 0.8 \end{bmatrix}^{-1}$$

We first find

$$r = ad - bc = (0.9)(0.8) - (-0.4)(-0.1) = 0.72 - 0.04 = 0.68$$

$$F = \begin{bmatrix} 0.9 & -0.1 \\ -0.4 & 0.8 \end{bmatrix}^{-1} = \begin{bmatrix} \dfrac{0.8}{0.68} & \dfrac{-(-0.1)}{0.68} \\ \dfrac{-(-0.4)}{0.68} & \dfrac{0.9}{0.68} \end{bmatrix} = \begin{bmatrix} 1.176 & 0.147 \\ 0.588 & 1.324 \end{bmatrix}$$

Now multiply the F matrix by the A matrix. This step is needed to determine how many students will be exempt from the course and how many will be required to take it. Multiplying the F matrix times the A matrix is fairly straightforward:

$$FA = \begin{bmatrix} 1.176 & 0.147 \\ 0.588 & 1.324 \end{bmatrix} \begin{bmatrix} 0.8 & 0 \\ 0.2 & 0.2 \end{bmatrix}$$

$$= \begin{bmatrix} 0.971 & 0.029 \\ 0.735 & 0.265 \end{bmatrix}$$

The final step is to multiply the results from the FA matrix by the M matrix, as shown here:

$$MFA = (200 \quad 50) \begin{bmatrix} 0.971 & 0.029 \\ 0.735 & 0.265 \end{bmatrix}$$

$$= (231 \quad 19)$$

As you can see, the MFA matrix consists of two numbers. The number of students who will be exempt from the course is 231. The number of students who will eventually have to take the course is 19.

⟶ SELF-TEST

■ Before taking the self-test, refer back to the learning objectives at the beginning of the chapter, the notes in the margins, and the glossary at the end of the chapter.

■ Use the key at the back of the book to correct your answers.

■ Restudy pages that correspond to any questions that you answered incorrectly or material you feel uncertain about.

1. If the states in a system or process are such that the system can only be in one state at a time, then the states are
   a. collectively exhaustive.
   b. mutually exclusive.
   c. absorbing.
   d. disappearing.

2. The product of a vector of state probabilities and the matrix of transition probabilities will yield
   a. another vector of state probabilities.
   b. a meaningless mess.
   c. the inverse of the equilibrium state matrix.
   d. all of the above.
   e. none of the above.

3. In the long run, the state probabilities will be 0 and 1
   a. in no instances.
   b. in all instances.
   c. in some instances.

4. To find equilibrium conditions
   a. the first vector of state probabilities must be known.
   b. the matrix of transition probabilities is unnecessary.
   c. the general terms in the vector of state probabilities are used on two occasions.
   d. the matrix of transition probabilities must be squared before it is inverted.
   e. none of the above.

5. Which of the following is not one of the assumptions of Markov analysis?
   a. There is a limited number of possible states.
   b. There is a limited number of possible future periods.
   c. A future state can be predicted from the previous state and the matrix of transition probabilities.
   d. The size and makeup of the system do not change during the analysis.
   e. All of the above are assumptions of Markov analysis.

6. In Markov analysis, the state probabilities must
   a. sum to 1.
   b. be less than 0.
   c. be less than 0.01.
   d. be greater than 1.
   e. be greater than 0.01.

7. If the state probabilities do not change from one period to the next, then
   a. the system is in equilibrium.
   b. each state probability must equal 0.
   c. each state probability must equal 1.
   d. the system is in its fundamental state.

8. In the matrix of transition probabilities,
   a. the sum of the probabilities in each row will equal 1.
   b. the sum of the probabilities in each column will equal 1.
   c. there must be at least one 0 in each row.
   d. there must be at least one 0 in each column.

9. It is necessary to use the fundamental matrix
   a. to find the equilibrium conditions when there are no absorbing states.
   b. to find the equilibrium conditions when there is one or more absorbing states.
   c. to find the matrix of transition probabilities.
   d. to find the inverse of a matrix.

10. In Markov analysis, the _____ allows us to get from a current state to a future state.

11. In Markov analysis, we assume that the state probabilities are both _____ and _____.

12. The _____ is the probability that the system is in a particular state.

DISCUSSION QUESTIONS AND PROBLEMS

Discussion Questions

16-1 List the assumptions that are made in Markov analysis.

16-2 What are the vector of state probabilities and the matrix of transition probabilities, and how can they be determined?

16-3 Describe how we can use Markov analysis to make future predictions.

16-4 What is an equilibrium condition? How do we know that we have an equilibrium condition, and how can we compute equilibrium conditions given the matrix of transition probabilities?

16-5 What is an absorbing state? Give several examples of absorbing states.

16-6 What is the fundamental matrix, and how is it used in determining equilibrium conditions?

Problems*

• 16-7 Find the inverse of each of the following matrices:

(a) $\begin{bmatrix} 0.9 & -0.1 \\ -0.2 & 0.7 \end{bmatrix}$

(b) $\begin{bmatrix} 0.8 & -0.1 \\ -0.3 & 0.9 \end{bmatrix}$

(c) $\begin{bmatrix} 0.7 & -0.2 \\ -0.2 & 0.9 \end{bmatrix}$

(d) $\begin{bmatrix} 0.8 & -0.2 \\ -0.1 & 0.7 \end{bmatrix}$

• 16-8 Ray Cahnman is the proud owner of a 1955 sports car. On any given day, Ray never knows whether his car will start. Ninety percent of the time it will start if it started the previous morning, and 70% of the time it will not start if it did not start the previous morning.

(a) Construct the matrix of transition probabilities.
(b) What is the probability that it will start tomorrow if it started today?
(c) What is the probability that it will start tomorrow if it did *not* start today?

• 16-9 Alan Resnik, a friend of Ray Cahnman, bet Ray $5 that Ray's car would not start five days from now (See Problem 16-8).

(a) What is the probability that it will not start five days from now if it started today?
(b) What is the probability that it will not start five days from now if it did not start today?
(c) What is the probability that it will start in the long run if the matrix of transition probabilities does not change?

16-10 Over any given month, Dress-Rite loses 10% of its customers to Fashion, Inc., and 20% of its market to Luxury Living. But Fashion, Inc., loses 5% of its market to Dress-Rite and 10% of its market to Luxury Living each month; and Luxury Living loses 5% of its market to Fashion, Inc., and 5% of its market to Dress-Rite. At the present time, each of these clothing stores has an equal share of the market. What do you think the market shares will be next month? What will they be in three months?

• 16-11 Draw a tree diagram to illustrate what the market shares would be next month for Problem 16-10.

16-12 Goodeating Dog Chow Company produces a variety of brands of dog chow. One of their best values is the 50-pound bag of Goodeating Dog Chow. George Hamilton, president of Goodeating, uses a very old machine to load 50 pounds of Goodeating Chow automatically into each bag. Unfortunately, because the machine is old, it occasionally over or under fills the bags. When the machine is *correctly* placing 50 pounds of dog chow into each bag, there is a 0.10 probability that the machine will only put 49 pounds in each bag the following day, and there is a 0.20 probability that 51 pounds will be placed in each bag the next day. If the machine is currently placing 49 pounds of dog chow in each bag, there is a 0.30 probability that it will put 50 pounds in each bag tomorrow and a 0.20 probability that it will put 51 pounds in each bag tomorrow. In addition, if the machine is placing 51 pounds in each bag today, there is a 0.40 probability that it will place 50 pounds in each bag tomorrow and a 0.10 probability that it will place 49 pounds in each bag tomorrow.

(a) If the machine is loading 50 pounds in each bag today, what is the probability that it will be placing 50 pounds in each bag tomorrow?
(b) Resolve part (a) when the machine is only placing 49 pounds in each bag today.
(c) Resolve part (a) when the machine is placing 51 pounds in each bag today.

16-13 Resolve Problem 16-12 (Goodeating Dog Chow) for five periods.

16-14 The University of South Wisconsin has had steady enrollments over the past five years. The school has its own bookstore, called University Book Store, but there are also three private bookstores in town: Bill's Book Store, College Book Store, and Battle's Book Store. The university is concerned about the large number of students who are switching to one of the private stores. As a result, South Wisconsin's president, Andy Lange, has decided to give a student three hours of university credit to look into the problem. The following matrix of transition probabilities was obtained:

	UNIVERSITY	BILL'S	COLLEGE	BATTLE'S
University	0.6	0.2	0.1	0.1
Bill's	0	0.7	0.2	0.1
College	0.1	0.1	0.8	0
Battle's	0.05	0.05	0.1	0.8

At the present time, each of the four bookstores has an equal share of the market. What will the market shares be for the next period?

16-15 Andy Lange, president of the University of South Wisconsin, is concerned with the declining business at the University Book Store. (See Problem 16-14 for details.) The students tell him that the prices are simply too high. Andy, however, has decided not to lower the prices. If the same conditions exist, what long-run market shares can Andy expect for the four bookstores?

---

* Note: 🜋 means the problem may be solved with QM for Windows; ✖ means the problem may be solved with Excel QM; and 🜋✖ means the problem may be solved with QM for Windows and/or Excel QM.

16-16 Hervis Rent-A-Car has three car rental locations in the greater Houston area: the Northside branch, the West End branch, and the Suburban branch. Customers can rent a car at any of these places and return it to any of the others without any additional fees. However, this can create a problem for Hervis if too many cars are taken to the popular Northside branch. For planning purposes, Hervis would like to predict where the cars will eventually be. Past data indicate that 80% of the cars rented at the Northside branch will be returned there, and the rest will be evenly distributed between the other two. For the West End branch, about 70% of the cars rented there will be returned there, and 20% will be returned to the Northside branch and the rest will go to the Suburban branch. Of the cars rented at the Suburban branch, 60% are returned there, 25% are returned to the Northside branch, and the other 15% are dropped off at the West End. If there are currently 100 cars being rented from Northside, 80 from West End, and 60 from the suburban branch, how many of these will be dropped off at each of the car rental locations?

16-17 A study of accounts receivables at the A&W Department Store indicates that bills are either current, one month overdue, two months overdue, written off as bad debts, or paid in full. Of those that are current, 80% are paid that month, and the rest become one month overdue. Of the one month overdue bills, 90% are paid, and the rest become two months overdue. Those that are two months overdue will either be paid (85%) or be listed as bad debts. If the sales each month average $150,000, determine how much the company expects to receive of this amount. How much will become bad debts?

16-18 The cellular phone industry is very competitive. Two companies in the greater Lubbock area, Horizon and Local Cellular, are constantly battling each other in an attempt to control the market. Each company has a one-year service agreement. At the end of each year, some customers will renew, while some will switch to the other company. Horizon customers tend to be loyal, and 80% renew, while 20% switch. About 70% of the Local Cellular customers renew with them and about 30% switch to Horizon. If there are currently 100,000 Horizon customers this year, and 80,000 Local Cellular customers, how many would we expect each company to have next year?

16-19 The personal computer industry is very fast moving and technology provides motivation for customers to upgrade with new computers every few years. Brand loyalty is very important and companies try to do things to keep their customers happy. However, some current customers will switch to a different company. Three particular brands, Doorway, Bell, and Kumpaq, hold the major shares of the market. People who own Doorway computers will buy another Doorway in their next purchase 80% of the time, while the rest will switch to the other companies in equal proportions. Owners of Bell computers will buy Bell again 90% of the time, while 5% will buy Doorway and 5% will buy Kumpaq. About 70% of the Kumpaq owners

will make Kumpaq their next purchase while 20% will buy Doorway and the rest will buy Bell. If each brand currently has 200,000 customers who plan to buy a new computer in the next year, how many computers of each type will be purchased?

16-20 In Section 16.7 we investigated an accounts receivable problem. How would the paid category and the bad debt category change with the following matrix of transition probabilities?

$$P = \begin{bmatrix} 1 & 0 & 0 & 0 \\ 0 & 1 & 0 & 0 \\ 0.7 & 0 & 0.2 & 0.1 \\ 0.4 & 0.2 & 0.2 & 0.2 \end{bmatrix}$$

16-21 Professor Green gives two-month computer programming courses during the summer term. Students must pass a number of exams to pass the course, and each student is given three chances to take the exams. The following states describe the possible situations that could occur:

1. *State 1:* pass all of the exams and pass the course
2. *State 2:* do not pass all of the exams by the third attempt and flunk the course
3. *State 3:* fail an exam in the first attempt
4. *State 4:* fail an exam in the second attempt

After observing several classes, Professor Green was able to obtain the following matrix of transition probabilities:

$$P = \begin{bmatrix} 1 & 0 & 0 & 0 \\ 0 & 1 & 0 & 0 \\ 0.6 & 0 & 0.1 & 0.3 \\ 0.3 & 0.3 & 0.2 & 0.2 \end{bmatrix}$$

At the present time there are 50 students who did not pass all exams on the first attempt, and there are 30 students who did not pass all remaining exams on the second attempt. How many students in these two groups will pass the course, and how many will fail the course?

16-22 Hicourt Industries is a commercial printing outfit in a medium-sized town in central Florida. Its only competitors are the Printing House and Gandy Printers. Last month, Hicourt Industries had approximately 30% of the market for the printing business in the area. The Printing House had 50% of the market, and Gandy Printers had 20% of the market. The association of printers, a locally run association, had recently determined how these three printers and smaller printing operations not involved in the commercial market were able to retain their customer base. Hicourt was the most successful in keeping its customers. Eighty percent of its customers for any one month remained customers for the next month. The Printing House, on the other hand, had only a 70% retention rate. Gandy Printers was in the worst condition. Only 60% of the customers for any one month remained with the firm. In one month, the market share had significantly changed. This was very exciting to George Hicourt, president of Hicourt Industries. This month, Hicourt Industries was able to obtain a 38% market share. The Printing House, on the other hand, lost market share. This month, it only had 42% of the market share. Gandy Printers remained the same; it kept its 20% of the market. Just looking at market share, George concluded that he was able to take 8% per month away from the Printing House. George estimated that in a few short months, he could basically run the Printing House out of business. His hope was to capture 80% of the total market, representing his original 30% along with the 50% share that the Printing House started off with. Will George be able to reach his goal? What do you think the long-term market shares will be for these three commercial printing operations? Will Hicourt Industries be able to run the Printing House completely out of business?

16-23 John Jones of Bayside Laundry has been providing cleaning and linen service for rental condominiums on the Gulf coast for over 10 years. Currently, John is servicing 26 condominium developments. John's two major competitors are Cleanco, which currently services 15 condominium developments, and Beach Services, which performs laundry and cleaning services for 11 condominium developments.

Recently, John contacted Bay Bank about a loan to expand his business operations. To justify the loan, John has kept detailed records of his customers and the customers that he received from his two major competitors. During the past year, he was able to keep 18 of his original 26 customers. During the same period, he was able to get 1 new customer from Cleanco and 2 new customers from Beach Services. Unfortunately, John lost 6 of his original customers to Cleanco and 2 of his original customers to Beach Services during the same year. John has also learned that Cleanco has kept 80% of its current customers. He also knows that Beach Services will keep at least 50% of its customers. For John to get the loan from Bay Bank, he needs to show the loan officer that he will maintain an adequate share of the market. The

officers of Bay Bank are concerned about the recent trends for market share, and they have decided not to give John a loan unless he will keep at least 35% of the market share in the long run. What types of equilibrium market shares can John expect? If you were an officer of Bay Bank, would you give John a loan?

16-24 Set up both the vector of state probabilities and the matrix of transition probabilities given the following information:

Store 1 currently has 40% of the market, store 2 currently has 60% of the market.

In each period, store 1 customers have an 80% chance of returning, 20% of switching to store 2.

In each period, store 2 customers have a 90% chance of returning, 10% of switching to store 1.

16-25 Find $\pi(2)$ for Problem 16-24.

16-26 Find the equilibrium conditions for Problem 16-24. Explain what it means.

16-27 As a result of a recent survey of students at the University of South Wisconsin, it was determined that the university owned bookstore currently has 40% of the market. (See Problem 16-14.) The other three bookstores, Bill's, College, and Battle's, each split the remaining initial market share. Given that the state probabilities are the same, what is the market share for the next period given the initial market shares? What impact do the initial market shares have on each store next period? What is the impact on the steady state market shares?

16-28 Sandy Sprunger is part owner in one of the largest quick-oil-change operations for a medium-sized city in the Midwest. Currently, the firm has 60% of the market. There are a total of 10 quick lubrication shops in the area. After performing some basic marketing research, Sandy has been able to capture the initial probabilities, or market shares, along with the matrix of transition, which represents probabilities that customers will switch from one quick lubrication shop to another. These values are shown in the table below:

Data for Problem 16-28

From	To									
	1	2	3	4	5	6	7	8	9	10
1	0.60	0.10	0.10	0.10	0.05	0.01	0.01	0.01	0.01	0.01
2	0.01	0.80	0.01	0.01	0.01	0.10	0.01	0.01	0.01	0.03
3	0.01	0.01	0.70	0.01	0.01	0.10	0.01	0.05	0.05	0.05
4	0.01	0.01	0.01	0.90	0.01	0.01	0.01	0.01	0.01	0.02
5	0.01	0.01	0.01	0.10	0.80	0.01	0.03	0.01	0.01	0.01
6	0.01	0.01	0.01	0.01	0.01	0.91	0.01	0.01	0.01	0.01
7	0.01	0.01	0.01	0.01	0.01	0.10	0.70	0.01	0.10	0.04
8	0.01	0.01	0.01	0.01	0.01	0.10	0.03	0.80	0.01	0.01
9	0.01	0.01	0.01	0.01	0.01	0.10	0.01	0.10	0.70	0.04
10	0.01	0.01	0.01	0.01	0.01	0.10	0.10	0.05	0.00	0.70

Initial probabilities, or market share, for shops 1 through 10 are 0.6, 0.1, 0.1, 0.1, 0.05, 0.01, 0.01, 0.01, 0.01, and 0.01.

(a) Given these data, determine market shares for the next period for each of the 10 shops.

(b) What are the equilibrium market shares?

(c) Sandy believes that the original estimates for market shares were wrong. She believes that shop 1 has 40% of the market, and shop 2 has 30%. All other values are the same. If this is the case, what is the impact on market shares for next-period and equilibrium shares?

(d) A marketing consultant believes that shop 1 has tremendous appeal. She believes that this shop will retain 99% of its current market share; 1% may switch to shop 2. If the consultant is correct, will shop 1 have 90% of the market in the long run?

16-29 During a recent trip to her favorite restaurant, Sandy (owner of shop 1) met Chris Talley (owner of shop 7) (see Problem 16-28). After an enjoyable lunch, Sandy and Chris had a heated discussion about market share for the quick-oil-change operations in their city. Here is their conversation:

Sandy: My operation is so superior that after someone changes oil at one of my shops, they will never do business with anyone else. On second thought, maybe 1 person out of 100 will try your shop after visiting one of my shops. In a month, I will have 99% of the market and you will have 1% of the market.

Chris: You have it completely reversed. In a month, I will have 99% of the market and you will only have 1% of the market. In fact, I will treat you to a meal at a restaurant of your choice if you are right. If I am right, you will treat me to one of those big steaks at David's Steak House. Do we have a deal?

Sandy: Yes! Get your checkbook or your credit card. You will have the privilege of paying for two very expensive meals at Anthony's Seafood Restaurant.

(a) Assume that Sandy is correct about customers visiting one of her quick-oil-change shops. Will she win the bet with Chris?

(b) Assume that Chris is correct about customers visiting one of his quick-oil-change shops. Will he win the bet?

(c) Describe what would happen if both Sandy and Chris are correct about customers visiting their quick-oil-change operations.

16-30 The first quick-oil-change store in Problem 16-28 retains 73% of its market share. This represents a probability of .73 in the first row and first column of the matrix of transition probabilities. The other probability values in the first row are equally distributed across the other stores (namely, 3% each). What impact does this have on the steady-state market shares for the quick-oil-change stores?

INTERNET HOMEWORK PROBLEMS

See our Internet home page at www.prenhall.com/render for additional problems 16-31 to 16-34.

⇒ CASE STUDY

Rentall Trucks

Jim Fox, an executive for Rentall Trucks, could not believe it. He had hired one of the town's best law firms, Folley, Smith, and Christensen. Their fee for drawing up the legal contracts was over $50,000. Folley, Smith, and Christensen had made one important omission from the contracts, and this blunder would more than likely cost Rentall Trucks millions of dollars. For the hundredth time, Jim carefully reconstructed the situation and pondered the inevitable.

Rentall Trucks was started by Robert (Bob) Renton more than 10 years ago. It specialized in renting trucks to businesses and private individuals. The company prospered, and Bob increased his net worth by millions of dollars. Bob was a legend in the rental business and was known all over the world for his keen business abilities.

Only a year and a half ago some of the executives of Rentall and some additional outside investors offered to buy Rentall from Bob. Bob was close to retirement, and the offer was unbelievable. His children and their children would be able to live in high style off the proceeds of the sale. Folley, Smith, and Christensen developed the contracts for the executives of Rentall and other investors, and the sale was made.

Being a perfectionist, it was only a matter of time until Bob was marching down to the Rentall headquarters, telling everyone the mistakes that Rentall was making and how to solve some of their problems. Pete Rosen, president of Rentall, became extremely angry about Bob's constant interference, and in a brief 10-minute meeting, Pete told Bob never to enter the Rentall offices again. It was at this time that Bob decided to reread the contracts, and it was also at this time that Bob and his lawyer discovered that there was no clause in the contracts that prevented Bob from competing directly with Rentall.

The brief 10-minute meeting with Pete Rosen was the beginning of Rentran. In less than six months, Bob Renton had lured some of the key executives away from Rentall and into his new business, Rentran, which would compete directly with Rentall Trucks in every way. After a few months of operation, Bob estimated that Rentran had about 5% of the total national market for truck rentals. Rentall had about 80% of the market, and another company, National Rentals, had the remaining 15% of the market.

Rentall's Jim Fox was in total shock. In a few months, Rentran had already captured 5% of the total market. At this rate, Rentran might completely dominate the market in a few short years. Pete Rosen even wondered if Rentall could maintain 50% of the market in the long run. As a result of these concerns, Pete hired a marketing research firm that analyzed a random sample of truck rental customers. The sample consisted of 1,000 existing or potential customers. The marketing research firm was very careful to make sure that the sample represented the true market conditions. The sample, taken in August, consisted of 800 customers of Rentall, 60 customers of Rentran, and the remainder National customers. The same sample was then analyzed the next month concerning the customers' propensity to switch companies. Of the original Rentall customers, 200 switched to Rentran, and 80 switched to National. Rentran was able to retain 51 of their original customers. Three customers switched to Rentall, and 6 customers switched to National. Finally, 14 customers switched from National to Rentall, and 35 customers switched from National to Rentran.

The board of directors meeting was only two weeks away, and there would be some difficult questions to answer—what happened, and what can be done about Rentran? In Jim Fox's opinion, nothing could be done about the costly omission made by Folley, Smith, and Christensen. The only solution was to take immediate corrective action that would curb Rentran's ability to lure customers away from Rentall.

After a careful analysis of Rentran, Rentall, and the truck rental business in general, Jim concluded that immediate changes would be needed in three areas: rental policy, advertising, and product line. Regarding rental policy, a number of changes were needed to make truck rental both easier and faster. Rentall could implement many of the techniques used by Hertz and other car rental agencies. In addition, changes in the product line were needed. Rentall's smaller trucks had to be more comfortable and easier to drive. Automatic transmission, comfortable bucket seats, air conditioners, quality radio and tape stereo systems, and cruise control should be included. Although expensive and difficult to maintain, these items could make a significant difference in market shares. Finally, Jim knew that additional advertising was needed. The advertising had to be immediate and aggressive. Television and journal advertising had to be increased, and a good advertising company was needed. If these new changes were implemented now, there would be a good chance that Rentall would be able to maintain close to its 80% of the market. To confirm Jim's perceptions, the same marketing research firm was employed to analyze the effect of these changes, using the same sample of 1,000 customers.

The marketing research firm, Meyers Marketing Research, Inc., performed a pilot test on the sample of 1,000 customers. The results of the analysis revealed that Rentall would only lose 100 of its original customers to Rentran and 20 to National if the new policies were implemented. In addition, Rentall would pick up customers from both Rentran and National. It was estimated that Rentall would now get 9 customers from Rentran and 28 customers from National.

Discussion Questions

1. What will the market shares be in one month if these changes are made? If no changes are made?
2. What will the market shares be in three months with the changes?
3. If market conditions remain the same, what market share would Rentall have in the long run? How does this compare with the market share that would result if the changes were not made?

INTERNET CASE STUDIES

See our Internet home page at **www.prenhall.com/render** for these additional case studies:

(1) St. Pierre Salt Company. This case involves the selection of centrifuges, which are used to separate recrystallized salt from brine solution.

(2) University of Texas—Austin. This case involves doctoral students at different stages of their graduate programs.

BIBLIOGRAPHY

Bowers, J. A. "Weather Risk in Offshore Projects," *Journal of the Operational Research Society* 45, 4 (April 1994): 409–418.

Ching, Wai. "Markov-Modulated Poisson Processes for Multi-Location Inventory Problems," *International Journal of Production Economics* (November 20, 1997): 217–224.

Desai, Vijay S. and Amit Gupta. "Determining Optimal Advertising Strategies: A Markov Decision Model Approach," *Decision Sciences* 27, 3 (Summer 1996): 569–588.

Freedman, D. *Markov Chains.* San Francisco: Holden-Day, Inc., 1971.

Gates, David. "Replacement of Train Wheels: An Application of Dynamic Reversal of a Markov Process," *Journal of Applied Probability* 31, 1 (March 1994): 1–8.

Rodrigo, V. et al. "A New Markov Description of the M/G/1 Retrial Queue," *European Journal of Operational Research* (January 1, 1998): 231–241.

Shearer, Mike et al. "Migration Analysis: Combining Approaches for Better Results," *Journal of Lending and Credit Risk Management* (April 1, 1998): 52–56.

APPENDIX 16.1: MARKOV ANALYSIS WITH QM FOR WINDOWS

Markov analysis can be used for a variety of practical problems, including market share, equilibrium conditions, and tracing patients through a medical system (see the "Modeling in the Real World" box on p. 661). The grocery store example is used to show how Markov analysis can be used to determine future market-share conditions. Programs 16.1 and 16.2 reveal how QM for Windows is used to compute market share and equilibrium conditions. Note that the initial conditions and the ending market share (probabilities) are also displayed.

Absorbing state analysis is also discussed in this chapter using a bill-paying example. Program 16.3 shows how QM for Windows is used to compute the amount paid and the amount of bad debt using absorbing state analysis.

PROGRAM 16.1

QM for Windows for Markov Analysis for the Three Grocery Stores

Markov Analysis - [Multiplications]

Number of transitions: 5

Market Share Solution			
	State 1	State 2	State 3
Period 0			
State 1	0.8	0.1	0.1
State 2	0.1	0.7	0.2
State 3	0.2	0.2	0.6
Ending Probability	0.4	0.3	0.3
Period 1			
State 1	0.67	0.17	0.16
State 2	0.19	0.54	0.27
State 3	0.3	0.28	0.42
Ending Probability	0.42	0.31	0.27
Period 2			
State 1	0.59	0.22	0.2
State 2	0.26	0.45	0.29

PROGRAM 16.2

Markov Analysis Results for the Grocery Example

Markov Analysis

Number of transitions: 5

Markov Analysis Results			
Market Share 5 step transition matrix			
	State 1	State 2	State 3
State 1	.468249	.286918	.244833
State 2	.371088	.349671	.279241
State 3	.405496	.321326	.273178
Ending probability	.420275	.316066	.263659
Steady State probability	.421054	.31579	.263158

PROGRAM 16.3

Output from Absorbing State Analysis on the Accounts Receivable Example of Section 16.7

Markov Analysis - [Matrices]

Number of transitions 2

Accounts Receivable Solution

Markov Matrix (sorted if	Paid	Bad Debt	Due < 1	Due 1-3
Paid	1.	0.	0.	0.
Bad Debt	0.	1.	0.	0.
Due < 1 month	0.6	0.	0.2	0.2
Due 1-3 months	0.4	0.1	0.3	0.2
B matrix	Due < 1	Due 1-3		
Due < 1 month	0.2	0.2		
Due 1-3 months	0.3	0.2		
F matrix (I-B)^-1	Due < 1	Due 1-3		
Due < 1 month	1.3793	0.3448		
Due 1-3 months	0.5172	1.3793		
FA matrix	Paid	Bad Debt		
Due < 1 month	0.9655	0.0345		
Due 1-3 months	0.8621	0.1379		

APPENDIX 16.2: MARKOV ANALYSIS WITH EXCEL

Performing the Markov analysis matrix operations is very easy with Excel, although the input process is different from most Excel operations. The two Excel functions that are most helpful with matrices are MMULT for matrix multiplication and MINVERSE for finding the inverse of the matrix. However, special procedures are used when these are entered in the spreadsheet. Matrix addition and subtraction is also easy in Excel using special procedures.

Using Excel to Predict Future Market Shares

In using Markov analysis to predict future market shares or future states, matrices are multiplied. To multiply matrices in Excel, we use MMULT as follows:

1. Highlight all the cells that will contain the resulting matrix.

2. Type =**MMULT**(**matrix1, matrix2**) where matrix 1 and matrix 2 are the cell ranges for the two matrices being multiplied.

3. Instead of just pressing ENTER, hold down the CTRL and SHIFT keys and then press ENTER.

Pressing CTRL-SHIFT-ENTER is used to indicate that a matrix operation is being performed so that all cells in the matrix are changed accordingly.

Program 16.4A shows the formulas for the three grocery example from Section 16.2. We have entered the time period in column A for reference only, as we will be computing the state probabilities through time

PROGRAM 16.4A

Excel Input and Formulas for the Three Grocery Example

Microsoft Excel - programc16

File Edit View Insert Format Tools Data Window Help

B7 = {=MMULT(B6:D6,$E$6:$G$8)}

	A	B	C	D	E	F	G	H
1	Three							
2			Enter the current state probabilities in B6, C6, and D6.		This is the matrix of transition probabilities.			
3								
4		American Food Store		Atlas Foods				
5	Time	#1	#2	#3	Matri			
6	0	0.4	0.3	0.3	0.8	0.1	0.1	
7	1	=MMULT(B6:D6,$E$6:$G$8)	=MMULT(B6:D6,$E$6:$G$8)	=MMULT(B6:D6,$E$6:$G$8)	0.1	0.7	0.2	
8	2	=MMULT(B7:D7,$E$6:$G$8)	=MMULT(B7:D7,$E$6:$G$8)	=MMULT(B7:D7,$E$6:$G$8)	0.2	0.2	0.6	
9	3	=MMULT(B8:D8,$E$6:$G$8)	=MMULT(B8:D8,$E$6:$G$8)	=MMULT(B8:D8,$E$6:$G$8)				
10	4	=MMULT(B9:D9,$E$6:$G$8)	=MMULT(B9:D9,$E$6:$G$8)	=MMULT(B9:D9,$E$6:$G$8)				
11	5	=MMULT(B10:D10,$E$6:$G$8)	=MMULT(B10:D10,$E$6:$G$8)	=MMULT(B10:D10,$E$6:$G$8)				
12	6	=MMULT(B11:D11,$E$6:$G$8)	=MMULT(B11:D11,$E$6:$G$8)	=MMULT(B11:D11,$E$6:$G$8)				
13								

The future state probabilities are in rows 7 to 12.

PROGRAM 16.4B

Excel Output for the Three Grocery Example

Microsoft Excel - programc16

File Edit View Insert Format Tools Data Window Help

B7   = {=MMULT(B6:D6,$E$6:$G$8)}

	A	B	C	D	E	F	G	H	I	J	K
1	Three Grocery Example										
2											
3			State Probilities								
4		Food Store	Food Mart	Atlas Foods							
5	Time	#1	#2	#3	Matrix of Transition Probabilities						
6	0	0.4	0.3	0.3	0.8	0.1	0.1				
7	1	0.4100	0.3100	0.2800	0.1	0.7	0.2				
8	2	0.4150	0.3140	0.2710	0.2	0.2	0.6				
9	3	0.4176	0.3155	0.2669							
10	4	0.4190	0.3160	0.2650							
11	5	0.4198	0.3161	0.2641							
12	6	0.4203	0.3161	0.2637							
13											

period 6. The state probabilities (cells B6 through D6) and the matrix of transition probabilities (cells E6 through G8) are entered as shown. We then use matrix multiplication to find the state probabilities for the next period. Highlight cells B7, C7, and D7 (this is where the resulting matrix will be) and type =MMULT(B6:D6,E6:G8), as shown in the table. Then press SHIFT-CTRL-ENTER (all at one time), and this formula is put in each of the three cells that were highlighted. When you have done this, Excel places {} around this formula in the box at the top of the screen. We then copy cells B7, C7, and D7 to rows 8 through 12 as shown. Program 16.4B shows the result and the state probabilities for the next six time periods.

Using Excel to Find the Fundamental Matrix and Absorbing States

Excel can be used to find the fundamental matrix that is used to predict future conditions when absorbing states exist. The MINVERSE function is used in the accounts receivable example from Section 16.7 of this chapter. Program 16.5A shows the formulas, and Program 16.5B provides the results. Remember that the entire range of the matrix (B18 through C19) is highlighted before the MINVERSE function is entered. Also recall that SHIFT-CTRL-ENTER are pressed all at once.

Matrix addition and subtraction can be handled in a fashion similar to the methods just described. In Program 16.5A, the *I–B* matrix was computed using a matrix method. First we highlighted the cells B14 through C15 (where the result is to be). Then we typed the formula seen in these cells and pressed the SHIFT-CTRL-ENTER keys (all at once), causing this formula to be entered in each of these cells. Excel then computes the appropriate values as shown in Program 16.5B.

PROGRAM 16.5A   **Excel Input and Formulas for Accounts Receivable Example**

Microsoft Excel - programc16

File Edit View Insert Format Tools Data Window Help

D15   = {=MMULT(D12:E13,D5:E6)}

This is the partitioned matrix of transition probabilities from Section 16.7.

	A	B	C	D	E	F
1	Acco					
2						
3			1	0	0	0
4	P=	I : 0	= 0	1	0	0
5		A : B	0.6	0	0.2	0.2
6			0.4	0.1	0.3	0.2
7						
8						
9	I - B =		=D3:E4-F5:G6	=D3:E4-F5:G6		
10			=D3:E4-F5:G6	=D3:E4-F5:G6		
11						
12	F = (I - B) inve		=MINVERSE(D9:E10)	=MINVERSE(D9:E10)		
13			=MINVERSE(D9:E10)	=MINVERSE(D9:E10)		
14						
15	FA =		=MMULT(D12:E13,D5:E6)	=MMULT(D12:E13,D5:E6)		
16			=MMULT(D12:E13,D5:E6)	=MMULT(D12:E13,D5:E6)		
17						

Compute the fundamental matrix (*F*) with the MINVERSE function.

Compute the *FA* matrix with the MMULT function.

PROGRAM 16.5B

**Excel Output for the
Accounts Receivable
Example**

Microsoft Excel - programc16							_ 8 X
File Edit View Insert Format Tools Data Window Help							_ 8 X
D15 ▼ = {=MMULT(D12:E13,D5:E6)}							

	A	B	C	D	E	F	G	H	I	J	K	L
1	Accounts Receivable Example											
2												
3				1	0	0	0					
4	P=	I : 0	=	0	1	0	0					
5		A : B		0.6	0	0.2	0.2					
6				0.4	0.1	0.3	0.2					
7												
8												
9		I - B =		0.8	-0.2							
10				-0.3	0.8							
11												
12		F = (I - B) inverse =		1.379	0.345							
13				0.517	1.379							
14												
15		FA =		0.966	0.034							
16				0.862	0.138							
17												

STATISTICAL QUALITY CONTROL

17.1 INTRODUCTION

For almost every product or service, there is more than one organization trying to make a sale. Price may be a major issue in whether a sale is made or lost, but another factor is *quality*. In fact, quality is often the major issue; and poor quality can be very expensive for both the producing firm and the customer.

Consequently, firms employ quality management tactics. Quality management, or as it is more commonly called, *quality control* (QC), is critical throughout the organization. One of the manager's major roles is to ensure that his or her firm can deliver a quality product at the right place, at the right time, and at the right price. Quality is not just of concern for manufactured products either; it is also important in services, from banking to hospital care to education.

Statistical process control uses statistical and probability tools to help control processes and produce consistent goods and services.

We begin this chapter with an attempt to define just what quality really is. Then we deal with the most important statistical methodology for quality management: *statistical process control* (SPC). SPC is the application of the statistical tools we discussed in Chapter 2 to the control of processes that result in products or services.

17.2 DEFINING QUALITY AND TQM

The quality of a product or service is the degree to which the product or service meets specifications.

To some people, a high-quality product is one that is stronger, will last longer, is built heavier, and is, in general, more durable than other products. In some cases this is a good definition of a quality product, but not always. A good circuit breaker, for example, is *not* one that lasts longer during periods of high current or voltage. So the *quality of a product* or *service* is the degree to which the product or service meets specifications. Increasingly, definitions of *quality* include an added emphasis on meeting the customer's needs. As you can see in Table 17.1, the first and second ones are similar to our definition.

Total quality management encompasses the whole organization.

Total quality management (TQM) refers to a quality emphasis that encompasses the entire organization, from supplier to customer. TQM emphasizes a commitment by management to have a companywide drive toward excellence in all aspects of the products and services that are important to the customer. Meeting the customer's expectations requires an emphasis on TQM if the firm is to compete as a leader in world markets.

TABLE 17.1	
Several Definitions of Quality	**"Quality is the degree to which a specific product conforms to a design or specification."**
	H. L. Gilmore. "Product Conformance Cost," *Quality Progress* (June 1974): 16.
	"Quality is the totality of features and characteristics of a product or service that bears on its ability to satisfy stated or implied needs."
	Ross Johnson and William O. Winchell. *Production and Quality.* Milwaukee, WI: American Society of Quality Control, 1989, p. 2.
	"Quality is fitness for use."
	J. M. Juran, ed. *Quality Control Handbook*, 3/e. New York: McGraw-Hill, 1974, p. 2.
	"Quality is defined by the customer; customers want products and services that, throughout their lives, meet customers' needs and expectations at a cost that represents value."
	Ford's definition as presented in William W. Scherkenbach. *Deming's Road to Continual Improvement.* Knoxville, TN: SPC Press, 1991, p. 161.
	"Even though quality cannot be defined, you know what it is."
	R. M. Pirsig. *Zen and the Art of Motorcycle Maintenance.* New York: Bantam Books, 1974, p. 213.

HISTORY   How Quality Control Has Evolved

In the early nineteenth century an individual skilled artisan started and finished a whole product. With the Industrial Revolution and the factory system, semiskilled workers, each making a small portion of the final product, became common. With this, responsibility for the quality of the final product tended to shift to supervisors, and pride of workmanship declined.

As organizations became larger in the twentieth century, inspection became more technical and organized. Inspectors were often grouped together; their job was to make sure that bad lots were not shipped to customers. Starting in the 1920s, major statistical QC tools were developed. W. Shewhart introduced control charts in 1924, and in 1930 H. F. Dodge and H. G. Romig designed acceptance sampling tables. Also at that time the important role of QC in all areas of the company's performance became recognized.

During and after World War II, the importance of quality grew, often with the encouragement of the U.S. government. Companies recognized that more than just inspection was needed to make a quality product. Quality needed to be built into the production process.

After World War II, an American, W. Edwards Deming, went to Japan to teach statistical QC concepts to the devastated Japanese manufacturing sector. A second pioneer, J. M. Juran, followed Deming to Japan, stressing top management support and involvement in the quality battle. In 1961 A. V. Feigenbaum wrote his classic book, *Total Quality Control*, which delivered a fundamental message: Make it right the first time! In 1979 Philip Crosby published *Quality Is Free*, stressing the need for management and employee commitment to the battle against poor quality. In 1988, the U.S. government presented its first awards for quality achievement. These are known as the Malcolm Baldrige National Quality Awards.

In recent years, a method of quality management called Six-Sigma was developed in the electronics industry. The goal of Six-Sigma is continuous improvement in performance to reduce and eliminate defects. Technically, to achieve six-sigma quality, there would have to be less than 3.4 defects per million opportunities. This approach to quality has been credited with achieving significant cost savings for a number of companies. General Electric estimated savings of $12 billion over a five-year period, and other firms have reported savings in the hundreds of millions of dollars.

17.3   STATISTICAL PROCESS CONTROL

Statistical process control helps set standards. It can also monitor, measure, and correct quality problems.

Statistical process control involves establishing standards, monitoring standards, making measurements, and taking corrective action as a product or service is being produced. Samples of process outputs are examined; if they are within acceptable limits, the process is permitted to continue. If they fall outside certain specific ranges, the process is stopped and, typically, the assignable cause is located and removed.

A control chart is a graphic way of presenting data over time.

Control charts are graphs that show upper and lower limits for the process we want to control. A *control chart* is a graphic presentation of data over time. Control charts are constructed in such a way that new data can quickly be compared with past performance. Upper and lower limits in a control chart can be in units of temperature, pressure, weight, length, and so on. We take samples of the process output and plot the average of these samples on a chart that has the limits on it.

Figure 17.1 graphically reveals the useful information that can be portrayed in control charts. When the average of the samples falls within the upper and lower control limits and no discernible pattern is present, the process is said to be in control; otherwise, the process is out of control or out of adjustment.

Variability in the Process

All processes are subject to a certain degree of variability. Walter Shewhart of Bell Laboratories, while studying process data in the 1920s, made the distinction between the common and special causes of variation. The key is keeping variations under control. So we now look at how to build control charts that help managers and workers develop a process that is capable of producing within established limits.

FIGURE 17.1

Patterns to Look for on Control Charts

(**Source:** Bertrand L. Hansen, *Quality Control: Theory and Applications*, © 1963, renewed 1991, p. 65. Reprinted by permission of Prentice Hall, Upper Saddle River, NJ.)

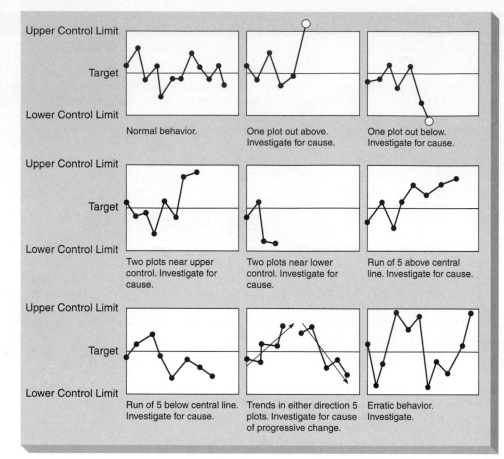

Building Control Charts When building control charts, averages of small samples (often of five items or parts) are used, as opposed to data on individual parts. Individual pieces tend to be too erratic to make trends quickly visible. The purpose of control charts is to help distinguish between *natural variations* and *variations due to assignable causes*.

IN ACTION   Statistical Process Control Helps DuPont and the Environment

DuPont has found that SPC is an excellent approach to solving environmental problems. With a goal of slashing manufacturing waste and hazardous waste disposals by 35%, DuPont brought together information from its quality control systems and its material management databases.

Diagrams and charts examining causes and effects revealed where major problems occurred. Then the company began reducing waste materials through improved SPC standards for production. Tying together shop-floor information-based monitoring systems with air-quality standards, DuPont identified ways to reduce emissions. Using a vendor evaluation system linked to just-in-time purchasing requirements, the company initiated controls over incoming hazardous materials.

DuPont now saves more than 15 million pounds of plastics annually by recycling them into products rather than dumping them into landfills. Through electronic purchasing the firm has reduced wastepaper to a trickle and, by using new packaging designs, has cut in-process material wastes by nearly 40%.

By integrating SPC with environmental compliance activities, DuPont has made major quality improvements that far exceed regulatory guidelines, and at the same time the company has realized huge cost savings.

Sources: *Automotive Industries* (June 1996): 93; and E. E. Dwinells and J. P. Sheffer. *APICS—The Performance Advantage* (March 1992): 30–31.

Natural variations are sources of variation in a process that is statistically in control.

Natural Variations Natural variations affect almost every production process and are to be expected. These variations are random and uncontrollable. *Natural variations* are the many sources of variation within a process that is in statistical control. They behave like a constant system of chance causes. Although individual measured values are all different, as a group they form a pattern that can be described as a distribution. When these distributions are *normal*, they are characterized by two parameters:

1. Mean, μ (the measure of central tendency, in this case, the average value)
2. Standard deviation, σ (variation, the amount by which the smaller values differ from the larger ones)

As long as the distribution (output precision) remains within specified limits, the process is said to be "in control," and the modest variations are tolerated.

Assignable variations in a process can be traced to a specific problem.

Assignable Variations When a process is not in control, we must detect and eliminate special (*assignable*) causes of *variation*. These variations are not random and can be controlled when the cause of the variation is determined. Factors such as machine wear, misadjusted equipment, fatigued or untrained workers, or new batches of raw material are all potential sources of assignable variations. Control charts such as those illustrated in Figure 17.1 help the manager pinpoint where a problem may lie.

The ability of a process to operate within statistical control is determined by the total variation that comes from natural causes—the minimum variation that can be achieved after all assignable causes have been eliminated. The objective of a process control system, then, is *to provide a statistical signal when assignable causes of variation are present*. Such a signal can quicken appropriate action to eliminate assignable causes.

17.4 CONTROL CHARTS FOR VARIABLES

$\bar{x}$-charts measure central tendency of a process.

Control charts for the mean, $\bar{x}$, and the range, R, are used to monitor processes that are measured in continuous units. Examples of these would be weight, height, and volume. The $\bar{x}$-(x-bar) *chart* tells us whether changes have occurred in the central tendency of a process. This might be due to such factors as tool wear, a gradual increase in temperature, a different method used on the second shift, or new and stronger materials. The *R-chart* values indicate that a gain or loss in uniformity has occurred. Such a change might be due to worn bearings, a loose tool part, an erratic flow of lubricants to a machine, or sloppiness on the part of a machine operator. The two types of charts go hand in hand when monitoring variables.

R-charts measure the range between the biggest (or heaviest) and smallest (or lightest) items in a random sample.

The Central Limit Theorem

The central limit theorem says that the distribution of sample means will follow a normal distribution as the sample size grows large.

The statistical foundation for $\bar{x}$-charts is the *central limit theorem*. In general terms, this theorem states that regardless of the distribution of the population of all parts or services, the distribution of $\bar{x}$'s (each of which is a mean of a sample drawn from the population) will tend to follow a normal curve as the sample size grows large. Fortunately, even if n is fairly small (say 4 or 5), the distributions of the averages will still roughly follow a normal curve. The theorem also states that (1) the mean of the distribution of the $\bar{x}$'s (called $\mu_{\bar{x}}$) will equal the mean of the overall population (called μ); and (2) the standard deviation of the sampling distribution, $\sigma_{\bar{x}}$, will be the population deviation, σ_x, divided by the square root of the sample size, n. In other words,

$$\mu_{\bar{x}} = \mu \quad \text{and} \quad \sigma_{\bar{x}} = \frac{\sigma_x}{\sqrt{n}}$$

Although there may be times when we may know $\mu_{\bar{x}}$ (and μ), often we must estimate this with the average of all the sample means (written as $\bar{\bar{x}}$).

FIGURE 17.2

**Population and Sampling
Distributions**

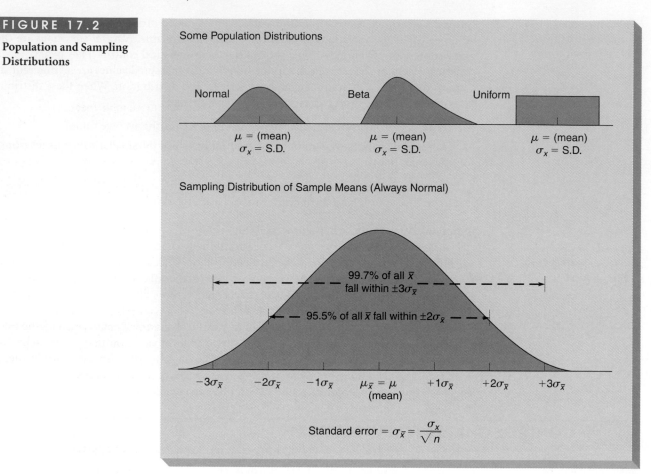

Figure 17.2 shows three possible population distributions, each with its own mean, μ, and standard deviation, σ_x. If a series of random samples ($\bar{x}_1, \bar{x}_2, \bar{x}_3, \bar{x}_4$, and so on) each of size n is drawn from any one of these, the resulting distribution of $\bar{x}_i$'s will appear as in the bottom graph of that figure. Because this is a normal distribution (as discussed in Chapter 2), we can state that

1. 99.7% of the time, the sample averages will fall within $\pm 3\sigma_{\bar{x}}$ of the population mean if the process has only random variations.

2. 95.5% of the time, the sample averages will fall within $\pm 2\sigma_{\bar{x}}$ of the population mean if the process has only random variations.

If a point on the control chart falls outside the $\pm 3\sigma_{\bar{x}}$ control limits, we are 99.7% sure that the process has changed. This is the theory behind control charts.

Setting $\bar{x}$-Chart Limits

If we know through historical data the standard deviation of the process population, $\sigma_{\bar{x}}$, we can set upper and lower control limits by these formulas:

$$\text{upper control limit (UCL)} = \bar{\bar{x}} + z\sigma_{\bar{x}} \qquad (17\text{-}1)$$

$$\text{lower control limit (LCL)} = \bar{\bar{x}} - z\sigma_{\bar{x}} \qquad (17\text{-}2)$$

where

$\bar{\bar{x}}$ = mean of the sample means

z = number of normal standard deviations (2 for 95.5% confidence, 3 for 99.7%)

$\sigma_{\bar{x}}$ = standard deviation of the sampling distribution of the sample means = $\dfrac{\sigma_x}{\sqrt{n}}$

Box-Filling Example   Let us say that a large production lot of boxes of cornflakes is sampled every hour. To set control limits that include 99.7% of the sample means, 36 boxes are randomly selected and weighed. The standard deviation of the overall population of boxes is estimated, through analysis of old records, to be 2 ounces. The average mean of all sam-

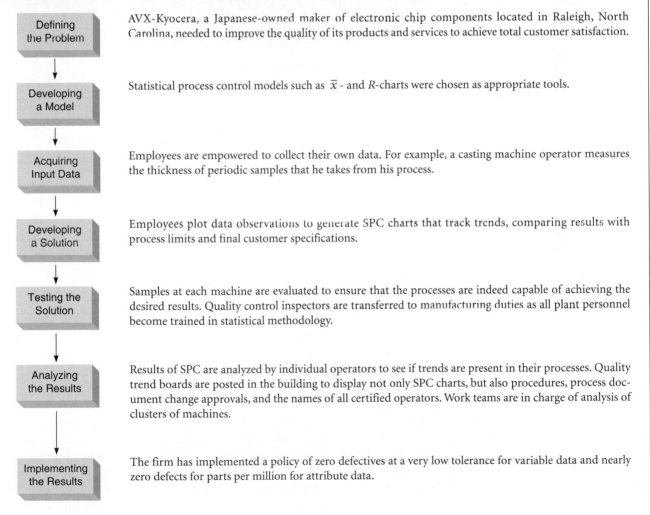

⏩ MODELING IN THE REAL WORLD · **Statistical Process Control at AVX-Kyocera**

Defining the Problem

AVX-Kyocera, a Japanese-owned maker of electronic chip components located in Raleigh, North Carolina, needed to improve the quality of its products and services to achieve total customer satisfaction.

Developing a Model

Statistical process control models such as $\bar{x}$- and R-charts were chosen as appropriate tools.

Acquiring Input Data

Employees are empowered to collect their own data. For example, a casting machine operator measures the thickness of periodic samples that he takes from his process.

Developing a Solution

Employees plot data observations to generate SPC charts that track trends, comparing results with process limits and final customer specifications.

Testing the Solution

Samples at each machine are evaluated to ensure that the processes are indeed capable of achieving the desired results. Quality control inspectors are transferred to manufacturing duties as all plant personnel become trained in statistical methodology.

Analyzing the Results

Results of SPC are analyzed by individual operators to see if trends are present in their processes. Quality trend boards are posted in the building to display not only SPC charts, but also procedures, process document change approvals, and the names of all certified operators. Work teams are in charge of analysis of clusters of machines.

Implementing the Results

The firm has implemented a policy of zero defectives at a very low tolerance for variable data and nearly zero defects for parts per million for attribute data.

Source: Basile A. Denisson. "War with Defects and Peace with Quality," *Quality Progress* (September 1993): 97–101.

ples taken is 16 ounces. We therefore have $\bar{\bar{x}} = 16$ ounces, $\sigma_x = 2$ ounces, $n = 36$, and $z = 3$. The control limits are

$$\text{UCL}_{\bar{x}} = \bar{\bar{x}} + z\sigma_{\bar{x}} = 16 + 3\left(\frac{2}{\sqrt{36}}\right) = 16 + 1 = 17 \text{ ounces}$$

$$\text{LCL}_{\bar{x}} = \bar{\bar{x}} - z\sigma_{\bar{x}} = 16 - 3\left(\frac{2}{\sqrt{36}}\right) = 16 - 1 = 15 \text{ ounces}$$

If the process standard deviation is not available or is difficult to compute, which is usually the case, these equations become impractical. In practice, the calculation of control limits is based on the average *range* rather than on standard deviations. We can use the equations

Control chart limits can be found using the range rather than the standard deviation.

$$\text{UCL}_{\bar{x}} = \bar{\bar{x}} + A_2\bar{R} \tag{17-3}$$

$$\text{LCL}_{\bar{x}} = \bar{\bar{x}} - A_2\bar{R} \tag{17-4}$$

where

$\bar{R}$ = average of the samples

A_2 = value found in Table 17.2 (which assumes that $Z = 3$)

$\bar{\bar{x}}$ = mean of the sample means

Super Cola Example Super Cola bottles soft drinks labeled "net weight 16 ounces." An overall process average of 16.01 ounces has been found by taking several batches of samples, in which each sample contained five bottles. The average range of the process is 0.25 ounce. We want to determine the upper and lower control limits for averages for this process.

Looking in Table 17.2 for a sample size of 5 in the mean factor A_2 column, we find the number 0.577. Thus, the upper and lower control chart limits are

$$\text{UCL}_{\bar{x}} = \bar{\bar{x}} + A_2\bar{R}$$

$$= 16.01 + (0.577)(0.25)$$

$$= 16.01 + 0.144$$

$$= 16.154$$

$$\text{LCL}_{\bar{x}} = \bar{\bar{x}} - A_2\bar{R}$$

$$= 16.01 - 0.144$$

$$= 15.866$$

The upper control limit is 16.154, and the lower control limit is 15.866.

Setting Range Chart Limits

We just determined the upper and lower control limits for the process *average*. In addition to being concerned with the process average, managers are interested in the *dispersion* or *variability*. Even though the process average is under control, the variability of the process may not be. For example, something may have worked itself loose in a piece of equipment. As a result, the average of the samples may remain the same, but the variation within the samples could be entirely too large. For this reason it is very common to find a control chart for *ranges* in order to monitor the process variability. The theory behind the control charts for ranges is the same for the process average. Limits are established that contain ±3

Dispersion or variability is also important. The central tendency can be under control, but ranges can be out of control.

TABLE 17.2	SAMPLE SIZE, n	MEAN FACTOR, A_2	UPPER RANGE, D_4	LOWER RANGE, D_3
Factors for Computing Control Chart Limits	2	1.880	3.268	0
	3	1.023	2.574	0
	4	0.729	2.282	0
	5	0.577	2.114	0
	6	0.483	2.004	0
	7	0.419	1.924	0.076
	8	0.373	1.864	0.136
	9	0.337	1.816	0.184
	10	0.308	1.777	0.223
	12	0.266	1.716	0.284
	14	0.235	1.671	0.329
	16	0.212	1.636	0.364
	18	0.194	1.608	0.392
	20	0.180	1.586	0.414
	25	0.153	1.541	0.459

Source: Reprinted by permission of the American Society for Testing and Materials, copyright 1951. Taken from Special Technical Publication 15-C, "Quality Control of Materials," pp. 63 and 72.

standard deviations of the distribution for the average range $\overline{R}$. With a few simplifying assumptions, we can set the upper and lower control limits for ranges:

$$\text{UCL}_R = D_4 \overline{R} \tag{17-5}$$

$$\text{LCL}_R = D_3 \overline{R} \tag{17-6}$$

where

$$\text{UCL}_R = \text{upper control chart limit for the range}$$

$$\text{LCL}_R = \text{lower control chart limit for the range}$$

$$D_4 \text{ and } D_3 = \text{values from Table 17.2}$$

Range Example As an example, consider a process in which the average *range* is 53 pounds. If the sample size is 5, we want to determine the upper and lower control chart limits.

Looking in Table 17.2 for a sample size of 5, we find that $D_4 = 2.114$ and $D_3 = 0$. The range control chart limits are

$$\text{UCL}_R = D_4 \overline{R}$$

$$= (2.114)(53 \text{ pounds})$$

$$= 112.042 \text{ pounds}$$

$$\text{LCL}_R = D_3 \overline{R}$$

$$= (0)(53 \text{ pounds})$$

$$= 0$$

A summary of the steps used for creating and using control charts for the mean and the range is provided in Table 17.3.

TABLE 17.3	
Five Steps to Follow in Using $\bar{x}$ and R-Charts	1. Collect 20 to 25 samples of $n = 4$ or $n = 5$ each from a stable process and compute the mean and range of each.
	2. Compute the overall means ($\bar{\bar{x}}$ and $\bar{R}$), set appropriate control limits, usually at the 99.7% level, and calculate the preliminary upper and lower control limits. If the process is not currently stable, use the desired mean, μ, instead of $\bar{\bar{x}}$ to calculate limits.
	3. Graph the sample means and ranges on their respective control charts and determine whether they fall outside the acceptable limits.
	4. Investigate points or patterns that indicate the process is out of control. Try to assign cases for the variation and then resume the process.
	5. Collect additional samples and, if necessary, revalidate the control limits using the new data.

17.5 CONTROL CHARTS FOR ATTRIBUTES

Sampling attributes differ from sampling variables.

Control charts for $\bar{x}$ and R do not apply when we are sampling *attributes*, which are typically classified as defective or nondefective. Measuring defectives involves counting them (e.g., number of bad lightbulbs in a given lot, or number of letters or data entry records typed with errors). There are two kinds of attribute control charts: (1) those that measure the percent defective in a sample, called *p-charts* and (2) those that count the number of defects, called *c-charts*.

p-Charts

p-chart limits are based on the binomial distribution and are easy to compute.

p-charts are the principal means of controlling attributes. Although attributes that are either good or bad follow the binomial distribution, the normal distribution can be used to calculate *p*-chart limits when sample sizes are large. The procedure resembles the $\bar{x}$-chart approach, which is also based on the central limit theorem.

The formulas for *p*-chart upper and lower control limits follow:

$$\text{UCL}_p = \bar{p} + z\sigma_p \tag{17-7}$$

$$\text{LCL}_p = \bar{p} - z\sigma_p \tag{17-8}$$

where

$\bar{p}$ = mean proportion or fraction defective in the sample

z = number of standard deviates ($z = 2$ for 95.5% limits; $z = 3$ for 99.7% limits)

σ_p = standard deviation of the sampling distribution

σ_p is estimated by $\hat{\sigma}_p$, which is

$$\hat{\sigma}_p = \sqrt{\frac{\bar{p}(1 - \bar{p})}{n}} \tag{17-9}$$

where n is the size of each sample.

IN ACTION   Unisys Corp.'s Costly Experiment in Health Care Services

In January 1996 things looked rosy for Unisys Corp.'s expansion into the computerized health care service business. It had just beat out Blue Cross/Blue Shield of Florida for an $86 million contract to serve Florida's state employee health insurance services. Its job was to handle the 215,000 Florida employees' claims processing—a seemingly simple and lucrative growth area for an old-line computer company like Unisys.

But one year later the contract was not only torn up, Unisys was fined over $500,000 for not meeting quality standards. Here are two of the measures of quality, both attributes (that is, either "defective" or "not defective") on which the firm was out of control:

1. **Percent of claims processed with errors.** An audit over a three-month period, by Coopers and Lybrand,

found that Unysis made errors in 8.5% of claims processed. The industry standard is 3.5% "defectives."

2. **Percent of claims processed within 30 days.** For this attribute measure, a "defect" is a processing time longer than the contract's time allowance. In one month's sample, 13% of the claims exceed the 30-day limit, far above the 5% allowed by the state of Florida.

The Florida contract was a migraine for Unisys, which underestimated the labor-intensiveness of health claims. Chief executive officer James Unruh pulled the plug on future ambitions in health care. Meanwhile, the State of Florida's Ron Poppel says, "We really need somebody that's in the insurance business."

Sources: *Business Week* (June 16, 1997): 6 and (July 15, 1996): 32; and *Information Week* (June 16, 1997): 144.

ARCO *p*-Chart Example Using a popular database software package, data-entry clerks at ARCO key in thousands of insurance records each day. Samples of the work of 20 clerks are shown in the following table. One hundred records entered by each clerk were carefully examined to determine if they contained any errors; the fraction defective in each sample was then computed.

SAMPLE NUMBER	NUMBER OF ERRORS	FRACTION DEFECTIVE	SAMPLE NUMBER	NUMBER OF ERRORS	FRACTION DEFECTIVE
1	6	0.06	11	6	0.06
2	5	0.05	12	1	0.01
3	0	0.00	13	8	0.08
4	1	0.01	14	7	0.07
5	4	0.04	15	5	0.05
6	2	0.02	16	4	0.04
7	5	0.05	17	11	0.11
8	3	0.03	18	3	0.03
9	3	0.03	19	0	0.00
10	2	0.02	20	4	0.04
				80	

We want to set control limits that include 99.7% of the random variation in the entry process when it is in control. Thus, $z = 3$.

$$\bar{p} = \frac{\text{total number of errors}}{\text{total number of records examined}} = \frac{80}{(100)(20)} = 0.04$$

$$\hat{\sigma}_p = \sqrt{\frac{(0.04)(1 - 0.04)}{100}} = 0.02$$

$\qquad\qquad$ *(Note:* 100 *is the size of each sample* $= n$)

$$\text{UCL}_p = \bar{p} + z\hat{\sigma}_p = 0.04 + 3(0.02) = 0.10$$

$$\text{LCL}_p = \bar{p} - z\hat{\sigma}_p = 0.04 - 3(0.02) = 0 \longleftarrow$$

$\qquad\qquad$ (since we cannot have a negative percent defective)

FIGURE 17.3

p-Chart for Data Entry
for ARCO

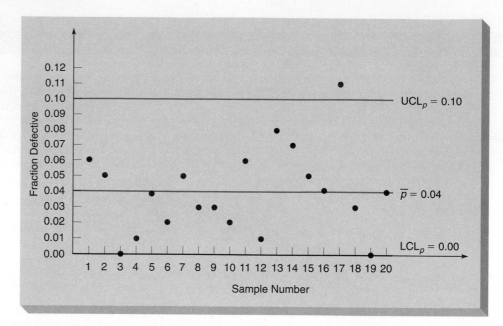

When we plot the control limits and the sample fraction defectives, we find that only one data-entry clerk (number 17) is out of control. The firm may wish to examine that person's work a bit more closely to see whether a serious problem exists (see Figure 17.3).

Using Excel QM for SPC Excel and other spreadsheets are extensively used in industry to maintain control charts. Excel QM's Quality Module can develop $\bar{x}$-charts, *p*-charts, and *c*-charts. Programs 17.1A and 17.1B illustrate Excel QM's spreadsheet approach to comput-

PROGRAM 17.1A

Excel QM's *p*-Chart Program Applied to the ARCO Data, Showing Input Data and Formulas

	A	B	C	D	E	F	G	H
1	**ARCO**			**Quality Control**				
2								
3	Number of samples	20		Enter the sample size then enter the number of defects in each sample.				
4	Sample size	100						
5								
6	Data					**Results**		
7		# Defects		% Defects		Total Sample Size	=B3*B4	
8	Sample 1	6		=B8/$B$4		Total Defects	=SUM(B8:B27)	
9	Sample 2	5		=B9/$B$4		Percentage defects	=G8/G7	
10	Sample 3	0		=B10/$B$4		Std dev of p-bar	=SQRT((((1-G9)*G9)/B4)	
11	Sample 4	1		=B11/$B$4				
12	Sample 5	4		=B12/$B$4		Upper Control Limit	=G9+3*G10	
13	Sample 6	2		=B13/$B$4		Center Line	=G9	
14	Sample 7	5		=B14/$B$4		Lower Control Limit	=IF(G9-3*G10>0,G9-3*G10,0)	
15	Sample 8	3		=B15/$B$4				
16	Sample 9	3		=B16/$B$4				
17	Sample 10	2		=B17/$B$4				
18	Sample 11	6		=B18/$B$4				
19	Sample 12	1		=B19/$B$4				
20	Sample 13	8		=B20/$B$4				
21	Sample 14	7		=B21/$B$4				
22	Sample 15	5		=B22/$B$4				
23	Sample 16	4		=B23/$B$4				
24	Sample 17	11		=B24/$B$4				
25	Sample 18	3		=B25/$B$4				
26	Sample 19	0		=B26/$B$4				
27	Sample 20	4		=B27/$B$4	=IF(D27>$G$12,"Above UCL",IF(D27<$G$14,"Below LCL",""))			

PROGRAM 17.1B

Output from Excel QM's *p*-Chart Analysis of the ARCO Data

	A	B	C	D	E	F	G	H	I	J
1	**ARCO**			Quality Control						
2										
3	Number of samples	20		Enter the sample size then enter the number of defects in						
4	Sample size	100								
5										
6	Data					Results				
7		# Defects		% Defects		Total Sample Size	2000			
8	Sample 1	6		0.06		Total Defects	80			
9	Sample 2	5		0.05		Percentage defects	0.04			
10	Sample 3	0		0		Std dev of p-bar	0.019596			
11	Sample 4	1		0.01						
12	Sample 5	4		0.04		Upper Control Limit	0.098788			
13	Sample 6	2		0.02		Center Line	0.04			
14	Sample 7	5		0.05		Lower Control Limit	0			
15	Sample 8	3		0.03						
16	Sample 9	3		0.03						
17	Sample 10	2		0.02						
18	Sample 11	6		0.06						
19	Sample 12	1		0.01						
20	Sample 13	8		0.08						
21	Sample 14	7		0.07						
22	Sample 15	5		0.05						
23	Sample 16	4		0.04						
24	Sample 17	11		0.11	Above UCL					
25	Sample 18	3		0.03						
26	Sample 19	0		0						
27	Sample 20	4		0.04						

ing the *p*-chart control limits for the ARCO example. Program 17.1A shows both the data input and formulas. Program 17.1B provides output. Excel also contains a built-in graphing ability with Chart Wizard.

c-Charts

c-charts count the number of defects, whereas p-charts track the percentage defective.

In the ARCO example discussed previously, we counted the number of defective database records entered. A defective record is one that was not exactly correct. A bad record may contain more than one defect, however. We use *c-charts* to control the *number* of defects per unit of output (or per insurance record in this case).

Control charts for defects are helpful for monitoring processes in which a large number of potential errors can occur but the actual number that do occur is relatively small. Defects may be mistyped words in a newspaper, blemishes on a table, or missing pickles on a fast-food hamburger.

The Poisson probability distribution, which has a variance equal to its mean, is the basis for *c*-charts. Since $\bar{c}$ is the mean number of defects per unit, the standard deviation is equal to $\sqrt{\bar{c}}$. To compute 99.7% control limits for *c*, we use the formula

$$\bar{c} \pm 3\sqrt{\bar{c}} \qquad (17\text{-}10)$$

Here is an example.

Red Top Cab Company *c*-Chart Example Red Top Cab Company receives several complaints per day about the behavior of its drivers. Over a nine-day period (in which days are the units of measure), the owner received the following number of calls from irate passengers: 3, 0, 8, 9, 6, 7, 4, 9, 8, for a total of 54 complaints.

To compute 99.7% control limits, we take

$$\bar{c} = \frac{54}{9} = 6 \text{ complaints per day}$$

Thus,

$$UCL_c = \bar{c} + 3\sqrt{\bar{c}} = 6 + 3\sqrt{6} = 6 + 3(2.45) = 13.35$$

$$LCL_c = \bar{c} - 3\sqrt{\bar{c}} = 6 - 3\sqrt{6} = 6 - 3(2.45) = 0 \longleftarrow$$

(because we cannot have a negative control limit)

After the owner plotted a control chart summarizing these data and posted it prominently in the drivers' locker room, the number of calls received dropped to an average of 3 per day. Can you explain why this may have occurred?

SUMMARY

To the manager of a firm producing goods or services, quality is the degree to which the product meets specifications. Quality control has become one of the most important precepts of business.

The expression "quality cannot be inspected into a product" is a central theme of organizations today. More and more world-class companies are following the ideas of Total Quality Management (TQM) which emphasizes the entire organization, from supplier to customer.

Statistical aspects of quality control date to the 1920s but are of special interest in our global marketplaces of this new century. Statistical process control tools described in this chapter include the $\bar{x}$- and R-charts for variable sampling and the p- and c-charts for attribute sampling.

GLOSSARY

Assignable Variation. Variation in the production process that can be traced to specific causes.

c-Chart. A quality control chart that is used to control the number of defects per unit of output.

Central Limit Theorem. The theoretical foundation for $\bar{x}$-charts. It states that regardless of the distribution of the population of all parts or services, the distribution of $\bar{x}$'s will tend to follow a normal curve as the sample size grows.

Control Chart. A graphic presentation of process data over time.

Natural Variations. Variabilities that affect almost every production process to some degree and are to be expected; also known as common causes.

p-Chart. A quality control chart that is used to control attributes.

Quality. The degree to which a product or service meets the specifications set for it.

R-Chart. A process control chart that tracks the "range" within a sample; indicates that a gain or loss of uniformity has occurred in a production process.

Total Quality Management (TQM). An emphasis on quality that encompasses the entire organization.

$\bar{x}$-Chart. A quality control chart for variables that indicates when changes occur in the central tendency of a production process.

KEY EQUATIONS

(17-1) Upper control limit (UCL) $= \bar{\bar{x}} + z\sigma_{\bar{x}}$

The upper limit for an $\bar{x}$-chart using standard deviations.

(17-2) Lower control limit (LCL) $= \bar{\bar{x}} - z\sigma_{\bar{x}}$

The lower control limit for an $\bar{x}$-chart using standard deviations.

(17-3) $UCL_{\bar{x}} = \bar{\bar{x}} + A_2\bar{R}$

The upper control limit for an $\bar{x}$-chart using tabled values and ranges.

(17-4) $LCL_{\bar{x}} = \bar{\bar{x}} - A_2\bar{R}$

The lower control limit for an $\bar{x}$-chart using tabled values and ranges.

(17-5) $UCL_R = D_4\bar{R}$

Upper control limit for a range chart.

(17-6) $LCL_R = D_3\bar{R}$

Lower control limit for a range chart.

(17-7) $UCL_p = \bar{p} + z\sigma_p$

Upper control unit for a p-chart.

(17-8) $\text{LCL}_p = \bar{p} - z\sigma_p$

Lower control limit for a p-chart.

(17-9) $\hat{\sigma}_p = \sqrt{\dfrac{\bar{p}(1 - \bar{p})}{n}}$

The estimated standard deviation of a binomial
distribution.

(17-10) $\bar{c} \pm 3\sqrt{\bar{c}}$

The upper and lower limits for a c-chart.

SOLVED PROBLEMS

Solved Problem 17-1

The manufacturer of precision parts for drill presses produces round shafts for use in the construction of
drill presses. The average diameter of a shaft is 0.56 inch. The inspection samples contain six shafts each.
The average range of these samples is 0.006 inch. Determine the upper and lower control chart limits.

Solution

The mean factor A_2 from Table 17.2, where the sample size is 6, is seen to be 0.483. With this factor, you
can obtain the upper and lower control limits:

$$\text{UCL}_{\bar{x}} = 0.56 + (0.483)(0.006) \qquad \text{LCL}_{\bar{x}} = 0.56 - 0.0029$$

$$= 0.56 + 0.0029 = 0.5629 \qquad\qquad = 0.5571$$

Solved Problem 17-2

Nocaf Drinks, Inc., a producer of decaffeinated coffee, bottles Nocaf. Each bottle should have a net
weight of 4 ounces. The machine that fills the bottles with coffee is new, and the operations manager
wants to make sure that it is properly adjusted. The operations manager takes a sample of $n = 8$ bottles
and records the average and range in ounces for each sample. The data for several samples are given in
the following table. Note that every sample consists of 8 bottles.

SAMPLE	SAMPLE RANGE	SAMPLE AVERAGE	SAMPLE	SAMPLE RANGE	SAMPLE AVERAGE
A	0.41	4.00	E	0.56	4.17
B	0.55	4.16	F	0.62	3.93
C	0.44	3.99	G	0.54	3.98
D	0.48	4.00	H	0.44	4.01

Is the machine properly adjusted and in control?

Solution

We first find that $\bar{\bar{x}} = 4.03$ and $\bar{R} = 0.51$. Then, using Table 17.2, we find

$$\text{UCL}_{\bar{x}} = \bar{\bar{x}} + A_2\bar{R} = 4.03 + (0.373)(0.51) = 4.22$$

$$\text{LCL}_{\bar{x}} = \bar{\bar{x}} - A_2\bar{R} = 4.03 - (0.373)(0.51) = 3.84$$

$$\text{UCL}_R = D_4\bar{R} = (1.864)(0.51) = 0.95$$

$$\text{LCL}_R = D_3\bar{R} = (0.136)(0.51) = 0.07$$

It appears that the process average and range are both in control.

Solved Problem 17-3

Crabill Electronics, Inc., makes resistors, and among the last 100 resistors inspected, the percent defective has been 0.05. Determine the upper and lower limits for this process for 99.7% confidence.

Solution

$$\text{UCL}_p = \bar{p} + 3\sqrt{\frac{\bar{p}(1 - \bar{p})}{n}} = 0.05 + 3\sqrt{\frac{(0.05)(1 - 0.05)}{100}}$$

$$= 0.05 + 3(0.0218) = 0.1154$$

$$\text{LCL}_p = \bar{p} - 3\sqrt{\frac{\bar{p}(1 - \bar{p})}{n}} = 0.05 - 3(0.0218)$$

$$= 0.05 - 0.0654 = 0 \text{ (since percent defective cannot be negative)}$$

SELF-TEST

■ Before taking the self-test, refer back to the learning objectives at the beginning of the chapter, the notes in the margins, and the glossary at the end of the chapter.

■ Use the key at the back of the book to correct your answers.

■ Restudy pages that correspond to any questions that you answered incorrectly or material you feel uncertain about.

1. The degree to which the product or service meets specifications is one definition of
   a. sigma.
   b. quality.
   c. range.
   d. process variability.

2. A control chart for monitoring processes in which values are measured in continuous units such as weight or volume is called a control chart for
   a. attributes.
   b. measurements.
   c. variables.
   d. quality.

3. The type of chart used to control the number of defects per unit of output is the
   a. $\bar{x}$ bar chart.
   b. R-chart.
   c. p-chart.
   d. c-chart.

4. Control charts for attributes are
   a. p-charts.
   b. m-charts.
   c. R-charts.
   d. $\bar{x}$-charts.

5. The Poisson distribution is often used with
   a. R-charts.
   b. p-charts.
   c. c-charts.
   d. x-charts.

6. A type of variability that indicates that a process is out of control is called
   a. natural variation.
   b. assignable variation.
   c. random variation.
   d. average variation.

7. A company is implementing a new quality control program. Items are sampled and classified as being defective or nondefective. The type of control chart that should be used is
   a. an R-chart.
   b. a control chart for variables.
   c. a control chart for attributes.
   d. a control limit chart.

8. After a control chart (for means) has been developed, samples are taken and the average is computed for each sample. The process could be considered out of control if
   a. one of the sample means is above the upper control limit.
   b. one of the sample means is below the lower control limit.
   c. five consecutive sample means show a consistent trend (either increasing or decreasing).
   d. all of the above were true.

9. A machine is supposed to fill soft drink cans to 12 ounces. It appears that although the average amount in the cans is about 12 ounces (based on sample means), there is a great deal of variability in each of the individual cans. The type of chart that would best detect this problem would be
   a. a p-chart.
   b. an R-chart.
   c. a c-chart.
   d. an attribute chart.

10. If a process only has random variations (it is in control), then 95.5% of the time the sample average will fall within
    a. 1 standard deviation of the population mean.
    b. 2 standard deviations of the population mean.
    c. 3 standard deviations of the population mean.
    d. 4 standard deviations of the population mean.

DISCUSSION QUESTIONS AND PROBLEMS

Discussion Questions

17-1 Why is the central limit theorem so important in SQC?

17-2 Why are $\bar{x}$- and R-charts usually used hand in hand?

17-3 Explain the difference between control charts for variables and control charts for attributes.

17-4 Explain the difference between c-charts and p-charts.

17-5 When using a control chart, what are some patterns that would indicate that the process is out of control?

17-6 What might cause a process to be out of control?

17-7 Explain why a process can be out of control even though all the samples fall within the upper and lower control limits.

Problems*

·17-8 Shader Storage Technologies produces refrigeration units for food producers and retail food establishments. The overall average temperature that these units maintain is 46° Fahrenheit. The average range is 2° Fahrenheit. Samples of 6 are taken to monitor the process. Determine the upper and lower control chart limits for averages and ranges for these refrigeration units.

·17-9 When set at the standard position, Autopitch can throw hard balls toward a batter at an average speed of 60 mph. Autopitch devices are made for both major- and minor-league teams to help them improve their batting averages. Autopitch executives take samples of 10 Autopitch devices at a time to monitor these devices and to maintain the highest quality. The average range is 3 mph. Using control-chart techniques, determine control-chart limits for averages and ranges for Autopitch.

·17-10 Zipper Products, Inc., produces granola cereal, granola bars, and other natural food products. Its natural granola cereal is sampled to ensure proper weight. Each sample contains eight boxes of cereal. The overall average for the samples is 17 ounces. The range is only 0.5 ounce. Determine the upper and lower control-chart limits for averages for the boxes of cereal.

:17-11 Small boxes of NutraFlakes cereal are labeled "net weight 10 ounces." Each hour, random samples of size $n = 4$ boxes are weighed to check process control. Five hours of observations yielded the following:

	WEIGHT			
TIME	BOX 1	BOX 2	BOX 3	BOX 4
9 A.M.	9.8	10.4	9.9	10.3
10 A.M.	10.1	10.2	9.9	9.8
11 A.M.	9.9	10.5	10.3	10.1
Noon	9.7	9.8	10.3	10.2
1 P.M.	9.7	10.1	9.9	9.9

Using these data, construct limits for $\bar{x}$- and R-charts. Is the process in control? What other steps should the QC department follow at this point?

:17-12 Sampling four pieces of precision-cut wire (to be used in computer assembly) every hour for the past 24 hours has produced the following results:

HOUR	$\bar{x}$	R	HOUR	$\bar{x}$	R
1	3.25″	0.71″	13	3.11″	0.85″
2	3.10	1.18	14	2.83	1.31
3	3.22	1.43	15	3.12	1.06
4	3.39	1.26	16	2.84	0.50
5	3.07	1.17	17	2.86	1.43
6	2.86	0.32	18	2.74	1.29
7	3.05	0.53	19	3.41	1.61
8	2.65	1.13	20	2.89	1.09
9	3.02	0.71	21	2.65	1.08
10	2.85	1.33	22	3.28	0.46
11	2.83	1.17	23	2.94	1.58
12	2.97	0.40	24	2.64	0.97

Develop appropriate control limits and determine whether there is any cause for concern in the cutting process.

:17-13 Due to the poor quality of various semiconductor products used in their manufacturing process, Microlaboratories has decided to develop a QC program. Because the semiconductor parts they get from suppliers are either good or defective, Milton Fisher has decided to develop control charts for attributes. The total number of semiconductors in every sample is 200. Furthermore, Milton would like to determine the upper control chart limit and the lower control chart limit for various values of the fraction defective (p) in the sample taken. To allow more flexibility, he has decided to develop a table that lists values for p, UCL, and LCL. The values for p should range from 0.01 to 0.10, incrementing by 0.01 each time. What are the UCLs and the LCLs for 99.7% confidence?

:17-14 For the past two months, Suzan Shader has been concerned about machine number 5 at the West Factory. To make sure that the machine is operating correctly, samples are taken, and the average and range for each sample is computed. Each sample consists of 12 items produced from the machine. Recently, 12 samples were taken, and for each, the sample range and average were computed. The sample range and sample average were 1.1 and 46 for the first sample, 1.31 and 45 for the second sample, 0.91 and 46 for the third sample, and 1.1 and 47 for the fourth sample. After the fourth sample, the sample averages increased. For

---

* Note: ⚲ means the problem may be solved with QM for Windows; ✖ means the problem may be solved with Excel QM; and ⚳ means the problem may be solved with QM for Windows and/or Excel QM.

the fifth sample, the range was 1.21 and the average was 48; for sample number 6 it was 0.82 and 47; for sample number 7, it was 0.86 and 50; and for the eighth sample, it was 1.11 and 49. After the eighth sample, the sample average continued to increase, never getting below 50. For sample number 9, the range and average were 1.12 and 51; for sample number 10, they were 0.99 and 52; for sample number 11, they were 0.86 and 50; and for sample number 12, they were 1.2 and 52.

Although Suzan's boss wasn't overly concerned about the process, Suzan was. During installation, the supplier set a value of 47 for the process average with an average range of 1.0. It was Suzan's feeling that something was definitely wrong with machine number 5. Do you agree?

: 17-15 Kitty Products caters to the growing market for cat supplies, with a full line of products, ranging from litter to toys to flea powder. One of its newer products, a tube of fluid that prevents hair balls in long-haired cats, is produced by an automated machine that is set to fill each tube with 63.5 grams of paste.

To keep this filling process under control, four tubes are pulled randomly from the assembly line every 4 hours. After several days, the data shown in the following table resulted. Set control limits for this process and graph the sample data for both the $\bar{x}$- and R-charts.

SAMPLE NO.	$\bar{x}$	R	SAMPLE NO.	$\bar{x}$	R	SAMPLE NO.	$\bar{x}$	R
1	63.5	2.0	10	63.5	1.3	18	63.6	1.8
2	63.6	1.0	11	63.3	1.8	19	63.8	1.3
3	63.7	1.7	12	63.2	1.0	20	63.5	1.6
4	63.9	0.9	13	63.6	1.8	21	63.9	1.0
5	63.4	1.2	14	63.3	1.5	22	63.2	1.8
6	63.0	1.6	15	63.4	1.7	23	63.3	1.7
7	63.2	1.8	16	63.4	1.4	24	64.0	2.0
8	63.3	1.3	17	63.5	1.1	25	63.4	1.5
9	63.7	1.6						

: 17-16 Colonel Electric is a large company that produces lightbulbs and other electrical products. One particular lightbulb is supposed to have an average life of about 1,000 hours before it burns out. Periodically the company will test 5 of these and measure the average time before these burn out. The following table gives the results of 10 such samples:

SAMPLE	1	2	3	4	5	6	7	8	9	10
Mean	979	1087	1080	934	1072	1007	952	986	1063	958
Range	50	94	57	65	135	134	101	98	145	84

(a) What is the overall average of these means? What is the average range?
(b) What are the upper and lower control limits for a 99.7% control chart for the mean?
(c) Does this process appear to be in control? Explain.

• 17-17 For Problem 17-16, develop upper and lower control limits for the range. Do these samples indicate that the process is in control?

: 17-18 Kate Drew has been hand-painting wooden Christmas ornaments for several years. Recently she has hired some friends to help her increase the volume of her business. In checking the quality of the work, she notices that some slight blemishes occasionally are apparent. A sample of 20 pieces of work resulted in the following number of blemishes on each piece: 0, 2, 1, 0, 0, 3, 2, 0, 4, 1, 2, 0, 0, 1, 2, 1, 0, 0, 0, 1. Develop upper and lower control limits for the number of blemishes on each piece.

: 17-19 A new president at Big State University has made student satisfaction with the enrollment and registration process one of her highest priorities. Students must see an advisor, sign up for classes, obtain a parking permit, pay tuition and fees, and buy textbooks and other supplies. During one registration period, 10 students every hour are sampled and asked about satisfaction with each of these areas. Twelve different groups of students were sampled, and the number in each group who had at least one complaint are as follows: 0, 2, 1, 0, 0, 1, 3, 0, 1, 2, 2, 0.

Develop upper and lower control limits (99.7%) for the proportion of students with complaints.

INTERNET HOMEWORK PROBLEMS

See our Internet home page at **www.prenhall.com/render** for additional homework problems 17-20 to 17-23.

⇒ CASE STUDY

Morristown *Daily Tribune*

In July 2001, the Morristown *Daily Tribune* published its first newspaper in direct competition with two other newspapers, the Morristown *Daily Ledger* and the *Clarion Herald*, a weekly publication. Presently, the *Ledger* is the most widely read newspaper in the area, with a total circulation of 38,500. The *Tribune*, however, has made significant inroads into the readership market since its inception. Total circulation of the *Tribune* now exceeds 27,000.

Rita Bornstein, editor of the *Tribune*, attributes the success of the newspaper to the accuracy of its contents, a strong editorial section, and the proper blending of local, regional, national, and international news items. In addition, the paper has been successful in getting the accounts of several major retailers who advertise extensively in the display section. Finally, experienced reporters, photographers, copy writers, typesetters, editors, and other personnel have formed a team dedicated to providing the most timely and accurate reporting of news in the area.

Of critical importance to good-quality newspaper printing is accurate typesetting. To assure quality in the final print, Ms. Bornstein has decided to develop a procedure for monitoring the performance of typesetters over a period of time. Such a proce-dure involves sampling output, establishing control limits, comparing the *Tribune*'s accuracy with that of the industry, and occasionally updating the information.

First, Ms. Bornstein randomly selected 30 newspapers published during the preceding 12 months. From each paper, 100 paragraphs were randomly chosen and were read for accuracy. The number of paragraphs with errors in each paper was recorded, and the fraction of paragraphs with errors in each sample was determined. The table below shows the results of the sampling.

Discussion Questions

1. Plot the overall fraction of errors ($\bar{p}$) and the upper and lower control limits on a control chart using a 95% confidence level.
2. Assume that the industry upper and lower control limits are 0.1000 and 0.0400, respectively. Plot them on the control chart.
3. Plot the fraction of errors in each sample. Do all fall within the firm's control limits? When one falls outside the control limits, what should be done?

Source: Professor Jerry Kinard, Western Carolina University.

SAMPLE	PARAGRAPHS WITH ERRORS IN THE SAMPLE	FRACTION OF PARAGRAPHS WITH ERRORS (PER 100)	SAMPLE	PARAGRAPHS WITH ERRORS IN THE SAMPLE	FRACTION OF PARAGRAPHS WITH ERRORS (PER 100)
1	2	0.02	16	2	0.02
2	4	0.04	17	3	0.03
3	10	0.10	18	7	0.07
4	4	0.04	19	3	0.03
5	1	0.01	20	2	0.02
6	1	0.01	21	3	0.03
7	13	0.13	22	7	0.07
8	9	0.09	23	4	0.04
9	11	0.11	24	3	0.03
10	0	0.00	25	2	0.02
11	3	0.03	26	2	0.02
12	4	0.04	27	0	0.00
13	2	0.02	28	1	0.01
14	2	0.02	29	3	0.03
15	8	0.08	30	4	0.04

INTERNET CASE STUDY

See our Internet home page at **www.prenhall.com/render** for this additional case study: Bayfield Mud Company. This case involves bags of mud-treating agents used in drilling for oil and natural gas.

BIBLIOGRAPHY

Berry, L. L., A. Parasuraman, and V. A. Zeithaml. "Improving Service Quality in America: Lessons Learned," *The Academy of Management Executive* 8, 2 (May 1994): 32–52.

Besterfield, D. H. *Quality Control*, 4/c. Upper Saddle River, NJ: Prentice Hall, 1994.

Carr, L. P. "Applying Cost of Quality to a Service Business," *Sloan Management Review* 33, 4 (Summer 1992): 72–78.

Crosby, P. B. *Quality Is Free*. New York: McGraw-Hill Book Company, 1979.

Curkovic, Sime, Shawnee Vickery, and Cornelia Droge. "Quality-Related Action Programs: Their Impact on Quality Performance and Firm Performance," *Decision Sciences* 31, 3 (Fall 2000): 885–906.

Das, Ajay, Robert B. Handfield, Roger J. Calantone, and Soumen Gosh. "A Contingent View of Quality Management—The Impact of International Competition on Quality," *Decision Sciences* 31, 3 (Summer 2000): 649–690.

Deming, W. E. *Out of the Crisis*. Cambridge, MA: MIT Center for Advanced Engineering Study, 1986.

DeVor, R. E., T. Chang, and J. W. Sutherland. *Statistical Quality Design and Control: Contemporary Concepts and Methods*. New York: Macmillan Publishing Co., Inc., 1992.

Easton, G. S. and S. L. Jarrell. "The Effects of Total Quality Management on Corporate Performance," *Journal of Business* 71, 2 (1998): 253–307.

Foster, S. Thomas. *Managing Quality: An Integrative Approach*. Upper Saddle River, NJ: Prentice Hall, 2001.

Juran, Joseph M. and A. Blanton Godfrey. *Juran's Quality Handbook*, 5/e. New York: McGraw-Hill Book Company, 1999.

Mitra, A. *Fundamentals of Quality Control and Improvement*, 2/e. Upper Saddle River, NJ: Prentice Hall, 1998.

Ravichandran, T. "Swiftness and Intensity of Administrative Innovation Adoption: An Empirical Study of TQM in Information Systems," *Decision Sciences* 31, 3 (Summer 2000): 691–724.

Wheeler, D. J. "Why Three Sigma Limits?" *Quality Digest* (August 1996): 63–64.

Wilson, Darryl D. and David A. Collier. "An Empirical Investigation of the Malcolm Baldrige National Quality Award Casual Model," *Decision Sciences* 31, 2 (Spring 2000): 361–390.

APPENDIX 17.1: USING QM FOR WINDOWS FOR SPC

QM for Windows' quality control module can compute most of the SPC control charts and limits introduced in this chapter. Once the module is selected, we select NEW and indicate which type of chart (*p*-chart, *x*-bar chart, and *c*-chart). In the next screen we indicate how many samples were taken. Then we are presented with the input screen where we indicate the number of items in each sample and input the appropriate numbers for each sample. Program 17.2 is the output screen for the *p*-chart data for ARCO found in Section 17.5. QM for Windows computes the average proportion (*p*-bar), the standard deviation, and upper and lower control limits. From this screen we can select WINDOW and select CONTROL CHART to actually view the chart and look for patterns that might indicate the process is out of control.

PROGRAM 17.2

QM for Windows Analysis of ARCO's Data to Compute *p*-chart Control Limits

QM for Windows - C:\Prentice\Data\Renstair\Arco.qua

Method		Sample Size	
3 sigma		◄	100

Quality Control Results

ARCO Insurance Records Solution					
Sample	Number of Defects	Fraction Defective			3 sigma
Sample 1	6.	0.06	Total Defects		80.
Sample 2	5.	0.05	Total units sampled		2,000.
Sample 3	0.	0.	Defect rate (pbar)		0.04
Sample 4	1.	0.01	Std dev of proportions		0.0196
Sample 5	4.	0.04			
Sample 6	2.	0.02	UCL (Upper control limit)		0.0988
Sample 7	5.	0.05	CL (Center line)		0.04
Sample 8	3.	0.03	LCL (Lower Control Limit)		0.
Sample 9	3.	0.03			
Sample 10	2.	0.02			
Sample 11	6.	0.06			
Sample 12	1.	0.01			
Sample 13	8.	0.08			
Sample 14	7.	0.07			
Sample 15	5.	0.05			

APPENDICES

APPENDIX A: AREAS UNDER THE STANDARD NORMAL CURVE

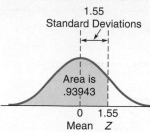

1.55
Standard Deviations

Area is
.93943

0   1.55
Mean   Z

Example: To find the area under the normal curve, you must know how many standard deviations that point is to the right of the mean. Then the area under the normal curve can be read directly from the normal table. For example, the total area under the normal curve for a point that is 1.55 standard deviations to the right of the mean is .93943.

	.00	.01	.02	.03	.04	.05	.06	.07	.08	.09
0.0	.50000	.50399	.50798	.51197	.51595	.51994	.52392	.52790	.53188	.53586
0.1	.53983	.54380	.54776	.55172	.55567	.55962	.56356	.56749	.57142	.57535
0.2	.57926	.58317	.58706	.59095	.59483	.59871	.60257	.60642	.61026	.61409
0.3	.61791	.62172	.62552	.62930	.63307	.63683	.64058	.64431	.64803	.65173
0.4	.65542	.65910	.66276	.66640	.67003	.67364	.67724	.68082	.68439	.68793
0.5	.69146	.69497	.69847	.70194	.70540	.70884	.71226	.71566	.71904	.72240
0.6	.72575	.72907	.73237	.73536	.73891	.74215	.74537	.74857	.75175	.75490
0.7	.75804	.76115	.76424	.76730	.77035	.77337	.77637	.77935	.78230	.78524
0.8	.78814	.79103	.79389	.79673	.79955	.80234	.80511	.80785	.81057	.81327
0.9	.81594	.81859	.82121	.82381	.82639	.82894	.83147	.83398	.83646	.83891
1.0	.84134	.84375	.84614	.84849	.85083	.85314	.85543	.85769	.85993	.86214
1.1	.86433	.86650	.86864	.87076	.87286	.87493	.87698	.87900	.88100	.88298
1.2	.88493	.88686	.88877	.89065	.89251	.89435	.89617	.89796	.89973	.90147
1.3	.90320	.90490	.90658	.90824	.90988	.91149	.91309	.91466	.91621	.91774
1.4	.91924	.92073	.92220	.92364	.92507	.92647	.92785	.92922	.93056	.93189
1.5	.93319	.93448	.93574	.93699	.93822	.93943	.94062	.94179	.94295	.94408
1.6	.94520	.94630	.94738	.94845	.94950	.95053	.95154	.95254	.95352	.95449
1.7	.95543	.95637	.95728	.95818	.95907	.95994	.96080	.96164	.96246	.96327
1.8	.96407	.96485	.96562	.96638	.96712	.96784	.96856	.96926	.96995	.97062
1.9	.97128	.97193	.97257	.97320	.97381	.97441	.97500	.97558	.97615	.97670
2.0	.97725	.97784	.97831	.97882	.97932	.97982	.98030	.98077	.98124	.98169
2.1	.98214	.98257	.98300	.98341	.98382	.98422	.98461	.98500	.98537	.98574
2.2	.98610	.98645	.98679	.98713	.98745	.98778	.98809	.98840	.98870	.98899
2.3	.98928	.98956	.98983	.99010	.99036	.99061	.99086	.99111	.99134	.99158
2.4	.99180	.99202	.99224	.99245	.99266	.99286	.99305	.99324	.99343	.99361
2.5	.99379	.99396	.99413	.99430	.99446	.99461	.99477	.99492	.99506	.99520
2.6	.99534	.99547	.99560	.99573	.99585	.99598	.99609	.99621	.99632	.99643
2.7	.99653	.99664	.99674	.99683	.99693	.99702	.99711	.99720	.99728	.99736
2.8	.99744	.99752	.99760	.99767	.99774	.99781	.99788	.99795	.99801	.99807
2.9	.99813	.99819	.99825	.99831	.99836	.99841	.99846	.99851	.99856	.99861
3.0	.99865	.99869	.99874	.99878	.99882	.99886	.99889	.99893	.99896	.99900
3.1	.99903	.99906	.99910	.99913	.99916	.99918	.99921	.99924	.99926	.99929
3.2	.99931	.99934	.99936	.99938	.99940	.99942	.99944	.99946	.99948	.99950

	.00	.01	.02	.03	.04	.05	.06	.07	.08	.09
3.3	.99952	.99953	.99955	.99957	.99958	.99960	.99961	.99962	.99964	.99965
3.4	.99966	.99968	.99969	.99970	.99971	.99972	.99973	.99974	.99975	.99976
3.5	.99977	.99978	.99978	.99979	.99980	.99981	.99981	.99982	.99983	.99983
3.6	.99984	.99985	.99985	.99986	.99986	.99987	.99987	.99998	.99988	.99989
3.7	.99989	.99990	.99990	.99990	.99991	.99991	.99992	.99992	.99992	.99992
3.8	.99993	.99993	.99993	.99994	.99994	.99994	.99994	.99995	.99995	.99995
3.9	.99995	.99995	.99996	.99996	.99996	.99996	.99996	.99996	.99997	.99997

Source: Reprinted from Robert O. Schlaifer, *Introduction to Statistics for Business Decisions*, published by McGraw-Hill Book Company, 1961, by permission of the copyright holder, the President and Fellows of Harvard College.

APPENDIX B: BINOMIAL PROBABILITIES

Probability of exactly r successes in n trials

n	r	0.05	0.10	0.15	0.20	0.25	0.30	0.35	0.40	0.45	0.50
1	0	0.9500	0.9000	0.8500	0.8000	0.7500	0.7000	0.6500	0.6000	0.5500	0.5000
	1	0.0500	0.1000	0.1500	0.2000	0.2500	0.3000	0.3500	0.4000	0.4500	0.5000
2	0	0.9025	0.8100	0.7225	0.6400	0.5625	0.4900	0.4225	0.3600	0.3025	0.2500
	1	0.0950	0.1800	0.2550	0.3200	0.3750	0.4200	0.4550	0.4800	0.4950	0.5000
	2	0.0025	0.0100	0.0225	0.0400	0.0625	0.0900	0.1225	0.1600	0.2025	0.2500
3	0	0.8574	0.7290	0.6141	0.5120	0.4219	0.3430	0.2746	0.2160	0.1664	0.1250
	1	0.1354	0.2430	0.3251	0.3840	0.4219	0.4410	0.4436	0.4320	0.4084	0.3750
	2	0.0071	0.0270	0.0574	0.0960	0.1406	0.1890	0.2389	0.2880	0.3341	0.3750
	3	0.0001	0.0010	0.0034	0.0080	0.0156	0.0270	0.0429	0.0640	0.0911	0.1250
4	0	0.8145	0.6561	0.5220	0.4096	0.3164	0.2401	0.1785	0.1296	0.0915	0.0625
	1	0.1715	0.2916	0.3685	0.4096	0.4219	0.4116	0.3845	0.3456	0.2995	0.2500
	2	0.0135	0.0486	0.0975	0.1536	0.2109	0.2646	0.3105	0.3456	0.3675	0.3750
	3	0.0005	0.0036	0.0115	0.0256	0.0469	0.0756	0.1115	0.1536	0.2005	0.2500
	4	0.0000	0.0001	0.0005	0.0016	0.0039	0.0081	0.0150	0.0256	0.0410	0.0625
5	0	0.7738	0.5905	0.4437	0.3277	0.2373	0.1681	0.1160	0.0778	0.0503	0.0313
	1	0.2036	0.3281	0.3915	0.4096	0.3955	0.3602	0.3124	0.2592	0.2059	0.1563
	2	0.0214	0.0729	0.1382	0.2048	0.2637	0.3087	0.3364	0.3456	0.3369	0.3125
	3	0.0011	0.0081	0.0244	0.0512	0.0879	0.1323	0.1811	0.2304	0.2757	0.3125
	4	0.0000	0.0005	0.0022	0.0064	0.0146	0.0284	0.0488	0.0768	0.1128	0.1563
	5	0.0000	0.0000	0.0001	0.0003	0.0010	0.0024	0.0053	0.0102	0.0185	0.0313
6	0	0.7351	0.5314	0.3771	0.2621	0.1780	0.1176	0.0754	0.0467	0.0277	0.0156
	1	0.2321	0.3543	0.3993	0.3932	0.3560	0.3025	0.2437	0.1866	0.1359	0.0938
	2	0.0305	0.0984	0.1762	0.2458	0.2966	0.3241	0.3280	0.3110	0.2780	0.2344
	3	0.0021	0.0146	0.0415	0.0819	0.1318	0.1852	0.2355	0.2765	0.3032	0.3125
	4	0.0001	0.0012	0.0055	0.0154	0.0330	0.0595	0.0951	0.1382	0.1861	0.2344
	5	0.0000	0.0001	0.0004	0.0015	0.0044	0.0102	0.0205	0.0369	0.0609	0.0938
	6	0.0000	0.0000	0.0000	0.0001	0.0002	0.0007	0.0018	0.0041	0.0083	0.0156
7	0	0.6983	0.4783	0.3206	0.2097	0.1335	0.0824	0.0490	0.0280	0.0152	0.0078
	1	0.2573	0.3720	0.3960	0.3670	0.3115	0.2471	0.1848	0.1306	0.0872	0.0547
	2	0.0406	0.1240	0.2097	0.2753	0.3115	0.3177	0.2985	0.2613	0.2140	0.1641
	3	0.0036	0.0230	0.0617	0.1147	0.1730	0.2269	0.2679	0.2903	0.2918	0.2734
	4	0.0002	0.0026	0.0109	0.0287	0.0577	0.0972	0.1442	0.1935	0.2388	0.2734
	5	0.0000	0.0002	0.0012	0.0043	0.0115	0.0250	0.0466	0.0774	0.1172	0.1641
	6	0.0000	0.0000	0.0001	0.0004	0.0013	0.0036	0.0084	0.0172	0.0320	0.0547
	7	0.0000	0.0000	0.0000	0.0000	0.0001	0.0002	0.0006	0.0016	0.0037	0.0078
8	0	0.6634	0.4305	0.2725	0.1678	0.1001	0.0576	0.0319	0.0168	0.0084	0.0039
	1	0.2793	0.3826	0.3847	0.3355	0.2670	0.1977	0.1373	0.0896	0.0548	0.0313
	2	0.0515	0.1488	0.2376	0.2936	0.3115	0.2965	0.2587	0.2090	0.1569	0.1094

| | | P | | | | | | | | | |
n	r	0.05	0.10	0.15	0.20	0.25	0.30	0.35	0.40	0.45	0.50
	3	0.0054	0.0331	0.0839	0.1468	0.2076	0.2541	0.2786	0.2787	0.2568	0.2188
	4	0.0004	0.0046	0.0185	0.0459	0.0865	0.1361	0.1875	0.2322	0.2627	0.2734
	5	0.0000	0.0004	0.0026	0.0092	0.0231	0.0467	0.0808	0.1239	0.1719	0.2188
	6	0.0000	0.0000	0.0002	0.0011	0.0038	0.0100	0.0217	0.0413	0.0703	0.1094
	7	0.0000	0.0000	0.0000	0.0001	0.0004	0.0012	0.0033	0.0079	0.0164	0.0313
	8	0.0000	0.0000	0.0000	0.0000	0.0000	0.0001	0.0002	0.0007	0.0017	0.0039
9	0	0.6302	0.3874	0.2316	0.1342	0.0751	0.0404	0.0207	0.0101	0.0046	0.0020
	1	0.2985	0.3874	0.3679	0.3020	0.2253	0.1556	0.1004	0.0605	0.0339	0.0176
	2	0.0629	0.1722	0.2597	0.3020	0.3003	0.2668	0.2162	0.1612	0.1110	0.0703
	3	0.0077	0.0446	0.1069	0.1762	0.2336	0.2668	0.2716	0.2508	0.2119	0.1641
	4	0.0006	0.0074	0.0283	0.0661	0.1168	0.1715	0.2194	0.2508	0.2600	0.2461
	5	0.0000	0.0008	0.0050	0.0165	0.0389	0.0735	0.1181	0.1672	0.2128	0.2461
	6	0.0000	0.0001	0.0006	0.0028	0.0087	0.0210	0.0424	0.0743	0.1160	0.1641
	7	0.0000	0.0000	0.0000	0.0003	0.0012	0.0039	0.0098	0.0212	0.0407	0.0703
	8	0.0000	0.0000	0.0000	0.0000	0.0001	0.0004	0.0013	0.0035	0.0083	0.0176
	9	0.0000	0.0000	0.0000	0.0000	0.0000	0.0000	0.0001	0.0003	0.0008	0.0020
10	0	0.5987	0.3487	0.1969	0.1074	0.0563	0.0282	0.0135	0.0060	0.0025	0.0010
	1	0.3151	0.3874	0.3474	0.2684	0.1877	0.1211	0.0725	0.0403	0.0207	0.0098
	2	0.0746	0.1937	0.2759	0.3020	0.2816	0.2335	0.1757	0.1209	0.0763	0.0439
	3	0.0105	0.0574	0.1298	0.2013	0.2503	0.2668	0.2522	0.2150	0.1665	0.1172
	4	0.0010	0.0112	0.0401	0.0881	0.1460	0.2001	0.2377	0.2508	0.2384	0.2051
	5	0.0001	0.0015	0.0085	0.0264	0.0584	0.1029	0.1536	0.2007	0.2340	0.2461
	6	0.0000	0.0001	0.0012	0.0055	0.0162	0.0368	0.0689	0.1115	0.1596	0.2051
	7	0.0000	0.0000	0.0001	0.0008	0.0031	0.0090	0.0212	0.0425	0.0746	0.1172
	8	0.0000	0.0000	0.0000	0.0001	0.0004	0.0014	0.0043	0.0106	0.0229	0.0439
	9	0.0000	0.0000	0.0000	0.0000	0.0000	0.0001	0.0005	0.0016	0.0042	0.0098
	10	0.0000	0.0000	0.0000	0.0000	0.0000	0.0000	0.0000	0.0001	0.0003	0.0010
15	0	0.4633	0.2059	0.0874	0.0352	0.0134	0.0047	0.0016	0.0005	0.0001	0.0000
	1	0.3658	0.3432	0.2312	0.1319	0.0668	0.0305	0.0126	0.0047	0.0016	0.0005
	2	0.1348	0.2669	0.2856	0.2309	0.1559	0.0916	0.0476	0.0219	0.0090	0.0032
	3	0.0307	0.1285	0.2184	0.2501	0.2252	0.1700	0.1110	0.0634	0.0318	0.0139
	4	0.0049	0.0428	0.1156	0.1876	0.2252	0.2186	0.1792	0.1268	0.0780	0.0417
	5	0.0006	0.0105	0.0449	0.1032	0.1651	0.2061	0.2123	0.1859	0.1404	0.0916
	6	0.0000	0.0019	0.0132	0.0430	0.0917	0.1472	0.1906	0.2066	0.1914	0.1527
	7	0.0000	0.0003	0.0030	0.0138	0.0393	0.0811	0.1319	0.1771	0.2013	0.1964
	8	0.0000	0.0000	0.0005	0.0035	0.0131	0.0348	0.0710	0.1181	0.1647	0.1964
	9	0.0000	0.0000	0.0001	0.0007	0.0034	0.0116	0.0298	0.0612	0.1048	0.1527
	10	0.0000	0.0000	0.0000	0.0001	0.0007	0.0030	0.0096	0.0245	0.0515	0.0916
	11	0.0000	0.0000	0.0000	0.0000	0.0001	0.0006	0.0024	0.0074	0.0191	0.0417
	12	0.0000	0.0000	0.0000	0.0000	0.0000	0.0001	0.0004	0.0016	0.0052	0.0139
	13	0.0000	0.0000	0.0000	0.0000	0.0000	0.0000	0.0001	0.0003	0.0010	0.0032
	14	0.0000	0.0000	0.0000	0.0000	0.0000	0.0000	0.0000	0.0000	0.0001	0.0005
	15	0.0000	0.0000	0.0000	0.0000	0.0000	0.0000	0.0000	0.0000	0.0000	0.0000

		P									
n	r	0.05	0.10	0.15	0.20	0.25	0.30	0.35	0.40	0.45	0.50
20	0	0.3585	0.1216	0.0388	0.0115	0.0032	0.0008	0.0002	0.0000	0.0000	0.0000
	1	0.3774	0.2702	0.1368	0.0576	0.0211	0.0068	0.0020	0.0005	0.0001	0.0000
	2	0.1887	0.2852	0.2293	0.1369	0.0669	0.0278	0.0100	0.0031	0.0008	0.0002
	3	0.0596	0.1901	0.2428	0.2054	0.1339	0.0716	0.0323	0.0123	0.0040	0.0011
	4	0.0133	0.0898	0.1821	0.2182	0.1897	0.1304	0.0738	0.0350	0.0139	0.0046
	5	0.0022	0.0319	0.1028	0.1746	0.2023	0.1789	0.1272	0.0746	0.0365	0.0148
	6	0.0003	0.0089	0.0454	0.1091	0.1686	0.1916	0.1712	0.1244	0.0746	0.0370
	7	0.0000	0.0020	0.0160	0.0545	0.1124	0.1643	0.1844	0.1659	0.1221	0.0739
	8	0.0000	0.0004	0.0046	0.0222	0.0609	0.1144	0.1614	0.1797	0.1623	0.1201
	9	0.0000	0.0001	0.0011	0.0074	0.0271	0.0654	0.1158	0.1597	0.1771	0.1602
	10	0.0000	0.0000	0.0002	0.0020	0.0099	0.0308	0.0686	0.1171	0.1593	0.1762
	11	0.0000	0.0000	0.0000	0.0005	0.0030	0.0120	0.0336	0.0710	0.1185	0.1602
	12	0.0000	0.0000	0.0000	0.0001	0.0008	0.0039	0.0136	0.0355	0.0727	0.1201
	13	0.0000	0.0000	0.0000	0.0000	0.0002	0.0010	0.0045	0.0146	0.0366	0.0739
	14	0.0000	0.0000	0.0000	0.0000	0.0000	0.0002	0.0012	0.0049	0.0150	0.0370
	15	0.0000	0.0000	0.0000	0.0000	0.0000	0.0000	0.0003	0.0013	0.0049	0.0148
	16	0.0000	0.0000	0.0000	0.0000	0.0000	0.0000	0.0000	0.0003	0.0013	0.0046
	17	0.0000	0.0000	0.0000	0.0000	0.0000	0.0000	0.0000	0.0000	0.0002	0.0011
	18	0.0000	0.0000	0.0000	0.0000	0.0000	0.0000	0.0000	0.0000	0.0000	0.0002
	19	0.0000	0.0000	0.0000	0.0000	0.0000	0.0000	0.0000	0.0000	0.0000	0.0000
	20	0.0000	0.0000	0.0000	0.0000	0.0000	0.0000	0.0000	0.0000	0.0000	0.0000

		P								
n	r	0.55	0.60	0.65	0.70	0.75	0.80	0.85	0.90	0.95
1	0	0.4500	0.4000	0.3500	0.3000	0.2500	0.2000	0.1500	0.1000	0.0500
	1	0.5500	0.6000	0.6500	0.7000	0.7500	0.8000	0.8500	0.9000	0.9500
2	0	0.2025	0.1600	0.1225	0.0900	0.0625	0.0400	0.0225	0.0100	0.0025
	1	0.4950	0.4800	0.4550	0.4200	0.3750	0.3200	0.2550	0.1800	0.0950
	2	0.3025	0.3600	0.4225	0.4900	0.5625	0.6400	0.7225	0.8100	0.9025
3	0	0.0911	0.0640	0.0429	0.0270	0.0156	0.0080	0.0034	0.0010	0.0001
	1	0.3341	0.2880	0.2389	0.1890	0.1406	0.0960	0.0574	0.0270	0.0071
	2	0.4084	0.4320	0.4436	0.4410	0.4219	0.3840	0.3251	0.2430	0.1354
	3	0.1664	0.2160	0.2746	0.3430	0.4219	0.5120	0.6141	0.7290	0.8574
4	0	0.0410	0.0256	0.0150	0.0081	0.0039	0.0016	0.0005	0.0001	0.0000
	1	0.2005	0.1536	0.1115	0.0756	0.0469	0.0256	0.0115	0.0036	0.0005
	2	0.3675	0.3456	0.3105	0.2646	0.2109	0.1536	0.0975	0.0486	0.0135
	3	0.2995	0.3456	0.3845	0.4116	0.4219	0.4096	0.3685	0.2916	0.1715
	4	0.0915	0.1296	0.1785	0.2401	0.3164	0.4096	0.5220	0.6561	0.8145
5	0	0.0185	0.0102	0.0053	0.0024	0.0010	0.0003	0.0001	0.0000	0.0000
	1	0.1128	0.0768	0.0488	0.0283	0.0146	0.0064	0.0022	0.0004	0.0000
	2	0.2757	0.2304	0.1811	0.1323	0.0879	0.0512	0.0244	0.0081	0.0011
	3	0.3369	0.3456	0.3364	0.3087	0.2637	0.2048	0.1382	0.0729	0.0214
	4	0.2059	0.2592	0.3124	0.3602	0.3955	0.4096	0.3915	0.3280	0.2036

		P								
n	r	0.55	0.60	0.65	0.70	0.75	0.80	0.85	0.90	0.95
	5	0.0503	0.0778	0.1160	0.1681	0.2373	0.3277	0.4437	0.5905	0.7738
6	0	0.0083	0.0041	0.0018	0.0007	0.0002	0.0001	0.0000	0.0000	0.0000
	1	0.0609	0.0369	0.0205	0.0102	0.0044	0.0015	0.0004	0.0001	0.0000
	2	0.1861	0.1382	0.0951	0.0595	0.0330	0.0154	0.0055	0.0012	0.0001
	3	0.3032	0.2765	0.2355	0.1852	0.1318	0.0819	0.0415	0.0146	0.0021
	4	0.2780	0.3110	0.3280	0.3241	0.2966	0.2458	0.1762	0.0984	0.0305
	5	0.1359	0.1866	0.2437	0.3025	0.3560	0.3932	0.3993	0.3543	0.2321
	6	0.0277	0.0467	0.0754	0.1176	0.1780	0.2621	0.3771	0.5314	0.7351
7	0	0.0037	0.0016	0.0006	0.0002	0.0001	0.0000	0.0000	0.0000	0.0000
	1	0.0320	0.0172	0.0084	0.0036	0.0013	0.0004	0.0001	0.0000	0.0000
	2	0.1172	0.0774	0.0466	0.0250	0.0115	0.0043	0.0012	0.0002	0.0000
	3	0.2388	0.1935	0.1442	0.0972	0.0577	0.0287	0.0109	0.0026	0.0002
	4	0.2918	0.2903	0.2679	0.2269	0.1730	0.1147	0.0617	0.0230	0.0036
	5	0.2140	0.2613	0.2985	0.3177	0.3115	0.2753	0.2097	0.1240	0.0406
	6	0.0872	0.1306	0.1848	0.2471	0.3115	0.3670	0.3960	0.3720	0.2573
	7	0.0152	0.0280	0.0490	0.0824	0.1335	0.2097	0.3206	0.4783	0.6983
8	0	0.0017	0.0007	0.0002	0.0001	0.0000	0.0000	0.0000	0.0000	0.0000
	1	0.0164	0.0079	0.0033	0.0012	0.0004	0.0001	0.0000	0.0000	0.0000
	2	0.0703	0.0413	0.0217	0.0100	0.0038	0.0011	0.0002	0.0000	0.0000
	3	0.1719	0.1239	0.0808	0.0467	0.0231	0.0092	0.0026	0.0004	0.0000
	4	0.2627	0.2322	0.1875	0.1361	0.0865	0.0459	0.0185	0.0046	0.0004
	5	0.2568	0.2787	0.2786	0.2541	0.2076	0.1468	0.0839	0.0331	0.0054
	6	0.1569	0.2090	0.2587	0.2965	0.3115	0.2936	0.2376	0.1488	0.0515
	7	0.0548	0.0896	0.1373	0.1977	0.2670	0.3355	0.3847	0.3826	0.2793
	8	0.0084	0.0168	0.0319	0.0576	0.1001	0.1678	0.2725	0.4305	0.6634
9	0	0.0008	0.0003	0.0001	0.0000	0.0000	0.0000	0.0000	0.0000	0.0000
	1	0.0083	0.0035	0.0013	0.0004	0.0001	0.0000	0.0000	0.0000	0.0000
	2	0.0407	0.0212	0.0098	0.0039	0.0012	0.0003	0.0000	0.0000	0.0000
	3	0.1160	0.0743	0.0424	0.0210	0.0087	0.0028	0.0006	0.0001	0.0000
	4	0.2128	0.1672	0.1181	0.0735	0.0389	0.0165	0.0050	0.0008	0.0000
	5	0.2600	0.2508	0.2194	0.1715	0.1168	0.0661	0.0283	0.0074	0.0006
	6	0.2119	0.2508	0.2716	0.2668	0.2336	0.1762	0.1069	0.0446	0.0077
	7	0.1110	0.1612	0.2162	0.2668	0.3003	0.3020	0.2597	0.1722	0.0629
	8	0.0339	0.0605	0.1004	0.1556	0.2253	0.3020	0.3679	0.3874	0.2985
	9	0.0046	0.0101	0.0207	0.0404	0.0751	0.1342	0.2316	0.3874	0.6302
10	0	0.0003	0.0001	0.0000	0.0000	0.0000	0.0000	0.0000	0.0000	0.0000
	1	0.0042	0.0016	0.0005	0.0001	0.0000	0.0000	0.0000	0.0000	0.0000
	2	0.0229	0.0106	0.0043	0.0014	0.0004	0.0001	0.0000	0.0000	0.0000
	3	0.0746	0.0425	0.0212	0.0090	0.0031	0.0008	0.0001	0.0000	0.0000
	4	0.1596	0.1115	0.0689	0.0368	0.0162	0.0055	0.0012	0.0001	0.0000
	5	0.2340	0.2007	0.1536	0.1029	0.0584	0.0264	0.0085	0.0015	0.0001
	6	0.2384	0.2508	0.2377	0.2001	0.1460	0.0881	0.0401	0.0112	0.0010

						P				
n	r	0.55	0.60	0.65	0.70	0.75	0.80	0.85	0.90	0.95
	7	0.1665	0.2150	0.2522	0.2668	0.2503	0.2013	0.1298	0.0574	0.0105
	8	0.0763	0.1209	0.1757	0.2335	0.2816	0.3020	0.2759	0.1937	0.0746
	9	0.0207	0.0403	0.0725	0.1211	0.1877	0.2684	0.3474	0.3874	0.3151
	10	0.0025	0.0060	0.0135	0.0282	0.0563	0.1074	0.1969	0.3487	0.5987
15	0	0.0000	0.0000	0.0000	0.0000	0.0000	0.0000	0.0000	0.0000	0.0000
	1	0.0001	0.0000	0.0000	0.0000	0.0000	0.0000	0.0000	0.0000	0.0000
	2	0.0010	0.0003	0.0001	0.0000	0.0000	0.0000	0.0000	0.0000	0.0000
	3	0.0052	0.0016	0.0004	0.0001	0.0000	0.0000	0.0000	0.0000	0.0000
	4	0.0191	0.0074	0.0024	0.0006	0.0001	0.0000	0.0000	0.0000	0.0000
	5	0.0515	0.0245	0.0096	0.0030	0.0007	0.0001	0.0000	0.0000	0.0000
	6	0.1048	0.0612	0.0298	0.0116	0.0034	0.0007	0.0001	0.0000	0.0000
	7	0.1647	0.1181	0.0710	0.0348	0.0131	0.0035	0.0005	0.0000	0.0000
	8	0.2013	0.1771	0.1319	0.0811	0.0393	0.0138	0.0030	0.0003	0.0000
	9	0.1914	0.2066	0.1906	0.1472	0.0917	0.0430	0.0132	0.0019	0.0000
	10	0.1404	0.1859	0.2123	0.2061	0.1651	0.1032	0.0449	0.0105	0.0006
	11	0.0780	0.1268	0.1792	0.2186	0.2252	0.1876	0.1156	0.0428	0.0049
	12	0.0318	0.0634	0.1110	0.1700	0.2252	0.2501	0.2184	0.1285	0.0307
	13	0.0090	0.0219	0.0476	0.0916	0.1559	0.2309	0.2856	0.2669	0.1348
	14	0.0016	0.0047	0.0126	0.0305	0.0668	0.1319	0.2312	0.3432	0.3658
	15	0.0001	0.0005	0.0016	0.0047	0.0134	0.0352	0.0874	0.2059	0.4633
20	0	0.0000	0.0000	0.0000	0.0000	0.0000	0.0000	0.0000	0.0000	0.0000
	1	0.0000	0.0000	0.0000	0.0000	0.0000	0.0000	0.0000	0.0000	0.0000
	2	0.0000	0.0000	0.0000	0.0000	0.0000	0.0000	0.0000	0.0000	0.0000
	3	0.0002	0.0000	0.0000	0.0000	0.0000	0.0000	0.0000	0.0000	0.0000
	4	0.0013	0.0003	0.0000	0.0000	0.0000	0.0000	0.0000	0.0000	0.0000
	5	0.0049	0.0013	0.0003	0.0000	0.0000	0.0000	0.0000	0.0000	0.0000
	6	0.0150	0.0049	0.0012	0.0002	0.0000	0.0000	0.0000	0.0000	0.0000
	7	0.0366	0.0146	0.0045	0.0010	0.0002	0.0000	0.0000	0.0000	0.0000
	8	0.0727	0.0355	0.0136	0.0039	0.0008	0.0001	0.0000	0.0000	0.0000
	9	0.1185	0.0710	0.0336	0.0120	0.0030	0.0005	0.0000	0.0000	0.0000
	10	0.1593	0.1171	0.0686	0.0308	0.0099	0.0020	0.0002	0.0000	0.0000
	11	0.1771	0.1597	0.1158	0.0654	0.0271	0.0074	0.0011	0.0001	0.0000
	12	0.1623	0.1797	0.1614	0.1144	0.0609	0.0222	0.0046	0.0004	0.0000
	13	0.1221	0.1659	0.1844	0.1643	0.1124	0.0545	0.0160	0.0020	0.0000
	14	0.0746	0.1244	0.1712	0.1916	0.1686	0.1091	0.0454	0.0089	0.0003
	15	0.0365	0.0746	0.1272	0.1789	0.2023	0.1746	0.1028	0.0319	0.0022
	16	0.0139	0.0350	0.0738	0.1304	0.1897	0.2182	0.1821	0.0898	0.0133
	17	0.0040	0.0123	0.0323	0.0716	0.1339	0.2054	0.2428	0.1901	0.0596
	18	0.0008	0.0031	0.0100	0.0278	0.0669	0.1369	0.2293	0.2852	0.1887
	19	0.0001	0.0005	0.0020	0.0068	0.0211	0.0576	0.1368	0.2702	0.3774
	20	0.0000	0.0000	0.0002	0.0008	0.0032	0.0115	0.0388	0.1216	0.3585

APPENDIX C: VALUES OF $e^{-\lambda}$ FOR USE IN THE POISSON DISTRIBUTION

λ	$e^{-\lambda}$	λ	$e^{-\lambda}$
0.0	1.0000	3.1	0.0450
0.1	0.9048	3.2	0.0408
0.2	0.8187	3.3	0.0369
0.3	0.7408	3.4	0.0334
0.4	0.6703	3.5	0.0302
0.5	0.6065	3.6	0.0273
0.6	0.5488	3.7	0.0247
0.7	0.4966	3.8	0.0224
0.8	0.4493	3.9	0.0202
0.9	0.4066	4.0	0.0183
1.0	0.3679	4.1	0.0166
1.1	0.3329	4.2	0.0150
1.2	0.3012	4.3	0.0136
1.3	0.2725	4.4	0.0123
1.4	0.2466	4.5	0.0111
1.5	0.2231	4.6	0.0101
1.6	0.2019	4.7	0.0091
1.7	0.1827	4.8	0.0082
1.8	0.1653	4.9	0.0074
1.9	0.1496	5.0	0.0067
2.0	0.1353	5.1	0.0061
2.1	0.1225	5.2	0.0055
2.2	0.1108	5.3	0.0050
2.3	0.1003	5.4	0.0045
2.4	0.0907	5.5	0.0041
2.5	0.0821	5.6	0.0037
2.6	0.0743	5.7	0.0033
2.7	0.0672	5.8	0.0030
2.8	0.0608	5.9	0.0027
2.9	0.0550	6.0	0.0025
3.0	0.0498		

APPENDIX D: USING QM FOR WINDOWS

Introduction

Welcome to QM for Windows. Along with its companion, Excel QM (see Appendix E), you have available to you the most user-friendly software available for the field of quantitative analysis/quantitative methods (QA/QM). QM for Windows is a package that has been designed to help you to better learn and understand this field. The software can be used to either solve problems or check answers that have been derived by hand. You will find that this software is exceptionally friendly due to the following features:

- Anyone familiar with any standard spreadsheet or word processor in Windows will easily be able to use QM for Windows. All modules have help screens that can be accessed at any time.

- Even though QM for Windows contains 19 modules and 40 submodules, the screens for every module are consistent, so that after you become accustomed to using one module you will have an easy time with the other modules.

- The spreadsheet-type data editor allows full screen editing.

- Files are opened and saved in the usual Windows fashion, and in addition, files are named by module, which makes it easy to find files saved previously.

- It is easy to change from one solution method to another to compare methods and answers.

- Graphs are easily displayed and printed.

Installing QM for Windows

For all Windows installations, including this one, it is best to be certain that no programs, including virus protection programs, are running while you are installing a new one:

1. Insert the Render/Stair/Hanna CD into the CD-ROM drive, which we assume is drive D:.
2. From the Windows Start button, select *Run, Browse*.
3. Change to the drive that contains the CD.
4. Select *Start* and press Return or click on OK.
5. Select *Install*.
6. Select *QM for Windows* from the next screen and follow the instructions on the screen.

Default values have been assigned in the setup program, but you may change them if you like. Help and upgrades to this software are available at *www.prenhall.com/weiss*.

QM for Windows requires some general information in order to operate. The first screen at registration is a software licensing agreement. In the second registration screen you should enter your name, university, course, and professor. The name is required. When you are finished, press [**OK**].

After the registration is complete, you will have a program group added to your program manager. The group will be called QM for Windows 2. In addition, a shortcut to the program will be placed on the desktop. To use the QM for Windows program, double-click on the shortcut on the desktop or use Start, QM for Windows 2, QM for Windows.

The screen that is displayed is the basic screen for the software and contains the assorted components that are part of most of the screens. This screen was displayed in chapter 1 as Program 1.1. The top of that screen is the standard Windows title bar for the window. Below the title bar is a standard Windows menu bar. The menu bar should be easy to use. The details of the eight menu options of File, Edit, View, Module, Format, Tools, Window, and Help are explained in this appendix. At the beginning of the program the only enabled menu options are File (to open a previously saved file or to exit the program), Module (to select the module), and Help. The other options will become enabled as a module is chosen or as a problem is started.

Below the menu are two toolbars: a standard toolbar and a format toolbar. The toolbars contain standard shortcuts for several of the menu commands. If you move the mouse over the button for about two seconds, an explanation of the button will be displayed on the screen.

The next bar contains an instruction. There is always an instruction here trying to help you to figure out what to do or what to enter. Currently, the instruction indicates to select a module or open a file. When data are to be entered into the data table, this instruction will explain what type of data (integer, real, positive, etc.) are to be entered.

In Program 1.1 in chapter 1 we showed the module list after clicking on Module. In some cases after selecting one of these modules a second menu of submodules will appear. The module list has 20 options, consisting of 19 QM modules and an Exit option.

Creating a New Problem

At this point the first option that will be chosen is File, followed by either New or Open to create a new data set or to load a previously saved data set. This is an option which will be chosen very often.

The top line of the creation screen contains a text box in which the title of the problem can be entered. For many modules it is necessary to enter the number of rows in the problem. Rows will have different names depending on the modules. For example, in linear programming, rows are constraints, whereas in forecasting, rows are past periods. At any rate, the number of rows can be chosen with either the scroll bar or the text box. In general, the maximum number of rows in any module is 90.

POM-QM for Windows has the capability to allow you different options for the default row and column names. Select one of the radio buttons to indicate which style of default naming should be used. In most modules the row names are not used for computations, but you should be careful because in some modules (most notably, Project Management) the names might relate to precedences.

Many modules require you to enter the number of columns. This is given in the same way as the number of rows. All row and column names can be changed in the data table.

Some modules will have an extra option box, such as for choosing minimize or maximize or selecting whether distances are symmetric. Select one of these options. In most cases this option can later be changed on the data screen.

When you are satisfied with your choices, click on the [**OK**] button or press the [**Return/Enter**] key. At this point a blank data screen will be displayed. Screens will differ module by module.

Entering and Editing Data

After a new data set has been created or an existing data set has been loaded, the data can be edited. Every entry is in a row and column position. You navigate through the spreadsheet using the cursor movement keys. These keys function in a regular way with one exception—the [**Return/Enter**] key.

The instruction bar on the screen will contain a brief instruction describing what is to be done. There are essentially three types of cells in the data table. One type is a regular data cell into which you enter either a name or a number. A second type is a cell that cannot be changed. A third type is a cell that contains a drop-down box. For example, the signs in a

---

Solving a problem
There are several ways to solve a problem. The easiest way is to press the Solve button on the standard toolbar. Alternatively, the function key [F9] may be used. Finally, if you press the enter key after the last piece of data is entered, the problem will be solved. After solving a problem, to return to editing the data press the Edit button, which has replaced the Solve button on the standard toolbar, or use [F9].

[Return/Enter]
This key moves from cell to cell in the order from left to right, from top to bottom, skipping the first column (which usually contains names). Therefore, when entering a table of data, if you start at the upper left and work your way to the lower right row by row, this key is exceptionally useful.

linear programming constraint are chosen from this type of box. To see all of the options, press the box with the arrow.

There is one more aspect to the data screen that needs to be considered. Some modules need extra data above that in the table. In most of these cases the data are contained in text/scrollbar combinations that appear on top of the data table.

Solution Displays

Numerical Formatting
Formatting is handled by the program automatically. For example, in most cases the number 1000 will automatically be formatted as 1,000. Do not type the comma. The program will prevent you from doing so!

At this point you can press the [**Solve**] button to begin the solution process. A new screen will be displayed.

An important thing to notice is that there is more solution information available. This can be seen by the icons given at the bottom. Click on these to view the information. Alternatively, notice that the Window option in the main menu is now enabled. It is always enabled at solution time. Even if the icons are covered by a window, the Window option will always allow you to view the other solution windows.

Now that we have examined how to create and solve a problem we explain all of the Menu options that are available.

File

File contains the usual options that one finds in Windows.

New As demonstrated before, this is chosen to begin a new problem/file.

Open This is used to open/load a previously saved file. File selection is the standard Windows common dialog type. Notice that the extension for files in the QM for Windows system is given by the first three letters of the module name. For example, all linear programming files have the extension *.lin. When you go to the open dialog, the default value is for the program to look for files of the type in this module. This can be changed at the bottom left where it says "Files of Type."

Deleting Files
It is not possible to delete a file using QM for Windows. Use the Windows file manager to do so.

The names that are legal are standard file names. Case (upper or lower) does not matter. In addition to the file name, you may preface the name with a drive letter (with its colon) or path designation. Examples of legal file names are

sample, test, a:sample, linear programming problem, chapter8.problem1.

You may type them in as uppercase, lowercase, or mixed. In all of the examples, QM for Windows will add the three-letter extension to the end of the file name. For example, linear programming problem will become *linear programming problem.lin* (assuming that it is indeed a linear programming problem).

In the event that there is a problem with the drive or file, an error message will be displayed to that effect.

Save Save will replace the file without asking you if you care about overwriting the previous version of this file. If you try to save and have not previously named the file, you will be asked to name this file.

Save as Save as will prompt you for a file name before saving. You can also specify the drive, such as C: or A:. This option is very similar to the option to load a data file. When you choose this option, the Windows Common Dialog Box for Files will be displayed. It is essentially identical to the one shown previously.

Save as Excel File Save as Excel File saves a file as an Excel file with both the data and appropriate formulas for the solutions and is available for some but not all of the modules.

Save as HTML Save as HTML saves the tables as an HTML formatted file that can immediately be placed on the Internet.

Print Print will display a print menu screen with four tabs. The Information tab allows you to select which of the output tables should be printed. The Page Header tab allows you to control the information displayed at the top of the page. The Layout tab controls the printing style. Information may be printed as plain ASCII text or as a table (grid) resembling the table on the screen. Try both types of printing and see which one you/your instructor prefers. The Printer tab allows certain print settings to be changed.

Exit the Program The last option on the File menu is Exit. This will exit the program if you are on the data screen or exit the solution screen and return to the data screen if you are on the solution screen. This can also be achieved by pressing the Edit command button on the solution screen.

Edit

The commands under Edit have three purposes. The first four commands are used to insert or delete rows or columns. The next command is used to copy an entry from one cell to all cells below it in the column. This is not often useful, but when it is useful it saves a great deal of work. The last two entries can be used to copy the data table to other Windows programs.

View

View has several options that enable you to customize the appearance of the screen. The toolbar can be displayed or not. The Instruction bar can be displayed at its default location above the data or below the data, as a floating window, or not at all. The Status bar can be displayed or not.

Colors can be set to monochrome (black and white) or from this state to their original colors.

Module

Module has been shown in chapter 1 as Program 1.1. The module selection contains a list of programs available with this book.

Format

Format also has several options for the display. The colors for the entire screen can be set, and the font type and size for the table can be set. Zeros can be set to display as blanks rather than zeros. The problem title that is displayed in the data table and was created at the creation screen can be changed. The table can be squeezed or expanded. That is, the column widths can be decreased or increased. The input can be checked or not.

Tools

The Tools menu option is an area available to annotate problems. If you want to write a note to yourself about the problem, select annotation; the note will be saved with the file if you save the file.

A normal distribution calculator is found in the Tools menu option.

A calculator is available for simple calculations, including square root. There is a normal distribution calculator that can be used for finding confidence intervals and the like.

Window

The Window menu option is enabled only at the solution screen.

Help

The first help option, module help, will give a small description of the module, the data required for input, the output results, and the options available in the module. It is worthwhile to look at this screen at least one time to be certain that there are no differences

APPENDICES

between your assumptions and the assumptions of the program. If there is anything to be warned about regarding the option, it will appear on the help screen as well as in the appropriate chapter of this book.

Help also contains a pointer to an online manual that is available for this software through www.prenhall.com/weiss. If you send mail, be sure to include the name of the program (QM for Windows), the version of the program (from Help, About), the module in which the problem is occurring, and a detailed explanation of the problem, and to attach the data file for which the problem occurs.

APPENDIX E: USING EXCEL QM

Excel QM

Excel QM has been designed to help you to better learn and understand both quantitative analysis and Excel. Even though the software contains many modules and submodules, the screens for every module are consistent and easy to use. The modules were illustrated in Program 1.2. This software is provided by means of the CD ROM in the back of this book at no cost to purchasers. No floppy disk drive is required, but Excel version 5 or better must be on your PC.

To install Excel QM, exit and reenter Windows; then follow these steps:

1. Insert the Render/Stair/Hanna CD into the CD-ROM drive, which we assume is drive D:.
2. From the Windows Start button, select *Run*, *Browse*.
3. Change to the drive that contains the CD.
4. Select *Start* and press Return or click on OK.
5. Select *Install*.
6. Select *Excel QM* from the next screen and follow the instructions on the screen.

Default values have been assigned in the setup program, but you may change them if you like. The default folder is C:\Program Files\ExcelQM. Generally speaking, it is simply necessary to click Next each time that the installation program asks a question. Help and upgrades to this software are available at *www.prenhall.com/weiss*.

Starting the Program

If you do not already have Excel open, then to start Excel QM click on Start, Programs, and then the Excel QM icon in order to use the software. In addition, the installation will create a shortcut and place it on your desktop. This can be used to start Excel QM. If you already have Excel open, then simply load the file ExcelQM.xla, which is in the default directory (C:ExcelQM or C:\Program Files\ExcelQM) if you did not change this at the time of installation.

It is also possible to install Excel QM as an add-in. This will load *Excel QM* each time that you start Excel. To do this, simply go to Tools, Addins, Browse and select Excel QM.xla.

Excel QM serves two purposes in the learning process. First, it can simply help you solve homework problems. You enter the appropriate data, and the program provides numerical solutions. QM for Windows operates on the same principle. But Excel QM allows for a second approach, that is, noting the Excel *formulas* used to develop solutions and modifying them to deal with a wider variety of problems. This "open" approach allows you to observe, understand, and even change the formulas underlying the Excel calculations, conveying Excel's power as a quantitative analysis tool.

Technical Support

If you have technical problems with either QM for Windows or Excel QM that your instructor cannot answer, send email to hweiss@sbm.temple.edu. If you send email be sure to include the name of the program (QM for Windows or Excel QM), the version of the program (from Help, About in QM for Windows; from QM About in Excel QM), the module in which the problem is occurring, and a detailed explanation of the problem, and to attach the data file for which the problem occurs (if appropriate).

APPENDIX F: SOLUTIONS TO SELECTED PROBLEMS

Chapter 1

1-14 (a) total revenue = $300; total variable cost = $160
(b) BEP = 50; total revenue = $750

1-16 BEP = 4.28

1-18 $5.80

1-20 BEP = 96; total revenue = $4,800

Chapter 2

2-14 0.30

2-16 (a) 0.10   (b) 0.04   (c) 0.25   (d) 0.40

2-18 (a) 0.20   (b) 0.09   (c) 0.31   (d) dependent

2-20 (a) 0.3   (b) 0.3   (c) 0.8   (d) 0.49   (e) 0.24
(f) 0.27

2-22 0.719

2-24 (a) 0.08   (b) 0.84   (c) 0.44   (d) 0.92

2-26 (a) 0.995   (b) 0.885
(c) Assumed events are independent

2-28 0.78

2-30 2.85

2-32 (a) 0.1172   (b) 0.0439   (c) 0.0098   (d) 0.0010
(e) 0.1719

2-34 0.328, 0.590

2-36 0.776

2-38 (a) 0.0548   (b) 0.6554   (c) 0.6554   (d) 0.2119

2-40 1829.27

2-42 (a) 0.5   (b) 0.27425   (c) 48.2

2-44 0.7365

2-46 0.162

Chapter 3

3-16 (a) decision making under uncertainty
(b) Maximax criterion   (c) Sub 100

3-18 (a) Maximize EMV   (b) Sub 100   (c) $292,857
(or $7,143 lower)

3-20 Stock market; minimum EOL = 21,500

3-22 (a) $200   (b) $80

3-24 (b) Stock 11 cases   (c) Stock 13 cases

3-26 (b) Produce 300 cases. EMV = $1,800

3-28 Construct clinic.

3-32 Do not gather information but build quadplex.

3-34 P(successful facility | favorable research) = 0.53
P(successful facility | unfavorable research) = 0.11

3-36 P(favorable market | favorable survey) = 0.78
P(favorable market | favorable study) = 0.89
Conduct survey EMV (with survey) = $24,160

3-38 0.923; 0.077; 0.25; 0.75

3-40 Do not conduct survey and do not construct clinic.
They are risk avoiders.

3-42 (a) Broad street, 27.5 minutes   (b) Expressway
(c) Risk avoider.

3-44 Do not conduct survey. Build medium-sized facility;
EMV = $670,000.

3-46 (a) Use information. EMV = $29,200
(b) EMV = $46,000
(c) Do not get information. EMV = $28,000
(d) Do not use information.
(e) Expected utility = 0.62. Risk seeker.
(f) Expected utility = 0.80. Risk avoider.

Chapter 4

4-10 (b) SST = 29.5   SSE = 12   SSR = 17.5
$\hat{Y} = 1 + 1.0X$ (c) $\hat{Y} = 7$

4-12 (a) $\hat{Y} = 18.99 + 0.74X$ (b) 80.41
(c) $r = 0.92$; $r^2 = 0.85$

4-14 (a) $83,502   (b) The model predicts the average
price for a house this size.
(c) Age, number of bedrooms, lot size   (d) 0.3969

4-16 $\hat{Y} = 1.02 + 0.00343X$; for $X = 450$, $\hat{Y} = 2.57$;
for $X = 800$, $\hat{Y} = 3.76$

4-20 The model with just *age* is best because it has the
highest r^2 (0.78).

4-22 $\hat{Y} = 82,185.6 + 25.94X_1 - 2151.74X_2 - 1711.54X_3$;
$X_1 = $ Sq. Ft., $X_2 = $ bedrooms, $X_3 = $ age
(a) $\hat{Y} = 82,185.6 + 25.94(2000) - 2151.74(3) - 1711.54(10) = $110,495$ (rounded)

4-24 Best model is $\hat{Y} = 1.518 + 0.669X$; $\hat{Y} = $ expenses
(millions), $X = $ admissions (100s). $r^2 = 0.974$.
The adjusted r^2 decreases when number of beds is
added, so only admissions should be used.

4-26 $\hat{Y} = 57.686 - 0.166X_1 - 0.005X_2$; $\hat{Y} = $ MPG,
$X_1 = $ horsepower, $X_2 = $ weight. This is better—
both r^2 and adjusted r^2 are higher.

4-28   The regression model with SAT by itself is significant indicating that schools with higher SAT scores do charge more, but $r^2 = 0.22$. When a dummy variable for public/private is used, r^2 goes up to 0.79. The coefficient indicates that private schools are more expensive.

Chapter 5

5-12 $F_{13} = 19$; MAD = 7.78

5-14 $F_{13} = 13.67$; MAD = 2.54 for 3-year moving average $F_{13} = 2.31$; MAD = 14 for 3-year weighted moving average

5-16   Trend equation has smallest MAD (1.39)

5-18   Year 1, 410.0; year 2, 422.0; year 3, 443.9; year 4, 466.1; year 5, 495.2; year 6, 521.8

5-20   MAD for $\alpha = 0.3$ is 74.56; MAD for $\alpha = 0.6$ is 51.8; MAD for $\alpha = 0.9$ is 38.1.

5-22   If years are coded 1–5, $Y = 421.2 + 33.6X$. Next year's sales = 622.8.

5-24   (a) 13.67   (b) 13.17   (c) MAD(3-Yr MA) = 2.20; MAD(3-Yr Wt. MA) = 2.72

5-26   (a) 46.9   (b) 57.6   (c) MAD is lower for $\alpha = 0.1$, but if sales = 85, the other forecast is closer.

5-28   67.4

5-30   (a) Quarter 1, 0.8825; Quarter 2, 0.9816; Quarter 3, 0.9712; Quarter 4, 1.1569
(b) $\hat{Y} = 237.75 + 3.67X$
(c) 300.066, 303.732, 307.398, 311.064
(d) 264.794, 298.158, 298.534, 359.872

5-32 $F_{11} = 6.26$; MAD = 0.58 for $\alpha = 0.8$ is lowest.

5-34   270, 390, 189, 351

Chapter 6

6-18   ROP = 4,000 screws

6-20   (a) 149.07   (b) ROP = 160   (c) 74.54, THC = $670.8   (d) 26.83, TOC = $670.8

6-22   141.4

6-24   (a) 250   (b) 125, THC = $187.5
(c) 10, TOC = $187.5   (d) $37,875
(e) 25 days   (f) 20

6-26   (a) 37,037.5   (b) ROP = 30   (c) order 1,000

6-28   Expand to 10,000 cu ft to hold 100 motors; expansion worth $250 per year

6-32   1,217 wheel bearings

6-34   30 units of safety stock

6-36   Item 33CP needs strict control; no strict control for the others.

6-38   (a) 547.7   (b) 717.9   (c) $273.85; $208.95

6-40   Order quantity = 852; total cost = $176

6-42   Order quantity = 51; total cost = $1,901.22

6-46   (a) 32   (b) 2   (c) 20; $2,400   (d) 336; 168
(e) $8,400 + $2,400

Chapter 7

7-14   40 air conditioners, 60 fans, profit = $1,900

7-16   175 radio ads, 10 TV ads

7-18   40 undergraduate, 20 graduate, $160,000

7-20 $20,000 Petrochemical; $30,000 Utilities; return = $4,200; risk = 6

7-22 $X = 18\frac{3}{4}$, $Y = 18\frac{3}{4}$, profit = $150

7-24   (1358.7, 1820.6), $3,179.3

7-26   (a) profit = $2,375   (b) 25 barrels pruned, 62.5 barrels regular   (c) 25 acres pruned, 125 acres regular

7-28   (a) Yes   (b) Doesn't change

7-34   (a) 25 units product 1, 0 units product 2
(b) 25 units resource 1, 75 units resource 2, 50 units resource 3   (c) 0, 0, and 25   (d) Resource 3. Up to $25 (dual price)   (e) Total profit would decrease by 5 (value of reduced cost).

7-36   24 coconuts, 12 skins; profit = 5,040 rupees

7-40   Make all MCA regular modems (27,750 of them)

Chapter 8

8-2   (b) $50,000 in LA bonds, $175,000 in Palmer Drugs, $25,000 in Happy Days

8-4   1.33 pounds of oat product per horse, 0 pounds of grain, 3.33 pounds of mineral product

8-6   Min. $C = 925X_1 + 2,000X_2$
$0.04X_1 + 0.05X_2 \geq 0.40$
$0.03X_1 + 0.03X_2 \geq 0.60$
$X_1 = 20$, $X_2 = 0$, $C = \$18,500$

8-10   Max. rolls = $20X_1 + 6.8X_2 + 12X_3 - 65,000X_4$
$X_1 + X_2 + X_3 \leq 17,000$
$X_1 \geq 3,000$
$X_2 - 0.05 X_3 \geq 0$
$X_4 \geq 0.20$
$X_4 \leq 0.45$; Sell 327,000 rolls

8-12 $X_1 = 497$, $X_2 = 1,241$, $P = \$195,505$

8-14   1,250 wheat in N parcel, 500 wheat in NW, 312.5 wheat in W, 137.5 wheat in SW, 131 alfalfa in SW, 600 barley in SE, 400 barley in N, profit = $337,862.10

Chapter 9

9-18   (b) $14X_1 + 4X_2 \leq 3,360$; $10X_1 + 12X_2 \leq 9,600$
(d) $S_1 = 3,360$, $S_2 = 9,600$ (e) X_2 (f) S_2
(g) 800 units of X_2 (h) 1,200,000

9-20 $X_1 = 2$, $X_2 = 6$, $S_1 = 0$, $S_2 = 0$, $P = \$36$

9-22 $X_1 = 14$, $X_2 = 33$, $C = \$221$

9-24   Unbounded

9-26   Degeneracy; $X_1 = 27$, $X_2 = 5$, $X_3 = 0$, $P = \$177$

9-28 (a) Min. $C = 9X_1 + 15X_2$
$X_1 + 2X_2 \geq 30$
$X_1 + 4X_2 \geq 40$
(b) $X_1 - 0, X_2 - 20, C = \$300$

9-30 8 coffee tables, 2 bookcases, profit = 96

9-34 (a) $\$7 \frac{1}{2}$ to infinity   (b) Negative infinity to $40
(c) $20   (d) $0

9-36 (a) 18 Model 102, 4 Model H23 (b) S_1 = slack time for soldering S_2 = slack time for inspection
(c) Yes—shadow price is $4   (d) No—the shadow price is less than $1.75.

9-38 (a) Negative infinity to $6 for phosphate;
$5 to infinity for potassium
(b) Basis won't change; but X_1, X_2, and S_2 will change.

9-40 max $P = 50U_1 + 4U_2$
$12U_1 + 1U_2 \leq 120$
$20U_1 + 3U_2 \leq 250$

Chapter 10

10-12 Des Moines to Albuquerque 200, Des Moines to Boston 50, Des Moines to Cleveland 50, Evansville to Boston 150, Ft. Lauderdale to Cleveland 250. Cost = $3,200. Initial solution is optimal.

10-16 25 units from Pineville to 3; 30 units from Oak Ridge to 2; 10 units from Oakville to 3; 30 units from Mapletown to 1. Cost = $230.

10-18 Total cost = $14,700.

10-20 Degeneracy; need to place a zero in an empty cell (such as 2-B)

10-22 Total interest cost = $28,300.

10-24 New Orleans' systems cost = $20,000; Houston's is $19,500, so Houston should be selected.

10-26 East St. Louis cost = 17,400; St. Louis cost – 17,250, St. Louis is $150 per week cheaper.

10-28 A12 to W, A15 to Z, B2 to Y, B9 to X, 50 hours

10-30 4,580 miles

10-32 Total rating = 335

10-34 Overall rating = 75.5

10-36 Total cost = $1.18

10-38 (a) 96   (b) 92   (c) Yes, score = 93

Chapter 11

11-13 (a) $X_i = 1$ if item i is selected, 0 otherwise. $X_1 = 1$, $X_2 = 1, X_4 = 1, X_5 = 1, X_6 = 1, X_7 = 1$, utility = 310
(b) $X_5 \leq X_3$

11-15 5 Boeing 757s, 8 Boeing 767s, passenger capacity = 1,273,000

11-17 Locations 2, 4, and 6 are used. The others are not.

11-19 Undertake apartment project and shopping center project. NPV = 33.

11-21 Generator 1 is used from 2-10 generating 2,400 megawatts. Generator 3 will be used during the entire 16 hours generating 3,200 megawatts from 6-2 and 3,300 megawatts from 2-10.

11-23 $X_1 = 0, X_2 = 3, P = \$9$

11-25 $X_1 = 500, X_2 = 400$

11-29 (b) $X_1 = 49, X_2 = 69, X_3 = 30, X_4 = 20$, All goals fully met.

11-31 (b) $X_1 = 18.3, X_2 = 10.8$, Revenue = $70,420

Chapter 12

12-8 200 on path 1-2-5-7-8, 200 on path 1-3-6-8, and 100 on path 1-4-8. Total = 500.

12-10 The minimum distance is 47 (4,700 feet).

12-12 Total distance is 177. Connect 1-2, 2-3, 3-4, 3-5, 5-6.

12-14 The total distance is 430. Route 1-3-5-7-10-13.

12-16 The minimal spanning tree length is 23.

12-18 The maximal flow is 17.

12-20 The maximal flow is 2,000 gallons.

12-22 The shortest route is 76. The path is 1–2–6–9–13–16.

12-24 (a) 1,200 miles (b) 1,000 miles.

12-26 Total distance = 40.

12-28 Maximum number = 190.

12-30 (a) The shortest distance is 49.
(b) The shortest distance is 55.
(c) The shortest distance is 64.

Chapter 13

13-18 (a) 0.50   (b) 0.50   (c) 0.97725   (d) 0.02275
(e) 43.84

13-20 (a) 0.0228   (b) 0.3085   (c) 0.8413   (d) 0.9772

13-24 14

13-28 (b) Critical path AC takes 20 weeks; path BD takes 18 weeks   (c) 0.222 for AC; 5 for BD   (d) 1.00
(e) 0.963   (f) path BD has more variability and has higher probability of exceeding 22 weeks.

13-34 Project completion time is 38.3 weeks.

13-36 Completion time is 25.7.

Chapter 14

14-10 Total cost for 1, 2, 3 and 4 clerks are $564, $428, $392, and $406 respectively.

14-12 (a) 4.167 cars   (b) .4167 hours   (c) 0.5 hours
(d) 0.8333   (e) 0.1667

14-14 (a) 0.512, 0.410, 0.328   (b) 0.2   (c) 0.8 minutes
(d) 3.2   (e) 4   (f) 0.429, 0.038 minutes, 0.15, 0.95

14-16 (a) 0.2687 hours   (b) 3.2
(c) Yes. Savings = $142.50 per hour.

14-18 (a) 0.0397 hours   (b) 0.9524   (c) 0.006 hours
(d) 0.1524   (e) 0.4286   (f) 0.4   (g) 0.137

14-20 With one person $L = 3$, $W = 1$ hour, $L_q = 2.25$, and $W_q = 0.75$ hour. With two people, $L = 0.6$, $W = 0.2$ hour, $L_q = 2.225$, and $W_q = 0.075$ hour.

14-22 No

14-24 (a) 0.1333 hours   (b) 1.333   (c) 0.2 hours
(d) 2   (e) 0.333

14-26 (a) 80 customers per day   (b) 10.66 hours, $266.50
(c) 0.664, $16.60   (d) 2 tellers, $208.60

14-30 (a) 0.576   (b) 1.24   (c) 0.344   (d) 0.217 hour
(e) 0.467 hour

Chapter 15

15-14 No

15-16 Expected value 6.35 (using formula). The average number is 7 in problem 15-15.

15-18 (b) Average number delayed = 0.40. Average number of arrivals = 2.07.

15-26 (a) Cost/hour is generally more expensive replacing 1 pen each time.
(b) Expected cost/hour with 1 pen policy = $1.38 (or $58/breakdown); expected cost/hour with 4-pen policy = $1.12 (or $132/breakdown).

Chapter 16

16-8 (b) 90%   (c) 30%

16-10 Next month 4/15, 5/15, 6/15. Three months 0.1952, 0.3252, 0.4796

16-12 (a) 70%   (b) 30%   (c) 40%

16-14 25% for Battles; 18.75% for University; 26.25% for Bill's; 30% for College

16-16 111 at Northside, 75 at West End, and 54 at Suburban

16-18 Horizon will have 104,000 customers and Local will have 76,000.

16-20 New MFA = (5,645.16, 1,354.84)

16-22 50% Hicourt, 30% Printing House, and 20% Gandy

16-26 Store 1 will have 1/3 of the customers and store 2 will have 2/3.

Chapter 17

17-8 45.034 to 46.966 for $\bar{x}$
0 to 4.008 for R

17-10 16.814 to 17.187 for $\bar{x}$
0.068 to 0.932 for R

17-12 2.236 to 3.728 for $\bar{x}$
0 to 2.336 for R
In control

17-16 (a) 1011.8 for $\bar{x}$ and 96.3 for R (b) 956.23 to 1067.37   (c) Process is out of control.

17-18 LCL = 0, UCL = 4

CD Module 1

M1-4 SUN − 0.80

M1-6 Lambda = 3.0445, Value of CI = 0.0223, RI = 0.58, CR = 0.0384

M1-8 Car 1, 0.4045

M1-10 University B has highest weighted average = 0.4995

CD Module 2

M2-6 1–2–6–7 with a total distance of 10 miles.

M2-8 Shortest route is 1–2–6–7 with a total distance of 14 miles.

M2-10 The shortest route is 1–2–5–8–9. Distance = 19 miles.

M2-12 4 units of item 1, 1 unit of item 2, and no units of items 3 and 4.

M2-14 Ship 6 units of item 1, 1 unit of item 2, and 1 unit of item 3.

M2-16 The shortest route is 1–3–6–11–15–17–19–20.

CD Module 3

M3-6 (a) OL = $8(20,000 − X)$ for $X \le 20,000$; OL = 0 otherwise   (b) $0.5716   (c) $0.5716
(d) 99.99%   (e) Print the book

M3-8 (a) BEP = 1,500   (b) Expected profit = $8,000

M3-10 (a) OL = $10(30 − X)$ for $X \le 30$; OL = 0 otherwise
(b) EOL = $59.34   (c) EVPI = $59.34

M3-12 (a) Use new process. New EMV = $283,000.
(b) Increase selling price. New EMV = $296,000.

M3-14 BEP = 4,955

M3-16 EVPI = $249.96

M3-18 EVPI = $51.24

CD Module 4

M4-8 Strategy for X:X_2; strategy for Y:Y_1; value of the game = 6

M4-10 $X_1 = {}^{35}\!/_{57}$; $X_2 = {}^{22}\!/_{57}$; $Y_1 = {}^{32}\!/_{57}$; $Y_2 = {}^{25}\!/_{57}$; value of game = 66.70

M4-12 (b) $Q = 41/72$, $1 − Q = 31/72$; $P = 55/72$. $1 − P = 17/72$

M4-14 Value of game = 9.33

M4-16 Saddle point exists. Shoe Town should invest $15,000 in advertising and Fancy Foot should invest $20,000 in advertising.

M4-18 Eliminate dominated strategy X_2. Then Y_3 is dominated and may be eliminated. The value of the game is 6.

M4-20 Always play strategy A_{14}. $3 million.

CD Module 5

M5-8 $X = -\frac{3}{2}$, $Y = \frac{1}{2}$; $Z = \frac{7}{2}$

M5-16 $\begin{pmatrix} -{}^{48}\!/_{60} & {}^{6}\!/_{60} & {}^{32}\!/_{60} \\ {}^{6}\!/_{60} & -{}^{12}\!/_{60} & {}^{6}\!/_{60} \\ {}^{12}\!/_{60} & {}^{6}\!/_{60} & -{}^{8}\!/_{60} \end{pmatrix}$

M5-18 $0X_1 + 4X_2 + 3X_3 = 28$; $1X_1 + 2X_2 + 2X_3 = 16$

CD Module 6

M6-6 (a) $Y'' = 12X - 6$ (b) $Y'' = 80X^3 + 12X$
(c) $Y'' = 6/X^4$ (d) $Y'' = 500/X^6$

M6-8 (a) $Y'' = 30X^4 - 1$ (b) $Y'' = 60X^2 + 24$
(c) $Y'' = 24/X^5$ (d) $Y'' = 250/X^6$

M6-10 $X = 5$ is point of inflection.
M6-12 $Q = 2,400$, $TR = 1,440,000$
M6-14 $P = 5.48$

APPENDIX G: SOLUTIONS TO SELF-TESTS

Chapter 1

1. c
2. d
3. b
4. b
5. c
6. c
7. d
8. c
9. d
10. a
11. a
12. Quantitative analysis
13. Defining the problem
14. schematic model
15. algorithm

Chapter 2

1. c
2. b
3. a
4. d
5. b
6. c
7. a
8. c
9. b
10. d
11. b
12. a
13. a
14. b
15. a

Chapter 3

1. b
2. c
3. c
4. a
5. c
6. b
7. a
8. c

9. a
10. d
11. b
12. c
13. a
14. c
15. b

Chapter 4

1. b
2. c
3. d
4. b
5. b
6. c
7. b
8. c
9. a
10. b
11. b
12. c

Chapter 5

1. b
2. a
3. d
4. c
5. b
6. b
7. d
8. b
9. d
10. b
11. a
12. d
13. b
14. c

Chapter 6

1. e
2. e
3. c
4. c

5. a
6. b
7. d
8. c
9. b
10. a
11. a

Chapter 7

1. b
2. a
3. b
4. c
5. a
6. b
7. c
8. c
9. b
10. c
11. a
12. a
13. a
14. a

Chapter 8

1. a
2. b
3. b
4. d
5. d
6. c
7. e
8. d
9. a
10. b
11. c
12. b

Chapter 9

1. a
2. d
3. d
4. a

5. a
6. d
7. a
8. d
9. b
10. a
11. a
12. b
13. c
14. c
15. d
16. a
17. b

Chapter 10

1. b
2. c
3. b
4. b
5. b
6. a
7. b
8. b
9. b
10. a
11. b
12. a

Chapter 11

1. a
2. b
3. a
4. a
5. a
6. b
7. b
8. b
9. d
10. b
11. e

Chapter 12

1. c
2. e
3. b
4. c
5. b
6. a
7. b
8. b
9. a
10. d

11. shortest route
12. maximal flow
13. minimal spanning tree

Chapter 13

1. e
2. c
3. a
4. d
5. b
6. c
7. b
8. a
9. b
10. b
11. d
12. a
13. Critical path (or critical)
14. program evaluation and review technique
15. linear programming model
16. optimistic, most likely, pessimistic
17. slack
18. monitor and control

Chapter 14

1. a
2. a
3. b
4. e
5. c
6. b
7. c
8. d
9. b
10. d
11. c
12. first-come, first-served
13. negative exponentially distributed
14. simulation

Chapter 15

1. b
2. b
3. a
4. c
5. b
6. a
7. a
8. d
9. a

10. b
11. a
12. b
13. d
14. d
15. c
16. c
17. e
18. (a) no, yes, no, no, no, yes, yes, yes, no, yes
    (b) yes, yes, yes, yes, no, yes, yes, no, no, no

Chapter 16

1. b
2. a
3. c
4. c
5. b
6. a
7. a
8. a
9. b
10. matrix of transition probabilities
11. collectively exhaustive, mutually exclusive
12. vector of state probabilities

Chapter 17

1. b
2. c
3. d
4. a
5. c
6. b
7. c
8. d
9. b
10. b

CD Module 1

1. a
2. d
3. b
4. b
5. c
6. b
7. b
8. b

CD Module 2

1. c
2. b

3. e
4. c
5. b
6. a
7. c
8. e
9. a
10. a
11. c
12. c
13. b
14. b

CD Module 3

1. c
2. d
3. b

4. a
5. b
6. b
7. c

CD Module 4

1. b
2. a
3. c
4. b
5. b
6. b
7. a

CD Module 5

1. c
2. a

3. b
4. c
5. b
6. a
7. e
8. d

CD Module 6

1. a
2. d
3. a
4. b
5. c
6. d
7. d

INDEX

Note: Any page number preceded by M means that topic is on your CD-ROM.

LICENSE AGREEMENT AND LIMITED WARRANTY

READ THIS LICENSE CAREFULLY BEFORE USING THIS PACKAGE. BY USING THIS PACKAGE, YOU ARE AGREEING TO THE TERMS AND CONDITIONS OF THIS LICENSE. IF YOU DO NOT AGREE, DO NOT USE THE PACKAGE. PROMPTLY RETURN THE UNUSED PACKAGE AND ALL ACCOMPANYING ITEMS TO THE PLACE YOU OBTAINED IT. *THESE TERMS APPLY TO ALL LICENSED SOFTWARE ON THE DISK EXCEPT THAT THE TERMS FOR USE OF ANY SHAREWARE OR FREEWARE ON THE DISKETTES ARE AS SET FORTH IN THE ELECTRONIC LICENSE LOCATED ON THE DISK:*

1. GRANT OF LICENSE and OWNERSHIP: The enclosed computer programs and data ("Software") are licensed, not sold, to you by Prentice-Hall, Inc. ("We" or the "Company") in consideration of your purchase or adoption of the accompanying Company textbooks and/or other materials, and your agreement to these terms. We reserve any rights not granted to you. You own only the disk(s) but we and/or licensors own the Software itself. This license allows individuals who have purchased the accompanying Company textbook to use and display their copy of the Software on a single computer (i.e., with a single CPU) at a single location for academic use only, so long as you comply with the terms of this Agreement. You may make one copy for back up, or transfer your copy to another CPU, provided that the Software is usable on only one computer. This license allows instructors at educational institutions [only] who have adopted the accompanying Company textbook to install, use and display the enclosed copy of the Software on individual computers in the computer lab designated for use by any students of a course requiring the accompanying Company textbook and only for as long as such textbook is a required text for such course, at a single campus or branch or geographic location of an educational institution, for academic use only, so long as you comply with the terms of this Agreement.

2. RESTRICTIONS: You may not transfer or distribute the Software or documentation to anyone else. You may not copy the documentation or the Software. You may not reverse engineer, disassemble, decompile, modify, adapt, translate, or create derivative works based on the Software or the Documentation. You may be held legally responsible for any copying or copyright infringement which is caused by your failure to abide by the terms of these restrictions.

3. TERMINATION: This license is effective until terminated. This license will terminate automatically without notice from the Company if you fail to comply with any provisions or limitations of this license. Upon termination, you shall destroy the Documentation and all copies of the Software. All provisions of this Agreement as to limitation and disclaimer of warranties, limitation of liability, remedies or damages, and our ownership rights shall survive termination.

4. LIMITED WARRANTY AND DISCLAIMER OF WARRANTY: Company warrants that for a period of 60 days from the date you purchase this Software (or purchase or adopt the accompanying textbook), the Software, when properly installed and used in accordance with the Documentation, will operate in substantial conformity with the description of the Software set forth in the Documentation, and that for a period of 30 days the disk(s) on which the Software is delivered shall be free from defects in materials and workmanship under normal use. The Company does not warrant that the Software will meet your requirements or that the operation of the Software will be uninterrupted or error-free. Your only remedy and the Company's only obligation under these limited warranties is, at the Company's option, return of the disk for a refund of any amounts paid for it by you or replacement of the disk. THIS LIMITED WARRANTY IS THE ONLY WARRANTY PROVIDED BY THE COMPANY AND ITS LICENSORS, AND THE COMPANY AND ITS LICENSORS DISCLAIM ALL OTHER WARRANTIES, EXPRESS OR IMPLIED, INCLUDING WITHOUT LIMITATION, THE IMPLIED WARRANTIES OF MERCHANTABILITY AND FITNESS FOR A PARTICULAR PURPOSE. THE COMPANY DOES NOT WARRANT, GUARANTEE OR MAKE ANY REPRESENTATION REGARDING THE ACCURACY, RELIABILITY, CURRENTNESS, USE, OR RESULTS OF USE, OF THE SOFTWARE.

5. LIMITATION OF REMEDIES AND DAMAGES: IN NO EVENT, SHALL THE COMPANY OR ITS EMPLOYEES, AGENTS, LICENSORS, OR CONTRACTORS BE LIABLE FOR ANY INCIDENTAL, INDIRECT, SPECIAL, OR CONSEQUENTIAL DAMAGES ARISING OUT OF OR IN CONNECTION WITH THIS LICENSE OR THE SOFTWARE, INCLUDING FOR LOSS OF USE, LOSS OF DATA, LOSS OF INCOME OR PROFIT, OR OTHER LOSSES, SUSTAINED AS A RESULT OF INJURY TO ANY PERSON, OR LOSS OF OR DAMAGE TO PROPERTY, OR CLAIMS OF THIRD PARTIES, EVEN IF THE COMPANY OR AN AUTHORIZED REPRESENTATIVE OF THE COMPANY HAS BEEN ADVISED OF THE POSSIBILITY OF SUCH DAMAGES. IN NO EVENT SHALL THE LIABILITY OF THE COMPANY FOR DAMAGES WITH RESPECT TO THE SOFTWARE EXCEED THE AMOUNTS ACTUALLY PAID BY YOU, IF ANY, FOR THE SOFTWARE OR THE ACCOMPANYING TEXTBOOK. SOME JURISDICTIONS DO NOT ALLOW THE LIMITATION OF LIABILITY IN CERTAIN CIRCUMSTANCES, THE ABOVE LIMITATIONS MAY NOT ALWAYS APPLY.

6. GENERAL: THIS AGREEMENT SHALL BE CONSTRUED IN ACCORDANCE WITH THE LAWS OF THE UNITED STATES OF AMERICA AND THE STATE OF NEW YORK, APPLICABLE TO CONTRACTS MADE IN NEW YORK, AND SHALL BENEFIT THE COMPANY, ITS AFFILIATES AND ASSIGNEES. This Agreement is the complete and exclusive statement of the agreement between you and the Company and supersedes all proposals, prior agreements, oral or written, and any other communications between you and the company or any of its representatives relating to the subject matter. If you are a U.S. Government user, this Software is licensed with "restricted rights" as set forth in subparagraphs (a)-(d) of the Commercial Computer-Restricted Rights clause at FAR 52.227-19 or in subparagraphs (c)(1)(ii) of the Rights in Technical Data and Computer Software clause at DFARS 252.227-7013, and similar clauses, as applicable.

Should you have any questions concerning this agreement or if you wish to contact the Company for any reason, please contact in writing:

Director, Media Production
Pearson Education
1 Lake Street
Upper Saddle River, NJ 07458